America
Votes™ 25

America Votes ™ 25

A HANDBOOK OF CONTEMPORARY AMERICAN ELECTION STATISTICS

RICHARD M. SCAMMON
ALICE V. McGILLIVRAY
RHODES COOK

2001—2002

CQ PRESS

A Division of Congressional Quarterly Inc.
Washington, D.C.

CQ Press

A Division of Congressional Quarterly Inc.

1255 22nd St., N.W., Suite 400

Washington, D.C. 20037

(202) 729-1900

Toll-free, 1-866-4CQ-PRESS (1-866-427-7737)

www.cqpress.com

Printed and bound in the United States of America

07   06   05   04   03   5   4   3   2   1

Electronic composition: TechBooks

ISBN: 1-56802-805-9
ISSN: 0065-678X

Contents

List of Maps

Introduction

In a sense, the election of 2002 was a second Republican revolution. It was not as historic or as expansive as the first one, when in 1994 Republicans gained control of both houses of Congress for the first time in forty years, taking a majority of the nation's governorships as well. The balloting on November 5, 2002, however, dispelled any lingering doubt as to whether the election eight years prior represented an interlude in the Democrats' long dominance of congressional and state-level politics or whether it launched a new political era with the GOP ascendant. The twenty-fifth volume of *America Votes* details in numerical form the sweep of the 2001–2002 election cycle, starting with the two 2001 gubernatorial elections in New Jersey and Virginia, proceeding through the 2002 primary season, and ending with the November 2002 general election for Congress and most of the nation's governorships.

Although the 2002 election was no landslide, its result was a clear affirmation of the verdict rendered in 1994. In short, the nation is closely divided politically, but it can be safely described as "leaning Republican." This is evident from a quick look at the vote in recent years for the U.S. House of Representatives, whose composition every two years can be aggregated into a semblance of a nationwide vote. In the elections of 1996, 1998, and 2000, the Republican advantage in House balloting was less than 1 million votes. In 2002, the GOP plurality swelled to more than 3.6 million. Even more compelling, however, has been the change in the vote-getting appeal of the two parties in recent years, as reflected in House voting. Since 1990, the year of the last midterm election in which Democrats won a majority of congressional seats, the nationwide vote for Democratic House candidates has increased by barely 1 million, while the Republican vote has increased by nearly 10 million. In other words, the Democratic congressional vote remained almost flat from 1990 to 2002, while the GOP House vote increased fully by a third.

The payoff for the GOP in 2002 was its most complete top-to-bottom victory since 1994. The party regained control of the Senate, which it had lost in 2001 with the defection of Sen. James M. Jeffords of Vermont to inde-

2002: Leaning Republican

There was not a large movement of seats in the midterm elections of 2002, but the incremental change that resulted was enough to create a Republican victory. While the president's party has historically lost ground in midterm elections, the GOP in 2002 regained control of the Senate, strengthened its advantage in the House of Representatives, and maintained a majority of the nation's governorships.

The chart below reflects partisan totals immediately before and after the 2002 general election. The preelection House totals include three Democratic vacancies—two seats in Ohio, one in Hawaii—that are credited to the Democrats in the preelection count.

	Preelection			Postelection		
	Rep.	Dem.	Other	Rep.	Dem.	Other
Governor	27	21	2	26	24	0
Senate	49	49	2	51	48	1
House	223	211	1	229	205	1

pendent status, strengthened its advantage in the House of Representatives, and maintained control of a majority of the nation's governorships. A number of factors can be credited in fashioning the outcome. President George W. Bush prominently inserted himself in election activities, raising tens of millions of dollars for the GOP and its candidates and lending his popularity to those candidates by campaigning hard on their behalf up to election eve. Meanwhile, the Democrats had no competing figure to promote their candidates nor, in the minds of many, a compelling agenda to woo undecided voters.

The result was a late surge to the GOP and a historic midterm showing by the president's party. Republicans gained six House and two Senate seats. It was the first time since 1934, when voters gave their stamp of approval to Franklin D. Roosevelt and the Democrats, that the president's party gained ground in both houses of Congress in a midterm election. The 2002 election was also apparently

Counting the 2002 Vote

In 2002, Republicans won a majority of the nationwide vote for the House of Representatives for the first time since 1994, when they scored their historic breakthrough that brought them control of both houses of Congress. For good measure, the GOP won a majority of the nationwide vote for the Senate in 2002, and fell just short of taking a majority of the gubernatorial vote for the 2001–2002 election cycle.

No blank or void ballots are included in the totals below. They are based on official results from 38 gubernatorial contests (36 held in 2002, two in 2001) and 34 races for the Senate, as well as two versions of the House vote. "All Races" feature the results from the 429 districts in which a vote was taken. There was no vote taken in six districts in Florida where candidates ran unopposed. "Contested Races" are those in which the Democrats and Republicans both fielded candidates. (For more information see table on page 528.)

Office	Total Vote	Republican	Democratic	Other	Rep.-Dem. Plurality	Percentage of Total Vote		
						Rep.	Dem.	Other
Governor	66,586,164	32,835,446	30,109,659	3,641,059	2,725,787 R	49.3%	45.2%	5.5%
Senate	43,027,668	21,566,157	19,861,824	1,599,687	1,704,333 R	50.1%	46.2%	3.7%
House								
All Races	73,449,133	37,360,424	33,758,288	2,330,421	3,602,136 R	50.9%	46.0%	3.2%
Contested Races	63,089,308	31,862,872	29,830,344	1,396,092	2,032,528 R	50.5%	47.3%	2.2%

2002: Close House Races

A total of 25 House members were elected to a seat in the 108th Congress in November 2002 with less than 52 percent of the total vote in their districts. The number of such close races was similar to the total in 2000, although unlike 2000, the list of vulnerable House members in 2002 was noticeably longer on the Democratic side. An asterisk (*) indicates candidates who won their first election to the House in November 2002. A pound sign (#) indicates that the House member was paired by redistricting against another incumbent in 2002.

Republicans (10)	2002 Winning Percentage	Democrats (15)	2002 Winning Percentage
Bob Beauprez, Colo. 7 *	47.3	Jim Matheson, Utah 2	49.4
Ginny Brown-Waite, Fla. 5 *	47.9	Rick Larsen, Wash. 2	50.1
Rick Renzi, Ariz. 1 *	49.2	Timothy H. Bishop, N.Y. 1 *	50.2
Mike D. Rogers, Ala. 3 *	50.3	Dennis Moore, Kan. 3	50.2
Chris Chocola, Ind. 2 *	50.5	Rodney Alexander, La. 5 *	50.3
John Hostettler, Ind. 8	51.3	Jim Marshall, Ga. 3 *	50.5
Jim Gerlach, Pa. 6 *	51.4	Joseph M. Hoeffel, Pa. 13	50.9
Henry Bonilla, Texas 23	51.5	Ken Lucas, Ky. 4	51.1
Phil Gingrey, Ga. 11 *	51.6	Tim Ryan, Ohio 17 *	51.1
Anne M. Northup, Ky. 3	51.6	Baron P. Hill, Ind. 9	51.2
		Dennis Cardoza, Calif. 18 *	51.3
		Tim Holden, Pa. 17 #	51.4
		Charles W. Stenholm, Texas 17	51.4
		Chet Edwards, Texas 11	51.6
		Chris Van Hollen, Md. 8 *	51.7

the first in which the president's party took control of the Senate in a midterm election, at least since the popular election of senators was instituted in 1913.

Giving additional luster to the Republicans' performance was the fact that they won the three most closely watched elements of the 2002 election: they took the Senate, they took the House, and the president's younger brother, Florida governor Jeb Bush—the *bête noire* of Democrats after the controversial finish to the 2000 presidential balloting in the Sunshine State—handily won reelection by a margin in excess of 600,000 votes.

Unlike 1994, in 2002 the GOP did not have to swing a large number of seats to reach its goals. The Republicans entered election day already possessing a majority of House seats and governorships and were only one seat down in the Senate. They hardly needed a tidal wave when a small ripple would do. That is essentially what they got.

In 1994, 56 of the 60 House seats that switched party hands went to the Republicans, as did all 8 Senate seats. In 2002, one could almost count on both hands the number of House seats that swung from one party to the other. The number of partisan seat switches in the Senate was just 4, with 3 going to the Republicans and 1 to the Democrats. In short, there was not the cascade of seats as in 1994, but a trickle that benefited the Republicans a bit more than the Democrats.

The House Since 1990: From Democratic to Republican

The House of Representatives went from Democratic to Republican in the 1990s, fueled by the GOP upsurge in the South. But since winning control of the House in 1994, Republicans steadily lost ground until 2002, when historic midterm election gains pushed them back close to their 1994 total. After both the 2000 and 2002 elections, Republicans held a majority of seats in the South and the Midwest. Democrats had the larger number in the East and West. Regions are defined below. An "I" indicates Independent.

	South				West			Midwest			East				Total House			
	R	D	I		R	D		R	D		R	D	I		R	D	I	
1990	44	85	0	D	37	48	D	45	68	D	41	66	1	D	167	267	1	D
1992	52	85	0	D	38	55	D	44	61	D	42	57	1	D	176	258	1	D
1994	73	64	0	R	53	40	R	59	46	R	45	54	1	D	230	204	1	R
1996	82	55	0	R	51	42	R	55	50	R	39	60	1	D	227	207	1	R
1998	82	55	0	R	49	44	R	54	51	R	38	61	1	D	223	211	1	R
2000	81	55	1	R	43	50	D	57	48	R	40	59	1	D	221	212	2	R
2002	85	57	0	R	46	52	D	61	39	R	37	57	1	D	229	205	1	R
Net Change in GOP Seats, 1990–2002	+41				+9			+16			−4				+62			

Note: Traditionally, Congressional Quarterly has defined the four regions as follows:

EAST—Connecticut, Delaware, Maine, Maryland, Massachusetts, New Hampshire, New Jersey, New York, Pennsylvania, Rhode Island, Vermont, West Virginia.
MIDWEST—Illinois, Indiana, Iowa, Kansas, Michigan, Minnesota, Missouri, Nebraska, North Dakota, Ohio, South Dakota, Wisconsin.
SOUTH—Alabama, Arkansas, Florida, Georgia, Kentucky, Louisiana, Mississippi, North Carolina, Oklahoma, South Carolina, Tennessee, Texas, Virginia.
WEST—Alaska, Arizona, California, Colorado, Hawaii, Idaho, Montana, Nevada, New Mexico, Oregon, Utah, Washington, Wyoming.

At the congressional level, the election of 2002 was ultimately as much about incumbency as anything else. When congressional districts were redrawn a decade earlier, the immediate impact was volatile. A total of 111 seats were won with less than 55 percent of the total vote in 1992, and 43 incumbents were defeated (19 in the primaries, 24 in the general election).

In 2002, however, the redistricting process resulted in a distinctly pro-incumbent cast. To be sure, there were overtones of partisan redistricting in Georgia and Maryland that aided the Democrats and in Michigan and Pennsylvania that boosted the Republicans. Yet the nationwide theme of congressional line drawing was incumbent protection. The result? Fewer than 50 winners won with less than 55 percent of the vote, and just 16 House incumbents were beaten (8 each in the primaries and general election). Half that number were paired against another House member in the same district.

It was such a pro-incumbent year that Democrat Patsy T. Mink of Hawaii was reelected more than a month after she had died—and with 56 percent of the vote. Virginia Republican Virgil H. Goode Jr., who had just switched to the party in August, won another term with 64 percent. Washington Democrat Jim McDermott, who made a controversial trip to Iraq shortly before the election, was reelected with 74 percent of the vote. California Democrat Barbara Lee, who shortly after the September 11 terrorist attacks cast the lone vote in Congress against granting President Bush authority to use military force against those responsible for them, won with 81 percent. Two House freshmen, Democrat Mike Ross of Arkansas and Republican Shelley Moore Capito of West Virginia, easily won with at least 60 percent of the vote against rivals they had narrowly beaten two years earlier.

Probably most indicative of the pro-incumbent nature of the year was the fate of the 57 "marginal" House members who had won their seats in 2000 with less than 55 percent of the total vote. Of this group, only three lost—Republican Constance A. Morella of Maryland and Democrats Bill Luther of Minnesota and Jim Maloney of

2002: Defeated Incumbents

While the election of 2002 was good for incumbents at all levels, the primaries turned out to be as challenging a hurdle for House members as the general election. Eight lost in each round, with four of the defeated incumbents in both the primaries and general election paired by redistricting against another incumbent. The losing "paired" incumbents are designated by a pound sign (#). The district listed with defeated House incumbents is the one in which they sought reelection in 2002.

The chart lists the gubernatorial, Senate, and House incumbents defeated in the 2002 primaries and general election, the number of terms they had served in that office before their loss in 2002, the percentage of the total vote they had received in the previous general election (1996 for senators, 1998 for governors, 2000 for House members) and their percentage of the total vote in the 2002 general election (for those who were not beaten in the primaries). A dash (—) indicates a candidate that was not elected to the position they held at the time of the 2002 election.

	Number of Terms	Previous Election Percentage	2002 Election Percentage
GOVERNORS			
Primaries			
(None)			
General Election			
(3 Democrats, 1 Republican)			
Roy Barnes, D-Ga.	1	52.5	46.2
Jim Hodges, D-S.C.	1	53.2	47.0
Scott McCallum, R-Wis.	—	—	41.4
Don Siegelman, D-Ala.	1	57.7	48.9
SENATORS			
Primaries			
(1 Republican)			
Robert C. Smith, R-N.H.	2	49.2	—
General Election			
(2 Democrats, 1 Republican)			
Jean Carnahan, D-Mo.	—	—	48.7
Max Cleland, D-Ga.	1	48.9	45.9
Tim Hutchinson, R-Ark.	1	52.7	46.1
REPRESENTATIVES			
Primaries			
(6 Democrats, 2 Republicans)			
Bob Barr, R-Ga. 7 #	4	55.3	—
Gary A. Condit, D-Calif. 18	6	67.1	—
Earl F. Hilliard, D-Ala. 7	5	74.6	—
Brian Kerns, R-Ind. 4 #	1	64.8	—
Frank R. Mascara, D-Pa. 12 #	4	64.4	—
Cynthia A. McKinney, D-Ga. 4	5	60.7	—
Lynn Rivers, D-Mich. 15 #	4	64.7	—
Tom Sawyer, D-Ohio 17	8	64.8	—
General Election			
(5 Democrats, 3 Republicans)			
George W. Gekas, R-Pa. 17 #	10	71.5	48.6
Felix J. Grucci Jr., R-N.Y. 1	1	55.5	48.6
Bill Luther, D-Minn. 2	4	49.6	42.2
Jim Maloney, D-Conn. 5 #	3	53.6	43.3
Constance A. Morella, R-Md. 8	8	52.0	47.5
David Phelps, D-Ill. 19 #	2	64.6	45.2
Karen L. Thurman, D-Fla. 5	5	64.3	46.2
Ronnie Shows, D-Miss. 3 #	2	58.1	34.8

Connecticut (the latter being paired in a new district with Republican Nancy L. Johnson).

The greatest volatility and competition in 2002 were in the races for governor. Of the 36 gubernatorial contests, 24 were won with less than 55 percent of the vote; 20 governorships switched party hands. Democrats picked up governors' chairs in some major battleground states, including Illinois, Michigan, and Pennsylvania, as well as in such unlikely places as Kansas, Oklahoma, and Wyoming. Republicans scored pickups on some similarly unlikely terrain, such as in Hawaii and Maryland, as well as holding on to governorships in the big southern linchpins of Florida and Texas.

The vast majority of governorships that switched party hands in 2002 were open seats, but a number of incumbent governors ran into trouble at the ballot box. Four of the 16 who sought reelection were defeated, including 3 Democrats in the Deep South states of Alabama, Georgia, and South Carolina. Even in victory, several gubernatorial heavyweights saw their vote shares decline noticeably from those in 1998. In California, Democrat Gray Davis won a second term with just 47 percent of the vote, down 11 percentage points from four years earlier. Republican George E. Pataki of New York won a third term with 49 percent, down 5 points, while in Texas, Republican Rick Perry won his first full term with 58 percent, down 10 points from the 1998 showing of his predecessor, George W. Bush. Among the big-name governors, Jeb Bush was a conspicuous exception. In spite of being a prime target of the Democrats in 2002, his 56 percent of the vote was 1 percentage point better than his showing in 1998.

If the congressional races were a place where voters could show their support for the national war on terrorism, the gubernatorial contests were the place to vent their dissatisfaction with economic problems and state budgetary decisions. Gubernatorial elections were also where third-party and independent candidacies were most likely to flourish in 2002. Former Democratic representative Timothy J. Penny drew 16 percent of the vote as the gubernatorial nominee of the Independence Party in Minnesota. A wealthy businessman, B. Thomas Golisano, polled 14 percent as the Independence Party candidate for governor in New York. Ed Thompson, the younger brother of former GOP governor Tommy Thompson, collected 10 percent of the vote as the Libertarian Party candidate for governor in Wisconsin. California voters gave 10 percent of their ballots to a collection of third-party candidates rather than choose between Davis and Republican Bill Simon.

There is no denying that the election of 2002 was a Republican victory. How big a victory depends on what benchmark is used:

- Compared to 1990, when Democrats still dominated at every level but the presidency, the GOP gains have been amazing.
- Compared to 1994, when Republicans scored their big breakthrough, the Republican showing in 2002 produced majorities that were not quite as decisive.
- Compared to 2000, when Democrats and Republicans played to "a perfect tie," Republican gains were incremental but significant.

In short, 2002 was an election that left the nation "leaning Republican."

The Method

The twenty-fifth volume of *America Votes* is different from its predecessors. It combines the traditional, detailed compilation of general election returns with expanded coverage of primary elections. County tables with general election results for major statewide offices have been a staple of *America Votes* in the past, but this volume for the first time includes county tables for contested primary races for governor and senator. In other respects, this *America Votes* follows the general pattern of the previous volumes in the series.

This introduction includes text and tables that tie together various aspects of the 2002 election cycle. The following section of summary tables provides the state-by-state voter turnout and vote for Senate, House, and governorship elections in the 2002 cycle. Also presented are a summary of special elections held after the general election of 2000 to fill vacancies in the 107th Congress and a list of changes in congressional membership in the 108th Congress that occurred between the 2002 general election and the end of July 2003.

Following this introductory material is the heart of the volume—50 chapters, one for each state. Each chapter begins with a list of the current governor, senators, and representatives, followed by tables of the statewide votes for president, governor, and senator from 1946 or 1948 to the present. Next is a map of the state showing counties, major population centers, and congressional districts for members of the House in the 108th Congress. Following the map are county-by-county tables of gubernatorial and Senate elections. With the exception of the governorships in New Jersey and Virginia, where voting was conducted in 2001, these tables cover the 2002 general election.

Virtually all the county tables for gubernatorial and Senate elections feature three columns representing Republican, Democratic, and Other. The exceptions are elections in which an individual independent or third-party candidate received at least 10 percent of the vote, in which case a column for their votes is also included. All the county tables include 2000 population numbers from the Census Bureau.

The county tables are followed by a list of votes cast for candidates for the House of Representatives, arranged by congressional district. The implementation of the 2000 Census for redistricting purposes led to changes in all multimember states before the 2002 election, with the exception of Maine, which drew new congressional district lines after 2002. Votes for House members are for the districts as defined for the 108th Congress. Results for elections before 2002 are included only for states with a single member in the House.

The last pages of each state chapter consist of two parts. The first part is the note section, containing a breakdown of votes cast in the general election for third-party, independent, and write-in candidates. For those major party candidates who also ran on a third-party ballot line, votes are aggregated as Democratic or Republican. Blank spaces by a contest indicate that there were no votes cast in these categories. The second part provides official results of the primary elections for governor, Senate, and House held in the 2002 election cycle, along with a new feature—county tables for contested gubernatorial and Senate primaries. As in the general election tables, these include all candidates who received at least 10 percent of the vote. In the chapters for New England states, tables list the votes for governor and senator by larger cities and towns as well as by counties. For Rhode Island, the results are listed for all cities and towns.

America Votes is compiled from official results obtained from election authorities in each state. Although complete accuracy is always the goal, it can sometimes prove elusive in a work such as this. On occasion, states may belatedly report changes in their vote totals after publication of the volume. Also on occasion, a particular return may not make sense. For instance, in the 2002 Republican gubernatorial primary in Arkansas, incumbent Mike Huckabee received at least 79.3 percent of the vote in every county except one, Ashley, where he collected a mere 9.8 percent of the vote against his little-known challenger. The vote was probably a transposition, but it was the result certified and therefore appears in this edition. As always, we want this book to be without peer in comprehensively meeting the needs of its users. Suggestions regarding new materials, together with any corrections of data, are welcome. Please direct comments to rhodescook@aol.com.

As in the preparation of *America Votes 23* and *America Votes 24*, thanks are in order to Eileen J. Canavan of the Federal Election Commission, with whom the author consulted in an effort to reconcile discrepancies in vote totals. Thanks also to Shana Wagger at CQ Press, along with several other CQ Press staff members: Gwenda Larsen and Joan Gossett, who helped edit and shepherd the day-to-day movement of copy with skill and good humor, and Grace Hill and January Layman-Wood, who researched election results in a number of troublesome states.

A special note of thanks is due David Tarr, the recently retired executive editor of CQ Press, who has been involved with *America Votes* longer than anyone except its original authors, Richard M. Scammon and Alice V. McGillivray. Over the years, David's good grace, keen eye, and deep knowledge of the electoral process have repeatedly steered these election volumes to successful completion.

Rhodes Cook
August 2003

ERRATA

America Votes 24

The following corrections should be made in the previous edition of *America Votes,* covering the 2000 election cycle.

Page x. The chart of "2000: Close House Races" should include Republican Mike Rogers, Mich. 8, who was elected with 48.8 percent of the total vote. His name should be accompanied by an asterisk (*), indicating that he won his first election to the House in 2000. With the addition of Rogers, 26 House members were elected in 2000 with less than 52 percent of the total vote.

Page 1. The voting age population excluding states without registration in 2000 was 199,360,000.

Page 6. Senate candidate Mel Carnahan (D) of Missouri was killed in a plane crash October 16, 2000.

Page 9. The far right-hand column of vote percentages in the 2000 presidential election should be labeled "Green."

Page 42. In the 2000 Texas Republican presidential primary, Steve Forbes received 2,865 votes (0.3 percent of the total), and "Other" received 13,876 votes (1.2 percent of the total).

Page 43. In the 2000 Oregon Republican presidential primary, 10,545 votes were received by "Other" (3.0 percent of the total), not Steve Forbes. The total nationwide vote received by Forbes in all the Republican presidential primaries in 2000 was 121,829, with 157,424 votes for "Other."

Page 51. In the Alabama 7th CD, the runner-up in the Democratic primary was "Artur" Davis.

Page 89. In the California 18th CD, the total number of votes cast for Democratic candidates in the primary was 86,685. Gary A. Condit received 92.1 percent of the votes; Rodger McAfee received 7.1 percent.

Page 238. In the Minnesota Senate results table, the last name of the Republican candidate in 2000 should be spelled "Grams."

Page 253. The last name of the Republican House candidate in the Mississippi 5th CD in 1998 and 2000 should be spelled "McDonnell."

Page 310. In the New York presidential results table, the Democrats carried the state by 1,704,323 votes in the 2000 election.

Page 468. In the Washington 7th CD, Jim McDermott received 100 percent of the vote in the Democratic primary.

VOTER TURNOUT

State	2002 Voting Age Population	Registration— General Electon	Percentage Voting Age Registered	U.S. House Vote	House Vote as Percent of		Senate	Governor	Largest Vote	Largest vote as Percent of Voting Age
					Voting Age Population	Registered Voters				
Alabama	3,397,000	2,356,423	69.4%	1,268,802	37.4%	53.8%	1,353,023	1,367,053	G	40.2%
Alaska	438,000	460,855	105.2%	227,725	52.0%	49.4%	229,548	231,484	G	52.9%
Arizona	3,960,000	2,229,180	56.3%	1,194,400	30.2%	53.6%	—	1,226,111	G	31.0%
Arkansas	2,031,000	1,579,254	77.8%	688,276	33.9%	43.6%	803,959	805,696	G	39.7%
California	25,849,000	15,167,159	58.7%	7,258,417	28.1%	47.9%	—	7,476,311	G	28.9%
Colorado	3,392,000	2,890,218	85.2%	1,397,070	41.2%	48.3%	1,416,082	1,412,602	S	41.7%
Connecticut	2,534,000	1,995,684	78.8%	989,309	39.0%	49.6%	—	1,022,998	G	40.4%
Delaware	608,000	519,727	85.5%	228,405	37.6%	43.9%	232,314	—	S	38.2%
Florida	12,789,000	9,302,360	72.7%	3,766,558	29.5%	40.5%	—	5,100,581	G	39.9%
Georgia	6,354,000	3,715,263	58.5%	1,918,297	30.2%	51.6%	2,030,608	2,027,177	S	32.0%
Hawaii	919,000	676,242	73.6%	359,984	39.2%	53.2%	—	382,110	G	41.6%
Idaho	986,000	679,535	68.9%	405,023	41.1%	59.6%	408,544	411,477	G	41.7%
Illinois	9,327,000	7,025,999	75.3%	3,429,136	36.8%	48.8%	3,486,851	3,538,891	G	37.9%
Indiana	4,576,000	4,144,703	90.6%	1,521,353	33.2%	36.7%	—	—	H	33.2%
Iowa	2,230,000	1,954,801	87.7%	1,012,622	45.4%	51.8%	1,023,075	1,025,802	G	46.0%
Kansas	2,013,000	1,615,699	80.3%	829,890	41.2%	51.4%	776,850	835,692	G	41.5%
Kentucky	3,143,000	2,649,084	84.3%	1,094,242	34.8%	41.3%	1,131,475	—	S	36.0%
Louisiana	3,299,000	2,806,202	85.1%	1,140,163	34.6%	40.6%	1,235,296	—	S	37.4%
Maine	993,000	950,059	95.7%	495,294	49.9%	52.1%	504,899	505,190	G	50.9%
Maryland	4,004,000	2,733,357	68.3%	1,661,918	41.5%	60.8%	—	1,706,179	G	42.6%
Massachusetts	4,897,000	3,972,651	81.1%	1,840,871	37.6%	46.3%	2,006,758	2,194,179	G	44.8%
Michigan	7,424,000	6,797,293	91.6%	3,055,897	41.2%	46.0%	3,129,287	3,177,565	G	42.8%
Minnesota	3,741,000	3,187,406	85.2%	2,201,638	58.9%	69.1%	2,254,639	2,252,473	S	60.3%
Mississippi	2,126,000	1,865,382	87.7%	677,636	31.9%	36.3%	630,495	—	H	31.9%
Missouri	4,257,000	3,681,844	86.5%	1,853,563	43.5%	50.3%	1,877,620	—	S	44.1%
Montana	686,000	624,548	91.0%	331,321	48.3%	53.0%	326,537	—	H	48.3%
Nebraska	1,277,000	1,083,544	84.9%	473,814	37.1%	43.7%	480,217	480,991	G	37.7%
Nevada	1,614,000	869,801	53.9%	499,908	31.0%	57.5%	—	504,079	G	31.2%
New Hampshire	956,000	690,159	72.2%	443,443	46.4%	64.3%	447,135	442,976	S	46.8%
New Jersey	6,433,000	4,655,852	72.4%	2,006,059	31.2%	43.1%	2,112,604	2,227,165	G	34.6%
New Mexico	1,339,000	949,044	70.9%	437,524	32.7%	46.1%	483,340	484,233	G	36.2%
New York	14,463,000	11,246,362	77.8%	3,821,613	26.4%	34.0%	—	4,579,078	G	31.7%
North Carolina	6,298,000	5,034,509	79.9%	2,244,149	35.6%	44.6%	2,331,181	—	S	37.0%
North Dakota	477,000			231,030	48.4%		—	—	H	48.4%
Ohio	8,521,000	7,104,549	83.4%	3,158,023	37.1%	44.5%	—	3,228,992	G	37.9%
Oklahoma	2,611,000	2,067,911	79.2%	1,001,852	38.4%	48.4%	1,018,424	1,035,620	G	39.7%
Oregon	2,654,000	1,872,615	70.6%	1,240,315	46.7%	66.2%	1,267,221	1,260,497	S	47.7%
Pennsylvania	9,356,000	7,835,775	83.8%	3,310,313	35.4%	42.2%	—	3,583,179	G	38.3%
Rhode Island	798,000	672,950	84.3%	328,646	41.2%	48.8%	323,912	332,655	G	41.7%
South Carolina	3,128,000	2,367,368	75.7%	985,434	31.5%	41.6%	1,102,948	1,107,725	G	35.4%
South Dakota	565,000	528,195	93.5%	336,807	59.6%	63.8%	337,508	334,559	S	59.7%
Tennessee	4,413,000	3,454,527	78.3%	1,529,309	34.7%	44.3%	1,642,421	1,653,167	G	37.5%
Texas	15,708,000	12,563,459	80.0%	4,295,210	27.3%	34.2%	4,514,012	4,553,987	G	29.0%
Utah	1,587,000	1,254,994	79.1%	557,153	35.1%	44.4%	—	—	H	35.1%
Vermont	475,000	418,718	88.2%	225,476	47.5%	53.8%	—	230,161	G	48.5%
Virginia	5,527,000	4,219,956	76.4%	1,516,482	27.4%	35.9%	1,489,422	1,886,721	G	34.1%
Washington	4,531,000	3,251,165	71.8%	1,739,116	38.4%	53.5%	—	—	H	38.4%
West Virginia	1,409,000	1,060,892	75.3%	399,949	28.4%	37.7%	436,183	—	S	31.0%
Wisconsin	4,073,000			1,637,546	40.2%		—	1,775,349	G	43.6%
Wyoming	371,000	241,200	65.0%	182,152	49.1%	75.5%	183,280	185,459	G	50.0%
	214,557,000	159,024,473	74.1%	73,449,133	34.2%	46.2%	43,027,668	66,586,164		

Voting age population excluding states without registration 210,007,000

Note: Registration and voting age population figures are for the fall of 2002. However, gubernatorial races in New Jersey and Virginia were held in fall 2001. The Louisiana Senate vote is for a runoff held December 7, 2002.

Sources: Registration figures—Committee for the Study of the American Electorate. Voting Age Population—U.S. Census Bureau

GUBERNATORIAL ELECTIONS 2001 AND 2002

State	Total Vote	Republican		Democratic		Other Vote	Rep.-Dem. Plurality	Percentage Total Vote Rep.	Dem.	Major Vote Rep.	Dem.
		Vote	Candidate	Vote	Candidate						
Alabama	1,367,053	672,225	Riley, Bob	669,105	Siegelman, Don	25,723	3,120 R	49.2%	48.9%	50.1%	49.9%
Alaska	231,484	129,279	Murkowski, Frank H.	94,216	Ulmer, Fran	7,989	35,063 R	55.8%	40.7%	57.8%	42.2%
Arizona	1,226,111	554,465	Salmon, Matt	566,284	Napolitano, Janet	105,362	11,819 D	45.2%	46.2%	49.5%	50.5%
Arkansas	805,696	427,082	Huckabee, Mike	378,250	Fisher, Jimmie Lou	364	48,832 R	53.0%	46.9%	53.0%	47.0%
California	7,476,311	3,169,801	Simon, Bill	3,533,490	Davis, Gray	773,020	363,689 D	42.4%	47.3%	47.3%	52.7%
Colorado	1,412,602	884,583	Owens, Bill	475,373	Heath, Rollie	52,646	409,210 R	62.6%	33.7%	65.0%	35.0%
Connecticut	1,022,998	573,958	Rowland, John G.	448,984	Curry, Bill	56	124,974 R	56.1%	43.9%	56.1%	43.9%
Florida	5,100,581	2,856,845	Bush, Jeb	2,201,427	McBride, Bill	42,309	655,418 R	56.0%	43.2%	56.5%	43.5%
Georgia	2,027,177	1,041,700	Perdue, Sonny	937,070	Barnes, Roy	48,407	104,630 R	51.4%	46.2%	52.6%	47.4%
Hawaii	382,110	197,009	Lingle, Linda	179,647	Hirono, Mazie K.	5,454	17,362 R	51.6%	47.0%	52.3%	47.7%
Idaho	411,477	231,566	Kempthorne, Dirk	171,711	Brady, Jerry M.	8,200	59,855 R	56.3%	41.7%	57.4%	42.6%
Ilinois	3,538,891	1,594,960	Ryan, Jim	1,847,040	Blagojevich, Rod R.	96,891	252,080 D	45.1%	52.2%	46.3%	53.7%
Iowa	1,025,802	456,612	Gross, Doug	540,449	Vilsack, Tom	28,741	83,837 D	44.5%	52.7%	45.8%	54.2%
Kansas	835,692	376,830	Shallenburger, Tim	441,858	Sebelius, Kathleen	17,004	65,028 D	45.1%	52.9%	46.0%	54.0%
Maine	505,190	209,496	Cianchette, Peter E.	238,179	Baldacci, John	57,515	28,683 D	41.5%	47.1%	46.8%	53.2%
Maryland	1,706,179	879,592	Ehrlich, Robert L. Jr.	813,422	Townsend, Kathleen Kennedy	13,165	66,170 R	51.6%	47.7%	52.0%	48.0%
Massachusetts	2,194,179	1,091,988	Romney, Mitt	985,981	O'Brien, Shannon P.	116,210	106,007 R	49.8%	44.9%	52.6%	47.4%
Michigan	3,177,565	1,506,104	Posthumus, Dick	1,633,796	Granholm, Jennifer M.	37,665	127,692 D	47.4%	51.4%	48.0%	52.0%
Minnesota	2,252,473	999,473	Pawlenty, Tim	821,268	Moe, Roger D.	431,732	178,205 R	44.4%	36.5%	54.9%	45.1%
Nebraska	480,991	330,349	Johanns, Mike	132,348	Dean, Stormy	18,294	198,001 R	68.7%	27.5%	71.4%	28.6%
Nevada	504,079	344,001	Guinn, Kenny	110,935	Neal, Joe	49,143	233,066 R	68.2%	22.0%	75.6%	24.4%
New Hampshire	442,976	259,663	Benson, Craig	169,277	Fernald, Mark	14,036	90,386 R	58.6%	38.2%	60.5%	39.5%
New Jersey (1)	2,227,165	928,174	Schundler, Bret	1,256,853	McGreevey, James E.	42,138	328,679 D	41.7%	56.4%	42.5%	57.5%
New Mexico	484,233	189,074	Sanchez, John A.	268,693	Richardson, Bill	26,466	79,619 D	39.0%	55.5%	41.3%	58.7%
New York	4,579,078	2,262,255	Pataki, George E.	1,534,064	McCall, H. Carl	782,759	728,191 R	49.4%	33.5%	59.6%	40.4%
Ohio	3,228,992	1,865,007	Taft, Bob	1,236,924	Hagan, Timothy	127,061	628,083 R	57.8%	38.3%	60.1%	39.9%
Oklahoma	1,035,620	441,277	Largent, Steve	448,143	Henry, Brad	146,200	6,866 D	42.6%	43.3%	49.6%	50.4%
Oregon	1,260,497	581,785	Mannix, Kevin L.	618,004	Kulongoski, Theodore R.	60,708	36,219 D	46.2%	49.0%	48.5%	51.5%
Pennsylvania	3,583,179	1,589,408	Fisher, Mike	1,913,235	Rendell, Edward G.	80,536	323,827 D	44.4%	53.4%	45.4%	54.6%
Rhode Island	332,655	181,827	Carcieri, Donald L.	150,229	York, Myrth	599	31,598 R	54.7%	45.2%	54.8%	45.2%
South Carolina	1,107,725	585,422	Sanford, Mark	521,140	Hodges, Jim	1,163	64,282 R	52.8%	47.0%	52.9%	47.1%
South Dakota	334,559	189,920	Rounds, Mike	140,263	Abbott, Jim	4,376	49,657 R	56.8%	41.9%	57.5%	42.5%
Tennessee	1,653,167	786,803	Hilleary, Van	837,284	Bredesen, Phil	29,080	50,481 D	47.6%	50.6%	48.4%	51.6%
Texas	4,553,987	2,632,591	Perry, Rick	1,819,798	Sanchez, Tony	101,598	812,793 R	57.8%	40.0%	59.1%	40.9%
Vermont	230,161	103,436	Douglas, Jim	97,565	Racine, Doug	29,160	5,871 R	44.9%	42.4%	51.5%	48.5%
Virginia (1)	1,886,721	887,234	Earley, Mark L.	984,177	Warner, Mark	15,310	96,943 D	47.0%	52.2%	47.4%	52.6%
Wisconsin	1,775,349	734,779	McCallum, Scott	800,515	Doyle, James E.	240,055	65,736 D	41.4%	45.1%	47.9%	52.1%
Wyoming	185,459	88,873	Bebout, Eli	92,662	Freudenthal, Dave	3,924	3,789 D	47.9%	50.0%	49.0%	51.0%
	66,586,164	32,835,446		30,109,659		3,641,059	2,725,787 R	49.3%	45.2%	52.2%	47.8%

(1) 2001 election

SENATE ELECTIONS 2002

State	Total Vote	Republican		Democratic		Other Vote	Rep.-Dem. Plurality	Percentage			
								Total Vote		Major Vote	
		Vote	Candidate	Vote	Candidate			Rep.	Dem.	Rep.	Dem.
Alabama	1,353,023	792,561	Sessions, Jeff	538,878	Parker, Susan	21,584	253,683 R	58.6%	39.8%	59.5%	40.5%
Alaska	229,548	179,438	Stevens, Ted	24,133	Vondersaar, Frank	25,977	155,305 R	78.2%	10.5%	88.1%	11.9%
Arkansas	803,959	370,653	Hutchinson, Tim	433,306	Pryor, Mark		62,653 D	46.1%	53.9%	46.1%	53.9%
Colorado	1,416,082	717,893	Allard, Wayne	648,130	Strickland, Tom	50,059	69,763 R	50.7%	45.8%	52.6%	47.4%
Delaware	232,314	94,793	Clatworthy, Raymond J.	135,253	Biden, Joseph R. Jr.	2,268	40,460 D	40.8%	58.2%	41.2%	58.8%
Georgia	2,030,608	1,071,464	Chambliss, Saxby	932,156	Cleland, Max	26,988	139,308 R	52.8%	45.9%	53.5%	46.5%
Idaho	408,544	266,215	Craig, Larry E.	132,975	Blinken, Alan	9,354	133,240 R	65.2%	32.5%	66.7%	33.3%
Illinois	3,486,851	1,325,703	Durkin, Jim	2,103,766	Durbin, Richard J.	57,382	778,063 D	38.0%	60.3%	38.7%	61.3%
Iowa	1,023,075	447,892	Ganske, Greg	554,278	Harkin, Tom	20,905	106,386 D	43.8%	54.2%	44.7%	55.3%
Kansas	776,850	641,075	Roberts, Pat		—	135,775	641,075 R	82.5%		100.0%	
Kentucky	1,131,475	731,679	McConnell, Mitch	399,634	Weinberg, Lois Combs	162	332,045 R	64.7%	35.3%	64.7%	35.3%
Louisiana	1,235,296	596,642	Terrell, Suzanne Haik	638,654	Landrieu, Mary L.		42,012 D	48.3%	51.7%	48.3%	51.7%
Maine	504,899	295,041	Collins, Susan	209,858	Pingree, Chellie		85,183 R	58.4%	41.6%	58.4%	41.6%
Massachusetts	2,006,758		—	1,605,976	Kerry, John	400,782	1,605,976 D		80.0%		100.0%
Michigan	3,129,287	1,185,545	Raczkowski, Andrew	1,896,614	Levin, Carl	47,128	711,069 D	37.9%	60.6%	38.5%	61.5%
Minnesota	2,254,639	1,116,697	Coleman, Norm	1,067,246	Mondale, Walter F.	70,696	49,451 R	49.5%	47.3%	51.1%	48.9%
Mississippi	630,495	533,269	Cochran, Thad		—	97,226	533,269 R	84.6%		100.0%	
Missouri (S)	1,877,620	935,032	Talent, Jim	913,778	Carnahan, Jean	28,810	21,254 R	49.8%	48.7%	50.6%	49.4%
Montana	326,537	103,611	Taylor, Mike	204,853	Baucus, Max	18,073	101,242 D	31.7%	62.7%	33.6%	66.4%
Nebraska	480,217	397,438	Hagel, Chuck	70,290	Matulka, Charlie A.	12,489	327,148 R	82.8%	14.6%	85.0%	15.0%
New Hampshire	447,135	227,229	Sununu, John E.	207,478	Shaheen, Jeanne	12,428	19,751 R	50.8%	46.4%	52.3%	47.7%
New Jersey	2,112,604	928,439	Forrester, Douglas R.	1,138,193	Lautenberg, Frank R.	45,972	209,754 D	43.9%	53.9%	44.9%	55.1%
New Mexico	483,340	314,301	Domenici, Pete V.	169,039	Tristani, Gloria		145,262 R	65.0%	35.0%	65.0%	35.0%
North Carolina	2,331,181	1,248,664	Dole, Elizabeth	1,047,983	Bowles, Erskine B.	34,534	200,681 R	53.6%	45.0%	54.4%	45.6%
Oklahoma	1,018,424	583,579	Inhofe, James M.	369,789	Walters, David	65,056	213,790 R	57.3%	36.3%	61.2%	38.8%
Oregon	1,267,221	712,287	Smith, Gordon H.	501,898	Bradbury, Bill	53,036	210,389 R	56.2%	39.6%	58.7%	41.3%
Rhode Island	323,912	69,881	Tingle, Robert G.	253,922	Reed, Jack	109	184,041 D	21.6%	78.4%	21.6%	78.4%
South Carolina	1,102,948	600,010	Graham, Lindsey	487,359	Sanders, Alex	15,579	112,651 R	54.4%	44.2%	55.2%	44.8%
South Dakota	337,508	166,957	Thune, John	167,481	Johnson, Tim	3,070	524 D	49.5%	49.6%	49.9%	50.1%
Tennessee	1,642,421	891,420	Alexander, Lamar	728,295	Clement, Bob	22,706	163,125 R	54.3%	44.3%	55.0%	45.0%
Texas	4,514,012	2,496,243	Cornyn, John	1,955,758	Kirk, Ron	62,011	540,485 R	55.3%	43.3%	56.1%	43.9%
Virginia	1,489,422	1,229,894	Warner, John W.		—	259,528	1,229,894 R	82.6%		100.0%	
West Virginia	436,183	160,902	Wolfe, Jay	275,281	Rockefeller, John D. IV		114,379 D	36.9%	63.1%	36.9%	63.1%
Wyoming	183,280	133,710	Enzi, Michael B.	49,570	Corcoran, Joyce Jansa		84,140 R	73.0%	27.0%	73.0%	27.0%
	43,027,668	21,566,157		19,861,824		1,599,687	1,704,333 R	50.1%	46.2%	52.1%	47.9%

S—Short term

Note: The Louisiana vote reflects the result of a runoff held December 7, 2002. No candidate received the majority required by state law in the first round of voting in November.

HOUSE ELECTIONS 2002

State	Seats Won		Total Vote	Republican	Democratic	Other	Rep.-Dem. Plurality	Percentage			
								Total Vote		Major Vote	
	Republican	Democratic						Rep.	Dem.	Rep.	Dem.
Alabama	5	2	1,268,802	694,606	507,117	67,079	187,489 R	54.7%	40.0%	57.8%	42.2%
Alaska	1		227,725	169,685	39,357	18,683	130,328 R	74.5%	17.3%	81.2%	18.8%
Arizona	6	2	1,194,400	681,922	472,135	40,343	209,787 R	57.1%	39.5%	59.1%	40.9%
Arkansas	1	3	688,276	283,739	392,086	12,451	108,347 D	41.2%	57.0%	42.0%	58.0%
California	20	33	7,258,417	3,225,666	3,731,081	301,670	505,415 D	44.4%	51.4%	46.4%	53.6%
Colorado	5	2	1,397,070	752,998	589,463	54,609	163,535 R	53.9%	42.2%	56.1%	43.9%
Connecticut	3	2	989,309	465,982	509,036	14,291	43,054 D	47.1%	51.5%	47.8%	52.2%
Delaware	1		228,405	164,605	61,011	2,789	103,594 R	72.1%	26.7%	73.0%	27.0%
Florida	18	7	3,766,558	2,161,349	1,537,124	68,085	624,225 R	57.4%	40.8%	58.4%	41.6%
Georgia	8	5	1,918,297	1,104,162	814,024	111	290,138 R	57.6%	42.4%	57.6%	42.4%
Hawaii		2	359,984	116,693	232,344	10,947	115,651 D	32.4%	64.5%	33.4%	66.6%
Idaho	2		405,023	256,348	138,038	10,637	118,310 R	63.3%	34.1%	65.0%	35.0%
Illinois	10	9	3,429,136	1,657,183	1,740,541	31,412	83,358 D	48.3%	50.8%	48.8%	51.2%
Indiana	6	3	1,521,353	840,694	640,568	40,091	200,126 R	55.3%	42.1%	56.8%	43.2%
Iowa	4	1	1,012,622	546,382	453,550	12,690	92,832 R	54.0%	44.8%	54.6%	45.4%
Kansas	3	1	829,890	536,026	259,911	33,953	276,115 R	64.6%	31.3%	67.3%	32.7%
Kentucky	5	1	1,094,242	693,860	350,924	49,458	342,936 R	63.4%	32.1%	66.4%	33.6%
Louisiana	4	3	1,140,163	640,205	358,027	141,931	282,178 R	56.2%	31.4%	64.1%	35.9%
Maine		2	495,294	205,780	289,514		83,734 D	41.5%	58.5%	41.5%	58.5%
Maryland	2	6	1,661,918	752,911	904,250	4,757	151,339 D	45.3%	54.4%	45.4%	54.6%
Massachusetts		10	1,840,871	290,484	1,528,634	21,753	1,238,150 D	15.8%	83.0%	16.0%	84.0%
Michigan	9	6	3,055,897	1,474,178	1,507,174	74,545	32,996 D	48.2%	49.3%	49.4%	50.6%
Minnesota	4	4	2,201,638	1,029,612	1,097,911	74,115	68,299 D	46.8%	49.9%	48.4%	51.6%
Mississippi	2	2	677,636	338,817	320,157	18,662	18,660 R	50.0%	47.2%	51.4%	48.6%
Missouri	5	4	1,853,563	985,905	829,177	38,481	156,728 R	53.2%	44.7%	54.3%	45.7%
Montana	1		331,321	214,100	108,233	8,988	105,867 R	64.6%	32.7%	66.4%	33.6%
Nebraska	3		473,814	386,869	46,843	40,102	340,026 R	81.6%	9.9%	89.2%	10.8%
Nevada	2	1	499,908	301,100	171,160	27,648	129,940 R	60.2%	34.2%	63.8%	36.2%
New Hampshire	2		443,443	254,797	175,905	12,741	78,892 R	57.5%	39.7%	59.2%	40.8%
New Jersey	6	7	2,006,059	933,964	1,030,204	41,891	96,240 D	46.6%	51.4%	47.6%	52.4%
New Mexico	2	1	437,524	175,342	262,100	82	86,758 D	40.1%	59.9%	40.1%	59.9%
New York	10	19	3,821,613	1,770,532	1,924,769	126,312	154,237 D	46.3%	50.4%	47.9%	52.1%
North Carolina	7	6	2,244,149	1,209,033	970,716	64,400	238,317 R	53.9%	43.3%	55.5%	44.5%
North Dakota		1	231,030	109,957	121,073		11,116 D	47.6%	52.4%	47.6%	52.4%
Ohio	12	6	3,158,023	1,775,555	1,331,614	50,854	443,941 R	56.2%	42.2%	57.1%	42.9%
Oklahoma	4	1	1,001,852	546,832	391,927	63,093	154,905 R	54.6%	39.1%	58.3%	41.7%
Oregon	1	4	1,240,315	528,997	676,920	34,398	147,923 D	42.7%	54.6%	43.9%	56.1%
Pennsylvania	12	7	3,310,313	1,859,270	1,348,665	102,378	510,605 R	56.2%	40.7%	58.0%	42.0%
Rhode Island		2	328,646	97,137	224,676	6,833	127,539 D	29.6%	68.4%	30.2%	69.8%
South Carolina	4	2	985,434	569,537	346,876	69,021	222,661 R	57.8%	35.2%	62.1%	37.9%
South Dakota	1		336,807	180,023	153,656	3,128	26,367 R	53.4%	45.6%	54.0%	46.0%
Tennessee	4	5	1,529,309	770,514	708,290	50,505	62,224 R	50.4%	46.3%	52.1%	47.9%
Texas	15	17	4,295,210	2,290,723	1,885,178	119,309	405,545 R	53.3%	43.9%	54.9%	45.1%
Utah	2	1	557,153	321,986	221,401	13,766	100,585 R	57.8%	39.7%	59.3%	40.7%
Vermont*			225,476	72,813		152,663	72,067 I	32.3%		64.3%	
Virginia	8	3	1,516,482	1,007,749	440,478	68,255	567,271 R	66.5%	29.0%	69.6%	30.4%
Washington	3	6	1,739,116	778,922	907,440	52,754	128,518 D	44.8%	52.2%	46.2%	53.8%
West Virginia	1	2	399,949	135,505	264,124	320	128,619 D	33.9%	66.0%	33.9%	66.1%
Wisconsin	4	4	1,637,546	889,146	676,925	71,475	212,221 R	54.3%	41.3%	56.8%	43.2%
Wyoming	1		182,152	110,229	65,961	5,962	44,268 R	60.5%	36.2%	62.6%	37.4%
	229	205	73,449,133	37,360,424	33,758,288	2,330,421	3,602,136 R	50.9%	46.0%	52.5%	47.5%

An asterisk (*) indicates that the lone House member elected by Vermont in 2002 was an Independent.

PARTY SWITCHES, SPECIAL ELECTIONS, AND POSTELECTION CHANGES 2001–2002

Between the general elections of 2000 and 2002, there were two party switches in Congress—one each in the Senate and the House of Representatives.

PARTY SWITCHES

SENATOR

Sen. James M. Jeffords of Vermont switched from Republican to Independent at the close of business on June 5, 2001.

REPRESENTATIVE

Rep. Virgil H. Goode Jr. of the Virginia 5th District switched from Independent to Republican on August 1, 2002.

SPECIAL ELECTIONS TO THE 107th CONGRESS

Between the general election of 2000 and the end of 2002, two appointments were made to fill vacancies in the Senate and nine special elections were held to fill vacancies in the House of Representatives. In addition, Democrat James A. Traficant Jr. of the Ohio 17th District was expelled from the House on July 24, 2002, after his conviction on bribery, tax evasion, and fraud charges, and Democrat Tony P. Hall of the Ohio 3rd District resigned his seat on September 9, 2002, to become U.S. ambassador to the United Nations' food and agriculture agencies. In neither case was there a special election. The Senate appointments and House special elections held to fill vacancies in the 107th Congress are listed below.

SENATORS

ALASKA

Frank H. Murkowski (R) resigned December 2, 2002, to become governor of Alaska. On December 20, 2002, he appointed his daughter, Lisa Murkowski (R), to fill the final two years of his term.

MINNESOTA

Paul Wellstone (D) died in a plane crash October 25, 2002. Dean Barkley (Independence Party) was appointed November 4, 2002, to fill the Senate seat for the remaining weeks of Wellstone's term.

REPRESENTATIVES

ARKANSAS 3rd CD

Asa Hutchinson (R) resigned August 6, 2001, to become head of the federal Drug Enforcement Administration (DEA). John Boozman (R) was elected November 20, 2001, to fill the remainder of the term.

September 25, 2001 Special Republican Primary

16,330 John Boozman; 10,431 Gunner DeLay; 9,403 Jim Hendren; 1,602 Brad Cates.

September 25, 2001 Special Democratic Primary

13,282 Mike Hathorn; 13,087 Jo Carson; 1,813 Norman "Bill" Williams Jr.

October 16, 2001 Special Republican Runoff

19,583 John Boozman; 15,029 Gunner DeLay.

October 16, 2001 Special Democratic Runoff

15,356 Mike Hathorn; 13,832 Jo Carson.

November 20, 2001 Special Election

53,308 John Boozman (R); 40,237 Mike Hathorn (D); 1,779 Sarah Marsh (Green); 420 Ralph Forbes (Freedom).

CALIFORNIA 32nd CD

Julian C. Dixon (D) died December 8, 2000. Diane Watson (D) was elected June 5, 2001, to fill the remainder of his term in the 107th Congress. The highest vote-getter in each party in the April 10, 2001, special election qualified for the June 5 voting.

April 10, 2001 Special Election (First Round)

29,524 Diane Watson (D); 23,697 Kevin Murray (D); 15,005 Nate Holden (D); 4,806 Noel Irwin Hentschel (R); 4,387 Leo James Terrell (D); 2,742 Philip A. Lowe (D); 2,315 Mike Schaefer (R); 1,407 Tad Daley (D); 1,167 Donna J. Warren (Green); 1,145 Jules Bagneris (D); 982 Mike Cyrus (R); 768 Kirsten Wonder Albrecht (D); 572 Wanda James (D); 558 Blair Hamilton Taylor (D); 514 Ezola Foster (Reform); 244 Frank Evans III (D).

CALIFORNIA 32nd CD (Continued)

June 5, 2001 Special Election Runoff

75,584 Diane Watson (D); 20,088 Noel Irwin Hentschel (R); 3,792 Donna J. Warren (Green); 1,557 Ezola Foster (Reform).

FLORiDA 1st CD

Joe Scarborough (R) resigned his seat September 6, 2001. Jeff Miller (R) was elected October 16, 2001, to fill the remainder of the term in the 107th Congress.

July 24, 2001 Special Republican Primary

24,217 Jeff Miller; 7,078 Michael C. Francisco; 6,536 Randy Knepper; 3,818 Bob Condon; 2,805 Robert "Bob" Pappas; 288 Ken Revell.

July 24, 2001 Special Democratic Primary

12,135 Steve Briese; 3,666 Chuck Lynch.

October 16, 2001 Special Election

53,247 Jeff Miller (R); 22,695 Steve Briese (D); 5,115 John G. Ralls Jr. (No Party Affiliation); 10 Tom Wells (write-in); 4 Floyd Miller (write-in).

HAWAII 2nd CD

Patsy T. Mink (D) died September 28, 2002. Ed Case (D) was elected November 30, 2002, to fill the remainder of her term in the 107th Congress.

November 30, 2002 Special Election

23,576 Ed Case (D); 16,624 John F. Mink (D); 1,933 John S. Carroll (R); 942 Whitney T. Anderson (R); 449 Mark McNett (Nonpartisan); 269 Kekoa D. Kaapu (D); 229 Richard H. Haake (R); 173 Doug Fairhurst (R); 149 Kimo Kaloi (R); 136 Nick Nikhilananda (Green); 116 Solomon Naluai (D); 94 Walter R. Barnes (R); 94 Carolyn Mart Golojuch (R); 86 Clifford P. Rhodes (R); 85 Timmy Yuen (R); 83 Joe Conner (R); 69 Joseph "Papa Joe" Payne (R); 67 Brian G. Cole (D); 66 John L. Baker (D); 62 Michael Gagne (D); 55 Bob Schieve (R); 54 Ron "Whodaguy" Jacobs (Nonpartisan); 51 Lillian Lai Lam Hong (Nonpartisan); 51 Art P. Reyes (D); 47 John Mayer (Nonpartisan); 33 Jeff Mallan (Libertarian); 32 Lawrence Duquesne (Libertarian); 28 Steve Tataii (D); 27 G. "Iimz" Goodwin (Green); 27 John Parker (Nonpartisan); 27 Bill Russell (Nonpartisan); 18 Chas Collins (D); 16 John "Jack" Randall (Nonpartisan); 15 Paul Britos (D); 15 Dan A. Cole (Nonpartisan); 11 Mike Rethman (Nonpartisan); 10 S. J. Harlan (Nonpartisan); 10 Robert M. Martin Jr. (Nonpartisan).

MASSACHUSETTS 9th CD

Joe Moakley (D) died May 28, 2001. Stephen F. Lynch (D) was elected October 16, 2001, to fill the remainder of the term in the 107th Congress.

September 11, 2001 Special Republican Primary

9,013 Jo Ann Sprague; 3,789 William D. McKinney; 265 write-in.

September 11, 2001 Special Democratic Primary

44,905 Stephen F. Lynch; 32,933 Cheryl Ann Jacques; 16,818 Brian A. Joyce; 15,009 Marc R. Pacheco; 3,110 William F. Sinnott; 767 John E. Taylor; 253 William A. Ferguson Jr.; 54 write-in.

October 16, 2001 Special Election

44,943 Stephen F. Lynch (D); 22,645 Jo Ann Sprague (R); 827 Susan C. Gallagher-Long (Conservative); 510 Brock R. Satter (Socialist Workers); 253 write-in.

OKLAHOMA 1st CD

Steve Largent (R) resigned February 15, 2002, to run for governor of Oklahoma in 2002. John Sullivan (R) was elected January 8, 2002, to fill the vacancy in the 107th Congress when Largent's resignation became effective.

December 11, 2001 Special Republican Primary

19,018 John Sullivan; 12,737 Cathy Keating; 9,513 Scott Pruitt; 296 George E. Banasky; 210 Evelyn L. Rogers.

December 11, 2001 Special Democratic Primary

12,516 Doug Dodd; 1,584 James E. Lamkin.

January 8, 2002 Special Election

61,694 John Sullivan (R); 50,850 Doug Dodd (D); 1,758 Neil Mavis (Independent); 388 David Fares (Independent).

PENNSYLVANIA 9th CD

Bud Shuster (R) resigned his seat effective February 3, 2001. His son, Bill Shuster (R), was elected May 15, 2001, to fill the remainder of the term in the 107th Congress. Candidates were nominated by district party convention or by a meeting of party leaders.

May 15, 2001 Special Election

55,670 Bill Shuster (R); 47,220 H. Scott Conklin (D); 4,437 Alanna K. Hartzok (Green); 321 write-in.

SOUTH CAROLINA 2nd CD

Floyd D. Spence (R) died August 16, 2001. Joe Wilson (R) was elected December 18, 2001, to fill the remainder of the term in the 107th Congress.

October 30, 2001 Special Republican Primary

34,646 Joe Wilson; 6,784 Joe Grimaud; 1,881 Stew Butler; 1,455 Richard Chalk; 1,115 Clyde T. Cobb.

October 30, 2001 Special Democratic Primary

Brent Weaver ran unopposed for the Democratic nomination.

December 18, 2001 Special Election

40,355 Joe Wilson (R); 14,034 Brent Weaver (D); 420 Warren Eilertson (Libertarian); 404 Steve Lefemine (Constitution); 1 write-in.

VIRGINIA 4th CD

Norman Sisisky (D) died March 29, 2001. J. Randy Forbes (R) was elected June 19, 2001, to fill the remainder of the term in the 107th Congress. Candidates were nominated by district party conventions.

June 19, 2001 Special Election

70,917 J. Randy Forbes (R); 65,190 L. Louise Lucas (D); 208 write-in.

2001–2002 SPECIAL HOUSE ELECTIONS: A SUMMARY

Nine special House elections were held to fill vacancies in the 108th Congress. But only one special election resulted in partisan change, with the Virginia 4th District switching from Democratic to Republican hands. The results below are based on the decisive round of voting in each special election when the new member was elected to Congress.

District	Former Member	New Member	Date Elected	Winning Percentage	Voter Turnout
Arkansas 3rd	Asa Hutchinson (R)	John Boozman (R)	November 20, 2001	55.7%	95,744
California 32nd	Julian C. Dixon (D)	Diane Watson (D)	June 5, 2001	74.8%	101,021
Florida 1st	Joe Scarborough (R)	Jeff Miller (R)	October 16, 2001	65.7%	81,071
Hawaii 2nd	Patsy T. Mink (D)	Ed Case (D)	November 30, 2002	51.4%	45,829
Massachusetts 9th	Joe Moakley (D)	Stephen F. Lynch (D)	October 16, 2001	65.0%	69,178
Oklahoma 1st	Steve Largent (R)	John Sullivan (R)	January 8, 2002	53.8%	114,690
Pennsylvania 9th	Bud Shuster (R)	Bill Shuster (R)	May 15, 2001	51.7%	107,648
South Carolina 2nd	Floyd D. Spence (R)	Joe Wilson (R)	December 18, 2001	73.1%	55,214
Virginia 4th	Norman Sisisky (D)	J. Randy Forbes (R)	June 19, 2001	52.0%	136,315

CHANGES FOLLOWING THE 2002 ELECTION

Following the 2002 general election, and through July 31, 2003, the following changes took place in the membership of the 108th Congress.

SENATOR

Alaska—Frank H. Murkowski (R) resigned December 2, 2002, to become governor of Alaska. On December 20, 2002, he appointed his daughter, Lisa Murkowski (R), to fill the final two years of his term.

REPRESENTATIVES

Hawaii 2nd CD—Patsy T. Mink (D) died September 28, 2002, but was posthumously elected in November 2002 to a seat in the 108th Congress. Ed Case (D) was elected January 4, 2003, to succeed her.

Texas 19th CD—Larry Combest (R) resigned May 31, 2003. Randy Neugebauer (R) was elected June 3, 2003, to succeed him.

UNITED STATES

POPULAR VOTE FOR PRESIDENT 1920 TO 2000

Year	Total Vote	Republican		Democratic		Other Vote	Plurality	Percentage			
								Total Vote		Major Vote	
		Vote	Candidate	Vote	Candidate			Rep.	Dem.	Rep.	Dem.
2000	105,396,627	50,455,156	Bush, George W.	50,992,335	Gore, Al	3,949,136	537,179 D	47.9%	48.4%	49.7%	50.3%
1996	96,277,872	39,198,755	Dole, Bob	47,402,357	Clinton, Bill	9,676,760	8,203,602 D	40.7%	49.2%	45.3%	54.7%
1992	104,425,014	39,103,882	Bush, George	44,909,326	Clinton, Bill	20,411,806	5,805,444 D	37.4%	43.0%	46.5%	53.5%
1988	91,594,809	48,886,097	Bush, George	41,809,074	Dukakis, Michael S.	899,638	7,077,023 R	53.4%	45.6%	53.9%	46.1%
1984	92,652,842	54,455,075	Reagan, Ronald	37,577,185	Mondale, Walter F.	620,582	16,877,890 R	58.8%	40.6%	59.2%	40.8%
1980	86,515,221	43,904,153	Reagan, Ronald	35,483,883	Carter, Jimmy	7,127,185	8,420,270 R	50.7%	41.0%	55.3%	44.7%
1976	81,555,889	39,147,793	Ford, Gerald R.	40,830,763	Carter, Jimmy	1,577,333	1,682,970 D	48.0%	50.1%	48.9%	51.1%
1972	77,718,554	47,169,911	Nixon, Richard M.	29,170,383	McGovern, George S.	1,378,260	17,999,528 R	60.7%	37.5%	61.8%	38.2%
1968	73,211,875	31,785,480	Nixon, Richard M.	31,275,166	Humphrey, Hubert H.	10,151,229	510,314 R	43.4%	42.7%	50.4%	49.6%
1964	70,644,592	27,178,188	Goldwater, Barry M.	43,129,566	Johnson, Lyndon B.	336,838	15,951,378 D	38.5%	61.1%	38.7%	61.3%
1960	68,838,219	34,108,157	Nixon, Richard M.	34,226,731	Kennedy, John F.	503,331	118,574 D	49.5%	49.7%	49.9%	50.1%
1956	62,026,908	35,590,472	Eisenhower, Dwight D.	26,022,752	Stevenson, Adlai E.	413,684	9,567,720 R	57.4%	42.0%	57.8%	42.2%
1952	61,550,918	33,936,234	Eisenhower, Dwight D.	27,314,992	Stevenson, Adlai E.	299,692	6,621,242 R	55.1%	44.4%	55.4%	44.6%
1948	48,793,826	21,991,291	Dewey, Thomas E.	24,179,345	Truman, Harry S.	2,623,190	2,188,054 D	45.1%	49.6%	47.6%	52.4%
1944	47,976,670	22,017,617	Dewey, Thomas E.	25,612,610	Roosevelt, Franklin D.	346,443	3,594,993 D	45.9%	53.4%	46.2%	53.8%
1940	49,900,418	22,348,480	Willkie, Wendell	27,313,041	Roosevelt, Franklin D.	238,897	4,964,561 D	44.8%	54.7%	45.0%	55.0%
1936	45,654,763	16,684,231	Landon, Alfred M.	27,757,333	Roosevelt, Franklin D.	1,213,199	11,073,102 D	36.5%	60.8%	37.5%	62.5%
1932	39,758,759	15,760,684	Hoover, Herbert C.	22,829,501	Roosevelt, Franklin D.	1,168,574	7,068,817 D	39.6%	57.4%	40.8%	59.2%
1928	36,805,951	21,437,277	Hoover, Herbert C.	15,007,698	Smith, Alfred E.	360,976	6,429,579 R	58.2%	40.8%	58.8%	41.2%
1924	29,095,023	15,719,921	Coolidge, Calvin	8,386,704	Davis, John W.	4,988,398	7,333,217 R	54.0%	28.8%	65.2%	34.8%
1920	26,768,613	16,153,115	Harding, Warren G.	9,133,092	Cox, James M.	1,482,406	7,020,023 R	60.3%	34.1%	63.9%	36.1%

For detail of Other Vote, see notes under "Postwar Vote for President" in each state chapter of the volume.

ELECTORAL COLLEGE VOTE 1920 TO 2000

Year	Total	Republican	Democratic	Other	
2000	538	271	266	1	(Blank)
1996	538	159	379	—	
1992	538	168	370	—	
1988	538	426	111	1	Bentsen
1984	538	525	13	—	
1980	538	489	49	—	
1976	538	240	297	1	Reagan
1972	538	520	17	1	Libertarian (Hospers)
1968	538	301	191	46	American Independent Party (Wallace)
1964	538	52	486	—	
1960	537	219	303	15	Byrd
1956	531	457	73	1	Jones
1952	531	442	89	—	
1948	531	189	303	39	States' Rights (Thurmond)
1944	531	99	432	—	
1940	531	82	449	—	
1936	531	8	523	—	
1932	531	59	472	—	
1928	531	444	87	—	
1924	531	382	136	13	Progressive (La Follette)
1920	531	404	127	—	

ALABAMA

GOVERNOR
Bob Riley (R). Elected 2002 to a four-year term.

SENATORS (2 Republicans)
Jeff Sessions (R). Reelected 2002 to a six-year term. Previously elected 1996.

Richard C. Shelby (R). Reelected 1998 to a six-year term. Previously elected 1992, 1986. Changed party affiliation from Democrat to Republican in November 1994.

REPRESENTATIVES (5 Republicans, 2 Democrats)
1. Jo Bonner (R)
2. Terry Everett (R)
3. Mike D. Rogers (R)
4. Robert B. Aderholt (R)
5. Robert E. "Bud" Cramer (D)
6. Spencer Bachus (R)
7. Artur Davis (D)

POSTWAR VOTE FOR PRESIDENT

Year	Total Vote	Republican Vote	Republican Candidate	Democratic Vote	Democratic Candidate	Other Vote	Plurality	Total Vote Rep.	Total Vote Dem.	Major Vote Rep.	Major Vote Dem.
2000**	1,666,272	941,173	Bush, George W.	692,611	Gore, Al	32,488	248,562 R	56.5%	41.6%	57.6%	42.4%
1996**	1,534,349	769,044	Dole, Bob	662,165	Clinton, Bill	103,140	106,879 R	50.1%	43.2%	53.7%	46.3%
1992**	1,688,060	804,283	Bush, George	690,080	Clinton, Bill	193,697	114,203 R	47.6%	40.9%	53.8%	46.2%
1988	1,378,476	815,576	Bush, George	549,506	Dukakis, Michael S.	13,394	266,070 R	59.2%	39.9%	59.7%	40.3%
1984	1,441,713	872,849	Reagan, Ronald	551,899	Mondale, Walter F.	16,965	320,950 R	60.5%	38.3%	61.3%	38.7%
1980**	1,341,929	654,192	Reagan, Ronald	636,730	Carter, Jimmy	51,007	17,462 R	48.8%	47.4%	50.7%	49.3%
1976	1,182,850	504,070	Ford, Gerald R.	659,170	Carter, Jimmy	19,610	155,100 D	42.6%	55.7%	43.3%	56.7%
1972	1,006,111	728,701	Nixon, Richard M.	256,923	McGovern, George S.	20,487	471,778 R	72.4%	25.5%	73.9%	26.1%
1968**	1,049,922	146,923	Nixon, Richard M.	196,579	Humphrey, Hubert H.	706,420	494,846 A	14.0%	18.7%	42.8%	57.2%
1964**	689,818	479,085	Goldwater, Barry M.		Johnson, Lyndon B.	210,733	268,353 R	69.5%		100.0%	
1960	570,225	237,981	Nixon, Richard M.	324,050	Kennedy, John F.	8,194	86,069 D	41.7%	56.8%	42.3%	57.7%
1956	496,861	195,694	Eisenhower, Dwight D.	280,844	Stevenson, Adlai E.	20,323	85,150 D	39.4%	56.5%	41.1%	58.9%
1952	426,120	149,231	Eisenhower, Dwight D.	275,075	Stevenson, Adlai E.	1,814	125,844 D	35.0%	64.6%	35.2%	64.8%
1948**	214,980	40,930	Dewey, Thomas E.		Truman, Harry S.	174,050	130,513 R	19.0%		100.0%	

In 2000 the other vote includes 18,323 votes cast for Green (Nader). In 1996 the other vote includes 92,149 votes cast for Perot. In 1992 the other vote includes 183,109 votes cast for Perot. In 1980 the other vote includes 16,481 votes for Independent (Anderson). In 1968 the other vote was 691,425 American Independent (Wallace); 10,960 American Independent of Alabama; 4,022 Prohibition and 13 scattered. In 1964 and 1948 the national Democratic candidates were not represented on the ballot. In 1964 the other vote was 210,732 Unpledged Democratic and 1 scattered. In 1948 other vote was 171,443 States Rights; 1,522 Progressive and 1,085 Prohibition.

ALABAMA

10

POSTWAR VOTE FOR GOVERNOR

Year	Total Vote	Republican Vote	Republican Candidate	Democratic Vote	Democratic Candidate	Other Vote	Rep.-Dem. Plurality	Total Vote Rep.	Total Vote Dem.	Major Vote Rep.	Major Vote Dem.
2002	1,367,053	672,225	Riley, Bob	669,105	Siegelman, Don	25,723	3,120 R	49.2%	48.9%	50.1%	49.9%
1998	1,317,842	554,746	James, Forrest H.	760,155	Siegelman, Don	2,941	205,409 D	42.1%	57.7%	42.2%	57.8%
1994	1,201,969	604,926	James, Forrest H.	594,169	Folsom, James E.	2,874	10,757 R	50.3%	49.4%	50.4%	49.6%
1990	1,216,250	633,519	Hunt, Guy	582,106	Hubbert, Paul R.	625	51,413 R	52.1%	47.9%	52.1%	47.9%
1986	1,236,230	696,203	Hunt, Guy	537,163	Baxley, Bill	2,864	159,040 R	56.3%	43.5%	56.4%	43.6%
1982	1,128,725	440,815	Folmar, Emory	650,538	Wallace, George C.	37,372	209,723 D	39.1%	57.6%	40.4%	59.6%
1978	760,474	196,963	Hunt, Guy	551,886	James, Forrest H.	11,625	354,923 D	25.9%	72.6%	26.3%	73.7%
1974	598,305	88,381	McCary, Elvin	497,574	Wallace, George C.	12,350	409,193 D	14.8%	83.2%	15.1%	84.9%
1970**	854,952		—	637,046	Wallace, George C.	217,906	637,046 D		74.5%		100.0%
1966	848,101	262,943	Martin, James D.	537,505	Wallace, Lurleen	47,653	274,562 D	31.0%	63.4%	32.8%	67.2%
1962	315,776		—	303,987	Wallace, George C.	11,789	303,987 D		96.3%		100.0%
1958	270,952	30,415	Longshore, W. L.	239,633	Patterson, John	904	209,218 D	11.2%	88.4%	11.3%	88.7%
1954	333,090	88,688	Amernethy, Tom	244,401	Folsom, James E.	1	155,713 D	26.6%	73.4%	26.6%	73.4%
1950	170,541	15,127	Crowder, John S.	155,414	Persons, Gordon		140,287 D	8.9%	91.1%	8.9%	91.1%
1946	197,324	22,362	Ward, Lyman	174,962	Folsom, James E.		152,600 D	11.3%	88.7%	11.3%	88.7%

In 1970 the other vote was 125,491 National Democratic Party of Alabama (Cashin); 75,679 Independent (Shelton); 9,705 Prohibition (Couch); 3,534 Independent (Walter) and 3,497 Whig (Watts).

POSTWAR VOTE FOR SENATOR

Year	Total Vote	Republican Vote	Republican Candidate	Democratic Vote	Democratic Candidate	Other Vote	Rep.-Dem. Plurality	Total Vote Rep.	Total Vote Dem.	Major Vote Rep.	Major Vote Dem.
2002	1,353,023	792,561	Sessions, Jeff	538,878	Parker, Susan	21,584	253,683 R	58.6%	39.8%	59.5%	40.5%
1998	1,293,405	817,973	Shelby, Richard C.	474,568	Suddith, Clayton	864	343,405 R	63.2%	36.7%	63.3%	36.7%
1996	1,499,393	786,436	Sessions, Jeff	681,651	Bedford, Roger	31,306	104,785 R	52.5%	45.5%	53.6%	46.4%
1992	1,577,799	522,015	Sellers, Richard	1,022,698	Shelby, Richard C.	33,086	500,683 D	33.1%	64.8%	33.8%	66.2%
1990	1,185,563	467,190	Cabaniss, Bill	717,814	Heflin, Howell	559	250,624 D	39.4%	60.5%	39.4%	60.6%
1986	1,211,953	602,537	Denton, Jeremiah	609,360	Shelby, Richard C.	56	6,823 D	49.7%	50.3%	49.7%	50.3%
1984	1,371,238	498,508	Smith, Albert L.	860,535	Heflin, Howell	12,195	362,027 D	36.4%	62.8%	36.7%	63.3%
1980	1,296,757	650,362	Denton, Jeremiah	610,175	Folsom, James E., Jr.	36,220	40,187 R	50.2%	47.1%	51.6%	48.4%
1978	582,025			547,054	Heflin, Howell	34,971	547,054 D		94.0%		100.0%
1978S	731,614	316,170	Martin, James D.	401,852	Stewart, Donald W.	13,592	85,682 D	43.2%	54.9%	44.0%	56.0%
1974	523,290		—	501,541	Allen, James B.	21,749	501,541 D		95.8%		100.0%
1972	1,051,099	347,523	Blount, Winston M.	654,491	Sparkman, John J.	49,085	306,968 D	33.1%	62.3%	34.7%	65.3%
1968	912,708	201,227	Hooper, Perry	638,774	Allen, James B.	72,707	437,547 D	22.0%	70.0%	24.0%	76.0%
1966	802,608	313,018	Grenier, John	482,138	Sparkman, John J.	7,452	169,120 D	39.0%	60.1%	39.4%	60.6%
1962	397,079	195,134	Martin, James D.	201,937	Hill, Lister	8	6,803 D	49.1%	50.9%	49.1%	50.9%
1960	554,081	164,868	Elgin, Julian	389,196	Sparkman, John J.	17	224,328 D	29.8%	70.2%	29.8%	70.2%
1956	330,191		—	330,182	Hill, Lister	9	330,182 D		100.0%		100.0%
1954	314,459	55,110	Guin, J. Foy	259,348	Sparkman, John J.	1	204,238 D	17.5%	82.5%	17.5%	82.5%
1950	164,011		—	125,534	Hill, Lister	38,477	125,534 D		76.5%		100.0%
1948	220,875	35,341	Parsons, Paul G.	185,534	Sparkman, John J.		150,193 D	16.0%	84.0%	16.0%	84.0%
1946S	163,217		—	163,217	Sparkman, John J.		163,217 D		100.0%		100.0%

One of the 1978 elections and the 1946 election were for short terms to fill vacancies.

ALABAMA

Congressional districts first established for elections held in 2002
7 members

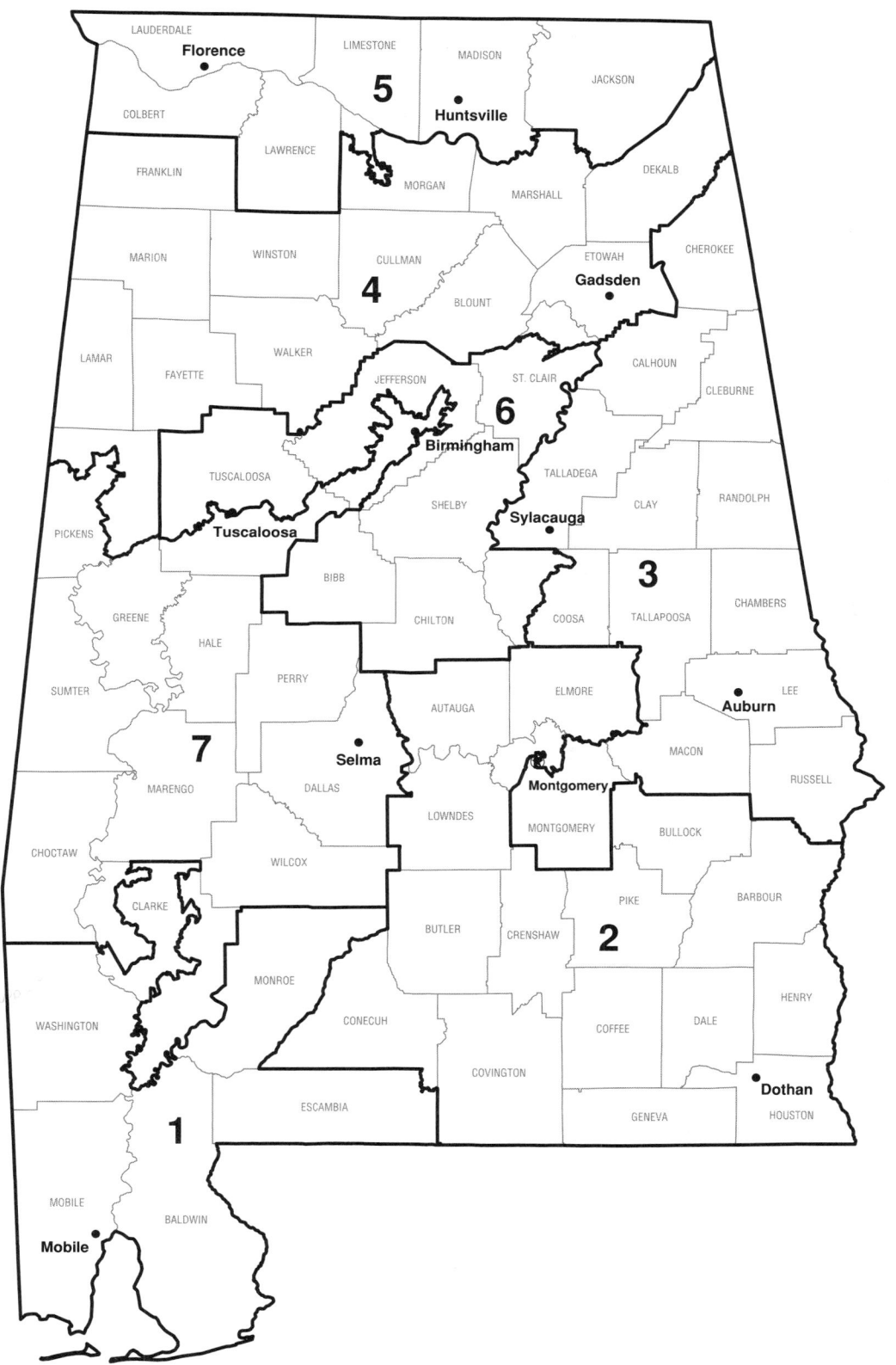

ALABAMA

GOVERNOR 2002

2000 Census Population	County	Total Vote	Republican	Democratic	Other	Rep.-Dem. Plurality	Percentage			
							Total Vote		Major Vote	
							Rep.	Dem.	Rep.	Dem.
43,671	AUTAUGA	14,800	9,345	5,137	318	4,208 R	63.1%	34.7%	64.5%	35.5%
140,415	BALDWIN	44,844	31,052	12,736	1,056	18,316 R	69.2%	28.4%	70.9%	29.1%
29,038	BARBOUR	8,153	3,183	4,858	112	1,675 D	39.0%	59.6%	39.6%	60.4%
20,826	BIBB	6,345	3,091	3,178	76	87 D	48.7%	50.1%	49.3%	50.7%
51,024	BLOUNT	15,677	8,866	6,393	418	2,473 R	56.6%	40.8%	58.1%	41.9%
11,714	BULLOCK	3,925	1,051	2,825	49	1,774 D	26.8%	72.0%	27.1%	72.9%
21,399	BUTLER	6,838	3,376	3,354	108	22 R	49.4%	49.0%	50.2%	49.8%
112,249	CALHOUN	33,418	15,190	17,718	510	2,528 D	45.5%	53.0%	46.2%	53.8%
36,583	CHAMBERS	9,724	4,837	4,767	120	70 R	49.7%	49.0%	50.4%	49.6%
23,988	CHEROKEE	6,096	2,489	3,500	107	1,011 D	40.8%	57.4%	41.6%	58.4%
39,593	CHILTON	13,698	7,787	5,679	232	2,108 R	56.8%	41.5%	57.8%	42.2%
15,922	CHOCTAW	5,104	2,287	2,780	37	493 D	44.8%	54.5%	45.1%	54.9%
27,867	CLARKE	8,895	4,563	4,245	87	318 R	51.3%	47.7%	51.8%	48.2%
14,254	CLAY	5,350	3,176	2,094	80	1,082 R	59.4%	39.1%	60.3%	39.7%
14,123	CLEBURNE	4,957	2,680	2,172	105	508 R	54.1%	43.8%	55.2%	44.8%
43,615	COFFEE	12,920	6,846	5,839	235	1,007 R	53.0%	45.2%	54.0%	46.0%
54,984	COLBERT	17,136	7,069	9,783	284	2,714 D	41.3%	57.1%	41.9%	58.1%
14,089	CONECUH	4,986	2,276	2,638	72	362 D	45.6%	52.9%	46.3%	53.7%
12,202	COOSA	4,406	1,812	2,521	73	709 D	41.1%	57.2%	41.8%	58.2%
37,631	COVINGTON	11,459	6,362	4,931	166	1,431 R	55.5%	43.0%	56.3%	43.7%
13,665	CRENSHAW	4,409	2,386	1,931	92	455 R	54.1%	43.8%	55.3%	44.7%
77,483	CULLMAN	25,859	14,049	10,974	836	3,075 R	54.3%	42.4%	56.1%	43.9%
49,129	DALE	12,006	6,717	5,106	183	1,611 R	55.9%	42.5%	56.8%	43.2%
46,365	DALLAS	16,082	5,663	10,285	134	4,622 D	35.2%	64.0%	35.5%	64.5%
64,452	DE KALB	18,390	9,502	8,547	341	955 R	51.7%	46.5%	52.6%	47.4%
65,874	ELMORE	21,220	13,834	6,830	556	7,004 R	65.2%	32.2%	66.9%	33.1%
38,440	ESCAMBIA	8,869	4,776	3,972	121	804 R	53.9%	44.8%	54.6%	45.4%
103,459	ETOWAH	31,954	13,371	17,942	641	4,571 D	41.8%	56.1%	42.7%	57.3%
18,495	FAYETTE	7,380	3,368	3,858	154	490 D	45.6%	52.3%	46.6%	53.4%
31,223	FRANKLIN	8,545	3,708	4,688	149	980 D	43.4%	54.9%	44.2%	55.8%
25,764	GENEVA	7,857	4,751	2,958	148	1,793 R	60.5%	37.6%	61.6%	38.4%
9,974	GREENE	4,266	666	3,576	24	2,910 D	15.6%	83.8%	15.7%	84.3%
17,185	HALE	6,391	1,945	4,407	39	2,462 D	30.4%	69.0%	30.6%	69.4%
16,310	HENRY	5,499	2,750	2,684	65	66 R	50.0%	48.8%	50.6%	49.4%
88,787	HOUSTON	25,492	16,183	9,018	291	7,165 R	63.5%	35.4%	64.2%	35.8%
53,926	JACKSON	12,475	5,216	7,007	252	1,791 D	41.8%	56.2%	42.7%	57.3%
662,047	JEFFERSON	215,449	92,079	119,918	3,452	27,839 D	42.7%	55.7%	43.4%	56.6%
15,904	LAMAR	5,805	2,826	2,908	71	82 D	48.7%	50.1%	49.3%	50.7%
87,966	LAUDERDALE	26,259	12,586	13,054	619	468 D	47.9%	49.7%	49.1%	50.9%
34,803	LAWRENCE	10,507	4,100	6,192	215	2,092 D	39.0%	58.9%	39.8%	60.2%
115,092	LEE	29,113	16,515	11,772	826	4,743 R	56.7%	40.4%	58.4%	41.6%
65,676	LIMESTONE	20,708	10,744	9,499	465	1,245 R	51.9%	45.9%	53.1%	46.9%
13,473	LOWNDES	5,480	1,347	4,084	49	2,737 D	24.6%	74.5%	24.8%	75.2%
24,105	MACON	6,986	919	5,987	80	5,068 D	13.2%	85.7%	13.3%	86.7%
276,700	MADISON	89,740	43,463	43,431	2,846	32 R	48.4%	48.4%	50.0%	50.0%
22,539	MARENGO	7,906	2,938	4,909	59	1,971 D	37.2%	62.1%	37.4%	62.6%
31,214	MARION	10,262	4,770	5,303	189	533 D	46.5%	51.7%	47.4%	52.6%
82,231	MARSHALL	23,543	12,508	10,426	609	2,082 R	53.1%	44.3%	54.5%	45.5%
399,843	MOBILE	109,437	56,577	50,782	2,078	5,795 R	51.7%	46.4%	52.7%	47.3%
24,324	MONROE	8,215	4,372	3,755	88	617 R	53.2%	45.7%	53.8%	46.2%
223,510	MONTGOMERY	70,504	32,254	37,109	1,141	4,855 D	45.7%	52.6%	46.5%	53.5%
111,064	MORGAN	36,268	19,461	15,983	824	3,478 R	53.7%	44.1%	54.9%	45.1%
11,861	PERRY	4,963	1,335	3,613	15	2,278 D	26.9%	72.8%	27.0%	73.0%
20,949	PICKENS	6,709	2,719	3,923	67	1,204 D	40.5%	58.5%	40.9%	59.1%
29,605	PIKE	8,336	4,357	3,846	133	511 R	52.3%	46.1%	53.1%	46.9%
22,380	RANDOLPH	7,612	4,210	3,302	100	908 R	55.3%	43.4%	56.0%	44.0%
49,756	RUSSELL	10,754	3,944	6,696	114	2,752 D	36.7%	62.3%	37.1%	62.9%
64,742	ST. CLAIR	19,835	11,443	8,026	366	3,417 R	57.7%	40.5%	58.8%	41.2%
143,293	SHELBY	49,568	33,536	14,964	1,068	18,572 R	67.7%	30.2%	69.1%	30.9%
14,798	SUMTER	5,084	1,176	3,868	40	2,692 D	23.1%	76.1%	23.3%	76.7%

ALABAMA

GOVERNOR 2002

2000 Census Population	County	Total Vote	Republican	Democratic	Other	Rep.-Dem. Plurality	Percentage			
							Total Vote		Major Vote	
							Rep.	Dem.	Rep.	Dem.
80,321	TALLADEGA	22,250	9,457	12,534	259	3,077 D	42.5%	56.3%	43.0%	57.0%
41,475	TALLAPOOSA	14,735	7,929	6,558	248	1,371 R	53.8%	44.5%	54.7%	45.3%
164,875	TUSCALOOSA	45,842	21,108	23,970	764	2,862 D	46.0%	52.3%	46.8%	53.2%
70,713	WALKER	20,847	8,595	11,857	395	3,262 D	41.2%	56.9%	42.0%	58.0%
18,097	WASHINGTON	6,228	2,814	3,323	91	509 D	45.2%	53.4%	45.9%	54.1%
13,183	WILCOX	4,614	1,302	3,284	28	1,982 D	28.2%	71.2%	28.4%	71.6%
24,843	WINSTON	8,069	4,618	3,298	153	1,320 R	57.2%	40.9%	58.3%	41.7%
4,447,100	TOTAL	1,367,053	672,225	669,105	25,723	3,120 R	49.2%	48.9%	50.1%	49.9%

ALABAMA

SENATOR 2002

2000 Census Population	County	Total Vote	Republican	Democratic	Other	Rep.-Dem. Plurality	Percentage			
							Total Vote		Major Vote	
							Rep.	Dem.	Rep.	Dem.
43,671	AUTAUGA	14,728	10,687	3,819	222	6,868 R	72.6%	35.7%	73.7%	26.3%
140,415	BALDWIN	44,758	34,327	9,525	906	24,802 R	76.7%	27.7%	78.3%	21.7%
29,038	BARBOUR	7,972	4,057	3,793	122	264 R	50.9%	93.5%	51.7%	48.3%
20,826	BIBB	6,297	3,667	2,553	77	1,114 R	58.2%	40.5%	59.0%	41.0%
51,024	BLOUNT	15,588	11,249	4,027	312	7,222 R	72.2%	25.8%	73.6%	26.4%
11,714	BULLOCK	3,560	1,141	2,372	47	1,231 D	32.1%	66.6%	32.5%	67.5%
21,399	BUTLER	6,769	3,845	2,833	91	1,012 R	56.8%	41.9%	57.6%	42.4%
112,249	CALHOUN	33,086	19,680	12,784	622	6,896 R	59.5%	38.6%	60.6%	39.4%
36,583	CHAMBERS	9,566	5,114	4,313	139	801 R	53.5%	45.1%	54.2%	45.8%
23,988	CHEROKEE	6,039	3,164	2,754	121	410 R	52.4%	45.6%	53.5%	46.5%
39,593	CHILTON	13,606	9,278	4,074	254	5,204 R	68.2%	29.9%	69.5%	30.5%
15,922	CHOCTAW	5,031	2,585	2,399	47	186 R	51.4%	47.7%	51.9%	48.1%
27,867	CLARKE	8,782	5,079	3,640	63	1,439 R	57.8%	41.4%	58.3%	41.7%
14,254	CLAY	5,212	3,329	1,791	92	1,538 R	63.9%	34.4%	65.0%	35.0%
14,123	CLEBURNE	4,751	2,931	1,656	164	1,275 R	61.7%	34.9%	63.9%	36.1%
43,615	COFFEE	12,893	9,018	3,664	211	5,354 R	69.9%	28.4%	71.1%	28.9%
54,984	COLBERT	17,089	8,377	8,446	266	69 D	49.0%	49.4%	49.8%	50.2%
14,089	CONECUH	4,882	2,442	2,345	95	97 R	50.0%	48.0%	51.0%	49.0%
12,202	COOSA	4,344	2,205	2,050	89	155 R	50.8%	47.2%	51.8%	48.2%
37,631	COVINGTON	11,355	8,011	3,149	195	4,862 R	70.6%	27.7%	71.8%	28.2%
13,665	CRENSHAW	4,364	2,722	1,585	57	1,137 R	62.4%	36.3%	63.2%	36.8%
77,483	CULLMAN	25,878	16,734	8,638	506	8,096 R	64.7%	33.4%	66.0%	34.0%
49,129	DALE	11,954	8,557	3,219	178	5,338 R	71.6%	26.9%	72.7%	27.3%
46,365	DALLAS	15,904	6,520	9,185	199	2,665 D	41.0%	57.8%	41.5%	58.5%
64,452	DE KALB	17,331	11,006	6,023	302	4,983 R	63.5%	34.8%	64.6%	35.4%
65,874	ELMORE	21,168	15,605	5,198	365	10,407 R	73.7%	24.6%	75.0%	25.0%
38,440	ESCAMBIA	8,809	5,556	3,135	118	2,421 R	63.1%	35.6%	63.9%	36.1%
103,459	ETOWAH	31,812	18,105	12,999	708	5,106 R	56.9%	40.9%	58.2%	41.8%
18,495	FAYETTE	7,263	3,998	3,104	161	894 R	55.0%	42.7%	56.3%	43.7%
31,223	FRANKLIN	8,492	4,422	3,952	118	470 R	52.1%	46.5%	52.8%	47.2%
25,764	GENEVA	7,812	6,014	1,654	144	4,360 R	77.0%	21.2%	78.4%	21.6%
9,974	GREENE	4,156	836	3,277	43	2,441 D	20.1%	78.8%	20.3%	79.7%
17,185	HALE	6,283	2,276	3,909	98	1,633 D	36.2%	62.2%	36.8%	63.2%
16,310	HENRY	5,432	3,449	1,885	98	1,564 R	63.5%	34.7%	64.7%	35.3%
88,787	HOUSTON	25,365	18,898	6,132	335	12,766 R	74.5%	24.2%	75.5%	24.5%
53,926	JACKSON	12,353	6,319	5,772	262	547 R	51.2%	46.7%	52.3%	47.7%
662,047	JEFFERSON	214,688	110,491	101,555	2,642	8,936 R	51.5%	47.3%	52.1%	47.9%
15,904	LAMAR	5,700	3,138	2,477	85	661 R	55.1%	43.5%	55.9%	44.1%
87,966	LAUDERDALE	26,230	14,183	11,669	378	2,514 R	54.1%	44.5%	54.9%	45.1%
34,803	LAWRENCE	10,491	4,542	5,793	156	1,251 D	43.3%	55.2%	43.9%	56.1%

ALABAMA

SENATOR 2002

2000 Census Population	County	Total Vote	Republican	Democratic	Other	Rep.-Dem. Plurality	Total Vote Rep.	Total Vote Dem.	Major Vote Rep.	Major Vote Dem.
115,092	LEE	28,983	17,577	10,832	574	6,745 R	60.6%	37.4%	61.9%	38.1%
65,676	LIMESTONE	20,687	11,873	8,508	306	3,365 R	57.4%	41.1%	58.3%	41.7%
13,473	LOWNDES	5,169	1,740	3,361	68	1,621 D	33.7%	65.0%	34.1%	65.9%
24,105	MACON	6,905	1,261	5,542	102	4,281 D	18.3%	80.3%	18.5%	81.5%
276,700	MADISON	89,447	55,229	32,476	1,742	22,753 R	61.7%	36.3%	63.0%	37.0%
22,539	MARENGO	7,818	3,663	4,074	81	411 D	46.9%	52.1%	47.3%	52.7%
31,214	MARION	10,206	5,760	4,265	181	1,495 R	56.4%	41.8%	57.5%	42.5%
82,231	MARSHALL	23,388	15,802	7,018	568	8,784 R	67.6%	30.0%	69.2%	30.8%
399,843	MOBILE	106,411	64,135	40,454	1,822	23,681 R	60.3%	38.0%	61.3%	38.7%
24,324	MONROE	8,132	4,972	3,058	102	1,914 R	61.1%	37.6%	61.9%	38.1%
223,510	MONTGOMERY	68,027	35,760	31,465	802	4,295 R	52.6%	46.3%	53.2%	46.8%
111,064	MORGAN	36,384	20,958	14,903	523	6,055 R	57.6%	41.0%	58.4%	41.6%
11,861	PERRY	4,903	1,417	3,455	31	2,038 D	28.9%	70.5%	29.1%	70.9%
20,949	PICKENS	6,652	3,254	3,300	98	46 D	48.9%	49.6%	49.6%	50.4%
29,605	PIKE	8,295	5,093	3,090	112	2,003 R	61.4%	37.3%	62.2%	37.8%
22,380	RANDOLPH	7,305	4,261	2,916	128	1,345 R	58.3%	39.9%	59.4%	40.6%
49,756	RUSSELL	10,540	4,382	5,976	182	1,594 D	41.6%	56.7%	42.3%	57.7%
64,742	ST. CLAIR	19,743	13,914	5,454	375	8,460 R	70.5%	27.6%	71.8%	28.2%
143,293	SHELBY	49,516	38,614	10,215	687	28,399 R	78.0%	20.6%	79.1%	20.9%
14,798	SUMTER	5,012	1,290	3,667	55	2,377 D	25.7%	73.2%	26.0%	74.0%
80,321	TALLADEGA	22,111	11,859	9,915	337	1,944 R	53.6%	44.8%	54.5%	45.5%
41,475	TALLAPOOSA	14,568	9,048	5,288	232	3,760 R	62.1%	36.3%	63.1%	36.9%
164,875	TUSCALOOSA	45,558	25,483	19,320	755	6,163 R	55.9%	42.4%	56.9%	43.1%
70,713	WALKER	20,776	11,079	9,379	318	1,700 R	53.3%	45.1%	54.2%	45.8%
18,097	WASHINGTON	6,160	3,412	2,647	101	765 R	55.4%	43.0%	56.3%	43.7%
13,183	WILCOX	4,541	1,572	2,928	41	1,356 D	34.6%	64.5%	34.9%	65.1%
24,843	WINSTON	7,993	5,596	2,224	173	3,372 R	70.0%	27.8%	71.6%	28.4%
4,447,100	TOTAL	1,353,023	792,561	538,878	21,584	253,683 R	58.6%	39.8%	59.5%	40.5%

ALABAMA

HOUSE OF REPRESENTATIVES

CD	Year	Total Vote	Republican Vote	Republican Candidate	Democratic Vote	Democratic Candidate	Other Vote	Rep.-Dem. Plurality	Total Vote Rep.	Total Vote Dem.	Major Vote Rep.	Major Vote Dem.
1	2002	178,687	108,102	Bonner, Jo	67,507	Belk, Judy McCain	3,078	40,595 R	60.5%	37.8%	61.6%	38.4%
2	2002	187,965	129,233	Everett, Terry*	55,495	Woods, Charles	3,237	73,738 R	68.8%	29.5%	70.0%	30.0%
3	2002	181,223	91,169	Rogers, Mike D.	87,351	Turnham, Joe	2,703	3,818 R	50.3%	48.2%	51.1%	48.9%
4	2002	161,101	139,705	Aderholt, Robert B.*			21,396	139,705 R	86.7%		100.0%	
5	2002	195,171	48,226	Engel, Stephen P.	143,029	Cramer, Robert E. "Bud"*	3,916	94,803 D	24.7%	73.3%	25.2%	74.8%
6	2002	198,346	178,171	Bachus, Spencer*			20,175	178,171 R	89.8%		100.0%	
7	2002	166,309			153,735	Davis, Artur	12,574	153,735 D		92.4%		100.0%
Total	2002	1,268,802	694,606		507,117		67,079	187,489 R	54.7%	40.0%	57.8%	42.2%

An asterisk (*) denotes incumbent.

ALABAMA

GENERAL AND PRIMARY ELECTIONS

2002 GENERAL ELECTIONS

Governor   Other vote was 23,272 Libertarian (John Peter Sophocleus); 2,451 scattered write-in.

Senator   Other vote was 20,234 Libertarian (Jeff Allen); 1,350 scattered write-in.

House   Other vote was:

CD 1   2,957 Libertarian (Dick Coffee); 121 scattered write-in.
CD 2   2,948 Libertarian (Floyd Shackelford); 289 scattered write-in.
CD 3   2,565 Libertarian (George Crispin); 138 scattered write-in.
CD 4   20,858 Libertarian (Tony Hughes McLendon); 538 scattered write-in.
CD 5   3,772 Libertarian (Alan F. Barksdale); 144 scattered write-in.
CD 6   19,639 Libertarian (J. Holden McAllister); 536 scattered write-in.
CD 7   12,100 Libertarian (Lauren Orth McCay); 474 scattered write-in.

2002 PRIMARY ELECTIONS

Primary   June 4, 2002   **Registration**   2,285,757   No Party Registration
(as of June 4, 2002)

Primary Runoff June 25, 2002

Primary Type   Open—Any registered voter could vote in the primary of either party, although any voter that participated in the Republican primary could not vote in the Democratic runoff. There was no such restriction on participation in the Republican runoff.

Note: An asterisk (*) denotes incumbent. The names of unopposed candidates did not appear on the ballot; therefore, no votes were cast for these candidates.

	REPUBLICAN PRIMARIES			DEMOCRATIC PRIMARIES		
Governor	Bob Riley	262,851	73.5%	Don Siegelman*	331,571	76.2%
	Steve Windom	63,775	17.8%	Charles Bishop	80,193	18.4%
	Tim James	30,871	8.6%	Mark "Rodeo Clown" Townsend	9,890	2.3%
				Gladys Riddle	9,246	2.1%
				Blake W. Harper III	4,410	1.0%
	TOTAL	357,497		TOTAL	435,310	
Senator	Jeff Sessions*	Unopposed		Susan Parker	190,978	48.0%
				Julian McPhillips	170,222	42.8%
				Wayne Sowell	36,719	9.2%
				TOTAL	397,919	
				PRIMARY RUNOFF		
				Susan Parker	176,582	65.1%
				Julian McPhillips	94,614	34.9%
				TOTAL	271,196	

ALABAMA

GENERAL AND PRIMARY ELECTIONS

	REPUBLICAN PRIMARIES			DEMOCRATIC PRIMARIES		
Congressional District 1	Jo Bonner	29,857	40.3%	Judy McCain Belk	14,213	36.0%
	Tom Young	15,087	20.3%	J. Don Foster	9,766	24.7%
	David Whetstone	10,997	14.8%	James O. Gordon	8,128	20.6%
	Albert Lipscomb	7,429	10.0%	Don Chamberlain	3,774	9.6%
	Chris Pringle	6,001	8.1%	Buzz Jordan	3,593	9.1%
	Rusty Glover	4,374	5.9%			
	Joe J. Gottler	411	0.6%			
	TOTAL	74,156		TOTAL	39,474	
	PRIMARY RUNOFF			PRIMARY RUNOFF		
	Jo Bonner	32,421	62.4%	Judy McCain Belk	13,007	58.4%
	Tom Young	19,501	37.6%	J. Don Foster	9,254	41.6%
	TOTAL	51,922		TOTAL	22,261	
Congressional District 2	Terry Everett*	Unopposed		Charles Woods	Unopposed	
Congressional District 3	Mike D. Rogers	28,113	76.1%	Joe Turnham	30,245	52.4%
	Jason Dial	4,681	12.7%	Gerald Willis	22,336	38.7%
	Jeff Fink	4,134	11.2%	Willie "Billy" Burnett	5,139	8.9%
	TOTAL	36,928		TOTAL	57,720	
Congressional District 4	Robert B. Aderholt*	Unopposed		No Democratic candidate		
Congressional District 5	Stephen P. Engel	13,971	55.9%	Robert E. "Bud" Cramer*	Unopposed	
	Michael Williams	11,040	44.1%			
	TOTAL	25,011				
Congressional District 6	Spencer Bachus*	79,509	87.8%	No Democratic candidate		
	Terry Reagin	11,042	12.2%			
	TOTAL	90,551				
Congressional District 7	No Republican candidate			Earl F. Hilliard*	46,224	45.7%
				Artur Davis	43,519	43.1%
				Sam Wiggins	11,315	11.2%
				TOTAL	101,058	
				PRIMARY RUNOFF		
				Artur Davis	52,394	56.0%
				Earl F. Hilliard*	41,162	44.0%
				TOTAL	93,556	

ALABAMA REPUBLICAN PRIMARY
GOVERNOR 2002

2000 Census Population	County	Total Vote	Riley	Windom	James	Winner	Percentage of Total Vote		
							Riley	Windom	James
43,671	AUTAUGA	7,151	5,450	961	740	Riley	76.2%	13.4%	10.3%
140,415	BALDWIN	25,496	16,974	5,497	3,025	Riley	66.6%	21.6%	11.9%
29,038	BARBOUR	396	276	87	33	Riley	69.7%	22.0%	8.3%
20,826	BIBB	1,764	1,496	152	116	Riley	84.8%	8.6%	6.6%
51,024	BLOUNT	6,768	4,869	1,235	664	Riley	71.9%	18.2%	9.8%
11,714	BULLOCK	62	51	6	5	Riley	82.3%	9.7%	8.1%
21,399	BUTLER	467	196	39	232	James	42.0%	8.4%	49.7%
112,249	CALHOUN	8,980	7,860	779	341	Riley	87.5%	8.7%	3.8%
36,583	CHAMBERS	1,464	1,274	73	117	Riley	87.0%	5.0%	8.0%
23,988	CHEROKEE	223	170	40	13	Riley	76.2%	17.9%	5.8%
39,593	CHILTON	5,970	4,902	571	497	Riley	82.1%	9.6%	8.3%
15,922	CHOCTAW	61	36	17	8	Riley	59.0%	27.9%	13.1%
27,867	CLARKE	1,243	707	379	157	Riley	56.9%	30.5%	12.6%
14,254	CLAY	2,481	2,341	76	64	Riley	94.4%	3.1%	2.6%
14,123	CLEBURNE	718	623	62	33	Riley	86.8%	8.6%	4.6%
43,615	COFFEE	2,595	1,565	596	434	Riley	60.3%	23.0%	16.7%
54,984	COLBERT	1,717	1,217	382	118	Riley	70.9%	22.2%	6.9%
14,089	CONECUH	213	121	68	24	Riley	56.8%	31.9%	11.3%
12,202	COOSA	721	638	41	42	Riley	88.5%	5.7%	5.8%
37,631	COVINGTON	2,164	1,427	497	240	Riley	65.9%	23.0%	11.1%
13,665	CRENSHAW	304	171	33	100	Riley	56.3%	10.9%	32.9%
77,483	CULLMAN	7,728	5,802	1,350	576	Riley	75.1%	17.5%	7.5%
49,129	DALE	2,462	1,567	544	351	Riley	63.6%	22.1%	14.3%
46,365	DALLAS	623	458	115	50	Riley	73.5%	18.5%	8.0%
64,452	DE KALB	2,765	2,050	514	201	Riley	74.1%	18.6%	7.3%
65,874	ELMORE	8,818	6,942	1,029	847	Riley	78.7%	11.7%	9.6%
38,440	ESCAMBIA	808	509	216	83	Riley	63.0%	26.7%	10.3%
103,459	ETOWAH	6,031	4,619	1,008	404	Riley	76.6%	16.7%	6.7%
18,495	FAYETTE	507	312	147	48	Riley	61.5%	29.0%	9.5%
31,223	FRANKLIN	394	290	78	26	Riley	73.6%	19.8%	6.6%
25,764	GENEVA	3,640	2,186	823	631	Riley	60.1%	22.6%	17.3%
9,974	GREENE	93	60	16	17	Riley	64.5%	17.2%	18.3%
17,185	HALE	96	74	17	5	Riley	77.1%	17.7%	5.2%
16,310	HENRY	368	229	96	43	Riley	62.2%	26.1%	11.7%
88,787	HOUSTON	6,272	4,031	1,482	759	Riley	64.3%	23.6%	12.1%
53,926	JACKSON	1,071	761	208	102	Riley	71.1%	19.4%	9.5%
662,047	JEFFERSON	61,598	46,094	11,247	4,257	Riley	74.8%	18.3%	6.9%
15,904	LAMAR	204	123	59	22	Riley	60.3%	28.9%	10.8%
87,966	LAUDERDALE	2,907	1,974	670	263	Riley	67.9%	23.0%	9.0%
34,803	LAWRENCE	387	280	64	43	Riley	72.4%	16.5%	11.1%
115,092	LEE	7,510	6,656	496	358	Riley	88.6%	6.6%	4.8%
65,676	LIMESTONE	3,389	2,397	650	342	Riley	70.7%	19.2%	10.1%
13,473	LOWNDES	306	196	44	66	Riley	64.1%	14.4%	21.6%
24,105	MACON	275	219	32	24	Riley	79.6%	11.6%	8.7%
276,700	MADISON	21,873	16,847	3,207	1,819	Riley	77.0%	14.7%	8.3%
22,539	MARENGO	500	361	111	28	Riley	72.2%	22.2%	5.6%
31,214	MARION	1,269	878	302	89	Riley	69.2%	23.8%	7.0%
82,231	MARSHALL	5,993	4,615	940	438	Riley	77.0%	15.7%	7.3%
399,843	MOBILE	44,716	26,686	13,440	4,590	Riley	59.7%	30.1%	10.3%
24,324	MONROE	2,073	1,272	540	261	Riley	61.4%	26.0%	12.6%
223,510	MONTGOMERY	21,659	17,350	2,505	1,804	Riley	80.1%	11.6%	8.3%
111,064	MORGAN	8,740	6,436	1,483	821	Riley	73.6%	17.0%	9.4%
11,861	PERRY	97	71	22	4	Riley	73.2%	22.7%	4.1%
20,949	PICKENS	225	160	39	26	Riley	71.1%	17.3%	11.6%
29,605	PIKE	2,015	1,633	235	147	Riley	81.0%	11.7%	7.3%
22,380	RANDOLPH	777	714	51	12	Riley	91.9%	6.6%	1.5%
49,756	RUSSELL	938	861	54	23	Riley	91.8%	5.8%	2.5%
64,742	ST. CLAIR	9,733	7,832	1,241	660	Riley	80.5%	12.8%	6.8%
143,293	SHELBY	20,997	16,058	3,531	1,408	Riley	76.5%	16.8%	6.7%
14,798	SUMTER	34	20	7	7	Riley	58.8%	20.6%	20.6%

ALABAMA REPUBLICAN PRIMARY

GOVERNOR 2002

2000 Census Population	County	Total Vote	Riley	Windom	James	Winner	Percentage of Total Vote		
							Riley	Windom	James
80,321	TALLADEGA	4,642	4,106	358	178	Riley	88.5%	7.7%	3.8%
41,475	TALLAPOOSA	3,980	3,615	216	149	Riley	90.8%	5.4%	3.7%
164,875	TUSCALOOSA	11,428	8,426	1,682	1,320	Riley	73.7%	14.7%	11.6%
70,713	WALKER	1,947	1,450	359	138	Riley	74.5%	18.4%	7.1%
18,097	WASHINGTON	328	170	107	51	Riley	51.8%	32.6%	15.5%
13,183	WILCOX	198	107	45	46	Riley	54.0%	22.7%	23.2%
24,843	WINSTON	4,125	2,990	804	331	Riley	72.5%	19.5%	8.0%
4,447,100	TOTAL	357,497	262,851	63,775	30,871	Riley	73.5%	17.8%	8.6%

ALABAMA DEMOCRATIC PRIMARY

GOVERNOR 2002

2000 Census Population	County	Total Vote	Siegelman	Bishop	Other	Winner	Percentage of Total Vote		
							Siegelman	Bishop	Other
43,671	AUTAUGA	2,463	1,987	360	116	Siegelman	80.7%	14.6%	4.7%
140,415	BALDWIN	3,815	3,130	484	201	Siegelman	82.0%	12.7%	5.3%
29,038	BARBOUR	5,624	3,964	1,345	315	Siegelman	70.5%	23.9%	5.6%
20,826	BIBB	2,502	1,889	490	123	Siegelman	75.5%	19.6%	4.9%
51,024	BLOUNT	1,485	1,257	172	56	Siegelman	84.6%	11.6%	3.8%
11,714	BULLOCK	3,954	2,912	815	227	Siegelman	73.6%	20.6%	5.7%
21,399	BUTLER	5,246	2,934	2,019	293	Siegelman	55.9%	38.5%	5.6%
112,249	CALHOUN	7,412	6,429	690	293	Siegelman	86.7%	9.3%	4.0%
36,583	CHAMBERS	3,779	2,767	716	296	Siegelman	73.2%	18.9%	7.8%
23,988	CHEROKEE	4,939	3,438	1,093	408	Siegelman	69.6%	22.1%	8.3%
39,593	CHILTON	2,607	2,223	277	107	Siegelman	85.3%	10.6%	4.1%
15,922	CHOCTAW	5,703	3,959	1,383	361	Siegelman	69.4%	24.3%	6.3%
27,867	CLARKE	5,714	3,714	1,612	388	Siegelman	65.0%	28.2%	6.8%
14,254	CLAY	1,660	1,363	191	106	Siegelman	82.1%	11.5%	6.4%
14,123	CLEBURNE	2,695	1,850	597	248	Siegelman	68.6%	22.2%	9.2%
43,615	COFFEE	4,252	2,979	1,054	219	Siegelman	70.1%	24.8%	5.2%
54,984	COLBERT	6,423	4,552	1,523	348	Siegelman	70.9%	23.7%	5.4%
14,089	CONECUH	4,023	2,132	1,703	188	Siegelman	53.0%	42.3%	4.7%
12,202	COOSA	2,714	2,015	506	193	Siegelman	74.2%	18.6%	7.1%
37,631	COVINGTON	3,734	2,261	1,271	202	Siegelman	60.6%	34.0%	5.4%
13,665	CRENSHAW	2,933	1,602	1,130	201	Siegelman	54.6%	38.5%	6.9%
77,483	CULLMAN	10,517	6,978	2,673	866	Siegelman	66.3%	25.4%	8.2%
49,129	DALE	2,481	1,964	400	117	Siegelman	79.2%	16.1%	4.7%
46,365	DALLAS	11,349	8,313	2,555	481	Siegelman	73.2%	22.5%	4.2%
64,452	DE KALB	5,832	4,290	1,211	331	Siegelman	73.6%	20.8%	5.7%
65,874	ELMORE	2,951	2,194	517	240	Siegelman	74.3%	17.5%	8.1%
38,440	ESCAMBIA	5,544	3,260	1,799	485	Siegelman	58.8%	32.4%	8.7%
103,459	ETOWAH	7,716	6,609	835	272	Siegelman	85.7%	10.8%	3.5%
18,495	FAYETTE	5,640	3,429	1,773	438	Siegelman	60.8%	31.4%	7.8%
31,223	FRANKLIN	6,888	4,264	2,092	532	Siegelman	61.9%	30.4%	7.7%
25,764	GENEVA	1,042	859	137	46	Siegelman	82.4%	13.1%	4.4%
9,974	GREENE	3,539	3,002	423	114	Siegelman	84.8%	12.0%	3.2%
17,185	HALE	5,707	4,333	1,138	236	Siegelman	75.9%	19.9%	4.1%
16,310	HENRY	3,799	2,655	864	280	Siegelman	69.9%	22.7%	7.4%
88,787	HOUSTON	6,265	4,766	1,175	324	Siegelman	76.1%	18.8%	5.2%
53,926	JACKSON	3,361	2,532	618	211	Siegelman	75.3%	18.4%	6.3%
662,047	JEFFERSON	54,891	48,942	4,686	1,263	Siegelman	89.2%	8.5%	2.3%
15,904	LAMAR	4,284	2,758	1,151	375	Siegelman	64.4%	26.9%	8.8%
87,966	LAUDERDALE	12,816	8,610	3,128	1,078	Siegelman	67.2%	24.4%	8.4%
34,803	LAWRENCE	7,890	5,363	1,896	631	Siegelman	68.0%	24.0%	8.0%

ALABAMA DEMOCRATIC PRIMARY

GOVERNOR 2002

2000 Census Population	County	Total Vote	Siegelman	Bishop	Other	Winner	Percentage of Total Vote		
							Siegelman	Bishop	Other
115,092	LEE	5,102	4,019	807	276	Siegelman	78.8%	15.8%	5.4%
65,676	LIMESTONE	6,588	4,471	1,667	450	Siegelman	67.9%	25.3%	6.8%
13,473	LOWNDES	3,927	2,815	955	157	Siegelman	71.7%	24.3%	4.0%
24,105	MACON	4,716	4,074	500	142	Siegelman	86.4%	10.6%	3.0%
276,700	MADISON	18,149	15,780	1,468	901	Siegelman	86.9%	8.1%	5.0%
22,539	MARENGO	5,503	3,994	1,244	265	Siegelman	72.6%	22.6%	4.8%
31,214	MARION	7,330	4,539	2,192	599	Siegelman	61.9%	29.9%	8.2%
82,231	MARSHALL	5,905	4,378	1,162	365	Siegelman	74.1%	19.7%	6.2%
399,843	MOBILE	23,883	20,257	2,601	1,025	Siegelman	84.8%	10.9%	4.3%
24,324	MONROE	2,996	2,078	802	116	Siegelman	69.4%	26.8%	3.9%
223,510	MONTGOMERY	18,277	15,081	2,482	714	Siegelman	82.5%	13.6%	3.9%
111,064	MORGAN	9,394	7,158	1,600	636	Siegelman	76.2%	17.0%	6.8%
11,861	PERRY	4,481	3,393	931	157	Siegelman	75.7%	20.8%	3.5%
20,949	PICKENS	5,117	3,558	1,060	499	Siegelman	69.5%	20.7%	9.8%
29,605	PIKE	1,627	1,269	306	52	Siegelman	78.0%	18.8%	3.2%
22,380	RANDOLPH	3,129	2,052	770	307	Siegelman	65.6%	24.6%	9.8%
49,756	RUSSELL	5,282	4,322	571	389	Siegelman	81.8%	10.8%	7.4%
64,742	ST. CLAIR	2,242	2,004	161	77	Siegelman	89.4%	7.2%	3.4%
143,293	SHELBY	3,286	2,943	253	90	Siegelman	89.6%	7.7%	2.7%
14,798	SUMTER	5,359	4,181	797	381	Siegelman	78.0%	14.9%	7.1%
80,321	TALLADEGA	7,026	6,065	660	301	Siegelman	86.3%	9.4%	4.3%
41,475	TALLAPOOSA	5,236	3,676	1,176	384	Siegelman	70.2%	22.5%	7.3%
164,875	TUSCALOOSA	10,615	8,920	1,251	444	Siegelman	84.0%	11.8%	4.2%
70,713	WALKER	12,639	7,838	3,893	908	Siegelman	62.0%	30.8%	7.2%
18,097	WASHINGTON	5,264	3,503	1,296	465	Siegelman	66.5%	24.6%	8.8%
13,183	WILCOX	5,077	3,973	938	166	Siegelman	78.3%	18.5%	3.3%
24,843	WINSTON	971	752	148	71	Siegelman	77.4%	15.2%	7.3%
4,447,100	TOTAL	435,310	331,571	80,193	23,546	Siegelman	76.2%	18.4%	5.4%

ALABAMA DEMOCRATIC PRIMARY

SENATOR 2002

2000 Census Population	County	Total Vote	Parker	McPhillips	Sowell	Winner	Percentage of Total Vote		
							Parker	McPhillips	Sowell
43,671	AUTAUGA	2,346	870	1,357	119	McPhillips	37.1%	57.8%	5.1%
140,415	BALDWIN	3,602	1,577	1,720	305	McPhillips	43.8%	47.8%	8.5%
29,038	BARBOUR	4,817	2,021	2,283	513	McPhillips	42.0%	47.4%	10.6%
20,826	BIBB	2,337	1,219	904	214	Parker	52.2%	38.7%	9.2%
51,024	BLOUNT	1,428	814	495	119	Parker	57.0%	34.7%	8.3%
11,714	BULLOCK	2,789	1,069	1,556	164	McPhillips	38.3%	55.8%	5.9%
21,399	BUTLER	5,147	1,973	2,882	292	McPhillips	38.3%	56.0%	5.7%
112,249	CALHOUN	6,817	3,537	2,742	538	Parker	51.9%	40.2%	7.9%
36,583	CHAMBERS	3,389	1,724	1,270	395	Parker	50.9%	37.5%	11.7%
23,988	CHEROKEE	4,397	2,324	1,378	695	Parker	52.9%	31.3%	15.8%
39,593	CHILTON	2,491	1,214	1,092	185	Parker	48.7%	43.8%	7.4%
15,922	CHOCTAW	4,689	2,393	1,665	631	Parker	51.0%	35.5%	13.5%
27,867	CLARKE	4,867	1,863	2,430	574	McPhillips	38.3%	49.9%	11.8%
14,254	CLAY	1,572	862	571	139	Parker	54.8%	36.3%	8.8%
14,123	CLEBURNE	2,340	1,269	580	491	Parker	54.2%	24.8%	21.0%
43,615	COFFEE	3,954	1,745	1,725	484	Parker	44.1%	43.6%	12.2%
54,984	COLBERT	5,789	3,099	2,099	591	Parker	53.5%	36.3%	10.2%
14,089	CONECUH	3,534	1,733	1,405	396	Parker	49.0%	39.8%	11.2%
12,202	COOSA	2,575	1,353	1,034	188	Parker	52.5%	40.2%	7.3%
37,631	COVINGTON	3,400	1,528	1,425	447	Parker	44.9%	41.9%	13.1%

20

ALABAMA DEMOCRATIC PRIMARY

SENATOR 2002

2000 Census Population	County	Total Vote	Parker	McPhillips	Sowell	Winner	Percentage of Total Vote Parker	McPhillips	Sowell
13,665	CRENSHAW	2,846	1,154	1,523	169	McPhillips	40.5%	53.5%	5.9%
77,483	CULLMAN	10,194	4,155	5,155	884	McPhillips	40.8%	50.6%	8.7%
49,129	DALE	2,333	1,090	967	276	Parker	46.7%	41.4%	11.8%
46,365	DALLAS	10,400	3,981	5,544	875	McPhillips	38.3%	53.3%	8.4%
64,452	DE KALB	4,907	2,635	1,455	817	Parker	53.7%	29.7%	16.6%
65,874	ELMORE	2,841	964	1,750	127	McPhillips	33.9%	61.6%	4.5%
38,440	ESCAMBIA	4,757	2,124	2,087	546	Parker	44.6%	43.9%	11.5%
103,459	ETOWAH	7,259	3,886	2,756	617	Parker	53.5%	38.0%	8.5%
18,495	FAYETTE	5,114	2,830	1,704	580	Parker	55.3%	33.3%	11.3%
31,223	FRANKLIN	6,010	3,754	1,225	1,031	Parker	62.5%	20.4%	17.2%
25,764	GENEVA	952	378	449	125	McPhillips	39.7%	47.2%	13.1%
9,974	GREENE	3,105	1,906	979	220	Parker	61.4%	31.5%	7.1%
17,185	HALE	5,302	2,206	2,830	266	McPhillips	41.6%	53.4%	5.0%
16,310	HENRY	3,420	1,365	1,508	547	McPhillips	39.9%	44.1%	16.0%
88,787	HOUSTON	5,730	1,924	2,927	879	McPhillips	33.6%	51.1%	15.3%
53,926	JACKSON	3,009	1,837	748	424	Parker	61.1%	24.9%	14.1%
662,047	JEFFERSON	52,606	24,219	23,884	4,503	Parker	46.0%	45.4%	8.6%
15,904	LAMAR	3,634	2,066	939	629	Parker	56.9%	25.8%	17.3%
87,966	LAUDERDALE	11,403	7,040	3,005	1,358	Parker	61.7%	26.4%	11.9%
34,803	LAWRENCE	7,488	5,037	1,582	869	Parker	67.3%	21.1%	11.6%
115,092	LEE	4,820	1,962	2,602	256	McPhillips	40.7%	54.0%	5.3%
65,676	LIMESTONE	6,415	4,660	1,152	603	Parker	72.6%	18.0%	9.4%
13,473	LOWNDES	3,488	1,028	2,304	156	McPhillips	29.5%	66.1%	4.5%
24,105	MACON	4,518	1,093	3,286	139	McPhillips	24.2%	72.7%	3.1%
276,700	MADISON	16,734	9,879	5,442	1,413	Parker	59.0%	32.5%	8.4%
22,539	MARENGO	4,807	2,372	1,982	453	Parker	49.3%	41.2%	9.4%
31,214	MARION	6,604	4,148	1,656	800	Parker	62.8%	25.1%	12.1%
82,231	MARSHALL	5,201	2,818	1,752	631	Parker	54.2%	33.7%	12.1%
399,843	MOBILE	20,482	6,689	12,540	1,253	McPhillips	32.7%	61.2%	6.1%
24,324	MONROE	2,741	991	1,410	340	McPhillips	36.2%	51.4%	12.4%
223,510	MONTGOMERY	16,710	4,193	12,090	427	McPhillips	25.1%	72.4%	2.6%
111,064	MORGAN	9,513	7,311	1,693	509	Parker	76.9%	17.8%	5.4%
11,861	PERRY	4,111	1,944	1,872	295	Parker	47.3%	45.5%	7.2%
20,949	PICKENS	4,710	2,722	1,453	535	Parker	57.8%	30.8%	11.4%
29,605	PIKE	1,505	608	808	89	McPhillips	40.4%	53.7%	5.9%
22,380	RANDOLPH	2,659	1,329	923	407	Parker	50.0%	34.7%	15.3%
49,756	RUSSELL	4,597	2,012	2,022	563	McPhillips	43.8%	44.0%	12.2%
64,742	ST. CLAIR	2,148	1,058	898	192	Parker	49.3%	41.8%	8.9%
143,293	SHELBY	3,152	1,854	1,077	221	Parker	58.8%	34.2%	7.0%
14,798	SUMTER	4,619	3,094	1,098	427	Parker	67.0%	23.8%	9.2%
80,321	TALLADEGA	6,595	3,787	2,424	384	Parker	57.4%	36.8%	5.8%
41,475	TALLAPOOSA	5,050	2,367	2,327	356	Parker	46.9%	46.1%	7.0%
164,875	TUSCALOOSA	9,604	4,938	3,962	704	Parker	51.4%	41.3%	7.3%
70,713	WALKER	11,741	5,640	4,833	1,268	Parker	48.0%	41.2%	10.8%
18,097	WASHINGTON	4,765	1,736	2,336	693	McPhillips	36.4%	49.0%	14.5%
13,183	WILCOX	4,148	1,519	2,333	296	McPhillips	36.6%	56.2%	7.1%
24,843	WINSTON	892	488	317	87	Parker	54.7%	35.5%	9.8%
4,447,100	TOTAL	397,919	190,978	170,222	36,719	Parker	48.0%	42.8%	9.2%

ALABAMA DEMOCRATIC PRIMARY RUNOFF
SENATOR 2002

2000 Census Population	County	Total Vote	Parker	McPhillips	Winner	Percentage of Total Vote Parker	McPhillips
43,671	AUTAUGA	1,176	575	601	McPhillips	48.9%	51.1%
140,415	BALDWIN	1,735	968	767	Parker	55.8%	44.2%
29,038	BARBOUR	1,117	658	459	Parker	58.9%	41.1%
20,826	BIBB	745	484	261	Parker	65.0%	35.0%
51,024	BLOUNT	513	414	99	Parker	80.7%	19.3%
11,714	BULLOCK	2,449	1,198	1,251	McPhillips	48.9%	51.1%
21,399	BUTLER	4,508	2,425	2,083	Parker	53.8%	46.2%
112,249	CALHOUN	2,643	2,100	543	Parker	79.5%	20.5%
36,583	CHAMBERS	1,807	1,126	681	Parker	62.3%	37.7%
23,988	CHEROKEE	4,070	2,950	1,120	Parker	72.5%	27.5%
39,593	CHILTON	994	643	351	Parker	64.7%	35.3%
15,922	CHOCTAW	4,166	2,800	1,366	Parker	67.2%	32.8%
27,867	CLARKE	3,367	1,620	1,747	McPhillips	48.1%	51.9%
14,254	CLAY	2,139	1,534	605	Parker	71.7%	28.3%
14,123	CLEBURNE	2,640	1,903	737	Parker	72.1%	27.9%
43,615	COFFEE	1,778	1,188	590	Parker	66.8%	33.2%
54,984	COLBERT	3,443	2,438	1,005	Parker	70.8%	29.2%
14,089	CONECUH	998	632	366	Parker	63.3%	36.7%
12,202	COOSA	1,561	1,072	489	Parker	68.7%	31.3%
37,631	COVINGTON	3,458	2,089	1,369	Parker	60.4%	39.6%
13,665	CRENSHAW	2,578	1,548	1,030	Parker	60.0%	40.0%
77,483	CULLMAN	2,154	1,539	615	Parker	71.4%	28.6%
49,129	DALE	1,246	810	436	Parker	65.0%	35.0%
46,365	DALLAS	10,178	5,975	4,203	Parker	58.7%	41.3%
64,452	DE KALB	4,134	2,973	1,161	Parker	71.9%	28.1%
65,874	ELMORE	1,485	686	799	McPhillips	46.2%	53.8%
38,440	ESCAMBIA	901	512	389	Parker	56.8%	43.2%
103,459	ETOWAH	3,622	2,648	974	Parker	73.1%	26.9%
18,495	FAYETTE	5,020	3,765	1,255	Parker	75.0%	25.0%
31,223	FRANKLIN	4,118	3,201	917	Parker	77.7%	22.3%
25,764	GENEVA	315	190	125	Parker	60.3%	39.7%
9,974	GREENE	3,059	2,397	662	Parker	78.4%	21.6%
17,185	HALE	4,178	1,857	2,321	McPhillips	44.4%	55.6%
16,310	HENRY	1,144	694	450	Parker	60.7%	39.3%
88,787	HOUSTON	1,132	726	406	Parker	64.1%	35.9%
53,926	JACKSON	1,223	932	291	Parker	76.2%	23.8%
662,047	JEFFERSON	49,158	33,792	15,366	Parker	68.7%	31.3%
15,904	LAMAR	1,871	1,400	471	Parker	74.8%	25.2%
87,966	LAUDERDALE	7,397	5,861	1,536	Parker	79.2%	20.8%
34,803	LAWRENCE	7,068	5,589	1,479	Parker	79.1%	20.9%
115,092	LEE	1,854	1,236	618	Parker	66.7%	33.3%
65,676	LIMESTONE	2,034	1,849	185	Parker	90.9%	9.1%
13,473	LOWNDES	3,688	1,541	2,147	McPhillips	41.8%	58.2%
24,105	MACON	3,188	1,149	2,039	McPhillips	36.0%	64.0%
276,700	MADISON	10,390	7,646	2,744	Parker	73.6%	26.4%
22,539	MARENGO	3,984	2,589	1,395	Parker	65.0%	35.0%
31,214	MARION	6,266	5,039	1,227	Parker	80.4%	19.6%
82,231	MARSHALL	2,489	1,844	645	Parker	74.1%	25.9%
399,843	MOBILE	11,406	5,030	6,376	McPhillips	44.1%	55.9%
24,324	MONROE	1,941	999	942	Parker	51.5%	48.5%
223,510	MONTGOMERY	13,899	5,114	8,785	McPhillips	36.8%	63.2%
111,064	MORGAN	5,706	4,916	790	Parker	86.2%	13.8%
11,861	PERRY	3,499	2,505	994	Parker	71.6%	28.4%
20,949	PICKENS	3,250	2,288	962	Parker	70.4%	29.6%
29,605	PIKE	846	437	409	Parker	51.7%	48.3%
22,380	RANDOLPH	2,167	1,524	643	Parker	70.3%	29.7%
49,756	RUSSELL	546	298	248	Parker	54.6%	45.4%
64,742	ST. CLAIR	801	572	229	Parker	71.4%	28.6%
143,293	SHELBY	1,407	1,148	259	Parker	81.6%	18.4%
14,798	SUMTER	3,894	3,021	873	Parker	77.6%	22.4%

ALABAMA DEMOCRATIC PRIMARY RUNOFF
SENATOR 2002

2000 Census Population	County	Total Vote	Parker	McPhillips	Winner	Percentage of Total Vote	
						Parker	McPhillips
80,321	TALLADEGA	2,131	1,606	525	Parker	75.4%	24.6%
41,475	TALLAPOOSA	1,579	1,034	545	Parker	65.5%	34.5%
164,875	TUSCALOOSA	10,008	7,091	2,917	Parker	70.9%	29.1%
70,713	WALKER	8,485	6,003	2,482	Parker	70.7%	29.3%
18,097	WASHINGTON	4,303	2,013	2,290	McPhillips	46.8%	53.2%
13,183	WILCOX	3,386	1,604	1,782	McPhillips	47.4%	52.6%
24,843	WINSTON	761	574	187	Parker	75.4%	24.6%
4,447,100	TOTAL	271,196	176,582	94,614	Parker	65.1%	34.9%

ALASKA

GOVERNOR
Frank H. Murkowski (R). Elected 2002 to a four-year term.

SENATORS (2 Republicans)
Ted Stevens (R). Reelected 2002 to a six-year term. Previously elected 1996, 1990, 1984, 1978, 1972, and in 1970 to fill out the term vacated by the death of Senator E. L. Bartlett; had been appointed December 1968 to fill this vacancy.

Lisa Murkowski (R). Appointed senator on Dec. 20, 2002, to fill the vacancy created by the resignation of her father, Frank H. Murkowski, to become governor of Alaska.

REPRESENTATIVE (1 Republican)
At Large. Don Young (R)

POSTWAR VOTE FOR PRESIDENT

| | | Republican | | Democratic | | | | Percentage | | | |
| | | | | | | Other | | Total Vote | | Major Vote | |
Year	Total Vote	Vote	Candidate	Vote	Candidate	Vote	Plurality	Rep.	Dem.	Rep.	Dem.
2000**	285,560	167,398	Bush, George W.	79,004	Gore, Al	39,158	88,394 R	58.6%	27.7%	67.9%	32.1%
1996**	241,620	122,746	Dole, Bob	80,380	Clinton, Bill	38,494	42,366 R	50.8%	33.3%	60.4%	39.6%
1992**	258,506	102,000	Bush, George	78,294	Clinton, Bill	78,212	23,706 R	39.5%	30.3%	56.6%	43.4%
1988	200,116	119,251	Bush, George	72,584	Dukakis, Michael S.	8,281	46,667 R	59.6%	36.3%	62.2%	37.8%
1984	207,605	138,377	Reagan, Ronald	62,007	Mondale, Walter F.	7,221	76,370 R	66.7%	29.9%	69.1%	30.9%
1980**	158,445	86,112	Reagan, Ronald	41,842	Carter, Jimmy	30,491	44,270 D	54.3%	26.4%	67.3%	32.7%
1976	123,574	71,555	Ford, Gerald R.	44,058	Carter, Jimmy	7,961	27,497 R	57.9%	35.7%	61.9%	38.1%
1972	95,219	55,349	Nixon, Richard M.	32,967	McGovern, George S.	6,903	22,382 R	58.1%	34.6%	62.7%	37.3%
1968	83,035	37,600	Nixon, Richard M.	35,411	Humphrey, Hubert H.	10,024	2,189 R	45.3%	42.6%	51.5%	48.5%
1964	67,259	22,930	Goldwater, Barry M.	44,329	Johnson, Lyndon B.		21,399 D	34.1%	65.9%	34.1%	65.9%
1960	60,762	30,953	Nixon, Richard M.	29,809	Kennedy, John F.		1,144 R	50.9%	49.1%	50.9%	49.1%

In 2000 the other vote column includes 28,747 votes cast for Green (Nader). In 1996 the other vote column includes 26,333 votes cast for Perot. In 1992 the other vote column includes 73,481 votes for Perot. In 1980 the other column includes 11,155 votes for Independent (Anderson). Alaska was formally admitted as a state in January 1959.

POSTWAR VOTE FOR GOVERNOR

| | | Republican | | Democratic | | | | Percentage | | | |
| | | | | | | Other | Rep.-Dem. | Total Vote | | Major Vote | |
Year	Total Vote	Vote	Candidate	Vote	Candidate	Vote	Plurality	Rep.	Dem.	Rep.	Dem.
2002	231,484	129,279	Murkowski, Frank H.	94,216	Ulmer, Fran	7,989	35,063 R	55.8%	40.7%	57.8%	42.2%
1998	220,177	39,331	Lindauer, John	112,879	Knowles, Tony	67,967	73,548 D	17.9%	51.3%	25.8%	74.2%
1994	213,435	87,157	Campbell, James O.	87,693	Knowles, Tony	38,585	536 D	40.8%	41.1%	49.8%	50.2%
1990**	194,750	50,991	Sturgulewski, Arliss	60,201	Knowles, Tony	83,558	15,520 I	26.2%	30.9%	45.9%	54.1%
1986	179,555	76,515	Sturgulewski, Arliss	84,943	Cowper, Steve	18,097	8,428 D	42.6%	47.3%	47.4%	52.6%
1982	194,885	72,291	Fink, Tom	89,918	Sheffield, Bill	32,676	17,627 D	37.1%	46.1%	44.6%	55.4%
1978**	126,910	49,580	Hammond, Jay S.	25,656	Croft, Chancy	51,674	23,924 R	39.1%	20.2%	65.9%	34.1%
1974	96,163	45,840	Hammond, Jay S.	45,553	Egan, William A.	4,770	287 R	47.7%	47.4%	50.2%	49.8%
1970	80,779	37,264	Miller, Keith	42,309	Egan, William A.	1,206	5,045 D	46.1%	52.4%	46.8%	53.2%
1966	66,294	33,145	Hickel, Walter J.	32,065	Egan, William A.	1,084	1,080 R	50.0%	48.4%	50.8%	49.2%
1962	56,681	27,054	Stepovich, Mike	29,627	Egan, William A.		2,573 D	47.7%	52.3%	47.7%	52.3%
1958	48,968	19,299	Butrovich, John	29,189	Egan, William A.	480	9,890 D	39.4%	59.6%	39.8%	60.2%

In 1990 Walter J. Hickel, the Alaskan Independence candidate, polled 75,721 votes (38.9% of the total vote) and won the election with a 15,520-vote plurality. In 1978 the other vote was 33,555 Walter J. Hickel (write-in); 15,656 Tom Kelly (Alaskans for Kelly) and 2,463 Donald R. Wright (Alaskan Independence).

ALASKA

POSTWAR VOTE FOR SENATOR

Year	Total Vote	Republican		Democratic		Other Vote	Rep.-Dem. Plurality	Percentage			
								Total Vote		Major Vote	
		Vote	Candidate	Vote	Candidate			Rep.	Dem.	Rep.	Dem.
2002	229,548	179,438	Stevens, Ted	24,133	Vondersaar, Frank	25,977	155,305 R	78.2%	10.5%	88.1%	11.9%
1998	221,807	165,227	Murkowski, Frank H.	43,743	Sonneman, Joseph	12,837	121,484 R	74.5%	19.7%	79.1%	20.9%
1996**	231,916	177,893	Stevens, Ted	23,977	Obermeyer, Theresa	30,046	153,916 R	76.7%	10.3%	88.1%	11.9%
1992	239,714	127,163	Murkowski, Frank H.	92,065	Smith, Tony	20,486	35,098 R	53.0%	38.4%	58.0%	42.0%
1990	189,957	125,806	Stevens, Ted	61,152	Beasley, Michael	2,999	64,654 R	66.2%	32.2%	67.3%	32.7%
1986	180,801	97,674	Murkowski, Frank H.	79,727	Olds, Glenn	3,400	17,947 R	54.0%	44.1%	55.1%	44.9%
1984	206,438	146,919	Stevens, Ted	58,804	Havelock, John E.	715	88,115 R	71.2%	28.5%	71.4%	28.6%
1980	156,762	84,159	Murkowski, Frank H.	72,007	Gruening, Clark S.	596	12,152 R	53.7%	45.9%	53.9%	46.1%
1978	122,741	92,783	Stevens, Ted	29,574	Hobbs, Donald W.	384	63,209 R	75.6%	24.1%	75.8%	24.2%
1974	93,275	38,914	Lewis, C. R.	54,361	Gravel, Mike		15,447 D	41.7%	58.3%	41.7%	58.3%
1972	96,007	74,216	Stevens, Ted	21,791	Guess, Gene		52,425 R	77.3%	22.7%	77.3%	22.7%
1970S	80,364	47,908	Stevens, Ted	32,456	Kay, Wendell P.		15,452 R	59.6%	40.4%	59.6%	40.4%
1968	80,931	30,286	Rasmuson, Elmer	36,527	Gravel, Mike	14,118	6,241 D	37.4%	45.1%	45.3%	54.7%
1966	65,250	15,961	McKinley, Lee L.	49,289	Bartlett, E. L.		33,328 D	24.5%	75.5%	24.5%	75.5%
1962	58,181	24,354	Stevens, Ted	33,827	Gruening, Ernest		9,473 D	41.9%	58.1%	41.9%	58.1%
1960	59,978	21,937	McKinley, Lee L.	38,041	Bartlett, E. L.		16,104 D	36.6%	63.4%	36.6%	63.4%
1958S	49,525	23,462	Stepovich, Mike	26,063	Gruening, Ernest		2,601 D	47.4%	52.6%	47.4%	52.6%
1958S	48,837	7,299	Robertson, R. E.	40,939	Bartlett, E. L.	599	33,640 D	14.9%	83.8%	15.1%	84.9%

In 1996 Green Party candidate Jed Whittaker finished second with 29,037 votes, a total of 148,856 behind Stevens. The 1970 election was for a short term to fill a vacancy. The two 1958 elections were held to indeterminate terms and the Senate later determined by lot that Senator Gruening would serve four years, Senator Bartlett two.

ALASKA

One member At Large

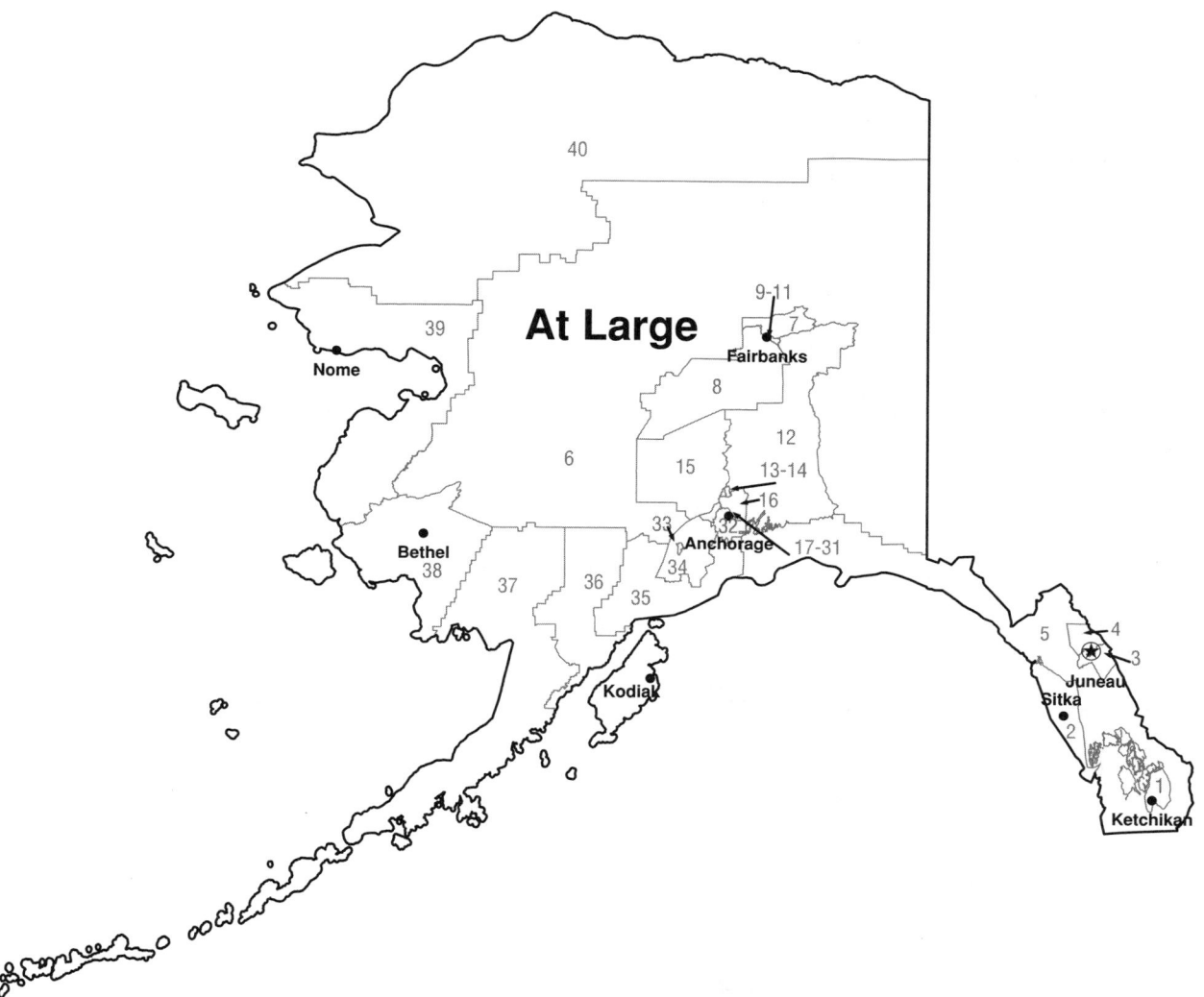

ALASKA

GOVERNOR 2002

2000 Census Population	District		Total Vote	Republican	Democratic	Other	Rep.-Dem. Plurality	Percentage			
								Total Vote		Major Vote	
								Rep.	Dem.	Rep.	Dem.
15,031	DISTRICT	1	5,329	3,711	1,460	158	2,251 R	69.6%	27.4%	71.8%	28.2%
14,991	DISTRICT	2	6,136	3,186	2,773	177	413 R	51.9%	45.2%	53.5%	46.5%
15,203	DISTRICT	3	8,051	2,778	5,111	162	2,333 D	34.5%	63.5%	35.2%	64.8%
15,508	DISTRICT	4	7,773	3,721	3,917	135	196 D	47.9%	50.4%	48.7%	51.3%
15,048	DISTRICT	5	5,994	2,880	2,887	227	7 D	48.0%	48.2%	49.9%	50.1%
14,905	DISTRICT	6	5,141	2,505	2,369	267	136 R	48.7%	46.1%	51.4%	48.6%
15,494	DISTRICT	7	8,077	4,519	3,257	301	1,262 R	55.9%	40.3%	58.1%	41.9%
15,552	DISTRICT	8	7,619	3,621	3,705	293	84 D	47.5%	48.6%	49.4%	50.6%
15,723	DISTRICT	9	5,580	3,198	2,157	225	1,041 R	57.3%	38.7%	59.7%	40.3%
15,599	DISTRICT	10	4,062	2,508	1,399	155	1,109 R	61.7%	34.4%	64.2%	35.8%
15,904	DISTRICT	11	6,447	4,871	1,354	222	3,517 R	75.6%	21.0%	78.2%	21.8%
16,303	DISTRICT	12	5,491	3,841	1,407	243	2,434 R	70.0%	25.6%	73.2%	26.8%
16,231	DISTRICT	13	6,794	4,545	2,005	244	2,540 R	66.9%	29.5%	69.4%	30.6%
16,119	DISTRICT	14	6,128	4,385	1,552	191	2,833 R	71.6%	25.3%	73.9%	26.1%
16,137	DISTRICT	15	6,128	4,115	1,692	321	2,423 R	67.2%	27.6%	70.9%	29.1%
16,104	DISTRICT	16	6,941	4,671	1,988	282	2,683 R	67.3%	28.6%	70.1%	29.9%
15,819	DISTRICT	17	6,678	4,412	2,063	203	2,349 R	66.1%	30.9%	68.1%	31.9%
15,639	DISTRICT	18	3,031	2,094	835	102	1,259 R	69.1%	27.5%	71.5%	28.5%
15,841	DISTRICT	19	5,063	2,872	1,991	200	881 R	56.7%	39.3%	59.1%	40.9%
15,837	DISTRICT	20	3,245	1,700	1,415	130	285 R	52.4%	43.6%	54.6%	45.4%
15,850	DISTRICT	21	6,409	3,625	2,631	153	994 R	56.6%	41.1%	57.9%	42.1%
15,831	DISTRICT	22	4,731	2,219	2,332	180	113 D	46.9%	49.3%	48.8%	51.2%
15,847	DISTRICT	23	5,184	2,110	2,895	179	785 D	40.7%	55.8%	42.2%	57.8%
15,812	DISTRICT	24	5,150	2,799	2,168	183	631 R	54.3%	42.1%	56.4%	43.6%
15,836	DISTRICT	25	4,939	2,352	2,350	237	2 R	47.6%	47.6%	50.0%	50.0%
15,823	DISTRICT	26	6,895	3,192	3,481	222	289 D	46.3%	50.5%	47.8%	52.2%
15,820	DISTRICT	27	5,940	3,520	2,249	171	1,271 R	59.3%	37.9%	61.0%	39.0%
15,839	DISTRICT	28	6,735	4,093	2,478	164	1,615 R	60.8%	36.8%	62.3%	37.7%
15,846	DISTRICT	29	4,759	2,790	1,801	168	989 R	58.6%	37.8%	60.8%	39.2%
15,839	DISTRICT	30	6,334	3,740	2,450	144	1,290 R	59.0%	38.7%	60.4%	39.6%
15,811	DISTRICT	31	7,594	4,535	2,909	150	1,626 R	59.7%	38.3%	60.9%	39.1%
15,329	DISTRICT	32	8,283	4,360	3,708	215	652 R	52.6%	44.8%	54.0%	46.0%
16,466	DISTRICT	33	6,119	4,102	1,773	244	2,329 R	67.0%	29.0%	69.8%	30.2%
16,409	DISTRICT	34	6,469	4,648	1,543	278	3,105 R	71.9%	23.9%	75.1%	24.9%
16,436	DISTRICT	35	6,470	3,301	2,925	244	376 R	51.0%	45.2%	53.0%	47.0%
14,928	DISTRICT	36	4,481	2,588	1,763	130	825 R	57.8%	39.3%	59.5%	40.5%
15,150	DISTRICT	37	3,678	1,789	1,734	155	55 R	48.6%	47.1%	50.8%	49.2%
14,921	DISTRICT	38	3,703	799	2,732	172	1,933 D	21.6%	73.8%	22.6%	77.4%
14,996	DISTRICT	39	4,155	1,248	2,719	188	1,471 D	30.0%	65.4%	31.5%	68.5%
15,155	DISTRICT	40	3,748	1,336	2,238	174	902 D	35.6%	59.7%	37.4%	62.6%
626,932	TOTAL		231,484	129,279	94,216	7,989	35,063 R	55.8%	40.7%	57.8%	42.2%

ALASKA

SENATOR 2002

2000 Census Population	District	Total Vote	Republican	Democratic	Other	Rep.-Dem. Plurality	Percentage			
							Total Vote		Major Vote	
							Rep.	Dem.	Rep.	Dem.
15,031	DISTRICT 1	5,287	4,296	509	482	3,787 R	81.3%	9.6%	89.4%	10.6%
14,991	DISTRICT 2	6,065	4,504	834	727	3,670 R	74.3%	13.8%	84.4%	15.6%
15,203	DISTRICT 3	7,841	4,818	1,569	1,454	3,249 R	61.4%	20.0%	75.4%	24.6%
15,508	DISTRICT 4	7,588	5,564	1,093	931	4,471 R	73.3%	14.4%	83.6%	16.4%
15,048	DISTRICT 5	5,912	4,071	923	918	3,148 R	68.9%	15.6%	81.5%	18.5%
14,905	DISTRICT 6	5,110	3,862	670	578	3,192 R	75.6%	13.1%	85.2%	14.8%
15,494	DISTRICT 7	7,991	5,849	832	1,310	5,017 R	73.2%	10.4%	87.5%	12.5%
15,552	DISTRICT 8	7,537	4,939	1,041	1,557	3,898 R	65.5%	13.8%	82.6%	17.4%
15,723	DISTRICT 9	5,541	4,241	774	526	3,467 R	76.5%	14.0%	84.6%	15.4%
15,599	DISTRICT 10	4,046	3,204	532	310	2,672 R	79.2%	13.1%	85.8%	14.2%
15,904	DISTRICT 11	6,422	5,591	406	425	5,185 R	87.1%	6.3%	93.2%	6.8%
16,303	DISTRICT 12	5,474	4,496	378	600	4,118 R	82.1%	6.9%	92.2%	7.8%
16,231	DISTRICT 13	6,760	5,670	407	683	5,263 R	83.9%	6.0%	93.3%	6.7%
16,119	DISTRICT 14	6,116	5,287	348	481	4,939 R	86.4%	5.7%	93.8%	6.2%
16,137	DISTRICT 15	6,101	4,867	409	825	4,458 R	79.8%	6.7%	92.2%	7.8%
16,104	DISTRICT 16	6,916	5,711	374	831	5,337 R	82.6%	5.4%	93.9%	6.1%
15,819	DISTRICT 17	6,631	5,738	415	478	5,323 R	86.5%	6.3%	93.3%	6.7%
15,639	DISTRICT 18	3,003	2,519	307	177	2,212 R	83.9%	10.2%	89.1%	10.9%
15,841	DISTRICT 19	5,013	3,998	565	450	3,433 R	79.8%	11.3%	87.6%	12.4%
15,837	DISTRICT 20	3,213	2,425	486	302	1,939 R	75.5%	15.1%	83.3%	16.7%
15,850	DISTRICT 21	6,374	5,153	684	537	4,469 R	80.8%	10.7%	88.3%	11.7%
15,831	DISTRICT 22	4,691	3,421	672	598	2,749 R	72.9%	14.3%	83.6%	16.4%
15,847	DISTRICT 23	5,113	3,511	805	797	2,706 R	68.7%	15.7%	81.3%	18.7%
15,812	DISTRICT 24	5,137	4,034	555	548	3,479 R	78.5%	10.8%	87.9%	12.1%
15,836	DISTRICT 25	4,896	3,576	636	684	2,940 R	73.0%	13.0%	84.9%	15.1%
15,823	DISTRICT 26	6,799	5,133	706	960	4,427 R	75.5%	10.4%	87.9%	12.1%
15,820	DISTRICT 27	5,911	4,900	497	514	4,403 R	82.9%	8.4%	90.8%	9.2%
15,839	DISTRICT 28	6,696	5,715	475	506	5,240 R	85.3%	7.1%	92.3%	7.7%
15,846	DISTRICT 29	4,737	3,938	437	362	3,501 R	83.1%	9.2%	90.0%	10.0%
15,839	DISTRICT 30	6,270	5,182	516	572	4,666 R	82.6%	8.2%	90.9%	9.1%
15,811	DISTRICT 31	7,561	6,391	515	655	5,876 R	84.5%	6.8%	92.5%	7.5%
15,329	DISTRICT 32	8,213	6,369	656	1,188	5,713 R	77.5%	8.0%	90.7%	9.3%
16,466	DISTRICT 33	6,086	5,080	476	530	4,604 R	83.5%	7.8%	91.4%	8.6%
16,409	DISTRICT 34	6,424	5,407	377	640	5,030 R	84.2%	5.9%	93.5%	6.5%
16,436	DISTRICT 35	6,416	4,552	686	1,178	3,866 R	70.9%	10.7%	86.9%	13.1%
14,928	DISTRICT 36	4,450	3,564	458	428	3,106 R	80.1%	10.3%	88.6%	11.4%
15,150	DISTRICT 37	3,658	3,001	358	299	2,643 R	82.0%	9.8%	89.3%	10.7%
14,921	DISTRICT 38	3,681	2,638	691	352	1,947 R	71.7%	18.8%	79.2%	20.8%
14,996	DISTRICT 39	4,137	3,322	519	296	2,803 R	80.3%	12.5%	86.5%	13.5%
15,155	DISTRICT 40	3,731	2,901	542	288	2,359 R	77.8%	14.5%	84.3%	15.7%
626,932	TOTAL	229,548	179,438	24,133	25,977	155,305 R	78.2%	10.5%	88.1%	11.9%

ALASKA
HOUSE OF REPRESENTATIVES

		Total	Republican		Democratic		Other	Rep.-Dem.	Total Vote		Major Vote	
CD	Year	Vote	Vote	Candidate	Vote	Candidate	Vote	Plurality	Rep.	Dem.	Rep.	Dem.
AL	2002	227,725	169,685	Young, Don*	39,357	Greene, Clifford	18,683	130,328 R	74.5%	17.3%	81.2%	18.8%
AL	2000	274,393	190,862	Young, Don*	45,372	Greene, Clifford	38,159	145,490 R	69.6%	16.5%	80.8%	19.2%
AL	1998	223,300	139,676	Young, Don*	77,232	Duncan, Jim	6,392	62,444 R	62.6%	34.6%	64.4%	35.6%
AL	1996	233,700	138,834	Young, Don*	85,114	Lincoln, Georgianna	9,752	53,720 R	59.4%	36.4%	62.0%	38.0%
AL	1994	208,240	118,537	Young, Don*	68,172	Smith, Tony	21,531	50,365 R	56.9%	32.7%	63.5%	36.5%
AL	1992	239,116	111,849	Young, Don*	102,378	Devens, John S.	24,889	9,471 R	46.8%	42.8%	52.2%	47.8%
AL	1990	191,647	99,003	Young, Don*	91,677	Devens, John S.	967	7,326 R	51.7%	47.8%	51.9%	48.1%
AL	1988	192,955	120,595	Young, Don*	71,881	Gruenstein, Peter	479	48,714 R	62.5%	37.3%	62.7%	37.3%
AL	1986	180,277	101,799	Young, Don*	74,053	Begich, Pegge	4,425	27,746 R	56.5%	41.1%	57.9%	42.1%
AL	1984	206,437	113,582	Young, Don*	86,052	Begich, Pegge	6,803	27,530 R	55.0%	41.7%	56.9%	43.1%
AL	1982	181,084	128,274	Young, Don*	52,011	Carlson, Dave	799	76,263 R	70.8%	28.7%	71.2%	28.8%
AL	1980	154,618	114,089	Young, Don*	39,922	Parnell, Kevin	607	74,167 R	73.8%	25.8%	74.1%	25.9%
AL	1978	124,187	68,811	Young, Don*	55,176	Rodney, Patrick	200	13,635 R	55.4%	44.4%	55.5%	44.5%
AL	1976	118,208	83,722	Young, Don*	34,194	Hopson, Eben	292	49,528 R	70.8%	28.9%	71.0%	29.0%
AL	1974	95,921	51,641	Young, Don*	44,280	Hensley, William L.		7,361 R	53.8%	46.2%	53.8%	46.2%
AL	1972	95,401	41,750	Young, Don	53,651	Begich, Nick*		11,901 D	43.8%	56.2%	43.8%	56.2%
AL	1970	80,084	35,947	Murkowski, Frank H	44,137	Begich, Nick		8,190 D	44.9%	55.1%	44.9%	55.1%
AL	1968	80,362	43,577	Pollock, Howard W.	36,785	Begich, Nick		6,792 R	54.2%	45.8%	54.2%	45.8%
AL	1966	65,907	34,040	Pollock, Howard W.	31,867	Rivers, Ralph J.*		2,173 R	51.6%	48.4%	51.6%	48.4%
AL	1964	67,146	32,556	Thomas, Lowell	34,590	Rivers, Ralph J.*		2,034 D	48.5%	51.5%	48.5%	51.5%
AL	1962	58,591	26,638	Thomas, Lowell	31,953	Rivers, Ralph J.*		5,315 D	45.5%	54.5%	45.5%	54.5%
AL	1960	59,063	25,517	Rettig, R. L.	33,546	Rivers, Ralph J.*		8,029 D	43.2%	56.8%	43.2%	56.8%
AL	1958	48,647	20,699	Benson, Henry A.	27,948	Rivers, Ralph J.*		7,249 D	42.5%	57.5%	42.5%	57.5%

An asterisk (*) denotes incumbent.

ALASKA
GENERAL AND PRIMARY ELECTIONS

2002 GENERAL ELECTIONS

Governor Other vote was 2,926 Green (Dian E. Benson); 2,185 Alaskan Independence (Don Wright); 1,506 Republican Moderate (Raymond Vinzant Sr.); 1,109 Libertarian (Billy Toien); 263 scattered write-in.

Senator Other vote was 16,608 Green (Jim Sykes); 6,724 Alaskan Independence (Jim Dore); 2,354 Libertarian (Leonard Karpinski); 291 scattered write-in.

House Other vote was;

At Large 14,435 Green (Russell deForest); 3,797 Libertarian (Bob Clift); 451 scattered write-in.

2002 PRIMARY ELECTIONS

Primary August 27, 2002

Registration (as of Aug. 27, 2002)

Republican	114,191
Democratic	71,318
Alaskan Independence	17,999
Libertarian	6,727
Green	4,582
Republican Moderate	2,909
Other Parties	4,304
Non-partisan	66,926
Undeclared	161,798
TOTAL	450,754

ALASKA

GENERAL AND PRIMARY ELECTIONS

2002 PRIMARY ELECTIONS

Primary Type   Semi-open—Voters registered with a recognized party in Alaska could vote only in their party's primary. Undeclared and non-partisan voters could participate in any party's primary. (Undeclared voters may be associated with a party, but have not declared which one. Non-partisan voters are not associated with any party.)

Note: An asterisk (*) denotes incumbent.

	REPUBLICAN PRIMARIES			DEMOCRATIC PRIMARIES		
Governor	Frank H. Murkowski	50,838	70.4%	Fran Ulmer	29,640	91.1%
	Wayne A. Ross	18,852	26.1%	Michael Beasley	1,704	5.2%
	Brad Snowden	1,637	2.3%	Bruce J. Lemke	1,203	3.7%
	Eric E. Wieler	921	1.3%			
	TOTAL	72,248			32,547	
Senator	Ted Stevens*	64,315	88.9%	Frank Vondersaar	18,256	66.3%
	Mike Aubrey	7,997	11.1%	Theresa Obermeyer	9,292	33.7%
	TOTAL	72,312		TOTAL	27,548	
House At Large	Don Young*	65,353	100.0%	Clifford Greene	15,467	64.5%
				Dae Miles	8,508	35.5%
				TOTAL	23,975	

ALASKA REPUBLICAN PRIMARY

GOVERNOR 2002

2000 Census Population	District	Total Vote	Murkowski	Ross	Other	Winner	Percentage of Total Vote		
							Murkowski	Ross	Other
15,031	DISTRICT 1	1,799	1,634	112	53	Murkowski	90.8%	6.2%	2.9%
14,991	DISTRICT 2	1,448	1,254	130	64	Murkowski	86.6%	9.0%	4.4%
15,203	DISTRICT 3	1,654	1,282	287	85	Murkowski	77.5%	17.4%	5.1%
15,508	DISTRICT 4	1,890	1,616	204	70	Murkowski	85.5%	10.8%	3.7%
15,048	DISTRICT 5	1,295	1,013	193	89	Murkowski	78.2%	14.9%	6.9%
14,905	DISTRICT 6	1,404	1,098	247	59	Murkowski	78.2%	17.6%	4.2%
15,494	DISTRICT 7	2,455	1,911	454	90	Murkowski	77.8%	18.5%	3.7%
15,552	DISTRICT 8	2,047	1,555	378	114	Murkowski	76.0%	18.5%	5.6%
15,723	DISTRICT 9	1,574	1,287	235	52	Murkowski	81.8%	14.9%	3.3%
15,599	DISTRICT 10	1,156	974	147	35	Murkowski	84.3%	12.7%	3.0%
15,904	DISTRICT 11	2,570	2,145	356	69	Murkowski	83.5%	13.9%	2.7%
16,303	DISTRICT 12	1,992	1,455	462	75	Murkowski	73.0%	23.2%	3.8%
16,231	DISTRICT 13	2,888	1,983	809	96	Murkowski	68.7%	28.0%	3.3%
16,119	DISTRICT 14	2,425	1,643	741	41	Murkowski	67.8%	30.6%	1.7%
16,137	DISTRICT 15	2,243	1,442	725	76	Murkowski	64.3%	32.3%	3.4%
16,104	DISTRICT 16	2,846	1,751	1,023	72	Murkowski	61.5%	35.9%	2.5%
15,819	DISTRICT 17	2,266	1,417	787	62	Murkowski	62.5%	34.7%	2.7%
15,639	DISTRICT 18	948	671	245	32	Murkowski	70.8%	25.8%	3.4%
15,841	DISTRICT 19	1,765	1,141	563	61	Murkowski	64.6%	31.9%	3.5%
15,837	DISTRICT 20	790	486	273	31	Murkowski	61.5%	34.6%	3.9%
15,850	DISTRICT 21	2,146	1,388	698	60	Murkowski	64.7%	32.5%	2.8%
15,831	DISTRICT 22	1,135	701	399	35	Murkowski	61.8%	35.2%	3.1%
15,847	DISTRICT 23	1,126	743	342	41	Murkowski	66.0%	30.4%	3.6%
15,812	DISTRICT 24	1,424	939	446	39	Murkowski	65.9%	31.3%	2.7%
15,836	DISTRICT 25	1,309	784	472	53	Murkowski	59.9%	36.1%	4.0%

ALASKA REPUBLICAN PRIMARY

GOVERNOR 2002

2000 Census Population	District	Total Vote	Murkowski	Ross	Other	Winner	Percentage of Total Vote		
							Murkowski	Ross	Other
15,823	DISTRICT 26	2,190	1,320	802	68	Murkowski	60.3%	36.6%	3.1%
15,820	DISTRICT 27	2,063	1,378	626	59	Murkowski	66.8%	30.3%	2.9%
15,839	DISTRICT 28	2,643	1,740	829	74	Murkowski	65.8%	31.4%	2.8%
15,846	DISTRICT 29	1,317	832	446	39	Murkowski	63.2%	33.9%	3.0%
15,839	DISTRICT 30	1,944	1,214	675	55	Murkowski	62.4%	34.7%	2.8%
15,811	DISTRICT 31	2,706	1,637	987	82	Murkowski	60.5%	36.5%	3.0%
15,329	DISTRICT 32	2,690	1,552	1,059	79	Murkowski	57.7%	39.4%	2.9%
16,466	DISTRICT 33	2,433	1,754	600	79	Murkowski	72.1%	24.7%	3.2%
16,409	DISTRICT 34	2,796	1,995	732	69	Murkowski	71.4%	26.2%	2.5%
16,436	DISTRICT 35	2,737	1,842	706	189	Murkowski	67.3%	25.8%	6.9%
14,928	DISTRICT 36	1,216	864	311	41	Murkowski	71.1%	25.6%	3.4%
15,150	DISTRICT 37	829	689	95	45	Murkowski	83.1%	11.5%	5.4%
14,921	DISTRICT 38	543	429	77	37	Murkowski	79.0%	14.2%	6.8%
14,996	DISTRICT 39	867	708	109	50	Murkowski	81.7%	12.6%	5.8%
15,155	DISTRICT 40	679	571	70	38	Murkowski	84.1%	10.3%	5.6%
626,932	TOTAL	72,248	50,838	18,852	2,558	Murkowski	70.4%	26.1%	3.5%

ALASKA DEMOCRATIC PRIMARY

GOVERNOR 2002

2000 Census Population	District	Total Vote	Ulmer	Other	Winner	Percentage of Total Vote	
						Ulmer	Other
15,031	DISTRICT 1	394	354	40	Ulmer	89.8%	10.2%
14,991	DISTRICT 2	982	898	84	Ulmer	91.4%	8.6%
15,203	DISTRICT 3	1,916	1,834	82	Ulmer	95.7%	4.3%
15,508	DISTRICT 4	1,236	1,172	64	Ulmer	94.8%	5.2%
15,048	DISTRICT 5	942	849	93	Ulmer	90.1%	9.9%
14,905	DISTRICT 6	1,018	872	146	Ulmer	85.7%	14.3%
15,494	DISTRICT 7	1,106	1,020	86	Ulmer	92.2%	7.8%
15,552	DISTRICT 8	1,268	1,193	75	Ulmer	94.1%	5.9%
15,723	DISTRICT 9	817	740	77	Ulmer	90.6%	9.4%
15,599	DISTRICT 10	479	417	62	Ulmer	87.1%	12.9%
15,904	DISTRICT 11	426	359	67	Ulmer	84.3%	15.7%
16,303	DISTRICT 12	361	322	39	Ulmer	89.2%	10.8%
16,231	DISTRICT 13	486	443	43	Ulmer	91.2%	8.8%
16,119	DISTRICT 14	439	395	44	Ulmer	90.0%	10.0%
16,137	DISTRICT 15	440	389	51	Ulmer	88.4%	11.6%
16,104	DISTRICT 16	490	441	49	Ulmer	90.0%	10.0%
15,819	DISTRICT 17	564	532	32	Ulmer	94.3%	5.7%
15,639	DISTRICT 18	210	172	38	Ulmer	81.9%	18.1%
15,841	DISTRICT 19	702	647	55	Ulmer	92.2%	7.8%
15,837	DISTRICT 20	490	449	41	Ulmer	91.6%	8.4%
15,850	DISTRICT 21	960	914	46	Ulmer	95.2%	4.8%
15,831	DISTRICT 22	856	795	61	Ulmer	92.9%	7.1%
15,847	DISTRICT 23	1,891	1,763	128	Ulmer	93.2%	6.8%
15,812	DISTRICT 24	724	681	43	Ulmer	94.1%	5.9%
15,836	DISTRICT 25	863	813	50	Ulmer	94.2%	5.8%
15,823	DISTRICT 26	1,380	1,323	57	Ulmer	95.9%	4.1%
15,820	DISTRICT 27	683	646	37	Ulmer	94.6%	5.4%
15,839	DISTRICT 28	763	714	49	Ulmer	93.6%	6.4%
15,846	DISTRICT 29	578	535	43	Ulmer	92.6%	7.4%
15,839	DISTRICT 30	733	705	28	Ulmer	96.2%	3.8%

ALASKA DEMOCRATIC PRIMARY

GOVERNOR 2002

2000 Census Population	District	Total Vote	Ulmer	Other	Winner	Percentage of Total Vote	
						Ulmer	Other
15,811	DISTRICT 31	837	792	45	Ulmer	94.6%	5.4%
15,329	DISTRICT 32	1,082	1,043	39	Ulmer	96.4%	3.6%
16,466	DISTRICT 33	590	516	74	Ulmer	87.5%	12.5%
16,409	DISTRICT 34	463	389	74	Ulmer	84.0%	16.0%
16,436	DISTRICT 35	637	586	51	Ulmer	92.0%	8.0%
14,928	DISTRICT 36	517	453	64	Ulmer	87.6%	12.4%
15,150	DISTRICT 37	653	534	119	Ulmer	81.8%	18.2%
14,921	DISTRICT 38	1,421	1,152	269	Ulmer	81.1%	18.9%
14,996	DISTRICT 39	1,154	959	195	Ulmer	83.1%	16.9%
15,155	DISTRICT 40	996	829	167	Ulmer	83.2%	16.8%
626,932	TOTAL	32,547	29,640	2,907	Ulmer	91.1%	8.9%

ALASKA REPUBLICAN PRIMARY

SENATOR 2002

2000 Census Population	District	Total Vote	Stevens	Aubrey	Winner	Percentage of Total Vote	
						Stevens	Aubrey
15,031	DISTRICT 1	1,796	1,644	152	Stevens	91.5%	8.5%
14,991	DISTRICT 2	1,445	1,286	159	Stevens	89.0%	11.0%
15,203	DISTRICT 3	1,628	1,372	256	Stevens	84.3%	15.7%
15,508	DISTRICT 4	1,885	1,667	218	Stevens	88.4%	11.6%
15,048	DISTRICT 5	1,294	1,123	171	Stevens	86.8%	13.2%
14,905	DISTRICT 6	1,406	1,241	165	Stevens	88.3%	11.7%
15,494	DISTRICT 7	2,460	2,132	328	Stevens	86.7%	13.3%
15,552	DISTRICT 8	2,038	1,728	310	Stevens	84.8%	15.2%
15,723	DISTRICT 9	1,574	1,389	185	Stevens	88.2%	11.8%
15,599	DISTRICT 10	1,161	1,062	99	Stevens	91.5%	8.5%
15,904	DISTRICT 11	2,574	2,320	254	Stevens	90.1%	9.9%
16,303	DISTRICT 12	1,991	1,733	258	Stevens	87.0%	13.0%
16,231	DISTRICT 13	2,905	2,594	311	Stevens	89.3%	10.7%
16,119	DISTRICT 14	2,419	2,178	241	Stevens	90.0%	10.0%
16,137	DISTRICT 15	2,252	1,938	314	Stevens	86.1%	13.9%
16,104	DISTRICT 16	2,844	2,494	350	Stevens	87.7%	12.3%
15,819	DISTRICT 17	2,269	2,086	183	Stevens	91.9%	8.1%
15,639	DISTRICT 18	961	880	81	Stevens	91.6%	8.4%
15,841	DISTRICT 19	1,780	1,590	190	Stevens	89.3%	10.7%
15,837	DISTRICT 20	789	680	109	Stevens	86.2%	13.8%
15,850	DISTRICT 21	2,144	1,931	213	Stevens	90.1%	9.9%
15,831	DISTRICT 22	1,139	1,004	135	Stevens	88.1%	11.9%
15,847	DISTRICT 23	1,131	1,026	105	Stevens	90.7%	9.3%
15,812	DISTRICT 24	1,430	1,304	126	Stevens	91.2%	8.8%
15,836	DISTRICT 25	1,300	1,136	164	Stevens	87.4%	12.6%
15,823	DISTRICT 26	2,177	1,954	223	Stevens	89.8%	10.2%
15,820	DISTRICT 27	2,068	1,885	183	Stevens	91.2%	8.8%
15,839	DISTRICT 28	2,654	2,453	201	Stevens	92.4%	7.6%
15,846	DISTRICT 29	1,313	1,183	130	Stevens	90.1%	9.9%
15,839	DISTRICT 30	1,949	1,782	167	Stevens	91.4%	8.6%
15,811	DISTRICT 31	2,713	2,436	277	Stevens	89.8%	10.2%
15,329	DISTRICT 32	2,683	2,356	327	Stevens	87.8%	12.2%
16,466	DISTRICT 33	2,438	2,128	310	Stevens	87.3%	12.7%
16,409	DISTRICT 34	2,801	2,437	364	Stevens	87.0%	13.0%
16,436	DISTRICT 35	2,756	2,347	409	Stevens	85.2%	14.8%
14,928	DISTRICT 36	1,193	1,062	131	Stevens	89.0%	11.0%
15,150	DISTRICT 37	835	779	56	Stevens	93.3%	6.7%
14,921	DISTRICT 38	545	501	44	Stevens	91.9%	8.1%
14,996	DISTRICT 39	887	831	56	Stevens	93.7%	6.3%
15,155	DISTRICT 40	685	643	42	Stevens	93.9%	6.1%
626,932	TOTAL	72,312	64,315	7,997	Stevens	88.9%	11.1%

ALASKA DEMOCRATIC PRIMARY

SENATOR 2002

2000 Census Population	District	Total Vote	Vondersaar	Obermeyer	Winner	Percentage of Total Vote	
						Vondersaar	Obermeyer
15,031	DISTRICT 1	319	139	180	Obermeyer	43.6%	56.4%
14,991	DISTRICT 2	688	323	365	Obermeyer	46.9%	53.1%
15,203	DISTRICT 3	1,317	700	617	Vondersaar	53.2%	46.8%
15,508	DISTRICT 4	856	394	462	Obermeyer	46.0%	54.0%
15,048	DISTRICT 5	769	399	370	Vondersaar	51.9%	48.1%
14,905	DISTRICT 6	915	578	337	Vondersaar	63.2%	36.8%
15,494	DISTRICT 7	809	393	416	Obermeyer	48.6%	51.4%
15,552	DISTRICT 8	999	501	498	Vondersaar	50.2%	49.8%
15,723	DISTRICT 9	684	311	373	Obermeyer	45.5%	54.5%
15,599	DISTRICT 10	412	137	275	Obermeyer	33.3%	66.7%
15,904	DISTRICT 11	380	135	245	Obermeyer	35.5%	64.5%
16,303	DISTRICT 12	321	196	125	Vondersaar	61.1%	38.9%
16,231	DISTRICT 13	432	341	91	Vondersaar	78.9%	21.1%
16,119	DISTRICT 14	392	300	92	Vondersaar	76.5%	23.5%
16,137	DISTRICT 15	403	310	93	Vondersaar	76.9%	23.1%
16,104	DISTRICT 16	436	348	88	Vondersaar	79.8%	20.2%
15,819	DISTRICT 17	491	381	110	Vondersaar	77.6%	22.4%
15,639	DISTRICT 18	200	113	87	Vondersaar	56.5%	43.5%
15,841	DISTRICT 19	612	436	176	Vondersaar	71.2%	28.8%
15,837	DISTRICT 20	445	295	150	Vondersaar	66.3%	33.7%
15,850	DISTRICT 21	849	655	194	Vondersaar	77.1%	22.9%
15,831	DISTRICT 22	767	559	208	Vondersaar	72.9%	27.1%
15,847	DISTRICT 23	1,647	1,221	426	Vondersaar	74.1%	25.9%
15,812	DISTRICT 24	634	472	162	Vondersaar	74.4%	25.6%
15,836	DISTRICT 25	739	580	159	Vondersaar	78.5%	21.5%
15,823	DISTRICT 26	1,133	915	218	Vondersaar	80.8%	19.2%
15,820	DISTRICT 27	617	494	123	Vondersaar	80.1%	19.9%
15,839	DISTRICT 28	671	543	128	Vondersaar	80.9%	19.1%
15,846	DISTRICT 29	515	386	129	Vondersaar	75.0%	25.0%
15,839	DISTRICT 30	639	514	125	Vondersaar	80.4%	19.6%
15,811	DISTRICT 31	744	628	116	Vondersaar	84.4%	15.6%
15,329	DISTRICT 32	927	785	142	Vondersaar	84.7%	15.3%
16,466	DISTRICT 33	513	362	151	Vondersaar	70.6%	29.4%
16,409	DISTRICT 34	408	293	115	Vondersaar	71.8%	28.2%
16,436	DISTRICT 35	533	387	146	Vondersaar	72.6%	27.4%
14,928	DISTRICT 36	435	255	180	Vondersaar	58.6%	41.4%
15,150	DISTRICT 37	585	385	200	Vondersaar	65.8%	34.2%
14,921	DISTRICT 38	1,329	812	517	Vondersaar	61.1%	38.9%
14,996	DISTRICT 39	1,046	671	375	Vondersaar	64.1%	35.9%
15,155	DISTRICT 40	937	609	328	Vondersaar	65.0%	35.0%
626,932	TOTAL	27,548	18,256	9,292	Vondersaar	66.3%	33.7%

ARIZONA

GOVERNOR
Janet Napolitano (D). Elected 2002 to a four-year term.

SENATORS (2 Republicans)
Jon Kyl (R). Reelected 2000 to a six-year term. Previously elected 1994.

John McCain (R). Reelected 1998 to a six-year term. Previously elected 1992, 1986.

REPRESENTATIVES (6 Republicans, 2 Democrats)
1. Rick Renzi (R)
2. Trent Franks (R)
3. John Shadegg (R)
4. Ed Pastor (D)
5. J. D. Hayworth (R)
6. Jeff Flake (R)
7. Raul M. Grijalva (D)
8. Jim Kolbe (R)

POSTWAR VOTE FOR PRESIDENT

| | | Republican | | Democratic | | | | Percentage | | | |
| | | | | | | | | Total Vote | | Major Vote | |
Year	Total Vote	Vote	Candidate	Vote	Candidate	Other Vote	Plurality	Rep.	Dem.	Rep.	Dem.
2000**	1,532,016	781,652	Bush, George W.	685,341	Gore, Al	65,023	96,311 R	51.0%	44.7%	53.3%	46.7%
1996**	1,404,405	622,073	Dole, Bob	653,288	Clinton, Bill	129,044	31,215 D	44.3%	46.5%	48.8%	51.2%
1992**	1,486,975	572,086	Bush, George	543,050	Clinton, Bill	371,839	29,036 R	38.5%	36.5%	51.3%	48.7%
1988	1,171,873	702,541	Bush, George	454,029	Dukakis, Michael S.	15,303	248,512 R	60.0%	38.7%	60.7%	39.3%
1984	1,025,897	681,416	Reagan, Ronald	333,854	Mondale, Walter F.	10,627	347,562 R	66.4%	32.5%	67.1%	32.9%
1980**	873,945	529,688	Reagan, Ronald	246,843	Carter, Jimmy	97,414	282,845 R	60.6%	28.2%	68.2%	31.8%
1976	742,719	418,642	Ford, Gerald R.	295,602	Carter, Jimmy	28,475	123,040 R	56.4%	39.8%	58.6%	41.4%
1972	622,926	402,812	Nixon, Richard M.	198,540	McGovern, George S.	21,574	204,272 R	64.7%	31.9%	67.0%	33.0%
1968	486,936	266,721	Nixon, Richard M.	170,514	Humphrey, Hubert H.	49,701	96,207 R	54.8%	35.0%	61.0%	39.0%
1964	480,770	242,535	Goldwater, Barry M.	237,753	Johnson, Lyndon B.	482	4,782 R	50.4%	49.5%	50.5%	49.5%
1960	398,491	221,241	Nixon, Richard M.	176,781	Kennedy, John F.	469	44,460 R	55.5%	44.4%	55.6%	44.4%
1956	290,173	176,990	Eisenhower, Dwight D.	112,880	Stevenson, Adlai E.	303	64,110 R	61.0%	38.9%	61.1%	38.9%
1952	260,570	152,042	Eisenhower, Dwight D.	108,528	Stevenson, Adlai E.		43,514 R	58.3%	41.7%	58.3%	41.7%
1948	177,065	77,597	Dewey, Thomas E.	95,251	Truman, Harry S.	4,217	17,654 D	43.8%	53.8%	44.9%	55.1%

In 2000 the other vote column includes 45,645 votes cast for Green (Nader). In 1996 the other vote column includes 112,072 votes cast for Perot. In 1992 the other vote column includes 353,741 votes cast for Perot. In 1980 the other column includes 76,952 votes for Independent (Anderson).

ARIZONA

POSTWAR VOTE FOR GOVERNOR

Year	Total Vote	Republican Vote	Republican Candidate	Democratic Vote	Democratic Candidate	Other Vote	Rep.-Dem. Plurality	Percentage Total Vote Rep.	Dem.	Major Vote Rep.	Dem.
2002	1,226,111	554,465	Salmon, Matt	566,284	Napolitano, Janet	105,362	11,819 D	45.2%	46.2%	49.5%	50.5%
1998	1,017,616	620,188	Hull, Jane Dee	361,552	Johnson, Paul	35,876	258,636 R	60.9%	35.5%	63.2%	36.8%
1994	1,129,607	593,492	Symington, Fife	500,702	Basha, Eddie	35,413	92,790 R	52.5%	44.3%	54.2%	45.8%
1990**	940,737	492,569	Symington, Fife	448,168	Goddard, Terry		44,401 R	52.4%	47.6%	52.4%	47.6%
1986**	866,984	343,913	Mecham, Evan	298,986	Warner, Carolyn	224,085	44,927 R	39.7%	34.5%	53.5%	46.5%
1982	726,364	235,877	Corbet, Leo	453,795	Babbitt, Bruce	36,692	217,918 D	32.5%	62.5%	34.2%	65.8%
1978	538,556	241,093	Mecham, Evan	282,605	Babbitt, Bruce	14,858	41,512 D	44.8%	52.5%	46.0%	54.0%
1974	552,202	273,674	Williams, Russell	278,375	Castro, Raul H.	153	4,701 D	49.6%	50.4%	49.6%	50.4%
1970**	411,409	209,522	Williams, John R.	201,887	Castro, Raul H.		7,635 R	50.9%	49.1%	50.9%	49.1%
1968	483,998	279,923	Williams, John R.	204,075	Goddard, Sam		75,848 R	57.8%	42.2%	57.8%	42.2%
1966	378,342	203,438	Williams, John R.	174,904	Goddard, Sam		28,534 R	53.8%	46.2%	53.8%	46.2%
1964	473,502	221,404	Kleindienst, Richard	252,098	Goddard, Sam		30,694 D	46.8%	53.2%	46.8%	53.2%
1962	365,841	200,578	Fannin, Paul	165,263	Goddard, Sam		35,315 R	54.8%	45.2%	54.8%	45.2%
1960	397,107	235,502	Fannin, Paul	161,605	Ackerman, Lee		73,897 R	59.3%	40.7%	59.3%	40.7%
1958	290,465	160,136	Fannin, Paul	130,329	Morrison, Robert		29,807 R	55.1%	44.9%	55.1%	44.9%
1956	288,592	116,744	Griffen, Horace B.	171,848	McFarland, Ernest W.		55,104 D	40.5%	59.5%	40.5%	59.5%
1954	243,970	115,866	Pyle, Howard	128,104	McFarland, Ernest W.		12,238 D	47.5%	52.5%	47.5%	52.5%
1952	260,285	156,592	Pyle, Howard	103,693	Haldiman, Joe C.		52,899 R	60.2%	39.8%	60.2%	39.8%
1950	195,227	99,109	Pyle, Howard	96,118	Frohmiller, Ana		2,991 R	50.8%	49.2%	50.8%	49.2%
1948	175,767	70,419	Brockett, Bruce	104,008	Garvey, Dan E.	1,340	33,589 D	40.1%	59.2%	40.4%	59.6%
1946	122,462	48,867	Brockett, Bruce	73,595	Osborn, Sidney P.		24,728 D	39.9%	60.1%	39.9%	60.1%

In 1990 neither major-party candidate won an absolute majority, therefore a runoff election was held February 26, 1991; the vote above is for the February runoff. In 1986 other vote was Bill Schulz (Independent). The term of office for Arizona's Governor was increased from two to four years effective with the 1970 election.

POSTWAR VOTE FOR SENATOR

Year	Total Vote	Republican Vote	Republican Candidate	Democratic Vote	Democratic Candidate	Other Vote	Rep.-Dem. Plurality	Percentage Total Vote Rep.	Dem.	Major Vote Rep.	Dem.
2000**	1,397,076	1,108,196	Kyl, Jon	—		288,880	1,108,196 R	79.3%		100.0%	
1998	1,013,280	696,577	McCain, John	275,224	Ranger, Ed	41,479	421,353 R	68.7%	27.2%	71.7%	28.3%
1994	1,119,060	600,999	Kyl, Jon	442,510	Coppersmith, Sam	75,551	158,489 R	53.7%	39.5%	57.6%	42.4%
1992	1,382,051	771,395	McCain, John	436,321	Sargent, Claire	174,335	335,074 R	55.8%	31.6%	63.9%	36.1%
1988	1,164,539	478,060	DeGreen, Keith	660,403	DeConcini, Dennis	26,076	182,343 D	41.1%	56.7%	42.0%	58.0%
1986	862,921	521,850	McCain, John	340,965	Kimball, Richard	106	180,885 R	60.5%	39.5%	60.5%	39.5%
1982	723,885	291,749	Dunn, Pete	411,970	DeConcini, Dennis	20,166	120,221 D	40.3%	56.9%	41.5%	58.5%
1980	874,238	432,371	Goldwater, Barry M.	422,972	Schulz, Bill	18,895	9,399 R	49.5%	48.4%	50.5%	49.5%
1976	741,210	321,236	Steiger, Sam	400,334	DeConcini, Dennis	19,640	79,098 D	43.3%	54.0%	44.5%	55.5%
1974	549,919	320,396	Goldwater, Barry M.	229,523	Marshall, Jonathan		90,873 R	58.3%	41.7%	58.3%	41.7%
1970	407,796	228,284	Fannin, Paul	179,512	Grossman, Sam		48,772 R	56.0%	44.0%	56.0%	44.0%
1968	479,945	274,607	Goldwater, Barry M.	205,338	Elson, Roy L.		69,269 R	57.2%	42.8%	57.2%	42.8%
1964	468,801	241,089	Fannin, Paul	227,712	Elson, Roy L.		13,377 R	51.4%	48.6%	51.4%	48.6%
1962	362,605	163,388	Mecham, Evan	199,217	Hayden, Carl		35,829 D	45.1%	54.9%	45.1%	54.9%
1958	293,623	164,593	Goldwater, Barry M.	129,030	McFarland, Ernest W.		35,563 R	56.1%	43.9%	56.1%	43.9%
1956	278,263	107,447	Jones, Ross F.	170,816	Hayden, Carl		63,369 D	38.6%	61.4%	38.6%	61.4%
1952	257,401	132,063	Goldwater, Barry M.	125,338	McFarland, Ernest W.		6,725 R	51.3%	48.7%	51.3%	48.7%
1950	185,092	68,846	Brockett, Bruce	116,246	Hayden, Carl		47,400 D	37.2%	62.8%	37.2%	62.8%
1946	116,239	35,022	Powers, Ward S.	80,415	McFarland, Ernest W.	802	45,393 D	30.1%	69.2%	30.3%	69.7%

The Democratic Party did not run a candidate in the 2000 Senate election.

ARIZONA

Congressional districts first established for elections held in 2002
8 members

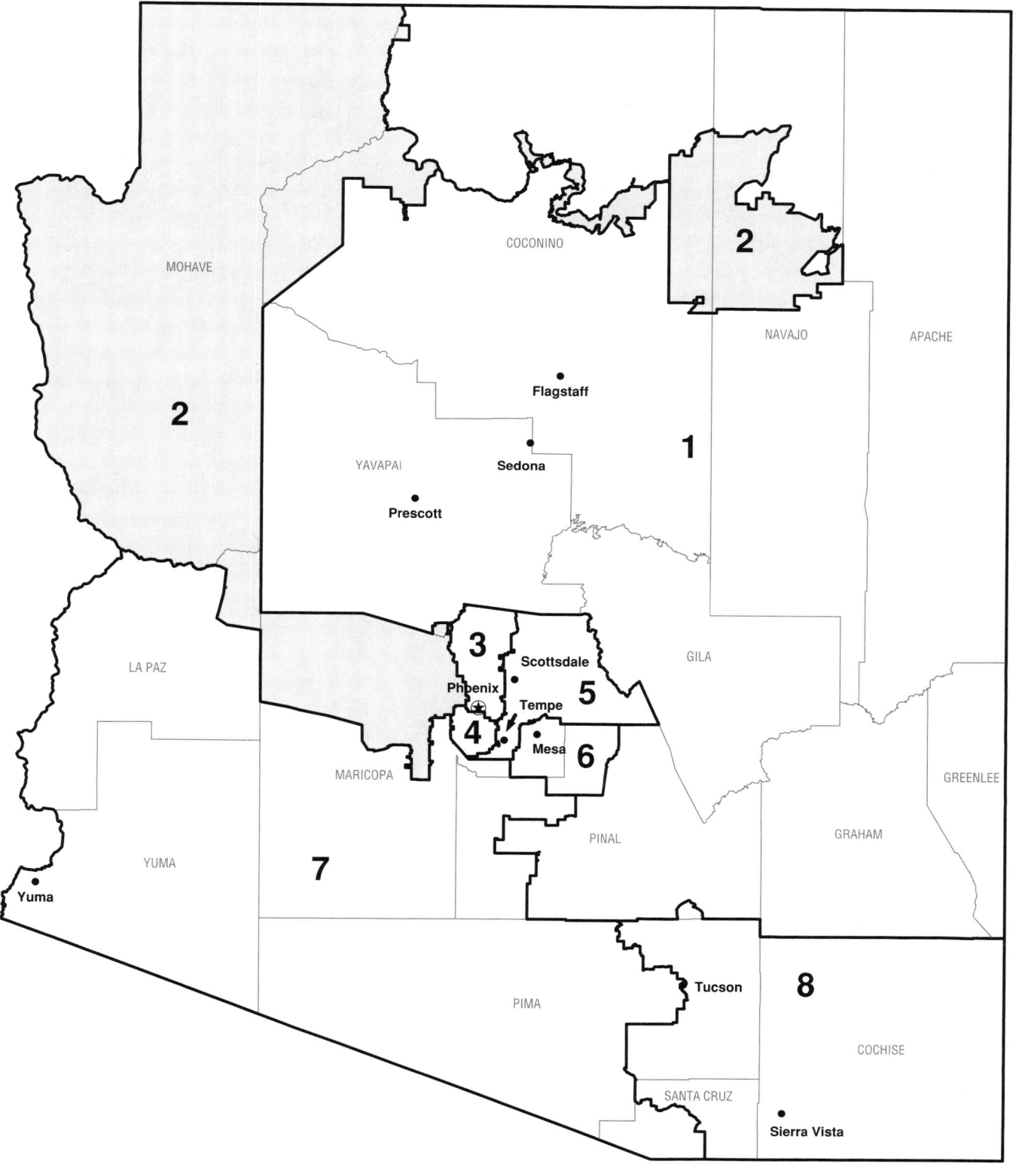

ARIZONA

GOVERNOR 2002

2000 Census Population	County	Total Vote	Republican	Democratic	Other	Rep.-Dem. Plurality	Total Vote Rep.	Total Vote Dem.	Major Vote Rep.	Major Vote Dem.
69,423	APACHE	17,850	4,041	10,927	2,882	6,886 D	22.6%	61.2%	27.0%	73.0%
117,755	COCHISE	27,754	13,210	11,401	3,143	1,809 R	47.6%	41.1%	53.7%	46.3%
116,320	COCONINO	34,485	11,585	18,928	3,972	7,343 D	33.6%	54.9%	38.0%	62.0%
51,335	GILA	15,452	6,336	7,331	1,785	995 D	41.0%	47.4%	46.4%	53.6%
33,489	GRAHAM	7,981	4,491	2,924	566	1,567 R	56.3%	36.6%	60.6%	39.4%
8,547	GREENLEE	2,151	955	966	230	11 D	44.4%	44.9%	49.7%	50.3%
19,715	LA PAZ	3,626	1,766	1,488	372	278 R	48.7%	41.0%	54.3%	45.7%
3,072,149	MARICOPA	704,750	337,954	313,107	53,689	24,847 R	48.0%	44.4%	51.9%	48.1%
155,032	MOHAVE	35,186	18,431	13,227	3,528	5,204 R	52.4%	37.6%	58.2%	41.8%
97,470	NAVAJO	23,458	9,423	11,669	2,366	2,246 D	40.2%	49.7%	44.7%	55.3%
843,746	PIMA	229,803	89,002	118,896	21,905	29,894 D	38.7%	51.7%	42.8%	57.2%
179,727	PINAL	38,023	16,380	18,300	3,343	1,920 D	43.1%	48.1%	47.2%	52.8%
38,381	SANTA CRUZ	6,344	2,069	3,675	600	1,606 D	32.6%	57.9%	36.0%	64.0%
167,517	YAVAPAI	57,376	28,245	23,238	5,893	5,007 R	49.2%	40.5%	54.9%	45.1%
160,026	YUMA	21,872	10,577	10,207	1,088	370 R	48.4%	46.7%	50.9%	49.1%
5,130,632	TOTAL	1,226,111	554,465	566,284	105,362	11,819 D	45.2%	46.2%	49.5%	50.5%

ARIZONA

HOUSE OF REPRESENTATIVES

CD	Year	Total Vote	Republican Vote	Republican Candidate	Democratic Vote	Democratic Candidate	Other Vote	Rep.-Dem. Plurality	Total Vote Rep.	Total Vote Dem.	Major Vote Rep.	Major Vote Dem.
1	2002	174,687	85,967	Renzi, Rick	79,730	Cordova, George	8,990	6,237 R	49.2%	45.6%	51.9%	48.1%
2	2002	167,502	100,359	Franks, Trent	61,217	Camacho, Randy	5,926	39,142 R	59.9%	36.5%	62.1%	37.9%
3	2002	155,751	104,847	Shadegg, John*	47,173	Hill, Charles	3,731	57,674 R	67.3%	30.3%	69.0%	31.0%
4	2002	66,065	18,381	Barnert, Jonathan	44,517	Pastor, Ed*	3,167	26,136 D	27.8%	67.4%	29.2%	70.8%
5	2002	169,812	103,870	Hayworth, J.D.*	61,559	Columbus, Craig	4,383	42,311 R	61.2%	36.3%	62.8%	37.2%
6	2002	156,337	103,094	Flake, Jeff*	49,355	Thomas, Deborah	3,888	53,739 R	65.9%	31.6%	67.6%	32.4%
7	2002	103,818	38,474	Hieb, Ross	61,256	Grijalva, Raul M.	4,088	22,782 D	37.1%	59.0%	38.6%	61.4%
8	2002	200,428	126,930	Kolbe, Jim*	67,328	Ryan, Mary Judge	6,170	59,602 R	63.3%	33.6%	65.3%	34.7%
Total	2002	1,194,400	681,922		472,135		40,343	209,787 R	57.1%	39.5%	59.1%	40.9%

An asterisk (*) denotes incumbent.

ARIZONA
GENERAL AND PRIMARY ELECTIONS

2002 GENERAL ELECTIONS

Governor Other vote was 84,947 Independent (Richard Mahoney); 20,356 Libertarian (Barry Hess); 29 write-in (Carlton Rahmani); 15 write-in (Tracey Sturgess); 5 write-in (Naida Axford); 5 write-in ("Rayj" Raymond Caplette); 4 write-in (D'Herrera Tapia); 1 write-in (L.D. "Denny" Talbow).

House Other vote was:

CD 1 8,990 Libertarian (Edwin Porr).
CD 2 5,919 Libertarian (Edward Carlson); 7 write-in (William Crum).
CD 3 3,731 Libertarian (Mark Yannone).
CD 4 3,167 Libertarian (Amy Gibbons).
CD 5 4,383 Libertarian (Warren Severin).
CD 6 3,888 Libertarian (Andy Wagner).
CD 7 4,088 Libertarian (John L. Nemeth).
CD 8 6,142 Libertarian (Joe Duarte); 28 write-in (Jim Dorrance).

2002 PRIMARY ELECTIONS

Primary September 10, 2002

Registration
(as of Sept. 10, 2002)

Republican	930,125
Democratic	798,375
Libertarian	14,119
Other	464,831
TOTAL	2,207,450

Primary Type Semi-open—Voters registered with a recognized party in Arizona could vote only in their party's primary. Other voters could participate in the primary of their choice.

Note: An asterisk (*) denotes incumbent.

	REPUBLICAN PRIMARIES			DEMOCRATIC PRIMARIES		
Governor	Matt Salmon	174,055	56.0%	Janet Napolitano	128,702	57.2%
	Betsey Bayless	92,473	29.7%	Alfredo Gutierrez	50,377	22.4%
	Carol Springer	44,333	14.3%	Mark Osterloh	31,422	14.0%
	Steve Moore (write-in)	16		Mike Newcomb	14,373	6.4%
	Diana Kennedy (write-in)	8				
	TOTAL	310,885		TOTAL	224,874	
Congressional District 1	Rick Renzi	11,379	24.4%	George Cordova	11,689	21.7%
	Lewis Noble Tenney	9,569	20.5%	Stephen Udall	10,690	19.9%
	Sydney Ann Hay	9,550	20.5%	Diane Prescott	9,629	17.9%
	Alan Everett	7,321	15.7%	Fred Duval	8,648	16.1%
	Bruce Whiting	6,872	14.8%	Derrick Watchman	7,326	13.6%
	David Stafford	1,894	4.1%	Sam Martinez	4,908	9.1%
				Roger Hartstone	922	1.7%
	TOTAL	46,585		TOTAL	53,812	
Congressional District 2	Trent Franks	14,749	27.7%	Randy Camacho	6,507	33.0%
	Lisa Atkins	13,952	26.2%	Elizabeth "Liz" Farley	5,994	30.4%
	John Keegan	10,560	19.8%	Sandy Reagan	3,857	19.6%
	Scott Bundgaard	8,701	16.3%	Linda Calvert	3,323	16.9%
	Dusko Jovicic	3,805	7.1%	Gene Scharer (write-in)	28	0.1%
	Mike Schaefer	933	1.7%			
	Dick Hensley	618	1.2%			
	TOTAL	53,318		TOTAL	19,709	

ARIZONA

GENERAL AND PRIMARY ELECTIONS

	REPUBLICAN PRIMARIES			DEMOCRATIC PRIMARIES		
Congressional District 3	John Shadegg*	36,500	100.0%	Charles Hill	14,336	100.0%
Congressional District 4	Jonathan Barnett	5,616	74.6%	Ed Pastor*	17,051	100.0%
	Don Karg	1,913	25.4%			
	TOTAL	7,529				
Congressional District 5	J.D. Hayworth*	37,325	100.0%	Craig Columbus	8,147	49.0%
				Larry King	4,903	29.5%
				Ronald E. Maynard	3,567	21.5%
				TOTAL	16,617	
Congressional District 6	Jeff Flake*	41,025	100.0%	Deborah Thomas	13,720	100.0%
Congressional District 7	Ross Hieb	6,426	40.7%	Raul M. Grijalva	14,835	40.8%
	Joseph Sweeney	4,781	30.3%	Elaine Richardson	7,589	20.9%
	Al Pina	2,372	15.0%	Jaime P. Gutierrez	5,401	14.9%
	Lori Lustig	2,207	14.0%	Lisa Otondo	2,302	6.3%
				Luis Armando Gonzales	2,105	5.8%
				Mark Fleisher	2,022	5.6%
				Sherry Smith	1,058	2.9%
				Jesus Romo	1,008	2.8%
	TOTAL	15,786		TOTAL	36,320	
Congressional District 8	Jim Kolbe*	35,546	72.5%	Mary Judge Ryan	32,322	100.0%
	James (Jim) Behnke	13,502	27.5%			
	TOTAL	49,048				

ARIZONA REPUBLICAN PRIMARY

GOVERNOR 2002

2000 Census Population	County	Total Vote	Salmon	Bayless	Springer	Other	Winner	Percentage of Total Vote Salmon	Bayless	Springer
69,423	APACHE	2,225	1,082	549	591	3	Salmon	48.6%	24.7%	26.6%
117,755	COCHISE	8,163	4,450	2,191	1,509	13	Salmon	54.5%	26.8%	18.5%
116,320	COCONINO	6,505	3,278	1,926	1,301		Salmon	50.4%	29.6%	20.0%
51,335	GILA	3,714	1,976	1,096	642		Salmon	53.2%	29.5%	17.3%
33,489	GRAHAM	2,162	1,494	382	286		Salmon	69.1%	17.7%	13.2%
8,547	GREENLEE	296	192	48	56		Salmon	64.9%	16.2%	18.9%
19,715	LA PAZ	967	422	367	178		Salmon	43.6%	38.0%	18.4%
3,072,149	MARICOPA	183,811	110,755	54,109	18,941	6	Salmon	60.3%	29.4%	10.3%
155,032	MOHAVE	12,544	6,631	3,304	2,609		Salmon	52.9%	26.3%	20.8%
97,470	NAVAJO	6,087	4,036	1,174	877		Salmon	66.3%	19.3%	14.4%
843,746	PIMA	46,337	21,468	17,250	7,619		Salmon	46.3%	37.2%	16.4%
179,727	PINAL	7,134	4,064	1,899	1,171		Salmon	57.0%	26.6%	16.4%
38,381	SANTA CRUZ	1,280	552	440	288		Salmon	43.1%	34.4%	22.5%
167,517	YAVAPAI	23,466	10,409	5,574	7,481	2	Salmon	44.4%	23.8%	31.9%
160,026	YUMA	6,194	3,246	2,164	784		Salmon	52.4%	34.9%	12.7%
5,130,632	TOTAL	310,885	174,055	92,473	44,333	24	Salmon	56.0%	29.7%	14.3%

ARIZONA DEMOCRATIC PRIMARY
GOVERNOR 2002

2000 Census Population	County	Total Vote	Napolitano	Gutierrez	Osterloh	Newcomb	Winner	Percentage of Total Vote			
								Napolitano	Gutierrez	Osterloh	Newcomb
69,423	APACHE	10,200	4,800	2,185	958	2,257	Napolitano	47.1%	21.4%	9.4%	22.1%
117,755	COCHISE	6,839	3,166	1,961	1,254	458	Napolitano	46.3%	28.7%	18.3%	6.7%
116,320	COCONINO	9,020	4,930	2,072	1,116	902	Napolitano	54.7%	23.0%	12.4%	10.0%
51,335	GILA	4,954	2,268	1,637	732	317	Napolitano	45.8%	33.0%	14.8%	6.4%
33,489	GRAHAM	2,458	979	770	482	227	Napolitano	39.8%	31.3%	19.6%	9.2%
8,547	GREENLEE	1,114	415	438	161	100	Gutierrez	37.3%	39.3%	14.5%	9.0%
19,715	LA PAZ	709	367	139	117	86	Napolitano	51.8%	19.6%	16.5%	12.1%
3,072,149	MARICOPA	93,084	57,753	20,059	11,189	4,083	Napolitano	62.0%	21.5%	12.0%	4.4%
155,032	MOHAVE	5,469	3,247	620	1,086	516	Napolitano	59.4%	11.3%	19.9%	9.4%
97,470	NAVAJO	7,623	3,881	1,666	969	1,107	Napolitano	50.9%	21.9%	12.7%	14.5%
843,746	PIMA	52,778	30,017	11,161	9,212	2,388	Napolitano	56.9%	21.1%	17.5%	4.5%
179,727	PINAL	10,479	5,244	3,009	1,580	646	Napolitano	50.0%	28.7%	15.1%	6.2%
38,381	SANTA CRUZ	3,870	2,014	1,417	283	156	Napolitano	52.0%	36.6%	7.3%	4.0%
167,517	YAVAPAI	10,292	6,561	1,630	1,537	564	Napolitano	63.7%	15.8%	14.9%	5.5%
160,026	YUMA	5,985	3,060	1,613	746	566	Napolitano	51.1%	27.0%	12.5%	9.5%
5,130,632	TOTAL	224,874	128,702	50,377	31,422	14,373	Napolitano	57.2%	22.4%	14.0%	6.4%

ARKANSAS

GOVERNOR
Mike Huckabee (R). Reelected 2002 to a four-year term. Had become Governor in July 1996 upon the resignation of Governor Jim Guy Tucker (D) who was convicted on fraud and conspiracy charges. Huckabee won his first full term in 1998.

SENATORS (2 Democrats)
Blanche Lincoln (D). Elected 1998 to a six-year term.

Mark Pryor (D). Elected 2002 to a six-year term.

REPRESENTATIVES (1 Republican, 3 Democrats)
1. Marion Berry (D)
2. Vic Snyder (D)
3. John Boozman (R)
4. Mike Ross (D)

POSTWAR VOTE FOR PRESIDENT

| | | Republican | | Democratic | | Other | | Percentage | | | |
| | | | | | | | | Total Vote | | Major Vote | |
Year	Total Vote	Vote	Candidate	Vote	Candidate	Vote	Plurality	Rep.	Dem.	Rep.	Dem.
2000**	921,781	472,940	Bush, George W.	422,768	Gore, Al	26,073	50,172 R	51.3%	45.9%	52.8%	47.2%
1996**	884,262	325,416	Dole, Bob	475,171	Clinton, Bill	83,675	149,755 D	36.8%	53.7%	40.6%	59.4%
1992**	950,653	337,324	Bush, George	505,823	Clinton, Bill	107,506	168,499 D	35.5%	53.2%	40.0%	60.0%
1988	827,738	466,578	Bush, George	349,237	Dukakis, Michael S.	11,923	117,341 R	56.4%	42.2%	57.2%	42.8%
1984	884,406	534,774	Reagan, Ronald	338,646	Mondale, Walter F.	10,986	196,128 R	60.5%	38.3%	61.2%	38.8%
1980**	837,582	403,164	Reagan, Ronald	398,041	Carter, Jimmy	36,377	5,123 R	48.1%	47.5%	50.3%	49.7%
1976	767,535	267,903	Ford, Gerald R.	498,604	Carter, Jimmy	1,028	230,701 D	34.9%	65.0%	35.0%	65.0%
1972	651,320	448,541	Nixon, Richard M.	199,892	McGovern, George S.	2,887	248,649 R	68.9%	30.7%	69.2%	30.8%
1968**	619,969	190,759	Nixon, Richard M.	188,228	Humphrey, Hubert H.	240,982	50,223 A	30.8%	30.4%	50.3%	49.7%
1964	560,426	243,264	Goldwater, Barry M.	314,197	Johnson, Lyndon B.	2,965	70,933 D	43.4%	56.1%	43.6%	56.4%
1960	428,509	184,508	Nixon, Richard M.	215,049	Kennedy, John F.	28,952	30,541 D	43.1%	50.2%	46.2%	53.8%
1956	406,572	186,287	Eisenhower, Dwight D.	213,277	Stevenson, Adlai E.	7,008	26,990 D	45.8%	52.5%	46.6%	53.4%
1952	404,800	177,155	Eisenhower, Dwight D.	226,300	Stevenson, Adlai E.	1,345	49,145 D	43.8%	55.9%	43.9%	56.1%
1948**	242,475	50,959	Dewey, Thomas E.	149,659	Truman, Harry S.	41,857	98,700 D	21.0%	61.7%	25.4%	74.6%

In 2000 the other vote column includes 13,421 votes cast for Green (Nader). In 1996 the other vote column includes 69,884 votes cast for Perot. In 1992 the other vote column includes 99,132 votes cast for Perot. In 1980 the other column includes 22,468 votes for Independent (Anderson). In 1968 other vote was American (Wallace). In 1948 other vote was 40,068 States Rights; 1,037 Socialist; 751 Progressive and 1 Prohibition.

ARKANSAS

POSTWAR VOTE FOR GOVERNOR

Year	Total Vote	Republican		Democratic		Other Vote	Rep.-Dem. Plurality	Percentage			
								Total Vote		Major Vote	
		Vote	Candidate	Vote	Candidate			Rep.	Dem.	Rep.	Dem.
2002	805,696	427,082	Huckabee, Mike	378,250	Fisher, Jimmie Lou	364	48,832 R	53.0%	46.9%	53.0%	47.0%
1998	706,011	421,989	Huckabee, Mike	272,923	Bristow, Bill	11,099	149,066 R	59.8%	38.7%	60.7%	39.3%
1994	716,840	287,904	Nelson, Sheffield	428,936	Tucker, Jim Guy		141,032 D	40.2%	59.8%	40.2%	59.8%
1990	696,412	295,925	Nelson, Sheffield	400,386	Clinton, Bill	101	104,461 D	42.5%	57.5%	42.5%	57.5%
1986**	688,551	248,427	White, Frank D.	439,882	Clinton, Bill	242	191,455 D	36.1%	63.9%	36.1%	63.9%
1984	886,548	331,987	Freeman, Woody	554,561	Clinton, Bill		222,574 D	37.4%	62.6%	37.4%	62.6%
1982	789,351	357,496	White, Frank D.	431,855	Clinton, Bill		74,359 D	45.3%	54.7%	45.3%	54.7%
1980	838,925	435,684	White, Frank D.	403,241	Clinton, Bill		32,443 R	51.9%	48.1%	51.9%	48.1%
1978	528,912	193,746	Lowe, A. Lynn	335,101	Clinton, Bill	65	141,355 D	36.6%	63.4%	36.6%	63.4%
1976	726,949	121,716	Griffith, Leon	605,083	Pryor, David H.	150	483,367 D	16.7%	83.2%	16.7%	83.3%
1974	545,974	187,872	Coon, Ken	358,018	Pryor, David H.	84	170,146 D	34.4%	65.6%	34.4%	65.6%
1972	648,069	159,177	Blaylock, Len E.	488,892	Bumpers, Dale		329,715 D	24.6%	75.4%	24.6%	75.4%
1970	609,198	197,418	Rockefeller, Winthrop	375,648	Bumpers, Dale	36,132	178,230 D	32.4%	61.7%	34.4%	65.6%
1968	615,595	322,782	Rockefeller, Winthrop	292,813	Crank, Marion		29,969 R	52.4%	47.6%	52.4%	47.6%
1966	563,527	306,324	Rockefeller, Winthrop	257,203	Johnson, James D.		49,121 R	54.4%	45.6%	54.4%	45.6%
1964	592,113	254,561	Rockefeller, Winthrop	337,489	Faubus, Orval E.	63	82,928 D	43.0%	57.0%	43.0%	57.0%
1962	308,092	82,349	Ricketts, Willis	225,743	Faubus, Orval E.		143,394 D	26.7%	73.3%	26.7%	73.3%
1960	421,985	129,921	Britt, Henry M.	292,064	Faubus, Orval E.		162,143 D	30.8%	69.2%	30.8%	69.2%
1958	286,886	50,288	Johnson, George W.	236,598	Faubus, Orval E.		186,310 D	17.5%	82.5%	17.5%	82.5%
1956	399,012	77,215	Mitchell, Roy	321,797	Faubus, Orval E.		244,582 D	19.4%	80.6%	19.4%	80.6%
1954	335,176	127,004	Remmel, Pratt C.	208,121	Faubus, Orval E.	51	81,117 D	37.9%	62.1%	37.9%	62.1%
1952	391,592	49,292	Speck, Jefferson W.	342,292	Cherry, Francis	8	293,000 D	12.6%	87.4%	12.6%	87.4%
1950	317,087	50,309	Speck, Jefferson W.	266,778	McMath, Sidney S.		216,469 D	15.9%	84.1%	15.9%	84.1%
1948	249,301	26,500	Black, Charles R.	222,801	McMath, Sidney S.		196,301 D	10.6%	89.4%	10.6%	89.4%
1946	152,162	24,133	Mills, W. T.	128,029	Laney, Ben T.		103,896 D	15.9%	84.1%	15.9%	84.1%

The term of office for Arkansas' Governor was increased from two to four years effective with the 1986 election.

POSTWAR VOTE FOR SENATOR

Year	Total Vote	Republican		Democratic		Other Vote	Rep.-Dem. Plurality	Percentage			
								Total Vote		Major Vote	
		Vote	Candidate	Vote	Candidate			Rep.	Dem.	Rep.	Dem.
2002	803,959	370,653	Hutchinson, Tim	433,306	Pryor, Mark		62,653 D	46.1%	53.9%	46.1%	53.9%
1998	700,644	295,870	Boozman, Fay	385,878	Lincoln, Blanche	18,896	90,008 D	42.2%	55.1%	43.4%	56.6%
1996	846,183	445,942	Hutchinson, Tim	400,241	Bryant, Winston		45,701 R	52.7%	47.3%	52.7%	47.3%
1992	920,008	366,373	Huckabee, Mike	553,635	Bumpers, Dale		187,262 D	39.8%	60.2%	39.8%	60.2%
1990**	494,735	—		493,910	Pryor, David H.	825	493,910 D		99.8%		100.0%
1986	695,487	262,313	Hutchinson, Asa	433,122	Bumpers, Dale	52	170,809 D	37.7%	62.3%	37.7%	62.3%
1984	875,956	373,615	Bethune, Ed	502,341	Pryor, David H.		128,726 D	42.7%	57.3%	42.7%	57.3%
1980	808,812	330,576	Clark, Bill	477,905	Bumpers, Dale	331	147,329 D	40.9%	59.1%	40.9%	59.1%
1978	522,239	84,722	Kelly, Tom	399,916	Pryor, David H.	37,601	315,194 D	16.2%	76.6%	17.5%	82.5%
1974	543,082	82,026	Jones, John H.	461,056	Bumpers, Dale		379,030 D	15.1%	84.9%	15.1%	84.9%
1972	634,636	248,238	Babbitt, Wayne H.	386,398	McClellan, John L.		138,160 D	39.1%	60.9%	39.1%	60.9%
1968	591,704	241,739	Bernard, Charles T.	349,965	Fulbright, J. W.		108,226 D	40.9%	59.1%	40.9%	59.1%
1966**		—			McClellan, John L.		D				
1962	312,880	98,013	Jones, Kenneth	214,867	Fulbright, J. W.		116,854 D	31.3%	68.7%	31.3%	68.7%
1960**		—			McClellan, John L.		D				
1956	399,695	68,016	Henley, Ben C.	331,679	Fulbright, J. W.		263,663 D	17.0%	83.0%	17.0%	83.0%
1954	291,058	—		291,058	McClellan, John L.		291,058 D		100.0%		100.0%
1950	302,582	—		302,582	Fulbright, J. W.		302,582 D		100.0%		100.0%
1948	216,401	—		216,401	McClellan, John L.		216,401 D		100.0%		100.0%

In 1990 Senator Pryor's vote was not canvassed in seven counties because he was unopposed. Senator McClellan was re-elected in 1966 and in 1960, but his vote was not canvassed in many counties.

42

ARKANSAS

Congressional districts first established for elections held in 2002
4 members

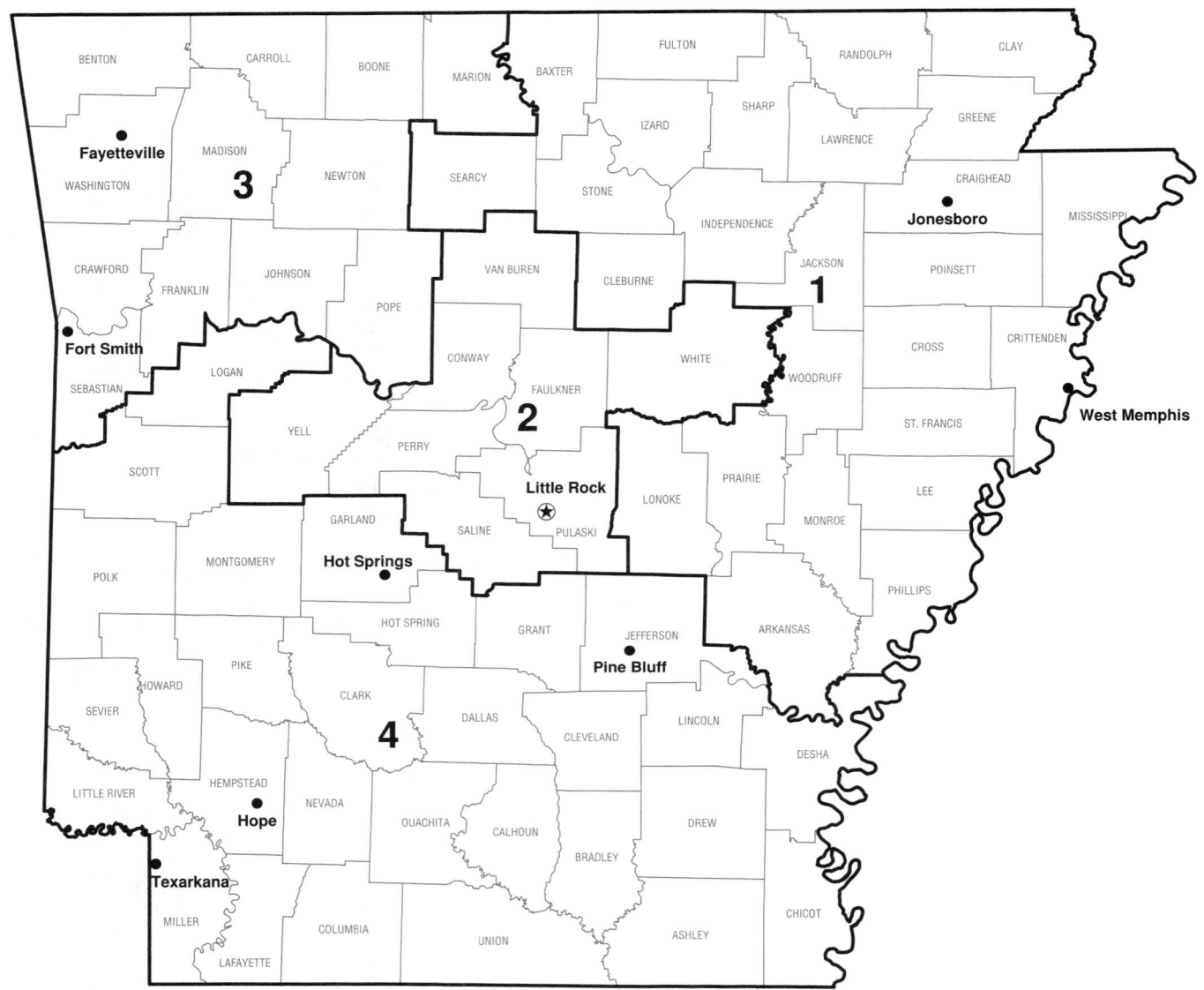

ARKANSAS
GOVERNOR 2002

2000 Census Population	County	Total Vote	Republican	Democratic	Other	Rep.-Dem. Plurality	Percentage Total Vote Rep.	Dem.	Major Vote Rep.	Dem.
20,749	ARKANSAS	6,020	3,186	2,834		352 R	52.9%	47.1%	52.9%	47.1%
24,209	ASHLEY	6,775	3,176	3,599		423 D	46.9%	53.1%	46.9%	53.1%
38,386	BAXTER	14,488	8,383	6,105		2,278 R	57.9%	42.1%	57.9%	42.1%
153,406	BENTON	45,770	31,077	14,693		16,384 R	67.9%	32.1%	67.9%	32.1%
33,948	BOONE	11,060	6,909	4,151		2,758 R	62.5%	37.5%	62.5%	37.5%
12,600	BRADLEY	3,470	1,545	1,925		380 D	44.5%	55.5%	44.5%	55.5%
5,744	CALHOUN	1,916	994	922		72 R	51.9%	48.1%	51.9%	48.1%
25,357	CARROLL	8,301	4,737	3,564		1,173 R	57.1%	42.9%	57.1%	42.9%
14,117	CHICOT	3,856	1,555	2,301		746 D	40.3%	59.7%	40.3%	59.7%
23,546	CLARK	7,599	3,431	4,167	1	736 D	45.2%	54.8%	45.2%	54.8%
17,609	CLAY	5,297	2,354	2,943		589 D	44.4%	55.6%	44.4%	55.6%
24,046	CLEBURNE	9,387	5,614	3,772	1	1,842 R	59.8%	40.2%	59.8%	40.2%
8,571	CLEVELAND	2,832	1,475	1,357		118 R	52.1%	47.9%	52.1%	47.9%
25,603	COLUMBIA	6,969	3,876	3,091	2	785 R	55.6%	44.4%	55.6%	44.4%
20,336	CONWAY	6,958	3,305	3,652	1	347 D	47.5%	52.5%	47.5%	52.5%
82,148	CRAIGHEAD	21,512	10,499	11,013		514 D	48.8%	51.2%	48.8%	51.2%
53,247	CRAWFORD	15,204	9,457	5,732	15	3,725 R	62.2%	37.7%	62.3%	37.7%
50,866	CRITTENDEN	11,659	5,523	6,136		613 D	47.4%	52.6%	47.4%	52.6%
19,526	CROSS	5,316	2,861	2,455		406 R	53.8%	46.2%	53.8%	46.2%
9,210	DALLAS	3,019	1,486	1,532	1	46 D	49.2%	50.7%	49.2%	50.8%
15,341	DESHA	3,939	1,754	2,185		431 D	44.5%	55.5%	44.5%	55.5%
18,723	DREW	5,270	2,683	2,587		96 R	50.9%	49.1%	50.9%	49.1%
86,014	FAULKNER	25,171	13,729	11,442		2,287 R	54.5%	45.5%	54.5%	45.5%
17,771	FRANKLIN	5,701	3,082	2,619		463 R	54.1%	45.9%	54.1%	45.9%
11,642	FULTON	3,650	1,707	1,942	1	235 D	46.8%	53.2%	46.8%	53.2%
88,068	GARLAND	34,751	17,473	17,270	8	203 R	50.3%	49.7%	50.3%	49.7%
16,464	GRANT	5,266	2,953	2,313		640 R	56.1%	43.9%	56.1%	43.9%
37,331	GREENE	11,180	4,722	6,458		1,736 D	42.2%	57.8%	42.2%	57.8%
23,587	HEMPSTEAD	5,840	2,862	2,976	2	114 D	49.0%	51.0%	49.0%	51.0%
30,353	HOT SPRING	9,768	4,701	5,067		366 D	48.1%	51.9%	48.1%	51.9%
14,300	HOWARD	3,715	1,935	1,780		155 R	52.1%	47.9%	52.1%	47.9%
34,233	INDEPENDENCE	10,308	5,836	4,472		1,364 R	56.6%	43.4%	56.6%	43.4%
13,249	IZARD	4,480	2,042	2,437	1	395 D	45.6%	54.4%	45.6%	54.4%
18,418	JACKSON	5,359	2,387	2,972		585 D	44.5%	55.5%	44.5%	55.5%
84,278	JEFFERSON	23,022	9,887	13,135		3,248 D	42.9%	57.1%	42.9%	57.1%
22,781	JOHNSON	6,405	3,484	2,921		563 R	54.4%	45.6%	54.4%	45.6%
8,559	LAFAYETTE	2,690	1,192	1,498		306 D	44.3%	55.7%	44.3%	55.7%
17,774	LAWRENCE	5,698	2,499	3,199		700 D	43.9%	56.1%	43.9%	56.1%
12,580	LEE	3,753	1,629	2,124		495 D	43.4%	56.6%	43.4%	56.6%
14,492	LINCOLN	3,400	1,646	1,746	8	100 D	48.4%	51.4%	48.5%	51.5%
13,628	LITTLE RIVER	4,416	1,964	2,452		488 D	44.5%	55.5%	44.5%	55.5%
22,486	LOGAN	7,220	3,830	3,389	1	441 R	53.0%	46.9%	53.1%	46.9%
52,828	LONOKE	16,493	9,985	6,508		3,477 R	60.5%	39.5%	60.5%	39.5%
14,243	MADISON	4,902	2,848	2,052	2	796 R	58.1%	41.9%	58.1%	41.9%
16,140	MARION	5,160	2,715	2,161	284	554 R	52.6%	41.9%	55.7%	44.3%
40,443	MILLER	10,857	5,882	4,971	4	911 R	54.2%	45.8%	54.2%	45.8%
51,979	MISSISSIPPI	10,882	5,319	5,563		244 D	48.9%	51.1%	48.9%	51.1%
10,254	MONROE	2,935	1,276	1,659		383 D	43.5%	56.5%	43.5%	56.5%
9,245	MONTGOMERY	3,173	1,939	1,234		705 R	61.1%	38.9%	61.1%	38.9%
9,955	NEVADA	3,087	1,354	1,733		379 D	43.9%	56.1%	43.9%	56.1%
8,608	NEWTON	3,525	2,153	1,372		781 R	61.1%	38.9%	61.1%	38.9%
28,790	OUACHITA	8,699	4,097	4,602		505 D	47.1%	52.9%	47.1%	52.9%
10,209	PERRY	3,498	1,806	1,691	1	115 R	51.6%	48.3%	51.6%	48.4%
26,445	PHILLIPS	7,815	3,883	3,932		49 D	49.7%	50.3%	49.7%	50.3%
11,303	PIKE	3,468	2,048	1,420		628 R	59.1%	40.9%	59.1%	40.9%
25,614	POINSETT	6,680	3,086	3,594		508 D	46.2%	53.8%	46.2%	53.8%
20,229	POLK	6,380	4,015	2,357	8	1,658 R	62.9%	36.9%	63.0%	37.0%
54,469	POPE	15,908	9,969	5,939		4,030 R	62.7%	37.3%	62.7%	37.3%
9,539	PRAIRIE	3,315	1,811	1,504		307 R	54.6%	45.4%	54.6%	45.4%
361,474	PULASKI	110,987	50,268	60,719		10,451 D	45.3%	54.7%	45.3%	54.7%

ARKANSAS

GOVERNOR 2002

2000 Census Population	County	Total Vote	Republican	Democratic	Other	Rep.-Dem. Plurality	Percentage Total Vote Rep.	Dem.	Major Vote Rep.	Dem.
18,195	RANDOLPH	5,224	2,255	2,969		714 D	43.2%	56.8%	43.2%	56.8%
29,329	ST. FRANCIS	7,580	2,934	4,646		1,712 D	38.7%	61.3%	38.7%	61.3%
83,529	SALINE	29,643	17,250	12,391	2	4,859 R	58.2%	41.8%	58.2%	41.8%
10,996	SCOTT	3,748	2,001	1,747		254 R	53.4%	46.6%	53.4%	46.6%
8,261	SEARCY	3,295	1,884	1,411		473 R	57.2%	42.8%	57.2%	42.8%
115,071	SEBASTIAN	33,502	20,264	13,238		7,026 R	60.5%	39.5%	60.5%	39.5%
15,757	SEVIER	3,629	1,759	1,869	1	110 D	48.5%	51.5%	48.5%	51.5%
17,119	SHARP	6,216	3,363	2,853		510 R	54.1%	45.9%	54.1%	45.9%
11,499	STONE	4,317	2,401	1,912	4	489 R	55.6%	44.3%	55.7%	44.3%
45,629	UNION	13,140	7,418	5,722		1,696 R	56.5%	43.5%	56.5%	43.5%
16,192	VAN BUREN	6,500	3,620	2,876	4	744 R	55.7%	44.2%	55.7%	44.3%
157,715	WASHINGTON	43,717	24,954	18,763		6,191 R	57.1%	42.9%	57.1%	42.9%
67,165	WHITE	20,635	13,085	7,541	9	5,544 R	63.4%	36.5%	63.4%	36.6%
8,741	WOODRUFF	2,884	1,202	1,682		480 D	41.7%	58.3%	41.7%	58.3%
21,139	YELL	5,492	2,798	2,691	3	107 R	50.9%	49.0%	51.0%	49.0%
2,673,400	TOTAL	805,696	427,082	378,250	364	48,832 R	53.0%	46.9%	53.0%	47.0%

ARKANSAS

SENATOR 2002

2000 Census Population	County	Total Vote	Republican	Democratic	Rep.-Dem. Plurality	Percentage Total Vote Rep.	Dem.	Major Vote Rep.	Dem.
20,749	ARKANSAS	6,068	2,422	3,646	1,224 D	39.9%	60.1%	39.9%	60.1%
24,209	ASHLEY	6,779	2,664	4,115	1,451 D	39.3%	60.7%	39.3%	60.7%
38,386	BAXTER	14,486	7,941	6,545	1,396 R	54.8%	45.2%	54.8%	45.2%
153,406	BENTON	45,936	29,237	16,699	12,538 R	63.6%	36.4%	63.6%	36.4%
33,948	BOONE	10,946	6,265	4,681	1,584 R	57.2%	42.8%	57.2%	42.8%
12,600	BRADLEY	3,494	1,269	2,225	956 D	36.3%	63.7%	36.3%	63.7%
5,744	CALHOUN	1,919	765	1,154	389 D	39.9%	60.1%	39.9%	60.1%
25,357	CARROLL	8,326	4,447	3,879	568 R	53.4%	46.6%	53.4%	46.6%
14,117	CHICOT	3,855	1,187	2,668	1,481 D	30.8%	69.2%	30.8%	69.2%
23,546	CLARK	7,633	2,610	5,023	2,413 D	34.2%	65.8%	34.2%	65.8%
17,609	CLAY	5,291	1,710	3,581	1,871 D	32.3%	67.7%	32.3%	67.7%
24,046	CLEBURNE	9,439	4,764	4,675	89 R	50.5%	49.5%	50.5%	49.5%
8,571	CLEVELAND	2,824	1,167	1,657	490 D	41.3%	58.7%	41.3%	58.7%
25,603	COLUMBIA	6,982	3,448	3,534	86 D	49.4%	50.6%	49.4%	50.6%
20,336	CONWAY	6,950	2,894	4,056	1,162 D	41.6%	58.4%	41.6%	58.4%
82,148	CRAIGHEAD	21,617	9,462	12,155	2,693 D	43.8%	56.2%	43.8%	56.2%
53,247	CRAWFORD	15,245	8,651	6,594	2,057 R	56.7%	43.3%	56.7%	43.3%
50,866	CRITTENDEN	11,629	4,482	7,147	2,665 D	38.5%	61.5%	38.5%	61.5%
19,526	CROSS	5,332	2,216	3,116	900 D	41.6%	58.4%	41.6%	58.4%
9,210	DALLAS	3,039	1,104	1,935	831 D	36.3%	63.7%	36.3%	63.7%
15,341	DESHA	3,829	1,131	2,698	1,567 D	29.5%	70.5%	29.5%	70.5%
18,723	DREW	5,287	2,111	3,176	1,065 D	39.9%	60.1%	39.9%	60.1%
86,014	FAULKNER	25,211	12,680	12,531	149 R	50.3%	49.7%	50.3%	49.7%
17,771	FRANKLIN	5,763	2,699	3,064	365 D	46.8%	53.2%	46.8%	53.2%
11,642	FULTON	3,661	1,486	2,175	689 D	40.6%	59.4%	40.6%	59.4%
88,068	GARLAND	30,677	14,713	15,964	1,251 D	48.0%	52.0%	48.0%	52.0%
16,464	GRANT	5,283	2,361	2,922	561 D	44.7%	55.3%	44.7%	55.3%
37,331	GREENE	11,217	4,414	6,803	2,389 D	39.4%	60.6%	39.4%	60.6%
23,587	HEMPSTEAD	5,828	2,310	3,518	1,208 D	39.6%	60.4%	39.6%	60.4%
30,353	HOT SPRING	9,617	3,561	6,056	2,495 D	37.0%	63.0%	37.0%	63.0%

ARKANSAS

SENATOR 2002

2000 Census Population	County	Total Vote	Republican	Democratic	Rep.-Dem. Plurality		Percentage			
							Total Vote		Major Vote	
							Rep.	Dem.	Rep.	Dem.
14,300	HOWARD	3,710	1,537	2,173	636	D	41.4%	58.6%	41.4%	58.6%
34,233	INDEPENDENCE	10,358	4,526	5,832	1,306	D	43.7%	56.3%	43.7%	56.3%
13,249	IZARD	4,528	1,842	2,686	844	D	40.7%	59.3%	40.7%	59.3%
18,418	JACKSON	5,411	1,711	3,700	1,989	D	31.6%	68.4%	31.6%	68.4%
84,278	JEFFERSON	23,085	6,791	16,294	9,503	D	29.4%	70.6%	29.4%	70.6%
22,781	JOHNSON	6,439	2,957	3,482	525	D	45.9%	54.1%	45.9%	54.1%
8,559	LAFAYETTE	2,709	1,062	1,647	585	D	39.2%	60.8%	39.2%	60.8%
17,774	LAWRENCE	5,726	2,088	3,638	1,550	D	36.5%	63.5%	36.5%	63.5%
12,580	LEE	3,756	1,193	2,563	1,370	D	31.8%	68.2%	31.8%	68.2%
14,492	LINCOLN	3,417	1,154	2,263	1,109	D	33.8%	66.2%	33.8%	66.2%
13,628	LITTLE RIVER	4,461	1,511	2,950	1,439	D	33.9%	66.1%	33.9%	66.1%
22,486	LOGAN	7,260	3,474	3,786	312	D	47.9%	52.1%	47.9%	52.1%
52,828	LONOKE	16,619	8,796	7,823	973	R	52.9%	47.1%	52.9%	47.1%
14,243	MADISON	4,963	2,648	2,315	333	R	53.4%	46.6%	53.4%	46.6%
16,140	MARION	5,141	2,847	2,294	553	R	55.4%	44.6%	55.4%	44.6%
40,443	MILLER	10,870	4,997	5,873	876	D	46.0%	54.0%	46.0%	54.0%
51,979	MISSISSIPPI	10,837	4,242	6,595	2,353	D	39.1%	60.9%	39.1%	60.9%
10,254	MONROE	2,954	998	1,956	958	D	33.8%	66.2%	33.8%	66.2%
9,245	MONTGOMERY	3,164	1,590	1,574	16	R	50.3%	49.7%	50.3%	49.7%
9,955	NEVADA	3,080	1,132	1,948	816	D	36.8%	63.2%	36.8%	63.2%
8,608	NEWTON	3,527	2,021	1,506	515	R	57.3%	42.7%	57.3%	42.7%
28,790	OUACHITA	8,742	3,026	5,716	2,690	D	34.6%	65.4%	34.6%	65.4%
10,209	PERRY	3,492	1,594	1,898	304	D	45.6%	54.4%	45.6%	54.4%
26,445	PHILLIPS	7,766	2,680	5,086	2,406	D	34.5%	65.5%	34.5%	65.5%
11,303	PIKE	3,484	1,603	1,881	278	D	46.0%	54.0%	46.0%	54.0%
25,614	POINSETT	6,709	2,305	4,404	2,099	D	34.4%	65.6%	34.4%	65.6%
20,229	POLK	6,363	3,756	2,607	1,149	R	59.0%	41.0%	59.0%	41.0%
54,469	POPE	15,964	8,723	7,241	1,482	R	54.6%	45.4%	54.6%	45.4%
9,539	PRAIRIE	3,337	1,316	2,021	705	D	39.4%	60.6%	39.4%	60.6%
361,474	PULASKI	111,695	45,287	66,408	21,121	D	40.5%	59.5%	40.5%	59.5%
18,195	RANDOLPH	5,256	2,076	3,180	1,104	D	39.5%	60.5%	39.5%	60.5%
29,329	ST. FRANCIS	7,590	2,525	5,065	2,540	D	33.3%	66.7%	33.3%	66.7%
83,529	SALINE	29,556	15,112	14,444	668	R	51.1%	48.9%	51.1%	48.9%
10,996	SCOTT	3,785	1,896	1,889	7	R	50.1%	49.9%	50.1%	49.9%
8,261	SEARCY	3,260	1,847	1,413	434	R	56.7%	43.3%	56.7%	43.3%
115,071	SEBASTIAN	33,707	18,731	14,976	3,755	R	55.6%	44.4%	55.6%	44.4%
15,757	SEVIER	3,602	1,545	2,057	512	D	42.9%	57.1%	42.9%	57.1%
17,119	SHARP	6,232	2,827	3,405	578	D	45.4%	54.6%	45.4%	54.6%
11,499	STONE	4,322	2,094	2,228	134	D	48.4%	51.6%	48.4%	51.6%
45,629	UNION	13,293	6,627	6,666	39	D	49.9%	50.1%	49.9%	50.1%
16,192	VAN BUREN	6,546	2,820	3,726	906	D	43.1%	56.9%	43.1%	56.9%
157,715	WASHINGTON	44,000	23,158	20,842	2,316	R	52.6%	47.4%	52.6%	47.4%
67,165	WHITE	20,649	10,700	9,949	751	R	51.8%	48.2%	51.8%	48.2%
8,741	WOODRUFF	2,893	724	2,169	1,445	D	25.0%	75.0%	25.0%	75.0%
21,139	YELL	5,538	2,393	3,145	752	D	43.2%	56.8%	43.2%	56.8%
2,673,400	TOTAL	803,959	370,653	433,306	62,653	D	46.1%	53.9%	46.1%	53.9%

ARKANSAS

HOUSE OF REPRESENTATIVES

CD	Year	Total Vote	Republican		Democratic		Other Vote	Rep.-Dem. Plurality	Percentage			
			Vote	Candidate	Vote	Candidate			Total Vote		Major Vote	
									Rep.	Dem.	Rep.	Dem.
1	2002	194,058	64,357	Robinson, Tommy F.	129,701	Berry, Marion*		65,344 D	33.2%	66.8%	33.2%	66.8%
2	2002	153,626			142,752	Snyder, Vic*	10,874	142,752 D		92.9%		100.0%
3	2002	143,055	141,478	Boozman, John*			1,577	141,478 R	98.9%		100.0%	
4	2002	197,537	77,904	Dickey, Jay	119,633	Ross, Mike*		41,729 D	39.4%	60.6%	39.4%	60.6%
Total	2002	688,276	283,739		392,086		12,451	108,347 D	41.2%	57.0%	42.0%	58.0%

An asterisk (*) denotes incumbent.

ARKANSAS

GENERAL AND PRIMARY ELECTIONS

2002 GENERAL ELECTIONS

Governor   Other vote was 160 write-in (Gene Mason); 154 write-in (Barry Emigh); 35 write-in (Oscar Stilley); 15 write-in (Elvis M. Nash).

Senator

House   Other vote was:

     CD 1
     CD 2   10,874 write-in (Ed Garner).
     CD 3   1,577 write-in (George N. Lyne).
     CD 4

2002 PRIMARY ELECTIONS

Primary   May 21, 2002   **Registration** (as of April 24, 2002)   1,550,505   No Party Registration required

Primary Type   Open—Any registered voter could vote in either the Democratic or Republican primary.

Note: An asterisk (*) denotes incumbent. The names of unopposed candidates did not appear on the primary ballot; therefore, no votes were cast for these candidates.

ARKANSAS

GENERAL AND PRIMARY ELECTIONS

	REPUBLICAN PRIMARIES			DEMOCRATIC PRIMARIES		
Governor	Mike Huckabee*	78,803	85.4%	Jimmie Lou Fisher	176,126	63.1%
	Doyle Cannady	13,434	14.6%	Joe Holmes	77,516	27.8%
				Jim Billie	25,455	9.1%
	TOTAL	92,237		TOTAL	279,097	
Senator	Tim Hutchinson*	71,576	77.7%	Mark Pryor	Unopposed	
	Jim Bob Duggar	20,546	22.3%			
	TOTAL	92,122				
Congressional District 1	Tommy F. Robinson	Unopposed		Marion Berry*	Unopposed	
Congressional District 2	No Republican candidate			Vic Snyder*	55,098	72.4%
				Jim B. Baker	21,033	27.6%
				TOTAL	76,131	
Congressional District 3	John Boozman*	Unopposed		No Democratic candidate		
Congressional District 4	Jay Dickey	10,608	86.3%	Mike Ross*	Unopposed	
	David "Bear" Stearns	1,689	13.7%			
	TOTAL	12,297				

ARKANSAS REPUBLICAN PRIMARY

GOVERNOR 2002

2000 Census Population	County	Total Vote	Huckabee	Cannady	Winner	Percentage of Total Vote	
						Huckabee	Cannady
20,749	ARKANSAS	94	88	6	Huckabee	93.6%	6.4%
24,209	ASHLEY	193	19	174	Cannady	9.8%	90.2%
38,386	BAXTER	3,884	3,244	640	Huckabee	83.5%	16.5%
153,406	BENTON	18,532	14,697	3,835	Huckabee	79.3%	20.7%
33,948	BOONE	1,913	1,735	178	Huckabee	90.7%	9.3%
12,600	BRADLEY	197	175	22	Huckabee	88.8%	11.2%
5,744	CALHOUN	24	23	1	Huckabee	95.8%	4.2%
25,357	CARROLL	1,240	1,085	155	Huckabee	87.5%	12.5%
14,117	CHICOT	21	21		Huckabee	100.0%	
23,546	CLARK	242	228	14	Huckabee	94.2%	5.8%
17,609	CLAY	87	78	9	Huckabee	89.7%	10.3%
24,046	CLEBURNE	1,009	917	92	Huckabee	90.9%	9.1%
8,571	CLEVELAND	221	210	11	Huckabee	95.0%	5.0%
25,603	COLUMBIA	302	283	19	Huckabee	93.7%	6.3%
20,336	CONWAY	285	271	14	Huckabee	95.1%	4.9%
82,148	CRAIGHEAD	1,369	1,253	116	Huckabee	91.5%	8.5%
53,247	CRAWFORD	1,962	1,700	262	Huckabee	86.6%	13.4%
50,866	CRITTENDEN	623	580	43	Huckabee	93.1%	6.9%
19,526	CROSS	21	19	2	Huckabee	90.5%	9.5%
9,210	DALLAS	17	16	1	Huckabee	94.1%	5.9%
15,341	DESHA	334	282	52	Huckabee	84.4%	15.6%
18,723	DREW	126	113	13	Huckabee	89.7%	10.3%
86,014	FAULKNER	2,585	2,315	270	Huckabee	89.6%	10.4%
17,771	FRANKLIN	394	341	53	Huckabee	86.5%	13.5%
11,642	FULTON	205	187	18	Huckabee	91.2%	8.8%
88,068	GARLAND	3,952	3,581	371	Huckabee	90.6%	9.4%
16,464	GRANT	326	293	33	Huckabee	89.9%	10.1%
37,331	GREENE	275	256	19	Huckabee	93.1%	6.9%
23,587	HEMPSTEAD	285	261	24	Huckabee	91.6%	8.4%
30,353	HOT SPRING	151	137	14	Huckabee	90.7%	9.3%

ARKANSAS REPUBLICAN PRIMARY

GOVERNOR 2002

2000 Census Population	County	Total Vote	Huckabee	Cannady	Winner	Percentage of Total Vote	
						Huckabee	Cannady
14,300	HOWARD	111	99	12	Huckabee	89.2%	10.8%
34,233	INDEPENDENCE	737	678	59	Huckabee	92.0%	8.0%
13,249	IZARD	385	341	44	Huckabee	88.6%	11.4%
18,418	JACKSON	99	85	14	Huckabee	85.9%	14.1%
84,278	JEFFERSON	1,903	1,756	147	Huckabee	92.3%	7.7%
22,781	JOHNSON	279	249	30	Huckabee	89.2%	10.8%
8,559	LAFAYETTE	213	195	18	Huckabee	91.5%	8.5%
17,774	LAWRENCE	163	144	19	Huckabee	88.3%	11.7%
12,580	LEE	49	41	8	Huckabee	83.7%	16.3%
14,492	LINCOLN	33	32	1	Huckabee	97.0%	3.0%
13,628	LITTLE RIVER	134	123	11	Huckabee	91.8%	8.2%
22,486	LOGAN	342	303	39	Huckabee	88.6%	11.4%
52,828	LONOKE	1,342	1,169	173	Huckabee	87.1%	12.9%
14,243	MADISON	396	362	34	Huckabee	91.4%	8.6%
16,140	MARION	702	628	74	Huckabee	89.5%	10.5%
40,443	MILLER	1,177	1,104	73	Huckabee	93.8%	6.2%
51,979	MISSISSIPPI	577	532	45	Huckabee	92.2%	7.8%
10,254	MONROE	68	65	3	Huckabee	95.6%	4.4%
9,245	MONTGOMERY	247	233	14	Huckabee	94.3%	5.7%
9,955	NEVADA	62	59	3	Huckabee	95.2%	4.8%
8,608	NEWTON	425	383	42	Huckabee	90.1%	9.9%
28,790	OUACHITA	200	187	13	Huckabee	93.5%	6.5%
10,209	PERRY	126	112	14	Huckabee	88.9%	11.1%
26,445	PHILLIPS	14	12	2	Huckabee	85.7%	14.3%
11,303	PIKE	126	119	7	Huckabee	94.4%	5.6%
25,614	POINSETT	157	140	17	Huckabee	89.2%	10.8%
20,229	POLK	421	380	41	Huckabee	90.3%	9.7%
54,469	POPE	1,161	1,075	86	Huckabee	92.6%	7.4%
9,539	PRAIRIE	110	103	7	Huckabee	93.6%	6.4%
361,474	PULASKI	13,663	11,984	1,679	Huckabee	87.7%	12.3%
18,195	RANDOLPH	135	128	7	Huckabee	94.8%	5.2%
29,329	ST. FRANCIS	9	9		Huckabee	100.0%	
83,529	SALINE	5,305	4,271	1,034	Huckabee	80.5%	19.5%
10,996	SCOTT	144	126	18	Huckabee	87.5%	12.5%
8,261	SEARCY	1,186	966	220	Huckabee	81.5%	18.5%
115,071	SEBASTIAN	5,554	4,551	1,003	Huckabee	81.9%	18.1%
15,757	SEVIER	296	255	41	Huckabee	86.1%	13.9%
17,119	SHARP	298	282	16	Huckabee	94.6%	5.4%
11,499	STONE	95	90	5	Huckabee	94.7%	5.3%
45,629	UNION	658	621	37	Huckabee	94.4%	5.6%
16,192	VAN BUREN	364	337	27	Huckabee	92.6%	7.4%
157,715	WASHINGTON	8,040	6,571	1,469	Huckabee	81.7%	18.3%
67,165	WHITE	3,711	3,356	355	Huckabee	90.4%	9.6%
8,741	WOODRUFF	22	22		Huckabee	100.0%	
21,139	YELL	129	117	12	Huckabee	90.7%	9.3%
2,673,400	TOTAL	92,237	78,803	13,434	Huckabee	85.4%	14.6%

ARKANSAS DEMOCRATIC PRIMARY
GOVERNOR 2002

2000 Census Population	County	Total Vote	Fisher	Holmes	Billie	Winner	Percentage of Total Vote		
							Fisher	Holmes	Billie
20,749	ARKANSAS	3,813	2,323	1,139	351	Fisher	60.9%	29.9%	9.2%
24,209	ASHLEY	3,349	1,967	876	506	Fisher	58.7%	26.2%	15.1%
38,386	BAXTER	1,272	795	402	75	Fisher	62.5%	31.6%	5.9%
153,406	BENTON	1,844	1,101	591	152	Fisher	59.7%	32.0%	8.2%
33,948	BOONE	2,182	1,371	672	139	Fisher	62.8%	30.8%	6.4%
12,600	BRADLEY	1,184	798	306	80	Fisher	67.4%	25.8%	6.8%
5,744	CALHOUN	1,763	950	627	186	Fisher	53.9%	35.6%	10.6%
25,357	CARROLL	1,504	927	426	151	Fisher	61.6%	28.3%	10.0%
14,117	CHICOT	2,470	1,638	577	255	Fisher	66.3%	23.4%	10.3%
23,546	CLARK	4,626	3,371	1,255		Fisher	72.9%	27.1%	
17,609	CLAY	2,078	1,663	313	102	Fisher	80.0%	15.1%	4.9%
24,046	CLEBURNE	4,407	2,312	1,552	543	Fisher	52.5%	35.2%	12.3%
8,571	CLEVELAND	1,308	403	861	44	Holmes	30.8%	65.8%	3.4%
25,603	COLUMBIA	3,815	2,222	1,018	575	Fisher	58.2%	26.7%	15.1%
20,336	CONWAY	3,472	2,090	1,067	315	Fisher	60.2%	30.7%	9.1%
82,148	CRAIGHEAD	10,889	8,291	2,052	546	Fisher	76.1%	18.8%	5.0%
53,247	CRAWFORD	4,821	2,748	1,569	504	Fisher	57.0%	32.5%	10.5%
50,866	CRITTENDEN	2,874	1,687	964	223	Fisher	58.7%	33.5%	7.8%
19,526	CROSS	3,945	2,716	876	353	Fisher	68.8%	22.2%	8.9%
9,210	DALLAS	2,752	1,418	1,048	286	Fisher	51.5%	38.1%	10.4%
15,341	DESHA	1,299	744	387	168	Fisher	57.3%	29.8%	12.9%
18,723	DREW	3,487	1,981	1,168	338	Fisher	56.8%	33.5%	9.7%
86,014	FAULKNER	8,659	5,235	2,284	1,140	Fisher	60.5%	26.4%	13.2%
17,771	FRANKLIN	3,452	2,009	1,129	314	Fisher	58.2%	32.7%	9.1%
11,642	FULTON	1,691	916	534	241	Fisher	54.2%	31.6%	14.3%
88,068	GARLAND	5,785	4,143	1,642		Fisher	71.6%	28.4%	
16,464	GRANT	1,733	1,018	572	143	Fisher	58.7%	33.0%	8.3%
37,331	GREENE	8,141	6,841	1,041	259	Fisher	84.0%	12.8%	3.2%
23,587	HEMPSTEAD	1,114	729	273	112	Fisher	65.4%	24.5%	10.1%
30,353	HOT SPRING	5,312	3,207	1,498	607	Fisher	60.4%	28.2%	11.4%
14,300	HOWARD	1,643	992	504	147	Fisher	60.4%	30.7%	8.9%
34,233	INDEPENDENCE	5,764	3,860	1,379	525	Fisher	67.0%	23.9%	9.1%
13,249	IZARD	1,577	1,122	302	153	Fisher	71.1%	19.2%	9.7%
18,418	JACKSON	3,864	2,492	946	426	Fisher	64.5%	24.5%	11.0%
84,278	JEFFERSON	6,708	2,462	3,821	425	Holmes	36.7%	57.0%	6.3%
22,781	JOHNSON	3,417	1,804	1,299	314	Fisher	52.8%	38.0%	9.2%
8,559	LAFAYETTE	1,722	846	601	275	Fisher	49.1%	34.9%	16.0%
17,774	LAWRENCE	3,726	2,673	786	267	Fisher	71.7%	21.1%	7.2%
12,580	LEE	2,306	1,313	624	369	Fisher	56.9%	27.1%	16.0%
14,492	LINCOLN	2,469	929	1,376	164	Holmes	37.6%	55.7%	6.6%
13,628	LITTLE RIVER	725	484	181	60	Fisher	66.8%	25.0%	8.3%
22,486	LOGAN	3,884	2,095	1,368	421	Fisher	53.9%	35.2%	10.8%
52,828	LONOKE	5,528	3,447	1,594	487	Fisher	62.4%	28.8%	8.8%
14,243	MADISON	1,947	1,174	529	244	Fisher	60.3%	27.2%	12.5%
16,140	MARION	1,554	674	663	217	Fisher	43.4%	42.7%	14.0%
40,443	MILLER	4,232	1,984	1,524	724	Fisher	46.9%	36.0%	17.1%
51,979	MISSISSIPPI	1,559	1,023	415	121	Fisher	65.6%	26.6%	7.8%
10,254	MONROE	1,768	1,104	484	180	Fisher	62.4%	27.4%	10.2%
9,245	MONTGOMERY	1,305	696	402	207	Fisher	53.3%	30.8%	15.9%
9,955	NEVADA	1,843	959	884		Fisher	52.0%	48.0%	
8,608	NEWTON	405	289	70	46	Fisher	71.4%	17.3%	11.4%
28,790	OUACHITA	5,577	3,708	1,361	508	Fisher	66.5%	24.4%	9.1%
10,209	PERRY	2,232	1,267	675	290	Fisher	56.8%	30.2%	13.0%
26,445	PHILLIPS	4,897	3,083	1,140	674	Fisher	63.0%	23.3%	13.8%
11,303	PIKE	1,270	774	343	153	Fisher	60.9%	27.0%	12.0%
25,614	POINSETT	3,472	2,269	965	238	Fisher	65.4%	27.8%	6.9%
20,229	POLK	2,705	1,309	1,017	379	Fisher	48.4%	37.6%	14.0%
54,469	POPE	6,268	3,925	1,673	670	Fisher	62.6%	26.7%	10.7%
9,539	PRAIRIE	1,847	1,096	580	171	Fisher	59.3%	31.4%	9.3%
361,474	PULASKI	36,149	26,696	6,955	2,498	Fisher	73.8%	19.2%	6.9%

50

ARKANSAS DEMOCRATIC PRIMARY

GOVERNOR 2002

2000 Census Population	County	Total Vote	Fisher	Holmes	Billie	Winner	Percentage of Total Vote		
							Fisher	Holmes	Billie
18,195	RANDOLPH	4,008	2,789	883	336	Fisher	69.6%	22.0%	8.4%
29,329	ST. FRANCIS	4,450	2,421	1,552	477	Fisher	54.4%	34.9%	10.7%
83,529	SALINE	5,302	3,877	934	491	Fisher	73.1%	17.6%	9.3%
10,996	SCOTT	1,990	1,121	562	307	Fisher	56.3%	28.2%	15.4%
8,261	SEARCY	221	146	15	60	Fisher	66.1%	6.8%	27.1%
115,071	SEBASTIAN	2,985	1,820	834	331	Fisher	61.0%	27.9%	11.1%
15,757	SEVIER	1,287	833	344	110	Fisher	64.7%	26.7%	8.5%
17,119	SHARP	3,833	2,278	1,146	409	Fisher	59.4%	29.9%	10.7%
11,499	STONE	2,662	1,528	715	419	Fisher	57.4%	26.9%	15.7%
45,629	UNION	4,197	2,211	1,574	412	Fisher	52.7%	37.5%	9.8%
16,192	VAN BUREN	3,942	2,151	1,157	634	Fisher	54.6%	29.4%	16.1%
157,715	WASHINGTON	4,539	3,125	1,232	182	Fisher	68.8%	27.1%	4.0%
67,165	WHITE	6,066	3,869	1,512	685	Fisher	63.8%	24.9%	11.3%
8,741	WOODRUFF	2,195	1,368	613	214	Fisher	62.3%	27.9%	9.7%
21,139	YELL	4,016	2,426	1,263	327	Fisher	60.4%	31.4%	8.1%
2,673,400	TOTAL	279,097	176,126	77,516	25,455	Fisher	63.1%	27.8%	9.1%

ARKANSAS REPUBLICAN PRIMARY

SENATOR 2002

2000 Census Population	County	Total Vote	Hutchinson	Duggar	Winner	Percentage of Total Vote	
						Hutchinson	Duggar
20,749	ARKANSAS	94	89	5	Hutchinson	94.7%	5.3%
24,209	ASHLEY	193	170	23	Hutchinson	88.1%	11.9%
38,386	BAXTER	3,870	3,276	594	Hutchinson	84.7%	15.3%
153,406	BENTON	18,799	12,297	6,502	Hutchinson	65.4%	34.6%
33,948	BOONE	1,948	1,590	358	Hutchinson	81.6%	18.4%
12,600	BRADLEY	196	174	22	Hutchinson	88.8%	11.2%
5,744	CALHOUN	24	20	4	Hutchinson	83.3%	16.7%
25,357	CARROLL	1,245	914	331	Hutchinson	73.4%	26.6%
14,117	CHICOT	21	21		Hutchinson	100.0%	
23,546	CLARK	241	218	23	Hutchinson	90.5%	9.5%
17,609	CLAY	87	79	8	Hutchinson	90.8%	9.2%
24,046	CLEBURNE	1,011	842	169	Hutchinson	83.3%	16.7%
8,571	CLEVELAND	221	194	27	Hutchinson	87.8%	12.2%
25,603	COLUMBIA	303	255	48	Hutchinson	84.2%	15.8%
20,336	CONWAY	278	238	40	Hutchinson	85.6%	14.4%
82,148	CRAIGHEAD	1,363	1,239	124	Hutchinson	90.9%	9.1%
53,247	CRAWFORD	1,971	1,442	529	Hutchinson	73.2%	26.8%
50,866	CRITTENDEN	601	540	61	Hutchinson	89.9%	10.1%
19,526	CROSS	21	21		Hutchinson	100.0%	
9,210	DALLAS	17	16	1	Hutchinson	94.1%	5.9%
15,341	DESHA	281	234	47	Hutchinson	83.3%	16.7%
18,723	DREW	126	116	10	Hutchinson	92.1%	7.9%
86,014	FAULKNER	2,492	1,835	657	Hutchinson	73.6%	26.4%
17,771	FRANKLIN	392	304	88	Hutchinson	77.6%	22.4%
11,642	FULTON	205	182	23	Hutchinson	88.8%	11.2%
88,068	GARLAND	3,943	3,258	685	Hutchinson	82.6%	17.4%
16,464	GRANT	326	269	57	Hutchinson	82.5%	17.5%
37,331	GREENE	274	255	19	Hutchinson	93.1%	6.9%
23,587	HEMPSTEAD	283	252	31	Hutchinson	89.0%	11.0%
30,353	HOT SPRING	146	125	21	Hutchinson	85.6%	14.4%

ARKANSAS REPUBLICAN PRIMARY

SENATOR 2002

2000 Census Population	County	Total Vote	Hutchinson	Duggar	Winner	Percentage of Total Vote	
						Hutchinson	Duggar
14,300	HOWARD	109	100	9	Hutchinson	91.7%	8.3%
34,233	INDEPENDENCE	728	635	93	Hutchinson	87.2%	12.8%
13,249	IZARD	363	322	41	Hutchinson	88.7%	11.3%
18,418	JACKSON	98	93	5	Hutchinson	94.9%	5.1%
84,278	JEFFERSON	1,767	1,502	265	Hutchinson	85.0%	15.0%
22,781	JOHNSON	282	240	42	Hutchinson	85.1%	14.9%
8,559	LAFAYETTE	212	199	13	Hutchinson	93.9%	6.1%
17,774	LAWRENCE	165	138	27	Hutchinson	83.6%	16.4%
12,580	LEE	50	44	6	Hutchinson	88.0%	12.0%
14,492	LINCOLN	33	31	2	Hutchinson	93.9%	6.1%
13,628	LITTLE RIVER	130	122	8	Hutchinson	93.8%	6.2%
22,486	LOGAN	343	279	64	Hutchinson	81.3%	18.7%
52,828	LONOKE	1,344	1,161	183	Hutchinson	86.4%	13.6%
14,243	MADISON	399	327	72	Hutchinson	82.0%	18.0%
16,140	MARION	700	623	77	Hutchinson	89.0%	11.0%
40,443	MILLER	1,158	1,035	123	Hutchinson	89.4%	10.6%
51,979	MISSISSIPPI	575	542	33	Hutchinson	94.3%	5.7%
10,254	MONROE	68	62	6	Hutchinson	91.2%	8.8%
9,245	MONTGOMERY	245	208	37	Hutchinson	84.9%	15.1%
9,955	NEVADA	62	58	4	Hutchinson	93.5%	6.5%
8,608	NEWTON	425	372	53	Hutchinson	87.5%	12.5%
28,790	OUACHITA	198	175	23	Hutchinson	88.4%	11.6%
10,209	PERRY	126	104	22	Hutchinson	82.5%	17.5%
26,445	PHILLIPS	14	13	1	Hutchinson	92.9%	7.1%
11,303	PIKE	125	106	19	Hutchinson	84.8%	15.2%
25,614	POINSETT	155	142	13	Hutchinson	91.6%	8.4%
20,229	POLK	421	364	57	Hutchinson	86.5%	13.5%
54,469	POPE	1,161	953	208	Hutchinson	82.1%	17.9%
9,539	PRAIRIE	109	97	12	Hutchinson	89.0%	11.0%
361,474	PULASKI	13,644	11,627	2,017	Hutchinson	85.2%	14.8%
18,195	RANDOLPH	132	121	11	Hutchinson	91.7%	8.3%
29,329	ST. FRANCIS	9	9		Hutchinson	100.0%	
83,529	SALINE	5,271	4,229	1,042	Hutchinson	80.2%	19.8%
10,996	SCOTT	145	111	34	Hutchinson	76.6%	23.4%
8,261	SEARCY	1,151	922	229	Hutchinson	80.1%	19.9%
115,071	SEBASTIAN	5,603	3,926	1,677	Hutchinson	70.1%	29.9%
15,757	SEVIER	292	264	28	Hutchinson	90.4%	9.6%
17,119	SHARP	295	280	15	Hutchinson	94.9%	5.1%
11,499	STONE	95	82	13	Hutchinson	86.3%	13.7%
45,629	UNION	659	613	46	Hutchinson	93.0%	7.0%
16,192	VAN BUREN	365	313	52	Hutchinson	85.8%	14.2%
157,715	WASHINGTON	8,104	5,377	2,727	Hutchinson	66.3%	33.7%
67,165	WHITE	3,670	3,063	607	Hutchinson	83.5%	16.5%
8,741	WOODRUFF	22	22		Hutchinson	100.0%	
21,139	YELL	128	105	23	Hutchinson	82.0%	18.0%
2,673,400	TOTAL	92,122	71,576	20,546	Hutchinson	77.7%	22.3%

CALIFORNIA

GOVERNOR
Gray Davis (D). Reelected 2002 to a four-year term. Previously elected 1998.

SENATORS (2 Democrats)
Barbara Boxer (D). Reelected 1998 to a six-year term. Previously elected 1992.

Dianne Feinstein (D). Reelected 2000 to a six-year term. Previously elected 1994 and 1992 to fill the remaining two years of the term vacated when Senator Pete Wilson (R) was elected Governor in November 1990.

REPRESENTATIVES (20 Republicans, 33 Democrats)
1. Mike Thompson (D)
2. Wally Herger (R)
3. Doug Ose (R)
4. John T. Doolittle (R)
5. Robert T. Matsui (D)
6. Lynn Woolsey (D)
7. George Miller (D)
8. Nancy Pelosi (D)
9. Barbara Lee (D)
10. Ellen O. Tauscher (D)
11. Richard W. Pombo (R)
12. Tom Lantos (D)
13. Pete Stark (D)
14. Anna G. Eshoo (D)
15. Michael M. Honda (D)
16. Zoe Lofgren (D)
17. Sam Farr (D)
18. Dennis Cardoza (D)
19. George P. Radanovich (R)
20. Cal Dooley (D)
21. Devin Nunes (R)
22. Bill Thomas (R)
23. Lois Capps (D)
24. Elton Gallegly (R)
25. Howard P. "Buck" McKeon (R)
26. David Dreier (R)
27. Brad Sherman (D)
28. Howard L. Berman (D)
29. Adam B. Schiff (D)
30. Henry A. Waxman (D)
31. Xavier Becerra (D)
32. Hilda L. Solis (D)
33. Diane Watson (D)
34. Lucille Roybal-Allard (D)
35. Maxine Waters (D)
36. Jane Harman (D)
37. Juanita Millender-McDonald (D)
38. Grace F. Napolitano (D)
39. Linda T. Sanchez (D)
40. Ed Royce (R)
41. Jerry Lewis (R)
42. Gary G. Miller (R)
43. Joe Baca (D)
44. Ken Calvert (R)
45. Mary Bono (R)
46. Dana Rohrabacher (R)
47. Loretta Sanchez (D)
48. Christopher Cox (R)
49. Darrell Issa (R)
50. Randy "Duke" Cunningham (R)
51. Bob Filner (D)
52. Duncan Hunter (R)
53. Susan A. Davis (D)

POSTWAR VOTE FOR PRESIDENT

Year	Total Vote	Republican Vote	Candidate	Democratic Vote	Candidate	Other Vote	Plurality	Total Vote Rep.	Total Vote Dem.	Major Vote Rep.	Major Vote Dem.
2000**	10,965,856	4,567,429	Bush, George W.	5,861,203	Gore, Al	537,224	1,293,774 D	41.7%	53.4%	43.8%	56.2%
1996**	10,019,484	3,828,380	Dole, Bob	5,119,835	Clinton, Bill	1,071,269	1,291,455 D	38.2%	51.1%	42.8%	57.2%
1992**	11,131,721	3,630,574	Bush, George	5,121,325	Clinton, Bill	2,379,822	1,490,751 D	32.6%	46.0%	41.5%	58.5%
1988	9,887,065	5,054,917	Bush, George	4,702,233	Dukakis, Michael S.	129,915	352,684 R	51.1%	47.6%	51.8%	48.2%
1984	9,505,423	5,467,009	Reagan, Ronald	3,922,519	Mondale, Walter F.	115,895	1,544,490 R	57.5%	41.3%	58.2%	41.8%
1980**	8,587,063	4,524,858	Reagan, Ronald	3,083,661	Carter, Jimmy	978,544	1,441,197 R	52.7%	35.9%	59.5%	40.5%
1976	7,867,117	3,882,244	Ford, Gerald R.	3,742,284	Carter, Jimmy	242,589	139,960 R	49.3%	47.6%	50.9%	49.1%
1972	8,367,862	4,602,096	Nixon, Richard M.	3,475,847	McGovern, George S.	289,919	1,126,249 R	55.0%	41.5%	57.0%	43.0%
1968	7,251,587	3,467,664	Nixon, Richard M.	3,244,318	Humphrey, Hubert H.	539,605	223,346 R	47.8%	44.7%	51.7%	48.3%
1964	7,057,586	2,879,108	Goldwater, Barry M.	4,171,877	Johnson, Lyndon B.	6,601	1,292,769 D	40.8%	59.1%	40.8%	59.2%
1960	6,506,578	3,259,722	Nixon, Richard M.	3,224,099	Kennedy, John F.	22,757	35,623 R	50.1%	49.6%	50.3%	49.7%
1956	5,466,355	3,027,668	Eisenhower, Dwight D.	2,420,135	Stevenson, Adlai E.	18,552	607,533 R	55.4%	44.3%	55.6%	44.4%
1952	5,141,849	2,897,310	Eisenhower, Dwight D.	2,197,548	Stevenson, Adlai E.	46,991	699,762 R	56.3%	42.7%	56.9%	43.1%
1948	4,021,538	1,895,269	Dewey, Thomas E.	1,913,134	Truman, Harry S.	213,135	17,865 D	47.1%	47.6%	49.8%	50.2%

In 2000 the other vote column includes 418,707 votes cast for Green (Nader). In 1996 the other vote column includes 697,847 votes cast for Perot. In 1992 the other vote column includes 2,296,006 votes cast for Perot. In 1980 the other column includes 739,833 votes for Independent (Anderson).

CALIFORNIA

POSTWAR VOTE FOR GOVERNOR

Year	Total Vote	Republican		Democratic		Other Vote	Rep.-Dem. Plurality	Percentage			
								Total Vote		Major Vote	
		Vote	Candidate	Vote	Candidate			Rep.	Dem.	Rep.	Dem.
2002	7,476,311	3,169,801	Simon, Bill	3,533,490	Davis, Gray	773,020	363,689 D	42.4%	47.3%	47.3%	52.7%
1998	8,385,196	3,218,030	Lungren, Dan	4,860,702	Davis, Gray	306,464	1,642,672 D	38.4%	58.0%	39.8%	60.2%
1994	8,665,375	4,781,766	Wilson, Pete	3,519,799	Brown, Kathleen	363,810	1,261,967 R	55.2%	40.6%	57.6%	42.4%
1990	7,699,467	3,791,904	Wilson, Pete	3,525,197	Feinstein, Dianne	382,366	266,707 R	49.2%	45.8%	51.8%	48.2%
1986	7,443,551	4,506,601	Deukmejian, George	2,781,714	Bradley, Tom	155,236	1,724,887 R	60.5%	37.4%	61.8%	38.2%
1982	7,876,698	3,881,014	Deukmejian, George	3,787,669	Bradley, Tom	208,015	93,345 R	49.3%	48.1%	50.6%	49.4%
1978	6,922,378	2,526,534	Younger, Evelle J.	3,878,812	Brown, Edmund G., Jr.	517,032	1,352,278 D	36.5%	56.0%	39.4%	60.6%
1974	6,248,070	2,952,954	Flournoy, Houston I.	3,131,648	Brown, Edmund G., Jr.	163,468	178,694 D	47.3%	50.1%	48.5%	51.5%
1970	6,510,072	3,439,664	Reagan, Ronald	2,938,607	Unruh, Jess	131,801	501,057 R	52.8%	45.1%	53.9%	46.1%
1966	6,503,445	3,742,913	Reagan, Ronald	2,749,174	Brown, Edmund G.	11,358	993,739 R	57.6%	42.3%	57.7%	42.3%
1962	5,853,270	2,740,351	Nixon, Richard M.	3,037,109	Brown, Edmund G.	75,810	296,758 D	46.8%	51.9%	47.4%	52.6%
1958	5,255,777	2,110,911	Knowland, William F.	3,140,076	Brown, Edmund G.	4,790	1,029,165 D	40.2%	59.7%	40.2%	59.8%
1954	4,030,368	2,290,519	Knight, Goodwin J.	1,739,368	Graves, Richard P.	481	551,151 R	56.8%	43.2%	56.8%	43.2%
1950	3,796,090	2,461,754	Warren, Earl	1,333,856	Roosevelt, James	480	1,127,898 R	64.8%	35.1%	64.9%	35.1%
1946**	2,558,399	2,344,542	Warren, Earl	—		213,857	2,344,542 R	91.6%		100.0%	

In 1946 the Republican candidate won both major party nominations.

POSTWAR VOTE FOR SENATOR

Year	Total Vote	Republican		Democratic		Other Vote	Rep.-Dem. Plurality	Percentage			
								Total Vote		Major Vote	
		Vote	Candidate	Vote	Candidate			Rep.	Dem.	Rep.	Dem.
2000	10,623,614	3,886,853	Campbell, Tom	5,932,522	Feinstein, Dianne	804,239	2,045,669 D	36.6%	55.8%	39.6%	60.4%
1998	8,314,953	3,576,351	Fong, Matt	4,411,705	Boxer, Barbara	326,897	835,354 D	43.0%	53.1%	44.8%	55.2%
1994	8,514,089	3,817,025	Huffington, Michael	3,979,152	Feinstein, Dianne	717,912	162,127 D	44.8%	46.7%	49.0%	51.0%
1992	10,799,703	4,644,182	Herschensohn, Bruce	5,173,467	Boxer, Barbara	982,054	529,285 D	43.0%	47.9%	47.3%	52.7%
1992S	10,782,743	4,093,501	Seymour, John	5,853,651	Feinstein, Dianne	835,591	1,760,150 D	38.0%	54.3%	41.2%	58.8%
1988	9,743,598	5,143,409	Wilson, Pete	4,287,253	McCarthy, Leo	312,936	856,156 R	52.8%	44.0%	54.5%	45.5%
1986	7,398,549	3,541,804	Zschau, Ed	3,646,672	Cranston, Alan	210,073	104,868 D	47.9%	49.3%	49.3%	50.7%
1982	7,805,538	4,022,565	Wilson, Pete	3,494,968	Brown, Edmund G., Jr.	288,005	527,597 R	51.5%	44.8%	53.5%	46.5%
1980	8,327,481	3,093,426	Gann, Paul	4,705,399	Cranston, Alan	528,656	1,611,973 D	37.1%	56.5%	39.7%	60.3%
1976	7,472,268	3,748,973	Hayakawa, S. I.	3,502,862	Tunney, John V.	220,433	246,111 R	50.2%	46.9%	51.7%	48.3%
1974	6,102,432	2,210,267	Richardson, H. L.	3,693,160	Cranston, Alan	199,005	1,482,893 D	36.2%	60.5%	37.4%	62.6%
1970	6,492,157	2,877,617	Murphy, George	3,496,558	Tunney, John V.	117,982	618,941 D	44.3%	53.9%	45.1%	54.9%
1968	7,102,465	3,329,148	Rafferty, Max	3,680,352	Cranston, Alan	92,965	351,204 D	46.9%	51.8%	47.5%	52.5%
1964	7,041,821	3,628,555	Murphy, George	3,411,912	Salinger, Pierre	1,354	216,643 R	51.5%	48.5%	51.5%	48.5%
1962	5,647,952	3,180,483	Kuchel, Thomas H.	2,452,839	Richards, Richard	14,630	727,644 R	56.3%	43.4%	56.5%	43.5%
1958	5,135,221	2,204,337	Knight, Goodwin J.	2,927,693	Engle, Clair	3,191	723,356 D	42.9%	57.0%	43.0%	57.0%
1956	5,361,467	2,892,918	Kuchel, Thomas H.	2,445,816	Richards, Richard	22,733	447,102 R	54.0%	45.6%	54.2%	45.8%
1954S	3,929,668	2,090,836	Kuchel, Thomas H.	1,788,071	Yorty, Samuel W.	50,761	302,765 R	53.2%	45.5%	53.9%	46.1%
1952**	4,542,548	3,982,448	Knowland, William F.	—		560,100	3,982,448 R	87.7%		100.0%	
1950	3,686,315	2,183,454	Nixon, Richard M.	1,502,507	Douglas, Helen	354	680,947 R	59.2%	40.8%	59.2%	40.8%
1946	2,639,465	1,428,067	Knowland, William F.	1,167,161	Rogers, Will	44,237	260,906 R	54.1%	44.2%	55.0%	45.0%

One of the 1992 elections was for a short term to fill a vacancy. The 1954 election was for a short term to fill a vacancy. In 1952 the Republican candidate won both major party nominations.

CALIFORNIA

Congressional districts first established for elections held in 2002
53 members

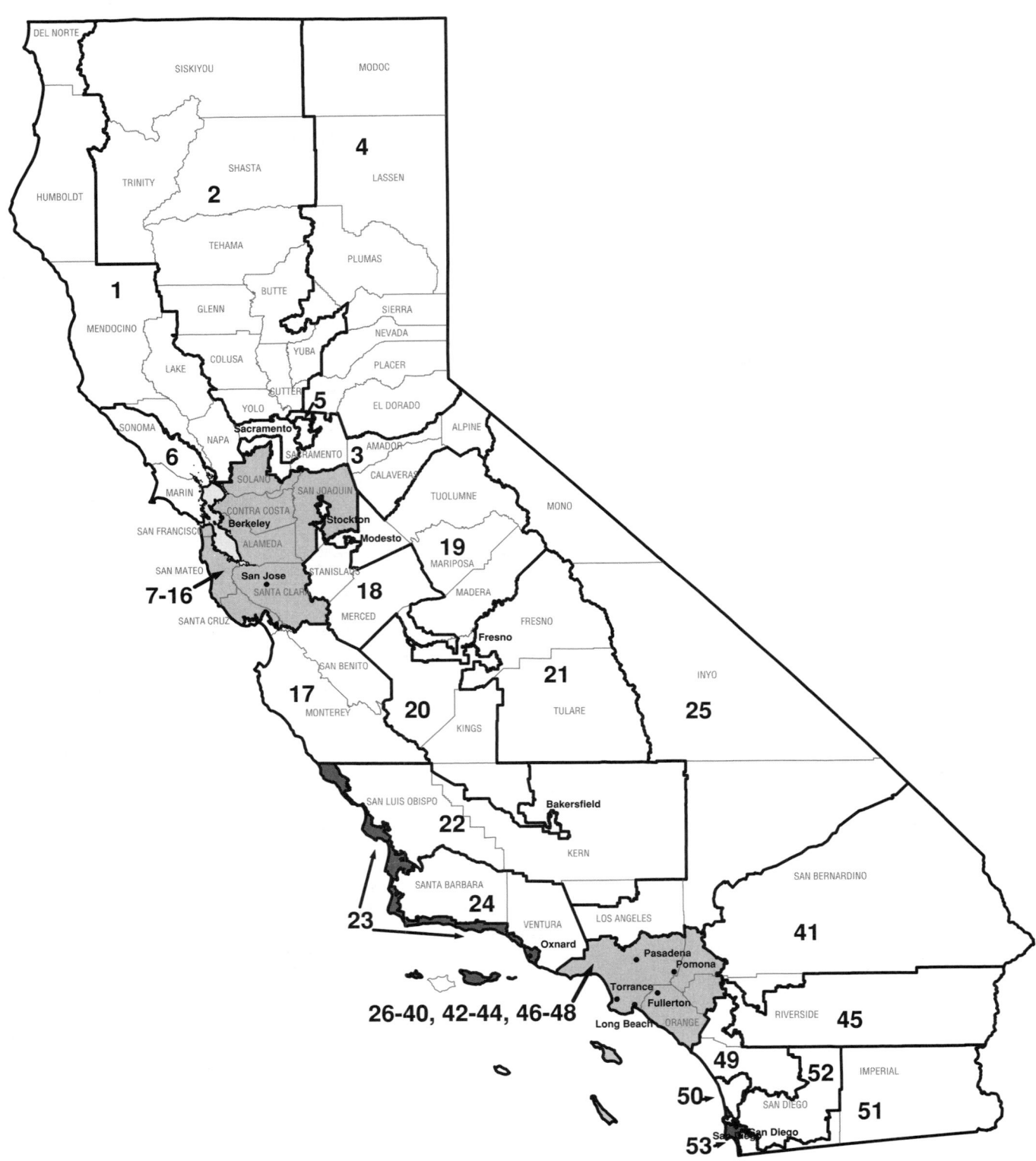

CALIFORNIA

San Francisco Bay Area

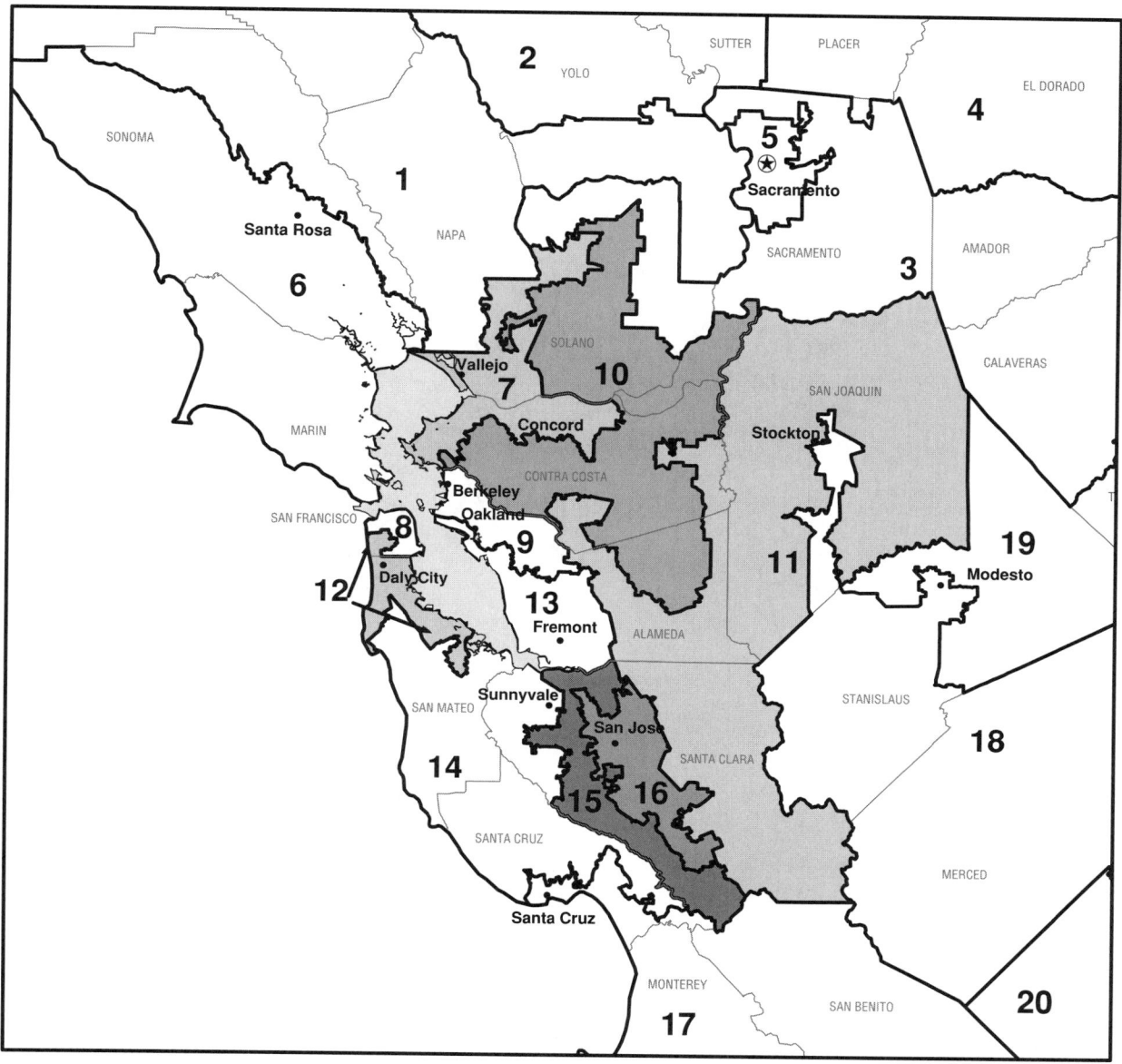

CALIFORNIA

Los Angeles, San Diego Areas

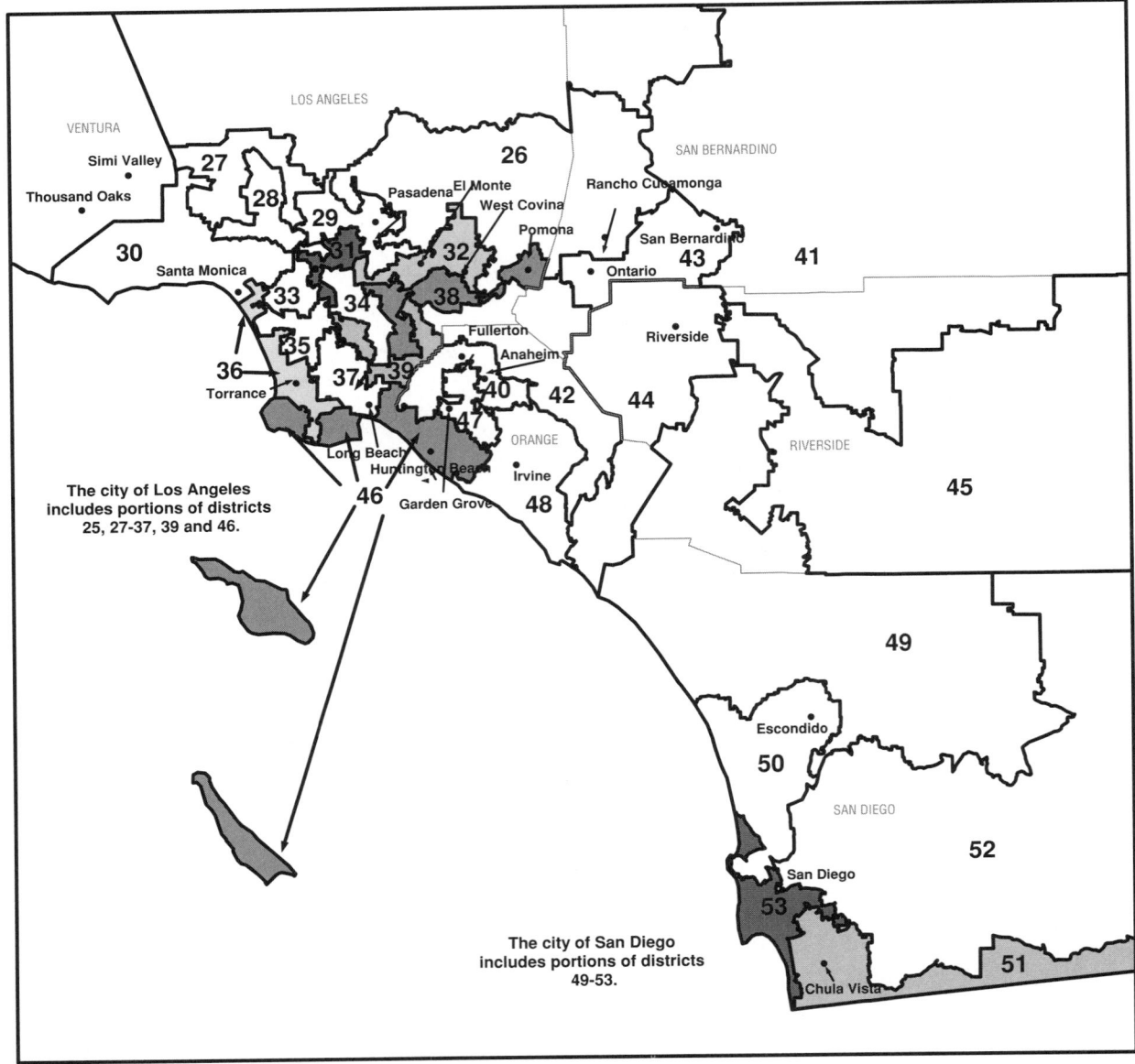

The city of Los Angeles
includes portions of districts
25, 27-37, 39 and 46.

The city of San Diego
includes portions of districts
49-53.

CALIFORNIA

GOVERNOR 2002

2000 Census Population	County	Total Vote	Republican	Democratic	Other	Rep.-Dem. Plurality	Percentage			
							Total Vote		Major Vote	
							Rep.	Dem.	Rep.	Dem.
1,443,741	ALAMEDA	343,901	76,407	216,058	51,436	139,651 D	22.2%	62.8%	26.1%	73.9%
1,208	ALPINE	560	247	229	84	18 R	44.1%	40.9%	51.9%	48.1%
35,100	AMADOR	12,978	6,997	4,437	1,544	2,560 R	53.9%	34.2%	61.2%	38.8%
203,171	BUTTE	61,457	32,706	19,437	9,314	13,269 R	53.2%	31.6%	62.7%	37.3%
40,554	CALAVERAS	15,194	8,104	5,052	2,038	3,052 R	53.3%	33.2%	61.6%	38.4%
18,804	COLUSA	4,575	2,996	1,243	336	1,753 R	65.5%	27.2%	70.7%	29.3%
948,816	CONTRA COSTA	264,870	94,487	140,975	29,408	46,488 D	35.7%	53.2%	40.1%	59.9%
27,507	DEL NORTE	6,750	3,093	2,922	735	171 R	45.8%	43.3%	51.4%	48.6%
156,299	EL DORADO	55,729	32,898	16,402	6,429	16,496 R	59.0%	29.4%	66.7%	33.3%
799,407	FRESNO	155,471	85,910	59,019	10,542	26,891 R	55.3%	38.0%	59.3%	40.7%
26,453	GLENN	6,517	4,268	1,685	564	2,583 R	65.5%	25.9%	71.7%	28.3%
126,518	HUMBOLDT	42,907	16,118	19,499	7,290	3,381 D	37.6%	45.4%	45.3%	54.7%
142,361	IMPERIAL	21,849	8,789	11,644	1,416	2,855 D	40.2%	53.3%	43.0%	57.0%
17,945	INYO	6,288	3,567	2,114	607	1,453 R	56.7%	33.6%	62.8%	37.2%
661,645	KERN	137,288	82,660	46,250	8,378	36,410 R	60.2%	33.7%	64.1%	35.9%
129,461	KINGS	21,215	12,212	7,776	1,227	4,436 R	57.6%	36.7%	61.1%	38.9%
58,309	LAKE	15,893	6,459	7,424	2,010	965 D	40.6%	46.7%	46.5%	53.5%
33,828	LASSEN	7,694	4,512	2,429	753	2,083 R	58.6%	31.6%	65.0%	35.0%
9,519,338	LOS ANGELES	1,706,059	594,748	953,162	158,149	358,414 D	34.9%	55.9%	38.4%	61.6%
123,109	MADERA	26,169	15,998	8,217	1,954	7,781 R	61.1%	31.4%	66.1%	33.9%
247,289	MARIN	88,055	24,520	49,512	14,023	24,992 D	27.8%	56.2%	33.1%	66.9%
17,130	MARIPOSA	6,485	3,720	2,126	639	1,594 R	57.4%	32.8%	63.6%	36.4%
86,265	MENDOCINO	24,904	8,331	10,832	5,741	2,501 D	33.5%	43.5%	43.5%	56.5%
210,554	MERCED	40,558	19,191	18,071	3,296	1,120 R	47.3%	44.6%	51.5%	48.5%
9,449	MODOC	3,381	2,161	900	320	1,261 R	63.9%	26.6%	70.6%	29.4%
12,853	MONO	2,956	1,552	1,064	340	488 R	52.5%	36.0%	59.3%	40.7%
401,762	MONTEREY	86,974	31,532	47,052	8,390	15,520 D	36.3%	54.1%	40.1%	59.9%
124,279	NAPA	36,672	13,483	17,516	5,673	4,033 D	36.8%	47.8%	43.5%	56.5%
92,033	NEVADA	39,315	20,573	13,338	5,404	7,235 R	52.3%	33.9%	60.7%	39.3%
2,846,289	ORANGE	641,008	368,152	222,149	50,707	146,003 R	57.4%	34.7%	62.4%	37.6%
248,399	PLACER	96,056	58,623	28,495	8,938	30,128 R	61.0%	29.7%	67.3%	32.7%
20,824	PLUMAS	7,858	4,310	2,598	950	1,712 R	54.8%	33.1%	62.4%	37.6%
1,545,387	RIVERSIDE	302,683	159,440	121,845	21,398	37,595 R	52.7%	40.3%	56.7%	43.3%
1,223,499	SACRAMENTO	316,397	147,456	129,143	39,798	18,313 R	46.6%	40.8%	53.3%	46.7%
53,234	SAN BENITO	12,373	5,163	6,049	1,161	886 D	41.7%	48.9%	46.0%	54.0%
1,709,434	SAN BERNARDINO	283,191	142,513	116,757	23,921	25,756 R	50.3%	41.2%	55.0%	45.0%
2,813,833	SAN DIEGO	661,298	342,095	268,278	50,925	73,817 R	51.7%	40.6%	56.0%	44.0%
776,733	SAN FRANCISCO	216,156	33,214	143,102	39,840	109,888 D	15.4%	66.2%	18.8%	81.2%
563,598	SAN JOAQUIN	123,443	58,239	53,747	11,457	4,492 R	47.2%	43.5%	52.0%	48.0%
246,681	SAN LUIS OBISPO	81,690	43,552	29,732	8,406	13,820 R	53.3%	36.4%	59.4%	40.6%
707,161	SAN MATEO	172,210	51,497	99,803	20,910	48,306 D	29.9%	58.0%	34.0%	66.0%
399,347	SANTA BARBARA	114,491	52,832	50,741	10,918	2,091 R	46.1%	44.3%	51.0%	49.0%
1,682,585	SANTA CLARA	360,396	116,862	199,399	44,135	82,537 D	32.4%	55.3%	37.0%	63.0%
255,602	SANTA CRUZ	77,584	20,598	43,469	13,517	22,871 D	26.5%	56.0%	32.2%	67.8%
163,256	SHASTA	48,559	28,625	15,292	4,642	13,333 R	58.9%	31.5%	65.2%	34.8%
3,555	SIERRA	1,438	805	420	213	385 R	56.0%	29.2%	65.7%	34.3%
44,301	SISKIYOU	15,603	9,112	4,972	1,519	4,140 R	58.4%	31.9%	64.7%	35.3%
394,542	SOLANO	88,522	33,516	46,385	8,621	12,869 D	37.9%	52.4%	41.9%	58.1%
458,614	SONOMA	145,028	43,408	73,079	28,541	29,671 D	29.9%	50.4%	37.3%	62.7%
446,997	STANISLAUS	96,194	46,091	41,908	8,195	4,183 R	47.9%	43.6%	52.4%	47.6%
78,930	SUTTER	19,370	12,024	5,782	1,564	6,242 R	62.1%	29.9%	67.5%	32.5%
56,039	TEHAMA	15,392	9,010	5,000	1,382	4,010 R	58.5%	32.5%	64.3%	35.7%
13,022	TRINITY	4,924	2,421	1,833	670	588 R	49.2%	37.2%	56.9%	43.1%
368,021	TULARE	62,498	37,172	21,294	4,032	15,878 R	59.5%	34.1%	63.6%	36.4%
54,501	TUOLUMNE	17,942	9,251	6,846	1,845	2,405 R	51.6%	38.2%	57.5%	42.5%
753,197	VENTURA	193,387	91,193	83,557	18,637	7,636 R	47.2%	43.2%	52.2%	47.8%
168,660	YOLO	46,353	17,484	21,983	6,886	4,499 D	37.7%	47.4%	44.3%	55.7%
60,219	YUBA	11,603	6,904	3,447	1,252	3,457 R	59.5%	29.7%	66.7%	33.3%
33,871,648	TOTAL	7,476,311	3,169,801	3,533,490	773,020	363,689 D	42.4%	47.3%	47.3%	52.7%

CALIFORNIA

HOUSE OF REPRESENTATIVES

			Republican		Democratic		Other	Rep.-Dem.	Percentage			
									Total Vote		Major Vote	
CD	Year	Total Vote	Vote	Candidate	Vote	Candidate	Vote	Plurality	Rep.	Dem.	Rep.	Dem.
1	2002	185,216	60,013	Wiesner, Lawrence R.	118,669	Thompson, Mike*	6,534	58,656 D	32.4%	64.1%	33.6%	66.4%
2	2002	178,985	117,747	Herger, Wally*	52,455	Johnson, Mike	8,783	65,292 R	65.8%	29.3%	69.2%	30.8%
3	2002	194,918	121,732	Ose, Doug*	67,136	Beeman, Howard	6,050	54,596 R	62.5%	34.4%	64.5%	35.5%
4	2002	228,506	147,997	Doolittle, John T.*	72,860	Norberg, Mark A.	7,649	75,137 R	64.8%	31.9%	67.0%	33.0%
5	2002	131,578	34,749	Frankhuizen, Richard	92,726	Matsui, Robert T.*	4,103	57,977 D	26.4%	70.5%	27.3%	72.7%
6	2002	209,563	62,052	Erickson, Paul L.	139,750	Woolsey, Lynn*	7,761	77,698 D	29.6%	66.7%	30.7%	69.3%
7	2002	138,376	36,584	Hargrave, Charles R.	97,849	Miller, George*	3,943	61,265 D	26.4%	70.7%	27.2%	72.8%
8	2002	160,441	20,063	German, G. Michael	127,684	Pelosi, Nancy*	12,694	107,621 D	12.5%	79.6%	13.6%	86.4%
9	2002	166,917	25,333	Udinsky, Jerry	135,893	Lee, Barbara*	5,691	110,560 D	15.2%	81.4%	15.7%	84.3%
10	2002	167,197			126,390	Tauscher, Ellen O.*	40,807	126,390 D		75.6%		100.0%
11	2002	173,956	104,921	Pombo, Richard W.*	69,035	Shaw, Elaine Dugger		35,886 R	60.3%	39.7%	60.3%	39.7%
12	2002	154,984	38,381	Moloney, Michael J.	105,597	Lantos, Tom*	11,006	67,216 D	24.8%	68.1%	26.7%	73.3%
13	2002	121,723	26,852	Mahmood, Syed R.	86,495	Stark, Pete*	8,376	59,643 D	22.1%	71.1%	23.7%	76.3%
14	2002	171,678	48,346	Nixon, Joseph H.	117,055	Eshoo, Anna G.*	6,277	68,709 D	28.2%	68.2%	29.2%	70.8%
15	2002	133,022	41,251	Hermann, Linda Rae	87,482	Honda, Michael M.*	4,289	46,231 D	31.0%	65.8%	32.0%	68.0%
16	2002	107,986	32,182	McNea, Douglas Adams	72,370	Lofgren, Zoe*	3,434	40,188 D	29.8%	67.0%	30.8%	69.2%
17	2002	149,296	40,334	Engler, Clint C.	101,632	Farr, Sam*	7,330	61,298 D	27.0%	68.1%	28.4%	71.6%
18	2002	109,593	47,528	Monteith, Dick	56,181	Cardoza, Dennis	5,884	8,653 D	43.4%	51.3%	45.8%	54.2%
19	2002	157,802	106,209	Radanovich, George P.*	47,403	Veen, John	4,190	58,806 R	67.3%	30.0%	69.1%	30.9%
20	2002	74,770	25,628	Minuth, Andre	47,627	Dooley, Cal*	1,515	21,999 D	34.3%	63.7%	35.0%	65.0%
21	2002	124,198	87,544	Nunes, Devin	32,584	LaPere, David G.	4,070	54,960 R	70.5%	26.2%	72.9%	27.1%
22	2002	164,285	120,473	Thomas, Bill*	38,988	Corvera, Jaime A.	4,824	81,485 R	73.3%	23.7%	75.6%	24.4%
23	2002	162,222	62,604	Rogers, Beth	95,752	Capps, Lois*	3,866	33,148 D	38.6%	59.0%	39.5%	60.5%
24	2002	185,006	120,585	Gallegly, Elton*	58,755	Rudin, Fern	5,666	61,830 R	65.2%	31.8%	67.2%	32.8%
25	2002	124,336	80,775	McKeon, Howard P. "Buck"*	38,674	Conaway, Bob	4,887	42,101 R	65.0%	31.1%	67.6%	32.4%
26	2002	149,530	95,360	Dreier, David*	50,081	Mikels, Marjorie Musser	4,089	45,279 R	63.8%	33.5%	65.6%	34.4%
27	2002	128,811	48,996	Levy, Robert M.	79,815	Sherman, Brad*		30,819 D	38.0%	62.0%	38.0%	62.0%
28	2002	103,326	23,926	Hernandez, Davis R., Jr.	73,771	Berman, Howard L.*	5,629	49,845 D	23.2%	71.4%	24.5%	75.5%
29	2002	121,541	40,616	Scileppi, Jim	76,036	Schiff, Adam B.*	4,889	35,420 D	33.4%	62.6%	34.8%	65.2%
30	2002	185,593	54,989	Goss, Tony D.	130,604	Waxman, Henry A.*		75,615 D	29.6%	70.4%	29.6%	70.4%
31	2002	67,243	12,674	Vega, Luis	54,569	Becerra, Xavier*		41,895 D	18.8%	81.2%	18.8%	81.2%
32	2002	85,079	23,366	Fischbeck, Emma E.	58,530	Solis, Hilda L.*	3,183	35,164 D	27.5%	68.8%	28.5%	71.5%
33	2002	118,449	16,699	Kim, Andrew	97,779	Watson, Diane*	3,971	81,080 D	14.1%	82.5%	14.6%	85.4%
34	2002	65,824	17,090	Miller, Wayne	48,734	Roybal-Allard, Lucille*		31,644 D	26.0%	74.0%	26.0%	74.0%
35	2002	93,407	18,094	Moen, Ross	72,401	Waters, Maxine*	2,912	54,307 D	19.4%	77.5%	20.0%	80.0%
36	2002	143,751	50,328	Johnson, Stuart	88,198	Harman, Jane*	5,225	37,870 D	35.0%	61.4%	36.3%	63.7%

CALIFORNIA
HOUSE OF REPRESENTATIVES

CD	Year	Total Vote	Republican Vote	Republican Candidate	Democratic Vote	Democratic Candidate	Other Vote	Rep.-Dem. Plurality	Total Vote Rep.	Total Vote Dem.	Major Vote Rep.	Major Vote Dem.
37	2002	87,012	20,154	Velasco, Oscar A.	63,445	Millender-McDonald, Juanita*	3,413	43,291 D	23.2%	72.9%	24.1%	75.9%
38	2002	88,027	23,126	Burrola, Alex A.	62,600	Napolitano, Grace F.*	2,301	39,474 D	26.3%	71.1%	27.0%	73.0%
39	2002	95,346	38,925	Escobar, Tim	52,256	Sanchez, Linda T.	4,165	13,331 D	40.8%	54.8%	42.7%	57.3%
40	2002	136,642	92,422	Royce, Ed*	40,265	Avalos, Christina	3,955	52,157 R	67.6%	29.5%	69.7%	30.3%
41	2002	135,533	91,326	Lewis, Jerry*	40,155	Johnson, Keith A.	4,052	51,171 R	67.4%	29.6%	69.5%	30.5%
42	2002	145,246	98,476	Miller, Gary G.*	42,090	Waldron, Richard	4,680	56,386 R	67.8%	29.0%	70.1%	29.9%
43	2002	68,340	20,821	Neighbor, Wendy C.	45,374	Baca, Joe*	2,145	24,553 D	30.5%	66.4%	31.5%	68.5%
44	2002	120,463	76,686	Calvert, Ken*	38,021	Vandenberg, Louis	5,756	38,665 R	63.7%	31.6%	66.9%	33.1%
45	2002	133,533	87,101	Bono, Mary*	43,692	Kurpiewski, Elle K.	2,740	43,409 R	65.2%	32.7%	66.6%	33.4%
46	2002	176,265	108,807	Rohrabacher, Dana*	60,890	Schipske, Gerrie	6,568	47,917 R	61.7%	34.5%	64.1%	35.9%
47	2002	70,178	24,346	Chavez, Jeff	42,501	Sanchez, Loretta*	3,331	18,155 D	34.7%	60.6%	36.4%	63.6%
48	2002	179,549	122,884	Cox, Christopher*	51,058	Graham, John	5,607	71,826 R	68.4%	28.4%	70.6%	29.4%
49	2002	122,497	94,594	Issa, Darrell*			27,903	94,594 R	77.2%		100.0%	
50	2002	172,701	111,095	Cunningham, Randy "Duke"*	55,855	Stewart, Del G.	5,751	55,240 R	64.3%	32.3%	66.5%	33.5%
51	2002	102,787	40,430	Garcia, Maria Guadalupe	59,541	Filner, Bob*	2,816	19,111 D	39.3%	57.9%	40.4%	59.6%
52	2002	169,010	118,561	Hunter, Duncan*	43,526	Moore-Kochlacs, Peter	6,923	75,035 R	70.2%	25.8%	73.1%	26.9%
53	2002	116,180	43,891	VanDeWeghe, Bill	72,252	Davis, Susan A.*	37	28,361 D	37.8%	62.2%	37.8%	62.2%
Total	2002	7,258,417	3,225,666		3,731,081		301,670	505,415 D	44.4%	51.4%	46.4%	53.6%

An asterisk (*) denotes incumbent.

CALIFORNIA
GENERAL AND PRIMARY ELECTIONS

2002 GENERAL ELECTIONS

Governor — Other vote was 393,036 Green (Peter Miguel Camejo); 161,203 Libertarian (Gary David Copeland); 128,035 American Independent (Reinhold Gulke); 88,415 Natural Law (Iris Adam); 1,789 write-in (Rob Marinko); 327 write-in (James F. Stewart); 55 write-in (Jim Mallon); 46 write-in (Nick Jesson); 37 write-in (Anselmo A. Chavez); 30 write-in (Debbie Jo Terzoli); 28 write-in (F. Nan Bailey); 13 write-in (Will B. King); 6 write-in (Nick Hoogoian).

House — Other vote was:

CD 1   6,534 Libertarian (Kevin Bastian).
CD 2   4,860 Natural Law (Patrice Thiessen); 3,923 Libertarian (Charles R. Martin).
CD 3   6,050 Libertarian (Douglas Arthur Tuma).
CD 4   7,247 Libertarian (Allen M. Roberts); 401 write-in (Bill Kirby); 1 write-in (Philip James Parisius).
CD 5   4,103 Libertarian (Timothy E. Roloff).
CD 6   4,936 Libertarian (Richard O. Barton); 2,825 Reform (Jeff Rainforth).
CD 7   3,943 Libertarian (Scott A. Wilson).
CD 8   10,033 Green (Jay Pond); 2,659 Libertarian (Ira Spivack); 2 write-in (Deborah Liatos).
CD 9   5,685 Libertarian (James M. Eyer); 6 write-in (Hector Reyna).
CD 10   40,807 Libertarian (Sonia E. Alonso Harden).

CALIFORNIA

GENERAL AND PRIMARY ELECTIONS

2002 GENERAL ELECTIONS

CD 11
CD 12   11,006 Libertarian (Maad Abu-Ghazalah).
CD 13   3,703 Libertarian (Mark W. Stroberg); 2,772 American Independent (Don J. Grundmann); 1,901 Reform (John J. Bambey).
CD 14   6,277 Libertarian (Andrew B. Carver).
CD 15   4,289 Libertarian (Jeff Landauer).
CD 16   3,434 Libertarian (Dennis Michael Umphress).
CD 17   4,885 Green (Ray Glock-Grueneich); 2,418 Libertarian (Jascha Lee); 27 write-in (Alan Shugart).
CD 18   3,641 American Independent (Kevin H. Cripe); 2,194 Libertarian (Linda De Groat); 49 write-in (Donna Crowder).
CD 19   4,190 Libertarian (Patrick Lee McHargue).
CD 20   1,515 Libertarian (Varrin Swearingen).
CD 21   4,070 Libertarian (Jonathan Richter).
CD 22   4,824 Libertarian (Frank Coates).
CD 23   3,866 Libertarian (James E. Hill).
CD 24   5,666 Libertarian (Gary Harber).
CD 25   4,887 Libertarian (Frank M. Consolo, Jr.).
CD 26   4,089 Libertarian (Randall Weissbuch).
CD 27
CD 28   5,629 Libertarian (Kelley L. Ross).
CD 29   4,889 Libertarian (Ted Brown).
CD 30
CD 31
CD 32   3,183 Libertarian (Michael "Mick" McGuire).
CD 33   3,971 Libertarian (Charles Tate).
CD 34
CD 35   2,912 American Independent (Gordon Michael Mego).
CD 36   5,225 Libertarian (Mark McSpadden).
CD 37   3,413 Libertarian (Herb Peters).
CD 38   2,301 Libertarian (Al Cuperus).
CD 39   4,165 Libertarian (Richard G. Newhouse).
CD 40   3,955 Libertarian (Charles R. "Chuck" McGlawn).
CD 41   4,052 Libertarian (Kevin Craig).
CD 42   4,680 Libertarian (Donald Yee).
CD 43   2,145 Libertarian (Ethel M. Mohler).
CD 44   5,756 Green (Phill Courtney).
CD 45   2,740 Libertarian (Rod Miller-Boyer).
CD 46   6,488 Libertarian (Keith Gann); 80 write-in (Thomas Lash).
CD 47   2,944 Libertarian (Paul Marsden); 382 write-in (Kenneth M. Valenzuela Fisher); 5 write-in (Michael J. Monge).
CD 48   5,607 Libertarian (Joe Michael Cobb).
CD 49   26,891 Libertarian (Karl W. Dietrich); 1,012 write-in (Michael P. Byron).
CD 50   5,751 Libertarian (Richard M. Fontanesi).
CD 51   2,816 Libertarian (Jeffrey S. Keup).
CD 52   6,923 Libertarian (Michael Benoit).
CD 53   37 write-in (Jim Dorenkott).

CALIFORNIA
GENERAL AND PRIMARY ELECTIONS

2002 PRIMARY ELECTIONS

Primary	March 5, 2002	

Registration
(as of Feb. 19, 2002)

Republican	5,354,358
Democratic	6,873,476
American Independent	309,174
Green	146,251
Libertarian	92,318
Reform	67,072
Natural Law	49,924
Miscellaneous	133,416
Non-Partisan	2,254,819
TOTAL	15,280,808

Primary Type Semi-open—Voters registered with a recognized party in California could vote only in their party's primary. Other voters could participate in the primary of the Democratic, Republican, American Independent or Natural Law parties.

Note: An asterisk (*) denotes incumbent.

	REPUBLICAN PRIMARIES			DEMOCRATIC PRIMARIES		
Governor	Bill Simon	1,129,973	49.4%	Gray Davis*	1,755,276	80.9%
	Richard J. Riordan	715,768	31.3%	Anselmo A. Chavez	179,301	8.3%
	Bill Jones	387,237	16.9%	Charles "Chuck" Pineda, Jr.	139,121	6.4%
	Nick Jesson	19,287	0.8%	Mosemarie Boyd	95,857	4.4%
	Edie Bukewihge	14,436	0.6%			
	Danney Ball	13,156	0.6%			
	Jim Dimov	5,595	0.2%			
	TOTAL	2,285,452		TOTAL	2,169,555	
Congressional District 1	Lawrence R. Wiesner	42,616	100.0%	Mike Thompson*	64,401	100.0%
Congressional District 2	Wally Herger*	71,028	88.8%	Mike Johnson	25,481	60.9%
	Al Thompson	6,616	8.3%	Raymond G. Hennemann	16,342	39.1%
	Bob Todd	2,370	3.0%			
	TOTAL	80,014		TOTAL	41,823	
Congressional District 3	Doug Ose*	67,277	100.0%	Howard Beeman	41,650	100.0%
Congressional District 4	John T. Doolittle*	79,575	77.5%	Mark A. Norberg	44,786	100.0%
	Bill Kirby	23,083	22.5%			
	TOTAL	102,658				
Congressional District 5	Richard Frankhuizen	23,691	100.0%	Robert T. Matsui*	48,355	100.0%
Congressional District 6	Paul L. Erickson	40,621	100.0%	Lynn Woolsey*	69,158	80.5%
				Mike Martini	16,770	19.5%
				TOTAL	85,928	
Congressional District 7	Charles R. Hargrave	22,031	100.0%	George Miller*	50,581	100.0%
Congressional District 8	G. Michael German	8,489	75.1%	Nancy Pelosi*	65,949	93.1%
	John Jenkel	2,816	24.9%	Paul McConnell	4,898	6.9%
	TOTAL	11,305		TOTAL	70,847	
Congressional District 9	Jerald Udinsky	8,106	61.8%	Barbara Lee*	68,550	84.8%
	Hector "Reno" Reyna	5,001	38.2%	Kevin A. Greene	12,257	15.2%
	TOTAL	13,107		TOTAL	80,807	
Congressional District 10	Gregory W. Ellis (write-in)	276	55.5%	Ellen O. Tauscher*	49,612	83.4%
	Anthony Rodriguez (write-in)	221	44.5%	Kurt Rasmussen	9,867	16.6%
	TOTAL	497		TOTAL	59,479	

CALIFORNIA

GENERAL AND PRIMARY ELECTIONS

	REPUBLICAN PRIMARIES			DEMOCRATIC PRIMARIES		
Congressional District 11	Richard W. Pombo*	53,525	87.0%	Elaine Dugger Shaw	24,738	63.9%
	Thomas A. "Tom" Benigno	7,982	13.0%	Robert L. Figueroa	13,956	36.1%
	TOTAL	61,507		TOTAL	38,694	
Congressional District 12	Michael J. Moloney	23,276	100.0%	Tom Lantos*	57,536	100.0%
Congressional District 13	Syed R. Mahmood	17,772	100.0%	Pete Stark*	40,981	100.0%
Congressional District 14	Joseph H. Nixon	32,911	100.0%	Anna G. Eshoo*	53,132	100.0%
Congressional District 15	Linda Rae Hermann	25,853	100.0%	Michael M. Honda*	38,636	100.0%
Congressional District 16	Douglas Adams McNea	19,008	100.0%	Zoe Lofgren*	34,247	100.0%
Congressional District 17	Clint C. Engler	21,710	63.2%	Sam Farr*	51,251	91.1%
	Ignacio Velazquez	12,660	36.8%	Art Dunn	5,008	8.9%
	TOTAL	34,370		TOTAL	56,259	
Congressional District 18	Dick Monteith	16,031	52.9%	Dennis Cardoza	22,879	53.2%
	Bill Conrad	9,543	31.5%	Gary A. Condit*	16,618	38.7%
	George R. House	3,885	12.8%	Ralph L. White	1,344	3.1%
	Park Yonker	849	2.8%	Sukhmander "Sukhi" Singh	963	2.2%
				Joseph Martin	740	1.7%
				Elvis Pringle	440	1.0%
	TOTAL	30,308		TOTAL	42,984	
Congressional District 19	George P. Radanovich*	61,724	100.0%	John Veen	34,274	100.0%
Congressional District 20	Andre Minuth	8,807	52.6%	Cal Dooley*	27,422	100.0%
	Ricky Martin	7,949	47.4%			
	TOTAL	16,756				
Congressional District 21	Devin Nunes	21,438	37.0%	David G. LaPere	24,595	100.0%
	Jim Patterson	19,099	33.0%			
	Mike Briggs	14,864	25.7%			
	Tom Wright	1,413	2.4%			
	Nathan Short	436	0.8%			
	Richard Morgan	369	0.6%			
	Greg Ingles	258	0.4%			
	TOTAL	57,877				
Congressional District 22	Bill Thomas*	70,738	100.0%	Jaime A. Corvera	29,949	100.0%
Congressional District 23	Beth Rogers	25,512	62.4%	Lois Capps*	43,324	100.0%
	Donald E. Regan	15,396	37.6%			
	Vincent Gillespie (write-in)	2				
	TOTAL	40,910				
Congressional District 24	Elton Gallegly*	62,239	100.0%	Fern Rudin	32,695	100.0%
Congressional District 25	Howard P. "Buck" McKeon*	37,000	84.5%	Bob Conaway	21,264	100.0%
	James O. "Jim" Aldrich	6,810	15.5%			
	TOTAL	43,810				
Congressional District 26	David Dreier*	53,123	100.0%	Marjorie Musser Mikels	25,671	100.0%
Congressional District 27	Robert M. Levy	25,011	100.0%	Brad Sherman*	33,718	100.0%
Congressional District 28	David R. Hernandez, Jr.	12,753	100.0%	Howard L. Berman*	34,864	100.0%
Congressional District 29	Jim Scileppi	26,978	100.0%	Adam B. Schiff*	29,852	100.0%

CALIFORNIA

GENERAL AND PRIMARY ELECTIONS

REPUBLICAN PRIMARIES			DEMOCRATIC PRIMARIES		
Congressional District 30	Tony D. Goss	29,520 100.0%	Henry A. Waxman*	52,785	89.6%
			Kevin Feldman	6,146	10.4%
			TOTAL	58,931	
Congressional District 31	Luis Vega	4,302 64.9%	Xavier Becerra*	24,231	100.0%
	Dino G. Pantazis	2,328 35.1%			
	TOTAL	6,630			
Congressional District 32	Emma E. Fischbeck	13,018 100.0%	Hilda L. Solis*	24,811	100.0%
Congressional District 33	Andrew Kim	7,911 100.0%	Diane Watson*	49,291	100.0%
Congressional District 34	Wayne Miller	8,727 100.0%	Lucille Roybal-Allard*	24,563	100.0%
Congressional District 35	Ross Moen	5,546 68.5%	Maxine Waters*	36,351	100.0%
	Michael Anthony Cyrus	2,554 31.5%			
	TOTAL	8,100			
Congressional District 36	Stuart Johnson	17,511 57.3%	Jane Harman*	35,638	100.0%
	Gloria Davis	13,056 42.7%			
	TOTAL	30,567			
Congressional District 37	Oscar A. Velasco	9,609 100.0%	Juanita Millender-McDonald*	25,302	77.7%
			Peter Mathews	7,269	22.3%
			TOTAL	32,571	
Congressional District 38	Alex A. Burrola	11,761 100.0%	Grace F. Napolitano*	21,815	65.0%
			Gregory Salcido	11,755	35.0%
			TOTAL	33,570	
Congressional District 39	Tim Escobar	12,894 70.4%	Linda T. Sanchez	10,804	33.5%
	Richard B. Owens	5,418 29.6%	Hector De La Torre	9,450	29.3%
			Sally M. Havice	6,223	19.3%
			Helen M. Rahder	2,698	8.4%
			Ken Graham	1,879	5.8%
			Cecy R. Groom	1,230	3.8%
	TOTAL	18,312	TOTAL	32,284	
Congressional District 40	Ed Royce*	54,439 100.0%	Christina Avalos	27,049	100.0%
Congressional District 41	Jerry Lewis*	45,833 100.0%	Keith A. Johnson	25,087	100.0%
Congressional District 42	Gary G. Miller*	59,065 100.0%	Richard Waldron	25,117	100.0%
Congressional District 43	Wendy C. Neighbor	11,691 100.0%	Joe Baca*	19,834	100.0%
Congressional District 44	Ken Calvert*	30,967 70.1%	Louis Vandenberg	21,871	100.0%
	Martin Collen	11,106 25.1%			
	Khalid Jafri	2,087 4.7%			
	TOTAL	44,160			
Congressional District 45	Mary Bono*	42,716 99.5%	Elle K. Kurpiewski	24,395	100.0%
	John Charles Baker (write-in)	200 0.5%			
	TOTAL	42,916			
Congressional District 46	Dana Rohrabacher*	65,748 100.0%	Gerrie Schipske	32,076	100.0%
Congressional District 47	Jeff Chavez	9,135 53.7%	Loretta Sanchez*	18,836	100.0%
	Kenneth M. Valenzuela Fisher	7,883 46.3%			
	TOTAL	17,018			
Congressional District 48	Christopher Cox*	84,229 89.4%	John Graham	33,354	100.0%
	David D. Cobert	6,367 6.8%			
	Dave Forman	3,654 3.9%			
	TOTAL	94,250			

CALIFORNIA

GENERAL AND PRIMARY ELECTIONS

REPUBLICAN PRIMARIES				DEMOCRATIC PRIMARIES		
Congressional District 49	Darrell Issa*	48,344	100.0%	Louis Garcia (write-in)	86	100.0%
Congressional District 50	Randy "Duke" Cunningham* James B. Hart TOTAL	54,491 8,354 62,845	86.7% 13.3%	Del G. Stewart	27,375	100.0%
Congressional District 51	Maria Guadalupe Garcia Guillermo "Willie" Durazo TOTAL	11,433 10,242 21,675	52.7% 47.3%	Bob Filner* Daniel C. "Danny" Ramirez TOTAL	25,179 10,584 35,763	70.4% 29.6%
Congressional District 52	Duncan Hunter*	60,793	100.0%	Peter Moore-Kochlacs	27,765	100.0%
Congressional District 53	Bill VanDeWeghe Tim Kane TOTAL	17,182 12,409 29,591	58.1% 41.9%	Susan A. Davis*	33,546	100.0%

CALIFORNIA REPUBLICAN PRIMARY

GOVERNOR 2002

2000 Census Population	County	Total Vote	Simon	Riordan	Jones	Other	Winner	Simon	Riordan	Jones	Other
1,443,741	ALAMEDA	55,928	30,963	15,046	8,314	1,605	Simon	55.4%	26.9%	14.9%	2.9%
1,208	ALPINE	234	96	53	72	13	Simon	41.0%	22.6%	30.8%	5.6%
35,100	AMADOR	5,307	2,732	1,067	1,417	91	Simon	51.5%	20.1%	26.7%	1.7%
203,171	BUTTE	26,668	15,120	4,091	6,847	610	Simon	56.7%	15.3%	25.7%	2.3%
40,554	CALAVERAS	6,511	3,430	1,097	1,789	195	Simon	52.7%	16.8%	27.5%	3.0%
18,804	COLUSA	2,443	1,163	475	743	62	Simon	47.6%	19.4%	30.4%	2.5%
948,816	CONTRA COSTA	74,914	40,317	19,606	13,527	1,464	Simon	53.8%	26.2%	18.1%	2.0%
27,507	DEL NORTE	2,492	1,274	437	613	168	Simon	51.1%	17.5%	24.6%	6.7%
156,299	EL DORADO	25,268	13,306	5,765	5,715	482	Simon	52.7%	22.8%	22.6%	1.9%
799,407	FRESNO	63,849	19,284	5,804	37,952	809	Jones	30.2%	9.1%	59.4%	1.3%
26,453	GLENN	3,036	1,662	351	927	96	Simon	54.7%	11.6%	30.5%	3.2%
126,518	HUMBOLDT	12,369	7,362	2,590	1,936	481	Simon	59.5%	20.9%	15.7%	3.9%
142,361	IMPERIAL	5,981	2,016	2,223	1,457	285	Riordan	33.7%	37.2%	24.4%	4.8%
17,945	INYO	3,071	1,378	988	597	108	Simon	44.9%	32.2%	19.4%	3.5%
661,645	KERN	60,370	30,765	13,343	14,929	1,333	Simon	51.0%	22.1%	24.7%	2.2%
129,461	KINGS	7,520	2,584	615	4,143	178	Jones	34.4%	8.2%	55.1%	2.4%
58,309	LAKE	4,992	2,746	970	1,095	181	Simon	55.0%	19.4%	21.9%	3.6%
33,828	LASSEN	3,869	1,686	848	1,086	249	Simon	43.6%	21.9%	28.1%	6.4%
9,519,338	LOS ANGELES	383,769	159,741	183,980	32,717	7,331	Riordan	41.6%	47.9%	8.5%	1.9%
123,109	MADERA	11,073	3,919	1,090	5,853	211	Jones	35.4%	9.8%	52.9%	1.9%
247,289	MARIN	20,940	10,095	7,924	2,553	368	Simon	48.2%	37.8%	12.2%	1.8%
17,130	MARIPOSA	3,100	1,326	371	1,338	65	Jones	42.8%	12.0%	43.2%	2.1%
86,265	MENDOCINO	6,719	3,201	1,764	1,447	307	Simon	47.6%	26.3%	21.5%	4.6%
210,554	MERCED	13,127	5,906	1,727	5,095	399	Simon	45.0%	13.2%	38.8%	3.0%
9,449	MODOC	1,685	666	280	632	107	Simon	39.5%	16.6%	37.5%	6.4%
12,853	MONO	1,280	572	420	237	51	Simon	44.7%	32.8%	18.5%	4.0%
401,762	MONTEREY	24,458	14,006	6,382	3,325	745	Simon	57.3%	26.1%	13.6%	3.0%
124,279	NAPA	11,174	6,153	2,506	2,147	368	Simon	55.1%	22.4%	19.2%	3.3%
92,033	NEVADA	17,133	9,618	3,641	3,565	309	Simon	56.1%	21.3%	20.8%	1.8%
2,846,289	ORANGE	300,848	152,111	113,176	29,025	6,536	Simon	50.6%	37.6%	9.6%	2.2%
248,399	PLACER	43,432	23,312	10,336	9,090	694	Simon	53.7%	23.8%	20.9%	1.6%
20,824	PLUMAS	3,588	1,806	709	977	96	Simon	50.3%	19.8%	27.2%	2.7%
1,545,387	RIVERSIDE	105,528	50,148	41,388	11,392	2,600	Simon	47.5%	39.2%	10.8%	2.5%
1,223,499	SACRAMENTO	104,263	52,906	25,506	23,788	2,063	Simon	50.7%	24.5%	22.8%	2.0%
53,234	SAN BENITO	3,920	2,322	783	666	149	Simon	59.2%	20.0%	17.0%	3.8%

CALIFORNIA REPUBLICAN PRIMARY

GOVERNOR 2002

2000 Census Population	County	Total Vote	Simon	Riordan	Jones	Other	Winner	Percentage of Total Vote			
								Simon	Riordan	Jones	Other
1,709,434	SAN BERNARDINO	89,819	43,990	34,368	8,917	2,544	Simon	49.0%	38.3%	9.9%	2.8%
2,813,833	SAN DIEGO	228,168	135,089	54,717	33,173	5,189	Simon	59.2%	24.0%	14.5%	2.3%
776,733	SAN FRANCISCO	23,499	10,309	9,582	3,054	554	Simon	43.9%	40.8%	13.0%	2.4%
563,598	SAN JOAQUIN	44,084	23,524	8,044	11,523	993	Simon	53.4%	18.2%	26.1%	2.3%
246,681	SAN LUIS OBISPO	31,466	16,248	10,040	4,561	617	Simon	51.6%	31.9%	14.5%	2.0%
707,161	SAN MATEO	39,530	20,437	12,783	5,550	760	Simon	51.7%	32.3%	14.0%	1.9%
399,347	SANTA BARBARA	36,285	17,791	13,541	4,337	616	Simon	49.0%	37.3%	12.0%	1.7%
1,682,585	SANTA CLARA	89,228	47,626	26,478	12,258	2,866	Simon	53.4%	29.7%	13.7%	3.2%
255,602	SANTA CRUZ	18,469	10,860	5,134	2,012	463	Simon	58.8%	27.8%	10.9%	2.5%
163,256	SHASTA	21,976	12,311	3,133	5,640	892	Simon	56.0%	14.3%	25.7%	4.1%
3,555	SIERRA	677	315	115	227	20	Simon	46.5%	17.0%	33.5%	3.0%
44,301	SISKIYOU	6,490	2,577	1,408	2,166	339	Simon	39.7%	21.7%	33.4%	5.2%
394,542	SOLANO	23,122	12,874	5,120	4,426	702	Simon	55.7%	22.1%	19.1%	3.0%
458,614	SONOMA	39,648	20,838	10,930	6,491	1,389	Simon	52.6%	27.6%	16.4%	3.5%
446,997	STANISLAUS	33,670	18,332	4,478	9,990	870	Simon	54.4%	13.3%	29.7%	2.6%
78,930	SUTTER	8,883	5,063	1,330	2,316	174	Simon	57.0%	15.0%	26.1%	2.0%
56,039	TEHAMA	7,260	3,930	977	2,069	284	Simon	54.1%	13.5%	28.5%	3.9%
13,022	TRINITY	2,049	927	378	601	143	Simon	45.2%	18.4%	29.3%	7.0%
368,021	TULARE	28,427	7,981	2,014	17,995	437	Jones	28.1%	7.1%	63.3%	1.5%
54,501	TUOLUMNE	7,326	4,103	1,107	1,984	132	Simon	56.0%	15.1%	27.1%	1.8%
753,197	VENTURA	66,237	30,169	28,286	6,525	1,257	Simon	45.5%	42.7%	9.9%	1.9%
168,660	YOLO	13,015	6,060	3,604	3,052	299	Simon	46.6%	27.7%	23.4%	2.3%
60,219	YUBA	5,265	2,927	849	1,364	125	Simon	55.6%	16.1%	25.9%	2.4%
33,871,648	TOTAL	2,285,452	1,129,973	715,768	387,237	52,474	Simon	49.4%	31.3%	16.9%	2.3%

CALIFORNIA DEMOCRATIC PRIMARY

GOVERNOR 2002

2000 Census Population	County	Total Vote	Davis	Other	Winner	Percentage of Total Vote	
						Davis	Other
1,443,741	ALAMEDA	131,013	111,369	19,644	Davis	85.0%	15.0%
1,208	ALPINE	184	155	29	Davis	84.2%	15.8%
35,100	AMADOR	3,582	2,701	881	Davis	75.4%	24.6%
203,171	BUTTE	17,680	13,498	4,182	Davis	76.3%	23.7%
40,554	CALAVERAS	4,383	3,314	1,069	Davis	75.6%	24.4%
18,804	COLUSA	1,517	1,007	510	Davis	66.4%	33.6%
948,816	CONTRA COSTA	88,583	73,512	15,071	Davis	83.0%	17.0%
27,507	DEL NORTE	2,220	1,594	626	Davis	71.8%	28.2%
156,299	EL DORADO	12,720	9,333	3,387	Davis	73.4%	26.6%
799,407	FRESNO	43,236	34,159	9,077	Davis	79.0%	21.0%
26,453	GLENN	1,627	1,127	500	Davis	69.3%	30.7%
126,518	HUMBOLDT	14,108	11,122	2,986	Davis	78.8%	21.2%
142,361	IMPERIAL	9,471	6,822	2,649	Davis	72.0%	28.0%
17,945	INYO	1,811	1,398	413	Davis	77.2%	22.8%
661,645	KERN	34,326	26,050	8,276	Davis	75.9%	24.1%
129,461	KINGS	5,689	4,230	1,459	Davis	74.4%	25.6%
58,309	LAKE	5,509	4,457	1,052	Davis	80.9%	19.1%
33,828	LASSEN	2,569	1,833	736	Davis	71.4%	28.6%
9,519,338	LOS ANGELES	530,529	436,970	93,559	Davis	82.4%	17.6%
123,109	MADERA	5,906	4,271	1,635	Davis	72.3%	27.7%
247,289	MARIN	30,207	25,333	4,874	Davis	83.9%	16.1%
17,130	MARIPOSA	1,769	1,362	407	Davis	77.0%	23.0%
86,265	MENDOCINO	9,605	7,311	2,294	Davis	76.1%	23.9%
210,554	MERCED	13,608	10,956	2,652	Davis	80.5%	19.5%
9,449	MODOC	1,026	703	323	Davis	68.5%	31.5%

CALIFORNIA DEMOCRATIC PRIMARY

GOVERNOR 2002

2000 Census Population	County	Total Vote	Davis	Other	Percentage of Total Vote		
					Winner	Davis	Other
12,853	MONO	762	612	150	Davis	80.3%	19.7%
401,762	MONTEREY	28,441	23,287	5,154	Davis	81.9%	18.1%
124,279	NAPA	12,104	9,550	2,554	Davis	78.9%	21.1%
92,033	NEVADA	9,033	7,079	1,954	Davis	78.4%	21.6%
2,846,289	ORANGE	146,748	113,971	32,777	Davis	77.7%	22.3%
248,399	PLACER	19,342	14,988	4,354	Davis	77.5%	22.5%
20,824	PLUMAS	2,380	1,760	620	Davis	73.9%	26.1%
1,545,387	RIVERSIDE	65,711	54,289	11,422	Davis	82.6%	17.4%
1,223,499	SACRAMENTO	91,779	70,774	21,005	Davis	77.1%	22.9%
53,234	SAN BENITO	4,291	3,407	884	Davis	79.4%	20.6%
1,709,434	SAN BERNARDINO	64,980	50,600	14,380	Davis	77.9%	22.1%
2,813,833	SAN DIEGO	146,020	118,013	28,007	Davis	80.8%	19.2%
776,733	SAN FRANCISCO	86,668	75,268	11,400	Davis	86.8%	13.2%
563,598	SAN JOAQUIN	36,815	29,404	7,411	Davis	79.9%	20.1%
246,681	SAN LUIS OBISPO	18,544	14,713	3,831	Davis	79.3%	20.7%
707,161	SAN MATEO	60,619	50,827	9,792	Davis	83.8%	16.2%
399,347	SANTA BARBARA	27,155	22,464	4,691	Davis	82.7%	17.3%
1,682,585	SANTA CLARA	112,099	92,084	20,015	Davis	82.1%	17.9%
255,602	SANTA CRUZ	31,189	25,349	5,840	Davis	81.3%	18.7%
163,256	SHASTA	12,153	8,854	3,299	Davis	72.9%	27.1%
3,555	SIERRA	471	328	143	Davis	69.6%	30.4%
44,301	SISKIYOU	4,292	2,972	1,320	Davis	69.2%	30.8%
394,542	SOLANO	29,551	23,922	5,629	Davis	81.0%	19.0%
458,614	SONOMA	58,323	45,896	12,427	Davis	78.7%	21.3%
446,997	STANISLAUS	30,988	24,369	6,619	Davis	78.6%	21.4%
78,930	SUTTER	4,073	2,826	1,247	Davis	69.4%	30.6%
56,039	TEHAMA	5,117	3,704	1,413	Davis	72.4%	27.6%
13,022	TRINITY	1,755	1,265	490	Davis	72.1%	27.9%
368,021	TULARE	14,845	11,421	3,424	Davis	76.9%	23.1%
54,501	TUOLUMNE	5,361	4,259	1,102	Davis	79.4%	20.6%
753,197	VENTURA	45,182	36,989	8,193	Davis	81.9%	18.1%
168,660	YOLO	16,392	13,006	3,386	Davis	79.3%	20.7%
60,219	YUBA	3,494	2,439	1,055	Davis	69.8%	30.2%
33,871,648	TOTAL	2,169,555	1,755,276	414,279	Davis	80.9%	19.1%

COLORADO

GOVERNOR
Bill Owens (R). Reelected 2002 to a four-year term. Previously elected 1998.

SENATORS (2 Republicans)
Wayne Allard (R). Reelected 2002 to a six-year term. Previously elected 1996.

Ben Nighthorse Campbell (R). Reelected 1998 to a six-year term. Previously elected 1992. Changed party affiliation from Democrat to Republican in March 1995.

REPRESENTATIVES (5 Republicans, 2 Democrats)
1. Diana DeGette (D)
2. Mark Udall (D)
3. Scott McInnis (R)
4. Marilyn Musgrave (R)
5. Joel Hefley (R)
6. Tom Tancredo (R)
7. Bob Beauprez (R)

POSTWAR VOTE FOR PRESIDENT

Year	Total Vote	Republican		Democratic		Other Vote	Plurality	Total Vote		Major Vote	
		Vote	Candidate	Vote	Candidate			Rep.	Dem.	Rep.	Dem.
2000**	1,741,368	883,748	Bush, George W.	738,227	Gore, Al	119,393	145,521 R	50.8%	42.4%	54.5%	45.5%
1996**	1,510,704	691,848	Dole, Bob	671,152	Clinton, Bill	147,704	20,696 R	45.8%	44.4%	50.8%	49.2%
1992**	1,569,180	562,850	Bush, George	629,681	Clinton, Bill	376,649	66,831 D	35.9%	40.1%	47.2%	52.8%
1988	1,372,394	728,177	Bush, George	621,453	Dukakis, Michael S.	22,764	106,724 R	53.1%	45.3%	54.0%	46.0%
1984	1,295,380	821,817	Reagan, Ronald	454,975	Mondale, Walter F.	18,588	366,842 R	63.4%	35.1%	64.4%	35.6%
1980**	1,184,415	652,264	Reagan, Ronald	367,973	Carter, Jimmy	164,178	284,291 R	55.1%	31.1%	63.9%	36.1%
1976	1,081,554	584,367	Ford, Gerald R.	460,353	Carter, Jimmy	36,834	124,014 R	54.0%	42.6%	55.9%	44.1%
1972	953,884	597,189	Nixon, Richard M.	329,980	McGovern, George S.	26,715	267,209 R	62.6%	34.6%	64.4%	35.6%
1968	811,199	409,345	Nixon, Richard M.	335,174	Humphrey, Hubert H.	66,680	74,171 R	50.5%	41.3%	55.0%	45.0%
1964	776,986	296,767	Goldwater, Barry M.	476,024	Johnson, Lyndon B.	4,195	179,257 D	38.2%	61.3%	38.4%	61.6%
1960	736,236	402,242	Nixon, Richard M.	330,629	Kennedy, John F.	3,365	71,613 R	54.6%	44.9%	54.9%	45.1%
1956	657,074	394,479	Eisenhower, Dwight D.	257,997	Stevenson, Adlai E.	4,598	136,482 R	60.0%	39.3%	60.5%	39.5%
1952	630,103	379,782	Eisenhower, Dwight D.	245,504	Stevenson, Adlai E.	4,817	134,278 R	60.3%	39.0%	60.7%	39.3%
1948	515,237	239,714	Dewey, Thomas E.	267,288	Truman, Harry S.	8,235	27,574 D	46.5%	51.9%	47.3%	52.7%

In 2000 the other vote column includes 91,434 votes cast for Green (Nader). In 1996 the other vote column includes 99,629 votes cast for Perot. In 1992 the other vote column includes 366,010 votes cast for Perot. In 1980 the other column includes 130,633 votes for Independent (Anderson).

COLORADO

POSTWAR VOTE FOR GOVERNOR

Year	Total Vote	Republican Vote	Republican Candidate	Democratic Vote	Democratic Candidate	Other Vote	Rep.-Dem. Plurality	Percentage Total Vote Rep.	Dem.	Major Vote Rep.	Dem.
2002	1,412,602	884,583	Owens, Bill	475,373	Heath, Rollie	52,646	409,210 R	62.6%	33.7%	65.0%	35.0%
1998	1,321,307	648,202	Owens, Bill	639,905	Schoettler, Gail	33,200	8,297 R	49.1%	48.4%	50.3%	49.7%
1994	1,116,307	432,042	Benson, Bruce	619,205	Romer, Roy	65,060	187,163 D	38.7%	55.5%	41.1%	58.9%
1990	1,011,272	358,403	Andrews, John	626,032	Romer, Roy	26,837	267,629 D	35.4%	61.9%	36.4%	63.6%
1986	1,058,928	434,420	Strickland, Ted	616,325	Romer, Roy	8,183	181,905 D	41.0%	58.2%	41.3%	58.7%
1982	956,021	302,740	Fuhr, John D.	627,960	Lamm, Richard D.	25,321	325,220 D	31.7%	65.7%	32.5%	67.5%
1978	823,807	317,292	Strickland, Ted	483,985	Lamm, Richard D.	22,530	166,693 D	38.5%	58.7%	39.6%	60.4%
1974	828,968	378,698	Vanderhoof, John D.	441,408	Lamm, Richard D.	8,862	62,710 D	45.7%	53.2%	46.2%	53.8%
1970	668,496	350,690	Love, John A.	302,432	Hogan, Mark	15,374	48,258 R	52.5%	45.2%	53.7%	46.3%
1966	660,063	356,730	Love, John A.	287,132	Knous, Robert L.	16,201	69,598 R	54.0%	43.5%	55.4%	44.6%
1962	616,481	349,342	Love, John A.	262,890	McNichols, Stephen	4,249	86,452 R	56.7%	42.6%	57.1%	42.9%
1958**	549,808	228,643	Burch, Palmer L.	321,165	McNichols, Stephen		92,522 D	41.6%	58.4%	41.6%	58.4%
1956	645,233	313,950	Brotzman, Donald G.	331,283	McNichols, Stephen		17,333 D	48.7%	51.3%	48.7%	51.3%
1954	489,540	227,335	Brotzman, Donald G.	262,205	Johnson, Ed C.		34,870 D	46.4%	53.6%	46.4%	53.6%
1952	613,034	349,924	Thornton, Dan	260,044	Metzger, John W.	3,066	89,880 R	57.1%	42.4%	57.4%	42.6%
1950	450,994	236,472	Thornton, Dan	212,976	Johnson, Walter	1,546	23,496 R	52.4%	47.2%	52.6%	47.4%
1948	501,680	168,928	Hamil, David A.	332,752	Knous, William Lee		163,824 D	33.7%	66.3%	33.7%	66.3%
1946	335,087	160,483	Lavington, Leon E.	174,604	Knous, William Lee		14,121 D	47.9%	52.1%	47.9%	52.1%

The term of office of Colorado's Governor was increased from two to four years effective with the 1958 election.

POSTWAR VOTE FOR SENATOR

Year	Total Vote	Republican Vote	Republican Candidate	Democratic Vote	Democratic Candidate	Other Vote	Rep.-Dem. Plurality	Percentage Total Vote Rep.	Dem.	Major Vote Rep.	Dem.
2002	1,416,082	717,893	Allard, Wayne	648,130	Strickland, Tom	50,059	69,763 R	50.7%	45.8%	52.6%	47.4%
1998	1,327,235	829,370	Campbell, Ben Nighthorse	464,754	Lamm, Dottie	33,111	364,616 R	62.5%	35.0%	64.1%	35.9%
1996	1,469,611	750,325	Allard, Wayne	677,600	Strickland, Tom	41,686	72,725 R	51.1%	46.1%	52.5%	47.5%
1992	1,552,289	662,893	Considine, Terry	803,725	Campbell, Ben Nighthorse	85,671	140,832 D	42.7%	51.8%	45.2%	54.8%
1990	1,022,027	569,048	Brown, Hank	425,746	Heath, Josie	27,233	143,302 R	55.7%	41.7%	57.2%	42.8%
1986	1,060,765	512,994	Kramer, Ken	529,449	Wirth, Timothy E.	18,322	16,455 D	48.4%	49.9%	49.2%	50.8%
1984	1,297,809	833,821	Armstrong, William L.	449,327	Dick, Nancy	14,661	384,494 R	64.2%	34.6%	65.0%	35.0%
1980	1,173,646	571,295	Buchanan, Mary E.	590,501	Hart, Gary W.	11,850	19,206 D	48.7%	50.3%	49.2%	50.8%
1978	819,150	480,596	Armstrong, William L.	330,247	Haskell, Floyd K.	8,307	150,349 R	58.7%	40.3%	59.3%	40.7%
1974	824,166	325,508	Dominick, Peter H.	471,691	Hart, Gary W.	26,967	146,183 D	39.5%	57.2%	40.8%	59.2%
1972	926,093	447,957	Allott, Gordon	457,545	Haskell, Floyd K.	20,591	9,588 D	48.4%	49.4%	49.5%	50.5%
1968	785,536	459,952	Dominick, Peter H.	325,584	McNichols, Stephen		134,368 R	58.6%	41.4%	58.6%	41.4%
1966	634,898	368,307	Allott, Gordon	266,259	Romer, Roy	332	102,048 R	58.0%	41.9%	58.0%	42.0%
1962	613,444	328,655	Dominick, Peter H.	279,586	Carroll, John A.	5,203	49,069 R	53.6%	45.6%	54.0%	46.0%
1960	727,633	389,428	Allott, Gordon	334,854	Knous, Robert L.	3,351	54,574 R	53.5%	46.0%	53.8%	46.2%
1956	636,974	317,102	Thornton, Dan	319,872	Carroll, John A.		2,770 D	49.8%	50.2%	49.8%	50.2%
1954	484,188	248,502	Allott, Gordon	235,686	Carroll, John A.		12,816 R	51.3%	48.7%	51.3%	48.7%
1950	450,176	239,734	Millikin, Eugene D.	210,442	Carroll, John A.		29,292 R	53.3%	46.7%	53.3%	46.7%
1948	510,121	165,069	Nicholson, W. F.	340,719	Johnson, Ed C.	4,333	175,650 D	32.4%	66.8%	32.6%	67.4%

COLORADO

Congressional districts first established for elections held in 2002
7 members

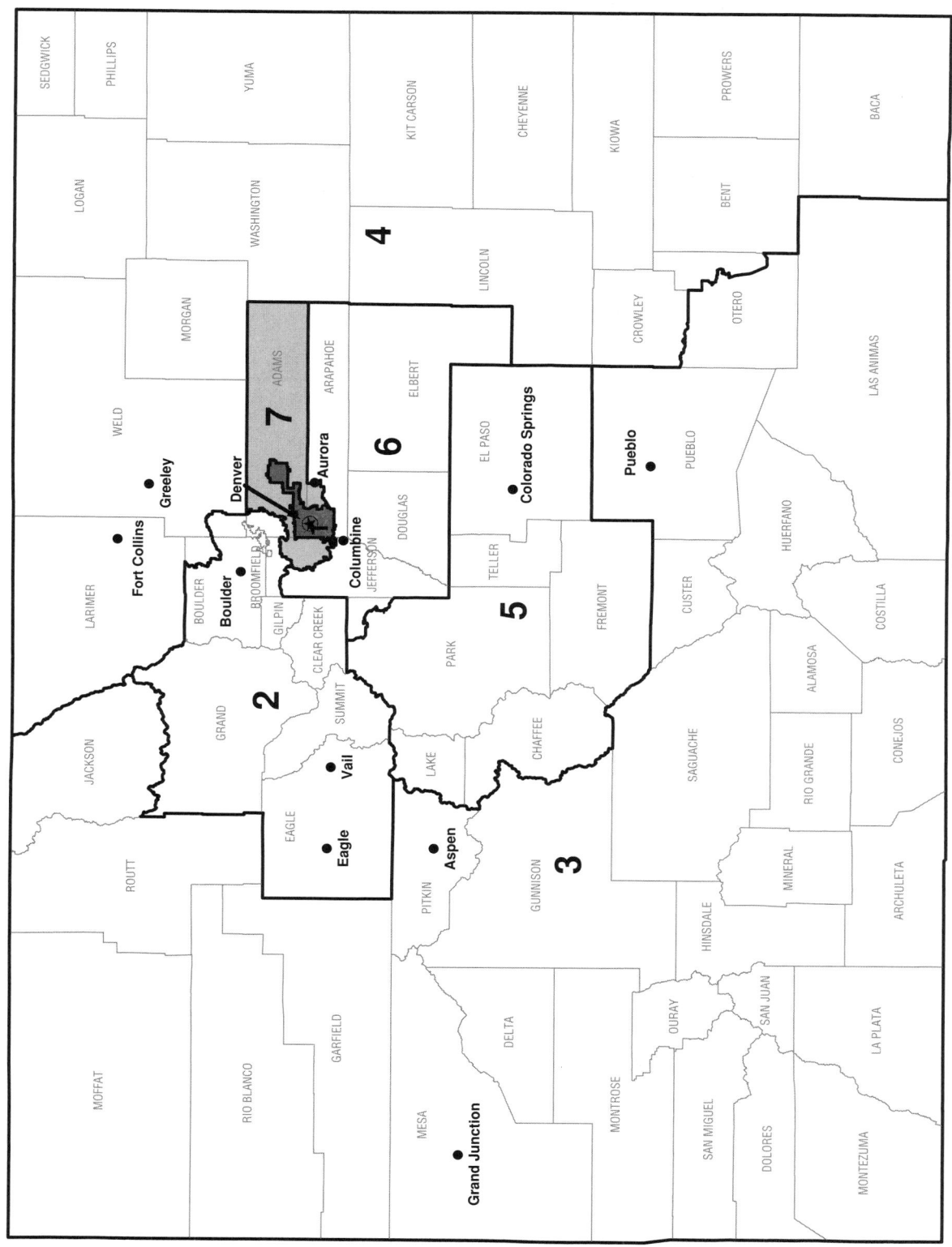

COLORADO

Denver Area

Congressional districts first established for elections held in 2002

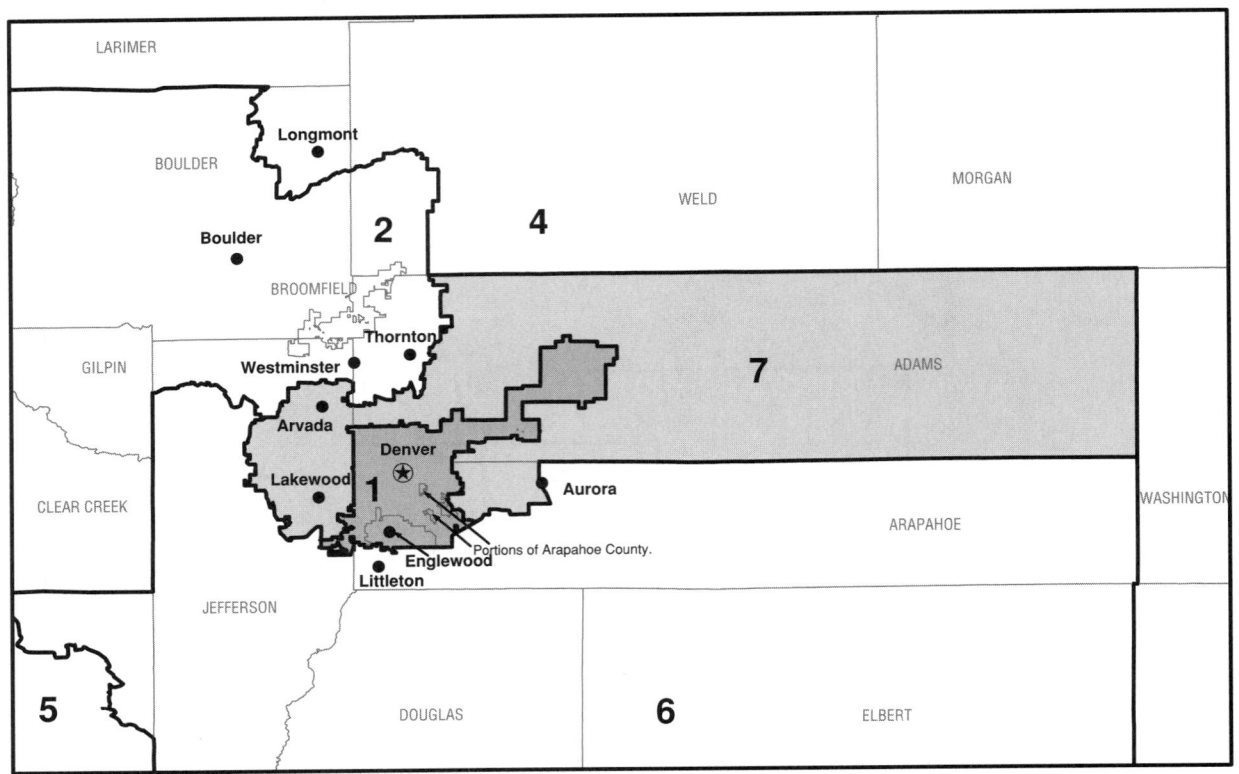

COLORADO

GOVERNOR 2002

2000 Census Population	County	Total Vote	Republican	Democratic	Other	Rep.-Dem. Plurality	Percentage			
							Total Vote		Major Vote	
							Rep.	Dem.	Rep.	Dem.
348,618	ADAMS	84,363	50,623	31,551	2,189	19,072 R	60.0%	37.4%	61.6%	38.4%
14,966	ALAMOSA	4,648	2,611	1,913	124	698 R	56.2%	41.2%	57.7%	42.3%
487,967	ARAPAHOE	151,574	101,542	46,260	3,772	55,282 R	67.0%	30.5%	68.7%	31.3%
9,898	ARCHULETA	3,981	2,885	994	102	1,891 R	72.5%	25.0%	74.4%	25.6%
4,517	BACA	2,177	1,653	501	23	1,152 R	75.9%	23.0%	76.7%	23.3%
5,998	BENT	1,927	1,266	630	31	636 R	65.7%	32.7%	66.8%	33.2%
269,814	BOULDER	106,436	46,964	50,829	8,643	3,865 D	44.1%	47.8%	48.0%	52.0%
38,272	BROOMFIELD*	14,200	9,307	4,414	479	4,893 R	65.5%	31.1%	67.8%	32.2%
16,242	CHAFFEE	6,880	4,187	2,394	299	1,793 R	60.9%	34.8%	63.6%	36.4%
2,231	CHEYENNE	1,065	890	165	10	725 R	83.6%	15.5%	84.4%	15.6%
9,322	CLEAR CREEK	4,045	2,348	1,466	231	882 R	58.0%	36.2%	61.6%	38.4%
8,400	CONEJOS	3,227	1,841	1,339	47	502 R	57.0%	41.5%	57.9%	42.1%
3,663	COSTILLA	1,598	780	762	56	18 R	48.8%	47.7%	50.6%	49.4%
5,518	CROWLEY	1,305	904	374	27	530 R	69.3%	28.7%	70.7%	29.3%
3,503	CUSTER	1,974	1,499	409	66	1,090 R	75.9%	20.7%	78.6%	21.4%
27,834	DELTA	11,238	7,925	2,738	575	5,187 R	70.5%	24.4%	74.3%	25.7%
554,636	DENVER	153,065	67,959	78,838	6,268	10,879 D	44.4%	51.5%	46.3%	53.7%
1,844	DOLORES	856	518	298	40	220 R	60.5%	34.8%	63.5%	36.5%
175,766	DOUGLAS	73,996	58,519	14,182	1,295	44,337 R	79.1%	19.2%	80.5%	19.5%
41,659	EAGLE	11,677	7,030	4,256	391	2,774 R	60.2%	36.4%	62.3%	37.7%
19,872	ELBERT	8,022	6,415	1,448	159	4,967 R	80.0%	18.1%	81.6%	18.4%
516,929	EL PASO	152,893	114,263	32,680	5,950	81,583 R	74.7%	21.4%	77.8%	22.2%
46,145	FREMONT	13,995	8,968	4,599	428	4,369 R	64.1%	32.9%	66.1%	33.9%
43,791	GARFIELD	13,883	8,856	4,438	589	4,418 R	63.8%	32.0%	66.6%	33.4%
4,757	GILPIN	2,291	1,277	831	183	446 R	55.7%	36.3%	60.6%	39.4%
12,442	GRAND	5,040	3,502	1,356	182	2,146 R	69.5%	26.9%	72.1%	27.9%
13,956	GUNNISON	5,429	2,634	2,428	367	206 R	48.5%	44.7%	52.0%	48.0%
790	HINSDALE	536	334	161	41	173 R	62.3%	30.0%	67.5%	32.5%
7,862	HUERFANO	2,810	1,602	1,131	77	471 R	57.0%	40.2%	58.6%	41.4%
1,577	JACKSON	844	654	165	25	489 R	77.5%	19.5%	79.9%	20.1%
525,507	JEFFERSON	189,099	122,356	60,656	6,087	61,700 R	64.7%	32.1%	66.9%	33.1%
1,622	KIOWA	916	721	188	7	533 R	78.7%	20.5%	79.3%	20.7%
8,011	KIT CARSON	3,080	2,520	520	40	2,000 R	81.8%	16.9%	82.9%	17.1%
7,812	LAKE	2,404	1,340	943	121	397 R	55.7%	39.2%	58.7%	41.3%
43,941	LA PLATA	15,954	9,022	5,952	980	3,070 R	56.6%	37.3%	60.3%	39.7%
251,494	LARIMER	93,673	60,727	27,931	5,015	32,796 R	64.8%	29.8%	68.5%	31.5%
15,207	LAS ANIMAS	5,161	2,690	2,363	108	327 R	52.1%	45.8%	53.2%	46.8%
6,087	LINCOLN	1,975	1,489	461	25	1,028 R	75.4%	23.3%	76.4%	23.6%
20,504	LOGAN	6,729	4,977	1,638	114	3,339 R	74.0%	24.3%	75.2%	24.8%
116,255	MESA	40,811	27,234	12,255	1,322	14,979 R	66.7%	30.0%	69.0%	31.0%
831	MINERAL	446	276	154	16	122 R	61.9%	34.5%	64.2%	35.8%
13,184	MOFFAT	4,523	3,318	1,091	114	2,227 R	73.4%	24.1%	75.3%	24.7%
23,830	MONTEZUMA	7,999	5,311	2,363	325	2,948 R	66.4%	29.5%	69.2%	30.8%
33,432	MONTROSE	12,320	8,644	3,217	459	5,427 R	70.2%	26.1%	72.9%	27.1%
27,171	MORGAN	7,670	5,657	1,884	129	3,773 R	73.8%	24.6%	75.0%	25.0%
20,311	OTERO	6,182	4,112	1,989	81	2,123 R	66.5%	32.2%	67.4%	32.6%
3,742	OURAY	1,895	1,177	621	97	556 R	62.1%	32.8%	65.5%	34.5%
14,523	PARK	5,912	4,057	1,505	350	2,552 R	68.6%	25.5%	72.9%	27.1%
4,480	PHILLIPS	1,919	1,516	376	27	1,140 R	79.0%	19.6%	80.1%	19.9%
14,872	PITKIN	6,054	3,096	2,613	345	483 R	51.1%	43.2%	54.2%	45.8%
14,483	PROWERS	4,014	2,898	1,071	45	1,827 R	72.2%	26.7%	73.0%	27.0%
141,472	PUEBLO	49,142	24,059	24,401	682	342 D	49.0%	49.7%	49.6%	50.4%
5,986	RIO BLANCO	2,454	1,922	482	50	1,440 R	78.3%	19.6%	80.0%	20.0%
12,413	RIO GRANDE	4,542	3,107	1,349	86	1,758 R	68.4%	29.7%	69.7%	30.3%
19,690	ROUTT	7,507	4,525	2,596	386	1,929 R	60.3%	34.6%	63.5%	36.5%

COLORADO

GOVERNOR 2002

2000 Census Population	County	Total Vote	Republican	Democratic	Other	Rep.-Dem. Plurality		Percentage			
								Total Vote		Major Vote	
								Rep.	Dem.	Rep.	Dem.
5,917	SAGUACHE	2,023	1,038	872	113	166	R	51.3%	43.1%	54.3%	45.7%
558	SAN JUAN	408	206	154	48	52	R	50.5%	37.7%	57.2%	42.8%
6,594	SAN MIGUEL	2,493	1,085	1,129	279	44	D	43.5%	45.3%	49.0%	51.0%
2,747	SEDGWICK	1,186	895	279	12	616	R	75.5%	23.5%	76.2%	23.8%
23,548	SUMMIT	8,164	4,395	3,241	528	1,154	R	53.8%	39.7%	57.6%	42.4%
20,555	TELLER	7,996	5,885	1,772	339	4,113	R	73.6%	22.2%	76.9%	23.1%
4,926	WASHINGTON	2,169	1,800	338	31	1,462	R	83.0%	15.6%	84.2%	15.8%
180,926	WELD	55,916	39,682	14,670	1,564	25,012	R	71.0%	26.2%	73.0%	27.0%
9,841	YUMA	3,891	3,090	749	52	2,341	R	79.4%	19.2%	80.5%	19.5%
4,301,261	TOTAL	1,412,602	884,583	475,373	52,646	409,210	R	62.6%	33.7%	65.0%	35.0%

* Note: Broomfield County was created effective 2001 out of portions of Adams, Boulder, Jefferson and Weld counties. The population figures in this table have been adjusted for each county using 2000 census data.

COLORADO

SENATOR 2002

2000 Census Population	County	Total Vote	Republican	Democratic	Other	Rep.-Dem. Plurality		Percentage			
								Total Vote		Major Vote	
								Rep.	Dem.	Rep.	Dem.
348,618	ADAMS	84,358	36,911	43,614	3,833	6,703	D	43.8%	51.7%	45.8%	54.2%
14,966	ALAMOSA	4,649	2,373	2,071	205	302	R	51.0%	44.5%	53.4%	46.6%
487,967	ARAPAHOE	152,563	79,176	68,673	4,714	10,503	R	51.9%	45.0%	53.6%	46.4%
9,898	ARCHULETA	3,958	2,401	1,404	153	997	R	60.7%	35.5%	63.1%	36.9%
4,517	BACA	2,185	1,476	629	80	847	R	67.6%	28.8%	70.1%	29.9%
5,998	BENT	1,883	1,009	777	97	232	R	53.6%	41.3%	56.5%	43.5%
269,814	BOULDER	106,433	36,911	66,407	3,115	29,496	D	34.7%	62.4%	35.7%	64.3%
38,272	BROOMFIELD*	14,174	7,376	6,327	471	1,049	R	52.0%	44.6%	53.8%	46.2%
16,242	CHAFFEE	6,917	3,862	2,797	258	1,065	R	55.8%	40.4%	58.0%	42.0%
2,231	CHEYENNE	1,070	787	242	41	545	R	73.6%	22.6%	76.5%	23.5%
9,322	CLEAR CREEK	4,031	1,877	1,962	192	85	D	46.6%	48.7%	48.9%	51.1%
8,400	CONEJOS	3,171	1,562	1,478	131	84	R	49.3%	46.6%	51.4%	48.6%
3,663	COSTILLA	1,557	499	957	101	458	D	32.0%	61.5%	34.3%	65.7%
5,518	CROWLEY	1,304	830	411	63	419	R	63.7%	31.5%	66.9%	33.1%
3,503	CUSTER	1,970	1,318	566	86	752	R	66.9%	28.7%	70.0%	30.0%
27,834	DELTA	11,065	6,776	3,734	555	3,042	R	61.2%	33.7%	64.5%	35.5%
554,636	DENVER	154,598	46,463	103,677	4,458	57,214	D	30.1%	67.1%	30.9%	69.1%
1,844	DOLORES	857	503	314	40	189	R	58.7%	36.6%	61.6%	38.4%
175,766	DOUGLAS	74,239	48,617	23,852	1,770	24,765	R	65.5%	32.1%	67.1%	32.9%
41,659	EAGLE	11,710	5,685	5,629	396	56	R	48.5%	48.1%	50.2%	49.8%
19,872	ELBERT	8,029	5,511	2,295	223	3,216	R	68.6%	28.6%	70.6%	29.4%
516,929	EL PASO	153,032	100,958	46,617	5,457	54,341	R	66.0%	30.5%	68.4%	31.6%
46,145	FREMONT	13,951	8,341	4,930	680	3,411	R	59.8%	35.3%	62.9%	37.1%
43,791	GARFIELD	13,840	7,057	6,223	560	834	R	51.0%	45.0%	53.1%	46.9%
4,757	GILPIN	2,289	892	1,209	188	317	D	39.0%	52.8%	42.5%	57.5%
12,442	GRAND	5,043	2,872	1,963	208	909	R	57.0%	38.9%	59.4%	40.6%
13,956	GUNNISON	5,445	2,322	2,844	279	522	D	42.6%	52.2%	44.9%	55.1%
790	HINSDALE	533	300	194	39	106	R	56.3%	36.4%	60.7%	39.3%
7,862	HUERFANO	2,776	1,272	1,384	120	112	D	45.8%	49.9%	47.9%	52.1%
1,577	JACKSON	855	611	200	44	411	R	71.5%	23.4%	75.3%	24.7%
525,507	JEFFERSON	189,402	95,680	86,278	7,444	9,402	R	50.5%	45.6%	52.6%	47.4%
1,622	KIOWA	936	664	252	20	412	R	70.9%	26.9%	72.5%	27.5%
8,011	KIT CARSON	3,098	2,125	860	113	1,265	R	68.6%	27.8%	71.2%	28.8%
7,812	LAKE	2,399	1,018	1,229	152	211	D	42.4%	51.2%	45.3%	54.7%
43,941	LA PLATA	16,111	7,609	8,016	486	407	D	47.2%	49.8%	48.7%	51.3%

COLORADO

SENATOR 2002

2000 Census Population	County	Total Vote	Republican	Democratic	Other	Rep.-Dem. Plurality	Total Vote Rep.	Total Vote Dem.	Major Vote Rep.	Major Vote Dem.
251,494	LARIMER	94,306	50,837	40,642	2,827	10,195 R	53.9%	43.1%	55.6%	44.4%
15,207	LAS ANIMAS	5,100	2,199	2,673	228	474 D	43.1%	52.4%	45.1%	54.9%
6,087	LINCOLN	1,964	1,365	550	49	815 R	69.5%	28.0%	71.3%	28.7%
20,504	LOGAN	6,770	4,425	2,139	206	2,286 R	65.4%	31.6%	67.4%	32.6%
116,255	MESA	40,958	24,030	14,710	2,218	9,320 R	58.7%	35.9%	62.0%	38.0%
831	MINERAL	439	235	183	21	52 R	53.5%	41.7%	56.2%	43.8%
13,184	MOFFAT	4,525	2,916	1,366	243	1,550 R	64.4%	30.2%	68.1%	31.9%
23,830	MONTEZUMA	8,052	4,886	2,924	242	1,962 R	60.7%	36.3%	62.6%	37.4%
33,432	MONTROSE	12,370	7,596	4,097	677	3,499 R	61.4%	33.1%	65.0%	35.0%
27,171	MORGAN	7,676	4,873	2,562	241	2,311 R	63.5%	33.4%	65.5%	34.5%
20,311	OTERO	6,096	3,470	2,423	203	1,047 R	56.9%	39.7%	58.9%	41.1%
3,742	OURAY	1,864	1,010	796	58	214 R	54.2%	42.7%	55.9%	44.1%
14,523	PARK	5,884	3,304	2,230	350	1,074 R	56.2%	37.9%	59.7%	40.3%
4,480	PHILLIPS	1,922	1,305	570	47	735 R	67.9%	29.7%	69.6%	30.4%
14,872	PITKIN	6,118	1,991	3,935	192	1,944 D	32.5%	64.3%	33.6%	66.4%
14,483	PROWERS	4,011	2,653	1,256	102	1,397 R	66.1%	31.3%	67.9%	32.1%
141,472	PUEBLO	48,888	20,254	26,870	1,764	6,616 D	41.4%	55.0%	43.0%	57.0%
5,986	RIO BLANCO	2,441	1,730	616	95	1,114 R	70.9%	25.2%	73.7%	26.3%
12,413	RIO GRANDE	4,515	2,670	1,655	190	1,015 R	59.1%	36.7%	61.7%	38.3%
19,690	ROUTT	7,511	3,364	3,889	258	525 D	44.8%	51.8%	46.4%	53.6%
5,917	SAGUACHE	1,985	877	1,016	92	139 D	44.2%	51.2%	46.3%	53.7%
558	SAN JUAN	417	194	186	37	8 R	46.5%	44.6%	51.1%	48.9%
6,594	SAN MIGUEL	2,529	782	1,644	103	862 D	30.9%	65.0%	32.2%	67.8%
2,747	SEDGWICK	1,118	716	360	42	356 R	64.0%	32.2%	66.5%	33.5%
23,548	SUMMIT	8,177	3,408	4,450	319	1,042 D	41.7%	54.4%	43.4%	56.6%
20,555	TELLER	7,995	5,191	2,456	348	2,735 R	64.9%	30.7%	67.9%	32.1%
4,926	WASHINGTON	2,160	1,637	468	55	1,169 R	75.8%	21.7%	77.8%	22.2%
180,926	WELD	55,984	33,582	20,413	1,989	13,169 R	60.0%	36.5%	62.2%	37.8%
9,841	YUMA	3,876	2,749	1,036	91	1,713 R	70.9%	26.7%	72.6%	27.4%
4,301,261	TOTAL	1,416,082	717,893	648,130	50,059	69,763 R	50.7%	45.8%	52.6%	47.4%

* Note: Broomfield County was created effective 2001 out of portions of Adams, Boulder, Jefferson and Weld counties. The population figures in this table have been adjusted for each county using 2000 census data.

COLORADO

HOUSE OF REPRESENTATIVES

CD	Year	Total Vote	Republican Vote	Republican Candidate	Democratic Vote	Democratic Candidate	Other Vote	Rep.-Dem. Plurality	Total Vote Rep.	Total Vote Dem.	Major Vote Rep.	Major Vote Dem.
1	2002	168,564	49,884	Chlouber, Ken	111,718	DeGette, Diana*	6,962	61,834 D	29.6%	66.3%	30.9%	69.1%
2	2002	205,522	75,564	Hume, Sandy	123,504	Udall, Mark*	6,454	47,940 D	36.8%	60.1%	38.0%	62.0%
3	2002	217,972	143,433	McInnis, Scott*	68,160	Berckefeldt, Denis	6,379	75,273 R	65.8%	31.3%	67.8%	32.2%
4	2002	209,955	115,359	Musgrave, Marilyn	87,499	Matsunaka, Stan	7,097	27,860 R	54.9%	41.7%	56.9%	43.1%
5	2002	184,677	128,118	Hefley, Joel*	45,587	Imrie, Curtis	10,972	82,531 R	69.4%	24.7%	73.8%	26.2%
6	2002	237,501	158,851	Tancredo, Tom*	71,327	Wright, Lance	7,323	87,524 R	66.9%	30.0%	69.0%	31.0%
7	2002	172,879	81,789	Beauprez, Bob	81,668	Feeley, Mike	9,422	121 R	47.3%	47.2%	50.0%	50.0%
Total	2002	1,397,070	752,998		589,463		54,609	163,535 R	53.9%	42.2%	56.1%	43.9%

An asterisk (*) denotes incumbent.

COLORADO

GENERAL AND PRIMARY ELECTIONS

2002 GENERAL ELECTIONS

Governor	Other vote was 32,099 Green (Ronald Forthofer); 20,547 Libertarian (Ralph Shnelvar).
Senator	Other vote was 21,547 American Constitution (Douglas "Dayhorse" Campbell); 20,776 Libertarian (Rick Stanley); 7,140 Concerns of the People (John Heckman); 596 write-in (Gary Cooper).
House	Other vote was:
CD 1	3,209 Green (Ken Seaman); 2,584 Libertarian (Kent Leonard); 1,169 American Constitution (George C. Lilly).
CD 2	3,579 Libertarian (Norm Olsen); 1,617 Natural Law (Patrick West); 1,258 American Constitution (Erik J. Brauer).
CD 3	4,370 Libertarian (J. Brent Shroyer); 1,903 Natural Law (Gary Swing); 106 write-in (Jason Alessio).
CD 4	7,097 Libertarian (John Volz).
CD 5	10,972 Libertarian (Biff Baker).
CD 6	7,323 Libertarian (Adam D. Katz).
CD 7	3,274 Green (Dave Chandler); 3,133 Reform (Victor Good); 2,906 Libertarian (G.T. "Bud" Martin); 109 write-in (Stanford E. Andress).

2002 PRIMARY ELECTIONS

Primary	August 13, 2002	**Registration** (as of Aug. 13, 2002)	
		Republican	1,037,738
		Democratic	855,553
		Libertarian	5,302
		Green	5,053
		Natural Law	999
		Reform	385
		American Constitution	136
		Concerns of the People	34
		Unaffiliated	939,244
		TOTAL	2,844,444

Primary Type	Semi-open—Registered Democrats and Republicans could vote only in their party's primary. "Unaffiliated" voters could vote in either primary.

Note: An asterisk (*) denotes incumbent.

COLORADO

GENERAL AND PRIMARY ELECTIONS

	REPUBLICAN PRIMARIES			DEMOCRATIC PRIMARIES		
Governor	Bill Owens*	189,705	100.0%	Rollie Heath	98,897	100.0%
Senator	Wayne Allard*	190,250	100.0%	Tom Strickland	110,309	100.0%
Congressional District 1	Ken Chlouber	14,516	100.0%	Diana DeGette* Ramona E. Martinez TOTAL	24,526 8,853 33,379	73.5% 26.5%
Congressional District 2	Sandy Hume Bob Vehar TOTAL	9,842 6,300 16,142	61.0% 39.0%	Mark Udall*	13,205	100.0%
Congressional District 3	Scott McInnis*	31,149	100.0%	Denis Berckefeldt	15,732	100.0%
Congressional District 4	Marilyn Musgrave Jeff Bedingfield TOTAL	28,683 15,743 44,426	64.6% 35.4%	Stan Matsunaka	12,235	100.0%
Congressional District 5	Joel Hefley*	26,133	100.0%	Curtis Imrie	4,108	100.0%
Congressional District 6	Tom Tancredo*	33,900	100.0%	Lance Wright	11,475	100.0%
Congressional District 7	Bob Beauprez Rick O'Donnell Sam H. Zakhem Joe Rogers TOTAL	10,172 8,213 4,848 3,430 26,663	38.2% 30.8% 18.2% 12.9%	Mike Feeley Dave Thomas TOTAL	11,265 8,690 19,955	56.5% 43.5%

CONNECTICUT

GOVERNOR

John G. Rowland (R). Reelected 2002 to a four-year term. Previously elected 1998, 1994.

SENATORS (2 Democrats)

Christopher J. Dodd (D). Reelected 1998 to a six-year term. Previously elected 1992, 1986, 1980.

Joseph I. Lieberman (D). Reelected 2000 to a six-year term. Previously elected 1994, 1988.

REPRESENTATIVES (3 Republicans, 2 Democrats)

1. John B. Larson (D)
2. Rob Simmons (R)
3. Rosa DeLauro (D)
4. Christopher Shays (R)
5. Nancy L. Johnson (R)

POSTWAR VOTE FOR PRESIDENT

Year	Total Vote	Republican		Democratic		Other Vote	Plurality	Percentage			
								Total Vote		Major Vote	
		Vote	Candidate	Vote	Candidate			Rep.	Dem.	Rep.	Dem.
2000**	1,459,525	561,094	Bush, George W.	816,015	Gore, Al	82,416	254,921 D	38.4%	55.9%	40.7%	59.3%
1996**	1,392,614	483,109	Dole, Bob	735,740	Clinton, Bill	173,765	252,631 D	34.7%	52.8%	39.6%	60.4%
1992**	1,616,332	578,313	Bush, George	682,318	Clinton, Bill	355,701	104,005 D	35.8%	42.2%	45.9%	54.1%
1988	1,443,394	750,241	Bush, George	676,584	Dukakis, Michael S.	16,569	73,657 R	52.0%	46.9%	52.6%	47.4%
1984	1,466,900	890,877	Reagan, Ronald	569,597	Mondale, Walter F.	6,426	321,280 R	60.7%	38.8%	61.0%	39.0%
1980**	1,406,285	677,210	Reagan, Ronald	541,732	Carter, Jimmy	187,343	135,478 R	48.2%	38.5%	55.6%	44.4%
1976	1,381,526	719,261	Ford, Gerald R.	647,895	Carter, Jimmy	14,370	71,366 R	52.1%	46.9%	52.6%	47.4%
1972	1,384,277	810,763	Nixon, Richard M.	555,498	McGovern, George S.	18,016	255,265 R	58.6%	40.1%	59.3%	40.7%
1968	1,256,232	556,721	Nixon, Richard M.	621,561	Humphrey, Hubert H.	77,950	64,840 D	44.3%	49.5%	47.2%	52.8%
1964	1,218,578	390,996	Goldwater, Barry M.	826,269	Johnson, Lyndon B.	1,313	435,273 D	32.1%	67.8%	32.1%	67.9%
1960	1,222,883	565,813	Nixon, Richard M.	657,055	Kennedy, John F.	15	91,242 D	46.3%	53.7%	46.3%	53.7%
1956	1,117,121	711,837	Eisenhower, Dwight D.	405,079	Stevenson, Adlai E.	205	306,758 R	63.7%	36.3%	63.7%	36.3%
1952	1,096,911	611,012	Eisenhower, Dwight D.	481,649	Stevenson, Adlai E.	4,250	129,363 R	55.7%	43.9%	55.9%	44.1%
1948	883,518	437,754	Dewey, Thomas E.	423,297	Truman, Harry S.	22,467	14,457 R	49.5%	47.9%	50.8%	49.2%

In 2000 the other vote column includes 64,452 votes cast for Green (Nader). In 1996 the other vote column includes 139,523 votes cast for Perot. In 1992 the other vote column includes 348,771 votes cast for Perot. In 1980 the other column includes 171,807 votes for Independent (Anderson).

CONNECTICUT

POSTWAR VOTE FOR GOVERNOR

Year	Total Vote	Republican Vote	Republican Candidate	Democratic Vote	Democratic Candidate	Other Vote	Rep.-Dem. Plurality	Percentage Total Vote Rep.	Dem.	Percentage Major Vote Rep.	Dem.
2002	1,022,998	573,958	Rowland, John G.	448,984	Curry, Bill	56	124,974 R	56.1%	43.9%	56.1%	43.9%
1998	999,537	628,707	Rowland, John G.	354,187	Kennelly, Barbara B.	16,643	274,520 R	62.9%	35.4%	64.0%	36.0%
1994**	1,147,084	415,201	Rowland, John G.	375,133	Curry, Bill	356,750	40,068 R	36.2%	32.7%	52.5%	47.5%
1990**	1,141,122	427,840	Rowland, John G.	236,641	Morrison, Bruce A.	476,641	32,736 C	37.5%	20.7%	64.4%	35.6%
1986	993,692	408,489	Belaga, Julie D.	575,638	O'Neill, William A.	9,565	167,149 D	41.1%	57.9%	41.5%	58.5%
1982	1,084,156	497,773	Rome, Lewis B.	578,264	O'Neill, William A.	8,119	80,491 D	45.9%	53.3%	46.3%	53.7%
1978	1,036,608	422,316	Sarasin, Ronald A.	613,109	Grasso, Ella T.	1,183	190,793 D	40.7%	59.1%	40.8%	59.2%
1974	1,102,773	440,169	Steele, Robert H.	643,490	Grasso, Ella T.	19,114	203,321 D	39.9%	58.4%	40.6%	59.4%
1970	1,082,797	582,160	Meskill, Thomas J.	500,561	Daddario, Emilio	76	81,599 R	53.8%	46.2%	53.8%	46.2%
1966	1,008,557	446,536	Gengras, E. Clayton	561,599	Dempsey, John N.	422	115,063 D	44.3%	55.7%	44.3%	55.7%
1962	1,031,902	482,852	Alsop, John	549,027	Dempsey, John N.	23	66,175 D	46.8%	53.2%	46.8%	53.2%
1958	974,509	360,644	Zeller, Fred R.	607,012	Ribicoff, Abraham A.	6,853	246,368 D	37.0%	62.3%	37.3%	62.7%
1954	936,753	460,528	Lodge, John D.	463,643	Ribicoff, Abraham A.	12,582	3,115 D	49.2%	49.5%	49.8%	50.2%
1950**	878,735	436,418	Lodge, John D.	419,404	Bowles, Chester	22,913	17,014 R	49.7%	47.7%	51.0%	49.0%
1948	875,170	429,071	Shannon, James C.	431,296	Bowles, Chester	14,803	2,225 D	49.0%	49.3%	49.9%	50.1%
1946	683,831	371,852	McConaughy, J. L.	276,335	Snow, Wilbert	35,644	95,517 R	54.4%	40.4%	57.4%	42.6%

In 1994 other vote was 216,585 Connecticut Party (Groark); 130,128 Independent (Scott); 10,007 Concerned Citizens (Zdonczyk); 30 write-ins. In 1990 Lowell P. Weicker, the Connecticut Party candidate, polled 460,576 votes (40.4% of the total vote) and won the election with a 32,736 plurality. The term of office for Connecticut's Governor was increased from two to four years effective with the 1950 election.

POSTWAR VOTE FOR SENATOR

Year	Total Vote	Republican Vote	Republican Candidate	Democratic Vote	Democratic Candidate	Other Vote	Rep.-Dem. Plurality	Percentage Total Vote Rep.	Dem.	Percentage Major Vote Rep.	Dem.
2000	1,311,261	448,077	Giordano, Philip A.	828,902	Lieberman, Joseph I.	34,282	380,825 D	34.2%	63.2%	35.1%	64.9%
1998	964,457	312,177	Franks, Gary A.	628,306	Dodd, Christopher J.	23,974	316,129 D	32.4%	65.1%	33.2%	66.8%
1994	1,079,767	334,833	Labriola, Jerry	723,842	Lieberman, Joseph I.	21,092	389,009 D	31.0%	67.0%	31.6%	68.4%
1992	1,500,709	572,036	Johnson, Brook	882,569	Dodd, Christopher J.	46,104	310,533 D	38.1%	58.8%	39.3%	60.7%
1988	1,383,526	678,454	Weicker, Lowell P.	688,499	Lieberman, Joseph I.	16,573	10,045 D	49.0%	49.8%	49.6%	50.4%
1986	976,933	340,438	Eddy, Roger W.	632,695	Dodd, Christopher J.	3,800	292,257 D	34.8%	64.8%	35.0%	65.0%
1982	1,083,613	545,987	Weicker, Lowell P.	499,146	Moffett, Anthony T.	38,480	46,841 R	50.4%	46.1%	52.2%	47.8%
1980	1,356,075	581,884	Buckley, James L.	763,969	Dodd, Christopher J.	10,222	182,085 D	42.9%	56.3%	43.2%	56.8%
1976	1,361,666	785,683	Weicker, Lowell P.	561,018	Schaffer, Gloria	14,965	224,665 R	57.7%	41.2%	58.3%	41.7%
1974	1,084,918	372,055	Brannen, James H.	690,820	Ribicoff, Abraham A.	22,043	318,765 D	34.3%	63.7%	35.0%	65.0%
1970	1,089,353	454,721	Weicker, Lowell P.	368,111	Duffey, Joseph D.	266,521	86,610 R	41.7%	33.8%	55.3%	44.7%
1968	1,206,537	551,455	May, Edwin H.	655,043	Ribicoff, Abraham A.	39	103,588 D	45.7%	54.3%	45.7%	54.3%
1964	1,208,163	426,939	Lodge, John D.	781,008	Dodd, Thomas J.	216	354,069 D	35.3%	64.6%	35.3%	64.7%
1962	1,029,301	501,694	Seely-Brown, Horace	527,522	Ribicoff, Abraham A.	85	25,828 D	48.7%	51.3%	48.7%	51.3%
1958	965,463	410,622	Purtell, William A.	554,841	Dodd, Thomas J.		144,219 D	42.5%	57.5%	42.5%	57.5%
1956	1,113,819	610,829	Bush, Prescott	479,460	Dodd, Thomas J.	23,530	131,369 R	54.8%	43.0%	56.0%	44.0%
1952	1,093,467	573,854	Purtell, William A.	485,066	Benton, William	34,547	88,788 R	52.5%	44.4%	54.2%	45.8%
1952S	1,093,268	559,465	Bush, Prescott	530,505	Ribicoff, Abraham A.	3,298	28,960 R	51.2%	48.5%	51.3%	48.7%
1950	877,827	409,053	Talbot, Joseph E.	453,646	McMahon, Brien	15,128	44,593 D	46.6%	51.7%	47.4%	52.6%
1950S	877,135	430,311	Bush, Prescott	431,413	Benton, William	15,411	1,102 D	49.1%	49.2%	49.9%	50.1%
1946	682,921	381,328	Baldwin, Raymond	276,424	Tone, Joseph M.	25,169	104,904 R	55.8%	40.5%	58.0%	42.0%

One each of the 1952 and 1950 elections was for a short term to fill a vacancy.

78

CONNECTICUT

Congressional districts first established for elections held in 2002
5 members

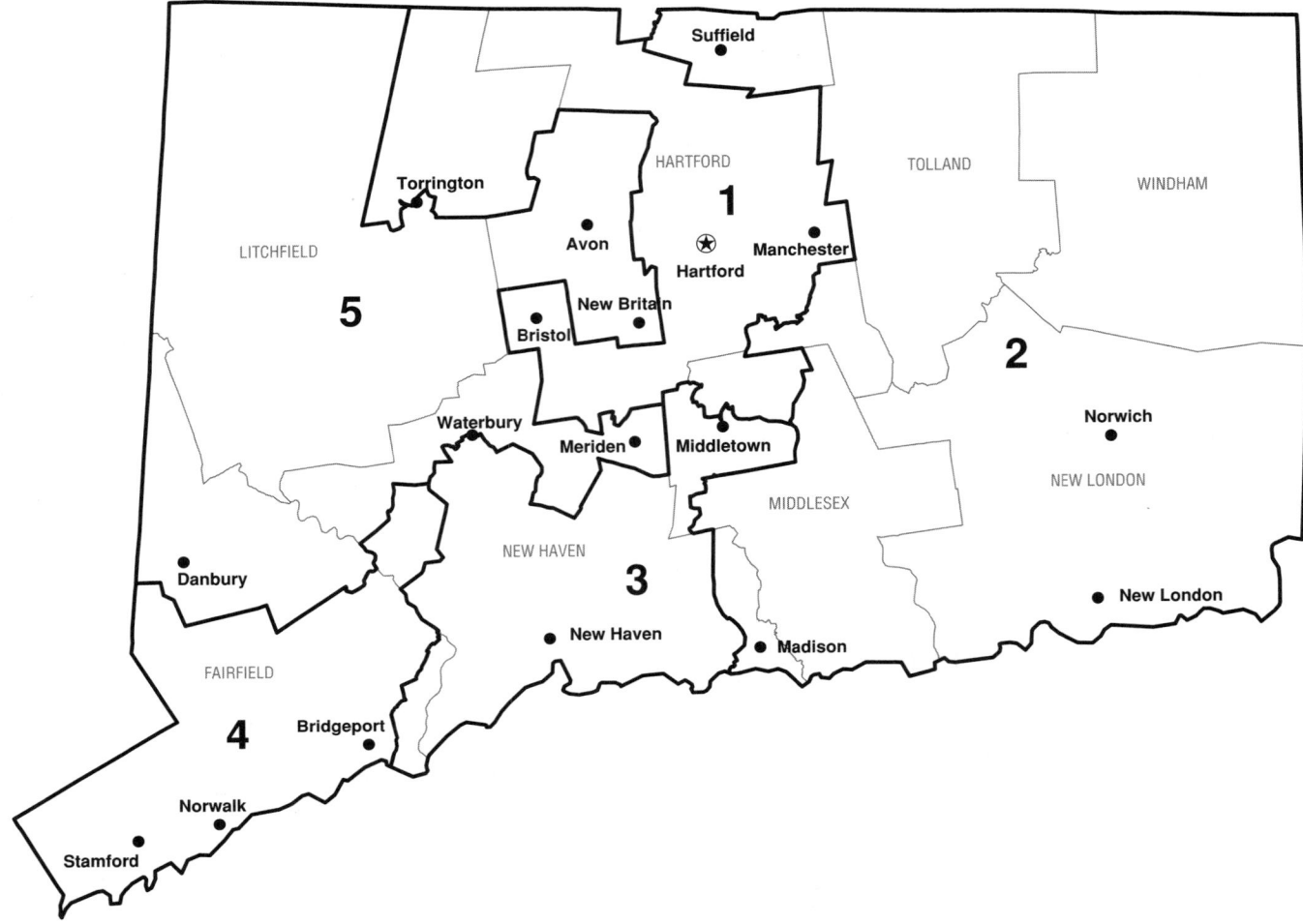

CONNECTICUT

GOVERNOR 2002

2000 Census Population	County	Total Vote	Republican	Democratic	Other	Rep.-Dem. Plurality	Percentage			
							Total Vote		Major Vote	
							Rep.	Dem.	Rep.	Dem.
882,567	FAIRFIELD	236,295	143,817	92,478		51,339 R	60.9%	39.1%	60.9%	39.1%
857,183	HARTFORD	269,800	143,316	126,484		16,832 R	53.1%	46.9%	53.1%	46.9%
182,193	LITCHFIELD	66,462	44,033	22,429		21,604 R	66.3%	33.7%	66.3%	33.7%
155,071	MIDDLESEX	56,835	31,153	25,682		5,471 R	54.8%	45.2%	54.8%	45.2%
824,008	NEW HAVEN	237,493	131,659	105,834		25,825 R	55.4%	44.6%	55.4%	44.6%
259,088	NEW LONDON	78,145	39,861	38,284		1,577 R	51.0%	49.0%	51.0%	49.0%
136,364	TOLLAND	46,980	25,915	21,065		4,850 R	55.2%	44.8%	55.2%	44.8%
109,091	WINDHAM	30,932	14,204	16,728		2,524 D	45.9%	54.1%	45.9%	54.1%
3,405,565	TOTAL	1,022,998	573,958	448,984	56	124,974 R	56.1%	43.9%	56.1%	43.9%

Note: There were 56 write-in votes in the official returns that were not assigned to any county.

	City/Town									
18,554	ANSONIA	4,688	2,552	2,136		416 R	54.4%	45.6%	54.4%	45.6%
19,587	BLOOMFIELD	7,236	2,397	4,839		2,442 D	33.1%	66.9%	33.1%	66.9%
28,683	BRANFORD	9,720	4,953	4,767		186 R	51.0%	49.0%	51.0%	49.0%
139,529	BRIDGEPORT	18,546	6,094	12,452		6,358 D	32.9%	67.1%	32.9%	67.1%
60,062	BRISTOL	16,334	8,993	7,341		1,652 R	55.1%	44.9%	55.1%	44.9%
28,543	CHESHIRE	10,733	7,065	3,668		3,397 R	65.8%	34.2%	65.8%	34.2%
74,848	DANBURY	15,534	9,037	6,497		2,540 R	58.2%	41.8%	58.2%	41.8%
19,607	DARIEN	6,663	5,029	1,634		3,395 R	75.5%	24.5%	75.5%	24.5%
49,575	EAST HARTFORD	12,565	5,600	6,965		1,365 D	44.6%	55.4%	44.6%	55.4%
28,289	EAST HAVEN	7,593	3,832	3,761		71 R	50.5%	49.5%	50.5%	49.5%
45,212	ENFIELD	13,490	7,464	6,026		1,438 R	55.3%	44.7%	55.3%	44.7%
57,340	FAIRFIELD	18,089	11,344	6,745		4,599 R	62.7%	37.3%	62.7%	37.3%
23,641	FARMINGTON	9,905	6,045	3,860		2,185 R	61.0%	39.0%	61.0%	39.0%
31,876	GLASTONBURY	14,756	9,620	5,136		4,484 R	65.2%	34.8%	65.2%	34.8%
61,101	GREENWICH	17,747	12,284	5,463		6,821 R	69.2%	30.8%	69.2%	30.8%
39,907	GROTON	9,476	4,986	4,490		496 R	52.6%	47.4%	52.6%	47.4%
21,398	GUILFORD	8,204	4,534	3,670		864 R	55.3%	44.7%	55.3%	44.7%
56,913	HAMDEN	17,327	7,681	9,646		1,965 D	44.3%	55.7%	44.3%	55.7%
121,578	HARTFORD	16,746	3,805	12,941		9,136 D	22.7%	77.3%	22.7%	77.3%
54,740	MANCHESTER	17,787	9,521	8,266		1,255 R	53.5%	46.5%	53.5%	46.5%
20,720	MANSFIELD	4,731	1,647	3,084		1,437 D	34.8%	65.2%	34.8%	65.2%
58,244	MERIDEN	15,410	8,004	7,406		598 R	51.9%	48.1%	51.9%	48.1%
43,167	MIDDLETOWN	12,831	5,786	7,045		1,259 D	45.1%	54.9%	45.1%	54.9%
52,305	MILFORD	16,416	9,655	6,761		2,894 R	58.8%	41.2%	58.8%	41.2%
30,989	NAUGATUCK	8,322	5,627	2,695		2,932 R	67.6%	32.4%	67.6%	32.4%
71,538	NEW BRITAIN	14,668	6,277	8,391		2,114 D	42.8%	57.2%	42.8%	57.2%
123,626	NEW HAVEN	21,442	5,417	16,025		10,608 D	25.3%	74.7%	25.3%	74.7%
25,671	NEW LONDON	4,842	2,124	2,718		594 D	43.9%	56.1%	43.9%	56.1%
27,121	NEW MILFORD	8,228	5,668	2,560		3,108 R	68.9%	31.1%	68.9%	31.1%
29,306	NEWINGTON	11,172	5,735	5,437		298 R	51.3%	48.7%	51.3%	48.7%
25,031	NEWTOWN	8,567	5,810	2,757		3,053 R	67.8%	32.2%	67.8%	32.2%
23,035	NORTH HAVEN	9,133	5,479	3,654		1,825 R	60.0%	40.0%	60.0%	40.0%
82,951	NORWALK	20,114	10,988	9,126		1,862 R	54.6%	45.4%	54.6%	45.4%
36,117	NORWICH	9,123	3,565	5,558		1,993 D	39.1%	60.9%	39.1%	60.9%
23,643	RIDGEFIELD	8,296	5,534	2,762		2,772 R	66.7%	33.3%	66.7%	33.3%
38,101	SHELTON	12,736	8,816	3,920		4,896 R	69.2%	30.8%	69.2%	30.8%
23,234	SIMSBURY	9,970	6,596	3,374		3,222 R	66.2%	33.8%	66.2%	33.8%
24,412	SOUTH WINDSOR	10,225	6,155	4,070		2,085 R	60.2%	39.8%	60.2%	39.8%
39,728	SOUTHINGTON	14,938	9,027	5,911		3,116 R	60.4%	39.6%	60.4%	39.6%
117,083	STAMFORD	28,000	14,988	13,012		1,976 R	53.5%	46.5%	53.5%	46.5%

80

CONNECTICUT

GOVERNOR 2002

2000 Census Population	City/Town	Total Vote	Republican	Democratic	Other	Rep.-Dem. Plurality	Total Vote Rep.	Total Vote Dem.	Major Vote Rep.	Major Vote Dem.
49,976	STRATFORD	14,697	8,624	6,073		2,551 R	58.7%	41.3%	58.7%	41.3%
35,202	TORRINGTON	11,156	7,286	3,870		3,416 R	65.3%	34.7%	65.3%	34.7%
34,243	TRUMBULL	12,679	8,537	4,142		4,395 R	67.3%	32.7%	67.3%	32.7%
28,063	VERNON	9,377	5,275	4,102		1,173 R	56.3%	43.7%	56.3%	43.7%
43,026	WALLINGFORD	14,831	8,492	6,339		2,153 R	57.3%	42.7%	57.3%	42.7%
107,271	WATERBURY	23,499	14,761	8,738		6,023 R	62.8%	37.2%	62.8%	37.2%
21,661	WATERTOWN	8,102	5,980	2,122		3,858 R	73.8%	26.2%	73.8%	26.2%
63,589	WEST HARTFORD	24,593	12,375	12,218		157 R	50.3%	49.7%	50.3%	49.7%
52,360	WEST HAVEN	12,695	5,635	7,060		1,425 D	44.4%	55.6%	44.4%	55.6%
25,749	WESTPORT	9,388	5,440	3,948		1,492 R	57.9%	42.1%	57.9%	42.1%
26,271	WETHERSFIELD	10,929	6,138	4,791		1,347 R	56.2%	43.8%	56.2%	43.8%
22,857	WINDHAM	5,346	2,056	3,290		1,234 D	38.5%	61.5%	38.5%	61.5%
28,237	WINDSOR	9,855	4,649	5,206		557 D	47.2%	52.8%	47.2%	52.8%

Note: There were 56 write-in votes in the official returns that were not assigned to any city or town.

CONNECTICUT

HOUSE OF REPRESENTATIVES

CD	Year	Total Vote	Rep. Vote	Rep. Candidate	Dem. Vote	Dem. Candidate	Other Vote	Rep.-Dem. Plurality	Total Vote Rep.	Total Vote Dem.	Major Vote Rep.	Major Vote Dem.
1	2002	201,688	66,968	Steele, Phil	134,698	Larson, John B.*	22	67,730 D	33.2%	66.8%	33.2%	66.8%
2	2002	217,108	117,434	Simmons, Rob*	99,674	Courtney, Joe		17,760 R	54.1%	45.9%	54.1%	45.9%
3	2002	185,364	54,757	Elser, Richter	121,557	DeLauro, Rosa*	9,050	66,800 D	29.5%	65.6%	31.1%	68.9%
4	2002	175,695	113,197	Shays, Christopher*	62,491	Sanchez, Stephanie H.	7	50,706 R	64.4%	35.6%	64.4%	35.6%
5	2002	209,454	113,626	Johnson, Nancy L.*	90,616	Maloney, Jim*	5,212	23,010 R	54.2%	43.3%	55.6%	44.4%
Total	2002	989,309	465,982		509,036		14,291	43,054 D	47.1%	51.5%	47.8%	52.2%

An asterisk (*) denotes incumbent.

CONNECTICUT

GENERAL AND PRIMARY ELECTIONS

2002 GENERAL ELECTIONS

Governor Other vote was 29 write-in (Philip Gosselin); 16 write-in (William M. Colonna); 9 write-in (Sylvester J. Pettway); 2 write-in (Maryellen Bousquet).

House Other vote was:

CD 1 18 write-in (Miriam J. Masullo); 4 write-in (Mark F. Welch).
CD 2
CD 3 9,050 Green (Charles A. Pillsbury).
CD 4 7 write-in (Carl E. Vassar).
CD 5 3,709 Concerned Citizens (Joseph A. Zdonczyk); 1,503 Libertarian (Walter J. Gengarelly).

CONNECTICUT

GENERAL AND PRIMARY ELECTIONS

2002 PRIMARY ELECTIONS

Primary   September 10, 2002

Registration
(as of Oct. 22, 2002—
no statewide totals tallied
at time of primary)

Republican	462,338
Democratic	682,478
Green	1,947
Libertarian	743
Concerned Citizens	254
Other Parties	2,397
Unaffiliated	845,527
TOTAL	1,995,684

Primary Type   Closed—Only registered Democrats and Republicans could vote in their party's primary.

Note: An asterisk (*) denotes incumbent. A gubernatorial or House candidate had to receive at least 15 percent of the vote in a pre-primary convention to force a primary.

	REPUBLICAN PRIMARIES			DEMOCRATIC PRIMARIES	
Governor	John G. Rowland*	Nominated by convention		Bill Curry	Nominated by convention
Congressional District 1	Phil Steele Miriam J. Masullo TOTAL	2,109 1,165 3,274	64.4% 35.6%	John B. Larson*	Nominated by convention
Congressional District 2	Rob Simmons*	Nominated by convention		Joe Courtney	Nominated by convention
Congressional District 3	Richter Elser	Nominated by convention		Rosa DeLauro*	Nominated by convention
Congressional District 4	Christopher Shays*	Nominated by convention		Stephanie H. Sanchez	Nominated by convention
Congressional District 5	Nancy L. Johnson*	Nominated by convention		Jim Maloney*	Nominated by convention

DELAWARE

GOVERNOR
Ruth Ann Minner (D). Elected 2000 to a four-year term.

SENATORS (2 Democrats)
Thomas R. Carper (D). Elected 2000 to a six-year term.

Joseph R. Biden Jr. (D). Reelected 2002 to a six-year term. Previously elected 1996, 1990, 1984, 1978, 1972.

REPRESENTATIVE (1 Republican)
At Large. Michael N. Castle (R)

POSTWAR VOTE FOR PRESIDENT

| | | Republican | | Democratic | | Other | | Percentage | | | |
| | Total | | | | | | | Total Vote | | Major Vote | |
Year	Vote	Vote	Candidate	Vote	Candidate	Vote	Plurality	Rep.	Dem.	Rep.	Dem.
2000**	327,622	137,288	Bush, George W.	180,068	Gore, Al	10,266	42,780 D	41.9%	55.0%	43.3%	56.7%
1996**	271,084	99,062	Dole, Bob	140,355	Clinton, Bill	31,667	41,293 D	36.5%	51.8%	41.4%	58.6%
1992**	289,735	102,313	Bush, George	126,054	Clinton, Bill	61,368	23,741 D	35.3%	43.5%	44.8%	55.2%
1988	249,891	139,639	Bush, George	108,647	Dukakis, Michael S.	1,605	30,992 R	55.9%	43.5%	56.2%	43.8%
1984	254,572	152,190	Reagan, Ronald	101,656	Mondale, Walter F.	726	50,534 R	59.8%	39.9%	60.0%	40.0%
1980**	235,900	111,252	Reagan, Ronald	105,754	Carter, Jimmy	18,894	5,498 R	47.2%	44.8%	51.3%	48.7%
1976	235,834	109,831	Ford, Gerald R.	122,596	Carter, Jimmy	3,407	12,765 D	46.6%	52.0%	47.3%	52.7%
1972	235,516	140,357	Nixon, Richard M.	92,283	McGovern, George S.	2,876	48,074 R	59.6%	39.2%	60.3%	39.7%
1968	214,367	96,714	Nixon, Richard M.	89,194	Humphrey, Hubert H.	28,459	7,520 R	45.1%	41.6%	52.0%	48.0%
1964	201,320	78,078	Goldwater, Barry M.	122,704	Johnson, Lyndon B.	538	44,626 D	38.8%	60.9%	38.9%	61.1%
1960	196,683	96,373	Nixon, Richard M.	99,590	Kennedy, John F.	720	3,217 D	49.0%	50.6%	49.2%	50.8%
1956	177,988	98,057	Eisenhower, Dwight D.	79,421	Stevenson, Adlai E.	510	18,636 R	55.1%	44.6%	55.3%	44.7%
1952	174,025	90,059	Eisenhower, Dwight D.	83,315	Stevenson, Adlai E.	651	6,744 R	51.8%	47.9%	51.9%	48.1%
1948	139,073	69,588	Dewey, Thomas E.	67,813	Truman, Harry S.	1,672	1,775 R	50.0%	48.8%	50.6%	49.4%

In 2000 the other vote column includes 8,307 votes cast for Green (Nader). In 1996 the other vote column includes 28,719 votes cast for Perot. In 1992 the other vote column includes 59,213 votes cast for Perot. In 1980 the other column includes 16,288 votes for Independent (Anderson).

POSTWAR VOTE FOR GOVERNOR

| | | Republican | | Democratic | | Other | Rep.-Dem. | Percentage | | | |
| | Total | | | | | | | Total Vote | | Major Vote | |
Year	Vote	Vote	Candidate	Vote	Candidate	Vote	Plurality	Rep.	Dem.	Rep.	Dem.
2000	323,688	128,603	Burris, John M.	191,695	Minner, Ruth Ann	3,390	63,092 D	39.7%	59.2%	40.2%	59.8%
1996	271,122	82,654	Rzewnicki, Janet	188,300	Carper, Thomas R.	168	105,646 D	30.5%	69.5%	30.5%	69.5%
1992	277,058	90,725	Scott, B. Gary	179,365	Carper, Thomas R.	6,968	88,640 D	32.7%	64.7%	33.6%	66.4%
1988	239,969	169,733	Castle, Michael N.	70,236	Kreshtoll, Jacob		99,497 R	70.7%	29.3%	70.7%	29.3%
1984	243,565	135,250	Castle, Michael N.	108,315	Quillen, William T.		26,935 R	55.5%	44.5%	55.5%	44.5%
1980	225,081	159,004	duPont, Pierre	64,217	Gordy, William J.	1,860	94,787 R	70.6%	28.5%	71.2%	28.8%
1976	229,563	130,531	duPont, Pierre	97,480	Tribbitt, Sherman W.	1,552	33,051 R	56.9%	42.5%	57.2%	42.8%
1972	228,722	109,583	Peterson, Russell W.	117,274	Tribbitt, Sherman W.	1,865	7,691 D	47.9%	51.3%	48.3%	51.7%
1968	206,834	104,474	Peterson, Russell W.	102,360	Terry, Charles L.		2,114 R	50.5%	49.5%	50.5%	49.5%
1964	200,171	97,374	Buckson, David P.	102,797	Terry, Charles L.		5,423 D	48.6%	51.4%	48.6%	51.4%
1960	194,835	94,043	Rollins, John W.	100,792	Carvel, Elbert N.		6,749 D	48.3%	51.7%	48.3%	51.7%
1956	177,012	91,965	Boggs, J. Caleb	85,047	McConnell, J. H. T.		6,918 R	52.0%	48.0%	52.0%	48.0%
1952	170,749	88,977	Boggs, J. Caleb	81,772	Carvel, Elbert N.		7,205 R	52.1%	47.9%	52.1%	47.9%
1948	140,335	64,996	George, Hyland P.	75,339	Carvel, Elbert N.		10,343 D	46.3%	53.7%	46.3%	53.7%

DELAWARE

POSTWAR VOTE FOR SENATOR

Year	Total Vote	Republican Vote	Republican Candidate	Democratic Vote	Democratic Candidate	Other Vote	Rep.-Dem. Plurality	Total Vote Rep.	Total Vote Dem.	Major Vote Rep.	Major Vote Dem.
2002	232,314	94,793	Clatworthy, Raymond J.	135,253	Biden, Joseph R. Jr.	2,268	40,460 D	40.8%	58.2%	41.2%	58.8%
2000	327,017	142,891	Roth, William V.	181,566	Carper, Thomas R.	2,560	38,675 D	43.7%	55.5%	44.0%	56.0%
1996	275,605	105,088	Clatworthy, Raymond J.	165,465	Biden, Joseph R. Jr.	5,052	60,377 D	38.1%	60.0%	38.8%	61.2%
1994	199,029	111,088	Roth, William V.	84,554	Oberly, Charles M.	3,387	26,534 R	55.8%	42.5%	56.8%	43.2%
1990	180,152	64,554	Brady, M. Jane	112,918	Biden, Joseph R. Jr.	2,680	48,364 D	35.8%	62.7%	36.4%	63.6%
1988	243,493	151,115	Roth, William V.	92,378	Woo, S. B.		58,737 R	62.1%	37.9%	62.1%	37.9%
1984	245,932	98,101	Burris, John M.	147,831	Biden, Joseph R. Jr.		49,730 D	39.9%	60.1%	39.9%	60.1%
1982	190,960	105,357	Roth, William V.	84,413	Levinson, David N.	1,190	20,944 R	55.2%	44.2%	55.5%	44.5%
1978	162,072	66,479	Baxter, James H.	93,930	Biden, Joseph R. Jr.	1,663	27,451 D	41.0%	58.0%	41.4%	58.6%
1976	224,859	125,502	Roth, William V.	98,055	Maloney, Thomas C.	1,302	27,447 R	55.8%	43.6%	56.1%	43.9%
1972	229,828	112,844	Boggs, J. Caleb	116,006	Biden, Joseph R. Jr.	978	3,162 D	49.1%	50.5%	49.3%	50.7%
1970	161,439	94,979	Roth, William V.	64,740	Zimmerman, Jacob	1,720	30,239 R	58.8%	40.1%	59.5%	40.5%
1966	164,549	97,268	Boggs, J. Caleb	67,281	Tunnell, James M., Jr.		29,987 R	59.1%	40.9%	59.1%	40.9%
1964	200,703	103,782	Williams, John J.	96,850	Carvel, Elbert N.	71	6,932 R	51.7%	48.3%	51.7%	48.3%
1960	194,964	98,874	Boggs, J. Caleb	96,090	Frear, J. Allen		2,784 R	50.7%	49.3%	50.7%	49.3%
1958	154,432	82,280	Williams, John J.	72,152	Carvel, Elbert N.		10,128 R	53.3%	46.7%	53.3%	46.7%
1954	144,900	62,389	Warburton, H. B.	82,511	Frear, J. Allen		20,122 D	43.1%	56.9%	43.1%	56.9%
1952	170,705	93,020	Williams, John J.	77,685	Bayard, A. I. duP.		15,335 R	54.5%	45.5%	54.5%	45.5%
1948	141,362	68,246	Buck, C. Douglas	71,888	Frear, J. Allen	1,228	3,642 D	48.3%	50.9%	48.7%	51.3%
1946	113,513	62,603	Williams, John J.	50,910	Tunnell, James M.		11,693 R	55.2%	44.8%	55.2%	44.8%

DELAWARE

One member At Large

DELAWARE

SENATOR 2002

2000 Census Population	County	Total Vote	Republican	Democratic	Other	Rep.-Dem. Plurality	Percentage			
							Total Vote		Major Vote	
							Rep.	Dem.	Rep.	Dem.
126,697	KENT	34,575	17,383	16,907	285	476 R	50.3%	48.9%	50.7%	49.3%
500,265	NEW CASTLE	145,247	52,133	91,516	1,598	39,383 D	35.9%	63.0%	36.3%	63.7%
156,638	SUSSEX	52,492	25,277	26,830	385	1,553 D	48.2%	51.1%	48.5%	51.5%
783,600	TOTAL	232,314	94,793	135,253	2,268	40,460 D	40.8%	58.2%	41.2%	58.8%

DELAWARE

HOUSE OF REPRESENTATIVES

CD	Year	Total Vote	Republican		Democratic		Other Vote	Rep.-Dem. Plurality	Percentage			
			Vote	Candidate	Vote	Candidate			Total Vote		Major Vote	
									Rep.	Dem.	Rep.	Dem.
AL	2002	228,405	164,605	Castle, Michael N.*	61,011	Miller, Micheal C.	2,789	103,594 R	72.1%	26.7%	73.0%	27.0%
AL	2000	313,126	211,797	Castle, Michael N.*	96,488	Miller, Micheal C.	4,841	115,309 R	67.6%	30.8%	68.7%	31.3%
AL	1998	180,527	119,811	Castle, Michael N.*	57,446	Williams, Dennis E.	3,270	62,365 R	66.4%	31.8%	67.6%	32.4%
AL	1996	266,836	185,576	Castle, Michael N.*	73,253	Williams, Dennis E.	8,007	112,323 R	69.5%	27.5%	71.7%	28.3%
AL	1994	195,037	137,960	Castle, Michael N.*	51,803	Desantis, Carol Ann	5,274	86,157 R	70.7%	26.6%	72.7%	27.3%
AL	1992	276,157	153,037	Castle, Michael N.*	117,426	Woo, S. B.	5,694	35,611 R	55.4%	42.5%	56.6%	43.4%
AL	1990	177,432	58,037	Williams, Ralph O.	116,274	Carper, Thomas R.*	3,121	58,237 D	32.7%	65.5%	33.3%	66.7%
AL	1988	234,517	76,179	Krapf, James P.	158,338	Carper, Thomas R.*		82,159 D	32.5%	67.5%	32.5%	67.5%
AL	1986	160,757	53,767	Neubergr, Thomas S.	106,351	Carper, Thomas R.*	639	52,584 D	33.4%	66.2%	33.6%	66.4%
AL	1984	243,014	100,650	DuPont, Pierre	142,070	Carper, Thomas R.*	294	41,420 D	41.4%	58.5%	41.5%	58.5%
AL	1982	188,064	87,153	Evans, Thomas B.*	98,533	Carper, Thomas R.	2,378	11,380 D	46.3%	52.4%	46.9%	53.1%
AL	1980	216,629	133,842	Evans, Thomas B.*	81,227	Maxwell, Robert L.	1,560	52,615 R	61.8%	37.5%	62.2%	37.8%
AL	1978	157,566	91,689	Evans, Thomas B.*	64,863	Hindes, Gary E.	1,014	26,826 R	58.2%	41.2%	58.6%	41.4%
AL	1976	214,799	110,677	Evans, Thomas B.	102,431	Shipley, Samuel L.	1,691	8,246 R	51.5%	47.7%	51.9%	48.1%
AL	1974	160,328	93,826	DuPont, Pierre*	63,490	Soles, James	3,012	30,336 R	58.5%	39.6%	59.6%	40.4%
AL	1972	225,851	141,237	DuPont, Pierre*	83,230	Handloff, Norma	1,384	58,007 R	62.5%	36.9%	62.9%	37.1%
AL	1970	160,313	86,125	DuPont, Pierre	71,429	Daniello, John D.	2,759	14,696 R	53.7%	44.6%	54.7%	45.3%
AL	1968	200,820	117,827	Roth, William V.*	82,993	McDowell, Harris B.		34,834 R	58.7%	41.3%	58.7%	41.3%
AL	1966	163,103	90,961	Roth, William V.	72,142	McDowell, Harris B.*		18,819 R	55.8%	44.2%	55.8%	44.2%
AL	1964	198,691	86,254	Snowden, James H.	112,361	McDowell, Harris B.*	76	26,107 D	43.4%	56.6%	43.4%	56.6%
AL	1962	153,356	71,934	Williams, Wilmer F.	81,166	McDowell, Harris B.*	256	9,232 D	46.9%	52.9%	47.0%	53.0%
AL	1960	194,564	96,337	McKinstry, James T.	98,227	McDowell, Harris B.*		1,890 D	49.5%	50.5%	49.5%	50.5%
AL	1958	152,896	76,099	Haskell, Harry G.*	76,797	McDowell, Harris B.		698 D	49.8%	50.2%	49.8%	50.2%
AL	1956	176,182	91,538	Haskell, Harry G.	84,644	McDowell, Harris B.*		6,894 R	52.0%	48.0%	52.0%	48.0%
AL	1954	144,236	65,035	Martin, Lilllian	79,201	McDowell, Harris B.		14,166 D	45.1%	54.9%	45.1%	54.9%
AL	1952	170,015	88,285	Warburton, H.B.	81,730	Scannell, Joseph S.		6,555 R	51.9%	48.1%	51.9%	48.1%
AL	1950	129,404	73,313	Boggs, J. Caleb*	56,091	Winchester, H.M.		17,222 R	56.7%	43.3%	56.7%	43.3%
AL	1948	140,535	71,127	Boggs, J. Caleb*	68,909	McGuigan, J. Carl	499	2,218 R	50.6%	49.0%	50.8%	49.2%
AL	1946	112,621	63,516	Boggs, J. Caleb	49,105	Traynor, Philip A.		14,411 R	56.4%	43.6%	56.4%	43.6%

An asterisk (*) denotes incumbent.

DELAWARE

GENERAL AND PRIMARY ELECTIONS

2002 GENERAL ELECTIONS

Senator Other vote was 996 Independent Party of Delaware (Maurice Barros); 922 Libertarian (Raymond T. Buranello); 350 Natural Law (Robert E. Mattson).

House Other vote was:

  At Large 2,789 Libertarian (Brad C. Thomas).

2002 PRIMARY ELECTIONS

Primary September 7, 2002

Registration (as of Sept. 1, 2002)

Republican	174,181
Democratic	222,351
Libertarian	753
Green	579
Natural Law	301
Reform	263
Constitution	262
Other Parties	1,126
Independent	116,552
TOTAL	516,368

Primary Type Closed—Only registered Democrats and Republicans could vote in their party's primary.

Note: An asterisk (*) denotes incumbent. The names of unopposed candidates did not appear on the primary ballot; therefore, no votes were cast for these candidates.

	REPUBLICAN PRIMARIES		DEMOCRATIC PRIMARIES		
Senator	Raymond J. Clatworthy	Unopposed	Biden, Joseph R. Jr.*	Unopposed	
House At Large	Michael N. Castle*	Unopposed	Micheal C. Miller	8,979	52.1%
			Steven L. Biener	8,244	47.9%
			TOTAL	17,223	

FLORIDA

GOVERNOR
Jeb Bush (R). Reelected 2002 to a four-year term. Previously elected 1998.

SENATORS (2 Democrats)
Bob Graham (D). Reelected 1998 to a six-year term. Previously elected 1992, 1986.

Bill Nelson (D). Elected 2000 to a six-year term.

REPRESENTATIVES (18 Republicans, 7 Democrats)
1. Jeff Miller (R)
2. Allen Boyd (D)
3. Corrine Brown (D)
4. Ander Crenshaw (R)
5. Ginny Brown-Waite (R)
6. Cliff Stearns (R)
7. John L. Mica (R)
8. Ric Keller (R)
9. Michael Bilirakis (R)
10. C.W. Bill Young (R)
11. Jim Davis (D)
12. Adam H. Putnam (R)
13. Katherine Harris (R)
14. Porter J. Goss (R)
15. Dave Weldon (R)
16. Mark Foley (R)
17. Kendrick B. Meek (D)
18. Ileana Ros-Lehtinen (R)
19. Robert Wexler (D)
20. Peter Deutsch (D)
21. Lincoln Diaz-Balart (R)
22. E. Clay Shaw Jr. (R)
23. Alcee L. Hastings (D)
24. Tom Feeney (R)
25. Mario Diaz-Balart (R)

POSTWAR VOTE FOR PRESIDENT

| Year | Total Vote | Republican | | Democratic | | Other Vote | Plurality | Percentage | | | |
| | | Vote | Candidate | Vote | Candidate | | | Total Vote | | Major Vote | |
								Rep.	Dem.	Rep.	Dem.
2000**	5,963,110	2,912,790	Bush, George W.	2,912,253	Gore, Al	138,067	537 R	48.8%	48.8%	50.0%	50.0%
1996**	5,303,794	2,244,536	Dole, Bob	2,546,870	Clinton, Bill	512,388	302,334 D	42.3%	48.0%	46.8%	53.2%
1992**	5,314,392	2,173,310	Bush, George	2,072,698	Clinton, Bill	1,068,384	100,612 R	40.9%	39.0%	51.2%	48.8%
1988	4,302,313	2,618,885	Bush, George	1,656,701	Dukakis, Michael S.	26,727	962,184 R	60.9%	38.5%	61.3%	38.7%
1984	4,180,051	2,730,350	Reagan, Ronald	1,448,816	Mondale, Walter F.	885	1,281,534 R	65.3%	34.7%	65.3%	34.7%
1980**	3,686,930	2,046,951	Reagan, Ronald	1,419,475	Carter, Jimmy	220,504	627,476 R	55.5%	38.5%	59.1%	40.9%
1976	3,150,631	1,469,531	Ford, Gerald R.	1,636,000	Carter, Jimmy	45,100	166,469 D	46.6%	51.9%	47.3%	52.7%
1972	2,583,283	1,857,759	Nixon, Richard M.	718,117	McGovern, George S.	7,407	1,139,642 R	71.9%	27.8%	72.1%	27.9%
1968**	2,187,805	886,804	Nixon, Richard M.	676,794	Humphrey, Hubert H.	624,207	210,010 R	40.5%	30.9%	56.7%	43.3%
1964	1,854,481	905,941	Goldwater, Barry M.	948,540	Johnson, Lyndon B.		42,599 D	48.9%	51.1%	48.9%	51.1%
1960	1,544,176	795,476	Nixon, Richard M.	748,700	Kennedy, John F.		46,776 R	51.5%	48.5%	51.5%	48.5%
1956	1,125,762	643,849	Eisenhower, Dwight D.	480,371	Stevenson, Adlai E.	1,542	163,478 R	57.2%	42.7%	57.3%	42.7%
1952	989,337	544,036	Eisenhower, Dwight D.	444,950	Stevenson, Adlai E.	351	99,086 R	55.0%	45.0%	55.0%	45.0%
1948	577,643	194,280	Dewey, Thomas E.	281,988	Truman, Harry S.	101,375	87,708 D	33.6%	48.8%	40.8%	59.2%

In 2000 the other vote column includes 97,488 votes cast for Green (Nader). In 1996 the other vote column includes 483,870 votes cast for Perot. In 1992 the other vote column includes 1,053,067 votes cast for Perot. In 1980 the other column includes 189,692 votes for Independent (Anderson). In 1968 other vote was George Wallace party.

FLORIDA

POSTWAR VOTE FOR GOVERNOR

Year	Total Vote	Republican		Democratic		Other Vote	Rep.-Dem. Plurality	Percentage			
								Total Vote		Major Vote	
		Vote	Candidate	Vote	Candidate			Rep.	Dem.	Rep.	Dem.
2002	5,100,581	2,856,845	Bush, Jeb	2,201,427	McBride, Bill	42,309	655,418 R	56.0%	43.2%	56.5%	43.5%
1998	3,964,441	2,191,105	Bush, Jeb	1,773,054	MacKay, Buddy	282	418,051 R	55.3%	44.7%	55.3%	44.7%
1994	4,206,659	2,071,068	Bush, Jeb	2,135,008	Chiles, Lawton	583	63,940 D	49.2%	50.8%	49.2%	50.8%
1990	3,530,871	1,535,068	Martinez, Bob	1,995,206	Chiles, Lawton	597	460,138 D	43.5%	56.5%	43.5%	56.5%
1986	3,386,171	1,847,525	Martinez, Bob	1,538,620	Pajcic, Steve	26	308,905 R	54.6%	45.4%	54.6%	45.4%
1982	2,688,566	949,013	Bafalis, L. A.	1,739,553	Graham, Bob		790,540 D	35.3%	64.7%	35.3%	64.7%
1978	2,530,468	1,123,888	Eckerd, Jack M.	1,406,580	Graham, Bob		282,692 D	44.4%	55.6%	44.4%	55.6%
1974	1,828,392	709,438	Thomas, Jerry	1,118,954	Askew, Reubin		409,516 D	38.8%	61.2%	38.8%	61.2%
1970	1,730,813	746,243	Kirk, Claude R.	984,305	Askew, Reubin	265	238,062 D	43.1%	56.9%	43.1%	56.9%
1966	1,489,661	821,190	Kirk, Claude R.	668,233	High, Robert King	238	152,957 R	55.1%	44.9%	55.1%	44.9%
1964S	1,663,481	686,297	Holley, Charles R.	933,554	Burns, Haydon	43,630	247,257 D	41.3%	56.1%	42.4%	57.6%
1960	1,419,343	569,936	Petersen, George C.	849,407	Bryant, Farris		279,471 D	40.2%	59.8%	40.2%	59.8%
1956	1,014,733	266,980	Washburne, W. A.	747,753	Collins, LeRoy		480,773 D	26.3%	73.7%	26.3%	73.7%
1954S	357,783	69,852	Watson, J. Tom	287,769	Collins, LeRoy	162	217,917 D	19.5%	80.4%	19.5%	80.5%
1952	834,518	210,009	Swan, Harry S.	624,463	McCarty, Dan	46	414,454 D	25.2%	74.8%	25.2%	74.8%
1948	457,638	76,153	Acker, Bert Lee	381,459	Warren, Fuller	26	305,306 D	16.6%	83.4%	16.6%	83.4%

The 1964 election was for a two-year term to permit shifting the vote for governor to non-presidential years. The 1954 election was for a short term to fill a vacancy.

POSTWAR VOTE FOR SENATOR

Year	Total Vote	Republican		Democratic		Other Vote	Rep.-Dem. Plurality	Percentage			
								Total Vote		Major Vote	
		Vote	Candidate	Vote	Candidate			Rep.	Dem.	Rep.	Dem.
2000	5,856,731	2,705,348	McCollum, Bill	2,989,487	Nelson, Bill	161,896	284,139 D	46.2%	51.0%	47.5%	52.5%
1998	3,900,162	1,463,755	Crist, Charlie	2,436,407	Graham, Bob		972,652 D	37.5%	62.5%	37.5%	62.5%
1994	4,106,176	2,894,726	Mack, Connie	1,210,412	Rodham, Hugh E.	1,038	1,684,314 R	70.5%	29.5%	70.5%	29.5%
1992	4,962,290	1,716,505	Grant, Bill	3,245,565	Graham, Bob	220	1,529,060 D	34.6%	65.4%	34.6%	65.4%
1988	4,068,209	2,051,071	Mack, Connie	2,016,553	MacKay, Buddy	585	34,518 R	50.4%	49.6%	50.4%	49.6%
1986	3,429,996	1,552,376	Hawkins, Paula	1,877,543	Graham, Bob	77	325,167 D	45.3%	54.7%	45.3%	54.7%
1982	2,653,419	1,015,330	Poole, Van B.	1,637,667	Chiles, Lawton	422	622,337 D	38.3%	61.7%	38.3%	61.7%
1980	3,528,028	1,822,460	Hawkins, Paula	1,705,409	Gunter, Bill	159	117,051 R	51.7%	48.3%	51.7%	48.3%
1976	2,857,534	1,057,886	Grady, John	1,799,518	Chiles, Lawton	130	741,632 D	37.0%	63.0%	37.0%	63.0%
1974	1,800,539	736,674	Eckerd, Jack M.	781,031	Stone, Richard	282,834	44,357 D	40.9%	43.4%	48.5%	51.5%
1970	1,675,378	772,817	Cramer, William C.	902,438	Chiles, Lawton	123	129,621 D	46.1%	53.9%	46.1%	53.9%
1968	2,024,136	1,131,499	Gurney, Edward J.	892,637	Collins, LeRoy		238,862 R	55.9%	44.1%	55.9%	44.1%
1964	1,560,337	562,212	Kirk, Claude R.	997,585	Holland, Spessard L.	540	435,373 D	36.0%	63.9%	36.0%	64.0%
1962	939,207	281,381	Rupert, Emerson H.	657,633	Smathers, George A.	193	376,252 D	30.0%	70.0%	30.0%	70.0%
1958	542,069	155,956	Hyzer, Leland	386,113	Holland, Spessard L.		230,157 D	28.8%	71.2%	28.8%	71.2%
1956	655,418		—	655,418	Smathers, George A.		655,418 D		100.0%		100.0%
1952	617,800		—	616,665	Holland, Spessard L.	1,135	616,665 D		99.8%		100.0%
1950	313,487	74,228	Booth, John P.	238,987	Smathers, George A.	272	164,759 D	23.7%	76.2%	23.7%	76.3%
1946	198,640	42,408	Schad, J. Harry	156,232	Holland, Spessard L.		113,824 D	21.3%	78.7%	21.3%	78.7%

FLORIDA

Congressional districts first established for elections held in 2002
25 members

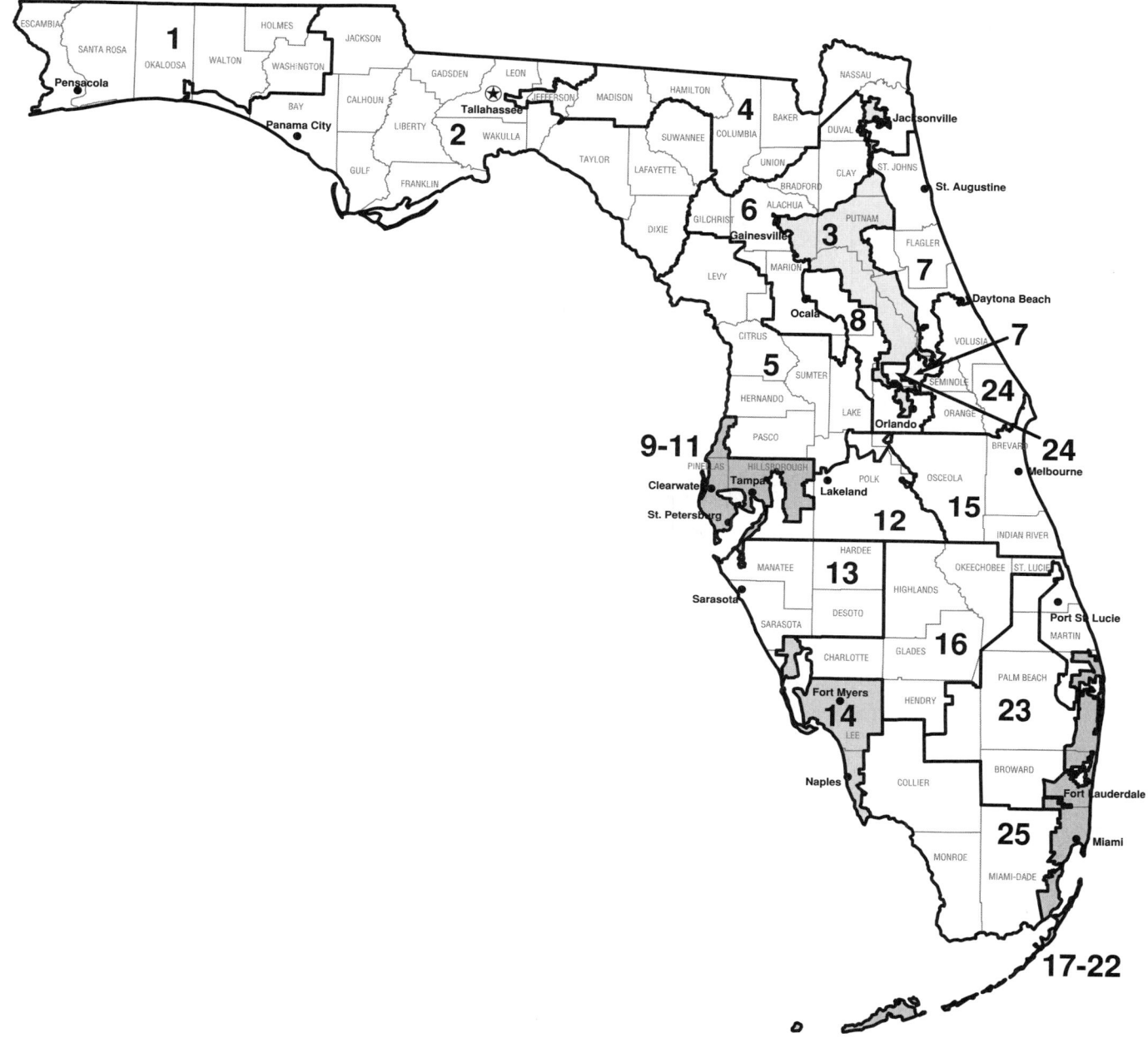

90

FLORIDA

St. Petersburg, Tampa, Fort Myers Areas

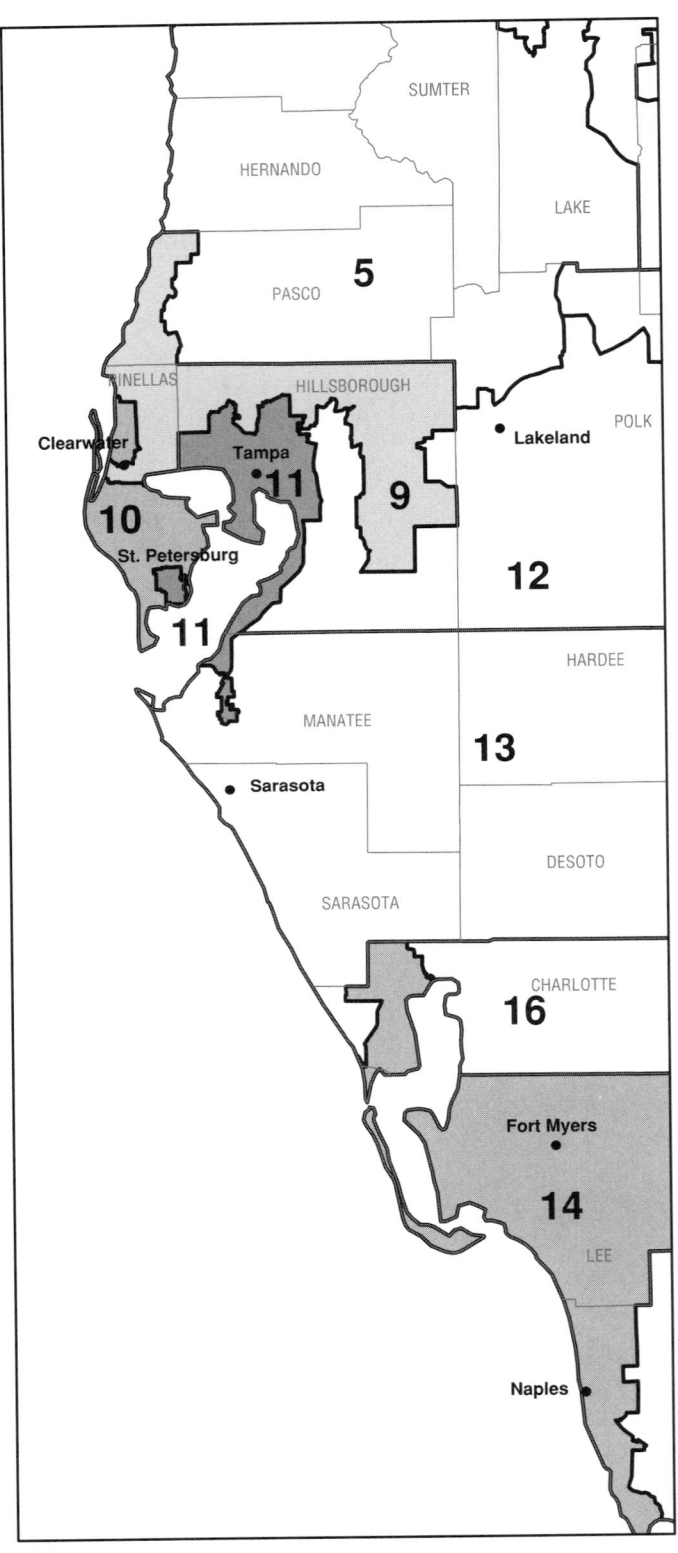

FLORIDA

Miami, Fort Lauderdale Areas

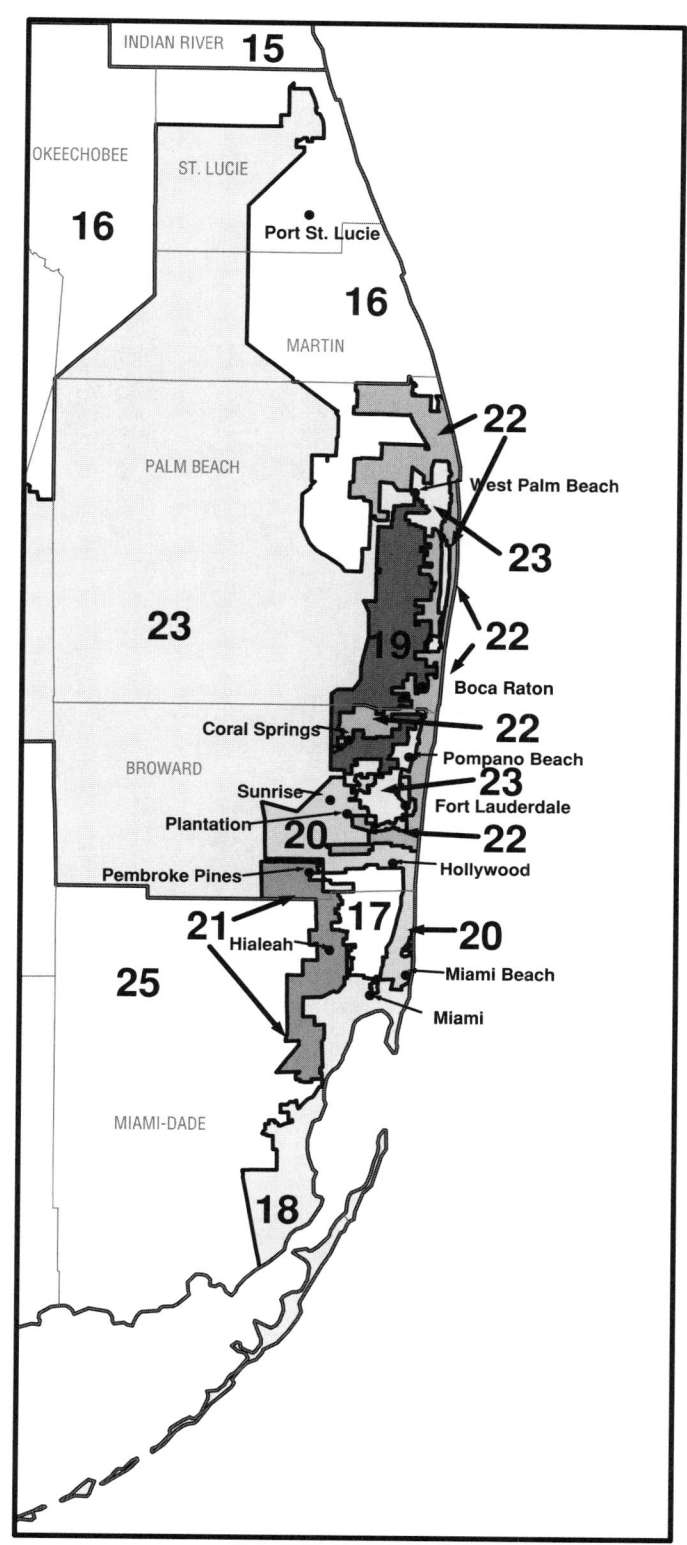

FLORIDA

GOVERNOR 2002

2000 Census Population	County	Total Vote	Republican	Democratic	Other	Rep.-Dem. Plurality	Percentage			
							Total Vote		Major Vote	
							Rep.	Dem.	Rep.	Dem.
217,955	ALACHUA	70,368	29,118	40,621	629	11,503 D	41.4%	57.7%	41.8%	58.2%
22,259	BAKER	6,523	4,515	1,961	47	2,554 R	69.2%	30.1%	69.7%	30.3%
148,217	BAY	48,709	34,107	14,258	344	19,849 R	70.0%	29.3%	70.5%	29.5%
26,088	BRADFORD	7,818	4,596	3,135	87	1,461 R	58.8%	40.1%	59.4%	40.6%
476,230	BREVARD	192,493	117,741	72,873	1,879	44,868 R	61.2%	37.9%	61.8%	38.2%
1,623,018	BROWARD	439,202	175,756	259,370	4,076	83,614 D	40.0%	59.1%	40.4%	59.6%
13,017	CALHOUN	4,251	1,917	2,274	60	357 D	45.1%	53.5%	45.7%	54.3%
141,627	CHARLOTTE	59,900	36,385	22,540	975	13,845 R	60.7%	37.6%	61.7%	38.3%
118,085	CITRUS	52,726	32,400	19,777	549	12,623 R	61.4%	37.5%	62.1%	37.9%
140,814	CLAY	50,852	39,347	11,233	272	28,114 R	77.4%	22.1%	77.8%	22.2%
251,377	COLLIER	83,479	61,555	21,237	687	40,318 R	73.7%	25.4%	74.3%	25.7%
56,513	COLUMBIA	16,331	9,554	6,603	174	2,951 R	58.5%	40.4%	59.1%	40.9%
2,253,362	DADE	502,454	266,107	233,469	2,878	32,638 R	53.0%	46.5%	53.3%	46.7%
32,209	DESOTO	7,254	3,951	3,212	91	739 R	54.5%	44.3%	55.2%	44.8%
13,827	DIXIE	4,057	2,273	1,722	62	551 R	56.0%	42.4%	56.9%	43.1%
778,879	DUVAL	242,742	148,923	92,263	1,556	56,660 R	61.4%	38.0%	61.7%	38.3%
294,410	ESCAMBIA	92,572	60,095	31,844	633	28,251 R	64.9%	34.4%	65.4%	34.6%
49,832	FLAGLER	25,739	14,407	11,133	199	3,274 R	56.0%	43.3%	56.4%	43.6%
11,057	FRANKLIN	3,805	1,819	1,931	55	112 D	47.8%	50.7%	48.5%	51.5%
45,087	GADSDEN	15,285	3,948	11,228	109	7,280 D	25.8%	73.5%	26.0%	74.0%
14,437	GILCHRIST	5,071	3,060	1,930	81	1,130 R	60.3%	38.1%	61.3%	38.7%
10,576	GLADES	2,959	1,698	1,223	38	475 R	57.4%	41.3%	58.1%	41.9%
13,332	GULF	5,421	3,026	2,349	46	677 R	55.8%	43.3%	56.3%	43.7%
13,327	HAMILTON	3,306	1,611	1,663	32	52 D	48.7%	50.3%	49.2%	50.8%
26,938	HARDEE	5,370	3,145	2,181	44	964 R	58.6%	40.6%	59.0%	41.0%
36,210	HENDRY	6,378	3,785	2,535	58	1,250 R	59.3%	39.7%	59.9%	40.1%
130,802	HERNANDO	57,686	33,736	23,357	593	10,379 R	58.5%	40.5%	59.1%	40.9%
87,366	HIGHLANDS	29,995	19,737	10,030	228	9,707 R	65.8%	33.4%	66.3%	33.7%
998,948	HILLSBOROUGH	312,066	175,630	134,276	2,160	41,354 R	56.3%	43.0%	56.7%	43.3%
18,564	HOLMES	5,624	3,580	1,986	58	1,594 R	63.7%	35.3%	64.3%	35.7%
112,947	INDIAN RIVER	44,346	29,560	14,448	338	15,112 R	66.7%	32.6%	67.2%	32.8%
46,755	JACKSON	14,823	6,868	7,815	140	947 D	46.3%	52.7%	46.8%	53.2%
12,902	JEFFERSON	5,762	2,141	3,569	52	1,428 D	37.2%	61.9%	37.5%	62.5%
7,022	LAFAYETTE	2,556	1,461	1,060	35	401 R	57.2%	41.5%	58.0%	42.0%
210,528	LAKE	81,496	51,736	27,785	1,975	23,951 R	63.5%	34.1%	65.1%	34.9%
440,888	LEE	162,515	109,183	51,682	1,650	57,501 R	67.2%	31.8%	67.9%	32.1%
239,452	LEON	94,017	32,551	60,771	695	28,220 D	34.6%	64.6%	34.9%	65.1%
34,450	LEVY	11,177	6,205	4,854	118	1,351 R	55.5%	43.4%	56.1%	43.9%
7,021	LIBERTY	2,386	932	1,433	21	501 D	39.1%	60.1%	39.4%	60.6%
18,733	MADISON	5,884	2,538	3,269	77	731 D	43.1%	55.6%	43.7%	56.3%
264,002	MANATEE	101,346	60,544	40,083	719	20,461 R	59.7%	39.6%	60.2%	39.8%
258,916	MARION	95,096	58,163	36,113	820	22,050 R	61.2%	38.0%	61.7%	38.3%
126,731	MARTIN	53,423	33,786	19,142	495	14,644 R	63.2%	35.8%	63.8%	36.2%
79,589	MONROE	25,667	13,567	11,832	268	1,735 R	52.9%	46.1%	53.4%	46.6%
57,663	NASSAU	21,255	15,593	5,483	179	10,110 R	73.4%	25.8%	74.0%	26.0%
170,498	OKALOOSA	56,618	43,587	12,563	468	31,024 R	77.0%	22.2%	77.6%	22.4%
35,910	OKEECHOBEE	8,547	4,646	3,823	78	823 R	54.4%	44.7%	54.9%	45.1%
896,344	ORANGE	240,754	137,070	102,134	1,550	34,936 R	56.9%	42.4%	57.3%	42.7%
172,493	OSCEOLA	48,012	29,017	18,591	404	10,426 R	60.4%	38.7%	60.9%	39.1%
1,131,184	PALM BEACH	376,633	160,581	213,649	2,403	53,068 D	42.6%	56.7%	42.9%	57.1%
344,765	PASCO	129,563	75,131	52,704	1,728	22,427 R	58.0%	40.7%	58.8%	41.2%
921,482	PINELLAS	334,436	185,467	146,136	2,833	39,331 R	55.5%	43.7%	55.9%	44.1%
483,924	POLK	142,554	87,322	54,299	933	33,023 R	61.3%	38.1%	61.7%	38.3%
70,423	PUTNAM	22,323	13,100	9,010	213	4,090 R	58.7%	40.4%	59.2%	40.8%
123,135	ST. JOHNS	55,932	40,056	15,512	364	24,544 R	71.6%	27.7%	72.1%	27.9%
192,695	ST. LUCIE	67,441	35,935	30,913	593	5,022 R	53.3%	45.8%	53.8%	46.2%
117,743	SANTA ROSA	43,739	32,754	10,648	337	22,106 R	74.9%	24.3%	75.5%	24.5%
325,957	SARASOTA	139,172	82,318	55,503	1,351	26,815 R	59.1%	39.9%	59.7%	40.3%
365,196	SEMINOLE	119,397	76,301	42,357	739	33,944 R	63.9%	35.5%	64.3%	35.7%
53,345	SUMTER	22,712	15,033	7,447	232	7,586 R	66.2%	32.8%	66.9%	33.1%

FLORIDA

GOVERNOR 2002

2000 Census Population	County	Total Vote	Republican	Democratic	Other	Rep.-Dem. Plurality	Percentage			
							Total Vote		Major Vote	
							Rep.	Dem.	Rep.	Dem.
34,844	SUWANNEE	11,099	7,068	3,911	120	3,157 R	63.7%	35.2%	64.4%	35.6%
19,256	TAYLOR	6,001	3,218	2,719	64	499 R	53.6%	45.3%	54.2%	45.8%
13,442	UNION	3,453	1,807	1,611	35	196 R	52.3%	46.7%	52.9%	47.1%
443,343	VOLUSIA	159,084	85,594	72,208	1,282	13,386 R	53.8%	45.4%	54.2%	45.8%
22,863	WAKULLA	8,466	3,700	4,664	102	964 D	43.7%	55.1%	44.2%	55.8%
40,601	WALTON	15,605	10,671	4,801	133	5,870 R	68.4%	30.8%	69.0%	31.0%
20,973	WASHINGTON	6,855	4,119	2,671	65	1,448 R	60.1%	39.0%	60.7%	39.3%
15,982,378	TOTAL	5,100,581	2,856,845	2,201,427	42,309	655,418 R	56.0%	43.2%	56.5%	43.5%

FLORIDA

HOUSE OF REPRESENTATIVES

CD	Year	Total Vote	Republican		Democratic		Other Vote	Rep.-Dem. Plurality	Percentage			
			Vote	Candidate	Vote	Candidate			Total Vote		Major Vote	
									Rep.	Dem.	Rep.	Dem.
1	2002	204,626	152,635	Miller, Jeff*	51,972	Oram, Bert	19	100,663 R	74.6%	25.4%	74.6%	25.4%
2	2002	227,439	75,275	McGurk, Tom	152,164	Boyd, Allen*		76,889 D	33.1%	66.9%	33.1%	66.9%
3	2002	149,213	60,747	Carroll, Jennifer	88,462	Brown, Corrine*	4	27,715 D	40.7%	59.3%	40.7%	59.3%
4	2002	171,661	171,152	Crenshaw, Ander*			509	171,152 R	99.7%		100.0%	
5	2002	254,671	121,998	Brown-Waite, Ginny	117,758	Thurman, Karen L.*	14,915	4,240 R	47.9%	46.2%	50.9%	49.1%
6	2002	216,616	141,570	Stearns, Cliff*	75,046	Bruderly, David E.		66,524 R	65.4%	34.6%	65.4%	34.6%
7	2002	238,591	142,147	Mica, John L.*	96,444	Hogan, Wayne		45,703 R	59.6%	40.4%	59.6%	40.4%
8	2002	189,596	123,497	Keller, Ric*	66,099	Diaz, Eddie		57,398 R	65.1%	34.9%	65.1%	34.9%
9	2002	237,008	169,369	Bilirakis, Michael *	67,623	Kalogianis, Chuck	16	101,746 R	71.5%	28.5%	71.5%	28.5%
10	2002			Young, C.W. Bill*				R				
11	2002					Davis, Jim*		D				
12	2002			Putnam, Adam H.*				R				
13	2002	253,809	139,048	Harris, Katherine	114,739	Schneider, Jan	22	24,309 R	54.8%	45.2%	54.8%	45.2%
14	2002			Goss, Porter J.*				R				
15	2002	231,857	146,414	Weldon, Dave*	85,433	Tso, Jim	10	60,981 R	63.1%	36.8%	63.2%	36.8%
16	2002	223,340	176,171	Foley, Mark*			47,169	176,171 R	78.9%		100.0%	
17	2002	113,822			113,749	Meek, Kendrick B.	73	113,749 D		99.9%		100.0%
18	2002	149,787	103,512	Ros-Lehtinen, Ileana*	42,852	Chote, Ray	3,423	60,660 R	69.1%	28.6%	70.7%	29.3%
19	2002	217,224	60,477	Merkl, Jack	156,747	Wexler, Robert*		96,270 D	27.8%	72.2%	27.8%	72.2%
20	2002					Deutsch, Peter*		D				
21	2002			Diaz-Balart, Lincoln*				R				

An asterisk (*) denotes incumbent. In Florida districts where a candidate had no opposition at all, including write-ins, no vote was taken.

FLORIDA

HOUSE OF REPRESENTATIVES

CD	Year	Total Vote	Republican		Democratic		Other Vote	Rep.-Dem. Plurality	Percentage			
									Total Vote		Major Vote	
			Vote	Candidate	Vote	Candidate			Rep.	Dem.	Rep.	Dem.
22	2002	217,115	131,930	Shaw, E. Clay Jr.*	83,265	Roberts, Carol A.	1,920	48,665 R	60.8%	38.4%	61.3%	38.7%
23	2002	124,338	27,986	Laurie, Charles	96,347	Hastings, Alcee L.*	5	68,361 D	22.5%	77.5%	22.5%	77.5%
24	2002	219,243	135,576	Feeney, Tom	83,667	Jacobs, Harry		51,909 R	61.8%	38.2%	61.8%	38.2%
25	2002	126,602	81,845	Diaz-Balart, Mario	44,757	Betancourt, Annie		37,088 R	64.6%	35.4%	64.6%	35.4%
Total	2002	3,766,558	2,161,349		1,537,124		68,085	624,225 R	57.4%	40.8%	58.4%	41.6%

An asterisk (*) denotes incumbent.

FLORIDA

GENERAL AND PRIMARY ELECTIONS

2002 GENERAL ELECTIONS

Governor   Other vote was 42,039 No Party Affiliation (Robert "Bob" Kunst); 172 write-in (John Wayne Smith); 44 write-in (Nancy Grant); 24 write-in (Rachele Fruit); 23 write-in (Terry Galloway AKA Mickee Faust); 7 write-in (C.C. Reed).

House   Other vote was:

CD 1   19 write-in (Tom Wells).
CD 2
CD 3   4 write-in (Jon Arnett).
CD 4   509 write-in (Charles S. Knause).
CD 5   8,639 No Party Affiliation (Jack Gargan); 6,223 No Party Affiliation (Brian Moore); 53 write-in (Werder).
CD 6
CD 7
CD 8
CD 9   16 write-in (Andrew Pasayan).
CD 10
CD 11
CD 12
CD 13   22 write-in (Wayne Genthner).
CD 14
CD 15   10 write-in (Donald Gibbons).
CD 16   47,169 Constitution Party of Florida (Jack McLain).
CD 17   73 write-in (Michael Italie).
CD 18   3,423 No Party Affiliation (Orin Opperman).
CD 19
CD 20
CD 21
CD 22   1,902 No Party Affiliation (Juan Xuna); 18 write-in (Stan Smilan).
CD 23   5 write-in (B.B.B.)
CD 24
CD 25

FLORIDA

GENERAL AND PRIMARY ELECTIONS

2002 PRIMARY ELECTIONS

Primary	September 10, 2002		Registration (as of Aug. 12, 2002)		

Registration (as of Aug. 12, 2002)	
Republican	3,553,349
Democratic	3,898,413
Independent Party	176,722
Libertarian	11,435
Green	5,184
Reform	4,680
Other Parties	6,961
No Party Affiliation	1,501,672
TOTAL	9,158,416

Primary Type   Closed—Only registered Democrats and Republicans could vote in their party's primary, with the exception of races where there were to be no other candidates (including write-ins) on the general election ballot. Then, the contested primary would be open to all voters. This exception, though, was not triggered in either the gubernatorial or congressional primaries in 2002.

Note: An asterisk (*) denotes incumbent. The names of unopposed candidates did not appear on the primary ballot; therefore, no votes were cast for these candidates.

	REPUBLICAN PRIMARIES			DEMOCRATIC PRIMARIES		
Governor	Jeb Bush*	Unopposed		Bill McBride	602,352	44.4%
				Janet Reno	597,558	44.0%
				Daryl L. Jones	157,107	11.6%
				TOTAL	1,357,017	
Congressional District 1	Jeff Miller*	41,990	64.4%	Bert Oram	Unopposed	
	Mike Francisco	23,164	35.6%			
	TOTAL	65,154				
Congressional District 2	Tom McGurk	Unopposed		Allen Boyd*	Unopposed	
Congressional District 3	Jennifer Carroll	Unopposed		Corrine Brown*	Unopposed	
Congressional District 4	Ander Crenshaw*	39,303	89.7%	No Democratic candidate		
	Deborah Katz Pueschel	4,509	10.3%			
	TOTAL	43,812				
Congressional District 5	Ginny Brown-Waite	31,242	57.6%	Karen L. Thurman*	Unopposed	
	Don Gessner	23,008	42.4%			
	TOTAL	54,250				
Congressional District 6	Cliff Stearns*	Unopposed		David E. Bruderly	29,541	59.4%
				James Francis Jude O'Neill	20,154	40.6%
				TOTAL	49,695	
Congressional District 7	John L. Mica*	Unopposed		Wayne Hogan	Unopposed	
Congressional District 8	Rick Keller*	Unopposed		Eddie Diaz	Unopposed	
Congressional District 9	Michael Bilirakis*	Unopposed		Chuck Kalogianis	Unopposed	
Congressional District 10	C.W. Bill Young*	Unopposed		No Democratic candidate		
Congressional District 11	No Republican candidate			Jim Davis*	Unopposed	
Congressional District 12	Adam H. Putnam*	Unopposed		No Democratic candidate		

FLORIDA

GENERAL AND PRIMARY ELECTIONS

	REPUBLICAN PRIMARIES			DEMOCRATIC PRIMARIES		
Congressional District 13	Katherine Harris	47,761	68.3%	Jan Schneider	20,205	44.4%
	John C. Hill	22,144	31.7%	Charles S. McKenzie Jr.	10,728	23.6%
				Candice Brown-McElyea	9,754	21.5%
				Patrick J. Feheley	4,771	10.5%
	TOTAL	69,905		TOTAL	45,458	
Congressional District 14	Porter J. Goss*	Unopposed		No Democratic candidate		
Congressional District 15	Dave Weldon*	46,086	83.5%	Jim Tso	Unopposed	
	Gerry L. Newby	9,126	16.5%			
	TOTAL	55,212				
Congressional District 16	Mark Foley*	Unopposed		No Democratic candidate		
Congressional District 17	No Republican candidate			Kendrick B. Meek	Unopposed	
Congressional District 18	Ileana Ros-Lehtinen*	38,885	88.0%	Ray Chote	Unopposed	
	May Chote	5,327	12.0%			
	TOTAL	44,212				
Congressional District 19	Jack Merkl	Unopposed		Robert Wexler*	Unopposed	
Congressional District 20	No Republican candidate			Peter Deutsch*	Unopposed	
Congressional District 21	Lincoln Diaz-Balart*	Unopposed		No Democratic candidate		
Congressional District 22	E. Clay Shaw Jr.*	Unopposed		Carol A. Roberts	Unopposed	
Congressional District 23	Charles Laurie	Unopposed		Alcee L. Hastings*	Unopposed	
Congressional District 24	Tom Feeney	Unopposed		Harry Jacobs	Unopposed	
Congressional District 25	Mario Diaz-Balart	Unopposed		Annie Betancourt	18,427	70.5%
				Lorna Virgili	7,709	29.5%
				TOTAL	26,136	

FLORIDA DEMOCRATIC PRIMARY

GOVERNOR 2002

2000 Census Population	County	Total Vote	McBride	Reno	Jones	Winner	Percentage of Total Vote		
							McBride	Reno	Jones
217,955	ALACHUA	26,361	16,453	7,789	2,119	McBride	62.4%	29.5%	8.0%
22,259	BAKER	3,562	2,195	776	591	McBride	61.6%	21.8%	16.6%
148,217	BAY	14,744	8,725	3,510	2,509	McBride	59.2%	23.8%	17.0%
26,088	BRADFORD	3,839	2,191	1,040	608	McBride	57.1%	27.1%	15.8%
476,230	BREVARD	36,256	17,290	14,546	4,420	McBride	47.7%	40.1%	12.2%
1,623,018	BROWARD	151,516	42,901	97,017	11,598	Reno	28.3%	64.0%	7.7%
13,017	CALHOUN	3,097	2,032	488	577	McBride	65.6%	15.8%	18.6%
141,627	CHARLOTTE	9,749	5,352	3,709	688	McBride	54.9%	38.0%	7.1%
118,085	CITRUS	11,958	6,619	4,361	978	McBride	55.4%	36.5%	8.2%
140,814	CLAY	6,262	3,072	2,319	871	McBride	49.1%	37.0%	13.9%

FLORIDA DEMOCRATIC PRIMARY

GOVERNOR 2002

2000 Census Population	County	Total Vote	McBride	Reno	Jones	Winner	Percentage of Total Vote		
							McBride	Reno	Jones
251,377	COLLIER	8,932	4,577	3,315	1,040	McBride	51.2%	37.1%	11.6%
56,513	COLUMBIA	8,273	5,009	1,990	1,274	McBride	60.5%	24.1%	15.4%
2,253,362	DADE	159,035	32,093	112,649	14,293	Reno	20.2%	70.8%	9.0%
32,209	DESOTO	3,071	1,714	948	409	McBride	55.8%	30.9%	13.3%
13,827	DIXIE	2,626	1,869	486	271	McBride	71.2%	18.5%	10.3%
778,879	DUVAL	74,238	28,111	29,182	16,945	Reno	37.9%	39.3%	22.8%
294,410	ESCAMBIA	23,241	13,089	6,541	3,611	McBride	56.3%	28.1%	15.5%
49,832	FLAGLER	7,206	3,317	3,033	856	McBride	46.0%	42.1%	11.9%
11,057	FRANKLIN	2,421	1,633	567	221	McBride	67.5%	23.4%	9.1%
45,087	GADSDEN	9,894	4,852	3,425	1,617	McBride	49.0%	34.6%	16.3%
14,437	GILCHRIST	2,588	1,742	517	329	McBride	67.3%	20.0%	12.7%
10,576	GLADES	1,574	794	555	225	McBride	50.4%	35.3%	14.3%
13,332	GULF	3,490	2,236	670	584	McBride	64.1%	19.2%	16.7%
13,327	HAMILTON	2,335	1,424	592	319	McBride	61.0%	25.4%	13.7%
26,938	HARDEE	2,938	1,798	576	564	McBride	61.2%	19.6%	19.2%
36,210	HENDRY	2,461	1,235	869	357	McBride	50.2%	35.3%	14.5%
130,802	HERNANDO	12,549	6,340	5,077	1,132	McBride	50.5%	40.5%	9.0%
87,366	HIGHLANDS	5,794	2,786	1,941	1,067	McBride	48.1%	33.5%	18.4%
998,948	HILLSBOROUGH	82,609	45,971	24,799	11,839	McBride	55.6%	30.0%	14.3%
18,564	HOLMES	3,789	2,729	555	505	McBride	72.0%	14.6%	13.3%
112,947	INDIAN RIVER	7,200	2,790	3,415	995	Reno	38.8%	47.4%	13.8%
46,755	JACKSON	8,232	4,975	1,471	1,786	McBride	60.4%	17.9%	21.7%
12,902	JEFFERSON	3,844	2,400	871	573	McBride	62.4%	22.7%	14.9%
7,022	LAFAYETTE	1,814	1,286	317	211	McBride	70.9%	17.5%	11.6%
210,528	LAKE	14,670	9,023	4,333	1,314	McBride	61.5%	29.5%	9.0%
440,888	LEE	23,100	11,538	9,507	2,055	McBride	49.9%	41.2%	8.9%
239,452	LEON	40,377	24,729	10,986	4,662	McBride	61.2%	27.2%	11.5%
34,450	LEVY	5,431	3,708	1,173	550	McBride	68.3%	21.6%	10.1%
7,021	LIBERTY	2,100	1,460	374	266	McBride	69.5%	17.8%	12.7%
18,733	MADISON	3,512	2,038	916	558	McBride	58.0%	26.1%	15.9%
264,002	MANATEE	19,696	10,281	7,490	1,925	McBride	52.2%	38.0%	9.8%
258,916	MARION	24,723	10,817	11,067	2,839	Reno	43.8%	44.8%	11.5%
126,731	MARTIN	8,305	3,045	4,537	723	Reno	36.7%	54.6%	8.7%
79,589	MONROE	6,665	1,989	4,004	672	Reno	29.8%	60.1%	10.1%
57,663	NASSAU	5,323	2,686	1,771	866	McBride	50.5%	33.3%	16.3%
170,498	OKALOOSA	8,019	4,910	2,047	1,062	McBride	61.2%	25.5%	13.2%
35,910	OKEECHOBEE	4,464	2,399	1,448	617	McBride	53.7%	32.4%	13.8%
896,344	ORANGE	65,313	33,896	23,018	8,399	McBride	51.9%	35.2%	12.9%
172,493	OSCEOLA	9,519	4,969	3,385	1,165	McBride	52.2%	35.6%	12.2%
1,131,184	PALM BEACH	108,000	35,624	64,445	7,931	Reno	33.0%	59.7%	7.3%
344,765	PASCO	29,472	15,615	11,069	2,788	McBride	53.0%	37.6%	9.5%
921,482	PINELLAS	77,306	40,214	30,349	6,743	McBride	52.0%	39.3%	8.7%
483,924	POLK	40,003	20,615	11,891	7,497	McBride	51.5%	29.7%	18.7%
70,423	PUTNAM	10,123	5,198	3,436	1,489	McBride	51.3%	33.9%	14.7%
123,135	ST. JOHNS	10,097	5,039	3,703	1,355	McBride	49.9%	36.7%	13.4%
192,695	ST. LUCIE	17,334	6,575	8,409	2,350	Reno	37.9%	48.5%	13.6%
117,743	SANTA ROSA	7,254	4,945	1,510	799	McBride	68.2%	20.8%	11.0%
325,957	SARASOTA	22,966	11,269	9,760	1,937	McBride	49.1%	42.5%	8.4%
365,196	SEMINOLE	17,937	10,537	5,277	2,123	McBride	58.7%	29.4%	11.8%
53,345	SUMTER	5,187	3,123	1,403	661	McBride	60.2%	27.0%	12.7%
34,844	SUWANNEE	4,965	2,931	1,336	698	McBride	59.0%	26.9%	14.1%
19,256	TAYLOR	3,306	2,085	757	464	McBride	63.1%	22.9%	14.0%
13,442	UNION	2,154	1,486	453	215	McBride	69.0%	21.0%	10.0%
443,343	VOLUSIA	38,742	19,352	14,858	4,532	McBride	50.0%	38.4%	11.7%
22,863	WAKULLA	4,741	3,121	1,152	468	McBride	65.8%	24.3%	9.9%
40,601	WALTON	5,081	3,167	1,197	717	McBride	62.3%	23.6%	14.1%
20,973	WASHINGTON	3,634	2,368	581	685	McBride	65.2%	16.0%	18.8%
15,982,378	TOTAL	1,357,017	602,352	597,558	157,107	McBride	44.4%	44.0%	11.6%

GEORGIA

GOVERNOR
Sonny Perdue (R). Elected 2002 to a four-year term.

SENATORS (1 Democrat, 1 Republican)
Saxby Chambliss (R). Elected 2002 to a six-year term.

Zell Miller (D). Elected 2000 to complete the term of Paul Coverdell (R), who died in July 2000. Miller previously elected governor.

REPRESENTATIVES (8 Republicans, 5 Democrats)
1. Jack Kingston (R)
2. Sanford D. Bishop Jr. (D)
3. Jim Marshall (D)
4. Denise L. Majette (D)
5. John Lewis (D)
6. Johnny Isakson (R)
7. John Linder (R)
8. Mac Collins (R)
9. Charlie Norwood (R)
10. Nathan Deal (R)
11. Phil Gingrey (R)
12. Max Burns (R)
13. David Scott (D)

POSTWAR VOTE FOR PRESIDENT

| Year | Total Vote | Republican | | Democratic | | Other Vote | Plurality | Percentage | | | |
| | | Vote | Candidate | Vote | Candidate | | | Total Vote | | Major Vote | |
								Rep.	Dem.	Rep.	Dem.
2000**	2,596,645	1,419,720	Bush, George W.	1,116,230	Gore, Al	60,695	303,490 R	54.7%	43.0%	56.0%	44.0%
1996**	2,299,071	1,080,843	Dole, Bob	1,053,849	Clinton, Bill	164,379	26,994 R	47.0%	45.8%	50.6%	49.4%
1992**	2,321,125	995,252	Bush, George	1,008,966	Clinton, Bill	316,907	13,714 D	42.9%	43.5%	49.7%	50.3%
1988	1,809,672	1,081,331	Bush, George	714,792	Dukakis, Michael S.	13,549	366,539 R	59.8%	39.5%	60.2%	39.8%
1984	1,776,120	1,068,722	Reagan, Ronald	706,628	Mondale, Walter F.	770	362,094 R	60.2%	39.8%	60.2%	39.8%
1980**	1,596,695	654,168	Reagan, Ronald	890,733	Carter, Jimmy	51,794	236,565 D	41.0%	55.8%	42.3%	57.7%
1976	1,467,458	483,743	Ford, Gerald R.	979,409	Carter, Jimmy	4,306	495,666 D	33.0%	66.7%	33.1%	66.9%
1972	1,174,772	881,496	Nixon, Richard M.	289,529	McGovern, George S.	3,747	591,967 R	75.0%	24.6%	75.3%	24.7%
1968**	1,250,266	380,111	Nixon, Richard M.	334,440	Humphrey, Hubert H.	535,715	155,439 A	30.4%	26.7%	53.2%	46.8%
1964	1,139,335	616,584	Goldwater, Barry M.	522,556	Johnson, Lyndon B.	195	94,028 R	54.1%	45.9%	54.1%	45.9%
1960	733,349	274,472	Nixon, Richard M.	458,638	Kennedy, John F.	239	184,166 D	37.4%	62.5%	37.4%	62.6%
1956	669,655	222,778	Eisenhower, Dwight D.	444,688	Stevenson, Adlai E.	2,189	221,910 D	33.3%	66.4%	33.4%	66.6%
1952	655,785	198,961	Eisenhower, Dwight D.	456,823	Stevenson, Adlai E.	1	257,862 D	30.3%	69.7%	30.3%	69.7%
1948**	418,844	76,691	Dewey, Thomas E.	254,646	Truman, Harry S.	87,507	169,511 D	18.3%	60.8%	23.1%	76.9%

In 2000 the other vote column includes 13,273 votes cast for Green (Nader). In 1996 the other vote column includes 146,337 votes cast for Perot. In 1992 the other vote column includes 309,657 votes cast for Perot. In 1980 the other column includes 36,055 votes for Independent (Anderson). In 1968 other vote was 535,550 American (Wallace) and 165 scattered. In 1948 other vote was 85,135 States Rights; 1,636 Progressive; 732 Prohibition; 3 Socialist and 1 scattered.

GEORGIA

POSTWAR VOTE FOR GOVERNOR

Year	Total Vote	Republican		Democratic		Other Vote	Rep.-Dem. Plurality	Percentage			
		Vote	Candidate	Vote	Candidate			Total Vote		Major Vote	
								Rep.	Dem.	Rep.	Dem.
2002	2,027,177	1,041,700	Perdue, Sonny	937,070	Barnes, Roy	48,407	104,630 R	51.4%	46.2%	52.6%	47.4%
1998	1,792,808	790,201	Millner, Guy	941,076	Barnes, Roy	61,531	150,875 D	44.1%	52.5%	45.6%	54.4%
1994	1,545,328	756,371	Millner, Guy	788,926	Miller, Zell	31	32,555 D	48.9%	51.1%	48.9%	51.1%
1990	1,449,682	645,625	Isakson, Johnny	766,662	Miller, Zell	37,395	121,037 D	44.5%	52.9%	45.7%	54.3%
1986	1,175,114	346,512	Davis, Guy	828,465	Harris, Joe Frank	137	481,953 D	29.5%	70.5%	29.5%	70.5%
1982	1,169,041	434,496	Bell, Robert H.	734,090	Harris, Joe Frank	455	299,594 D	37.2%	62.8%	37.2%	62.8%
1978	662,862	128,139	Cook, Rodney M.	534,572	Busbee, George	151	406,433 D	19.3%	80.6%	19.3%	80.7%
1974	936,438	289,113	Thompson, Ronnie	646,777	Busbee, George	548	357,664 D	30.9%	69.1%	30.9%	69.1%
1970	1,046,663	424,983	Suit, Hal	620,419	Carter, Jimmy	1,261	195,436 D	40.6%	59.3%	40.7%	59.3%
1966**	975,019	453,665	Callaway, Howard H.	450,626	Maddox, Lester	70,728	3,039 R	46.5%	46.2%	50.2%	49.8%
1962	311,691		—	311,524	Sanders, Carl E.	167	311,524 D		99.9%		100.0%
1958	168,497		—	168,414	Vandiver, Ernest	83	168,414 D		100.0%		100.0%
1954	331,966		—	331,899	Griffin, Marvin	67	331,899 D		100.0%		100.0%
1950	234,430		—	230,771	Talmadge, Herman	3,659	230,771 D		98.4%		100.0%
1948S	363,763		—	354,711	Talmadge, Herman	9,052	354,711 D		97.5%		100.0%
1946	145,403		—	143,279	Talmadge, Herman	2,124	143,279 D		98.5%		100.0%

In 1966 in the absence of a majority for any candidate, the State Legislature elected Lester Maddox to a four-year term. The 1948 election was for a short term to fill a vacancy.

POSTWAR VOTE FOR SENATOR

Year	Total Vote	Republican		Democratic		Other Vote	Rep.-Dem. Plurality	Percentage			
		Vote	Candidate	Vote	Candidate			Total Vote		Major Vote	
								Rep.	Dem.	Rep.	Dem.
2002	2,030,608	1,071,464	Chambliss, Saxby	932,156	Cleland, Max	26,988	139,308 R	52.8%	45.9%	53.5%	46.5%
2000S	2,428,510	920,478	Mattingly, Mack	1,413,224	Miller, Zell	94,808	492,746 D	37.9%	58.2%	39.4%	60.6%
1998	1,753,911	918,540	Coverdell, Paul	791,904	Coles, Michael	43,467	126,636 R	52.4%	45.2%	53.7%	46.3%
1996	2,259,232	1,073,969	Millner, Guy	1,103,993	Cleland, Max	81,270	30,024 D	47.5%	48.9%	49.3%	50.7%
1992**	1,253,991	635,114	Coverdell, Paul	618,877	Fowler, Wyche		16,237 R	50.6%	49.4%	50.6%	49.4%
1990	1,033,517		—	1,033,439	Nunn, Sam	78	1,033,439 D		100.0%		100.0%
1986	1,225,008	601,241	Mattingly, Mack	623,707	Fowler, Wyche	60	22,466 D	49.1%	50.9%	49.1%	50.9%
1984	1,681,344	337,196	Hicks, Jon Michael	1,344,104	Nunn, Sam	44	1,006,908 D	20.1%	79.9%	20.1%	79.9%
1980	1,580,340	803,686	Mattingly, Mack	776,143	Talmadge, Herman	511	27,543 R	50.9%	49.1%	50.9%	49.1%
1978	645,164	108,808	Stokes, John W.	536,320	Nunn, Sam	36	427,512 D	16.9%	83.1%	16.9%	83.1%
1974	874,555	246,866	Johnson, Jerry R.	627,376	Talmadge, Herman	313	380,510 D	28.2%	71.7%	28.2%	71.8%
1972	1,178,708	542,331	Thompson, Fletcher	635,970	Nunn, Sam	407	93,639 D	46.0%	54.0%	46.0%	54.0%
1968	1,141,889	256,796	Patton, E. Earl	885,093	Talmadge, Herman		628,297 D	22.5%	77.5%	22.5%	77.5%
1966	622,371		—	622,043	Russell, Richard B.	328	622,043 D		99.9%		100.0%
1962	306,250		—	306,250	Talmadge, Herman		306,250 D		100.0%		100.0%
1960	576,495		—	576,140	Russell, Richard B.	355	576,140 D		99.9%		100.0%
1956	541,267		—	541,094	Talmadge, Herman	173	541,094 D		100.0%		100.0%
1954	333,936		—	333,917	Russell, Richard B.	19	333,917 D		100.0%		100.0%
1950	261,293		—	261,290	George, Walter F.	3	261,290 D		100.0%		100.0%
1948	362,504		—	362,104	Russell, Richard B.	400	362,104 D		99.9%		100.0%

The 2000 election was for a short term to fill a vacancy. In 1992 the figures in the table are for the runoff election held November 24 as no candidate received a majority of the vote in the November 3 General Election. The vote in the November 3 election was 1,073,282 (47.7%) Republican (Coverdell); 1,108,416 (49.2%) Democratic (Fowler) and 69,889 (3.1%) other.

GEORGIA

Congressional districts first established for elections held in 2002
13 members

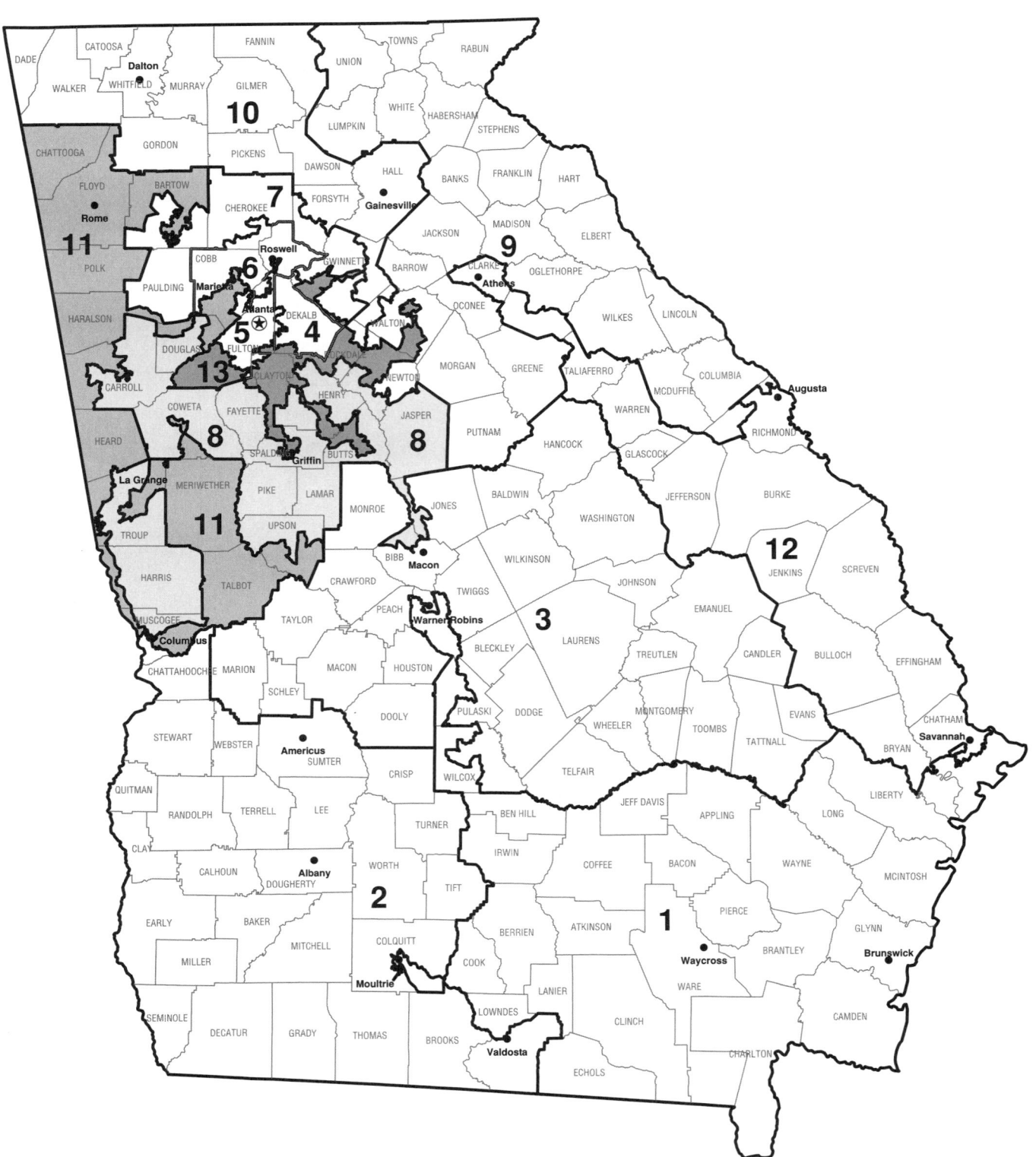

GEORGIA

Atlanta Area

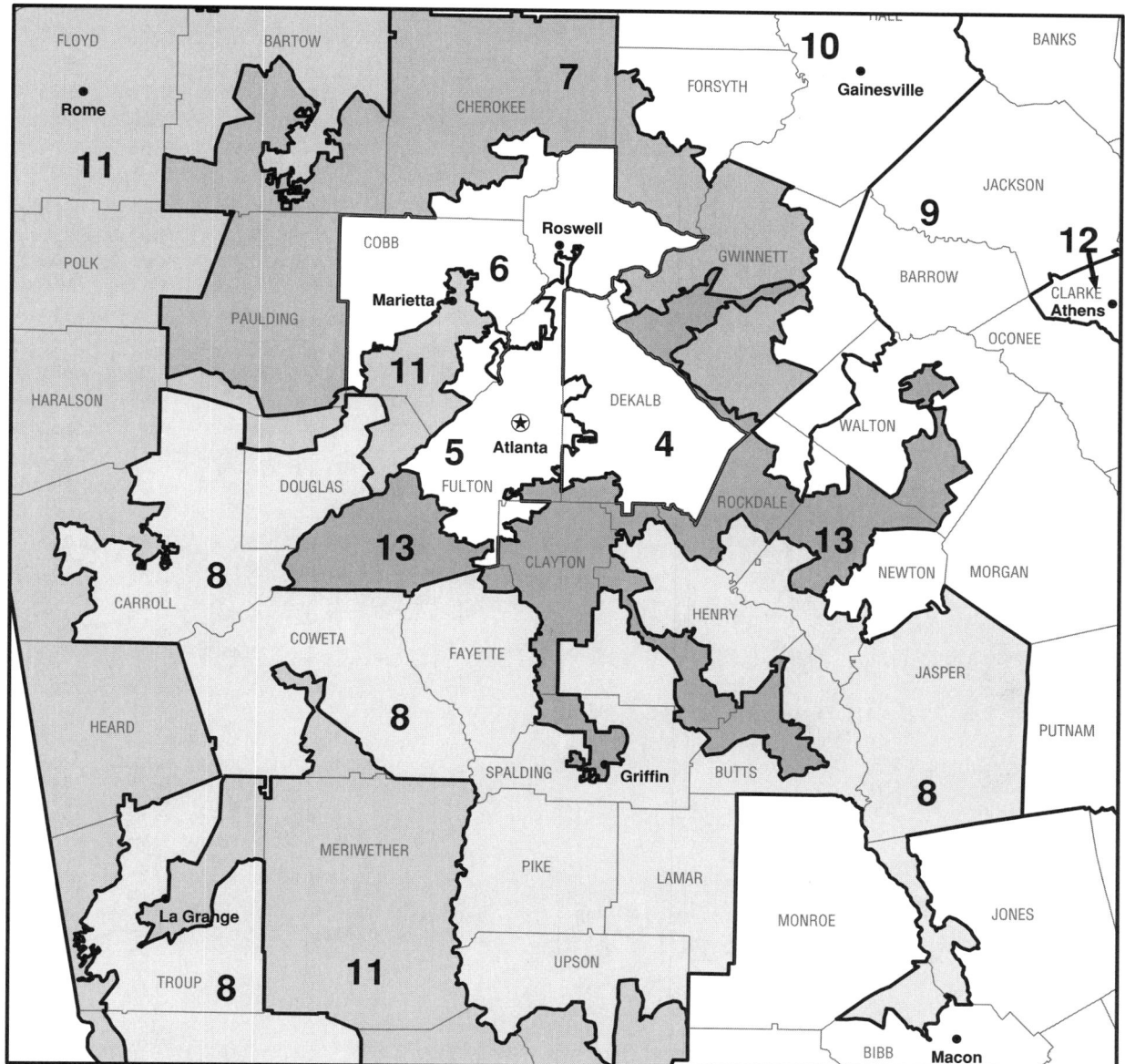

GEORGIA

GOVERNOR 2002

2000 Census Population	County	Total Vote	Republican	Democratic	Other	Rep.-Dem. Plurality	Percentage			
							Total Vote		Major Vote	
							Rep.	Dem.	Rep.	Dem.
17,419	APPLING	4,557	2,987	1,500	70	1,487 R	65.5%	32.9%	66.6%	33.4%
7,609	ATKINSON	1,587	997	562	28	435 R	62.8%	35.4%	64.0%	36.0%
10,103	BACON	2,475	1,577	865	33	712 R	63.7%	34.9%	64.6%	35.4%
4,074	BAKER	1,053	416	622	15	206 D	39.5%	59.1%	40.1%	59.9%
44,700	BALDWIN	9,584	4,900	4,523	161	377 R	51.1%	47.2%	52.0%	48.0%
14,422	BANKS	3,546	2,354	1,117	75	1,237 R	66.4%	31.5%	67.8%	32.2%
46,144	BARROW	9,675	6,242	3,071	362	3,171 R	64.5%	31.7%	67.0%	33.0%
76,019	BARTOW	18,109	11,183	6,413	513	4,770 R	61.8%	35.4%	63.6%	36.4%
17,484	BEN HILL	3,684	1,920	1,703	61	217 R	52.1%	46.2%	53.0%	47.0%
16,235	BERRIEN	3,606	2,171	1,377	58	794 R	60.2%	38.2%	61.2%	38.8%
153,887	BIBB	39,605	18,685	20,311	609	1,626 D	47.2%	51.3%	47.9%	52.1%
11,666	BLECKLEY	3,269	2,408	825	36	1,583 R	73.7%	25.2%	74.5%	25.5%
14,629	BRANTLEY	3,282	2,432	757	93	1,675 R	74.1%	23.1%	76.3%	23.7%
16,450	BROOKS	2,956	1,397	1,511	48	114 D	47.3%	51.1%	48.0%	52.0%
23,417	BRYAN	5,696	3,744	1,866	86	1,878 R	65.7%	32.8%	66.7%	33.3%
55,983	BULLOCH	12,005	6,858	4,956	191	1,902 R	57.1%	41.3%	58.0%	42.0%
22,243	BURKE	5,674	2,627	2,966	81	339 D	46.3%	52.3%	47.0%	53.0%
19,522	BUTTS	4,759	2,761	1,888	110	873 R	58.0%	39.7%	59.4%	40.6%
6,320	CALHOUN	1,467	547	906	14	359 D	37.3%	61.8%	37.6%	62.4%
43,664	CAMDEN	7,457	4,180	3,114	163	1,066 R	56.1%	41.8%	57.3%	42.7%
9,577	CANDLER	2,031	1,205	789	37	416 R	59.3%	38.8%	60.4%	39.6%
87,268	CARROLL	20,744	13,339	6,887	518	6,452 R	64.3%	33.2%	65.9%	34.1%
53,282	CATOOSA	12,104	7,578	4,313	213	3,265 R	62.6%	35.6%	63.7%	36.3%
10,282	CHARLTON	1,785	1,101	656	28	445 R	61.7%	36.8%	62.7%	37.3%
232,048	CHATHAM	59,260	26,444	32,052	764	5,608 D	44.6%	54.1%	45.2%	54.8%
14,882	CHATTAHOOCHEE	688	271	410	7	139 D	39.4%	59.6%	39.8%	60.2%
25,470	CHATTOOGA	4,493	2,457	1,919	117	538 R	54.7%	42.7%	56.1%	43.9%
141,903	CHEROKEE	41,693	28,613	11,718	1,362	16,895 R	68.6%	28.1%	70.9%	29.1%
101,489	CLARKE	21,671	8,173	12,419	1,079	4,246 D	37.7%	57.3%	39.7%	60.3%
3,357	CLAY	892	259	624	9	365 D	29.0%	70.0%	29.3%	70.7%
236,517	CLAYTON	43,934	12,209	30,557	1,168	18,348 D	27.8%	69.6%	28.5%	71.5%
6,878	CLINCH	1,250	597	636	17	39 D	47.8%	50.9%	48.4%	51.6%
607,751	COBB	177,433	92,684	79,278	5,471	13,406 R	52.2%	44.7%	53.9%	46.1%
37,413	COFFEE	7,857	4,699	3,041	117	1,658 R	59.8%	38.7%	60.7%	39.3%
42,053	COLQUITT	8,025	5,119	2,764	142	2,355 R	63.8%	34.4%	64.9%	35.1%
89,288	COLUMBIA	28,600	19,187	9,061	352	10,126 R	67.1%	31.7%	67.9%	32.1%
15,771	COOK	2,998	1,587	1,352	59	235 R	52.9%	45.1%	54.0%	46.0%
89,215	COWETA	25,005	16,208	8,197	600	8,011 R	64.8%	32.8%	66.4%	33.6%
12,495	CRAWFORD	2,896	1,710	1,144	42	566 R	59.0%	39.5%	59.9%	40.1%
21,996	CRISP	4,680	2,606	2,006	68	600 R	55.7%	42.9%	56.5%	43.5%
15,154	DADE	3,267	1,858	1,342	67	516 R	56.9%	41.1%	58.1%	41.9%
15,999	DAWSON	5,038	3,558	1,301	179	2,257 R	70.6%	25.8%	73.2%	26.8%
28,240	DECATUR	5,481	2,580	2,790	111	210 D	47.1%	50.9%	48.0%	52.0%
665,865	DEKALB	170,211	39,854	125,324	5,033	85,470 D	23.4%	73.6%	24.1%	75.9%
19,171	DODGE	4,612	3,016	1,528	68	1,488 R	65.4%	33.1%	66.4%	33.6%
11,525	DOOLY	2,758	1,357	1,357	44		49.2%	49.2%	50.0%	50.0%
96,065	DOUGHERTY	22,893	8,261	14,400	232	6,139 D	36.1%	62.9%	36.5%	63.5%
92,174	DOUGLAS	23,155	13,441	9,148	566	4,293 R	58.0%	39.5%	59.5%	40.5%
12,354	EARLY	2,652	1,243	1,373	36	130 D	46.9%	51.8%	47.5%	52.5%
3,754	ECHOLS	596	369	211	16	158 R	61.9%	35.4%	63.6%	36.4%
37,535	EFFINGHAM	11,254	7,550	3,532	172	4,018 R	67.1%	31.4%	68.1%	31.9%
20,511	ELBERT	4,704	2,369	2,235	100	134 R	50.4%	47.5%	51.5%	48.5%
21,837	EMANUEL	4,872	2,843	1,957	72	886 R	58.4%	40.2%	59.2%	40.8%
10,495	EVANS	2,346	1,286	1,021	39	265 R	54.8%	43.5%	55.7%	44.3%
19,798	FANNIN	6,754	4,269	2,280	205	1,989 R	63.2%	33.8%	65.2%	34.8%
91,263	FAYETTE	33,793	21,655	11,378	760	10,277 R	64.1%	33.7%	65.6%	34.4%
90,565	FLOYD	21,472	12,710	8,187	575	4,523 R	59.2%	38.1%	60.8%	39.2%
98,407	FORSYTH	32,767	24,542	7,178	1,047	17,364 R	74.9%	21.9%	77.4%	22.6%
20,285	FRANKLIN	4,663	2,779	1,752	132	1,027 R	59.6%	37.6%	61.3%	38.7%
816,006	FULTON	201,446	70,446	125,885	5,115	55,439 D	35.0%	62.5%	35.9%	64.1%

GEORGIA

GOVERNOR 2002

2000 Census Population	County	Total Vote	Republican	Democratic	Other	Rep.-Dem. Plurality	Percentage			
							Total Vote		Major Vote	
							Rep.	Dem.	Rep.	Dem.
23,456	GILMER	6,025	3,959	1,917	149	2,042 R	65.7%	31.8%	67.4%	32.6%
2,556	GLASCOCK	659	449	203	7	246 R	68.1%	30.8%	68.9%	31.1%
67,568	GLYNN	17,154	10,725	6,212	217	4,513 R	62.5%	36.2%	63.3%	36.7%
44,104	GORDON	9,800	6,074	3,468	258	2,606 R	62.0%	35.4%	63.7%	36.3%
23,659	GRADY	4,998	2,268	2,651	79	383 D	45.4%	53.0%	46.1%	53.9%
14,406	GREENE	4,591	2,436	2,093	62	343 R	53.1%	45.6%	53.8%	46.2%
588,448	GWINNETT	142,922	85,387	52,495	5,040	32,892 R	59.7%	36.7%	61.9%	38.1%
35,902	HABERSHAM	8,180	5,450	2,525	205	2,925 R	66.6%	30.9%	68.3%	31.7%
139,277	HALL	30,251	20,587	8,860	804	11,727 R	68.1%	29.3%	69.9%	30.1%
10,076	HANCOCK	2,240	449	1,761	30	1,312 D	20.0%	78.6%	20.3%	79.7%
25,690	HARALSON	7,185	4,502	2,458	225	2,044 R	62.7%	34.2%	64.7%	35.3%
23,695	HARRIS	6,841	4,021	2,724	96	1,297 R	58.8%	39.8%	59.6%	40.4%
22,997	HART	6,206	3,277	2,793	136	484 R	52.8%	45.0%	54.0%	46.0%
11,012	HEARD	2,508	1,371	1,066	71	305 R	54.7%	42.5%	56.3%	43.7%
119,341	HENRY	34,455	21,352	12,171	932	9,181 R	62.0%	35.3%	63.7%	36.3%
110,765	HOUSTON	30,233	20,311	9,564	358	10,747 R	67.2%	31.6%	68.0%	32.0%
9,931	IRWIN	2,610	1,539	1,043	28	496 R	59.0%	40.0%	59.6%	40.4%
41,589	JACKSON	9,092	6,102	2,742	248	3,360 R	67.1%	30.2%	69.0%	31.0%
11,426	JASPER	3,073	1,817	1,185	71	632 R	59.1%	38.6%	60.5%	39.5%
12,684	JEFF DAVIS	3,380	2,219	1,101	60	1,118 R	65.7%	32.6%	66.8%	33.2%
17,266	JEFFERSON	4,352	1,872	2,424	56	552 D	43.0%	55.7%	43.6%	56.4%
8,575	JENKINS	2,116	1,130	960	26	170 R	53.4%	45.4%	54.1%	45.9%
8,560	JOHNSON	2,177	1,454	693	30	761 R	66.8%	31.8%	67.7%	32.3%
23,639	JONES	6,749	4,065	2,582	102	1,483 R	60.2%	38.3%	61.2%	38.8%
15,912	LAMAR	4,345	2,312	1,938	95	374 R	53.2%	44.6%	54.4%	45.6%
7,241	LANIER	1,352	685	643	24	42 R	50.7%	47.6%	51.6%	48.4%
44,874	LAURENS	11,564	6,938	4,468	158	2,470 R	60.0%	38.6%	60.8%	39.2%
24,757	LEE	6,301	4,172	2,048	81	2,124 R	66.2%	32.5%	67.1%	32.9%
61,610	LIBERTY	7,303	2,934	4,230	139	1,296 D	40.2%	57.9%	41.0%	59.0%
8,348	LINCOLN	2,262	1,232	1,002	28	230 R	54.5%	44.3%	55.1%	44.9%
10,304	LONG	1,669	929	714	26	215 R	55.7%	42.8%	56.5%	43.5%
92,115	LOWNDES	18,330	9,640	8,418	272	1,222 R	52.6%	45.9%	53.4%	46.6%
21,016	LUMPKIN	5,138	3,327	1,627	184	1,700 R	64.8%	31.7%	67.2%	32.8%
21,231	MCDUFFIE	5,141	2,899	2,173	69	726 R	56.4%	42.3%	57.2%	42.8%
10,847	MCINTOSH	3,289	1,404	1,833	52	429 D	42.7%	55.7%	43.4%	56.6%
14,074	MACON	3,553	1,349	2,161	43	812 D	38.0%	60.8%	38.4%	61.6%
25,730	MADISON	6,065	4,179	1,702	184	2,477 R	68.9%	28.1%	71.1%	28.9%
7,144	MARION	1,918	908	971	39	63 D	47.3%	50.6%	48.3%	51.7%
22,534	MERIWETHER	5,439	2,551	2,789	99	238 D	46.9%	51.3%	47.8%	52.2%
6,383	MILLER	1,390	743	627	20	116 R	53.5%	45.1%	54.2%	45.8%
23,932	MITCHELL	4,830	2,081	2,692	57	611 D	43.1%	55.7%	43.6%	56.4%
21,757	MONROE	6,801	4,140	2,535	126	1,605 R	60.9%	37.3%	62.0%	38.0%
8,270	MONTGOMERY	2,110	1,419	658	33	761 R	67.3%	31.2%	68.3%	31.7%
15,457	MORGAN	4,817	2,880	1,827	110	1,053 R	59.8%	37.9%	61.2%	38.8%
36,506	MURRAY	6,266	3,912	2,153	201	1,759 R	62.4%	34.4%	64.5%	35.5%
186,291	MUSCOGEE	37,145	14,083	22,573	489	8,490 D	37.9%	60.8%	38.4%	61.6%
62,001	NEWTON	15,601	8,816	6,320	465	2,496 R	56.5%	40.5%	58.2%	41.8%
26,225	OCONEE	10,353	6,819	3,252	282	3,567 R	65.9%	31.4%	67.7%	32.3%
12,635	OGLETHORPE	3,389	2,002	1,270	117	732 R	59.1%	37.5%	61.2%	38.8%
81,678	PAULDING	20,541	13,848	6,127	566	7,721 R	67.4%	29.8%	69.3%	30.7%
23,668	PEACH	5,630	3,027	2,525	78	502 R	53.8%	44.8%	54.5%	45.5%
22,983	PICKENS	6,360	4,254	1,922	184	2,332 R	66.9%	30.2%	68.9%	31.1%
15,636	PIERCE	4,068	3,068	963	37	2,105 R	75.4%	23.7%	76.1%	23.9%
13,688	PIKE	4,140	2,823	1,232	85	1,591 R	68.2%	29.8%	69.6%	30.4%
38,127	POLK	8,611	5,058	3,327	226	1,731 R	58.7%	38.6%	60.3%	39.7%
9,588	PULASKI	2,463	1,622	818	23	804 R	65.9%	33.2%	66.5%	33.5%
18,812	PUTNAM	5,181	3,077	2,012	92	1,065 R	59.4%	38.8%	60.5%	39.5%
2,598	QUITMAN	575	147	407	21	260 D	25.6%	70.8%	26.5%	73.5%
15,050	RABUN	4,525	2,530	1,895	100	635 R	55.9%	41.9%	57.2%	42.8%
7,791	RANDOLPH	2,105	725	1,351	29	626 D	34.4%	64.2%	34.9%	65.1%

GEORGIA

GOVERNOR 2002

2000 Census Population	County	Total Vote	Republican	Democratic	Other	Rep.-Dem. Plurality	Percentage			
							Total Vote		Major Vote	
							Rep.	Dem.	Rep.	Dem.
199,775	RICHMOND	47,795	18,015	29,148	632	11,133 D	37.7%	61.0%	38.2%	61.8%
70,111	ROCKDALE	19,369	11,040	7,688	641	3,352 R	57.0%	39.7%	58.9%	41.1%
3,766	SCHLEY	936	565	352	19	213 R	60.4%	37.6%	61.6%	38.4%
15,374	SCREVEN	3,984	2,093	1,842	49	251 R	52.5%	46.2%	53.2%	46.8%
9,369	SEMINOLE	1,999	989	958	52	31 R	49.5%	47.9%	50.8%	49.2%
58,417	SPALDING	12,715	7,718	4,759	238	2,959 R	60.7%	37.4%	61.9%	38.1%
25,435	STEPHENS	5,956	3,455	2,386	115	1,069 R	58.0%	40.1%	59.2%	40.8%
5,252	STEWART	1,218	380	823	15	443 D	31.2%	67.6%	31.6%	68.4%
33,200	SUMTER	7,522	3,249	4,153	120	904 D	43.2%	55.2%	43.9%	56.1%
6,498	TALBOT	2,024	635	1,362	27	727 D	31.4%	67.3%	31.8%	68.2%
2,077	TALIAFERRO	561	172	384	5	212 D	30.7%	68.4%	30.9%	69.1%
22,305	TATTNALL	4,582	2,888	1,639	55	1,249 R	63.0%	35.8%	63.8%	36.2%
8,815	TAYLOR	2,287	1,212	1,023	52	189 R	53.0%	44.7%	54.2%	45.8%
11,794	TELFAIR	2,711	1,588	1,092	31	496 R	58.6%	40.3%	59.3%	40.7%
10,970	TERRELL	2,699	1,217	1,464	18	247 D	45.1%	54.2%	45.4%	54.6%
42,737	THOMAS	9,833	5,237	4,430	166	807 R	53.3%	45.1%	54.2%	45.8%
38,407	TIFT	7,745	4,802	2,824	119	1,978 R	62.0%	36.5%	63.0%	37.0%
26,067	TOOMBS	6,174	4,219	1,863	92	2,356 R	68.3%	30.2%	69.4%	30.6%
9,319	TOWNS	3,233	1,818	1,350	65	468 R	56.2%	41.8%	57.4%	42.6%
6,854	TREUTLEN	1,577	931	622	24	309 R	59.0%	39.4%	59.9%	40.1%
58,779	TROUP	12,792	7,743	4,853	196	2,890 R	60.5%	37.9%	61.5%	38.5%
9,504	TURNER	1,958	1,106	831	21	275 R	56.5%	42.4%	57.1%	42.9%
10,590	TWIGGS	2,930	1,407	1,466	57	59 D	48.0%	50.0%	49.0%	51.0%
17,289	UNION	5,547	3,348	2,071	128	1,277 R	60.4%	37.3%	61.8%	38.2%
27,597	UPSON	6,745	3,849	2,790	106	1,059 R	57.1%	41.4%	58.0%	42.0%
61,053	WALKER	12,805	7,875	4,639	291	3,236 R	61.5%	36.2%	62.9%	37.1%
60,687	WALTON	15,899	10,612	4,841	446	5,771 R	66.7%	30.4%	68.7%	31.3%
35,483	WARE	7,512	5,010	2,415	87	2,595 R	66.7%	32.1%	67.5%	32.5%
6,336	WARREN	1,627	689	912	26	223 D	42.3%	56.1%	43.0%	57.0%
21,176	WASHINGTON	5,182	2,558	2,559	65	1 D	49.4%	49.4%	50.0%	50.0%
26,565	WAYNE	6,389	3,992	2,304	93	1,688 R	62.5%	36.1%	63.4%	36.6%
2,390	WEBSTER	744	363	373	8	10 D	48.8%	50.1%	49.3%	50.7%
6,179	WHEELER	1,358	802	550	6	252 R	59.1%	40.5%	59.3%	40.7%
19,944	WHITE	5,980	3,806	2,036	138	1,770 R	63.6%	34.0%	65.1%	34.9%
83,525	WHITFIELD	16,379	11,363	4,675	341	6,688 R	69.4%	28.5%	70.9%	29.1%
8,577	WILCOX	1,999	1,248	730	21	518 R	62.4%	36.5%	63.1%	36.9%
10,687	WILKES	3,292	1,526	1,714	52	188 D	46.4%	52.1%	47.1%	52.9%
10,220	WILKINSON	2,934	1,392	1,501	41	109 D	47.4%	51.2%	48.1%	51.9%
21,967	WORTH	4,967	2,998	1,891	78	1,107 R	60.4%	38.1%	61.3%	38.7%
8,186,453	TOTAL	2,027,145	1,041,677	937,062	48,406	104,615 R	51.4%	46.2%	52.6%	47.4%

Note: The results from the gubernatorial election were amended as follows: 1,041,700 Republican; 937,070 Democratic; 48,407 Other. The changes came too late to be reflected in the county table.

GEORGIA
SENATOR 2002

2000 Census Population	County	Total Vote	Republican	Democratic	Other	Rep.-Dem. Plurality		Percentage			
								Total Vote		Major Vote	
								Rep.	Dem.	Rep.	Dem.
17,419	APPLING	4,550	2,793	1,699	58	1,094	R	61.4%	37.3%	62.2%	37.8%
7,609	ATKINSON	1,576	982	565	29	417	R	62.3%	35.9%	63.5%	36.5%
10,103	BACON	2,478	1,536	920	22	616	R	62.0%	37.1%	62.5%	37.5%
4,074	BAKER	1,054	414	630	10	216	D	39.3%	59.8%	39.7%	60.3%
44,700	BALDWIN	9,605	4,556	4,958	91	402	D	47.4%	51.6%	47.9%	52.1%
14,422	BANKS	3,552	2,232	1,268	52	964	R	62.8%	35.7%	63.8%	36.2%
46,144	BARROW	9,692	6,287	3,220	185	3,067	R	64.9%	33.2%	66.1%	33.9%
76,019	BARTOW	18,139	11,012	6,784	343	4,228	R	60.7%	37.4%	61.9%	38.1%
17,484	BEN HILL	3,711	1,803	1,858	50	55	D	48.6%	50.1%	49.2%	50.8%
16,235	BERRIEN	3,607	1,976	1,574	57	402	R	54.8%	43.6%	55.7%	44.3%
153,887	BIBB	39,795	19,151	20,356	288	1,205	D	48.1%	51.2%	48.5%	51.5%
11,666	BLECKLEY	3,296	2,125	1,139	32	986	R	64.5%	34.6%	65.1%	34.9%
14,629	BRANTLEY	3,296	2,087	1,147	62	940	R	63.3%	34.8%	64.5%	35.5%
16,450	BROOKS	2,952	1,403	1,506	43	103	D	47.5%	51.0%	48.2%	51.8%
23,417	BRYAN	5,689	3,611	2,013	65	1,598	R	63.5%	35.4%	64.2%	35.8%
55,983	BULLOCH	12,043	6,881	5,052	110	1,829	R	57.1%	41.9%	57.7%	42.3%
22,243	BURKE	5,657	2,576	3,014	67	438	D	45.5%	53.3%	46.1%	53.9%
19,522	BUTTS	4,767	2,705	2,011	51	694	R	56.7%	42.2%	57.4%	42.6%
6,320	CALHOUN	1,466	538	919	9	381	D	36.7%	62.7%	36.9%	63.1%
43,664	CAMDEN	7,454	4,069	3,258	127	811	R	54.6%	43.7%	55.5%	44.5%
9,577	CANDLER	2,016	1,067	918	31	149	R	52.9%	45.5%	53.8%	46.2%
87,268	CARROLL	20,785	12,426	8,031	328	4,395	R	59.8%	38.6%	60.7%	39.3%
53,282	CATOOSA	12,143	7,460	4,518	165	2,942	R	61.4%	37.2%	62.3%	37.7%
10,282	CHARLTON	1,777	1,143	617	17	526	R	64.3%	34.7%	64.9%	35.1%
232,048	CHATHAM	59,314	27,927	30,840	547	2,913	D	47.1%	52.0%	47.5%	52.5%
14,882	CHATTAHOOCHEE	687	291	383	13	92	D	42.4%	55.7%	43.2%	56.8%
25,470	CHATTOOGA	4,506	2,277	2,161	68	116	R	50.5%	48.0%	51.3%	48.7%
141,903	CHEROKEE	41,738	30,211	10,828	699	19,383	R	72.4%	25.9%	73.6%	26.4%
101,489	CLARKE	21,806	8,638	12,809	359	4,171	D	39.6%	58.7%	40.3%	59.7%
3,357	CLAY	893	268	611	14	343	D	30.0%	68.4%	30.5%	69.5%
236,517	CLAYTON	44,051	12,635	30,760	656	18,125	D	28.7%	69.8%	29.1%	70.9%
6,878	CLINCH	1,255	733	510	12	223	R	58.4%	40.6%	59.0%	41.0%
607,751	COBB	177,623	105,750	69,082	2,791	36,668	R	59.5%	38.9%	60.5%	39.5%
37,413	COFFEE	7,853	4,661	3,098	94	1,563	R	59.4%	39.4%	60.1%	39.9%
42,053	COLQUITT	8,064	5,146	2,844	74	2,302	R	63.8%	35.3%	64.4%	35.6%
89,288	COLUMBIA	28,583	20,015	8,333	235	11,682	R	70.0%	29.2%	70.6%	29.4%
15,771	COOK	3,003	1,557	1,418	28	139	R	51.8%	47.2%	52.3%	47.7%
89,215	COWETA	25,038	16,665	8,067	306	8,598	R	66.6%	32.2%	67.4%	32.6%
12,495	CRAWFORD	2,902	1,690	1,186	26	504	R	58.2%	40.9%	58.8%	41.2%
21,996	CRISP	4,670	2,576	2,044	50	532	R	55.2%	43.8%	55.8%	44.2%
15,154	DADE	3,259	1,952	1,253	54	699	R	59.9%	38.4%	60.9%	39.1%
15,999	DAWSON	5,055	3,595	1,349	111	2,246	R	71.1%	26.7%	72.7%	27.3%
28,240	DECATUR	5,482	2,627	2,777	78	150	D	47.9%	50.7%	48.6%	51.4%
665,865	DEKALB	170,845	44,759	123,747	2,339	78,988	D	26.2%	72.4%	26.6%	73.4%
19,171	DODGE	4,621	2,742	1,826	53	916	R	59.3%	39.5%	60.0%	40.0%
11,525	DOOLY	2,759	1,324	1,407	28	83	D	48.0%	51.0%	48.5%	51.5%
96,065	DOUGHERTY	23,042	8,834	14,066	142	5,232	D	38.3%	61.0%	38.6%	61.4%
92,174	DOUGLAS	23,173	13,536	9,306	331	4,230	R	58.4%	40.2%	59.3%	40.7%
12,354	EARLY	2,652	1,226	1,400	26	174	D	46.2%	52.8%	46.7%	53.3%
3,754	ECHOLS	595	337	251	7	86	R	56.6%	42.2%	57.3%	42.7%
37,535	EFFINGHAM	11,240	7,162	3,945	133	3,217	R	63.7%	35.1%	64.5%	35.5%
20,511	ELBERT	4,713	2,191	2,460	62	269	D	46.5%	52.2%	47.1%	52.9%
21,837	EMANUEL	4,862	2,547	2,256	59	291	R	52.4%	46.4%	53.0%	47.0%
10,495	EVANS	2,351	1,209	1,109	33	100	R	51.4%	47.2%	52.2%	47.8%
19,798	FANNIN	6,762	4,052	2,576	134	1,476	R	59.9%	38.1%	61.1%	38.9%
91,263	FAYETTE	33,852	22,092	11,364	396	10,728	R	65.3%	33.6%	66.0%	34.0%
90,565	FLOYD	21,539	11,824	9,379	336	2,445	R	54.9%	43.5%	55.8%	44.2%
98,407	FORSYTH	32,812	25,336	6,976	500	18,360	R	77.2%	21.3%	78.4%	21.6%
20,285	FRANKLIN	4,664	2,431	2,163	70	268	R	52.1%	46.4%	52.9%	47.1%
816,006	FULTON	201,813	81,441	117,859	2,513	36,418	D	40.4%	58.4%	40.9%	59.1%

GEORGIA

SENATOR 2002

2000 Census Population	County	Total Vote	Republican	Democratic	Other	Rep.-Dem. Plurality	Percentage			
							Total Vote		Major Vote	
							Rep.	Dem.	Rep.	Dem.
23,456	GILMER	6,025	3,869	2,056	100	1,813 R	64.2%	34.1%	65.3%	34.7%
2,556	GLASCOCK	662	426	231	5	195 R	64.4%	34.9%	64.8%	35.2%
67,568	GLYNN	17,194	10,720	6,294	180	4,426 R	62.3%	36.6%	63.0%	37.0%
44,104	GORDON	9,811	5,845	3,810	156	2,035 R	59.6%	38.8%	60.5%	39.5%
23,659	GRADY	5,024	2,170	2,812	42	642 D	43.2%	56.0%	43.6%	56.4%
14,406	GREENE	4,589	2,559	1,990	40	569 R	55.8%	43.4%	56.3%	43.7%
588,448	GWINNETT	143,176	91,604	49,093	2,479	42,511 R	64.0%	34.3%	65.1%	34.9%
35,902	HABERSHAM	8,180	5,342	2,719	119	2,623 R	65.3%	33.2%	66.3%	33.7%
139,277	HALL	30,303	21,029	8,859	415	12,170 R	69.4%	29.2%	70.4%	29.6%
10,076	HANCOCK	2,228	481	1,714	33	1,233 D	21.6%	76.9%	21.9%	78.1%
25,690	HARALSON	7,187	4,055	3,001	131	1,054 R	56.4%	41.8%	57.5%	42.5%
23,695	HARRIS	6,849	4,050	2,715	84	1,335 R	59.1%	39.6%	59.9%	40.1%
22,997	HART	6,196	2,841	3,269	86	428 D	45.9%	52.8%	46.5%	53.5%
11,012	HEARD	2,505	1,291	1,161	53	130 R	51.5%	46.3%	52.7%	47.3%
119,341	HENRY	34,510	21,552	12,440	518	9,112 R	62.5%	36.0%	63.4%	36.6%
110,765	HOUSTON	30,222	19,109	10,856	257	8,253 R	63.2%	35.9%	63.8%	36.2%
9,931	IRWIN	2,602	1,409	1,157	36	252 R	54.2%	44.5%	54.9%	45.1%
41,589	JACKSON	9,097	6,026	2,939	132	3,087 R	66.2%	32.3%	67.2%	32.8%
11,426	JASPER	3,075	1,754	1,279	42	475 R	57.0%	41.6%	57.8%	42.2%
12,684	JEFF DAVIS	3,386	2,099	1,234	53	865 R	62.0%	36.4%	63.0%	37.0%
17,266	JEFFERSON	4,346	1,786	2,526	34	740 D	41.1%	58.1%	41.4%	58.6%
8,575	JENKINS	2,112	1,052	1,032	28	20 R	49.8%	48.9%	50.5%	49.5%
8,560	JOHNSON	2,174	1,318	836	20	482 R	60.6%	38.5%	61.2%	38.8%
23,639	JONES	6,776	3,914	2,794	68	1,120 R	57.8%	41.2%	58.3%	41.7%
15,912	LAMAR	4,357	2,309	1,989	59	320 R	53.0%	45.7%	53.7%	46.3%
7,241	LANIER	1,352	723	606	23	117 R	53.5%	44.8%	54.4%	45.6%
44,874	LAURENS	11,578	6,643	4,821	114	1,822 R	57.4%	41.6%	57.9%	42.1%
24,757	LEE	6,319	4,281	1,982	56	2,299 R	67.7%	31.4%	68.4%	31.6%
61,610	LIBERTY	7,335	2,813	4,442	80	1,629 D	38.4%	60.6%	38.8%	61.2%
8,348	LINCOLN	2,262	1,178	1,054	30	124 R	52.1%	46.6%	52.8%	47.2%
10,304	LONG	1,676	823	831	22	8 D	49.1%	49.6%	49.8%	50.2%
92,115	LOWNDES	18,371	9,992	8,194	185	1,798 R	54.4%	44.6%	54.9%	45.1%
21,016	LUMPKIN	5,155	3,254	1,798	103	1,456 R	63.1%	34.9%	64.4%	35.6%
21,231	MCDUFFIE	4,544	2,529	1,965	50	564 R	55.7%	43.2%	56.3%	43.7%
10,847	MCINTOSH	3,292	1,305	1,934	53	629 D	39.6%	58.7%	40.3%	59.7%
14,074	MACON	3,585	1,293	2,251	41	958 D	36.1%	62.8%	36.5%	63.5%
25,730	MADISON	6,057	3,950	2,012	95	1,938 R	65.2%	33.2%	66.3%	33.7%
7,144	MARION	1,902	850	1,022	30	172 D	44.7%	53.7%	45.4%	54.6%
22,534	MERIWETHER	5,420	2,306	3,037	77	731 D	42.5%	56.0%	43.2%	56.8%
6,383	MILLER	1,394	744	627	23	117 R	53.4%	45.0%	54.3%	45.7%
23,932	MITCHELL	4,856	2,086	2,727	43	641 D	43.0%	56.2%	43.3%	56.7%
21,757	MONROE	6,817	4,083	2,663	71	1,420 R	59.9%	39.1%	60.5%	39.5%
8,270	MONTGOMERY	2,103	1,265	820	18	445 R	60.2%	39.0%	60.7%	39.3%
15,457	MORGAN	4,825	2,839	1,921	65	918 R	58.8%	39.8%	59.6%	40.4%
36,506	MURRAY	6,272	3,689	2,449	134	1,240 R	58.8%	39.0%	60.1%	39.9%
186,291	MUSCOGEE	37,201	15,269	21,581	351	6,312 D	41.0%	58.0%	41.4%	58.6%
62,001	NEWTON	15,620	8,937	6,454	229	2,483 R	57.2%	41.3%	58.1%	41.9%
26,225	OCONEE	10,384	6,821	3,418	145	3,403 R	65.7%	32.9%	66.6%	33.4%
12,635	OGLETHORPE	3,395	1,954	1,381	60	573 R	57.6%	40.7%	58.6%	41.4%
81,678	PAULDING	20,573	13,890	6,372	311	7,518 R	67.5%	31.0%	68.6%	31.4%
23,668	PEACH	5,666	2,878	2,734	54	144 R	50.8%	48.3%	51.3%	48.7%
22,983	PICKENS	6,379	4,196	2,095	88	2,101 R	65.8%	32.8%	66.7%	33.3%
15,636	PIERCE	4,067	2,945	1,091	31	1,854 R	72.4%	26.8%	73.0%	27.0%
13,688	PIKE	4,148	2,686	1,419	43	1,267 R	64.8%	34.2%	65.4%	34.6%
38,127	POLK	8,631	4,526	3,954	151	572 R	52.4%	45.8%	53.4%	46.6%
9,588	PULASKI	2,469	1,439	1,011	19	428 R	58.3%	40.9%	58.7%	41.3%
18,812	PUTNAM	5,176	2,981	2,137	58	844 R	57.6%	41.3%	58.2%	41.8%
2,598	QUITMAN	565	182	374	9	192 D	32.2%	66.2%	32.7%	67.3%
15,050	RABUN	4,540	2,468	1,992	80	476 R	54.4%	43.9%	55.3%	44.7%
7,791	RANDOLPH	2,131	710	1,397	24	687 D	33.3%	65.6%	33.7%	66.3%

GEORGIA

SENATOR 2002

2000 Census Population	County	Total Vote	Republican	Democratic	Other	Rep.-Dem. Plurality	Percentage			
							Total Vote		Major Vote	
							Rep.	Dem.	Rep.	Dem.
199,775	RICHMOND	47,709	19,275	27,929	505	8,654 D	40.4%	58.5%	40.8%	59.2%
70,111	ROCKDALE	19,426	11,422	7,690	314	3,732 R	58.8%	39.6%	59.8%	40.2%
3,766	SCHLEY	944	567	368	9	199 R	60.1%	39.0%	60.6%	39.4%
15,374	SCREVEN	3,989	1,905	2,035	49	130 D	47.8%	51.0%	48.4%	51.6%
9,369	SEMINOLE	2,008	900	1,083	25	183 D	44.8%	53.9%	45.4%	54.6%
58,417	SPALDING	12,709	7,356	5,203	150	2,153 R	57.9%	40.9%	58.6%	41.4%
25,435	STEPHENS	5,956	3,451	2,419	86	1,032 R	57.9%	40.6%	58.8%	41.2%
5,252	STEWART	1,206	370	816	20	446 D	30.7%	67.7%	31.2%	68.8%
33,200	SUMTER	7,497	3,453	3,972	72	519 D	46.1%	53.0%	46.5%	53.5%
6,498	TALBOT	2,022	598	1,394	30	796 D	29.6%	68.9%	30.0%	70.0%
2,077	TALIAFERRO	555	182	363	10	181 D	32.8%	65.4%	33.4%	66.6%
22,305	TATTNALL	4,589	2,482	2,051	56	431 R	54.1%	44.7%	54.8%	45.2%
8,815	TAYLOR	2,301	1,118	1,174	9	56 D	48.6%	51.0%	48.8%	51.2%
11,794	TELFAIR	2,719	1,368	1,321	30	47 R	50.3%	48.6%	50.9%	49.1%
10,970	TERRELL	2,679	1,135	1,517	27	382 D	42.4%	56.6%	42.8%	57.2%
42,737	THOMAS	9,836	5,017	4,715	104	302 R	51.0%	47.9%	51.6%	48.4%
38,407	TIFT	7,769	4,802	2,898	69	1,904 R	61.8%	37.3%	62.4%	37.6%
26,067	TOOMBS	6,196	3,865	2,262	69	1,603 R	62.4%	36.5%	63.1%	36.9%
9,319	TOWNS	3,253	1,880	1,335	38	545 R	57.8%	41.0%	58.5%	41.5%
6,854	TREUTLEN	1,583	842	726	15	116 R	53.2%	45.9%	53.7%	46.3%
58,779	TROUP	12,790	7,369	5,295	126	2,074 R	57.6%	41.4%	58.2%	41.8%
9,504	TURNER	1,967	996	958	13	38 R	50.6%	48.7%	51.0%	49.0%
10,590	TWIGGS	2,962	1,279	1,640	43	361 D	43.2%	55.4%	43.8%	56.2%
17,289	UNION	5,605	3,327	2,183	95	1,144 R	59.4%	38.9%	60.4%	39.6%
27,597	UPSON	6,763	3,838	2,848	77	990 R	56.7%	42.1%	57.4%	42.6%
61,053	WALKER	12,794	7,527	5,072	195	2,455 R	58.8%	39.6%	59.7%	40.3%
60,687	WALTON	15,913	10,672	4,992	249	5,680 R	67.1%	31.4%	68.1%	31.9%
35,483	WARE	7,506	4,939	2,505	62	2,434 R	65.8%	33.4%	66.3%	33.7%
6,336	WARREN	1,627	681	925	21	244 D	41.9%	56.9%	42.4%	57.6%
21,176	WASHINGTON	5,171	2,339	2,776	56	437 D	45.2%	53.7%	45.7%	54.3%
26,565	WAYNE	6,402	3,583	2,750	69	833 R	56.0%	43.0%	56.6%	43.4%
2,390	WEBSTER	740	289	444	7	155 D	39.1%	60.0%	39.4%	60.6%
6,179	WHEELER	1,362	746	608	8	138 R	54.8%	44.6%	55.1%	44.9%
19,944	WHITE	5,997	3,821	2,104	72	1,717 R	63.7%	35.1%	64.5%	35.5%
83,525	WHITFIELD	16,402	10,696	5,467	239	5,229 R	65.2%	33.3%	66.2%	33.8%
8,577	WILCOX	2,011	1,121	875	15	246 R	55.7%	43.5%	56.2%	43.8%
10,687	WILKES	3,284	1,527	1,715	42	188 D	46.5%	52.2%	47.1%	52.9%
10,220	WILKINSON	2,946	1,279	1,633	34	354 D	43.4%	55.4%	43.9%	56.1%
21,967	WORTH	4,980	2,908	2,006	66	902 R	58.4%	40.3%	59.2%	40.8%
8,186,453		2,029,991	1,071,153	931,857	26,981	139,296 R	52.8%	45.9%	53.5%	46.5%

Note: The results from the Senate election were amended as follows: 1,071,464 Republican; 932,156 Democratic; 26,988 Other. The changes came too late to be reflected in the county table.

GEORGIA

HOUSE OF REPRESENTATIVES

CD	Year	Total Vote	Republican		Democratic		Other Vote	Rep.-Dem. Plurality	Percentage			
									Total Vote		Major Vote	
			Vote	Candidate	Vote	Candidate			Rep.	Dem.	Rep.	Dem.
1	2002	143,700	103,661	Kingston, Jack*	40,026	Smart, Don	13	63,635 R	72.1%	27.9%	72.1%	27.9%
2	2002	102,925			102,925	Bishop, Sanford D. Jr.*		102,925 D		100.0%		100.0%
3	2002	149,260	73,866	Clay, Calder	75,394	Marshall, Jim		1,528 D	49.5%	50.5%	49.5%	50.5%
4	2002	153,247	35,202	Van Auken, Cynthia	118,045	Majette, Denise L.		82,843 D	23.0%	77.0%	23.0%	77.0%
5	2002	116,230			116,230	Lewis, John*		116,230 D		100.0%		100.0%
6	2002	204,252	163,209	Isakson, Johnny*	41,043	Weisberger, Jeff		122,166 R	79.9%	20.1%	79.9%	20.1%
7	2002	176,170	139,019	Linder, John *	37,127	Berlon, Mike	24	101,892 R	78.9%	21.1%	78.9%	21.1%
8	2002	181,927	142,505	Collins, Mac*	39,422	Petrakopoulos, Angelos		103,083 R	78.3%	21.7%	78.3%	21.7%
9	2002	169,287	123,313	Norwood, Charlie*	45,974	Irwin, Barry		77,339 R	72.8%	27.2%	72.8%	27.2%
10	2002	129,242	129,242	Deal, Nathan*				129,242 R	100.0%		100.0%	
11	2002	134,184	69,261	Gingrey, Phil	64,923	Kahn, Roger		4,338 R	51.6%	48.4%	51.6%	48.4%
12	2002	140,457	77,479	Burns, Max	62,904	Walker, Champ	74	14,575 R	55.2%	44.8%	55.2%	44.8%
13	2002	117,416	47,405	Cox, Clay	70,011	Scott, David		22,606 D	40.4%	59.6%	40.4%	59.6%
Total	2002	1,918,297	1,104,162		814,024		111	290,138 R	57.6%	42.4%	57.6%	42.4%

An asterisk (*) denotes incumbent.

GEORGIA

GENERAL AND PRIMARY ELECTIONS

2002 GENERAL ELECTIONS

Governor   Other vote was 47,123 Libertarian (Gary Hayes); 1,198 write-in (Nan Garrett); 62 write-in (Sam Hay); 15 write-in (David C. Byrne); 9 write-in (Bill Bolton).

Senator   Other vote was 26,988 Libertarian (Sandy Thomas).

House   Other vote was:

CD 1   13 write-in (Joyce Griggs).
CD 2
CD 3
CD 4
CD 5
CD 6
CD 7   12 write-in (Al Herman); 12 write-in (John F. Sugg).
CD 8
CD 9
CD 10
CD 11
CD 12
CD 13   74 write-in (Marc Smith).

GEORGIA

GENERAL AND PRIMARY ELECTIONS

2002 PRIMARY ELECTIONS

Primary August 20, 2002

Registration
(as of Aug. 20, 2002—
includes 1,016,965
inactive registrants) 4,667,555 No Party Registration

Primary Runoff September 10, 2002

Primary Type Open—Any registered voter could participate in either the Democratic or Republican primary, although if they voted in one party's primary they could not participate in a primary runoff of the other party.

Note: An asterisk (*) denotes incumbent.

	REPUBLICAN PRIMARIES			DEMOCRATIC PRIMARIES		
Governor	Sonny Perdue	259,966	50.8%	Roy Barnes*	434,892	100.0%
	Linda Schrenko	142,911	27.9%			
	Bill Byrne	108,586	21.2%			
	TOTAL	511,463				
Senator	Saxby Chambliss	300,371	61.1%	Max Cleland*	454,733	100.0%
	Bob Irvin	132,132	26.9%			
	Robert "Bob" Brown	59,109	12.0%			
	TOTAL	491,612				
Congressional District 1	Jack Kingston*	30,878	100.0%	Don Smart	21,818	100.0%
Congressional District 2	No Republican candidate			Sanford D. Bishop Jr.*	47,567	100.0%
Congressional District 3	Calder Clay	21,149	100.0%	Jim Marshall	26,614	53.6%
				Chuck Byrd	16,542	33.3%
				Joe Lester	5,663	11.4%
				Sig Dayan	851	1.7%
				TOTAL	49,670	
Congressional District 4	Cynthia Van Auken	2,169	38.8%	Denise L. Majette	68,612	58.3%
	Catherine Davis	1,910	34.1%	Cynthia McKinney*	49,058	41.7%
	Barbara Pereira	1,515	27.1%			
	TOTAL	5,594		TOTAL	117,670	
	PRIMARY RUNOFF					
	Cynthia Van Auken	1,292	61.3%			
	Catherine Davis	816	38.7%			
	TOTAL	2,108				
Congressional District 5	No Republican candidate			John Lewis*	49,842	100.0%
Congressional District 6	Johnny Isakson*	59,186	100.0%	Jeff Weisberger	11,408	100.0%
Congressional District 7	John Linder*	56,892	64.5%	Mike Berlon	9,618	100.0%
	Bob Barr*	31,374	35.5%			
	TOTAL	88,266				
Congressional District 8	Mac Collins*	53,691	100.0%	Angelos Petrakopoulos	16,922	100.0%
Congressional District 9	Charlie Norwood*	42,452	81.7%	Barry Irwin	24,792	100.0%
	Lee Dickerson	9,522	18.3%			
	TOTAL	51,974				
Congressional District 10	Nathan Deal*	43,874	100.0%	No Democratic candidate		

GEORGIA

GENERAL AND PRIMARY ELECTIONS

REPUBLICAN PRIMARIES			DEMOCRATIC PRIMARIES		
Congressional District 11	Phil Gingrey	12,377	40.1%	Roger Kahn	20,410	52.3%
	Cecil Staton	9,750	31.6%	Buddy Darden	18,623	47.7%
	Bob Herriott	8,717	28.3%			
	TOTAL	30,844		TOTAL	39,033	
	PRIMARY RUNOFF					
	Phil Gingrey	9,930	63.6%			
	Cecil Staton	5,692	36.4%			
	TOTAL	15,622				
Congressional District 12	Max Burns	13,956	50.5%	Champ Walker	14,011	33.3%
	Barbara Dooley	13,700	49.5%	Ben Allen	5,703	13.6%
				Tony Center	5,547	13.2%
				Merwyn Scott	4,619	11.0%
				Chuck Pardue	4,463	10.6%
				Bob Finch	4,385	10.4%
				Denise Freeman	3,332	7.9%
	TOTAL	27,656		TOTAL	42,060	
				PRIMARY RUNOFF		
				Champ Walker	16,405	54.2%
				Ben Allen	13,877	45.8%
				TOTAL	30,282	
Congressional District 13	Clay Cox	16,543		David Scott	22,624	53.8%
				Greg Hecht	8,384	19.9%
				David Worley	5,568	13.2%
				Donzella James	4,703	11.2%
				Embry Malone	762	1.8%
				TOTAL	42,041	

GEORGIA REPUBLICAN PRIMARY

GOVERNOR 2002

2000 Census Population	County	Total Vote	Perdue	Schrenko	Byrne	Winner	Percentage of Total Vote		
							Perdue	Schrenko	Byrne
17,419	APPLING	1,079	776	198	105	Perdue	71.9%	18.4%	9.7%
7,609	ATKINSON	377	227	99	51	Perdue	60.2%	26.3%	13.5%
10,103	BACON	275	207	47	21	Perdue	75.3%	17.1%	7.6%
4,074	BAKER	103	58	28	17	Perdue	56.3%	27.2%	16.5%
44,700	BALDWIN	1,393	1,022	254	117	Perdue	73.4%	18.2%	8.4%
14,422	BANKS	980	499	307	174	Perdue	50.9%	31.3%	17.8%
46,144	BARROW	4,301	2,173	1,277	851	Perdue	50.5%	29.7%	19.8%
76,019	BARTOW	6,270	2,803	1,992	1,475	Perdue	44.7%	31.8%	23.5%
17,484	BEN HILL	768	606	106	56	Perdue	78.9%	13.8%	7.3%
16,235	BERRIEN	346	223	86	37	Perdue	64.5%	24.9%	10.7%
153,887	BIBB	8,763	7,486	847	430	Perdue	85.4%	9.7%	4.9%
11,666	BLECKLEY	1,356	1,187	144	25	Perdue	87.5%	10.6%	1.8%
14,629	BRANTLEY	744	458	151	135	Perdue	61.6%	20.3%	18.1%
16,450	BROOKS	237	112	86	39	Perdue	47.3%	36.3%	16.5%
23,417	BRYAN	1,269	698	335	236	Perdue	55.0%	26.4%	18.6%
55,983	BULLOCH	3,283	1,916	928	439	Perdue	58.4%	28.3%	13.4%
22,243	BURKE	1,373	531	687	155	Schrenko	38.7%	50.0%	11.3%
19,522	BUTTS	1,018	563	273	182	Perdue	55.3%	26.8%	17.9%
6,320	CALHOUN	75	37	19	19	Perdue	49.3%	25.3%	25.3%
43,664	CAMDEN	1,301	540	325	436	Perdue	41.5%	25.0%	33.5%

GEORGIA REPUBLICAN PRIMARY

GOVERNOR 2002

2000 Census Population	County	Total Vote	Perdue	Schrenko	Byrne	Winner	Percentage of Total Vote Perdue	Schrenko	Byrne
9,577	CANDLER	413	222	129	62	Perdue	53.8%	31.2%	15.0%
87,268	CARROLL	5,501	3,289	1,400	812	Perdue	59.8%	25.4%	14.8%
53,282	CATOOSA	2,547	1,783	403	361	Perdue	70.0%	15.8%	14.2%
10,282	CHARLTON	360	292	40	28	Perdue	81.1%	11.1%	7.8%
232,048	CHATHAM	12,427	7,832	2,832	1,763	Perdue	63.0%	22.8%	14.2%
14,882	CHATTAHOOCHEE	73	25	29	19	Schrenko	34.2%	39.7%	26.0%
25,470	CHATTOOGA	583	289	184	110	Perdue	49.6%	31.6%	18.9%
141,903	CHEROKEE	21,724	9,446	5,744	6,534	Perdue	43.5%	26.4%	30.1%
101,489	CLARKE	3,550	2,035	835	680	Perdue	57.3%	23.5%	19.2%
3,357	CLAY	33	16	7	10	Perdue	48.5%	21.2%	30.3%
236,517	CLAYTON	4,902	2,115	1,809	978	Perdue	43.1%	36.9%	20.0%
6,878	CLINCH	153	98	40	15	Perdue	64.1%	26.1%	9.8%
607,751	COBB	54,358	19,103	11,395	23,860	Byrne	35.1%	21.0%	43.9%
37,413	COFFEE	966	737	151	78	Perdue	76.3%	15.6%	8.1%
42,053	COLQUITT	2,629	1,605	599	425	Perdue	61.0%	22.8%	16.2%
89,288	COLUMBIA	11,268	2,700	7,627	941	Schrenko	24.0%	67.7%	8.4%
15,771	COOK	428	284	94	50	Perdue	66.4%	22.0%	11.7%
89,215	COWETA	7,915	4,038	2,467	1,410	Perdue	51.0%	31.2%	17.8%
12,495	CRAWFORD	639	533	65	41	Perdue	83.4%	10.2%	6.4%
21,996	CRISP	1,086	754	258	74	Perdue	69.4%	23.8%	6.8%
15,154	DADE	999	537	241	221	Perdue	53.8%	24.1%	22.1%
15,999	DAWSON	2,179	1,093	595	491	Perdue	50.2%	27.3%	22.5%
28,240	DECATUR	419	211	105	103	Perdue	50.4%	25.1%	24.6%
665,865	DEKALB	6,355	2,626	1,958	1,771	Perdue	41.3%	30.8%	27.9%
19,171	DODGE	1,434	1,229	144	61	Perdue	85.7%	10.0%	4.3%
11,525	DOOLY	550	442	68	40	Perdue	80.4%	12.4%	7.3%
96,065	DOUGHERTY	1,801	883	514	404	Perdue	49.0%	28.5%	22.4%
92,174	DOUGLAS	8,722	4,079	2,594	2,049	Perdue	46.8%	29.7%	23.5%
12,354	EARLY	255	100	95	60	Perdue	39.2%	37.3%	23.5%
3,754	ECHOLS	10	7	2	1	Perdue	70.0%	20.0%	10.0%
37,535	EFFINGHAM	3,804	2,196	910	698	Perdue	57.7%	23.9%	18.3%
20,511	ELBERT	565	329	151	85	Perdue	58.2%	26.7%	15.0%
21,837	EMANUEL	994	508	387	99	Perdue	51.1%	38.9%	10.0%
10,495	EVANS	463	317	82	64	Perdue	68.5%	17.7%	13.8%
19,798	FANNIN	2,493	1,189	797	507	Perdue	47.7%	32.0%	20.3%
91,263	FAYETTE	11,653	5,840	3,665	2,148	Perdue	50.1%	31.5%	18.4%
90,565	FLOYD	5,461	2,471	1,887	1,103	Perdue	45.2%	34.6%	20.2%
98,407	FORSYTH	15,664	7,532	4,476	3,656	Perdue	48.1%	28.6%	23.3%
20,285	FRANKLIN	790	304	254	232	Perdue	38.5%	32.2%	29.4%
816,006	FULTON	32,814	15,472	8,999	8,343	Perdue	47.2%	27.4%	25.4%
23,456	GILMER	2,298	1,164	656	478	Perdue	50.7%	28.5%	20.8%
2,556	GLASCOCK	238	35	191	12	Schrenko	14.7%	80.3%	5.0%
67,568	GLYNN	6,317	3,568	1,582	1,167	Perdue	56.5%	25.0%	18.5%
44,104	GORDON	2,418	1,429	569	420	Perdue	59.1%	23.5%	17.4%
23,659	GRADY	446	253	91	102	Perdue	56.7%	20.4%	22.9%
14,406	GREENE	941	584	199	158	Perdue	62.1%	21.1%	16.8%
588,448	GWINNETT	59,470	26,973	18,542	13,955	Perdue	45.4%	31.2%	23.5%
35,902	HABERSHAM	2,005	1,011	576	418	Perdue	50.4%	28.7%	20.8%
139,277	HALL	13,051	6,245	3,936	2,870	Perdue	47.9%	30.2%	22.0%
10,076	HANCOCK	87	54	25	8	Perdue	62.1%	28.7%	9.2%
25,690	HARALSON	1,569	766	444	359	Perdue	48.8%	28.3%	22.9%
23,695	HARRIS	1,776	778	710	288	Perdue	43.8%	40.0%	16.2%
22,997	HART	1,135	722	249	164	Perdue	63.6%	21.9%	14.4%
11,012	HEARD	550	292	184	74	Perdue	53.1%	33.5%	13.5%
119,341	HENRY	10,681	5,495	3,060	2,126	Perdue	51.4%	28.6%	19.9%
110,765	HOUSTON	12,500	11,628	544	328	Perdue	93.0%	4.4%	2.6%
9,931	IRWIN	635	524	64	47	Perdue	82.5%	10.1%	7.4%
41,589	JACKSON	3,619	2,009	1,052	558	Perdue	55.5%	29.1%	15.4%
11,426	JASPER	764	464	177	123	Perdue	60.7%	23.2%	16.1%
12,684	JEFF DAVIS	502	403	53	46	Perdue	80.3%	10.6%	9.2%

GEORGIA REPUBLICAN PRIMARY

GOVERNOR 2002

2000 Census Population	County	Total Vote	Perdue	Schrenko	Byrne	Winner	Percentage of Total Vote		
							Perdue	Schrenko	Byrne
17,266	JEFFERSON	536	171	303	62	Schrenko	31.9%	56.5%	11.6%
8,575	JENKINS	415	250	129	36	Perdue	60.2%	31.1%	8.7%
8,560	JOHNSON	689	447	194	48	Perdue	64.9%	28.2%	7.0%
23,639	JONES	1,381	1,118	172	91	Perdue	81.0%	12.5%	6.6%
15,912	LAMAR	1,296	762	368	166	Perdue	58.8%	28.4%	12.8%
7,241	LANIER	122	65	43	14	Perdue	53.3%	35.2%	11.5%
44,874	LAURENS	2,448	1,790	463	195	Perdue	73.1%	18.9%	8.0%
24,757	LEE	2,184	959	696	529	Perdue	43.9%	31.9%	24.2%
61,610	LIBERTY	583	301	156	126	Perdue	51.6%	26.8%	21.6%
8,348	LINCOLN	747	164	504	79	Schrenko	22.0%	67.5%	10.6%
10,304	LONG	183	109	45	29	Perdue	59.6%	24.6%	15.8%
92,115	LOWNDES	3,761	2,182	1,124	455	Perdue	58.0%	29.9%	12.1%
21,016	LUMPKIN	2,208	1,081	691	436	Perdue	49.0%	31.3%	19.7%
21,231	MCDUFFIE	1,276	465	705	106	Schrenko	36.4%	55.3%	8.3%
10,847	MCINTOSH	308	178	68	62	Perdue	57.8%	22.1%	20.1%
14,074	MACON	289	237	32	20	Perdue	82.0%	11.1%	6.9%
25,730	MADISON	1,776	1,049	475	252	Perdue	59.1%	26.7%	14.2%
7,144	MARION	191	95	63	33	Perdue	49.7%	33.0%	17.3%
22,534	MERIWETHER	749	338	307	104	Perdue	45.1%	41.0%	13.9%
6,383	MILLER	76	21	33	22	Schrenko	27.6%	43.4%	28.9%
23,932	MITCHELL	542	327	144	71	Perdue	60.3%	26.6%	13.1%
21,757	MONROE	2,160	1,596	354	210	Perdue	73.9%	16.4%	9.7%
8,270	MONTGOMERY	605	494	78	33	Perdue	81.7%	12.9%	5.5%
15,457	MORGAN	1,353	892	300	161	Perdue	65.9%	22.2%	11.9%
36,506	MURRAY	1,828	949	470	409	Perdue	51.9%	25.7%	22.4%
186,291	MUSCOGEE	10,573	3,831	4,928	1,814	Schrenko	36.2%	46.6%	17.2%
62,001	NEWTON	4,430	2,418	1,294	718	Perdue	54.6%	29.2%	16.2%
26,225	OCONEE	4,112	2,756	796	560	Perdue	67.0%	19.4%	13.6%
12,635	OGLETHORPE	1,354	811	310	233	Perdue	59.9%	22.9%	17.2%
81,678	PAULDING	9,263	3,695	2,525	3,043	Perdue	39.9%	27.3%	32.9%
23,668	PEACH	1,436	1,249	119	68	Perdue	87.0%	8.3%	4.7%
22,983	PICKENS	1,762	806	469	487	Perdue	45.7%	26.6%	27.6%
15,636	PIERCE	1,416	1,184	169	63	Perdue	83.6%	11.9%	4.4%
13,688	PIKE	1,942	1,202	499	241	Perdue	61.9%	25.7%	12.4%
38,127	POLK	1,308	585	395	328	Perdue	44.7%	30.2%	25.1%
9,588	PULASKI	831	793	28	10	Perdue	95.4%	3.4%	1.2%
18,812	PUTNAM	1,199	817	230	152	Perdue	68.1%	19.2%	12.7%
2,598	QUITMAN	1			1	Byrne			100.0%
15,050	RABUN	767	423	197	147	Perdue	55.1%	25.7%	19.2%
7,791	RANDOLPH	41	14	13	14		34.1%	31.7%	34.1%
199,775	RICHMOND	8,652	2,094	5,748	810	Schrenko	24.2%	66.4%	9.4%
70,111	ROCKDALE	6,327	3,222	1,816	1,289	Perdue	50.9%	28.7%	20.4%
3,766	SCHLEY	96	54	30	12	Perdue	56.3%	31.3%	12.5%
15,374	SCREVEN	1,290	684	440	166	Perdue	53.0%	34.1%	12.9%
9,369	SEMINOLE	125	51	44	30	Perdue	40.8%	35.2%	24.0%
58,417	SPALDING	4,077	2,751	806	520	Perdue	67.5%	19.8%	12.8%
25,435	STEPHENS	707	273	236	198	Perdue	38.6%	33.4%	28.0%
5,252	STEWART	105	62	39	4	Perdue	59.0%	37.1%	3.8%
33,200	SUMTER	790	472	170	148	Perdue	59.7%	21.5%	18.7%
6,498	TALBOT	192	96	68	28	Perdue	50.0%	35.4%	14.6%
2,077	TALIAFERRO	86	53	24	9	Perdue	61.6%	27.9%	10.5%
22,305	TATTNALL	478	297	98	83	Perdue	62.1%	20.5%	17.4%
8,815	TAYLOR	306	240	43	23	Perdue	78.4%	14.1%	7.5%
11,794	TELFAIR	508	398	58	52	Perdue	78.3%	11.4%	10.2%
10,970	TERRELL	357	254	61	42	Perdue	71.1%	17.1%	11.8%
42,737	THOMAS	1,694	1,048	370	276	Perdue	61.9%	21.8%	16.3%
38,407	TIFT	2,097	1,327	525	245	Perdue	63.3%	25.0%	11.7%
26,067	TOOMBS	1,897	1,526	235	136	Perdue	80.4%	12.4%	7.2%
9,319	TOWNS	884	489	236	159	Perdue	55.3%	26.7%	18.0%
6,854	TREUTLEN	283	232	34	17	Perdue	82.0%	12.0%	6.0%

GEORGIA REPUBLICAN PRIMARY

GOVERNOR 2002

2000 Census Population	County	Total Vote	Perdue	Schrenko	Byrne	Winner	Percentage of Total Vote		
							Perdue	Schrenko	Byrne
58,779	TROUP	3,950	1,861	1,551	538	Perdue	47.1%	39.3%	13.6%
9,504	TURNER	228	149	58	21	Perdue	65.4%	25.4%	9.2%
10,590	TWIGGS	306	260	25	21	Perdue	85.0%	8.2%	6.9%
17,289	UNION	965	532	255	178	Perdue	55.1%	26.4%	18.4%
27,597	UPSON	1,551	970	427	154	Perdue	62.5%	27.5%	9.9%
61,053	WALKER	2,648	1,775	487	386	Perdue	67.0%	18.4%	14.6%
60,687	WALTON	6,800	3,947	1,687	1,166	Perdue	58.0%	24.8%	17.1%
35,483	WARE	2,101	1,780	229	92	Perdue	84.7%	10.9%	4.4%
6,336	WARREN	264	106	121	37	Schrenko	40.2%	45.8%	14.0%
21,176	WASHINGTON	307	220	53	34	Perdue	71.7%	17.3%	11.1%
26,565	WAYNE	663	430	159	74	Perdue	64.9%	24.0%	11.2%
2,390	WEBSTER	94	52	32	10	Perdue	55.3%	34.0%	10.6%
6,179	WHEELER	230	191	20	19	Perdue	83.0%	8.7%	8.3%
19,944	WHITE	1,178	582	383	213	Perdue	49.4%	32.5%	18.1%
83,525	WHITFIELD	3,755	2,416	854	485	Perdue	64.3%	22.7%	12.9%
8,577	WILCOX	559	454	81	24	Perdue	81.2%	14.5%	4.3%
10,687	WILKES	177	73	80	24	Schrenko	41.2%	45.2%	13.6%
10,220	WILKINSON	297	239	39	19	Perdue	80.5%	13.1%	6.4%
21,967	WORTH	1,005	602	275	128	Perdue	59.9%	27.4%	12.7%
8,186,453	TOTAL	511,463	259,966	142,911	108,586	Perdue	50.8%	27.9%	21.2%

GEORGIA REPUBLICAN PRIMARY

SENATOR 2002

2000 Census Population	County	Total Vote	Chambliss	Irvin	Brown	Winner	Percentage of Total Vote		
							Chambliss	Irvin	Brown
17,419	APPLING	1,070	950	64	56	Chambliss	88.8%	6.0%	5.2%
7,609	ATKINSON	374	311	36	27	Chambliss	83.2%	9.6%	7.2%
10,103	BACON	271	237	11	23	Chambliss	87.5%	4.1%	8.5%
4,074	BAKER	107	92	10	5	Chambliss	86.0%	9.3%	4.7%
44,700	BALDWIN	1,354	1,157	106	91	Chambliss	85.5%	7.8%	6.7%
14,422	BANKS	924	462	300	162	Chambliss	50.0%	32.5%	17.5%
46,144	BARROW	4,126	1,969	1,500	657	Chambliss	47.7%	36.4%	15.9%
76,019	BARTOW	5,908	3,115	1,810	983	Chambliss	52.7%	30.6%	16.6%
17,484	BEN HILL	769	654	79	36	Chambliss	85.0%	10.3%	4.7%
16,235	BERRIEN	344	303	24	17	Chambliss	88.1%	7.0%	4.9%
153,887	BIBB	8,800	8,207	350	243	Chambliss	93.3%	4.0%	2.8%
11,666	BLECKLEY	1,244	1,066	138	40	Chambliss	85.7%	11.1%	3.2%
14,629	BRANTLEY	706	502	91	113	Chambliss	71.1%	12.9%	16.0%
16,450	BROOKS	239	183	29	27	Chambliss	76.6%	12.1%	11.3%
23,417	BRYAN	1,171	703	249	219	Chambliss	60.0%	21.3%	18.7%
55,983	BULLOCH	3,222	2,335	561	326	Chambliss	72.5%	17.4%	10.1%
22,243	BURKE	1,216	701	309	206	Chambliss	57.6%	25.4%	16.9%
19,522	BUTTS	979	566	289	124	Chambliss	57.8%	29.5%	12.7%
6,320	CALHOUN	66	61	5		Chambliss	92.4%	7.6%	
43,664	CAMDEN	1,264	673	272	319	Chambliss	53.2%	21.5%	25.2%
9,577	CANDLER	389	275	64	50	Chambliss	70.7%	16.5%	12.9%
87,268	CARROLL	5,254	2,549	1,889	816	Chambliss	48.5%	36.0%	15.5%
53,282	CATOOSA	2,320	1,066	644	610	Chambliss	45.9%	27.8%	26.3%
10,282	CHARLTON	366	330	16	20	Chambliss	90.2%	4.4%	5.5%
232,048	CHATHAM	12,100	8,731	2,086	1,283	Chambliss	72.2%	17.2%	10.6%
14,882	CHATTAHOOCHEE	71	40	13	18	Chambliss	56.3%	18.3%	25.4%
25,470	CHATTOOGA	563	271	174	118	Chambliss	48.1%	30.9%	21.0%
141,903	CHEROKEE	20,797	11,497	6,672	2,628	Chambliss	55.3%	32.1%	12.6%
101,489	CLARKE	3,315	2,122	764	429	Chambliss	64.0%	23.0%	12.9%
3,357	CLAY	30	20	5	5	Chambliss	66.7%	16.7%	16.7%

GEORGIA REPUBLICAN PRIMARY

SENATOR 2002

2000 Census Population	County	Total Vote	Chambliss	Irvin	Brown	Winner	Percentage of Total Vote		
							Chambliss	Irvin	Brown
236,517	CLAYTON	4,739	2,432	1,577	730	Chambliss	51.3%	33.3%	15.4%
6,878	CLINCH	149	133	8	8	Chambliss	89.3%	5.4%	5.4%
607,751	COBB	52,344	32,632	14,971	4,741	Chambliss	62.3%	28.6%	9.1%
37,413	COFFEE	979	876	63	40	Chambliss	89.5%	6.4%	4.1%
42,053	COLQUITT	2,781	2,534	146	101	Chambliss	91.1%	5.2%	3.6%
89,288	COLUMBIA	10,398	5,741	2,620	2,037	Chambliss	55.2%	25.2%	19.6%
15,771	COOK	431	380	35	16	Chambliss	88.2%	8.1%	3.7%
89,215	COWETA	7,635	4,420	2,201	1,014	Chambliss	57.9%	28.8%	13.3%
12,495	CRAWFORD	632	570	27	35	Chambliss	90.2%	4.3%	5.5%
21,996	CRISP	1,073	885	144	44	Chambliss	82.5%	13.4%	4.1%
15,154	DADE	872	327	225	320	Chambliss	37.5%	25.8%	36.7%
15,999	DAWSON	2,079	1,103	677	299	Chambliss	53.1%	32.6%	14.4%
28,240	DECATUR	416	270	73	73	Chambliss	64.9%	17.5%	17.5%
665,865	DEKALB	6,241	3,343	1,942	956	Chambliss	53.6%	31.1%	15.3%
19,171	DODGE	1,365	1,235	63	67	Chambliss	90.5%	4.6%	4.9%
11,525	DOOLY	554	498	30	26	Chambliss	89.9%	5.4%	4.7%
96,065	DOUGHERTY	1,816	1,577	180	59	Chambliss	86.8%	9.9%	3.2%
92,174	DOUGLAS	8,286	4,482	2,820	984	Chambliss	54.1%	34.0%	11.9%
12,354	EARLY	255	194	30	31	Chambliss	76.1%	11.8%	12.2%
3,754	ECHOLS	10	8	2		Chambliss	80.0%	20.0%	
37,535	EFFINGHAM	3,590	2,270	701	619	Chambliss	63.2%	19.5%	17.2%
20,511	ELBERT	539	222	196	121	Chambliss	41.2%	36.4%	22.4%
21,837	EMANUEL	869	576	176	117	Chambliss	66.3%	20.3%	13.5%
10,495	EVANS	429	296	75	58	Chambliss	69.0%	17.5%	13.5%
19,798	FANNIN	2,316	1,017	907	392	Chambliss	43.9%	39.2%	16.9%
91,263	FAYETTE	11,231	6,341	3,533	1,357	Chambliss	56.5%	31.5%	12.1%
90,565	FLOYD	5,120	2,781	1,623	716	Chambliss	54.3%	31.7%	14.0%
98,407	FORSYTH	15,062	7,951	5,407	1,704	Chambliss	52.8%	35.9%	11.3%
20,285	FRANKLIN	761	311	296	154	Chambliss	40.9%	38.9%	20.2%
816,006	FULTON	32,284	17,727	11,841	2,716	Chambliss	54.9%	36.7%	8.4%
23,456	GILMER	1,983	1,016	656	311	Chambliss	51.2%	33.1%	15.7%
2,556	GLASCOCK	164	67	63	34	Chambliss	40.9%	38.4%	20.7%
67,568	GLYNN	6,118	4,033	1,093	992	Chambliss	65.9%	17.9%	16.2%
44,104	GORDON	2,193	1,096	673	424	Chambliss	50.0%	30.7%	19.3%
23,659	GRADY	421	285	75	61	Chambliss	67.7%	17.8%	14.5%
14,406	GREENE	928	666	188	74	Chambliss	71.8%	20.3%	8.0%
588,448	GWINNETT	57,266	31,552	17,747	7,967	Chambliss	55.1%	31.0%	13.9%
35,902	HABERSHAM	1,890	888	751	251	Chambliss	47.0%	39.7%	13.3%
139,277	HALL	12,681	7,082	3,942	1,657	Chambliss	55.8%	31.1%	13.1%
10,076	HANCOCK	75	58	12	5	Chambliss	77.3%	16.0%	6.7%
25,690	HARALSON	1,490	784	493	213	Chambliss	52.6%	33.1%	14.3%
23,695	HARRIS	1,672	926	392	354	Chambliss	55.4%	23.4%	21.2%
22,997	HART	1,014	475	299	240	Chambliss	46.8%	29.5%	23.7%
11,012	HEARD	520	266	153	101	Chambliss	51.2%	29.4%	19.4%
119,341	HENRY	10,242	5,643	3,236	1,363	Chambliss	55.1%	31.6%	13.3%
110,765	HOUSTON	12,292	11,269	661	362	Chambliss	91.7%	5.4%	2.9%
9,931	IRWIN	631	501	101	29	Chambliss	79.4%	16.0%	4.6%
41,589	JACKSON	3,478	1,842	1,174	462	Chambliss	53.0%	33.8%	13.3%
11,426	JASPER	745	526	137	82	Chambliss	70.6%	18.4%	11.0%
12,684	JEFF DAVIS	491	445	19	27	Chambliss	90.6%	3.9%	5.5%
17,266	JEFFERSON	426	200	164	62	Chambliss	46.9%	38.5%	14.6%
8,575	JENKINS	376	232	71	73	Chambliss	61.7%	18.9%	19.4%
8,560	JOHNSON	632	552	36	44	Chambliss	87.3%	5.7%	7.0%
23,639	JONES	1,380	1,256	72	52	Chambliss	91.0%	5.2%	3.8%
15,912	LAMAR	1,307	1,065	154	88	Chambliss	81.5%	11.8%	6.7%
7,241	LANIER	135	112	13	10	Chambliss	83.0%	9.6%	7.4%
44,874	LAURENS	2,395	2,160	125	110	Chambliss	90.2%	5.2%	4.6%
24,757	LEE	2,223	1,928	217	78	Chambliss	86.7%	9.8%	3.5%
61,610	LIBERTY	548	322	104	122	Chambliss	58.8%	19.0%	22.3%
8,348	LINCOLN	651	278	203	170	Chambliss	42.7%	31.2%	26.1%

GEORGIA REPUBLICAN PRIMARY
SENATOR 2002

2000 Census Population	County	Total Vote	Chambliss	Irvin	Brown	Winner	Percentage of Total Vote		
							Chambliss	Irvin	Brown
10,304	LONG	169	91	36	42	Chambliss	53.8%	21.3%	24.9%
92,115	LOWNDES	3,779	3,233	363	183	Chambliss	85.6%	9.6%	4.8%
21,016	LUMPKIN	2,054	971	713	370	Chambliss	47.3%	34.7%	18.0%
21,231	MCDUFFIE	1,186	633	334	219	Chambliss	53.4%	28.2%	18.5%
10,847	MCINTOSH	296	167	58	71	Chambliss	56.4%	19.6%	24.0%
14,074	MACON	281	257	11	13	Chambliss	91.5%	3.9%	4.6%
25,730	MADISON	1,600	783	532	285	Chambliss	48.9%	33.3%	17.8%
7,144	MARION	183	114	36	33	Chambliss	62.3%	19.7%	18.0%
22,534	MERIWETHER	707	355	236	116	Chambliss	50.2%	33.4%	16.4%
6,383	MILLER	75	56	11	8	Chambliss	74.7%	14.7%	10.7%
23,932	MITCHELL	542	490	38	14	Chambliss	90.4%	7.0%	2.6%
21,757	MONROE	2,165	1,918	132	115	Chambliss	88.6%	6.1%	5.3%
8,270	MONTGOMERY	572	496	37	39	Chambliss	86.7%	6.5%	6.8%
15,457	MORGAN	1,310	835	338	137	Chambliss	63.7%	25.8%	10.5%
36,506	MURRAY	1,674	531	585	558	Irvin	31.7%	34.9%	33.3%
186,291	MUSCOGEE	10,280	5,173	3,528	1,579	Chambliss	50.3%	34.3%	15.4%
62,001	NEWTON	4,320	2,503	1,338	479	Chambliss	57.9%	31.0%	11.1%
26,225	OCONEE	3,927	2,368	967	592	Chambliss	60.3%	24.6%	15.1%
12,635	OGLETHORPE	1,281	681	408	192	Chambliss	53.2%	31.9%	15.0%
81,678	PAULDING	8,754	4,748	2,804	1,202	Chambliss	54.2%	32.0%	13.7%
23,668	PEACH	1,406	1,272	84	50	Chambliss	90.5%	6.0%	3.6%
22,983	PICKENS	1,671	972	502	197	Chambliss	58.2%	30.0%	11.8%
15,636	PIERCE	1,301	1,125	85	91	Chambliss	86.5%	6.5%	7.0%
13,688	PIKE	1,803	1,130	449	224	Chambliss	62.7%	24.9%	12.4%
38,127	POLK	1,208	624	364	220	Chambliss	51.7%	30.1%	18.2%
9,588	PULASKI	790	727	35	28	Chambliss	92.0%	4.4%	3.5%
18,812	PUTNAM	1,166	915	167	84	Chambliss	78.5%	14.3%	7.2%
2,598	QUITMAN	1	1			Chambliss	100.0%		
15,050	RABUN	737	303	306	128	Irvin	41.1%	41.5%	17.4%
7,791	RANDOLPH	42	34	7	1	Chambliss	81.0%	16.7%	2.4%
199,775	RICHMOND	8,036	4,760	2,151	1,125	Chambliss	59.2%	26.8%	14.0%
70,111	ROCKDALE	6,117	3,504	2,042	571	Chambliss	57.3%	33.4%	9.3%
3,766	SCHLEY	93	71	13	9	Chambliss	76.3%	14.0%	9.7%
15,374	SCREVEN	1,139	659	271	209	Chambliss	57.9%	23.8%	18.3%
9,369	SEMINOLE	125	82	21	22	Chambliss	65.6%	16.8%	17.6%
58,417	SPALDING	3,762	2,164	1,079	519	Chambliss	57.5%	28.7%	13.8%
25,435	STEPHENS	677	281	270	126	Chambliss	41.5%	39.9%	18.6%
5,252	STEWART	93	68	14	11	Chambliss	73.1%	15.1%	11.8%
33,200	SUMTER	782	669	74	39	Chambliss	85.5%	9.5%	5.0%
6,498	TALBOT	173	109	30	34	Chambliss	63.0%	17.3%	19.7%
2,077	TALIAFERRO	74	36	27	11	Chambliss	48.6%	36.5%	14.9%
22,305	TATTNALL	458	303	81	74	Chambliss	66.2%	17.7%	16.2%
8,815	TAYLOR	296	243	20	33	Chambliss	82.1%	6.8%	11.1%
11,794	TELFAIR	542	483	34	25	Chambliss	89.1%	6.3%	4.6%
10,970	TERRELL	362	192	153	17	Chambliss	53.0%	42.3%	4.7%
42,737	THOMAS	1,692	1,354	221	117	Chambliss	80.0%	13.1%	6.9%
38,407	TIFT	2,214	1,930	171	113	Chambliss	87.2%	7.7%	5.1%
26,067	TOOMBS	1,715	1,355	184	176	Chambliss	79.0%	10.7%	10.3%
9,319	TOWNS	839	418	298	123	Chambliss	49.8%	35.5%	14.7%
6,854	TREUTLEN	280	254	18	8	Chambliss	90.7%	6.4%	2.9%
58,779	TROUP	3,732	1,933	1,116	683	Chambliss	51.8%	29.9%	18.3%
9,504	TURNER	244	192	32	20	Chambliss	78.7%	13.1%	8.2%
10,590	TWIGGS	307	278	12	17	Chambliss	90.6%	3.9%	5.5%
17,289	UNION	920	486	327	107	Chambliss	52.8%	35.5%	11.6%
27,597	UPSON	1,547	1,303	144	100	Chambliss	84.2%	9.3%	6.5%
61,053	WALKER	2,416	1,124	667	625	Chambliss	46.5%	27.6%	25.9%
60,687	WALTON	6,548	3,756	2,039	753	Chambliss	57.4%	31.1%	11.5%
35,483	WARE	2,065	1,882	109	74	Chambliss	91.1%	5.3%	3.6%
6,336	WARREN	226	123	60	43	Chambliss	54.4%	26.5%	19.0%
21,176	WASHINGTON	284	229	23	32	Chambliss	80.6%	8.1%	11.3%

GEORGIA REPUBLICAN PRIMARY

SENATOR 2002

2000 Census Population	County	Total Vote	Chambliss	Irvin	Brown	Winner	Percentage of Total Vote		
							Chambliss	Irvin	Brown
26,565	WAYNE	631	424	111	96	Chambliss	67.2%	17.6%	15.2%
2,390	WEBSTER	91	64	20	7	Chambliss	70.3%	22.0%	7.7%
6,179	WHEELER	230	207	16	7	Chambliss	90.0%	7.0%	3.0%
19,944	WHITE	1,139	632	386	121	Chambliss	55.5%	33.9%	10.6%
83,525	WHITFIELD	3,467	1,803	991	673	Chambliss	52.0%	28.6%	19.4%
8,577	WILCOX	555	460	63	32	Chambliss	82.9%	11.4%	5.8%
10,687	WILKES	173	85	57	31	Chambliss	49.1%	32.9%	17.9%
10,220	WILKINSON	299	270	11	18	Chambliss	90.3%	3.7%	6.0%
21,967	WORTH	1,007	874	99	34	Chambliss	86.8%	9.8%	3.4%
8,186,453	TOTAL	491,612	300,371	132,132	59,109	Chambliss	61.1%	26.9%	12.0%

HAWAII

GOVERNOR
Linda Lingle (R). Elected 2002 to a four-year term.

SENATORS (2 Democrats)
Daniel K. Akaka (D). Reelected 2000 to a six-year term. Previously elected 1994 and 1990 to fill out the remaining four years of the term vacated by the death of Senator Spark M. Matsunaga (D); had been appointed May 1990 to fill this vacancy.

Daniel K. Inouye (D). Reelected 1998 to a six-year term. Previously elected 1992, 1986, 1980, 1974, 1968, 1962.

REPRESENTATIVES (2 Democrats)
1. Neil Abercrombie (D)   2. Ed Case (D)*

Note: The asterisk (*) indicates that Ed Case won a special election in January 2003 to fill the seat of Patsy T. Mink (D) in the 108th Congress. Mink died in September 2002, but was posthumously reelected in November 2002.

POSTWAR VOTE FOR PRESIDENT

| | | Republican | | Democratic | | | | Percentage | | | |
| | | | | | | | | Total Vote | | Major Vote | |
Year	Total Vote	Vote	Candidate	Vote	Candidate	Other Vote	Plurality	Rep.	Dem.	Rep.	Dem.
2000**	367,951	137,845	Bush, George W.	205,286	Gore, Al	24,820	67,441 D	37.5%	55.8%	40.2%	59.8%
1996**	360,120	113,943	Dole, Bob	205,012	Clinton, Bill	41,165	91,069 D	31.6%	56.9%	35.7%	64.3%
1992**	372,842	136,822	Bush, George	179,310	Clinton, Bill	56,710	42,488 D	36.7%	48.1%	43.3%	56.7%
1988	354,461	158,625	Bush, George	192,364	Dukakis, Michael S.	3,472	33,739 D	44.8%	54.3%	45.2%	54.8%
1984	335,846	185,050	Reagan, Ronald	147,154	Mondale, Walter F.	3,642	37,896 R	55.1%	43.8%	55.7%	44.3%
1980**	303,287	130,112	Reagan, Ronald	135,879	Carter, Jimmy	37,296	5,767 D	42.9%	44.8%	48.9%	51.1%
1976	291,301	140,003	Ford, Gerald R.	147,375	Carter, Jimmy	3,923	7,372 D	48.1%	50.6%	48.7%	51.3%
1972	270,274	168,865	Nixon, Richard M.	101,409	McGovern, George S.		67,456 R	62.5%	37.5%	62.5%	37.5%
1968	236,218	91,425	Nixon, Richard M.	141,324	Humphrey, Hubert H.	3,469	49,899 D	38.7%	59.8%	39.3%	60.7%
1964	207,271	44,022	Goldwater, Barry M.	163,249	Johnson, Lyndon B.		119,227 D	21.2%	78.8%	21.2%	78.8%
1960	184,705	92,295	Nixon, Richard M.	92,410	Kennedy, John F.		115 D	50.0%	50.0%	50.0%	50.0%

In 2000 the other vote column includes 21,623 votes cast for Green (Nader). In 1996 the other vote column includes 27,358 votes cast for Perot. In 1992 the other vote column includes 53,003 votes cast for Perot. In 1980 the other column includes 32,021 votes for Independent (Anderson). Hawaii was formally admitted as a state in August 1959.

HAWAII

POSTWAR VOTE FOR GOVERNOR

Year	Total Vote	Republican Vote	Republican Candidate	Democratic Vote	Democratic Candidate	Other Vote	Rep.-Dem. Plurality	Total Vote Rep.	Total Vote Dem.	Major Vote Rep.	Major Vote Dem.
2002	382,110	197,009	Lingle, Linda	179,647	Hirono, Mazie K.	5,454	17,362 R	51.6%	47.0%	52.3%	47.7%
1998	407,556	198,952	Lingle, Linda	204,206	Cayetano, Benjamin J.	4,398	5,254 D	48.8%	50.1%	49.3%	50.7%
1994**	369,013	107,908	Saiki, Patricia	134,978	Cayetano, Benjamin J.	126,127	27,070 D	29.2%	36.6%	44.4%	55.6%
1990	340,132	131,310	Hemmings, Fred	203,491	Waihee, John	5,331	72,181 D	38.6%	59.8%	39.2%	60.8%
1986	334,115	160,460	Anderson, D. G.	173,655	Waihee, John		13,195 D	48.0%	52.0%	48.0%	52.0%
1982**	311,853	81,507	Anderson, D. G.	141,043	Ariyoshi, George R.	89,303	59,536 D	26.1%	45.2%	36.6%	63.4%
1978	281,587	124,610	Leopold, John	153,394	Ariyoshi, George R.	3,583	28,784 D	44.3%	54.5%	44.8%	55.2%
1974	249,650	113,388	Crossley, Randolph	136,262	Ariyoshi, George R.		22,874 D	45.4%	54.6%	45.4%	54.6%
1970	239,061	101,249	King, Samuel P.	137,812	Burns, John A.		36,563 D	42.4%	57.6%	42.4%	57.6%
1966	213,164	104,324	Crossley, Randolph	108,840	Burns, John A.		4,516 D	48.9%	51.1%	48.9%	51.1%
1962	196,015	81,707	Quinn, William F.	114,308	Burns, John A.		32,601 D	41.7%	58.3%	41.7%	58.3%
1959S	168,662	86,213	Quinn, William F.	82,074	Burns, John A.	375	4,139 R	51.1%	48.7%	51.2%	48.8%

In 1994 the Best Party candidate (Frank F. Fasi) ran second with 113,158 votes (30.7% of the total vote) and the plurality of the three-party vote was 21,820 (D). In 1982 other vote was for Independent Democrat (Frank F. Fasi) who ran second with 89,303 votes (28.6% of the total vote) and the plurality of the three-party vote was 51,740 (D). The 1959 election was for a short term pending the regular vote in 1962.

POSTWAR VOTE FOR SENATOR

Year	Total Vote	Republican Vote	Republican Candidate	Democratic Vote	Democratic Candidate	Other Vote	Rep.-Dem. Plurality	Total Vote Rep.	Total Vote Dem.	Major Vote Rep.	Major Vote Dem.
2000	345,623	84,701	Carroll, John S.	251,215	Akaka, Daniel K.	9,707	166,514 D	24.5%	72.7%	25.2%	74.8%
1998	398,124	70,964	Young, Crystal	315,252	Inouye, Daniel K.	11,908	244,288 D	17.8%	79.2%	18.4%	81.6%
1994	356,902	86,320	Hustace, Maria M.	256,189	Akaka, Daniel K.	14,393	169,869 D	24.2%	71.8%	25.2%	74.8%
1992	363,662	97,928	Reed, Rick	208,266	Inouye, Daniel K.	57,468	110,338 D	26.9%	57.3%	32.0%	68.0%
1990S	349,666	155,978	Saiki, Patricia	188,901	Akaka, Daniel K.	4,787	32,923 D	44.6%	54.0%	45.2%	54.8%
1988	323,876	66,987	Hustace, Maria M.	247,941	Matsunaga, Spark M.	8,948	180,954 D	20.7%	76.6%	21.3%	78.7%
1986	328,797	86,910	Hutchinson, Frank	241,887	Inouye, Daniel K.		154,977 D	26.4%	73.6%	26.4%	73.6%
1982	306,410	52,071	Brown, Clarence J.	245,386	Matsunaga, Spark M.	8,953	193,315 D	17.0%	80.1%	17.5%	82.5%
1980	288,006	53,068	Brown, Cooper	224,485	Inouye, Daniel K.	10,453	171,417 D	18.4%	77.9%	19.1%	80.9%
1976	302,092	122,724	Quinn, William F.	162,305	Matsunaga, Spark M.	17,063	39,581 D	40.6%	53.7%	43.1%	56.9%
1974	250,221		—	207,454	Inouye, Daniel K.	42,767	207,454 D		82.9%		100.0%
1970	240,760	124,163	Fong, Hiram L.	116,597	Heftel, Cecil		7,566 R	51.6%	48.4%	51.6%	48.4%
1968	226,927	34,008	Thiessen, Wayne C.	189,248	Inouye, Daniel K.	3,671	155,240 D	15.0%	83.4%	15.2%	84.8%
1964	208,814	110,747	Fong, Hiram L.	96,789	Gill, Thomas P.	1,278	13,958 R	53.0%	46.4%	53.4%	46.6%
1962	196,361	60,067	Dillingham, Ben F.	136,294	Inouye, Daniel K.		76,227 D	30.6%	69.4%	30.6%	69.4%
1959**	164,808	87,161	Fong, Hiram L.	77,647	Fasi, Frank F.		9,514 R	52.9%	47.1%	52.9%	47.1%
1959S	163,875	79,123	Tsukiyama, W. C.	83,700	Long, Oren E.	1,052	4,577 D	48.3%	51.1%	48.6%	51.4%

The 1990 election was for a short term to fill a vacancy. The two 1959 elections were held to indeterminate terms and the Senate later determined by lot that Senator Long would serve a short term, Senator Fong a long term.

HAWAII

Congressional districts first established for elections held in 2002
2 members

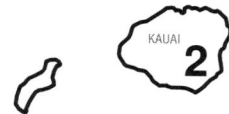

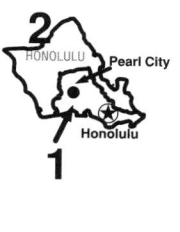

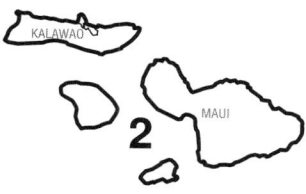

HAWAII

GOVERNOR 2002

2000 Census Population	County	Total Vote	Republican	Democratic	Other	Rep.-Dem. Plurality	Percentage Total Vote Rep.	Dem.	Major Vote Rep.	Dem.
148,677	HAWAII	49,968	25,530	23,602	836	1,928 R	51.1%	47.2%	52.0%	48.0%
876,156	HONOLULU	267,894	141,315	123,180	3,399	18,135 R	52.8%	46.0%	53.4%	46.6%
58,463	KAUAI	23,104	9,426	13,352	326	3,926 D	40.8%	57.8%	41.4%	58.6%
128,094	MAUI	41,144	20,738	19,513	893	1,225 R	50.4%	47.4%	51.5%	48.5%
1,211,537	TOTAL	382,110	197,009	179,647	5,454	17,362 R	51.6%	47.0%	52.3%	47.7%

Note: The 2000 Census includes 147 people in Kalawao County; their votes are part of the Maui County results.

HAWAII

HOUSE OF REPRESENTATIVES

CD	Year	Total Vote	Republican Vote	Candidate	Democratic Vote	Candidate	Other Vote	Rep.-Dem. Plurality	Percentage Total Vote Rep.	Dem.	Major Vote Rep.	Dem.
1	2002	180,733	45,032	Terry, Mark	131,673	Abercrombie, Neil*	4,028	86,641 D	24.9%	72.9%	25.5%	74.5%
2	2002	179,251	71,661	McDermott, Bob	100,671	Mink, Patsy T.*	6,919	29,010 D	40.0%	56.2%	41.6%	58.4%
Total	2002	359,984	116,693		232,344		10,947	115,651 D	32.4%	64.5%	33.4%	66.6%

An asterisk (*) denotes incumbent.

HAWAII

GENERAL AND PRIMARY ELECTIONS

2002 GENERAL ELECTIONS

Governor   Other vote was 2,561 Natural Law (Kau`i "Bu La`ia" Hill); 1,364 Libertarian (Tracy Ahn Ryan); 1,147 Non Partisan (Jim Brewer); 382 Free Energy (Daniel H. Cunningham).

House   Other vote was:

CD 1   4,028 Libertarian (James H. Bracken).
CD 2   4,719 Libertarian (Jeff Mallan); 2,200 Natural Law (Nicholas Bedworth).

2002 PRIMARY ELECTIONS

Primary   September 21, 2002   **Registration**   667,679   No Party Registration
(as of Aug. 30, 2002)

Primary Type   Open—Any registered voter could vote in the party primary of their choice.

Note: An asterisk (*) denotes incumbent.

HAWAII
GENERAL AND PRIMARY ELECTIONS

REPUBLICAN PRIMARIES			DEMOCRATIC PRIMARIES		
Governor	Linda Lingle	70,808	89.8%	Mazie K. Hirono	76,709	41.2%
	John Carroll	7,616	9.7%	Ed Case	74,096	39.8%
	Crystal Young	454	0.6%	D.G. "Andy" Anderson	33,384	17.9%
				George Nitta Jr.	747	0.4%
				Art P. Reyes	568	0.3%
				Joe Fernandez	491	0.3%
	TOTAL	78,878		TOTAL	185,995	
Congressional District 1	Mark Terry	8,826	38.2%	Neil Abercrombie*	69,222	100.0%
	Stephen N. Bischoff	8,065	34.9%			
	Harry J. Friel	3,957	17.1%			
	Opassi White	2,266	9.8%			
	TOTAL	23,114				
Congressional District 2	Bob McDermott	20,180	71.7%	Patsy T. Mink*	67,246	82.6%
	James M. "The Ump" Donovan	7,948	28.3%	Steve Tataii	14,178	17.4%
	TOTAL	28,128		TOTAL	81,424	

HAWAII REPUBLICAN PRIMARY

GOVERNOR 2002

2000 Census Population	County	Total Vote	Lingle	Other	Winner	Percentage of Total Vote	
						Lingle	Other
148,677	HAWAII	9,346	8,636	710	Lingle	92.4%	7.6%
876,156	HONOLULU	57,398	50,843	6,555	Lingle	88.6%	11.4%
58,463	KAUAI	3,494	3,250	244	Lingle	93.0%	7.0%
128,094	MAUI	8,640	8,079	561	Lingle	93.5%	6.5%
1,211,537	TOTAL	78,878	70,808	8,070	Lingle	89.8%	10.2%

Note: The 2000 Census includes 147 people in Kalawao County; their votes are part of the Maui County returns.

HAWAII DEMOCRATIC PRIMARY

GOVERNOR 2002

2000 Census Population	County	Total Vote	Hirono	Case	Anderson	Other	Winner	Percentage of Total Vote			
								Hirono	Case	Anderson	Other
148,677	HAWAII	25,133	11,052	10,680	3,166	235	Hirono	44.0%	42.5%	12.6%	0.9%
876,156	HONOLULU	128,779	51,245	53,108	23,183	1,243	Case	39.8%	41.2%	18.0%	1.0%
58,463	KAUAI	14,009	6,584	5,093	2,208	124	Hirono	47.0%	36.4%	15.8%	0.9%
128,094	MAUI	18,074	7,828	5,215	4,827	204	Hirono	43.3%	28.9%	26.7%	1.1%
1,211,537	TOTAL	185,995	76,709	74,096	33,384	1,806	Hironi	41.2%	39.8%	17.9%	1.0%

Note: The 2000 Census includes 147 people in Kalawao County; their votes are part of the Maui County returns.

IDAHO

GOVERNOR
Dirk Kempthorne (R). Reelected 2002 to a four-year term. Previously elected 1998.

SENATORS (2 Republicans)
Larry E. Craig (R). Reelected 2002 to a six-year term. Previously elected 1996, 1990.

Michael D. Crapo (R). Elected 1998 to a six-year term.

REPRESENTATIVES (2 Republicans)
1. C. L. "Butch" Otter (R)   2. Mike Simpson (R)

POSTWAR VOTE FOR PRESIDENT

| | | Republican | | Democratic | | Other | | Percentage | | | |
| | | | | | | | | Total Vote | | Major Vote | |
Year	Total Vote	Vote	Candidate	Vote	Candidate	Vote	Plurality	Rep.	Dem.	Rep.	Dem.
2000**	501,621	336,937	Bush, George W.	138,637	Gore, Al	26,047	198,300 R	67.2%	27.6%	70.8%	29.2%
1996**	491,719	256,595	Dole, Bob	165,443	Clinton, Bill	69,681	91,152 R	52.2%	33.6%	60.8%	39.2%
1992**	482,142	202,645	Bush, George	137,013	Clinton, Bill	142,484	65,632 R	42.0%	28.4%	59.7%	40.3%
1988	408,968	253,881	Bush, George	147,272	Dukakis, Michael S.	7,815	106,609 R	62.1%	36.0%	63.3%	36.7%
1984	411,144	297,523	Reagan, Ronald	108,510	Mondale, Walter F.	5,111	189,013 R	72.4%	26.4%	73.3%	26.7%
1980**	437,431	290,699	Reagan, Ronald	110,192	Carter, Jimmy	36,540	180,507 R	66.5%	25.2%	72.5%	27.5%
1976	344,071	204,151	Ford, Gerald R.	126,549	Carter, Jimmy	13,371	77,602 R	59.3%	36.8%	61.7%	38.3%
1972	310,379	199,384	Nixon, Richard M.	80,826	McGovern, George S.	30,169	118,558 R	64.2%	26.0%	71.2%	28.8%
1968	291,183	165,369	Nixon, Richard M.	89,273	Humphrey, Hubert H.	36,541	76,096 R	56.8%	30.7%	64.9%	35.1%
1964	292,477	143,557	Goldwater, Barry M.	148,920	Johnson, Lyndon B.		5,363 D	49.1%	50.9%	49.1%	50.9%
1960	300,450	161,597	Nixon, Richard M.	138,853	Kennedy, John F.		22,744 R	53.8%	46.2%	53.8%	46.2%
1956	272,989	166,979	Eisenhower, Dwight D.	105,868	Stevenson, Adlai E.	142	61,111 R	61.2%	38.8%	61.2%	38.8%
1952	276,254	180,707	Eisenhower, Dwight D.	95,081	Stevenson, Adlai E.	466	85,626 R	65.4%	34.4%	65.5%	34.5%
1948	214,816	101,514	Dewey, Thomas E.	107,370	Truman, Harry S.	5,932	5,856 D	47.3%	50.0%	48.6%	51.4%

In 2000 the other vote column includes 12,292 votes cast for Green (Nader). In 1996 the other vote column includes 62,518 votes cast for Perot. In 1992 the other vote column includes 130,395 votes cast for Perot. In 1980 the other column includes 27,058 votes for Independent (Anderson).

IDAHO

POSTWAR VOTE FOR GOVERNOR

Year	Total Vote	Republican		Democratic		Other Vote	Rep.-Dem. Plurality	Percentage			
								Total Vote		Major Vote	
		Vote	Candidate	Vote	Candidate			Rep.	Dem.	Rep.	Dem.
2002	411,477	231,566	Kempthorne, Dirk	171,711	Brady, Jerry M.	8,200	59,855 R	56.3%	41.7%	57.4%	42.6%
1998	381,248	258,095	Kempthorne, Dirk	110,815	Huntley, Robert C.	12,338	147,280 R	67.7%	29.1%	70.0%	30.0%
1994	413,346	216,123	Batt, Phil	181,363	EchoHawk, Larry	15,860	34,760 R	52.3%	43.9%	54.4%	45.6%
1990	320,610	101,937	Fairchild, Roger	218,673	Andrus, Cecil D.		116,736 D	31.8%	68.2%	31.8%	68.2%
1986	387,426	189,794	Leroy, David H.	193,429	Andrus, Cecil D.	4,203	3,635 D	49.0%	49.9%	49.5%	50.5%
1982	326,522	161,157	Batt, Philip	165,365	Evans, John V.		4,208 D	49.4%	50.6%	49.4%	50.6%
1978	288,566	114,149	Larsen, Allan	169,540	Evans, John V.	4,877	55,391 D	39.6%	58.8%	40.2%	59.8%
1974	259,632	68,731	Murphy, Jack M.	184,142	Andrus, Cecil D.	6,759	115,411 D	26.5%	70.9%	27.2%	72.8%
1970	245,112	117,108	Samuelson, Don	128,004	Andrus, Cecil D.		10,896 D	47.8%	52.2%	47.8%	52.2%
1966	252,593	104,586	Samuelson, Don	93,744	Andrus, Cecil D.	54,263	10,842 R	41.4%	37.1%	52.7%	47.3%
1962	255,454	139,578	Smylie, Robert E.	115,876	Smith, Vernon K.		23,702 R	54.6%	45.4%	54.6%	45.4%
1958	239,046	121,810	Smylie, Robert E.	117,236	Derr, A. M.		4,574 R	51.0%	49.0%	51.0%	49.0%
1954	228,685	124,038	Smylie, Robert E.	104,647	Hamilton, Clark		19,391 R	54.2%	45.8%	54.2%	45.8%
1950	204,792	107,642	Jordan, Len B.	97,150	Wright, Calvin E.		10,492 R	52.6%	47.4%	52.6%	47.4%
1946	181,364	102,233	Robins, C. A.	79,131	Williams, Arnold		23,102 R	56.4%	43.6%	56.4%	43.6%

POSTWAR VOTE FOR SENATOR

Year	Total Vote	Republican		Democratic		Other Vote	Rep.-Dem. Plurality	Percentage			
								Total Vote		Major Vote	
		Vote	Candidate	Vote	Candidate			Rep.	Dem.	Rep.	Dem.
2002	408,544	266,215	Craig, Larry E.	132,975	Blinken, Alan	9,354	133,240 R	65.2%	32.5%	66.7%	33.3%
1998	378,174	262,966	Crapo, Michael D.	107,375	Mauk, Bill	7,833	155,591 R	69.5%	28.4%	71.0%	29.0%
1996	497,233	283,532	Craig, Larry E.	198,422	Minnick, Walt	15,279	85,110 R	57.0%	39.9%	58.8%	41.2%
1992	478,522	270,468	Kempthorne, Dirk	208,036	Stallings, Richard	18	62,432 R	56.5%	43.5%	56.5%	43.5%
1990	315,936	193,641	Craig, Larry E.	122,295	Twilegar, Ron J.		71,346 R	61.3%	38.7%	61.3%	38.7%
1986	382,024	196,958	Symms, Steven D.	185,066	Evans, John V.		11,892 R	51.6%	48.4%	51.6%	48.4%
1984	406,168	293,193	McClure, James A.	105,591	Busch, Peter M.	7,384	187,602 R	72.2%	26.0%	73.5%	26.5%
1980	439,647	218,701	Symms, Steven D.	214,439	Church, Frank	6,507	4,262 R	49.7%	48.8%	50.5%	49.5%
1978	284,047	194,412	McClure, James A.	89,635	Jensen, Dwight		104,777 R	68.4%	31.6%	68.4%	31.6%
1974	258,847	109,072	Smith, Robert L.	145,140	Church, Frank	4,635	36,068 D	42.1%	56.1%	42.9%	57.1%
1972	309,602	161,804	McClure, James A.	140,913	Davis, William E.	6,885	20,891 R	52.3%	45.5%	53.5%	46.5%
1968	287,876	114,394	Hansen, George V.	173,482	Church, Frank		59,088 D	39.7%	60.3%	39.7%	60.3%
1966	252,456	139,819	Jordan, Len B.	112,637	Harding, Ralph R.		27,182 R	55.4%	44.6%	55.4%	44.6%
1962	258,786	117,129	Hawley, Jack	141,657	Church, Frank		24,528 D	45.3%	54.7%	45.3%	54.7%
1962S	257,677	131,279	Jordan, Len B.	126,398	Pfost, Gracie		4,881 R	50.9%	49.1%	50.9%	49.1%
1960	292,096	152,648	Dworshak, Henry C.	139,448	McLaughlin, Bob		13,200 R	52.3%	47.7%	52.3%	47.7%
1956	265,292	102,781	Welker, Herman	149,096	Church, Frank	13,415	46,315 D	38.7%	56.2%	40.8%	59.2%
1954	226,408	142,269	Dworshak, Henry C.	84,139	Taylor, Glen H.		58,130 R	62.8%	37.2%	62.8%	37.2%
1950	201,417	124,237	Welker, Herman	77,180	Clark, D. Worth		47,057 R	61.7%	38.3%	61.7%	38.3%
1950S	201,970	104,068	Dworshak, Henry C.	97,902	Burtenshaw, Claude		6,166 R	51.5%	48.5%	51.5%	48.5%
1948	214,188	103,868	Dworshak, Henry C.	107,000	Miller, Bert H.	3,320	3,132 D	48.5%	50.0%	49.3%	50.7%
1946S	180,152	105,523	Dworshak, Henry C.	74,629	Donart, George E.		30,894 R	58.6%	41.4%	58.6%	41.4%

One each of the 1962 and 1950 elections and the 1946 election were for short terms to fill vacancies.

IDAHO

Congressional districts first established for elections held in 2002
2 members

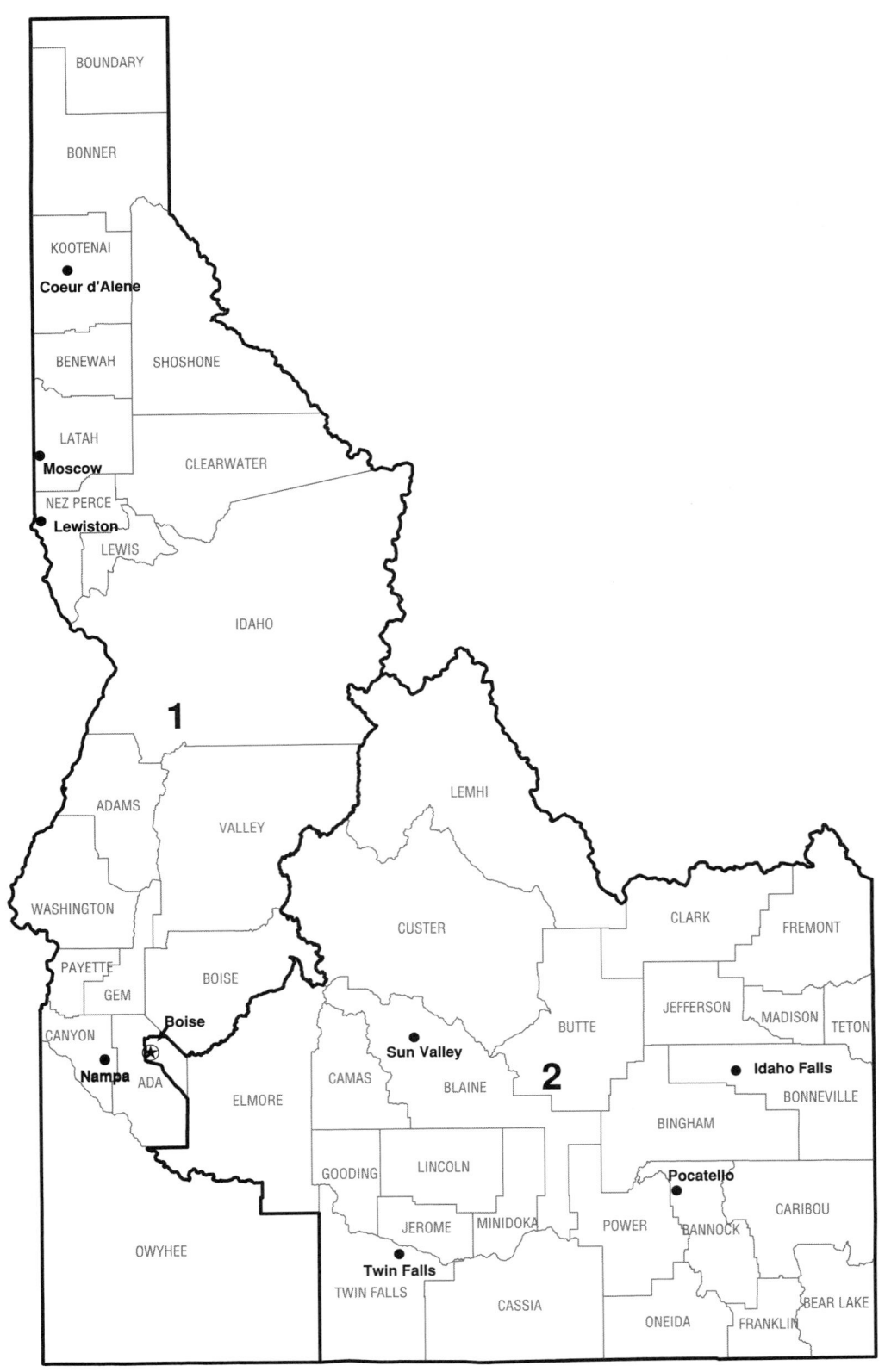

IDAHO

GOVERNOR 2002

2000 Census Population	County	Total Vote	Republican	Democratic	Other	Rep.-Dem. Plurality	Percentage			
							Total Vote		Major Vote	
							Rep.	Dem.	Rep.	Dem.
300,904	ADA	105,424	51,258	52,360	1,806	1,102 D	48.6%	49.7%	49.5%	50.5%
3,476	ADAMS	1,601	1,009	547	45	462 R	63.0%	34.2%	64.8%	35.2%
75,565	BANNOCK	24,989	11,416	13,070	503	1,654 D	45.7%	52.3%	46.6%	53.4%
6,411	BEAR LAKE	2,433	1,663	734	36	929 R	68.4%	30.2%	69.4%	30.6%
9,171	BENEWAH	3,243	1,919	1,227	97	692 R	59.2%	37.8%	61.0%	39.0%
41,735	BINGHAM	12,307	7,659	4,389	259	3,270 R	62.2%	35.7%	63.6%	36.4%
18,991	BLAINE	6,276	2,693	3,403	180	710 D	42.9%	54.2%	44.2%	55.8%
6,670	BOISE	2,669	1,394	1,184	91	210 R	52.2%	44.4%	54.1%	45.9%
36,835	BONNER	10,988	5,797	4,932	259	865 R	52.8%	44.9%	54.0%	46.0%
82,522	BONNEVILLE	28,480	17,520	10,380	580	7,140 R	61.5%	36.4%	62.8%	37.2%
9,871	BOUNDARY	2,781	1,766	941	74	825 R	63.5%	33.8%	65.2%	34.8%
2,899	BUTTE	1,310	814	469	27	345 R	62.1%	35.8%	63.4%	36.6%
991	CAMAS	405	258	136	11	122 R	63.7%	33.6%	65.5%	34.5%
131,441	CANYON	37,084	22,536	13,795	753	8,741 R	60.8%	37.2%	62.0%	38.0%
7,304	CARIBOU	2,526	1,642	846	38	796 R	65.0%	33.5%	66.0%	34.0%
21,416	CASSIA	5,989	4,377	1,479	133	2,898 R	73.1%	24.7%	74.7%	25.3%
1,022	CLARK	306	226	72	8	154 R	73.9%	23.5%	75.8%	24.2%
8,930	CLEARWATER	3,126	1,635	1,423	68	212 R	52.3%	45.5%	53.5%	46.5%
4,342	CUSTER	1,778	1,248	480	50	768 R	70.2%	27.0%	72.2%	27.8%
29,130	ELMORE	5,305	3,131	2,082	92	1,049 R	59.0%	39.2%	60.1%	39.9%
11,329	FRANKLIN	3,271	2,611	588	72	2,023 R	79.8%	18.0%	81.6%	18.4%
11,819	FREMONT	3,964	2,749	1,110	105	1,639 R	69.3%	28.0%	71.2%	28.8%
15,181	GEM	5,320	3,014	2,182	124	832 R	56.7%	41.0%	58.0%	42.0%
14,155	GOODING	4,114	2,543	1,487	84	1,056 R	61.8%	36.1%	63.1%	36.9%
15,511	IDAHO	6,517	4,252	2,075	190	2,177 R	65.2%	31.8%	67.2%	32.8%
19,155	JEFFERSON	6,685	4,902	1,661	122	3,241 R	73.3%	24.8%	74.7%	25.3%
18,342	JEROME	4,579	3,065	1,427	87	1,638 R	66.9%	31.2%	68.2%	31.8%
108,685	KOOTENAI	32,160	18,967	12,547	646	6,420 R	59.0%	39.0%	60.2%	39.8%
34,935	LATAH	11,683	4,963	6,456	264	1,493 D	42.5%	55.3%	43.5%	56.5%
7,806	LEMHI	3,502	2,533	873	96	1,660 R	72.3%	24.9%	74.4%	25.6%
3,747	LEWIS	1,395	754	618	23	136 R	54.1%	44.3%	55.0%	45.0%
4,044	LINCOLN	1,346	807	508	31	299 R	60.0%	37.7%	61.4%	38.6%
27,467	MADISON	7,178	5,280	1,771	127	3,509 R	73.6%	24.7%	74.9%	25.1%
20,174	MINIDOKA	5,319	3,569	1,630	120	1,939 R	67.1%	30.6%	68.6%	31.4%
37,410	NEZ PERCE	12,573	5,867	6,523	183	656 D	46.7%	51.9%	47.4%	52.6%
4,125	ONEIDA	1,284	955	299	30	656 R	74.4%	23.3%	76.2%	23.8%
10,644	OWYHEE	2,637	1,771	785	81	986 R	67.2%	29.8%	69.3%	30.7%
20,578	PAYETTE	5,573	3,530	1,930	113	1,600 R	63.3%	34.6%	64.7%	35.3%
7,538	POWER	2,281	1,324	932	25	392 R	58.0%	40.9%	58.7%	41.3%
13,771	SHOSHONE	4,285	1,802	2,378	105	576 D	42.1%	55.5%	43.1%	56.9%
5,999	TETON	2,329	1,245	1,043	41	202 R	53.5%	44.8%	54.4%	45.6%
64,284	TWIN FALLS	17,929	11,187	6,433	309	4,754 R	62.4%	35.9%	63.5%	36.5%
7,651	VALLEY	3,326	1,803	1,463	60	340 R	54.2%	44.0%	55.2%	44.8%
9,977	WASHINGTON	3,207	2,112	1,043	52	1,069 R	65.9%	32.5%	66.9%	33.1%
1,293,953	TOTAL	411,477	231,566	171,711	8,200	59,855 R	56.3%	41.7%	57.4%	42.6%

IDAHO

SENATOR 2002

2000 Census Population	County	Total Vote	Republican	Democratic	Other	Rep.-Dem. Plurality	Percentage			
							Total Vote		Major Vote	
							Rep.	Dem.	Rep.	Dem.
300,904	ADA	104,430	61,113	40,741	2,576	20,372 R	58.5%	39.0%	60.0%	40.0%
3,476	ADAMS	1,602	1,184	360	58	824 R	73.9%	22.5%	76.7%	23.3%
75,565	BANNOCK	24,941	14,499	9,833	609	4,666 R	58.1%	39.4%	59.6%	40.4%
6,411	BEAR LAKE	2,412	1,877	499	36	1,378 R	77.8%	20.7%	79.0%	21.0%
9,171	BENEWAH	3,239	2,109	1,047	83	1,062 R	65.1%	32.3%	66.8%	33.2%
41,735	BINGHAM	12,263	9,049	2,954	260	6,095 R	73.8%	24.1%	75.4%	24.6%
18,991	BLAINE	6,106	2,636	3,225	245	589 D	43.2%	52.8%	45.0%	55.0%
6,670	BOISE	2,663	1,764	813	86	951 R	66.2%	30.5%	68.5%	31.5%
36,835	BONNER	10,961	6,524	4,174	263	2,350 R	59.5%	38.1%	61.0%	39.0%
82,522	BONNEVILLE	28,203	21,088	6,390	725	14,698 R	74.8%	22.7%	76.7%	23.3%
9,871	BOUNDARY	2,750	1,893	788	69	1,105 R	68.8%	28.7%	70.6%	29.4%
2,899	BUTTE	1,303	929	352	22	577 R	71.3%	27.0%	72.5%	27.5%
991	CAMAS	404	298	95	11	203 R	73.8%	23.5%	75.8%	24.2%
131,441	CANYON	36,589	25,251	10,562	776	14,689 R	69.0%	28.9%	70.5%	29.5%
7,304	CARIBOU	2,529	1,966	523	40	1,443 R	77.7%	20.7%	79.0%	21.0%
21,416	CASSIA	5,952	4,753	1,102	97	3,651 R	79.9%	18.5%	81.2%	18.8%
1,022	CLARK	301	236	56	9	180 R	78.4%	18.6%	80.8%	19.2%
8,930	CLEARWATER	3,103	2,087	969	47	1,118 R	67.3%	31.2%	68.3%	31.7%
4,342	CUSTER	1,782	1,353	391	38	962 R	75.9%	21.9%	77.6%	22.4%
29,130	ELMORE	5,309	3,483	1,724	102	1,759 R	65.6%	32.5%	66.9%	33.1%
11,329	FRANKLIN	3,221	2,749	418	54	2,331 R	85.3%	13.0%	86.8%	13.2%
11,819	FREMONT	3,956	3,209	662	85	2,547 R	81.1%	16.7%	82.9%	17.1%
15,181	GEM	5,330	3,615	1,598	117	2,017 R	67.8%	30.0%	69.3%	30.7%
14,155	GOODING	4,117	2,881	1,153	83	1,728 R	70.0%	28.0%	71.4%	28.6%
15,511	IDAHO	6,510	4,968	1,380	162	3,588 R	76.3%	21.2%	78.3%	21.7%
19,155	JEFFERSON	6,607	5,393	1,045	169	4,348 R	81.6%	15.8%	83.8%	16.2%
18,342	JEROME	4,569	3,260	1,230	79	2,030 R	71.4%	26.9%	72.6%	27.4%
108,685	KOOTENAI	32,121	20,276	11,140	705	9,136 R	63.1%	34.7%	64.5%	35.5%
34,935	LATAH	11,599	5,838	5,426	335	412 R	50.3%	46.8%	51.8%	48.2%
7,806	LEMHI	3,489	2,658	748	83	1,910 R	76.2%	21.4%	78.0%	22.0%
3,747	LEWIS	1,400	962	414	24	548 R	68.7%	29.6%	69.9%	30.1%
4,044	LINCOLN	1,338	869	436	33	433 R	64.9%	32.6%	66.6%	33.4%
27,467	MADISON	7,160	6,166	883	111	5,283 R	86.1%	12.3%	87.5%	12.5%
20,174	MINIDOKA	5,238	3,747	1,366	125	2,381 R	71.5%	26.1%	73.3%	26.7%
37,410	NEZ PERCE	12,457	7,040	5,229	188	1,811 R	56.5%	42.0%	57.4%	42.6%
4,125	ONEIDA	1,275	1,017	236	22	781 R	79.8%	18.5%	81.2%	18.8%
10,644	OWYHEE	2,633	1,960	614	59	1,346 R	74.4%	23.3%	76.1%	23.9%
20,578	PAYETTE	5,494	3,930	1,435	129	2,495 R	71.5%	26.1%	73.3%	26.7%
7,538	POWER	2,272	1,541	696	35	845 R	67.8%	30.6%	68.9%	31.1%
13,771	SHOSHONE	4,229	2,124	2,008	97	116 R	50.2%	47.5%	51.4%	48.6%
5,999	TETON	2,300	1,425	813	62	612 R	62.0%	35.3%	63.7%	36.3%
64,284	TWIN FALLS	17,851	12,102	5,430	319	6,672 R	67.8%	30.4%	69.0%	31.0%
7,651	VALLEY	3,335	2,064	1,187	84	877 R	61.9%	35.6%	63.5%	36.5%
9,977	WASHINGTON	3,201	2,329	830	42	1,499 R	72.8%	25.9%	73.7%	26.3%
1,293,953	TOTAL	408,544	266,215	132,975	9,354	133,240 R	65.2%	32.5%	66.7%	33.3%

IDAHO

HOUSE OF REPRESENTATIVES

			Republican		Democratic				Percentage			
		Total					Other	Rep.-Dem.	Total Vote		Major Vote	
CD	Year	Vote	Vote	Candidate	Vote	Candidate	Vote	Plurality	Rep.	Dem.	Rep.	Dem.
1	2002	206,141	120,743	Otter, C. L. "Butch"*	80,269	Richardson, Betty	5,129	40,474 R	58.6%	38.9%	60.1%	39.9%
2	2002	198,882	135,605	Simpson, Mike*	57,769	Kinghorn, Edward	5,508	77,836 R	68.2%	29.0%	70.1%	29.9%
Total	2002	405,023	256,348		138,038		10,637	118,310 R	63.3%	34.1%	65.0%	35.0%

An asterisk (*) denotes incumbent.

IDAHO

GENERAL AND PRIMARY ELECTIONS

2002 GENERAL ELECTIONS

Governor   Other vote was 8,187 Libertarian (Daniel L.J. Adams); 13 write-in (Kevin Powers).

Senator   Other vote was 9,354 Libertarian (Donovan Bramwell).

House   Other vote was:

CD 1   5,129 Libertarian (Steve Gothard).
CD 2   5,508 Libertarian (John A. Lewis).

2002 PRIMARY ELECTIONS

Primary   May 28, 2002   **Registration**   626,592   No Party Registration
(as of May 28, 2002)

Primary Type   Open—Any registered voter could vote in the party primary of their choice.

Note: An asterisk (*) denotes incumbent.

	REPUBLICAN PRIMARIES			DEMOCRATIC PRIMARIES		
Governor	Dirk Kempthorne*	95,882	65.9%	Jerry M. Brady	33,285	87.4%
	Milt Erhart	37,523	25.8%	Rue T. Stears	4,798	12.6%
	Walter L. Bayes	6,873	4.7%			
	Raynelle J. George	5,271	3.6%			
	TOTAL	145,549		TOTAL	38,083	
Senator	Larry E. Craig*	130,126	100.0%	Alan Blinken	26,346	70.9%
				D.P. "Dave" Sneddon	10,812	29.1%
				TOTAL	37,158	
Congressional District 1	C.L. "Butch" Otter*	60,352	100.0%	Betty Richardson	17,764	100.0%
Congressional District 2	Mike Simpson*	60,092	100.0%	Edward W. Kinghorn	15,600	100.0%

IDAHO REPUBLICAN PRIMARY

GOVERNOR 2002

2000 Census Population	County	Total Vote	Kempthorne	Erhart	Other	Winner	Percentage of Total Vote		
							Kempthorne	Erhart	Other
300,904	ADA	34,934	19,882	12,162	2,890	Kempthorne	56.9%	34.8%	8.3%
3,476	ADAMS	914	549	257	108	Kempthorne	60.1%	28.1%	11.8%
75,565	BANNOCK	5,892	3,695	1,679	518	Kempthorne	62.7%	28.5%	8.8%
6,411	BEAR LAKE	1,489	1,124	263	102	Kempthorne	75.5%	17.7%	6.9%
9,171	BENEWAH	563	496	31	36	Kempthorne	88.1%	5.5%	6.4%
41,735	BINGHAM	5,779	3,556	1,847	376	Kempthorne	61.5%	32.0%	6.5%
18,991	BLAINE	566	484	50	32	Kempthorne	85.5%	8.8%	5.7%
6,670	BOISE	978	533	325	120	Kempthorne	54.5%	33.2%	12.3%
36,835	BONNER	3,329	2,815	199	315	Kempthorne	84.6%	6.0%	9.5%
82,522	BONNEVILLE	8,581	5,151	2,807	623	Kempthorne	60.0%	32.7%	7.3%
9,871	BOUNDARY	1,364	1,098	115	151	Kempthorne	80.5%	8.4%	11.1%
2,899	BUTTE	701	478	172	51	Kempthorne	68.2%	24.5%	7.3%
991	CAMAS	161	97	54	10	Kempthorne	60.2%	33.5%	6.2%
131,441	CANYON	13,935	8,388	4,371	1,176	Kempthorne	60.2%	31.4%	8.4%
7,304	CARIBOU	914	638	210	66	Kempthorne	69.8%	23.0%	7.2%
21,416	CASSIA	3,508	2,468	728	312	Kempthorne	70.4%	20.8%	8.9%
1,022	CLARK	299	216	55	28	Kempthorne	72.2%	18.4%	9.4%
8,930	CLEARWATER	1,252	999	91	162	Kempthorne	79.8%	7.3%	12.9%
4,342	CUSTER	1,056	796	164	96	Kempthorne	75.4%	15.5%	9.1%
29,130	ELMORE	2,121	1,409	518	194	Kempthorne	66.4%	24.4%	9.1%
11,329	FRANKLIN	2,330	1,922	249	159	Kempthorne	82.5%	10.7%	6.8%
11,819	FREMONT	2,117	1,375	565	177	Kempthorne	65.0%	26.7%	8.4%
15,181	GEM	3,008	1,785	929	294	Kempthorne	59.3%	30.9%	9.8%
14,155	GOODING	1,754	1,130	488	136	Kempthorne	64.4%	27.8%	7.8%
15,511	IDAHO	3,413	2,688	304	421	Kempthorne	78.8%	8.9%	12.3%
19,155	JEFFERSON	2,850	1,819	818	213	Kempthorne	63.8%	28.7%	7.5%
18,342	JEROME	1,377	1,008	286	83	Kempthorne	73.2%	20.8%	6.0%
108,685	KOOTENAI	11,382	9,389	1,048	945	Kempthorne	82.5%	9.2%	8.3%
34,935	LATAH	1,691	1,253	256	182	Kempthorne	74.1%	15.1%	10.8%
7,806	LEMHI	1,641	1,254	273	114	Kempthorne	76.4%	16.6%	6.9%
3,747	LEWIS	422	335	37	50	Kempthorne	79.4%	8.8%	11.8%
4,044	LINCOLN	506	307	149	50	Kempthorne	60.7%	29.4%	9.9%
27,467	MADISON	3,513	2,298	954	261	Kempthorne	65.4%	27.2%	7.4%
20,174	MINIDOKA	2,013	1,339	535	139	Kempthorne	66.5%	26.6%	6.9%
37,410	NEZ PERCE	2,061	1,649	212	200	Kempthorne	80.0%	10.3%	9.7%
4,125	ONEIDA	751	651	59	41	Kempthorne	86.7%	7.9%	5.5%
10,644	OWYHEE	1,260	752	382	126	Kempthorne	59.7%	30.3%	10.0%
20,578	PAYETTE	3,108	1,950	902	256	Kempthorne	62.7%	29.0%	8.2%
7,538	POWER	740	520	171	49	Kempthorne	70.3%	23.1%	6.6%
13,771	SHOSHONE	669	543	60	66	Kempthorne	81.2%	9.0%	9.9%
5,999	TETON	1,044	738	208	98	Kempthorne	70.7%	19.9%	9.4%
64,284	TWIN FALLS	6,101	4,056	1,584	461	Kempthorne	66.5%	26.0%	7.6%
7,651	VALLEY	1,584	1,004	451	129	Kempthorne	63.4%	28.5%	8.1%
9,977	WASHINGTON	1,878	1,245	505	128	Kempthorne	66.3%	26.9%	6.8%
1,293,953	TOTAL	145,549	95,882	37,523	12,144	Kempthorne	65.9%	25.8%	8.3%

IDAHO DEMOCRATIC PRIMARY

GOVERNOR 2002

2000 Census Population	County	Total Vote	Brady	Stears	Winner	Percentage of Total Vote	
						Brady	Stears
300,904	ADA	12,193	11,268	925	Brady	92.4%	7.6%
3,476	ADAMS	79	72	7	Brady	91.1%	8.9%
75,565	BANNOCK	4,113	3,669	444	Brady	89.2%	10.8%
6,411	BEAR LAKE	156	133	23	Brady	85.3%	14.7%
9,171	BENEWAH	599	462	137	Brady	77.1%	22.9%
41,735	BINGHAM	641	529	112	Brady	82.5%	17.5%
18,991	BLAINE	855	775	80	Brady	90.6%	9.4%
6,670	BOISE	199	168	31	Brady	84.4%	15.6%
36,835	BONNER	1,371	1,096	275	Brady	79.9%	20.1%
82,522	BONNEVILLE	1,670	1,497	173	Brady	89.6%	10.4%
9,871	BOUNDARY	139	114	25	Brady	82.0%	18.0%
2,899	BUTTE	55	50	5	Brady	90.9%	9.1%
991	CAMAS	22	17	5	Brady	77.3%	22.7%
131,441	CANYON	2,176	1,896	280	Brady	87.1%	12.9%
7,304	CARIBOU	99	82	17	Brady	82.8%	17.2%
21,416	CASSIA	169	146	23	Brady	86.4%	13.6%
1,022	CLARK	2	2		Brady	100.0%	
8,930	CLEARWATER	538	461	77	Brady	85.7%	14.3%
4,342	CUSTER	51	40	11	Brady	78.4%	21.6%
29,130	ELMORE	565	489	76	Brady	86.5%	13.5%
11,329	FRANKLIN	86	55	31	Brady	64.0%	36.0%
11,819	FREMONT	124	107	17	Brady	86.3%	13.7%
15,181	GEM	490	429	61	Brady	87.6%	12.4%
14,155	GOODING	292	261	31	Brady	89.4%	10.6%
15,511	IDAHO	342	259	83	Brady	75.7%	24.3%
19,155	JEFFERSON	206	164	42	Brady	79.6%	20.4%
18,342	JEROME	222	190	32	Brady	85.6%	14.4%
108,685	KOOTENAI	2,700	2,146	554	Brady	79.5%	20.5%
34,935	LATAH	1,336	1,191	145	Brady	89.1%	10.9%
7,806	LEMHI	71	65	6	Brady	91.5%	8.5%
3,747	LEWIS	224	182	42	Brady	81.3%	18.8%
4,044	LINCOLN	120	98	22	Brady	81.7%	18.3%
27,467	MADISON	162	144	18	Brady	88.9%	11.1%
20,174	MINIDOKA	258	176	82	Brady	68.2%	31.8%
37,410	NEZ PERCE	2,048	1,757	291	Brady	85.8%	14.2%
4,125	ONEIDA	40	34	6	Brady	85.0%	15.0%
10,644	OWYHEE	147	122	25	Brady	83.0%	17.0%
20,578	PAYETTE	358	307	51	Brady	85.8%	14.2%
7,538	POWER	185	164	21	Brady	88.6%	11.4%
13,771	SHOSHONE	1,303	1,017	286	Brady	78.1%	21.9%
5,999	TETON	238	194	44	Brady	81.5%	18.5%
64,284	TWIN FALLS	927	816	111	Brady	88.0%	12.0%
7,651	VALLEY	271	235	36	Brady	86.7%	13.3%
9,977	WASHINGTON	241	206	35	Brady	85.5%	14.5%
1,293,953	TOTAL	38,083	33,285	4,798	Brady	87.4%	12.6%

IDAHO DEMOCRATIC PRIMARY

SENATOR 2002

2000 Census Population	County	Total Vote	Blinken	Sneddon	Winner	Percentage of Total Vote	
						Blinken	Sneddon
300,904	ADA	11,821	9,431	2,390	Blinken	79.8%	20.2%
3,476	ADAMS	78	60	18	Blinken	76.9%	23.1%
75,565	BANNOCK	4,033	2,844	1,189	Blinken	70.5%	29.5%
6,411	BEAR LAKE	154	62	92	Sneddon	40.3%	59.7%
9,171	BENEWAH	617	263	354	Sneddon	42.6%	57.4%
41,735	BINGHAM	607	420	187	Blinken	69.2%	30.8%
18,991	BLAINE	940	815	125	Blinken	86.7%	13.3%
6,670	BOISE	193	128	65	Blinken	66.3%	33.7%
36,835	BONNER	1,389	702	687	Blinken	50.5%	49.5%
82,522	BONNEVILLE	1,477	993	484	Blinken	67.2%	32.8%
9,871	BOUNDARY	141	77	64	Blinken	54.6%	45.4%
2,899	BUTTE	51	36	15	Blinken	70.6%	29.4%
991	CAMAS	23	15	8	Blinken	65.2%	34.8%
131,441	CANYON	2,045	1,398	647	Blinken	68.4%	31.6%
7,304	CARIBOU	102	55	47	Blinken	53.9%	46.1%
21,416	CASSIA	172	107	65	Blinken	62.2%	37.8%
1,022	CLARK	2	2		Blinken	100.0%	
8,930	CLEARWATER	544	386	158	Blinken	71.0%	29.0%
4,342	CUSTER	51	24	27	Sneddon	47.1%	52.9%
29,130	ELMORE	557	388	169	Blinken	69.7%	30.3%
11,329	FRANKLIN	84	42	42		50.0%	50.0%
11,819	FREMONT	113	81	32	Blinken	71.7%	28.3%
15,181	GEM	479	320	159	Blinken	66.8%	33.2%
14,155	GOODING	295	190	105	Blinken	64.4%	35.6%
15,511	IDAHO	347	229	118	Blinken	66.0%	34.0%
19,155	JEFFERSON	197	139	58	Blinken	70.6%	29.4%
18,342	JEROME	220	167	53	Blinken	75.9%	24.1%
108,685	KOOTENAI	2,689	1,679	1,010	Blinken	62.4%	37.6%
34,935	LATAH	1,290	973	317	Blinken	75.4%	24.6%
7,806	LEMHI	68	38	30	Blinken	55.9%	44.1%
3,747	LEWIS	222	135	87	Blinken	60.8%	39.2%
4,044	LINCOLN	127	96	31	Blinken	75.6%	24.4%
27,467	MADISON	155	112	43	Blinken	72.3%	27.7%
20,174	MINIDOKA	261	152	109	Blinken	58.2%	41.8%
37,410	NEZ PERCE	1,966	1,317	649	Blinken	67.0%	33.0%
4,125	ONEIDA	44	26	18	Blinken	59.1%	40.9%
10,644	OWYHEE	150	96	54	Blinken	64.0%	36.0%
20,578	PAYETTE	353	247	106	Blinken	70.0%	30.0%
7,538	POWER	178	125	53	Blinken	70.2%	29.8%
13,771	SHOSHONE	1,277	802	475	Blinken	62.8%	37.2%
5,999	TETON	202	131	71	Blinken	64.9%	35.1%
64,284	TWIN FALLS	932	681	251	Blinken	73.1%	26.9%
7,651	VALLEY	269	188	81	Blinken	69.9%	30.1%
9,977	WASHINGTON	243	174	69	Blinken	71.6%	28.4%
1,293,953	TOTAL	37,158	26,346	10,812	Blinken	70.9%	29.1%

ILLINOIS

GOVERNOR
Rod R. Blagojevich (D). Elected 2002 to a four-year term.

SENATORS (1 Democrat, 1 Republican)
Richard J. Durbin (D). Reelected 2002 to a six-year term. Previously elected 1996.

Peter G. Fitzgerald (R). Elected 1998 to a six-year term.

REPRESENTATIVES (10 Republicans, 9 Democrats)
1. Bobby L. Rush (D)
2. Jesse L. Jackson Jr. (D)
3. William O. Lipinski (D)
4. Luis V. Gutierrez (D)
5. Rahm Emanuel (D)
6. Henry J. Hyde (R)
7. Danny K. Davis (D)
8. Philip M. Crane (R)
9. Jan Schakowsky (D)
10. Mark Steven Kirk (R)
11. Jerry Weller (R)
12. Jerry F. Costello (D)
13. Judy Biggert (R)
14. J. Dennis Hastert (R)
15. Timothy V. Johnson (R)
16. Donald Manzullo (R)
17. Lane Evans (D)
18. Ray LaHood (R)
19. John Shimkus (R)

POSTWAR VOTE FOR PRESIDENT

Year	Total Vote	Republican		Democratic		Other Vote	Plurality	Percentage			
								Total Vote		Major Vote	
		Vote	Candidate	Vote	Candidate			Rep.	Dem.	Rep.	Dem.
2000**	4,742,123	2,019,421	Bush, George W.	2,589,026	Gore, Al	133,676	569,605 D	42.6%	54.6%	43.8%	56.2%
1996**	4,311,391	1,587,021	Dole, Bob	2,341,744	Clinton, Bill	382,626	754,723 D	36.8%	54.3%	40.4%	59.6%
1992**	5,050,157	1,734,096	Bush, George	2,453,350	Clinton, Bill	862,711	719,254 D	34.3%	48.6%	41.4%	58.6%
1988	4,559,120	2,310,939	Bush, George	2,215,940	Dukakis, Michael S.	32,241	94,999 R	50.7%	48.6%	51.0%	49.0%
1984	4,819,088	2,707,103	Reagan, Ronald	2,086,499	Mondale, Walter F.	25,486	620,604 R	56.2%	43.3%	56.5%	43.5%
1980**	4,749,721	2,358,049	Reagan, Ronald	1,981,413	Carter, Jimmy	410,259	376,636 R	49.6%	41.7%	54.3%	45.7%
1976	4,718,914	2,364,269	Ford, Gerald R.	2,271,295	Carter, Jimmy	83,350	92,974 R	50.1%	48.1%	51.0%	49.0%
1972	4,723,236	2,788,179	Nixon, Richard M.	1,913,472	McGovern, George S.	21,585	874,707 R	59.0%	40.5%	59.3%	40.7%
1968	4,619,749	2,174,774	Nixon, Richard M.	2,039,814	Humphrey, Hubert H.	405,161	134,960 R	47.1%	44.2%	51.6%	48.4%
1964	4,702,841	1,905,946	Goldwater, Barry M.	2,796,833	Johnson, Lyndon B.	62	890,887 D	40.5%	59.5%	40.5%	59.5%
1960	4,757,409	2,368,988	Nixon, Richard M.	2,377,846	Kennedy, John F.	10,575	8,858 D	49.8%	50.0%	49.9%	50.1%
1956	4,407,407	2,623,327	Eisenhower, Dwight D.	1,775,682	Stevenson, Adlai E.	8,398	847,645 R	59.5%	40.3%	59.6%	40.4%
1952	4,481,058	2,457,327	Eisenhower, Dwight D.	2,013,920	Stevenson, Adlai E.	9,811	443,407 R	54.8%	44.9%	55.0%	45.0%
1948	3,984,046	1,961,103	Dewey, Thomas E.	1,994,715	Truman, Harry S.	28,228	33,612 D	49.2%	50.1%	49.6%	50.4%

In 2000 the other vote column includes 103,759 votes cast for Green (Nader). In 1996 the other vote column includes 346,408 votes cast for Perot. In 1992 the other vote column includes 840,515 votes cast for Perot. In 1980 the other column includes 346,754 votes for Independent (Anderson).

ILLINOIS

POSTWAR VOTE FOR GOVERNOR

Year	Total Vote	Republican		Democratic		Other Vote	Rep.-Dem. Plurality	Percentage			
								Total Vote		Major Vote	
		Vote	Candidate	Vote	Candidate			Rep.	Dem.	Rep.	Dem.
2002	3,538,891	1,594,960	Ryan, Jim	1,847,040	Blagojevich, Rod R.	96,891	252,080 D	45.1%	52.2%	46.3%	53.7%
1998	3,358,705	1,714,094	Ryan, George H.	1,594,191	Poshard, Glenn	50,420	119,903 R	51.0%	47.5%	51.8%	48.2%
1994	3,106,566	1,984,318	Edgar, Jim	1,069,850	Netsch, Dawn C.	52,398	914,468 R	63.9%	34.4%	65.0%	35.0%
1990	3,257,410	1,653,126	Edgar, Jim	1,569,217	Hartigan, Neil F.	35,067	83,909 R	50.7%	48.2%	51.3%	48.7%
1986**	3,143,978	1,655,849	Thompson, James R.	208,830	[See note below]	1,279,299	1,447,019 R	52.7%	6.6%	88.8%	11.2%
1982	3,673,681	1,816,101	Thompson, James R.	1,811,027	Stevenson, Adlai E., III	46,553	5,074 R	49.4%	49.3%	50.1%	49.9%
1978	3,150,095	1,859,684	Thompson, James R.	1,263,134	Bakalis, Michael	27,277	596,550 R	59.0%	40.1%	59.6%	40.4%
1976S	4,638,997	3,000,395	Thompson, James R.	1,610,258	Howlett, Michael J.	28,344	1,390,137 R	64.7%	34.7%	65.1%	34.9%
1972	4,678,804	2,293,809	Ogilvie, Richard B.	2,371,303	Walker, Daniel	13,692	77,494 D	49.0%	50.7%	49.2%	50.8%
1968	4,506,000	2,307,295	Ogilvie, Richard B.	2,179,501	Shapiro, Samuel H.	19,204	127,794 R	51.2%	48.4%	51.4%	48.6%
1964	4,657,500	2,239,095	Percy, Charles H.	2,418,394	Kerner, Otto	11	179,299 D	48.1%	51.9%	48.1%	51.9%
1960	4,674,187	2,070,479	Stratton, William G.	2,594,731	Kerner, Otto	8,977	524,252 D	44.3%	55.5%	44.4%	55.6%
1956	4,314,611	2,171,786	Stratton, William G.	2,134,909	Austin, Richard B.	7,916	36,877 R	50.3%	49.5%	50.4%	49.6%
1952	4,415,864	2,317,363	Stratton, William G.	2,089,721	Dixon, Sherwood	8,780	227,642 R	52.5%	47.3%	52.6%	47.4%
1948	3,940,257	1,678,007	Green, Dwight H.	2,250,074	Stevenson, Adlai E.	12,176	572,067 D	42.6%	57.1%	42.7%	57.3%

In 1986 there was no Democratic candidate for Governor on the ballot. Mark Fairchild, a supporter of Lyndon H. LaRouche Jr., was the "paired" Democratic candidate for Lt. Governor and the Democratic vote above was cast for this ticket of "no name" and Fairchild. Other vote in this election was 1,256,626 Adlai E. Stevenson III (Solidarity) who received 40.0% of the total vote and came in second; 15,646 Gary L. Shilts (Libertarian); 6,843 Diane Roling (Socialist Workers) and 184 scattered. The 1976 vote was for a two-year term to permit shifting the vote for Governor to non-Presidential years.

POSTWAR VOTE FOR SENATOR

Year	Total Vote	Republican		Democratic		Other Vote	Rep.-Dem. Plurality	Percentage			
								Total Vote		Major Vote	
		Vote	Candidate	Vote	Candidate			Rep.	Dem.	Rep.	Dem.
2002	3,486,851	1,325,703	Durkin, Jim	2,103,766	Durbin, Richard J.	57,382	778,063 D	38.0%	60.3%	38.7%	61.3%
1998	3,394,521	1,709,041	Fitzgerald, Peter G.	1,610,496	Moseley-Braun, Carol	74,984	98,545 R	50.3%	47.4%	51.5%	48.5%
1996	4,250,722	1,728,824	Salvi, Al	2,384,028	Durbin, Richard J.	137,870	655,204 D	40.7%	56.1%	42.0%	58.0%
1992	4,939,558	2,126,833	Williamson, Richard S.	2,631,229	Moseley-Braun, Carol	181,496	504,396 D	43.1%	53.3%	44.7%	55.3%
1990	3,251,005	1,135,628	Martin, Lynn	2,115,377	Simon, Paul		979,749 D	34.9%	65.1%	34.9%	65.1%
1986	3,122,883	1,053,734	Koehler, Judy	2,033,783	Dixon, Alan J.	35,366	980,049 D	33.7%	65.1%	34.1%	65.9%
1984	4,787,473	2,308,039	Percy, Charles H.	2,397,303	Simon, Paul	82,131	89,264 D	48.2%	50.1%	49.1%	50.9%
1980	4,580,029	1,946,296	O'Neal, David C.	2,565,302	Dixon, Alan J.	68,431	619,006 D	42.5%	56.0%	43.1%	56.9%
1978	3,184,764	1,698,711	Percy, Charles H.	1,448,187	Seith, Alex	37,866	250,524 R	53.3%	45.5%	54.0%	46.0%
1974	2,914,666	1,084,884	Burditt, George M.	1,811,496	Stevenson, Adlai E., III	18,286	726,612 D	37.2%	62.2%	37.5%	62.5%
1972	4,608,380	2,867,078	Percy, Charles H.	1,721,031	Pucinski, Roman C.	20,271	1,146,047 R	62.2%	37.3%	62.5%	37.5%
1970S	3,599,272	1,519,718	Smith, Ralph T.	2,065,054	Stevenson, Adlai E., III	14,500	545,336 D	42.2%	57.4%	42.4%	57.6%
1968	4,449,757	2,358,947	Dirksen, Everett M.	2,073,242	Clark, William G.	17,568	285,705 R	53.0%	46.6%	53.2%	46.8%
1966	3,822,725	2,100,449	Percy, Charles H.	1,678,147	Douglas, Paul H.	44,129	422,302 R	54.9%	43.9%	55.6%	44.4%
1962	3,709,216	1,961,202	Dirksen, Everett M.	1,748,007	Yates, Sidney R.	7	213,195 R	52.9%	47.1%	52.9%	47.1%
1960	4,632,796	2,093,846	Witwer, Samuel W.	2,530,943	Douglas, Paul H.	8,007	437,097 D	45.2%	54.6%	45.3%	54.7%
1956	4,264,830	2,307,352	Dirksen, Everett M.	1,949,883	Stengel, Richard	7,595	357,469 R	54.1%	45.7%	54.2%	45.8%
1954	3,368,025	1,563,683	Meek, Joseph T.	1,804,338	Douglas, Paul H.	4	240,655 D	46.4%	53.6%	46.4%	53.6%
1950	3,622,673	1,951,984	Dirksen, Everett M.	1,657,630	Lucas, Scott W.	13,059	294,354 R	53.9%	45.8%	54.1%	45.9%
1948	3,900,285	1,740,026	Brooks, C. Wayland	2,147,754	Douglas, Paul H.	12,505	407,728 D	44.6%	55.1%	44.8%	55.2%

The 1970 election was for a short term to fill a vacancy.

ILLINOIS

Congressional districts first established for elections held in 2002
19 members

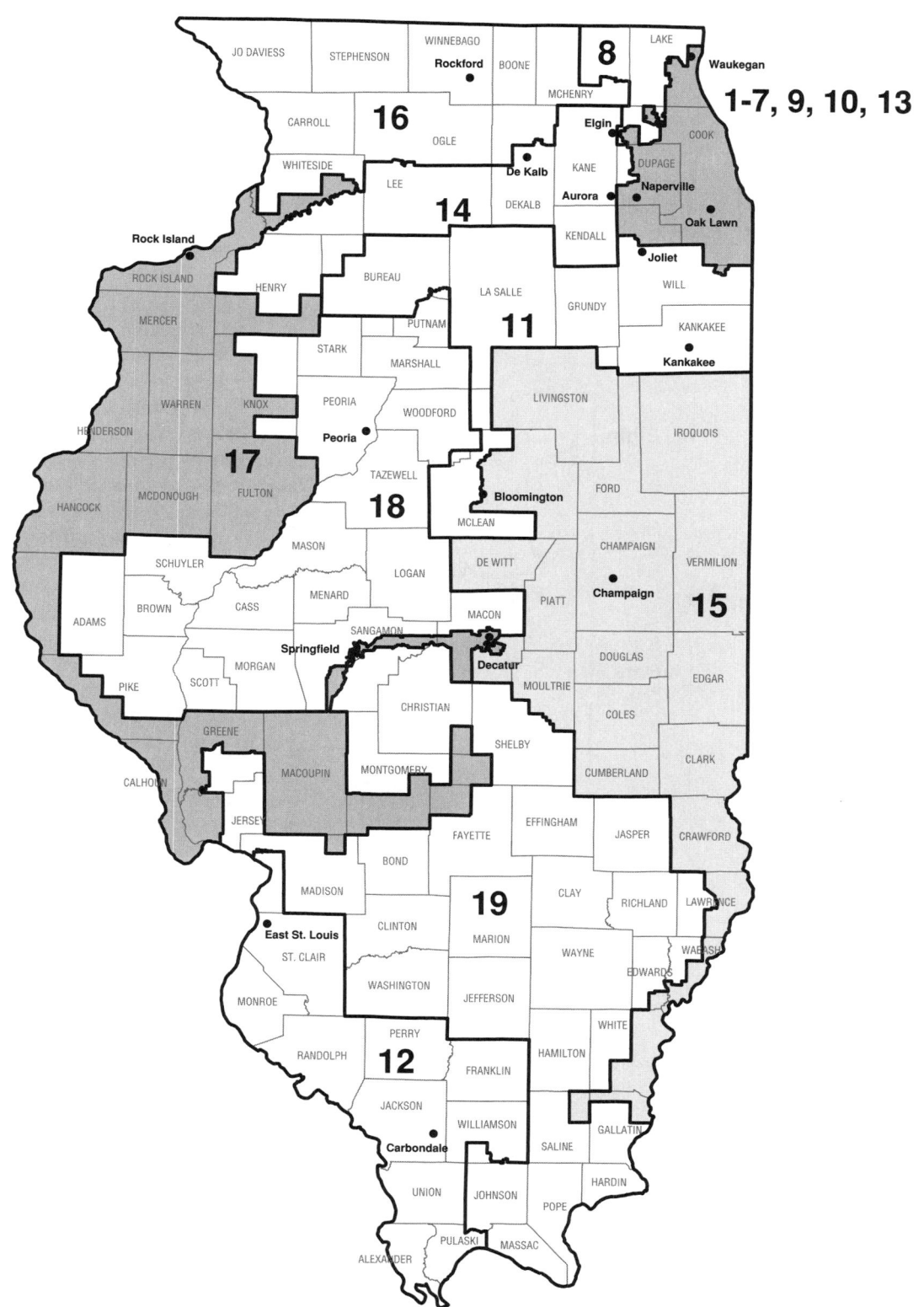

1-7, 9, 10, 13

ILLINOIS

Chicago Area

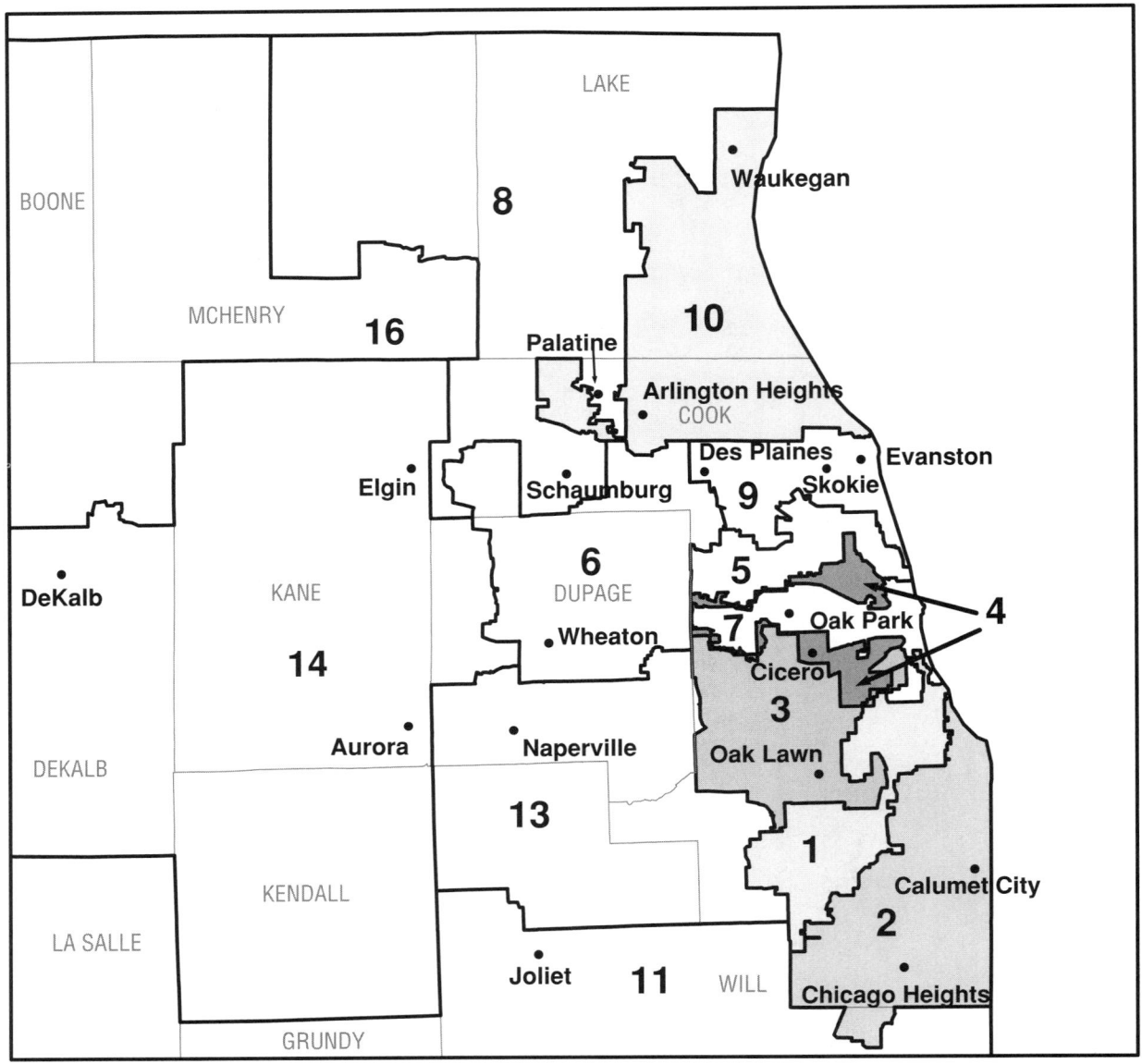

ILLINOIS
GOVERNOR 2002

2000 Census Population	County	Total Vote	Republican	Democratic	Other	Rep.-Dem. Plurality	Percentage			
							Total Vote		Major Vote	
							Rep.	Dem.	Rep.	Dem.
68,277	ADAMS	24,590	15,307	8,819	464	6,488 R	62.2%	35.9%	63.4%	36.6%
9,590	ALEXANDER	3,177	1,110	2,018	49	908 D	34.9%	63.5%	35.5%	64.5%
17,633	BOND	5,758	2,865	2,784	109	81 R	49.8%	48.4%	50.7%	49.3%
41,786	BOONE	11,309	6,123	4,657	529	1,466 R	54.1%	41.2%	56.8%	43.2%
6,950	BROWN	2,200	1,232	931	37	301 R	56.0%	42.3%	57.0%	43.0%
35,503	BUREAU	13,323	6,953	5,788	582	1,165 R	52.2%	43.4%	54.6%	45.4%
5,084	CALHOUN	2,275	966	1,268	41	302 D	42.5%	55.7%	43.2%	56.8%
16,674	CARROLL	5,865	3,054	2,560	251	494 R	52.1%	43.6%	54.4%	45.6%
13,695	CASS	5,340	2,581	2,630	129	49 D	48.3%	49.3%	49.5%	50.5%
179,669	CHAMPAIGN	52,411	27,406	23,271	1,734	4,135 R	52.3%	44.4%	54.1%	45.9%
35,372	CHRISTIAN	12,195	5,658	6,252	285	594 D	46.4%	51.3%	47.5%	52.5%
17,008	CLARK	6,417	3,624	2,645	148	979 R	56.5%	41.2%	57.8%	42.2%
14,560	CLAY	5,258	3,072	2,035	151	1,037 R	58.4%	38.7%	60.2%	39.8%
35,535	CLINTON	12,267	5,859	6,142	266	283 D	47.8%	50.1%	48.8%	51.2%
53,196	COLES	14,799	8,085	6,334	380	1,751 R	54.6%	42.8%	56.1%	43.9%
5,376,741	COOK	1,372,945	436,214	905,188	31,543	468,974 D	31.8%	65.9%	32.5%	67.5%
20,452	CRAWFORD	7,292	3,729	3,406	157	323 R	51.1%	46.7%	52.3%	47.7%
11,253	CUMBERLAND	4,051	2,367	1,534	150	833 R	58.4%	37.9%	60.7%	39.3%
88,969	DE KALB	24,455	13,100	10,249	1,106	2,851 R	53.6%	41.9%	56.1%	43.9%
16,798	DE WITT	5,428	2,914	2,373	141	541 R	53.7%	43.7%	55.1%	44.9%
19,922	DOUGLAS	6,110	3,572	2,369	169	1,203 R	58.5%	38.8%	60.1%	39.9%
904,161	DU PAGE	270,959	171,386	91,753	7,820	79,633 R	63.3%	33.9%	65.1%	34.9%
19,704	EDGAR	7,627	4,219	3,179	229	1,040 R	55.3%	41.7%	57.0%	43.0%
6,971	EDWARDS	2,695	1,899	753	43	1,146 R	70.5%	27.9%	71.6%	28.4%
34,264	EFFINGHAM	12,658	8,150	3,967	541	4,183 R	64.4%	31.3%	67.3%	32.7%
21,802	FAYETTE	7,951	4,024	3,678	249	346 R	50.6%	46.3%	52.2%	47.8%
14,241	FORD	4,738	3,004	1,599	135	1,405 R	63.4%	33.7%	65.3%	34.7%
39,018	FRANKLIN	14,687	5,872	8,566	249	2,694 D	40.0%	58.3%	40.7%	59.3%
38,250	FULTON	12,806	5,336	7,046	424	1,710 D	41.7%	55.0%	43.1%	56.9%
6,445	GALLATIN	3,067	1,108	1,888	71	780 D	36.1%	61.6%	37.0%	63.0%
14,761	GREENE	4,839	2,293	2,407	139	114 D	47.4%	49.7%	48.8%	51.2%
37,535	GRUNDY	13,530	7,422	5,638	470	1,784 R	54.9%	41.7%	56.8%	43.2%
8,621	HAMILTON	4,180	1,966	2,144	70	178 D	47.0%	51.3%	47.8%	52.2%
20,121	HANCOCK	7,936	4,743	2,951	242	1,792 R	59.8%	37.2%	61.6%	38.4%
4,800	HARDIN	2,330	1,039	1,249	42	210 D	44.6%	53.6%	45.4%	54.6%
8,213	HENDERSON	3,244	1,609	1,528	107	81 R	49.6%	47.1%	51.3%	48.7%
51,020	HENRY	16,529	9,002	7,107	420	1,895 R	54.5%	43.0%	55.9%	44.1%
31,334	IROQUOIS	10,626	6,741	3,516	369	3,225 R	63.4%	33.1%	65.7%	34.3%
59,612	JACKSON	16,085	7,402	8,135	548	733 D	46.0%	50.6%	47.6%	52.4%
10,117	JASPER	4,110	2,291	1,588	231	703 R	55.7%	38.6%	59.1%	40.9%
40,045	JEFFERSON	12,992	6,289	6,435	268	146 D	48.4%	49.5%	49.4%	50.6%
21,668	JERSEY	7,728	3,592	3,922	214	330 D	46.5%	50.8%	47.8%	52.2%
22,289	JO DAVIESS	8,279	4,774	3,205	300	1,569 R	57.7%	38.7%	59.8%	40.2%
12,878	JOHNSON	4,804	2,717	2,005	82	712 R	56.6%	41.7%	57.5%	42.5%
404,119	KANE	105,960	60,999	40,877	4,084	20,122 R	57.6%	38.6%	59.9%	40.1%
103,833	KANKAKEE	29,121	14,895	13,428	798	1,467 R	51.1%	46.1%	52.6%	47.4%
54,544	KENDALL	20,066	12,365	6,950	751	5,415 R	61.6%	34.6%	64.0%	36.0%
55,836	KNOX	18,595	10,073	8,076	446	1,997 R	54.2%	43.4%	55.5%	44.5%
644,356	LAKE	173,888	91,889	76,188	5,811	15,701 R	52.8%	43.8%	54.7%	45.3%
111,509	LA SALLE	36,805	16,643	18,477	1,685	1,834 D	45.2%	50.2%	47.4%	52.6%
15,452	LAWRENCE	5,387	2,591	2,678	118	87 D	48.1%	49.7%	49.2%	50.8%
36,062	LEE	11,687	6,192	5,080	415	1,112 R	53.0%	43.5%	54.9%	45.1%
39,678	LIVINGSTON	11,747	7,180	4,275	292	2,905 R	61.1%	36.4%	62.7%	37.3%
31,183	LOGAN	11,026	6,350	4,440	236	1,910 R	57.6%	40.3%	58.9%	41.1%
32,913	MCDONOUGH	10,787	6,236	4,197	354	2,039 R	57.8%	38.9%	59.8%	40.2%
260,077	MCHENRY	76,681	45,494	26,815	4,372	18,679 R	59.3%	35.0%	62.9%	37.1%
150,433	MCLEAN	41,857	24,233	16,480	1,144	7,753 R	57.9%	39.4%	59.5%	40.5%
114,706	MACON	37,264	18,197	18,416	651	219 D	48.8%	49.4%	49.7%	50.3%
49,019	MACOUPIN	15,966	6,692	8,865	409	2,173 D	41.9%	55.5%	43.0%	57.0%
258,941	MADISON	78,584	33,052	43,980	1,552	10,928 D	42.1%	56.0%	42.9%	57.1%

ILLINOIS

GOVERNOR 2002

2000 Census Population	County	Total Vote	Republican	Democratic	Other	Rep.-Dem. Plurality	Percentage			
							Total Vote		Major Vote	
							Rep.	Dem.	Rep.	Dem.
41,691	MARION	12,909	5,525	7,039	345	1,514 D	42.8%	54.5%	44.0%	56.0%
13,180	MARSHALL	4,929	2,745	2,014	170	731 R	55.7%	40.9%	57.7%	42.3%
16,038	MASON	5,893	2,781	2,952	160	171 D	47.2%	50.1%	48.5%	51.5%
15,161	MASSAC	5,284	2,391	2,835	58	444 D	45.2%	53.7%	45.8%	54.2%
12,486	MENARD	5,641	3,424	2,103	114	1,321 R	60.7%	37.3%	62.0%	38.0%
16,957	MERCER	6,830	3,498	3,131	201	367 R	51.2%	45.8%	52.8%	47.2%
27,619	MONROE	10,365	5,342	4,823	200	519 R	51.5%	46.5%	52.6%	47.4%
30,652	MONTGOMERY	10,209	4,375	5,613	221	1,238 D	42.9%	55.0%	43.8%	56.2%
36,616	MORGAN	12,096	6,288	5,465	343	823 R	52.0%	45.2%	53.5%	46.5%
14,287	MOULTRIE	5,127	2,715	2,276	136	439 R	53.0%	44.4%	54.4%	45.6%
51,032	OGLE	15,325	8,838	5,739	748	3,099 R	57.7%	37.4%	60.6%	39.4%
183,433	PEORIA	55,146	29,399	24,370	1,377	5,029 R	53.3%	44.2%	54.7%	45.3%
23,094	PERRY	8,505	3,691	4,572	242	881 D	43.4%	53.8%	44.7%	55.3%
16,365	PIATT	6,358	3,594	2,605	159	989 R	56.5%	41.0%	58.0%	42.0%
17,384	PIKE	6,943	3,785	2,978	180	807 R	54.5%	42.9%	56.0%	44.0%
4,413	POPE	2,053	1,008	1,010	35	2 D	49.1%	49.2%	50.0%	50.0%
7,348	PULASKI	2,850	1,268	1,533	49	265 D	44.5%	53.8%	45.3%	54.7%
6,086	PUTNAM	2,590	1,138	1,330	122	192 D	43.9%	51.4%	46.1%	53.9%
33,893	RANDOLPH	11,410	4,461	6,780	169	2,319 D	39.1%	59.4%	39.7%	60.3%
16,149	RICHLAND	6,055	3,285	2,639	131	646 R	54.3%	43.6%	55.5%	44.5%
149,374	ROCK ISLAND	42,679	18,382	23,193	1,104	4,811 D	43.1%	54.3%	44.2%	55.8%
256,082	ST. CLAIR	66,598	27,324	38,164	1,110	10,840 D	41.0%	57.3%	41.7%	58.3%
26,733	SALINE	9,852	4,620	5,062	170	442 D	46.9%	51.4%	47.7%	52.3%
188,951	SANGAMON	80,114	43,996	34,561	1,557	9,435 R	54.9%	43.1%	56.0%	44.0%
7,189	SCHUYLER	3,722	2,108	1,509	105	599 R	56.6%	40.5%	58.3%	41.7%
5,537	SCOTT	2,363	1,269	1,021	73	248 R	53.7%	43.2%	55.4%	44.6%
22,893	SHELBY	8,250	4,714	3,289	247	1,425 R	57.1%	39.9%	58.9%	41.1%
6,332	STARK	2,282	1,371	839	72	532 R	60.1%	36.8%	62.0%	38.0%
48,979	STEPHENSON	14,006	8,047	5,358	601	2,689 R	57.5%	38.3%	60.0%	40.0%
128,485	TAZEWELL	40,765	23,448	16,149	1,168	7,299 R	57.5%	39.6%	59.2%	40.8%
18,293	UNION	6,775	3,264	3,335	176	71 D	48.2%	49.2%	49.5%	50.5%
83,919	VERMILION	23,906	11,742	11,517	647	225 R	49.1%	48.2%	50.5%	49.5%
12,937	WABASH	4,233	2,755	1,414	64	1,341 R	65.1%	33.4%	66.1%	33.9%
18,735	WARREN	6,095	3,604	2,332	159	1,272 R	59.1%	38.3%	60.7%	39.3%
15,148	WASHINGTON	5,969	3,169	2,681	119	488 R	53.1%	44.9%	54.2%	45.8%
17,151	WAYNE	7,283	4,865	2,246	172	2,619 R	66.8%	30.8%	68.4%	31.6%
15,371	WHITE	6,902	3,668	3,085	149	583 R	53.1%	44.7%	54.3%	45.7%
60,653	WHITESIDE	16,727	8,020	8,214	493	194 D	47.9%	49.1%	49.4%	50.6%
502,266	WILL	145,421	77,091	63,888	4,442	13,203 R	53.0%	43.9%	54.7%	45.3%
61,296	WILLIAMSON	21,197	11,054	9,627	516	1,427 R	52.1%	45.4%	53.5%	46.5%
278,418	WINNEBAGO	77,288	36,798	37,060	3,430	262 D	47.6%	48.0%	49.8%	50.2%
35,469	WOODFORD	12,660	8,350	3,955	355	4,395 R	66.0%	31.2%	67.9%	32.1%
12,419,293	TOTAL	3,538,891	1,594,960	1,847,040	96,891	252,080 D	45.1%	52.2%	46.3%	53.7%

ILLINOIS

SENATOR 2002

2000 Census Population	County	Total Vote	Republican	Democratic	Other	Rep.-Dem. Plurality	Percentage			
							Total Vote		Major Vote	
							Rep.	Dem.	Rep.	Dem.
68,277	ADAMS	24,613	9,974	14,353	286	4,379 D	40.5%	58.3%	41.0%	59.0%
9,590	ALEXANDER	2,902	948	1,892	62	944 D	32.7%	65.2%	33.4%	66.6%
17,633	BOND	5,630	2,472	3,048	110	576 D	43.9%	54.1%	44.8%	55.2%
41,786	BOONE	11,213	5,565	5,391	257	174 R	49.6%	48.1%	50.8%	49.2%
6,950	BROWN	2,187	844	1,306	37	462 D	38.6%	59.7%	39.3%	60.7%
35,503	BUREAU	13,112	5,351	7,482	279	2,131 D	40.8%	57.1%	41.7%	58.3%
5,084	CALHOUN	2,206	729	1,438	39	709 D	33.0%	65.2%	33.6%	66.4%
16,674	CARROLL	5,832	2,950	2,771	111	179 R	50.6%	47.5%	51.6%	48.4%
13,695	CASS	5,306	1,990	3,248	68	1,258 D	37.5%	61.2%	38.0%	62.0%
179,669	CHAMPAIGN	52,550	21,142	30,302	1,106	9,160 D	40.2%	57.7%	41.1%	58.9%
35,372	CHRISTIAN	12,143	4,012	7,930	201	3,918 D	33.0%	65.3%	33.6%	66.4%
17,008	CLARK	6,265	3,351	2,792	122	559 R	53.5%	44.6%	54.5%	45.5%
14,560	CLAY	5,089	2,460	2,543	86	83 D	48.3%	50.0%	49.2%	50.8%
35,535	CLINTON	12,062	5,438	6,425	199	987 D	45.1%	53.3%	45.8%	54.2%
53,196	COLES	14,770	6,427	8,118	225	1,691 D	43.5%	55.0%	44.2%	55.8%
5,376,741	COOK	1,337,436	365,335	953,233	18,868	587,898 D	27.3%	71.3%	27.7%	72.3%
20,452	CRAWFORD	7,031	3,465	3,386	180	79 R	49.3%	48.2%	50.6%	49.4%
11,253	CUMBERLAND	3,987	1,807	2,092	88	285 D	45.3%	52.5%	46.3%	53.7%
88,969	DE KALB	24,329	10,718	13,040	571	2,322 D	44.1%	53.6%	45.1%	54.9%
16,798	DE WITT	5,393	2,258	3,055	80	797 D	41.9%	56.6%	42.5%	57.5%
19,922	DOUGLAS	6,094	2,705	3,312	77	607 D	44.4%	54.3%	45.0%	55.0%
904,161	DU PAGE	271,073	147,227	119,485	4,361	27,742 R	54.3%	44.1%	55.2%	44.8%
19,704	EDGAR	7,422	3,395	3,860	167	465 D	45.7%	52.0%	46.8%	53.2%
6,971	EDWARDS	2,537	1,593	908	36	685 R	62.8%	35.8%	63.7%	36.3%
34,264	EFFINGHAM	12,299	6,023	6,003	273	20 R	49.0%	48.8%	50.1%	49.9%
21,802	FAYETTE	7,873	3,387	4,338	148	951 D	43.0%	55.1%	43.8%	56.2%
14,241	FORD	4,675	2,399	2,202	74	197 R	51.3%	47.1%	52.1%	47.9%
39,018	FRANKLIN	14,370	4,519	9,646	205	5,127 D	31.4%	67.1%	31.9%	68.1%
38,250	FULTON	12,765	3,912	8,607	246	4,695 D	30.6%	67.4%	31.2%	68.8%
6,445	GALLATIN	2,947	818	2,078	51	1,260 D	27.8%	70.5%	28.2%	71.8%
14,761	GREENE	4,836	1,966	2,763	107	797 D	40.7%	57.1%	41.6%	58.4%
37,535	GRUNDY	13,347	5,700	7,408	239	1,708 D	42.7%	55.5%	43.5%	56.5%
8,621	HAMILTON	3,988	1,455	2,472	61	1,017 D	36.5%	62.0%	37.1%	62.9%
20,121	HANCOCK	7,881	3,420	4,304	157	884 D	43.4%	54.6%	44.3%	55.7%
4,800	HARDIN	2,184	883	1,269	32	386 D	40.4%	58.1%	41.0%	59.0%
8,213	HENDERSON	3,163	1,283	1,811	69	528 D	40.6%	57.3%	41.5%	58.5%
51,020	HENRY	16,245	7,013	8,961	271	1,948 D	43.2%	55.2%	43.9%	56.1%
31,334	IROQUOIS	10,457	5,868	4,372	217	1,496 R	56.1%	41.8%	57.3%	42.7%
59,612	JACKSON	15,915	6,109	9,420	386	3,311 D	38.4%	59.2%	39.3%	60.7%
10,117	JASPER	3,962	1,868	2,021	73	153 D	47.1%	51.0%	48.0%	52.0%
40,045	JEFFERSON	12,831	5,227	7,416	188	2,189 D	40.7%	57.8%	41.3%	58.7%
21,668	JERSEY	7,570	2,959	4,426	185	1,467 D	39.1%	58.5%	40.1%	59.9%
22,289	JO DAVIESS	7,963	4,232	3,583	148	649 R	53.1%	45.0%	54.2%	45.8%
12,878	JOHNSON	4,603	2,369	2,145	89	224 R	51.5%	46.6%	52.5%	47.5%
404,119	KANE	105,288	52,770	50,086	2,432	2,684 R	50.1%	47.6%	51.3%	48.7%
103,833	KANKAKEE	28,844	11,550	16,805	489	5,255 D	40.0%	58.3%	40.7%	59.3%
54,544	KENDALL	19,941	11,045	8,471	425	2,574 R	55.4%	42.5%	56.6%	43.4%
55,836	KNOX	18,408	7,164	10,912	332	3,748 D	38.9%	59.3%	39.6%	60.4%
644,356	LAKE	173,277	77,511	92,936	2,830	15,425 D	44.7%	53.6%	45.5%	54.5%
111,509	LA SALLE	36,765	13,173	22,710	882	9,537 D	35.8%	61.8%	36.7%	63.3%
15,452	LAWRENCE	5,215	2,569	2,509	137	60 R	49.3%	48.1%	50.6%	49.4%
36,062	LEE	11,620	5,357	6,037	226	680 D	46.1%	52.0%	47.0%	53.0%
39,678	LIVINGSTON	11,588	6,278	5,157	153	1,121 R	54.2%	44.5%	54.9%	45.1%
31,183	LOGAN	10,951	4,813	5,978	160	1,165 D	44.0%	54.6%	44.6%	55.4%
32,913	MCDONOUGH	10,702	4,594	5,901	207	1,307 D	42.9%	55.1%	43.8%	56.2%
260,077	MCHENRY	75,948	38,394	35,820	1,734	2,574 R	50.6%	47.2%	51.7%	48.3%
150,433	MCLEAN	41,958	19,701	21,568	689	1,867 D	47.0%	51.4%	47.7%	52.3%
114,706	MACON	37,374	13,728	23,179	467	9,451 D	36.7%	62.0%	37.2%	62.8%
49,019	MACOUPIN	15,821	5,516	10,002	303	4,486 D	34.9%	63.2%	35.5%	64.5%
258,941	MADISON	77,971	29,644	46,786	1,541	17,142 D	38.0%	60.0%	38.8%	61.2%

ILLINOIS

SENATOR 2002

2000 Census Population	County	Total Vote	Republican	Democratic	Other	Rep.-Dem. Plurality	Percentage			
							Total Vote		Major Vote	
							Rep.	Dem.	Rep.	Dem.
41,691	MARION	12,839	4,978	7,617	244	2,639 D	38.8%	59.3%	39.5%	60.5%
13,180	MARSHALL	4,804	1,987	2,688	129	701 D	41.4%	56.0%	42.5%	57.5%
16,038	MASON	5,826	1,887	3,835	104	1,948 D	32.4%	65.8%	33.0%	67.0%
15,161	MASSAC	5,126	2,267	2,782	77	515 D	44.2%	54.3%	44.9%	55.1%
12,486	MENARD	5,592	2,495	3,024	73	529 D	44.6%	54.1%	45.2%	54.8%
16,957	MERCER	6,747	2,737	3,872	138	1,135 D	40.6%	57.4%	41.4%	58.6%
27,619	MONROE	10,182	5,162	4,858	162	304 R	50.7%	47.7%	51.5%	48.5%
30,652	MONTGOMERY	10,160	3,337	6,678	145	3,341 D	32.8%	65.7%	33.3%	66.7%
36,616	MORGAN	12,004	4,704	7,130	170	2,426 D	39.2%	59.4%	39.7%	60.3%
14,287	MOULTRIE	5,106	1,828	3,189	89	1,361 D	35.8%	62.5%	36.4%	63.6%
51,032	OGLE	15,125	7,673	7,134	318	539 R	50.7%	47.2%	51.8%	48.2%
183,433	PEORIA	55,046	22,920	31,197	929	8,277 D	41.6%	56.7%	42.4%	57.6%
23,094	PERRY	8,229	3,057	5,051	121	1,994 D	37.1%	61.4%	37.7%	62.3%
16,365	PIATT	6,309	2,612	3,603	94	991 D	41.4%	57.1%	42.0%	58.0%
17,384	PIKE	6,957	2,790	4,066	101	1,276 D	40.1%	58.4%	40.7%	59.3%
4,413	POPE	1,946	867	1,051	28	184 D	44.6%	54.0%	45.2%	54.8%
7,348	PULASKI	2,707	1,129	1,535	43	406 D	41.7%	56.7%	42.4%	57.6%
6,086	PUTNAM	2,559	951	1,557	51	606 D	37.2%	60.8%	37.9%	62.1%
33,893	RANDOLPH	11,112	4,249	6,727	136	2,478 D	38.2%	60.5%	38.7%	61.3%
16,149	RICHLAND	5,785	2,995	2,654	136	341 R	51.8%	45.9%	53.0%	47.0%
149,374	ROCK ISLAND	42,757	15,096	26,998	663	11,902 D	35.3%	63.1%	35.9%	64.1%
256,082	ST. CLAIR	65,689	24,772	39,848	1,069	15,076 D	37.7%	60.7%	38.3%	61.7%
26,733	SALINE	9,489	3,597	5,750	142	2,153 D	37.9%	60.6%	38.5%	61.5%
188,951	SANGAMON	80,503	32,616	46,943	944	14,327 D	40.5%	58.3%	41.0%	59.0%
7,189	SCHUYLER	3,675	1,563	2,054	58	491 D	42.5%	55.9%	43.2%	56.8%
5,537	SCOTT	2,333	947	1,357	29	410 D	40.6%	58.2%	41.1%	58.9%
22,893	SHELBY	8,229	3,207	4,900	122	1,693 D	39.0%	59.5%	39.6%	60.4%
6,332	STARK	2,259	1,114	1,097	48	17 R	49.3%	48.6%	50.4%	49.6%
48,979	STEPHENSON	13,824	6,914	6,656	254	258 R	50.0%	48.1%	51.0%	49.0%
128,485	TAZEWELL	40,620	19,129	20,755	736	1,626 D	47.1%	51.1%	48.0%	52.0%
18,293	UNION	6,625	2,531	3,989	105	1,458 D	38.2%	60.2%	38.8%	61.2%
83,919	VERMILION	23,855	9,436	13,966	453	4,530 D	39.6%	58.5%	40.3%	59.7%
12,937	WABASH	4,097	2,287	1,734	76	553 R	55.8%	42.3%	56.9%	43.1%
18,735	WARREN	6,012	2,792	3,115	105	323 D	46.4%	51.8%	47.3%	52.7%
15,148	WASHINGTON	5,805	3,103	2,611	91	492 R	53.5%	45.0%	54.3%	45.7%
17,151	WAYNE	7,003	4,095	2,745	163	1,350 R	58.5%	39.2%	59.9%	40.1%
15,371	WHITE	6,443	2,828	3,505	110	677 D	43.9%	54.4%	44.7%	55.3%
60,653	WHITESIDE	16,698	7,303	9,079	316	1,776 D	43.7%	54.4%	44.6%	55.4%
502,266	WILL	144,110	65,764	75,814	2,532	10,050 D	45.6%	52.6%	46.5%	53.5%
61,296	WILLIAMSON	20,681	8,856	11,498	327	2,642 D	42.8%	55.6%	43.5%	56.5%
278,418	WINNEBAGO	76,655	32,520	42,442	1,693	9,922 D	42.4%	55.4%	43.4%	56.6%
35,469	WOODFORD	12,601	7,235	5,150	216	2,085 R	57.4%	40.9%	58.4%	41.6%
12,419,293	TOTAL	3,486,851	1,325,703	2,103,766	57,382	778,063 D	38.0%	60.3%	38.7%	61.3%

ILLINOIS

HOUSE OF REPRESENTATIVES

CD	Year	Total Vote	Republican Vote	Republican Candidate	Democratic Vote	Democratic Candidate	Other Vote	Rep.-Dem. Plurality	Total Vote Rep.	Total Vote Dem.	Major Vote Rep.	Major Vote Dem.
1	2002	183,656	29,776	Wardingley, Raymond G.	149,068	Rush, Bobby L.*	4,812	119,292 D	16.2%	81.2%	16.6%	83.4%
2	2002	184,010	32,567	Nelson, Doug	151,443	Jackson, Jesse L. Jr.*		118,876 D	17.7%	82.3%	17.7%	82.3%
3	2002	156,042			156,042	Lipinski, William O.*		156,042 D		100.0%		100.0%
4	2002	84,513	12,778	Lopez-Cisneros, Anthony J. "Tony"	67,339	Gutierrez, Luis V.*	4,396	54,561 D	15.1%	79.7%	15.9%	84.1%
5	2002	159,435	46,008	Augusti, Mark A.	106,514	Emanuel, Rahm	6,913	60,506 D	28.9%	66.8%	30.2%	69.8%
6	2002	173,872	113,174	Hyde, Henry J.*	60,698	Berry, Tom		52,476 R	65.1%	34.9%	65.1%	34.9%
7	2002	165,756	25,280	Tunney, Mark	137,933	Davis, Danny K.*	2,543	112,653 D	15.3%	83.2%	15.5%	84.5%
8	2002	165,926	95,275	Crane, Philip M.*	70,626	Bean, Melissa L.	25	24,649 R	57.4%	42.6%	57.4%	42.6%
9	2002	168,836	45,307	Duric, Nicholas M.	118,642	Schakowsky, Jan*	4,887	73,335 D	26.8%	70.3%	27.6%	72.4%
10	2002	186,911	128,611	Kirk, Mark Steven*	58,300	Perritt, Henry H. "Hank"		70,311 R	68.8%	31.2%	68.8%	31.2%
11	2002	193,085	124,192	Weller, Jerry*	68,893	Van Duyne, Keith S.		55,299 R	64.3%	35.7%	64.3%	35.7%
12	2002	190,020	58,440	Sadler, David	131,580	Costello, Jerry F.*		73,140 D	30.8%	69.2%	30.8%	69.2%
13	2002	198,615	139,546	Biggert, Judy*	59,069	Mason, Tom		80,477 R	70.3%	29.7%	70.3%	29.7%
14	2002	182,363	135,198	Hastert, J. Dennis*	47,165	Quick, Laurence J.		88,033 R	74.1%	25.9%	74.1%	25.9%
15	2002	206,617	134,650	Johnson, Timothy V.*	64,131	Hartke, Joshua T.	7,836	70,519 R	65.2%	31.0%	67.7%	32.3%
16	2002	188,827	133,339	Manzullo, Donald*	55,488	Kutsch, John		77,851 R	70.6%	29.4%	70.6%	29.4%
17	2002	203,612	76,519	Calderone, Peter	127,093	Evans, Lane*		50,574 D	37.6%	62.4%	37.6%	62.4%
18	2002	192,567	192,567	LaHood, Ray*				192,567 R	100.0%		100.0%	
19	2002	244,473	133,956	Shimkus, John*	110,517	Phelps, David*		23,439 R	54.8%	45.2%	54.8%	45.2%
Total	2002	3,429,136	1,657,183		1,740,541		31,412	83,358 D	48.3%	50.8%	48.8%	51.2%

An asterisk (*) denotes incumbent.

ILLINOIS

GENERAL AND PRIMARY ELECTIONS

2002 GENERAL ELECTIONS

Governor	Other vote was 73,794 Libertarian (Cal Skinner); 23,089 Independent (Marisellis Brown); 8 write-in (Peter Dale Kauss).
Senator	Other vote was 57,382 Libertarian (Steven Burgauer).
House	Other vote was:

CD 1	4,812 Libertarian (Dorothy G. Tsatsos).
CD 2	
CD 3	
CD 4	4,396 Libertarian (Maggie Kohls).
CD 5	6,913 Libertarian (Frank Gonzalez).
CD 6	
CD 7	2,543 Libertarian (Martin Pankau).
CD 8	25 write-in (Chuck Kelecic).
CD 9	4,887 Libertarian (Stephanie "vs. the Machine" Sailor).
CD 10	
CD 11	
CD 12	
CD 13	
CD 14	
CD 15	7,836 Illinois Green (Carl Estabrook).
CD 16	
CD 17	
CD 18	
CD 19	

2002 PRIMARY ELECTIONS

Primary	March 19, 2002	**Registration** (as of March 19, 2002)	7,069,886	No Party Registration

Primary Type Open—Any registered voter could participate in the primary of either party.

Note: An asterisk (*) denotes incumbent.

	REPUBLICAN PRIMARIES			DEMOCRATIC PRIMARIES		
Governor	Jim Ryan	410,074	44.7%	Rod R. Blagojevich	457,197	36.5%
	Patrick J. O'Malley	260,860	28.4%	Paul G. Vallas	431,728	34.5%
	Corinne Wood	246,825	26.9%	Roland W. Burris	363,591	29.0%
	Shannon Renken (write-in)	69				
	TOTAL	917,828		TOTAL	1,252,516	
Senator	Jim Durkin	378,010	45.8%	Richard J. Durbin*	918,467	100.0%
	James D. Oberweis	259,515	31.4%			
	John Cox	187,706	22.7%			
	TOTAL	825,231				
Congressional District 1	Raymond G. Wardingley	9,430	100.0%	Bobby L. Rush*	111,462	100.0%
Congressional District 2	Doug Nelson	10,494	100.0%	Jesse L. Jackson Jr.*	100,370	85.3%
				Yvonne L. Christian-Williams	11,757	10.0%
				Anthony W. Williams	5,501	4.7%
				TOTAL	117,628	

ILLINOIS

GENERAL AND PRIMARY ELECTIONS

REPUBLICAN PRIMARIES			DEMOCRATIC PRIMARIES		
Congressional District 3	No Republican candidate		William O. Lipinski*	90,051	100.0%
Congressional District 4	Anthony J. "Tony" Lopez-Cisneros	5,721	100.0%	Luis V. Gutierrez*	38,338	68.2%
				Martin R. Castro	12,008	21.4%
				John Joseph Holowinski	5,849	10.4%
				TOTAL	56,195	
Congressional District 5	Mark A. Augusti	5,753	40.9%	Rahm Emanuel	46,774	50.5%
	William F. Hurley	5,678	40.3%	Nancy Kaszak	35,716	38.6%
	Gene Urbaszewski	2,632	18.7%	Peter Dagher	4,145	4.5%
	Gene Koprowski (write-in)	14	0.1%	Stanley Niziolek	1,698	1.8%
				Mark A. Fredrickson	1,202	1.3%
				Ray "The Angel" Lear	1,094	1.2%
				Paul A. Rauner	1,043	1.1%
				Joseph Slovinec	953	1.0%
	TOTAL	14,077		TOTAL	92,625	
Congressional District 6	Henry J. Hyde*	66,584	100.0%	Tom Berry	26,791	100.0%
Congressional District 7	Mark Tunney	5,445	58.4%	Danny K. Davis*	92,960	100.0%
	Byron F. Reed	2,048	22.0%			
	Robert Dallas	1,823	19.6%			
	TOTAL	9,316				
Congressional District 8	Philip M. Crane*	59,051	100.0%	Melissa L. Bean	26,382	100.0%
Congressional District 9	*No Republican candidate filed for the primary. Nicholas M. Duric was subsequently named to fill the vacancy on the general election ballot.*			Jan Schakowsky*	69,020	100.0%
Congressional District 10	Mark Steven Kirk*	47,477	100.0%	Henry H. "Hank" Perritt Jr.	39,323	100.0%
Congressional District 11	Jerry Weller*	52,459	100.0%	Keith S. Van Duyne	35,005	100.0%
				Charles M. Hughes (write-in)	13	
				TOTAL	35,018	
Congressional District 12	David Sadler	15,019	66.1%	Jerry F. Costello*	58,195	100.0%
	Patricia Elaine Beard	7,706	33.9%			
	TOTAL	22,725				
Congressional District 13	Judy Biggert*	70,691	100.0%	*No Democratic candidate filed for the primary. Tom Mason was subsequently named to fill the vacancy on the general election ballot.*		
Congressional District 14	J. Dennis Hastert*	74,976	100.0%	*No Democratic candidate filed for the primary. Laurence J. Quick was subsequently named to fill the vacancy on the general election ballot.*		
Congressional District 15	Timothy V. Johnson*	70,510	100.0%	*No Democratic candidate filed for the primary. Joshua T. Hartke was subsequently named to fill the vacancy on the general election ballot.*		
Congressional District 16	Donald Manzullo*	69,476	100.0%	John Kutsch	27,702	100.0%
Congressional District 17	Peter Calderone	22,435	58.3%	Lane Evans*	48,583	100.0%
	Tony Rees	16,048	41.7%			
	TOTAL	38,483				
Congressional District 18	Ray LaHood*	74,092	100.0%	No Democratic candidate		
Congressional District 19	John Shimkus*	52,191	100.0%	David Phelps*	48,154	83.4%
				Vic Roberts	9,607	16.6%
				TOTAL	57,761	

ILLINOIS REPUBLICAN PRIMARY

GOVERNOR 2002

2000 Census Population	County	Total Vote	Ryan	O'Malley	Wood	Other	Winner	Percentage of Total Vote		
								Ryan	O'Malley	Wood
68,277	ADAMS	7,379	2,098	3,292	1,989		O'Malley	28.4%	44.6%	27.0%
9,590	ALEXANDER	311	207	87	17		Ryan	66.6%	28.0%	5.5%
17,633	BOND	1,239	603	489	147		Ryan	48.7%	39.5%	11.9%
41,786	BOONE	5,165	1,944	1,517	1,704		Ryan	37.6%	29.4%	33.0%
6,950	BROWN	610	278	221	111		Ryan	45.6%	36.2%	18.2%
35,503	BUREAU	5,212	1,813	1,570	1,829		Wood	34.8%	30.1%	35.1%
5,084	CALHOUN	365	112	194	59		O'Malley	30.7%	53.2%	16.2%
16,674	CARROLL	3,345	1,055	845	1,445		Wood	31.5%	25.3%	43.2%
13,695	CASS	1,822	794	598	430		Ryan	43.6%	32.8%	23.6%
179,669	CHAMPAIGN	18,071	7,624	5,259	5,187	1	Ryan	42.2%	29.1%	28.7%
35,372	CHRISTIAN	2,255	1,027	916	312		Ryan	45.5%	40.6%	13.8%
17,008	CLARK	2,870	997	1,258	615		O'Malley	34.7%	43.8%	21.4%
14,560	CLAY	943	226	640	77		O'Malley	24.0%	67.9%	8.2%
35,535	CLINTON	2,148	681	1,214	253		O'Malley	31.7%	56.5%	11.8%
53,196	COLES	4,382	1,966	1,302	1,114		Ryan	44.9%	29.7%	25.4%
5,376,741	COOK	182,811	82,222	46,706	53,882	1	Ryan	45.0%	25.5%	29.5%
20,452	CRAWFORD	2,313	757	1,242	314		O'Malley	32.7%	53.7%	13.6%
11,253	CUMBERLAND	1,172	489	488	195		Ryan	41.7%	41.6%	16.6%
88,969	DE KALB	10,025	4,312	2,760	2,953		Ryan	43.0%	27.5%	29.5%
16,798	DE WITT	3,472	1,382	1,018	1,072		Ryan	39.8%	29.3%	30.9%
19,922	DOUGLAS	2,703	1,189	805	709		Ryan	44.0%	29.8%	26.2%
904,161	DU PAGE	125,027	68,293	24,329	32,404	1	Ryan	54.6%	19.5%	25.9%
19,704	EDGAR	3,272	1,229	1,025	1,018		Ryan	37.6%	31.3%	31.1%
6,971	EDWARDS	1,256	722	402	132		Ryan	57.5%	32.0%	10.5%
34,264	EFFINGHAM	3,277	919	2,009	349		O'Malley	28.0%	61.3%	10.6%
21,802	FAYETTE	1,950	771	956	223		O'Malley	39.5%	49.0%	11.4%
14,241	FORD	2,396	942	763	688	3	Ryan	39.3%	31.8%	28.7%
39,018	FRANKLIN	2,204	1,347	644	213		Ryan	61.1%	29.2%	9.7%
38,250	FULTON	2,143	901	625	617		Ryan	42.0%	29.2%	28.8%
6,445	GALLATIN	271	177	72	22		Ryan	65.3%	26.6%	8.1%
14,761	GREENE	1,162	316	689	157		O'Malley	27.2%	59.3%	13.5%
37,535	GRUNDY	3,493	1,484	1,188	821		Ryan	42.5%	34.0%	23.5%
8,621	HAMILTON	696	375	275	46		Ryan	53.9%	39.5%	6.6%
20,121	HANCOCK	2,457	887	808	762		Ryan	36.1%	32.9%	31.0%
4,800	HARDIN	784	513	208	63		Ryan	65.4%	26.5%	8.0%
8,213	HENDERSON	946	404	195	347		Ryan	42.7%	20.6%	36.7%
51,020	HENRY	4,151	1,899	1,047	1,205		Ryan	45.7%	25.2%	29.0%
31,334	IROQUOIS	4,893	1,959	1,460	1,474		Ryan	40.0%	29.8%	30.1%
59,612	JACKSON	2,621	1,417	930	274		Ryan	54.1%	35.5%	10.5%
10,117	JASPER	728	193	470	65		O'Malley	26.5%	64.6%	8.9%
40,045	JEFFERSON	1,749	861	741	147		Ryan	49.2%	42.4%	8.4%
21,668	JERSEY	1,617	396	1,044	177		O'Malley	24.5%	64.6%	10.9%
22,289	JO DAVIESS	3,070	1,190	772	1,108		Ryan	38.8%	25.1%	36.1%
12,878	JOHNSON	1,708	1,050	521	137		Ryan	61.5%	30.5%	8.0%
404,119	KANE	48,670	22,302	11,632	14,734	2	Ryan	45.8%	23.9%	30.3%
103,833	KANKAKEE	7,881	3,368	2,366	2,146	1	Ryan	42.7%	30.0%	27.2%
54,544	KENDALL	11,133	5,012	2,671	3,450		Ryan	45.0%	24.0%	31.0%
55,836	KNOX	4,925	2,936	1,026	963		Ryan	59.6%	20.8%	19.6%
644,356	LAKE	69,602	27,454	15,718	26,424	6	Ryan	39.4%	22.6%	38.0%
111,509	LA SALLE	8,482	3,822	2,562	2,098		Ryan	45.1%	30.2%	24.7%
15,452	LAWRENCE	1,815	762	808	243	2	O'Malley	42.0%	44.5%	13.4%
36,062	LEE	3,854	1,341	1,327	1,186		Ryan	34.8%	34.4%	30.8%
39,678	LIVINGSTON	7,159	2,969	1,781	2,392	17	Ryan	41.5%	24.9%	33.4%
31,183	LOGAN	5,947	2,403	2,307	1,235	2	Ryan	40.4%	38.8%	20.8%
32,913	MCDONOUGH	5,120	1,894	1,250	1,976		Wood	37.0%	24.4%	38.6%
260,077	MCHENRY	30,155	12,616	7,387	10,150	2	Ryan	41.8%	24.5%	33.7%
150,433	MCLEAN	18,691	6,856	6,292	5,532	11	Ryan	36.7%	33.7%	29.6%
114,706	MACON	9,651	5,727	2,292	1,632		Ryan	59.3%	23.7%	16.9%
49,019	MACOUPIN	2,239	818	1,122	299		O'Malley	36.5%	50.1%	13.4%
258,941	MADISON	12,841	3,844	7,385	1,612		O'Malley	29.9%	57.5%	12.6%

ILLINOIS REPUBLICAN PRIMARY

GOVERNOR 2002

2000 Census Population	County	Total Vote	Ryan	O'Malley	Wood	Other	Winner	Percentage of Total Vote		
								Ryan	O'Malley	Wood
41,691	MARION	2,464	807	1,326	331		O'Malley	32.8%	53.8%	13.4%
13,180	MARSHALL	1,923	786	565	572		Ryan	40.9%	29.4%	29.7%
16,038	MASON	1,363	620	379	364		Ryan	45.5%	27.8%	26.7%
15,161	MASSAC	1,666	596	941	129		O'Malley	35.8%	56.5%	7.7%
12,486	MENARD	3,210	1,667	934	609		Ryan	51.9%	29.1%	19.0%
16,957	MERCER	1,407	528	453	426		Ryan	37.5%	32.2%	30.3%
27,619	MONROE	1,741	622	875	244		O'Malley	35.7%	50.3%	14.0%
30,652	MONTGOMERY	1,883	881	748	254		Ryan	46.8%	39.7%	13.5%
36,616	MORGAN	5,090	2,449	1,534	1,107		Ryan	48.1%	30.1%	21.7%
14,287	MOULTRIE	1,447	722	397	328		Ryan	49.9%	27.4%	22.7%
51,032	OGLE	8,770	3,004	3,145	2,621		O'Malley	34.3%	35.9%	29.9%
183,433	PEORIA	15,000	7,679	3,740	3,580	1	Ryan	51.2%	24.9%	23.9%
23,094	PERRY	1,982	1,022	725	235		Ryan	51.6%	36.6%	11.9%
16,365	PIATT	2,786	1,169	791	826		Ryan	42.0%	28.4%	29.6%
17,384	PIKE	1,772	577	799	396		O'Malley	32.6%	45.1%	22.3%
4,413	POPE	798	410	261	127		Ryan	51.4%	32.7%	15.9%
7,348	PULASKI	1,043	633	291	119		Ryan	60.7%	27.9%	11.4%
6,086	PUTNAM	499	205	160	134		Ryan	41.1%	32.1%	26.9%
33,893	RANDOLPH	1,257	479	682	96		O'Malley	38.1%	54.3%	7.6%
16,149	RICHLAND	976	261	586	129		O'Malley	26.7%	60.0%	13.2%
149,374	ROCK ISLAND	6,367	2,474	2,187	1,706		Ryan	38.9%	34.3%	26.8%
256,082	ST. CLAIR	8,439	1,930	5,522	987		O'Malley	22.9%	65.4%	11.7%
26,733	SALINE	1,702	1,066	475	161		Ryan	62.6%	27.9%	9.5%
188,951	SANGAMON	30,671	18,100	7,726	4,845		Ryan	59.0%	25.2%	15.8%
7,189	SCHUYLER	1,013	398	341	274		Ryan	39.3%	33.7%	27.0%
5,537	SCOTT	1,264	463	464	337		O'Malley	36.6%	36.7%	26.7%
22,893	SHELBY	1,907	839	839	229			44.0%	44.0%	12.0%
6,332	STARK	817	428	171	218		Ryan	52.4%	20.9%	26.7%
48,979	STEPHENSON	8,382	3,023	2,298	3,060	1	Wood	36.1%	27.4%	36.5%
128,485	TAZEWELL	13,046	5,764	4,502	2,780		Ryan	44.2%	34.5%	21.3%
18,293	UNION	1,267	833	346	88		Ryan	65.7%	27.3%	6.9%
83,919	VERMILION	7,693	3,657	1,968	2,067	1	Ryan	47.5%	25.6%	26.9%
12,937	WABASH	912	449	340	123		Ryan	49.2%	37.3%	13.5%
18,735	WARREN	3,252	1,475	661	1,116		Ryan	45.4%	20.3%	34.3%
15,148	WASHINGTON	1,420	492	749	179		O'Malley	34.6%	52.7%	12.6%
17,151	WAYNE	3,491	1,397	1,587	507		O'Malley	40.0%	45.5%	14.5%
15,371	WHITE	1,128	560	438	130		Ryan	49.6%	38.8%	11.5%
60,653	WHITESIDE	4,023	1,243	1,128	1,652		Wood	30.9%	28.0%	41.1%
502,266	WILL	49,041	21,187	15,146	12,692	16	Ryan	43.2%	30.9%	25.9%
61,296	WILLIAMSON	3,646	1,959	1,412	275		Ryan	53.7%	38.7%	7.5%
278,418	WINNEBAGO	26,276	10,436	9,657	6,183		Ryan	39.7%	36.8%	23.5%
35,469	WOODFORD	6,345	2,639	2,051	1,654	1	Ryan	41.6%	32.3%	26.1%
12,419,293	TOTAL	917,828	410,074	260,860	246,825	69	Ryan	44.7%	28.4%	26.9%

144

ILLINOIS DEMOCRATIC PRIMARY
GOVERNOR 2002

2000 Census Population	County	Total Vote	Blagojevich	Vallas	Burris	Winner	Percentage of Total Vote		
							Blagojevich	Vallas	Burris
68,277	ADAMS	4,756	1,892	1,620	1,244	Blagojevich	39.8%	34.1%	26.2%
9,590	ALEXANDER	1,906	865	391	650	Blagojevich	45.4%	20.5%	34.1%
17,633	BOND	1,135	724	215	196	Blagojevich	63.8%	18.9%	17.3%
41,786	BOONE	1,452	995	263	194	Blagojevich	68.5%	18.1%	13.4%
6,950	BROWN	452	276	52	124	Blagojevich	61.1%	11.5%	27.4%
35,503	BUREAU	2,219	1,266	522	431	Blagojevich	57.1%	23.5%	19.4%
5,084	CALHOUN	788	583	86	119	Blagojevich	74.0%	10.9%	15.1%
16,674	CARROLL	603	426	80	97	Blagojevich	70.6%	13.3%	16.1%
13,695	CASS	1,134	647	227	260	Blagojevich	57.1%	20.0%	22.9%
179,669	CHAMPAIGN	9,549	4,070	2,807	2,672	Blagojevich	42.6%	29.4%	28.0%
35,372	CHRISTIAN	4,948	2,928	1,268	752	Blagojevich	59.2%	25.6%	15.2%
17,008	CLARK	1,190	796	179	215	Blagojevich	66.9%	15.0%	18.1%
14,560	CLAY	803	474	136	193	Blagojevich	59.0%	16.9%	24.0%
35,535	CLINTON	1,790	1,107	322	361	Blagojevich	61.8%	18.0%	20.2%
53,196	COLES	2,949	1,521	896	532	Blagojevich	51.6%	30.4%	18.0%
5,376,741	COOK	747,410	213,028	268,514	265,868	Vallas	28.5%	35.9%	35.6%
20,452	CRAWFORD	1,673	1,278	155	240	Blagojevich	76.4%	9.3%	14.3%
11,253	CUMBERLAND	1,480	685	414	381	Blagojevich	46.3%	28.0%	25.7%
88,969	DE KALB	5,131	2,222	2,031	878	Blagojevich	43.3%	39.6%	17.1%
16,798	DE WITT	734	426	149	159	Blagojevich	58.0%	20.3%	21.7%
19,922	DOUGLAS	941	562	204	175	Blagojevich	59.7%	21.7%	18.6%
904,161	DU PAGE	53,158	16,260	30,678	6,220	Vallas	30.6%	57.7%	11.7%
19,704	EDGAR	1,264	726	305	233	Blagojevich	57.4%	24.1%	18.4%
6,971	EDWARDS	282	129	29	124	Blagojevich	45.7%	10.3%	44.0%
34,264	EFFINGHAM	2,265	1,104	748	413	Blagojevich	48.7%	33.0%	18.2%
21,802	FAYETTE	1,746	1,195	282	269	Blagojevich	68.4%	16.2%	15.4%
14,241	FORD	432	243	110	79	Blagojevich	56.3%	25.5%	18.3%
39,018	FRANKLIN	6,341	3,493	1,942	906	Blagojevich	55.1%	30.6%	14.3%
38,250	FULTON	4,054	2,157	1,007	890	Blagojevich	53.2%	24.8%	22.0%
6,445	GALLATIN	2,617	1,317	738	562	Blagojevich	50.3%	28.2%	21.5%
14,761	GREENE	1,969	1,307	275	387	Blagojevich	66.4%	14.0%	19.7%
37,535	GRUNDY	2,385	970	1,146	269	Vallas	40.7%	48.1%	11.3%
8,621	HAMILTON	1,623	889	449	285	Blagojevich	54.8%	27.7%	17.6%
20,121	HANCOCK	1,308	497	367	444	Blagojevich	38.0%	28.1%	33.9%
4,800	HARDIN	834	576	166	92	Blagojevich	69.1%	19.9%	11.0%
8,213	HENDERSON	599	378	86	135	Blagojevich	63.1%	14.4%	22.5%
51,020	HENRY	2,590	1,770	425	395	Blagojevich	68.3%	16.4%	15.3%
31,334	IROQUOIS	977	493	262	222	Blagojevich	50.5%	26.8%	22.7%
59,612	JACKSON	4,506	1,729	1,678	1,099	Blagojevich	38.4%	37.2%	24.4%
10,117	JASPER	1,012	583	219	210	Blagojevich	57.6%	21.6%	20.8%
40,045	JEFFERSON	5,004	2,424	1,426	1,154	Blagojevich	48.4%	28.5%	23.1%
21,668	JERSEY	1,878	1,288	281	309	Blagojevich	68.6%	15.0%	16.5%
22,289	JO DAVIESS	844	472	197	175	Blagojevich	55.9%	23.3%	20.7%
12,878	JOHNSON	1,021	581	306	134	Blagojevich	56.9%	30.0%	13.1%
404,119	KANE	21,815	8,273	9,629	3,913	Vallas	37.9%	44.1%	17.9%
103,833	KANKAKEE	6,250	2,232	2,185	1,833	Blagojevich	35.7%	35.0%	29.3%
54,544	KENDALL	3,015	1,324	1,261	430	Blagojevich	43.9%	41.8%	14.3%
55,836	KNOX	3,418	1,940	738	740	Blagojevich	56.8%	21.6%	21.7%
644,356	LAKE	46,668	15,160	23,284	8,224	Vallas	32.5%	49.9%	17.6%
111,509	LA SALLE	7,366	3,858	2,267	1,241	Blagojevich	52.4%	30.8%	16.8%
15,452	LAWRENCE	1,612	1,036	138	438	Blagojevich	64.3%	8.6%	27.2%
36,062	LEE	1,790	1,239	247	304	Blagojevich	69.2%	13.8%	17.0%
39,678	LIVINGSTON	1,153	634	299	220	Blagojevich	55.0%	25.9%	19.1%
31,183	LOGAN	1,262	584	475	203	Blagojevich	46.3%	37.6%	16.1%
32,913	MCDONOUGH	1,371	592	468	311	Blagojevich	43.2%	34.1%	22.7%
260,077	MCHENRY	10,798	4,202	5,422	1,174	Vallas	38.9%	50.2%	10.9%
150,433	MCLEAN	6,063	3,160	1,504	1,399	Blagojevich	52.1%	24.8%	23.1%
114,706	MACON	10,274	5,158	2,572	2,544	Blagojevich	50.2%	25.0%	24.8%
49,019	MACOUPIN	4,928	3,223	1,147	558	Blagojevich	65.4%	23.3%	11.3%
258,941	MADISON	25,711	17,794	4,258	3,659	Blagojevich	69.2%	16.6%	14.2%

ILLINOIS DEMOCRATIC PRIMARY

GOVERNOR 2002

2000 Census Population	County	Total Vote	Blagojevich	Vallas	Burris	Winner	Percentage of Total Vote		
							Blagojevich	Vallas	Burris
41,691	MARION	5,970	2,586	1,349	2,035	Blagojevich	43.3%	22.6%	34.1%
13,180	MARSHALL	934	473	263	198	Blagojevich	50.6%	28.2%	21.2%
16,038	MASON	2,401	1,173	595	633	Blagojevich	48.9%	24.8%	26.4%
15,161	MASSAC	1,172	744	229	199	Blagojevich	63.5%	19.5%	17.0%
12,486	MENARD	629	283	254	92	Blagojevich	45.0%	40.4%	14.6%
16,957	MERCER	1,324	878	210	236	Blagojevich	66.3%	15.9%	17.8%
27,619	MONROE	1,565	1,156	236	173	Blagojevich	73.9%	15.1%	11.1%
30,652	MONTGOMERY	2,866	1,872	676	318	Blagojevich	65.3%	23.6%	11.1%
36,616	MORGAN	2,276	1,151	652	473	Blagojevich	50.6%	28.6%	20.8%
14,287	MOULTRIE	1,762	920	557	285	Blagojevich	52.2%	31.6%	16.2%
51,032	OGLE	1,875	1,308	294	273	Blagojevich	69.8%	15.7%	14.6%
183,433	PEORIA	13,776	6,273	3,534	3,969	Blagojevich	45.5%	25.7%	28.8%
23,094	PERRY	2,762	1,812	563	387	Blagojevich	65.6%	20.4%	14.0%
16,365	PIATT	960	552	249	159	Blagojevich	57.5%	25.9%	16.6%
17,384	PIKE	2,012	1,411	202	399	Blagojevich	70.1%	10.0%	19.8%
4,413	POPE	712	433	175	104	Blagojevich	60.8%	24.6%	14.6%
7,348	PULASKI	801	393	151	257	Blagojevich	49.1%	18.9%	32.1%
6,086	PUTNAM	754	431	180	143	Blagojevich	57.2%	23.9%	19.0%
33,893	RANDOLPH	6,069	4,534	818	717	Blagojevich	74.7%	13.5%	11.8%
16,149	RICHLAND	917	669	103	145	Blagojevich	73.0%	11.2%	15.8%
149,374	ROCK ISLAND	14,663	10,150	2,081	2,432	Blagojevich	69.2%	14.2%	16.6%
256,082	ST. CLAIR	21,882	12,993	1,920	6,969	Blagojevich	59.4%	8.8%	31.8%
26,733	SALINE	4,291	2,298	1,362	631	Blagojevich	53.6%	31.7%	14.7%
188,951	SANGAMON	14,497	6,911	5,141	2,445	Blagojevich	47.7%	35.5%	16.9%
7,189	SCHUYLER	496	256	79	161	Blagojevich	51.6%	15.9%	32.5%
5,537	SCOTT	347	207	51	89	Blagojevich	59.7%	14.7%	25.6%
22,893	SHELBY	2,281	885	956	440	Vallas	38.8%	41.9%	19.3%
6,332	STARK	301	171	77	53	Blagojevich	56.8%	25.6%	17.6%
48,979	STEPHENSON	2,056	1,442	197	417	Blagojevich	70.1%	9.6%	20.3%
128,485	TAZEWELL	9,178	5,109	2,278	1,791	Blagojevich	55.7%	24.8%	19.5%
18,293	UNION	2,600	1,362	867	371	Blagojevich	52.4%	33.3%	14.3%
83,919	VERMILION	4,509	2,501	705	1,303	Blagojevich	55.5%	15.6%	28.9%
12,937	WABASH	616	344	63	209	Blagojevich	55.8%	10.2%	33.9%
18,735	WARREN	815	477	163	175	Blagojevich	58.5%	20.0%	21.5%
15,148	WASHINGTON	990	764	111	115	Blagojevich	77.2%	11.2%	11.6%
17,151	WAYNE	1,349	697	235	417	Blagojevich	51.7%	17.4%	30.9%
15,371	WHITE	3,312	1,165	795	1,352	Burris	35.2%	24.0%	40.8%
60,653	WHITESIDE	3,131	2,264	431	436	Blagojevich	72.3%	13.8%	13.9%
502,266	WILL	40,324	13,431	17,782	9,111	Vallas	33.3%	44.1%	22.6%
61,296	WILLIAMSON	7,025	3,178	2,793	1,054	Blagojevich	45.2%	39.8%	15.0%
278,418	WINNEBAGO	19,764	13,017	2,492	4,255	Blagojevich	65.9%	12.6%	21.5%
35,469	WOODFORD	1,306	762	312	232	Blagojevich	58.3%	23.9%	17.8%
12,419,293	TOTAL	1,252,516	457,197	431,728	363,591	Blagojevich	36.5%	34.5%	29.0%

ILLINOIS REPUBLICAN PRIMARY

SENATOR 2002

2000 Census Population	County	Total Vote	Durkin	Oberweis	Cox	Winner	Percentage of Total Vote		
							Durkin	Oberweis	Cox
68,277	ADAMS	6,233	3,345	839	2,049	Durkin	53.7%	13.5%	32.9%
9,590	ALEXANDER	272	153	46	73	Durkin	56.3%	16.9%	26.8%
17,633	BOND	1,023	616	188	219	Durkin	60.2%	18.4%	21.4%
41,786	BOONE	4,769	1,492	1,288	1,989	Cox	31.3%	27.0%	41.7%
6,950	BROWN	534	360	61	113	Durkin	67.4%	11.4%	21.2%
35,503	BUREAU	4,361	2,281	1,023	1,057	Durkin	52.3%	23.5%	24.2%
5,084	CALHOUN	282	139	38	105	Durkin	49.3%	13.5%	37.2%
16,674	CARROLL	2,931	1,401	450	1,080	Durkin	47.8%	15.4%	36.8%
13,695	CASS	1,539	840	244	455	Durkin	54.6%	15.9%	29.6%
179,669	CHAMPAIGN	15,892	6,851	4,674	4,367	Durkin	43.1%	29.4%	27.5%
35,372	CHRISTIAN	1,977	663	482	832	Cox	33.5%	24.4%	42.1%
17,008	CLARK	2,464	1,211	313	940	Durkin	49.1%	12.7%	38.1%
14,560	CLAY	829	350	127	352	Cox	42.2%	15.3%	42.5%
35,535	CLINTON	1,855	976	363	516	Durkin	52.6%	19.6%	27.8%
53,196	COLES	3,768	1,655	720	1,393	Durkin	43.9%	19.1%	37.0%
5,376,741	COOK	165,989	85,707	52,004	28,278	Durkin	51.6%	31.3%	17.0%
20,452	CRAWFORD	2,051	1,149	351	551	Durkin	56.0%	17.1%	26.9%
11,253	CUMBERLAND	1,000	506	148	346	Durkin	50.6%	14.8%	34.6%
88,969	DE KALB	8,976	2,693	4,586	1,697	Oberweis	30.0%	51.1%	18.9%
16,798	DE WITT	2,953	1,110	556	1,287	Cox	37.6%	18.8%	43.6%
19,922	DOUGLAS	2,341	991	616	734	Durkin	42.3%	26.3%	31.4%
904,161	DU PAGE	116,361	55,443	44,572	16,346	Durkin	47.6%	38.3%	14.0%
19,704	EDGAR	2,732	1,343	451	938	Durkin	49.2%	16.5%	34.3%
6,971	EDWARDS	998	495	111	392	Durkin	49.6%	11.1%	39.3%
34,264	EFFINGHAM	2,796	1,141	480	1,175	Cox	40.8%	17.2%	42.0%
21,802	FAYETTE	1,716	928	322	466	Durkin	54.1%	18.8%	27.2%
14,241	FORD	2,048	884	618	546	Durkin	43.2%	30.2%	26.7%
39,018	FRANKLIN	1,847	987	300	560	Durkin	53.4%	16.2%	30.3%
38,250	FULTON	1,958	990	372	596	Durkin	50.6%	19.0%	30.4%
6,445	GALLATIN	231	121	46	64	Durkin	52.4%	19.9%	27.7%
14,761	GREENE	989	565	201	223	Durkin	57.1%	20.3%	22.5%
37,535	GRUNDY	3,161	1,176	1,235	750	Oberweis	37.2%	39.1%	23.7%
8,621	HAMILTON	565	323	50	192	Durkin	57.2%	8.8%	34.0%
20,121	HANCOCK	2,120	1,353	322	445	Durkin	63.8%	15.2%	21.0%
4,800	HARDIN	615	387	49	179	Durkin	62.9%	8.0%	29.1%
8,213	HENDERSON	799	545	113	141	Durkin	68.2%	14.1%	17.6%
51,020	HENRY	3,704	2,079	807	818	Durkin	56.1%	21.8%	22.1%
31,334	IROQUOIS	4,226	1,949	1,097	1,180	Durkin	46.1%	26.0%	27.9%
59,612	JACKSON	2,338	1,440	401	497	Durkin	61.6%	17.2%	21.3%
10,117	JASPER	631	304	64	263	Durkin	48.2%	10.1%	41.7%
40,045	JEFFERSON	1,554	902	315	337	Durkin	58.0%	20.3%	21.7%
21,668	JERSEY	1,379	748	348	283	Durkin	54.2%	25.2%	20.5%
22,289	JO DAVIESS	2,847	1,012	456	1,379	Cox	35.5%	16.0%	48.4%
12,878	JOHNSON	1,377	868	172	337	Durkin	63.0%	12.5%	24.5%
404,119	KANE	45,465	13,229	25,625	6,611	Oberweis	29.1%	56.4%	14.5%
103,833	KANKAKEE	7,003	3,511	1,564	1,928	Durkin	50.1%	22.3%	27.5%
54,544	KENDALL	10,340	2,635	6,349	1,356	Oberweis	25.5%	61.4%	13.1%
55,836	KNOX	4,219	2,473	855	891	Durkin	58.6%	20.3%	21.1%
644,356	LAKE	62,198	30,099	20,554	11,545	Durkin	48.4%	33.0%	18.6%
111,509	LA SALLE	7,622	3,140	2,558	1,924	Durkin	41.2%	33.6%	25.2%
15,452	LAWRENCE	1,602	835	217	550	Durkin	52.1%	13.5%	34.3%
36,062	LEE	3,524	1,233	1,127	1,164	Durkin	35.0%	32.0%	33.0%
39,678	LIVINGSTON	6,040	3,004	1,287	1,749	Durkin	49.7%	21.3%	29.0%
31,183	LOGAN	5,147	2,222	1,314	1,611	Durkin	43.2%	25.5%	31.3%
32,913	MCDONOUGH	4,388	3,165	564	659	Durkin	72.1%	12.9%	15.0%
260,077	MCHENRY	27,131	10,778	9,814	6,539	Durkin	39.7%	36.2%	24.1%
150,433	MCLEAN	16,553	6,761	5,785	4,007	Durkin	40.8%	34.9%	24.2%
114,706	MACON	8,522	3,341	1,432	3,749	Cox	39.2%	16.8%	44.0%
49,019	MACOUPIN	2,039	972	495	572	Durkin	47.7%	24.3%	28.1%
258,941	MADISON	10,947	6,150	1,952	2,845	Durkin	56.2%	17.8%	26.0%

ILLINOIS REPUBLICAN PRIMARY

SENATOR 2002

2000 Census Population	County	Total Vote	Durkin	Oberweis	Cox	Winner	Percentage of Total Vote		
							Durkin	Oberweis	Cox
41,691	MARION	2,185	1,143	395	647	Durkin	52.3%	18.1%	29.6%
13,180	MARSHALL	1,672	724	430	518	Durkin	43.3%	25.7%	31.0%
16,038	MASON	1,218	606	240	372	Durkin	49.8%	19.7%	30.5%
15,161	MASSAC	1,296	747	147	402	Durkin	57.6%	11.3%	31.0%
12,486	MENARD	2,857	1,297	828	732	Durkin	45.4%	29.0%	25.6%
16,957	MERCER	1,263	742	213	308	Durkin	58.7%	16.9%	24.4%
27,619	MONROE	1,526	833	357	336	Durkin	54.6%	23.4%	22.0%
30,652	MONTGOMERY	1,645	600	498	547	Durkin	36.5%	30.3%	33.3%
36,616	MORGAN	4,328	2,334	834	1,160	Durkin	53.9%	19.3%	26.8%
14,287	MOULTRIE	1,246	435	193	618	Cox	34.9%	15.5%	49.6%
51,032	OGLE	7,909	2,435	1,593	3,881	Cox	30.8%	20.1%	49.1%
183,433	PEORIA	13,407	6,275	3,891	3,241	Durkin	46.8%	29.0%	24.2%
23,094	PERRY	1,619	929	263	427	Durkin	57.4%	16.2%	26.4%
16,365	PIATT	2,454	835	501	1,118	Cox	34.0%	20.4%	45.6%
17,384	PIKE	1,483	860	243	380	Durkin	58.0%	16.4%	25.6%
4,413	POPE	619	393	67	159	Durkin	63.5%	10.8%	25.7%
7,348	PULASKI	818	534	135	149	Durkin	65.3%	16.5%	18.2%
6,086	PUTNAM	420	156	109	155	Durkin	37.1%	26.0%	36.9%
33,893	RANDOLPH	1,056	582	178	296	Durkin	55.1%	16.9%	28.0%
16,149	RICHLAND	833	456	82	295	Durkin	54.7%	9.8%	35.4%
149,374	ROCK ISLAND	5,748	3,482	856	1,410	Durkin	60.6%	14.9%	24.5%
256,082	ST. CLAIR	7,426	3,682	1,413	2,331	Durkin	49.6%	19.0%	31.4%
26,733	SALINE	1,390	809	156	425	Durkin	58.2%	11.2%	30.6%
188,951	SANGAMON	27,801	12,144	8,981	6,676	Durkin	43.7%	32.3%	24.0%
7,189	SCHUYLER	888	525	190	173	Durkin	59.1%	21.4%	19.5%
5,537	SCOTT	1,039	630	168	241	Durkin	60.6%	16.2%	23.2%
22,893	SHELBY	1,638	651	261	726	Cox	39.7%	15.9%	44.3%
6,332	STARK	692	348	158	186	Durkin	50.3%	22.8%	26.9%
48,979	STEPHENSON	7,797	2,813	1,187	3,797	Cox	36.1%	15.2%	48.7%
128,485	TAZEWELL	11,601	4,799	3,460	3,342	Durkin	41.4%	29.8%	28.8%
18,293	UNION	1,086	602	185	299	Durkin	55.4%	17.0%	27.5%
83,919	VERMILION	6,587	2,834	1,219	2,534	Durkin	43.0%	18.5%	38.5%
12,937	WABASH	803	386	75	342	Durkin	48.1%	9.3%	42.6%
18,735	WARREN	2,745	1,812	440	493	Durkin	66.0%	16.0%	18.0%
15,148	WASHINGTON	1,192	723	227	242	Durkin	60.7%	19.0%	20.3%
17,151	WAYNE	2,854	1,450	407	997	Durkin	50.8%	14.3%	34.9%
15,371	WHITE	966	517	155	294	Durkin	53.5%	16.0%	30.4%
60,653	WHITESIDE	3,584	1,696	895	993	Durkin	47.3%	25.0%	27.7%
502,266	WILL	44,949	19,097	17,631	8,221	Durkin	42.5%	39.2%	18.3%
61,296	WILLIAMSON	3,195	1,537	482	1,176	Durkin	48.1%	15.1%	36.8%
278,418	WINNEBAGO	24,204	8,137	4,756	11,311	Cox	33.6%	19.6%	46.7%
35,469	WOODFORD	5,421	2,400	1,505	1,516	Durkin	44.3%	27.8%	28.0%
12,419,293	TOTAL	825,231	378,010	259,515	187,706	Durkin	45.8%	31.4%	22.7%

INDIANA

GOVERNOR
Joe Kernan (D). Assumed office September 13, 2003, upon the death of Frank L. O'Bannon (D).

SENATORS (1 Democrat, 1 Republican)
Evan Bayh (D). Elected 1998 to a six-year term.

Richard G. Lugar (R). Reelected 2000 to a six-year term. Previously elected 1994, 1988, 1982, 1976.

REPRESENTATIVES (6 Republicans, 3 Democrats)
1. Peter J. Visclosky (D)
2. Chris Chocola (R)
3. Mark Souder (R)
4. Steve Buyer (R)
5. Dan Burton (R)
6. Mike Pence (R)
7. Julia Carson (D)
8. John Hostettler (R)
9. Baron P. Hill (D)

POSTWAR VOTE FOR PRESIDENT

Year	Total Vote	Republican Vote	Republican Candidate	Democratic Vote	Democratic Candidate	Other Vote	Plurality	Total Vote Rep.	Total Vote Dem.	Major Vote Rep.	Major Vote Dem.
2000**	2,199,302	1,245,836	Bush, George W.	901,980	Gore, Al	51,486	343,856 R	56.6%	41.0%	58.0%	42.0%
1996**	2,135,842	1,006,693	Dole, Bob	887,424	Clinton, Bill	241,725	119,269 R	47.1%	41.5%	53.1%	46.9%
1992**	2,305,871	989,375	Bush, George	848,420	Clinton, Bill	468,076	140,955 R	42.9%	36.8%	53.8%	46.2%
1988	2,168,621	1,297,763	Bush, George	860,643	Dukakis, Michael S.	10,215	437,120 R	59.8%	39.7%	60.1%	39.9%
1984	2,233,069	1,377,230	Reagan, Ronald	841,481	Mondale, Walter F.	14,358	535,749 R	61.7%	37.7%	62.1%	37.9%
1980**	2,242,033	1,255,656	Reagan, Ronald	844,197	Carter, Jimmy	142,180	411,459 R	56.0%	37.7%	59.8%	40.2%
1976	2,220,362	1,183,958	Ford, Gerald R.	1,014,714	Carter, Jimmy	21,690	169,244 R	53.3%	45.7%	53.8%	46.2%
1972	2,125,529	1,405,154	Nixon, Richard M.	708,568	McGovern, George S.	11,807	696,586 R	66.1%	33.3%	66.5%	33.5%
1968	2,123,597	1,067,885	Nixon, Richard M.	806,659	Humphrey, Hubert H.	249,053	261,226 R	50.3%	38.0%	57.0%	43.0%
1964	2,091,606	911,118	Goldwater, Barry M.	1,170,848	Johnson, Lyndon B.	9,640	259,730 D	43.6%	56.0%	43.8%	56.2%
1960	2,135,360	1,175,120	Nixon, Richard M.	952,358	Kennedy, John F.	7,882	222,762 R	55.0%	44.6%	55.2%	44.8%
1956	1,974,607	1,182,811	Eisenhower, Dwight D.	783,908	Stevenson, Adlai E.	7,888	398,903 R	59.9%	39.7%	60.1%	39.9%
1952	1,955,049	1,136,259	Eisenhower, Dwight D.	801,530	Stevenson, Adlai E.	17,260	334,729 R	58.1%	41.0%	58.6%	41.4%
1948	1,656,212	821,079	Dewey, Thomas E.	807,831	Truman, Harry S.	27,302	13,248 R	49.6%	48.8%	50.4%	49.6%

In 2000 the other vote column includes 18,531 votes cast for Green (Nader). In 1996 the other vote column includes 224,299 votes cast for Perot. In 1992 the other vote column includes 455,934 votes cast for Perot. In 1980 the other column includes 111,639 votes for Independent (Anderson).

INDIANA

POSTWAR VOTE FOR GOVERNOR

Year	Total Vote	Republican		Democratic		Other Vote	Rep.-Dem. Plurality	Percentage			
		Vote	Candidate	Vote	Candidate			Total Vote		Major Vote	
								Rep.	Dem.	Rep.	Dem.
2000	2,179,413	908,285	McIntosh, David M.	1,232,525	O'Bannon, Frank L.	38,603	324,240 D	41.7%	56.6%	42.4%	57.6%
1996	2,110,047	986,982	Goldsmith, Stephen	1,087,128	O'Bannon, Frank L.	35,937	100,146 D	46.8%	51.5%	47.6%	52.4%
1992	2,229,116	822,533	Pearson, Linley E.	1,382,151	Bayh, Evan	24,432	559,618 D	36.9%	62.0%	37.3%	62.7%
1988	2,140,781	1,002,207	Mutz, John M.	1,138,574	Bayh, Evan		136,367 D	46.8%	53.2%	46.8%	53.2%
1984	2,197,988	1,146,497	Orr, Robert D.	1,036,922	Townsend, W. Wayne	14,569	109,575 R	52.2%	47.2%	52.5%	47.5%
1980	2,178,403	1,257,383	Orr, Robert D.	913,116	Hillenbrand, John A.	7,904	344,267 R	57.7%	41.9%	57.9%	42.1%
1976	2,175,324	1,236,555	Bowen, Otis R.	927,243	Conrad, Larry A.	11,526	309,312 R	56.8%	42.6%	57.1%	42.9%
1972	2,120,847	1,203,903	Bowen, Otis R.	900,489	Welsh, Matthew E.	16,455	303,414 R	56.8%	42.5%	57.2%	42.8%
1968	2,049,072	1,080,271	Whitcomb, Edgar D.	965,816	Rock, Robert L.	2,985	114,455 R	52.7%	47.1%	52.8%	47.2%
1964	2,072,915	901,342	Ristine, Richard O.	1,164,620	Branigin, Roger D.	6,953	263,278 D	43.5%	56.2%	43.6%	56.4%
1960	2,128,965	1,049,540	Parker, Crawford F.	1,072,717	Welsh, Matthew E.	6,708	23,177 D	49.3%	50.4%	49.5%	50.5%
1956	1,954,290	1,086,868	Handley, Harold W.	859,393	Tucker, Ralph	8,029	227,475 R	55.6%	44.0%	55.8%	44.2%
1952	1,931,869	1,075,685	Craig, George N.	841,984	Watkins, John A.	14,200	233,701 R	55.7%	43.6%	56.1%	43.9%
1948	1,652,321	745,892	Creighton, Hobart	884,995	Schricker, Henry F.	21,434	139,103 D	45.1%	53.6%	45.7%	54.3%

POSTWAR VOTE FOR SENATOR

Year	Total Vote	Republican		Democratic		Other Vote	Rep.-Dem. Plurality	Percentage			
		Vote	Candidate	Vote	Candidate			Total Vote		Major Vote	
								Rep.	Dem.	Rep.	Dem.
2000	2,145,209	1,427,944	Lugar, Richard G.	683,273	Johnson, David L.	33,992	744,671 R	66.6%	31.9%	67.6%	32.4%
1998	1,588,617	552,732	Helmke, Paul	1,012,244	Bayh, Evan	23,641	459,512 D	34.8%	63.7%	35.3%	64.7%
1994	1,543,568	1,039,625	Lugar, Richard G.	470,799	Jontz, Jim	33,144	568,826 R	67.4%	30.5%	68.8%	31.2%
1992	2,211,426	1,267,972	Coats, Daniel R.	900,148	Hogsett, Joseph H.	43,306	367,824 R	57.3%	40.7%	58.5%	41.5%
1990S	1,504,302	806,048	Coats, Daniel R.	696,639	Hill, Baron P.	1,615	109,409 R	53.6%	46.3%	53.6%	46.4%
1988	2,099,303	1,430,525	Lugar, Richard G.	668,778	Wickes, Jack		761,747 R	68.1%	31.9%	68.1%	31.9%
1986	1,545,563	936,143	Quayle, J. Danforth	595,192	Long, Jill L.	14,228	340,951 R	60.6%	38.5%	61.1%	38.9%
1982	1,817,287	978,301	Lugar, Richard G.	828,400	Fithian, Floyd	10,586	149,901 R	53.8%	45.6%	54.1%	45.9%
1980	2,198,376	1,182,414	Quayle, J. Danforth	1,015,962	Bayh, Birch		166,452 R	53.8%	46.2%	53.8%	46.2%
1976	2,171,187	1,275,833	Lugar, Richard G.	878,522	Hartke, R. Vance	16,832	397,311 R	58.8%	40.5%	59.2%	40.8%
1974	1,752,978	814,117	Lugar, Richard G.	889,269	Bayh, Birch	49,592	75,152 D	46.4%	50.7%	47.8%	52.2%
1970	1,737,697	866,707	Roudebush, Richard	870,990	Hartke, R. Vance		4,283 D	49.9%	50.1%	49.9%	50.1%
1968	2,053,118	988,571	Ruckelshaus, William	1,060,456	Bayh, Birch	4,091	71,885 D	48.1%	51.7%	48.2%	51.8%
1964	2,076,963	941,519	Bontrager, D. Russell	1,128,505	Hartke, R. Vance	6,939	186,986 D	45.3%	54.3%	45.5%	54.5%
1962	1,800,038	894,547	Capehart, Homer E.	905,491	Bayh, Birch		10,944 D	49.7%	50.3%	49.7%	50.3%
1958	1,724,598	731,635	Handley, Harold W.	973,636	Hartke, R. Vance	19,327	242,001 D	42.4%	56.5%	42.9%	57.1%
1956	1,963,986	1,084,262	Capehart, Homer E.	871,781	Wickard, Claude	7,943	212,481 R	55.2%	44.4%	55.4%	44.6%
1952	1,946,118	1,020,605	Jenner, William E.	911,169	Schricker, Henry F.	14,344	109,436 R	52.4%	46.8%	52.8%	47.2%
1950	1,598,724	844,303	Capehart, Homer E.	741,025	Campbell, Alex M.	13,396	103,278 R	52.8%	46.4%	53.3%	46.7%
1946	1,347,434	739,809	Jenner, William E.	584,288	Townsend, M. Clifford	23,337	155,521 R	54.9%	43.4%	55.9%	44.1%

The 1990 election was for a short term to fill a vacancy.

INDIANA

Congressional districts first established for elections held in 2002
9 members

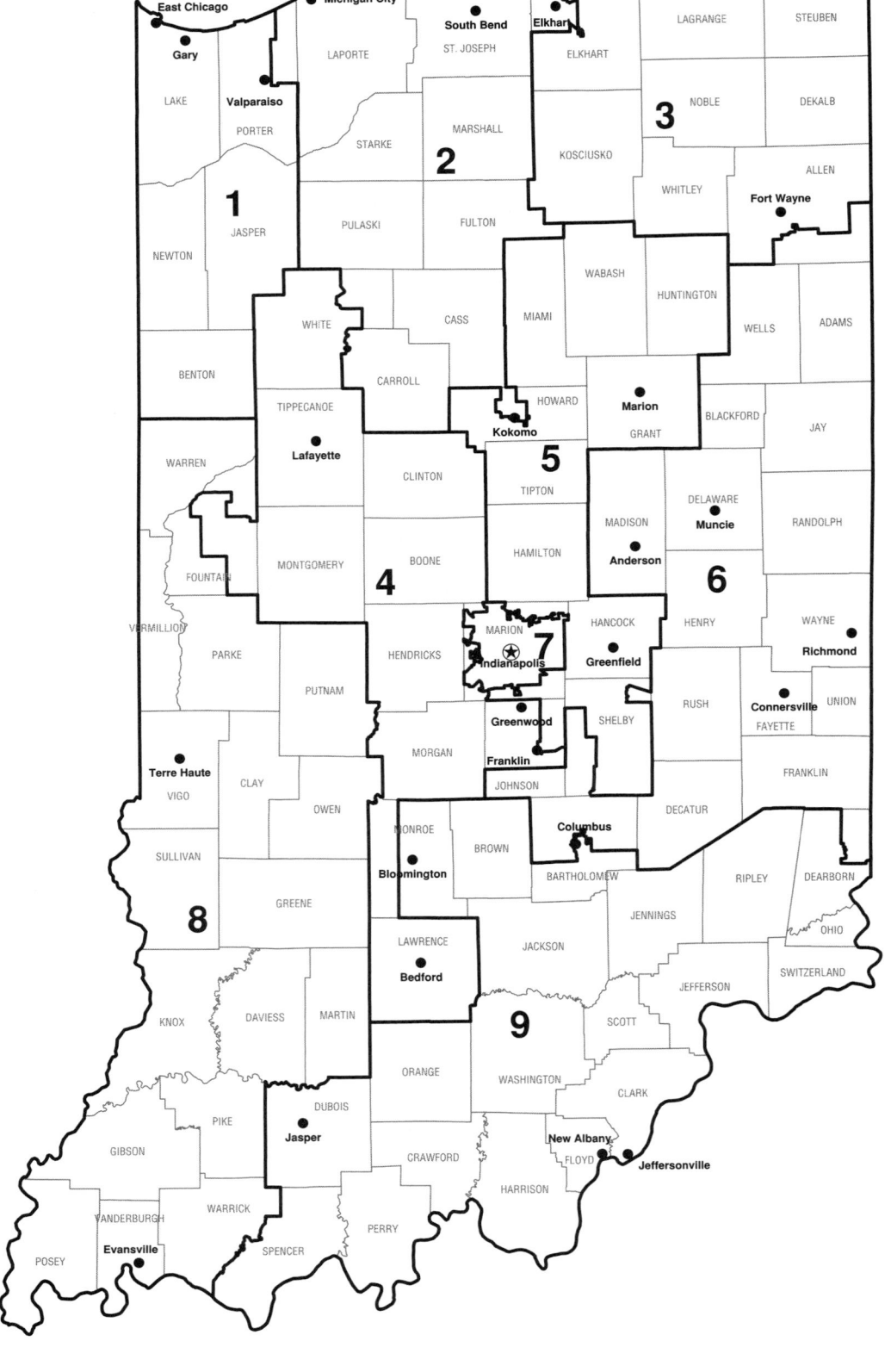

INDIANA

HOUSE OF REPRESENTATIVES

CD	Year	Total Vote	Republican		Democratic		Other Vote	Rep.-Dem. Plurality	Percentage			
									Total Vote		Major Vote	
			Vote	Candidate	Vote	Candidate			Rep.	Dem.	Rep.	Dem.
1	2002	135,111	41,909	Leyva, Mark J.	90,443	Visclosky, Peter J.*	2,759	48,534 D	31.0%	66.9%	31.7%	68.3%
2	2002	188,458	95,081	Chocola, Chris	86,253	Thompson, Jill Long	7,124	8,828 R	50.5%	45.8%	52.4%	47.6%
3	2002	146,606	92,566	Souder, Mark*	50,509	Rigdon, Jay	3,531	42,057 R	63.1%	34.5%	64.7%	35.3%
4	2002	158,008	112,760	Buyer, Steve*	41,314	Abbott, Bill	3,934	71,446 R	71.4%	26.1%	73.2%	26.8%
5	2002	179,855	129,442	Burton, Dan*	45,283	Carr, Katherine Fox	5,130	84,159 R	72.0%	25.2%	74.1%	25.9%
6	2002	185,653	118,436	Pence, Mike*	63,871	Fox, Melina Ann	3,346	54,565 R	63.8%	34.4%	65.0%	35.0%
7	2002	145,840	64,379	McVey, Brose A.	77,478	Carson, Julia*	3,983	13,099 D	44.1%	53.1%	45.4%	54.6%
8	2002	192,865	98,952	Hostettler, John *	88,763	Hartke, Bryan L.	5,150	10,189 R	51.3%	46.0%	52.7%	47.3%
9	2002	188,957	87,169	Sodrel, Mike	96,654	Hill, Baron P.*	5,134	9,485 D	46.1%	51.2%	47.4%	52.6%
Total	2002	1,521,353	840,694		640,568		40,091	200,126 R	55.3%	42.1%	56.8%	43.2%

An asterisk (*) denotes incumbent.

INDIANA

GENERAL AND PRIMARY ELECTIONS

2002 GENERAL ELECTIONS

House   Other vote was:

CD 1   2,759 Libertarian (Timothy P. Brennan).
CD 2   7,112 Libertarian (Sharon Metheny); 6 write-in (M. Myer Blatt); 6 write-in (James A. Mello).
CD 3   3,531 Libertarian (Mike Donlan).
CD 4   3,934 Libertarian (Jerry L. Susong).
CD 5   5,130 Libertarian (Christopher Adkins).
CD 6   3,346 Libertarian (Doris Robertson).
CD 7   3,919 Libertarian (Andrew M. Horning); 64 write-in (James "Jim" Kell Jeffries).
CD 8   5,150 Libertarian (Pam Williams).
CD 9   2,745 Green (Jeff Melton); 2,389 Libertarian (Al Cox).

2002 PRIMARY ELECTIONS

Primary   May 7, 2002   **Registration**   3,939,103   No Party Registration
                                          (as of May 7, 2002)

Primary Type   Open—Any registered voter could participate in the primary of either party.

Note: An asterisk (*) denotes incumbent.

INDIANA

GENERAL AND PRIMARY ELECTIONS

	REPUBLICAN PRIMARIES			DEMOCRATIC PRIMARIES		
Congressional District 1	Mark J. Levya	9,546	59.6%	Peter J. Visclosky*	57,099	85.6%
	Cyril B. "Cy" Huerter	6,465	40.4%	Ralph Spelbring	9,621	14.4%
	TOTAL	16,011		TOTAL	66,720	
Congressional District 2	Chris Chocola	30,176	78.2%	Jill Long Thompson	19,628	52.5%
	Lewis F. "Farmer" Hass	8,417	21.8%	Mark J. Meissner	7,151	19.1%
				William E. Alexa	5,546	14.8%
				Kathy Cekanski Farrand	2,792	7.5%
				Steven W. Osborn	2,273	6.1%
	TOTAL	38,593		TOTAL	37,390	
Congressional District 3	Mark Souder*	53,186	59.6%	Jay Rigdon	9,217	100.0%
	Paul Helmke	33,038	37.0%			
	William R. Larsen	3,079	3.4%			
	TOTAL	89,303				
Congressional District 4	Steve Buyer*	44,608	54.6%	*No candidate filed for the Democratic primary.*		
	Brian Kerns*	24,443	29.9%	*Bill Abbott was subsequently named to fill*		
	R. Michael Young	6,605	8.1%	*the vacancy on the general election ballot.*		
	Thomas J. Herr	2,684	3.3%			
	Tim Baynard	1,754	2.1%			
	Bob Smith	1,589	1.9%			
	TOTAL	81,683				
Congressional District 5	Dan Burton*	65,022	83.8%	Katherine Fox Carr	5,349	37.5%
	George Thomas Holland	12,560	16.2%	Jerry Hall	3,758	26.3%
				Mike Brinegar	3,635	25.5%
				Darin Patrick Griesey	1,532	10.7%
	TOTAL	77,582		TOTAL	14,274	
Congressional District 6	Mike Pence*	55,142	100.0%	Melina Ann Fox	29,450	100.0%
Congressional District 7	Brose A. McVey	17,875	68.9%	Julia Carson*	24,807	90.8%
	Jack Reynolds	8,054	31.1%	Bob "Citizen Kern" Hidalgo	2,515	9.2%
	TOTAL	25,929		TOTAL	27,322	
Congressional District 8	John Hostettler*	29,673	100.0%	Bryan L. Hartke	40,174	69.3%
				Michael Graf	17,831	30.7%
				TOTAL	58,005	
Congressional District 9	Mike Sodrel	15,109	44.5%	Baron P. Hill*	49,910	100.0%
	Chris Redmon	9,380	27.6%			
	Jeff Ellington	6,684	19.7%			
	David Fowler	2,757	8.1%			
	TOTAL	33,930				

IOWA

GOVERNOR
Tom Vilsack (D). Reelected 2002 to a four-year term. Previously elected 1998.

SENATORS (1 Democrat, 1 Republican)
Charles E. Grassley (R). Reelected 1998 to a six-year term. Previously elected 1992, 1986, 1980.

Tom Harkin (D). Reelected 2002 to a six-year term. Previously elected 1996, 1990, 1984.

REPRESENTATIVES (4 Republicans, 1 Democrat)
1. Jim Nussle (R)
2. Jim Leach (R)
3. Leonard L. Boswell (D)
4. Tom Latham (R)
5. Steve King (R)

POSTWAR VOTE FOR PRESIDENT

| | | Republican | | Democratic | | | | Percentage | | | |
| | | | | | | | | Total Vote | | Major Vote | |
Year	Total Vote	Vote	Candidate	Vote	Candidate	Other Vote	Plurality	Rep.	Dem.	Rep.	Dem.
2000**	1,315,563	634,373	Bush, George W.	638,517	Gore, Al	42,673	4,144 D	48.2%	48.5%	49.8%	50.2%
1996**	1,234,075	492,644	Dole, Bob	620,258	Clinton, Bill	121,173	127,614 D	39.9%	50.3%	44.3%	55.7%
1992**	1,354,607	504,891	Bush, George	586,353	Clinton, Bill	263,363	81,462 D	37.3%	43.3%	46.3%	53.7%
1988	1,225,614	545,355	Bush, George	670,557	Dukakis, Michael S.	9,702	125,202 D	44.5%	54.7%	44.9%	55.1%
1984	1,319,805	703,088	Reagan, Ronald	605,620	Mondale, Walter F.	11,097	97,468 R	53.3%	45.9%	53.7%	46.3%
1980**	1,317,661	676,026	Reagan, Ronald	508,672	Carter, Jimmy	132,963	167,354 R	51.3%	38.6%	57.1%	42.9%
1976	1,279,306	632,863	Ford, Gerald R.	619,931	Carter, Jimmy	26,512	12,932 R	49.5%	48.5%	50.5%	49.5%
1972	1,225,944	706,207	Nixon, Richard M.	496,206	McGovern, George S.	23,531	210,001 R	57.6%	40.5%	58.7%	41.3%
1968	1,167,931	619,106	Nixon, Richard M.	476,699	Humphrey, Hubert H.	72,126	142,407 R	53.0%	40.8%	56.5%	43.5%
1964	1,184,539	449,148	Goldwater, Barry M.	733,030	Johnson, Lyndon B.	2,361	283,882 D	37.9%	61.9%	38.0%	62.0%
1960	1,273,810	722,381	Nixon, Richard M.	550,565	Kennedy, John F.	864	171,816 R	56.7%	43.2%	56.7%	43.3%
1956	1,234,564	729,187	Eisenhower, Dwight D.	501,858	Stevenson, Adlai E.	3,519	227,329 R	59.1%	40.7%	59.2%	40.8%
1952	1,268,773	808,906	Eisenhower, Dwight D.	451,513	Stevenson, Adlai E.	8,354	357,393 R	63.8%	35.6%	64.2%	35.8%
1948	1,038,264	494,018	Dewey, Thomas E.	522,380	Truman, Harry S.	21,866	28,362 D	47.6%	50.3%	48.6%	51.4%

In 2000 the other vote column includes 29,374 votes cast for Green (Nader). In 1996 the other vote column includes 105,159 votes cast for Perot. In 1992 the other vote column includes 253,468 votes cast for Perot. In 1980 the other column includes 115,633 votes for Independent (Anderson).

IOWA

POSTWAR VOTE FOR GOVERNOR

Year	Total Vote	Republican		Democratic		Other Vote	Rep.-Dem. Plurality	Percentage			
								Total Vote		Major Vote	
		Vote	Candidate	Vote	Candidate			Rep.	Dem.	Rep.	Dem.
2002	1,025,802	456,612	Gross, Doug	540,449	Vilsack, Tom	28,741	83,837 D	44.5%	52.7%	45.8%	54.2%
1998	956,418	444,787	Lightfoot, Jim Ross	500,231	Vilsack, Tom	11,400	55,444 D	46.5%	52.3%	47.1%	52.9%
1994	997,248	566,395	Branstad, Terry E.	414,453	Campbell, Bonnie J.	16,400	151,942 R	56.8%	41.6%	57.7%	42.3%
1990	976,483	591,852	Branstad, Terry E.	379,372	Avenson, Donald D.	5,259	212,480 R	60.6%	38.9%	60.9%	39.1%
1986	910,623	472,712	Branstad, Terry E.	436,987	Junkins, Lowell L.	924	35,725 R	51.9%	48.0%	52.0%	48.0%
1982	1,038,229	548,313	Branstad, Terry E.	483,291	Conlin, Roxanne	6,625	65,022 R	52.8%	46.5%	53.2%	46.8%
1978	843,190	491,713	Ray, Robert	345,519	Fitzgerald, Jerome D.	5,958	146,194 R	58.3%	41.0%	58.7%	41.3%
1974**	920,458	534,518	Ray, Robert	377,553	Schaben, James, F.	8,387	156,965 R	58.1%	41.0%	58.6%	41.4%
1972	1,210,222	707,177	Ray, Robert	487,282	Franzenburg, Paul	15,763	219,895 R	58.4%	40.3%	59.2%	40.8%
1970	791,241	403,394	Ray, Robert	368,911	Fulton, Robert	18,936	34,483 R	51.0%	46.6%	52.2%	47.8%
1968	1,136,489	614,328	Ray, Robert	521,216	Franzenburg, Paul	945	93,112 R	54.1%	45.9%	54.1%	45.9%
1966	893,175	394,518	Murray, William G.	494,259	Hughes, Harold E.	4,398	99,741 D	44.2%	55.3%	44.4%	55.6%
1964	1,167,734	365,131	Hultman, Evan	794,610	Hughes, Harold E.	7,993	429,479 D	31.3%	68.0%	31.5%	68.5%
1962	819,854	388,955	Erbe, Norman A.	430,899	Hughes, Harold E.		41,944 D	47.4%	52.6%	47.4%	52.6%
1960	1,237,089	645,026	Erbe, Norman A.	592,063	McManus, E. J.		52,963 R	52.1%	47.9%	52.1%	47.9%
1958	859,095	394,071	Murray, William G.	465,024	Loveless, Herschel C.		70,953 D	45.9%	54.1%	45.9%	54.1%
1956	1,204,235	587,383	Hoegh, Leo A.	616,852	Loveless, Herschel C.		29,469 D	48.8%	51.2%	48.8%	51.2%
1954	848,592	435,944	Hoegh, Leo A.	410,255	Herring, Clyde E.	2,393	25,689 R	51.4%	48.3%	51.5%	48.5%
1952	1,230,045	638,388	Beardsley, William	587,671	Loveless, Herschel C.	3,986	50,717 R	51.9%	47.8%	52.1%	47.9%
1950	857,213	506,642	Beardsley, William	347,176	Gillette, Lester S.	3,395	159,466 R	59.1%	40.5%	59.3%	40.7%
1948	994,833	553,900	Beardsley, William	434,432	Switzer, Carroll O.	6,501	119,468 R	55.7%	43.7%	56.0%	44.0%
1946	631,681	362,592	Blue, Robert D.	266,190	Miles, Frank	2,899	96,402 R	57.4%	42.1%	57.7%	42.3%

The term of office of Iowa's Governor was increased from two to four years effective with the 1974 election.

POSTWAR VOTE FOR SENATOR

Year	Total Vote	Republican		Democratic		Other Vote	Rep.-Dem. Plurality	Percentage			
								Total Vote		Major Vote	
		Vote	Candidate	Vote	Candidate			Rep.	Dem.	Rep.	Dem.
2002	1,023,075	447,892	Ganske, Greg	554,278	Harkin, Tom	20,905	106,386 D	43.8%	54.2%	44.7%	55.3%
1998	947,907	648,480	Grassley, Charles E.	289,049	Osterberg, David	10,378	359,431 R	68.4%	30.5%	69.2%	30.8%
1996	1,224,054	571,807	Lightfoot, Jim Ross	634,166	Harkin, Tom	18,081	62,359 D	46.7%	51.8%	47.4%	52.6%
1992	1,292,494	899,761	Grassley, Charles E.	351,561	Lloyd-Jones, Jean	41,172	548,200 R	69.6%	27.2%	71.9%	28.1%
1990	983,933	446,869	Tauke, Tom	535,975	Harkin, Tom	1,089	89,106 D	45.4%	54.5%	45.5%	54.5%
1986	891,762	588,880	Grassley, Charles E.	299,406	Roehrick, John P.	3,476	289,474 R	66.0%	33.6%	66.3%	33.7%
1984	1,292,700	564,381	Jepsen, Roger W.	716,883	Harkin, Tom	11,436	152,502 D	43.7%	55.5%	44.0%	56.0%
1980	1,277,034	683,014	Grassley, Charles E.	581,545	Culver, John C.	12,475	101,469 R	53.5%	45.5%	54.0%	46.0%
1978	824,654	421,598	Jepsen, Roger W.	395,066	Clark, Richard	7,990	26,532 R	51.1%	47.9%	51.6%	48.4%
1974	889,561	420,546	Stanley, David M.	462,947	Culver, John C.	6,068	42,401 D	47.3%	52.0%	47.6%	52.4%
1972	1,203,333	530,525	Miller, Jack	662,637	Clark, Richard	10,171	132,112 D	44.1%	55.1%	44.5%	55.5%
1968	1,144,086	568,469	Stanley, David M.	574,884	Hughes, Harold E.	733	6,415 D	49.7%	50.2%	49.7%	50.3%
1966	857,496	522,339	Miller, Jack	324,114	Smith, E. B.	11,043	198,225 R	60.9%	37.8%	61.7%	38.3%
1962	807,972	431,364	Hickenlooper, Bourke B.	376,602	Smith, E. B.	6	54,762 R	53.4%	46.6%	53.4%	46.6%
1960	1,237,582	642,463	Miller, Jack	595,119	Loveless, Herschel C.		47,344 R	51.9%	48.1%	51.9%	48.1%
1956	1,178,655	635,499	Hickenlooper, Bourke B.	543,156	Evans, R. M.		92,343 R	53.9%	46.1%	53.9%	46.1%
1954	847,355	442,409	Martin, Thomas E.	402,712	Gillette, Guy	2,234	39,697 R	52.2%	47.5%	52.3%	47.7%
1950	858,523	470,613	Hickenlooper, Bourke B.	383,766	Loveland, A. J.	4,144	86,847 R	54.8%	44.7%	55.1%	44.9%
1948	1,000,412	415,778	Wilson, George A.	578,226	Gillette, Guy	6,408	162,448 D	41.6%	57.8%	41.8%	58.2%

155

IOWA

Congressional districts first established for elections held in 2002
5 members

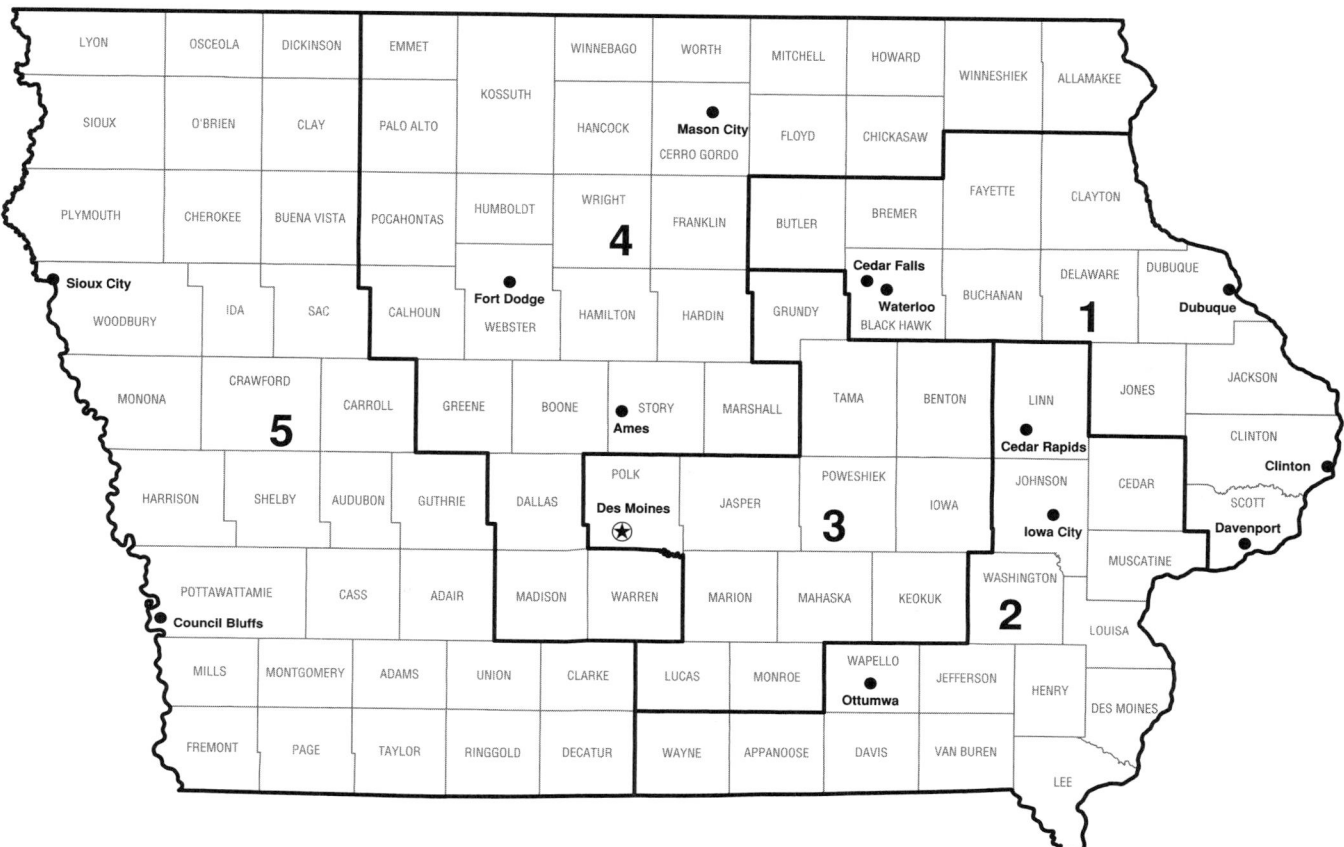

156

IOWA

GOVERNOR 2002

| 2000 Census Population | County | Total Vote | Republican | Democratic | Other | Rep.-Dem. Plurality | Percentage | | | |
| | | | | | | | Total Vote | | Major Vote | |
							Rep.	Dem.	Rep.	Dem.
8,243	ADAIR	3,278	1,440	1,728	110	288 D	43.9%	52.7%	45.5%	54.5%
4,482	ADAMS	1,740	829	867	44	38 D	47.6%	49.8%	48.9%	51.1%
14,675	ALLAMAKEE	4,948	2,520	2,228	200	292 R	50.9%	45.0%	53.1%	46.9%
13,721	APPANOOSE	4,800	2,211	2,490	99	279 D	46.1%	51.9%	47.0%	53.0%
6,830	AUDUBON	2,554	1,183	1,310	61	127 D	46.3%	51.3%	47.5%	52.5%
25,308	BENTON	9,173	4,137	4,758	278	621 D	45.1%	51.9%	46.5%	53.5%
128,012	BLACK HAWK	41,687	17,038	23,501	1,148	6,463 D	40.9%	56.4%	42.0%	58.0%
26,224	BOONE	9,984	3,802	5,939	243	2,137 D	38.1%	59.5%	39.0%	61.0%
23,325	BREMER	8,439	4,061	4,066	312	5 D	48.1%	48.2%	50.0%	50.0%
21,093	BUCHANAN	7,289	2,970	4,079	240	1,109 D	40.7%	56.0%	42.1%	57.9%
20,411	BUENA VISTA	5,899	2,940	2,837	122	103 R	49.8%	48.1%	50.9%	49.1%
15,305	BUTLER	4,909	2,475	2,232	202	243 R	50.4%	45.5%	52.6%	47.4%
11,115	CALHOUN	4,058	1,843	2,112	103	269 D	45.4%	52.0%	46.6%	53.4%
21,421	CARROLL	7,491	3,548	3,799	144	251 D	47.4%	50.7%	48.3%	51.7%
14,684	CASS	5,386	3,084	2,197	105	887 R	57.3%	40.8%	58.4%	41.6%
18,187	CEDAR	6,471	3,064	3,205	202	141 D	47.3%	49.5%	48.9%	51.1%
46,447	CERRO GORDO	16,280	6,439	9,354	487	2,915 D	39.6%	57.5%	40.8%	59.2%
13,035	CHEROKEE	4,834	2,253	2,433	148	180 D	46.6%	50.3%	48.1%	51.9%
13,095	CHICKASAW	5,099	2,161	2,755	183	594 D	42.4%	54.0%	44.0%	56.0%
9,133	CLARKE	3,763	1,531	2,097	135	566 D	40.7%	55.7%	42.2%	57.8%
17,372	CLAY	5,769	2,880	2,763	126	117 R	49.9%	47.9%	51.0%	49.0%
18,678	CLAYTON	6,906	3,107	3,525	274	418 D	45.0%	51.0%	46.8%	53.2%
50,149	CLINTON	16,131	7,074	8,701	356	1,627 D	43.9%	53.9%	44.8%	55.2%
16,942	CRAWFORD	4,874	2,921	1,879	74	1,042 R	59.9%	38.6%	60.9%	39.1%
40,750	DALLAS	16,459	7,819	8,241	399	422 D	47.5%	50.1%	48.7%	51.3%
8,541	DAVIS	3,074	1,412	1,581	81	169 D	45.9%	51.4%	47.2%	52.8%
8,689	DECATUR	2,939	1,318	1,520	101	202 D	44.8%	51.7%	46.4%	53.6%
18,404	DELAWARE	6,313	3,023	3,107	183	84 D	47.9%	49.2%	49.3%	50.7%
42,351	DES MOINES	15,236	5,853	8,935	448	3,082 D	38.4%	58.6%	39.6%	60.4%
16,424	DICKINSON	6,656	3,275	3,255	126	20 R	49.2%	48.9%	50.2%	49.8%
89,143	DUBUQUE	32,277	12,612	18,912	753	6,300 D	39.1%	58.6%	40.0%	60.0%
11,027	EMMET	3,364	1,496	1,806	62	310 D	44.5%	53.7%	45.3%	54.7%
22,008	FAYETTE	7,847	3,590	4,092	165	502 D	45.7%	52.1%	46.7%	53.3%
16,900	FLOYD	5,496	2,187	3,150	159	963 D	39.8%	57.3%	41.0%	59.0%
10,704	FRANKLIN	4,101	1,717	2,117	267	400 D	41.9%	51.6%	44.8%	55.2%
8,010	FREMONT	2,594	1,406	1,132	56	274 R	54.2%	43.6%	55.4%	44.6%
10,366	GREENE	3,933	1,548	2,283	102	735 D	39.4%	58.0%	40.4%	59.6%
12,369	GRUNDY	4,732	2,654	1,970	108	684 R	56.1%	41.6%	57.4%	42.6%
11,353	GUTHRIE	4,327	1,935	2,274	118	339 D	44.7%	52.6%	46.0%	54.0%
16,438	HAMILTON	6,171	2,713	3,289	169	576 D	44.0%	53.3%	45.2%	54.8%
12,100	HANCOCK	4,201	2,130	1,944	127	186 R	50.7%	46.3%	52.3%	47.7%
18,812	HARDIN	6,974	3,051	3,719	204	668 D	43.7%	53.3%	45.1%	54.9%
15,666	HARRISON	4,933	2,636	2,190	107	446 R	53.4%	44.4%	54.6%	45.4%
20,336	HENRY	6,856	2,973	3,723	160	750 D	43.4%	54.3%	44.4%	55.6%
9,932	HOWARD	3,343	1,471	1,765	107	294 D	44.0%	52.8%	45.5%	54.5%
10,381	HUMBOLDT	3,668	1,700	1,887	81	187 D	46.3%	51.4%	47.4%	52.6%
7,837	IDA	2,580	1,339	1,172	69	167 R	51.9%	45.4%	53.3%	46.7%
15,671	IOWA	5,822	2,853	2,746	223	107 R	49.0%	47.2%	51.0%	49.0%
20,296	JACKSON	6,358	2,776	3,449	133	673 D	43.7%	54.2%	44.6%	55.4%
37,213	JASPER	14,687	5,837	8,506	344	2,669 D	39.7%	57.9%	40.7%	59.3%
16,181	JEFFERSON	5,981	2,571	2,324	1,086	247 R	43.0%	38.9%	52.5%	47.5%
111,006	JOHNSON	38,622	12,377	24,278	1,967	11,901 D	32.0%	62.9%	33.8%	66.2%
20,221	JONES	7,279	3,214	3,832	233	618 D	44.2%	52.6%	45.6%	54.4%
11,400	KEOKUK	3,952	1,980	1,898	74	82 R	50.1%	48.0%	51.1%	48.9%
17,163	KOSSUTH	7,678	3,399	4,087	192	688 D	44.3%	53.2%	45.4%	54.6%
38,052	LEE	13,281	4,514	8,255	512	3,741 D	34.0%	62.2%	35.4%	64.6%
191,701	LINN	73,452	30,500	41,008	1,944	10,508 D	41.5%	55.8%	42.7%	57.3%
12,183	LOUISA	3,451	1,751	1,601	99	150 R	50.7%	46.4%	52.2%	47.8%
9,422	LUCAS	3,161	1,435	1,665	61	230 D	45.4%	52.7%	46.3%	53.7%
11,763	LYON	4,264	3,112	1,103	49	2,009 R	73.0%	25.9%	73.8%	26.2%

IOWA

GOVERNOR 2002

2000 Census Population	County	Total Vote	Republican	Democratic	Other	Rep.-Dem. Plurality	Percentage			
							Total Vote		Major Vote	
							Rep.	Dem.	Rep.	Dem.
14,019	MADISON	5,837	2,775	2,894	168	119 D	47.5%	49.6%	49.0%	51.0%
22,335	MAHASKA	7,197	4,018	3,078	101	940 R	55.8%	42.8%	56.6%	43.4%
32,052	MARION	11,498	5,973	5,318	207	655 R	51.9%	46.3%	52.9%	47.1%
39,311	MARSHALL	14,217	6,256	7,624	337	1,368 D	44.0%	53.6%	45.1%	54.9%
14,547	MILLS	4,218	2,412	1,718	88	694 R	57.2%	40.7%	58.4%	41.6%
10,874	MITCHELL	3,729	1,648	1,971	110	323 D	44.2%	52.9%	45.5%	54.5%
10,020	MONONA	3,510	1,644	1,777	89	133 D	46.8%	50.6%	48.1%	51.9%
8,016	MONROE	2,736	1,153	1,508	75	355 D	42.1%	55.1%	43.3%	56.7%
11,771	MONTGOMERY	3,494	2,099	1,323	72	776 R	60.1%	37.9%	61.3%	38.7%
41,722	MUSCATINE	11,296	5,371	5,604	321	233 D	47.5%	49.6%	48.9%	51.1%
15,102	O'BRIEN	5,272	3,359	1,814	99	1,545 R	63.7%	34.4%	64.9%	35.1%
7,003	OSCEOLA	2,279	1,494	737	48	757 R	65.6%	32.3%	67.0%	33.0%
16,976	PAGE	4,964	3,064	1,817	83	1,247 R	61.7%	36.6%	62.8%	37.2%
10,147	PALO ALTO	3,571	1,534	1,971	66	437 D	43.0%	55.2%	43.8%	56.2%
24,849	PLYMOUTH	7,540	4,062	3,264	214	798 R	53.9%	43.3%	55.4%	44.6%
8,662	POCAHONTAS	3,088	1,399	1,575	114	176 D	45.3%	51.0%	47.0%	53.0%
374,601	POLK	142,310	59,408	79,785	3,117	20,377 D	41.7%	56.1%	42.7%	57.3%
87,704	POTTAWATTAMIE	25,689	12,997	12,090	602	907 R	50.6%	47.1%	51.8%	48.2%
18,815	POWESHIEK	6,813	2,948	3,654	211	706 D	43.3%	53.6%	44.7%	55.3%
5,469	RINGGOLD	2,221	986	1,191	44	205 D	44.4%	53.6%	45.3%	54.7%
11,529	SAC	3,821	1,825	1,890	106	65 D	47.8%	49.5%	49.1%	50.9%
158,668	SCOTT	52,342	23,234	27,412	1,696	4,178 D	44.4%	52.4%	45.9%	54.1%
13,173	SHELBY	4,882	3,375	1,434	73	1,941 R	69.1%	29.4%	70.2%	29.8%
31,589	SIOUX	11,247	9,110	2,043	94	7,067 R	81.0%	18.2%	81.7%	18.3%
79,981	STORY	28,611	11,263	16,211	1,137	4,948 D	39.4%	56.7%	41.0%	59.0%
18,103	TAMA	6,297	2,779	3,357	161	578 D	44.1%	53.3%	45.3%	54.7%
6,958	TAYLOR	2,614	1,257	1,287	70	30 D	48.1%	49.2%	49.4%	50.6%
12,309	UNION	4,431	1,866	2,421	144	555 D	42.1%	54.6%	43.5%	56.5%
7,809	VAN BUREN	2,813	1,581	1,118	114	463 R	56.2%	39.7%	58.6%	41.4%
36,051	WAPELLO	13,270	4,928	7,967	375	3,039 D	37.1%	60.0%	38.2%	61.8%
40,671	WARREN	16,177	6,891	8,931	355	2,040 D	42.6%	55.2%	43.6%	56.4%
20,670	WASHINGTON	7,125	3,497	3,425	203	72 R	49.1%	48.1%	50.5%	49.5%
6,730	WAYNE	2,332	1,099	1,180	53	81 D	47.1%	50.6%	48.2%	51.8%
40,235	WEBSTER	13,259	5,463	7,554	242	2,091 D	41.2%	57.0%	42.0%	58.0%
11,723	WINNEBAGO	4,211	1,954	2,134	123	180 D	46.4%	50.7%	47.8%	52.2%
21,310	WINNESHIEK	7,408	3,659	3,450	299	209 R	49.4%	46.6%	51.5%	48.5%
103,877	WOODBURY	28,150	13,230	14,231	689	1,001 D	47.0%	50.6%	48.2%	51.8%
7,909	WORTH	2,995	1,176	1,697	122	521 D	39.3%	56.7%	40.9%	59.1%
14,334	WRIGHT	4,514	2,137	2,323	54	186 D	47.3%	51.5%	47.9%	52.1%
2,926,324	TOTAL	1,025,802	456,612	540,449	28,741	83,837 D	44.5%	52.7%	45.8%	54.2%

IOWA

SENATOR 2002

2000 Census Population	County	Total Vote	Republican	Democratic	Other	Rep.-Dem. Plurality	Percentage			
							Total Vote		Major Vote	
							Rep.	Dem.	Rep.	Dem.
8,243	ADAIR	3,279	1,450	1,753	76	303 D	44.2%	53.5%	45.3%	54.7%
4,482	ADAMS	1,734	764	937	33	173 D	44.1%	54.0%	44.9%	55.1%
14,675	ALLAMAKEE	4,922	2,334	2,463	125	129 D	47.4%	50.0%	48.7%	51.3%
13,721	APPANOOSE	4,821	2,127	2,618	76	491 D	44.1%	54.3%	44.8%	55.2%
6,830	AUDUBON	2,528	1,130	1,363	35	233 D	44.7%	53.9%	45.3%	54.7%
25,308	BENTON	9,116	4,031	4,901	184	870 D	44.2%	53.8%	45.1%	54.9%
128,012	BLACK HAWK	41,592	16,475	24,302	815	7,827 D	39.6%	58.4%	40.4%	59.6%
26,224	BOONE	9,945	3,852	5,902	191	2,050 D	38.7%	59.3%	39.5%	60.5%
23,325	BREMER	8,426	3,969	4,307	150	338 D	47.1%	51.1%	48.0%	52.0%
21,093	BUCHANAN	7,264	2,838	4,285	141	1,447 D	39.1%	59.0%	39.8%	60.2%
20,411	BUENA VISTA	5,900	2,779	3,023	98	244 D	47.1%	51.2%	47.9%	52.1%
15,305	BUTLER	4,906	2,510	2,290	106	220 R	51.2%	46.7%	52.3%	47.7%
11,115	CALHOUN	4,048	1,911	2,047	90	136 D	47.2%	50.6%	48.3%	51.7%
21,421	CARROLL	7,444	3,317	3,992	135	675 D	44.6%	53.6%	45.4%	54.6%
14,684	CASS	5,414	3,044	2,306	64	738 R	56.2%	42.6%	56.9%	43.1%
18,187	CEDAR	6,458	2,892	3,423	143	531 D	44.8%	53.0%	45.8%	54.2%
46,447	CERRO GORDO	16,220	6,295	9,406	519	3,111 D	38.8%	58.0%	40.1%	59.9%
13,035	CHEROKEE	4,830	2,199	2,509	122	310 D	45.5%	51.9%	46.7%	53.3%
13,095	CHICKASAW	5,096	1,920	3,028	148	1,108 D	37.7%	59.4%	38.8%	61.2%
9,133	CLARKE	3,745	1,385	2,269	91	884 D	37.0%	60.6%	37.9%	62.1%
17,372	CLAY	5,706	2,772	2,822	112	50 D	48.6%	49.5%	49.6%	50.4%
18,678	CLAYTON	6,895	2,864	3,861	170	997 D	41.5%	56.0%	42.6%	57.4%
50,149	CLINTON	16,187	6,309	9,581	297	3,272 D	39.0%	59.2%	39.7%	60.3%
16,942	CRAWFORD	4,606	2,285	2,275	46	10 R	49.6%	49.4%	50.1%	49.9%
40,750	DALLAS	16,417	7,978	8,165	274	187 D	48.6%	49.7%	49.4%	50.6%
8,541	DAVIS	3,048	1,270	1,714	64	444 D	41.7%	56.2%	42.6%	57.4%
8,689	DECATUR	2,916	1,222	1,618	76	396 D	41.9%	55.5%	43.0%	57.0%
18,404	DELAWARE	6,320	3,148	3,096	76	52 R	49.8%	49.0%	50.4%	49.6%
42,351	DES MOINES	15,099	5,662	9,080	357	3,418 D	37.5%	60.1%	38.4%	61.6%
16,424	DICKINSON	6,645	3,133	3,397	115	264 D	47.1%	51.1%	48.0%	52.0%
89,143	DUBUQUE	32,244	12,237	19,383	624	7,146 D	38.0%	60.1%	38.7%	61.3%
11,027	EMMET	3,326	1,395	1,855	76	460 D	41.9%	55.8%	42.9%	57.1%
22,008	FAYETTE	7,684	3,339	4,238	107	899 D	43.5%	55.2%	44.1%	55.9%
16,900	FLOYD	5,487	2,135	3,187	165	1,052 D	38.9%	58.1%	40.1%	59.9%
10,704	FRANKLIN	4,094	1,906	2,082	106	176 D	46.6%	50.9%	47.8%	52.2%
8,010	FREMONT	2,590	1,495	1,056	39	439 R	57.7%	40.8%	58.6%	41.4%
10,366	GREENE	3,921	1,556	2,306	59	750 D	39.7%	58.8%	40.3%	59.7%
12,369	GRUNDY	4,737	2,705	1,972	60	733 R	57.1%	41.6%	57.8%	42.2%
11,353	GUTHRIE	4,317	1,901	2,350	66	449 D	44.0%	54.4%	44.7%	55.3%
16,438	HAMILTON	6,162	2,750	3,283	129	533 D	44.6%	53.3%	45.6%	54.4%
12,100	HANCOCK	4,171	2,018	2,036	117	18 D	48.4%	48.8%	49.8%	50.2%
18,812	HARDIN	6,960	3,217	3,613	130	396 D	46.2%	51.9%	47.1%	52.9%
15,666	HARRISON	4,934	2,711	2,128	95	583 R	54.9%	43.1%	56.0%	44.0%
20,336	HENRY	6,789	3,146	3,500	143	354 D	46.3%	51.6%	47.3%	52.7%
9,932	HOWARD	3,315	1,320	1,920	75	600 D	39.8%	57.9%	40.7%	59.3%
10,381	HUMBOLDT	3,661	1,771	1,834	56	63 D	48.4%	50.1%	49.1%	50.9%
7,837	IDA	2,621	1,255	1,304	62	49 D	47.9%	49.8%	49.0%	51.0%
15,671	IOWA	5,797	2,701	2,960	136	259 D	46.6%	51.1%	47.7%	52.3%
20,296	JACKSON	6,401	2,531	3,753	117	1,222 D	39.5%	58.6%	40.3%	59.7%
37,213	JASPER	14,663	5,947	8,500	216	2,553 D	40.6%	58.0%	41.2%	58.8%
16,181	JEFFERSON	5,906	2,414	3,119	373	705 D	40.9%	52.8%	43.6%	56.4%
111,006	JOHNSON	38,619	12,315	24,965	1,339	12,650 D	31.9%	64.6%	33.0%	67.0%
20,221	JONES	7,242	3,085	3,983	174	898 D	42.6%	55.0%	43.6%	56.4%
11,400	KEOKUK	3,884	1,864	1,978	42	114 D	48.0%	50.9%	48.5%	51.5%
17,163	KOSSUTH	7,610	3,232	4,206	172	974 D	42.5%	55.3%	43.5%	56.5%
38,052	LEE	13,221	4,670	8,093	458	3,423 D	35.3%	61.2%	36.6%	63.4%
191,701	LINN	73,322	30,436	41,380	1,506	10,944 D	41.5%	56.4%	42.4%	57.6%
12,183	LOUISA	3,443	1,559	1,783	101	224 D	45.3%	51.8%	46.6%	53.4%
9,422	LUCAS	3,165	1,399	1,707	59	308 D	44.2%	53.9%	45.0%	55.0%
11,763	LYON	4,245	2,933	1,271	41	1,662 R	69.1%	29.9%	69.8%	30.2%

IOWA

SENATOR 2002

2000 Census Population	County	Total Vote	Republican	Democratic	Other	Rep.-Dem. Plurality	Total Vote Rep.	Total Vote Dem.	Major Vote Rep.	Major Vote Dem.
14,019	MADISON	5,842	2,790	2,960	92	170 D	47.8%	50.7%	48.5%	51.5%
22,335	MAHASKA	7,214	4,005	3,124	85	881 R	55.5%	43.3%	56.2%	43.8%
32,052	MARION	11,391	5,819	5,437	135	382 R	51.1%	47.7%	51.7%	48.3%
39,311	MARSHALL	14,186	6,047	7,908	231	1,861 D	42.6%	55.7%	43.3%	56.7%
14,547	MILLS	4,230	2,609	1,547	74	1,062 R	61.7%	36.6%	62.8%	37.2%
10,874	MITCHELL	3,703	1,584	2,019	100	435 D	42.8%	54.5%	44.0%	56.0%
10,020	MONONA	3,493	1,492	1,883	118	391 D	42.7%	53.9%	44.2%	55.8%
8,016	MONROE	2,722	1,099	1,566	57	467 D	40.4%	57.5%	41.2%	58.8%
11,771	MONTGOMERY	3,512	2,213	1,230	69	983 R	63.0%	35.0%	64.3%	35.7%
41,722	MUSCATINE	11,217	4,988	5,972	257	984 D	44.5%	53.2%	45.5%	54.5%
15,102	O'BRIEN	5,270	3,258	1,936	76	1,322 R	61.8%	36.7%	62.7%	37.3%
7,003	OSCEOLA	2,274	1,441	783	50	658 R	63.4%	34.4%	64.8%	35.2%
16,976	PAGE	4,955	3,114	1,779	62	1,335 R	62.8%	35.9%	63.6%	36.4%
10,147	PALO ALTO	3,536	1,415	2,003	118	588 D	40.0%	56.6%	41.4%	58.6%
24,849	PLYMOUTH	7,475	3,990	3,307	178	683 R	53.4%	44.2%	54.7%	45.3%
8,662	POCAHONTAS	3,092	1,434	1,576	82	142 D	46.4%	51.0%	47.6%	52.4%
374,601	POLK	142,173	60,119	79,774	2,280	19,655 D	42.3%	56.1%	43.0%	57.0%
87,704	POTTAWATTAMIE	25,807	13,557	11,798	452	1,759 R	52.5%	45.7%	53.5%	46.5%
18,815	POWESHIEK	6,646	2,895	3,609	142	714 D	43.6%	54.3%	44.5%	55.5%
5,469	RINGGOLD	2,196	866	1,295	35	429 D	39.4%	59.0%	40.1%	59.9%
11,529	SAC	3,785	1,764	1,951	70	187 D	46.6%	51.5%	47.5%	52.5%
158,668	SCOTT	52,284	22,346	28,907	1,031	6,561 D	42.7%	55.3%	43.6%	56.4%
13,173	SHELBY	4,822	2,810	1,939	73	871 R	58.3%	40.2%	59.2%	40.8%
31,589	SIOUX	11,208	9,045	2,103	60	6,942 R	80.7%	18.8%	81.1%	18.9%
79,981	STORY	28,611	11,532	16,395	684	4,863 D	40.3%	57.3%	41.3%	58.7%
18,103	TAMA	6,274	2,686	3,470	118	784 D	42.8%	55.3%	43.6%	56.4%
6,958	TAYLOR	2,595	1,172	1,381	42	209 D	45.2%	53.2%	45.9%	54.1%
12,309	UNION	4,425	1,865	2,467	93	602 D	42.1%	55.8%	43.1%	56.9%
7,809	VAN BUREN	2,790	1,389	1,324	77	65 R	49.8%	47.5%	51.2%	48.8%
36,051	WAPELLO	13,210	4,707	8,200	303	3,493 D	35.6%	62.1%	36.5%	63.5%
40,671	WARREN	16,227	6,819	9,145	263	2,326 D	42.0%	56.4%	42.7%	57.3%
20,670	WASHINGTON	7,097	3,441	3,518	138	77 D	48.5%	49.6%	49.4%	50.6%
6,730	WAYNE	2,338	1,060	1,241	37	181 D	45.3%	53.1%	46.1%	53.9%
40,235	WEBSTER	13,195	5,539	7,433	223	1,894 D	42.0%	56.3%	42.7%	57.3%
11,723	WINNEBAGO	4,184	1,862	2,224	98	362 D	44.5%	53.2%	45.6%	54.4%
21,310	WINNESHIEK	7,381	3,283	3,893	205	610 D	44.5%	52.7%	45.7%	54.3%
103,877	WOODBURY	28,136	12,722	14,643	771	1,921 D	45.2%	52.0%	46.5%	53.5%
7,909	WORTH	2,976	1,080	1,793	103	713 D	36.3%	60.2%	37.6%	62.4%
14,334	WRIGHT	4,545	2,227	2,267	51	40 D	49.0%	49.9%	49.6%	50.4%
2,926,324	TOTAL	1,023,075	447,892	554,278	20,905	106,386 D	43.8%	54.2%	44.7%	55.3%

IOWA

HOUSE OF REPRESENTATIVES

CD	Year	Total Vote	Republican Vote	Republican Candidate	Democratic Vote	Democratic Candidate	Other Vote	Rep.-Dem. Plurality	Total Vote Rep.	Total Vote Dem.	Major Vote Rep.	Major Vote Dem.
1	2002	196,455	112,280	Nussle, Jim*	83,779	Hutchinson, Ann	396	28,501 R	57.2%	42.6%	57.3%	42.7%
2	2002	207,171	108,130	Leach, Jim*	94,767	Thomas, Julie	4,274	13,363 R	52.2%	45.7%	53.3%	46.7%
3	2002	215,985	97,285	Thompson, Stan	115,367	Boswell, Leonard L.*	3,333	18,082 D	45.0%	53.4%	45.7%	54.3%
4	2002	210,774	115,430	Latham, Tom*	90,784	Norris, John	4,560	24,646 R	54.8%	43.1%	56.0%	44.0%
5	2002	182,237	113,257	King, Steve	68,853	Shomshor, Paul	127	44,404 R	62.1%	37.8%	62.2%	37.8%
Total	2002	1,012,622	546,382		453,550		12,690	92,832 R	54.0%	44.8%	54.6%	45.4%

An asterisk (*) denotes incumbent.

IOWA

GENERAL AND PRIMARY ELECTIONS

2002 GENERAL ELECTIONS

Governor   Other vote was 14,628 Iowa Green (Jay Robinson); 13,098 Libertarian (Clyde Cleveland); 1,015 write-in.

Senator   Other vote was 11,340 Iowa Green (Timothy A. Harthan); 8,864 Libertarian (Richard J. Moore); 701 write-in.

House   Other vote was:

CD 1   396 write-in.
CD 2   4,178 Libertarian (Kevin Litten); 96 write-in.
CD 3   2,689 Libertarian (Jeffrey J. Smith); 569 Socialist Workers (Edwin B. Fruit); 75 write-in.
CD 4   2,952 Libertarian (Terry L. Wilson); 1,544 One Earth (Jim Hennager); 64 write-in.
CD 5   127 write-in.

2002 PRIMARY ELECTIONS

Primary   June 4, 2002

Registration (as of May 25, 2002— includes 106,932 inactive registrants)		
	Republican	591,573
	Democratic	561,855
	Green	1,153
	No Party	790,640
	TOTAL	1,945,221

Primary Type   Semi-open—Registered Democrats and Republicans could vote only in their party's primary, although any registered voter could participate in either party's primary by changing their registration to that party on primary day.

Note: An asterisk (*) denotes incumbent. State law requires a candidate to attain at least 35 percent of the primary vote to win their party's nomination. In the Iowa 5th District, none of the Republican candidates did so, and Steve King was subsequently nominated by convention.

IOWA

GENERAL AND PRIMARY ELECTIONS

	REPUBLICAN PRIMARIES			DEMOCRATIC PRIMARIES		
Governor	Doug Gross	71,478	35.9%	Tom Vilsack*	79,277	98.6%
	Steve Sukup	64,490	32.4%	Write-in	1,166	1.4%
	Bob Vander Plaats	63,077	31.7%			
	Write-in	189	0.1%			
	TOTAL	199,234		TOTAL	80,443	
Senator	Greg Ganske	116,229	59.0%	Tom Harkin*	83,505	99.3%
	Bill Salier	80,700	40.9%	Write-in	555	0.7%
	Write-in	167	0.1%			
	TOTAL	197,096		TOTAL	84,060	
Congressional District 1	Jim Nussle*	26,648	99.5%	Ann Hutchinson	12,235	58.8%
	Write-in	135	0.5%	Dave Nagle	7,799	37.5%
				Denny Heath	740	3.6%
				Write-in	34	0.2%
	TOTAL	26,783		TOTAL	20,808	
Congressional District 2	Jim Leach*	24,441	99.4%	Julie Thomas	14,367	99.6%
	Write-in	155	0.6%	Write-in	60	0.4%
	TOTAL	24,596		TOTAL	14,427	
Congressional District 3	Stan Thompson	29,530	99.6%	Leonard L. Boswell*	21,623	99.4%
	Write-in	123	0.4%	Write-in	126	0.6%
	TOTAL	29,653		TOTAL	21,749	
Congressional District 4	Tom Latham*	38,321	88.5%	John Norris	13,905	99.7%
	Gail E. Boliver	4,956	11.4%	Write-in	41	0.3%
	Write-in	17				
	TOTAL	43,294		TOTAL	13,946	
Congressional District 5	Steve King	16,503	30.3%	Paul Shomshor	7,122	99.6%
	John Redwine	13,428	24.6%	Write-in	32	0.4%
	Brent Siegrist	12,978	23.8%			
	Jeff Ballenger	11,563	21.2%			
	Write-in	22				
	TOTAL	54,494		TOTAL	7,154	

IOWA REPUBLICAN PRIMARY

GOVERNOR 2002

2000 Census Population	County	Total Vote	Gross	Sukup	Vander Plaats	Other	Winner	Percentage of Total Vote			
								Gross	Sukup	Vander Plaats	Other
8,243	ADAIR	927	299	430	198		Sukup	32.3%	46.4%	21.4%	
4,482	ADAMS	356	168	133	55		Gross	47.2%	37.4%	15.4%	
14,675	ALLAMAKEE	1,441	440	467	534		Vander Plaats	30.5%	32.4%	37.1%	
13,721	APPANOOSE	724	320	267	137		Gross	44.2%	36.9%	18.9%	
6,830	AUDUBON	557	271	159	127		Gross	48.7%	28.5%	22.8%	
25,308	BENTON	1,260	398	453	408	1	Sukup	31.6%	36.0%	32.4%	0.1%
128,012	BLACK HAWK	6,986	2,853	2,458	1,669	6	Gross	40.8%	35.2%	23.9%	0.1%
26,224	BOONE	1,865	730	523	609	3	Gross	39.1%	28.0%	32.7%	0.2%
23,325	BREMER	1,613	482	704	427		Sukup	29.9%	43.6%	26.5%	
21,093	BUCHANAN	1,246	355	422	468	1	Vander Plaats	28.5%	33.9%	37.6%	0.1%
20,411	BUENA VISTA	1,500	483	475	539	3	Vander Plaats	32.2%	31.7%	35.9%	0.2%
15,305	BUTLER	2,116	336	1,308	472		Sukup	15.9%	61.8%	22.3%	
11,115	CALHOUN	1,007	336	383	286	2	Sukup	33.4%	38.0%	28.4%	0.2%
21,421	CARROLL	1,132	614	320	197	1	Gross	54.2%	28.3%	17.4%	0.1%
14,684	CASS	2,076	1,069	567	440		Gross	51.5%	27.3%	21.2%	
18,187	CEDAR	853	275	311	265	2	Sukup	32.2%	36.5%	31.1%	0.2%
46,447	CERRO GORDO	3,690	517	2,723	449	1	Sukup	14.0%	73.8%	12.2%	
13,035	CHEROKEE	1,247	372	301	574		Vander Plaats	29.8%	24.1%	46.0%	
13,095	CHICKASAW	890	248	333	309		Sukup	27.9%	37.4%	34.7%	
9,133	CLARKE	781	338	280	163		Gross	43.3%	35.9%	20.9%	
17,372	CLAY	1,255	544	235	475	1	Gross	43.3%	18.7%	37.8%	0.1%
18,678	CLAYTON	1,081	317	451	313		Sukup	29.3%	41.7%	29.0%	
50,149	CLINTON	2,143	1,032	603	507	1	Gross	48.2%	28.1%	23.7%	
16,942	CRAWFORD	1,482	884	432	166		Gross	59.6%	29.1%	11.2%	
40,750	DALLAS	2,889	1,323	872	694		Gross	45.8%	30.2%	24.0%	
8,541	DAVIS	526	162	182	179	3	Sukup	30.8%	34.6%	34.0%	0.6%
8,689	DECATUR	582	230	205	147		Gross	39.5%	35.2%	25.3%	
18,404	DELAWARE	1,209	377	512	320		Sukup	31.2%	42.3%	26.5%	
42,351	DES MOINES	1,489	394	127	967	1	Vander Plaats	26.5%	8.5%	64.9%	0.1%
16,424	DICKINSON	1,388	579	298	508	3	Gross	41.7%	21.5%	36.6%	0.2%
89,143	DUBUQUE	3,021	1,243	1,145	627	6	Gross	41.1%	37.9%	20.8%	0.2%
11,027	EMMET	330	170	94	66		Gross	51.5%	28.5%	20.0%	
22,008	FAYETTE	1,744	613	549	582		Gross	35.1%	31.5%	33.4%	
16,900	FLOYD	1,053	244	634	164	11	Sukup	23.2%	60.2%	15.6%	1.0%
10,704	FRANKLIN	2,309	178	1,931	200		Sukup	7.7%	83.6%	8.7%	
8,010	FREMONT	603	229	172	202		Gross	38.0%	28.5%	33.5%	
10,366	GREENE	876	292	276	307	1	Vander Plaats	33.3%	31.5%	35.0%	0.1%
12,369	GRUNDY	1,661	471	623	566	1	Sukup	28.4%	37.5%	34.1%	0.1%
11,353	GUTHRIE	1,179	493	444	238	4	Gross	41.8%	37.7%	20.2%	0.3%
16,438	HAMILTON	1,673	508	823	339	3	Sukup	30.4%	49.2%	20.3%	0.2%
12,100	HANCOCK	1,573	274	995	303	1	Sukup	17.4%	63.3%	19.3%	0.1%
18,812	HARDIN	2,361	352	1,602	406	1	Sukup	14.9%	67.9%	17.2%	
15,666	HARRISON	775	453	184	135	3	Gross	58.5%	23.7%	17.4%	0.4%
20,336	HENRY	1,169	518	235	415	1	Gross	44.3%	20.1%	35.5%	0.1%
9,932	HOWARD	514	139	194	181		Sukup	27.0%	37.7%	35.2%	
10,381	HUMBOLDT	912	253	375	284		Sukup	27.7%	41.1%	31.1%	
7,837	IDA	824	256	339	229		Sukup	31.1%	41.1%	27.8%	
15,671	IOWA	1,140	380	498	262		Sukup	33.3%	43.7%	23.0%	
20,296	JACKSON	624	242	178	203	1	Gross	38.8%	28.5%	32.5%	0.2%
37,213	JASPER	2,290	900	636	754		Gross	39.3%	27.8%	32.9%	
16,181	JEFFERSON	1,091	530	195	363	3	Gross	48.6%	17.9%	33.3%	0.3%
111,006	JOHNSON	3,317	1,341	1,032	941	3	Gross	40.4%	31.1%	28.4%	0.1%
20,221	JONES	1,138	389	542	206	1	Sukup	34.2%	47.6%	18.1%	0.1%
11,400	KEOKUK	1,001	395	380	226		Gross	39.5%	38.0%	22.6%	
17,163	KOSSUTH	1,130	430	456	242	2	Sukup	38.1%	40.4%	21.4%	0.2%
38,052	LEE	1,160	236	141	782	1	Vander Plaats	20.3%	12.2%	67.4%	0.1%
191,701	LINN	10,557	3,645	3,675	3,229	8	Sukup	34.5%	34.8%	30.6%	0.1%
12,183	LOUISA	572	237	147	188		Gross	41.4%	25.7%	32.9%	
9,422	LUCAS	603	205	207	191		Sukup	34.0%	34.3%	31.7%	
11,763	LYON	2,197	519	226	1,452		Vander Plaats	23.6%	10.3%	66.1%	

IOWA REPUBLICAN PRIMARY

GOVERNOR 2002

2000 Census Population	County	Total Vote	Gross	Sukup	Vander Plaats	Other	Winner	Percentage of Total Vote			
								Gross	Sukup	Vander Plaats	Other
14,019	MADISON	1,343	517	451	373	2	Gross	38.5%	33.6%	27.8%	0.1%
22,335	MAHASKA	1,990	509	508	973		Vander Plaats	25.6%	25.5%	48.9%	
32,052	MARION	2,724	699	540	1,485		Vander Plaats	25.7%	19.8%	54.5%	
39,311	MARSHALL	2,767	1,149	913	703	2	Gross	41.5%	33.0%	25.4%	0.1%
14,547	MILLS	1,382	482	640	256	4	Sukup	34.9%	46.3%	18.5%	0.3%
10,874	MITCHELL	998	178	674	146		Sukup	17.8%	67.5%	14.6%	
10,020	MONONA	603	234	154	214	1	Gross	38.8%	25.5%	35.5%	0.2%
8,016	MONROE	392	167	143	81	1	Gross	42.6%	36.5%	20.7%	0.3%
11,771	MONTGOMERY	1,621	804	512	302	3	Gross	49.6%	31.6%	18.6%	0.2%
41,722	MUSCATINE	2,468	898	1,052	517	1	Sukup	36.4%	42.6%	20.9%	
15,102	O'BRIEN	2,568	301	212	2,053	2	Vander Plaats	11.7%	8.3%	79.9%	0.1%
7,003	OSCEOLA	1,013	207	129	675	2	Vander Plaats	20.4%	12.7%	66.6%	0.2%
16,976	PAGE	1,437	579	382	476		Gross	40.3%	26.6%	33.1%	
10,147	PALO ALTO	675	276	176	223		Gross	40.9%	26.1%	33.0%	
24,849	PLYMOUTH	2,208	497	404	1,307		Vander Plaats	22.5%	18.3%	59.2%	
8,662	POCAHONTAS	530	160	200	170		Sukup	30.2%	37.7%	32.1%	
374,601	POLK	25,097	12,222	6,717	6,128	30	Gross	48.7%	26.8%	24.4%	0.1%
87,704	POTTAWATTAMIE	5,956	3,305	1,183	1,453	15	Gross	55.5%	19.9%	24.4%	0.3%
18,815	POWESHIEK	1,698	608	638	449	3	Sukup	35.8%	37.6%	26.4%	0.2%
5,469	RINGGOLD	748	289	320	138	1	Sukup	38.6%	42.8%	18.4%	0.1%
11,529	SAC	1,663	596	661	406		Sukup	35.8%	39.7%	24.4%	
158,668	SCOTT	7,722	3,436	2,482	1,781	23	Gross	44.5%	32.1%	23.1%	0.3%
13,173	SHELBY	1,835	1,282	207	346		Gross	69.9%	11.3%	18.9%	
31,589	SIOUX	7,811	674	572	6,565		Vander Plaats	8.6%	7.3%	84.0%	
79,981	STORY	4,813	1,750	1,443	1,619	1	Gross	36.4%	30.0%	33.6%	
18,103	TAMA	1,133	408	420	304	1	Sukup	36.0%	37.1%	26.8%	0.1%
6,958	TAYLOR	493	195	218	80		Sukup	39.6%	44.2%	16.2%	
12,309	UNION	961	379	360	222		Gross	39.4%	37.5%	23.1%	
7,809	VAN BUREN	760	236	107	416	1	Vander Plaats	31.1%	14.1%	54.7%	0.1%
36,051	WAPELLO	1,250	516	376	353	5	Gross	41.3%	30.1%	28.2%	0.4%
40,671	WARREN	2,294	951	646	696	1	Gross	41.5%	28.2%	30.3%	
20,670	WASHINGTON	1,266	496	470	300		Gross	39.2%	37.1%	23.7%	
6,730	WAYNE	506	195	208	103		Sukup	38.5%	41.1%	20.4%	
40,235	WEBSTER	2,633	904	1,156	572	1	Sukup	34.3%	43.9%	21.7%	
11,723	WINNEBAGO	858	243	482	133		Sukup	28.3%	56.2%	15.5%	
21,310	WINNESHIEK	1,291	410	450	431		Sukup	31.8%	34.9%	33.4%	
103,877	WOODBURY	5,794	1,372	1,092	3,321	9	Vander Plaats	23.7%	18.8%	57.3%	0.2%
7,909	WORTH	1,004	171	675	158		Sukup	17.0%	67.2%	15.7%	
14,334	WRIGHT	1,221	302	655	264		Sukup	24.7%	53.6%	21.6%	
2,926,324	TOTAL	199,234	71,478	64,490	63,077	189	Gross	35.9%	32.4%	31.7%	0.1%

IOWA REPUBLICAN PRIMARY

SENATOR 2002

2000 Census Population	County	Total Vote	Ganske	Salier	Other	Winner	Percentage of Total Vote		
							Ganske	Salier	Other
8,243	ADAIR	930	557	373		Ganske	59.9%	40.1%	
4,482	ADAMS	357	249	107	1	Ganske	69.7%	30.0%	0.3%
14,675	ALLAMAKEE	1,425	671	754		Salier	47.1%	52.9%	
13,721	APPANOOSE	729	533	196		Ganske	73.1%	26.9%	
6,830	AUDUBON	562	376	185	1	Ganske	66.9%	32.9%	0.2%
25,308	BENTON	1,247	578	668	1	Salier	46.4%	53.6%	0.1%
128,012	BLACK HAWK	6,995	3,865	3,119	11	Ganske	55.3%	44.6%	0.2%
26,224	BOONE	1,855	1,074	775	6	Ganske	57.9%	41.8%	0.3%
23,325	BREMER	1,597	906	690	1	Ganske	56.7%	43.2%	0.1%
21,093	BUCHANAN	1,236	508	727	1	Salier	41.1%	58.8%	0.1%
20,411	BUENA VISTA	1,468	903	564	1	Ganske	61.5%	38.4%	0.1%
15,305	BUTLER	2,027	1,046	981		Ganske	51.6%	48.4%	
11,115	CALHOUN	1,009	599	409	1	Ganske	59.4%	40.5%	0.1%
21,421	CARROLL	1,111	785	325	1	Ganske	70.7%	29.3%	0.1%
14,684	CASS	2,103	1,633	469	1	Ganske	77.7%	22.3%	
18,187	CEDAR	830	436	393	1	Ganske	52.5%	47.3%	0.1%
46,447	CERRO GORDO	3,626	1,747	1,874	5	Salier	48.2%	51.7%	0.1%
13,035	CHEROKEE	1,205	785	420		Ganske	65.1%	34.9%	
13,095	CHICKASAW	896	323	573		Salier	36.0%	64.0%	
9,133	CLARKE	768	491	277		Ganske	63.9%	36.1%	
17,372	CLAY	1,184	840	343	1	Ganske	70.9%	29.0%	0.1%
18,678	CLAYTON	1,070	602	466	2	Ganske	56.3%	43.6%	0.2%
50,149	CLINTON	2,125	1,308	817		Ganske	61.6%	38.4%	
16,942	CRAWFORD	1,359	965	394		Ganske	71.0%	29.0%	
40,750	DALLAS	2,889	1,732	1,155	2	Ganske	60.0%	40.0%	0.1%
8,541	DAVIS	535	287	247	1	Ganske	53.6%	46.2%	0.2%
8,689	DECATUR	577	394	183		Ganske	68.3%	31.7%	
18,404	DELAWARE	1,164	712	452		Ganske	61.2%	38.8%	
42,351	DES MOINES	1,472	907	563	2	Ganske	61.6%	38.2%	0.1%
16,424	DICKINSON	1,377	1,116	261		Ganske	81.0%	19.0%	
89,143	DUBUQUE	2,980	1,833	1,144	3	Ganske	61.5%	38.4%	0.1%
11,027	EMMET	330	220	110		Ganske	66.7%	33.3%	
22,008	FAYETTE	1,718	833	885		Salier	48.5%	51.5%	
16,900	FLOYD	1,003	423	578	2	Salier	42.2%	57.6%	0.2%
10,704	FRANKLIN	2,165	1,108	1,056	1	Ganske	51.2%	48.8%	
8,010	FREMONT	622	442	178	2	Ganske	71.1%	28.6%	0.3%
10,366	GREENE	873	577	296		Ganske	66.1%	33.9%	
12,369	GRUNDY	1,637	779	858		Salier	47.6%	52.4%	
11,353	GUTHRIE	1,175	712	462	1	Ganske	60.6%	39.3%	0.1%
16,438	HAMILTON	1,679	847	830	2	Ganske	50.4%	49.4%	0.1%
12,100	HANCOCK	1,546	743	803		Salier	48.1%	51.9%	
18,812	HARDIN	2,306	1,016	1,287	3	Salier	44.1%	55.8%	0.1%
15,666	HARRISON	799	617	181	1	Ganske	77.2%	22.7%	0.1%
20,336	HENRY	1,159	691	467	1	Ganske	59.6%	40.3%	0.1%
9,932	HOWARD	504	256	247	1	Ganske	50.8%	49.0%	0.2%
10,381	HUMBOLDT	899	538	361		Ganske	59.8%	40.2%	
7,837	IDA	775	486	289		Ganske	62.7%	37.3%	
15,671	IOWA	1,132	599	533		Ganske	52.9%	47.1%	
20,296	JACKSON	614	376	238		Ganske	61.2%	38.8%	
37,213	JASPER	2,290	1,278	1,011	1	Ganske	55.8%	44.1%	
16,181	JEFFERSON	1,075	616	457	2	Ganske	57.3%	42.5%	0.2%
111,006	JOHNSON	3,358	1,766	1,591	1	Ganske	52.6%	47.4%	0.0%
20,221	JONES	1,134	517	615	2	Salier	45.6%	54.2%	0.2%
11,400	KEOKUK	947	614	333		Ganske	64.8%	35.2%	
17,163	KOSSUTH	1,125	745	380		Ganske	66.2%	33.8%	
38,052	LEE	1,218	400	816	2	Salier	32.8%	67.0%	0.2%
191,701	LINN	10,598	5,092	5,500	6	Salier	48.0%	51.9%	0.1%
12,183	LOUISA	560	373	187		Ganske	66.6%	33.4%	
9,422	LUCAS	599	301	298		Ganske	50.3%	49.7%	
11,763	LYON	2,011	1,214	797		Ganske	60.4%	39.6%	

IOWA REPUBLICAN PRIMARY

SENATOR 2002

2000 Census Population	County	Total Vote	Ganske	Salier	Other	Winner	Percentage of Total Vote		
							Ganske	Salier	Other
14,019	MADISON	1,359	827	529	3	Ganske	60.9%	38.9%	0.2%
22,335	MAHASKA	1,904	1,043	860	1	Ganske	54.8%	45.2%	0.1%
32,052	MARION	2,706	1,176	1,529	1	Salier	43.5%	56.5%	
39,311	MARSHALL	2,770	1,602	1,168		Ganske	57.8%	42.2%	
14,547	MILLS	1,465	1,159	305	1	Ganske	79.1%	20.8%	0.1%
10,874	MITCHELL	1,006	290	716		Salier	28.8%	71.2%	
10,020	MONONA	595	333	262		Ganske	56.0%	44.0%	
8,016	MONROE	385	231	154		Ganske	60.0%	40.0%	
11,771	MONTGOMERY	1,709	1,210	497	2	Ganske	70.8%	29.1%	0.1%
41,722	MUSCATINE	2,399	1,535	863	1	Ganske	64.0%	36.0%	
15,102	O'BRIEN	2,347	1,544	799	4	Ganske	65.8%	34.0%	0.2%
7,003	OSCEOLA	908	640	268		Ganske	70.5%	29.5%	
16,976	PAGE	1,458	958	500		Ganske	65.7%	34.3%	
10,147	PALO ALTO	658	438	220		Ganske	66.6%	33.4%	
24,849	PLYMOUTH	2,112	1,235	877		Ganske	58.5%	41.5%	
8,662	POCAHONTAS	528	321	207		Ganske	60.8%	39.2%	
374,601	POLK	25,229	16,192	9,012	25	Ganske	64.2%	35.7%	0.1%
87,704	POTTAWATTAMIE	6,331	5,308	1,006	17	Ganske	83.8%	15.9%	0.3%
18,815	POWESHIEK	1,680	1,019	661		Ganske	60.7%	39.3%	
5,469	RINGGOLD	746	498	248		Ganske	66.8%	33.2%	
11,529	SAC	1,602	1,046	556		Ganske	65.3%	34.7%	
158,668	SCOTT	7,720	4,479	3,231	10	Ganske	58.0%	41.9%	0.1%
13,173	SHELBY	1,749	1,266	479	4	Ganske	72.4%	27.4%	0.2%
31,589	SIOUX	7,255	3,739	3,516		Ganske	51.5%	48.5%	
79,981	STORY	4,850	2,940	1,906	4	Ganske	60.6%	39.3%	0.1%
18,103	TAMA	1,124	606	517	1	Ganske	53.9%	46.0%	0.1%
6,958	TAYLOR	501	363	138		Ganske	72.5%	27.5%	
12,309	UNION	953	592	361		Ganske	62.1%	37.9%	
7,809	VAN BUREN	759	333	425	1	Salier	43.9%	56.0%	0.1%
36,051	WAPELLO	1,248	775	469	4	Ganske	62.1%	37.6%	0.3%
40,671	WARREN	2,295	1,303	991	1	Ganske	56.8%	43.2%	
20,670	WASHINGTON	1,241	722	519		Ganske	58.2%	41.8%	
6,730	WAYNE	500	308	192		Ganske	61.6%	38.4%	
40,235	WEBSTER	2,606	1,591	1,013	2	Ganske	61.1%	38.9%	0.1%
11,723	WINNEBAGO	841	404	436	1	Salier	48.0%	51.8%	0.1%
21,310	WINNESHIEK	1,266	788	477	1	Ganske	62.2%	37.7%	0.1%
103,877	WOODBURY	5,582	3,294	2,276	12	Ganske	59.0%	40.8%	0.2%
7,909	WORTH	987	545	442		Ganske	55.2%	44.8%	
14,334	WRIGHT	1,163	636	527		Ganske	54.7%	45.3%	
2,926,324	TOTAL	197,096	116,229	80,700	167	Ganske	59.0%	40.9%	0.1%

KANSAS

GOVERNOR
Kathleen Sebelius (D). Elected 2002 to a four-year term.

SENATORS (2 Republicans)
Sam Brownback (R). Reelected 1998 to a six-year term. Had been elected 1996 to fill out the remaining two years of the term vacated when Senator Robert Dole (R) resigned to run for president.

Pat Roberts (R). Reelected 2002 to a six-year term. Previously elected 1996.

REPRESENTATIVES (3 Republicans, 1 Democrat)
1. Jerry Moran (R)
2. Jim Ryun (R)
3. Dennis Moore (D)
4. Todd Tiahrt (R)

POSTWAR VOTE FOR PRESIDENT

Year	Total Vote	Republican Vote	Republican Candidate	Democratic Vote	Democratic Candidate	Other Vote	Plurality	Percentage Total Vote Rep.	Percentage Total Vote Dem.	Percentage Major Vote Rep.	Percentage Major Vote Dem.
2000**	1,072,218	622,332	Bush, George W.	399,276	Gore, Al	50,610	223,056 R	58.0%	37.2%	60.9%	39.1%
1996**	1,074,300	583,245	Dole, Bob	387,659	Clinton, Bill	103,396	195,586 R	54.3%	36.1%	60.1%	39.9%
1992**	1,157,335	449,951	Bush, George	390,434	Clinton, Bill	316,950	59,517 R	38.9%	33.7%	53.5%	46.5%
1988	993,044	554,049	Bush, George	422,636	Dukakis, Michael S.	16,359	131,413 R	55.8%	42.6%	56.7%	43.3%
1984	1,021,991	677,296	Reagan, Ronald	333,149	Mondale, Walter F.	11,546	344,147 R	66.3%	32.6%	67.0%	33.0%
1980**	979,795	566,812	Reagan, Ronald	326,150	Carter, Jimmy	86,833	240,662 R	57.9%	33.3%	63.5%	36.5%
1976	957,845	502,752	Ford, Gerald R.	430,421	Carter, Jimmy	24,672	72,331 R	52.5%	44.9%	53.9%	46.1%
1972	916,095	619,812	Nixon, Richard M.	270,287	McGovern, George S.	25,996	349,525 R	67.7%	29.5%	69.6%	30.4%
1968	872,783	478,674	Nixon, Richard M.	302,996	Humphrey, Hubert H.	91,113	175,678 R	54.8%	34.7%	61.2%	38.8%
1964	857,901	386,579	Goldwater, Barry M.	464,028	Johnson, Lyndon B.	7,294	77,449 D	45.1%	54.1%	45.4%	54.6%
1960	928,825	561,474	Nixon, Richard M.	363,213	Kennedy, John F.	4,138	198,261 R	60.4%	39.1%	60.7%	39.3%
1956	866,243	566,878	Eisenhower, Dwight D.	296,317	Stevenson, Adlai E.	3,048	270,561 R	65.4%	34.2%	65.7%	34.3%
1952	896,166	616,302	Eisenhower, Dwight D.	273,296	Stevenson, Adlai E.	6,568	343,006 R	68.8%	30.5%	69.3%	30.7%
1948	788,819	423,039	Dewey, Thomas E.	351,902	Truman, Harry S.	13,878	71,137 R	53.6%	44.6%	54.6%	45.4%

In 2000 the other vote column includes 36,086 votes cast for Green (Nader). In 1996 the other vote column includes 92,639 votes cast for Perot. In 1992 the other vote column includes 312,358 votes cast for Perot. In 1980 the other vote column includes 68,231 votes for Independent (Anderson).

KANSAS

POSTWAR VOTE FOR GOVERNOR

Year	Total Vote	Republican Vote	Republican Candidate	Democratic Vote	Democratic Candidate	Other Vote	Rep.-Dem. Plurality	Total Vote Rep.	Total Vote Dem.	Major Vote Rep.	Major Vote Dem.
2002	835,692	376,830	Shallenburger, Tim	441,858	Sebelius, Kathleen	17,004	65,028 D	45.1%	52.9%	46.0%	54.0%
1998	742,665	544,882	Graves, Bill	168,243	Sawyer, Tom	29,540	376,639 R	73.4%	22.7%	76.4%	23.6%
1994	821,030	526,113	Graves, Bill	294,733	Slattery, Jim	184	231,380 R	64.1%	35.9%	64.1%	35.9%
1990	783,325	333,589	Hayden, Mike	380,609	Finney, Joan	69,127	47,020 D	42.6%	48.6%	46.7%	53.3%
1986	840,605	436,267	Hayden, Mike	404,338	Docking, Thomas R.		31,929 R	51.9%	48.1%	51.9%	48.1%
1982	763,263	339,356	Hardage, Sam	405,772	Carlin, John	18,135	66,416 D	44.5%	53.2%	45.5%	54.5%
1978	736,246	348,015	Bennett, Robert F.	363,835	Carlin, John	24,396	15,820 D	47.3%	49.4%	48.9%	51.1%
1974**	783,875	387,792	Bennett, Robert F.	384,115	Miller, Vern	11,968	3,677 R	49.5%	49.0%	50.2%	49.8%
1972	921,552	341,440	Kay, Morris	571,256	Docking, Robert	8,856	229,816 D	37.1%	62.0%	37.4%	62.6%
1970	745,196	333,227	Frizzell, Kent	404,611	Docking, Robert	7,358	71,384 D	44.7%	54.3%	45.2%	54.8%
1968	862,473	410,673	Harman, Rick	447,269	Docking, Robert	4,531	36,596 D	47.6%	51.9%	47.9%	52.1%
1966	692,955	304,325	Avery, William H.	380,030	Docking, Robert	8,600	75,705 D	43.9%	54.8%	44.5%	55.5%
1964	850,414	432,667	Avery, William H.	400,264	Wiles, Harry G.	17,483	32,403 R	50.9%	47.1%	51.9%	48.1%
1962	638,798	341,257	Anderson, John	291,285	Saffels, Dale E.	6,256	49,972 R	53.4%	45.6%	54.0%	46.0%
1960	922,522	511,534	Anderson, John	402,261	Docking, George	8,727	109,273 R	55.4%	43.6%	56.0%	44.0%
1958	735,939	313,036	Reed, Clyde M.	415,506	Docking, George	7,397	102,470 D	42.5%	56.5%	43.0%	57.0%
1956	864,935	364,340	Shaw, Warren W.	479,701	Docking, George	20,894	115,361 D	42.1%	55.5%	43.2%	56.8%
1954	622,633	329,868	Hall, Fred	286,218	Docking, George	6,547	43,650 R	53.0%	46.0%	53.5%	46.5%
1952	872,139	491,338	Arn, Edward F.	363,482	Rooney, Charles	17,319	127,856 R	56.3%	41.7%	57.5%	42.5%
1950	619,310	333,001	Arn, Edward F.	275,494	Anderson, Kenneth	10,815	57,507 R	53.8%	44.5%	54.7%	45.3%
1948	760,407	433,396	Carlson, Frank	307,485	Carpenter, Randolph	19,526	125,911 R	57.0%	40.4%	58.5%	41.5%
1946	577,694	309,064	Carlson, Frank	254,283	Woodring, Harry H.	14,347	54,781 R	53.5%	44.0%	54.9%	45.1%

The term of office of Kansas' Governor was increased from two to four years effective with the 1974 election.

POSTWAR VOTE FOR SENATOR

Year	Total Vote	Republican Vote	Republican Candidate	Democratic Vote	Democratic Candidate	Other Vote	Rep.-Dem. Plurality	Total Vote Rep.	Total Vote Dem.	Major Vote Rep.	Major Vote Dem.
2002	776,850	641,075	Roberts, Pat	—		135,775	641,075 R	82.5%		100.0%	
1998	727,236	474,639	Brownback, Sam	229,718	Feleciano, Paul, Jr.	22,879	244,921 R	65.3%	31.6%	67.4%	32.6%
1996	1,052,300	652,677	Roberts, Pat	362,380	Thompson, Sally	37,243	290,297 R	62.0%	34.4%	64.3%	35.7%
1996S	1,064,716	574,021	Brownback, Sam	461,344	Docking, Jill	29,351	112,677 R	53.9%	43.3%	55.4%	44.6%
1992	1,126,447	706,246	Dole, Robert	349,525	O'Dell, Gloria	70,676	356,721 R	62.7%	31.0%	66.9%	33.1%
1990	786,235	578,605	Kassebaum, Nancy Landon	207,491	Williams, Dick	139	371,114 R	73.6%	26.4%	73.6%	26.4%
1986	823,566	576,902	Dole, Robert	246,664	MacDonald, Guy		330,238 R	70.0%	30.0%	70.0%	30.0%
1984	996,729	757,402	Kassebaum, Nancy Landon	211,664	Maher, James	27,663	545,738 R	76.0%	21.2%	78.2%	21.8%
1980	938,957	598,686	Dole, Robert	340,271	Simpson, John		258,415 R	63.8%	36.2%	63.8%	36.2%
1978	748,839	403,354	Kassebaum, Nancy Landon	317,602	Roy, William R.	27,883	85,752 R	53.9%	42.4%	55.9%	44.1%
1974	794,437	403,983	Dole, Robert	390,451	Roy, William R.	3	13,532 R	50.9%	49.1%	50.9%	49.1%
1972	871,722	622,591	Pearson, James B.	200,764	Tetzlaff, Arch O.	48,367	421,827 R	71.4%	23.0%	75.6%	24.4%
1968	817,096	490,911	Dole, Robert	315,911	Robinson, William I.	10,274	175,000 R	60.1%	38.7%	60.8%	39.2%
1966	671,345	350,077	Pearson, James B.	303,223	Breeding, J. Floyd	18,045	46,854 R	52.1%	45.2%	53.6%	46.4%
1962	622,232	388,500	Carlson, Frank	223,630	Smith, K. L.	10,102	164,870 R	62.4%	35.9%	63.5%	36.5%
1962S	613,250	344,689	Pearson, James B.	260,756	Aylward, Paul L.	7,805	83,933 R	56.2%	42.5%	56.9%	43.1%
1960	888,592	485,499	Schoeppel, Andrew F.	388,895	Theis, Frank	14,198	96,604 R	54.6%	43.8%	55.5%	44.5%
1956	825,280	477,822	Carlson, Frank	333,939	Hart, George	13,519	143,883 R	57.9%	40.5%	58.9%	41.1%
1954	618,063	348,144	Schoeppel, Andrew F.	258,575	McGill, George	11,344	89,569 R	56.3%	41.8%	57.4%	42.6%
1950	619,104	335,880	Carlson, Frank	271,365	Aiken, Paul	11,859	64,515 R	54.3%	43.8%	55.3%	44.7%
1948	716,342	393,412	Schoeppel, Andrew F.	305,987	McGill, George	16,943	87,425 R	54.9%	42.7%	56.3%	43.7%

One of the 1996 and 1962 elections was for a short term to fill a vacancy.

KANSAS

Congressional districts first established for elections held in 2002
4 members

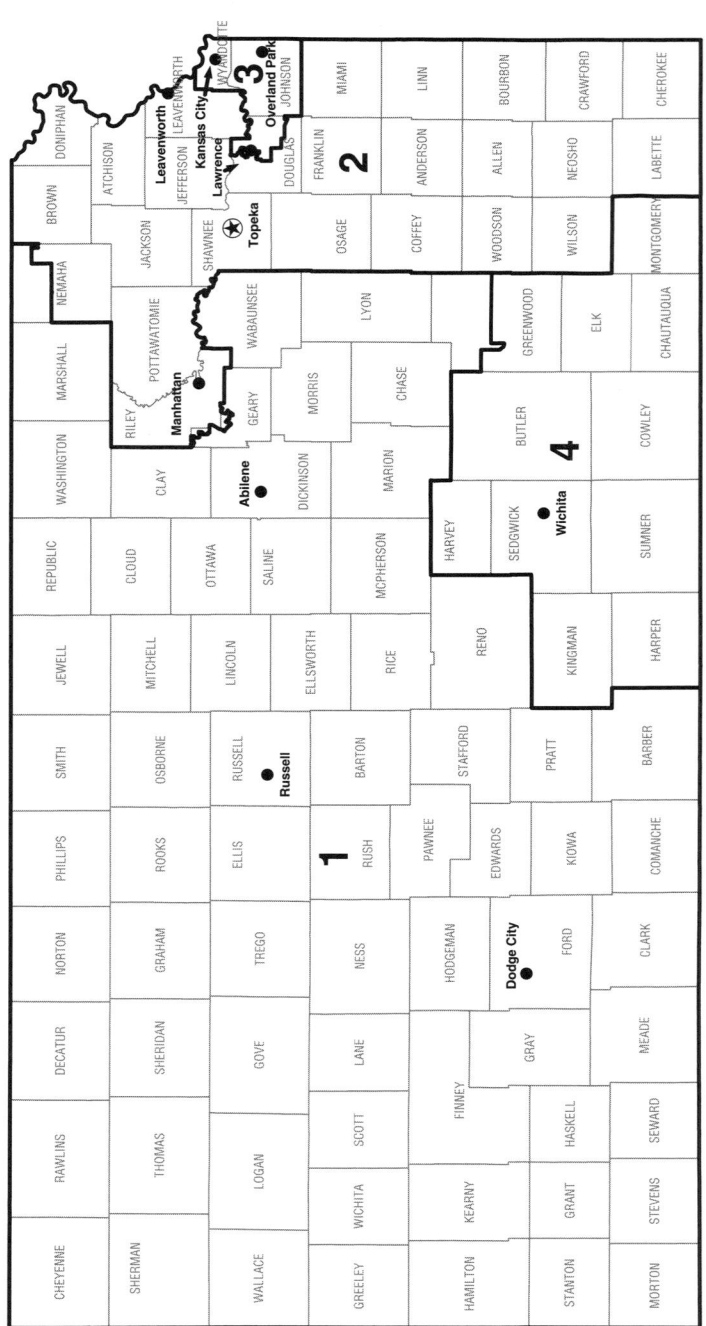

KANSAS

GOVERNOR 2002

2000 Census Population	County	Total Vote	Republican	Democratic	Other	Rep.-Dem. Plurality	Percentage			
							Total Vote		Major Vote	
							Rep.	Dem.	Rep.	Dem.
14,385	ALLEN	4,386	1,842	2,441	103	599 D	42.0%	55.7%	43.0%	57.0%
8,110	ANDERSON	2,767	1,137	1,562	68	425 D	41.1%	56.5%	42.1%	57.9%
16,774	ATCHISON	5,083	1,936	3,037	110	1,101 D	38.1%	59.7%	38.9%	61.1%
5,307	BARBER	1,847	968	848	31	120 R	52.4%	45.9%	53.3%	46.7%
28,205	BARTON	8,959	4,231	4,570	158	339 D	47.2%	51.0%	48.1%	51.9%
15,379	BOURBON	4,466	2,220	2,159	87	61 R	49.7%	48.3%	50.7%	49.3%
10,724	BROWN	3,528	1,540	1,896	92	356 D	43.7%	53.7%	44.8%	55.2%
59,482	BUTLER	17,781	9,108	8,320	353	788 R	51.2%	46.8%	52.3%	47.7%
3,030	CHASE	1,124	496	605	23	109 D	44.1%	53.8%	45.0%	55.0%
4,359	CHAUTAUQUA	1,235	788	423	24	365 R	63.8%	34.3%	65.1%	34.9%
22,605	CHEROKEE	6,638	3,614	2,921	103	693 R	54.4%	44.0%	55.3%	44.7%
3,165	CHEYENNE	1,241	740	483	18	257 R	59.6%	38.9%	60.5%	39.5%
2,390	CLARK	1,041	577	438	26	139 R	55.4%	42.1%	56.8%	43.2%
8,822	CLAY	3,241	1,573	1,618	50	45 D	48.5%	49.9%	49.3%	50.7%
10,268	CLOUD	3,360	1,591	1,697	72	106 D	47.4%	50.5%	48.4%	51.6%
8,865	COFFEY	3,415	1,618	1,714	83	96 D	47.4%	50.2%	48.6%	51.4%
1,967	COMANCHE	779	401	359	19	42 R	51.5%	46.1%	52.8%	47.2%
36,291	COWLEY	11,090	4,709	6,180	201	1,471 D	42.5%	55.7%	43.2%	56.8%
38,242	CRAWFORD	11,533	4,438	6,890	205	2,452 D	38.5%	59.7%	39.2%	60.8%
3,472	DECATUR	1,410	643	743	24	100 D	45.6%	52.7%	46.4%	53.6%
19,344	DICKINSON	6,846	3,014	3,682	150	668 D	44.0%	53.8%	45.0%	55.0%
8,249	DONIPHAN	2,444	1,380	986	78	394 R	56.5%	40.3%	58.3%	41.7%
99,962	DOUGLAS	31,139	8,973	21,594	572	12,621 D	28.8%	69.3%	29.4%	70.6%
3,449	EDWARDS	1,199	573	586	40	13 D	47.8%	48.9%	49.4%	50.6%
3,261	ELK	1,196	639	530	27	109 R	53.4%	44.3%	54.7%	45.3%
27,507	ELLIS	9,357	3,320	5,843	194	2,523 D	35.5%	62.4%	36.2%	63.8%
6,525	ELLSWORTH	2,616	881	1,684	51	803 D	33.7%	64.4%	34.3%	65.7%
40,523	FINNEY	7,130	3,714	3,285	131	429 R	52.1%	46.1%	53.1%	46.9%
32,458	FORD	6,818	3,231	3,381	206	150 D	47.4%	49.6%	48.9%	51.1%
24,784	FRANKLIN	7,538	3,471	3,904	163	433 D	46.0%	51.8%	47.1%	52.9%
27,947	GEARY	4,901	1,817	2,977	107	1,160 D	37.1%	60.7%	37.9%	62.1%
3,068	GOVE	1,281	710	539	32	171 R	55.4%	42.1%	56.8%	43.2%
2,946	GRAHAM	1,079	441	614	24	173 D	40.9%	56.9%	41.8%	58.2%
7,909	GRANT	2,037	1,135	852	50	283 R	55.7%	41.8%	57.1%	42.9%
5,904	GRAY	1,704	962	710	32	252 R	56.5%	41.7%	57.5%	42.5%
1,534	GREELEY	578	325	248	5	77 R	56.2%	42.9%	56.7%	43.3%
7,673	GREENWOOD	2,620	1,263	1,294	63	31 D	48.2%	49.4%	49.4%	50.6%
2,670	HAMILTON	905	444	443	18	1 R	49.1%	49.0%	50.1%	49.9%
6,536	HARPER	2,320	1,153	1,125	42	28 R	49.7%	48.5%	50.6%	49.4%
32,869	HARVEY	11,555	5,324	6,034	197	710 D	46.1%	52.2%	46.9%	53.1%
4,307	HASKELL	1,300	779	485	36	294 R	59.9%	37.3%	61.6%	38.4%
2,085	HODGEMAN	841	517	302	22	215 R	61.5%	35.9%	63.1%	36.9%
12,657	JACKSON	4,233	1,610	2,441	182	831 D	38.0%	57.7%	39.7%	60.3%
18,426	JEFFERSON	6,474	2,572	3,628	274	1,056 D	39.7%	56.0%	41.5%	58.5%
3,791	JEWELL	1,416	723	652	41	71 R	51.1%	46.0%	52.6%	47.4%
451,086	JOHNSON	166,095	86,936	76,943	2,216	9,993 R	52.3%	46.3%	53.0%	47.0%
4,531	KEARNY	1,148	636	503	9	133 R	55.4%	43.8%	55.8%	44.2%
8,673	KINGMAN	2,981	1,566	1,342	73	224 R	52.5%	45.0%	53.9%	46.1%
3,278	KIOWA	1,235	714	497	24	217 R	57.8%	40.2%	59.0%	41.0%
22,835	LABETTE	7,026	2,902	3,996	128	1,094 D	41.3%	56.9%	42.1%	57.9%
2,155	LANE	841	413	407	21	6 R	49.1%	48.4%	50.4%	49.6%
68,691	LEAVENWORTH	16,651	7,327	8,912	412	1,585 D	44.0%	53.5%	45.1%	54.9%
3,578	LINCOLN	1,422	700	700	22		49.2%	49.2%	50.0%	50.0%
9,570	LINN	3,168	1,546	1,536	86	10 R	48.8%	48.5%	50.2%	49.8%
3,046	LOGAN	1,206	641	536	29	105 R	53.2%	44.4%	54.5%	45.5%
35,935	LYON	10,207	3,542	6,429	236	2,887 D	34.7%	63.0%	35.5%	64.5%
29,554	MCPHERSON	10,139	5,072	4,903	164	169 R	50.0%	48.4%	50.8%	49.2%
13,361	MARION	4,841	2,622	2,113	106	509 R	54.2%	43.6%	55.4%	44.6%
10,965	MARSHALL	4,194	1,685	2,403	106	718 D	40.2%	57.3%	41.2%	58.8%
4,631	MEADE	1,603	944	639	20	305 R	58.9%	39.9%	59.6%	40.4%

KANSAS

GOVERNOR 2002

2000 Census Population	County	Total Vote	Republican	Democratic	Other	Rep.-Dem. Plurality	Percentage			
							Total Vote		Major Vote	
							Rep.	Dem.	Rep.	Dem.
28,351	MIAMI	9,149	4,496	4,513	140	17 D	49.1%	49.3%	49.9%	50.1%
6,932	MITCHELL	2,624	1,309	1,279	36	30 R	49.9%	48.7%	50.6%	49.4%
36,252	MONTGOMERY	10,096	5,210	4,720	166	490 R	51.6%	46.8%	52.5%	47.5%
6,104	MORRIS	2,483	1,021	1,404	58	383 D	41.1%	56.5%	42.1%	57.9%
3,496	MORTON	1,104	621	466	17	155 R	56.3%	42.2%	57.1%	42.9%
10,717	NEMAHA	4,722	2,206	2,382	134	176 D	46.7%	50.4%	48.1%	51.9%
16,997	NEOSHO	5,055	2,322	2,669	64	347 D	45.9%	52.8%	46.5%	53.5%
3,454	NESS	1,445	715	700	30	15 R	49.5%	48.4%	50.5%	49.5%
5,953	NORTON	2,096	922	1,134	40	212 D	44.0%	54.1%	44.8%	55.2%
16,712	OSAGE	5,579	2,138	3,247	194	1,109 D	38.3%	58.2%	39.7%	60.3%
4,452	OSBORNE	1,676	803	843	30	40 D	47.9%	50.3%	48.8%	51.2%
6,163	OTTAWA	2,594	1,270	1,270	54		49.0%	49.0%	50.0%	50.0%
7,233	PAWNEE	2,332	956	1,340	36	384 D	41.0%	57.5%	41.6%	58.4%
6,001	PHILLIPS	2,029	991	993	45	2 D	48.8%	48.9%	49.9%	50.1%
18,209	POTTAWATOMIE	6,742	2,999	3,199	544	200 D	44.5%	47.4%	48.4%	51.6%
9,647	PRATT	3,304	1,424	1,821	59	397 D	43.1%	55.1%	43.9%	56.1%
2,966	RAWLINS	1,573	960	576	37	384 R	61.0%	36.6%	62.5%	37.5%
64,790	RENO	20,177	9,829	9,937	411	108 D	48.7%	49.2%	49.7%	50.3%
5,835	REPUBLIC	2,264	1,188	1,023	53	165 R	52.5%	45.2%	53.7%	46.3%
10,761	RICE	3,637	1,749	1,824	64	75 D	48.1%	50.2%	49.0%	51.0%
62,843	RILEY	13,688	5,333	8,094	261	2,761 D	39.0%	59.1%	39.7%	60.3%
5,685	ROOKS	2,075	999	1,033	43	34 D	48.1%	49.8%	49.2%	50.8%
3,551	RUSH	1,437	538	862	37	324 D	37.4%	60.0%	38.4%	61.6%
7,370	RUSSELL	2,840	1,240	1,539	61	299 D	43.7%	54.2%	44.6%	55.4%
53,597	SALINE	18,428	6,951	11,050	427	4,099 D	37.7%	60.0%	38.6%	61.4%
5,120	SCOTT	1,813	1,097	684	32	413 R	60.5%	37.7%	61.6%	38.4%
452,869	SEDGWICK	122,724	59,598	60,777	2,349	1,179 D	48.6%	49.5%	49.5%	50.5%
22,510	SEWARD	3,639	2,000	1,580	59	420 R	55.0%	43.4%	55.9%	44.1%
169,871	SHAWNEE	62,698	20,393	40,578	1,727	20,185 D	32.5%	64.7%	33.4%	66.6%
2,813	SHERIDAN	1,151	584	548	19	36 R	50.7%	47.6%	51.6%	48.4%
6,760	SHERMAN	2,032	995	990	47	5 R	49.0%	48.7%	50.1%	49.9%
4,536	SMITH	1,791	864	894	33	30 D	48.2%	49.9%	49.1%	50.9%
4,789	STAFFORD	1,705	858	818	29	40 R	50.3%	48.0%	51.2%	48.8%
2,406	STANTON	686	381	288	17	93 R	55.5%	42.0%	57.0%	43.0%
5,463	STEVENS	1,600	1,003	570	27	433 R	62.7%	35.6%	63.8%	36.2%
25,946	SUMNER	8,281	3,807	4,302	172	495 D	46.0%	52.0%	46.9%	53.1%
8,180	THOMAS	2,896	1,559	1,271	66	288 R	53.8%	43.9%	55.1%	44.9%
3,319	TREGO	1,473	480	969	24	489 D	32.6%	65.8%	33.1%	66.9%
6,885	WABAUNSEE	2,948	1,216	1,579	153	363 D	41.2%	53.6%	43.5%	56.5%
1,749	WALLACE	700	467	216	17	251 R	66.7%	30.9%	68.4%	31.6%
6,483	WASHINGTON	2,585	1,435	1,091	59	344 R	55.5%	42.2%	56.8%	43.2%
2,531	WICHITA	797	524	264	9	260 R	65.7%	33.1%	66.5%	33.5%
10,332	WILSON	3,281	1,768	1,447	66	321 R	53.9%	44.1%	55.0%	45.0%
3,788	WOODSON	1,265	629	609	27	20 R	49.7%	48.1%	50.8%	49.2%
157,882	WYANDOTTE	35,270	8,595	25,883	792	17,288 D	24.4%	73.4%	24.9%	75.1%
2,688,418	TOTAL	835,692	376,830	441,858	17,004	65,028 D	45.1%	52.9%	46.0%	54.0%

KANSAS

SENATOR 2002

2000 Census Population	County	Total Vote	Republican	Democratic	Other	Rep.-Dem. Plurality	Total Vote Rep.	Total Vote Dem.	Major Vote Rep.	Major Vote Dem.
14,385	ALLEN	4,263	3,570		693	3,570 R	83.7%		100.0%	
8,110	ANDERSON	2,592	2,119		473	2,119 R	81.8%		100.0%	
16,774	ATCHISON	4,562	3,480		1,082	3,480 R	76.3%		100.0%	
5,307	BARBER	1,808	1,628		180	1,628 R	90.0%		100.0%	
28,205	BARTON	8,802	8,090		712	8,090 R	91.9%		100.0%	
15,379	BOURBON	4,142	3,393		749	3,393 R	81.9%		100.0%	
10,724	BROWN	3,406	2,963		443	2,963 R	87.0%		100.0%	
59,482	BUTLER	16,892	14,320		2,572	14,320 R	84.8%		100.0%	
3,030	CHASE	1,068	932		136	932 R	87.3%		100.0%	
4,359	CHAUTAUQUA	1,162	996		166	996 R	85.7%		100.0%	
22,605	CHEROKEE	6,124	4,720		1,404	4,720 R	77.1%		100.0%	
3,165	CHEYENNE	1,186	1,104		82	1,104 R	93.1%		100.0%	
2,390	CLARK	1,037	951		86	951 R	91.7%		100.0%	
8,822	CLAY	3,187	2,982		205	2,982 R	93.6%		100.0%	
10,268	CLOUD	3,207	2,886		321	2,886 R	90.0%		100.0%	
8,865	COFFEY	3,254	2,889		365	2,889 R	88.8%		100.0%	
1,967	COMANCHE	758	678		80	678 R	89.4%		100.0%	
36,291	COWLEY	10,449	8,540		1,909	8,540 R	81.7%		100.0%	
38,242	CRAWFORD	10,304	7,791		2,513	7,791 R	75.6%		100.0%	
3,472	DECATUR	1,372	1,283		89	1,283 R	93.5%		100.0%	
19,344	DICKINSON	6,634	5,926		708	5,926 R	89.3%		100.0%	
8,249	DONIPHAN	2,308	1,949		359	1,949 R	84.4%		100.0%	
99,962	DOUGLAS	27,778	19,825		7,953	19,825 R	71.4%		100.0%	
3,449	EDWARDS	1,183	1,102		81	1,102 R	93.2%		100.0%	
3,261	ELK	1,139	951		188	951 R	83.5%		100.0%	
27,507	ELLIS	8,699	7,703		996	7,703 R	88.6%		100.0%	
6,525	ELLSWORTH	2,483	2,246		237	2,246 R	90.5%		100.0%	
40,523	FINNEY	6,958	6,332		626	6,332 R	91.0%		100.0%	
32,458	FORD	6,729	6,301		428	6,301 R	93.6%		100.0%	
24,784	FRANKLIN	7,095	5,811		1,284	5,811 R	81.9%		100.0%	
27,947	GEARY	4,635	3,907		728	3,907 R	84.3%		100.0%	
3,068	GOVE	1,252	1,162		90	1,162 R	92.8%		100.0%	
2,946	GRAHAM	1,031	935		96	935 R	90.7%		100.0%	
7,909	GRANT	1,985	1,881		104	1,881 R	94.8%		100.0%	
5,904	GRAY	1,672	1,592		80	1,592 R	95.2%		100.0%	
1,534	GREELEY	563	529		34	529 R	94.0%		100.0%	
7,673	GREENWOOD	2,483	2,124		359	2,124 R	85.5%		100.0%	
2,670	HAMILTON	866	818		48	818 R	94.5%		100.0%	
6,536	HARPER	2,251	1,961		290	1,961 R	87.1%		100.0%	
32,869	HARVEY	10,887	9,361		1,526	9,361 R	86.0%		100.0%	
4,307	HASKELL	1,275	1,211		64	1,211 R	95.0%		100.0%	
2,085	HODGEMAN	831	793		38	793 R	95.4%		100.0%	
12,657	JACKSON	4,078	3,525		553	3,525 R	86.4%		100.0%	
18,426	JEFFERSON	6,138	5,099		1,039	5,099 R	83.1%		100.0%	
3,791	JEWELL	1,387	1,272		115	1,272 R	91.7%		100.0%	
451,086	JOHNSON	154,638	123,682		30,956	123,682 R	80.0%		100.0%	
4,531	KEARNY	1,126	1,070		56	1,070 R	95.0%		100.0%	
8,673	KINGMAN	2,883	2,627		256	2,627 R	91.1%		100.0%	
3,278	KIOWA	1,207	1,146		61	1,146 R	94.9%		100.0%	
22,835	LABETTE	6,469	5,283		1,186	5,283 R	81.7%		100.0%	
2,155	LANE	818	772		46	772 R	94.4%		100.0%	
68,691	LEAVENWORTH	15,465	12,019		3,446	12,019 R	77.7%		100.0%	
3,578	LINCOLN	1,383	1,281		102	1,281 R	92.6%		100.0%	
9,570	LINN	2,958	2,405		553	2,405 R	81.3%		100.0%	
3,046	LOGAN	1,184	1,103		81	1,103 R	93.2%		100.0%	
35,935	LYON	9,671	8,269		1,402	8,269 R	85.5%		100.0%	
29,554	MCPHERSON	9,790	8,796		994	8,796 R	89.8%		100.0%	
13,361	MARION	4,657	4,209		448	4,209 R	90.4%		100.0%	
10,965	MARSHALL	3,983	3,544		439	3,544 R	89.0%		100.0%	
4,631	MEADE	1,568	1,467		101	1,467 R	93.6%		100.0%	

KANSAS

SENATOR 2002

2000 Census Population	County	Total Vote	Republican	Democratic	Other	Rep.-Dem. Plurality	Percentage			
							Total Vote		Major Vote	
							Rep.	Dem.	Rep.	Dem.
28,351	MIAMI	8,557	7,007		1,550	7,007 R	81.9%		100.0%	
6,932	MITCHELL	2,540	2,369		171	2,369 R	93.3%		100.0%	
36,252	MONTGOMERY	9,540	7,797		1,743	7,797 R	81.7%		100.0%	
6,104	MORRIS	2,368	2,141		227	2,141 R	90.4%		100.0%	
3,496	MORTON	1,087	1,026		61	1,026 R	94.4%		100.0%	
10,717	NEMAHA	4,425	3,948		477	3,948 R	89.2%		100.0%	
16,997	NEOSHO	4,737	3,921		816	3,921 R	82.8%		100.0%	
3,454	NESS	1,411	1,337		74	1,337 R	94.8%		100.0%	
5,953	NORTON	2,037	1,885		152	1,885 R	92.5%		100.0%	
16,712	OSAGE	5,217	4,295		922	4,295 R	82.3%		100.0%	
4,452	OSBORNE	1,614	1,480		134	1,480 R	91.7%		100.0%	
6,163	OTTAWA	2,520	2,303		217	2,303 R	91.4%		100.0%	
7,233	PAWNEE	2,277	2,127		150	2,127 R	93.4%		100.0%	
6,001	PHILLIPS	1,976	1,817		159	1,817 R	92.0%		100.0%	
18,209	POTTAWATOMIE	6,415	5,499		916	5,499 R	85.7%		100.0%	
9,647	PRATT	3,186	2,866		320	2,866 R	90.0%		100.0%	
2,966	RAWLINS	1,544	1,449		95	1,449 R	93.8%		100.0%	
64,790	RENO	19,503	16,869		2,634	16,869 R	86.5%		100.0%	
5,835	REPUBLIC	2,181	2,033		148	2,033 R	93.2%		100.0%	
10,761	RICE	3,527	3,194		333	3,194 R	90.6%		100.0%	
62,843	RILEY	13,027	10,947		2,080	10,947 R	84.0%		100.0%	
5,685	ROOKS	2,015	1,826		189	1,826 R	90.6%		100.0%	
3,551	RUSH	1,395	1,266		129	1,266 R	90.8%		100.0%	
7,370	RUSSELL	2,740	2,502		238	2,502 R	91.3%		100.0%	
53,597	SALINE	17,809	15,508		2,301	15,508 R	87.1%		100.0%	
5,120	SCOTT	1,786	1,656		130	1,656 R	92.7%		100.0%	
452,869	SEDGWICK	110,675	90,646		20,029	90,646 R	81.9%		100.0%	
22,510	SEWARD	3,541	3,211		330	3,211 R	90.7%		100.0%	
169,871	SHAWNEE	58,189	46,876		11,313	46,876 R	80.6%		100.0%	
2,813	SHERIDAN	1,106	1,038		68	1,038 R	93.9%		100.0%	
6,760	SHERMAN	1,959	1,815		144	1,815 R	92.6%		100.0%	
4,536	SMITH	1,703	1,552		151	1,552 R	91.1%		100.0%	
4,789	STAFFORD	1,660	1,535		125	1,535 R	92.5%		100.0%	
2,406	STANTON	668	632		36	632 R	94.6%		100.0%	
5,463	STEVENS	1,551	1,483		68	1,483 R	95.6%		100.0%	
25,946	SUMNER	7,922	6,551		1,371	6,551 R	82.7%		100.0%	
8,180	THOMAS	2,796	2,585		211	2,585 R	92.5%		100.0%	
3,319	TREGO	1,400	1,268		132	1,268 R	90.6%		100.0%	
6,885	WABAUNSEE	2,846	2,486		360	2,486 R	87.4%		100.0%	
1,749	WALLACE	684	663		21	663 R	96.9%		100.0%	
6,483	WASHINGTON	2,478	2,291		187	2,291 R	92.5%		100.0%	
2,531	WICHITA	773	731		42	731 R	94.6%		100.0%	
10,332	WILSON	3,101	2,642		459	2,642 R	85.2%		100.0%	
3,788	WOODSON	1,206	1,022		184	1,022 R	84.7%		100.0%	
157,882	WYANDOTTE	27,443	15,676		11,767	15,676 R	57.1%		100.0%	
2,688,418	TOTAL	776,850	641,075		135,775	641,075 R	82.5%		100.0%	

KANSAS

HOUSE OF REPRESENTATIVES

CD	Year	Total Vote	Republican Vote	Republican Candidate	Democratic Vote	Democratic Candidate	Other Vote	Rep.-Dem. Plurality	Total Vote Rep.	Total Vote Dem.	Major Vote Rep.	Major Vote Dem.
1	2002	208,561	189,976	Moran, Jerry*			18,585	189,976 R	91.1%		100.0%	
2	2002	210,977	127,477	Ryun, Jim*	79,160	Lykins, Dan	4,340	48,317 R	60.4%	37.5%	61.7%	38.3%
3	2002	219,389	102,882	Taff, Adam	110,095	Moore, Dennis*	6,412	7,213 D	46.9%	50.2%	48.3%	51.7%
4	2002	190,963	115,691	Tiahrt, Todd*	70,656	Nolla, Carlos	4,616	45,035 R	60.6%	37.0%	62.1%	37.9%
Total	2002	829,890	536,026		259,911		33,953	276,115 R	64.6%	31.3%	67.3%	32.7%

An asterisk (*) denotes incumbent.

KANSAS

GENERAL AND PRIMARY ELECTIONS

2002 GENERAL ELECTIONS

Governor Other vote was 8,907 Reform (Ted Pettibone); 8,097 Libertarian (Dennis Hawver).

Senator Other vote was 70,725 Libertarian (Steven A. Rosile); 65,050 Reform (George Cook).

House Other vote was:

CD 1 18,585 Libertarian (Jack Warner).
CD 2 4,340 Libertarian (Art Clack).
CD 3 5,046 Reform (Dawn Bly); 1,366 Libertarian (Douglas Martin).
CD 4 4,616 Libertarian (Maike Warren).

2002 PRIMARY ELECTIONS

Primary August 6, 2002

Registration (as of July 22, 2002)

Republican	719,758
Democratic	431,996
Libertarian	9,348
Reform	1,854
Unaffiliated	425,872
TOTAL	1,588,859

(The statewide registration total is reported as the number above but adds to 1,588,828.)

Primary Type Semi-open—Registered Democrats and Republicans could vote only in their party's primary. "Unaffiliated" voters could participate in either primary if they changed their registration to that party on primary day.

Note: An asterisk (*) denotes incumbent.

KANSAS

GENERAL AND PRIMARY ELECTIONS

	REPUBLICAN PRIMARIES			DEMOCRATIC PRIMARIES		
Governor	Tim Shallenburger	122,713	41.4%	Kathleen Sebelius	87,850	100.0%
	Dave Kerr	87,494	29.5%			
	Bob Knight	78,118	26.4%			
	Dan Bloom	7,769	2.6%			
	TOTAL	296,094				
Senator	Pat Roberts*	234,779	83.7%	No Democratic candidate		
	Tom Oyler	45,638	16.3%			
	TOTAL	280,417				
Congressional District 1	Jerry Moran*	78,272	100.0%	No Democratic candidate		
Congressional District 2	Jim Ryun*	55,647	100.0%	Dan Lykins	21,290	100.0%
Congressional District 3	Adam Taff	40,609	51.8%	Dennis Moore*	22,991	100.0%
	Jeff Colyer	37,771	48.2%			
	TOTAL	78,380				
Congressional District 4	Todd Tiahrt*	53,237	100.0%	Carlos Nolla	15,582	75.3%
				Patrick Quaney	5,110	24.7%
				TOTAL	20,692	

KANSAS REPUBLICAN PRIMARY

GOVERNOR 2002

2000 Census Population	County	Total Vote	Shallenburger	Kerr	Knight	Bloom	Winner	Percentage of Total Vote			
								Shallenburger	Kerr	Knight	Bloom
14,385	ALLEN	1,404	498	466	402	38	Shallenburger	35.5%	33.2%	28.6%	2.7%
8,110	ANDERSON	741	343	139	224	35	Shallenburger	46.3%	18.8%	30.2%	4.7%
16,774	ATCHISON	1,038	541	208	238	51	Shallenburger	52.1%	20.0%	22.9%	4.9%
5,307	BARBER	804	208	260	324	12	Knight	25.9%	32.3%	40.3%	1.5%
28,205	BARTON	4,180	1,151	1,617	1,338	74	Kerr	27.5%	38.7%	32.0%	1.8%
15,379	BOURBON	1,264	672	256	306	30	Shallenburger	53.2%	20.3%	24.2%	2.4%
10,724	BROWN	1,330	567	275	401	87	Shallenburger	42.6%	20.7%	30.2%	6.5%
59,482	BUTLER	6,247	2,896	868	2,360	123	Shallenburger	46.4%	13.9%	37.8%	2.0%
3,030	CHASE	446	177	131	126	12	Shallenburger	39.7%	29.4%	28.3%	2.7%
4,359	CHAUTAUQUA	572	317	64	179	12	Shallenburger	55.4%	11.2%	31.3%	2.1%
22,605	CHEROKEE	1,824	1,334	182	284	24	Shallenburger	73.1%	10.0%	15.6%	1.3%
3,165	CHEYENNE	614	325	192	82	15	Shallenburger	52.9%	31.3%	13.4%	2.4%
2,390	CLARK	537	259	160	111	7	Shallenburger	48.2%	29.8%	20.7%	1.3%
8,822	CLAY	1,902	958	371	509	64	Shallenburger	50.4%	19.5%	26.8%	3.4%
10,268	CLOUD	1,106	473	295	310	28	Shallenburger	42.8%	26.7%	28.0%	2.5%
8,865	COFFEY	1,640	719	369	479	73	Shallenburger	43.8%	22.5%	29.2%	4.5%
1,967	COMANCHE	399	131	168	92	8	Kerr	32.8%	42.1%	23.1%	2.0%
36,291	COWLEY	3,413	1,109	440	1,823	41	Knight	32.5%	12.9%	53.4%	1.2%
38,242	CRAWFORD	2,001	1,113	402	431	55	Shallenburger	55.6%	20.1%	21.5%	2.7%
3,472	DECATUR	612	236	226	139	11	Shallenburger	38.6%	36.9%	22.7%	1.8%
19,344	DICKINSON	3,237	1,241	925	977	94	Shallenburger	38.3%	28.6%	30.2%	2.9%
8,249	DONIPHAN	1,208	589	281	190	148	Shallenburger	48.8%	23.3%	15.7%	12.3%
99,962	DOUGLAS	7,560	2,425	2,199	2,440	496	Knight	32.1%	29.1%	32.3%	6.6%
3,449	EDWARDS	630	185	313	123	9	Kerr	29.4%	49.7%	19.5%	1.4%
3,261	ELK	509	252	91	159	7	Shallenburger	49.5%	17.9%	31.2%	1.4%
27,507	ELLIS	1,679	612	584	462	21	Shallenburger	36.5%	34.8%	27.5%	1.3%
6,525	ELLSWORTH	765	175	308	261	21	Kerr	22.9%	40.3%	34.1%	2.7%
40,523	FINNEY	2,224	895	766	537	26	Shallenburger	40.2%	34.4%	24.1%	1.2%
32,458	FORD	1,963	865	547	517	34	Shallenburger	44.1%	27.9%	26.3%	1.7%
24,784	FRANKLIN	2,405	996	501	788	120	Shallenburger	41.4%	20.8%	32.8%	5.0%

KANSAS REPUBLICAN PRIMARY
GOVERNOR 2002

2000 Census Population	County	Total Vote	Shallenburger	Kerr	Knight	Bloom	Winner	Percentage of Total Vote			
								Shallenburger	Kerr	Knight	Bloom
27,947	GEARY	1,600	584	331	643	42	Knight	36.5%	20.7%	40.2%	2.6%
3,068	GOVE	469	206	179	77	7	Shallenburger	43.9%	38.2%	16.4%	1.5%
2,946	GRAHAM	483	176	179	116	12	Kerr	36.4%	37.1%	24.0%	2.5%
7,909	GRANT	840	301	369	164	6	Kerr	35.8%	43.9%	19.5%	0.7%
5,904	GRAY	527	296	126	94	11	Shallenburger	56.2%	23.9%	17.8%	2.1%
1,534	GREELEY	212	70	96	39	7	Kerr	33.0%	45.3%	18.4%	3.3%
7,673	GREENWOOD	1,206	537	242	400	27	Shallenburger	44.5%	20.1%	33.2%	2.2%
2,670	HAMILTON	390	144	176	68	2	Kerr	36.9%	45.1%	17.4%	0.5%
6,536	HARPER	922	349	170	396	7	Knight	37.9%	18.4%	43.0%	0.8%
32,869	HARVEY	4,454	1,823	747	1,806	78	Shallenburger	40.9%	16.8%	40.5%	1.8%
4,307	HASKELL	597	288	183	120	6	Shallenburger	48.2%	30.7%	20.1%	1.0%
2,085	HODGEMAN	335	157	113	55	10	Shallenburger	46.9%	33.7%	16.4%	3.0%
12,657	JACKSON	1,522	660	447	330	85	Shallenburger	43.4%	29.4%	21.7%	5.6%
18,426	JEFFERSON	2,113	936	444	572	161	Shallenburger	44.3%	21.0%	27.1%	7.6%
3,791	JEWELL	524	173	235	99	17	Kerr	33.0%	44.8%	18.9%	3.2%
451,086	JOHNSON	71,674	29,041	31,603	9,611	1,419	Kerr	40.5%	44.1%	13.4%	2.0%
4,531	KEARNY	611	221	276	108	6	Kerr	36.2%	45.2%	17.7%	1.0%
8,673	KINGMAN	1,216	435	340	409	32	Shallenburger	35.8%	28.0%	33.6%	2.6%
3,278	KIOWA	621	207	297	106	11	Kerr	33.3%	47.8%	17.1%	1.8%
22,835	LABETTE	1,578	618	608	340	12	Shallenburger	39.2%	38.5%	21.5%	0.8%
2,155	LANE	485	139	235	103	8	Kerr	28.7%	48.5%	21.2%	1.6%
68,691	LEAVENWORTH	3,744	1,700	859	1,035	150	Shallenburger	45.4%	22.9%	27.6%	4.0%
3,578	LINCOLN	994	341	351	269	33	Kerr	34.3%	35.3%	27.1%	3.3%
9,570	LINN	1,186	666	201	295	24	Shallenburger	56.2%	16.9%	24.9%	2.0%
3,046	LOGAN	470	228	148	87	7	Shallenburger	48.5%	31.5%	18.5%	1.5%
35,935	LYON	2,903	1,131	877	809	86	Shallenburger	39.0%	30.2%	27.9%	3.0%
29,554	MCPHERSON	4,115	1,857	994	1,182	82	Shallenburger	45.1%	24.2%	28.7%	2.0%
13,361	MARION	1,925	753	475	659	38	Shallenburger	39.1%	24.7%	34.2%	2.0%
10,965	MARSHALL	1,194	355	411	367	61	Kerr	29.7%	34.4%	30.7%	5.1%
4,631	MEADE	710	417	160	120	13	Shallenburger	58.7%	22.5%	16.9%	1.8%
28,351	MIAMI	2,730	1,417	488	719	106	Shallenburger	51.9%	17.9%	26.3%	3.9%
6,932	MITCHELL	1,112	377	441	249	45	Kerr	33.9%	39.7%	22.4%	4.0%
36,252	MONTGOMERY	3,903	2,117	828	884	74	Shallenburger	54.2%	21.2%	22.6%	1.9%
6,104	MORRIS	1,229	429	364	391	45	Shallenburger	34.9%	29.6%	31.8%	3.7%
3,496	MORTON	529	189	213	119	8	Kerr	35.7%	40.3%	22.5%	1.5%
10,717	NEMAHA	1,504	632	329	471	72	Shallenburger	42.0%	21.9%	31.3%	4.8%
16,997	NEOSHO	1,539	612	470	435	22	Shallenburger	39.8%	30.5%	28.3%	1.4%
3,454	NESS	532	160	256	110	6	Kerr	30.1%	48.1%	20.7%	1.1%
5,953	NORTON	942	369	303	239	31	Shallenburger	39.2%	32.2%	25.4%	3.3%
16,712	OSAGE	1,735	686	405	522	122	Shallenburger	39.5%	23.3%	30.1%	7.0%
4,452	OSBORNE	616	192	259	152	13	Kerr	31.2%	42.0%	24.7%	2.1%
6,163	OTTAWA	899	378	285	223	13	Shallenburger	42.0%	31.7%	24.8%	1.4%
7,233	PAWNEE	1,351	380	574	367	30	Kerr	28.1%	42.5%	27.2%	2.2%
6,001	PHILLIPS	948	396	346	179	27	Shallenburger	41.8%	36.5%	18.9%	2.8%
18,209	POTTAWATOMIE	2,763	1,505	482	678	98	Shallenburger	54.5%	17.4%	24.5%	3.5%
9,647	PRATT	1,394	386	599	382	27	Kerr	27.7%	43.0%	27.4%	1.9%
2,966	RAWLINS	1,000	363	388	226	23	Kerr	36.3%	38.8%	22.6%	2.3%
64,790	RENO	8,855	3,264	3,425	2,025	141	Kerr	36.9%	38.7%	22.9%	1.6%
5,835	REPUBLIC	899	361	319	192	27	Shallenburger	40.2%	35.5%	21.4%	3.0%
10,761	RICE	1,580	576	540	434	30	Shallenburger	36.5%	34.2%	27.5%	1.9%
62,843	RILEY	4,507	1,678	1,059	1,702	68	Knight	37.2%	23.5%	37.8%	1.5%
5,685	ROOKS	1,131	426	477	207	21	Kerr	37.7%	42.2%	18.3%	1.9%
3,551	RUSH	642	179	276	171	16	Kerr	27.9%	43.0%	26.6%	2.5%
7,370	RUSSELL	1,373	387	575	382	29	Kerr	28.2%	41.9%	27.8%	2.1%
53,597	SALINE	5,990	2,177	1,798	1,864	151	Shallenburger	36.3%	30.0%	31.1%	2.5%
5,120	SCOTT	823	321	310	186	6	Shallenburger	39.0%	37.7%	22.6%	0.7%
452,869	SEDGWICK	42,154	18,626	4,742	18,174	612	Shallenburger	44.2%	11.2%	43.1%	1.5%
22,510	SEWARD	1,594	801	373	398	22	Shallenburger	50.3%	23.4%	25.0%	1.4%
169,871	SHAWNEE	20,655	8,670	6,249	4,566	1,170	Shallenburger	42.0%	30.3%	22.1%	5.7%
2,813	SHERIDAN	407	158	158	78	13		38.8%	38.8%	19.2%	3.2%

KANSAS REPUBLICAN PRIMARY

GOVERNOR 2002

2000 Census Population	County	Total Vote	Shallenburger	Kerr	Knight	Bloom	Winner	Percentage of Total Vote			
								Shallenburger	Kerr	Knight	Bloom
6,760	SHERMAN	737	291	315	121	10	Kerr	39.5%	42.7%	16.4%	1.4%
4,536	SMITH	677	314	232	104	27	Shallenburger	46.4%	34.3%	15.4%	4.0%
4,789	STAFFORD	766	247	325	181	13	Kerr	32.2%	42.4%	23.6%	1.7%
2,406	STANTON	248	76	120	52		Kerr	30.6%	48.4%	21.0%	
5,463	STEVENS	686	365	240	79	2	Shallenburger	53.2%	35.0%	11.5%	0.3%
25,946	SUMNER	2,561	1,017	346	1,152	46	Knight	39.7%	13.5%	45.0%	1.8%
8,180	THOMAS	1,153	467	435	241	10	Shallenburger	40.5%	37.7%	20.9%	0.9%
3,319	TREGO	521	146	238	126	11	Kerr	28.0%	45.7%	24.2%	2.1%
6,885	WABAUNSEE	1,356	582	381	325	68	Shallenburger	42.9%	28.1%	24.0%	5.0%
1,749	WALLACE	377	196	138	35	8	Shallenburger	52.0%	36.6%	9.3%	2.1%
6,483	WASHINGTON	1,287	595	377	278	37	Shallenburger	46.2%	29.3%	21.6%	2.9%
2,531	WICHITA	301	174	77	47	3	Shallenburger	57.8%	25.6%	15.6%	1.0%
10,332	WILSON	1,766	787	346	572	61	Shallenburger	44.6%	19.6%	32.4%	3.5%
3,788	WOODSON	583	268	126	174	15	Shallenburger	46.0%	21.6%	29.8%	2.6%
157,882	WYANDOTTE	3,865	1,905	991	815	154	Shallenburger	49.3%	25.6%	21.1%	4.0%
2,688,418	TOTAL	296,094	122,713	87,494	78,118	7,769	Shallenburger	41.4%	29.5%	26.4%	2.6%

KANSAS REPUBLICAN PRIMARY

SENATOR 2002

2000 Census Population	County	Total Vote	Roberts	Oyler	Winner	Percentage of Total Vote	
						Roberts	Oyler
14,385	ALLEN	1,351	1,062	289	Roberts	78.6%	21.4%
8,110	ANDERSON	711	566	145	Roberts	79.6%	20.4%
16,774	ATCHISON	1,000	832	168	Roberts	83.2%	16.8%
5,307	BARBER	811	733	78	Roberts	90.4%	9.6%
28,205	BARTON	4,139	3,818	321	Roberts	92.2%	7.8%
15,379	BOURBON	1,213	957	256	Roberts	78.9%	21.1%
10,724	BROWN	1,327	1,176	151	Roberts	88.6%	11.4%
59,482	BUTLER	5,959	4,849	1,110	Roberts	81.4%	18.6%
3,030	CHASE	443	383	60	Roberts	86.5%	13.5%
4,359	CHAUTAUQUA	548	426	122	Roberts	77.7%	22.3%
22,605	CHEROKEE	1,719	1,308	411	Roberts	76.1%	23.9%
3,165	CHEYENNE	574	535	39	Roberts	93.2%	6.8%
2,390	CLARK	533	496	37	Roberts	93.1%	6.9%
8,822	CLAY	1,903	1,749	154	Roberts	91.9%	8.1%
10,268	CLOUD	1,077	966	111	Roberts	89.7%	10.3%
8,865	COFFEY	1,598	1,352	246	Roberts	84.6%	15.4%
1,967	COMANCHE	401	368	33	Roberts	91.8%	8.2%
36,291	COWLEY	3,272	2,655	617	Roberts	81.1%	18.9%
38,242	CRAWFORD	1,908	1,418	490	Roberts	74.3%	25.7%
3,472	DECATUR	618	580	38	Roberts	93.9%	6.1%
19,344	DICKINSON	3,189	2,774	415	Roberts	87.0%	13.0%
8,249	DONIPHAN	1,197	988	209	Roberts	82.5%	17.5%
99,962	DOUGLAS	7,174	5,683	1,491	Roberts	79.2%	20.8%
3,449	EDWARDS	621	587	34	Roberts	94.5%	5.5%
3,261	ELK	501	389	112	Roberts	77.6%	22.4%
27,507	ELLIS	1,648	1,470	178	Roberts	89.2%	10.8%
6,525	ELLSWORTH	754	688	66	Roberts	91.2%	8.8%
40,523	FINNEY	2,175	1,996	179	Roberts	91.8%	8.2%
32,458	FORD	1,968	1,862	106	Roberts	94.6%	5.4%
24,784	FRANKLIN	2,258	1,765	493	Roberts	78.2%	21.8%

KANSAS REPUBLICAN PRIMARY

SENATOR 2002

2000 Census Population	County	Total Vote	Roberts	Oyler	Winner	Percentage of Total Vote Roberts	Oyler
27,947	GEARY	1,574	1,373	201	Roberts	87.2%	12.8%
3,068	GOVE	474	448	26	Roberts	94.5%	5.5%
2,946	GRAHAM	475	415	60	Roberts	87.4%	12.6%
7,909	GRANT	846	814	32	Roberts	96.2%	3.8%
5,904	GRAY	527	508	19	Roberts	96.4%	3.6%
1,534	GREELEY	210	200	10	Roberts	95.2%	4.8%
7,673	GREENWOOD	1,164	959	205	Roberts	82.4%	17.6%
2,670	HAMILTON	392	376	16	Roberts	95.9%	4.1%
6,536	HARPER	890	785	105	Roberts	88.2%	11.8%
32,869	HARVEY	4,273	3,611	662	Roberts	84.5%	15.5%
4,307	HASKELL	588	564	24	Roberts	95.9%	4.1%
2,085	HODGEMAN	338	318	20	Roberts	94.1%	5.9%
12,657	JACKSON	1,528	1,348	180	Roberts	88.2%	11.8%
18,426	JEFFERSON	2,066	1,758	308	Roberts	85.1%	14.9%
3,791	JEWELL	529	482	47	Roberts	91.1%	8.9%
451,086	JOHNSON	66,464	51,986	14,478	Roberts	78.2%	21.8%
4,531	KEARNY	615	578	37	Roberts	94.0%	6.0%
8,673	KINGMAN	1,191	1,020	171	Roberts	85.6%	14.4%
3,278	KIOWA	605	575	30	Roberts	95.0%	5.0%
22,835	LABETTE	1,515	1,189	326	Roberts	78.5%	21.5%
2,155	LANE	471	444	27	Roberts	94.3%	5.7%
68,691	LEAVENWORTH	3,626	2,912	714	Roberts	80.3%	19.7%
3,578	LINCOLN	985	894	91	Roberts	90.8%	9.2%
9,570	LINN	1,133	900	233	Roberts	79.4%	20.6%
3,046	LOGAN	467	444	23	Roberts	95.1%	4.9%
35,935	LYON	2,827	2,462	365	Roberts	87.1%	12.9%
29,554	MCPHERSON	4,015	3,594	421	Roberts	89.5%	10.5%
13,361	MARION	1,870	1,714	156	Roberts	91.7%	8.3%
10,965	MARSHALL	1,201	1,069	132	Roberts	89.0%	11.0%
4,631	MEADE	695	652	43	Roberts	93.8%	6.2%
28,351	MIAMI	2,648	2,023	625	Roberts	76.4%	23.6%
6,932	MITCHELL	1,118	1,041	77	Roberts	93.1%	6.9%
36,252	MONTGOMERY	3,827	2,816	1,011	Roberts	73.6%	26.4%
6,104	MORRIS	1,205	1,098	107	Roberts	91.1%	8.9%
3,496	MORTON	534	503	31	Roberts	94.2%	5.8%
10,717	NEMAHA	1,463	1,310	153	Roberts	89.5%	10.5%
16,997	NEOSHO	1,439	1,147	292	Roberts	79.7%	20.3%
3,454	NESS	517	486	31	Roberts	94.0%	6.0%
5,953	NORTON	968	893	75	Roberts	92.3%	7.7%
16,712	OSAGE	1,673	1,430	243	Roberts	85.5%	14.5%
4,452	OSBORNE	609	562	47	Roberts	92.3%	7.7%
6,163	OTTAWA	883	798	85	Roberts	90.4%	9.6%
7,233	PAWNEE	1,360	1,291	69	Roberts	94.9%	5.1%
6,001	PHILLIPS	954	878	76	Roberts	92.0%	8.0%
18,209	POTTAWATOMIE	2,630	2,315	315	Roberts	88.0%	12.0%
9,647	PRATT	1,376	1,268	108	Roberts	92.2%	7.8%
2,966	RAWLINS	942	883	59	Roberts	93.7%	6.3%
64,790	RENO	8,555	7,557	998	Roberts	88.3%	11.7%
5,835	REPUBLIC	920	855	65	Roberts	92.9%	7.1%
10,761	RICE	1,563	1,421	142	Roberts	90.9%	9.1%
62,843	RILEY	4,334	3,916	418	Roberts	90.4%	9.6%
5,685	ROOKS	1,131	1,027	104	Roberts	90.8%	9.2%
3,551	RUSH	649	612	37	Roberts	94.3%	5.7%
7,370	RUSSELL	1,362	1,267	95	Roberts	93.0%	7.0%
53,597	SALINE	5,957	5,239	718	Roberts	87.9%	12.1%
5,120	SCOTT	821	780	41	Roberts	95.0%	5.0%
452,869	SEDGWICK	36,881	29,810	7,071	Roberts	80.8%	19.2%
22,510	SEWARD	1,581	1,482	99	Roberts	93.7%	6.3%
169,871	SHAWNEE	19,480	16,844	2,636	Roberts	86.5%	13.5%
2,813	SHERIDAN	399	365	34	Roberts	91.5%	8.5%

KANSAS REPUBLICAN PRIMARY

SENATOR 2002

2000 Census Population	County	Total Vote	Roberts	Oyler	Winner	Percentage of Total Vote Roberts	Oyler
6,760	SHERMAN	742	685	57	Roberts	92.3%	7.7%
4,536	SMITH	694	645	49	Roberts	92.9%	7.1%
4,789	STAFFORD	750	696	54	Roberts	92.8%	7.2%
2,406	STANTON	252	242	10	Roberts	96.0%	4.0%
5,463	STEVENS	680	653	27	Roberts	96.0%	4.0%
25,946	SUMNER	2,502	2,049	453	Roberts	81.9%	18.1%
8,180	THOMAS	1,127	1,045	82	Roberts	92.7%	7.3%
3,319	TREGO	527	483	44	Roberts	91.7%	8.3%
6,885	WABAUNSEE	1,350	1,199	151	Roberts	88.8%	11.2%
1,749	WALLACE	378	361	17	Roberts	95.5%	4.5%
6,483	WASHINGTON	1,266	1,164	102	Roberts	91.9%	8.1%
2,531	WICHITA	290	278	12	Roberts	95.9%	4.1%
10,332	WILSON	1,692	1,283	409	Roberts	75.8%	24.2%
3,788	WOODSON	593	486	107	Roberts	82.0%	18.0%
157,882	WYANDOTTE	3,651	2,770	881	Roberts	75.9%	24.1%
2,688,418	TOTAL	280,417	234,779	45,638	Roberts	83.7%	16.3%

KENTUCKY

GOVERNOR

Paul E. Patton (D). Reelected 1999 to a four-year term. Previously elected 1995.

SENATORS (2 Republicans)

Jim Bunning (R). Elected 1998 to a six-year term.

Mitch McConnell (R). Reelected 2002 to a six-year term. Previously elected 1996, 1990, 1984.

REPRESENTATIVES (5 Republicans, 1 Democrat)

1. Edward Whitfield (R)
2. Ron Lewis (R)
3. Anne M. Northup (R)
4. Ken Lucas (D)
5. Harold Rogers (R)
6. Ernie Fletcher (R)

POSTWAR VOTE FOR PRESIDENT

Year	Total Vote	Republican		Democratic		Other Vote	Plurality	Percentage			
								Total Vote		Major Vote	
		Vote	Candidate	Vote	Candidate			Rep.	Dem.	Rep.	Dem.
2000**	1,544,187	872,492	Bush, George W.	638,898	Gore, Al	32,797	233,594 R	56.5%	41.4%	57.7%	42.3%
1996**	1,388,708	623,283	Dole, Bob	636,614	Clinton, Bill	128,811	13,331 D	44.9%	45.8%	49.5%	50.5%
1992**	1,492,900	617,178	Bush, George	665,104	Clinton, Bill	210,618	47,926 D	41.3%	44.6%	48.1%	51.9%
1988	1,322,517	734,281	Bush, George	580,368	Dukakis, Michael S.	7,868	153,913 R	55.5%	43.9%	55.9%	44.1%
1984	1,369,345	821,702	Reagan, Ronald	539,539	Mondale, Walter F.	8,104	282,163 R	60.0%	39.4%	60.4%	39.6%
1980**	1,294,627	635,274	Reagan, Ronald	616,417	Carter, Jimmy	42,936	18,857 R	49.1%	47.6%	50.8%	49.2%
1976	1,167,142	531,852	Ford, Gerald R.	615,717	Carter, Jimmy	19,573	83,865 D	45.6%	52.8%	46.3%	53.7%
1972	1,067,499	676,446	Nixon, Richard M.	371,159	McGovern, George S.	19,894	305,287 R	63.4%	34.8%	64.6%	35.4%
1968	1,055,893	462,411	Nixon, Richard M.	397,541	Humphrey, Hubert H.	195,941	64,870 R	43.8%	37.6%	53.8%	46.2%
1964	1,046,105	372,977	Goldwater, Barry M.	669,659	Johnson, Lyndon B.	3,469	296,682 D	35.7%	64.0%	35.8%	64.2%
1960	1,124,462	602,607	Nixon, Richard M.	521,855	Kennedy, John F.		80,752 R	53.6%	46.4%	53.6%	46.4%
1956	1,053,805	572,192	Eisenhower, Dwight D.	476,453	Stevenson, Adlai E.	5,160	95,739 R	54.3%	45.2%	54.6%	45.4%
1952	993,148	495,029	Eisenhower, Dwight D.	495,729	Stevenson, Adlai E.	2,390	700 D	49.8%	49.9%	50.0%	50.0%
1948	822,658	341,210	Dewey, Thomas E.	466,756	Truman, Harry S.	14,692	125,546 D	41.5%	56.7%	42.2%	57.8%

In 2000 the other vote column includes 23,192 votes cast for Green (Nader). In 1996 the other vote column includes 120,396 votes cast for Perot. In 1992 the other vote column includes 203,944 votes cast for Perot. In 1980 the other column includes 31,127 votes for Independent (Anderson).

KENTUCKY

POSTWAR VOTE FOR GOVERNOR

Year	Total Vote	Republican		Democratic		Other Vote	Rep.-Dem. Plurality	Percentage			
								Total Vote		Major Vote	
		Vote	Candidate	Vote	Candidate			Rep.	Dem.	Rep.	Dem.
1999**	580,074	128,788	Martin, Peppy	352,099	Patton, Paul E.	99,187	223,311 D	22.2%	60.7%	26.8%	73.2%
1995	983,979	479,227	Forgy, Larry	500,787	Patton, Paul E.	3,965	21,560 D	48.7%	50.9%	48.9%	51.1%
1991	834,920	294,452	Hopkins, Larry J.	540,468	Jones, Brereton C.		246,016 D	35.3%	64.7%	35.3%	64.7%
1987	777,815	273,141	Harper, John	504,674	Wilkinson, Wallace G.		231,533 D	35.1%	64.9%	35.1%	64.9%
1983	1,030,671	454,650	Bunning, Jim	561,674	Collins, Martha Layne	14,347	107,024 D	44.1%	54.5%	44.7%	55.3%
1979	939,366	381,278	Nunn, Louie B.	558,088	Brown, J. Y., Jr.		176,810 D	40.6%	59.4%	40.6%	59.4%
1975	748,157	277,998	Gable, Robert E.	470,159	Carroll, Julian		192,161 D	37.2%	62.8%	37.2%	62.8%
1971	930,790	412,653	Emberton, Thomas	470,720	Ford, Wendell H.	47,417	58,067 D	44.3%	50.6%	46.7%	53.3%
1967	886,946	454,123	Nunn, Louie B.	425,674	Ward, Henry	7,149	28,449 R	51.2%	48.0%	51.6%	48.4%
1963	886,047	436,496	Nunn, Louie B.	449,551	Breathitt, Edward T.		13,055 D	49.3%	50.7%	49.3%	50.7%
1959	853,005	336,456	Robsion, John M.	516,549	Combs, Bert T.		180,093 D	39.4%	60.6%	39.4%	60.6%
1955	778,488	322,671	Denney, Edwin R.	451,647	Chandler, Albert B.	4,170	128,976 D	41.4%	58.0%	41.7%	58.3%
1951	634,359	288,014	Siler, Eugene	346,345	Wetherby, Lawrence		58,331 D	45.4%	54.6%	45.4%	54.6%
1947	672,372	287,130	Dummit, Eldon S.	385,242	Clements, Earle C.		98,112 D	42.7%	57.3%	42.7%	57.3%

In 1999 the other vote column includes 88,930 votes cast for Reform (Galbraith).

POSTWAR VOTE FOR SENATOR

Year	Total Vote	Republican		Democratic		Other Vote	Rep.-Dem. Plurality	Percentage			
								Total Vote		Major Vote	
		Vote	Candidate	Vote	Candidate			Rep.	Dem.	Rep.	Dem.
2002	1,131,475	731,679	McConnell, Mitch	399,634	Weinberg, Lois Combs	162	332,045 R	64.7%	35.3%	64.7%	35.3%
1998	1,145,414	569,817	Bunning, Jim	563,051	Baesler, Scotty	12,546	6,766 R	49.7%	49.2%	50.3%	49.7%
1996	1,307,046	724,794	McConnell, Mitch	560,012	Beshear, Steven L.	22,240	164,782 R	55.5%	42.8%	56.4%	43.6%
1992	1,330,858	476,604	Williams, David L.	836,888	Ford, Wendell H.	17,366	360,284 D	35.8%	62.9%	36.3%	63.7%
1990	916,010	478,034	McConnell, Mitch	437,976	Sloane, Harvey		40,058 R	52.2%	47.8%	52.2%	47.8%
1986	677,280	173,330	Andrews, Jackson M.	503,775	Ford, Wendell H.	175	330,445 D	25.6%	74.4%	25.6%	74.4%
1984	1,292,407	644,990	McConnell, Mitch	639,721	Huddleston, Walter	7,696	5,269 R	49.9%	49.5%	50.2%	49.8%
1980	1,106,890	386,029	Foust, Mary Louise	720,861	Ford, Wendell H.		334,832 D	34.9%	65.1%	34.9%	65.1%
1978	476,783	175,766	Guenthner, Louie	290,730	Huddleston, Walter	10,287	114,964 D	36.9%	61.0%	37.7%	62.3%
1974	745,994	328,982	Cook, Marlow W.	399,406	Ford, Wendell H.	17,606	70,424 D	44.1%	53.5%	45.2%	54.8%
1972	1,037,861	494,337	Nunn, Louie B.	528,550	Huddleston, Walter	14,974	34,213 D	47.6%	50.9%	48.3%	51.7%
1968	942,865	484,260	Cook, Marlow W.	448,960	Peden, Katherine	9,645	35,300 R	51.4%	47.6%	51.9%	48.1%
1966	749,884	483,805	Cooper, John Sherman	266,079	Brown, J. Y.		217,726 R	64.5%	35.5%	64.5%	35.5%
1962	820,088	432,648	Morton, Thruston B.	387,440	Wyatt, Wilson W.		45,208 R	52.8%	47.2%	52.8%	47.2%
1960	1,088,377	644,087	Cooper, John Sherman	444,290	Johnson, Keen		199,797 R	59.2%	40.8%	59.2%	40.8%
1956	1,006,825	506,903	Morton, Thruston B.	499,922	Clements, Earle C.		6,981 R	50.3%	49.7%	50.3%	49.7%
1956S	1,011,645	538,505	Cooper, John Sherman	473,140	Wetherby, Lawrence		65,365 R	53.2%	46.8%	53.2%	46.8%
1954	797,057	362,948	Cooper, John Sherman	434,109	Barkley, Alben W.		71,161 D	45.5%	54.5%	45.5%	54.5%
1952S	960,228	494,576	Cooper, John Sherman	465,652	Underwood, Thomas R.		28,924 R	51.5%	48.5%	51.5%	48.5%
1950	612,617	278,368	Dawson, Charles L.	334,249	Clements, Earle C.		55,881 D	45.4%	54.6%	45.4%	54.6%
1948	794,469	383,776	Cooper, John Sherman	408,256	Chapman, Virgil	2,437	24,480 D	48.3%	51.4%	48.5%	51.5%
1946S	615,119	327,652	Cooper, John Sherman	285,829	Brown, J. Y.	1,638	41,823 R	53.3%	46.5%	53.4%	46.6%

One of the 1956 elections and those in 1952 and 1946 were for short terms to fill vacancies.

KENTUCKY

Congressional districts first established for elections held in 2002
6 members

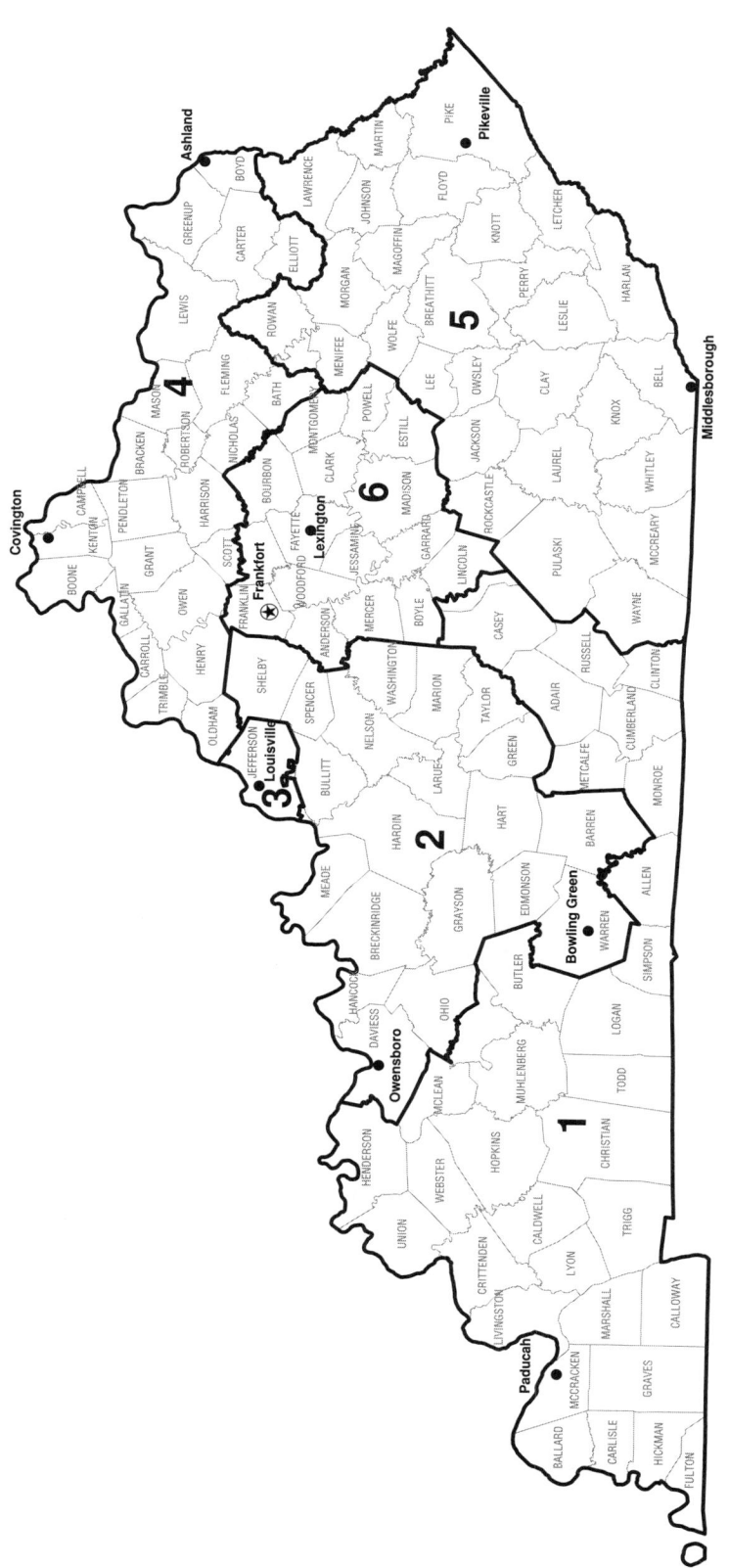

KENTUCKY

SENATOR 2002

2000 Census Population	County	Total Vote	Republican	Democratic	Other	Rep.-Dem. Plurality	Percentage			
							Total Vote		Major Vote	
							Rep.	Dem.	Rep.	Dem.
17,244	ADAIR	5,815	4,712	1,103		3,609 R	81.0%	19.0%	81.0%	19.0%
17,800	ALLEN	5,073	3,984	1,089		2,895 R	78.5%	21.5%	78.5%	21.5%
19,111	ANDERSON	5,620	3,637	1,983		1,654 R	64.7%	35.3%	64.7%	35.3%
8,286	BALLARD	2,951	1,743	1,208		535 R	59.1%	40.9%	59.1%	40.9%
38,033	BARREN	10,016	7,575	2,441		5,134 R	75.6%	24.4%	75.6%	24.4%
11,085	BATH	3,360	1,796	1,564		232 R	53.5%	46.5%	53.5%	46.5%
30,060	BELL	8,225	5,542	2,683		2,859 R	67.4%	32.6%	67.4%	32.6%
85,991	BOONE	21,437	16,986	4,451		12,535 R	79.2%	20.8%	79.2%	20.8%
19,360	BOURBON	4,704	2,981	1,723		1,258 R	63.4%	36.6%	63.4%	36.6%
49,752	BOYD	13,248	7,545	5,702	1	1,843 R	57.0%	43.0%	57.0%	43.0%
27,697	BOYLE	8,997	5,894	3,102	1	2,792 R	65.5%	34.5%	65.5%	34.5%
8,279	BRACKEN	2,209	1,632	577		1,055 R	73.9%	26.1%	73.9%	26.1%
16,100	BREATHITT	4,407	1,817	2,590		773 D	41.2%	58.8%	41.2%	58.8%
18,648	BRECKINRIDGE	6,740	4,812	1,928		2,884 R	71.4%	28.6%	71.4%	28.6%
61,236	BULLITT	15,161	10,050	5,111		4,939 R	66.3%	33.7%	66.3%	33.7%
13,010	BUTLER	3,942	3,120	822		2,298 R	79.1%	20.9%	79.1%	20.9%
13,060	CALDWELL	3,977	2,757	1,220		1,537 R	69.3%	30.7%	69.3%	30.7%
34,177	CALLOWAY	8,779	5,777	3,002		2,775 R	65.8%	34.2%	65.8%	34.2%
88,616	CAMPBELL	21,760	15,726	6,034		9,692 R	72.3%	27.7%	72.3%	27.7%
5,351	CARLISLE	1,690	1,084	606		478 R	64.1%	35.9%	64.1%	35.9%
10,155	CARROLL	2,210	1,293	917		376 R	58.5%	41.5%	58.5%	41.5%
26,889	CARTER	7,092	4,220	2,872		1,348 R	59.5%	40.5%	59.5%	40.5%
15,447	CASEY	4,115	3,352	763		2,589 R	81.5%	18.5%	81.5%	18.5%
72,265	CHRISTIAN	11,484	7,976	3,508		4,468 R	69.5%	30.5%	69.5%	30.5%
33,144	CLARK	9,062	5,792	3,270		2,522 R	63.9%	36.1%	63.9%	36.1%
24,556	CLAY	4,454	3,049	1,405		1,644 R	68.5%	31.5%	68.5%	31.5%
9,634	CLINTON	3,768	3,055	713		2,342 R	81.1%	18.9%	81.1%	18.9%
9,384	CRITTENDEN	3,032	2,136	896		1,240 R	70.4%	29.6%	70.4%	29.6%
7,147	CUMBERLAND	2,300	1,898	402		1,496 R	82.5%	17.5%	82.5%	17.5%
91,545	DAVIESS	26,439	17,502	8,936	1	8,566 R	66.2%	33.8%	66.2%	33.8%
11,644	EDMONSON	3,928	2,996	932		2,064 R	76.3%	23.7%	76.3%	23.7%
6,748	ELLIOTT	1,738	703	1,035		332 D	40.4%	59.6%	40.4%	59.6%
15,307	ESTILL	4,478	2,958	1,520		1,438 R	66.1%	33.9%	66.1%	33.9%
260,512	FAYETTE	72,145	42,863	29,281	1	13,582 R	59.4%	40.6%	59.4%	40.6%
13,792	FLEMING	4,947	3,248	1,699		1,549 R	65.7%	34.3%	65.7%	34.3%
42,441	FLOYD	11,646	4,634	7,012		2,378 D	39.8%	60.2%	39.8%	60.2%
47,687	FRANKLIN	15,849	8,237	7,612		625 R	52.0%	48.0%	52.0%	48.0%
7,752	FULTON	1,803	1,152	651		501 R	63.9%	36.1%	63.9%	36.1%
7,870	GALLATIN	1,795	1,060	735		325 R	59.1%	40.9%	59.1%	40.9%
14,792	GARRARD	4,247	3,086	1,161		1,925 R	72.7%	27.3%	72.7%	27.3%
22,384	GRANT	4,018	2,744	1,274		1,470 R	68.3%	31.7%	68.3%	31.7%
37,028	GRAVES	10,915	7,078	3,837		3,241 R	64.8%	35.2%	64.8%	35.2%
24,053	GRAYSON	7,497	5,668	1,829		3,839 R	75.6%	24.4%	75.6%	24.4%
11,518	GREEN	4,184	3,341	843		2,498 R	79.9%	20.1%	79.9%	20.1%
36,891	GREENUP	9,237	5,120	4,117		1,003 R	55.4%	44.6%	55.4%	44.6%
8,392	HANCOCK	3,094	1,919	1,175		744 R	62.0%	38.0%	62.0%	38.0%
94,174	HARDIN	20,387	14,149	6,237	1	7,912 R	69.4%	30.6%	69.4%	30.6%
33,202	HARLAN	8,501	5,294	3,207		2,087 R	62.3%	37.7%	62.3%	37.7%
17,983	HARRISON	4,829	2,941	1,888		1,053 R	60.9%	39.1%	60.9%	39.1%
17,445	HART	4,508	3,153	1,355		1,798 R	69.9%	30.1%	69.9%	30.1%
44,829	HENDERSON	11,931	7,241	4,690		2,551 R	60.7%	39.3%	60.7%	39.3%
15,060	HENRY	4,323	2,843	1,480		1,363 R	65.8%	34.2%	65.8%	34.2%
5,262	HICKMAN	1,544	961	583		378 R	62.2%	37.8%	62.2%	37.8%
46,519	HOPKINS	11,380	7,602	3,778		3,824 R	66.8%	33.2%	66.8%	33.2%
13,495	JACKSON	2,262	1,882	380		1,502 R	83.2%	16.8%	83.2%	16.8%
693,604	JEFFERSON	230,037	136,504	93,394	139	43,110 R	59.3%	40.6%	59.4%	40.6%
39,041	JESSAMINE	9,982	6,994	2,988		4,006 R	70.1%	29.9%	70.1%	29.9%
23,445	JOHNSON	7,174	4,882	2,292		2,590 R	68.1%	31.9%	68.1%	31.9%
151,464	KENTON	34,807	25,252	9,555		15,697 R	72.5%	27.5%	72.5%	27.5%
17,649	KNOTT	6,221	2,106	4,115		2,009 D	33.9%	66.1%	33.9%	66.1%

KENTUCKY

SENATOR 2002

2000 Census Population	County	Total Vote	Republican	Democratic	Other	Rep.-Dem. Plurality	Percentage Total Vote		Percentage Major Vote	
							Rep.	Dem.	Rep.	Dem.
31,795	KNOX	8,827	6,537	2,289	1	4,248 R	74.1%	25.9%	74.1%	25.9%
13,373	LARUE	3,756	2,573	1,183		1,390 R	68.5%	31.5%	68.5%	31.5%
52,715	LAUREL	12,656	10,022	2,631	3	7,391 R	79.2%	20.8%	79.2%	20.8%
15,569	LAWRENCE	5,052	3,035	2,017		1,018 R	60.1%	39.9%	60.1%	39.9%
7,916	LEE	2,687	1,890	795	2	1,095 R	70.3%	29.6%	70.4%	29.6%
12,401	LESLIE	4,312	3,355	956	1	2,399 R	77.8%	22.2%	77.8%	22.2%
25,277	LETCHER	7,246	4,031	3,215		816 R	55.6%	44.4%	55.6%	44.4%
14,092	LEWIS	3,205	2,481	724		1,757 R	77.4%	22.6%	77.4%	22.6%
23,361	LINCOLN	5,642	3,763	1,879		1,884 R	66.7%	33.3%	66.7%	33.3%
9,804	LIVINGSTON	2,697	1,546	1,151		395 R	57.3%	42.7%	57.3%	42.7%
26,573	LOGAN	6,750	4,573	2,177		2,396 R	67.7%	32.3%	67.7%	32.3%
8,080	LYON	2,342	1,386	956		430 R	59.2%	40.8%	59.2%	40.8%
65,514	MCCRACKEN	18,507	12,679	5,828		6,851 R	68.5%	31.5%	68.5%	31.5%
17,080	MCCREARY	3,614	2,815	799		2,016 R	77.9%	22.1%	77.9%	22.1%
9,938	MCLEAN	3,445	2,260	1,185		1,075 R	65.6%	34.4%	65.6%	34.4%
70,872	MADISON	16,153	10,102	6,051		4,051 R	62.5%	37.5%	62.5%	37.5%
13,332	MAGOFFIN	4,928	2,470	2,458		12 R	50.1%	49.9%	50.1%	49.9%
18,212	MARION	5,414	3,194	2,217	3	977 R	59.0%	40.9%	59.0%	41.0%
30,125	MARSHALL	10,418	6,819	3,599		3,220 R	65.5%	34.5%	65.5%	34.5%
12,578	MARTIN	4,786	3,528	1,258		2,270 R	73.7%	26.3%	73.7%	26.3%
16,800	MASON	3,783	2,499	1,284		1,215 R	66.1%	33.9%	66.1%	33.9%
26,349	MEADE	7,001	4,482	2,518	1	1,964 R	64.0%	36.0%	64.0%	36.0%
6,556	MENIFEE	1,991	1,187	804		383 R	59.6%	40.4%	59.6%	40.4%
20,817	MERCER	6,530	4,455	2,075		2,380 R	68.2%	31.8%	68.2%	31.8%
10,037	METCALFE	3,091	2,283	808		1,475 R	73.9%	26.1%	73.9%	26.1%
11,756	MONROE	4,482	3,875	607		3,268 R	86.5%	13.5%	86.5%	13.5%
22,554	MONTGOMERY	5,269	3,196	2,073		1,123 R	60.7%	39.3%	60.7%	39.3%
13,948	MORGAN	3,183	1,715	1,468		247 R	53.9%	46.1%	53.9%	46.1%
31,839	MUHLENBERG	10,031	5,829	4,202		1,627 R	58.1%	41.9%	58.1%	41.9%
37,477	NELSON	8,448	5,308	3,140		2,168 R	62.8%	37.2%	62.8%	37.2%
6,813	NICHOLAS	1,542	907	635		272 R	58.8%	41.2%	58.8%	41.2%
22,916	OHIO	6,988	4,817	2,171		2,646 R	68.9%	31.1%	68.9%	31.1%
46,178	OLDHAM	16,254	12,361	3,893		8,468 R	76.0%	24.0%	76.0%	24.0%
10,547	OWEN	3,242	2,150	1,092		1,058 R	66.3%	33.7%	66.3%	33.7%
4,858	OWSLEY	2,036	1,535	501		1,034 R	75.4%	24.6%	75.4%	24.6%
14,390	PENDLETON	3,533	2,538	995		1,543 R	71.8%	28.2%	71.8%	28.2%
29,390	PERRY	9,646	5,120	4,526		594 R	53.1%	46.9%	53.1%	46.9%
68,736	PIKE	17,901	8,554	9,346	1	792 D	47.8%	52.2%	47.8%	52.2%
13,237	POWELL	3,635	1,773	1,862		89 D	48.8%	51.2%	48.8%	51.2%
56,217	PULASKI	12,421	9,776	2,645		7,131 R	78.7%	21.3%	78.7%	21.3%
2,266	ROBERTSON	772	500	272		228 R	64.8%	35.2%	64.8%	35.2%
16,582	ROCKCASTLE	3,738	3,053	685		2,368 R	81.7%	18.3%	81.7%	18.3%
22,094	ROWAN	5,530	2,898	2,632		266 R	52.4%	47.6%	52.4%	47.6%
16,315	RUSSELL	5,601	4,455	1,146		3,309 R	79.5%	20.5%	79.5%	20.5%
33,061	SCOTT	8,613	5,454	3,159		2,295 R	63.3%	36.7%	63.3%	36.7%
33,337	SHELBY	10,714	7,569	3,145		4,424 R	70.6%	29.4%	70.6%	29.4%
16,405	SIMPSON	4,217	2,920	1,297		1,623 R	69.2%	30.8%	69.2%	30.8%
11,766	SPENCER	4,348	3,065	1,283		1,782 R	70.5%	29.5%	70.5%	29.5%
22,927	TAYLOR	7,424	5,632	1,792		3,840 R	75.9%	24.1%	75.9%	24.1%
11,971	TODD	2,957	2,084	869	4	1,215 R	70.5%	29.4%	70.6%	29.4%
12,597	TRIGG	3,944	2,660	1,284		1,376 R	67.4%	32.6%	67.4%	32.6%
8,125	TRIMBLE	2,772	1,793	979		814 R	64.7%	35.3%	64.7%	35.3%
15,637	UNION	3,756	2,281	1,475		806 R	60.7%	39.3%	60.7%	39.3%
92,522	WARREN	24,488	17,747	6,741		11,006 R	72.5%	27.5%	72.5%	27.5%
10,916	WASHINGTON	3,173	2,225	948		1,277 R	70.1%	29.9%	70.1%	29.9%
19,923	WAYNE	4,951	3,527	1,424		2,103 R	71.2%	28.8%	71.2%	28.8%
14,120	WEBSTER	3,231	1,778	1,453		325 R	55.0%	45.0%	55.0%	45.0%
35,865	WHITLEY	8,078	5,968	2,108	2	3,860 R	73.9%	26.1%	73.9%	26.1%
7,065	WOLFE	2,336	1,039	1,297		258 D	44.5%	55.5%	44.5%	55.5%
23,208	WOODFORD	5,914	3,558	2,356		1,202 R	60.2%	39.8%	60.2%	39.8%
4,041,769	TOTAL	1,131,475	731,679	399,634	162	332,045 R	64.7%	35.3%	64.7%	35.3%

KENTUCKY

HOUSE OF REPRESENTATIVES

CD	Year	Total Vote	Republican		Democratic		Other Vote	Rep.-Dem. Plurality	Percentage			
									Total Vote		Major Vote	
			Vote	Candidate	Vote	Candidate			Rep.	Dem.	Rep.	Dem.
1	2002	180,217	117,600	Whitfield, Edward*	62,617	Alexander, Klint		54,983 R	65.3%	34.7%	65.3%	34.7%
2	2002	176,288	122,773	Lewis, Ron*	51,431	Williams, David L.	2,084	71,342 R	69.6%	29.2%	70.5%	29.5%
3	2002	229,074	118,228	Northup, Anne M.*	110,846	Conway, Jack		7,382 R	51.6%	48.4%	51.6%	48.4%
4	2002	171,735	81,651	Davis, Geoff	87,776	Lucas, Ken*	2,308	6,125 D	47.5%	51.1%	48.2%	51.8%
5	2002	176,240	137,986	Rogers, Harold*	38,254	Bailey, Sidney Jane		99,732 R	78.3%	21.7%	78.3%	21.7%
6	2002	160,688	115,622	Fletcher, Ernie*			45,066	115,622 R	72.0%		100.0%	
Total	2002	1,094,242	693,860		350,924		49,458	342,936 R	63.4%	32.1%	66.4%	33.6%

An asterisk (*) denotes incumbent.

KENTUCKY

GENERAL AND PRIMARY ELECTIONS

2002 GENERAL ELECTIONS

Senator   Other vote was 115 write-in (Ralph H. Stewart); 47 write-in (Andrew Ellis Overby, Sr.).

House   Other vote was:

CD 1
CD 2   2,084 Libertarian (Robert Guy Dyer).
CD 3
CD 4   2,308 Libertarian (John Grote).
CD 5
CD 6   41,753 Independent (Gatewood Galbraith); 3,313 Libertarian (Mark Gailey).

2002 PRIMARY ELECTIONS

Primary	May 28, 2002	**Registration** (as of May 28, 2002)	Republican	902,915
			Democratic	1,573,293
			Other	172,238
			TOTAL	2,648,446

Primary Type   Closed—Only registered Democrats and Republicans could vote in their party's primary.

Note: An asterisk (*) denotes incumbent. The names of unopposed candidates did not appear on the primary ballot; therefore, no votes were cast for these candidates.

KENTUCKY

GENERAL AND PRIMARY ELECTIONS

	REPUBLICAN PRIMARIES			DEMOCRATIC PRIMARIES		
Senator	Mitch McConnell*	Unopposed		Lois Combs Weinberg Tom Barlow TOTAL	231,013 230,055 461,068	50.1% 49.9%
Congressional District 1	Edward Whitfield*	Unopposed		Klint Alexander	Unopposed	
Congressional District 2	Ron Lewis*	Unopposed		David L. Williams Pete Tabb TOTAL	57,104 17,478 74,582	76.6% 23.4%
Congressional District 3	Anne M. Northup*	Unopposed		Jack Conway	Unopposed	
Congressional District 4	Geoff Davis Roger Thoney TOTAL	17,088 4,784 21,872	78.1% 21.9%	Ken Lucas*	Unopposed	
Congressional District 5	Harold Rogers* Billy Ray Wilson TOTAL	77,615 6,948 84,563	91.8% 8.2%	Sidney Jane Bailey	Unopposed	
Congressional District 6	Ernie Fletcher*	Unopposed		No Democratic candidate		

KENTUCKY DEMOCRATIC PRIMARY

SENATOR 2002

2000 Census Population	County	Total Vote	Weinberg	Barlow	Winner	Percentage of Total Vote	
						Weinberg	Barlow
17,244	ADAIR	1,001	333	668	Barlow	33.3%	66.7%
17,800	ALLEN	1,361	234	1,127	Barlow	17.2%	82.8%
19,111	ANDERSON	3,456	1,896	1,560	Weinberg	54.9%	45.1%
8,286	BALLARD	2,409	475	1,934	Barlow	19.7%	80.3%
38,033	BARREN	5,334	1,443	3,891	Barlow	27.1%	72.9%
11,085	BATH	2,736	1,466	1,270	Weinberg	53.6%	46.4%
30,060	BELL	2,164	1,110	1,054	Weinberg	51.3%	48.7%
85,991	BOONE	1,642	937	705	Weinberg	57.1%	42.9%
19,360	BOURBON	3,569	2,084	1,485	Weinberg	58.4%	41.6%
49,752	BOYD	5,127	2,872	2,255	Weinberg	56.0%	44.0%
27,697	BOYLE	4,190	2,132	2,058	Weinberg	50.9%	49.1%
8,279	BRACKEN	2,050	928	1,122	Barlow	45.3%	54.7%
16,100	BREATHITT	4,514	2,740	1,774	Weinberg	60.7%	39.3%
18,648	BRECKINRIDGE	3,018	1,335	1,683	Barlow	44.2%	55.8%
61,236	BULLITT	7,640	3,708	3,932	Barlow	48.5%	51.5%
13,010	BUTLER	308	79	229	Barlow	25.6%	74.4%
13,060	CALDWELL	2,945	822	2,123	Barlow	27.9%	72.1%
34,177	CALLOWAY	5,794	1,979	3,815	Barlow	34.2%	65.8%
88,616	CAMPBELL	3,152	1,616	1,536	Weinberg	51.3%	48.7%
5,351	CARLISLE	1,996	498	1,498	Barlow	24.9%	75.1%
10,155	CARROLL	2,520	1,176	1,344	Barlow	46.7%	53.3%
26,889	CARTER	2,942	1,613	1,329	Weinberg	54.8%	45.2%
15,447	CASEY	445	216	229	Barlow	48.5%	51.5%
72,265	CHRISTIAN	4,955	1,366	3,589	Barlow	27.6%	72.4%
33,144	CLARK	4,783	3,013	1,770	Weinberg	63.0%	37.0%

KENTUCKY DEMOCRATIC PRIMARY
SENATOR 2002

2000 Census Population	County	Total Vote	Weinberg	Barlow	Winner	Percentage of Total Vote Weinberg	Barlow
24,556	CLAY	412	315	97	Weinberg	76.5%	23.5%
9,634	CLINTON	872	250	622	Barlow	28.7%	71.3%
9,384	CRITTENDEN	814	223	591	Barlow	27.4%	72.6%
7,147	CUMBERLAND	272	96	176	Barlow	35.3%	64.7%
91,545	DAVIESS	8,998	2,828	6,170	Barlow	31.4%	68.6%
11,644	EDMONSON	586	175	411	Barlow	29.9%	70.1%
6,748	ELLIOTT	2,117	1,297	820	Weinberg	61.3%	38.7%
15,307	ESTILL	1,118	711	407	Weinberg	63.6%	36.4%
260,512	FAYETTE	24,630	18,493	6,137	Weinberg	75.1%	24.9%
13,792	FLEMING	2,300	1,298	1,002	Weinberg	56.4%	43.6%
42,441	FLOYD	12,233	7,925	4,308	Weinberg	64.8%	35.2%
47,687	FRANKLIN	11,959	6,928	5,031	Weinberg	57.9%	42.1%
7,752	FULTON	1,440	399	1,041	Barlow	27.7%	72.3%
7,870	GALLATIN	1,465	702	763	Barlow	47.9%	52.1%
14,792	GARRARD	794	470	324	Weinberg	59.2%	40.8%
22,384	GRANT	2,612	1,251	1,361	Barlow	47.9%	52.1%
37,028	GRAVES	7,363	2,308	5,055	Barlow	31.3%	68.7%
24,053	GRAYSON	1,367	592	775	Barlow	43.3%	56.7%
11,518	GREEN	1,165	476	689	Barlow	40.9%	59.1%
36,891	GREENUP	3,796	2,117	1,679	Weinberg	55.8%	44.2%
8,392	HANCOCK	1,754	437	1,317	Barlow	24.9%	75.1%
94,174	HARDIN	10,025	5,175	4,850	Weinberg	51.6%	48.4%
33,202	HARLAN	4,944	2,524	2,420	Weinberg	51.1%	48.9%
17,983	HARRISON	2,988	1,646	1,342	Weinberg	55.1%	44.9%
17,445	HART	2,605	932	1,673	Barlow	35.8%	64.2%
44,829	HENDERSON	8,032	2,149	5,883	Barlow	26.8%	73.2%
15,060	HENRY	2,609	1,448	1,161	Weinberg	55.5%	44.5%
5,262	HICKMAN	1,636	404	1,232	Barlow	24.7%	75.3%
46,519	HOPKINS	7,592	1,714	5,878	Barlow	22.6%	77.4%
13,495	JACKSON	116	70	46	Weinberg	60.3%	39.7%
693,604	JEFFERSON	64,628	41,484	23,144	Weinberg	64.2%	35.8%
39,041	JESSAMINE	3,575	1,917	1,658	Weinberg	53.6%	46.4%
23,445	JOHNSON	1,676	927	749	Weinberg	55.3%	44.7%
151,464	KENTON	4,068	2,565	1,503	Weinberg	63.1%	36.9%
17,649	KNOTT	7,065	5,366	1,699	Weinberg	76.0%	24.0%
31,795	KNOX	1,840	972	868	Weinberg	52.8%	47.2%
13,373	LARUE	2,601	1,029	1,572	Barlow	39.6%	60.4%
52,715	LAUREL	1,170	691	479	Weinberg	59.1%	40.9%
15,569	LAWRENCE	1,844	919	925	Barlow	49.8%	50.2%
7,916	LEE	702	440	262	Weinberg	62.7%	37.3%
12,401	LESLIE	146	90	56	Weinberg	61.6%	38.4%
25,277	LETCHER	4,321	2,827	1,494	Weinberg	65.4%	34.6%
14,092	LEWIS	386	213	173	Weinberg	55.2%	44.8%
23,361	LINCOLN	2,292	1,172	1,120	Weinberg	51.1%	48.9%
9,804	LIVINGSTON	3,206	941	2,265	Barlow	29.4%	70.6%
26,573	LOGAN	4,405	781	3,624	Barlow	17.7%	82.3%
8,080	LYON	2,188	697	1,491	Barlow	31.9%	68.1%
65,514	MCCRACKEN	5,612	2,043	3,569	Barlow	36.4%	63.6%
17,080	MCCREARY	800	355	445	Barlow	44.4%	55.6%
9,938	MCLEAN	2,116	398	1,718	Barlow	18.8%	81.2%
70,872	MADISON	7,106	4,365	2,741	Weinberg	61.4%	38.6%
13,332	MAGOFFIN	2,682	1,628	1,054	Weinberg	60.7%	39.3%
18,212	MARION	4,127	2,055	2,072	Barlow	49.8%	50.2%
30,125	MARSHALL	7,143	2,077	5,066	Barlow	29.1%	70.9%
12,578	MARTIN	761	404	357	Weinberg	53.1%	46.9%

KENTUCKY DEMOCRATIC PRIMARY
SENATOR 2002

2000 Census Population	County	Total Vote	Weinberg	Barlow	Winner	Percentage of Total Vote	
						Weinberg	Barlow
16,800	MASON	1,664	902	762	Weinberg	54.2%	45.8%
26,349	MEADE	4,289	2,171	2,118	Weinberg	50.6%	49.4%
6,556	MENIFEE	1,478	769	709	Weinberg	52.0%	48.0%
20,817	MERCER	3,159	1,613	1,546	Weinberg	51.1%	48.9%
10,037	METCALFE	1,466	385	1,081	Barlow	26.3%	73.7%
11,756	MONROE	475	170	305	Barlow	35.8%	64.2%
22,554	MONTGOMERY	4,186	2,591	1,595	Weinberg	61.9%	38.1%
13,948	MORGAN	2,718	1,426	1,292	Weinberg	52.5%	47.5%
31,839	MUHLENBERG	5,848	1,191	4,657	Barlow	20.4%	79.6%
37,477	NELSON	5,481	2,375	3,106	Barlow	43.3%	56.7%
6,813	NICHOLAS	1,776	996	780	Weinberg	56.1%	43.9%
22,916	OHIO	2,258	537	1,721	Barlow	23.8%	76.2%
46,178	OLDHAM	2,918	1,828	1,090	Weinberg	62.6%	37.4%
10,547	OWEN	1,632	839	793	Weinberg	51.4%	48.6%
4,858	OWSLEY	331	191	140	Weinberg	57.7%	42.3%
14,390	PENDLETON	2,051	939	1,112	Barlow	45.8%	54.2%
29,390	PERRY	6,010	3,882	2,128	Weinberg	64.6%	35.4%
68,736	PIKE	13,118	7,301	5,817	Weinberg	55.7%	44.3%
13,237	POWELL	2,586	1,821	765	Weinberg	70.4%	29.6%
56,217	PULASKI	1,529	825	704	Weinberg	54.0%	46.0%
2,266	ROBERTSON	776	349	427	Barlow	45.0%	55.0%
16,582	ROCKCASTLE	283	161	122	Weinberg	56.9%	43.1%
22,094	ROWAN	2,719	1,712	1,007	Weinberg	63.0%	37.0%
16,315	RUSSELL	627	242	385	Barlow	38.6%	61.4%
33,061	SCOTT	4,046	2,522	1,524	Weinberg	62.3%	37.7%
33,337	SHELBY	4,476	2,292	2,184	Weinberg	51.2%	48.8%
16,405	SIMPSON	2,343	407	1,936	Barlow	17.4%	82.6%
11,766	SPENCER	2,485	1,093	1,392	Barlow	44.0%	56.0%
22,927	TAYLOR	2,066	1,016	1,050	Barlow	49.2%	50.8%
11,971	TODD	2,759	533	2,226	Barlow	19.3%	80.7%
12,597	TRIGG	2,841	663	2,178	Barlow	23.3%	76.7%
8,125	TRIMBLE	1,984	943	1,041	Barlow	47.5%	52.5%
15,637	UNION	3,540	605	2,935	Barlow	17.1%	82.9%
92,522	WARREN	8,313	2,370	5,943	Barlow	28.5%	71.5%
10,916	WASHINGTON	1,757	851	906	Barlow	48.4%	51.6%
19,923	WAYNE	997	519	478	Weinberg	52.1%	47.9%
14,120	WEBSTER	3,362	653	2,709	Barlow	19.4%	80.6%
35,865	WHITLEY	993	516	477	Weinberg	52.0%	48.0%
7,065	WOLFE	1,607	973	634	Weinberg	60.5%	39.5%
23,208	WOODFORD	2,996	2,061	935	Weinberg	68.8%	31.2%
4,041,769	TOTAL	461,068	231,013	230,055	Weinberg	50.1%	49.9%

188

LOUISIANA

GOVERNOR
Mike Foster (R). Reelected 1999 to a four-year term. Previously elected 1995.

SENATORS (2 Democrats)
John B. Breaux (D). Reelected 1998 to a six-year term. Previously elected 1992, 1986.

Mary L. Landrieu (D). Reelected 2002 to a six-year term. Previously elected 1996.

REPRESENTATIVES (4 Republicans, 3 Democrats)
1. David Vitter (R)
2. William J. Jefferson (D)
3. Billy Tauzin (R)
4. Jim McCrery (R)
5. Rodney Alexander (D)
6. Richard H. Baker (R)
7. Chris John (D)

POSTWAR VOTE FOR PRESIDENT

| | | Republican | | Democratic | | Other | | Percentage | | | |
| | | | | | | | | Total Vote | | Major Vote | |
Year	Total Vote	Vote	Candidate	Vote	Candidate	Vote	Plurality	Rep.	Dem.	Rep.	Dem.
2000**	1,765,656	927,871	Bush, George W.	792,344	Gore, Al	45,441	135,527 R	52.6%	44.9%	53.9%	46.1%
1996**	1,783,959	712,586	Dole, Bob	927,837	Clinton, Bill	143,536	215,251 D	39.9%	52.0%	43.4%	56.6%
1992**	1,790,017	733,386	Bush, George	815,971	Clinton, Bill	240,660	82,585 D	41.0%	45.6%	47.3%	52.7%
1988	1,628,202	883,702	Bush, George	717,460	Dukakis, Michael S.	27,040	166,242 R	54.3%	44.1%	55.2%	44.8%
1984	1,706,822	1,037,299	Reagan, Ronald	651,586	Mondale, Walter F.	17,937	385,713 R	60.8%	38.2%	61.4%	38.6%
1980**	1,548,591	792,853	Reagan, Ronald	708,453	Carter, Jimmy	47,285	84,400 R	51.2%	45.7%	52.8%	47.2%
1976	1,278,439	587,446	Ford, Gerald R.	661,365	Carter, Jimmy	29,628	73,919 D	46.0%	51.7%	47.0%	53.0%
1972	1,051,491	686,852	Nixon, Richard M.	298,142	McGovern, George S.	66,497	388,710 R	65.3%	28.4%	69.7%	30.3%
1968**	1,097,450	257,535	Nixon, Richard M.	309,615	Humphrey, Hubert H.	530,300	220,685 A	23.5%	28.2%	45.4%	54.6%
1964	896,293	509,225	Goldwater, Barry M.	387,068	Johnson, Lyndon B.		122,157 R	56.8%	43.2%	56.8%	43.2%
1960	807,891	230,980	Nixon, Richard M.	407,339	Kennedy, John F.	169,572	176,359 D	28.6%	50.4%	36.2%	63.8%
1956	617,544	329,047	Eisenhower, Dwight D.	243,977	Stevenson, Adlai E.	44,520	85,070 R	53.3%	39.5%	57.4%	42.6%
1952	651,952	306,925	Eisenhower, Dwight D.	345,027	Stevenson, Adlai E.		38,102 D	47.1%	52.9%	47.1%	52.9%
1948**	416,336	72,657	Dewey, Thomas E.	136,344	Truman, Harry S.	207,335	67,946 SR	17.5%	32.7%	34.8%	65.2%

In 2000 the other vote column includes 20,473 votes cast for Green (Nader). In 1996 the other vote column includes 123,293 votes cast for Perot. In 1992 the other vote column includes 211,478 votes cast for Perot. In 1980 the other vote column includes 26,345 votes for Independent (Anderson). In 1968 the other vote was American (Wallace). In 1948 the other vote was 204,290 States Rights; 3,035 Progressive and 10 scattered.

LOUISIANA

POSTWAR VOTE FOR GOVERNOR

Year	Total Vote	Republican Vote	Republican Candidate	Democratic Vote	Democratic Candidate	Other Vote	Rep.-Dem. Plurality	Total Vote Rep.	Total Vote Dem.	Major Vote Rep.	Major Vote Dem.
1999	1,295,205	805,203	Foster, Mike	382,445	Jefferson, William J.	107,557	422,758 R	62.2%	29.5%	67.8%	32.2%
1995*	1,550,360	984,499	Foster, Mike	565,861	Fields, Cleo		418,638 R	63.5%	36.5%	63.5%	36.5%
1991*	1,728,040	671,009	Duke, David E.	1,057,031	Edwards, Edwin W.		386,022 D	38.8%	61.2%	38.8%	61.2%
1987**	1,558,730	287,780	Livingston, Robert L.	516,078	Roemer, Charles	754,872	78,277 D	18.5%	33.1%		
1983	1,615,905	588,508	Treen, David C.	1,006,561	Edwards, Edwin W.	20,836	418,053 D	36.4%	62.3%	36.9%	63.1%
1979*	1,371,825	690,691	Treen, David C.	681,134	Lambert, Louis		9,557 R	50.3%	49.7%	50.3%	49.7%
1975	430,095		—	430,095	Edwards, Edwin W.		430,095 D		100.0%		100.0%
1972	1,121,570	480,424	Treen, David C.	641,146	Edwards, Edwin W.		160,722 D	42.8%	57.2%	42.8%	57.2%
1968	372,762		—	372,762	McKeithen, John J.		372,762 D		100.0%		100.0%
1964	773,390	297,753	Lyons, C. H.	469,589	McKeithen, John J.	6,048	171,836 D	38.5%	60.7%	38.8%	61.2%
1960	506,562	86,135	Grevemberg, F. C.	407,907	Davis, Jimmie H.	12,520	321,772 D	17.0%	80.5%	17.4%	82.6%
1956	172,291		—	172,291	Long, Earl K.		172,291 D		100.0%		100.0%
1952	123,681	4,958	Bagwell, Harrison G.	118,723	Kennon, Robert F.		113,765 D	4.0%	96.0%	4.0%	96.0%
1948	76,566		—	76,566	Long, Earl K.		76,566 D		100.0%		100.0%

Since 1978 Louisiana has had a two-tier election system in which all candidates, regardless of party, run together in a first-round, open primary. A candidate that wins a majority of the vote in the first round is elected. If no candidate receives 50 percent, a runoff is held between the top two finishers. An asterisk (*) indicates gubernatorial elections that were decided in a runoff, with the runoff results listed. In elections that did not require a runoff, the leading Democratic and Republican candidates are listed with their first-round votes. The votes for other candidates are listed in the "Other" column, regardless of whether they were Democratic, Republican, or independent. In 1987, Democrat Edwin W. Edwards withdrew after finishing second in the initial round of voting. Democrat Charles Roemer finished first with 33.1 percent, 78,277 votes ahead of Edwards. With Edwards' withdrawal, no runoff was held.

POSTWAR VOTE FOR SENATOR

Year	Total Vote	Republican Vote	Republican Candidate	Democratic Vote	Democratic Candidate	Other Vote	Rep.-Dem. Plurality	Total Vote Rep.	Total Vote Dem.	Major Vote Rep.	Major Vote Dem.
2002*	1,235,296	596,642	Terrell, Suzanne Haik	638,654	Landrieu, Mary L.		42,012 D	48.3%	51.7%	48.3%	51.7%
1998	969,165	306,616	Donelon, Jim	620,502	Breaux, John B.	42,047	313,886 D	31.6%	64.0%	33.1%	66.9%
1996*	1,700,102	847,157	Jenkins, Louis	852,945	Landrieu, Mary L.		5,788 D	49.8%	50.2%	49.8%	50.2%
1992	843,037	69,986	Stockstill, Lyle	616,021	Breaux, John B.	157,030	541,236 D	8.3%	73.1%		
1990	1,396,113	607,391	Duke, David E.	752,902	Johnston, J. Bennett	35,820	145,511 D	43.5%	53.9%	44.7%	55.3%
1986*	1,369,897	646,311	Moore, W. Henson	723,586	Breaux, John B.		77,275 D	47.2%	52.8%	47.2%	52.8%
1984	977,473	86,546	Robert M. Ross	838,181	Johnston, J. Bennett	52,746	751,635 D	8.9%	85.7%		
1980	841,013	13,739	Bardwell, Jerry C.	484,770	Long, Russell B.	342,504	158,848 D	1.6%	57.6%		
1978	839,669		—	498,773	Johnston, J. Bennett	340,896	157,877 D		59.4%		
1974	434,643		—	434,643	Long, Russell B.		434,643 D		100.0%		100.0%
1972**	1,084,904	206,846	Toledano, Ben C.	598,987	Johnston, J. Bennett	279,071	392,141 D	19.1%	55.2%	25.7%	74.3%
1968	518,586		—	518,586	Long, Russell B.		518,586 D		100.0%		100.0%
1966	437,695		—	437,695	Ellender, Allen J.		437,695 D		100.0%		100.0%
1962	421,904	103,066	O'Hearn, Taylor W.	318,838	Long, Russell B.		215,772 D	24.4%	75.6%	24.4%	75.6%
1960	541,928	109,698	Reese, George W.	432,228	Ellender, Allen J.	2	322,530 D	20.2%	79.8%	20.2%	79.8%
1956	335,564		—	335,564	Long, Russell B.		335,564 D		100.0%		100.0%
1954	207,115		—	207,115	Ellender, Allen J.		207,115 D		100.0%		100.0%
1950	251,838	30,931	Gerth, Charles S.	220,907	Long, Russell B.		189,976 D	12.3%	87.7%	12.3%	87.7%
1948	330,124		—	330,115	Ellender, Allen J.	9	330,115 D		100.0%		100.0%
1948S	408,667	102,331	Clarke, Clem S.	306,336	Long, Russell B.		204,005 D	25.0%	75.0%	25.0%	75.0%

An asterisk (*) indicates Senate elections since 1978 that have been decided in a runoff, with the runoff results listed. In elections that did not require a runoff, the leading Democratic and Republican candidates are listed with their first-round votes. The votes for other candidates are listed in the "Other" column, regardless of whether they were Democratic, Republican, or independent. In 1972 the other vote includes 250,161 votes for John J. McKeithen (Independent). One of the 1948 elections was for a short term to fill a vacancy.

LOUISIANA

Congressional districts first established for elections held in 2002
7 members

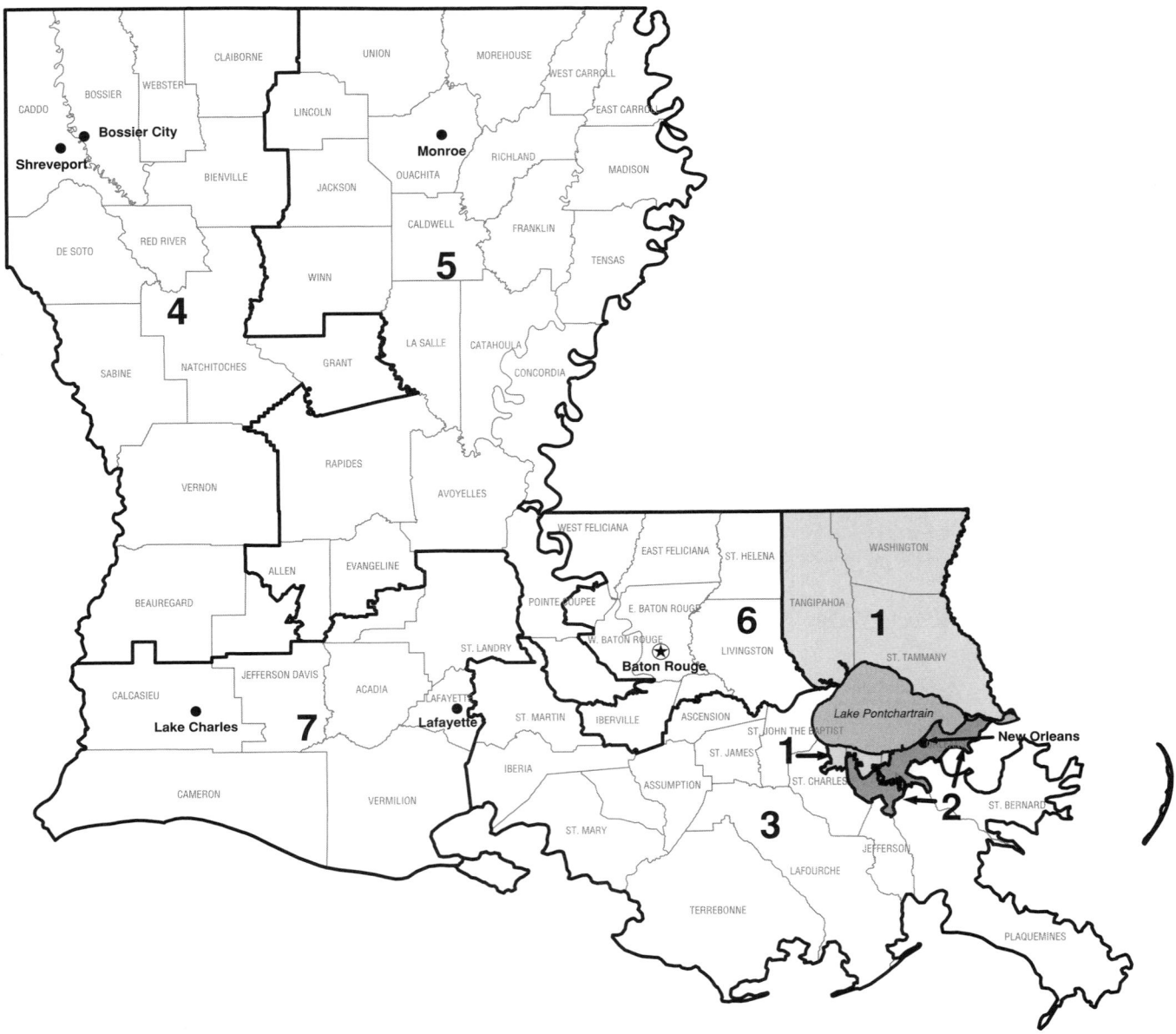

LOUISIANA

SENATOR 2002 (FIRST ROUND)

2000 Census Population	Parish	Total Vote	Landrieu (D)	Terrell (R)	Cooksey (R)	Other	Winner	Percentage of Total Vote Landrieu (D)	Terrell (R)	Cooksey (R)	Other
58,861	ACADIA	16,626	6,991	4,619	2,516	2,500	Landrieu	42.0%	27.8%	15.1%	15.0%
25,440	ALLEN	5,899	2,637	1,133	880	1,249	Landrieu	44.7%	19.2%	14.9%	21.2%
76,627	ASCENSION	23,649	10,547	6,973	1,627	4,502	Landrieu	44.6%	29.5%	6.9%	19.0%
23,388	ASSUMPTION	7,354	4,097	1,704	423	1,130	Landrieu	55.7%	23.2%	5.8%	15.4%
41,481	AVOYELLES	10,661	4,721	1,512	3,158	1,270	Landrieu	44.3%	14.2%	29.6%	11.9%
32,986	BEAUREGARD	8,205	2,692	1,919	1,258	2,336	Landrieu	32.8%	23.4%	15.3%	28.5%
15,752	BIENVILLE	5,077	2,573	1,086	838	580	Landrieu	50.7%	21.4%	16.5%	11.4%
98,310	BOSSIER	26,993	10,871	8,504	4,580	3,038	Landrieu	40.3%	31.5%	17.0%	11.3%
252,161	CADDO	70,294	36,767	18,045	8,830	6,652	Landrieu	52.3%	25.7%	12.6%	9.5%
183,577	CALCASIEU	52,926	24,073	13,126	4,635	11,092	Landrieu	45.5%	24.8%	8.8%	21.0%
10,560	CALDWELL	4,076	1,206	595	1,922	353	Cooksey	29.6%	14.6%	47.2%	8.7%
9,991	CAMERON	3,181	1,417	792	368	604	Landrieu	44.5%	24.9%	11.6%	19.0%
10,920	CATAHOULA	4,724	1,898	505	1,772	549	Landrieu	40.2%	10.7%	37.5%	11.6%
16,851	CLAIBORNE	4,227	1,945	968	863	451	Landrieu	46.0%	22.9%	20.4%	10.7%
20,247	CONCORDIA	6,844	2,795	687	2,624	738	Landrieu	40.8%	10.0%	38.3%	10.8%
25,494	DE SOTO	7,080	3,642	1,747	971	720	Landrieu	51.4%	24.7%	13.7%	10.2%
412,852	EAST BATON ROUGE	122,291	55,609	34,421	8,606	23,655	Landrieu	45.5%	28.1%	7.0%	19.3%
9,421	EAST CARROLL	2,525	1,250	281	659	335	Landrieu	49.5%	11.1%	26.1%	13.3%
21,360	EAST FELICIANA	7,240	3,605	1,552	517	1,566	Landrieu	49.8%	21.4%	7.1%	21.6%
35,434	EVANGELINE	9,693	3,971	2,144	2,242	1,336	Landrieu	41.0%	22.1%	23.1%	13.8%
21,263	FRANKLIN	6,294	2,134	1,246	2,211	703	Cooksey	33.9%	19.8%	35.1%	11.2%
18,698	GRANT	4,958	1,537	774	1,901	746	Cooksey	31.0%	15.6%	38.3%	15.0%
73,266	IBERIA	17,844	6,528	5,750	2,412	3,154	Landrieu	36.6%	32.2%	13.5%	17.7%
33,320	IBERVILLE	11,713	6,676	2,462	675	1,900	Landrieu	57.0%	21.0%	5.8%	16.2%
15,397	JACKSON	5,850	2,275	1,095	1,823	657	Landrieu	38.9%	18.7%	31.2%	11.2%
455,466	JEFFERSON	116,199	48,207	47,291	11,647	9,054	Landrieu	41.5%	40.7%	10.0%	7.8%
31,435	JEFFERSON DAVIS	8,168	3,397	2,118	1,070	1,583	Landrieu	41.6%	25.9%	13.1%	19.4%
190,503	LAFAYETTE	54,966	19,945	17,297	8,525	9,199	Landrieu	36.3%	31.5%	15.5%	16.7%
89,974	LAFOURCHE	23,870	11,621	7,400	1,957	2,892	Landrieu	48.7%	31.0%	8.2%	12.1%
14,282	LA SALLE	4,717	993	459	2,906	359	Cooksey	21.1%	9.7%	61.6%	7.6%
42,509	LINCOLN	12,081	4,786	2,373	3,569	1,353	Landrieu	39.6%	19.6%	29.5%	11.2%
91,814	LIVINGSTON	27,581	8,801	8,591	2,564	7,625	Landrieu	31.9%	31.1%	9.3%	27.6%
13,728	MADISON	3,464	1,511	547	969	437	Landrieu	43.6%	15.8%	28.0%	12.6%
31,021	MOREHOUSE	8,578	3,251	1,369	3,040	918	Landrieu	37.9%	16.0%	35.4%	10.7%
39,080	NATCHITOCHES	10,259	4,945	2,145	1,784	1,385	Landrieu	48.2%	20.9%	17.4%	13.5%
484,674	ORLEANS	126,375	94,811	21,170	4,469	5,925	Landrieu	75.0%	16.8%	3.5%	4.7%
147,250	OUACHITA	41,888	14,139	7,784	15,745	4,220	Cooksey	33.8%	18.6%	37.6%	10.1%
26,757	PLAQUEMINES	9,561	4,711	3,466	581	803	Landrieu	49.3%	36.3%	6.1%	8.4%
22,763	POINTE COUPEE	7,725	4,099	1,660	625	1,341	Landrieu	53.1%	21.5%	8.1%	17.4%
126,337	RAPIDES	37,574	14,667	5,997	12,295	4,615	Landrieu	39.0%	16.0%	32.7%	12.3%
9,622	RED RIVER	3,575	1,926	749	387	513	Landrieu	53.9%	21.0%	10.8%	14.3%
20,981	RICHLAND	6,422	2,315	1,380	2,081	646	Landrieu	36.0%	21.5%	32.4%	10.1%
23,459	SABINE	5,571	1,983	1,061	1,641	886	Landrieu	35.6%	19.0%	29.5%	15.9%
67,229	ST. BERNARD	17,806	7,792	7,430	1,285	1,299	Landrieu	43.8%	41.7%	7.2%	7.3%
48,072	ST. CHARLES	14,017	6,034	5,187	1,505	1,291	Landrieu	43.0%	37.0%	10.7%	9.2%
10,525	ST. HELENA	4,038	2,228	683	384	743	Landrieu	55.2%	16.9%	9.5%	18.4%
21,216	ST. JAMES	8,329	5,035	1,799	461	1,034	Landrieu	60.5%	21.6%	5.5%	12.4%
43,044	ST. JOHN THE BAPTIST	11,297	5,892	3,063	607	1,735	Landrieu	52.2%	27.1%	5.4%	15.4%
87,700	ST. LANDRY	24,162	12,622	6,392	2,600	2,548	Landrieu	52.2%	26.5%	10.8%	10.5%
48,583	ST. MARTIN	13,556	6,075	3,405	1,764	2,312	Landrieu	44.8%	25.1%	13.0%	17.1%
53,500	ST. MARY	14,288	6,430	3,813	1,906	2,139	Landrieu	45.0%	26.7%	13.3%	15.0%
191,268	ST. TAMMANY	58,006	17,444	26,955	7,196	6,411	Terrell	30.1%	46.5%	12.4%	11.1%
100,588	TANGIPAHOA	24,388	10,448	8,284	2,533	3,123	Landrieu	42.8%	34.0%	10.4%	12.8%
6,618	TENSAS	2,066	913	351	568	234	Landrieu	44.2%	17.0%	27.5%	11.3%
104,503	TERREBONNE	24,377	10,833	8,157	2,239	3,148	Landrieu	44.4%	33.5%	9.2%	12.9%

LOUISIANA

SENATOR 2002 (FIRST ROUND)

2000 Census Population	Parish	Total Vote	Landrieu (D)	Terrell (R)	Cooksey (R)	Other	Winner	Percentage of Total Vote Landrieu (D)	Terrell (R)	Cooksey (R)	Other
22,803	UNION	7,026	2,263	1,290	2,810	663	Cooksey	32.2%	18.4%	40.0%	9.4%
53,807	VERMILION	14,767	6,461	3,969	2,356	1,981	Landrieu	43.8%	26.9%	16.0%	13.4%
52,531	VERNON	9,778	4,118	1,625	2,177	1,858	Landrieu	42.1%	16.6%	22.3%	19.0%
43,926	WASHINGTON	11,318	5,391	3,047	1,316	1,564	Landrieu	47.6%	26.9%	11.6%	13.8%
41,831	WEBSTER	12,991	6,425	3,372	1,778	1,416	Landrieu	49.5%	26.0%	13.7%	10.9%
21,601	WEST BATON ROUGE	6,858	3,541	1,892	405	1,020	Landrieu	51.6%	27.6%	5.9%	14.9%
12,314	WEST CARROLL	3,325	889	656	1,441	339	Cooksey	26.7%	19.7%	43.3%	10.2%
15,111	WEST FELICIANA	4,363	2,061	1,003	469	830	Landrieu	47.2%	23.0%	10.7%	19.0%
16,894	WINN	4,779	1,887	636	1,786	470	Landrieu	39.5%	13.3%	37.4%	9.8%
4,468,976	TOTAL	1,246,333	573,347	339,506	171,752	161,728	Landrieu	46.0%	27.2%	13.8%	13.0%

LOUISIANA

SENATOR 2002 (RUNOFF)

2000 Census Population	Parish	Total Vote	Republican (Terrell)	Democratic (Landrieu)	Other	Rep.-Dem. Plurality	Percentage Total Vote Rep.	Dem.	Major Vote Rep.	Dem.
58,861	ACADIA	15,409	8,214	7,195		1,019 R	53.3%	46.7%	53.3%	46.7%
25,440	ALLEN	5,312	2,201	3,111		910 D	41.4%	58.6%	41.4%	58.6%
76,627	ASCENSION	22,663	11,336	11,327		9 R	50.0%	50.0%	50.0%	50.0%
23,388	ASSUMPTION	7,380	2,414	4,966		2,552 D	32.7%	67.3%	32.7%	67.3%
41,481	AVOYELLES	11,361	4,897	6,464		1,567 D	43.1%	56.9%	43.1%	56.9%
32,986	BEAUREGARD	7,914	4,638	3,276		1,362 R	58.6%	41.4%	58.6%	41.4%
15,752	BIENVILLE	5,195	2,120	3,075		955 D	40.8%	59.2%	40.8%	59.2%
98,310	BOSSIER	25,482	15,005	10,477		4,528 R	58.9%	41.1%	58.9%	41.1%
252,161	CADDO	70,742	31,073	39,669		8,596 D	43.9%	56.1%	43.9%	56.1%
183,577	CALCASIEU	48,464	22,546	25,918		3,372 D	46.5%	53.5%	46.5%	53.5%
10,560	CALDWELL	2,872	1,635	1,237		398 R	56.9%	43.1%	56.9%	43.1%
9,991	CAMERON	2,556	1,277	1,279		2 D	50.0%	50.0%	50.0%	50.0%
10,920	CATAHOULA	3,010	1,410	1,600		190 D	46.8%	53.2%	46.8%	53.2%
16,851	CLAIBORNE	4,425	2,074	2,351		277 D	46.9%	53.1%	46.9%	53.1%
20,247	CONCORDIA	5,344	2,491	2,853		362 D	46.6%	53.4%	46.6%	53.4%
25,494	DE SOTO	7,610	3,318	4,292		974 D	43.6%	56.4%	43.6%	56.4%
412,852	EAST BATON ROUGE	124,647	61,229	63,418		2,189 D	49.1%	50.9%	49.1%	50.9%
9,421	EAST CARROLL	2,161	801	1,360		559 D	37.1%	62.9%	37.1%	62.9%
21,360	EAST FELICIANA	6,621	2,976	3,645		669 D	44.9%	55.1%	44.9%	55.1%
35,434	EVANGELINE	9,303	4,563	4,740		177 D	49.0%	51.0%	49.0%	51.0%
21,263	FRANKLIN	5,754	3,150	2,604		546 R	54.7%	45.3%	54.7%	45.3%
18,698	GRANT	4,452	2,677	1,775		902 R	60.1%	39.9%	60.1%	39.9%
73,266	IBERIA	18,489	10,274	8,215		2,059 R	55.6%	44.4%	55.6%	44.4%
33,320	IBERVILLE	10,821	3,431	7,390		3,959 D	31.7%	68.3%	31.7%	68.3%
15,397	JACKSON	5,477	2,786	2,691		95 R	50.9%	49.1%	50.9%	49.1%
455,466	JEFFERSON	126,558	70,473	56,085		14,388 R	55.7%	44.3%	55.7%	44.3%
31,435	JEFFERSON DAVIS	7,959	3,780	4,179		399 D	47.5%	52.5%	47.5%	52.5%
190,503	LAFAYETTE	51,712	30,568	21,144		9,424 R	59.1%	40.9%	59.1%	40.9%
89,974	LAFOURCHE	23,395	10,557	12,838		2,281 D	45.1%	54.9%	45.1%	54.9%
14,282	LA SALLE	3,783	2,530	1,253		1,277 R	66.9%	33.1%	66.9%	33.1%
42,509	LINCOLN	11,632	6,327	5,305		1,022 R	54.4%	45.6%	54.4%	45.6%
91,814	LIVINGSTON	26,218	16,897	9,321		7,576 R	64.4%	35.6%	64.4%	35.6%
13,728	MADISON	3,092	1,333	1,759		426 D	43.1%	56.9%	43.1%	56.9%
31,021	MOREHOUSE	7,983	3,974	4,009		35 D	49.8%	50.2%	49.8%	50.2%
39,080	NATCHITOCHES	9,916	4,517	5,399		882 D	45.6%	54.4%	45.6%	54.4%
484,674	ORLEANS	132,660	26,880	105,780		78,900 D	20.3%	79.7%	20.3%	79.7%
147,250	OUACHITA	41,780	24,450	17,330		7,120 R	58.5%	41.5%	58.5%	41.5%
26,757	PLAQUEMINES	7,427	3,774	3,653		121 R	50.8%	49.2%	50.8%	49.2%
22,763	POINTE COUPEE	7,975	2,998	4,977		1,979 D	37.6%	62.4%	37.6%	62.4%
126,337	RAPIDES	33,329	17,983	15,346		2,637 R	54.0%	46.0%	54.0%	46.0%

LOUISIANA

SENATOR 2002 (RUNOFF)

2000 Census Population	Parish	Total Vote	Republican (Terrell)	Democratic (Landrieu)	Other	Rep.-Dem. Plurality	Total Vote Rep.	Dem.	Major Vote Rep.	Dem.
9,622	RED RIVER	3,301	1,269	2,032		763 D	38.4%	61.6%	38.4%	61.6%
20,981	RICHLAND	6,048	3,368	2,680		688 R	55.7%	44.3%	55.7%	44.3%
23,459	SABINE	5,720	3,438	2,282		1,156 R	60.1%	39.9%	60.1%	39.9%
67,229	ST. BERNARD	19,032	10,101	8,931		1,170 R	53.1%	46.9%	53.1%	46.9%
48,072	ST. CHARLES	15,048	7,874	7,174		700 R	52.3%	47.7%	52.3%	47.7%
10,525	ST. HELENA	4,006	1,292	2,714		1,422 D	32.3%	67.7%	32.3%	67.7%
21,216	ST. JAMES	7,865	2,512	5,353		2,841 D	31.9%	68.1%	31.9%	68.1%
43,044	ST. JOHN THE BAPTIST	12,446	4,944	7,502		2,558 D	39.7%	60.3%	39.7%	60.3%
87,700	ST. LANDRY	22,813	9,648	13,165		3,517 D	42.3%	57.7%	42.3%	57.7%
48,583	ST. MARTIN	13,550	6,005	7,545		1,540 D	44.3%	55.7%	44.3%	55.7%
53,500	ST. MARY	13,507	6,762	6,745		17 R	50.1%	49.9%	50.1%	49.9%
191,268	ST. TAMMANY	61,645	41,995	19,650		22,345 R	68.1%	31.9%	68.1%	31.9%
100,588	TANGIPAHOA	23,709	12,841	10,868		1,973 R	54.2%	45.8%	54.2%	45.8%
6,618	TENSAS	2,117	847	1,270		423 D	40.0%	60.0%	40.0%	60.0%
104,503	TERREBONNE	23,822	12,167	11,655		512 R	51.1%	48.9%	51.1%	48.9%
22,803	UNION	6,895	4,181	2,714		1,467 R	60.6%	39.4%	60.6%	39.4%
53,807	VERMILION	14,400	7,042	7,358		316 D	48.9%	51.1%	48.9%	51.1%
52,531	VERNON	8,492	4,591	3,901		690 R	54.1%	45.9%	54.1%	45.9%
43,926	WASHINGTON	11,609	5,401	6,208		807 D	46.5%	53.5%	46.5%	53.5%
41,831	WEBSTER	11,801	5,746	6,055		309 D	48.7%	51.3%	48.7%	51.3%
21,601	WEST BATON ROUGE	7,212	3,025	4,187		1,162 D	41.9%	58.1%	41.9%	58.1%
12,314	WEST CARROLL	3,163	2,028	1,135		893 R	64.1%	35.9%	64.1%	35.9%
15,111	WEST FELICIANA	3,927	1,741	2,186		445 D	44.3%	55.7%	44.3%	55.7%
16,894	WINN	4,285	2,247	2,038		209 R	52.4%	47.6%	52.4%	47.6%
4,468,976	TOTAL	1,235,296	596,642	638,654		42,012 D	48.3%	51.7%	48.3%	51.7%

LOUISIANA

HOUSE OF REPRESENTATIVES

CD	Year	Total Vote	Republican Vote	Candidate	Democratic Vote	Candidate	Other Vote	Rep.-Dem. Plurality	Total Vote Rep.	Dem.	Major Vote Rep.	Dem.
1	2002	180,570	147,117	Vitter, David*			33,453	147,117 R	81.5%		100.0%	
2	2002	142,156	15,440	Sullivan, "Silky"	90,310	Jefferson, William J.*	36,406	74,870 D	10.9%	63.5%	14.6%	85.4%
3	2002	150,342	130,323	Tauzin, Billy*			20,019	130,323 R	86.7%		100.0%	
4	2002	160,093	114,649	McCrery, Jim*	42,340	Milkovich, John	3,104	72,309 R	71.6%	26.4%	73.0%	27.0%
5	2002	172,462	85,744	Fletcher, Lee	86,718	Alexander, Rodney		974 D	49.7%	50.3%	49.7%	50.3%
6	2002	174,830	146,932	Baker, Richard H.*			27,898	146,932 R	84.0%	0.0%	100.0%	0.0%
7	2002	159,710			138,659	John, Chris*	21,051	138,659 D		86.8%		100.0%
Total	2002	1,140,163	640,205		358,027		141,931	282,178 R	56.2%	31.4%	64.1%	35.9%

Note: Louisiana has a unique two-tier electoral system, with a first round of voting that features candidates from all parties running on the same ballot. A candidate that wins a majority of the vote in the first round is elected. Otherwise, the top two finishers meet in a runoff. In 2002, a U.S. House runoff was required only in District 5. The returns in the table are from that election, held Dec. 7, 2002. House members were elected in the first round of voting in the other six districts, on Nov. 5, 2002. In elections that did not require a runoff, the leading Democratic and Republican candidates are listed with their first-round votes. The votes for other candidates are listed in the "Other" column, regardless of whether they were Democratic, Republican, or unaffiliated with either party.

An asterisk (*) denotes incumbent.

LOUISIANA

PRIMARY ELECTIONS

2002 PRIMARY ELECTIONS

Open Election	November 5, 2002	**Registration** (as of Nov. 5, 2002)	Republican 646,418
			Democratic 1,620,577
Runoff Election	December 7, 2002		Other 539,207
			TOTAL 2,806,202

Primary Type Louisiana has a two-tier electoral system open to all voters, with a first round of voting (sometimes called an open primary) that features candidates from all parties running on the same ballot. A candidate that wins a majority of the vote in the first round is elected. Otherwise, there is a runoff held several weeks later between the top two finishers. Runoffs for the Senate and one House seat were necessary in 2002.

Note: An asterisk (*) denotes incumbent. An "O" indicates "Other," the designation for a candidate in Louisiana who does not file as a Democrat or Republican. A pound sign (#) indicates candidate qualified for a runoff.

FIRST ROUND VOTE (NOV. 5, 2002)

Senator	Mary L. Landrieu (D)*#	573,347	46.0%
	Suzanne Haik Terrell (R)#	339,506	27.2%
	John Cooksey (R)	171,752	13.8%
	"Tony" Perkins (R)	119,776	9.6%
	Raymond Brown (D)	23,553	1.9%
	Patrick E. "Live Wire" Landry (O)	10,442	0.8%
	James Lemann (O)	3,866	0.3%
	Gary D. Robbins (O)	2,423	0.2%
	Ernest Edward Skillman Jr. (R)	1,668	0.1%
	TOTAL	1,246,333	
Congressional District 1	David Vitter (R)*	147,117	81.5%
	Monica L. Monica (R)	20,268	11.2%
	Robert Namer (R)	7,229	4.0%
	Ian P. Hawxhurst (O)	5,956	3.3%
	TOTAL	180,570	
Congressional District 2	William J. Jefferson (D)*	90,310	63.5%
	Irma Muse Dixon (D)	28,480	20.0%
	"Silky" Sullivan (R)	15,440	10.9%
	Clarence "Buddy" Hunt (D)	4,137	2.9%
	Wayne E. Clement (O)	3,789	2.7%
	TOTAL	142,156	
Congressional District 3	Billy Tauzin (R)*	130,323	86.7%
	William Beier (O)	12,964	8.6%
	David Iwancio (O)	7,055	4.7%
	TOTAL	150,342	
Congressional District 4	Jim McCrery (R)*	114,649	71.6%
	John Milkovich (D)	42,340	26.4%
	"Bill" Jacobs (O)	3,104	1.9%
	TOTAL	160,093	
Congressional District 5	Rodney Alexander (D)#	52,952	28.7%
	Lee Fletcher (R)#	45,278	24.5%
	Clyde C. Holloway (R)	42,573	23.1%
	Robert J. Barham (R)	34,533	18.7%
	Sam Houston Melton Jr. (D)	4,595	2.5%
	Jack Wright (R)	3,581	1.9%
	Vinson Mouser (O)	1,145	0.6%
	TOTAL	184,657	
Congressional District 6	Richard H. Baker (R)*	146,932	84.0%
	"Rick" Moscatello (O)	27,898	16.0%
	TOTAL	174,830	
Congressional District 7	Chris John (D)*	138,659	86.8%
	Roberto Valletta (O)	21,051	13.2%
	TOTAL	159,710	

MAINE

GOVERNOR
John Baldacci (D). Elected 2002 to a four-year term.

SENATORS (2 Republicans)
Susan Collins (R). Reelected 2002 to a six-year term. Previously elected 1996.

Olympia J. Snowe (R). Reelected 2000 to a six-year term. Previously elected 1994.

REPRESENTATIVES (2 Democrats)
1. Tom Allen (D)
2. Michael H. Michaud (D)

POSTWAR VOTE FOR PRESIDENT

| | | Republican | | Democratic | | | | | Percentage | | | |
| | | | | | | | | | Total Vote | | Major Vote | |
Year	Total Vote	Vote	Candidate	Vote	Candidate	Other Vote	Plurality		Rep.	Dem.	Rep.	Dem.
2000**	651,817	286,616	Bush, George W.	319,951	Gore, Al	45,250	33,335	D	44.0%	49.1%	47.3%	52.7%
1996**	605,897	186,378	Dole, Bob	312,788	Clinton, Bill	106,731	126,410	D	30.8%	51.6%	37.3%	62.7%
1992**	679,499	206,504	Bush, George	263,420	Clinton, Bill	209,575	56,600	D	30.4%	38.8%	43.9%	56.1%
1988	555,035	307,131	Bush, George	243,569	Dukakis, Michael S.	4,335	63,562	R	55.3%	43.9%	55.8%	44.2%
1984	553,144	336,500	Reagan, Ronald	214,515	Mondale, Walter F.	2,129	121,985	R	60.8%	38.8%	61.1%	38.9%
1980**	523,011	238,522	Reagan, Ronald	220,974	Carter, Jimmy	63,515	17,548	R	45.6%	42.3%	51.9%	48.1%
1976	483,216	236,320	Ford, Gerald R.	232,279	Carter, Jimmy	14,617	4,041	R	48.9%	48.1%	50.4%	49.6%
1972	417,042	256,458	Nixon, Richard M.	160,584	McGovern, George S.		95,874	R	61.5%	38.5%	61.5%	38.5%
1968	392,936	169,254	Nixon, Richard M.	217,312	Humphrey, Hubert H.	6,370	48,058	D	43.1%	55.3%	43.8%	56.2%
1964	380,965	118,701	Goldwater, Barry M.	262,264	Johnson, Lyndon B.		143,563	D	31.2%	68.8%	31.2%	68.8%
1960	421,767	240,608	Nixon, Richard M.	181,159	Kennedy, John F.		59,449	R	57.0%	43.0%	57.0%	43.0%
1956	351,706	249,238	Eisenhower, Dwight D.	102,468	Stevenson, Adlai E.		146,770	R	70.9%	29.1%	70.9%	29.1%
1952	351,786	232,353	Eisenhower, Dwight D.	118,806	Stevenson, Adlai E.	627	113,547	R	66.0%	33.8%	66.2%	33.8%
1948	264,787	150,234	Dewey, Thomas E.	111,916	Truman, Harry S.	2,637	38,318	R	56.7%	42.3%	57.3%	42.7%

In 2000 the other vote column includes 37,127 votes cast for Green (Nader). In 1996 the other vote column includes 85,970 votes cast for Perot. In 1992 the other vote column includes 206,820 votes cast for Perot, who came in second statewide. In 1980 the other vote column includes 53,327 votes for Independent (Anderson).

MAINE

POSTWAR VOTE FOR GOVERNOR

Year	Total Vote	Republican Vote	Candidate	Democratic Vote	Candidate	Other Vote	Rep.-Dem. Plurality	Percentage Total Vote Rep.	Dem.	Major Vote Rep.	Dem.
2002	505,190	209,496	Cianchette, Peter E.	238,179	Baldacci, John	57,515	28,683 D	41.5%	47.1%	46.8%	53.2%
1998**	421,009	79,716	Longley, James B., Jr.	50,506	Connolly, Thomas J.	290,787	167,056 I	18.9%	12.0%	61.2%	38.8%
1994**	511,308	117,990	Collins, Susan	172,951	Brennan, Joseph E.	220,367	7,878 I	23.1%	33.8%	40.6%	59.4%
1990	522,492	243,766	McKernan, John R.	230,038	Brennan, Joseph E.	48,688	13,728 R	46.7%	44.0%	51.4%	48.6%
1986**	426,861	170,312	McKernan, John R.	128,744	Tierney, James	127,805	41,568 R	39.9%	30.2%	56.9%	43.1%
1982	460,295	172,949	Cragin, Charles L.	281,066	Brennan, Joseph E.	6,280	108,117 D	37.6%	61.1%	38.1%	61.9%
1978	370,258	126,862	Palmer, Linwood E.	176,493	Brennan, Joseph E.	66,903	49,631 D	34.3%	47.7%	41.8%	58.2%
1974**	363,945	84,176	Erwin, James S.	132,219	Mitchell, George J.	147,550	10,245 I	23.1%	36.3%	38.9%	61.1%
1970	325,386	162,248	Erwin, James S.	163,138	Curtis, Kenneth M.		890 D	49.9%	50.1%	49.9%	50.1%
1966	323,838	151,802	Reed, John H.	172,036	Curtis, Kenneth M.		20,234 D	46.9%	53.1%	46.9%	53.1%
1962	292,725	146,604	Reed, John H.	146,121	Dolloff, Maynard C.		483 R	50.1%	49.9%	50.1%	49.9%
1960S	417,315	219,768	Reed, John H.	197,547	Coffin, Frank M.		22,221 R	52.7%	47.3%	52.7%	47.3%
1958**	280,295	134,572	Hildreth, Horace A.	145,723	Clauson, Clinton A.		11,151 D	48.0%	52.0%	48.0%	52.0%
1956	304,649	124,395	Trafton, Willis A.	180,254	Muskie, Edmund S.		55,859 D	40.8%	59.2%	40.8%	59.2%
1954	248,971	113,298	Cross, Burton M.	135,673	Muskie, Edmund S.		22,375 D	45.5%	54.5%	45.5%	54.5%
1952	248,441	128,532	Cross, Burton M.	82,538	Oliver, James C.	37,371	45,994 R	51.7%	33.2%	60.9%	39.1%
1950	241,177	145,823	Payne, Frederick G.	94,304	Grant, Earl S.	1,050	51,519 R	60.5%	39.1%	60.7%	39.3%
1948	222,500	145,956	Payne, Frederick G.	76,544	Lausier, Louis B.		69,412 R	65.6%	34.4%	65.6%	34.4%
1946	179,951	110,327	Hildreth, Horace A.	69,624	Clark, F. Davis		40,703 R	61.3%	38.7%	61.3%	38.7%

In 1998 Angus King received 246,772 votes (58.6% of the total vote) as an Independent and won by a plurality of 167,056 votes. In 1994 Angus King, as an Independent candidate, polled 180,829 votes (35.4% of the total vote) and won the election with a 7,878-vote plurality. In 1986 the other vote was 64,317 Sherry F. Huber (Independent); 63,474 John E. Menario (Independent) and 14 scattered. In 1974 James B. Longley, an Independent candidate, polled 142,464 votes (39.1% of the total vote) and won the election with a 10,245-vote plurality. The 1960 election was for a short term to fill a vacancy. The term of office of Maine's Governor was increased from two to four years effective with the 1958 election.

POSTWAR VOTE FOR SENATOR

Year	Total Vote	Republican Vote	Candidate	Democratic Vote	Candidate	Other Vote	Rep.-Dem. Plurality	Percentage Total Vote Rep.	Dem.	Major Vote Rep.	Dem.
2002	504,899	295,041	Collins, Susan	209,858	Pingree, Chellie		85,183 R	58.4%	41.6%	58.4%	41.6%
2000	634,872	437,689	Snowe, Olympia J.	197,183	Lawrence, Mark		240,506 R	68.9%	31.1%	68.9%	31.1%
1996	606,777	298,422	Collins, Susan	266,226	Brennan, Joseph E.	42,129	32,196 R	49.2%	43.9%	52.9%	47.1%
1994	511,733	308,244	Snowe, Olympia J.	186,042	Andrews, Thomas H.	17,447	122,202 R	60.2%	36.4%	62.4%	37.6%
1990	520,320	319,167	Cohen, William S.	201,053	Rolde, Neil	100	118,114 R	61.3%	38.6%	61.4%	38.6%
1988	557,375	104,758	Wyman, Jasper S.	452,590	Mitchell, George J.	27	347,832 D	18.8%	81.2%	18.8%	81.2%
1984	551,406	404,414	Cohen, William S.	142,626	Mitchell, Elizabeth H.	4,366	261,788 R	73.3%	25.9%	73.9%	26.1%
1982	459,715	179,882	Emery, David F.	279,819	Mitchell, George J.	14	99,937 D	39.1%	60.9%	39.1%	60.9%
1978	375,172	212,294	Cohen, William S.	127,327	Hathaway, William D.	35,551	84,967 R	56.6%	33.9%	62.5%	37.5%
1976	486,254	193,489	Monks, Robert A. G.	292,704	Muskie, Edmund S.	61	99,215 D	39.8%	60.2%	39.8%	60.2%
1972	421,310	197,040	Smith, Margaret Chase	224,270	Hathaway, William D.		27,230 D	46.8%	53.2%	46.8%	53.2%
1970	323,860	123,906	Bishop, Neil S.	199,954	Muskie, Edmund S.		76,048 D	38.3%	61.7%	38.3%	61.7%
1966	319,535	188,291	Smith, Margaret Chase	131,136	Violette, Elmer H.	108	57,155 R	58.9%	41.0%	58.9%	41.1%
1964	380,551	127,040	McIntire, Clifford	253,511	Muskie, Edmund S.		126,471 D	33.4%	66.6%	33.4%	66.6%
1960	416,699	256,890	Smith, Margaret Chase	159,809	Cormier, Lucia M.		97,081 R	61.6%	38.4%	61.6%	38.4%
1958	284,226	111,522	Payne, Frederick G.	172,704	Muskie, Edmund S.		61,182 D	39.2%	60.8%	39.2%	60.8%
1954	246,605	144,530	Smith, Margaret Chase	102,075	Fullam, Paul A.		42,455 R	58.6%	41.4%	58.6%	41.4%
1952	237,164	139,205	Payne, Frederick G.	82,665	Dube, Roger P.	15,294	56,540 R	58.7%	34.9%	62.7%	37.3%
1948	223,256	159,182	Smith, Margaret Chase	64,074	Scolten, Adrian H.		95,108 R	71.3%	28.7%	71.3%	28.7%
1946	175,014	111,215	Brewster, Owen	63,799	MacDonald, Peter		47,416 R	63.5%	36.5%	63.5%	36.5%

MAINE

Congressional districts established for elections held from 1994 through 2002
2 members

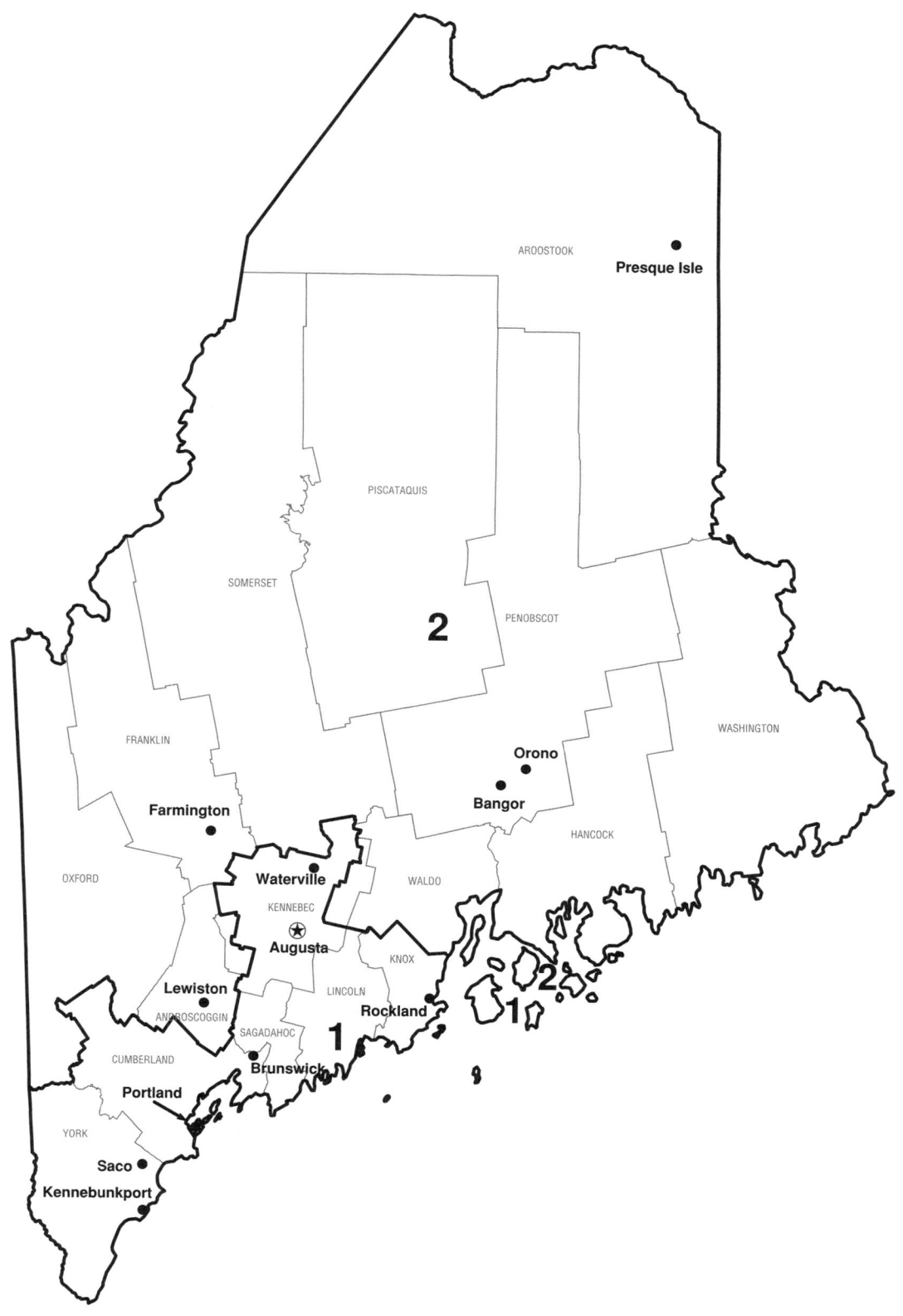

MAINE

GOVERNOR 2002

2000 Census Population	County	Total Vote	Republican	Democratic	Other	Rep.-Dem. Plurality	Percentage			
							Total Vote		Major Vote	
							Rep.	Dem.	Rep.	Dem.
103,793	ANDROSCOGGIN	36,735	15,069	17,064	4,602	1,995 D	41.0%	46.5%	46.9%	53.1%
73,938	AROOSTOOK	26,089	8,401	15,785	1,903	7,384 D	32.2%	60.5%	34.7%	65.3%
265,612	CUMBERLAND	114,268	50,095	49,900	14,273	195 R	43.8%	43.7%	50.1%	49.9%
29,467	FRANKLIN	11,335	4,711	5,147	1,477	436 D	41.6%	45.4%	47.8%	52.2%
51,791	HANCOCK	23,336	8,600	12,132	2,604	3,532 D	36.9%	52.0%	41.5%	58.5%
117,114	KENNEBEC	46,377	19,047	22,159	5,171	3,112 D	41.1%	47.8%	46.2%	53.8%
39,618	KNOX	16,390	7,266	6,636	2,488	630 R	44.3%	40.5%	52.3%	47.7%
33,616	LINCOLN	16,333	7,512	6,325	2,496	1,187 R	46.0%	38.7%	54.3%	45.7%
54,755	OXFORD	20,615	8,815	9,275	2,525	460 D	42.8%	45.0%	48.7%	51.3%
144,919	PENOBSCOT	55,758	20,861	31,619	3,278	10,758 D	37.4%	56.7%	39.8%	60.2%
17,235	PISCATAQUIS	7,106	3,045	3,583	478	538 D	42.9%	50.4%	45.9%	54.1%
35,214	SAGADAHOC	14,510	6,253	6,186	2,071	67 R	43.1%	42.6%	50.3%	49.7%
50,888	SOMERSET	18,073	7,932	8,475	1,666	543 D	43.9%	46.9%	48.3%	51.7%
36,280	WALDO	14,754	5,944	7,002	1,808	1,058 D	40.3%	47.5%	45.9%	54.1%
33,941	WASHINGTON	11,690	3,902	7,013	775	3,111 D	33.4%	60.0%	35.7%	64.3%
186,742	YORK	71,821	32,043	29,878	9,900	2,165 R	44.6%	41.6%	51.7%	48.3%
1,274,923	TOTAL	505,190	209,496	238,179	57,515	28,683 D	41.5%	47.1%	46.8%	53.2%
	City/Town									
23,203	AUBURN	8,580	3,501	3,924	1,155	423 D	40.8%	45.7%	47.2%	52.8%
18,560	AUGUSTA	7,168	2,657	3,786	725	1,129 D	37.1%	52.8%	41.2%	58.8%
31,473	BANGOR	11,249	3,627	6,986	636	3,359 D	32.2%	62.1%	34.2%	65.8%
9,266	BATH	3,532	1,361	1,670	501	309 D	38.5%	47.3%	44.9%	55.1%
6,381	BELFAST	2,746	988	1,418	340	430 D	36.0%	51.6%	41.1%	58.9%
6,353	BERWICK	1,781	855	702	224	153 R	48.0%	39.4%	54.9%	45.1%
20,942	BIDDEFORD	7,678	2,720	4,060	898	1,340 D	35.4%	52.9%	40.1%	59.9%
8,987	BREWER	3,836	1,545	2,087	204	542 D	40.3%	54.4%	42.5%	57.5%
21,172	BRUNSWICK	7,977	3,011	3,871	1,095	860 D	37.7%	48.5%	43.8%	56.2%
7,452	BUXTON	2,902	1,397	1,087	418	310 R	48.1%	37.5%	56.2%	43.8%
5,254	CAMDEN	2,639	1,017	1,192	430	175 D	38.5%	45.2%	46.0%	54.0%
9,068	CAPE ELIZABETH	5,083	2,478	2,046	559	432 R	48.8%	40.3%	54.8%	45.2%
8,312	CARIBOU	2,663	923	1,533	207	610 D	34.7%	57.6%	37.6%	62.4%
7,159	CUMBERLAND TOWN	3,867	2,196	1,313	358	883 R	56.8%	34.0%	62.6%	37.4%
5,954	ELIOT	2,477	1,178	951	348	227 R	47.6%	38.4%	55.3%	44.7%
6,456	ELLSWORTH	2,832	1,262	1,336	234	74 D	44.6%	47.2%	48.6%	51.4%
6,573	FAIRFIELD	2,309	891	1,171	247	280 D	38.6%	50.7%	43.2%	56.8%
10,310	FALMOUTH	5,684	3,095	2,104	485	991 R	54.5%	37.0%	59.5%	40.5%
7,410	FARMINGTON	2,538	1,046	1,121	371	75 D	41.2%	44.2%	48.3%	51.7%
7,800	FREEPORT	3,810	1,633	1,591	586	42 R	42.9%	41.8%	50.7%	49.3%
6,198	GARDINER	2,332	920	1,114	298	194 D	39.5%	47.8%	45.2%	54.8%
14,141	GORHAM	5,537	2,699	2,244	594	455 R	48.7%	40.5%	54.6%	45.4%
6,820	GRAY	2,903	1,612	1,009	282	603 R	55.5%	34.8%	61.5%	38.5%
6,327	HAMPDEN	3,012	1,298	1,556	158	258 D	43.1%	51.7%	45.5%	54.5%
5,239	HARPSWELL	2,742	1,239	1,100	403	139 R	45.2%	40.1%	53.0%	47.0%
6,476	HOULTON	1,990	765	1,130	95	365 D	38.4%	56.8%	40.4%	59.6%
4,985	JAY	1,924	572	1,176	176	604 D	29.7%	61.1%	32.7%	67.3%
10,476	KENNEBUNK	4,946	2,462	1,733	751	729 R	49.8%	35.0%	58.7%	41.3%
9,543	KITTERY	3,508	1,377	1,481	650	104 D	39.3%	42.2%	48.2%	51.8%
35,690	LEWISTON	11,770	4,040	6,393	1,337	2,353 D	34.3%	54.3%	38.7%	61.3%
2,361	LIMESTONE	620	189	387	44	198 D	30.5%	62.4%	32.8%	67.2%
5,221	LINCOLN TOWN	1,855	732	1,033	90	301 D	39.5%	55.7%	41.5%	58.5%
9,077	LISBON	3,168	1,401	1,369	398	32 R	44.2%	43.2%	50.6%	49.4%
5,203	MILLINOCKET	2,417	753	1,571	93	818 D	31.2%	65.0%	32.4%	67.6%
5,959	OAKLAND	2,082	927	963	192	36 D	44.5%	46.3%	49.0%	51.0%

MAINE

GOVERNOR 2002

2000 Census Population	City/Town	Total Vote	Republican	Democratic	Other	Rep.-Dem. Plurality		Percentage			
								Total Vote		Major Vote	
								Rep.	Dem.	Rep.	Dem.
8,856	OLD ORCHARD BEACH	3,561	1,461	1,633	467	172	D	41.0%	45.9%	47.2%	52.8%
8,130	OLD TOWN	3,038	844	1,987	207	1,143	D	27.8%	65.4%	29.8%	70.2%
9,112	ORONO	2,808	724	1,725	359	1,001	D	25.8%	61.4%	29.6%	70.4%
62,249	PORTLAND	24,955	7,295	13,518	4,142	6,223	D	29.2%	54.2%	35.1%	64.9%
9,511	PRESQUE ISLE	3,060	1,151	1,692	217	541	D	37.6%	55.3%	40.5%	59.5%
7,609	ROCKLAND	2,537	1,098	1,083	356	15	R	43.3%	42.7%	50.3%	49.7%
6,472	RUMFORD	2,490	719	1,573	198	854	D	28.9%	63.2%	31.4%	68.6%
16,822	SACO	6,566	2,616	3,234	716	618	D	39.8%	49.3%	44.7%	55.3%
20,806	SANFORD	7,131	2,875	3,403	853	528	D	40.3%	47.7%	45.8%	54.2%
16,970	SCARBOROUGH	7,996	4,389	2,954	653	1,435	R	54.9%	36.9%	59.8%	40.2%
8,824	SKOWHEGAN	2,982	1,129	1,600	253	471	D	37.9%	53.7%	41.4%	58.6%
6,671	SOUTH BERWICK	2,306	1,120	871	315	249	R	48.6%	37.8%	56.3%	43.7%
23,324	SOUTH PORTLAND	9,875	4,007	4,748	1,120	741	D	40.6%	48.1%	45.8%	54.2%
9,285	STANDISH	3,766	1,916	1,432	418	484	R	50.9%	38.0%	57.2%	42.8%
9,100	TOPSHAM	3,616	1,645	1,546	425	99	R	45.5%	42.8%	51.6%	48.4%
15,605	WATERVILLE	4,889	1,515	2,844	530	1,329	D	31.0%	58.2%	34.8%	65.2%
9,400	WELLS	3,844	1,895	1,454	495	441	R	49.3%	37.8%	56.6%	43.4%
16,142	WESTBROOK	6,453	2,712	3,098	643	386	D	42.0%	48.0%	46.7%	53.3%
14,904	WINDHAM	5,858	2,951	2,269	638	682	R	50.4%	38.7%	56.5%	43.5%
7,743	WINSLOW	3,217	1,307	1,651	259	344	D	40.6%	51.3%	44.2%	55.8%
6,232	WINTHROP	2,664	1,223	1,177	264	46	R	45.9%	44.2%	51.0%	49.0%
8,360	YARMOUTH	4,349	2,231	1,636	482	595	R	51.3%	37.6%	57.7%	42.3%
12,854	YORK TOWN	5,605	2,750	2,016	839	734	R	49.1%	36.0%	57.7%	42.3%

MAINE

SENATOR 2002

2000 Census Population	County	Total Vote	Republican	Democratic	Other	Rep.-Dem. Plurality		Percentage			
								Total Vote		Major Vote	
								Rep.	Dem.	Rep.	Dem.
103,793	ANDROSCOGGIN	36,407	20,095	16,312		3,783	R	55.2%	44.8%	55.2%	44.8%
73,938	AROOSTOOK	26,156	17,869	8,287		9,582	R	68.3%	31.7%	68.3%	31.7%
265,612	CUMBERLAND	114,218	64,123	50,095		14,028	R	56.1%	43.9%	56.1%	43.9%
29,467	FRANKLIN	11,328	6,555	4,773		1,782	R	57.9%	42.1%	57.9%	42.1%
51,791	HANCOCK	23,284	13,399	9,885		3,514	R	57.5%	42.5%	57.5%	42.5%
117,114	KENNEBEC	46,339	24,724	21,615		3,109	R	53.4%	46.6%	53.4%	46.6%
39,618	KNOX	16,522	8,691	7,831		860	R	52.6%	47.4%	52.6%	47.4%
33,616	LINCOLN	16,198	9,609	6,589		3,020	R	59.3%	40.7%	59.3%	40.7%
54,755	OXFORD	20,609	11,821	8,788		3,033	R	57.4%	42.6%	57.4%	42.6%
144,919	PENOBSCOT	55,529	35,024	20,505		14,519	R	63.1%	36.9%	63.1%	36.9%
17,235	PISCATAQUIS	7,092	4,633	2,459		2,174	R	65.3%	34.7%	65.3%	34.7%
35,214	SAGADAHOC	14,787	8,403	6,384		2,019	R	56.8%	43.2%	56.8%	43.2%
50,888	SOMERSET	18,038	10,353	7,685		2,668	R	57.4%	42.6%	57.4%	42.6%
36,280	WALDO	14,727	8,489	6,238		2,251	R	57.6%	42.4%	57.6%	42.4%
33,941	WASHINGTON	11,747	7,697	4,050		3,647	R	65.5%	34.5%	65.5%	34.5%
186,742	YORK	71,918	43,556	28,362		15,194	R	60.6%	39.4%	60.6%	39.4%
1,274,923	TOTAL	504,899	295,041	209,858		85,183	R	58.4%	41.6%	58.4%	41.6%

MAINE

SENATOR 2002

2000 Census Population	City/Town	Total Vote	Republican	Democratic	Other	Rep.-Dem. Plurality	Total Vote Rep.	Total Vote Dem.	Major Vote Rep.	Major Vote Dem.
23,203	AUBURN	8,237	4,430	3,807		623 R	53.8%	46.2%	53.8%	46.2%
18,560	AUGUSTA	7,189	3,804	3,385		419 R	52.9%	47.1%	52.9%	47.1%
31,473	BANGOR	11,184	6,825	4,359		2,466 R	61.0%	39.0%	61.0%	39.0%
9,266	BATH	3,537	1,827	1,710		117 R	51.7%	48.3%	51.7%	48.3%
6,381	BELFAST	2,747	1,500	1,247		253 R	54.6%	45.4%	54.6%	45.4%
6,353	BERWICK	1,789	1,246	543		703 R	69.6%	30.4%	69.6%	30.4%
20,942	BIDDEFORD	7,677	4,124	3,553		571 R	53.7%	46.3%	53.7%	46.3%
8,987	BREWER	3,824	2,583	1,241		1,342 R	67.5%	32.5%	67.5%	32.5%
21,172	BRUNSWICK	7,999	3,958	4,041		83 D	49.5%	50.5%	49.5%	50.5%
7,452	BUXTON	2,905	1,862	1,043		819 R	64.1%	35.9%	64.1%	35.9%
5,254	CAMDEN	2,657	1,183	1,474		291 D	44.5%	55.5%	44.5%	55.5%
9,068	CAPE ELIZABETH	5,070	2,971	2,099		872 R	58.6%	41.4%	58.6%	41.4%
8,312	CARIBOU	2,678	1,988	690		1,298 R	74.2%	25.8%	74.2%	25.8%
7,159	CUMBERLAND TOWN	3,862	2,549	1,313		1,236 R	66.0%	34.0%	66.0%	34.0%
5,954	ELIOT	2,470	1,555	915		640 R	63.0%	37.0%	63.0%	37.0%
6,456	ELLSWORTH	2,832	1,883	949		934 R	66.5%	33.5%	66.5%	33.5%
6,573	FAIRFIELD	2,315	1,147	1,168		21 D	49.5%	50.5%	49.5%	50.5%
10,310	FALMOUTH	5,692	3,727	1,965		1,762 R	65.5%	34.5%	65.5%	34.5%
7,410	FARMINGTON	2,523	1,463	1,060		403 R	58.0%	42.0%	58.0%	42.0%
7,800	FREEPORT	3,810	2,035	1,775		260 R	53.4%	46.6%	53.4%	46.6%
6,198	GARDINER	2,320	1,253	1,067		186 R	54.0%	46.0%	54.0%	46.0%
14,141	GORHAM	5,514	3,516	1,998		1,518 R	63.8%	36.2%	63.8%	36.2%
6,820	GRAY	2,959	2,040	919		1,121 R	68.9%	31.1%	68.9%	31.1%
6,327	HAMPDEN	2,991	2,051	940		1,111 R	68.6%	31.4%	68.6%	31.4%
5,239	HARPSWELL	2,749	1,555	1,194		361 R	56.6%	43.4%	56.6%	43.4%
6,476	HOULTON	1,997	1,493	504		989 R	74.8%	25.2%	74.8%	25.2%
4,985	JAY	1,936	867	1,069		202 D	44.8%	55.2%	44.8%	55.2%
10,476	KENNEBUNK	4,935	3,084	1,851		1,233 R	62.5%	37.5%	62.5%	37.5%
9,543	KITTERY	3,529	1,958	1,571		387 R	55.5%	44.5%	55.5%	44.5%
35,690	LEWISTON	11,815	5,769	6,046		277 D	48.8%	51.2%	48.8%	51.2%
2,361	LIMESTONE	627	424	203		221 R	67.6%	32.4%	67.6%	32.4%
5,221	LINCOLN TOWN	1,833	1,250	583		667 R	68.2%	31.8%	68.2%	31.8%
9,077	LISBON	3,162	1,921	1,241		680 R	60.8%	39.2%	60.8%	39.2%
5,203	MILLINOCKET	2,417	1,344	1,073		271 R	55.6%	44.4%	55.6%	44.4%
5,959	OAKLAND	2,080	1,110	970		140 R	53.4%	46.6%	53.4%	46.6%
8,856	OLD ORCHARD BEACH	3,557	1,942	1,615		327 R	54.6%	45.4%	54.6%	45.4%
8,130	OLD TOWN	3,015	1,557	1,458		99 R	51.6%	48.4%	51.6%	48.4%
9,112	ORONO	2,796	1,305	1,491		186 D	46.7%	53.3%	46.7%	53.3%
62,249	PORTLAND	24,919	10,239	14,680		4,441 D	41.1%	58.9%	41.1%	58.9%
9,511	PRESQUE ISLE	3,037	2,175	862		1,313 R	71.6%	28.4%	71.6%	28.4%
7,609	ROCKLAND	2,546	1,273	1,273			50.0%	50.0%	50.0%	50.0%
6,472	RUMFORD	2,498	1,072	1,426		354 D	42.9%	57.1%	42.9%	57.1%
16,822	SACO	6,558	3,678	2,880		798 R	56.1%	43.9%	56.1%	43.9%
20,806	SANFORD	7,150	4,136	3,014		1,122 R	57.8%	42.2%	57.8%	42.2%
16,970	SCARBOROUGH	7,965	5,276	2,689		2,587 R	66.2%	33.8%	66.2%	33.8%
8,824	SKOWHEGAN	3,001	1,543	1,458		85 R	51.4%	48.6%	51.4%	48.6%
6,671	SOUTH BERWICK	2,308	1,494	814		680 R	64.7%	35.3%	64.7%	35.3%
23,324	SOUTH PORTLAND	9,862	5,098	4,764		334 R	51.7%	48.3%	51.7%	48.3%
9,285	STANDISH	3,750	2,487	1,263		1,224 R	66.3%	33.7%	66.3%	33.7%
9,100	TOPSHAM	3,929	2,461	1,468		993 R	62.6%	37.4%	62.6%	37.4%
15,605	WATERVILLE	4,864	1,936	2,928		992 D	39.8%	60.2%	39.8%	60.2%
9,400	WELLS	3,846	2,472	1,374		1,098 R	64.3%	35.7%	64.3%	35.7%
16,142	WESTBROOK	6,480	3,769	2,711		1,058 R	58.2%	41.8%	58.2%	41.8%
14,904	WINDHAM	5,855	3,825	2,030		1,795 R	65.3%	34.7%	65.3%	34.7%
7,743	WINSLOW	3,243	1,529	1,714		185 D	47.1%	52.9%	47.1%	52.9%
6,232	WINTHROP	2,645	1,619	1,026		593 R	61.2%	38.8%	61.2%	38.8%
8,360	YARMOUTH	4,342	2,700	1,642		1,058 R	62.2%	37.8%	62.2%	37.8%
12,854	YORK TOWN	5,622	3,474	2,148		1,326 R	61.8%	38.2%	61.8%	38.2%

MAINE

HOUSE OF REPRESENTATIVES

			Republican		Democratic		Other	Rep.-Dem.	Total Vote		Major Vote	
									Percentage			
CD	Year	Total Vote	Vote	Candidate	Vote	Candidate	Vote	Plurality	Rep.	Dem.	Rep.	Dem.
1	2002	270,577	97,931	Joyce, Steven	172,646	Allen, Tom*		74,715 D	36.2%	63.8%	36.2%	63.8%
2	2002	224,717	107,849	Raye, Kevin L.	116,868	Michaud, Michael H.		9,019 D	48.0%	52.0%	48.0%	52.0%
Total	2002	495,294	205,780		289,514			83,734 D	41.5%	58.5%	41.5%	58.5%

An asterisk (*) denotes incumbent.

MAINE

GENERAL AND PRIMARY ELECTIONS

2002 GENERAL ELECTIONS

Governor   Other vote was 46,903 Green Independent (Jonathan K. Carter); 10,612 Independent (John M. Michael).

Senator

House   Other vote was:

  CD 1
  CD 2

2002 PRIMARY ELECTIONS

Primary   June 11, 2002

Registration
(as of June 11, 2002)

Republican	269,237
Democratic	288,524
Green Independent	13,272
Unenrolled	341,061
TOTAL	912,094

Primary Type   Semi-open—Registered Democrats and Republicans can participate only in their party's primary. "Unenrolled" and new voters can vote in either party's primary by enrolling in that party on primary day.

Note: An asterisk (*) denotes incumbent.

REPUBLICAN PRIMARIES				DEMOCRATIC PRIMARIES		
Governor	Peter E. Cianchette	52,692	66.9%	John Baldacci	71,735	100.0%
	James D. Libby	26,091	33.1%			
	TOTAL	78,783				
Senator	Susan Collins*	74,643	100.0%	Chellie Pingree	59,732	100.0%
Congressional District 1	Steven Joyce	34,291	100.0%	Tom Allen*	32,085	100.0%
Congressional District 2	Kevin L. Raye	11,861	30.6%	Michael H. Michaud	12,230	31.4%
	Timothy C. Woodcock	11,542	29.7%	Susan W. Longley	10,800	27.7%
	Stavros J. Mendros	8,022	20.7%	Sean Faircloth	7,829	20.1%
	Richard H. Campbell	7,383	19.0%	John M. Nutting	4,751	12.2%
				David Costello	1,773	4.5%
				Lori M. Handrahan	1,623	4.2%
	TOTAL	38,808		TOTAL	39,006	

MAINE REPUBLICAN PRIMARY

GOVERNOR 2002

2000 Census Population	County	Total Vote	Cianchette	Libby	Winner	Percentage of Total Vote Cianchette	Libby
103,793	ANDROSCOGGIN	4,177	2,734	1,443	Cianchette	65.5%	34.5%
73,938	AROOSTOOK	2,912	1,897	1,015	Cianchette	65.1%	34.9%
265,612	CUMBERLAND	16,688	11,352	5,336	Cianchette	68.0%	32.0%
29,467	FRANKLIN	2,035	1,396	639	Cianchette	68.6%	31.4%
51,791	HANCOCK	4,513	3,196	1,317	Cianchette	70.8%	29.2%
117,114	KENNEBEC	6,353	4,474	1,879	Cianchette	70.4%	29.6%
39,618	KNOX	3,186	2,269	917	Cianchette	71.2%	28.8%
33,616	LINCOLN	3,322	2,145	1,177	Cianchette	64.6%	35.4%
54,755	OXFORD	3,434	2,282	1,152	Cianchette	66.5%	33.5%
144,919	PENOBSCOT	10,143	7,601	2,542	Cianchette	74.9%	25.1%
17,235	PISCATAQUIS	1,285	879	406	Cianchette	68.4%	31.6%
35,214	SAGADAHOC	2,213	1,523	690	Cianchette	68.8%	31.2%
50,888	SOMERSET	3,211	2,461	750	Cianchette	76.6%	23.4%
36,280	WALDO	2,714	1,956	758	Cianchette	72.1%	27.9%
33,941	WASHINGTON	1,989	1,317	672	Cianchette	66.2%	33.8%
186,742	YORK	10,608	5,210	5,398	Libby	49.1%	50.9%
1,274,923	TOTAL	78,783	52,692	26,091	Cianchette	66.9%	33.1%

	City/Town						
23,203	AUBURN	1,096	758	338	Cianchette	69.2%	30.8%
18,560	AUGUSTA	882	610	272	Cianchette	69.2%	30.8%
31,473	BANGOR	2,150	1,691	459	Cianchette	78.7%	21.3%
9,266	BATH	570	441	129	Cianchette	77.4%	22.6%
6,381	BELFAST	501	388	113	Cianchette	77.4%	22.6%
6,353	BERWICK	167	101	66	Cianchette	60.5%	39.5%
20,942	BIDDEFORD	296	175	121	Cianchette	59.1%	40.9%
8,987	BREWER	1,007	789	218	Cianchette	78.4%	21.6%
21,172	BRUNSWICK	786	573	213	Cianchette	72.9%	27.1%
7,452	BUXTON	720	126	594	Libby	17.5%	82.5%
5,254	CAMDEN	512	389	123	Cianchette	76.0%	24.0%
9,068	CAPE ELIZABETH	852	677	175	Cianchette	79.5%	20.5%
8,312	CARIBOU	345	228	117	Cianchette	66.1%	33.9%
7,159	CUMBERLAND TOWN	1,000	803	197	Cianchette	80.3%	19.7%
5,954	ELIOT	477	307	170	Cianchette	64.4%	35.6%
6,456	ELLSWORTH	801	590	211	Cianchette	73.7%	26.3%
6,573	FAIRFIELD	287	218	69	Cianchette	76.0%	24.0%
10,310	FALMOUTH	1,355	1,028	327	Cianchette	75.9%	24.1%
7,410	FARMINGTON	510	376	134	Cianchette	73.7%	26.3%
7,800	FREEPORT	452	322	130	Cianchette	71.2%	28.8%
6,198	GARDINER	357	255	102	Cianchette	71.4%	28.6%
14,141	GORHAM	777	388	389	Libby	49.9%	50.1%
6,820	GRAY	437	287	150	Cianchette	65.7%	34.3%
6,327	HAMPDEN	689	545	144	Cianchette	79.1%	20.9%
5,239	HARPSWELL	421	302	119	Cianchette	71.7%	28.3%
6,476	HOULTON	250	168	82	Cianchette	67.2%	32.8%
4,985	JAY	144	86	58	Cianchette	59.7%	40.3%
10,476	KENNEBUNK	1,325	842	483	Cianchette	63.5%	36.5%
9,543	KITTERY	790	528	262	Cianchette	66.8%	33.2%
35,690	LEWISTON	1,030	739	291	Cianchette	71.7%	28.3%
2,361	LIMESTONE	140	89	51	Cianchette	63.6%	36.4%
5,221	LINCOLN TOWN	374	272	102	Cianchette	72.7%	27.3%
9,077	LISBON	384	228	156	Cianchette	59.4%	40.6%
5,203	MILLINOCKET	303	233	70	Cianchette	76.9%	23.1%
5,959	OAKLAND	247	186	61	Cianchette	75.3%	24.7%

MAINE REPUBLICAN PRIMARY

GOVERNOR 2002

2000 Census Population	City/Town	Total Vote	Cianchette	Libby	Winner	Percentage of Total Vote	
						Cianchette	Libby
8,856	OLD ORCHARD BEACH	178	114	64	Cianchette	64.0%	36.0%
8,130	OLD TOWN	408	296	112	Cianchette	72.5%	27.5%
9,112	ORONO	360	282	78	Cianchette	78.3%	21.7%
62,249	PORTLAND	2,226	1,543	683	Cianchette	69.3%	30.7%
9,511	PRESQUE ISLE	442	337	105	Cianchette	76.2%	23.8%
7,609	ROCKLAND	482	350	132	Cianchette	72.6%	27.4%
6,472	RUMFORD	270	210	60	Cianchette	77.8%	22.2%
16,822	SACO	497	264	233	Cianchette	53.1%	46.9%
20,806	SANFORD	699	329	370	Libby	47.1%	52.9%
16,970	SCARBOROUGH	1,120	761	359	Cianchette	67.9%	32.1%
8,824	SKOWHEGAN	452	358	94	Cianchette	79.2%	20.8%
6,671	SOUTH BERWICK	302	200	102	Cianchette	66.2%	33.8%
23,324	SOUTH PORTLAND	1,289	953	336	Cianchette	73.9%	26.1%
9,285	STANDISH	1,010	467	543	Libby	46.2%	53.8%
9,100	TOPSHAM	418	298	120	Cianchette	71.3%	28.7%
15,605	WATERVILLE	487	379	108	Cianchette	77.8%	22.2%
9,400	WELLS	583	388	195	Cianchette	66.6%	33.4%
16,142	WESTBROOK	714	452	262	Cianchette	63.3%	36.7%
14,904	WINDHAM	935	590	345	Cianchette	63.1%	36.9%
7,743	WINSLOW	264	204	60	Cianchette	77.3%	22.7%
6,232	WINTHROP	378	259	119	Cianchette	68.5%	31.5%
8,360	YARMOUTH	1,045	816	229	Cianchette	78.1%	21.9%
12,854	YORK TOWN	442	302	140	Cianchette	68.3%	31.7%

MARYLAND

GOVERNOR
Robert L. Ehrlich Jr. (R). Elected 2002 to a four-year term.

SENATORS (2 Democrats)
Barbara A. Mikulski (D). Reelected 1998 to a six-year term. Previously elected 1992, 1986.

Paul S. Sarbanes (D). Reelected 2000 to a six-year term. Previously elected 1994, 1988, 1982, 1976.

REPRESENTATIVES (6 Democrats, 2 Republicans)
1. Wayne T. Gilchrest (R)
2. C.A. Dutch Ruppersberger (D)
3. Benjamin L. Cardin (D)
4. Albert R. Wynn (D)
5. Steny H. Hoyer (D)
6. Roscoe G. Bartlett (R)
7. Elijah E. Cummings (D)
8. Chris Van Hollen (D)

POSTWAR VOTE FOR PRESIDENT

| | | Republican | | Democratic | | Other | | Percentage | | | |
| | | | | | | | | Total Vote | | Major Vote | |
Year	Total Vote	Vote	Candidate	Vote	Candidate	Vote	Plurality	Rep.	Dem.	Rep.	Dem.
2000**	2,020,480	813,797	Bush, George W.	1,140,782	Gore, Al	65,901	326,985 D	40.3%	56.5%	41.6%	58.4%
1996**	1,780,870	681,530	Dole, Bob	966,207	Clinton, Bill	133,133	284,677 D	38.3%	54.3%	41.4%	58.6%
1992**	1,985,046	707,094	Bush, George	988,571	Clinton, Bill	289,381	281,477 D	35.6%	49.8%	41.7%	58.3%
1988	1,714,358	876,167	Bush, George	826,304	Dukakis, Michael S.	11,887	49,863 R	51.1%	48.2%	51.5%	48.5%
1984	1,675,873	879,918	Reagan, Ronald	787,935	Mondale, Walter F.	8,020	91,983 R	52.5%	47.0%	52.8%	47.2%
1980**	1,540,496	680,606	Reagan, Ronald	726,161	Carter, Jimmy	133,729	45,555 D	44.2%	47.1%	48.4%	51.6%
1976	1,439,897	672,661	Ford, Gerald R.	759,612	Carter, Jimmy	7,624	86,951 D	46.7%	52.8%	47.0%	53.0%
1972	1,353,812	829,305	Nixon, Richard M.	505,781	McGovern, George S.	18,726	323,524 R	61.3%	37.4%	62.1%	37.9%
1968	1,235,039	517,995	Nixon, Richard M.	538,310	Humphrey, Hubert H.	178,734	20,315 D	41.9%	43.6%	49.0%	51.0%
1964	1,116,457	385,495	Goldwater, Barry M.	730,912	Johnson, Lyndon B.	50	345,417 D	34.5%	65.5%	34.5%	65.5%
1960	1,055,349	489,538	Nixon, Richard M.	565,808	Kennedy, John F.	3	76,270 D	46.4%	53.6%	46.4%	53.6%
1956	932,827	559,738	Eisenhower, Dwight D.	372,613	Stevenson, Adlai E.	476	187,125 R	60.0%	39.9%	60.0%	40.0%
1952	902,074	499,424	Eisenhower, Dwight D.	395,337	Stevenson, Adlai E.	7,313	104,087 R	55.4%	43.8%	55.8%	44.2%
1948	596,748	294,814	Dewey, Thomas E.	286,521	Truman, Harry S.	15,413	8,293 R	49.4%	48.0%	50.7%	49.3%

In 2000 the other vote column includes 53,768 votes cast for Green (Nader). In 1996 the other vote column includes 115,812 votes cast for Perot. In 1992 the other vote column includes 281,414 votes cast for Perot. In 1980 the other column includes 119,537 votes for Independent (Anderson).

MARYLAND

POSTWAR VOTE FOR GOVERNOR

Year	Total Vote	Republican Vote	Candidate	Democratic Vote	Candidate	Other Vote	Rep.-Dem. Plurality	Total Vote Rep.	Total Vote Dem.	Major Vote Rep.	Major Vote Dem.
2002	1,706,179	879,592	Ehrlich, Robert L. Jr.	813,422	Townsend, Kathleen Kennedy	13,165	66,170 R	51.6%	47.7%	52.0%	48.0%
1998	1,535,978	688,357	Sauerbrey, Ellen R.	846,972	Glendening, Parris N.	649	158,615 D	44.8%	55.1%	44.8%	55.2%
1994	1,410,300	702,101	Sauerbrey, Ellen R.	708,094	Glendening, Parris N.	105	5,993 D	49.8%	50.2%	49.8%	50.2%
1990	1,111,088	446,980	Shepard, William S.	664,015	Schaefer, William D.	93	217,035 D	40.2%	59.8%	40.2%	59.8%
1986	1,101,476	194,185	Mooney, Thomas J.	907,291	Schaefer, William D.		713,106 D	17.6%	82.4%	17.6%	82.4%
1982	1,139,149	432,826	Pascal, Robert A.	705,910	Hughes, Harry	413	273,084 D	38.0%	62.0%	38.0%	62.0%
1978	1,011,963	293,635	Beall, J. Glenn, Jr.	718,328	Hughes, Harry		424,693 D	29.0%	71.0%	29.0%	71.0%
1974	949,097	346,449	Gore, Louise	602,648	Mandel, Marvin		256,199 D	36.5%	63.5%	36.5%	63.5%
1970	973,099	314,336	Blain, C. Stanley	639,579	Mandel, Marvin	19,184	325,243 D	32.3%	65.7%	33.0%	67.0%
1966	918,761	455,318	Agnew, Spiro T.	373,543	Mahoney, George P.	89,900	81,775 R	49.6%	40.7%	54.9%	45.1%
1962	775,101	343,051	Small, Frank	432,045	Tawes, J. Millard	5	88,994 D	44.3%	55.7%	44.3%	55.7%
1958	763,234	278,173	Devereux, James	485,061	Tawes, J. Millard		206,888 D	36.4%	63.6%	36.4%	63.6%
1954	700,484	381,451	McKeldin, Theodore	319,033	Byrd, Harry C.		62,418 R	54.5%	45.5%	54.5%	45.5%
1950	645,631	369,807	McKeldin, Theodore	275,824	Lane, William P.		93,983 R	57.3%	42.7%	57.3%	42.7%
1946	489,836	221,752	McKeldin, Theodore	268,084	Lane, William P.		46,332 D	45.3%	54.7%	45.3%	54.7%

POSTWAR VOTE FOR SENATOR

Year	Total Vote	Republican Vote	Candidate	Democratic Vote	Candidate	Other Vote	Rep.-Dem. Plurality	Total Vote Rep.	Total Vote Dem.	Major Vote Rep.	Major Vote Dem.
2000	1,946,898	715,178	Rappaport, Paul	1,230,013	Sarbanes, Paul S.	1,707	514,835 D	36.7%	63.2%	36.8%	63.2%
1998	1,507,447	444,637	Pierpont, Ross Z.	1,062,810	Mikulski, Barbara A.		618,173 D	29.5%	70.5%	29.5%	70.5%
1994	1,369,104	559,908	Brock, William E.	809,125	Sarbanes, Paul S.	71	249,217 D	40.9%	59.1%	40.9%	59.1%
1992	1,841,735	533,688	Keyes, Alan L.	1,307,610	Mikulski, Barbara A.	437	773,922 D	29.0%	71.0%	29.0%	71.0%
1988	1,617,065	617,537	Keyes, Alan L.	999,166	Sarbanes, Paul S.	362	381,629 D	38.2%	61.8%	38.2%	61.8%
1986	1,112,637	437,411	Chavez, Linda	675,225	Mikulski, Barbara A.	1	237,814 D	39.3%	60.7%	39.3%	60.7%
1982	1,114,690	407,334	Hogan, Lawrence J.	707,356	Sarbanes, Paul S.		300,022 D	36.5%	63.5%	36.5%	63.5%
1980	1,286,088	850,970	Mathias, Charles	435,118	Conroy, Edward T.		415,852 R	66.2%	33.8%	66.2%	33.8%
1976	1,365,568	530,439	Beall, J. Glenn, Jr.	772,101	Sarbanes, Paul S.	63,028	241,662 D	38.8%	56.5%	40.7%	59.3%
1974	877,786	503,223	Mathias, Charles	374,563	Mikulski, Barbara A.		128,660 R	57.3%	42.7%	57.3%	42.7%
1970	956,370	484,960	Beall, J. Glenn, Jr.	460,422	Tydings, Joseph D.	10,988	24,538 R	50.7%	48.1%	51.3%	48.7%
1968	1,133,727	541,893	Mathias, Charles	443,367	Brewster, Daniel B.	148,467	98,526 R	47.8%	39.1%	55.0%	45.0%
1964	1,081,049	402,393	Beall, J. Glenn	678,649	Tydings, Joseph D.	7	276,256 D	37.2%	62.8%	37.2%	62.8%
1962	714,248	270,312	Miller, Edward T.	443,935	Brewster, Daniel B.	1	173,623 D	37.8%	62.2%	37.8%	62.2%
1958	749,291	382,021	Beall, J. Glenn	367,270	D'Alesandro, Thomas		14,751 R	51.0%	49.0%	51.0%	49.0%
1956	892,167	473,059	Butler, John Marshall	419,108	Mahoney, George P.		53,951 R	53.0%	47.0%	53.0%	47.0%
1952	856,193	449,823	Beall, J. Glenn	406,370	Mahoney, George P.		43,453 R	52.5%	47.5%	52.5%	47.5%
1950	615,614	326,291	Butler, John Marshall	283,180	Tydings, Millard E.	6,143	43,111 R	53.0%	46.0%	53.5%	46.5%
1946	472,232	235,000	Markey, David John	237,232	O'Conor, Herbert R.		2,232 D	49.8%	50.2%	49.8%	50.2%

MARYLAND

Congressional districts first established for elections held in 2002
8 members

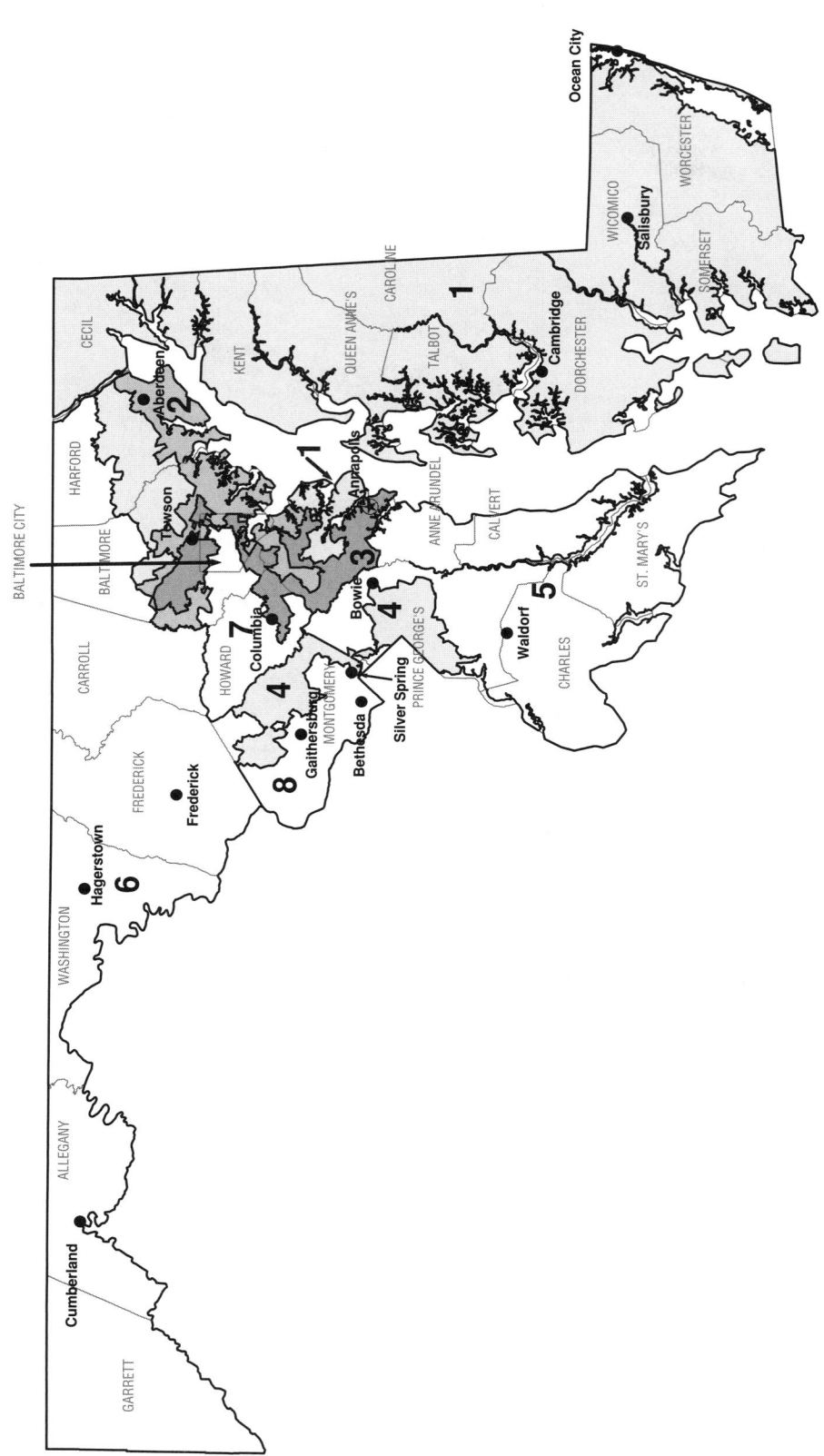

MARYLAND

Baltimore, Washington, D.C., Area

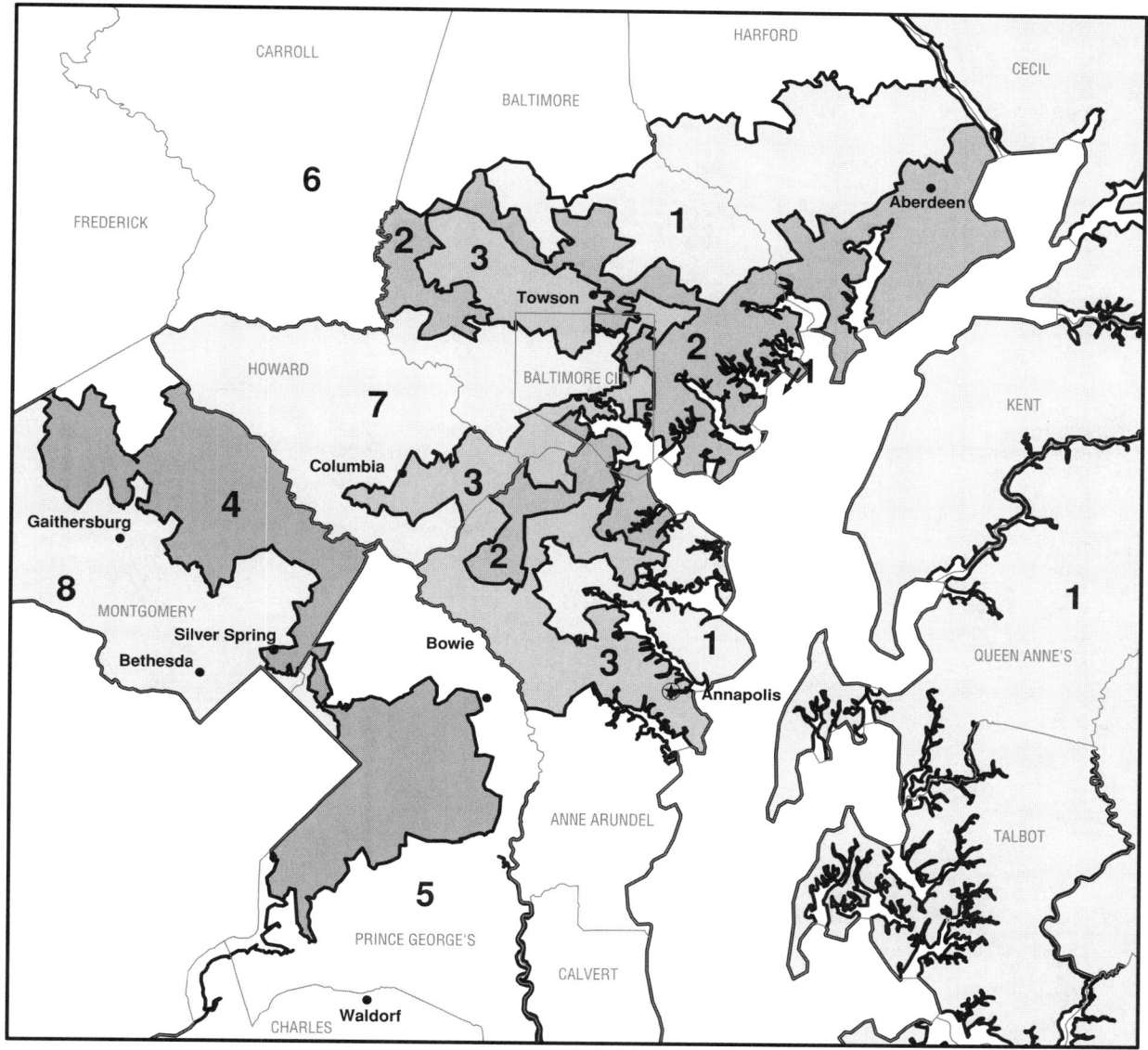

MARYLAND

GOVERNOR 2002

2000 Census Population	County	Total Vote	Republican	Democratic	Other	Rep.-Dem. Plurality	Percentage Total Vote Rep.	Total Vote Dem.	Major Vote Rep.	Major Vote Dem.
74,930	ALLEGANY	22,448	14,416	7,831	201	6,585 R	64.2%	34.9%	64.8%	35.2%
489,656	ANNE ARUNDEL	176,179	113,968	60,753	1,458	53,215 R	64.7%	34.5%	65.2%	34.8%
651,154	BALTIMORE CITY	160,106	38,838	120,070	1,198	81,232 D	24.3%	75.0%	24.4%	75.6%
754,292	BALTIMORE COUNTY	279,387	170,920	106,195	2,272	64,725 R	61.2%	38.0%	61.7%	38.3%
74,563	CALVERT	26,255	16,193	9,854	208	6,339 R	61.7%	37.5%	62.2%	37.8%
29,772	CAROLINE	8,418	6,286	2,069	63	4,217 R	74.7%	24.6%	75.2%	24.8%
150,897	CARROLL	59,946	47,328	12,107	511	35,221 R	79.0%	20.2%	79.6%	20.4%
85,951	CECIL	24,891	16,956	7,668	267	9,288 R	68.1%	30.8%	68.9%	31.1%
120,546	CHARLES	35,100	19,695	15,149	256	4,546 R	56.1%	43.2%	56.5%	43.5%
30,674	DORCHESTER	10,325	6,941	3,316	68	3,625 R	67.2%	32.1%	67.7%	32.3%
195,277	FREDERICK	66,155	43,646	21,913	596	21,733 R	66.0%	33.1%	66.6%	33.4%
29,846	GARRETT	9,019	6,604	2,355	60	4,249 R	73.2%	26.1%	73.7%	26.3%
218,590	HARFORD	85,503	63,553	21,246	704	42,307 R	74.3%	24.8%	74.9%	25.1%
247,842	HOWARD	96,508	53,260	42,438	810	10,822 R	55.2%	44.0%	55.7%	44.3%
19,197	KENT	7,710	5,012	2,641	57	2,371 R	65.0%	34.3%	65.5%	34.5%
873,341	MONTGOMERY	296,524	113,680	180,576	2,268	66,896 D	38.3%	60.9%	38.6%	61.4%
801,515	PRINCE GEORGES	197,194	45,193	150,927	1,074	105,734 D	22.9%	76.5%	23.0%	77.0%
40,563	QUEEN ANNES	16,642	12,341	4,190	111	8,151 R	74.2%	25.2%	74.7%	25.3%
86,211	ST. MARYS	25,299	15,986	9,048	265	6,938 R	63.2%	35.8%	63.9%	36.1%
24,747	SOMERSET	6,608	4,516	2,052	40	2,464 R	68.3%	31.1%	68.8%	31.2%
33,812	TALBOT	14,305	10,002	4,225	78	5,777 R	69.9%	29.5%	70.3%	29.7%
131,923	WASHINGTON	38,345	26,312	11,719	314	14,593 R	68.6%	30.6%	69.2%	30.8%
84,644	WICOMICO	24,995	16,054	8,775	166	7,279 R	64.2%	35.1%	64.7%	35.3%
46,543	WORCESTER	18,317	11,892	6,305	120	5,587 R	64.9%	34.4%	65.4%	34.6%
5,296,486	TOTAL	1,706,179	879,592	813,422	13,165	66,170 R	51.6%	47.7%	52.0%	48.0%

MARYLAND

HOUSE OF REPRESENTATIVES

CD	Year	Total Vote	Republican Vote	Republican Candidate	Democratic Vote	Democratic Candidate	Other Vote	Rep.-Dem. Plurality	Total Vote Rep.	Total Vote Dem.	Major Vote Rep.	Major Vote Dem.
1	2002	250,413	192,004	Gilchrest, Wayne T.*	57,986	Tamlyn, Ann D.	423	134,018 R	76.7%	23.2%	76.8%	23.2%
2	2002	195,202	88,954	Bentley, Helen Delich	105,718	Ruppersberger, C.A. Dutch	530	16,764 D	45.6%	54.2%	45.7%	54.3%
3	2002	221,543	75,721	Conwell, Scott	145,589	Cardin, Benjamin L.*	233	69,868 D	34.2%	65.7%	34.2%	65.8%
4	2002	167,555	34,890	Kimble, John B.	131,644	Wynn, Albert R.*	1,021	96,754 D	20.8%	78.6%	21.0%	79.0%
5	2002	199,087	60,758	Crawford, Joseph T.	137,903	Hoyer, Steny H.*	426	77,145 D	30.5%	69.3%	30.6%	69.4%
6	2002	223,611	147,825	Bartlett, Roscoe G.*	75,575	DeArmon, Donald M.	211	72,250 R	66.1%	33.8%	66.2%	33.8%
7	2002	186,394	49,172	Ward, Joseph E.	137,047	Cummings, Elijah E.*	175	87,875 D	26.4%	73.5%	26.4%	73.6%
8	2002	218,113	103,587	Morella, Constance A.*	112,788	Van Hollen, Chris	1,738	9,201 D	47.5%	51.7%	47.9%	52.1%
Total	2002	1,661,918	752,911		904,250		4,757	151,339 D	45.3%	54.4%	45.4%	54.6%

An asterisk (*) denotes incumbent.

MARYLAND
GENERAL AND PRIMARY ELECTIONS

2002 GENERAL ELECTIONS

Governor   Other vote was 11,546 Libertarian (Spear Lancaster); 201 write-in/Democratic (Ralph Jaffe); 61 write-in/Democratic (James T. Lynch Jr.); 1,357 scattered write-in. Write-in candidates could designate a party affiliation.

House   Other vote was:

CD 1   423 scattered write-in.
CD 2   530 scattered write-in.
CD 3   233 scattered write-in.
CD 4   162 write-in/Democratic (Mignon Davis); 33 write-in/Republican (Floyd W. Anderson Jr.); 826 scattered write-in.
CD 5   186 write-in/Green (B. Auerbach); 240 scattered write-in.
CD 6   211 scattered write-in.
CD 7   175 scattered write-in.
CD 8   1,599 Unaffiliated (Stephen Bassett); 139 scattered write-in.

2002 PRIMARY ELECTIONS

Primary   September 10, 2002

Registration (as of Aug. 20, 2002)		
Republican	823,425
Democratic	1,539,595
Libertarian	6,226
Green	3,899
Reform	1,163
Constitution	262
Declined and Others	373,573
TOTAL	2,748,143

Primary Type   Closed—Only registered Democrats and Republicans could vote in their party's primary.

Note: An asterisk (*) denotes incumbent.

	REPUBLICAN PRIMARIES			DEMOCRATIC PRIMARIES		
Governor	Robert L. Ehrlich Jr.	229,927	92.9%	Kathleen Kennedy Townsend	434,948	80.0%
	James J. Sheridan	9,181	3.7%	Robert Raymond Fustero	108,659	20.0%
	Ross Z. Pierpont	8,458	3.4%			
	TOTAL	247,566		TOTAL	543,607	
Congressional District 1	Wayne T. Gilchrest*	35,599	60.0%	Ann D. Tamlyn	40,008	100.0%
	Dave Fischer	21,524	36.3%			
	Brad McClanahan	2,185	3.7%			
	TOTAL	59,308				
Congressional District 2	Helen Delich Bentley	19,590	80.0%	C.A. Dutch Ruppersberger	32,974	50.3%
	Scot Michael Young	4,891	20.0%	Oz Bengur	23,729	36.2%
				Kenneth T. Bosley	5,104	7.8%
				Brian Hollister Davis	2,285	3.5%
				James Edward DeLoach Jr.	1,508	2.3%
	TOTAL	24,481		TOTAL	65,600	
Congressional District 3	Scott Conwell	17,307	78.8%	Benjamin L. Cardin*	62,938	90.0%
	Michael Jackson	4,649	21.2%	John Rea	6,986	10.0%
	TOTAL	21,956		TOTAL	69,924	
Congressional District 4	John B. Kimble	3,428	34.6%	Albert R. Wynn*	66,225	83.3%
	Floyd W. Anderson Jr.	3,325	33.6%	Don Williams	13,299	16.7%
	John F. Jamele	2,097	21.2%			
	ReNita Michon Jefferson	1,055	10.7%			
	TOTAL	9,905		TOTAL	79,524	

MARYLAND

GENERAL AND PRIMARY ELECTIONS

REPUBLICAN PRIMARIES				DEMOCRATIC PRIMARIES		
Congressional District 5	Joseph T. Crawford	20,692	100.0%	Steny H. Hoyer*	62,512	100.0%
Congressional District 6	Roscoe G. Bartlett*	50,276	100.0%	Donald M. DeArmon	17,067	52.3%
				Kevin M. Shaffer	15,542	47.7%
				TOTAL	32,609	
Congressional District 7	Joseph E. Ward	12,357	100.0%	Elijah E. Cummings*	67,938	89.3%
				A. Robert Kaufman	4,905	6.4%
				Charles U. Smith	1,757	2.3%
				Charles C. McPeek	1,453	1.9%
				TOTAL	76,053	
Congressional District 8	Constance A. Morella*	20,465	100.0%	Chris Van Hollen	37,494	43.5%
				Mark K. Shriver	35,022	40.6%
				Ira S. Shapiro	10,956	12.7%
				Deborah A. Vollmer	2,149	2.5%
				Anthony Jaworski	660	0.8%
				TOTAL	86,281	

MARYLAND REPUBLICAN PRIMARY

GOVERNOR 2002

2000 Census Population	County	Total Vote	Ehrlich	Other	Winner	Percentage of Total Vote	
						Ehrlich	Other
74,930	ALLEGANY	6,889	6,008	881	Ehrlich	87.2%	12.8%
489,656	ANNE ARUNDEL	33,028	31,542	1,486	Ehrlich	95.5%	4.5%
651,154	BALTIMORE CITY	5,514	5,038	476	Ehrlich	91.4%	8.6%
754,292	BALTIMORE COUNTY	37,908	36,754	1,154	Ehrlich	97.0%	3.0%
74,563	CALVERT	5,041	4,639	402	Ehrlich	92.0%	8.0%
29,772	CAROLINE	1,801	1,728	73	Ehrlich	95.9%	4.1%
150,897	CARROLL	17,245	16,331	914	Ehrlich	94.7%	5.3%
85,951	CECIL	4,735	4,151	584	Ehrlich	87.7%	12.3%
120,546	CHARLES	5,088	4,517	571	Ehrlich	88.8%	11.2%
30,674	DORCHESTER	2,365	2,221	144	Ehrlich	93.9%	6.1%
195,277	FREDERICK	14,485	13,122	1,363	Ehrlich	90.6%	9.4%
29,846	GARRETT	3,985	3,234	751	Ehrlich	81.2%	18.8%
218,590	HARFORD	18,738	18,189	549	Ehrlich	97.1%	2.9%
247,842	HOWARD	14,455	13,577	878	Ehrlich	93.9%	6.1%
19,197	KENT	1,829	1,776	53	Ehrlich	97.1%	2.9%
873,341	MONTGOMERY	31,834	28,227	3,607	Ehrlich	88.7%	11.3%
801,515	PRINCE GEORGES	9,894	8,529	1,365	Ehrlich	86.2%	13.8%
40,563	QUEEN ANNES	4,688	4,506	182	Ehrlich	96.1%	3.9%
86,211	ST. MARYS	5,757	5,099	658	Ehrlich	88.6%	11.4%
24,747	SOMERSET	1,535	1,461	74	Ehrlich	95.2%	4.8%
33,812	TALBOT	3,803	3,681	122	Ehrlich	96.8%	3.2%
131,923	WASHINGTON	7,064	6,417	647	Ehrlich	90.8%	9.2%
84,644	WICOMICO	5,732	5,314	418	Ehrlich	92.7%	7.3%
46,543	WORCESTER	4,153	3,866	287	Ehrlich	93.1%	6.9%
5,296,486	TOTAL	247,566	229,927	17,639	Ehrlich	92.9%	7.1%

MARYLAND DEMOCRATIC PRIMARY

GOVERNOR 2002

2000 Census Population	County	Total Vote	Townsend	Fustero	Winner	Percentage of Total Vote	
						Townsend	Fustero
74,930	ALLEGANY	5,819	4,476	1,343	Townsend	76.9%	23.1%
489,656	ANNE ARUNDEL	39,593	27,423	12,170	Townsend	69.3%	30.7%
651,154	BALTIMORE CITY	79,720	69,102	10,618	Townsend	86.7%	13.3%
754,292	BALTIMORE COUNTY	84,379	55,340	29,039	Townsend	65.6%	34.4%
74,563	CALVERT	6,327	5,092	1,235	Townsend	80.5%	19.5%
29,772	CAROLINE	1,751	1,085	666	Townsend	62.0%	38.0%
150,897	CARROLL	9,171	5,431	3,740	Townsend	59.2%	40.8%
85,951	CECIL	6,020	4,067	1,953	Townsend	67.6%	32.4%
120,546	CHARLES	7,842	6,411	1,431	Townsend	81.8%	18.2%
30,674	DORCHESTER	3,738	2,540	1,198	Townsend	68.0%	32.0%
195,277	FREDERICK	11,336	9,198	2,138	Townsend	81.1%	18.9%
29,846	GARRETT	1,447	1,108	339	Townsend	76.6%	23.4%
218,590	HARFORD	16,615	9,761	6,854	Townsend	58.7%	41.3%
247,842	HOWARD	22,678	18,302	4,376	Townsend	80.7%	19.3%
19,197	KENT	2,312	1,575	737	Townsend	68.1%	31.9%
873,341	MONTGOMERY	105,895	94,492	11,403	Townsend	89.2%	10.8%
801,515	PRINCE GEORGES	104,645	95,031	9,614	Townsend	90.8%	9.2%
40,563	QUEEN ANNES	4,011	2,590	1,421	Townsend	64.6%	35.4%
86,211	ST. MARYS	7,412	5,401	2,011	Townsend	72.9%	27.1%
24,747	SOMERSET	2,137	1,304	833	Townsend	61.0%	39.0%
33,812	TALBOT	2,920	2,091	829	Townsend	71.6%	28.4%
131,923	WASHINGTON	6,360	4,599	1,761	Townsend	72.3%	27.7%
84,644	WICOMICO	6,488	4,897	1,591	Townsend	75.5%	24.5%
46,543	WORCESTER	4,991	3,632	1,359	Townsend	72.8%	27.2%
5,296,486	TOTAL	543,607	434,948	108,659	Townsend	80.0%	20.0%

MASSACHUSETTS

GOVERNOR
Mitt Romney (R). Elected 2002 to a four-year term.

SENATORS (2 Democrats)
Edward M. Kennedy (D). Reelected 2000 to a six-year term. Previously elected 1994, 1988, 1982, 1976, 1970, 1964 and in 1962 to fill out the term vacated by the December 1960 resignation of Senator John F. Kennedy, who was elected President in November 1960.

John Kerry (D). Reelected 2002 to a six-year term. Previously elected 1996, 1990, 1984.

REPRESENTATIVES (10 Democrats)
1. John W. Olver (D)
2. Richard E. Neal (D)
3. Jim McGovern (D)
4. Barney Frank (D)
5. Martin T. Meehan (D)
6. John F. Tierney (D)
7. Edward J. Markey (D)
8. Michael E. Capuano (D)
9. Stephen F. Lynch (D)
10. Bill Delahunt (D)

POSTWAR VOTE FOR PRESIDENT

| | | Republican | | Democratic | | Other | | Percentage | | | |
| | | | | | | | | Total Vote | | Major Vote | |
Year	Total Vote	Vote	Candidate	Vote	Candidate	Vote	Plurality	Rep.	Dem.	Rep.	Dem.
2000**	2,702,984	878,502	Bush, George W.	1,616,487	Gore, Al	207,995	737,985 D	32.5%	59.8%	35.2%	64.8%
1996**	2,556,785	718,107	Dole, Bob	1,571,763	Clinton, Bill	266,915	853,656 D	28.1%	61.5%	31.4%	68.6%
1992**	2,773,700	805,049	Bush, George	1,318,662	Clinton, Bill	649,989	513,613 D	29.0%	47.5%	37.9%	62.1%
1988	2,632,805	1,194,635	Bush, George	1,401,415	Dukakis, Michael S.	36,755	206,780 D	45.4%	53.2%	46.0%	54.0%
1984	2,559,453	1,310,936	Reagan, Ronald	1,239,606	Mondale, Walter F.	8,911	71,330 R	51.2%	48.4%	51.4%	48.6%
1980**	2,524,298	1,057,631	Reagan, Ronald	1,053,802	Carter, Jimmy	412,865	3,829 R	41.9%	41.7%	50.1%	49.9%
1976	2,547,558	1,030,276	Ford, Gerald R.	1,429,475	Carter, Jimmy	87,807	399,199 D	40.4%	56.1%	41.9%	58.1%
1972	2,458,756	1,112,078	Nixon, Richard M.	1,332,540	McGovern, George S.	14,138	220,462 D	45.2%	54.2%	45.5%	54.5%
1968	2,331,752	766,844	Nixon, Richard M.	1,469,218	Humphrey, Hubert H.	95,690	702,374 D	32.9%	63.0%	34.3%	65.7%
1964	2,344,798	549,727	Goldwater, Barry M.	1,786,422	Johnson, Lyndon B.	8,649	1,236,695 D	23.4%	76.2%	23.5%	76.5%
1960	2,469,480	976,750	Nixon, Richard M.	1,487,174	Kennedy, John F.	5,556	510,424 D	39.6%	60.2%	39.6%	60.4%
1956	2,348,506	1,393,197	Eisenhower, Dwight D.	948,190	Stevenson, Adlai E.	7,119	445,007 R	59.3%	40.4%	59.5%	40.5%
1952	2,383,398	1,292,325	Eisenhower, Dwight D.	1,083,525	Stevenson, Adlai E.	7,548	208,800 R	54.2%	45.5%	54.4%	45.6%
1948	2,107,146	909,370	Dewey, Thomas E.	1,151,788	Truman, Harry S.	45,988	242,418 D	43.2%	54.7%	44.1%	55.9%

In 2000 the other vote column includes 173,564 votes cast for Green (Nader). In 1996 the other vote column includes 227,217 votes cast for Perot. In 1992 the other vote column includes 630,731 votes cast for Perot. In 1980 the other vote column includes 382,539 votes for Independent (Anderson).

MASSACHUSETTS

POSTWAR VOTE FOR GOVERNOR

Year	Total Vote	Republican		Democratic		Other Vote	Rep.-Dem. Plurality	Percentage			
								Total Vote		Major Vote	
		Vote	Candidate	Vote	Candidate			Rep.	Dem.	Rep.	Dem.
2002	2,194,179	1,091,988	Romney, Mitt	985,981	O'Brien, Shannon P.	116,210	106,007 R	49.8%	44.9%	52.6%	47.4%
1998	1,903,336	967,160	Cellucci, Paul	901,843	Harshbarger, Scott	34,333	65,317 R	50.8%	47.4%	51.7%	48.3%
1994	2,164,318	1,533,430	Weld, William F.	611,650	Roosevelt, Mark	19,238	921,780 R	70.9%	28.3%	71.5%	28.5%
1990	2,342,927	1,175,817	Weld, William F.	1,099,878	Silber, John	67,232	75,939 R	50.2%	46.9%	51.7%	48.3%
1986	1,684,079	525,364	Kariotis, George	1,157,786	Dukakis, Michael S.	929	632,422 D	31.2%	68.7%	31.2%	68.8%
1982	2,050,254	749,679	Sears, John W.	1,219,109	Dukakis, Michael S.	81,466	469,430 D	36.6%	59.5%	38.1%	61.9%
1978	1,962,251	926,072	Hatch, Francis W.	1,030,294	King, Edward J.	5,885	104,222 D	47.2%	52.5%	47.3%	52.7%
1974	1,854,798	784,353	Sargent, Francis W.	992,284	Dukakis, Michael S.	78,161	207,931 D	42.3%	53.5%	44.1%	55.9%
1970	1,867,906	1,058,623	Sargent, Francis W.	799,269	White, Kevin H.	10,014	259,354 R	56.7%	42.8%	57.0%	43.0%
1966**	2,041,177	1,277,358	Volpe, John A.	752,720	McCormack, Edward J.	11,099	524,638 R	62.6%	36.9%	62.9%	37.1%
1964	2,340,130	1,176,462	Volpe, John A.	1,153,416	Bellotti, Francis X.	10,252	23,046 R	50.3%	49.3%	50.5%	49.5%
1962	2,109,089	1,047,891	Volpe, John A.	1,053,322	Peabody, Endicott	7,876	5,431 D	49.7%	49.9%	49.9%	50.1%
1960	2,417,133	1,269,295	Volpe, John A.	1,130,810	Ward, Joseph D.	17,028	138,485 R	52.5%	46.8%	52.9%	47.1%
1958	1,899,117	818,463	Gibbons, Charles	1,067,020	Furcolo, Foster	13,634	248,557 D	43.1%	56.2%	43.4%	56.6%
1956	2,339,884	1,096,759	Whittier, Sumner G.	1,234,618	Furcolo, Foster	8,507	137,859 D	46.9%	52.8%	47.0%	53.0%
1954	1,903,774	985,339	Herter, Christian A.	910,087	Murphy, Robert F.	8,348	75,252 R	51.8%	47.8%	52.0%	48.0%
1952	2,356,298	1,175,955	Herter, Christian A.	1,161,499	Dever, Paul A.	18,844	14,456 R	49.9%	49.3%	50.3%	49.7%
1950	1,910,180	824,069	Coolidge, Arthur W.	1,074,570	Dever, Paul A.	11,541	250,501 D	43.1%	56.3%	43.4%	56.6%
1948	2,099,250	849,895	Bradford, Robert F.	1,239,247	Dever, Paul A.	10,108	389,352 D	40.5%	59.0%	40.7%	59.3%
1946	1,683,452	911,152	Bradford, Robert F.	762,743	Tobin, Maurice	9,557	148,409 R	54.1%	45.3%	54.4%	45.6%

The term of office of Massachusetts' Governor was increased from two to four years effective with the 1966 election.

POSTWAR VOTE FOR SENATOR

Year	Total Vote	Republican		Democratic		Other Vote	Rep.-Dem. Plurality	Percentage			
								Total Vote		Major Vote	
		Vote	Candidate	Vote	Candidate			Rep.	Dem.	Rep.	Dem.
2002**	2,006,758	—		1,605,976	Kerry, John	400,782	1,605,976 D		80.0%		100.0%
2000	2,599,420	334,341	Robinson, Jack E.	1,889,494	Kennedy, Edward M.	375,585	1,555,153 D	12.9%	72.7%	15.0%	85.0%
1996	2,555,886	1,142,837	Weld, William F.	1,334,345	Kerry, John	78,704	191,508 D	44.7%	52.2%	46.1%	53.9%
1994	2,179,964	894,005	Romney, Mitt	1,266,011	Kennedy, Edward M.	19,948	372,006 D	41.0%	58.1%	41.4%	58.6%
1990	2,316,212	992,917	Rappaport, Jim	1,321,712	Kerry, John	1,583	328,795 D	42.9%	57.1%	42.9%	57.1%
1988	2,606,225	884,267	Malone, Joseph	1,693,344	Kennedy, Edward M.	28,614	809,077 D	33.9%	65.0%	34.3%	65.7%
1984	2,530,195	1,136,806	Shamie, Raymond	1,392,981	Kerry, John	408	256,175 D	44.9%	55.1%	44.9%	55.1%
1982	2,050,769	784,602	Shamie, Raymond	1,247,084	Kennedy, Edward M.	19,083	462,482 D	38.3%	60.8%	38.6%	61.4%
1978	1,985,700	890,584	Brooke, Edward W.	1,093,283	Tsongas, Paul E.	1,833	202,699 D	44.8%	55.1%	44.9%	55.1%
1976	2,491,255	722,641	Robertson, Michael	1,726,657	Kennedy, Edward M.	41,957	1,004,016 D	29.0%	69.3%	29.5%	70.5%
1972	2,370,676	1,505,932	Brooke, Edward W.	823,278	Droney, John J.	41,466	682,654 R	63.5%	34.7%	64.7%	35.3%
1970	1,935,607	715,978	Spaulding, Josiah A.	1,202,856	Kennedy, Edward M.	16,773	486,878 D	37.0%	62.1%	37.3%	62.7%
1966	1,999,949	1,213,473	Brooke, Edward W.	774,761	Peabody, Endicott	11,715	438,712 R	60.7%	38.7%	61.0%	39.0%
1964	2,312,028	587,663	Whitmore, Howard	1,716,907	Kennedy, Edward M.	7,458	1,129,244 D	25.4%	74.3%	25.5%	74.5%
1962S	2,097,085	877,669	Lodge, George C.	1,162,611	Kennedy, Edward M.	56,805	284,942 D	41.9%	55.4%	43.0%	57.0%
1960	2,417,813	1,358,556	Saltonstall, Leverett	1,050,725	O'Connor, Thomas J.	8,532	307,831 R	56.2%	43.5%	56.4%	43.6%
1958	1,862,041	488,318	Celeste, Vincent J.	1,362,926	Kennedy, John F.	10,797	874,608 D	26.2%	73.2%	26.4%	73.6%
1954	1,892,710	956,605	Saltonstall, Leverett	927,899	Furcolo, Foster	8,206	28,706 R	50.5%	49.0%	50.8%	49.2%
1952	2,360,425	1,141,247	Lodge, Henry Cabot	1,211,984	Kennedy, John F.	7,194	70,737 D	48.3%	51.3%	48.5%	51.5%
1948	2,055,798	1,088,475	Saltonstall, Leverett	954,398	Fitzgerald, John I.	12,925	134,077 R	52.9%	46.4%	53.3%	46.7%
1946	1,662,063	989,736	Lodge, Henry Cabot	660,200	Walsh, David I.	12,127	329,536 R	59.5%	39.7%	60.0%	40.0%

The Republican Party did not run a candidate in the 2002 Senate election. The 1962 election was for a short term to fill a vacancy.

MASSACHUSETTS

Congressional districts first established for elections held in 2002
10 members

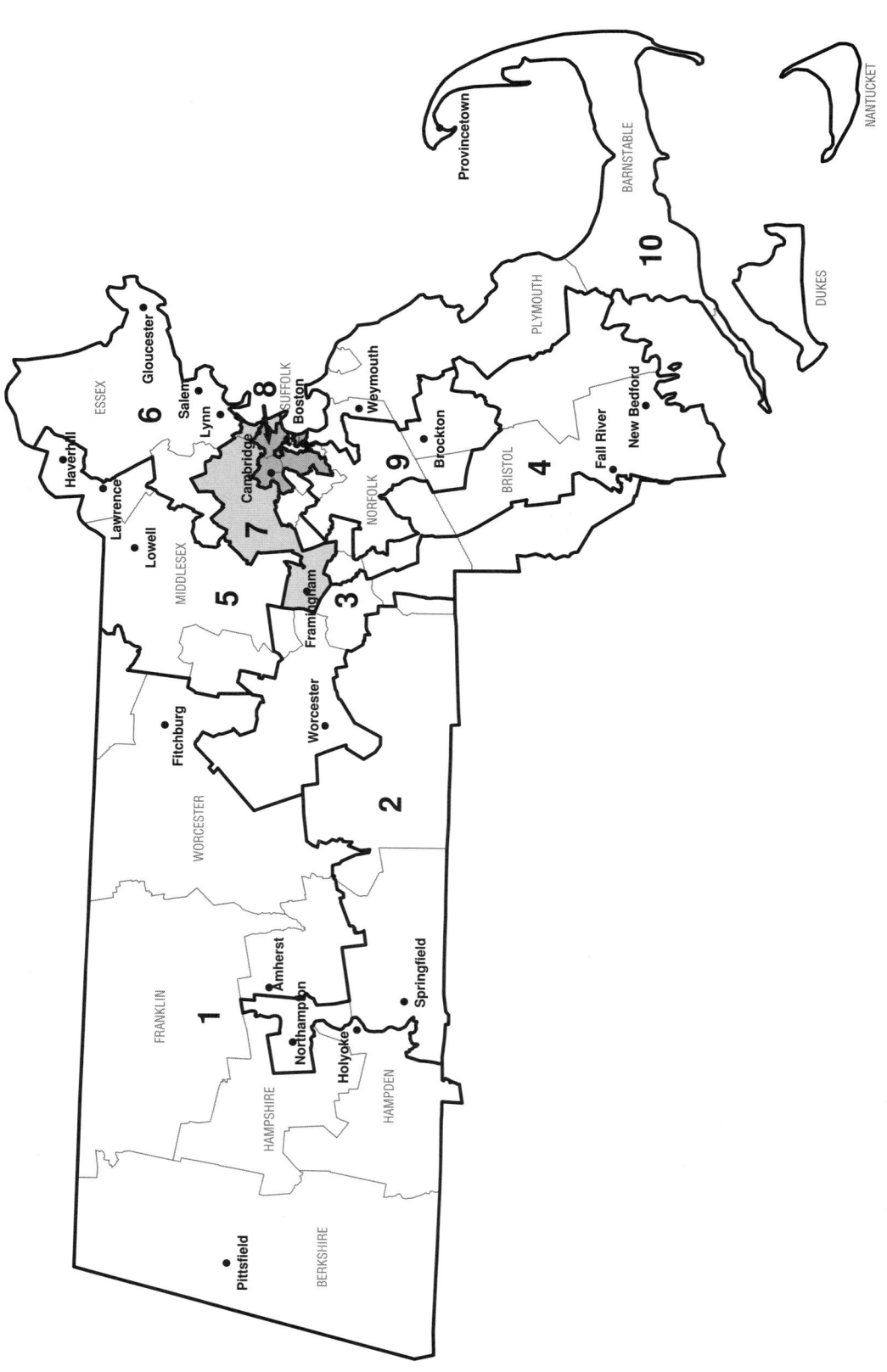

MASSACHUSETTS

Boston Area

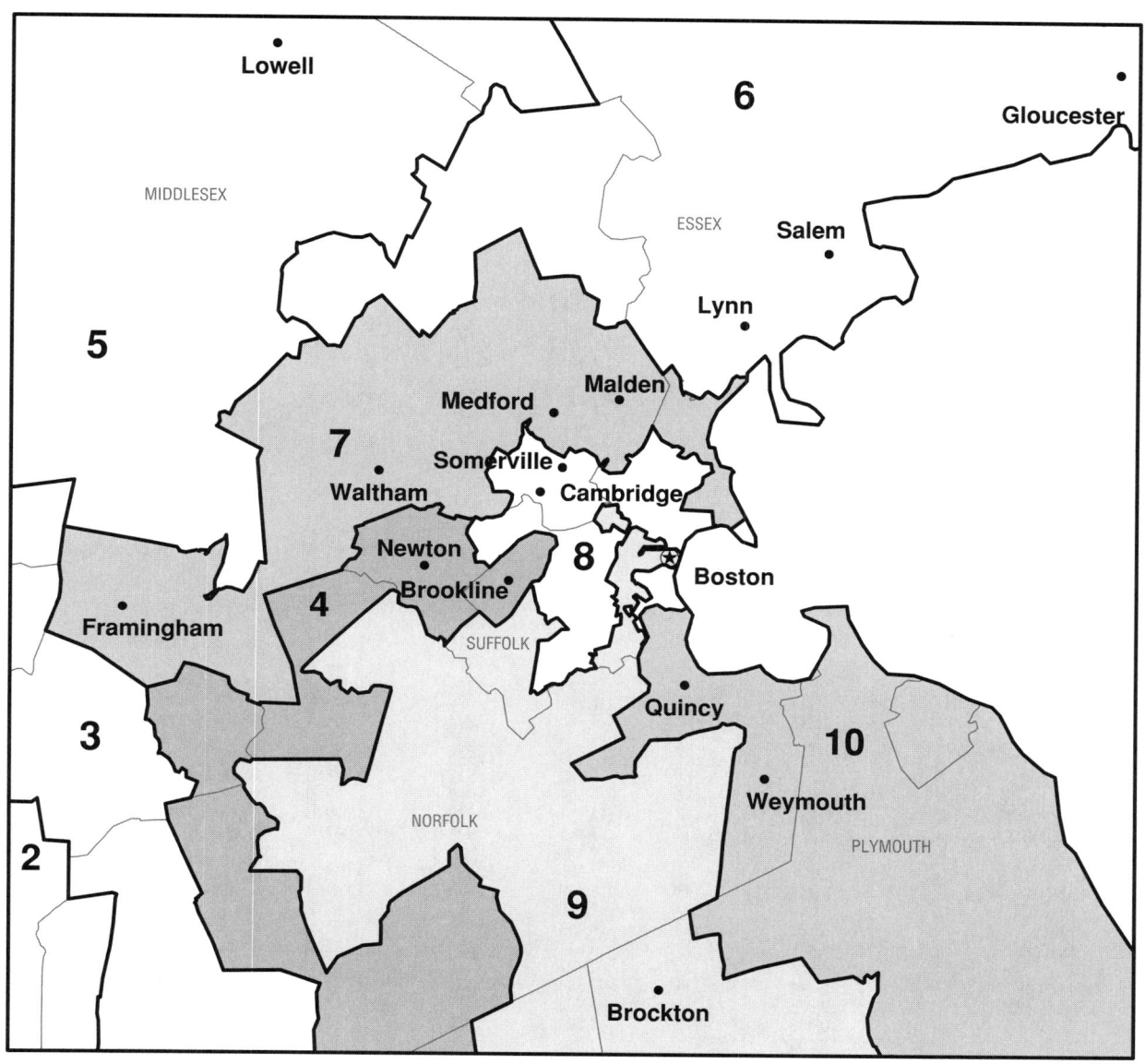

MASSACHUSETTS

GOVERNOR 2002

2000 Census Population	County	Total Vote	Republican	Democratic	Other	Rep.-Dem. Plurality	Percentage Total Vote Rep.	Total Vote Dem.	Major Vote Rep.	Major Vote Dem.
222,230	BARNSTABLE	101,993	57,466	39,640	4,887	17,826 R	56.3%	38.9%	59.2%	40.8%
134,953	BERKSHIRE	43,141	13,897	26,963	2,281	13,066 D	32.2%	62.5%	34.0%	66.0%
534,678	BRISTOL	158,324	71,189	80,275	6,860	9,086 D	45.0%	50.7%	47.0%	53.0%
14,987	DUKES	6,961	2,815	3,688	458	873 D	40.4%	53.0%	43.3%	56.7%
723,419	ESSEX	255,546	141,932	100,798	12,816	41,134 R	55.5%	39.4%	58.5%	41.5%
71,535	FRANKLIN	26,274	9,381	14,438	2,455	5,057 D	35.7%	55.0%	39.4%	60.6%
456,228	HAMPDEN	135,376	66,114	63,470	5,792	2,644 R	48.8%	46.9%	51.0%	49.0%
152,251	HAMPSHIRE	54,505	18,358	32,229	3,918	13,871 D	33.7%	59.1%	36.3%	63.7%
1,465,396	MIDDLESEX	541,931	267,579	241,934	32,418	25,645 R	49.4%	44.6%	52.5%	47.5%
9,520	NANTUCKET	3,924	1,974	1,746	204	228 R	50.3%	44.5%	53.1%	46.9%
650,308	NORFOLK	262,918	140,440	110,198	12,280	30,242 R	53.4%	41.9%	56.0%	44.0%
472,822	PLYMOUTH	173,764	100,029	65,978	7,757	34,051 R	57.6%	38.0%	60.3%	39.7%
689,807	SUFFOLK	175,679	60,623	105,280	9,776	44,657 D	34.5%	59.9%	36.5%	63.5%
750,963	WORCESTER	253,843	140,191	99,344	14,308	40,847 R	55.2%	39.1%	58.5%	41.5%
6,349,097	TOTAL	2,194,179	1,091,988	985,981	116,210	106,007 R	49.8%	44.9%	52.6%	47.4%

2000 Census Population	City/Town	Total Vote	Republican	Democratic	Other	Rep.-Dem. Plurality	Percentage Total Vote Rep.	Total Vote Dem.	Major Vote Rep.	Major Vote Dem.
20,331	ACTON	8,876	4,582	3,677	617	905 R	51.6%	41.4%	55.5%	44.5%
28,144	AGAWAM	9,709	5,403	3,862	444	1,541 R	55.6%	39.8%	58.3%	41.7%
34,874	AMHERST	8,006	1,462	5,722	822	4,260 D	18.3%	71.5%	20.4%	79.6%
31,247	ANDOVER	13,676	8,628	4,382	666	4,246 R	63.1%	32.0%	66.3%	33.7%
42,389	ARLINGTON	20,386	7,992	10,939	1,455	2,947 D	39.2%	53.7%	42.2%	57.8%
42,068	ATTLEBORO	11,661	6,835	4,291	535	2,544 R	58.6%	36.8%	61.4%	38.6%
47,821	BARNSTABLE	19,939	11,756	7,270	913	4,486 R	59.0%	36.5%	61.8%	38.2%
24,194	BELMONT	11,902	6,337	4,934	631	1,403 R	53.2%	41.5%	56.2%	43.8%
39,862	BEVERLY	15,354	8,513	6,045	796	2,468 R	55.4%	39.4%	58.5%	41.5%
38,981	BILLERICA	13,259	7,750	4,786	723	2,964 R	58.5%	36.1%	61.8%	38.2%
589,141	BOSTON	149,629	48,785	92,309	8,535	43,524 D	32.6%	61.7%	34.6%	65.4%
33,828	BRAINTREE	14,737	8,073	6,130	534	1,943 R	54.8%	41.6%	56.8%	43.2%
94,304	BROCKTON	21,623	10,051	10,600	972	549 D	46.5%	49.0%	48.7%	51.3%
57,107	BROOKLINE	20,183	6,437	12,457	1,289	6,020 D	31.9%	61.7%	34.1%	65.9%
22,876	BURLINGTON	9,279	5,400	3,458	421	1,942 R	58.2%	37.3%	61.0%	39.0%
101,355	CAMBRIDGE	32,111	7,117	22,061	2,933	14,944 D	22.2%	68.7%	24.4%	75.6%
20,775	CANTON	8,953	5,163	3,419	371	1,744 R	57.7%	38.2%	60.2%	39.8%
33,858	CHELMSFORD	14,848	9,027	5,040	781	3,987 R	60.8%	33.9%	64.2%	35.8%
54,653	CHICOPEE	16,783	7,592	8,453	738	861 D	45.2%	50.4%	47.3%	52.7%
16,993	CONCORD	8,411	4,003	3,811	597	192 R	47.6%	45.3%	51.2%	48.8%
25,212	DANVERS	10,344	6,338	3,586	420	2,752 R	61.3%	34.7%	63.9%	36.1%
30,666	DARTMOUTH	9,878	4,016	5,403	459	1,387 D	40.7%	54.7%	42.6%	57.4%
23,464	DEDHAM	10,363	5,510	4,393	460	1,117 R	53.2%	42.4%	55.6%	44.4%
28,562	DRACUT	10,135	5,981	3,666	488	2,315 R	59.0%	36.2%	62.0%	38.0%
22,299	EASTON	8,790	5,372	3,039	379	2,333 R	61.1%	34.6%	63.9%	36.1%
38,037	EVERETT	10,458	4,677	5,314	467	637 D	44.7%	50.8%	46.8%	53.2%
91,938	FALL RIVER	20,808	6,058	13,938	812	7,880 D	29.1%	67.0%	30.3%	69.7%
32,660	FALMOUTH	14,902	7,643	6,492	767	1,151 R	51.3%	43.6%	54.1%	45.9%
39,102	FITCHBURG	10,262	5,062	4,656	544	406 R	49.3%	45.4%	52.1%	47.9%
66,910	FRAMINGHAM	21,222	10,869	9,227	1,126	1,642 R	51.2%	43.5%	54.1%	45.9%
29,560	FRANKLIN	11,264	6,972	3,785	507	3,187 R	61.9%	33.6%	64.8%	35.2%
30,273	GLOUCESTER	11,080	5,470	4,948	662	522 R	49.4%	44.7%	52.5%	47.5%
58,969	HAVERHILL	17,841	9,905	7,023	913	2,882 R	55.5%	39.4%	58.5%	41.5%
19,882	HINGHAM	9,812	6,215	3,147	450	3,068 R	63.3%	32.1%	66.4%	33.6%
39,838	HOLYOKE	10,919	4,259	6,100	560	1,841 D	39.0%	55.9%	41.1%	58.9%
72,043	LAWRENCE	11,363	4,211	6,459	693	2,248 D	37.1%	56.8%	39.5%	60.5%
41,303	LEOMINSTER	13,355	7,282	5,340	733	1,942 R	54.5%	40.0%	57.7%	42.3%
30,355	LEXINGTON	14,627	6,262	7,360	1,005	1,098 D	42.8%	50.3%	46.0%	54.0%
105,167	LOWELL	21,256	9,997	10,085	1,174	88 D	47.0%	47.4%	49.8%	50.2%
89,050	LYNN	20,973	9,455	10,602	916	1,147 D	45.1%	50.6%	47.1%	52.9%

MASSACHUSETTS

GOVERNOR 2002

2000 Census Population	City/Town	Total Vote	Republican	Democratic	Other	Rep.-Dem. Plurality	Percentage Total Vote Rep.	Dem.	Major Vote Rep.	Dem.
56,340	MALDEN	15,233	6,305	8,076	852	1,771 D	41.4%	53.0%	43.8%	56.2%
20,377	MARBLEHEAD	10,045	6,002	3,564	479	2,438 R	59.8%	35.5%	62.7%	37.3%
36,255	MARLBOROUGH	12,223	7,214	4,405	604	2,809 R	59.0%	36.0%	62.1%	37.9%
24,324	MARSHFIELD	10,287	6,193	3,642	452	2,551 R	60.2%	35.4%	63.0%	37.0%
55,765	MEDFORD	20,310	9,114	10,090	1,106	976 D	44.9%	49.7%	47.5%	52.5%
27,134	MELROSE	12,446	6,511	5,304	631	1,207 R	52.3%	42.6%	55.1%	44.9%
43,789	METHUEN	13,807	8,198	4,909	700	3,289 R	59.4%	35.6%	62.5%	37.5%
26,799	MILFORD	8,495	4,863	3,289	343	1,574 R	57.2%	38.7%	59.7%	40.3%
26,062	MILTON	12,445	6,144	5,730	571	414 R	49.4%	46.0%	51.7%	48.3%
32,170	NATICK	13,872	7,295	5,800	777	1,495 R	52.6%	41.8%	55.7%	44.3%
28,911	NEEDHAM	14,410	7,754	5,935	721	1,819 R	53.8%	41.2%	56.6%	43.4%
93,768	NEW BEDFORD	23,007	5,857	16,133	1,017	10,276 D	25.5%	70.1%	26.6%	73.4%
83,829	NEWTON	35,292	13,630	19,556	2,106	5,926 D	38.6%	55.4%	41.1%	58.9%
27,202	NORTH ANDOVER	10,798	7,047	3,212	539	3,835 R	65.3%	29.7%	68.7%	31.3%
27,143	NORTH ATTLEBOROUGH	9,069	5,802	2,874	393	2,928 R	64.0%	31.7%	66.9%	33.1%
28,978	NORTHAMPTON	11,730	2,594	8,065	1,071	5,471 D	22.1%	68.8%	24.3%	75.7%
28,587	NORWOOD	11,090	6,048	4,538	504	1,510 R	54.5%	40.9%	57.1%	42.9%
48,129	PEABODY	19,761	10,520	8,397	844	2,123 R	53.2%	42.5%	55.6%	44.4%
45,793	PITTSFIELD	13,213	4,182	8,470	561	4,288 D	31.7%	64.1%	33.1%	66.9%
51,701	PLYMOUTH	18,982	11,088	6,942	952	4,146 R	58.4%	36.6%	61.5%	38.5%
88,025	QUINCY	30,810	14,666	14,665	1,479	1 R	47.6%	47.6%	50.0%	50.0%
30,963	RANDOLPH	10,269	4,353	5,474	442	1,121 D	42.4%	53.3%	44.3%	55.7%
23,708	READING	10,740	6,231	4,031	478	2,200 R	58.0%	37.5%	60.7%	39.3%
47,283	REVERE	13,180	6,207	6,404	569	197 D	47.1%	48.6%	49.2%	50.8%
40,407	SALEM	14,089	6,384	6,895	810	511 D	45.3%	48.9%	48.1%	51.9%
26,078	SAUGUS	10,411	5,816	4,163	432	1,653 R	55.9%	40.0%	58.3%	41.7%
17,863	SCITUATE	9,004	5,477	3,126	401	2,351 R	60.8%	34.7%	63.7%	36.3%
31,640	SHREWSBURY	12,851	7,848	4,490	513	3,358 R	61.1%	34.9%	63.6%	36.4%
77,478	SOMERVILLE	22,183	6,299	13,607	2,277	7,308 D	28.4%	61.3%	31.6%	68.4%
152,082	SPRINGFIELD	33,194	12,566	19,364	1,264	6,798 D	37.9%	58.3%	39.4%	60.6%
22,219	STONEHAM	9,050	4,951	3,690	409	1,261 R	54.7%	40.8%	57.3%	42.7%
27,149	STOUGHTON	10,087	5,282	4,326	479	956 R	52.4%	42.9%	55.0%	45.0%
55,976	TAUNTON	15,476	7,027	7,814	635	787 D	45.4%	50.5%	47.3%	52.7%
28,851	TEWKSBURY	11,132	6,666	3,945	521	2,721 R	59.9%	35.4%	62.8%	37.2%
24,804	WAKEFIELD	10,993	6,249	4,252	492	1,997 R	56.8%	38.7%	59.5%	40.5%
22,824	WALPOLE	9,979	6,338	3,233	408	3,105 R	63.5%	32.4%	66.2%	33.8%
59,226	WALTHAM	17,327	8,742	7,525	1,060	1,217 R	50.5%	43.4%	53.7%	46.3%
32,986	WATERTOWN	12,144	5,026	6,379	739	1,353 D	41.4%	52.5%	44.1%	55.9%
26,613	WELLESLEY	11,861	6,937	4,390	534	2,547 R	58.5%	37.0%	61.2%	38.8%
27,899	WEST SPRINGFIELD	8,512	4,688	3,430	394	1,258 R	55.1%	40.3%	57.7%	42.3%
40,072	WESTFIELD	13,224	7,134	5,484	606	1,650 R	53.9%	41.5%	56.5%	43.5%
53,988	WEYMOUTH	21,385	11,402	9,093	890	2,309 R	53.3%	42.5%	55.6%	44.4%
20,810	WINCHESTER	10,259	5,930	3,788	541	2,142 R	57.8%	36.9%	61.0%	39.0%
37,258	WOBURN	13,851	7,707	5,508	636	2,199 R	55.6%	39.8%	58.3%	41.7%
172,648	WORCESTER	43,875	18,306	23,024	2,545	4,718 D	41.7%	52.5%	44.3%	55.7%
24,807	YARMOUTH	11,272	6,524	4,294	454	2,230 R	57.9%	38.1%	60.3%	39.7%

MASSACHUSETTS

SENATOR 2002

2000 Census Population	County	Total Vote	Republican	Democratic	Libertarian	Other	Rep.-Dem. Plurality	Percentage of Total Vote		
								Rep.	Dem.	Lib.
222,230	BARNSTABLE	92,061		70,393	20,696	972	70,393 D		76.5%	22.5%
134,953	BERKSHIRE	40,343		34,521	5,424	398	34,521 D		85.6%	13.4%
534,678	BRISTOL	147,097		122,104	24,489	504	122,104 D		83.0%	16.6%
14,987	DUKES	6,512		5,487	864	161	5,487 D		84.3%	13.3%
723,419	ESSEX	234,181		186,309	45,956	1,916	186,309 D		79.6%	19.6%
71,535	FRANKLIN	24,361		18,654	3,757	1,950	18,654 D		76.6%	15.4%
456,228	HAMPDEN	123,090		100,616	21,696	778	100,616 D		81.7%	17.6%
152,251	HAMPSHIRE	50,540		39,448	7,398	3,694	39,448 D		78.1%	14.6%
1,465,396	MIDDLESEX	500,141		395,087	91,951	13,103	395,087 D		79.0%	18.4%
9,520	NANTUCKET	3,641		3,008	604	29	3,008 D		82.6%	16.6%
650,308	NORFOLK	240,657		192,342	45,235	3,080	192,342 D		79.9%	18.8%
472,822	PLYMOUTH	159,032		123,597	34,623	812	123,597 D		77.7%	21.8%
689,807	SUFFOLK	151,898		129,026	20,634	2,238	129,026 D		84.9%	13.6%
750,963	WORCESTER	233,204		185,384	46,480	1,340	185,384 D		79.5%	19.9%
6,349,097	TOTAL	2,006,758		1,605,976	369,807	30,975	1,605,976 D		80.0%	18.4%
	City/Town									
20,331	ACTON	8,234		6,533	1,483	218	6,533 D		79.3%	18.0%
28,144	AGAWAM	8,697		6,823	1,866	8	6,823 D		78.5%	21.5%
34,874	AMHERST	7,483		5,617	682	1,184	5,617 D		75.1%	9.1%
31,247	ANDOVER	12,222		9,090	2,983	149	9,090 D		74.4%	24.4%
42,389	ARLINGTON	18,840		15,186	2,687	967	15,186 D		80.6%	14.3%
42,068	ATTLEBORO	10,765		8,522	2,186	57	8,522 D		79.2%	20.3%
47,821	BARNSTABLE	17,929		13,724	4,080	125	13,724 D		76.5%	22.8%
24,194	BELMONT	10,588		8,292	1,921	375	8,292 D		78.3%	18.1%
39,862	BEVERLY	13,994		11,298	2,587	109	11,298 D		80.7%	18.5%
38,981	BILLERICA	12,428		9,430	2,920	78	9,430 D		75.9%	23.5%
589,141	BOSTON	127,932		108,953	16,887	2,092	108,953 D		85.2%	13.2%
33,828	BRAINTREE	13,535		10,855	2,642	38	10,855 D		80.2%	19.5%
94,304	BROCKTON	20,075		16,684	3,363	28	16,684 D		83.1%	16.8%
57,107	BROOKLINE	18,702		15,374	2,064	1,264	15,374 D		82.2%	11.0%
22,876	BURLINGTON	8,607		6,665	1,870	72	6,665 D		77.4%	21.7%
101,355	CAMBRIDGE	30,286		23,551	2,897	3,838	23,551 D		77.8%	9.6%
20,775	CANTON	8,151		6,553	1,559	39	6,553 D		80.4%	19.1%
33,858	CHELMSFORD	13,619		10,179	3,359	81	10,179 D		74.7%	24.7%
54,653	CHICOPEE	15,806		13,131	2,568	107	13,131 D		83.1%	16.2%
16,993	CONCORD	7,554		5,730	1,440	384	5,730 D		75.9%	19.1%
25,212	DANVERS	9,395		7,483	1,865	47	7,483 D		79.6%	19.9%
30,666	DARTMOUTH	9,051		7,669	1,336	46	7,669 D		84.7%	14.8%
23,464	DEDHAM	9,417		7,522	1,791	104	7,522 D		79.9%	19.0%
28,562	DRACUT	9,622		7,437	2,142	43	7,437 D		77.3%	22.3%
22,299	EASTON	7,933		6,069	1,829	35	6,069 D		76.5%	23.1%
38,037	EVERETT	9,391		7,801	1,585	5	7,801 D		83.1%	16.9%
91,938	FALL RIVER	19,534		17,300	2,193	41	17,300 D		88.6%	11.2%
32,660	FALMOUTH	13,553		10,638	2,661	254	10,638 D		78.5%	19.6%
39,102	FITCHBURG	9,611		7,904	1,673	34	7,904 D		82.2%	17.4%
66,910	FRAMINGHAM	19,848		15,901	3,704	243	15,901 D		80.1%	18.7%
29,560	FRANKLIN	10,327		8,188	2,079	60	8,188 D		79.3%	20.1%
30,273	GLOUCESTER	10,244		8,307	1,693	244	8,307 D		81.1%	16.5%
58,969	HAVERHILL	16,503		13,131	3,318	54	13,131 D		79.6%	20.1%
19,882	HINGHAM	8,835		6,762	1,959	114	6,762 D		76.5%	22.2%
39,838	HOLYOKE	10,031		8,429	1,523	79	8,429 D		84.0%	15.2%
72,043	LAWRENCE	10,653		8,926	1,723	4	8,926 D		83.8%	16.2%
41,303	LEOMINSTER	12,328		9,921	2,347	60	9,921 D		80.5%	19.0%
30,355	LEXINGTON	13,299		10,650	2,151	498	10,650 D		80.1%	16.2%
105,167	LOWELL	20,025		16,395	3,509	121	16,395 D		81.9%	17.5%
89,050	LYNN	19,690		16,841	2,724	125	16,841 D		85.5%	13.8%

MASSACHUSETTS

SENATOR 2002

2000 Census Population	City/Town	Total Vote	Republican	Democratic	Libertarian	Other	Rep.-Dem. Plurality	Percentage of Total Vote		
								Rep.	Dem.	Lib.
56,340	MALDEN	14,237		12,028	2,054	155	12,028 D		84.5%	14.4%
20,377	MARBLEHEAD	9,042		7,113	1,783	146	7,113 D		78.7%	19.7%
36,255	MARLBOROUGH	11,388		8,988	2,328	72	8,988 D		78.9%	20.4%
24,324	MARSHFIELD	9,505		7,322	2,157	26	7,322 D		77.0%	22.7%
55,765	MEDFORD	18,866		15,588	2,883	395	15,588 D		82.6%	15.3%
27,134	MELROSE	11,381		9,280	1,948	153	9,280 D		81.5%	17.1%
43,789	METHUEN	12,624		9,750	2,854	20	9,750 D		77.2%	22.6%
26,799	MILFORD	7,766		6,325	1,435	6	6,325 D		81.4%	18.5%
26,062	MILTON	11,249		8,981	2,180	88	8,981 D		79.8%	19.4%
32,170	NATICK	12,882		10,223	2,473	186	10,223 D		79.4%	19.2%
28,911	NEEDHAM	13,081		10,611	2,249	221	10,611 D		81.1%	17.2%
93,768	NEW BEDFORD	21,858		19,659	2,128	71	19,659 D		89.9%	9.7%
83,829	NEWTON	32,380		26,814	4,596	970	26,814 D		82.8%	14.2%
27,202	NORTH ANDOVER	9,692		7,285	2,343	64	7,285 D		75.2%	24.2%
27,143	NORTH ATTLEBOROUGH	8,329		6,346	1,940	43	6,346 D		76.2%	23.3%
28,978	NORTHAMPTON	10,953		8,263	1,241	1,449	8,263 D		75.4%	11.3%
28,587	NORWOOD	10,153		8,118	1,971	64	8,118 D		80.0%	19.4%
48,129	PEABODY	18,570		15,452	3,052	66	15,452 D		83.2%	16.4%
45,793	PITTSFIELD	12,412		10,694	1,702	16	10,694 D		86.2%	13.7%
51,701	PLYMOUTH	17,448		13,506	3,848	94	13,506 D		77.4%	22.1%
88,025	QUINCY	28,495		23,320	4,931	244	23,320 D		81.8%	17.3%
30,963	RANDOLPH	9,650		8,299	1,301	50	8,299 D		86.0%	13.5%
23,708	READING	9,758		7,731	1,950	77	7,731 D		79.2%	20.0%
47,283	REVERE	12,091		10,194	1,848	49	10,194 D		84.3%	15.3%
40,407	SALEM	13,240		11,078	2,037	125	11,078 D		83.7%	15.4%
26,078	SAUGUS	9,531		7,804	1,712	15	7,804 D		81.9%	18.0%
17,863	SCITUATE	8,125		6,171	1,867	87	6,171 D		76.0%	23.0%
31,640	SHREWSBURY	11,684		9,312	2,313	59	9,312 D		79.7%	19.8%
77,478	SOMERVILLE	21,029		17,032	2,551	1,446	17,032 D		81.0%	12.1%
152,082	SPRINGFIELD	30,152		26,141	3,790	221	26,141 D		86.7%	12.6%
22,219	STONEHAM	8,321		6,729	1,535	57	6,729 D		80.9%	18.4%
27,149	STOUGHTON	9,353		7,658	1,660	35	7,658 D		81.9%	17.7%
55,976	TAUNTON	14,215		11,888	2,292	35	11,888 D		83.6%	16.1%
28,851	TEWKSBURY	10,400		8,118	2,235	47	8,118 D		78.1%	21.5%
24,804	WAKEFIELD	10,046		8,056	1,917	73	8,056 D		80.2%	19.1%
22,824	WALPOLE	8,918		6,941	1,935	42	6,941 D		77.8%	21.7%
59,226	WALTHAM	15,549		12,315	3,071	163	12,315 D		79.2%	19.8%
32,986	WATERTOWN	11,274		9,185	1,721	368	9,185 D		81.5%	15.3%
26,613	WELLESLEY	10,497		8,056	2,208	233	8,056 D		76.7%	21.0%
27,899	WEST SPRINGFIELD	7,686		5,940	1,735	11	5,940 D		77.3%	22.6%
40,072	WESTFIELD	11,960		9,524	2,360	76	9,524 D		79.6%	19.7%
53,988	WEYMOUTH	19,732		15,874	3,739	119	15,874 D		80.4%	18.9%
20,810	WINCHESTER	9,005		6,866	2,000	139	6,866 D		76.2%	22.2%
37,258	WOBURN	12,677		10,192	2,412	73	10,192 D		80.4%	19.0%
172,648	WORCESTER	40,600		34,414	5,878	308	34,414 D		84.8%	14.5%
24,807	YARMOUTH	10,091		7,732	2,302	57	7,732 D		76.6%	22.8%

MASSACHUSETTS

HOUSE OF REPRESENTATIVES

CD	Year	Total Vote	Republican		Democratic		Other Vote	Rep.-Dem. Plurality	Percentage			
									Total Vote		Major Vote	
			Vote	Candidate	Vote	Candidate			Rep.	Dem.	Rep.	Dem.
1	2002	204,019	66,061	Kinnaman, Matthew W.	137,841	Olver, John W.*	117	71,780 D	32.4%	67.6%	32.4%	67.6%
2	2002	154,728		—	153,387	Neal, Richard E.*	1,341	153,387 D		99.1%		100.0%
3	2002	157,545		—	155,697	McGovern, Jim*	1,848	155,697 D		98.8%		100.0%
4	2002	167,816		—	166,125	Frank, Barney*	1,691	166,125 D		99.0%		100.0%
5	2002	203,777	69,337	McCarthy, Charles	122,562	Meehan, Martin T.*	11,878	53,225 D	34.0%	60.1%	36.1%	63.9%
6	2002	238,615	75,462	Smith, Mark C.	162,900	Tierney, John F.*	253	87,438 D	31.6%	68.3%	31.7%	68.3%
7	2002	174,037		—	170,968	Markey, Edward J.*	3,069	170,968 D		98.2%		100.0%
8	2002	112,356		—	111,861	Capuano, Michael E.*	495	111,861 D		99.6%		100.0%
9	2002	168,976		—	168,055	Lynch, Stephen F.*	921	168,055 D		99.5%		100.0%
10	2002	259,002	79,624	Gonzaga, Luiz	179,238	Delahunt, Bill*	140	99,614 D	30.7%	69.2%	30.8%	69.2%
Total	2002	1,840,871	290,484		1,528,634		21,753	1,238,150 D	15.8%	83.0%	16.0%	84.0%

An asterisk (*) denotes incumbent.

MASSACHUSETTS

GENERAL AND PRIMARY ELECTIONS

2002 GENERAL ELECTIONS

Governor Other vote was 76,530 Green (Jill E. Stein); 23,044 Libertarian (Carla A. Howell); 15,335 Independent (Barbara C. Johnson); 1,301 scattered write-in.

Senator Other vote was 369,807 Libertarian (Michael E. Cloud); 24,898 write-in (Randall Forsberg); 6,077 scattered write-in. (The Libertarian vote is listed in the county and city/town tables for the 2002 Senate election in Massachusetts. The party's nominee received 18.4 percent of the total vote.)

House Other vote was:

CD 1	117 scattered write-in.
CD 2	1,341 scattered write-in.
CD 3	1,848 scattered write-in.
CD 4	1,691 scattered write-in.
CD 5	11,729 Libertarian (Ilana Freedman); 149 scattered write-in.
CD 6	253 scattered write-in.
CD 7	863 write-in (Daniel Melnechuk); 2,206 scattered write-in.
CD 8	495 scattered write-in.
CD 9	921 scattered write-in.
CD 10	140 scattered write-in.

MASSACHUSETTS

GENERAL AND PRIMARY ELECTIONS

2002 PRIMARY ELECTIONS

Primary	September 17, 2002	**Registration** (as of Sept. 17, 2002)	Republican	526,787
			Democratic	1,430,277
			Libertarian	20,004
			Green	5,741
			Miscellaneous	6,673
			Unenrolled	1,932,930
			TOTAL	3,922,412

Primary Type Semi-open—Registered Democrats and Republicans could vote only in their party's primary. "Unenrolled" voters could participate in either party's primary.

Note: An asterisk (*) denotes incumbent.

	REPUBLICAN PRIMARIES			DEMOCRATIC PRIMARIES		
Governor	Mitt Romney	227,960	99.2%	Shannon P. O'Brien	243,039	32.5%
	Write-in	1,834	0.8%	Robert B. Reich	185,315	24.8%
				Thomas F. Birmingham	179,703	24.0%
				Warren E. Tolman	132,157	17.7%
				Steven Grossman	5,976	0.8%
				Write-in	1,113	0.1%
	TOTAL	229,794		TOTAL	747,303	
Senator	No Republican candidate filed for the primary. There were 11,504 scattered write-in votes and 1,441 write-in votes for Jack E. Robinson.			John Kerry*	615,517	99.4%
				Write-in	3,979	0.6%
				TOTAL	619,496	
Congressional District 1	Matthew W. Kinnaman	13,780	99.6%	John W. Olver*	49,907	99.7%
	Write-in	55	0.4%	Write-in	168	0.3%
	TOTAL	13,835		TOTAL	50,075	
Congressional District 2	No Republican candidate filed for the primary. There were 524 scattered write-in votes.			Richard E. Neal*	47,369	99.5%
				Write-in	260	0.5%
				TOTAL	47,629	
Congressional District 3	No Republican candidate filed for the primary. There were 721 scattered write-in votes.			Jim McGovern*	44,515	99.6%
				Write-in	188	0.4%
				TOTAL	44,703	
Congressional District 4	No Republican candidate filed for the primary. There were 485 scattered write-in votes.			Barney Frank*	66,057	99.7%
				Write-in	169	0.3%
				TOTAL	66,226	
Congressional District 5	Charles McCarthy	13,068	56.4%	Martin T. Meehan*	49,041	99.5%
	Thomas P. Tierney	10,046	43.4%	Write-in	261	0.5%
	Write-in	46	0.2%			
	TOTAL	23,160		TOTAL	49,302	
Congressional District 6	Mark C. Smith	22,117	99.4%	John F. Tierney*	68,992	99.7%
	Write-in	128	0.6%	Write-in	222	0.3%
	TOTAL	22,245		TOTAL	69,214	
Congressional District 7	No Republican candidate filed for the primary. There were 986 scattered write-in votes.			Edward J. Markey*	73,014	84.9%
				James O. Hall	12,964	15.1%
				Write-in	66	0.1%
				TOTAL	86,044	
Congressional District 8	No Republican candidate filed for the primary. There were 87 scattered write-in votes.			Michael E. Capuano*	49,451	99.7%
				Write-in	144	0.3%
				TOTAL	49,595	

MASSACHUSETTS

GENERAL AND PRIMARY ELECTIONS

	REPUBLICAN PRIMARIES			DEMOCRATIC PRIMARIES		
Congressional District 9	No Republican candidate filed for the primary. There were 545 scattered write-in votes.			Stephen F. Lynch*	69,244	80.6%
				William A. Ferguson Jr.	16,643	19.4%
				Write-in	54	0.1%
				TOTAL	85,941	
Congressional District 10	Luiz Gonzaga	24,851	99.5%	Bill Delahunt*	64,686	99.7%
	Write-in	124	0.5%	Write-in	190	0.3%
	TOTAL	24,975		TOTAL	64,876	

MASSACHUSETTS DEMOCRATIC PRIMARY

GOVERNOR 2002

2000 Census Population	County	Total Vote	O'Brien	Reich	Birmingham	Tolman	Other	Winner	Percentage of Total Vote				
									O'Brien	Reich	Birmingham	Tolman	Other
222,230	BARNSTABLE	25,483	9,812	7,024	3,994	4,498	155	O'Brien	38.5%	27.6%	15.7%	17.7%	0.6%
134,953	BERKSHIRE	11,901	4,410	4,541	1,555	1,271	124	Reich	37.1%	38.2%	13.1%	10.7%	1.0%
534,678	BRISTOL	49,557	15,300	7,440	18,953	7,132	732	Birmingham	30.9%	15.0%	38.2%	14.4%	1.5%
14,987	DUKES	1,878	631	771	247	204	25	Reich	33.6%	41.1%	13.2%	10.9%	1.3%
723,419	ESSEX	89,274	27,664	22,304	22,525	15,656	1,125	O'Brien	31.0%	25.0%	25.2%	17.5%	1.3%
71,535	FRANKLIN	11,097	3,480	4,600	1,070	1,885	62	Reich	31.4%	41.5%	9.6%	17.0%	0.6%
456,228	HAMPDEN	36,832	16,054	6,144	7,690	6,621	323	O'Brien	43.6%	16.7%	20.9%	18.0%	0.9%
152,251	HAMPSHIRE	22,690	9,586	7,980	2,086	2,921	117	O'Brien	42.2%	35.2%	9.2%	12.9%	0.5%
1,465,396	MIDDLESEX	197,415	57,145	56,633	43,268	39,034	1,335	O'Brien	28.9%	28.7%	21.9%	19.8%	0.7%
9,520	NANTUCKET	796	280	343	72	93	8	Reich	35.2%	43.1%	9.0%	11.7%	1.0%
650,308	NORFOLK	99,894	33,228	25,240	22,683	17,838	905	O'Brien	33.3%	25.3%	22.7%	17.9%	0.9%
472,822	PLYMOUTH	47,088	17,723	8,934	11,692	8,405	334	O'Brien	37.6%	19.0%	24.8%	17.8%	0.7%
689,807	SUFFOLK	88,185	25,145	19,155	29,412	13,640	833	Birmingham	28.5%	21.7%	33.4%	15.5%	0.9%
750,963	WORCESTER	65,213	22,581	14,206	14,456	12,959	1,011	O'Brien	34.6%	21.8%	22.2%	19.9%	1.6%
6,349,097	TOTAL	747,303	243,039	185,315	179,703	132,157	7,089	O'Brien	32.5%	24.8%	24.0%	17.7%	0.9%
	City/Town												
20,331	ACTON	2,859	1,004	1,048	259	521	27	Reich	35.1%	36.7%	9.1%	18.2%	0.9%
28,144	AGAWAM	1,895	761	298	417	409	10	O'Brien	40.2%	15.7%	22.0%	21.6%	0.5%
34,874	AMHERST	3,489	756	1,909	315	500	9	Reich	21.7%	54.7%	9.0%	14.3%	0.3%
31,247	ANDOVER	3,925	1,276	1,547	527	549	26	Reich	32.5%	39.4%	13.4%	14.0%	0.7%
42,389	ARLINGTON	9,699	2,966	3,315	1,665	1,698	55	Reich	30.6%	34.2%	17.2%	17.5%	0.6%
42,068	ATTLEBORO	2,013	744	356	413	481	19	O'Brien	37.0%	17.7%	20.5%	23.9%	0.9%
47,821	BARNSTABLE	4,588	1,827	1,138	754	836	33	O'Brien	39.8%	24.8%	16.4%	18.2%	0.7%
24,194	BELMONT	4,852	1,257	1,381	498	1,691	25	Tolman	25.9%	28.5%	10.3%	34.9%	0.5%
39,862	BEVERLY	5,800	2,074	1,385	1,063	1,232	46	O'Brien	35.8%	23.9%	18.3%	21.2%	0.8%
38,981	BILLERICA	3,652	1,179	660	1,011	783	19	O'Brien	32.3%	18.1%	27.7%	21.4%	0.5%
589,141	BOSTON	74,264	22,687	17,310	21,357	12,207	703	O'Brien	30.5%	23.3%	28.8%	16.4%	0.9%
33,828	BRAINTREE	6,255	2,145	1,039	1,792	1,236	43	O'Brien	34.3%	16.6%	28.6%	19.8%	0.7%
94,304	BROCKTON	7,904	2,784	1,336	2,211	1,487	86	O'Brien	35.2%	16.9%	28.0%	18.8%	1.1%
57,107	BROOKLINE	9,276	2,685	4,325	1,185	1,005	76	Reich	28.9%	46.6%	12.8%	10.8%	0.8%
22,876	BURLINGTON	2,659	903	572	649	522	13	O'Brien	34.0%	21.5%	24.4%	19.6%	0.5%
101,355	CAMBRIDGE	16,798	4,158	7,515	2,695	2,327	103	Reich	24.8%	44.7%	16.0%	13.9%	0.6%
20,775	CANTON	3,324	1,060	846	765	634	19	O'Brien	31.9%	25.5%	23.0%	19.1%	0.6%
33,858	CHELMSFORD	3,620	1,186	898	746	760	30	O'Brien	32.8%	24.8%	20.6%	21.0%	0.8%
54,653	CHICOPEE	5,473	2,642	686	993	1,103	49	O'Brien	48.3%	12.5%	18.1%	20.2%	0.9%
16,993	CONCORD	2,849	1,029	1,173	226	412	9	Reich	36.1%	41.2%	7.9%	14.5%	0.3%

MASSACHUSETTS DEMOCRATIC PRIMARY
GOVERNOR 2002

2000 Census Population	City/Town	Total Vote	O'Brien	Reich	Birmingham	Tolman	Other	Winner	Percentage of Total Vote				
									O'Brien	Reich	Birmingham	Tolman	Other
25,212	DANVERS	3,011	1,046	642	731	569	23	O'Brien	34.7%	21.3%	24.3%	18.9%	0.8%
30,666	DARTMOUTH	2,840	828	547	1,102	344	19	Birmingham	29.2%	19.3%	38.8%	12.1%	0.7%
23,464	DEDHAM	5,817	1,906	1,086	1,484	1,270	71	O'Brien	32.8%	18.7%	25.5%	21.8%	1.2%
28,562	DRACUT	3,112	899	445	1,055	683	30	Birmingham	28.9%	14.3%	33.9%	21.9%	1.0%
22,299	EASTON	2,220	735	524	571	377	13	O'Brien	33.1%	23.6%	25.7%	17.0%	0.6%
38,037	EVERETT	6,615	1,044	587	4,156	787	41	Birmingham	15.8%	8.9%	62.8%	11.9%	0.6%
91,938	FALL RIVER	10,589	3,150	1,288	4,485	1,426	240	Birmingham	29.7%	12.2%	42.4%	13.5%	2.3%
32,660	FALMOUTH	4,707	1,898	1,233	759	787	30	O'Brien	40.3%	26.2%	16.1%	16.7%	0.6%
39,102	FITCHBURG	3,079	1,170	585	624	667	33	O'Brien	38.0%	19.0%	20.3%	21.7%	1.1%
66,910	FRAMINGHAM	7,611	2,348	2,437	1,190	1,574	62	Reich	30.9%	32.0%	15.6%	20.7%	0.8%
29,560	FRANKLIN	2,332	781	519	502	518	12	O'Brien	33.5%	22.3%	21.5%	22.2%	0.5%
30,273	GLOUCESTER	3,284	1,017	1,447	398	405	17	Reich	31.0%	44.1%	12.1%	12.3%	0.5%
58,969	HAVERHILL	5,317	1,900	1,159	1,153	1,061	44	O'Brien	35.7%	21.8%	21.7%	20.0%	0.8%
19,882	HINGHAM	2,535	948	693	451	436	7	O'Brien	37.4%	27.3%	17.8%	17.2%	0.3%
39,838	HOLYOKE	4,004	1,780	686	877	634	27	O'Brien	44.5%	17.1%	21.9%	15.8%	0.7%
72,043	LAWRENCE	5,115	1,708	731	1,675	744	257	O'Brien	33.4%	14.3%	32.7%	14.5%	5.0%
41,303	LEOMINSTER	2,944	1,233	598	547	553	13	O'Brien	41.9%	20.3%	18.6%	18.8%	0.4%
30,355	LEXINGTON	5,931	1,980	2,485	584	868	14	Reich	33.4%	41.9%	9.8%	14.6%	0.2%
105,167	LOWELL	8,056	2,024	1,190	3,428	1,333	81	Birmingham	25.1%	14.8%	42.6%	16.5%	1.0%
89,050	LYNN	10,367	2,814	1,815	3,880	1,656	202	Birmingham	27.1%	17.5%	37.4%	16.0%	1.9%
56,340	MALDEN	6,232	1,645	1,129	2,397	1,008	53	Birmingham	26.4%	18.1%	38.5%	16.2%	0.9%
20,377	MARBLEHEAD	3,078	918	1,245	485	389	41	Reich	29.8%	40.4%	15.8%	12.6%	1.3%
36,255	MARLBOROUGH	3,661	1,174	744	814	888	41	O'Brien	32.1%	20.3%	22.2%	24.3%	1.1%
24,324	MARSHFIELD	2,790	981	571	679	548	11	O'Brien	35.2%	20.5%	24.3%	19.6%	0.4%
55,765	MEDFORD	9,011	2,213	1,969	3,284	1,482	63	Birmingham	24.6%	21.9%	36.4%	16.4%	0.7%
27,134	MELROSE	4,421	1,340	1,025	1,256	777	23	O'Brien	30.3%	23.2%	28.4%	17.6%	0.5%
43,789	METHUEN	4,093	1,333	821	1,041	836	62	O'Brien	32.6%	20.1%	25.4%	20.4%	1.5%
26,799	MILFORD	1,958	756	449	347	396	10	O'Brien	38.6%	22.9%	17.7%	20.2%	0.5%
26,062	MILTON	7,004	2,480	1,589	1,769	1,111	55	O'Brien	35.4%	22.7%	25.3%	15.9%	0.8%
32,170	NATICK	4,493	1,458	1,397	648	954	36	O'Brien	32.5%	31.1%	14.4%	21.2%	0.8%
28,911	NEEDHAM	5,146	1,706	1,993	659	755	33	Reich	33.2%	38.7%	12.8%	14.7%	0.6%
93,768	NEW BEDFORD	11,112	2,819	1,549	5,097	1,380	267	Birmingham	25.4%	13.9%	45.9%	12.4%	2.4%
83,829	NEWTON	16,808	5,050	7,014	1,939	2,642	163	Reich	30.0%	41.7%	11.5%	15.7%	1.0%
27,202	NORTH ANDOVER	3,118	1,015	849	615	616	23	O'Brien	32.6%	27.2%	19.7%	19.8%	0.7%
27,143	NORTH ATTLEBOROUGH	1,362	502	239	334	280	7	O'Brien	36.9%	17.5%	24.5%	20.6%	0.5%
28,978	NORTHAMPTON	6,253	2,355	2,793	390	686	29	Reich	37.7%	44.7%	6.2%	11.0%	0.5%
28,587	NORWOOD	4,269	1,372	841	1,175	842	39	O'Brien	32.1%	19.7%	27.5%	19.7%	0.9%
48,129	PEABODY	9,353	2,495	1,904	3,119	1,730	105	Birmingham	26.7%	20.4%	33.3%	18.5%	1.1%
45,793	PITTSFIELD	3,688	1,361	1,276	640	376	35	O'Brien	36.9%	34.6%	17.4%	10.2%	0.9%
51,701	PLYMOUTH	4,482	1,579	907	1,148	827	21	O'Brien	35.2%	20.2%	25.6%	18.5%	0.5%
88,025	QUINCY	14,938	4,875	2,610	4,478	2,793	182	O'Brien	32.6%	17.5%	30.0%	18.7%	1.2%
30,963	RANDOLPH	4,891	1,649	1,231	1,099	845	67	O'Brien	33.7%	25.2%	22.5%	17.3%	1.4%
23,708	READING	3,129	1,084	853	673	508	11	O'Brien	34.6%	27.3%	21.5%	16.2%	0.4%
47,283	REVERE	6,971	1,230	994	3,896	781	70	Birmingham	17.6%	14.3%	55.9%	11.2%	1.0%
40,407	SALEM	6,779	2,101	1,590	1,503	1,491	94	O'Brien	31.0%	23.5%	22.2%	22.0%	1.4%
26,078	SAUGUS	4,507	1,049	702	2,006	722	28	Birmingham	23.3%	15.6%	44.5%	16.0%	0.6%
17,863	SCITUATE	2,492	923	594	496	457	22	O'Brien	37.0%	23.8%	19.9%	18.3%	0.9%
31,640	SHREWSBURY	2,915	1,096	724	601	485	9	O'Brien	37.6%	24.8%	20.6%	16.6%	0.3%
77,478	SOMERVILLE	10,346	2,503	3,534	2,734	1,489	86	Reich	24.2%	34.2%	26.4%	14.4%	0.8%
152,082	SPRINGFIELD	11,375	4,939	1,639	2,754	1,907	136	O'Brien	43.4%	14.4%	24.2%	16.8%	1.2%
22,219	STONEHAM	2,965	873	566	964	540	22	Birmingham	29.4%	19.1%	32.5%	18.2%	0.7%
27,149	STOUGHTON	3,817	1,209	984	816	752	56	O'Brien	31.7%	25.8%	21.4%	19.7%	1.5%
55,976	TAUNTON	4,865	1,808	566	1,876	583	32	Birmingham	37.2%	11.6%	38.6%	12.0%	0.7%
28,851	TEWKSBURY	3,433	1,024	540	1,168	668	33	Birmingham	29.8%	15.7%	34.0%	19.5%	1.0%
24,804	WAKEFIELD	4,073	1,254	771	1,270	757	21	Birmingham	30.8%	18.9%	31.2%	18.6%	0.5%

MASSACHUSETTS DEMOCRATIC PRIMARY

GOVERNOR 2002

2000 Census Population	City/Town	Total Vote	O'Brien	Reich	Birmingham	Tolman	Other	Winner	Percentage of Total Vote				
									O'Brien	Reich	Birmingham	Tolman	Other
22,824	WALPOLE	2,749	935	594	653	556	11	O'Brien	34.0%	21.6%	23.8%	20.2%	0.4%
59,226	WALTHAM	6,297	1,812	1,524	959	1,957	45	Tolman	28.8%	24.2%	15.2%	31.1%	0.7%
32,986	WATERTOWN	6,636	980	1,095	454	4,091	16	Tolman	14.8%	16.5%	6.8%	61.6%	0.2%
26,613	WELLESLEY	4,014	1,548	1,425	443	561	37	O'Brien	38.6%	35.5%	11.0%	14.0%	0.9%
27,899	WEST SPRINGFIELD	1,819	834	342	313	316	14	O'Brien	45.8%	18.8%	17.2%	17.4%	0.8%
40,072	WESTFIELD	2,962	1,421	419	579	520	23	O'Brien	48.0%	14.1%	19.5%	17.6%	0.8%
53,988	WEYMOUTH	8,000	2,659	1,419	2,472	1,413	37	O'Brien	33.2%	17.7%	30.9%	17.7%	0.5%
20,810	WINCHESTER	3,195	1,035	995	595	558	12	O'Brien	32.4%	31.1%	18.6%	17.5%	0.4%
37,258	WOBURN	4,805	1,665	891	1,166	1,049	34	O'Brien	34.7%	18.5%	24.3%	21.8%	0.7%
172,648	WORCESTER	15,110	4,523	3,462	4,093	2,449	583	O'Brien	29.9%	22.9%	27.1%	16.2%	3.9%
24,807	YARMOUTH	2,656	1,015	675	460	494	12	O'Brien	38.2%	25.4%	17.3%	18.6%	0.5%

MICHIGAN

GOVERNOR
Jennifer M. Granholm (D). Elected 2002 to a four-year term.

SENATORS (2 Democrats)
Carl Levin (D). Reelected 2002 to a six-year term. Previously elected 1996, 1990, 1984, 1978.

Debbie Stabenow (D). Elected 2000 to a six-year term.

REPRESENTATIVES (9 Republicans, 6 Democrats)
1. Bart Stupak (D)
2. Peter Hoekstra (R)
3. Vernon J. Ehlers (R)
4. Dave Camp (R)
5. Dale E. Kildee (D)
6. Fred Upton (R)
7. Nick Smith (R)
8. Mike Rogers (R)
9. Joe Knollenberg (R)
10. Candice S. Miller (R)
11. Thaddeus McCotter (R)
12. Sander M. Levin (D)
13. Carolyn Cheeks Kilpatrick (D)
14. John Conyers Jr. (D)
15. John D. Dingell (D)

POSTWAR VOTE FOR PRESIDENT

| | | Republican | | Democratic | | Other | | Percentage | | | |
| | | | | | | | | Total Vote | | Major Vote | |
Year	Total Vote	Vote	Candidate	Vote	Candidate	Vote	Plurality	Rep.	Dem.	Rep.	Dem.
2000**	4,232,711	1,953,139	Bush, George W.	2,170,418	Gore, Al	109,154	217,279 D	46.1%	51.3%	47.4%	52.6%
1996**	3,848,844	1,481,212	Dole, Bob	1,989,653	Clinton, Bill	377,979	508,441 D	38.5%	51.7%	42.7%	57.3%
1992**	4,274,673	1,554,940	Bush, George	1,871,182	Clinton, Bill	848,551	316,242 D	36.4%	43.8%	45.4%	54.6%
1988	3,669,163	1,965,486	Bush, George	1,675,783	Dukakis, Michael S.	27,894	289,703 R	53.6%	45.7%	54.0%	46.0%
1984	3,801,658	2,251,571	Reagan, Ronald	1,529,638	Mondale, Walter F.	20,449	721,933 R	59.2%	40.2%	59.5%	40.5%
1980**	3,909,725	1,915,225	Reagan, Ronald	1,661,532	Carter, Jimmy	332,968	253,693 R	49.0%	42.5%	53.5%	46.5%
1976	3,653,749	1,893,742	Ford, Gerald R.	1,696,714	Carter, Jimmy	63,293	197,028 R	51.8%	46.4%	52.7%	47.3%
1972	3,489,727	1,961,721	Nixon, Richard M.	1,459,435	McGovern, George S.	68,571	502,286 R	56.2%	41.8%	57.3%	42.7%
1968	3,306,250	1,370,665	Nixon, Richard M.	1,593,082	Humphrey, Hubert H.	342,503	222,417 D	41.5%	48.2%	46.2%	53.8%
1964	3,203,102	1,060,152	Goldwater, Barry M.	2,136,615	Johnson, Lyndon B.	6,335	1,076,463 D	33.1%	66.7%	33.2%	66.8%
1960	3,318,097	1,620,428	Nixon, Richard M.	1,687,269	Kennedy, John F.	10,400	66,841 D	48.8%	50.9%	49.0%	51.0%
1956	3,080,468	1,713,647	Eisenhower, Dwight D.	1,359,898	Stevenson, Adlai E.	6,923	353,749 R	55.6%	44.1%	55.8%	44.2%
1952	2,798,592	1,551,529	Eisenhower, Dwight D.	1,230,657	Stevenson, Adlai E.	16,406	320,872 R	55.4%	44.0%	55.8%	44.2%
1948	2,109,609	1,038,595	Dewey, Thomas E.	1,003,448	Truman, Harry S.	67,566	35,147 R	49.2%	47.6%	50.9%	49.1%

In 2000 the other vote column includes 84,165 votes cast for Green (Nader). In 1996 the other vote column includes 336,670 votes cast for Perot. In 1992 the other vote column includes 824,813 votes cast for Perot. In 1980 the other vote column includes 275,223 votes for Independent (Anderson).

MICHIGAN

POSTWAR VOTE FOR GOVERNOR

Year	Total Vote	Republican Vote	Republican Candidate	Democratic Vote	Democratic Candidate	Other Vote	Rep.-Dem. Plurality	Total Vote Rep.	Total Vote Dem.	Major Vote Rep.	Major Vote Dem.
2002	3,177,565	1,506,104	Posthumus, Dick	1,633,796	Granholm, Jennifer M.	37,665	127,692 D	47.4%	51.4%	48.0%	52.0%
1998	3,027,104	1,883,005	Engler, John	1,143,574	Fieger, Geoffrey	525	739,431 R	62.2%	37.8%	62.2%	37.8%
1994	3,089,077	1,899,101	Engler, John	1,188,438	Wolpe, Howard	1,538	710,663 R	61.5%	38.5%	61.5%	38.5%
1990	2,564,563	1,276,134	Engler, John	1,258,539	Blanchard, James J.	29,890	17,595 R	49.8%	49.1%	50.3%	49.7%
1986	2,396,564	753,647	Lucas, William	1,632,138	Blanchard, James J.	10,779	878,491 D	31.4%	68.1%	31.6%	68.4%
1982	3,040,008	1,369,582	Headlee, Richard H.	1,561,291	Blanchard, James J.	109,135	191,709 D	45.1%	51.4%	46.7%	53.3%
1978	2,867,212	1,628,485	Milliken, William G.	1,237,256	Fitzgerald, William	1,471	391,229 R	56.8%	43.2%	56.8%	43.2%
1974	2,657,017	1,356,865	Milliken, William G.	1,242,247	Levin, Sander	57,905	114,618 R	51.1%	46.8%	52.2%	47.8%
1970	2,656,162	1,339,047	Milliken, William G.	1,294,638	Levin, Sander	22,477	44,409 R	50.4%	48.7%	50.8%	49.2%
1966**	2,461,909	1,490,430	Romney, George W.	963,383	Ferency, Zolton A.	8,096	527,047 R	60.5%	39.1%	60.7%	39.3%
1964	3,158,102	1,764,355	Romney, George W.	1,381,442	Staebler, Neil	12,305	382,913 R	55.9%	43.7%	56.1%	43.9%
1962	2,764,839	1,420,086	Romney, George W.	1,339,513	Swainson, John B.	5,240	80,573 R	51.4%	48.4%	51.5%	48.5%
1960	3,255,991	1,602,022	Bagwell, Paul D.	1,643,634	Swainson, John B.	10,335	41,612 D	49.2%	50.5%	49.4%	50.6%
1958	2,312,184	1,078,089	Bagwell, Paul D.	1,225,533	Williams, G. Mennen	8,562	147,444 D	46.6%	53.0%	46.8%	53.2%
1956	3,049,651	1,376,376	Cobo, Albert E.	1,666,689	Williams, G. Mennen	6,586	290,313 D	45.1%	54.7%	45.2%	54.8%
1954	2,187,027	963,300	Leonard, Donald S.	1,216,308	Williams, G. Mennen	7,419	253,008 D	44.0%	55.6%	44.2%	55.8%
1952	2,865,980	1,423,275	Alger, Fred M.	1,431,893	Williams, G. Mennen	10,812	8,618 D	49.7%	50.0%	49.8%	50.2%
1950	1,879,382	933,998	Kelly, Harry F.	935,152	Williams, G. Mennen	10,232	1,154 D	49.7%	49.8%	50.0%	50.0%
1948	2,113,122	964,810	Sigler, Kim	1,128,664	Williams, G. Mennen	19,648	163,854 D	45.7%	53.4%	46.1%	53.9%
1946	1,665,475	1,003,878	Sigler, Kim	644,540	Van Wagoner, Murray	17,057	359,338 R	60.3%	38.7%	60.9%	39.1%

The term of office of Michigan's Governor was increased from two to four years effective with the 1966 election.

POSTWAR VOTE FOR SENATOR

Year	Total Vote	Republican Vote	Republican Candidate	Democratic Vote	Democratic Candidate	Other Vote	Rep.-Dem. Plurality	Total Vote Rep.	Total Vote Dem.	Major Vote Rep.	Major Vote Dem.
2002	3,129,287	1,185,545	Raczkowski, Andrew	1,896,614	Levin, Carl	47,128	711,069 D	37.9%	60.6%	38.5%	61.5%
2000	4,167,685	1,994,693	Abraham, Spencer	2,061,952	Stabenow, Debbie	111,040	67,259 D	47.9%	49.5%	49.2%	50.8%
1996	3,762,575	1,500,106	Romney, Ronna	2,195,738	Levin, Carl	66,731	695,632 D	39.9%	58.4%	40.6%	59.4%
1994	3,043,385	1,578,770	Abraham, Spencer	1,300,960	Carr, M. Robert	163,655	277,810 R	51.9%	42.7%	54.8%	45.2%
1990	2,560,494	1,055,695	Schuette, Bill	1,471,753	Levin, Carl	33,046	416,058 D	41.2%	57.5%	41.8%	58.2%
1988	3,505,985	1,348,219	Dunn, Jim	2,116,865	Riegle, Donald W.	40,901	768,646 D	38.5%	60.4%	38.9%	61.1%
1984	3,700,938	1,745,302	Lousma, Jack	1,915,831	Levin, Carl	39,805	170,529 D	47.2%	51.8%	47.7%	52.3%
1982	2,994,334	1,223,288	Ruppe, Philip E.	1,728,793	Riegle, Donald W.	42,253	505,505 D	40.9%	57.7%	41.4%	58.6%
1978	2,846,630	1,362,165	Griffin, Robert P.	1,484,193	Levin, Carl	272	122,028 D	47.9%	52.1%	47.9%	52.1%
1976	3,490,664	1,635,087	Esch, Marvin L.	1,831,031	Riegle, Donald W.	24,546	195,944 D	46.8%	52.5%	47.2%	52.8%
1972	3,406,906	1,781,065	Griffin, Robert P.	1,577,178	Kelley, Frank J.	48,663	203,887 R	52.3%	46.3%	53.0%	47.0%
1970	2,610,839	858,470	Romney, Lenore	1,744,716	Hart, Philip A.	7,653	886,246 D	32.9%	66.8%	33.0%	67.0%
1966	2,439,365	1,363,530	Griffin, Robert P.	1,069,484	Williams, G. Mennen	6,351	294,046 R	55.9%	43.8%	56.0%	44.0%
1964	3,101,667	1,096,272	Peterson, Elly M.	1,996,912	Hart, Philip A.	8,483	900,640 D	35.3%	64.4%	35.4%	64.6%
1960	3,226,647	1,548,873	Bentley, Alvin M.	1,669,179	McNamara, Patrick V.	8,595	120,306 D	48.0%	51.7%	48.1%	51.9%
1958	2,271,644	1,046,963	Potter, Charles E.	1,216,966	Hart, Philip A.	7,715	170,003 D	46.1%	53.6%	46.2%	53.8%
1954	2,144,840	1,049,420	Ferguson, Homer	1,088,550	McNamara, Patrick V.	6,870	39,130 D	48.9%	50.8%	49.1%	50.9%
1952	2,821,133	1,428,352	Potter, Charles E.	1,383,416	Moody, Blair	9,365	44,936 R	50.6%	49.0%	50.8%	49.2%
1948	2,062,097	1,045,156	Ferguson, Homer	1,000,329	Hook, Frank E.	16,612	44,827 R	50.7%	48.5%	51.1%	48.9%
1946	1,618,720	1,085,570	Vandenberg, Arthur	517,923	Lee, James H.	15,227	567,647 R	67.1%	32.0%	67.7%	32.3%

MICHIGAN

Congressional districts first established for elections held in 2002
15 members

MICHIGAN

Detroit Area

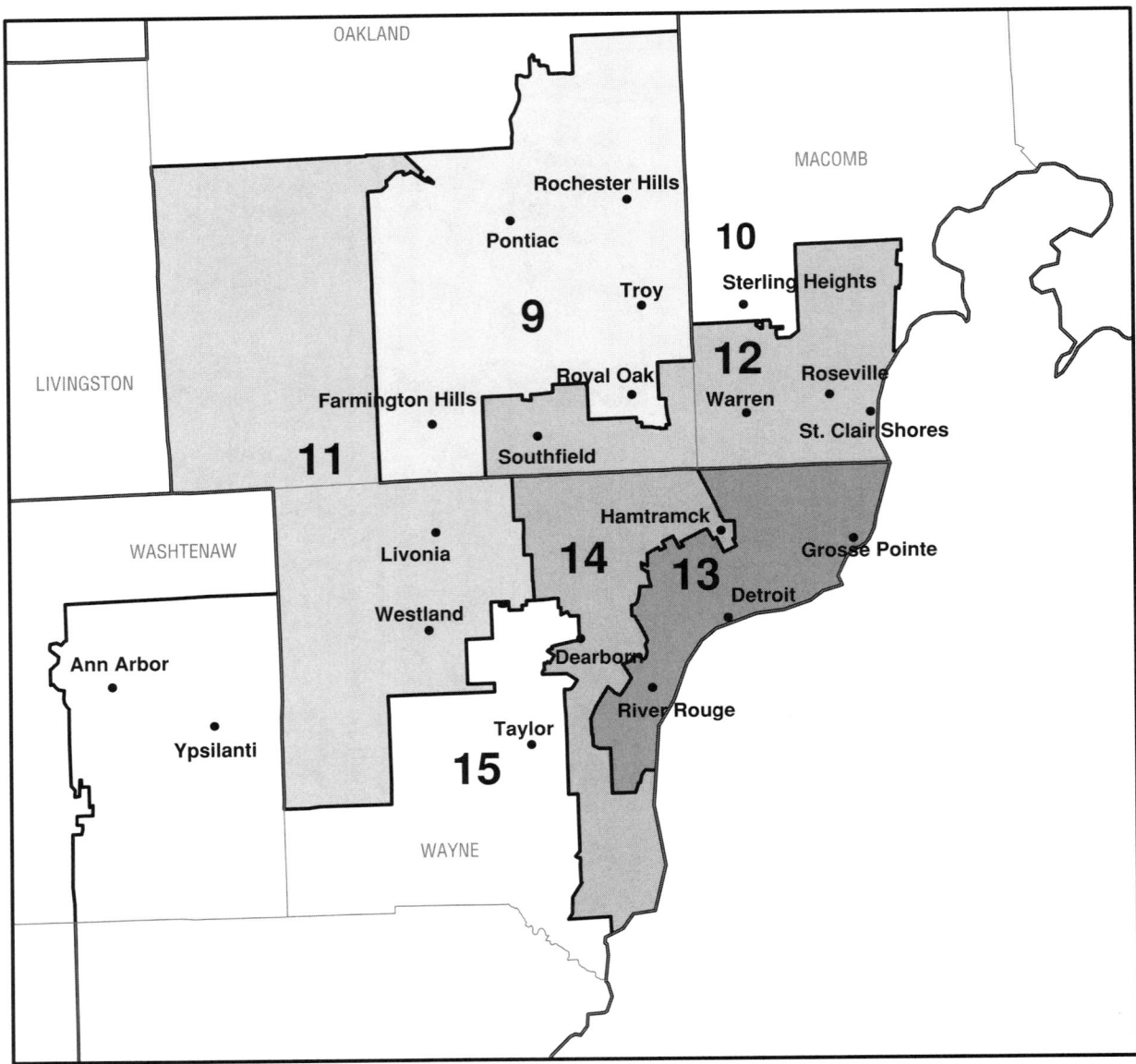

MICHIGAN
GOVERNOR 2002

2000 Census Population	County	Total Vote	Republican	Democratic	Other	Rep.-Dem. Plurality	Percentage			
							Total Vote		Major Vote	
							Rep.	Dem.	Rep.	Dem.
11,719	ALCONA	4,587	2,387	2,165	35	222 R	52.0%	47.2%	52.4%	47.6%
9,862	ALGER	3,527	1,623	1,855	49	232 D	46.0%	52.6%	46.7%	53.3%
105,665	ALLEGAN	34,836	21,695	12,772	369	8,923 R	62.3%	36.7%	62.9%	37.1%
31,314	ALPENA	11,223	4,722	6,391	110	1,669 D	42.1%	56.9%	42.5%	57.5%
23,110	ANTRIM	9,457	5,576	3,752	129	1,824 R	59.0%	39.7%	59.8%	40.2%
17,269	ARENAC	5,516	2,611	2,821	84	210 D	47.3%	51.1%	48.1%	51.9%
8,746	BARAGA	2,480	1,170	1,263	47	93 D	47.2%	50.9%	48.1%	51.9%
56,755	BARRY	20,266	11,943	8,136	187	3,807 R	58.9%	40.1%	59.5%	40.5%
110,157	BAY	39,762	18,001	21,190	571	3,189 D	45.3%	53.3%	45.9%	54.1%
15,998	BENZIE	6,625	3,480	3,036	109	444 R	52.5%	45.8%	53.4%	46.6%
162,453	BERRIEN	40,845	23,378	17,094	373	6,284 R	57.2%	41.9%	57.8%	42.2%
45,787	BRANCH	11,104	6,012	5,001	91	1,011 R	54.1%	45.0%	54.6%	45.4%
137,985	CALHOUN	40,496	18,789	21,298	409	2,509 D	46.4%	52.6%	46.9%	53.1%
51,104	CASS	12,729	6,845	5,741	143	1,104 R	53.8%	45.1%	54.4%	45.6%
26,090	CHARLEVOIX	9,617	5,608	3,836	173	1,772 R	58.3%	39.9%	59.4%	40.6%
26,448	CHEBOYGAN	9,487	5,268	4,107	112	1,161 R	55.5%	43.3%	56.2%	43.8%
38,543	CHIPPEWA	10,898	5,357	5,428	113	71 D	49.2%	49.8%	49.7%	50.3%
31,252	CLARE	9,428	4,578	4,719	131	141 D	48.6%	50.1%	49.2%	50.8%
64,753	CLINTON	26,060	13,711	12,070	279	1,641 R	52.6%	46.3%	53.2%	46.8%
14,273	CRAWFORD	4,892	2,566	2,233	93	333 R	52.5%	45.6%	53.5%	46.5%
38,520	DELTA	13,624	6,590	6,862	172	272 D	48.4%	50.4%	49.0%	51.0%
27,472	DICKINSON	8,353	4,358	3,882	113	476 R	52.2%	46.5%	52.9%	47.1%
103,655	EATON	39,040	18,247	20,395	398	2,148 D	46.7%	52.2%	47.2%	52.8%
31,437	EMMET	11,653	7,111	4,330	212	2,781 R	61.0%	37.2%	62.2%	37.8%
436,141	GENESEE	134,215	51,828	80,687	1,700	28,859 D	38.6%	60.1%	39.1%	60.9%
26,023	GLADWIN	9,031	4,569	4,350	112	219 R	50.6%	48.2%	51.2%	48.8%
17,370	GOGEBIC	5,686	2,308	3,292	86	984 D	40.6%	57.9%	41.2%	58.8%
77,654	GRAND TRAVERSE	30,130	17,382	12,330	418	5,052 R	57.7%	40.9%	58.5%	41.5%
42,285	GRATIOT	11,577	6,252	5,203	122	1,049 R	54.0%	44.9%	54.6%	45.4%
46,527	HILLSDALE	12,428	7,498	4,778	152	2,720 R	60.3%	38.4%	61.1%	38.9%
36,016	HOUGHTON	10,350	5,119	5,026	205	93 R	49.5%	48.6%	50.5%	49.5%
36,079	HURON	12,135	7,218	4,783	134	2,435 R	59.5%	39.4%	60.1%	39.9%
279,320	INGHAM	91,177	34,414	55,571	1,192	21,157 D	37.7%	60.9%	38.2%	61.8%
61,518	IONIA	18,311	10,232	7,919	160	2,313 R	55.9%	43.2%	56.4%	43.6%
27,339	IOSCO	9,999	4,817	5,031	151	214 D	48.2%	50.3%	48.9%	51.1%
13,138	IRON	4,539	2,017	2,429	93	412 D	44.4%	53.5%	45.4%	54.6%
63,351	ISABELLA	15,221	7,428	7,534	259	106 D	48.8%	49.5%	49.6%	50.4%
158,422	JACKSON	46,965	24,344	22,036	585	2,308 R	51.8%	46.9%	52.5%	47.5%
238,603	KALAMAZOO	74,758	34,795	39,090	873	4,295 D	46.5%	52.3%	47.1%	52.9%
16,571	KALKASKA	5,316	3,010	2,234	72	776 R	56.6%	42.0%	57.4%	42.6%
574,335	KENT	194,212	117,755	74,823	1,634	42,932 R	60.6%	38.5%	61.1%	38.9%
2,301	KEWEENAW	1,048	545	482	21	63 R	52.0%	46.0%	53.1%	46.9%
11,333	LAKE	3,645	1,671	1,904	70	233 D	45.8%	52.2%	46.7%	53.3%
87,904	LAPEER	28,891	17,040	11,384	467	5,656 R	59.0%	39.4%	59.9%	40.1%
21,119	LEELANAU	9,875	5,501	4,241	133	1,260 R	55.7%	42.9%	56.5%	43.5%
98,890	LENAWEE	28,251	14,650	13,314	287	1,336 R	51.9%	47.1%	52.4%	47.6%
156,951	LIVINGSTON	59,330	36,699	22,006	625	14,693 R	61.9%	37.1%	62.5%	37.5%
7,024	LUCE	1,944	889	1,016	39	127 D	45.7%	52.3%	46.7%	53.3%
11,943	MACKINAC	4,666	2,425	2,206	35	219 R	52.0%	47.3%	52.4%	47.6%
788,149	MACOMB	256,730	132,583	121,065	3,082	11,518 R	51.6%	47.2%	52.3%	47.7%
24,527	MANISTEE	8,900	4,401	4,389	110	12 R	49.4%	49.3%	50.1%	49.9%
64,634	MARQUETTE	22,150	8,906	12,779	465	3,873 D	40.2%	57.7%	41.1%	58.9%
28,274	MASON	10,536	5,594	4,802	140	792 R	53.1%	45.6%	53.8%	46.2%
40,553	MECOSTA	11,338	6,197	5,020	121	1,177 R	54.7%	44.3%	55.2%	44.8%
25,326	MENOMINEE	7,035	3,576	3,335	124	241 R	50.8%	47.4%	51.7%	48.3%
82,874	MIDLAND	29,874	17,156	12,342	376	4,814 R	57.4%	41.3%	58.2%	41.8%
14,478	MISSAUKEE	5,237	3,462	1,724	51	1,738 R	66.1%	32.9%	66.8%	33.2%
145,945	MONROE	41,558	21,266	19,845	447	1,421 R	51.2%	47.8%	51.7%	48.3%
61,266	MONTCALM	17,571	9,689	7,763	119	1,926 R	55.1%	44.2%	55.5%	44.5%
10,315	MONTMORENCY	4,010	2,231	1,722	57	509 R	55.6%	42.9%	56.4%	43.6%

MICHIGAN

GOVERNOR 2002

2000 Census Population	County	Total Vote	Republican	Democratic	Other	Rep.-Dem. Plurality	Percentage Total Vote		Major Vote	
							Rep.	Dem.	Rep.	Dem.
170,200	MUSKEGON	52,904	22,600	29,884	420	7,284 D	42.7%	56.5%	43.1%	56.9%
47,874	NEWAYGO	15,347	8,910	6,268	169	2,642 R	58.1%	40.8%	58.7%	41.3%
1,194,156	OAKLAND	435,611	210,414	220,082	5,115	9,668 D	48.3%	50.5%	48.9%	51.1%
26,873	OCEANA	8,601	4,637	3,886	78	751 R	53.9%	45.2%	54.4%	45.6%
21,645	OGEMAW	7,523	3,689	3,727	107	38 D	49.0%	49.5%	49.7%	50.3%
7,818	ONTONAGON	2,689	1,334	1,301	54	33 R	49.6%	48.4%	50.6%	49.4%
23,197	OSCEOLA	7,439	4,399	2,973	67	1,426 R	59.1%	40.0%	59.7%	40.3%
9,418	OSCODA	2,968	1,669	1,242	57	427 R	56.2%	41.8%	57.3%	42.7%
23,301	OTSEGO	8,473	4,982	3,346	145	1,636 R	58.8%	39.5%	59.8%	40.2%
238,314	OTTAWA	87,701	62,464	24,654	583	37,810 R	71.2%	28.1%	71.7%	28.3%
14,411	PRESQUE ISLE	5,643	2,862	2,717	64	145 R	50.7%	48.1%	51.3%	48.7%
25,469	ROSCOMMON	10,260	5,223	4,909	128	314 R	50.9%	47.8%	51.5%	48.5%
210,039	SAGINAW	72,277	33,440	38,051	786	4,611 D	46.3%	52.6%	46.8%	53.2%
164,235	ST. CLAIR	52,403	27,647	23,813	943	3,834 R	52.8%	45.4%	53.7%	46.3%
62,422	ST. JOSEPH	15,514	9,014	6,341	159	2,673 R	58.1%	40.9%	58.7%	41.3%
44,547	SANILAC	14,081	8,581	5,265	235	3,316 R	60.9%	37.4%	62.0%	38.0%
8,903	SCHOOLCRAFT	3,218	1,468	1,701	49	233 D	45.6%	52.9%	46.3%	53.7%
71,687	SHIAWASSEE	25,173	12,971	11,843	359	1,128 R	51.5%	47.0%	52.3%	47.7%
58,266	TUSCOLA	19,219	10,824	8,097	298	2,727 R	56.3%	42.1%	57.2%	42.8%
76,263	VAN BUREN	21,400	10,685	10,518	197	167 R	49.9%	49.1%	50.4%	49.6%
322,895	WASHTENAW	107,474	39,659	65,995	1,820	26,336 D	36.9%	61.4%	37.5%	62.5%
2,061,162	WAYNE	566,498	175,899	384,121	6,478	208,222 D	31.1%	67.8%	31.4%	68.6%
30,484	WEXFORD	10,005	5,640	4,230	135	1,410 R	56.4%	42.3%	57.1%	42.9%
9,938,444	TOTAL	3,177,565	1,506,104	1,633,796	37,665	127,692 D	47.4%	51.4%	48.0%	52.0%

MICHIGAN

SENATOR 2002

2000 Census Population	County	Total Vote	Republican	Democratic	Other	Rep.-Dem. Plurality	Percentage Total Vote		Major Vote	
							Rep.	Dem.	Rep.	Dem.
11,719	ALCONA	4,404	1,861	2,506	37	645 D	42.3%	56.9%	42.6%	57.4%
9,862	ALGER	3,443	1,099	2,304	40	1,205 D	31.9%	66.9%	32.3%	67.7%
105,665	ALLEGAN	34,405	19,068	14,819	518	4,249 R	55.4%	43.1%	56.3%	43.7%
31,314	ALPENA	10,867	3,302	7,442	123	4,140 D	30.4%	68.5%	30.7%	69.3%
23,110	ANTRIM	9,368	4,472	4,742	154	270 D	47.7%	50.6%	48.5%	51.5%
17,269	ARENAC	5,419	1,751	3,575	93	1,824 D	32.3%	66.0%	32.9%	67.1%
8,746	BARAGA	2,435	822	1,583	30	761 D	33.8%	65.0%	34.2%	65.8%
56,755	BARRY	20,023	9,925	9,748	350	177 R	49.6%	48.7%	50.4%	49.6%
110,157	BAY	39,283	11,368	27,361	554	15,993 D	28.9%	69.7%	29.4%	70.6%
15,998	BENZIE	6,398	2,736	3,549	113	813 D	42.8%	55.5%	43.5%	56.5%
162,453	BERRIEN	40,348	21,197	18,596	555	2,601 R	52.5%	46.1%	53.3%	46.7%
45,787	BRANCH	10,783	5,106	5,540	137	434 D	47.4%	51.4%	48.0%	52.0%
137,985	CALHOUN	40,127	14,864	24,689	574	9,825 D	37.0%	61.5%	37.6%	62.4%
51,104	CASS	12,483	6,181	6,077	225	104 R	49.5%	48.7%	50.4%	49.6%
26,090	CHARLEVOIX	9,531	4,240	5,085	206	845 D	44.5%	53.4%	45.5%	54.5%
26,448	CHEBOYGAN	9,332	3,811	5,396	125	1,585 D	40.8%	57.8%	41.4%	58.6%
38,543	CHIPPEWA	10,780	3,772	6,874	134	3,102 D	35.0%	63.8%	35.4%	64.6%
31,252	CLARE	9,393	3,181	6,056	156	2,875 D	33.9%	64.5%	34.4%	65.6%
64,753	CLINTON	25,529	11,511	13,594	424	2,083 D	45.1%	53.2%	45.9%	54.1%
14,273	CRAWFORD	4,827	1,894	2,851	82	957 D	39.2%	59.1%	39.9%	60.1%
38,520	DELTA	13,482	4,529	8,798	155	4,269 D	33.6%	65.3%	34.0%	66.0%
27,472	DICKINSON	8,339	3,047	5,190	102	2,143 D	36.5%	62.2%	37.0%	63.0%
103,655	EATON	38,374	15,587	22,134	653	6,547 D	40.6%	57.7%	41.3%	58.7%
31,437	EMMET	11,562	5,305	6,021	236	716 D	45.9%	52.1%	46.8%	53.2%
436,141	GENESEE	133,197	39,030	92,057	2,110	53,027 D	29.3%	69.1%	29.8%	70.2%

MICHIGAN

SENATOR 2002

2000 Census Population	County	Total Vote	Republican	Democratic	Other	Rep.-Dem. Plurality	Total Vote Rep.	Total Vote Dem.	Major Vote Rep.	Major Vote Dem.
26,023	GLADWIN	8,959	3,227	5,603	129	2,376 D	36.0%	62.5%	36.5%	63.5%
17,370	GOGEBIC	5,638	1,604	3,921	113	2,317 D	28.4%	69.5%	29.0%	71.0%
77,654	GRAND TRAVERSE	29,809	14,003	15,288	518	1,285 D	47.0%	51.3%	47.8%	52.2%
42,285	GRATIOT	11,297	4,929	6,235	133	1,306 D	43.6%	55.2%	44.2%	55.8%
46,527	HILLSDALE	11,777	6,258	5,373	146	885 R	53.1%	45.6%	53.8%	46.2%
36,016	HOUGHTON	10,167	3,885	6,114	168	2,229 D	38.2%	60.1%	38.9%	61.1%
36,079	HURON	11,820	5,097	6,572	151	1,475 D	43.1%	55.6%	43.7%	56.3%
279,320	INGHAM	90,221	28,406	59,651	2,164	31,245 D	31.5%	66.1%	32.3%	67.7%
61,518	IONIA	17,293	8,205	8,900	188	695 D	47.4%	51.5%	48.0%	52.0%
27,339	IOSCO	9,829	3,429	6,173	227	2,744 D	34.9%	62.8%	35.7%	64.3%
13,138	IRON	4,520	1,346	3,099	75	1,753 D	29.8%	68.6%	30.3%	69.7%
63,351	ISABELLA	15,079	5,601	9,157	321	3,556 D	37.1%	60.7%	38.0%	62.0%
158,422	JACKSON	46,347	19,753	25,807	787	6,054 D	42.6%	55.7%	43.4%	56.6%
238,603	KALAMAZOO	73,964	30,856	41,910	1,198	11,054 D	41.7%	56.7%	42.4%	57.6%
16,571	KALKASKA	5,055	2,247	2,727	81	480 D	44.5%	53.9%	45.2%	54.8%
574,335	KENT	191,482	99,253	89,797	2,432	9,456 R	51.8%	46.9%	52.5%	47.5%
2,301	KEWEENAW	1,046	384	636	26	252 D	36.7%	60.8%	37.6%	62.4%
11,333	LAKE	3,592	1,148	2,378	66	1,230 D	32.0%	66.2%	32.6%	67.4%
87,904	LAPEER	28,448	13,194	14,689	565	1,495 D	46.4%	51.6%	47.3%	52.7%
21,119	LEELANAU	9,802	4,502	5,128	172	626 D	45.9%	52.3%	46.7%	53.3%
98,890	LENAWEE	27,564	11,959	15,202	403	3,243 D	43.4%	55.2%	44.0%	56.0%
156,951	LIVINGSTON	58,513	30,585	27,023	905	3,562 R	52.3%	46.2%	53.1%	46.9%
7,024	LUCE	1,917	686	1,194	37	508 D	35.8%	62.3%	36.5%	63.5%
11,943	MACKINAC	4,598	1,684	2,856	58	1,172 D	36.6%	62.1%	37.1%	62.9%
788,149	MACOMB	251,606	97,062	151,107	3,437	54,045 D	38.6%	60.1%	39.1%	60.9%
24,527	MANISTEE	8,677	3,246	5,324	107	2,078 D	37.4%	61.4%	37.9%	62.1%
64,634	MARQUETTE	22,039	5,827	15,877	335	10,050 D	26.4%	72.0%	26.8%	73.2%
28,274	MASON	10,454	4,231	6,058	165	1,827 D	40.5%	57.9%	41.1%	58.9%
40,553	MECOSTA	10,879	4,797	5,906	176	1,109 D	44.1%	54.3%	44.8%	55.2%
25,326	MENOMINEE	6,904	2,635	4,146	123	1,511 D	38.2%	60.1%	38.9%	61.1%
82,874	MIDLAND	29,565	13,821	15,266	478	1,445 D	46.7%	51.6%	47.5%	52.5%
14,478	MISSAUKEE	5,191	2,752	2,390	49	362 R	53.0%	46.0%	53.5%	46.5%
145,945	MONROE	40,993	14,791	25,600	602	10,809 D	36.1%	62.4%	36.6%	63.4%
61,266	MONTCALM	16,770	7,974	8,657	139	683 D	47.5%	51.6%	47.9%	52.1%
10,315	MONTMORENCY	3,929	1,518	2,360	51	842 D	38.6%	60.1%	39.1%	60.9%
170,200	MUSKEGON	51,490	17,096	33,806	588	16,710 D	33.2%	65.7%	33.6%	66.4%
47,874	NEWAYGO	14,991	7,154	7,598	239	444 D	47.7%	50.7%	48.5%	51.5%
1,194,156	OAKLAND	429,985	172,891	250,657	6,437	77,766 D	40.2%	58.3%	40.8%	59.2%
26,873	OCEANA	8,196	3,522	4,592	82	1,070 D	43.0%	56.0%	43.4%	56.6%
21,645	OGEMAW	7,476	2,436	4,900	140	2,464 D	32.6%	65.5%	33.2%	66.8%
7,818	ONTONAGON	2,686	811	1,820	55	1,009 D	30.2%	67.8%	30.8%	69.2%
23,197	OSCEOLA	7,172	3,363	3,724	85	361 D	46.9%	51.9%	47.5%	52.5%
9,418	OSCODA	2,939	1,316	1,568	55	252 D	44.8%	53.4%	45.6%	54.4%
23,301	OTSEGO	8,357	3,664	4,555	138	891 D	43.8%	54.5%	44.6%	55.4%
238,314	OTTAWA	86,609	56,102	29,605	902	26,497 R	64.8%	34.2%	65.5%	34.5%
14,411	PRESQUE ISLE	5,634	1,919	3,659	56	1,740 D	34.1%	64.9%	34.4%	65.6%
25,469	ROSCOMMON	10,138	3,595	6,382	161	2,787 D	35.5%	63.0%	36.0%	64.0%
210,039	SAGINAW	71,221	23,400	46,944	877	23,544 D	32.9%	65.9%	33.3%	66.7%
164,235	ST. CLAIR	51,575	20,124	30,505	946	10,381 D	39.0%	59.1%	39.7%	60.3%
62,422	ST. JOSEPH	15,175	7,737	7,182	256	555 R	51.0%	47.3%	51.9%	48.1%
44,547	SANILAC	13,814	6,688	6,844	282	156 D	48.4%	49.5%	49.4%	50.6%
8,903	SCHOOLCRAFT	3,196	925	2,215	56	1,290 D	28.9%	69.3%	29.5%	70.5%
71,687	SHIAWASSEE	24,657	9,731	14,551	375	4,820 D	39.5%	59.0%	40.1%	59.9%
58,266	TUSCOLA	18,838	7,448	11,023	367	3,575 D	39.5%	58.5%	40.3%	59.7%
76,263	VAN BUREN	20,167	9,005	10,935	227	1,930 D	44.7%	54.2%	45.2%	54.8%
322,895	WASHTENAW	106,484	33,001	71,130	2,353	38,129 D	31.0%	66.8%	31.7%	68.3%
2,061,162	WAYNE	558,722	128,893	422,155	7,674	293,262 D	23.1%	75.6%	23.4%	76.6%
30,484	WEXFORD	9,889	4,170	5,553	166	1,383 D	42.2%	56.2%	42.9%	57.1%
9,938,444	TOTAL	3,129,287	1,185,545	1,896,614	47,128	711,069 D	37.9%	60.6%	38.5%	61.5%

MICHIGAN

HOUSE OF REPRESENTATIVES

CD	Year	Total Vote	Republican Vote	Republican Candidate	Democratic Vote	Democratic Candidate	Other Vote	Rep.-Dem. Plurality	Total Vote Rep.	Total Vote Dem.	Major Vote Rep.	Major Vote Dem.
1	2002	222,687	69,254	Hooper, Don	150,701	Stupak, Bart*	2,732	81,447 D	31.1%	67.7%	31.5%	68.5%
2	2002	222,907	156,937	Hoekstra, Peter*	61,749	Wrisley, Jeff	4,221	95,188 R	70.4%	27.7%	71.8%	28.2%
3	2002	218,855	153,131	Ehlers, Vernon J.*	61,987	Lynnes, Kathryn	3,737	91,144 R	70.0%	28.3%	71.2%	28.8%
4	2002	218,573	149,090	Camp, Dave*	65,950	Hollenbeck, Lawrence	3,533	83,140 R	68.2%	30.2%	69.3%	30.7%
5	2002	173,339			158,709	Kildee, Dale E.*	14,630	158,709 D		91.6%		100.0%
6	2002	183,517	126,936	Upton, Fred*	53,793	Giguere, Gary, Jr.	2,788	73,143 R	69.2%	29.3%	70.2%	29.8%
7	2002	203,069	121,142	Smith, Nick*	78,412	Simpson, Mike	3,515	42,730 R	59.7%	38.6%	60.7%	39.3%
8	2002	230,597	156,525	Rogers, Mike*	70,920	McAlpine, Frank	3,152	85,605 R	67.9%	30.8%	68.8%	31.2%
9	2002	242,880	141,102	Knollenberg, Joe*	96,856	Fink, David	4,922	44,246 R	58.1%	39.9%	59.3%	40.7%
10	2002	216,928	137,339	Miller, Candice S.	77,053	Marlinga, Carl	2,536	60,286 R	63.3%	35.5%	64.1%	35.9%
11	2002	220,405	126,050	McCotter, Thaddeus	87,402	Kelley, Kevin	6,953	38,648 R	57.2%	39.7%	59.1%	40.9%
12	2002	206,528	61,502	Dean, Harvey	140,970	Levin, Sander M.*	4,056	79,468 D	29.8%	68.3%	30.4%	69.6%
13	2002	131,941			120,869	Kilpatrick, Carolyn Cheeks*	11,072	120,869 D		91.6%		100.0%
14	2002	174,608	26,544	Stone, Dave	145,285	Conyers, John, Jr.*	2,779	118,741 D	15.2%	83.2%	15.4%	84.6%
15	2002	189,063	48,626	Kaltenbach, Martin	136,518	Dingell, John D.*	3,919	87,892 D	25.7%	72.2%	26.3%	73.7%
Total	2002	3,055,897	1,474,178		1,507,174		74,545	32,996 D	48.2%	49.3%	49.4%	50.6%

An asterisk (*) denotes incumbent.

MICHIGAN

GENERAL AND PRIMARY ELECTIONS

2002 GENERAL ELECTIONS

Governor   Other vote was 25,236 Green (Douglas Campbell); 12,411 U.S. Taxpayers (Joseph Pilchak); 7 write-in (Don Mackle); 6 write-in (Mark McFarlin); 5 write-in (Angelo Brown).

Senator   Other vote was 23,931 Green (Eric Borregard); 12,831 Reform (John Mangopoulos); 10,366 Natural Law (Doug Dern).

House   Other vote was:

CD 1   2,732 Libertarian (John Loosemore).
CD 2   2,680 Libertarian (Laurie Aleck); 1,541 U.S. Taxpayers (Ronald Graeser).
CD 3   2,613 Libertarian (Tom Quinn); 1,124 Reform (Richard Lucey).
CD 4   2,261 Green (Sterling Johnson); 1,272 Libertarian (Al Chia Jr.).
CD 5   9,344 Libertarian (Clint Foster); 5,188 Green (Harley Mikkelson); 97 write-in (Thom Moffitt); 1 write-in (William Fuzi).
CD 6   2,788 Reform (Richard Overton).
CD 7   3,515 Libertarian (Ken Proctor).
CD 8   3,152 Libertarian (Thomas Yeutter).
CD 9   4,922 Libertarian (Robert Schubring).

MICHIGAN

GENERAL AND PRIMARY ELECTIONS

2002 GENERAL ELECTIONS

CD 10	2,536 Libertarian (Renae Coon).
CD 11	4,243 Green (William Boyd); 2,710 U.S. Taxpayers (Dan Malone).
CD 12	2,694 Libertarian (Dick Gach); 1,362 U.S. Taxpayers (Steven Revis).
CD 13	11,072 Libertarian (Raymond Warner).
CD 14	1,532 Libertarian (Francis Schorr); 1,247 Green (John Litle).
CD 15	3,919 Libertarian (Gregory Stempfle).

2002 PRIMARY ELECTIONS

Primary   August 6, 2002

Registration   6,807,837   No Party Registration
(as of July 8, 2002)

Primary Type   Open—Any registered voter could participate in the primary of either party.

Note: An asterisk (*) denotes incumbent.

	REPUBLICAN PRIMARIES			DEMOCRATIC PRIMARIES		
Governor	Dick Posthumus	474,804	81.4%	Jennifer M. Granholm	499,129	47.7%
	John Schwarz	108,581	18.6%	David E. Bonior	292,958	28.0%
	Angelo Brown (write-in)	6		James Blanchard	254,586	24.3%
				Tracey Stevenson	7	
	TOTAL	583,391		TOTAL	1,046,680	
Senator	Andrew Raczkowski	445,876	100.0%	Carl Levin*	889,517	100.0%
Congressional District 1	Don Hooper	13,640	51.1%	Bart Stupak*	62,103	100.0%
	Don Birgel	13,059	48.9%			
	TOTAL	26,699				
Congressional District 2	Peter Hoekstra*	57,882	100.0%	Jeffrey Wrisley	30,432	100.0%
Congressional District 3	Vernon J. Ehlers*	49,090	100.0%	Kathryn Lynnes	29,631	100.0%
Congressional District 4	Dave Camp*	49,649	100.0%	Lawrence Hollenbeck	34,038	100.0%
Congressional District 5	Thom Moffitt (write-in)	226	100.0%	Dale E. Kildee*	58,249	99.9%
				Robert Mavis Jr. (write-in)	45	0.1%
	There was no Republican candidate on the general election ballot.			TOTAL	58,294	
Congressional District 6	Fred Upton*	44,487	66.0%	Gary Giguere Jr.	23,464	100.0%
	Dale Shugars	21,580	32.0%			
	Gloria Ham	1,321	2.0%			
	TOTAL	67,388				
Congressional District 7	Nick Smith*	36,071	100.0%	Mike Simpson	35,072	100.0%
Congressional District 8	Mike Rogers*	39,924	100.0%	Frank McAlpine	32,376	100.0%
Congressional District 9	Joe Knollenberg*	45,696	86.6%	David Fink	56,997	100.0%
	Bart Baron	7,044	13.4%			
	TOTAL	52,740				
Congressional District 10	Candice S. Miller	41,454	100.0%	Carl Marlinga	50,335	100.0%
Congressional District 11	Thaddeus McCotter	25,940	69.1%	Kevin Kelley	57,493	100.0%
	David Hagerty	11,619	30.9%			
	TOTAL	37,559				

MICHIGAN

GENERAL AND PRIMARY ELECTIONS

	REPUBLICAN PRIMARIES			DEMOCRATIC PRIMARIES		
Congressional District 12	Harvey Dean	8,390	42.8%	Sander M. Levin*	71,881	78.8%
	Charles Frangie	5,942	30.3%	William Callahan	16,926	18.5%
	Jamie Morgan	5,268	26.9%	Mario Fundarski	2,444	2.7%
	TOTAL	19,600		TOTAL	91,251	
Congressional District 13	Jim Gram (write-in)	3	100.0%	Carolyn Cheeks Kilpatrick*	69,317	100.0%
				Sam Thomas (write-in)	1	
	There was no Republican candidate on the general election ballot.			TOTAL	69,318	
Congressional District 14	Dave Stone	6,246	100.0%	John Conyers Jr.*	94,904	100.0%
Congressional District 15	Martin Kaltenbach	14,463	100.0%	John D. Dingell*	58,120	58.7%
				Lynn Rivers*	40,832	41.3%
				TOTAL	98,952	

MICHIGAN REPUBLICAN PRIMARY

GOVERNOR 2002

2000 Census Population	County	Total Vote	Posthumus	Schwarz	Other	Winner	Percentage of Total Vote Posthumus	Schwarz
11,719	ALCONA	1,260	1,006	254		Posthumus	79.8%	20.2%
9,862	ALGER	361	315	46		Posthumus	87.3%	12.7%
105,665	ALLEGAN	12,799	10,996	1,803		Posthumus	85.9%	14.1%
31,314	ALPENA	2,093	1,610	483		Posthumus	76.9%	23.1%
23,110	ANTRIM	2,422	1,986	436		Posthumus	82.0%	18.0%
17,269	ARENAC	812	671	141		Posthumus	82.6%	17.4%
8,746	BARAGA	194	166	28		Posthumus	85.6%	14.4%
56,755	BARRY	5,104	4,330	774		Posthumus	84.8%	15.2%
110,157	BAY	4,899	3,966	933		Posthumus	81.0%	19.0%
15,998	BENZIE	2,121	1,488	633		Posthumus	70.2%	29.8%
162,453	BERRIEN	15,501	11,746	3,755		Posthumus	75.8%	24.2%
45,787	BRANCH	3,666	2,691	975		Posthumus	73.4%	26.6%
137,985	CALHOUN	9,211	5,342	3,869		Posthumus	58.0%	42.0%
51,104	CASS	4,065	3,049	1,016		Posthumus	75.0%	25.0%
26,090	CHARLEVOIX	1,920	1,509	411		Posthumus	78.6%	21.4%
26,448	CHEBOYGAN	1,751	1,447	304		Posthumus	82.6%	17.4%
38,543	CHIPPEWA	1,388	1,182	206		Posthumus	85.2%	14.8%
31,252	CLARE	1,489	1,304	185		Posthumus	87.6%	12.4%
64,753	CLINTON	6,526	5,185	1,341		Posthumus	79.5%	20.5%
14,273	CRAWFORD	1,637	1,309	328		Posthumus	80.0%	20.0%
38,520	DELTA	1,471	1,259	212		Posthumus	85.6%	14.4%
27,472	DICKINSON	563	472	91		Posthumus	83.8%	16.2%
103,655	EATON	7,252	4,963	2,289		Posthumus	68.4%	31.6%
31,437	EMMET	1,997	1,502	495		Posthumus	75.2%	24.8%
436,141	GENESEE	11,388	9,723	1,665		Posthumus	85.4%	14.6%
26,023	GLADWIN	1,391	1,253	138		Posthumus	90.1%	9.9%
17,370	GOGEBIC	272	229	43		Posthumus	84.2%	15.8%
77,654	GRAND TRAVERSE	7,744	6,047	1,697		Posthumus	78.1%	21.9%
42,285	GRATIOT	2,304	2,014	290		Posthumus	87.4%	12.6%
46,527	HILLSDALE	4,210	3,332	878		Posthumus	79.1%	20.9%
36,016	HOUGHTON	946	796	150		Posthumus	84.1%	15.9%
36,079	HURON	4,184	3,509	675		Posthumus	83.9%	16.1%
279,320	INGHAM	11,588	8,460	3,128		Posthumus	73.0%	27.0%
61,518	IONIA	3,938	3,392	546		Posthumus	86.1%	13.9%
27,339	IOSCO	1,860	1,541	319		Posthumus	82.8%	17.2%

MICHIGAN REPUBLICAN PRIMARY
GOVERNOR 2002

2000 Census Population	County	Total Vote	Posthumus	Schwarz	Other	Winner	Percentage of Total Vote	
							Posthumus	Schwarz
13,138	IRON	312	271	41		Posthumus	86.9%	13.1%
63,351	ISABELLA	2,809	2,299	510		Posthumus	81.8%	18.2%
158,422	JACKSON	7,928	6,597	1,331		Posthumus	83.2%	16.8%
238,603	KALAMAZOO	24,944	18,472	6,472		Posthumus	74.1%	25.9%
16,571	KALKASKA	1,090	903	187		Posthumus	82.8%	17.2%
574,335	KENT	46,871	42,919	3,952		Posthumus	91.6%	8.4%
2,301	KEWEENAW	196	166	30		Posthumus	84.7%	15.3%
11,333	LAKE	672	586	86		Posthumus	87.2%	12.8%
87,904	LAPEER	8,176	6,759	1,417		Posthumus	82.7%	17.3%
21,119	LEELANAU	3,379	2,599	780		Posthumus	76.9%	23.1%
98,890	LENAWEE	4,986	4,209	777		Posthumus	84.4%	15.6%
156,951	LIVINGSTON	12,995	10,720	2,275		Posthumus	82.5%	17.5%
7,024	LUCE	405	323	82		Posthumus	79.8%	20.2%
11,943	MACKINAC	713	595	118		Posthumus	83.5%	16.5%
788,149	MACOMB	40,731	34,564	6,167		Posthumus	84.9%	15.1%
24,527	MANISTEE	2,375	1,936	439		Posthumus	81.5%	18.5%
64,634	MARQUETTE	1,492	1,292	200		Posthumus	86.6%	13.4%
28,274	MASON	2,182	1,820	362		Posthumus	83.4%	16.6%
40,553	MECOSTA	3,298	2,811	487		Posthumus	85.2%	14.8%
25,326	MENOMINEE	1,271	959	312		Posthumus	75.5%	24.5%
82,874	MIDLAND	7,592	6,134	1,458		Posthumus	80.8%	19.2%
14,478	MISSAUKEE	1,945	1,737	208		Posthumus	89.3%	10.7%
145,945	MONROE	5,387	4,420	967		Posthumus	82.0%	18.0%
61,266	MONTCALM	5,469	4,554	915		Posthumus	83.3%	16.7%
10,315	MONTMORENCY	1,358	986	372		Posthumus	72.6%	27.4%
170,200	MUSKEGON	7,597	6,776	821		Posthumus	89.2%	10.8%
47,874	NEWAYGO	4,966	4,131	835		Posthumus	83.2%	16.8%
1,194,156	OAKLAND	88,372	68,288	20,084		Posthumus	77.3%	22.7%
26,873	OCEANA	2,357	2,020	337		Posthumus	85.7%	14.3%
21,645	OGEMAW	1,042	875	167		Posthumus	84.0%	16.0%
7,818	ONTONAGON	175	137	38		Posthumus	78.3%	21.7%
23,197	OSCEOLA	2,379	2,044	335		Posthumus	85.9%	14.1%
9,418	OSCODA	708	620	88		Posthumus	87.6%	12.4%
23,301	OTSEGO	2,157	1,773	384		Posthumus	82.2%	17.8%
238,314	OTTAWA	29,290	26,538	2,747	5	Posthumus	90.6%	9.4%
14,411	PRESQUE ISLE	964	798	166		Posthumus	82.8%	17.2%
25,469	ROSCOMMON	3,032	2,526	506		Posthumus	83.3%	16.7%
210,039	SAGINAW	10,382	8,962	1,420		Posthumus	86.3%	13.7%
164,235	ST. CLAIR	10,268	7,191	3,077		Posthumus	70.0%	30.0%
62,422	ST. JOSEPH	6,053	4,643	1,410		Posthumus	76.7%	23.3%
44,547	SANILAC	3,746	3,038	708		Posthumus	81.1%	18.9%
8,903	SCHOOLCRAFT	341	266	75		Posthumus	78.0%	22.0%
71,687	SHIAWASSEE	6,044	5,142	902		Posthumus	85.1%	14.9%
58,266	TUSCOLA	2,981	2,645	336		Posthumus	88.7%	11.3%
76,263	VAN BUREN	5,498	4,532	966		Posthumus	82.4%	17.6%
322,895	WASHTENAW	10,059	7,905	2,154		Posthumus	78.6%	21.4%
2,061,162	WAYNE	53,240	43,132	10,107	1	Posthumus	81.0%	19.0%
30,484	WEXFORD	2,837	2,401	436		Posthumus	84.6%	15.4%
9,938,444	TOTAL	583,391	474,804	108,581	6	Posthumus	81.4%	18.6%

MICHIGAN DEMOCRATIC PRIMARY

GOVERNOR 2002

2000 Census Population	County	Total Vote	Granholm	Bonior	Blanchard	Other	Winner	Percentage of Total Vote		
								Granholm	Bonior	Blanchard
11,719	ALCONA	1,201	599	377	225		Granholm	49.9%	31.4%	18.7%
9,862	ALGER	1,666	761	439	466		Granholm	45.7%	26.4%	28.0%
105,665	ALLEGAN	5,120	4,123	513	484		Granholm	80.5%	10.0%	9.5%
31,314	ALPENA	3,838	2,245	947	646		Granholm	58.5%	24.7%	16.8%
23,110	ANTRIM	2,072	1,235	420	417		Granholm	59.6%	20.3%	20.1%
17,269	ARENAC	1,976	849	554	573		Granholm	43.0%	28.0%	29.0%
8,746	BARAGA	974	452	253	269		Granholm	46.4%	26.0%	27.6%
56,755	BARRY	3,747	2,869	527	351		Granholm	76.6%	14.1%	9.4%
110,157	BAY	17,213	7,704	4,796	4,713		Granholm	44.8%	27.9%	27.4%
15,998	BENZIE	1,234	667	252	315		Granholm	54.1%	20.4%	25.5%
162,453	BERRIEN	4,982	2,133	1,069	1,780		Granholm	42.8%	21.5%	35.7%
45,787	BRANCH	1,637	1,145	236	256		Granholm	69.9%	14.4%	15.6%
137,985	CALHOUN	9,638	7,158	1,109	1,369	2	Granholm	74.3%	11.5%	14.2%
51,104	CASS	1,758	911	305	542		Granholm	51.8%	17.3%	30.8%
26,090	CHARLEVOIX	1,530	878	323	329		Granholm	57.4%	21.1%	21.5%
26,448	CHEBOYGAN	2,136	1,176	478	482		Granholm	55.1%	22.4%	22.6%
38,543	CHIPPEWA	2,785	1,488	672	625		Granholm	53.4%	24.1%	22.4%
31,252	CLARE	2,079	1,079	540	460		Granholm	51.9%	26.0%	22.1%
64,753	CLINTON	5,783	3,845	1,199	739		Granholm	66.5%	20.7%	12.8%
14,273	CRAWFORD	835	441	209	185		Granholm	52.8%	25.0%	22.2%
38,520	DELTA	6,917	3,878	1,347	1,692		Granholm	56.1%	19.5%	24.5%
27,472	DICKINSON	2,178	941	588	649		Granholm	43.2%	27.0%	29.8%
103,655	EATON	9,554	6,416	1,681	1,457		Granholm	67.2%	17.6%	15.3%
31,437	EMMET	1,611	986	285	340		Granholm	61.2%	17.7%	21.1%
436,141	GENESEE	47,593	19,061	16,006	12,526		Granholm	40.1%	33.6%	26.3%
26,023	GLADWIN	2,352	1,092	704	556		Granholm	46.4%	29.9%	23.6%
17,370	GOGEBIC	2,355	1,043	422	890		Granholm	44.3%	17.9%	37.8%
77,654	GRAND TRAVERSE	5,347	3,451	976	920		Granholm	64.5%	18.3%	17.2%
42,285	GRATIOT	2,667	1,379	682	606		Granholm	51.7%	25.6%	22.7%
46,527	HILLSDALE	1,716	963	344	409		Granholm	56.1%	20.0%	23.8%
36,016	HOUGHTON	3,286	1,838	664	784		Granholm	55.9%	20.2%	23.9%
36,079	HURON	2,369	1,062	647	660		Granholm	44.8%	27.3%	27.9%
279,320	INGHAM	31,935	20,916	5,697	5,322		Granholm	65.5%	17.8%	16.7%
61,518	IONIA	3,680	2,495	681	504		Granholm	67.8%	18.5%	13.7%
27,339	IOSCO	3,153	1,530	872	751		Granholm	48.5%	27.7%	23.8%
13,138	IRON	2,235	1,016	554	665		Granholm	45.5%	24.8%	29.8%
63,351	ISABELLA	2,778	1,653	630	495		Granholm	59.5%	22.7%	17.8%
158,422	JACKSON	10,311	5,939	1,998	2,374		Granholm	57.6%	19.4%	23.0%
238,603	KALAMAZOO	16,309	12,896	1,718	1,695		Granholm	79.1%	10.5%	10.4%
16,571	KALKASKA	1,053	535	284	234		Granholm	50.8%	27.0%	22.2%
574,335	KENT	38,671	30,797	4,401	3,473		Granholm	79.6%	11.4%	9.0%
2,301	KEWEENAW	428	221	80	127		Granholm	51.6%	18.7%	29.7%
11,333	LAKE	1,072	531	268	273		Granholm	49.5%	25.0%	25.5%
87,904	LAPEER	6,278	2,919	2,174	1,185		Granholm	46.5%	34.6%	18.9%
21,119	LEELANAU	1,622	1,113	251	258		Granholm	68.6%	15.5%	15.9%
98,890	LENAWEE	6,713	3,211	1,505	1,997		Granholm	47.8%	22.4%	29.7%
156,951	LIVINGSTON	11,294	6,663	2,505	2,126		Granholm	59.0%	22.2%	18.8%
7,024	LUCE	713	332	141	240		Granholm	46.6%	19.8%	33.7%
11,943	MACKINAC	1,159	647	269	243		Granholm	55.8%	23.2%	21.0%
788,149	MACOMB	98,571	38,050	43,136	17,385		Bonior	38.6%	43.8%	17.6%
24,527	MANISTEE	1,821	918	523	380		Granholm	50.4%	28.7%	20.9%
64,634	MARQUETTE	10,766	4,983	3,172	2,611		Granholm	46.3%	29.5%	24.3%
28,274	MASON	1,926	1,254	360	312		Granholm	65.1%	18.7%	16.2%
40,553	MECOSTA	2,556	1,661	489	406		Granholm	65.0%	19.1%	15.9%
25,326	MENOMINEE	1,986	878	371	737		Granholm	44.2%	18.7%	37.1%
82,874	MIDLAND	4,894	2,501	1,273	1,120		Granholm	51.1%	26.0%	22.9%
14,478	MISSAUKEE	832	374	211	247		Granholm	45.0%	25.4%	29.7%
145,945	MONROE	17,926	7,123	4,901	5,902		Granholm	39.7%	27.3%	32.9%
61,266	MONTCALM	3,308	2,241	598	469		Granholm	67.7%	18.1%	14.2%
10,315	MONTMORENCY	957	512	248	197		Granholm	53.5%	25.9%	20.6%

MICHIGAN DEMOCRATIC PRIMARY

GOVERNOR 2002

2000 Census Population	County	Total Vote	Granholm	Bonior	Blanchard	Other	Winner	Percentage of Total Vote		
								Granholm	Bonior	Blanchard
170,200	MUSKEGON	16,846	11,910	2,506	2,430		Granholm	70.7%	14.9%	14.4%
47,874	NEWAYGO	2,733	2,047	374	312		Granholm	74.9%	13.7%	11.4%
1,194,156	OAKLAND	141,745	71,980	33,495	36,270		Granholm	50.8%	23.6%	25.6%
26,873	OCEANA	1,866	1,257	306	303		Granholm	67.4%	16.4%	16.2%
21,645	OGEMAW	2,652	1,216	736	700		Granholm	45.9%	27.8%	26.4%
7,818	ONTONAGON	1,021	435	282	304		Granholm	42.6%	27.6%	29.8%
23,197	OSCEOLA	1,256	653	313	290		Granholm	52.0%	24.9%	23.1%
9,418	OSCODA	797	368	247	182		Granholm	46.2%	31.0%	22.8%
23,301	OTSEGO	1,777	987	426	364		Granholm	55.5%	24.0%	20.5%
238,314	OTTAWA	10,888	8,773	1,150	960	5	Granholm	80.6%	10.6%	8.8%
14,411	PRESQUE ISLE	1,611	874	377	360		Granholm	54.3%	23.4%	22.3%
25,469	ROSCOMMON	2,799	1,411	788	600		Granholm	50.4%	28.2%	21.4%
210,039	SAGINAW	20,865	8,861	6,746	5,258		Granholm	42.5%	32.3%	25.2%
164,235	ST. CLAIR	18,060	5,083	10,598	2,379		Bonior	28.1%	58.7%	13.2%
62,422	ST. JOSEPH	2,083	1,520	311	252		Granholm	73.0%	14.9%	12.1%
44,547	SANILAC	3,655	1,504	1,322	829		Granholm	41.1%	36.2%	22.7%
8,903	SCHOOLCRAFT	1,341	628	322	391		Granholm	46.8%	24.0%	29.2%
71,687	SHIAWASSEE	5,384	2,936	1,379	1,069		Granholm	54.5%	25.6%	19.9%
58,266	TUSCOLA	5,032	2,226	1,582	1,224		Granholm	44.2%	31.4%	24.3%
76,263	VAN BUREN	3,805	2,875	435	495		Granholm	75.6%	11.4%	13.0%
322,895	WASHTENAW	46,903	26,105	11,651	9,147		Granholm	55.7%	24.8%	19.5%
2,061,162	WAYNE	306,784	106,794	98,377	101,613		Granholm	34.8%	32.1%	33.1%
30,484	WEXFORD	1,681	909	361	411		Granholm	54.1%	21.5%	24.4%
9,938,444	TOTAL	1,046,680	499,129	292,958	254,586	7	Granholm	47.7%	28.0%	24.3%

MINNESOTA

GOVERNOR
Tim Pawlenty (R). Elected 2002 to a four-year term.

SENATORS (1 Democrat, 1 Republican)
Norm Coleman (R). Elected 2002 to a six-year term.

Mark Dayton (D). Elected 2000 to a six-year term.

REPRESENTATIVES (4 Democrats, 4 Republicans)
1. Gil Gutknecht (R)
2. John Kline (R)
3. Jim Ramstad (R)
4. Betty McCollum (D)
5. Martin Olav Sabo (D)
6. Mark Kennedy (R)
7. Collin C. Peterson (D)
8. James L. Oberstar (D)

POSTWAR VOTE FOR PRESIDENT

Year	Total Vote	Republican		Democratic		Other Vote	Plurality	Percentage			
								Total Vote		Major Vote	
		Vote	Candidate	Vote	Candidate			Rep.	Dem.	Rep.	Dem.
2000**	2,438,685	1,109,659	Bush, George W.	1,168,266	Gore, Al	160,760	58,607 D	45.5%	47.9%	48.7%	51.3%
1996**	2,192,640	766,476	Dole, Bob	1,120,438	Clinton, Bill	305,726	353,962 D	35.0%	51.1%	40.6%	59.4%
1992**	2,347,948	747,841	Bush, George	1,020,997	Clinton, Bill	579,110	273,156 D	31.9%	43.5%	42.3%	57.7%
1988	2,096,790	962,337	Bush, George	1,109,471	Dukakis, Michael S.	24,982	147,134 D	45.9%	52.9%	46.4%	53.6%
1984	2,084,449	1,032,603	Reagan, Ronald	1,036,364	Mondale, Walter F.	15,482	3,761 D	49.5%	49.7%	49.9%	50.1%
1980**	2,051,980	873,268	Reagan, Ronald	954,174	Carter, Jimmy	224,538	80,906 D	42.6%	46.5%	47.8%	52.2%
1976	1,949,931	819,395	Ford, Gerald R.	1,070,440	Carter, Jimmy	60,096	251,045 D	42.0%	54.9%	43.4%	56.6%
1972	1,741,652	898,269	Nixon, Richard M.	802,346	McGovern, George S.	41,037	95,923 R	51.6%	46.1%	52.8%	47.2%
1968	1,588,506	658,643	Nixon, Richard M.	857,738	Humphrey, Hubert H.	72,125	199,095 D	41.5%	54.0%	43.4%	56.6%
1964	1,554,462	559,624	Goldwater, Barry M.	991,117	Johnson, Lyndon B.	3,721	431,493 D	36.0%	63.8%	36.1%	63.9%
1960	1,541,887	757,915	Nixon, Richard M.	779,933	Kennedy, John F.	4,039	22,018 D	49.2%	50.6%	49.3%	50.7%
1956	1,340,005	719,302	Eisenhower, Dwight D.	617,525	Stevenson, Adlai E.	3,178	101,777 R	53.7%	46.1%	53.8%	46.2%
1952	1,379,483	763,211	Eisenhower, Dwight D.	608,458	Stevenson, Adlai E.	7,814	154,753 R	55.3%	44.1%	55.6%	44.4%
1948	1,212,226	483,617	Dewey, Thomas E.	692,966	Truman, Harry S.	35,643	209,349 D	39.9%	57.2%	41.1%	58.9%

In 2000 the other vote column includes 126,696 votes cast for Green (Nader). In 1996 the other vote column includes 257,704 votes cast for Perot. In 1992 the other vote column includes 562,506 votes cast for Perot. In 1980 the other vote column includes 174,990 votes for Independent (Anderson).

MINNESOTA

POSTWAR VOTE FOR GOVERNOR

Year	Total Vote	Republican		Democratic		Other Vote	Rep.-Dem. Plurality	Percentage			
		Vote	Candidate	Vote	Candidate			Total Vote		Major Vote	
								Rep.	Dem.	Rep.	Dem.
2002**	2,252,473	999,473	Pawlenty, Tim	821,268	Moe, Roger D.	431,732	178,205 R	44.4%	36.5%	54.9%	45.1%
1998**	2,090,518	716,880	Coleman, Norm	587,060	Humphrey, Hubert H., III	786,578	56,523 V	34.3%	28.1%	55.0%	45.0%
1994	1,765,590	1,094,165	Carlson, Arne	589,344	Marty, John	82,081	504,821 R	62.0%	33.4%	65.0%	35.0%
1990	1,806,777	895,988	Carlson, Arne	836,218	Perpich, Rudy	74,571	59,770 R	49.6%	46.3%	51.7%	48.3%
1986	1,415,989	606,755	Ludeman, Cal R.	790,138	Perpich, Rudy	19,096	183,383 D	42.9%	55.8%	43.4%	56.6%
1982	1,789,539	715,796	Whitney, Wheelock	1,049,104	Perpich, Rudy	24,639	333,308 D	40.0%	58.6%	40.6%	59.4%
1978	1,585,702	830,019	Quie, Albert H.	718,244	Perpich, Rudy	37,439	111,775 R	52.3%	45.3%	53.6%	46.4%
1974	1,252,898	367,722	Johnson, John W.	786,787	Anderson, Wendell R.	98,389	419,065 D	29.3%	62.8%	31.9%	68.1%
1970	1,365,443	621,780	Head, Douglas M.	737,921	Anderson, Wendell R.	5,742	116,141 D	45.5%	54.0%	45.7%	54.3%
1966	1,295,058	680,593	LeVander, Harold	607,943	Rolvaag, Karl F.	6,522	72,650 R	52.6%	46.9%	52.8%	47.2%
1962**	1,246,904	619,751	Andersen, Elmer L.	619,842	Rolvaag, Karl F.	7,311	91 D	49.7%	49.7%	50.0%	50.0%
1960	1,550,265	783,813	Andersen, Elmer L.	760,934	Freeman, Orville L.	5,518	22,879 R	50.6%	49.1%	50.7%	49.3%
1958	1,159,915	490,731	MacKinnon, George	658,326	Freeman, Orville L.	10,858	167,595 D	42.3%	56.8%	42.7%	57.3%
1956	1,422,161	685,196	Nelsen, Ancher	731,180	Freeman, Orville L.	5,785	45,984 D	48.2%	51.4%	48.4%	51.6%
1954	1,151,417	538,865	Anderson, C. Elmer	607,099	Freeman, Orville L.	5,453	68,234 D	46.8%	52.7%	47.0%	53.0%
1952	1,418,869	785,125	Anderson, C. Elmer	624,480	Freeman, Orville L.	9,264	160,645 R	55.3%	44.0%	55.7%	44.3%
1950	1,046,632	635,800	Youngdahl, Luther	400,637	Peterson, Harry H.	10,195	235,163 R	60.7%	38.3%	61.3%	38.7%
1948	1,210,894	643,572	Youngdahl, Luther	545,766	Halsted, Charles L.	21,556	97,806 R	53.1%	45.1%	54.1%	45.9%
1946	880,348	519,067	Youngdahl, Luther	349,565	Barker, Harold H.	11,716	169,502 R	59.0%	39.7%	59.8%	40.2%

In 2002 Timothy J. Penny, the Independence Party candidate, received 364,534 votes (16.2 percent of the total vote). In 1998 Jesse Ventura, the Reform Party candidate, received 773,403 votes (37.0 percent of the total vote) and was elected with a plurality of 56,523 votes. The term of office of Minnesota's Governor was increased from two to four years effective with the 1962 election.

POSTWAR VOTE FOR SENATOR

Year	Total Vote	Republican		Democratic		Other Vote	Rep.-Dem. Plurality	Percentage			
		Vote	Candidate	Vote	Candidate			Total Vote		Major Vote	
								Rep.	Dem.	Rep.	Dem.
2002**	2,254,639	1,116,697	Coleman, Norm	1,067,246	Mondale, Walter F.	70,696	49,451 R	49.5%	47.3%	51.1%	48.9%
2000	2,419,520	1,047,474	Grams, Rod	1,181,553	Dayton, Mark	190,493	134,079 D	43.3%	48.8%	47.0%	53.0%
1996	2,183,062	901,282	Boschwitz, Rudy	1,098,493	Wellstone, Paul	183,287	197,211 D	41.3%	50.3%	45.1%	54.9%
1994	1,772,929	869,653	Grams, Rod	781,860	Wynia, Ann	121,416	87,793 R	49.1%	44.1%	52.7%	47.3%
1990	1,808,045	864,375	Boschwitz, Rudy	911,999	Wellstone, Paul	31,671	47,624 D	47.8%	50.4%	48.7%	51.3%
1988	2,093,953	1,176,210	Durenberger, David	856,694	Humphrey, Hubert H., III	61,049	319,516 R	56.2%	40.9%	57.9%	42.1%
1984	2,066,143	1,199,926	Boschwitz, Rudy	852,844	Growe, Joan Anderson	13,373	347,082 R	58.1%	41.3%	58.5%	41.5%
1982	1,804,675	949,207	Durenberger, David	840,401	Dayton, Mark	15,067	108,806 R	52.6%	46.6%	53.0%	47.0%
1978	1,580,778	894,092	Boschwitz, Rudy	638,375	Anderson, Wendell R.	48,311	255,717 R	56.6%	40.4%	58.3%	41.7%
1978S	1,560,724	957,908	Durenberger, David	538,675	Short, Robert E.	64,141	419,233 R	61.4%	34.5%	64.0%	36.0%
1976	1,912,068	478,611	Brekke, Gerald W.	1,290,736	Humphrey, Hubert H.	142,721	812,125 D	25.0%	67.5%	27.1%	72.9%
1972	1,731,653	742,121	Hansen, Philip	981,340	Mondale, Walter F.	8,192	239,219 D	42.9%	56.7%	43.1%	56.9%
1970	1,364,887	568,025	MacGregor, Clark	788,256	Humphrey, Hubert H.	8,606	220,231 D	41.6%	57.8%	41.9%	58.1%
1966	1,271,426	574,868	Forsythe, Robert A.	685,840	Mondale, Walter F.	10,718	110,972 D	45.2%	53.9%	45.6%	54.4%
1964	1,543,590	605,933	Whitney, Wheelock	931,353	McCarthy, Eugene J.	6,304	325,420 D	39.3%	60.3%	39.4%	60.6%
1960	1,536,839	648,586	Peterson, P. K.	884,168	Humphrey, Hubert H.	4,085	235,582 D	42.2%	57.5%	42.3%	57.7%
1958	1,150,883	536,629	Thye, Edward J.	608,847	McCarthy, Eugene J.	5,407	72,218 D	46.6%	52.9%	46.8%	53.2%
1954	1,138,952	479,619	Bjornson, Val	642,193	Humphrey, Hubert H.	17,140	162,574 D	42.1%	56.4%	42.8%	57.2%
1952	1,387,419	785,649	Thye, Edward J.	590,011	Carlson, William E.	11,759	195,638 R	56.6%	42.5%	57.1%	42.9%
1948	1,220,250	485,801	Ball, Joseph H.	729,494	Humphrey, Hubert H.	4,955	243,693 D	39.8%	59.8%	40.0%	60.0%
1946	878,731	517,775	Thye, Edward J.	349,520	Jorgenson, Theodore	11,436	168,255 R	58.9%	39.8%	59.7%	40.3%

In 2002 the Democratic incumbent, Paul Wellstone, was killed in an airplane crash in October. Walter F. Mondale was named to replace him on the general election ballot. One of the 1978 elections was for a short term to fill a vacancy.

MINNESOTA

Congressional districts first established for elections held in 2002
8 members

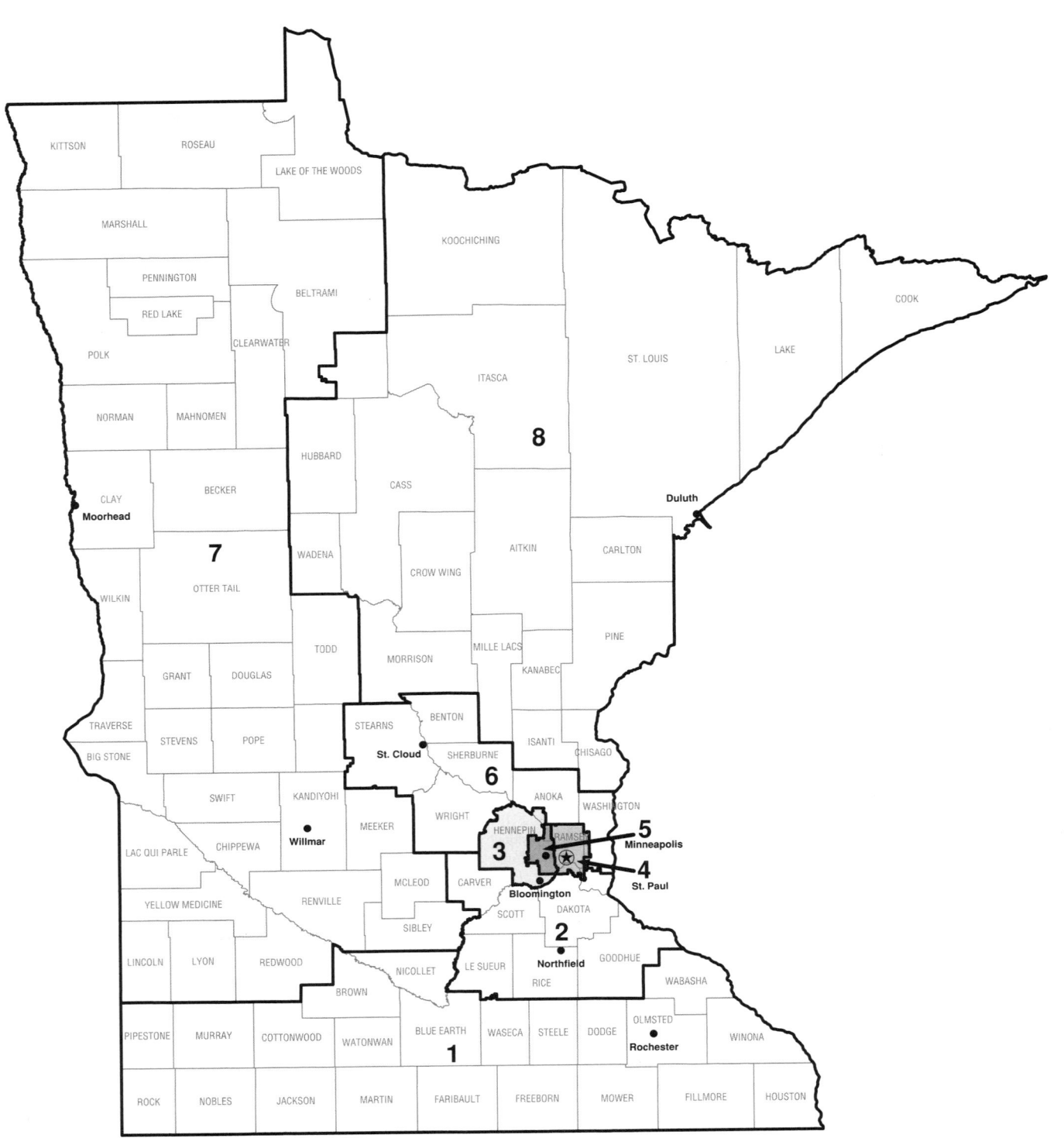

MINNESOTA

Minneapolis-St. Paul Area

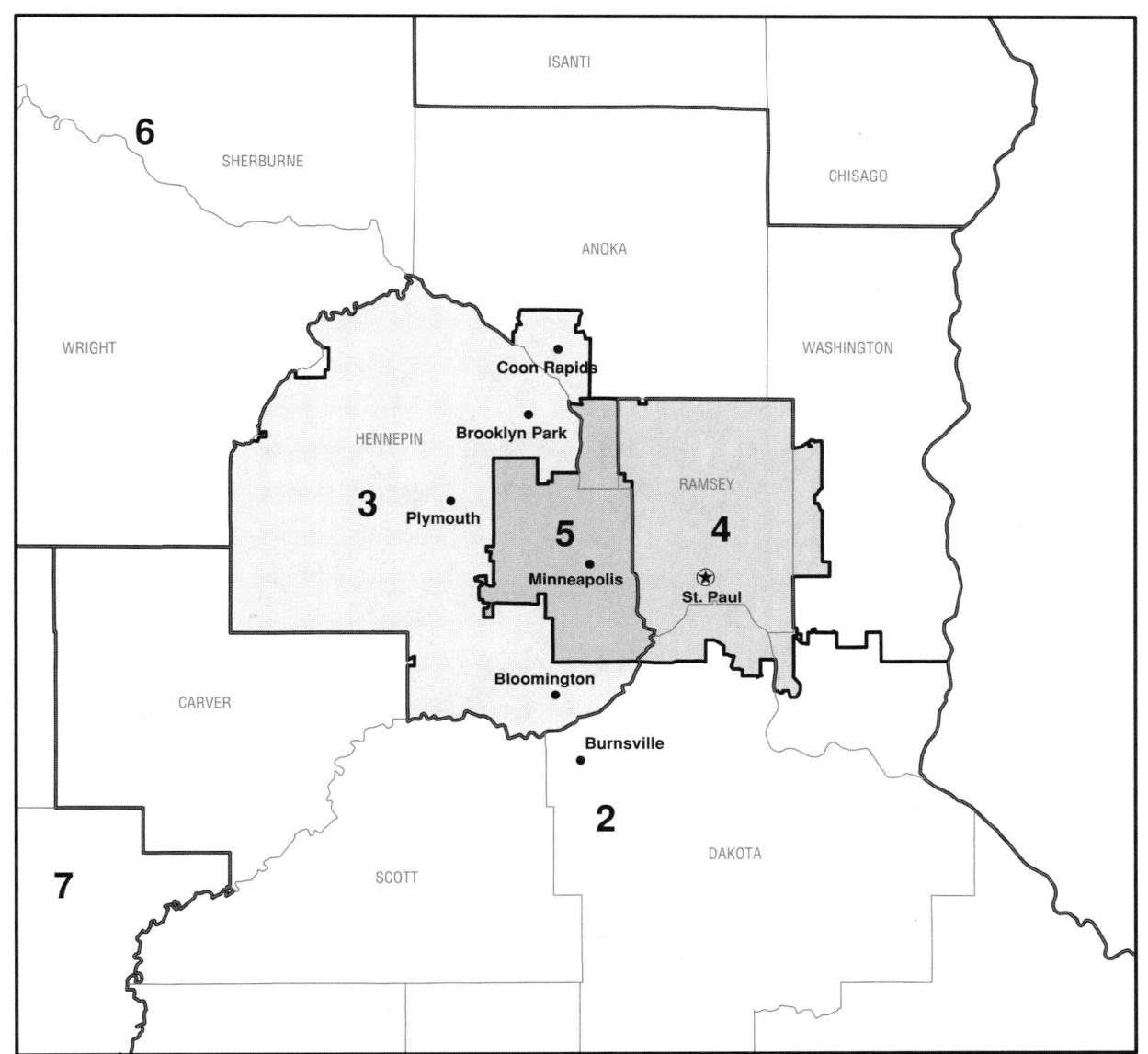

MINNESOTA

GOVERNOR 2002

2000 Census Population	County	Total Vote	Republican	Democratic	Independence (Penny)	Other	Plurality		Percentage		
									Rep.	Dem.	Independence
15,301	AITKIN	7,948	3,341	3,064	1,346	197	277	R	42.0%	38.6%	16.9%
298,084	ANOKA	139,054	71,169	45,553	19,161	3,171	25,616	R	51.2%	32.8%	13.8%
30,000	BECKER	13,191	6,145	5,384	1,392	270	761	R	46.6%	40.8%	10.6%
39,650	BELTRAMI	14,998	6,395	6,720	1,250	633	325	D	42.6%	44.8%	8.3%
34,226	BENTON	13,415	6,524	4,336	2,129	426	2,188	R	48.6%	32.3%	15.9%
5,820	BIG STONE	2,682	1,116	1,192	315	59	76	D	41.6%	44.4%	11.7%
55,941	BLUE EARTH	24,000	8,925	6,333	8,001	741	924	R	37.2%	26.4%	33.3%
26,911	BROWN	11,364	5,833	2,731	2,586	214	3,102	R	51.3%	24.0%	22.8%
31,671	CARLTON	14,224	4,267	8,198	1,489	270	3,931	D	30.0%	57.6%	10.5%
70,205	CARVER	34,733	21,396	7,848	4,826	663	13,548	R	61.6%	22.6%	13.9%
27,150	CASS	12,477	6,115	4,174	1,843	345	1,941	R	49.0%	33.5%	14.8%
13,088	CHIPPEWA	5,862	2,250	2,394	1,117	101	144	D	38.4%	40.8%	19.1%
41,101	CHISAGO	21,973	11,791	6,755	2,879	548	5,036	R	53.7%	30.7%	13.1%
51,229	CLAY	20,407	8,292	9,956	1,707	452	1,664	D	40.6%	48.8%	8.4%
8,423	CLEARWATER	3,660	1,597	1,705	273	85	108	D	43.6%	46.6%	7.5%
5,168	COOK	2,835	962	1,228	441	204	266	D	33.9%	43.3%	15.6%
12,167	COTTONWOOD	5,554	2,638	1,813	992	111	825	R	47.5%	32.6%	17.9%
55,099	CROW WING	26,551	12,970	8,984	3,952	645	3,986	R	48.8%	33.8%	14.9%
355,904	DAKOTA	169,659	90,534	53,440	22,156	3,529	37,094	R	53.4%	31.5%	13.1%
17,731	DODGE	8,088	3,203	1,383	3,382	120	179	I	39.6%	17.1%	41.8%
32,821	DOUGLAS	15,413	8,092	4,790	2,206	325	3,302	R	52.5%	31.1%	14.3%
16,181	FARIBAULT	7,617	2,626	1,209	3,689	93	1,063	I	34.5%	15.9%	48.4%
21,122	FILLMORE	9,272	2,959	1,733	4,432	148	1,473	I	31.9%	18.7%	47.8%
32,584	FREEBORN	15,756	4,530	2,827	8,189	210	3,659	I	28.8%	17.9%	52.0%
44,127	GOODHUE	20,630	8,749	5,229	6,260	392	2,489	R	42.4%	25.3%	30.3%
6,289	GRANT	3,285	1,464	1,313	434	74	151	R	44.6%	40.0%	13.2%
1,116,200	HENNEPIN	515,978	210,140	213,147	71,010	21,681	3,007	D	40.7%	41.3%	13.8%
19,718	HOUSTON	8,600	3,358	2,007	3,060	175	298	R	39.0%	23.3%	35.6%
18,376	HUBBARD	9,080	4,562	3,246	1,010	262	1,316	R	50.2%	35.7%	11.1%
31,287	ISANTI	14,771	7,827	4,745	1,820	379	3,082	R	53.0%	32.1%	12.3%
43,992	ITASCA	19,511	6,770	9,917	2,273	551	3,147	D	34.7%	50.8%	11.6%
11,268	JACKSON	4,984	2,161	1,719	986	118	442	R	43.4%	34.5%	19.8%
14,996	KANABEC	6,464	3,302	2,177	815	170	1,125	R	51.1%	33.7%	12.6%
41,203	KANDIYOHI	18,002	8,332	6,879	2,483	308	1,453	R	46.3%	38.2%	13.8%
5,285	KITTSON	2,425	735	1,470	189	31	735	D	30.3%	60.6%	7.8%
14,355	KOOCHICHING	5,978	2,186	2,866	776	150	680	D	36.6%	47.9%	13.0%
8,067	LAC QUI PARLE	4,041	1,511	1,797	644	89	286	D	37.4%	44.5%	15.9%
11,058	LAKE	6,030	1,792	3,333	730	175	1,541	D	29.7%	55.3%	12.1%
4,522	LAKE OF THE WOODS	2,146	888	944	254	60	56	D	41.4%	44.0%	11.8%
25,426	LE SUEUR	11,847	5,038	2,824	3,739	246	1,299	R	42.5%	23.8%	31.6%
6,429	LINCOLN	3,032	1,240	1,278	436	78	38	D	40.9%	42.2%	14.4%
25,425	LYON	9,944	4,896	3,349	1,477	222	1,547	R	49.2%	33.7%	14.9%
34,898	MCLEOD	14,356	8,010	3,583	2,419	344	4,427	R	55.8%	25.0%	16.9%
5,190	MAHNOMEN	2,343	926	1,100	226	91	174	D	39.5%	46.9%	9.6%
10,155	MARSHALL	4,809	1,975	2,348	398	88	373	D	41.1%	48.8%	8.3%
21,802	MARTIN	9,386	4,437	2,389	2,399	161	2,038	R	47.3%	25.5%	25.6%
22,644	MEEKER	10,346	5,182	3,128	1,753	283	2,054	R	50.1%	30.2%	16.9%
22,330	MILLE LACS	10,172	5,190	3,205	1,510	267	1,985	R	51.0%	31.5%	14.8%
31,712	MORRISON	14,204	7,838	3,985	2,014	367	3,853	R	55.2%	28.1%	14.2%
38,603	MOWER	16,162	4,656	4,361	6,875	270	2,219	I	28.8%	27.0%	42.5%
9,165	MURRAY	4,636	2,042	1,730	734	130	312	R	44.0%	37.3%	15.8%
29,771	NICOLLET	14,460	5,783	4,207	4,142	328	1,576	R	40.0%	29.1%	28.6%
20,832	NOBLES	8,341	3,735	3,132	1,264	210	603	R	44.8%	37.5%	15.2%
7,442	NORMAN	3,332	1,093	1,921	279	39	828	D	32.8%	57.7%	8.4%
124,277	OLMSTED	53,038	20,889	10,458	20,904	787	15	I	39.4%	19.7%	39.4%
57,159	OTTER TAIL	26,052	13,676	9,101	2,760	515	4,575	R	52.5%	34.9%	10.6%
13,584	PENNINGTON	5,477	2,130	2,739	507	101	609	D	38.9%	50.0%	9.3%
26,530	PINE	11,319	4,939	4,501	1,534	345	438	R	43.6%	39.8%	13.6%
9,895	PIPESTONE	4,455	2,158	1,460	711	126	698	R	48.4%	32.8%	16.0%
31,369	POLK	12,673	4,521	7,153	840	159	2,632	D	35.7%	56.4%	6.6%

MINNESOTA

GOVERNOR 2002

2000 Census Population	County	Total Vote	Republican	Democratic	Independence (Penny)	Other	Plurality	Percentage		
								Rep.	Dem.	Independence
11,236	POPE	5,630	2,436	2,215	828	151	221 R	43.3%	39.3%	14.7%
511,035	RAMSEY	225,135	86,200	101,924	27,507	9,504	15,724 D	38.3%	45.3%	12.2%
4,299	RED LAKE	1,914	717	990	172	35	273 D	37.5%	51.7%	9.0%
16,815	REDWOOD	6,985	3,671	1,891	1,275	148	1,780 R	52.6%	27.1%	18.3%
17,154	RENVILLE	7,335	3,252	2,589	1,341	153	663 R	44.3%	35.3%	18.3%
56,665	RICE	24,809	9,334	8,380	6,038	1,057	954 R	37.6%	33.8%	24.3%
9,721	ROCK	4,478	2,195	1,727	452	104	468 R	49.0%	38.6%	10.1%
16,338	ROSEAU	6,353	3,158	2,701	352	142	457 R	49.7%	42.5%	5.5%
200,528	ST. LOUIS	94,500	25,059	56,568	10,019	2,854	31,509 D	26.5%	59.9%	10.6%
89,498	SCOTT	44,753	26,074	10,898	6,884	897	15,176 R	58.3%	24.4%	15.4%
64,417	SHERBURNE	29,705	17,293	7,975	3,758	679	9,318 R	58.2%	26.8%	12.7%
15,356	SIBLEY	7,067	3,592	1,684	1,656	135	1,908 R	50.8%	23.8%	23.4%
133,166	STEARNS	56,933	28,849	17,362	8,648	2,074	11,487 R	50.7%	30.5%	15.2%
33,680	STEELE	15,648	6,425	2,615	6,354	254	71 R	41.1%	16.7%	40.6%
10,053	STEVENS	5,363	2,454	1,923	703	283	531 R	45.8%	35.9%	13.1%
11,956	SWIFT	5,050	1,883	2,403	667	97	520 D	37.3%	47.6%	13.2%
24,426	TODD	10,333	5,363	3,218	1,474	278	2,145 R	51.9%	31.1%	14.3%
4,134	TRAVERSE	1,905	788	826	253	38	38 D	41.4%	43.4%	13.3%
21,610	WABASHA	10,043	3,998	2,133	3,735	177	263 R	39.8%	21.2%	37.2%
13,713	WADENA	6,015	3,213	1,979	669	154	1,234 R	53.4%	32.9%	11.1%
19,526	WASECA	8,583	2,565	887	5,022	109	2,457 I	29.9%	10.3%	58.5%
201,130	WASHINGTON	104,003	54,792	33,968	12,808	2,435	20,824 R	52.7%	32.7%	12.3%
11,876	WATONWAN	4,941	1,985	1,436	1,414	106	549 R	40.2%	29.1%	28.6%
7,138	WILKIN	2,849	1,452	1,079	258	60	373 R	51.0%	37.9%	9.1%
49,985	WINONA	19,683	7,385	5,413	6,103	782	1,282 R	37.5%	27.5%	31.0%
89,986	WRIGHT	44,605	25,575	11,962	6,011	1,057	13,613 R	57.3%	26.8%	13.5%
11,080	YELLOW MEDICINE	4,813	1,964	2,031	715	103	67 D	40.8%	42.2%	14.9%
4,919,479	TOTAL	2,252,473	999,473	821,268	364,534	67,198	178,205 R	44.4%	36.5%	16.2%

Note: The plurality is based on the margin of victory by the winner over the runner-up. The Independence Party candidate, Timothy J. Penny, finished first or second in several counties.

MINNESOTA

SENATOR 2002

2000 Census Population	County	Total Vote	Republican	Democratic	Other	Rep.-Dem. Plurality	Percentage			
							Total Vote		Major Vote	
							Rep.	Dem.	Rep.	Dem.
15,301	AITKIN	8,012	3,711	3,855	446	144 D	46.3%	48.1%	49.0%	51.0%
298,084	ANOKA	139,574	78,176	57,511	3,887	20,665 R	56.0%	41.2%	57.6%	42.4%
30,000	BECKER	13,287	6,845	5,841	601	1,004 R	51.5%	44.0%	54.0%	46.0%
39,650	BELTRAMI	15,099	7,243	7,433	423	190 D	48.0%	49.2%	49.4%	50.6%
34,226	BENTON	13,534	7,193	5,807	534	1,386 R	53.1%	42.9%	55.3%	44.7%
5,820	BIG STONE	2,703	1,173	1,337	193	164 D	43.4%	49.5%	46.7%	53.3%
55,941	BLUE EARTH	24,188	11,615	11,435	1,138	180 R	48.0%	47.3%	50.4%	49.6%
26,911	BROWN	11,457	6,564	4,404	489	2,160 R	57.3%	38.4%	59.8%	40.2%
31,671	CARLTON	14,214	5,083	8,529	602	3,446 D	35.8%	60.0%	37.3%	62.7%
70,205	CARVER	34,854	22,966	11,072	816	11,894 R	65.9%	31.8%	67.5%	32.5%
27,150	CASS	12,497	6,697	5,006	794	1,691 R	53.6%	40.1%	57.2%	42.8%
13,088	CHIPPEWA	5,848	2,488	3,173	187	685 D	42.5%	54.3%	43.9%	56.1%
41,101	CHISAGO	21,915	12,567	8,660	688	3,907 R	57.3%	39.5%	59.2%	40.8%
51,229	CLAY	20,438	9,365	10,454	619	1,089 D	45.8%	51.1%	47.3%	52.7%
8,423	CLEARWATER	3,678	1,790	1,746	142	44 R	48.7%	47.5%	50.6%	49.4%
5,168	COOK	2,787	1,180	1,240	367	60 D	42.3%	44.5%	48.8%	51.2%
12,167	COTTONWOOD	5,536	2,779	2,606	151	173 R	50.2%	47.1%	51.6%	48.4%
55,099	CROW WING	26,484	14,222	10,883	1,379	3,339 R	53.7%	41.1%	56.7%	43.3%
355,904	DAKOTA	168,798	96,149	68,742	3,907	27,407 R	57.0%	40.7%	58.3%	41.7%
17,731	DODGE	8,205	4,234	3,592	379	642 R	51.6%	43.8%	54.1%	45.9%
32,821	DOUGLAS	15,367	8,639	6,021	707	2,618 R	56.2%	39.2%	58.9%	41.1%
16,181	FARIBAULT	7,651	3,734	3,627	290	107 R	48.8%	47.4%	50.7%	49.3%
21,122	FILLMORE	9,394	4,088	4,908	398	820 D	43.5%	52.2%	45.4%	54.6%
32,584	FREEBORN	15,806	6,542	8,418	846	1,876 D	41.4%	53.3%	43.7%	56.3%
44,127	GOODHUE	20,719	10,791	9,169	759	1,622 R	52.1%	44.3%	54.1%	45.9%
6,289	GRANT	3,262	1,551	1,594	117	43 D	47.5%	48.9%	49.3%	50.7%
1,116,200	HENNEPIN	516,005	233,779	268,504	13,722	34,725 D	45.3%	52.0%	46.5%	53.5%
19,718	HOUSTON	8,670	4,234	4,110	326	124 R	48.8%	47.4%	50.7%	49.3%
18,376	HUBBARD	9,086	4,944	3,758	384	1,186 R	54.4%	41.4%	56.8%	43.2%
31,287	ISANTI	14,823	8,365	6,019	439	2,346 R	56.4%	40.6%	58.2%	41.8%
43,992	ITASCA	19,715	7,849	10,928	938	3,079 D	39.8%	55.4%	41.8%	58.2%
11,268	JACKSON	5,068	2,356	2,526	186	170 D	46.5%	49.8%	48.3%	51.7%
14,996	KANABEC	6,508	3,508	2,755	245	753 R	53.9%	42.3%	56.0%	44.0%
41,203	KANDIYOHI	18,150	9,345	8,245	560	1,100 R	51.5%	45.4%	53.1%	46.9%
5,285	KITTSON	2,381	937	1,212	232	275 D	39.4%	50.9%	43.6%	56.4%
14,355	KOOCHICHING	6,076	2,735	3,106	235	371 D	45.0%	51.1%	46.8%	53.2%
8,067	LAC QUI PARLE	4,069	1,653	2,236	180	583 D	40.6%	55.0%	42.5%	57.5%
11,058	LAKE	6,037	2,229	3,542	266	1,313 D	36.9%	58.7%	38.6%	61.4%
4,522	LAKE OF THE WOODS	2,173	1,125	754	294	371 R	51.8%	34.7%	59.9%	40.1%
25,426	LE SUEUR	11,943	6,152	5,302	489	850 R	51.5%	44.4%	53.7%	46.3%
6,429	LINCOLN	3,095	1,298	1,660	137	362 D	41.9%	53.6%	43.9%	56.1%
25,425	LYON	10,111	5,109	4,632	370	477 R	50.5%	45.8%	52.4%	47.6%
34,898	MCLEOD	14,130	8,469	5,087	574	3,382 R	59.9%	36.0%	62.5%	37.5%
5,190	MAHNOMEN	2,367	1,039	1,218	110	179 D	43.9%	51.5%	46.0%	54.0%
10,155	MARSHALL	4,811	2,173	2,439	199	266 D	45.2%	50.7%	47.1%	52.9%
21,802	MARTIN	9,396	5,024	4,039	333	985 R	53.5%	43.0%	55.4%	44.6%
22,644	MEEKER	10,453	5,704	4,274	475	1,430 R	54.6%	40.9%	57.2%	42.8%
22,330	MILLE LACS	10,189	5,454	4,355	380	1,099 R	53.5%	42.7%	55.6%	44.4%
31,712	MORRISON	14,546	7,839	6,039	668	1,800 R	53.9%	41.5%	56.5%	43.5%
38,603	MOWER	16,206	6,122	9,497	587	3,375 D	37.8%	58.6%	39.2%	60.8%
9,165	MURRAY	4,722	2,164	2,351	207	187 D	45.8%	49.8%	47.9%	52.1%
29,771	NICOLLET	14,321	7,012	6,811	498	201 R	49.0%	47.6%	50.7%	49.3%
20,832	NOBLES	8,483	4,170	3,979	334	191 R	49.2%	46.9%	51.2%	48.8%
7,442	NORMAN	3,347	1,286	1,941	120	655 D	38.4%	58.0%	39.9%	60.1%
124,277	OLMSTED	52,078	27,564	22,791	1,723	4,773 R	52.9%	43.8%	54.7%	45.3%
57,159	OTTER TAIL	26,361	14,766	10,690	905	4,076 R	56.0%	40.6%	58.0%	42.0%
13,584	PENNINGTON	5,553	2,500	2,869	184	369 D	45.0%	51.7%	46.6%	53.4%
26,530	PINE	11,381	5,278	5,640	463	362 D	46.4%	49.6%	48.3%	51.7%
9,895	PIPESTONE	4,486	2,309	2,004	173	305 R	51.5%	44.7%	53.5%	46.5%
31,369	POLK	12,731	5,854	6,407	470	553 D	46.0%	50.3%	47.7%	52.3%

MINNESOTA

SENATOR 2002

2000 Census Population	County	Total Vote	Republican	Democratic	Other	Rep.-Dem. Plurality		Percentage			
								Total Vote		Major Vote	
								Rep.	Dem.	Rep.	Dem.
11,236	POPE	5,683	2,599	2,870	214	271	D	45.7%	50.5%	47.5%	52.5%
511,035	RAMSEY	224,664	94,582	124,752	5,330	30,170	D	42.1%	55.5%	43.1%	56.9%
4,299	RED LAKE	1,930	839	991	100	152	D	43.5%	51.3%	45.8%	54.2%
16,815	REDWOOD	7,059	3,948	2,798	313	1,150	R	55.9%	39.6%	58.5%	41.5%
17,154	RENVILLE	7,398	3,533	3,532	333	1	R	47.8%	47.7%	50.0%	50.0%
56,665	RICE	24,694	11,012	12,892	790	1,880	D	44.6%	52.2%	46.1%	53.9%
9,721	ROCK	4,565	2,373	2,019	173	354	R	52.0%	44.2%	54.0%	46.0%
16,338	ROSEAU	6,446	3,589	2,630	227	959	R	55.7%	40.8%	57.7%	42.3%
200,528	ST. LOUIS	94,909	29,998	62,090	2,821	32,092	D	31.6%	65.4%	32.6%	67.4%
89,498	SCOTT	44,543	28,102	15,308	1,133	12,794	R	63.1%	34.4%	64.7%	35.3%
64,417	SHERBURNE	29,764	18,478	10,330	956	8,148	R	62.1%	34.7%	64.1%	35.9%
15,356	SIBLEY	7,084	3,900	2,819	365	1,081	R	55.1%	39.8%	58.0%	42.0%
133,166	STEARNS	57,497	31,945	23,520	2,032	8,425	R	55.6%	40.9%	57.6%	42.4%
33,680	STEELE	15,300	8,165	6,552	583	1,613	R	53.4%	42.8%	55.5%	44.5%
10,053	STEVENS	5,362	2,625	2,566	171	59	R	49.0%	47.9%	50.6%	49.4%
11,956	SWIFT	5,083	1,999	2,907	177	908	D	39.3%	57.2%	40.7%	59.3%
24,426	TODD	10,606	5,644	4,460	502	1,184	R	53.2%	42.1%	55.9%	44.1%
4,134	TRAVERSE	1,946	853	1,016	77	163	D	43.8%	52.2%	45.6%	54.4%
21,610	WABASHA	9,829	4,905	4,549	375	356	R	49.9%	46.3%	51.9%	48.1%
13,713	WADENA	6,077	3,377	2,462	238	915	R	55.6%	40.5%	57.8%	42.2%
19,526	WASECA	8,542	4,369	3,687	486	682	R	51.1%	43.2%	54.2%	45.8%
201,130	WASHINGTON	103,875	59,269	42,249	2,357	17,020	R	57.1%	40.7%	58.4%	41.6%
11,876	WATONWAN	4,991	2,362	2,346	283	16	R	47.3%	47.0%	50.2%	49.8%
7,138	WILKIN	2,877	1,555	1,219	103	336	R	54.0%	42.4%	56.1%	43.9%
49,985	WINONA	19,684	9,219	9,755	710	536	D	46.8%	49.6%	48.6%	51.4%
89,986	WRIGHT	44,596	27,626	15,590	1,380	12,036	R	61.9%	35.0%	63.9%	36.1%
11,080	YELLOW MEDICINE	4,857	2,101	2,554	202	453	D	43.3%	52.6%	45.1%	54.9%
4,919,479	TOTAL	2,254,639	1,116,697	1,067,246	70,696	49,451	R	49.5%	47.3%	51.1%	48.9%

MINNESOTA

HOUSE OF REPRESENTATIVES

CD	Year	Total Vote	Republican		Democratic		Other Vote	Rep.-Dem. Plurality		Percentage			
			Vote	Candidate	Vote	Candidate				Total Vote		Major Vote	
										Rep.	Dem.	Rep.	Dem.
1	2002	265,982	163,570	Gutknecht, Gil*	92,165	Andreasen, Steve	10,247	71,405	R	61.5%	34.7%	64.0%	36.0%
2	2002	286,860	152,970	Kline, John	121,121	Luther, Bill*	12,769	31,849	R	53.3%	42.2%	55.8%	44.2%
3	2002	296,218	213,334	Ramstad, Jim*	82,575	Stanton, Darryl	309	130,759	R	72.0%	27.9%	72.1%	27.9%
4	2002	264,540	89,705	Billington, Clyde	164,597	McCollum, Betty*	10,238	74,892	D	33.9%	62.2%	35.3%	64.7%
5	2002	255,982	66,271	Mathias, Daniel Nielsen	171,572	Sabo, Martin Olav*	18,139	105,301	D	25.9%	67.0%	27.9%	72.1%
6	2002	287,312	164,747	Kennedy, Mark*	100,738	Robert, Janet	21,827	64,009	R	57.3%	35.1%	62.1%	37.9%
7	2002	260,813	90,342	Stevens, Dan	170,234	Peterson, Collin C.*	237	79,892	D	34.6%	65.3%	34.7%	65.3%
8	2002	283,931	88,673	Lemen, Bob	194,909	Oberstar, James L.*	349	106,236	D	31.2%	68.6%	31.3%	68.7%
Total	2002	2,201,638	1,029,612		1,097,911		74,115	68,299	D	46.8%	49.9%	48.4%	51.6%

An asterisk (*) denotes incumbent.

MINNESOTA

GENERAL AND PRIMARY ELECTIONS

2002 GENERAL ELECTIONS

Governor Other vote was 50,589 Green (Ken Pentel); 9,698 Independent (Booker T. Hodges IV); 3,026 Socialist Workers (Kari J. Sachs); 2,537 Constitution (Lawrence Michael Aeshliman); 1,340 scattered write-in; 4 write-in (Richard A. Klatte); 2 write-in (Bill Dahn); 2 write-in (Lealand Vettleson). (The Independence Party candidate, Timothy J. Penny, received 364,534 votes, 16.2 percent of the total vote. The Independence Party vote is listed in the county table for the 2002 gubernatorial election in Minnesota.)

Senator Other vote was 45,139 Independence (Jim Moore); 11,381 Democratic (Paul Wellstone); 10,119 Green (Ray Tricomo); 2,254 Constitution (Miro Drago Kovatchevich); 1,790 scattered write-in; 7 write-in (Ed McGaa); 3 write-in ("Dick" Franson); 3 write-in (Michelle Marie Harbeck). (Although Wellstone died in October, his name appeared on some absentee ballots.)

House Other vote was:

CD 1	9,964 Green (Greg Mikkelson); 283 scattered write-in.
CD 2	12,430 No New Taxes (Samuel D. Garst); 339 scattered write-in.
CD 3	309 scattered write-in.
CD 4	9,919 Green (Scott J. Raskiewicz); 319 scattered write-in.
CD 5	17,825 Green (Tim Davis); 314 scattered write-in.
CD 6	21,484 Independence (Dan Becker); 343 scattered write-in.
CD 7	237 scattered write-in.
CD 8	349 scattered write-in.

2002 PRIMARY ELECTIONS

Primary September 10, 2002   **Registration** (as of Sept. 9, 2002)   2,591,449   No Party Registration

Primary Type Open—Any registered voter could participate in the primary of either party.

Note: An asterisk (*) denotes incumbent.

	REPUBLICAN PRIMARIES			DEMOCRATIC PRIMARIES		
Governor	Tim Pawlenty	172,927	88.6%	Roger D. Moe	199,103	88.8%
	Leslie Davis	22,172	11.4%	Ole' Savior	25,135	11.2%
	TOTAL	195,099		TOTAL	224,238	
Senator	Norm Coleman	195,630	94.4%	Paul Wellstone*	222,839	92.6%
	Jack Shepard	11,678	5.6%	"Dick" Franson	11,884	4.9%
				Alve Erickson	6,052	2.5%
	TOTAL	207,308		TOTAL	240,775	
				Wellstone was killed in a plane crash in October. He was replaced on the November ballot by Walter F. Mondale		
Congressional District 1	Gil Gutknecht*	25,978	100.0%	Steve Andreasen	19,394	100.0%
Congressional District 2	John Kline	22,596	100.0%	Bill Luther*	14,437	100.0%
Congressional District 3	Jim Ramstad*	26,275	100.0%	Darryl Stanton	14,837	100.0%
Congressional District 4	Clyde Billington	14,052	100.0%	Betty McCollum*	30,878	100.0%
Congressional District 5	Daniel Nielsen Mathias	9,947	100.0%	Martin Olav Sabo*	33,310	100.0%

MINNESOTA

GENERAL AND PRIMARY ELECTIONS

	REPUBLICAN PRIMARIES			DEMOCRATIC PRIMARIES		
Congressional District 6	Mark Kennedy*	22,239	100.0%	Janet Robert	16,204	100.0%
Congressional District 7	Dan Stevens	29,855	100.0%	Collin C. Peterson*	35,130	100.0%
Congressional District 8	Bob Lemen	13,422	50.5%	James L. Oberstar*	50,582	100.0%
	Warren L. Nelson	13,132	49.5%			
	TOTAL	26,554				

MINNESOTA REPUBLICAN PRIMARY

GOVERNOR 2002

2000 Census Population	County	Total Vote	Pawlenty	Davis	Winner	Percentage of Total Vote Pawlenty	Davis
15,301	AITKIN	1,434	1,191	243	Pawlenty	83.1%	16.9%
298,084	ANOKA	12,623	11,269	1,354	Pawlenty	89.3%	10.7%
30,000	BECKER	1,823	1,509	314	Pawlenty	82.8%	17.2%
39,650	BELTRAMI	1,292	1,156	136	Pawlenty	89.5%	10.5%
34,226	BENTON	1,143	962	181	Pawlenty	84.2%	15.8%
5,820	BIG STONE	269	229	40	Pawlenty	85.1%	14.9%
55,941	BLUE EARTH	1,648	1,449	199	Pawlenty	87.9%	12.1%
26,911	BROWN	1,211	1,113	98	Pawlenty	91.9%	8.1%
31,671	CARLTON	1,023	842	181	Pawlenty	82.3%	17.7%
70,205	CARVER	4,729	4,265	464	Pawlenty	90.2%	9.8%
27,150	CASS	1,854	1,629	225	Pawlenty	87.9%	12.1%
13,088	CHIPPEWA	761	668	93	Pawlenty	87.8%	12.2%
41,101	CHISAGO	1,458	1,301	157	Pawlenty	89.2%	10.8%
51,229	CLAY	2,972	2,536	436	Pawlenty	85.3%	14.7%
8,423	CLEARWATER	383	302	81	Pawlenty	78.9%	21.1%
5,168	COOK	368	312	56	Pawlenty	84.8%	15.2%
12,167	COTTONWOOD	489	424	65	Pawlenty	86.7%	13.3%
55,099	CROW WING	3,248	2,887	361	Pawlenty	88.9%	11.1%
355,904	DAKOTA	14,482	13,455	1,027	Pawlenty	92.9%	7.1%
17,731	DODGE	800	693	107	Pawlenty	86.6%	13.4%
32,821	DOUGLAS	1,998	1,769	229	Pawlenty	88.5%	11.5%
16,181	FARIBAULT	523	462	61	Pawlenty	88.3%	11.7%
21,122	FILLMORE	701	570	131	Pawlenty	81.3%	18.7%
32,584	FREEBORN	2,506	2,123	383	Pawlenty	84.7%	15.3%
44,127	GOODHUE	1,573	1,446	127	Pawlenty	91.9%	8.1%
6,289	GRANT	264	231	33	Pawlenty	87.5%	12.5%
1,116,200	HENNEPIN	35,507	32,517	2,990	Pawlenty	91.6%	8.4%
19,718	HOUSTON	609	490	119	Pawlenty	80.5%	19.5%
18,376	HUBBARD	1,134	981	153	Pawlenty	86.5%	13.5%
31,287	ISANTI	1,474	1,328	146	Pawlenty	90.1%	9.9%
43,992	ITASCA	2,106	1,708	398	Pawlenty	81.1%	18.9%
11,268	JACKSON	351	317	34	Pawlenty	90.3%	9.7%
14,996	KANABEC	551	479	72	Pawlenty	86.9%	13.1%
41,203	KANDIYOHI	2,222	2,063	159	Pawlenty	92.8%	7.2%
5,285	KITTSON	285	231	54	Pawlenty	81.1%	18.9%
14,355	KOOCHICHING	1,146	918	228	Pawlenty	80.1%	19.9%
8,067	LAC QUI PARLE	314	257	57	Pawlenty	81.8%	18.2%
11,058	LAKE	415	326	89	Pawlenty	78.6%	21.4%
4,522	LAKE OF THE WOODS	426	284	142	Pawlenty	66.7%	33.3%
25,426	LE SUEUR	647	608	39	Pawlenty	94.0%	6.0%

MINNESOTA REPUBLICAN PRIMARY

GOVERNOR 2002

2000 Census Population	County	Total Vote	Pawlenty	Davis	Winner	Percentage of Total Vote	
						Pawlenty	Davis
6,429	LINCOLN	184	146	38	Pawlenty	79.3%	20.7%
25,425	LYON	844	774	70	Pawlenty	91.7%	8.3%
34,898	MCLEOD	3,567	3,206	361	Pawlenty	89.9%	10.1%
5,190	MAHNOMEN	408	317	91	Pawlenty	77.7%	22.3%
10,155	MARSHALL	604	474	130	Pawlenty	78.5%	21.5%
21,802	MARTIN	1,002	905	97	Pawlenty	90.3%	9.7%
22,644	MEEKER	1,853	1,597	256	Pawlenty	86.2%	13.8%
22,330	MILLE LACS	1,453	1,286	167	Pawlenty	88.5%	11.5%
31,712	MORRISON	1,229	1,101	128	Pawlenty	89.6%	10.4%
38,603	MOWER	1,547	1,268	279	Pawlenty	82.0%	18.0%
9,165	MURRAY	239	194	45	Pawlenty	81.2%	18.8%
29,771	NICOLLET	1,551	1,407	144	Pawlenty	90.7%	9.3%
20,832	NOBLES	435	359	76	Pawlenty	82.5%	17.5%
7,442	NORMAN	469	395	74	Pawlenty	84.2%	15.8%
124,277	OLMSTED	5,065	4,430	635	Pawlenty	87.5%	12.5%
57,159	OTTER TAIL	4,850	3,955	895	Pawlenty	81.5%	18.5%
13,584	PENNINGTON	227	189	38	Pawlenty	83.3%	16.7%
26,530	PINE	1,248	1,085	163	Pawlenty	86.9%	13.1%
9,895	PIPESTONE	770	569	201	Pawlenty	73.9%	26.1%
31,369	POLK	1,045	876	169	Pawlenty	83.8%	16.2%
11,236	POPE	432	383	49	Pawlenty	88.7%	11.3%
511,035	RAMSEY	14,035	12,856	1,179	Pawlenty	91.6%	8.4%
4,299	RED LAKE	137	105	32	Pawlenty	76.6%	23.4%
16,815	REDWOOD	1,187	1,112	75	Pawlenty	93.7%	6.3%
17,154	RENVILLE	607	549	58	Pawlenty	90.4%	9.6%
56,665	RICE	1,281	1,140	141	Pawlenty	89.0%	11.0%
9,721	ROCK	605	460	145	Pawlenty	76.0%	24.0%
16,338	ROSEAU	507	389	118	Pawlenty	76.7%	23.3%
200,528	ST. LOUIS	7,114	5,749	1,365	Pawlenty	80.8%	19.2%
89,498	SCOTT	4,287	3,928	359	Pawlenty	91.6%	8.4%
64,417	SHERBURNE	1,862	1,651	211	Pawlenty	88.7%	11.3%
15,356	SIBLEY	1,265	1,114	151	Pawlenty	88.1%	11.9%
133,166	STEARNS	5,880	5,169	711	Pawlenty	87.9%	12.1%
33,680	STEELE	944	853	91	Pawlenty	90.4%	9.6%
10,053	STEVENS	502	425	77	Pawlenty	84.7%	15.3%
11,956	SWIFT	507	421	86	Pawlenty	83.0%	17.0%
24,426	TODD	918	815	103	Pawlenty	88.8%	11.2%
4,134	TRAVERSE	135	111	24	Pawlenty	82.2%	17.8%
21,610	WABASHA	809	697	112	Pawlenty	86.2%	13.8%
13,713	WADENA	1,374	1,173	201	Pawlenty	85.4%	14.6%
19,526	WASECA	902	786	116	Pawlenty	87.1%	12.9%
201,130	WASHINGTON	6,182	5,757	425	Pawlenty	93.1%	6.9%
11,876	WATONWAN	1,103	896	207	Pawlenty	81.2%	18.8%
7,138	WILKIN	226	190	36	Pawlenty	84.1%	15.9%
49,985	WINONA	1,630	1,364	266	Pawlenty	83.7%	16.3%
89,986	WRIGHT	3,003	2,729	274	Pawlenty	90.9%	9.1%
11,080	YELLOW MEDICINE	313	272	41	Pawlenty	86.9%	13.1%
4,919,479	TOTAL	195,099	172,927	22,172	Pawlenty	88.6%	11.4%

MINNESOTA DEMOCRATIC PRIMARY
GOVERNOR 2002

2000 Census Population	County	Total Vote	Moe	Savior	Winner	Percentage of Total Vote	
						Moe	Savior
15,301	AITKIN	1,594	1,338	256	Moe	83.9%	16.1%
298,084	ANOKA	13,096	11,044	2,052	Moe	84.3%	15.7%
30,000	BECKER	1,980	1,734	246	Moe	87.6%	12.4%
39,650	BELTRAMI	1,752	1,606	146	Moe	91.7%	8.3%
34,226	BENTON	1,034	842	192	Moe	81.4%	18.6%
5,820	BIG STONE	469	429	40	Moe	91.5%	8.5%
55,941	BLUE EARTH	2,526	2,112	414	Moe	83.6%	16.4%
26,911	BROWN	419	386	33	Moe	92.1%	7.9%
31,671	CARLTON	2,383	2,110	273	Moe	88.5%	11.5%
70,205	CARVER	985	853	132	Moe	86.6%	13.4%
27,150	CASS	1,478	1,292	186	Moe	87.4%	12.6%
13,088	CHIPPEWA	1,083	953	130	Moe	88.0%	12.0%
41,101	CHISAGO	2,122	1,756	366	Moe	82.8%	17.2%
51,229	CLAY	4,110	3,769	341	Moe	91.7%	8.3%
8,423	CLEARWATER	723	621	102	Moe	85.9%	14.1%
5,168	COOK	1,025	851	174	Moe	83.0%	17.0%
12,167	COTTONWOOD	411	368	43	Moe	89.5%	10.5%
55,099	CROW WING	2,415	2,144	271	Moe	88.8%	11.2%
355,904	DAKOTA	10,013	8,937	1,076	Moe	89.3%	10.7%
17,731	DODGE	503	432	71	Moe	85.9%	14.1%
32,821	DOUGLAS	1,631	1,418	213	Moe	86.9%	13.1%
16,181	FARIBAULT	426	380	46	Moe	89.2%	10.8%
21,122	FILLMORE	471	416	55	Moe	88.3%	11.7%
32,584	FREEBORN	2,105	1,816	289	Moe	86.3%	13.7%
44,127	GOODHUE	1,235	1,099	136	Moe	89.0%	11.0%
6,289	GRANT	369	313	56	Moe	84.8%	15.2%
1,116,200	HENNEPIN	45,132	41,499	3,633	Moe	92.0%	8.0%
19,718	HOUSTON	367	318	49	Moe	86.6%	13.4%
18,376	HUBBARD	1,046	928	118	Moe	88.7%	11.3%
31,287	ISANTI	1,461	1,251	210	Moe	85.6%	14.4%
43,992	ITASCA	4,600	3,958	642	Moe	86.0%	14.0%
11,268	JACKSON	406	367	39	Moe	90.4%	9.6%
14,996	KANABEC	504	422	82	Moe	83.7%	16.3%
41,203	KANDIYOHI	2,598	2,391	207	Moe	92.0%	8.0%
5,285	KITTSON	551	519	32	Moe	94.2%	5.8%
14,355	KOOCHICHING	2,270	1,974	296	Moe	87.0%	13.0%
8,067	LAC QUI PARLE	569	509	60	Moe	89.5%	10.5%
11,058	LAKE	2,058	1,725	333	Moe	83.8%	16.2%
4,522	LAKE OF THE WOODS	688	576	112	Moe	83.7%	16.3%
25,426	LE SUEUR	582	508	74	Moe	87.3%	12.7%
6,429	LINCOLN	189	171	18	Moe	90.5%	9.5%
25,425	LYON	646	590	56	Moe	91.3%	8.7%
34,898	MCLEOD	1,999	1,754	245	Moe	87.7%	12.3%
5,190	MAHNOMEN	665	515	150	Moe	77.4%	22.6%
10,155	MARSHALL	1,128	996	132	Moe	88.3%	11.7%
21,802	MARTIN	594	537	57	Moe	90.4%	9.6%
22,644	MEEKER	553	470	83	Moe	85.0%	15.0%
22,330	MILLE LACS	974	797	177	Moe	81.8%	18.2%
31,712	MORRISON	940	801	139	Moe	85.2%	14.8%
38,603	MOWER	2,181	1,916	265	Moe	87.8%	12.2%
9,165	MURRAY	316	283	33	Moe	89.6%	10.4%
29,771	NICOLLET	2,097	1,775	322	Moe	84.6%	15.4%
20,832	NOBLES	480	426	54	Moe	88.8%	11.2%
7,442	NORMAN	978	869	109	Moe	88.9%	11.1%
124,277	OLMSTED	2,945	2,602	343	Moe	88.4%	11.6%
57,159	OTTER TAIL	3,599	3,198	401	Moe	88.9%	11.1%
13,584	PENNINGTON	414	366	48	Moe	88.4%	11.6%
26,530	PINE	1,597	1,344	253	Moe	84.2%	15.8%
9,895	PIPESTONE	771	681	90	Moe	88.3%	11.7%
31,369	POLK	1,951	1,758	193	Moe	90.1%	9.9%

MINNESOTA DEMOCRATIC PRIMARY

GOVERNOR 2002

2000 Census Population	County	Total Vote	Moe	Savior	Winner	Moe	Savior
						Percentage of Total Vote	
11,236	POPE	442	384	58	Moe	86.9%	13.1%
511,035	RAMSEY	27,742	25,101	2,641	Moe	90.5%	9.5%
4,299	RED LAKE	264	236	28	Moe	89.4%	10.6%
16,815	REDWOOD	637	575	62	Moe	90.3%	9.7%
17,154	RENVILLE	621	557	64	Moe	89.7%	10.3%
56,665	RICE	1,539	1,372	167	Moe	89.1%	10.9%
9,721	ROCK	458	413	45	Moe	90.2%	9.8%
16,338	ROSEAU	449	403	46	Moe	89.8%	10.2%
200,528	ST. LOUIS	22,546	20,207	2,339	Moe	89.6%	10.4%
89,498	SCOTT	2,503	2,132	371	Moe	85.2%	14.8%
64,417	SHERBURNE	1,717	1,446	271	Moe	84.2%	15.8%
15,356	SIBLEY	949	818	131	Moe	86.2%	13.8%
133,166	STEARNS	4,541	3,950	591	Moe	87.0%	13.0%
33,680	STEELE	558	481	77	Moe	86.2%	13.8%
10,053	STEVENS	605	521	84	Moe	86.1%	13.9%
11,956	SWIFT	957	863	94	Moe	90.2%	9.8%
24,426	TODD	1,086	935	151	Moe	86.1%	13.9%
4,134	TRAVERSE	174	154	20	Moe	88.5%	11.5%
21,610	WABASHA	522	454	68	Moe	87.0%	13.0%
13,713	WADENA	1,014	872	142	Moe	86.0%	14.0%
19,526	WASECA	493	387	106	Moe	78.5%	21.5%
201,130	WASHINGTON	5,517	4,923	594	Moe	89.2%	10.8%
11,876	WATONWAN	1,092	935	157	Moe	85.6%	14.4%
7,138	WILKIN	229	198	31	Moe	86.5%	13.5%
49,985	WINONA	1,404	1,245	159	Moe	88.7%	11.3%
89,986	WRIGHT	1,505	1,312	193	Moe	87.2%	12.8%
11,080	YELLOW MEDICINE	467	416	51	Moe	89.1%	10.9%
4,919,479	TOTAL	224,238	199,103	25,135	Moe	88.8%	11.2%

MINNESOTA REPUBLICAN PRIMARY

SENATOR 2002

2000 Census Population	County	Total Vote	Coleman	Shepard	Winner	Coleman	Shepard
						Percentage of Total Vote	
15,301	AITKIN	1,551	1,431	120	Coleman	92.3%	7.7%
298,084	ANOKA	13,528	12,901	627	Coleman	95.4%	4.6%
30,000	BECKER	1,955	1,845	110	Coleman	94.4%	5.6%
39,650	BELTRAMI	1,367	1,281	86	Coleman	93.7%	6.3%
34,226	BENTON	1,271	1,176	95	Coleman	92.5%	7.5%
5,820	BIG STONE	283	260	23	Coleman	91.9%	8.1%
55,941	BLUE EARTH	1,775	1,655	120	Coleman	93.2%	6.8%
26,911	BROWN	1,252	1,176	76	Coleman	93.9%	6.1%
31,671	CARLTON	1,092	1,031	61	Coleman	94.4%	5.6%
70,205	CARVER	4,877	4,523	354	Coleman	92.7%	7.3%
27,150	CASS	1,970	1,849	121	Coleman	93.9%	6.1%
13,088	CHIPPEWA	823	768	55	Coleman	93.3%	6.7%
41,101	CHISAGO	1,555	1,490	65	Coleman	95.8%	4.2%
51,229	CLAY	3,231	3,020	211	Coleman	93.5%	6.5%
8,423	CLEARWATER	413	378	35	Coleman	91.5%	8.5%
5,168	COOK	393	356	37	Coleman	90.6%	9.4%
12,167	COTTONWOOD	526	501	25	Coleman	95.2%	4.8%
55,099	CROW WING	3,458	3,262	196	Coleman	94.3%	5.7%
355,904	DAKOTA	14,795	13,942	853	Coleman	94.2%	5.8%
17,731	DODGE	856	804	52	Coleman	93.9%	6.1%

MINNESOTA REPUBLICAN PRIMARY

SENATOR 2002

2000 Census Population	County	Total Vote	Coleman	Shepard	Winner	Percentage of Total Vote	
						Coleman	Shepard
32,821	DOUGLAS	2,112	1,995	117	Coleman	94.5%	5.5%
16,181	FARIBAULT	542	506	36	Coleman	93.4%	6.6%
21,122	FILLMORE	756	682	74	Coleman	90.2%	9.8%
32,584	FREEBORN	2,743	2,560	183	Coleman	93.3%	6.7%
44,127	GOODHUE	1,651	1,562	89	Coleman	94.6%	5.4%
6,289	GRANT	278	268	10	Coleman	96.4%	3.6%
1,116,200	HENNEPIN	37,436	35,668	1,768	Coleman	95.3%	4.7%
19,718	HOUSTON	640	597	43	Coleman	93.3%	6.7%
18,376	HUBBARD	1,223	1,150	73	Coleman	94.0%	6.0%
31,287	ISANTI	1,596	1,530	66	Coleman	95.9%	4.1%
43,992	ITASCA	2,338	2,182	156	Coleman	93.3%	6.7%
11,268	JACKSON	375	347	28	Coleman	92.5%	7.5%
14,996	KANABEC	581	549	32	Coleman	94.5%	5.5%
41,203	KANDIYOHI	2,353	2,242	111	Coleman	95.3%	4.7%
5,285	KITTSON	302	280	22	Coleman	92.7%	7.3%
14,355	KOOCHICHING	1,260	1,181	79	Coleman	93.7%	6.3%
8,067	LAC QUI PARLE	326	303	23	Coleman	92.9%	7.1%
11,058	LAKE	442	415	27	Coleman	93.9%	6.1%
4,522	LAKE OF THE WOODS	478	413	65	Coleman	86.4%	13.6%
25,426	LE SUEUR	671	633	38	Coleman	94.3%	5.7%
6,429	LINCOLN	193	180	13	Coleman	93.3%	6.7%
25,425	LYON	887	837	50	Coleman	94.4%	5.6%
34,898	MCLEOD	3,809	3,611	198	Coleman	94.8%	5.2%
5,190	MAHNOMEN	437	405	32	Coleman	92.7%	7.3%
10,155	MARSHALL	655	622	33	Coleman	95.0%	5.0%
21,802	MARTIN	1,062	1,011	51	Coleman	95.2%	4.8%
22,644	MEEKER	1,929	1,707	222	Coleman	88.5%	11.5%
22,330	MILLE LACS	1,519	1,447	72	Coleman	95.3%	4.7%
31,712	MORRISON	1,345	1,282	63	Coleman	95.3%	4.7%
38,603	MOWER	1,655	1,553	102	Coleman	93.8%	6.2%
9,165	MURRAY	240	208	32	Coleman	86.7%	13.3%
29,771	NICOLLET	1,666	1,578	88	Coleman	94.7%	5.3%
20,832	NOBLES	482	426	56	Coleman	88.4%	11.6%
7,442	NORMAN	500	451	49	Coleman	90.2%	9.8%
124,277	OLMSTED	5,474	5,159	315	Coleman	94.2%	5.8%
57,159	OTTER TAIL	5,316	4,958	358	Coleman	93.3%	6.7%
13,584	PENNINGTON	238	218	20	Coleman	91.6%	8.4%
26,530	PINE	1,336	1,271	65	Coleman	95.1%	4.9%
9,895	PIPESTONE	876	749	127	Coleman	85.5%	14.5%
31,369	POLK	1,158	1,085	73	Coleman	93.7%	6.3%
11,236	POPE	455	427	28	Coleman	93.8%	6.2%
511,035	RAMSEY	14,817	14,178	639	Coleman	95.7%	4.3%
4,299	RED LAKE	149	143	6	Coleman	96.0%	4.0%
16,815	REDWOOD	1,238	1,170	68	Coleman	94.5%	5.5%
17,154	RENVILLE	637	599	38	Coleman	94.0%	6.0%
56,665	RICE	1,373	1,295	78	Coleman	94.3%	5.7%
9,721	ROCK	626	557	69	Coleman	89.0%	11.0%
16,338	ROSEAU	561	516	45	Coleman	92.0%	8.0%
200,528	ST. LOUIS	7,822	7,348	474	Coleman	93.9%	6.1%
89,498	SCOTT	4,504	4,310	194	Coleman	95.7%	4.3%
64,417	SHERBURNE	2,028	1,935	93	Coleman	95.4%	4.6%
15,356	SIBLEY	1,333	1,234	99	Coleman	92.6%	7.4%
133,166	STEARNS	6,362	5,975	387	Coleman	93.9%	6.1%
33,680	STEELE	1,019	970	49	Coleman	95.2%	4.8%
10,053	STEVENS	543	500	43	Coleman	92.1%	7.9%
11,956	SWIFT	539	498	41	Coleman	92.4%	7.6%
24,426	TODD	1,003	944	59	Coleman	94.1%	5.9%
4,134	TRAVERSE	139	128	11	Coleman	92.1%	7.9%
21,610	WABASHA	860	789	71	Coleman	91.7%	8.3%
13,713	WADENA	1,500	1,391	109	Coleman	92.7%	7.3%

MINNESOTA REPUBLICAN PRIMARY

SENATOR 2002

2000 Census Population	County	Total Vote	Coleman	Shepard	Winner	Percentage of Total Vote	
						Coleman	Shepard
19,526	WASECA	987	945	42	Coleman	95.7%	4.3%
201,130	WASHINGTON	6,391	6,143	248	Coleman	96.1%	3.9%
11,876	WATONWAN	1,175	1,105	70	Coleman	94.0%	6.0%
7,138	WILKIN	237	225	12	Coleman	94.9%	5.1%
49,985	WINONA	1,736	1,600	136	Coleman	92.2%	7.8%
89,986	WRIGHT	3,106	2,943	163	Coleman	94.8%	5.2%
11,080	YELLOW MEDICINE	317	292	25	Coleman	92.1%	7.9%
4,919,479	TOTAL	207,308	195,630	11,678	Coleman	94.4%	5.6%

MINNESOTA DEMOCRATIC PRIMARY

SENATOR 2002

2000 Census Population	County	Total Vote	Wellstone	Other	Winner	Percentage of Total Vote	
						Wellstone	Other
15,301	AITKIN	1,715	1,507	208	Wellstone	87.9%	12.1%
298,084	ANOKA	14,016	12,710	1,306	Wellstone	90.7%	9.3%
30,000	BECKER	2,061	1,894	167	Wellstone	91.9%	8.1%
39,650	BELTRAMI	1,777	1,654	123	Wellstone	93.1%	6.9%
34,226	BENTON	1,170	1,046	124	Wellstone	89.4%	10.6%
5,820	BIG STONE	500	469	31	Wellstone	93.8%	6.2%
55,941	BLUE EARTH	2,731	2,410	321	Wellstone	88.2%	11.8%
26,911	BROWN	441	428	13	Wellstone	97.1%	2.9%
31,671	CARLTON	2,503	2,290	213	Wellstone	91.5%	8.5%
70,205	CARVER	1,094	1,020	74	Wellstone	93.2%	6.8%
27,150	CASS	1,564	1,449	115	Wellstone	92.6%	7.4%
13,088	CHIPPEWA	1,186	1,126	60	Wellstone	94.9%	5.1%
41,101	CHISAGO	2,300	2,005	295	Wellstone	87.2%	12.8%
51,229	CLAY	4,253	3,959	294	Wellstone	93.1%	6.9%
8,423	CLEARWATER	731	627	104	Wellstone	85.8%	14.2%
5,168	COOK	1,122	870	252	Wellstone	77.5%	22.5%
12,167	COTTONWOOD	441	415	26	Wellstone	94.1%	5.9%
55,099	CROW WING	2,566	2,339	227	Wellstone	91.2%	8.8%
355,904	DAKOTA	10,726	10,116	610	Wellstone	94.3%	5.7%
17,731	DODGE	557	510	47	Wellstone	91.6%	8.4%
32,821	DOUGLAS	1,766	1,633	133	Wellstone	92.5%	7.5%
16,181	FARIBAULT	482	446	36	Wellstone	92.5%	7.5%
21,122	FILLMORE	527	492	35	Wellstone	93.4%	6.6%
32,584	FREEBORN	2,366	2,212	154	Wellstone	93.5%	6.5%
44,127	GOODHUE	1,371	1,278	93	Wellstone	93.2%	6.8%
6,289	GRANT	387	360	27	Wellstone	93.0%	7.0%
1,116,200	HENNEPIN	48,351	46,462	1,889	Wellstone	96.1%	3.9%
19,718	HOUSTON	395	353	42	Wellstone	89.4%	10.6%
18,376	HUBBARD	1,101	1,021	80	Wellstone	92.7%	7.3%
31,287	ISANTI	1,575	1,436	139	Wellstone	91.2%	8.8%
43,992	ITASCA	5,025	4,372	653	Wellstone	87.0%	13.0%
11,268	JACKSON	445	420	25	Wellstone	94.4%	5.6%
14,996	KANABEC	539	483	56	Wellstone	89.6%	10.4%
41,203	KANDIYOHI	2,706	2,538	168	Wellstone	93.8%	6.2%
5,285	KITTSON	567	539	28	Wellstone	95.1%	4.9%
14,355	KOOCHICHING	2,362	1,953	409	Wellstone	82.7%	17.3%
8,067	LAC QUI PARLE	591	545	46	Wellstone	92.2%	7.8%
11,058	LAKE	2,179	1,806	373	Wellstone	82.9%	17.1%
4,522	LAKE OF THE WOODS	724	623	101	Wellstone	86.0%	14.0%
25,426	LE SUEUR	638	589	49	Wellstone	92.3%	7.7%

MINNESOTA DEMOCRATIC PRIMARY

SENATOR 2002

2000 Census Population	County	Total Vote	Wellstone	Other	Winner	Percentage of Total Vote	
						Wellstone	Other
6,429	LINCOLN	204	186	18	Wellstone	91.2%	8.8%
25,425	LYON	695	651	44	Wellstone	93.7%	6.3%
34,898	MCLEOD	2,214	2,060	154	Wellstone	93.0%	7.0%
5,190	MAHNOMEN	698	601	97	Wellstone	86.1%	13.9%
10,155	MARSHALL	1,200	1,084	116	Wellstone	90.3%	9.7%
21,802	MARTIN	657	623	34	Wellstone	94.8%	5.2%
22,644	MEEKER	586	559	27	Wellstone	95.4%	4.6%
22,330	MILLE LACS	1,046	951	95	Wellstone	90.9%	9.1%
31,712	MORRISON	1,043	943	100	Wellstone	90.4%	9.6%
38,603	MOWER	2,396	2,213	183	Wellstone	92.4%	7.6%
9,165	MURRAY	336	308	28	Wellstone	91.7%	8.3%
29,771	NICOLLET	2,260	1,986	274	Wellstone	87.9%	12.1%
20,832	NOBLES	532	476	56	Wellstone	89.5%	10.5%
7,442	NORMAN	983	913	70	Wellstone	92.9%	7.1%
124,277	OLMSTED	3,268	3,053	215	Wellstone	93.4%	6.6%
57,159	OTTER TAIL	3,823	3,527	296	Wellstone	92.3%	7.7%
13,584	PENNINGTON	436	396	40	Wellstone	90.8%	9.2%
26,530	PINE	1,705	1,509	196	Wellstone	88.5%	11.5%
9,895	PIPESTONE	886	771	115	Wellstone	87.0%	13.0%
31,369	POLK	2,000	1,846	154	Wellstone	92.3%	7.7%
11,236	POPE	488	459	29	Wellstone	94.1%	5.9%
511,035	RAMSEY	29,965	28,520	1,445	Wellstone	95.2%	4.8%
4,299	RED LAKE	273	245	28	Wellstone	89.7%	10.3%
16,815	REDWOOD	687	629	58	Wellstone	91.6%	8.4%
17,154	RENVILLE	672	628	44	Wellstone	93.5%	6.5%
56,665	RICE	1,688	1,591	97	Wellstone	94.3%	5.7%
9,721	ROCK	504	463	41	Wellstone	91.9%	8.1%
16,338	ROSEAU	475	436	39	Wellstone	91.8%	8.2%
200,528	ST. LOUIS	24,085	21,511	2,574	Wellstone	89.3%	10.7%
89,498	SCOTT	2,781	2,559	222	Wellstone	92.0%	8.0%
64,417	SHERBURNE	1,855	1,663	192	Wellstone	89.6%	10.4%
15,356	SIBLEY	1,062	947	115	Wellstone	89.2%	10.8%
133,166	STEARNS	4,931	4,520	411	Wellstone	91.7%	8.3%
33,680	STEELE	608	567	41	Wellstone	93.3%	6.7%
10,053	STEVENS	640	602	38	Wellstone	94.1%	5.9%
11,956	SWIFT	1,000	949	51	Wellstone	94.9%	5.1%
24,426	TODD	1,193	1,056	137	Wellstone	88.5%	11.5%
4,134	TRAVERSE	185	169	16	Wellstone	91.4%	8.6%
21,610	WABASHA	588	548	40	Wellstone	93.2%	6.8%
13,713	WADENA	1,116	1,020	96	Wellstone	91.4%	8.6%
19,526	WASECA	574	523	51	Wellstone	91.1%	8.9%
201,130	WASHINGTON	5,847	5,535	312	Wellstone	94.7%	5.3%
11,876	WATONWAN	1,199	1,114	85	Wellstone	92.9%	7.1%
7,138	WILKIN	248	220	28	Wellstone	88.7%	11.3%
49,985	WINONA	1,522	1,418	104	Wellstone	93.2%	6.8%
89,986	WRIGHT	1,583	1,458	125	Wellstone	92.1%	7.9%
11,080	YELLOW MEDICINE	487	428	59	Wellstone	87.9%	12.1%
4,919,479	TOTAL	240,775	222,839	17,936	Wellstone	92.6%	7.4%

MISSISSIPPI

GOVERNOR

Ronnie Musgrove (D). Elected 2000 to a four-year term by the Mississippi House after neither the Republican nor Democratic candidate won a majority in the November 1999 election.

SENATORS (2 Republicans)

Thad Cochran (R). Reelected 2002 to a six-year term. Previously elected 1996, 1990, 1984, 1978.

Trent Lott (R). Reelected 2000 to a six-year term. Previously elected 1994, 1988.

REPRESENTATIVES (2 Democrats, 2 Republicans)

1. Roger Wicker (R)
2. Bennie Thompson (D)
3. Charles W. "Chip" Pickering Jr. (R)
4. Gene Taylor (D)

POSTWAR VOTE FOR PRESIDENT

| | | Republican | | Democratic | | Other | | Percentage | | | |
| | | | | | | | | Total Vote | | Major Vote | |
Year	Total Vote	Vote	Candidate	Vote	Candidate	Vote	Plurality	Rep.	Dem.	Rep.	Dem.
2000**	994,184	572,844	Bush, George W.	404,614	Gore, Al	16,726	168,230 R	57.6%	40.7%	58.6%	41.4%
1996**	893,857	439,838	Dole, Bob	394,022	Clinton, Bill	59,997	45,816 R	49.2%	44.1%	52.7%	47.3%
1992**	981,793	487,793	Bush, George	400,258	Clinton, Bill	93,742	87,535 R	49.7%	40.8%	54.9%	45.1%
1988	931,527	557,890	Bush, George	363,921	Dukakis, Michael S.	9,716	193,969 R	59.9%	39.1%	60.5%	39.5%
1984	941,104	582,377	Reagan, Ronald	352,192	Mondale, Walter F.	6,535	230,185 R	61.9%	37.4%	62.3%	37.7%
1980**	892,620	441,089	Reagan, Ronald	429,281	Carter, Jimmy	22,250	11,808 R	49.4%	48.1%	50.7%	49.3%
1976	769,361	366,846	Ford, Gerald R.	381,309	Carter, Jimmy	21,206	14,463 D	47.7%	49.6%	49.0%	51.0%
1972	645,963	505,125	Nixon, Richard M.	126,782	McGovern, George S.	14,056	378,343 R	78.2%	19.6%	79.9%	20.1%
1968**	654,509	88,516	Nixon, Richard M.	150,644	Humphrey, Hubert H.	415,349	264,705 A	13.5%	23.0%	37.0%	63.0%
1964	409,146	356,528	Goldwater, Barry M.	52,618	Johnson, Lyndon B.		303,910 R	87.1%	12.9%	87.1%	12.9%
1960**	298,171	73,561	Nixon, Richard M.	108,362	Kennedy, John F.	116,248	7,886 U	24.7%	36.3%	40.4%	59.6%
1956	248,104	60,685	Eisenhower, Dwight D.	144,453	Stevenson, Adlai E.	42,966	83,768 D	24.5%	58.2%	29.6%	70.4%
1952	285,532	112,966	Eisenhower, Dwight D.	172,566	Stevenson, Adlai E.		59,600 D	39.6%	60.4%	39.6%	60.4%
1948**	192,190	5,043	Dewey, Thomas E.	19,384	Truman, Harry S.	167,763	148,154 SR	2.6%	10.1%	20.6%	79.4%

In 2000 the other vote column includes 8,122 votes cast for Green (Nader). In 1996 the other vote column includes 52,222 votes cast for Perot. In 1992 the other vote column includes 85,626 votes cast for Perot. In 1980 the other column includes 12,036 votes for Independent (Anderson). In 1968 other vote was Independent (Wallace). In 1960 other vote was Unpledged Independent Democratic. In 1948 other vote was 167,538 States Rights and 225 Progressive.

MISSISSIPPI

POSTWAR VOTE FOR GOVERNOR

Year	Total Vote	Republican Vote	Republican Candidate	Democratic Vote	Democratic Candidate	Other Vote	Rep.-Dem. Plurality	Percentage Total Vote Rep.	Dem.	Major Vote Rep.	Dem.
1999**	763,938	370,691	Parker, Mike	379,034	Musgrove, Ronnie	14,213	8,343 D	48.5%	49.6%	49.4%	50.6%
1995	819,471	455,261	Fordice, Kirk	364,210	Molpus, Dick		91,051 R	55.6%	44.4%	55.6%	44.4%
1991	711,188	361,500	Fordice, Kirk	338,435	Mabus, Ray	11,253	23,065 R	50.8%	47.6%	51.6%	48.4%
1987	721,695	336,006	Reed, Jack	385,689	Mabus, Ray		49,683 D	46.6%	53.4%	46.6%	53.4%
1983	742,737	288,764	Bramlett, Leon	409,209	Allain, William A.	44,764	120,445 D	38.9%	55.1%	41.4%	58.6%
1979	677,322	263,702	Carmichael, Gil	413,620	Winter, William F.		149,918 D	38.9%	61.1%	38.9%	61.1%
1975	708,033	319,632	Carmichael, Gil	369,568	Finch, Cliff	18,833	49,936 D	45.1%	52.2%	46.4%	53.6%
1971	780,537		—	601,122	Waller, William L.	179,415	601,122 D		77.0%		100.0%
1967	448,697	133,379	Phillips, Rubel L.	315,318	Williams, John Bell		181,939 D	29.7%	70.3%	29.7%	70.3%
1963	363,971	138,515	Phillips, Rubel L.	225,456	Johnson, Paul B.		86,941 D	38.1%	61.9%	38.1%	61.9%
1959	57,671		—	57,671	Barnett, Ross R.		57,671 D		100.0%		100.0%
1955	40,707		—	40,707	Coleman, James P.		40,707 D		100.0%		100.0%
1951	43,422		—	43,422	White, Hugh		43,422 D		100.0%		100.0%
1947	166,095		—	161,993	Wright, Fielding L.	4,102	161,993 D		97.5%		100.0%

In 1999 no candidate received a majority of the vote. Democrat Musgrove was elected in January 2000 by the Mississippi House of Representatives.

POSTWAR VOTE FOR SENATOR

Year	Total Vote	Republican Vote	Republican Candidate	Democratic Vote	Democratic Candidate	Other Vote	Rep.-Dem. Plurality	Percentage Total Vote Rep.	Dem.	Major Vote Rep.	Dem.
2002	630,495	533,269	Cochran, Thad		—	97,226	533,269 R	84.6%		100.0%	
2000	994,144	654,941	Lott, Trent	314,090	Brown, Troy	25,113	340,851 R	65.9%	31.6%	67.6%	32.4%
1996	878,662	624,154	Cochran, Thad	240,647	Hunt, James W.	13,861	383,507 R	71.0%	27.4%	72.2%	27.8%
1994	608,085	418,333	Lott, Trent	189,752	Harper, Ken		228,581 R	68.8%	31.2%	68.8%	31.2%
1990	274,244	274,244	Cochran, Thad		—		274,244 R	100.0%		100.0%	
1988	946,719	510,380	Lott, Trent	436,339	Dowdy, Wayne		74,041 R	53.9%	46.1%	53.9%	46.1%
1984	952,240	580,314	Cochran, Thad	371,926	Winter, William F.		208,388 R	60.9%	39.1%	60.9%	39.1%
1982	645,026	230,927	Barbour, Haley	414,099	Stennis, John		183,172 D	35.8%	64.2%	35.8%	64.2%
1978	583,936	263,089	Cochran, Thad	185,454	Dantin, Maurice	135,393	77,635 R	45.1%	31.8%	58.7%	41.3%
1976	554,433		—	554,433	Stennis, John		554,433 D		100.0%		100.0%
1972	645,746	249,779	Carmichael, Gil	375,102	Eastland, James O.	20,865	125,323 D	38.7%	58.1%	40.0%	60.0%
1970	324,215		—	286,622	Stennis, John	37,593	286,622 D		88.4%		100.0%
1966	393,900	105,150	Walker, Prentiss	258,248	Eastland, James O.	30,502	153,098 D	26.7%	65.6%	28.9%	71.1%
1964	343,364		—	343,364	Stennis, John		343,364 D		100.0%		100.0%
1960	266,148	21,807	Moore, Joe A.	244,341	Eastland, James O.		222,534 D	8.2%	91.8%	8.2%	91.8%
1958	61,039		—	61,039	Stennis, John		61,039 D		100.0%		100.0%
1954	105,526	4,678	White, James A.	100,848	Eastland, James O.		96,170 D	4.4%	95.6%	4.4%	95.6%
1952	233,919		—	233,919	Stennis, John		233,919 D		100.0%		100.0%
1948	151,478		—	151,478	Eastland, James O.		151,478 D		100.0%		100.0%
1947S	193,709		[See note below]				D				
1946	46,747		—	46,747	Bilbo, Theodore		46,747 D		100.0%		100.0%

The 1947 election was for a short term to fill a vacancy and was held without party designation or nomination; John Stennis polled 52,068 votes (26.9% of the total vote) and won the election with a 6,343-vote plurality. Other candidate votes in this election were 45,725 W. M. Colmer; 43,642 Forrest B. Jackson; 27,159 Paul B. Johnson; 24,492 John E. Rankin and 623 R. L. Collins.

MISSISSIPPI

Congressional districts first established for elections held in 2002
4 members

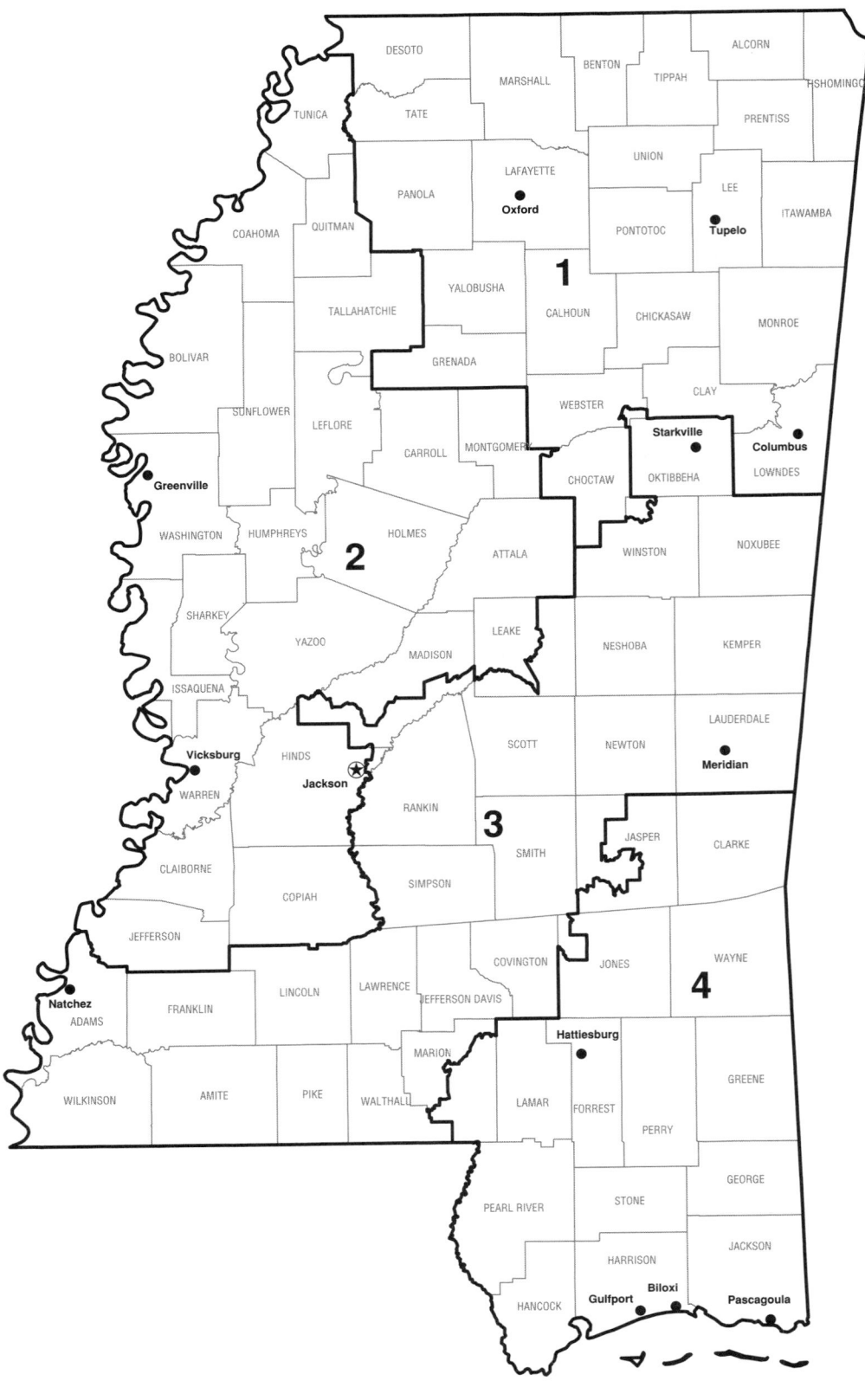

MISSISSIPPI
SENATOR 2002

2000 Census Population	County	Total Vote	Republican	Democratic	Other	Rep.-Dem. Plurality	Total Vote Rep.	Total Vote Dem.	Major Vote Rep.	Major Vote Dem.
34,340	ADAMS	8,665	6,621		2,044	6,621 R	76.4%		100.0%	
34,558	ALCORN	3,710	3,284		426	3,284 R	88.5%		100.0%	
13,599	AMITE	5,786	3,811		1,975	3,811 R	65.9%		100.0%	
19,661	ATTALA	5,654	4,810		844	4,810 R	85.1%		100.0%	
8,026	BENTON	1,569	1,272		297	1,272 R	81.1%		100.0%	
40,633	BOLIVAR	6,797	5,660		1,137	5,660 R	83.3%		100.0%	
15,069	CALHOUN	3,028	2,614		414	2,614 R	86.3%		100.0%	
10,769	CARROLL	2,655	2,215		440	2,215 R	83.4%		100.0%	
19,440	CHICKASAW	4,141	3,299		842	3,299 R	79.7%		100.0%	
9,758	CHOCTAW	1,946	1,698		248	1,698 R	87.3%		100.0%	
11,831	CLAIBORNE	2,155	1,386		769	1,386 R	64.3%		100.0%	
17,955	CLARKE	4,504	3,755		749	3,755 R	83.4%		100.0%	
21,979	CLAY	6,046	4,356		1,690	4,356 R	72.0%		100.0%	
30,622	COAHOMA	3,402	3,036		366	3,036 R	89.2%		100.0%	
28,757	COPIAH	6,707	5,315		1,392	5,315 R	79.2%		100.0%	
19,407	COVINGTON	5,573	4,685		888	4,685 R	84.1%		100.0%	
107,199	DE SOTO	11,780	10,431		1,349	10,431 R	88.5%		100.0%	
72,604	FORREST	15,651	13,771		1,880	13,771 R	88.0%		100.0%	
8,448	FRANKLIN	2,945	2,475		470	2,475 R	84.0%		100.0%	
19,144	GEORGE	4,123	3,717		406	3,717 R	90.2%		100.0%	
13,299	GREENE	2,529	2,256		273	2,256 R	89.2%		100.0%	
23,263	GRENADA	5,567	4,675		892	4,675 R	84.0%		100.0%	
42,967	HANCOCK	8,194	7,034		1,160	7,034 R	85.8%		100.0%	
189,601	HARRISON	41,770	35,954		5,816	35,954 R	86.1%		100.0%	
250,800	HINDS	56,825	46,687		10,138	46,687 R	82.2%		100.0%	
21,609	HOLMES	4,019	2,732		1,287	2,732 R	68.0%		100.0%	
11,206	HUMPHREYS	2,444	1,797		647	1,797 R	73.5%		100.0%	
2,274	ISSAQUENA	542	422		120	422 R	77.9%		100.0%	
22,770	ITAWAMBA	5,105	4,424		681	4,424 R	86.7%		100.0%	
131,420	JACKSON	28,361	25,305		3,056	25,305 R	89.2%		100.0%	
18,149	JASPER	4,722	3,564		1,158	3,564 R	75.5%		100.0%	
9,740	JEFFERSON	1,940	1,225		715	1,225 R	63.1%		100.0%	
13,962	JEFFERSON DAVIS	3,846	2,964		882	2,964 R	77.1%		100.0%	
64,958	JONES	15,214	13,463		1,751	13,463 R	88.5%		100.0%	
10,453	KEMPER	3,243	2,701		542	2,701 R	83.3%		100.0%	
38,744	LAFAYETTE	6,553	5,605		948	5,605 R	85.5%		100.0%	
39,070	LAMAR	10,851	10,069		782	10,069 R	92.8%		100.0%	
78,161	LAUDERDALE	19,596	17,398		2,198	17,398 R	88.8%		100.0%	
13,258	LAWRENCE	5,026	4,186		840	4,186 R	83.3%		100.0%	
20,940	LEAKE	5,101	4,326		775	4,326 R	84.8%		100.0%	
75,755	LEE	14,179	12,585		1,594	12,585 R	88.8%		100.0%	
37,947	LEFLORE	5,751	4,553		1,198	4,553 R	79.2%		100.0%	
33,166	LINCOLN	10,088	8,708		1,380	8,708 R	86.3%		100.0%	
61,586	LOWNDES	12,204	10,268		1,936	10,268 R	84.1%		100.0%	
74,674	MADISON	22,888	20,109		2,779	20,109 R	87.9%		100.0%	
25,595	MARION	6,930	5,988		942	5,988 R	86.4%		100.0%	
34,993	MARSHALL	5,227	4,068		1,159	4,068 R	77.8%		100.0%	
38,014	MONROE	6,324	5,204		1,120	5,204 R	82.3%		100.0%	
12,189	MONTGOMERY	3,204	2,813		391	2,813 R	87.8%		100.0%	
28,684	NESHOBA	7,579	6,864		715	6,864 R	90.6%		100.0%	
21,838	NEWTON	6,021	5,491		530	5,491 R	91.2%		100.0%	
12,548	NOXUBEE	3,123	2,194		929	2,194 R	70.3%		100.0%	
42,902	OKTIBBEHA	9,781	7,793		1,988	7,793 R	79.7%		100.0%	
34,274	PANOLA	6,343	5,058		1,285	5,058 R	79.7%		100.0%	
48,621	PEARL RIVER	8,243	7,212		1,031	7,212 R	87.5%		100.0%	
12,138	PERRY	3,045	2,695		350	2,695 R	88.5%		100.0%	
38,940	PIKE	11,204	8,776		2,428	8,776 R	78.3%		100.0%	
26,726	PONTOTOC	5,060	4,530		530	4,530 R	89.5%		100.0%	
25,556	PRENTISS	5,656	4,951		705	4,951 R	87.5%		100.0%	
10,117	QUITMAN	1,489	1,088		401	1,088 R	73.1%		100.0%	

MISSISSIPPI

SENATOR 2002

2000 Census Population	County	Total Vote	Republican	Democratic	Other	Rep.-Dem. Plurality	Percentage			
							Total Vote		Major Vote	
							Rep.	Dem.	Rep.	Dem.
115,327	RANKIN	33,521	31,180		2,341	31,180 R	93.0%		100.0%	
28,423	SCOTT	6,563	5,501		1,062	5,501 R	83.8%		100.0%	
6,580	SHARKEY	1,566	1,233		333	1,233 R	78.7%		100.0%	
27,639	SIMPSON	7,121	5,823		1,298	5,823 R	81.8%		100.0%	
16,182	SMITH	5,537	5,075		462	5,075 R	91.7%		100.0%	
13,622	STONE	3,489	3,132		357	3,132 R	89.8%		100.0%	
34,369	SUNFLOWER	4,719	3,479		1,240	3,479 R	73.7%		100.0%	
14,903	TALLAHATCHIE	3,028	2,261		767	2,261 R	74.7%		100.0%	
25,370	TATE	3,954	3,363		591	3,363 R	85.1%		100.0%	
20,826	TIPPAH	4,239	3,646		593	3,646 R	86.0%		100.0%	
19,163	TISHOMINGO	4,032	3,344		688	3,344 R	82.9%		100.0%	
9,227	TUNICA	809	551		258	551 R	68.1%		100.0%	
25,362	UNION	5,146	4,672		474	4,672 R	90.8%		100.0%	
15,156	WALTHALL	4,349	3,530		819	3,530 R	81.2%		100.0%	
49,644	WARREN	12,720	11,036		1,684	11,036 R	86.8%		100.0%	
62,977	WASHINGTON	10,934	8,263		2,671	8,263 R	75.6%		100.0%	
21,216	WAYNE	5,232	4,384		848	4,384 R	83.8%		100.0%	
10,294	WEBSTER	3,179	2,829		350	2,829 R	89.0%		100.0%	
10,312	WILKINSON	2,321	1,403		918	1,403 R	60.4%		100.0%	
20,160	WINSTON	6,859	5,661		1,198	5,661 R	82.5%		100.0%	
13,051	YALOBUSHA	2,821	2,205		616	2,205 R	78.2%		100.0%	
28,149	YAZOO	5,732	4,752		980	4,752 R	82.9%		100.0%	
2,844,658	TOTAL	630,495	533,269		97,226	533,269 R	84.6%		100.0%	

MISSISSIPPI

HOUSE OF REPRESENTATIVES

CD	Year	Total Vote	Republican Vote	Republican Candidate	Democratic Vote	Democratic Candidate	Other Vote	Rep.-Dem. Plurality	Total Vote Rep.	Total Vote Dem.	Major Vote Rep.	Major Vote Dem.
1	2002	133,567	95,404	Wicker, Roger*	32,318	Weathers, Rex N.	5,845	63,086 R	71.4%	24.2%	74.7%	25.3%
2	2002	163,050	69,711	LeSueur, Clinton B.	89,913	Thompson, Bennie*	3,426	20,202 D	42.8%	55.1%	43.7%	56.3%
3	2002	219,151	139,329	Pickering, Charles W. "Chip" Jr.*	76,184	Shows, Ronnie*	3,638	63,145 R	63.6%	34.8%	64.6%	35.4%
4	2002	161,868	34,373	Mertz, Karl Cleveland	121,742	Taylor, Gene*	5,753	87,369 D	21.2%	75.2%	22.0%	78.0%
Total	2002	677,636	338,817		320,157		18,662	18,660 R	50.0%	47.2%	51.4%	48.6%

An asterisk (*) denotes incumbent.

MISSISSIPPI

GENERAL AND PRIMARY ELECTIONS

2002 GENERAL ELECTIONS

Senator	Other vote was 97,226 Reform (Shawn O'Hara).
House	Other vote was:

CD 1	3,477 Reform (Brenda Blackburn); 2,368 Libertarian (Harold M. Taylor).
CD 2	3,426 Reform (Lee Dilworth).
CD 3	1,431 Independent (Jim Giles); 949 Independent (Harvey L. Darden); 760 Libertarian (Brad A. McDonald); 498 Reform (Carroll Grantham).
CD 4	3,311 Libertarian (Wayne L. Parker); 2,442 Reform (Thomas Huffmaster).

2002 PRIMARY ELECTIONS

Primary	June 4, 2002	**Registration** (as of December 31, 2002)	1,865,382	No Party Registration

Note: Mississippi has compiled statewide voter registration totals on a biennial basis in recent years. The previous total from the end of 2000 showed 2,008,381 registered voters, but preceded a significant purge of names in many counties.

Primary Type Open—Any registered voter could participate in the primary of either party.

Note: An asterisk (*) denotes incumbent. The names of unopposed candidates did not appear on the primary ballot; therefore, no votes were cast for these candidates.

	REPUBLICAN PRIMARIES			DEMOCRATIC PRIMARIES		
Senator	Thad Cochran*	Unopposed		Steven Douglas Turney	30,808	52.2%
				James W. "Bootie" Hunt	28,176	47.8%
				TOTAL	58,984	
				Note: Steven Douglas Turney withdrew from the race after the primary. There was no Democratic candidate in the general election.		
Congressional District 1	Roger Wicker*	Unopposed		Rex N. Weathers	Unopposed	
Congressional District 2	Clinton B. LeSueur	6,376	55.1%	Bennie Thompson*	47,893	73.5%
	Charlotte Reeves	5,198	44.9%	George E. Irvin	17,277	26.5%
	Write-in	7	0.1%			
	TOTAL	11,581		TOTAL	65,170	
Congressional District 3	Charles W. "Chip" Pickering Jr.*	Unopposed		Ronnie Shows*	Unopposed	
Congressional District 4	Karl Cleveland Mertz	Unopposed		Gene Taylor*	Unopposed	

MISSISSIPPI DEMOCRATIC PRIMARY

SENATOR 2002

2000 Census Population	County	Total Vote	Turney	Hunt	Winner	Percentage of Total Vote	
						Turney	Hunt
34,340	ADAMS	413	127	286	Hunt	30.8%	69.2%
34,558	ALCORN	201	97	104	Hunt	48.3%	51.7%
13,599	AMITE	362	163	199	Hunt	45.0%	55.0%
19,661	ATTALA	1,379	644	735	Hunt	46.7%	53.3%
8,026	BENTON	162	76	86	Hunt	46.9%	53.1%
40,633	BOLIVAR	1,880	1,021	859	Turney	54.3%	45.7%
15,069	CALHOUN	180	64	116	Hunt	35.6%	64.4%
10,769	CARROLL	797	429	368	Turney	53.8%	46.2%
19,440	CHICKASAW	120	49	71	Hunt	40.8%	59.2%
9,758	CHOCTAW	208	102	106	Hunt	49.0%	51.0%
11,831	CLAIBORNE	1,211	539	672	Hunt	44.5%	55.5%
17,955	CLARKE	453	241	212	Turney	53.2%	46.8%
21,979	CLAY	221	119	102	Turney	53.8%	46.2%
30,622	COAHOMA	691	380	311	Turney	55.0%	45.0%
28,757	COPIAH	1,848	949	899	Turney	51.4%	48.6%
19,407	COVINGTON	170	99	71	Turney	58.2%	41.8%
107,199	DE SOTO	161	100	61	Turney	62.1%	37.9%
72,604	FORREST	551	299	252	Turney	54.3%	45.7%
8,448	FRANKLIN	295	96	199	Hunt	32.5%	67.5%
19,144	GEORGE	320	152	168	Hunt	47.5%	52.5%
13,299	GREENE	160	60	100	Hunt	37.5%	62.5%
23,263	GRENADA	174	71	103	Hunt	40.8%	59.2%
42,967	HANCOCK	185	105	80	Turney	56.8%	43.2%
189,601	HARRISON	483	259	224	Turney	53.6%	46.4%
250,800	HINDS	13,791	8,352	5,439	Turney	60.6%	39.4%
21,609	HOLMES	2,061	971	1,090	Hunt	47.1%	52.9%
11,206	HUMPHREYS	1,474	782	692	Turney	53.1%	46.9%
2,274	ISSAQUENA	334	165	169	Hunt	49.4%	50.6%
22,770	ITAWAMBA	310	138	172	Hunt	44.5%	55.5%
131,420	JACKSON	537	232	305	Hunt	43.2%	56.8%
18,149	JASPER	335	164	171	Hunt	49.0%	51.0%
9,740	JEFFERSON	864	299	565	Hunt	34.6%	65.4%
13,962	JEFFERSON DAVIS	468	212	256	Hunt	45.3%	54.7%
64,958	JONES	433	192	241	Hunt	44.3%	55.7%
10,453	KEMPER	286	107	179	Hunt	37.4%	62.6%
38,744	LAFAYETTE	218	101	117	Hunt	46.3%	53.7%
39,070	LAMAR	161	91	70	Turney	56.5%	43.5%
78,161	LAUDERDALE	329	150	179	Hunt	45.6%	54.4%
13,258	LAWRENCE	409	210	199	Turney	51.3%	48.7%
20,940	LEAKE	919	418	501	Hunt	45.5%	54.5%
75,755	LEE	432	190	242	Hunt	44.0%	56.0%
37,947	LEFLORE	877	520	357	Turney	59.3%	40.7%
33,166	LINCOLN	418	227	191	Turney	54.3%	45.7%
61,586	LOWNDES	78	30	48	Hunt	38.5%	61.5%
74,674	MADISON	2,098	1,286	812	Turney	61.3%	38.7%
25,595	MARION	481	151	330	Hunt	31.4%	68.6%
34,993	MARSHALL	240	101	139	Hunt	42.1%	57.9%
38,014	MONROE	367	165	202	Hunt	45.0%	55.0%
12,189	MONTGOMERY	859	376	483	Hunt	43.8%	56.2%
28,684	NESHOBA	511	326	185	Turney	63.8%	36.2%
21,838	NEWTON	261	124	137	Hunt	47.5%	52.5%
12,548	NOXUBEE	259	90	169	Hunt	34.7%	65.3%
42,902	OKTIBBEHA	340	187	153	Turney	55.0%	45.0%
34,274	PANOLA	320	144	176	Hunt	45.0%	55.0%
48,621	PEARL RIVER	326	191	135	Turney	58.6%	41.4%
12,138	PERRY	155	87	68	Turney	56.1%	43.9%
38,940	PIKE	309	153	156	Hunt	49.5%	50.5%
26,726	PONTOTOC	290	144	146	Hunt	49.7%	50.3%
25,556	PRENTISS	133	95	38	Turney	71.4%	28.6%
10,117	QUITMAN	564	263	301	Hunt	46.6%	53.4%

MISSISSIPPI DEMOCRATIC PRIMARY

SENATOR 2002

2000 Census Population	County	Total Vote	Turney	Hunt	Winner	Percentage of Total Vote	
						Turney	Hunt
115,327	RANKIN	598	325	273	Turney	54.3%	45.7%
28,423	SCOTT	411	160	251	Hunt	38.9%	61.1%
6,580	SHARKEY	986	481	505	Hunt	48.8%	51.2%
27,639	SIMPSON	606	228	378	Hunt	37.6%	62.4%
16,182	SMITH	290	110	180	Hunt	37.9%	62.1%
13,622	STONE	138	49	89	Hunt	35.5%	64.5%
34,369	SUNFLOWER	1,926	956	970	Hunt	49.6%	50.4%
14,903	TALLAHATCHIE	1,080	584	496	Turney	54.1%	45.9%
25,370	TATE	205	96	109	Hunt	46.8%	53.2%
20,826	TIPPAH	208	102	106	Hunt	49.0%	51.0%
19,163	TISHOMINGO	143	61	82	Hunt	42.7%	57.3%
9,227	TUNICA	304	168	136	Turney	55.3%	44.7%
25,362	UNION	294	180	114	Turney	61.2%	38.8%
15,156	WALTHALL	278	113	165	Hunt	40.6%	59.4%
49,644	WARREN	2,618	1,391	1,227	Turney	53.1%	46.9%
62,977	WASHINGTON	3,013	1,675	1,338	Turney	55.6%	44.4%
21,216	WAYNE	271	107	164	Hunt	39.5%	60.5%
10,294	WEBSTER	188	99	89	Turney	52.7%	47.3%
10,312	WILKINSON	172	66	106	Hunt	38.4%	61.6%
20,160	WINSTON	254	128	126	Turney	50.4%	49.6%
13,051	YALOBUSHA	129	54	75	Hunt	41.9%	58.1%
28,149	YAZOO						
2,844,658	TOTAL	58,984	30,808	28,176	Turney	52.2%	47.8%

Note: No vote was reported from Yazoo County. Turney withdrew from the race after the primary. There was no Democratic Senate candidate in the general election.

MISSOURI

GOVERNOR
Bob Holden (D). Elected 2000 to a four-year term.

SENATORS (2 Republicans)
Christopher S. Bond (R). Reelected 1998 to a six-year term. Previously elected 1992, 1986.

Jim Talent (R). Elected 2002 to fill the remaining four years of the term won by the late Mel Carnahan in 2000. Carnahan died in a plane crash in October 2000, but his name remained on the ballot. His widow, Jean Carnahan, was appointed to fill the seat until a special election could be held in 2002.

REPRESENTATIVES (5 Republicans, 4 Democrats)
1. William Lacy Clay (D)
2. Todd Akin (R)
3. Richard A. Gephardt (D)
4. Ike Skelton (D)
5. Karen McCarthy (D)
6. Sam Graves (R)
7. Roy Blunt (R)
8. Jo Ann Emerson (R)
9. Kenny Hulshof (R)

POSTWAR VOTE FOR PRESIDENT

| | | Republican | | Democratic | | Other | | Percentage | | | |
| | | | | | | | | Total Vote | | Major Vote | |
Year	Total Vote	Vote	Candidate	Vote	Candidate	Vote	Plurality	Rep.	Dem.	Rep.	Dem.
2000**	2,359,892	1,189,924	Bush, George W.	1,111,138	Gore, Al	58,830	78,786 R	50.4%	47.1%	51.7%	48.3%
1996**	2,158,065	890,016	Dole, Bob	1,025,935	Clinton, Bill	242,114	135,919 D	41.2%	47.5%	46.5%	53.5%
1992**	2,391,565	811,159	Bush, George	1,053,873	Clinton, Bill	526,533	242,714 D	33.9%	44.1%	43.5%	56.5%
1988	2,093,713	1,084,953	Bush, George	1,001,619	Dukakis, Michael S.	7,141	83,334 R	51.8%	47.8%	52.0%	48.0%
1984	2,122,783	1,274,188	Reagan, Ronald	848,583	Mondale, Walter F.	12	425,605 R	60.0%	40.0%	60.0%	40.0%
1980**	2,099,824	1,074,181	Reagan, Ronald	931,182	Carter, Jimmy	94,461	142,999 R	51.2%	44.3%	53.6%	46.4%
1976	1,953,600	927,443	Ford, Gerald R.	998,387	Carter, Jimmy	27,770	70,944 D	47.5%	51.1%	48.2%	51.8%
1972	1,855,803	1,153,852	Nixon, Richard M.	697,147	McGovern, George S.	4,804	456,705 R	62.2%	37.6%	62.3%	37.7%
1968	1,809,502	811,932	Nixon, Richard M.	791,444	Humphrey, Hubert H.	206,126	20,488 R	44.9%	43.7%	50.6%	49.4%
1964	1,817,879	653,535	Goldwater, Barry M.	1,164,344	Johnson, Lyndon B.		510,809 D	36.0%	64.0%	36.0%	64.0%
1960	1,934,422	962,221	Nixon, Richard M.	972,201	Kennedy, John F.		9,980 D	49.7%	50.3%	49.7%	50.3%
1956	1,832,562	914,289	Eisenhower, Dwight D.	918,273	Stevenson, Adlai E.		3,984 D	49.9%	50.1%	49.9%	50.1%
1952	1,892,062	959,429	Eisenhower, Dwight D.	929,830	Stevenson, Adlai E.	2,803	29,599 R	50.7%	49.1%	50.8%	49.2%
1948	1,578,628	655,039	Dewey, Thomas E.	917,315	Truman, Harry S.	6,274	262,276 D	41.5%	58.1%	41.7%	58.3%

In 2000 the other vote column includes 38,515 votes cast for Green (Nader). In 1996 the other vote column includes 217,188 votes cast for Perot. In 1992 the other vote column includes 518,741 votes cast for Perot. In 1980 the other vote column includes 77,920 votes for Independent (Anderson).

MISSOURI

POSTWAR VOTE FOR GOVERNOR

Year	Total Vote	Republican		Democratic		Other Vote	Rep.-Dem. Plurality	Percentage			
								Total Vote		Major Vote	
		Vote	Candidate	Vote	Candidate			Rep.	Dem.	Rep.	Dem.
2000	2,346,830	1,131,307	Talent, Jim	1,152,752	Holden, Bob	62,771	21,445 D	48.2%	49.1%	49.5%	50.5%
1996	2,142,518	866,268	Kelly, Margaret	1,224,801	Carnahan, Mel	51,449	358,533 D	40.4%	57.2%	41.4%	58.6%
1992	2,344,121	968,574	Webster, William L.	1,375,425	Carnahan, Mel	122	406,851 D	41.3%	58.7%	41.3%	58.7%
1988	2,085,928	1,339,531	Ashcroft, John	724,919	Hearnes, Betty C.	21,478	614,612 R	64.2%	34.8%	64.9%	35.1%
1984	2,108,210	1,194,506	Ashcroft, John	913,700	Rothman, Kenneth J.	4	280,806 R	56.7%	43.3%	56.7%	43.3%
1980	2,088,028	1,098,950	Bond, Christopher S.	981,884	Teasdale, Joseph P.	7,194	117,066 R	52.6%	47.0%	52.8%	47.2%
1976	1,933,575	958,110	Bond, Christopher S.	971,184	Teasdale, Joseph P.	4,281	13,074 D	49.6%	50.2%	49.7%	50.3%
1972	1,865,683	1,029,451	Bond, Christopher S.	832,751	Dowd, Edward L.	3,481	196,700 R	55.2%	44.6%	55.3%	44.7%
1968	1,764,602	691,797	Roos, Lawrence K.	1,072,805	Hearnes, Warren E.		381,008 D	39.2%	60.8%	39.2%	60.8%
1964	1,789,600	678,949	Shepley, Ethan	1,110,651	Hearnes, Warren E.		431,702 D	37.9%	62.1%	37.9%	62.1%
1960	1,887,331	792,131	Farmer, Edward G.	1,095,200	Dalton, John M.		303,069 D	42.0%	58.0%	42.0%	58.0%
1956	1,808,338	866,810	Hocker, Lon	941,528	Blair, James T.		74,718 D	47.9%	52.1%	47.9%	52.1%
1952	1,871,095	886,370	Elliott, Howard	983,166	Donnelly, Phil M.	1,559	96,796 D	47.4%	52.5%	47.4%	52.6%
1948	1,567,338	670,064	Thompson, Murray	893,092	Smith, Forrest	4,182	223,028 D	42.8%	57.0%	42.9%	57.1%

POSTWAR VOTE FOR SENATOR

Year	Total Vote	Republican		Democratic		Other Vote	Rep.-Dem. Plurality	Percentage			
								Total Vote		Major Vote	
		Vote	Candidate	Vote	Candidate			Rep.	Dem.	Rep.	Dem.
2002S	1,877,620	935,032	Talent, Jim	913,778	Carnahan, Jean	28,810	21,254 R	49.8%	48.7%	50.6%	49.4%
2000**	2,361,586	1,142,852	Ashcroft, John	1,191,812	Carnahan, Mel	26,922	48,960 D	48.4%	50.5%	49.0%	51.0%
1998	1,576,857	830,625	Bond, Christopher S.	690,208	Nixon, Jeremiah W.	56,024	140,417 R	52.7%	43.8%	54.6%	45.4%
1994	1,775,116	1,060,149	Ashcroft, John	633,697	Wheat, Alan	81,270	426,452 R	59.7%	35.7%	62.6%	37.4%
1992	2,354,925	1,221,901	Bond, Christopher S.	1,057,967	Rothman-Serot, Geri	75,057	163,934 R	51.9%	44.9%	53.6%	46.4%
1988	2,078,875	1,407,416	Danforth, John C.	660,045	Nixon, Jeremiah W.	11,414	747,371 R	67.7%	31.8%	68.1%	31.9%
1986	1,477,327	777,612	Bond, Christopher S.	699,624	Woods, Harriett	91	77,988 R	52.6%	47.4%	52.6%	47.4%
1982	1,543,521	784,876	Danforth, John C.	758,629	Woods, Harriett	16	26,247 R	50.8%	49.1%	50.9%	49.1%
1980	2,066,965	985,399	McNary, Gene	1,074,859	Eagleton, Thomas F.	6,707	89,460 D	47.7%	52.0%	47.8%	52.2%
1976	1,914,777	1,090,067	Danforth, John C.	813,571	Hearnes, Warren E.	11,139	276,496 R	56.9%	42.5%	57.3%	42.7%
1974	1,224,303	480,900	Curtis, Thomas B.	735,433	Eagleton, Thomas F.	7,970	254,533 D	39.3%	60.1%	39.5%	60.5%
1970	1,283,912	617,903	Danforth, John C.	655,431	Symington, Stuart	10,578	37,528 D	48.1%	51.0%	48.5%	51.5%
1968	1,737,958	850,544	Curtis, Thomas B.	887,414	Eagleton, Thomas F.		36,870 D	48.9%	51.1%	48.9%	51.1%
1964	1,783,043	596,377	Bradshaw, Jean P.	1,186,666	Symington, Stuart		590,289 D	33.4%	66.6%	33.4%	66.6%
1962	1,222,259	555,330	Kemper, Crosby	666,929	Long, Edward V.		111,599 D	45.4%	54.6%	45.4%	54.6%
1960S	1,880,232	880,576	Hocker, Lon	999,656	Long, Edward V.		119,080 D	46.8%	53.2%	46.8%	53.2%
1958	1,173,903	393,847	Palmer, Hazel	780,056	Symington, Stuart		386,209 D	33.6%	66.4%	33.6%	66.4%
1956	1,800,984	785,048	Douglas, Herbert	1,015,936	Hennings, Thomas C.		230,888 D	43.6%	56.4%	43.6%	56.4%
1952	1,868,083	858,170	Kem, James P.	1,008,523	Symington, Stuart	1,390	150,353 D	45.9%	54.0%	46.0%	54.0%
1950	1,279,414	592,922	Donnell, Forrest C.	685,732	Hennings, Thomas C.	760	92,810 D	46.3%	53.6%	46.4%	53.6%
1946	1,084,100	572,556	Kem, James P.	511,544	Briggs, Frank P.		61,012 R	52.8%	47.2%	52.8%	47.2%

In the 2000 election, the Democratic candidate, Mel Carnahan, was killed in an airplane crash in October but his name remained on the ballot and he won the election in November. Subsequently, his widow, Jean Carnahan, was appointed to fill the seat until an election could be held in 2002 for the remaining four years of the term. The 1960 election was for a short term to fill a vacancy.

MISSOURI

Congressional districts first established for elections held in 2002
9 members

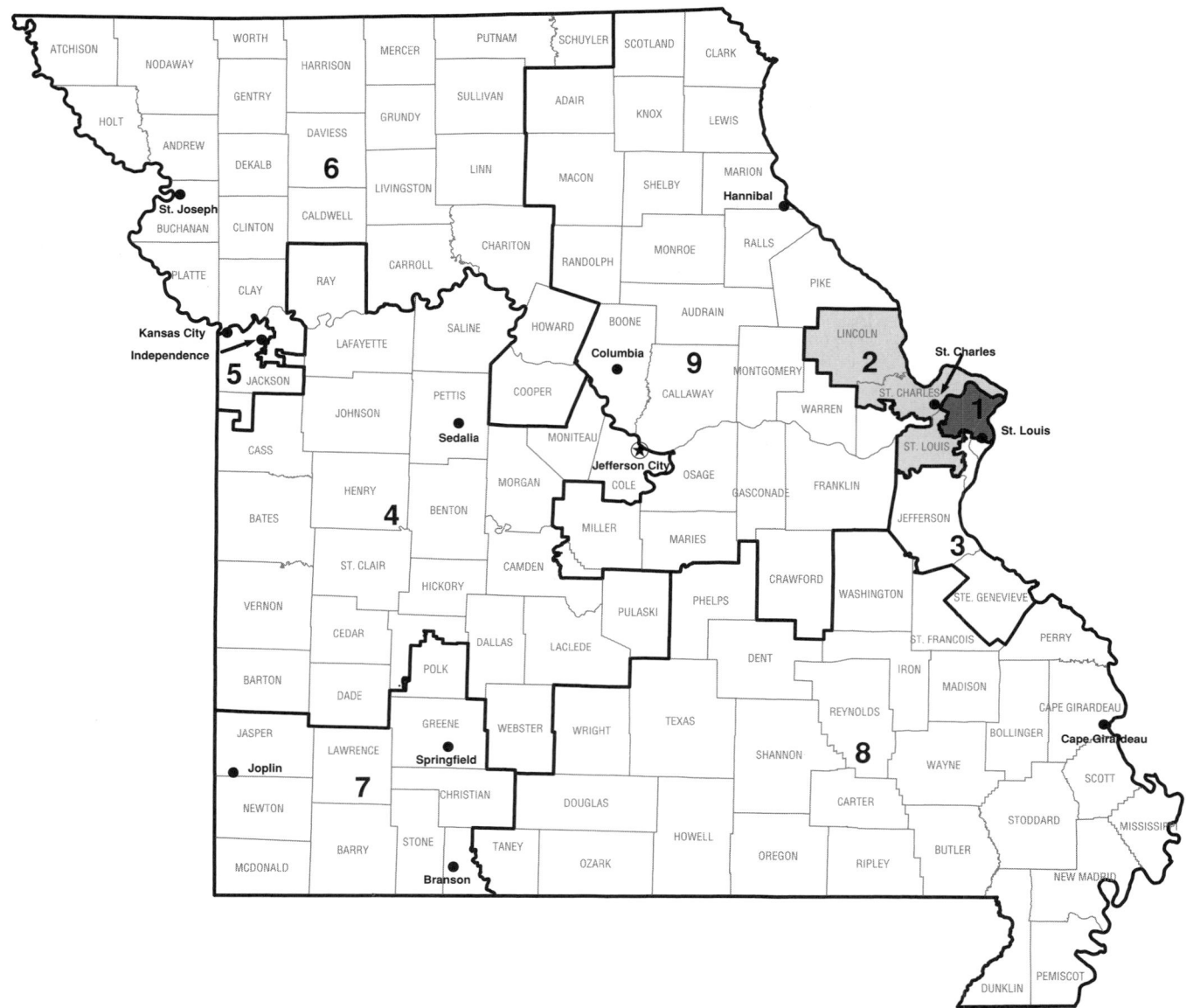

MISSOURI
SENATOR 2002

2000 Census Population	County	Total Vote	Republican	Democratic	Other	Rep.-Dem. Plurality	Percentage			
							Total Vote		Major Vote	
							Rep.	Dem.	Rep.	Dem.
24,977	ADAIR	7,757	4,165	3,455	137	710 R	53.7%	44.5%	54.7%	45.3%
16,492	ANDREW	5,747	3,284	2,331	132	953 R	57.1%	40.6%	58.5%	41.5%
6,430	ATCHISON	2,358	1,390	939	29	451 R	58.9%	39.8%	59.7%	40.3%
25,853	AUDRAIN	8,427	4,265	3,997	165	268 R	50.6%	47.4%	51.6%	48.4%
34,010	BARRY	10,188	6,449	3,542	197	2,907 R	63.3%	34.8%	64.5%	35.5%
12,541	BARTON	4,353	3,222	1,063	68	2,159 R	74.0%	24.4%	75.2%	24.8%
16,653	BATES	6,584	3,175	3,287	122	112 D	48.2%	49.9%	49.1%	50.9%
17,180	BENTON	6,449	3,464	2,901	84	563 R	53.7%	45.0%	54.4%	45.6%
12,029	BOLLINGER	4,346	2,811	1,480	55	1,331 R	64.7%	34.1%	65.5%	34.5%
135,454	BOONE	48,761	23,379	23,867	1,515	488 D	47.9%	48.9%	49.5%	50.5%
85,998	BUCHANAN	26,831	12,425	13,702	704	1,277 D	46.3%	51.1%	47.6%	52.4%
40,867	BUTLER	10,494	6,578	3,793	123	2,785 R	62.7%	36.1%	63.4%	36.6%
8,969	CALDWELL	3,147	1,584	1,496	67	88 R	50.3%	47.5%	51.4%	48.6%
40,766	CALLAWAY	12,467	6,427	5,796	244	631 R	51.6%	46.5%	52.6%	47.4%
37,051	CAMDEN	14,240	8,429	5,587	224	2,842 R	59.2%	39.2%	60.1%	39.9%
68,693	CAPE GIRARDEAU	22,986	15,774	6,858	354	8,916 R	68.6%	29.8%	69.7%	30.3%
10,285	CARROLL	3,591	1,941	1,597	53	344 R	54.1%	44.5%	54.9%	45.1%
5,941	CARTER	2,213	1,216	968	29	248 R	54.9%	43.7%	55.7%	44.3%
82,092	CASS	29,139	15,288	13,409	442	1,879 R	52.5%	46.0%	53.3%	46.7%
13,733	CEDAR	4,855	2,926	1,811	118	1,115 R	60.3%	37.3%	61.8%	38.2%
8,438	CHARITON	3,241	1,630	1,573	38	57 R	50.3%	48.5%	50.9%	49.1%
54,285	CHRISTIAN	20,105	12,791	6,955	359	5,836 R	63.6%	34.6%	64.8%	35.2%
7,416	CLARK	3,087	1,501	1,552	34	51 D	48.6%	50.3%	49.2%	50.8%
184,006	CLAY	59,080	27,497	30,684	899	3,187 D	46.5%	51.9%	47.3%	52.7%
18,979	CLINTON	6,614	3,007	3,492	115	485 D	45.5%	52.8%	46.3%	53.7%
71,397	COLE	28,428	17,178	10,860	390	6,318 R	60.4%	38.2%	61.3%	38.7%
16,670	COOPER	5,362	3,137	2,104	121	1,033 R	58.5%	39.2%	59.9%	40.1%
22,804	CRAWFORD	6,883	3,574	3,208	101	366 R	51.9%	46.6%	52.7%	47.3%
7,923	DADE	3,058	2,016	993	49	1,023 R	65.9%	32.5%	67.0%	33.0%
15,661	DALLAS	5,305	3,129	2,037	139	1,092 R	59.0%	38.4%	60.6%	39.4%
8,016	DAVIESS	3,018	1,504	1,450	64	54 R	49.8%	48.0%	50.9%	49.1%
11,597	DE KALB	3,522	1,875	1,568	79	307 R	53.2%	44.5%	54.5%	45.5%
14,927	DENT	5,031	3,019	1,918	94	1,101 R	60.0%	38.1%	61.2%	38.8%
13,084	DOUGLAS	4,459	2,963	1,409	87	1,554 R	66.4%	31.6%	67.8%	32.2%
33,155	DUNKLIN	7,378	3,828	3,506	44	322 R	51.9%	47.5%	52.2%	47.8%
93,807	FRANKLIN	33,171	17,949	14,754	468	3,195 R	54.1%	44.5%	54.9%	45.1%
15,342	GASCONADE	5,378	3,299	1,997	82	1,302 R	61.3%	37.1%	62.3%	37.7%
6,861	GENTRY	2,586	1,329	1,191	66	138 R	51.4%	46.1%	52.7%	47.3%
240,391	GREENE	83,892	49,164	33,144	1,584	16,020 R	58.6%	39.5%	59.7%	40.3%
10,432	GRUNDY	3,866	2,112	1,647	107	465 R	54.6%	42.6%	56.2%	43.8%
8,850	HARRISON	3,220	1,823	1,316	81	507 R	56.6%	40.9%	58.1%	41.9%
21,997	HENRY	8,238	3,980	4,134	124	154 D	48.3%	50.2%	49.1%	50.9%
8,940	HICKORY	3,857	1,908	1,847	102	61 R	49.5%	47.9%	50.8%	49.2%
5,351	HOLT	1,971	1,225	710	36	515 R	62.2%	36.0%	63.3%	36.7%
10,212	HOWARD	4,027	2,039	1,858	130	181 R	50.6%	46.1%	52.3%	47.7%
37,238	HOWELL	10,666	6,501	3,986	179	2,515 R	61.0%	37.4%	62.0%	38.0%
10,697	IRON	3,351	1,490	1,823	38	333 D	44.5%	54.4%	45.0%	55.0%
654,880	JACKSON	200,394	74,689	123,058	2,647	48,369 D	37.3%	61.4%	37.8%	62.2%
104,686	JASPER	29,577	20,108	8,984	485	11,124 R	68.0%	30.4%	69.1%	30.9%
198,099	JEFFERSON	62,384	29,018	32,497	869	3,479 D	46.5%	52.1%	47.2%	52.8%
48,258	JOHNSON	13,010	6,423	6,305	282	118 R	49.4%	48.5%	50.5%	49.5%
4,361	KNOX	1,733	994	730	9	264 R	57.4%	42.1%	57.7%	42.3%
32,513	LACLEDE	10,846	6,893	3,707	246	3,186 R	63.6%	34.2%	65.0%	35.0%
32,960	LAFAYETTE	11,491	5,559	5,751	181	192 D	48.4%	50.0%	49.2%	50.8%
35,204	LAWRENCE	11,103	6,907	3,911	285	2,996 R	62.2%	35.2%	63.8%	36.2%
10,494	LEWIS	3,481	1,857	1,590	34	267 R	53.3%	45.7%	53.9%	46.1%
38,944	LINCOLN	13,812	6,999	6,618	195	381 R	50.7%	47.9%	51.4%	48.6%
13,754	LINN	4,306	2,019	2,232	55	213 D	46.9%	51.8%	47.5%	52.5%
14,558	LIVINGSTON	4,503	2,269	2,158	76	111 R	50.4%	47.9%	51.3%	48.7%
21,681	MCDONALD	5,530	3,568	1,840	122	1,728 R	64.5%	33.3%	66.0%	34.0%

MISSOURI
SENATOR 2002

2000 Census Population	County	Total Vote	Republican	Democratic	Other	Rep.-Dem. Plurality	Percentage			
							Total Vote		Major Vote	
							Rep.	Dem.	Rep.	Dem.
15,762	MACON	5,579	3,007	2,492	80	515 R	53.9%	44.7%	54.7%	45.3%
11,800	MADISON	3,421	1,774	1,599	48	175 R	51.9%	46.7%	52.6%	47.4%
8,903	MARIES	3,336	1,820	1,446	70	374 R	54.6%	43.3%	55.7%	44.3%
28,289	MARION	9,150	5,145	3,899	106	1,246 R	56.2%	42.6%	56.9%	43.1%
3,757	MERCER	1,506	916	567	23	349 R	60.8%	37.6%	61.8%	38.2%
23,564	MILLER	7,622	4,711	2,757	154	1,954 R	61.8%	36.2%	63.1%	36.9%
13,427	MISSISSIPPI	4,039	1,971	2,041	27	70 D	48.8%	50.5%	49.1%	50.9%
14,827	MONITEAU	5,215	3,198	1,898	119	1,300 R	61.3%	36.4%	62.8%	37.2%
9,311	MONROE	3,297	1,628	1,616	53	12 R	49.4%	49.0%	50.2%	49.8%
12,136	MONTGOMERY	4,394	2,434	1,897	63	537 R	55.4%	43.2%	56.2%	43.8%
19,309	MORGAN	6,934	3,770	2,976	188	794 R	54.4%	42.9%	55.9%	44.1%
19,760	NEW MADRID	5,381	2,534	2,818	29	284 D	47.1%	52.4%	47.3%	52.7%
52,636	NEWTON	16,586	11,273	5,071	242	6,202 R	68.0%	30.6%	69.0%	31.0%
21,912	NODAWAY	7,009	3,629	3,209	171	420 R	51.8%	45.8%	53.1%	46.9%
10,344	OREGON	3,816	1,933	1,834	49	99 R	50.7%	48.1%	51.3%	48.7%
13,062	OSAGE	5,283	3,418	1,782	83	1,636 R	64.7%	33.7%	65.7%	34.3%
9,542	OZARK	3,354	2,019	1,248	87	771 R	60.2%	37.2%	61.8%	38.2%
20,047	PEMISCOT	3,639	1,548	2,057	34	509 D	42.5%	56.5%	42.9%	57.1%
18,132	PERRY	5,799	3,795	1,921	83	1,874 R	65.4%	33.1%	66.4%	33.6%
39,403	PETTIS	12,589	7,158	5,194	237	1,964 R	56.9%	41.3%	58.0%	42.0%
39,825	PHELPS	13,400	7,237	5,952	211	1,285 R	54.0%	44.4%	54.9%	45.1%
18,351	PIKE	5,711	2,744	2,908	59	164 D	48.0%	50.9%	48.5%	51.5%
73,781	PLATTE	26,534	13,320	12,832	382	488 R	50.2%	48.4%	50.9%	49.1%
26,992	POLK	8,617	5,378	3,061	178	2,317 R	62.4%	35.5%	63.7%	36.3%
41,165	PULASKI	7,952	4,423	3,360	169	1,063 R	55.6%	42.3%	56.8%	43.2%
5,223	PUTNAM	1,661	1,131	518	12	613 R	68.1%	31.2%	68.6%	31.4%
9,626	RALLS	3,889	1,999	1,846	44	153 R	51.4%	47.5%	52.0%	48.0%
24,663	RANDOLPH	7,733	3,894	3,671	168	223 R	50.4%	47.5%	51.5%	48.5%
23,354	RAY	7,640	3,020	4,531	89	1,511 D	39.5%	59.3%	40.0%	60.0%
6,689	REYNOLDS	2,501	1,154	1,306	41	152 D	46.1%	52.2%	46.9%	53.1%
13,509	RIPLEY	4,150	2,361	1,736	53	625 R	56.9%	41.8%	57.6%	42.4%
283,883	ST. CHARLES	105,699	60,528	43,917	1,254	16,611 R	57.3%	41.5%	58.0%	42.0%
9,652	ST. CLAIR	4,052	2,167	1,787	98	380 R	53.5%	44.1%	54.8%	45.2%
55,641	ST. FRANCOIS	15,347	6,916	8,258	173	1,342 D	45.1%	53.8%	45.6%	54.4%
1,016,315	ST. LOUIS COUNTY	391,186	185,923	200,985	4,278	15,062 D	47.5%	51.4%	48.1%	51.9%
348,189	ST. LOUIS CITY	95,103	19,546	73,822	1,735	54,276 D	20.6%	77.6%	20.9%	79.1%
17,842	STE. GENEVIEVE	5,806	2,572	3,138	96	566 D	44.3%	54.0%	45.0%	55.0%
23,756	SALINE	7,361	3,199	4,026	136	827 D	43.5%	54.7%	44.3%	55.7%
4,170	SCHUYLER	1,640	795	821	24	26 D	48.5%	50.1%	49.2%	50.8%
4,983	SCOTLAND	1,854	962	877	15	85 R	51.9%	47.3%	52.3%	47.7%
40,422	SCOTT	12,116	7,123	4,885	108	2,238 R	58.8%	40.3%	59.3%	40.7%
8,324	SHANNON	2,972	1,433	1,491	48	58 D	48.2%	50.2%	49.0%	51.0%
6,799	SHELBY	2,716	1,459	1,241	16	218 R	53.7%	45.7%	54.0%	46.0%
29,705	STODDARD	9,510	5,638	3,798	74	1,840 R	59.3%	39.9%	59.7%	40.3%
28,658	STONE	9,965	6,367	3,415	183	2,952 R	63.9%	34.3%	65.1%	34.9%
7,219	SULLIVAN	2,621	1,418	1,154	49	264 R	54.1%	44.0%	55.1%	44.9%
39,703	TANEY	12,199	7,842	4,136	221	3,706 R	64.3%	33.9%	65.5%	34.5%
23,003	TEXAS	8,438	4,589	3,620	229	969 R	54.4%	42.9%	55.9%	44.1%
20,454	VERNON	6,993	3,796	3,054	143	742 R	54.3%	43.7%	55.4%	44.6%
24,525	WARREN	9,057	5,053	3,911	93	1,142 R	55.8%	43.2%	56.4%	43.6%
23,344	WASHINGTON	6,744	2,819	3,819	106	1,000 D	41.8%	56.6%	42.5%	57.5%
13,259	WAYNE	4,666	2,523	2,085	58	438 R	54.1%	44.7%	54.8%	45.2%
31,045	WEBSTER	10,683	6,407	4,053	223	2,354 R	60.0%	37.9%	61.3%	38.7%
2,382	WORTH	999	535	450	14	85 R	53.6%	45.0%	54.3%	45.7%
17,955	WRIGHT	6,259	4,117	2,016	126	2,101 R	65.8%	32.2%	67.1%	32.9%
5,595,211	TOTAL	1,877,620	935,032	913,778	28,810	21,254 R	49.8%	48.7%	50.6%	49.4%

MISSOURI

HOUSE OF REPRESENTATIVES

CD	Year	Total Vote	Republican		Democratic		Other Vote	Rep.-Dem. Plurality	Percentage			
									Total Vote		Major Vote	
			Vote	Candidate	Vote	Candidate			Rep.	Dem.	Rep.	Dem.
1	2002	191,055	51,755	Schwadron, Richard	133,946	Clay, William Lacy*	5,354	82,191 D	27.1%	70.1%	27.9%	72.1%
2	2002	248,828	167,057	Akin, Todd*	77,223	Hogan, John	4,548	89,834 R	67.1%	31.0%	68.4%	31.6%
3	2002	206,878	80,551	Enz, Catherine S.	122,181	Gephardt, Richard A.*	4,146	41,630 D	38.9%	59.1%	39.7%	60.3%
4	2002	210,238	64,451	Noland, James A. "Jim"	142,204	Skelton, Ike*	3,583	77,753 D	30.7%	67.6%	31.2%	68.8%
5	2002	186,167	60,245	Gordon, Steve	122,645	McCarthy, Karen*	3,277	62,400 D	32.4%	65.9%	32.9%	67.1%
6	2002	208,088	131,151	Graves, Sam*	73,202	Rinehart, Cathy	3,735	57,949 R	63.0%	35.2%	64.2%	35.8%
7	2002	199,863	149,519	Blunt, Roy*	45,964	Lapham, Ron	4,380	103,555 R	74.8%	23.0%	76.5%	23.5%
8	2002	188,321	135,144	Emerson, Jo Ann*	50,686	Curtis, Gene	2,491	84,458 R	71.8%	26.9%	72.7%	27.3%
9	2002	214,125	146,032	Hulshof, Kenny*	61,126	Deichman, Donald M. "Don"	6,967	84,906 R	68.2%	28.5%	70.5%	29.5%
Total	2002	1,853,563	985,905		829,177		38,481	156,728 R	53.2%	44.7%	54.3%	45.7%

An asterisk (*) denotes incumbent.

MISSOURI

GENERAL AND PRIMARY ELECTIONS

2002 GENERAL ELECTIONS

Senator   Other vote was 18,345 Libertarian (Tamara A. Millay); 10,465 Green (Daniel "Digger" Romano).

House   Other vote was:

CD 1   5,354 Libertarian (Jim Higgins).
CD 2   4,548 Libertarian (Darla R. Maloney).
CD 3   4,146 Libertarian (Daniel "Dan" Byington).
CD 4   3,583 Libertarian (Daniel Roy Nelson).
CD 5   3,277 Libertarian (Jeanne Bojarksi).
CD 6   3,735 Libertarian (Erik Buck).
CD 7   4,378 Libertarian (Doug Burlison); 2 write-in (Steven L. Reed).
CD 8   2,491 Libertarian (Eric Van Oostrom).
CD 9   4,262 Green (Keith Brekhus); 2,705 Libertarian (John Mruzik).

2002 PRIMARY ELECTIONS

Primary   August 6, 2002   **Registration**   3,664,881   No Party Registration
                                        (as of Aug. 6, 2002)

Primary Type   Open—Any registered voter could participate in the primary of either party.

Note: An asterisk (*) denotes incumbent.

MISSOURI

GENERAL AND PRIMARY ELECTIONS

	REPUBLICAN PRIMARIES			DEMOCRATIC PRIMARIES		
Senator	Jim Talent	395,994	89.6%	Jean Carnahan*	368,149	83.2%
	Joseph A. May	18,525	4.2%	Darrel D. Day	74,237	16.8%
	Doris Bass Landfather	14,074	3.2%			
	Scott Craig Babbitt	7,705	1.7%			
	Martin Lindstedt	5,773	1.3%			
	TOTAL	442,071		TOTAL	442,386	
Congressional District 1	Richard Schwadron	15,522	100.0%	William Lacy Clay*	41,405	74.3%
				Carl E. Harris	14,322	25.7%
				TOTAL	55,727	
Congressional District 2	Todd Akin*	55,728	100.0%	John Hogan	26,299	100.0%
Congressional District 3	Catherine S. Enz	13,573	58.5%	Richard A. Gephardt*	44,535	73.6%
	Mike Steger	9,620	41.5%	Michael Bram	16,014	26.4%
	TOTAL	23,193		TOTAL	60,549	
Congressional District 4	James A. "Jim" Noland	40,485	67.3%	Ike Skelton*	54,631	100.0%
	Bob Brown	14,822	24.6%			
	Chuck Liffick	4,828	8.0%			
	TOTAL	60,135				
Congressional District 5	Steve Gordon	8,215	33.6%	Karen McCarthy*	40,532	86.3%
	Ronald "Ron" Harris	7,693	31.5%	Charles Lindsey	6,460	13.7%
	Chet Southworth	4,009	16.4%			
	Joyce P. Lea	2,896	11.9%			
	Annalisa Zapien-Pina	1,612	6.6%			
	TOTAL	24,425		TOTAL	46,992	
Congressional District 6	Sam Graves*	46,107	100.0%	Cathy Rinehart	33,887	67.1%
				Ed Mitchell	10,755	21.3%
				David P. Gilstrap	5,851	11.6%
				TOTAL	50,493	
Congressional District 7	Roy Blunt*	70,693	100.0%	Ron Lapham	17,507	100.0%
Congressional District 8	Jo Ann Emerson*	50,605	87.1%	Gene Curtis	33,939	100.0%
	Richard Allen Kline	7,499	12.9%			
	TOTAL	58,104				
Congressional District 9	Kenny Hulshof*	54,239	100.0%	Donald M. "Don" Deichman	45,856	100.0%

MISSOURI REPUBLICAN PRIMARY

SENATOR 2002

2000 Census Population	County	Total Vote	Talent	Other	Winner	Percentage of Total Vote	
						Talent	Other
24,977	ADAIR	1,080	995	85	Talent	92.1%	7.9%
16,492	ANDREW	3,471	2,928	543	Talent	84.4%	15.6%
6,430	ATCHISON	757	589	168	Talent	77.8%	22.2%
25,853	AUDRAIN	1,511	1,419	92	Talent	93.9%	6.1%
34,010	BARRY	5,340	4,643	697	Talent	86.9%	13.1%
12,541	BARTON	2,581	2,293	288	Talent	88.8%	11.2%
16,653	BATES	833	758	75	Talent	91.0%	9.0%
17,180	BENTON	2,985	2,567	418	Talent	86.0%	14.0%
12,029	BOLLINGER	1,720	1,558	162	Talent	90.6%	9.4%
135,454	BOONE	10,486	9,852	634	Talent	94.0%	6.0%
85,998	BUCHANAN	4,924	4,484	440	Talent	91.1%	8.9%
40,867	BUTLER	4,047	3,497	550	Talent	86.4%	13.6%
8,969	CALDWELL	1,457	1,204	253	Talent	82.6%	17.4%
40,766	CALLAWAY	2,172	2,048	124	Talent	94.3%	5.7%
37,051	CAMDEN	6,119	5,196	923	Talent	84.9%	15.1%
68,693	CAPE GIRARDEAU	9,390	8,406	984	Talent	89.5%	10.5%
10,285	CARROLL	1,073	995	78	Talent	92.7%	7.3%
5,941	CARTER	957	768	189	Talent	80.3%	19.7%
82,092	CASS	4,994	4,566	428	Talent	91.4%	8.6%
13,733	CEDAR	2,293	1,966	327	Talent	85.7%	14.3%
8,438	CHARITON	266	240	26	Talent	90.2%	9.8%
54,285	CHRISTIAN	7,692	6,542	1,150	Talent	85.0%	15.0%
7,416	CLARK	880	769	111	Talent	87.4%	12.6%
184,006	CLAY	9,856	8,961	895	Talent	90.9%	9.1%
18,979	CLINTON	1,112	983	129	Talent	88.4%	11.6%
71,397	COLE	6,917	6,460	457	Talent	93.4%	6.6%
16,670	COOPER	1,935	1,750	185	Talent	90.4%	9.6%
22,804	CRAWFORD	1,595	1,460	135	Talent	91.5%	8.5%
7,923	DADE	2,181	1,870	311	Talent	85.7%	14.3%
15,661	DALLAS	2,762	2,312	450	Talent	83.7%	16.3%
8,016	DAVIESS	624	546	78	Talent	87.5%	12.5%
11,597	DE KALB	711	652	59	Talent	91.7%	8.3%
14,927	DENT	1,504	1,357	147	Talent	90.2%	9.8%
13,084	DOUGLAS	2,449	2,097	352	Talent	85.6%	14.4%
33,155	DUNKLIN	1,105	986	119	Talent	89.2%	10.8%
93,807	FRANKLIN	12,964	11,615	1,349	Talent	89.6%	10.4%
15,342	GASCONADE	2,462	2,216	246	Talent	90.0%	10.0%
6,861	GENTRY	400	364	36	Talent	91.0%	9.0%
240,391	GREENE	21,757	19,642	2,115	Talent	90.3%	9.7%
10,432	GRUNDY	1,834	1,565	269	Talent	85.3%	14.7%
8,850	HARRISON	1,968	1,636	332	Talent	83.1%	16.9%
21,997	HENRY	1,412	1,265	147	Talent	89.6%	10.4%
8,940	HICKORY	1,942	1,608	334	Talent	82.8%	17.2%
5,351	HOLT	789	669	120	Talent	84.8%	15.2%
10,212	HOWARD	398	368	30	Talent	92.5%	7.5%
37,238	HOWELL	4,454	3,893	561	Talent	87.4%	12.6%
10,697	IRON	257	241	16	Talent	93.8%	6.2%
654,880	JACKSON	33,402	29,529	3,873	Talent	88.4%	11.6%
104,686	JASPER	13,060	11,552	1,508	Talent	88.5%	11.5%
198,099	JEFFERSON	7,782	7,252	530	Talent	93.2%	6.8%
48,258	JOHNSON	3,168	2,794	374	Talent	88.2%	11.8%
4,361	KNOX	391	365	26	Talent	93.4%	6.6%
32,513	LACLEDE	6,449	5,524	925	Talent	85.7%	14.3%
32,960	LAFAYETTE	2,316	2,119	197	Talent	91.5%	8.5%
35,204	LAWRENCE	4,998	4,193	805	Talent	83.9%	16.1%
10,494	LEWIS	529	491	38	Talent	92.8%	7.2%
38,944	LINCOLN	2,691	2,488	203	Talent	92.5%	7.5%
13,754	LINN	505	448	57	Talent	88.7%	11.3%
14,558	LIVINGSTON	1,381	1,267	114	Talent	91.7%	8.3%
21,681	MCDONALD	2,003	1,705	298	Talent	85.1%	14.9%

MISSOURI REPUBLICAN PRIMARY

SENATOR 2002

2000 Census Population	County	Total Vote	Talent	Other	Winner	Percentage of Total Vote	
						Talent	Other
15,762	MACON	1,233	1,155	78	Talent	93.7%	6.3%
11,800	MADISON	776	705	71	Talent	90.9%	9.1%
8,903	MARIES	874	816	58	Talent	93.4%	6.6%
28,289	MARION	1,661	1,563	98	Talent	94.1%	5.9%
3,757	MERCER	633	563	70	Talent	88.9%	11.1%
23,564	MILLER	3,870	3,418	452	Talent	88.3%	11.7%
13,427	MISSISSIPPI	609	573	36	Talent	94.1%	5.9%
14,827	MONITEAU	2,716	2,358	358	Talent	86.8%	13.2%
9,311	MONROE	237	221	16	Talent	93.2%	6.8%
12,136	MONTGOMERY	2,391	2,089	302	Talent	87.4%	12.6%
19,309	MORGAN	2,933	2,577	356	Talent	87.9%	12.1%
19,760	NEW MADRID	380	350	30	Talent	92.1%	7.9%
52,636	NEWTON	9,343	8,236	1,107	Talent	88.2%	11.8%
21,912	NODAWAY	1,748	1,414	334	Talent	80.9%	19.1%
10,344	OREGON	610	531	79	Talent	87.0%	13.0%
13,062	OSAGE	2,330	2,156	174	Talent	92.5%	7.5%
9,542	OZARK	2,246	1,880	366	Talent	83.7%	16.3%
20,047	PEMISCOT	37	32	5	Talent	86.5%	13.5%
18,132	PERRY	3,233	2,873	360	Talent	88.9%	11.1%
39,403	PETTIS	5,414	4,769	645	Talent	88.1%	11.9%
39,825	PHELPS	2,457	2,163	294	Talent	88.0%	12.0%
18,351	PIKE	465	434	31	Talent	93.3%	6.7%
73,781	PLATTE	4,793	4,327	466	Talent	90.3%	9.7%
26,992	POLK	3,871	3,281	590	Talent	84.8%	15.2%
41,165	PULASKI	1,312	1,208	104	Talent	92.1%	7.9%
5,223	PUTNAM	1,207	999	208	Talent	82.8%	17.2%
9,626	RALLS	384	360	24	Talent	93.8%	6.3%
24,663	RANDOLPH	1,014	943	71	Talent	93.0%	7.0%
23,354	RAY	716	614	102	Talent	85.8%	14.2%
6,689	REYNOLDS	94	82	12	Talent	87.2%	12.8%
13,509	RIPLEY	1,160	999	161	Talent	86.1%	13.9%
283,883	ST. CHARLES	27,785	25,207	2,578	Talent	90.7%	9.3%
9,652	ST. CLAIR	1,565	1,393	172	Talent	89.0%	11.0%
55,641	ST. FRANCOIS	2,238	2,102	136	Talent	93.9%	6.1%
1,016,315	ST. LOUIS COUNTY	68,648	64,566	4,082	Talent	94.1%	5.9%
348,189	ST. LOUIS CITY	3,319	3,035	284	Talent	91.4%	8.6%
17,842	STE. GENEVIEVE	753	702	51	Talent	93.2%	6.8%
23,756	SALINE	431	385	46	Talent	89.3%	10.7%
4,170	SCHUYLER	518	447	71	Talent	86.3%	13.7%
4,983	SCOTLAND	407	369	38	Talent	90.7%	9.3%
40,422	SCOTT	1,474	1,371	103	Talent	93.0%	7.0%
8,324	SHANNON	167	151	16	Talent	90.4%	9.6%
6,799	SHELBY	175	163	12	Talent	93.1%	6.9%
29,705	STODDARD	1,613	1,520	93	Talent	94.2%	5.8%
28,658	STONE	4,778	3,959	819	Talent	82.9%	17.1%
7,219	SULLIVAN	717	642	75	Talent	89.5%	10.5%
39,703	TANEY	6,535	5,437	1,098	Talent	83.2%	16.8%
23,003	TEXAS	3,759	3,211	548	Talent	85.4%	14.6%
20,454	VERNON	860	752	108	Talent	87.4%	12.6%
24,525	WARREN	3,781	3,372	409	Talent	89.2%	10.8%
23,344	WASHINGTON	1,085	994	91	Talent	91.6%	8.4%
13,259	WAYNE	1,069	984	85	Talent	92.0%	8.0%
31,045	WEBSTER	6,112	5,210	902	Talent	85.2%	14.8%
2,382	WORTH	131	115	16	Talent	87.8%	12.2%
17,955	WRIGHT	4,313	3,692	621	Talent	85.6%	14.4%
5,595,211	TOTAL	442,071	395,994	46,077	Talent	89.6%	10.4%

MISSOURI DEMOCRATIC PRIMARY

SENATOR 2002

2000 Census Population	County	Total Vote	Carnahan	Day	Winner	Percentage of Total Vote	
						Carnahan	Day
24,977	ADAIR	2,683	1,973	710	Carnahan	73.5%	26.5%
16,492	ANDREW	715	622	93	Carnahan	87.0%	13.0%
6,430	ATCHISON	719	561	158	Carnahan	78.0%	22.0%
25,853	AUDRAIN	3,253	2,461	792	Carnahan	75.7%	24.3%
34,010	BARRY	1,124	947	177	Carnahan	84.3%	15.7%
12,541	BARTON	442	373	69	Carnahan	84.4%	15.6%
16,653	BATES	3,340	2,484	856	Carnahan	74.4%	25.6%
17,180	BENTON	1,277	1,135	142	Carnahan	88.9%	11.1%
12,029	BOLLINGER	692	591	101	Carnahan	85.4%	14.6%
135,454	BOONE	12,054	10,752	1,302	Carnahan	89.2%	10.8%
85,998	BUCHANAN	11,918	9,005	2,913	Carnahan	75.6%	24.4%
40,867	BUTLER	1,078	919	159	Carnahan	85.3%	14.7%
8,969	CALDWELL	565	496	69	Carnahan	87.8%	12.2%
40,766	CALLAWAY	3,775	2,892	883	Carnahan	76.6%	23.4%
37,051	CAMDEN	2,073	1,803	270	Carnahan	87.0%	13.0%
68,693	CAPE GIRARDEAU	1,997	1,705	292	Carnahan	85.4%	14.6%
10,285	CARROLL	677	591	86	Carnahan	87.3%	12.7%
5,941	CARTER	299	270	29	Carnahan	90.3%	9.7%
82,092	CASS	7,960	6,373	1,587	Carnahan	80.1%	19.9%
13,733	CEDAR	822	683	139	Carnahan	83.1%	16.9%
8,438	CHARITON	2,250	1,540	710	Carnahan	68.4%	31.6%
54,285	CHRISTIAN	1,760	1,519	241	Carnahan	86.3%	13.7%
7,416	CLARK	1,043	849	194	Carnahan	81.4%	18.6%
184,006	CLAY	13,849	11,760	2,089	Carnahan	84.9%	15.1%
18,979	CLINTON	3,219	2,519	700	Carnahan	78.3%	21.7%
71,397	COLE	8,885	6,454	2,431	Carnahan	72.6%	27.4%
16,670	COOPER	823	706	117	Carnahan	85.8%	14.2%
22,804	CRAWFORD	1,128	1,003	125	Carnahan	88.9%	11.1%
7,923	DADE	171	150	21	Carnahan	87.7%	12.3%
15,661	DALLAS	652	548	104	Carnahan	84.0%	16.0%
8,016	DAVIESS	1,202	914	288	Carnahan	76.0%	24.0%
11,597	DE KALB	1,312	949	363	Carnahan	72.3%	27.7%
14,927	DENT	1,300	1,011	289	Carnahan	77.8%	22.2%
13,084	DOUGLAS	185	153	32	Carnahan	82.7%	17.3%
33,155	DUNKLIN	1,773	1,488	285	Carnahan	83.9%	16.1%
93,807	FRANKLIN	6,196	5,419	777	Carnahan	87.5%	12.5%
15,342	GASCONADE	541	478	63	Carnahan	88.4%	11.6%
6,861	GENTRY	1,591	1,144	447	Carnahan	71.9%	28.1%
240,391	GREENE	11,386	10,165	1,221	Carnahan	89.3%	10.7%
10,432	GRUNDY	409	351	58	Carnahan	85.8%	14.2%
8,850	HARRISON	343	302	41	Carnahan	88.0%	12.0%
21,997	HENRY	4,490	3,418	1,072	Carnahan	76.1%	23.9%
8,940	HICKORY	628	557	71	Carnahan	88.7%	11.3%
5,351	HOLT	330	275	55	Carnahan	83.3%	16.7%
10,212	HOWARD	2,377	1,702	675	Carnahan	71.6%	28.4%
37,238	HOWELL	1,039	946	93	Carnahan	91.0%	9.0%
10,697	IRON	1,955	1,474	481	Carnahan	75.4%	24.6%
654,880	JACKSON	47,454	42,329	5,125	Carnahan	89.2%	10.8%
104,686	JASPER	2,324	1,957	367	Carnahan	84.2%	15.8%
198,099	JEFFERSON	17,720	13,231	4,489	Carnahan	74.7%	25.3%
48,258	JOHNSON	2,839	2,429	410	Carnahan	85.6%	14.4%
4,361	KNOX	465	398	67	Carnahan	85.6%	14.4%
32,513	LACLEDE	947	812	135	Carnahan	85.7%	14.3%
32,960	LAFAYETTE	4,660	3,643	1,017	Carnahan	78.2%	21.8%
35,204	LAWRENCE	959	808	151	Carnahan	84.3%	15.7%
10,494	LEWIS	1,654	1,284	370	Carnahan	77.6%	22.4%
38,944	LINCOLN	5,224	3,927	1,297	Carnahan	75.2%	24.8%
13,754	LINN	2,264	1,689	575	Carnahan	74.6%	25.4%
14,558	LIVINGSTON	1,391	1,198	193	Carnahan	86.1%	13.9%
21,681	MCDONALD	780	636	144	Carnahan	81.5%	18.5%

MISSOURI DEMOCRATIC PRIMARY

SENATOR 2002

2000 Census Population	County	Total Vote	Carnahan	Day	Winner	Percentage of Total Vote Carnahan	Day
15,762	MACON	2,243	1,652	591	Carnahan	73.7%	26.3%
11,800	MADISON	1,010	825	185	Carnahan	81.7%	18.3%
8,903	MARIES	1,400	1,077	323	Carnahan	76.9%	23.1%
28,289	MARION	3,864	2,822	1,042	Carnahan	73.0%	27.0%
3,757	MERCER	154	129	25	Carnahan	83.8%	16.2%
23,564	MILLER	670	616	54	Carnahan	91.9%	8.1%
13,427	MISSISSIPPI	1,939	1,492	447	Carnahan	76.9%	23.1%
14,827	MONITEAU	516	470	46	Carnahan	91.1%	8.9%
9,311	MONROE	2,363	1,725	638	Carnahan	73.0%	27.0%
12,136	MONTGOMERY	617	562	55	Carnahan	91.1%	8.9%
19,309	MORGAN	1,580	1,368	212	Carnahan	86.6%	13.4%
19,760	NEW MADRID	2,152	1,600	552	Carnahan	74.3%	25.7%
52,636	NEWTON	953	785	168	Carnahan	82.4%	17.6%
21,912	NODAWAY	2,638	1,987	651	Carnahan	75.3%	24.7%
10,344	OREGON	1,993	1,534	459	Carnahan	77.0%	23.0%
13,062	OSAGE	1,132	929	203	Carnahan	82.1%	17.9%
9,542	OZARK	151	142	9	Carnahan	94.0%	6.0%
20,047	PEMISCOT	2,741	2,168	573	Carnahan	79.1%	20.9%
18,132	PERRY	400	357	43	Carnahan	89.3%	10.8%
39,403	PETTIS	1,795	1,528	267	Carnahan	85.1%	14.9%
39,825	PHELPS	2,870	2,336	534	Carnahan	81.4%	18.6%
18,351	PIKE	3,796	2,745	1,051	Carnahan	72.3%	27.7%
73,781	PLATTE	4,297	3,801	496	Carnahan	88.5%	11.5%
26,992	POLK	857	750	107	Carnahan	87.5%	12.5%
41,165	PULASKI	3,524	2,469	1,055	Carnahan	70.1%	29.9%
5,223	PUTNAM	78	73	5	Carnahan	93.6%	6.4%
9,626	RALLS	2,608	1,773	835	Carnahan	68.0%	32.0%
24,663	RANDOLPH	2,655	1,954	701	Carnahan	73.6%	26.4%
23,354	RAY	5,001	3,903	1,098	Carnahan	78.0%	22.0%
6,689	REYNOLDS	1,991	1,527	464	Carnahan	76.7%	23.3%
13,509	RIPLEY	1,277	990	287	Carnahan	77.5%	22.5%
283,883	ST. CHARLES	12,834	11,628	1,206	Carnahan	90.6%	9.4%
9,652	ST. CLAIR	1,228	979	249	Carnahan	79.7%	20.3%
55,641	ST. FRANCOIS	5,764	4,681	1,083	Carnahan	81.2%	18.8%
1,016,315	ST. LOUIS COUNTY	71,748	64,671	7,077	Carnahan	90.1%	9.9%
348,189	ST. LOUIS CITY	40,688	35,240	5,448	Carnahan	86.6%	13.4%
17,842	STE. GENEVIEVE	2,563	1,967	596	Carnahan	76.7%	23.3%
23,756	SALINE	4,944	3,711	1,233	Carnahan	75.1%	24.9%
4,170	SCHUYLER	525	438	87	Carnahan	83.4%	16.6%
4,983	SCOTLAND	856	675	181	Carnahan	78.9%	21.1%
40,422	SCOTT	4,211	2,898	1,313	Carnahan	68.8%	31.2%
8,324	SHANNON	2,424	1,799	625	Carnahan	74.2%	25.8%
6,799	SHELBY	2,112	1,420	692	Carnahan	67.2%	32.8%
29,705	STODDARD	1,740	1,410	330	Carnahan	81.0%	19.0%
28,658	STONE	858	725	133	Carnahan	84.5%	15.5%
7,219	SULLIVAN	1,104	905	199	Carnahan	82.0%	18.0%
39,703	TANEY	872	744	128	Carnahan	85.3%	14.7%
23,003	TEXAS	1,609	1,346	263	Carnahan	83.7%	16.3%
20,454	VERNON	3,334	2,347	987	Carnahan	70.4%	29.6%
24,525	WARREN	1,096	1,015	81	Carnahan	92.6%	7.4%
23,344	WASHINGTON	2,322	1,989	333	Carnahan	85.7%	14.3%
13,259	WAYNE	1,336	1,122	214	Carnahan	84.0%	16.0%
31,045	WEBSTER	966	825	141	Carnahan	85.4%	14.6%
2,382	WORTH	687	487	200	Carnahan	70.9%	29.1%
17,955	WRIGHT	319	267	52	Carnahan	83.7%	16.3%
5,595,211	TOTAL	442,386	368,149	74,237	Carnahan	83.2%	16.8%

MONTANA

GOVERNOR
Judy Martz (R). Elected 2000 to a four-year term.

SENATORS (1 Democrat, 1 Republican)
Max Baucus (D). Reelected 2002 to a six-year term. Previously elected 1996, 1990, 1984, 1978.

Conrad Burns (R). Reelected 2000 to a six-year term. Previously elected 1994, 1988.

REPRESENTATIVE (1 Republican)
At Large. Denny Rehberg (R)

POSTWAR VOTE FOR PRESIDENT

| | | Republican | | Democratic | | Other | | Percentage | | | |
| | | | | | | | | Total Vote | | Major Vote | |
Year	Total Vote	Vote	Candidate	Vote	Candidate	Vote	Plurality	Rep.	Dem.	Rep.	Dem.
2000**	410,997	240,178	Bush, George W.	137,126	Gore, Al	33,693	103,052 R	58.4%	33.4%	63.7%	36.3%
1996**	407,261	179,652	Dole, Bob	167,922	Clinton, Bill	59,687	11,730 R	44.1%	41.2%	51.7%	48.3%
1992**	410,611	144,207	Bush, George	154,507	Clinton, Bill	111,897	10,300 D	35.1%	37.6%	48.3%	51.7%
1988	365,674	190,412	Bush, George	168,936	Dukakis, Michael S.	6,326	21,476 R	52.1%	46.2%	53.0%	47.0%
1984	384,377	232,450	Reagan, Ronald	146,742	Mondale, Walter F.	5,185	85,708 R	60.5%	38.2%	61.3%	38.7%
1980**	363,952	206,814	Reagan, Ronald	118,032	Carter, Jimmy	39,106	88,782 R	56.8%	32.4%	63.7%	36.3%
1976	328,734	173,703	Ford, Gerald R.	149,259	Carter, Jimmy	5,772	24,444 R	52.8%	45.4%	53.8%	46.2%
1972	317,603	183,976	Nixon, Richard M.	120,197	McGovern, George S.	13,430	63,779 R	57.9%	37.8%	60.5%	39.5%
1968	274,404	138,835	Nixon, Richard M.	114,117	Humphrey, Hubert H.	21,452	24,718 R	50.6%	41.6%	54.9%	45.1%
1964	278,628	113,032	Goldwater, Barry M.	164,246	Johnson, Lyndon B.	1,350	51,214 D	40.6%	58.9%	40.8%	59.2%
1960	277,579	141,841	Nixon, Richard M.	134,891	Kennedy, John F.	847	6,950 R	51.1%	48.6%	51.3%	48.7%
1956	271,171	154,933	Eisenhower, Dwight D.	116,238	Stevenson, Adlai E.		38,695 R	57.1%	42.9%	57.1%	42.9%
1952	265,037	157,394	Eisenhower, Dwight D.	106,213	Stevenson, Adlai E.	1,430	51,181 R	59.4%	40.1%	59.7%	40.3%
1948	224,278	96,770	Dewey, Thomas E.	119,071	Truman, Harry S.	8,437	22,301 D	43.1%	53.1%	44.8%	55.2%

In 2000 the other vote column includes 24,437 votes cast for Green (Nader). In 1996 the other vote column includes 55,229 votes cast for Perot. In 1992 the other vote column includes 107,225 votes cast for Perot. In 1980 the other vote column includes 29,281 votes for Independent (Anderson).

MONTANA

POSTWAR VOTE FOR GOVERNOR

Year	Total Vote	Republican Vote	Republican Candidate	Democratic Vote	Democratic Candidate	Other Vote	Rep.-Dem. Plurality	Total Vote Rep.	Total Vote Dem.	Major Vote Rep.	Major Vote Dem.
2000	410,192	209,135	Martz, Judy	193,131	O'Keefe, Mark	7,926	16,004 R	51.0%	47.1%	52.0%	48.0%
1996**	405,175	320,768	Racicot, Marc	84,407	Jacobson, Judy		236,361 R	79.2%	20.8%	79.2%	20.8%
1992	407,842	209,401	Racicot, Marc	198,421	Bradley, Dorothy	20	10,980 R	51.3%	48.7%	51.3%	48.7%
1988	367,021	190,604	Stephens, Stan	169,313	Judge, Thomas L.	7,104	21,291 R	51.9%	46.1%	53.0%	47.0%
1984	378,970	100,070	Goodover, Pat M.	266,578	Schwinden, Ted	12,322	166,508 D	26.4%	70.3%	27.3%	72.7%
1980	360,466	160,892	Ramirez, Jack	199,574	Schwinden, Ted		38,682 D	44.6%	55.4%	44.6%	55.4%
1976	316,720	115,848	Woodahl, Robert	195,420	Judge, Thomas L.	5,452	79,572 D	36.6%	61.7%	37.2%	62.8%
1972	318,754	146,231	Smith, Ed	172,523	Judge, Thomas L.		26,292 D	45.9%	54.1%	45.9%	54.1%
1968	278,112	116,432	Babcock, Tim M.	150,481	Anderson, Forrest H.	11,199	34,049 D	41.9%	54.1%	43.6%	56.4%
1964	280,975	144,113	Babcock, Tim M.	136,862	Renne, Roland		7,251 R	51.3%	48.7%	51.3%	48.7%
1960	279,881	154,230	Nutter, Donald G.	125,651	Cannon, Paul		28,579 R	55.1%	44.9%	55.1%	44.9%
1956	270,366	138,878	Aronson, J. Hugo	131,488	Olsen, Arnold H.		7,390 R	51.4%	48.6%	51.4%	48.6%
1952	263,792	134,423	Aronson, J. Hugo	129,369	Bonner, John W.		5,054 R	51.0%	49.0%	51.0%	49.0%
1948	222,964	97,792	Ford, Sam C.	124,267	Bonner, John W.	905	26,475 D	43.9%	55.7%	44.0%	56.0%

In 1996, the Democratic vote total included 7,936 absentee ballots cast for the party's initial gubernatorial candidate, Chet Blaylock, who died in October 1996.

POSTWAR VOTE FOR SENATOR

Year	Total Vote	Republican Vote	Republican Candidate	Democratic Vote	Democratic Candidate	Other Vote	Rep.-Dem. Plurality	Total Vote Rep.	Total Vote Dem.	Major Vote Rep.	Major Vote Dem.
2002	326,537	103,611	Taylor, Mike	204,853	Baucus, Max	18,073	101,242 D	31.7%	62.7%	33.6%	66.4%
2000	411,601	208,082	Burns, Conrad	194,430	Schweitzer, Brian	9,089	13,652 R	50.6%	47.2%	51.7%	48.3%
1996	407,490	182,111	Rehberg, Denny	201,935	Baucus, Max	23,444	19,824 D	44.7%	49.6%	47.4%	52.6%
1994	350,409	218,542	Burns, Conrad	131,845	Mudd, Jack	22	86,697 R	62.4%	37.6%	62.4%	37.6%
1990	319,336	93,836	Kolstad, Allen C.	217,563	Baucus, Max	7,937	123,727 D	29.4%	68.1%	30.1%	69.9%
1988	365,254	189,445	Burns, Conrad	175,809	Melcher, John		13,636 R	51.9%	48.1%	51.9%	48.1%
1984	379,155	154,308	Cozzens, Chuck	215,704	Baucus, Max	9,143	61,396 D	40.7%	56.9%	41.7%	58.3%
1982	321,062	133,789	Williams, Larry	174,861	Melcher, John	12,412	41,072 D	41.7%	54.5%	43.3%	56.7%
1978	287,942	127,589	Williams, Larry	160,353	Baucus, Max		32,764 D	44.3%	55.7%	44.3%	55.7%
1976	321,445	115,213	Burger, Stanley C.	206,232	Melcher, John		91,019 D	35.8%	64.2%	35.8%	64.2%
1972	314,925	151,316	Hibbard, Henry S.	163,609	Metcalf, Lee		12,293 D	48.0%	52.0%	48.0%	52.0%
1970	247,869	97,809	Wallace, Harold E.	150,060	Mansfield, Mike		52,251 D	39.5%	60.5%	39.5%	60.5%
1966	259,863	121,697	Babcock, Tim M.	138,166	Metcalf, Lee		16,469 D	46.8%	53.2%	46.8%	53.2%
1964	280,010	99,367	Blewett, Alex	180,643	Mansfield, Mike		81,276 D	35.5%	64.5%	35.5%	64.5%
1960	276,612	136,281	Fjare, Orvin B.	140,331	Metcalf, Lee		4,050 D	49.3%	50.7%	49.3%	50.7%
1958	229,483	54,573	Welch, Lou W.	174,910	Mansfield, Mike		120,337 D	23.8%	76.2%	23.8%	76.2%
1954	227,454	112,863	D'Ewart, Wesley A.	114,591	Murray, James E.		1,728 D	49.6%	50.4%	49.6%	50.4%
1952	262,297	127,360	Ecton, Zales N.	133,109	Mansfield, Mike	1,828	5,749 D	48.6%	50.7%	48.9%	51.1%
1948	221,003	94,458	David, Tom J.	125,193	Murray, James E.	1,352	30,735 D	42.7%	56.6%	43.0%	57.0%
1946	190,566	101,901	Ecton, Zales N.	86,476	Erickson, Leif	2,189	15,425 R	53.5%	45.4%	54.1%	45.9%

MONTANA

One member At Large

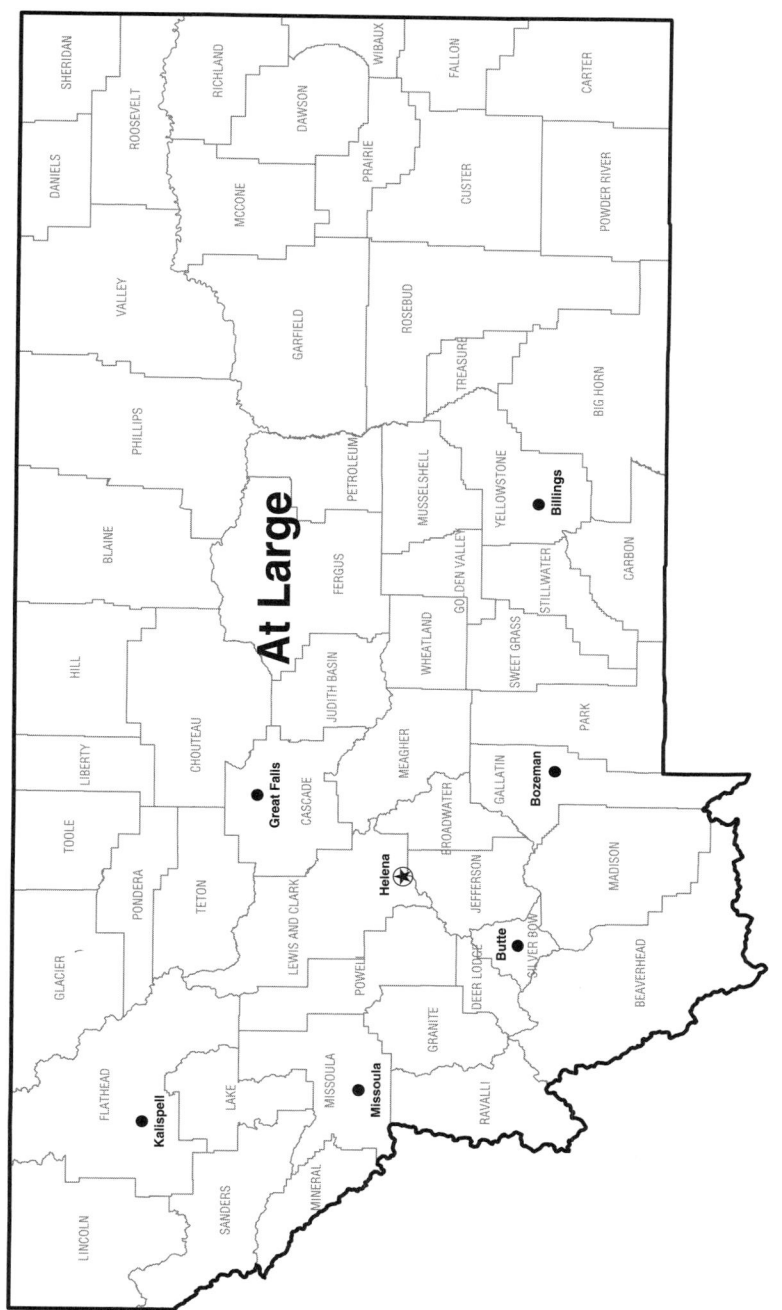

MONTANA

SENATOR 2002

2000 Census Population	County	Total Vote	Republican	Democratic	Other	Rep.-Dem. Plurality	Percentage			
							Total Vote		Major Vote	
							Rep.	Dem.	Rep.	Dem.
9,202	BEAVERHEAD	3,127	1,378	1,587	162	209 D	44.1%	50.8%	46.5%	53.5%
12,671	BIG HORN	3,977	835	2,970	172	2,135 D	21.0%	74.7%	21.9%	78.1%
7,009	BLAINE	2,370	578	1,704	88	1,126 D	24.4%	71.9%	25.3%	74.7%
4,385	BROADWATER	1,828	693	1,028	107	335 D	37.9%	56.2%	40.3%	59.7%
9,552	CARBON	4,293	1,306	2,737	250	1,431 D	30.4%	63.8%	32.3%	67.7%
1,360	CARTER	616	342	258	16	84 R	55.5%	41.9%	57.0%	43.0%
80,357	CASCADE	25,320	6,378	17,491	1,451	11,113 D	25.2%	69.1%	26.7%	73.3%
5,970	CHOUTEAU	2,585	766	1,697	122	931 D	29.6%	65.6%	31.1%	68.9%
11,696	CUSTER	3,967	1,114	2,679	174	1,565 D	28.1%	67.5%	29.4%	70.6%
2,017	DANIELS	1,031	380	607	44	227 D	36.9%	58.9%	38.5%	61.5%
9,059	DAWSON	3,595	1,199	2,286	110	1,087 D	33.4%	63.6%	34.4%	65.6%
9,417	DEER LODGE	3,784	439	3,169	176	2,730 D	11.6%	83.7%	12.2%	87.8%
2,837	FALLON	1,250	561	661	28	100 D	44.9%	52.9%	45.9%	54.1%
11,893	FERGUS	4,968	2,252	2,452	264	200 D	45.3%	49.4%	47.9%	52.1%
74,471	FLATHEAD	25,580	11,069	13,011	1,500	1,942 D	43.3%	50.9%	46.0%	54.0%
67,831	GALLATIN	24,266	8,091	14,498	1,677	6,407 D	33.3%	59.7%	35.8%	64.2%
1,279	GARFIELD	564	221	323	20	102 D	39.2%	57.3%	40.6%	59.4%
13,247	GLACIER	3,415	656	2,619	140	1,963 D	19.2%	76.7%	20.0%	80.0%
1,042	GOLDEN VALLEY	433	185	223	25	38 D	42.7%	51.5%	45.3%	54.7%
2,830	GRANITE	1,284	585	604	95	19 D	45.6%	47.0%	49.2%	50.8%
16,673	HILL	5,293	1,215	3,819	259	2,604 D	23.0%	72.2%	24.1%	75.9%
10,049	JEFFERSON	4,293	1,440	2,593	260	1,153 D	33.5%	60.4%	35.7%	64.3%
2,329	JUDITH BASIN	1,127	361	716	50	355 D	32.0%	63.5%	33.5%	66.5%
26,507	LAKE	9,242	3,568	5,145	529	1,577 D	38.6%	55.7%	41.0%	59.0%
55,716	LEWIS AND CLARK	22,523	5,764	15,543	1,216	9,779 D	25.6%	69.0%	27.1%	72.9%
2,158	LIBERTY	1,014	295	661	58	366 D	29.1%	65.2%	30.9%	69.1%
18,837	LINCOLN	6,759	3,026	3,428	305	402 D	44.8%	50.7%	46.9%	53.1%
1,977	MCCONE	1,061	388	647	26	259 D	36.6%	61.0%	37.5%	62.5%
6,851	MADISON	3,079	1,291	1,624	164	333 D	41.9%	52.7%	44.3%	55.7%
1,932	MEAGHER	758	310	416	32	106 D	40.9%	54.9%	42.7%	57.3%
3,884	MINERAL	1,373	569	724	80	155 D	41.4%	52.7%	44.0%	56.0%
95,802	MISSOULA	33,327	8,806	22,111	2,410	13,305 D	26.4%	66.3%	28.5%	71.5%
4,497	MUSSELSHELL	1,837	719	1,018	100	299 D	39.1%	55.4%	41.4%	58.6%
15,694	PARK	6,078	2,061	3,657	360	1,596 D	33.9%	60.2%	36.0%	64.0%
493	PETROLEUM	245	91	132	22	41 D	37.1%	53.9%	40.8%	59.2%
4,601	PHILLIPS	1,764	665	1,024	75	359 D	37.7%	58.0%	39.4%	60.6%
6,424	PONDERA	2,463	794	1,557	112	763 D	32.2%	63.2%	33.8%	66.2%
1,858	POWDER RIVER	930	414	472	44	58 D	44.5%	50.8%	46.7%	53.3%
7,180	POWELL	2,352	893	1,349	110	456 D	38.0%	57.4%	39.8%	60.2%
1,199	PRAIRIE	670	264	390	16	126 D	39.4%	58.2%	40.4%	59.6%
36,070	RAVALLI	13,656	6,270	6,640	746	370 D	45.9%	48.6%	48.6%	51.4%
9,667	RICHLAND	3,582	1,341	2,166	75	825 D	37.4%	60.5%	38.2%	61.8%
10,620	ROOSEVELT	3,042	722	2,244	76	1,522 D	23.7%	73.8%	24.3%	75.7%
9,383	ROSEBUD	3,004	720	2,138	146	1,418 D	24.0%	71.2%	25.2%	74.8%
10,227	SANDERS	4,064	1,785	2,068	211	283 D	43.9%	50.9%	46.3%	53.7%
4,105	SHERIDAN	1,673	465	1,162	46	697 D	27.8%	69.5%	28.6%	71.4%
34,606	SILVER BOW	12,234	1,692	9,881	661	8,189 D	13.8%	80.8%	14.6%	85.4%
8,195	STILLWATER	3,265	1,207	1,888	170	681 D	37.0%	57.8%	39.0%	61.0%
3,609	SWEET GRASS	1,473	711	699	63	12 R	48.3%	47.5%	50.4%	49.6%
6,445	TETON	2,798	893	1,754	151	861 D	31.9%	62.7%	33.7%	66.3%
5,267	TOOLE	1,949	594	1,225	130	631 D	30.5%	62.9%	32.7%	67.3%
861	TREASURE	416	127	266	23	139 D	30.5%	63.9%	32.3%	67.7%
7,675	VALLEY	3,482	845	2,520	117	1,675 D	24.3%	72.4%	25.1%	74.9%
2,259	WHEATLAND	813	290	491	32	201 D	35.7%	60.4%	37.1%	62.9%
1,068	WIBAUX	538	191	331	16	140 D	35.5%	61.5%	36.6%	63.4%
129,352	YELLOWSTONE	46,107	13,796	29,750	2,561	15,954 D	29.9%	64.5%	31.7%	68.3%
902,195	TOTAL	326,537	103,611	204,853	18,073	101,242 D	31.7%	62.7%	33.6%	66.4%

MONTANA

HOUSE OF REPRESENTATIVES

CD	Year	Total Vote	Republican Vote	Republican Candidate	Democratic Vote	Democratic Candidate	Other Vote	Rep.-Dem. Plurality	Rep.	Dem.	Rep.	Dem.
AL	2002	331,321	214,100	Rehberg, Denny*	108,233	Kelly, Steve	8,988	105,867 R	64.6%	32.7%	66.4%	33.6%
AL	2000	410,523	211,418	Rehberg, Denny	189,971	Keenan, Nancy	9,134	21,447 R	51.5%	46.3%	52.7%	47.3%
AL	1998	331,551	175,748	Hill, Rick*	147,073	Deschamps, Dusty	8,730	28,675 R	53.0%	44.4%	54.4%	45.6%
AL	1996	404,426	211,975	Hill, Rick	174,516	Yellowtail, Bill	17,935	37,459 R	52.4%	43.2%	54.8%	45.2%
AL	1994	352,133	148,715	Jamison, Cy	171,372	Williams, Pat*	32,046	22,657 D	42.2%	48.7%	46.5%	53.5%
AL	1992	403,735	189,570	Marlenee, Ron	203,711	Williams, Pat*	10,454	14,141 D	47.0%	50.5%	48.2%	51.8%

(Percentage columns: Total Vote — Rep., Dem.; Major Vote — Rep., Dem.)

An asterisk (*) denotes incumbent.

MONTANA

GENERAL AND PRIMARY ELECTIONS

2002 GENERAL ELECTIONS

Senator Other vote was 10,420 Libertarian (Stan Jones); 7,653 Green (Bob Kelleher).

House Other vote was:

At Large 8,988 Libertarian (Mike Fellows).

2002 PRIMARY ELECTIONS

Primary June 4, 2002

Registration (as of June 4, 2002) 606,147 No Party Registration

Primary Type Open—Any registered voter could participate in the primary of either party.

Note: An asterisk (*) denotes incumbent.

	REPUBLICAN PRIMARIES			DEMOCRATIC PRIMARIES		
Senator	Mike Taylor	48,169	60.2%	Max Baucus*	66,713	100.0%
	Bradley S. Johnson	14,252	17.8%			
	John K. McDonald	10,116	12.6%			
	Melvin Hanson	7,536	9.4%			
	TOTAL	80,073				
Congressional At Large	Denny Rehberg*	83,617	100.0%	Steve Kelly	40,441	74.3%
				Robert Candee	14,003	25.7%
				TOTAL	54,444	

MONTANA REPUBLICAN PRIMARY

SENATOR 2002

2000 Census Population	County	Total Vote	Taylor	Johnson	McDonald	Hanson	Winner	Percentage of Total Vote			
								Taylor	Johnson	McDonald	Hanson
9,202	BEAVERHEAD	1,779	1,108	268	207	196	Taylor	62.3%	15.1%	11.6%	11.0%
12,671	BIG HORN	857	633	91	74	59	Taylor	73.9%	10.6%	8.6%	6.9%
7,009	BLAINE	119	69	20	14	16	Taylor	58.0%	16.8%	11.8%	13.4%
4,385	BROADWATER	797	456	165	106	70	Taylor	57.2%	20.7%	13.3%	8.8%
9,552	CARBON	1,227	865	137	131	94	Taylor	70.5%	11.2%	10.7%	7.7%
1,360	CARTER	232	161	26	21	24	Taylor	69.4%	11.2%	9.1%	10.3%
80,357	CASCADE	5,016	2,865	897	903	351	Taylor	57.1%	17.9%	18.0%	7.0%
5,970	CHOUTEAU	1,330	791	258	192	89	Taylor	59.5%	19.4%	14.4%	6.7%
11,696	CUSTER	993	726	130	89	48	Taylor	73.1%	13.1%	9.0%	4.8%
2,017	DANIELS	224	160	21	22	21	Taylor	71.4%	9.4%	9.8%	9.4%
9,059	DAWSON	1,352	804	193	191	164	Taylor	59.5%	14.3%	14.1%	12.1%
9,417	DEER LODGE	324	161	76	48	39	Taylor	49.7%	23.5%	14.8%	12.0%
2,837	FALLON	580	343	54	90	93	Taylor	59.1%	9.3%	15.5%	16.0%
11,893	FERGUS	1,748	1,291	231	153	73	Taylor	73.9%	13.2%	8.8%	4.2%
74,471	FLATHEAD	8,824	4,686	1,940	918	1,280	Taylor	53.1%	22.0%	10.4%	14.5%
67,831	GALLATIN	4,859	3,025	1,036	513	285	Taylor	62.3%	21.3%	10.6%	5.9%
1,279	GARFIELD	378	263	31	66	18	Taylor	69.6%	8.2%	17.5%	4.8%
13,247	GLACIER	209	110	41	41	17	Taylor	52.6%	19.6%	19.6%	8.1%
1,042	GOLDEN VALLEY	187	120	28	32	7	Taylor	64.2%	15.0%	17.1%	3.7%
2,830	GRANITE	704	345	145	128	86	Taylor	49.0%	20.6%	18.2%	12.2%
16,673	HILL	686	390	104	94	98	Taylor	56.9%	15.2%	13.7%	14.3%
10,049	JEFFERSON	1,221	761	241	121	98	Taylor	62.3%	19.7%	9.9%	8.0%
2,329	JUDITH BASIN	724	446	85	164	29	Taylor	61.6%	11.7%	22.7%	4.0%
26,507	LAKE	2,851	2,091	385	218	157	Taylor	73.3%	13.5%	7.6%	5.5%
55,716	LEWIS AND CLARK	5,097	3,121	971	678	327	Taylor	61.2%	19.1%	13.3%	6.4%
2,158	LIBERTY	528	341	79	73	35	Taylor	64.6%	15.0%	13.8%	6.6%
18,837	LINCOLN	1,540	896	275	188	181	Taylor	58.2%	17.9%	12.2%	11.8%
1,977	MCCONE	416	295	39	52	30	Taylor	70.9%	9.4%	12.5%	7.2%
6,851	MADISON	818	461	152	126	79	Taylor	56.4%	18.6%	15.4%	9.7%
1,932	MEAGHER	596	374	86	81	55	Taylor	62.8%	14.4%	13.6%	9.2%
3,884	MINERAL	290	87	58	76	69	Taylor	30.0%	20.0%	26.2%	23.8%
95,802	MISSOULA	2,611	1,629	451	345	186	Taylor	62.4%	17.3%	13.2%	7.1%
4,497	MUSSELSHELL	907	545	147	130	85	Taylor	60.1%	16.2%	14.3%	9.4%
15,694	PARK	1,915	1,299	229	265	122	Taylor	67.8%	12.0%	13.8%	6.4%
493	PETROLEUM	87	39	14	23	11	Taylor	44.8%	16.1%	26.4%	12.6%
4,601	PHILLIPS	623	428	67	74	54	Taylor	68.7%	10.8%	11.9%	8.7%
6,424	PONDERA	854	527	161	120	46	Taylor	61.7%	18.9%	14.1%	5.4%
1,858	POWDER RIVER	294	201	31	34	28	Taylor	68.4%	10.5%	11.6%	9.5%
7,180	POWELL	1,013	481	261	163	108	Taylor	47.5%	25.8%	16.1%	10.7%
1,199	PRAIRIE	352	242	44	38	28	Taylor	68.8%	12.5%	10.8%	8.0%
36,070	RAVALLI	5,399	3,116	1,092	592	599	Taylor	57.7%	20.2%	11.0%	11.1%
9,667	RICHLAND	792	461	167	101	63	Taylor	58.2%	21.1%	12.8%	8.0%
10,620	ROOSEVELT	292	183	37	36	36	Taylor	62.7%	12.7%	12.3%	12.3%
9,383	ROSEBUD	490	309	65	77	39	Taylor	63.1%	13.3%	15.7%	8.0%
10,227	SANDERS	1,024	494	171	147	212	Taylor	48.2%	16.7%	14.4%	20.7%
4,105	SHERIDAN	252	202	20	20	10	Taylor	80.2%	7.9%	7.9%	4.0%
34,606	SILVER BOW	1,378	693	364	183	138	Taylor	50.3%	26.4%	13.3%	10.0%
8,195	STILLWATER	1,717	1,084	220	252	161	Taylor	63.1%	12.8%	14.7%	9.4%
3,609	SWEET GRASS	945	619	121	117	88	Taylor	65.5%	12.8%	12.4%	9.3%
6,445	TETON	896	550	184	113	49	Taylor	61.4%	20.5%	12.6%	5.5%
5,267	TOOLE	733	456	118	90	69	Taylor	62.2%	16.1%	12.3%	9.4%
861	TREASURE	146	84	21	21	20	Taylor	57.5%	14.4%	14.4%	13.7%
7,675	VALLEY	759	512	74	91	82	Taylor	67.5%	9.7%	12.0%	10.8%
2,259	WHEATLAND	356	212	52	64	28	Taylor	59.6%	14.6%	18.0%	7.9%
1,068	WIBAUX	118	58	15	20	25	Taylor	49.2%	12.7%	16.9%	21.2%
129,352	YELLOWSTONE	9,614	5,500	1,863	1,190	1,061	Taylor	57.2%	19.4%	12.4%	11.0%
902,195	TOTAL	80,073	48,169	14,252	10,116	7,536	Taylor	60.2%	17.8%	12.6%	9.4%

NEBRASKA

GOVERNOR
Mike Johanns (R). Reelected 2002 to a four-year term. Previously elected 1998.

SENATORS (1 Democrat, 1 Republican)
Chuck Hagel (R). Reelected 2002 to a six-year term. Previously elected 1996.

Ben Nelson (D). Elected 2000 to a six-year term.

REPRESENTATIVES (3 Republicans)
1. Doug Bereuter (R)
2. Lee Terry (R)
3. Tom Osborne (R)

POSTWAR VOTE FOR PRESIDENT

Year	Total Vote	Republican		Democratic		Other Vote	Plurality	Percentage			
								Total Vote		Major Vote	
		Vote	Candidate	Vote	Candidate			Rep.	Dem.	Rep.	Dem.
2000**	697,019	433,862	Bush, George W.	231,780	Gore, Al	31,377	202,082 R	62.2%	33.3%	65.2%	34.8%
1996**	677,415	363,467	Dole, Bob	236,761	Clinton, Bill	77,187	126,706 R	53.7%	35.0%	60.6%	39.4%
1992**	737,546	343,678	Bush, George	216,864	Clinton, Bill	177,004	126,814 R	46.6%	29.4%	61.3%	38.7%
1988	661,465	397,956	Bush, George	259,235	Dukakis, Michael S.	4,274	138,721 R	60.2%	39.2%	60.6%	39.4%
1984	652,090	460,054	Reagan, Ronald	187,866	Mondale, Walter F.	4,170	272,188 R	70.6%	28.8%	71.0%	29.0%
1980**	640,854	419,937	Reagan, Ronald	166,851	Carter, Jimmy	54,066	253,086 R	65.5%	26.0%	71.6%	28.4%
1976	607,668	359,705	Ford, Gerald R.	233,692	Carter, Jimmy	14,271	126,013 R	59.2%	38.5%	60.6%	39.4%
1972	576,289	406,298	Nixon, Richard M.	169,991	McGovern, George S.		236,307 R	70.5%	29.5%	70.5%	29.5%
1968	536,851	321,163	Nixon, Richard M.	170,784	Humphrey, Hubert H.	44,904	150,379 R	59.8%	31.8%	65.3%	34.7%
1964	584,154	276,847	Goldwater, Barry M.	307,307	Johnson, Lyndon B.		30,460 D	47.4%	52.6%	47.4%	52.6%
1960	613,095	380,553	Nixon, Richard M.	232,542	Kennedy, John F.		148,011 R	62.1%	37.9%	62.1%	37.9%
1956	577,137	378,108	Eisenhower, Dwight D.	199,029	Stevenson, Adlai E.		179,079 R	65.5%	34.5%	65.5%	34.5%
1952	609,660	421,603	Eisenhower, Dwight D.	188,057	Stevenson, Adlai E.		233,546 R	69.2%	30.8%	69.2%	30.8%
1948	488,940	264,774	Dewey, Thomas E.	224,165	Truman, Harry S.	1	40,609 R	54.2%	45.8%	54.2%	45.8%

In 2000 the other vote column includes 24,540 votes cast for Green (Nader). In 1996 the other vote column includes 71,278 votes cast for Perot. In 1992 the other vote column includes 174,104 votes cast for Perot. In 1980 the other vote column includes 44,993 votes for Independent (Anderson).

NEBRASKA

POSTWAR VOTE FOR GOVERNOR

Year	Total Vote	Republican Vote	Republican Candidate	Democratic Vote	Democratic Candidate	Other Vote	Rep.-Dem. Plurality	Percentage Total Vote Rep.	Total Vote Dem.	Major Vote Rep.	Major Vote Dem.
2002	480,991	330,349	Johanns, Mike	132,348	Dean, Stormy	18,294	198,001 R	68.7%	27.5%	71.4%	28.6%
1998	545,238	293,910	Johanns, Mike	250,678	Hoppner, Bill	650	43,232 R	53.9%	46.0%	54.0%	46.0%
1994	579,561	148,230	Spence, Gene	423,270	Nelson, Ben	8,061	275,040 D	25.6%	73.0%	25.9%	74.1%
1990	586,542	288,741	Orr, Kay	292,771	Nelson, Ben	5,030	4,030 D	49.2%	49.9%	49.7%	50.3%
1986	564,422	298,325	Orr, Kay	265,156	Boosalis, Helen	941	33,169 R	52.9%	47.0%	52.9%	47.1%
1982	547,902	270,203	Thone, Charles	277,436	Kerrey, Bob	263	7,233 D	49.3%	50.6%	49.3%	50.7%
1978	492,423	275,473	Thone, Charles	216,754	Whelan, Gerald T.	196	58,719 R	55.9%	44.0%	56.0%	44.0%
1974	451,306	159,780	Marvel, Richard D.	267,012	Exon, J. J.	24,514	107,232 D	35.4%	59.2%	37.4%	62.6%
1970	461,619	201,994	Tiemann, Norbert T.	248,552	Exon, J. J.	11,073	46,558 D	43.8%	53.8%	44.8%	55.2%
1966**	486,396	299,245	Tiemann, Norbert T.	186,985	Sorensen, Philip C.	166	112,260 R	61.5%	38.4%	61.5%	38.5%
1964	578,090	231,029	Burney, Dwight W.	347,026	Morrison, Frank B.	35	115,997 D	40.0%	60.0%	40.0%	60.0%
1962	464,585	221,885	Seaton, Fred A.	242,669	Morrison, Frank B.	31	20,784 D	47.8%	52.2%	47.8%	52.2%
1960	598,971	287,302	Cooper, John R.	311,344	Morrison, Frank B.	325	24,042 D	48.0%	52.0%	48.0%	52.0%
1958	421,067	209,705	Anderson, Victor E.	211,345	Brooks, Ralph G.	17	1,640 D	49.8%	50.2%	49.8%	50.2%
1956	567,933	308,293	Anderson, Victor E.	228,048	Sorrell, Frank	31,592	80,245 R	54.3%	40.2%	57.5%	42.5%
1954	414,841	250,080	Anderson, Victor E.	164,753	Ritchie, William	8	85,327 R	60.3%	39.7%	60.3%	39.7%
1952	595,714	366,009	Crosby, Robert B.	229,700	Raecke, Walter R.	5	136,309 R	61.4%	38.6%	61.4%	38.6%
1950	449,720	247,081	Peterson, Val	202,638	Raecke, Walter R.	1	44,443 R	54.9%	45.1%	54.9%	45.1%
1948	476,352	286,119	Peterson, Val	190,214	Sorrell, Frank	19	95,905 R	60.1%	39.9%	60.1%	39.9%
1946	380,835	249,468	Peterson, Val	131,367	Sorrell, Frank		118,101 R	65.5%	34.5%	65.5%	34.5%

The term of office of Nebraska's Governor was increased from two to four years effective with the 1966 election.

POSTWAR VOTE FOR SENATOR

Year	Total Vote	Republican Vote	Republican Candidate	Democratic Vote	Democratic Candidate	Other Vote	Rep.-Dem. Plurality	Percentage Total Vote Rep.	Total Vote Dem.	Major Vote Rep.	Major Vote Dem.
2002	480,217	397,438	Hagel, Chuck	70,290	Matulka, Charlie A.	12,489	327,148 R	82.8%	14.6%	85.0%	15.0%
2000	692,344	337,967	Stenberg, Don	353,097	Nelson, Ben	1,280	15,130 D	48.8%	51.0%	48.9%	51.1%
1996	676,789	379,933	Hagel, Chuck	281,904	Nelson, Ben	14,952	98,029 R	56.1%	41.7%	57.4%	42.6%
1994	579,205	260,668	Stoney, Jan	317,297	Kerrey, Bob	1,240	56,629 D	45.0%	54.8%	45.1%	54.9%
1990	593,828	243,013	Daub, Harold J.	349,779	Exon, J. J.	1,036	106,766 D	40.9%	58.9%	41.0%	59.0%
1988	667,860	278,250	Karnes, David	378,717	Kerrey, Bob	10,893	100,467 D	41.7%	56.7%	42.4%	57.6%
1984	639,668	307,147	Hoch, Nancy	332,217	Exon, J. J.	304	25,070 D	48.0%	51.9%	48.0%	52.0%
1982	545,647	155,760	Keck, Jim	363,350	Zorinsky, Edward	26,537	207,590 D	28.5%	66.6%	30.0%	70.0%
1978	494,368	159,806	Shasteen, Donald	334,276	Exon, J. J.	286	174,470 D	32.3%	67.6%	32.3%	67.7%
1976	598,314	284,284	McCollister, John Y.	313,809	Zorinsky, Edward	221	29,525 D	47.5%	52.4%	47.5%	52.5%
1972	568,580	301,841	Curtis, Carl T.	265,922	Carpenter, Terry	817	35,919 R	53.1%	46.8%	53.2%	46.8%
1970	458,966	240,894	Hruska, Roman L.	217,681	Morrison, Frank B.	391	23,213 R	52.5%	47.4%	52.5%	47.5%
1966	485,101	296,116	Curtis, Carl T.	187,950	Morrison, Frank B.	1,035	108,166 R	61.0%	38.7%	61.2%	38.8%
1964	563,401	345,772	Hruska, Roman L.	217,605	Arndt, Raymond W.	24	128,167 R	61.4%	38.6%	61.4%	38.6%
1960	598,743	352,748	Curtis, Carl T.	245,837	Conrad, Robert	158	106,911 R	58.9%	41.1%	58.9%	41.1%
1958	417,385	232,227	Hruska, Roman L.	185,152	Morrison, Frank B.	6	47,075 R	55.6%	44.4%	55.6%	44.4%
1954	418,691	255,695	Curtis, Carl T.	162,990	Neville, Keith	6	92,705 R	61.1%	38.9%	61.1%	38.9%
1954S	411,225	250,341	Hruska, Roman L.	160,881	Green, James F.	3	89,460 R	60.9%	39.1%	60.9%	39.1%
1952	591,749	408,971	Butler, Hugh	164,660	Long, Stanley D.	18,118	244,311 R	69.1%	27.8%	71.3%	28.7%
1952S	581,750	369,841	Griswold, Dwight	211,898	Ritchie, William	11	157,943 R	63.6%	36.4%	63.6%	36.4%
1948	471,895	267,575	Wherry, Kenneth S.	204,320	Carpenter, Terry		63,255 R	56.7%	43.3%	56.7%	43.3%
1946	382,958	271,208	Butler, Hugh	111,750	Mekota, John E.		159,458 R	70.8%	29.2%	70.8%	29.2%

One each of the 1954 and 1952 elections was for a short term to fill a vacancy.

NEBRASKA

Congressional districts first established for elections held in 2002
3 members

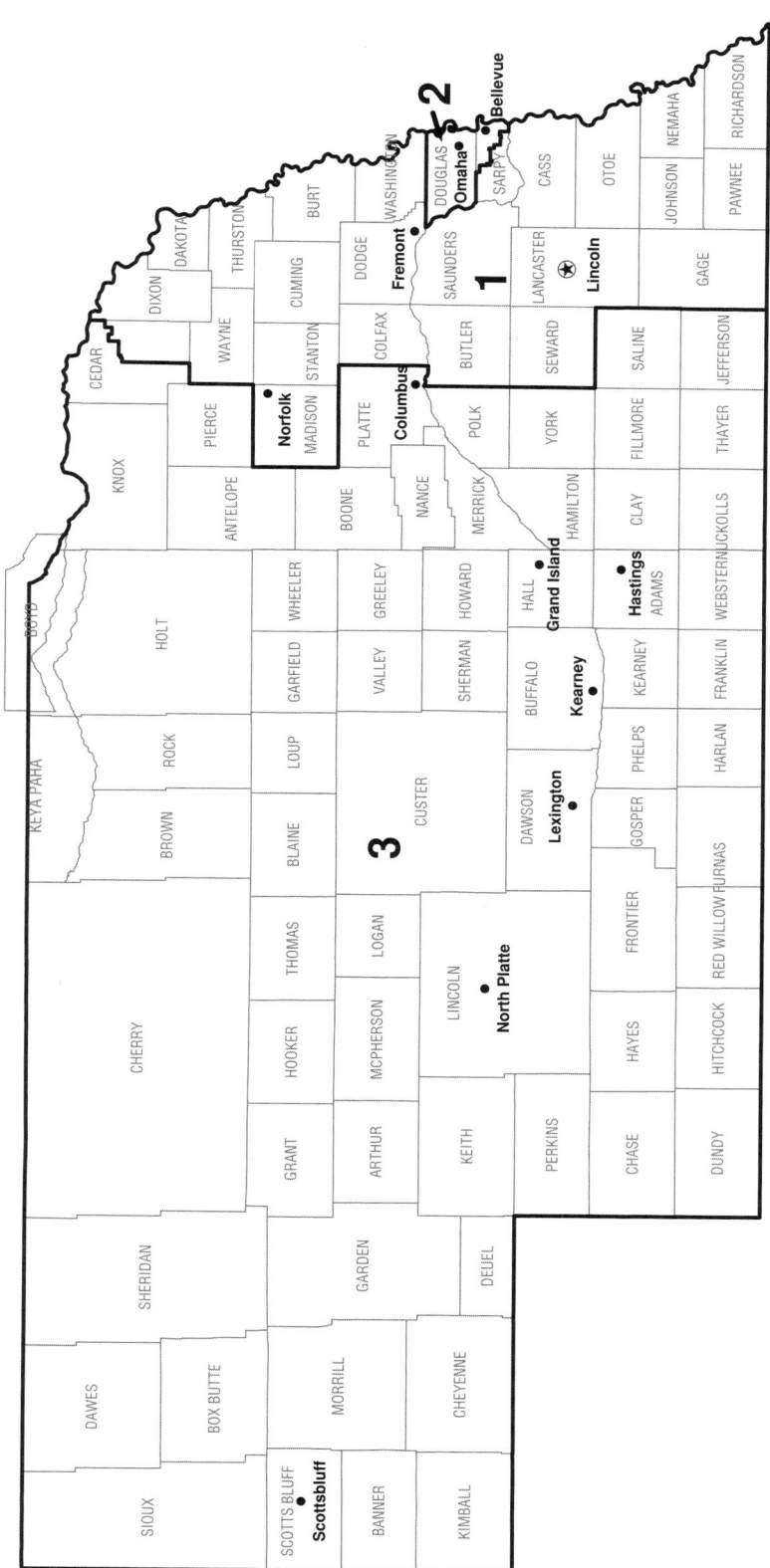

NEBRASKA

GOVERNOR 2002

2000 Census Population	County	Total Vote	Republican	Democratic	Other	Rep.-Dem. Plurality	Total Vote Rep.	Dem.	Major Vote Rep.	Dem.
31,151	ADAMS	8,509	5,552	2,459	498	3,093 R	65.2%	28.9%	69.3%	30.7%
7,452	ANTELOPE	2,237	1,771	465	1	1,306 R	79.2%	20.8%	79.2%	20.8%
444	ARTHUR	251	199	33	19	166 R	79.3%	13.1%	85.8%	14.2%
819	BANNER	371	317	39	15	278 R	85.4%	10.5%	89.0%	11.0%
583	BLAINE	346	277	56	13	221 R	80.1%	16.2%	83.2%	16.8%
6,259	BOONE	2,719	1,987	567	165	1,420 R	73.1%	20.9%	77.8%	22.2%
12,158	BOX BUTTE	3,803	2,670	912	221	1,758 R	70.2%	24.0%	74.5%	25.5%
2,438	BOYD	935	675	195	65	480 R	72.2%	20.9%	77.6%	22.4%
3,525	BROWN	1,493	1,119	295	79	824 R	74.9%	19.8%	79.1%	20.9%
42,259	BUFFALO	10,035	7,353	2,239	443	5,114 R	73.3%	22.3%	76.7%	23.3%
7,791	BURT	2,559	1,703	747	109	956 R	66.5%	29.2%	69.5%	30.5%
8,767	BUTLER	2,837	1,952	736	149	1,216 R	68.8%	25.9%	72.6%	27.4%
24,334	CASS	6,909	4,499	2,104	306	2,395 R	65.1%	30.5%	68.1%	31.9%
9,615	CEDAR	3,568	2,648	666	254	1,982 R	74.2%	18.7%	79.9%	20.1%
4,068	CHASE	1,384	1,145	170	69	975 R	82.7%	12.3%	87.1%	12.9%
6,148	CHERRY	2,211	1,747	404	60	1,343 R	79.0%	18.3%	81.2%	18.8%
9,830	CHEYENNE	2,806	2,247	464	95	1,783 R	80.1%	16.5%	82.9%	17.1%
7,039	CLAY	2,258	1,539	583	136	956 R	68.2%	25.8%	72.5%	27.5%
10,441	COLFAX	2,881	2,121	631	129	1,490 R	73.6%	21.9%	77.1%	22.9%
10,203	CUMING	3,001	2,405	467	129	1,938 R	80.1%	15.6%	83.7%	16.3%
11,793	CUSTER	4,459	3,377	862	220	2,515 R	75.7%	19.3%	79.7%	20.3%
20,253	DAKOTA	4,261	2,802	1,299	160	1,503 R	65.8%	30.5%	68.3%	31.7%
9,060	DAWES	2,633	1,818	683	132	1,135 R	69.0%	25.9%	72.7%	27.3%
24,365	DAWSON	5,226	3,915	1,086	225	2,829 R	74.9%	20.8%	78.3%	21.7%
2,098	DEUEL	827	690	107	30	583 R	83.4%	12.9%	86.6%	13.4%
6,339	DIXON	2,106	1,559	441	106	1,118 R	74.0%	20.9%	78.0%	22.1%
36,160	DODGE	9,770	6,767	2,649	354	4,118 R	69.3%	27.1%	71.9%	28.1%
463,585	DOUGLAS	119,325	77,294	39,288	2,743	38,006 R	64.8%	32.9%	66.3%	33.7%
2,292	DUNDY	829	588	187	54	401 R	70.9%	22.6%	75.9%	24.1%
6,634	FILLMORE	2,391	1,761	551	79	1,210 R	73.7%	23.0%	76.2%	23.8%
3,574	FRANKLIN	1,320	951	305	64	646 R	72.0%	23.1%	75.7%	24.3%
3,099	FRONTIER	1,130	841	227	62	614 R	74.4%	20.1%	78.7%	21.3%
5,324	FURNAS	2,127	1,659	387	81	1,272 R	78.0%	18.2%	81.1%	18.9%
22,993	GAGE	7,085	4,598	2,118	369	2,480 R	64.9%	29.9%	68.5%	31.5%
2,292	GARDEN	959	774	137	48	637 R	80.7%	14.3%	85.0%	15.0%
1,902	GARFIELD	721	528	155	38	373 R	73.2%	21.5%	77.3%	22.7%
2,143	GOSPER	881	668	188	25	480 R	75.8%	21.3%	78.0%	22.0%
747	GRANT	337	288	37	12	251 R	85.5%	11.0%	88.6%	11.4%
2,714	GREELEY	1,135	707	349	79	358 R	62.3%	30.7%	67.0%	33.0%
53,534	HALL	13,149	8,869	3,741	539	5,128 R	67.4%	28.5%	70.3%	29.7%
9,403	HAMILTON	3,461	2,607	713	141	1,894 R	75.3%	20.6%	78.5%	21.5%
3,786	HARLAN	1,336	988	294	54	694 R	74.0%	22.0%	77.1%	22.9%
1,068	HAYES	506	378	51	77	327 R	74.7%	10.1%	88.1%	11.9%
3,111	HITCHCOCK	1,152	882	212	58	670 R	76.6%	18.4%	80.6%	19.4%
11,551	HOLT	4,113	3,190	725	198	2,465 R	77.6%	17.6%	81.5%	18.5%
783	HOOKER	362	277	72	13	205 R	76.5%	19.9%	79.4%	20.6%
6,567	HOWARD	2,308	1,507	684	117	823 R	65.3%	29.6%	68.8%	31.2%
8,333	JEFFERSON	3,259	2,102	979	178	1,123 R	64.5%	30.0%	68.2%	31.8%
4,488	JOHNSON	1,911	1,180	617	114	563 R	61.7%	32.3%	65.7%	34.3%
6,882	KEARNEY	2,296	1,678	478	140	1,200 R	73.1%	20.8%	77.8%	22.2%
8,875	KEITH	3,097	2,390	542	165	1,848 R	77.2%	17.5%	81.5%	18.5%
983	KEYA PAHA	547	419	103	25	316 R	76.6%	18.8%	80.3%	19.7%
4,089	KIMBALL	1,178	952	176	50	776 R	80.8%	14.9%	84.4%	15.6%
9,374	KNOX	3,657	2,534	754	369	1,780 R	69.3%	20.6%	77.1%	22.9%
250,291	LANCASTER	67,247	41,289	23,626	2,332	17,663 R	61.4%	35.1%	63.6%	36.4%
34,632	LINCOLN	9,960	6,888	2,625	447	4,263 R	69.2%	26.4%	72.4%	27.6%
774	LOGAN	369	298	52	19	246 R	80.8%	14.1%	85.1%	14.9%
712	LOUP	317	229	73	15	156 R	72.2%	23.0%	75.8%	24.2%
533	MCPHERSON	199	161	31	7	130 R	80.9%	15.6%	83.9%	16.1%
35,226	MADISON	8,433	6,551	1,466	416	5,085 R	77.7%	17.4%	81.7%	18.3%

NEBRASKA
GOVERNOR 2002

2000 Census Population	County	Total Vote	Republican	Democratic	Other	Rep.-Dem. Plurality	Percentage			
							Total Vote		Major Vote	
							Rep.	Dem.	Rep.	Dem.
8,204	MERRICK	2,456	1,734	597	125	1,137 R	70.6%	24.3%	74.4%	25.6%
5,440	MORRILL	1,676	1,267	296	113	971 R	75.6%	17.7%	81.1%	18.9%
4,038	NANCE	1,344	896	355	93	541 R	66.7%	26.4%	71.6%	28.4%
7,576	NEMAHA	3,005	2,150	729	126	1,421 R	71.5%	24.3%	74.7%	25.3%
5,057	NUCKOLLS	1,848	1,350	415	83	935 R	73.1%	22.5%	76.5%	23.5%
15,396	OTOE	4,559	3,159	1,181	219	1,978 R	69.3%	25.9%	72.8%	27.2%
3,087	PAWNEE	1,190	761	359	70	402 R	63.9%	30.2%	67.9%	32.1%
3,200	PERKINS	1,198	926	216	56	710 R	77.3%	18.0%	81.1%	18.9%
9,747	PHELPS	3,370	2,604	650	116	1,954 R	77.3%	19.3%	80.0%	20.0%
7,857	PIERCE	2,256	1,806	324	126	1,482 R	80.1%	14.4%	84.8%	15.2%
31,662	PLATTE	9,920	7,844	1,758	318	6,086 R	79.1%	17.7%	81.7%	18.3%
5,639	POLK	2,044	1,487	475	82	1,012 R	72.7%	23.2%	75.8%	24.2%
11,448	RED WILLOW	3,674	2,792	719	163	2,073 R	76.0%	19.6%	79.5%	20.5%
9,531	RICHARDSON	3,134	2,241	712	181	1,529 R	71.5%	22.7%	75.9%	24.1%
1,756	ROCK	782	504	254	24	250 R	64.5%	32.5%	66.5%	33.5%
13,843	SALINE	4,108	2,411	1,470	227	941 R	58.7%	35.8%	62.1%	37.9%
122,595	SARPY	28,801	20,402	7,681	718	12,721 R	70.8%	26.7%	72.6%	27.4%
19,830	SAUNDERS	6,900	4,609	1,977	314	2,632 R	66.8%	28.7%	70.0%	30.0%
36,951	SCOTTS BLUFF	8,804	6,936	1,602	266	5,334 R	78.8%	18.2%	81.2%	18.8%
16,496	SEWARD	5,320	3,728	1,276	316	2,452 R	70.1%	24.0%	74.5%	25.5%
6,198	SHERIDAN	1,927	1,504	294	129	1,210 R	78.0%	15.3%	83.6%	16.4%
3,318	SHERMAN	1,352	850	451	51	399 R	62.9%	33.4%	65.3%	34.7%
1,475	SIOUX	534	430	81	23	349 R	80.5%	15.2%	84.1%	15.9%
6,455	STANTON	1,756	1,349	275	132	1,074 R	76.8%	15.7%	83.1%	16.9%
6,055	THAYER	2,237	1,636	500	101	1,136 R	73.1%	22.4%	76.6%	23.4%
729	THOMAS	400	308	73	19	235 R	77.0%	18.3%	80.8%	19.2%
7,171	THURSTON	1,548	979	480	89	499 R	63.2%	31.0%	67.1%	32.9%
4,647	VALLEY	2,099	1,496	542	61	954 R	71.3%	25.8%	73.4%	26.6%
18,780	WASHINGTON	6,010	4,363	1,432	215	2,931 R	72.6%	23.8%	75.3%	24.7%
9,851	WAYNE	2,901	2,158	595	148	1,563 R	74.4%	20.5%	78.4%	21.6%
4,061	WEBSTER	1,617	1,095	436	86	659 R	67.7%	27.0%	71.5%	28.5%
886	WHEELER	380	281	69	30	212 R	73.9%	18.2%	80.3%	19.7%
14,598	YORK	4,349	3,413	772	164	2,641 R	78.5%	17.8%	81.6%	18.4%
1,711,263	TOTAL	480,991	330,349	132,348	18,294	198,001 R	68.7%	27.5%	71.4%	28.6%

NEBRASKA
SENATOR 2002

2000 Census Population	County	Total Vote	Republican	Democratic	Other	Rep.-Dem. Plurality	Percentage			
							Total Vote		Major Vote	
							Rep.	Dem.	Rep.	Dem.
31,151	ADAMS	8,518	7,260	1,050	208	6,210 R	85.2%	12.3%	87.4%	12.6%
7,452	ANTELOPE	2,382	2,081	235	66	1,846 R	87.4%	9.9%	89.9%	10.1%
444	ARTHUR	245	226	16	3	210 R	92.2%	6.5%	93.4%	6.6%
819	BANNER	373	348	14	11	334 R	93.3%	3.8%	96.1%	3.9%
583	BLAINE	340	314	22	4	292 R	92.4%	6.5%	93.5%	6.5%
6,259	BOONE	2,703	2,417	228	58	2,189 R	89.4%	8.4%	91.4%	8.6%
12,158	BOX BUTTE	3,808	3,052	653	103	2,399 R	80.1%	17.1%	82.4%	17.6%
2,438	BOYD	893	746	116	31	630 R	83.5%	13.0%	86.5%	13.5%
3,525	BROWN	1,508	1,384	79	45	1,305 R	91.8%	5.2%	94.6%	5.4%
42,259	BUFFALO	10,062	8,880	938	244	7,942 R	88.3%	9.3%	90.4%	9.6%
7,791	BURT	2,545	2,105	384	56	1,721 R	82.7%	15.1%	84.6%	15.4%
8,767	BUTLER	2,807	2,313	432	62	1,881 R	82.4%	15.4%	84.3%	15.7%
24,334	CASS	6,894	5,607	1,054	233	4,553 R	81.3%	15.3%	84.2%	15.8%
9,615	CEDAR	3,474	2,880	523	71	2,357 R	82.9%	15.1%	84.6%	15.4%
4,068	CHASE	1,384	1,248	101	35	1,147 R	90.2%	7.3%	92.5%	7.5%
6,148	CHERRY	2,181	1,926	223	32	1,703 R	88.3%	10.2%	89.6%	10.4%
9,830	CHEYENNE	2,807	2,398	344	65	2,054 R	85.4%	12.3%	87.5%	12.5%
7,039	CLAY	2,278	1,990	231	57	1,759 R	87.4%	10.1%	89.6%	10.4%
10,441	COLFAX	2,873	2,445	316	112	2,129 R	85.1%	11.0%	88.6%	11.4%
10,203	CUMING	2,977	2,701	231	45	2,470 R	90.7%	7.8%	92.1%	7.9%
11,793	CUSTER	4,459	4,004	379	76	3,625 R	89.8%	8.5%	91.4%	8.6%
20,253	DAKOTA	4,218	2,878	1,225	115	1,653 R	68.2%	29.0%	70.1%	29.9%
9,060	DAWES	2,639	2,176	400	63	1,776 R	82.5%	15.2%	84.5%	15.5%
24,365	DAWSON	5,199	4,582	502	115	4,080 R	88.1%	9.7%	90.1%	9.9%
2,098	DEUEL	897	718	159	20	559 R	80.0%	17.7%	81.9%	18.1%
6,339	DIXON	2,096	1,701	324	71	1,377 R	81.2%	15.5%	84.0%	16.0%
36,160	DODGE	9,532	7,948	1,361	223	6,587 R	83.4%	14.3%	85.4%	14.6%
463,585	DOUGLAS	118,893	93,092	21,867	3,934	71,225 R	78.3%	18.4%	81.0%	19.0%
2,292	DUNDY	807	715	70	22	645 R	88.6%	8.7%	91.1%	8.9%
6,634	FILLMORE	2,396	2,082	276	38	1,806 R	86.9%	11.5%	88.3%	11.7%
3,574	FRANKLIN	1,322	1,154	136	32	1,018 R	87.3%	10.3%	89.5%	10.5%
3,099	FRONTIER	1,124	1,005	99	20	906 R	89.4%	8.8%	91.0%	9.0%
5,324	FURNAS	2,134	1,904	193	37	1,711 R	89.2%	9.0%	90.8%	9.2%
22,993	GAGE	7,122	5,804	1,147	171	4,657 R	81.5%	16.1%	83.5%	16.5%
2,292	GARDEN	950	846	81	23	765 R	89.1%	8.5%	91.3%	8.7%
1,902	GARFIELD	712	638	58	16	580 R	89.6%	8.1%	91.7%	8.3%
2,143	GOSPER	875	804	62	9	742 R	91.9%	7.1%	92.8%	7.2%
747	GRANT	332	304	21	7	283 R	91.6%	6.3%	93.5%	6.5%
2,714	GREELEY	1,099	929	146	24	783 R	84.5%	13.3%	86.4%	13.6%
53,534	HALL	13,093	11,096	1,687	310	9,409 R	84.7%	12.9%	86.8%	13.2%
9,403	HAMILTON	3,457	3,119	275	63	2,844 R	90.2%	8.0%	91.9%	8.1%
3,786	HARLAN	1,322	1,162	135	25	1,027 R	87.9%	10.2%	89.6%	10.4%
1,068	HAYES	492	449	26	17	423 R	91.3%	5.3%	94.5%	5.5%
3,111	HITCHCOCK	1,148	998	123	27	875 R	86.9%	10.7%	89.0%	11.0%
11,551	HOLT	3,973	3,488	389	96	3,099 R	87.8%	9.8%	90.0%	10.0%
783	HOOKER	367	317	45	5	272 R	86.4%	12.3%	87.6%	12.4%
6,567	HOWARD	2,284	1,951	270	63	1,681 R	85.4%	11.8%	87.8%	12.2%
8,333	JEFFERSON	3,244	2,618	551	75	2,067 R	80.7%	17.0%	82.6%	17.4%
4,488	JOHNSON	1,896	1,558	295	43	1,263 R	82.2%	15.6%	84.1%	15.9%
6,882	KEARNEY	2,290	2,009	224	57	1,785 R	87.7%	9.8%	90.0%	10.0%
8,875	KEITH	3,080	2,730	278	72	2,452 R	88.6%	9.0%	90.8%	9.2%
983	KEYA PAHA	537	477	45	15	432 R	88.8%	8.4%	91.4%	8.6%
4,089	KIMBALL	1,181	1,008	144	29	864 R	85.4%	12.2%	87.5%	12.5%
9,374	KNOX	3,580	3,059	449	72	2,610 R	85.4%	12.5%	87.2%	12.8%
250,291	LANCASTER	67,789	53,855	12,156	1,778	41,699 R	79.4%	17.9%	81.6%	18.4%
34,632	LINCOLN	9,972	8,143	1,576	253	6,567 R	81.7%	15.8%	83.8%	16.2%
774	LOGAN	373	334	32	7	302 R	89.5%	8.6%	91.3%	8.7%
712	LOUP	308	274	29	5	245 R	89.0%	9.4%	90.4%	9.6%
533	MCPHERSON	198	178	19	1	159 R	89.9%	9.6%	90.4%	9.6%
35,226	MADISON	8,445	7,495	764	186	6,731 R	88.8%	9.0%	90.7%	9.3%

NEBRASKA

SENATOR 2002

2000 Census Population	County	Total Vote	Republican	Democratic	Other	Rep.-Dem. Plurality	Total Vote Rep.	Total Vote Dem.	Major Vote Rep.	Major Vote Dem.
8,204	MERRICK	2,456	2,151	261	44	1,890 R	87.6%	10.6%	89.2%	10.8%
5,440	MORRILL	1,657	1,439	174	44	1,265 R	86.8%	10.5%	89.2%	10.8%
4,038	NANCE	1,337	1,114	191	32	923 R	83.3%	14.3%	85.4%	14.6%
7,576	NEMAHA	2,994	2,560	375	59	2,185 R	85.5%	12.5%	87.2%	12.8%
5,057	NUCKOLLS	1,838	1,587	206	45	1,381 R	86.3%	11.2%	88.5%	11.5%
15,396	OTOE	4,583	3,837	651	95	3,186 R	83.7%	14.2%	85.5%	14.5%
3,087	PAWNEE	1,168	912	218	38	694 R	78.1%	18.7%	80.7%	19.3%
3,200	PERKINS	1,185	1,024	119	42	905 R	86.4%	10.0%	89.6%	10.4%
9,747	PHELPS	3,374	3,050	276	48	2,774 R	90.4%	8.2%	91.7%	8.3%
7,857	PIERCE	2,242	2,061	150	31	1,911 R	91.9%	6.7%	93.2%	6.8%
31,662	PLATTE	9,922	8,886	873	163	8,013 R	89.6%	8.8%	91.1%	8.9%
5,639	POLK	2,032	1,780	221	31	1,559 R	87.6%	10.9%	89.0%	11.0%
11,448	RED WILLOW	3,682	3,221	369	92	2,852 R	87.5%	10.0%	89.7%	10.3%
9,531	RICHARDSON	3,085	2,476	517	92	1,959 R	80.3%	16.8%	82.7%	17.3%
1,756	ROCK	754	712	36	6	676 R	94.4%	4.8%	95.2%	4.8%
13,843	SALINE	4,083	3,200	807	76	2,393 R	78.4%	19.8%	79.9%	20.1%
122,595	SARPY	28,766	24,309	3,738	719	20,571 R	84.5%	13.0%	86.7%	13.3%
19,830	SAUNDERS	6,938	5,619	1,145	174	4,474 R	81.0%	16.5%	83.1%	16.9%
36,951	SCOTTS BLUFF	8,838	7,655	1,013	170	6,642 R	86.6%	11.5%	88.3%	11.7%
16,496	SEWARD	5,344	4,502	712	130	3,790 R	84.2%	13.3%	86.3%	13.7%
6,198	SHERIDAN	1,933	1,735	161	37	1,574 R	89.8%	8.3%	91.5%	8.5%
3,318	SHERMAN	1,335	1,132	170	33	962 R	84.8%	12.7%	86.9%	13.1%
1,475	SIOUX	521	464	46	11	418 R	89.1%	8.8%	91.0%	9.0%
6,455	STANTON	1,748	1,554	155	39	1,399 R	88.9%	8.9%	90.9%	9.1%
6,055	THAYER	2,225	1,964	227	34	1,737 R	88.3%	10.2%	89.6%	10.4%
729	THOMAS	404	363	29	12	334 R	89.9%	7.2%	92.6%	7.4%
7,171	THURSTON	1,528	1,138	345	45	793 R	74.5%	22.6%	76.7%	23.3%
4,647	VALLEY	2,086	1,818	223	45	1,595 R	87.2%	10.7%	89.1%	10.9%
18,780	WASHINGTON	6,016	5,084	748	184	4,336 R	84.5%	12.4%	87.2%	12.8%
9,851	WAYNE	2,906	2,530	319	57	2,211 R	87.1%	11.0%	88.8%	11.2%
4,061	WEBSTER	1,604	1,352	221	31	1,131 R	84.3%	13.8%	86.0%	14.0%
886	WHEELER	380	340	32	8	308 R	89.5%	8.4%	91.4%	8.6%
14,598	YORK	4,366	3,946	354	66	3,592 R	90.4%	8.1%	91.8%	8.2%
1,711,263	TOTAL	480,217	397,438	70,290	12,489	327,148 R	82.8%	14.6%	85.0%	15.0%

NEBRASKA

HOUSE OF REPRESENTATIVES

CD	Year	Total Vote	Republican Vote	Republican Candidate	Democratic Vote	Democratic Candidate	Other Vote	Rep.-Dem. Plurality	Total Vote Rep.	Total Vote Dem.	Major Vote Rep.	Major Vote Dem.
1	2002	155,844	133,013	Bereuter, Doug*			22,831	133,013 R	85.4%		100.0%	
2	2002	142,014	89,917	Terry, Lee*	46,843	Simon, Jim	5,254	43,074 R	63.3%	33.0%	65.7%	34.3%
3	2002	175,956	163,939	Osborne, Tom*			12,017	163,939 R	93.2%		100.0%	
Total	2002	473,814	386,869		46,843		40,102	340,026 R	81.6%	9.9%	89.2%	10.8%

An asterisk (*) denotes incumbent.

NEBRASKA

GENERAL AND PRIMARY ELECTIONS

2002 GENERAL ELECTIONS

Governor   Other vote was 18,294 Nebraska Party (Paul A. Rosberg).

Senator   Other vote was 7,423 Libertarian (John J. Graziano); 5,066 By Petition (Phil Chase).

House   Other vote was:

CD 1   22,831 Libertarian (Robert Eckerson).
CD 2   3,236 Green (Doug Paterson); 2,018 Libertarian (Dave Stock).
CD 3   12,017 Libertarian (Jerry Hickman).

2002 PRIMARY ELECTIONS

Primary   May 14, 2002

Registration (as of May 14, 2002)		
Republican	537,870
Democratic	379,583
Libertarian	2,992
Nebraska Party	284
Green	26
Nonpartisan	149,724
TOTAL	1,070,479

Primary Type   Semi-open—Registered Democrats and Republicans could vote only in their party's primary. Voters registered as nonpartisan could participate in either party's primary for the Senate and House (but not governor).

Note: An asterisk (*) denotes incumbent. Ballots cast by nonpartisan voters in primaries for the House and Senate were tallied separately but were included in the overall totals, which are listed below. Official results from Nebraska election officials gave the vote for Democrat Jim Simon in the 2nd Congressional District as 16,337, but his total of Democratic and nonpartisan primary votes adds to 16,377.

	REPUBLICAN PRIMARIES			**DEMOCRATIC PRIMARIES**		
Governor	Mike Johanns*	128,277	86.8%	Stormy Dean	47,369	77.3%
	Robert J. Wicht	19,441	13.2%	Luis R. Calvillo	13,943	22.7%
	TOTAL	147,718		TOTAL	61,312	
Senator	Chuck Hagel*	144,160	100.0%	Charlie A. Matulka	33,922	59.3%
				Al Hamburg	23,272	40.7%
				TOTAL	57,194	
Congressional District 1	Doug Bereuter*	40,911	100.0%	No Democratic candidate		
Congressional District 2	Lee Terry*	24,193	100.0%	Jim Simon	16,377	100.0%
Congressional District 3	Tom Osborne*	78,297	100.0%	No Democratic candidate		

NEBRASKA REPUBLICAN PRIMARY

GOVERNOR 2002

2000 Census Population	County	Total Vote	Johanns	Wicht	Winner	Percentage of Total Vote Johanns	Wicht
31,151	ADAMS	2,930	1,996	934	Johanns	68.1%	31.9%
7,452	ANTELOPE	1,314	1,141	173	Johanns	86.8%	13.2%
444	ARTHUR	163	149	14	Johanns	91.4%	8.6%
819	BANNER	353	321	32	Johanns	90.9%	9.1%
583	BLAINE	198	175	23	Johanns	88.4%	11.6%
6,259	BOONE	1,330	1,132	198	Johanns	85.1%	14.9%
12,158	BOX BUTTE	1,989	1,692	297	Johanns	85.1%	14.9%
2,438	BOYD	310	270	40	Johanns	87.1%	12.9%
3,525	BROWN	781	704	77	Johanns	90.1%	9.9%
42,259	BUFFALO	5,122	4,372	750	Johanns	85.4%	14.6%
7,791	BURT	836	716	120	Johanns	85.6%	14.4%
8,767	BUTLER	1,227	1,054	173	Johanns	85.9%	14.1%
24,334	CASS	2,043	1,741	302	Johanns	85.2%	14.8%
9,615	CEDAR	1,035	905	130	Johanns	87.4%	12.6%
4,068	CHASE	870	777	93	Johanns	89.3%	10.7%
6,148	CHERRY	1,629	1,458	171	Johanns	89.5%	10.5%
9,830	CHEYENNE	1,024	912	112	Johanns	89.1%	10.9%
7,039	CLAY	1,322	1,047	275	Johanns	79.2%	20.8%
10,441	COLFAX	819	734	85	Johanns	89.6%	10.4%
10,203	CUMING	1,029	926	103	Johanns	90.0%	10.0%
11,793	CUSTER	2,377	2,089	288	Johanns	87.9%	12.1%
20,253	DAKOTA	676	597	79	Johanns	88.3%	11.7%
9,060	DAWES	1,116	976	140	Johanns	87.5%	12.5%
24,365	DAWSON	2,234	1,952	282	Johanns	87.4%	12.6%
2,098	DEUEL	741	667	74	Johanns	90.0%	10.0%
6,339	DIXON	471	422	49	Johanns	89.6%	10.4%
36,160	DODGE	2,913	2,531	382	Johanns	86.9%	13.1%
463,585	DOUGLAS	19,614	17,670	1,944	Johanns	90.1%	9.9%
2,292	DUNDY	384	335	49	Johanns	87.2%	12.8%
6,634	FILLMORE	876	767	109	Johanns	87.6%	12.4%
3,574	FRANKLIN	625	515	110	Johanns	82.4%	17.6%
3,099	FRONTIER	620	523	97	Johanns	84.4%	15.6%
5,324	FURNAS	1,049	902	147	Johanns	86.0%	14.0%
22,993	GAGE	1,571	1,344	227	Johanns	85.6%	14.4%
2,292	GARDEN	758	663	95	Johanns	87.5%	12.5%
1,902	GARFIELD	396	347	49	Johanns	87.6%	12.4%
2,143	GOSPER	582	513	69	Johanns	88.1%	11.9%
747	GRANT	196	172	24	Johanns	87.8%	12.2%
2,714	GREELEY	226	189	37	Johanns	83.6%	16.4%
53,534	HALL	5,411	4,530	881	Johanns	83.7%	16.3%
9,403	HAMILTON	1,840	1,609	231	Johanns	87.4%	12.6%
3,786	HARLAN	644	551	93	Johanns	85.6%	14.4%
1,068	HAYES	142	122	20	Johanns	85.9%	14.1%
3,111	HITCHCOCK	387	324	63	Johanns	83.7%	16.3%
11,551	HOLT	1,910	1,712	198	Johanns	89.6%	10.4%
783	HOOKER	344	287	57	Johanns	83.4%	16.6%
6,567	HOWARD	832	645	187	Johanns	77.5%	22.5%
8,333	JEFFERSON	1,072	930	142	Johanns	86.8%	13.2%
4,488	JOHNSON	867	700	167	Johanns	80.7%	19.3%
6,882	KEARNEY	972	823	149	Johanns	84.7%	15.3%
8,875	KEITH	1,376	1,205	171	Johanns	87.6%	12.4%
983	KEYA PAHA	347	321	26	Johanns	92.5%	7.5%
4,089	KIMBALL	713	646	67	Johanns	90.6%	9.4%
9,374	KNOX	1,278	1,110	168	Johanns	86.9%	13.1%
250,291	LANCASTER	14,322	12,291	2,031	Johanns	85.8%	14.2%
34,632	LINCOLN	4,092	3,490	602	Johanns	85.3%	14.7%
774	LOGAN	191	162	29	Johanns	84.8%	15.2%
712	LOUP	244	212	32	Johanns	86.9%	13.1%
533	MCPHERSON	135	121	14	Johanns	89.6%	10.4%
35,226	MADISON	3,029	2,619	410	Johanns	86.5%	13.5%

NEBRASKA REPUBLICAN PRIMARY

GOVERNOR 2002

2000 Census Population	County	Total Vote	Johanns	Wicht	Winner	Percentage of Total Vote	
						Johanns	Wicht
8,204	MERRICK	918	788	130	Johanns	85.8%	14.2%
5,440	MORRILL	793	689	104	Johanns	86.9%	13.1%
4,038	NANCE	512	440	72	Johanns	85.9%	14.1%
7,576	NEMAHA	1,024	890	134	Johanns	86.9%	13.1%
5,057	NUCKOLLS	770	660	110	Johanns	85.7%	14.3%
15,396	OTOE	1,318	1,145	173	Johanns	86.9%	13.1%
3,087	PAWNEE	529	457	72	Johanns	86.4%	13.6%
3,200	PERKINS	364	318	46	Johanns	87.4%	12.6%
9,747	PHELPS	1,747	1,542	205	Johanns	88.3%	11.7%
7,857	PIERCE	931	801	130	Johanns	86.0%	14.0%
31,662	PLATTE	3,416	3,047	369	Johanns	89.2%	10.8%
5,639	POLK	776	674	102	Johanns	86.9%	13.1%
11,448	RED WILLOW	1,288	1,135	153	Johanns	88.1%	11.9%
9,531	RICHARDSON	1,094	988	106	Johanns	90.3%	9.7%
1,756	ROCK	408	372	36	Johanns	91.2%	8.8%
13,843	SALINE	953	791	162	Johanns	83.0%	17.0%
122,595	SARPY	5,955	5,372	583	Johanns	90.2%	9.8%
19,830	SAUNDERS	1,690	1,440	250	Johanns	85.2%	14.8%
36,951	SCOTTS BLUFF	5,456	4,929	527	Johanns	90.3%	9.7%
16,496	SEWARD	1,426	1,257	169	Johanns	88.1%	11.9%
6,198	SHERIDAN	1,074	881	193	Johanns	82.0%	18.0%
3,318	SHERMAN	684	568	116	Johanns	83.0%	17.0%
1,475	SIOUX	336	304	32	Johanns	90.5%	9.5%
6,455	STANTON	938	815	123	Johanns	86.9%	13.1%
6,055	THAYER	855	774	81	Johanns	90.5%	9.5%
729	THOMAS	241	205	36	Johanns	85.1%	14.9%
7,171	THURSTON	347	273	74	Johanns	78.7%	21.3%
4,647	VALLEY	897	757	140	Johanns	84.4%	15.6%
18,780	WASHINGTON	2,115	1,890	225	Johanns	89.4%	10.6%
9,851	WAYNE	1,718	1,470	248	Johanns	85.6%	14.4%
4,061	WEBSTER	681	536	145	Johanns	78.7%	21.3%
886	WHEELER	261	227	34	Johanns	87.0%	13.0%
14,598	YORK	2,306	2,036	270	Johanns	88.3%	11.7%
1,711,263	TOTAL	147,718	128,277	19,441	Johanns	86.8%	13.2%

NEBRASKA DEMOCRATIC PRIMARY
GOVERNOR 2002

2000 Census Population	County	Total Vote	Dean	Calvillo	Winner	Percentage of Total Vote Dean	Calvillo
31,151	ADAMS	1,207	868	339	Dean	71.9%	28.1%
7,452	ANTELOPE	348	260	88	Dean	74.7%	25.3%
444	ARTHUR	27	18	9	Dean	66.7%	33.3%
819	BANNER	15	14	1	Dean	93.3%	6.7%
583	BLAINE	25	16	9	Dean	64.0%	36.0%
6,259	BOONE	332	242	90	Dean	72.9%	27.1%
12,158	BOX BUTTE	459	358	101	Dean	78.0%	22.0%
2,438	BOYD	103	84	19	Dean	81.6%	18.4%
3,525	BROWN	122	94	28	Dean	77.0%	23.0%
42,259	BUFFALO	1,386	1,151	235	Dean	83.0%	17.0%
7,791	BURT	313	259	54	Dean	82.7%	17.3%
8,767	BUTLER	406	326	80	Dean	80.3%	19.7%
24,334	CASS	981	772	209	Dean	78.7%	21.3%
9,615	CEDAR	680	488	192	Dean	71.8%	28.2%
4,068	CHASE	226	179	47	Dean	79.2%	20.8%
6,148	CHERRY	227	166	61	Dean	73.1%	26.9%
9,830	CHEYENNE	255	168	87	Dean	65.9%	34.1%
7,039	CLAY	327	247	80	Dean	75.5%	24.5%
10,441	COLFAX	503	416	87	Dean	82.7%	17.3%
10,203	CUMING	252	190	62	Dean	75.4%	24.6%
11,793	CUSTER	643	508	135	Dean	79.0%	21.0%
20,253	DAKOTA	365	274	91	Dean	75.1%	24.9%
9,060	DAWES	231	158	73	Dean	68.4%	31.6%
24,365	DAWSON	682	529	153	Dean	77.6%	22.4%
2,098	DEUEL	58	38	20	Dean	65.5%	34.5%
6,339	DIXON	198	143	55	Dean	72.2%	27.8%
36,160	DODGE	1,202	954	248	Dean	79.4%	20.6%
463,585	DOUGLAS	13,960	10,528	3,432	Dean	75.4%	24.6%
2,292	DUNDY	78	65	13	Dean	83.3%	16.7%
6,634	FILLMORE	331	247	84	Dean	74.6%	25.4%
3,574	FRANKLIN	177	133	44	Dean	75.1%	24.9%
3,099	FRONTIER	131	98	33	Dean	74.8%	25.2%
5,324	FURNAS	285	203	82	Dean	71.2%	28.8%
22,993	GAGE	890	688	202	Dean	77.3%	22.7%
2,292	GARDEN	85	49	36	Dean	57.6%	42.4%
1,902	GARFIELD	64	48	16	Dean	75.0%	25.0%
2,143	GOSPER	85	67	18	Dean	78.8%	21.2%
747	GRANT	28	18	10	Dean	64.3%	35.7%
2,714	GREELEY	339	274	65	Dean	80.8%	19.2%
53,534	HALL	2,413	1,912	501	Dean	79.2%	20.8%
9,403	HAMILTON	359	281	78	Dean	78.3%	21.7%
3,786	HARLAN	222	176	46	Dean	79.3%	20.7%
1,068	HAYES	27	15	12	Dean	55.6%	44.4%
3,111	HITCHCOCK	131	85	46	Dean	64.9%	35.1%
11,551	HOLT	473	323	150	Dean	68.3%	31.7%
783	HOOKER	33	25	8	Dean	75.8%	24.2%
6,567	HOWARD	455	346	109	Dean	76.0%	24.0%
8,333	JEFFERSON	443	341	102	Dean	77.0%	23.0%
4,488	JOHNSON	260	209	51	Dean	80.4%	19.6%
6,882	KEARNEY	354	290	64	Dean	81.9%	18.1%
8,875	KEITH	308	230	78	Dean	74.7%	25.3%
983	KEYA PAHA	51	37	14	Dean	72.5%	27.5%
4,089	KIMBALL	97	76	21	Dean	78.4%	21.6%
9,374	KNOX	543	369	174	Dean	68.0%	32.0%
250,291	LANCASTER	8,540	7,065	1,475	Dean	82.7%	17.3%
34,632	LINCOLN	2,170	1,706	464	Dean	78.6%	21.4%
774	LOGAN	20	14	6	Dean	70.0%	30.0%
712	LOUP	29	22	7	Dean	75.9%	24.1%
533	MCPHERSON	21	18	3	Dean	85.7%	14.3%
35,226	MADISON	589	472	117	Dean	80.1%	19.9%

NEBRASKA DEMOCRATIC PRIMARY

GOVERNOR 2002

2000 Census Population	County	Total Vote	Dean	Calvillo	Winner	Percentage of Total Vote	
						Dean	Calvillo
8,204	MERRICK	302	236	66	Dean	78.1%	21.9%
5,440	MORRILL	192	136	56	Dean	70.8%	29.2%
4,038	NANCE	240	188	52	Dean	78.3%	21.7%
7,576	NEMAHA	501	378	123	Dean	75.4%	24.6%
5,057	NUCKOLLS	315	231	84	Dean	73.3%	26.7%
15,396	OTOE	538	397	141	Dean	73.8%	26.2%
3,087	PAWNEE	200	156	44	Dean	78.0%	22.0%
3,200	PERKINS	121	98	23	Dean	81.0%	19.0%
9,747	PHELPS	390	290	100	Dean	74.4%	25.6%
7,857	PIERCE	154	109	45	Dean	70.8%	29.2%
31,662	PLATTE	1,235	936	299	Dean	75.8%	24.2%
5,639	POLK	221	176	45	Dean	79.6%	20.4%
11,448	RED WILLOW	415	299	116	Dean	72.0%	28.0%
9,531	RICHARDSON	609	446	163	Dean	73.2%	26.8%
1,756	ROCK	65	59	6	Dean	90.8%	9.2%
13,843	SALINE	1,278	1,068	210	Dean	83.6%	16.4%
122,595	SARPY	2,949	2,217	732	Dean	75.2%	24.8%
19,830	SAUNDERS	1,013	774	239	Dean	76.4%	23.6%
36,951	SCOTTS BLUFF	897	678	219	Dean	75.6%	24.4%
16,496	SEWARD	627	486	141	Dean	77.5%	22.5%
6,198	SHERIDAN	171	121	50	Dean	70.8%	29.2%
3,318	SHERMAN	275	219	56	Dean	79.6%	20.4%
1,475	SIOUX	44	29	15	Dean	65.9%	34.1%
6,455	STANTON	155	124	31	Dean	80.0%	20.0%
6,055	THAYER	294	232	62	Dean	78.9%	21.1%
729	THOMAS	25	20	5	Dean	80.0%	20.0%
7,171	THURSTON	501	317	184	Dean	63.3%	36.7%
4,647	VALLEY	322	265	57	Dean	82.3%	17.7%
18,780	WASHINGTON	609	498	111	Dean	81.8%	18.2%
9,851	WAYNE	357	273	84	Dean	76.5%	23.5%
4,061	WEBSTER	240	174	66	Dean	72.5%	27.5%
886	WHEELER	49	39	10	Dean	79.6%	20.4%
14,598	YORK	444	350	94	Dean	78.8%	21.2%
1,711,263	TOTAL	61,312	47,369	13,943	Dean	77.3%	22.7%

NEBRASKA DEMOCRATIC PRIMARY
SENATOR 2002

2000 Census Population	County	Total Vote	Matulka	Hamburg	Winner	Percentage of Total Vote Matulka	Hamburg
31,151	ADAMS	1,092	519	573	Hamburg	47.5%	52.5%
7,452	ANTELOPE	335	130	205	Hamburg	38.8%	61.2%
444	ARTHUR	30	16	14	Matulka	53.3%	46.7%
819	BANNER	17	11	6	Matulka	64.7%	35.3%
583	BLAINE	24	13	11	Matulka	54.2%	45.8%
6,259	BOONE	318	146	172	Hamburg	45.9%	54.1%
12,158	BOX BUTTE	462	257	205	Matulka	55.6%	44.4%
2,438	BOYD	88	44	44		50.0%	50.0%
3,525	BROWN	117	44	73	Hamburg	37.6%	62.4%
42,259	BUFFALO	1,162	612	550	Matulka	52.7%	47.3%
7,791	BURT	261	130	131	Hamburg	49.8%	50.2%
8,767	BUTLER	431	340	91	Matulka	78.9%	21.1%
24,334	CASS	937	548	389	Matulka	58.5%	41.5%
9,615	CEDAR	650	267	383	Hamburg	41.1%	58.9%
4,068	CHASE	188	63	125	Hamburg	33.5%	66.5%
6,148	CHERRY	223	110	113	Hamburg	49.3%	50.7%
9,830	CHEYENNE	250	121	129	Hamburg	48.4%	51.6%
7,039	CLAY	305	127	178	Hamburg	41.6%	58.4%
10,441	COLFAX	518	370	148	Matulka	71.4%	28.6%
10,203	CUMING	222	98	124	Hamburg	44.1%	55.9%
11,793	CUSTER	571	271	300	Hamburg	47.5%	52.5%
20,253	DAKOTA	334	108	226	Hamburg	32.3%	67.7%
9,060	DAWES	223	113	110	Matulka	50.7%	49.3%
24,365	DAWSON	588	242	346	Hamburg	41.2%	58.8%
2,098	DEUEL	59	30	29	Matulka	50.8%	49.2%
6,339	DIXON	197	78	119	Hamburg	39.6%	60.4%
36,160	DODGE	1,145	613	532	Matulka	53.5%	46.5%
463,585	DOUGLAS	12,764	8,442	4,322	Matulka	66.1%	33.9%
2,292	DUNDY	73	27	46	Hamburg	37.0%	63.0%
6,634	FILLMORE	346	198	148	Matulka	57.2%	42.8%
3,574	FRANKLIN	164	69	95	Hamburg	42.1%	57.9%
3,099	FRONTIER	123	48	75	Hamburg	39.0%	61.0%
5,324	FURNAS	260	102	158	Hamburg	39.2%	60.8%
22,993	GAGE	912	578	334	Matulka	63.4%	36.6%
2,292	GARDEN	79	42	37	Matulka	53.2%	46.8%
1,902	GARFIELD	63	34	29	Matulka	54.0%	46.0%
2,143	GOSPER	81	41	40	Matulka	50.6%	49.4%
747	GRANT	28	14	14		50.0%	50.0%
2,714	GREELEY	285	146	139	Matulka	51.2%	48.8%
53,534	HALL	2,218	1,364	854	Matulka	61.5%	38.5%
9,403	HAMILTON	338	156	182	Hamburg	46.2%	53.8%
3,786	HARLAN	195	100	95	Matulka	51.3%	48.7%
1,068	HAYES	30	12	18	Hamburg	40.0%	60.0%
3,111	HITCHCOCK	121	53	68	Hamburg	43.8%	56.2%
11,551	HOLT	469	200	269	Hamburg	42.6%	57.4%
783	HOOKER	32	13	19	Hamburg	40.6%	59.4%
6,567	HOWARD	437	226	211	Matulka	51.7%	48.3%
8,333	JEFFERSON	430	259	171	Matulka	60.2%	39.8%
4,488	JOHNSON	249	160	89	Matulka	64.3%	35.7%
6,882	KEARNEY	299	134	165	Hamburg	44.8%	55.2%
8,875	KEITH	298	148	150	Hamburg	49.7%	50.3%
983	KEYA PAHA	50	18	32	Hamburg	36.0%	64.0%
4,089	KIMBALL	108	64	44	Matulka	59.3%	40.7%
9,374	KNOX	511	218	293	Hamburg	42.7%	57.3%
250,291	LANCASTER	7,709	5,493	2,216	Matulka	71.3%	28.7%
34,632	LINCOLN	2,055	897	1,158	Hamburg	43.6%	56.4%
774	LOGAN	17	5	12	Hamburg	29.4%	70.6%
712	LOUP	26	9	17	Hamburg	34.6%	65.4%
533	MCPHERSON	20	11	9	Matulka	55.0%	45.0%
35,226	MADISON	564	296	268	Matulka	52.5%	47.5%

NEBRASKA DEMOCRATIC PRIMARY

SENATOR 2002

2000 Census Population	County	Total Vote	Matulka	Hamburg	Winner	Percentage of Total Vote Matulka	Hamburg
8,204	MERRICK	277	145	132	Matulka	52.3%	47.7%
5,440	MORRILL	187	104	83	Matulka	55.6%	44.4%
4,038	NANCE	208	114	94	Matulka	54.8%	45.2%
7,576	NEMAHA	454	255	199	Matulka	56.2%	43.8%
5,057	NUCKOLLS	293	133	160	Hamburg	45.4%	54.6%
15,396	OTOE	503	310	193	Matulka	61.6%	38.4%
3,087	PAWNEE	188	121	67	Matulka	64.4%	35.6%
3,200	PERKINS	109	45	64	Hamburg	41.3%	58.7%
9,747	PHELPS	372	169	203	Hamburg	45.4%	54.6%
7,857	PIERCE	150	61	89	Hamburg	40.7%	59.3%
31,662	PLATTE	1,234	869	365	Matulka	70.4%	29.6%
5,639	POLK	217	147	70	Matulka	67.7%	32.3%
11,448	RED WILLOW	386	160	226	Hamburg	41.5%	58.5%
9,531	RICHARDSON	591	284	307	Hamburg	48.1%	51.9%
1,756	ROCK	42	20	22	Hamburg	47.6%	52.4%
13,843	SALINE	1,174	750	424	Matulka	63.9%	36.1%
122,595	SARPY	2,784	1,657	1,127	Matulka	59.5%	40.5%
19,830	SAUNDERS	1,087	826	261	Matulka	76.0%	24.0%
36,951	SCOTTS BLUFF	950	612	338	Matulka	64.4%	35.6%
16,496	SEWARD	609	465	144	Matulka	76.4%	23.6%
6,198	SHERIDAN	174	83	91	Hamburg	47.7%	52.3%
3,318	SHERMAN	268	154	114	Matulka	57.5%	42.5%
1,475	SIOUX	43	23	20	Matulka	53.5%	46.5%
6,455	STANTON	146	76	70	Matulka	52.1%	47.9%
6,055	THAYER	281	142	139	Matulka	50.5%	49.5%
729	THOMAS	25	20	5	Matulka	80.0%	20.0%
7,171	THURSTON	468	193	275	Hamburg	41.2%	58.8%
4,647	VALLEY	314	174	140	Matulka	55.4%	44.6%
18,780	WASHINGTON	508	287	221	Matulka	56.5%	43.5%
9,851	WAYNE	342	146	196	Hamburg	42.7%	57.3%
4,061	WEBSTER	237	109	128	Hamburg	46.0%	54.0%
886	WHEELER	46	15	31	Hamburg	32.6%	67.4%
14,598	YORK	426	255	171	Matulka	59.9%	40.1%
1,711,263	TOTAL	57,194	33,922	23,272	Matulka	59.3%	40.7%

NEVADA

GOVERNOR
Kenny Guinn (R). Reelected 2002 to a four-year term. Previously elected 1998.

SENATORS (1 Democrat, 1 Republican)
John Ensign (R). Elected 2000 to a six-year term.

Harry Reid (D). Reelected 1998 to a six-year term. Previously elected 1992, 1986.

REPRESENTATIVES (2 Republicans, 1 Democrat)
1. Shelley Berkley (D)
2. Jim Gibbons (R)
3. Jon Porter (R)

POSTWAR VOTE FOR PRESIDENT

Year	Total Vote	Republican Vote	Republican Candidate	Democratic Vote	Democratic Candidate	Other Vote	Plurality	Total Vote Rep.	Total Vote Dem.	Major Vote Rep.	Major Vote Dem.
2000**	608,970	301,575	Bush, George W.	279,978	Gore, Al	27,417	21,597 R	49.5%	46.0%	51.9%	48.1%
1996**	464,279	199,244	Dole, Bob	203,974	Clinton, Bill	61,061	4,730 D	42.9%	43.9%	49.4%	50.6%
1992**	506,318	175,828	Bush, George	189,148	Clinton, Bill	141,342	13,320 D	34.7%	37.4%	48.2%	51.8%
1988	350,067	206,040	Bush, George	132,738	Dukakis, Michael S.	11,289	73,302 R	58.9%	37.9%	60.8%	39.2%
1984	286,667	188,770	Reagan, Ronald	91,655	Mondale, Walter F.	6,242	97,115 R	65.8%	32.0%	67.3%	32.7%
1980**	247,885	155,017	Reagan, Ronald	66,666	Carter, Jimmy	26,202	88,351 R	62.5%	26.9%	69.9%	30.1%
1976	201,876	101,273	Ford, Gerald R.	92,479	Carter, Jimmy	8,124	8,794 R	50.2%	45.8%	52.3%	47.7%
1972	181,766	115,750	Nixon, Richard M.	66,016	McGovern, George S.		49,734 R	63.7%	36.3%	63.7%	36.3%
1968	154,218	73,188	Nixon, Richard M.	60,598	Humphrey, Hubert H.	20,432	12,590 R	47.5%	39.3%	54.7%	45.3%
1964	135,433	56,094	Goldwater, Barry M.	79,339	Johnson, Lyndon B.		23,245 D	41.4%	58.6%	41.4%	58.6%
1960	107,267	52,387	Nixon, Richard M.	54,880	Kennedy, John F.		2,493 D	48.8%	51.2%	48.8%	51.2%
1956	96,689	56,049	Eisenhower, Dwight D.	40,640	Stevenson, Adlai E.		15,409 R	58.0%	42.0%	58.0%	42.0%
1952	82,190	50,502	Eisenhower, Dwight D.	31,688	Stevenson, Adlai E.		18,814 R	61.4%	38.6%	61.4%	38.6%
1948	62,117	29,357	Dewey, Thomas E.	31,291	Truman, Harry S.	1,469	1,934 D	47.3%	50.4%	48.4%	51.6%

In 2000 the other vote column includes 15,008 votes cast for Green (Nader). In 1996 the other vote column includes 43,986 votes cast for Perot. In 1992 the other vote column includes 132,580 votes cast for Perot. In 1980 the other vote column includes 17,651 votes for Independent (Anderson).

POSTWAR VOTE FOR GOVERNOR

Year	Total Vote	Republican Vote	Republican Candidate	Democratic Vote	Democratic Candidate	Other Vote	Rep.-Dem. Plurality	Total Vote Rep.	Total Vote Dem.	Major Vote Rep.	Major Vote Dem.
2002	504,079	344,001	Guinn, Kenny	110,935	Neal, Joe	49,143	233,066 R	68.2%	22.0%	75.6%	24.4%
1998	433,630	223,892	Guinn, Kenny	182,281	Jones, Jan Laverty	27,457	41,611 R	51.6%	42.0%	55.1%	44.9%
1994	379,676	156,875	Gibbons, Jim	200,026	Miller, Robert J.	22,775	43,151 D	41.3%	52.7%	44.0%	56.0%
1990	320,743	95,789	Gallaway, Jim	207,878	Miller, Robert J.	17,076	112,089 D	29.9%	64.8%	31.5%	68.5%
1986	260,375	65,081	Cafferata, Patty	187,268	Bryan, Richard H.	8,026	122,187 D	25.0%	71.9%	25.8%	74.2%
1982	239,751	100,104	List, Robert F.	128,132	Bryan, Richard H.	11,515	28,028 D	41.8%	53.4%	43.9%	56.1%
1978	192,445	108,097	List, Robert F.	76,361	Rose, Robert E.	7,987	31,736 R	56.2%	39.7%	58.6%	41.4%
1974	169,358	28,959	Crumpler, Shirley	114,114	O'Callaghan, Mike	26,285	85,155 D	17.1%	67.4%	20.2%	79.8%
1970	146,991	64,400	Fike, Ed	70,697	O'Callaghan, Mike	11,894	6,297 D	43.8%	48.1%	47.7%	52.3%
1966	137,677	71,807	Laxalt, Paul	65,870	Sawyer, Grant		5,937 R	52.2%	47.8%	52.2%	47.8%
1962	96,929	32,145	Gragson, Oran K.	64,784	Sawyer, Grant		32,639 D	33.2%	66.8%	33.2%	66.8%
1958	84,889	34,025	Russell, Charles H.	50,864	Sawyer, Grant		16,839 D	40.1%	59.9%	40.1%	59.9%
1954	78,462	41,665	Russell, Charles H.	36,797	Pittman, Vail		4,868 R	53.1%	46.9%	53.1%	46.9%
1950	61,773	35,609	Russell, Charles H.	26,164	Pittman, Vail		9,445 R	57.6%	42.4%	57.6%	42.4%
1946	49,902	21,247	Jepson, Melvin E.	28,655	Pittman, Vail		7,408 D	42.6%	57.4%	42.6%	57.4%

NEVADA

POSTWAR VOTE FOR SENATOR

Year	Total Vote	Republican Vote	Candidate	Democratic Vote	Candidate	Other Vote	Rep.-Dem. Plurality	Total Vote Rep.	Dem.	Major Vote Rep.	Dem.
2000	600,250	330,687	Ensign, John	238,260	Bernstein, Ed	31,303	92,427 R	55.1%	39.7%	58.1%	41.9%
1998	435,790	208,222	Ensign, John	208,650	Reid, Harry	18,918	428 D	47.8%	47.9%	49.9%	50.1%
1994	380,530	156,020	Furman, Hal	193,804	Bryan, Richard H.	30,706	37,784 D	41.0%	50.9%	44.6%	55.4%
1992	495,887	199,413	Dahl, Demar	253,150	Reid, Harry	43,324	53,737 D	40.2%	51.0%	44.1%	55.9%
1988	349,649	161,336	Hecht, Chic	175,548	Bryan, Richard H.	12,765	14,212 D	46.1%	50.2%	47.9%	52.1%
1986	261,932	116,606	Santini, James	130,955	Reid, Harry	14,371	14,349 D	44.5%	50.0%	47.1%	52.9%
1982	240,394	120,377	Hecht, Chic	114,720	Cannon, Howard W.	5,297	5,657 R	50.1%	47.7%	51.2%	48.8%
1980	246,436	144,224	Laxalt, Paul	92,129	Gojack, Mary	10,083	52,095 R	58.5%	37.4%	61.0%	39.0%
1976	201,980	63,471	Towell, David	127,295	Cannon, Howard W.	11,214	63,824 D	31.4%	63.0%	33.3%	66.7%
1974	169,473	79,605	Laxalt, Paul	78,981	Reid, Harry	10,887	624 R	47.0%	46.6%	50.2%	49.8%
1970	147,768	60,838	Raggio, William J.	85,187	Cannon, Howard W.	1,743	24,349 D	41.2%	57.6%	41.7%	58.3%
1968	152,690	69,068	Fike, Ed	83,622	Bible, Alan		14,554 D	45.2%	54.8%	45.2%	54.8%
1964	134,624	67,288	Laxalt, Paul	67,336	Cannon, Howard W.		48 D	50.0%	50.0%	50.0%	50.0%
1962	97,192	33,749	Wright, William B.	63,443	Bible, Alan		29,694 D	34.7%	65.3%	34.7%	65.3%
1958	84,492	35,760	Malone, George W.	48,732	Cannon, Howard W.		12,972 D	42.3%	57.7%	42.3%	57.7%
1956	96,389	45,712	Young, Clifton	50,677	Bible, Alan		4,965 D	47.4%	52.6%	47.4%	52.6%
1954S	77,513	32,470	Brown, Ernest S.	45,043	Bible, Alan		12,573 D	41.9%	58.1%	41.9%	58.1%
1952	81,090	41,906	Malone, George W.	39,184	Mechling, Thomas B.		2,722 R	51.7%	48.3%	51.7%	48.3%
1950	61,762	25,933	Marshall, George E.	35,829	McCarran, Pat		9,896 D	42.0%	58.0%	42.0%	58.0%
1946	50,354	27,801	Malone, George W.	22,553	Bunker, Berkeley		5,248 R	55.2%	44.8%	55.2%	44.8%

The 1954 election was for a short term to fill a vacancy.

NEVADA

Congressional districts first established for elections held in 2002
3 members

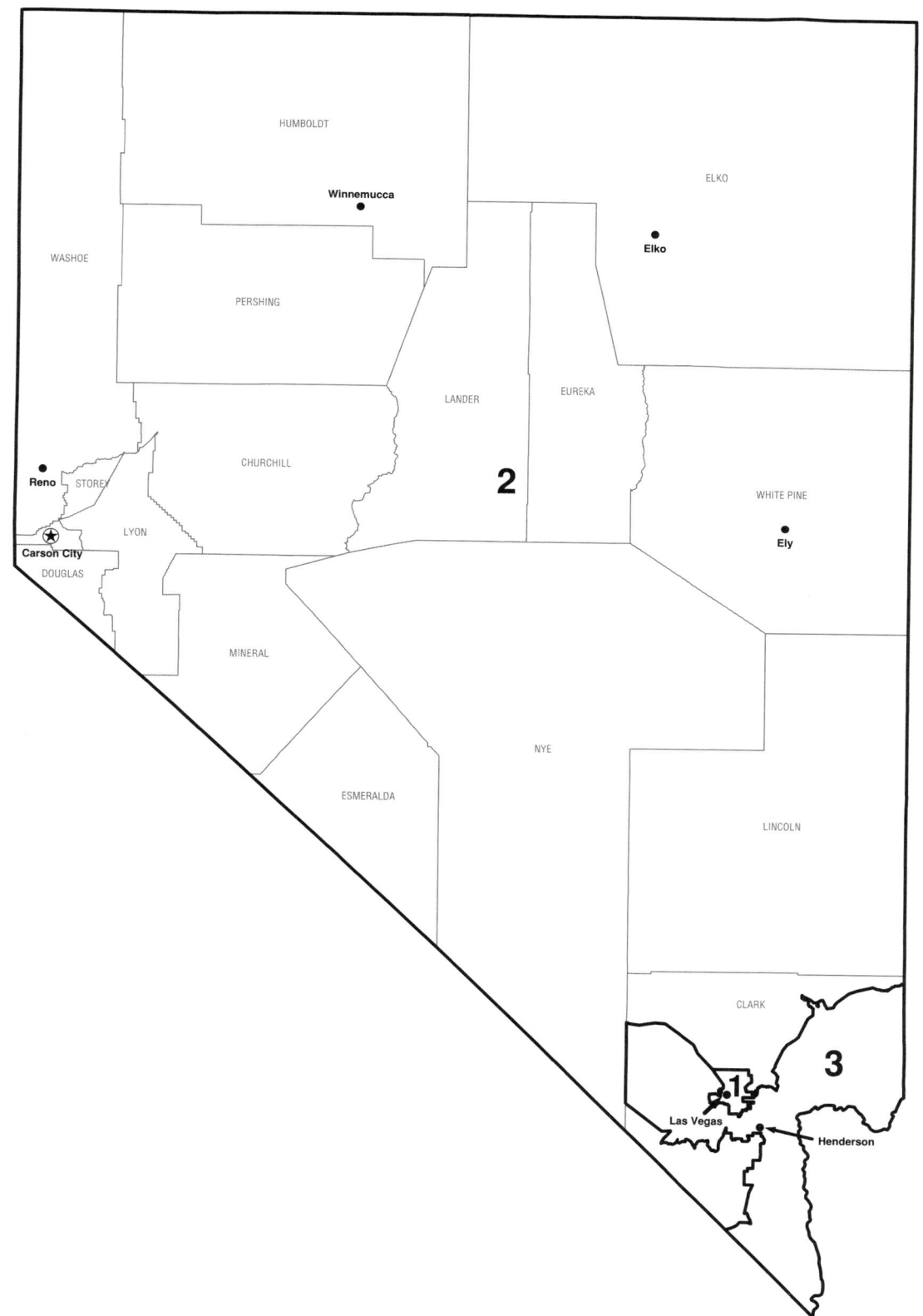

NEVADA

GOVERNOR 2002

2000 Census Population	County	Total Vote	Republican	Democratic	Other	Rep.-Dem. Plurality		Percentage			
								Total Vote		Major Vote	
								Rep.	Dem.	Rep.	Dem.
52,457	CARSON CITY	17,272	12,051	3,448	1,773	8,603 R		69.8%	20.0%	77.8%	22.2%
23,982	CHURCHILL	7,376	5,867	952	557	4,915 R		79.5%	12.9%	86.0%	14.0%
1,375,765	CLARK	307,003	200,157	74,378	32,468	125,779 R		65.2%	24.2%	72.9%	27.1%
41,259	DOUGLAS	16,758	12,977	2,520	1,261	10,457 R		77.4%	15.0%	83.7%	16.3%
45,291	ELKO	11,038	8,568	1,386	1,084	7,182 R		77.6%	12.6%	86.1%	13.9%
971	ESMERALDA	439	286	87	66	199 R		65.1%	19.8%	76.7%	23.3%
1,651	EUREKA	687	525	85	77	440 R		76.4%	12.4%	86.1%	13.9%
16,106	HUMBOLDT	4,307	3,446	522	339	2,924 R		80.0%	12.1%	86.8%	13.2%
5,794	LANDER	1,863	1,503	231	129	1,272 R		80.7%	12.4%	86.7%	13.3%
4,165	LINCOLN	1,732	1,266	279	187	987 R		73.1%	16.1%	81.9%	18.1%
34,501	LYON	10,892	8,169	1,796	927	6,373 R		75.0%	16.5%	82.0%	18.0%
5,071	MINERAL	2,032	1,290	508	234	782 R		63.5%	25.0%	71.7%	28.3%
32,485	NYE	10,779	7,349	2,226	1,204	5,123 R		68.2%	20.7%	76.8%	23.2%
6,693	PERSHING	1,668	1,254	236	178	1,018 R		75.2%	14.1%	84.2%	15.8%
3,399	STOREY	1,648	1,198	300	150	898 R		72.7%	18.2%	80.0%	20.0%
339,486	WASHOE	105,560	76,059	21,244	8,257	54,815 R		72.1%	20.1%	78.2%	21.8%
9,181	WHITE PINE	3,025	2,036	737	252	1,299 R		67.3%	24.4%	73.4%	26.6%
1,998,257	TOTAL	504,079	344,001	110,935	49,143	233,066 R		68.2%	22.0%	75.6%	24.4%

NEVADA

HOUSE OF REPRESENTATIVES

CD	Year	Total Vote	Republican		Democratic		Other Vote	Rep.-Dem. Plurality	Percentage			
			Vote	Candidate	Vote	Candidate			Total Vote		Major Vote	
									Rep.	Dem.	Rep.	Dem.
1	2002	119,714	51,148	Boggs-McDonald, Lynette Maria	64,312	Berkley, Shelley*	4,254	13,164 D	42.7%	53.7%	44.3%	55.7%
2	2002	201,200	149,574	Gibbons, Jim*	40,189	Souza, Travis O.	11,437	109,385 R	74.3%	20.0%	78.8%	21.2%
3	2002	178,994	100,378	Porter, Jon	66,659	Herrera, Dario	11,957	33,719 R	56.1%	37.2%	60.1%	39.9%
Total	2002	499,908	301,100		171,160		27,648	129,940 R	60.2%	34.2%	63.8%	36.2%

An asterisk (*) denotes incumbent.

NEVADA

GENERAL AND PRIMARY ELECTIONS

2002 GENERAL ELECTIONS

Governor Other vote was 23,674 "None of These Candidates"; 8,104 Libertarian (Dick Geyer); 7,047 Independent American (David G. Holmgren); 5,543 Independent (Jerry L. Norton); 4,775 Green (Charles Laws).

House Other vote was:

CD 1 2,861 Independent American (Steven "Capt. Truth" Dempsey); 1,393 Green (W. Lane Startin).

CD 2 7,240 Independent American (Janine Hansen); 3,413 Libertarian (Brendan Trainor); 784 Natural Law (Robert "Stickerman" Winquist).

CD 3 6,842 Independent (Pete O'Neil); 3,421 Libertarian (Neil Scott); 1,694 Independent American (Richard Wayne Odell).

2002 PRIMARY ELECTIONS

Primary September 3, 2002

Registration (as of July 31, 2002)

Republican	351,022
Democratic	339,691
Independent American	14,518
Libertarian	4,479
Green	1,933
Natural Law	597
Reform	587
Other	1,156
Nonpartisan	115,639
TOTAL	829,622

Primary Type Closed—Only registered Democrats and Republicans could vote in their party's primary.

Note: An asterisk (*) denotes incumbent. The names of unopposed candidates did not appear on the primary ballot; therefore, no votes were cast for these candidates.

	REPUBLICAN PRIMARIES			DEMOCRATIC PRIMARIES		
Governor	Kenny Guinn*	97,367	82.9%	Joe Neal	31,805	35.7%
	Shirley Cook	7,717	6.6%	None of These Candidates	21,875	24.6%
	None of These Candidates	7,195	6.1%	Barbara Scott	18,974	21.3%
	Bruce Westcott	2,507	2.1%	Dan Meyer	11,403	12.8%
	Bill Hiett	1,167	1.0%	Christopher J. Petrella	4,917	5.5%
	Stanleigh Harold Lusak	566	0.5%			
	James K. Prevot	560	0.5%			
	Poliak	395	0.3%			
	TOTAL	117,474		TOTAL	88,974	
Congressional District 1	Lynette Maria Boggs-McDonald	16,838	78.9%	Shelley Berkley*	Unopposed	
	Alfred Ordunez	4,506	21.1%			
	TOTAL	21,344				
Congressional District 2	Jim Gibbons*	Unopposed		Travis O. Souza	Unopposed	
Congresional District 3	Jon Porter	25,446	68.6%	Dario Herrera	20,773	68.8%
	Barry D. Bilbray	6,179	16.7%	Mark J. Budetich Jr.	9,419	31.2%
	Susan Kiger	3,407	9.2%			
	Bob Daily	2,052	5.5%			
	TOTAL	37,084		TOTAL	30,192	

NEVADA REPUBLICAN PRIMARY

GOVERNOR 2002

2000 Census Population	County	Total Vote	Guinn	Other	Winner	Percentage of Total Vote	
						Guinn	Other
52,457	CARSON CITY	5,706	4,708	998	Guinn	82.5%	17.5%
23,982	CHURCHILL	1,901	1,665	236	Guinn	87.6%	12.4%
1,375,765	CLARK	61,902	49,884	12,018	Guinn	80.6%	19.4%
41,259	DOUGLAS	4,020	3,531	489	Guinn	87.8%	12.2%
45,291	ELKO	3,663	3,083	580	Guinn	84.2%	15.8%
971	ESMERALDA	152	103	49	Guinn	67.8%	32.2%
1,651	EUREKA	433	349	84	Guinn	80.6%	19.4%
16,106	HUMBOLDT	1,613	1,379	234	Guinn	85.5%	14.5%
5,794	LANDER	757	626	131	Guinn	82.7%	17.3%
4,165	LINCOLN	631	510	121	Guinn	80.8%	19.2%
34,501	LYON	3,310	2,809	501	Guinn	84.9%	15.1%
5,071	MINERAL	550	422	128	Guinn	76.7%	23.3%
32,485	NYE	3,547	2,881	666	Guinn	81.2%	18.8%
6,693	PERSHING	649	535	114	Guinn	82.4%	17.6%
3,399	STOREY	644	537	107	Guinn	83.4%	16.6%
339,486	WASHOE	27,214	23,689	3,525	Guinn	87.0%	13.0%
9,181	WHITE PINE	782	656	126	Guinn	83.9%	16.1%
1,998,257	TOTAL	117,474	97,367	20,107	Guinn	82.9%	17.1%

NEVADA DEMOCRATIC PRIMARY

GOVERNOR 2002

2000 Census Population	County	Total Vote	Neal	"None"	Scott	Meyer	Petrella	Winner	Percentage of Total Vote				
									Neal	"None"	Scott	Meyer	Petrella
52,457	CARSON CITY	3,166	1,233	839	670	319	105	Neal	38.9%	26.5%	21.2%	10.1%	3.3%
23,982	CHURCHILL	747	219	232	195	78	23	"None"	29.3%	31.1%	26.1%	10.4%	3.1%
1,375,765	CLARK	57,092	21,855	12,884	11,288	7,523	3,542	Neal	38.3%	22.6%	19.8%	13.2%	6.2%
41,259	DOUGLAS	1,251	420	276	342	151	62	Neal	33.6%	22.1%	27.3%	12.1%	5.0%
45,291	ELKO	1,413	316	474	379	191	53	"None"	22.4%	33.5%	26.8%	13.5%	3.8%
971	ESMERALDA	92	17	33	27	7	8	"None"	18.5%	35.9%	29.3%	7.6%	8.7%
1,651	EUREKA	145	24	63	36	19	3	"None"	16.6%	43.4%	24.8%	13.1%	2.1%
16,106	HUMBOLDT	928	172	347	222	142	45	"None"	18.5%	37.4%	23.9%	15.3%	4.8%
5,794	LANDER	458	80	168	91	97	22	"None"	17.5%	36.7%	19.9%	21.2%	4.8%
4,165	LINCOLN	417	131	138	67	68	13	"None"	31.4%	33.1%	16.1%	16.3%	3.1%
34,501	LYON	1,864	454	510	590	233	77	Scott	24.4%	27.4%	31.7%	12.5%	4.1%
5,071	MINERAL	802	212	268	207	78	37	"None"	26.4%	33.4%	25.8%	9.7%	4.6%
32,485	NYE	2,778	620	909	708	380	161	"None"	22.3%	32.7%	25.5%	13.7%	5.8%
6,693	PERSHING	500	97	207	120	55	21	"None"	19.4%	41.4%	24.0%	11.0%	4.2%
3,399	STOREY	410	125	120	88	62	15	Neal	30.5%	29.3%	21.5%	15.1%	3.7%
339,486	WASHOE	15,844	5,563	4,001	3,751	1,888	641	Neal	35.1%	25.3%	23.7%	11.9%	4.0%
9,181	WHITE PINE	1,067	267	406	193	112	89	"None"	25.0%	38.1%	18.1%	10.5%	8.3%
1,998,257	TOTAL	88,974	31,805	21,875	18,974	11,403	4,917	Neal	35.7%	24.6%	21.3%	12.8%	5.5%

NEW HAMPSHIRE

GOVERNOR
Craig Benson (R). Elected 2002 to a two-year term.

SENATORS (2 Republicans)
Judd Gregg (R). Reelected 1998 to a six-year term. Previously elected 1992.

John E. Sununu (R). Elected 2002 to a six-year term.

REPRESENTATIVES (2 Republicans)
1. Jeb Bradley (R)
2. Charles Bass (R)

POSTWAR VOTE FOR PRESIDENT

Year	Total Vote	Republican		Democratic		Other Vote	Plurality	Percentage			
								Total Vote		Major Vote	
		Vote	Candidate	Vote	Candidate			Rep.	Dem.	Rep.	Dem.
2000**	569,081	273,559	Bush, George W.	266,348	Gore, Al	29,174	7,211 R	48.1%	46.8%	50.7%	49.3%
1996**	499,175	196,532	Dole, Bob	246,214	Clinton, Bill	56,429	49,682 D	39.4%	49.3%	44.4%	55.6%
1992**	537,943	202,484	Bush, George	209,040	Clinton, Bill	126,419	6,556 D	37.6%	38.9%	44.4%	55.6%
1988	451,074	281,537	Bush, George	163,696	Dukakis, Michael S.	5,841	117,841 R	62.4%	36.3%	63.2%	36.8%
1984	389,066	267,051	Reagan, Ronald	120,395	Mondale, Walter F.	1,620	146,656 R	68.6%	30.9%	68.9%	31.1%
1980**	383,990	221,705	Reagan, Ronald	108,864	Carter, Jimmy	53,421	112,841 R	57.7%	28.4%	67.1%	32.9%
1976	339,618	185,935	Ford, Gerald R.	147,635	Carter, Jimmy	6,048	38,300 R	54.7%	43.5%	55.7%	44.3%
1972	334,055	213,724	Nixon, Richard M.	116,435	McGovern, George S.	3,896	97,289 R	64.0%	34.9%	64.7%	35.3%
1968	297,298	154,903	Nixon, Richard M.	130,589	Humphrey, Hubert H.	11,806	24,314 R	52.1%	43.9%	54.3%	45.7%
1964	288,093	104,029	Goldwater, Barry M.	184,064	Johnson, Lyndon B.		80,035 D	36.1%	63.9%	36.1%	63.9%
1960	295,761	157,989	Nixon, Richard M.	137,772	Kennedy, John F.		20,217 R	53.4%	46.6%	53.4%	46.6%
1956	266,994	176,519	Eisenhower, Dwight D.	90,364	Stevenson, Adlai E.	111	86,155 R	66.1%	33.8%	66.1%	33.9%
1952	272,950	166,287	Eisenhower, Dwight D.	106,663	Stevenson, Adlai E.		59,624 R	60.9%	39.1%	60.9%	39.1%
1948	231,440	121,299	Dewey, Thomas E.	107,995	Truman, Harry S.	2,146	13,304 R	52.4%	46.7%	52.9%	47.1%

In 2000 the other vote column includes 22,198 votes cast for Green (Nader). In 1996 the other vote column includes 48,390 votes cast for Perot. In 1992 the other vote column includes 121,337 votes cast for Perot. In 1980 the other vote column includes 49,693 votes for Independent (Anderson).

NEW HAMPSHIRE

POSTWAR VOTE FOR GOVERNOR

Year	Total Vote	Republican		Democratic		Other Vote	Rep.-Dem. Plurality	Percentage			
		Vote	Candidate	Vote	Candidate			Total Vote		Major Vote	
								Rep.	Dem.	Rep.	Dem.
2002	442,976	259,663	Benson, Craig	169,277	Fernald, Mark	14,036	90,386 R	58.6%	38.2%	60.5%	39.5%
2000	564,953	246,952	Humphrey, Gordon J.	275,038	Shaheen, Jeanne	42,963	28,086 D	43.7%	48.7%	47.3%	52.7%
1998	318,940	98,473	Lucas, Jay	210,769	Shaheen, Jeanne	9,698	112,296 D	30.9%	66.1%	31.8%	68.2%
1996	497,040	196,321	Lamontagne, Ovide	284,175	Shaheen, Jeanne	16,544	87,854 D	39.5%	57.2%	40.9%	59.1%
1994	311,882	218,134	Merrill, Steve	79,686	King, Wayne D.	14,062	138,448 R	69.9%	25.6%	73.2%	26.8%
1992	516,170	289,170	Merrill, Steve	206,232	Arnesen, Deborah A.	20,768	82,938 R	56.0%	40.0%	58.4%	41.6%
1990	295,018	177,773	Gregg, Judd	101,923	Grandmaison, J. Joseph	15,322	75,850 R	60.3%	34.5%	63.6%	36.4%
1988	441,923	267,064	Gregg, Judd	172,543	McEachern, Paul	2,316	94,521 R	60.4%	39.0%	60.8%	39.2%
1986	251,107	134,824	Sununu, John H.	116,142	McEachern, Paul	141	18,682 R	53.7%	46.3%	53.7%	46.3%
1984	383,910	256,574	Sununu, John H.	127,156	Spirou, Chris	180	129,418 R	66.8%	33.1%	66.9%	33.1%
1982	282,588	145,389	Sununu, John H.	132,317	Gallen, Hugh J.	4,882	13,072 R	51.4%	46.8%	52.4%	47.6%
1980	384,031	156,178	Thomson, Meldrim	226,436	Gallen, Hugh J.	1,417	70,258 D	40.7%	59.0%	40.8%	59.2%
1978	269,587	122,464	Thomson, Meldrim	133,133	Gallen, Hugh J.	13,990	10,669 D	45.4%	49.4%	47.9%	52.1%
1976	342,669	197,589	Thomson, Meldrim	145,015	Spanos, Harry V.	65	52,574 R	57.7%	42.3%	57.7%	42.3%
1974	226,665	115,933	Thomson, Meldrim	110,591	Leonard, Richard W.	141	5,342 R	51.1%	48.8%	51.2%	48.8%
1972	323,102	133,702	Thomson, Meldrim	126,107	Crowley, Roger J.	63,293	7,595 R	41.4%	39.0%	51.5%	48.5%
1970	222,441	102,298	Peterson, Walter R.	98,098	Crowley, Roger J.	22,045	4,200 R	46.0%	44.1%	51.0%	49.0%
1968	285,342	149,902	Peterson, Walter R.	135,378	Bussiere, Emile R.	62	14,524 R	52.5%	47.4%	52.5%	47.5%
1966	233,642	107,259	Gregg, Hugh	125,882	King, John W.	501	18,623 D	45.9%	53.9%	46.0%	54.0%
1964	285,863	94,824	Pillsbury, John	190,863	King, John W.	176	96,039 D	33.2%	66.8%	33.2%	66.8%
1962	230,048	94,567	Pillsbury, John	135,481	King, John W.		40,914 D	41.1%	58.9%	41.1%	58.9%
1960	290,527	161,123	Powell, Wesley	129,404	Boutin, Bernard L.		31,719 R	55.5%	44.5%	55.5%	44.5%
1958	206,745	106,790	Powell, Wesley	99,955	Boutin, Bernard L.		6,835 R	51.7%	48.3%	51.7%	48.3%
1956	258,695	141,578	Dwinell, Lane	117,117	Shaw, John		24,461 R	54.7%	45.3%	54.7%	45.3%
1954	194,631	107,287	Dwinell, Lane	87,344	Shaw, John		19,943 R	55.1%	44.9%	55.1%	44.9%
1952	265,715	167,791	Gregg, Hugh	97,924	Craig, William H.		69,867 R	63.1%	36.9%	63.1%	36.9%
1950	191,239	108,907	Adams, Sherman	82,258	Bingham, Robert P.	74	26,649 R	56.9%	43.0%	57.0%	43.0%
1948	222,571	116,212	Adams, Sherman	105,207	Hill, Herbert W.	1,152	11,005 R	52.2%	47.3%	52.5%	47.5%
1946	163,451	103,204	Dale, Charles M.	60,247	Keefe, F. Clyde		42,957 R	63.1%	36.9%	63.1%	36.9%

POSTWAR VOTE FOR SENATOR

Year	Total Vote	Republican		Democratic		Other Vote	Rep.-Dem. Plurality	Percentage			
		Vote	Candidate	Vote	Candidate			Total Vote		Major Vote	
								Rep.	Dem.	Rep.	Dem.
2002	447,135	227,229	Sununu, John E.	207,478	Shaheen, Jeanne	12,428	19,751 R	50.8%	46.4%	52.3%	47.7%
1998	314,956	213,477	Gregg, Judd	88,883	Condodemetraky, George	12,596	124,594 R	67.8%	28.2%	70.6%	29.4%
1996	492,598	242,304	Smith, Robert C.	227,397	Swett, Dick	22,897	14,907 R	49.2%	46.2%	51.6%	48.4%
1992	518,416	249,591	Gregg, Judd	234,982	Rauh, John	33,843	14,609 R	48.1%	45.3%	51.5%	48.5%
1990	291,393	189,792	Smith, Robert C.	91,299	Durkin, John A.	10,302	98,493 R	65.1%	31.3%	67.5%	32.5%
1986	244,797	154,090	Rudman, Warren	79,225	Peabody, Endicott	11,482	74,865 R	62.9%	32.4%	66.0%	34.0%
1984	384,406	225,828	Humphrey, Gordon J.	157,447	D'Amours, Norman E.	1,131	68,381 R	58.7%	41.0%	58.9%	41.1%
1980	375,064	195,563	Rudman, Warren	179,455	Durkin, John A.	46	16,108 R	52.1%	47.8%	52.1%	47.9%
1978	263,779	133,745	Humphrey, Gordon J.	127,945	McIntyre, Thomas J.	2,089	5,800 R	50.7%	48.5%	51.1%	48.9%
1975S	262,682	113,007	Wyman, Louis C.	140,778	Durkin, John A.	8,897	27,771 D	43.0%	53.6%	44.5%	55.5%
1974**	223,363	110,926	Wyman, Louis C.	110,924	Durkin, John A.	1,513	2 R	49.7%	49.7%	50.0%	50.0%
1972	324,354	139,852	Powell, Wesley	184,495	McIntyre, Thomas J.	7	44,643 D	43.1%	56.9%	43.1%	56.9%
1968	286,989	170,163	Cotton, Norris	116,816	King, John W.	10	53,347 R	59.3%	40.7%	59.3%	40.7%
1966	229,305	105,241	Thyng, Harrison R.	123,888	McIntyre, Thomas J.	176	18,647 D	45.9%	54.0%	45.9%	54.1%
1962	224,479	134,035	Cotton, Norris	90,444	Catalfo, Alfred		43,591 R	59.7%	40.3%	59.7%	40.3%
1962S	224,811	107,199	Bass, Perkins	117,612	McIntyre, Thomas J.		10,413 D	47.7%	52.3%	47.7%	52.3%
1960	287,545	173,521	Bridges, Styles	114,024	Hill, Herbert W.		59,497 R	60.3%	39.7%	60.3%	39.7%
1956	251,943	161,424	Cotton, Norris	90,519	Pickett, Laurence M.		70,905 R	64.1%	35.9%	64.1%	35.9%
1954	194,536	117,150	Bridges, Styles	77,386	Morin, Gerard L.		39,764 R	60.2%	39.8%	60.2%	39.8%
1954S	189,558	114,068	Cotton, Norris	75,490	Bentley, Stanley J.		38,578 R	60.2%	39.8%	60.2%	39.8%
1950	190,573	106,142	Tobey, Charles W.	72,473	Kelley, Emmet J.	11,958	33,669 R	55.7%	38.0%	59.4%	40.6%
1948	222,898	129,600	Bridges, Styles	91,760	Fortin, Alfred E.	1,538	37,840 R	58.1%	41.2%	58.5%	41.5%

Following the 1974 election, neither candidate was seated and the 1975 special election was held for the remaining years of that term. One each of the 1962 and 1954 elections were for short terms to fill vacancies.

NEW HAMPSHIRE

Congressional districts first established for elections held in 2002
2 members

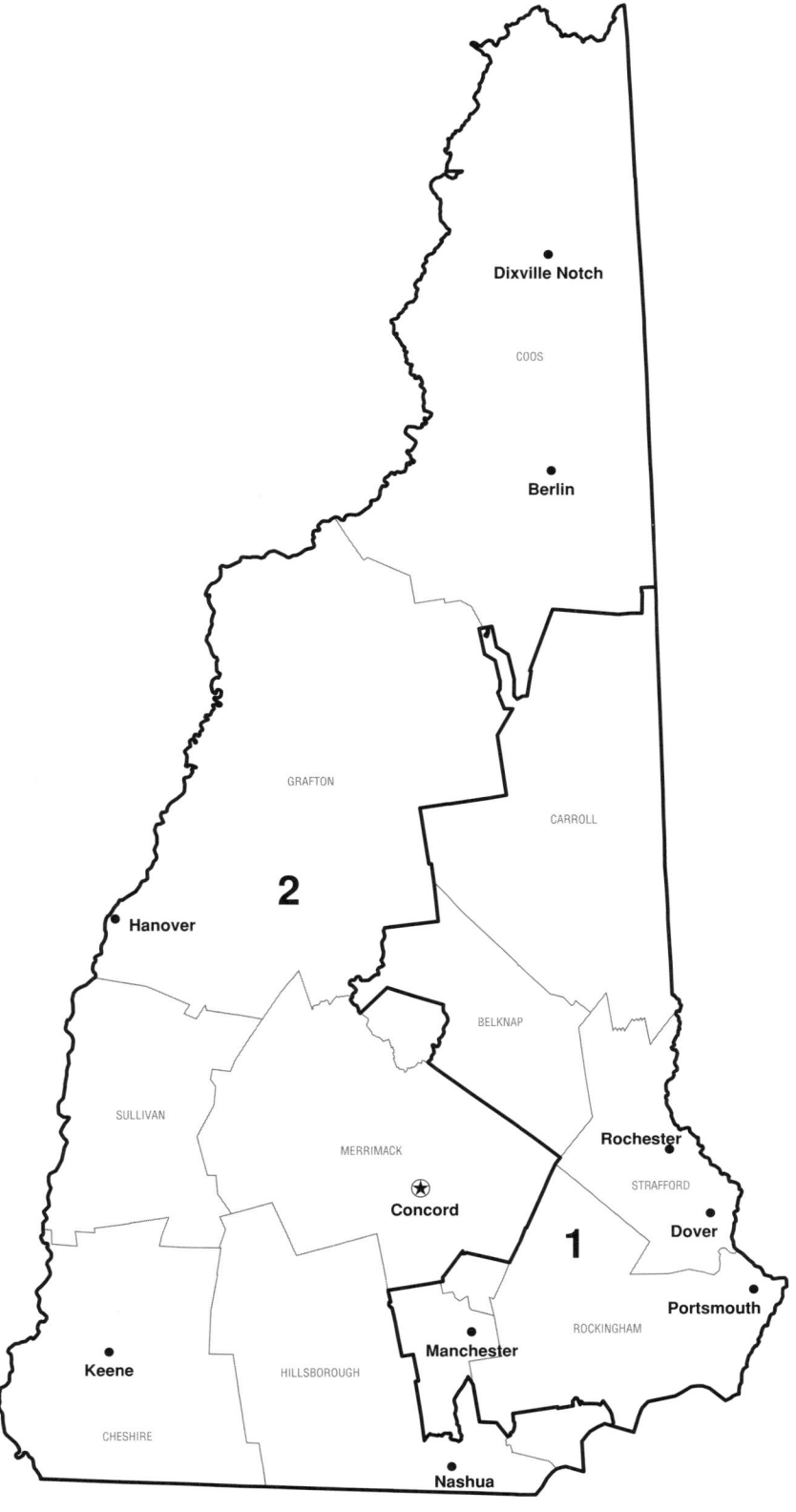

NEW HAMPSHIRE

GOVERNOR 2002

2000 Census Population	County	Total Vote	Republican	Democratic	Other	Rep.-Dem. Plurality	Percentage			
							Total Vote		Major Vote	
							Rep.	Dem.	Rep.	Dem.
56,325	BELKNAP	21,675	14,691	6,385	599	8,306 R	67.8%	29.5%	69.7%	30.3%
43,666	CARROLL	19,067	12,596	5,930	541	6,666 R	66.1%	31.1%	68.0%	32.0%
73,825	CHESHIRE	25,719	11,595	13,320	804	1,725 D	45.1%	51.8%	46.5%	53.5%
33,111	COOS	11,063	6,890	3,823	350	3,067 R	62.3%	34.6%	64.3%	35.7%
81,743	GRAFTON	29,786	16,182	12,607	997	3,575 R	54.3%	42.3%	56.2%	43.8%
380,841	HILLSBOROUGH	127,843	78,305	45,324	4,214	32,981 R	61.3%	35.5%	63.3%	36.7%
136,225	MERRIMACK	53,109	27,773	23,711	1,625	4,062 R	52.3%	44.6%	53.9%	46.1%
277,359	ROCKINGHAM	101,964	62,542	36,342	3,080	26,200 R	61.3%	35.6%	63.2%	36.8%
112,233	STRAFFORD	38,223	21,352	15,461	1,410	5,891 R	55.9%	40.4%	58.0%	42.0%
40,458	SULLIVAN	14,527	7,737	6,374	416	1,363 R	53.3%	43.9%	54.8%	45.2%
1,235,786	TOTAL	442,976	259,663	169,277	14,036	90,386 R	58.6%	38.2%	60.5%	39.5%
	City/Town									
10,769	AMHERST	5,007	3,100	1,767	140	1,333 R	61.9%	35.3%	63.7%	36.3%
6,178	ATKINSON	2,825	1,898	840	87	1,058 R	67.2%	29.7%	69.3%	30.7%
7,475	BARRINGTON	2,845	1,623	1,084	138	539 R	57.0%	38.1%	60.0%	40.0%
18,274	BEDFORD	8,835	6,591	2,076	168	4,515 R	74.6%	23.5%	76.0%	24.0%
6,716	BELMONT	2,109	1,455	596	58	859 R	69.0%	28.3%	70.9%	29.1%
10,331	BERLIN	3,524	1,996	1,408	120	588 R	56.6%	40.0%	58.6%	41.4%
7,138	BOW	3,514	1,910	1,491	113	419 R	54.4%	42.4%	56.2%	43.8%
13,151	CLAREMONT	3,916	1,978	1,843	95	135 R	50.5%	47.1%	51.8%	48.2%
40,687	CONCORD	14,749	6,299	7,999	451	1,700 D	42.7%	54.2%	44.1%	55.9%
8,604	CONWAY	3,009	1,830	1,095	84	735 R	60.8%	36.4%	62.6%	37.4%
34,021	DERRY	8,384	5,272	2,897	215	2,375 R	62.9%	34.6%	64.5%	35.5%
26,884	DOVER	9,769	5,167	4,231	371	936 R	52.9%	43.3%	55.0%	45.0%
12,664	DURHAM	3,786	1,384	2,277	125	893 D	36.6%	60.1%	37.8%	62.2%
5,476	EPPING	1,941	1,203	657	81	546 R	62.0%	33.8%	64.7%	35.3%
14,058	EXETER	5,582	2,871	2,549	162	322 R	51.4%	45.7%	53.0%	47.0%
5,774	FARMINGTON	1,708	1,111	502	95	609 R	65.0%	29.4%	68.9%	31.1%
8,405	FRANKLIN	2,421	1,497	856	68	641 R	61.8%	35.4%	63.6%	36.4%
6,803	GILFORD	3,221	2,316	837	68	1,479 R	71.9%	26.0%	73.5%	26.5%
16,929	GOFFSTOWN	5,893	3,936	1,778	179	2,158 R	66.8%	30.2%	68.9%	31.1%
8,297	HAMPSTEAD	3,182	2,164	929	89	1,235 R	68.0%	29.2%	70.0%	30.0%
14,937	HAMPTON	6,461	3,843	2,443	175	1,400 R	59.5%	37.8%	61.1%	38.9%
10,850	HANOVER	4,241	1,270	2,894	77	1,624 D	29.9%	68.2%	30.5%	69.5%
7,015	HOLLIS	3,337	2,022	1,207	108	815 R	60.6%	36.2%	62.6%	37.4%
11,721	HOOKSETT	4,306	2,936	1,252	118	1,684 R	68.2%	29.1%	70.1%	29.9%
22,928	HUDSON	6,823	4,316	2,276	231	2,040 R	63.3%	33.4%	65.5%	34.5%
5,476	JAFFREY	1,891	904	932	55	28 D	47.8%	49.3%	49.2%	50.8%
22,563	KEENE	7,625	2,888	4,475	262	1,587 D	37.9%	58.7%	39.2%	60.8%
5,862	KINGSTON	2,098	1,305	711	82	594 R	62.2%	33.9%	64.7%	35.3%
16,411	LACONIA	5,422	3,660	1,629	133	2,031 R	67.5%	30.0%	69.2%	30.8%
12,568	LEBANON	4,266	1,882	2,270	114	388 D	44.1%	53.2%	45.3%	54.7%
7,360	LITCHFIELD	2,449	1,654	717	78	937 R	67.5%	29.3%	69.8%	30.2%
5,845	LITTLETON	1,936	1,354	539	43	815 R	69.9%	27.8%	71.5%	28.5%
23,236	LONDONDERRY	7,680	5,110	2,347	223	2,763 R	66.5%	30.6%	68.5%	31.5%
107,006	MANCHESTER	31,053	19,125	10,983	945	8,142 R	61.6%	35.4%	63.5%	36.5%
25,119	MERRIMACK TOWN	9,510	6,119	3,008	383	3,111 R	64.3%	31.6%	67.0%	33.0%
13,535	MILFORD	4,698	2,743	1,809	146	934 R	58.4%	38.5%	60.3%	39.7%
86,605	NASHUA	24,875	14,071	9,882	922	4,189 R	56.6%	39.7%	58.7%	41.3%
8,027	NEWMARKET	3,114	1,503	1,474	137	29 R	48.3%	47.3%	50.5%	49.5%
6,269	NEWPORT	1,822	1,095	683	44	412 R	60.1%	37.5%	61.6%	38.4%
10,914	PELHAM	3,595	2,352	1,131	112	1,221 R	65.4%	31.5%	67.5%	32.5%
6,897	PEMBROKE	2,529	1,373	1,082	74	291 R	54.3%	42.8%	55.9%	44.1%
5,883	PETERBOROUGH	2,734	1,152	1,504	78	352 D	42.1%	55.0%	43.4%	56.6%
7,747	PLAISTOW	2,436	1,587	793	56	794 R	65.1%	32.6%	66.7%	33.3%
5,892	PLYMOUTH	1,662	837	723	102	114 R	50.4%	43.5%	53.7%	46.3%
20,784	PORTSMOUTH	8,530	3,701	4,562	267	861 D	43.4%	53.5%	44.8%	55.2%

NEW HAMPSHIRE

GOVERNOR 2002

2000 Census Population	City/Town	Total Vote	Republican	Democratic	Other	Rep.-Dem. Plurality	Percentage			
							Total Vote		Major Vote	
							Rep.	Dem.	Rep.	Dem.
9,674	RAYMOND	2,744	1,746	863	135	883 R	63.6%	31.5%	66.9%	33.1%
28,461	ROCHESTER	8,990	5,846	2,866	278	2,980 R	65.0%	31.9%	67.1%	32.9%
28,112	SALEM	8,857	5,814	2,846	197	2,968 R	65.6%	32.1%	67.1%	32.9%
7,934	SEABROOK	2,333	1,510	733	90	777 R	64.7%	31.4%	67.3%	32.7%
11,477	SOMERSWORTH	3,439	1,958	1,357	124	601 R	56.9%	39.5%	59.1%	40.9%
6,800	SWANZEY	2,180	1,062	1,057	61	5 R	48.7%	48.5%	50.1%	49.9%
7,776	WEARE	2,716	1,736	867	113	869 R	63.9%	31.9%	66.7%	33.3%
10,709	WINDHAM	4,429	3,158	1,160	111	1,998 R	71.3%	26.2%	73.1%	26.9%

NEW HAMPSHIRE

SENATOR 2002

2000 Census Population	County	Total Vote	Republican	Democratic	Other	Rep.-Dem. Plurality	Percentage			
							Total Vote		Major Vote	
							Rep.	Dem.	Rep.	Dem.
56,325	BELKNAP	21,942	12,658	8,765	519	3,893 R	57.7%	39.9%	59.1%	40.9%
43,666	CARROLL	19,287	10,650	8,134	503	2,516 R	55.2%	42.2%	56.7%	43.3%
73,825	CHESHIRE	25,855	10,737	14,200	918	3,463 D	41.5%	54.9%	43.1%	56.9%
33,111	COOS	11,328	5,055	5,957	316	902 D	44.6%	52.6%	45.9%	54.1%
81,743	GRAFTON	30,120	14,081	15,266	773	1,185 D	46.7%	50.7%	48.0%	52.0%
380,841	HILLSBOROUGH	128,972	68,320	57,354	3,298	10,966 R	53.0%	44.5%	54.4%	45.6%
136,225	MERRIMACK	53,527	25,263	26,898	1,366	1,635 D	47.2%	50.3%	48.4%	51.6%
277,359	ROCKINGHAM	102,777	55,710	43,968	3,099	11,742 R	54.2%	42.8%	55.9%	44.1%
112,233	STRAFFORD	38,676	17,418	20,109	1,149	2,691 D	45.0%	52.0%	46.4%	53.6%
40,458	SULLIVAN	14,651	7,337	6,827	487	510 R	50.1%	46.6%	51.8%	48.2%
1,235,786	TOTAL	447,135	227,229	207,478	12,428	19,751 R	50.8%	46.4%	52.3%	47.7%

2000 Census Population	City/Town	Total Vote	Republican	Democratic	Other	Rep.-Dem. Plurality	Rep.	Dem.	Rep.	Dem.
10,769	AMHERST	5,078	2,840	2,132	106	708 R	55.9%	42.0%	57.1%	42.9%
6,178	ATKINSON	2,850	1,651	1,112	87	539 R	57.9%	39.0%	59.8%	40.2%
7,475	BARRINGTON	2,871	1,351	1,422	98	71 D	47.1%	49.5%	48.7%	51.3%
18,274	BEDFORD	8,860	6,051	2,733	76	3,318 R	68.3%	30.8%	68.9%	31.1%
6,716	BELMONT	2,179	1,164	960	55	204 R	53.4%	44.1%	54.8%	45.2%
10,331	BERLIN	3,650	1,109	2,452	89	1,343 D	30.4%	67.2%	31.1%	68.9%
7,138	BOW	3,553	1,825	1,664	64	161 R	51.4%	46.8%	52.3%	47.7%
13,151	CLAREMONT	3,963	1,868	1,949	146	81 D	47.1%	49.2%	48.9%	51.1%
40,687	CONCORD	14,861	5,807	8,707	347	2,900 D	39.1%	58.6%	40.0%	60.0%
8,604	CONWAY	3,042	1,378	1,578	86	200 D	45.3%	51.9%	46.6%	53.4%
34,021	DERRY	8,451	4,670	3,580	201	1,090 R	55.3%	42.4%	56.6%	43.4%
26,884	DOVER	9,881	4,362	5,268	251	906 D	44.1%	53.3%	45.3%	54.7%
12,664	DURHAM	3,848	1,227	2,560	61	1,333 D	31.9%	66.5%	32.4%	67.6%
5,476	EPPING	1,956	1,029	861	66	168 R	52.6%	44.0%	54.4%	45.6%
14,058	EXETER	5,645	2,616	2,896	133	280 D	46.3%	51.3%	47.5%	52.5%
5,774	FARMINGTON	1,723	862	763	98	99 R	50.0%	44.3%	53.0%	47.0%
8,405	FRANKLIN	2,435	1,143	1,223	69	80 D	46.9%	50.2%	48.3%	51.7%
6,803	GILFORD	3,260	2,020	1,185	55	835 R	62.0%	36.3%	63.0%	37.0%
16,929	GOFFSTOWN	5,962	3,499	2,312	151	1,187 R	58.7%	38.8%	60.2%	39.8%
8,297	HAMPSTEAD	3,211	1,941	1,197	73	744 R	60.4%	37.3%	61.9%	38.1%
14,937	HAMPTON	6,543	3,456	2,873	214	583 R	52.8%	43.9%	54.6%	45.4%
10,850	HANOVER	4,345	1,140	3,171	34	2,031 D	26.2%	73.0%	26.4%	73.6%
7,015	HOLLIS	3,376	1,794	1,507	75	287 R	53.1%	44.6%	54.3%	45.7%
11,721	HOOKSETT	4,366	2,622	1,636	108	986 R	60.1%	37.5%	61.6%	38.4%
22,928	HUDSON	6,894	3,578	3,106	210	472 R	51.9%	45.1%	53.5%	46.5%

NEW HAMPSHIRE

SENATOR 2002

2000 Census Population	City/Town	Total Vote	Republican	Democratic	Other	Rep.-Dem. Plurality	Total Vote Rep.	Total Vote Dem.	Major Vote Rep.	Major Vote Dem.
5,476	JAFFREY	1,889	910	910	69		48.2%	48.2%	50.0%	50.0%
22,563	KEENE	7,680	2,796	4,620	264	1,824 D	36.4%	60.2%	37.7%	62.3%
5,862	KINGSTON	2,121	1,166	864	91	302 R	55.0%	40.7%	57.4%	42.6%
16,411	LACONIA	5,494	3,141	2,235	118	906 R	57.2%	40.7%	58.4%	41.6%
12,568	LEBANON	4,295	1,693	2,513	89	820 D	39.4%	58.5%	40.3%	59.7%
7,360	LITCHFIELD	2,476	1,400	1,025	51	375 R	56.5%	41.4%	57.7%	42.3%
5,845	LITTLETON	1,967	1,124	818	25	306 R	57.1%	41.6%	57.9%	42.1%
23,236	LONDONDERRY	7,741	4,518	3,059	164	1,459 R	58.4%	39.5%	59.6%	40.4%
107,006	MANCHESTER	31,343	16,581	14,118	644	2,463 R	52.9%	45.0%	54.0%	46.0%
25,119	MERRIMACK TOWN	9,599	5,237	4,061	301	1,176 R	54.6%	42.3%	56.3%	43.7%
13,535	MILFORD	4,712	2,476	2,107	129	369 R	52.5%	44.7%	54.0%	46.0%
86,605	NASHUA	25,146	11,511	12,947	688	1,436 D	45.8%	51.5%	47.1%	52.9%
8,027	NEWMARKET	3,133	1,309	1,729	95	420 D	41.8%	55.2%	43.1%	56.9%
6,269	NEWPORT	1,837	954	824	59	130 R	51.9%	44.9%	53.7%	46.3%
10,914	PELHAM	3,646	1,999	1,490	157	509 R	54.8%	40.9%	57.3%	42.7%
6,897	PEMBROKE	2,534	1,245	1,215	74	30 R	49.1%	47.9%	50.6%	49.4%
5,883	PETERBOROUGH	2,744	1,199	1,483	62	284 D	43.7%	54.0%	44.7%	55.3%
7,747	PLAISTOW	2,421	1,403	942	76	461 R	58.0%	38.9%	59.8%	40.2%
5,892	PLYMOUTH	1,684	712	902	70	190 D	42.3%	53.6%	44.1%	55.9%
20,784	PORTSMOUTH	8,546	3,356	4,888	302	1,532 D	39.3%	57.2%	40.7%	59.3%
9,674	RAYMOND	2,765	1,541	1,093	131	448 R	55.7%	39.5%	58.5%	41.5%
28,461	ROCHESTER	9,085	4,470	4,330	285	140 R	49.2%	47.7%	50.8%	49.2%
28,112	SALEM	8,984	4,846	3,853	285	993 R	53.9%	42.9%	55.7%	44.3%
7,934	SEABROOK	2,358	1,353	881	124	472 R	57.4%	37.4%	60.6%	39.4%
11,477	SOMERSWORTH	3,488	1,530	1,862	96	332 D	43.9%	53.4%	45.1%	54.9%
6,800	SWANZEY	2,188	965	1,157	66	192 D	44.1%	52.9%	45.5%	54.5%
7,776	WEARE	2,745	1,508	1,147	90	361 R	54.9%	41.8%	56.8%	43.2%
10,709	WINDHAM	4,471	2,767	1,610	94	1,157 R	61.9%	36.0%	63.2%	36.8%

NEW HAMPSHIRE

HOUSE OF REPRESENTATIVES

CD	Year	Total Vote	Republican Vote	Republican Candidate	Democratic Vote	Democratic Candidate	Other Vote	Rep.-Dem. Plurality	Total Vote Rep.	Total Vote Dem.	Major Vote Rep.	Major Vote Dem.
1	2002	221,987	128,993	Bradley, Jeb	85,426	Clark, Martha Fuller	7,568	43,567 R	58.1%	38.5%	60.2%	39.8%
2	2002	221,456	125,804	Bass, Charles*	90,479	Swett, Katrina	5,173	35,325 R	56.8%	40.9%	58.2%	41.8%
Total	2002	443,443	254,797		175,905		12,741	78,892 R	57.5%	39.7%	59.2%	40.8%

An asterisk (*) denotes incumbent.

NEW HAMPSHIRE
GENERAL AND PRIMARY ELECTIONS

2002 GENERAL ELECTIONS

Governor   Other vote was 13,028 Libertarian (John J. Babiarz); 1,008 scattered write-in.

Senator   Other vote was 9,835 Libertarian (Kenneth E. Blevens); 2,396 write-in (Robert C. Smith); 197 scattered write-in.

House   Other vote was:

CD 1   7,387 Libertarian (Dan Belforti); 181 scattered write-in.
CD 2   5,051 Libertarian (Rosalie Babiarz); 122 scattered write-in.

2002 PRIMARY ELECTIONS

Primary   September 10, 2002

Registration (as of Sept. 10, 2002)

Republican	245,791
Democratic	170,405
Undeclared	242,028
TOTAL	658,224

Primary Type   Semi-open—Registered Democrats and Republicans could vote only in their party's primary. "Undeclared" voters could participate in either party's primary.

Note: An asterisk (*) denotes incumbent.

REPUBLICAN PRIMARIES			DEMOCRATIC PRIMARIES		
Governor					
Craig Benson	56,099	36.7%	Mark Fernald	34,683	53.3%
Bruce Keough	51,461	33.6%	Bev Hollingworth	27,777	42.7%
Gordon J. Humphrey	42,698	27.9%	Write-in	2,632	4.0%
Robert Kingsbury	877	0.6%			
Joseph S. Haas	759	0.5%			
Robert Howard Kroepel	578	0.4%			
Write-in	575	0.4%			
TOTAL	153,047		TOTAL	65,092	
Senator					
John E. Sununu	81,920	53.3%	Jeanne Shaheen	57,995	95.9%
Robert C. Smith*	68,608	44.7%	Write-in	2,488	4.1%
Kenneth Scot Stremsky	2,694	1.8%			
Write-in	363	0.2%			
TOTAL	153,585		TOTAL	60,483	
Congressional District 1					
Jeb Bradley	23,012	31.4%	Martha Fuller Clark	26,317	83.9%
John A. Stephen	16,956	23.1%	Sean Patrick Dean	4,717	15.0%
Sean Mahoney	13,861	18.9%	Write-in	330	1.1%
Vivian Clark	6,889	9.4%			
Wayne Barrows	6,008	8.2%			
Francine "Fran" Wendelboe	4,947	6.7%			
Gary Scott Hoffman	1,101	1.5%			
"Bob" Bevill	547	0.7%			
Write-in	80	0.1%			
TOTAL	73,401		TOTAL	31,364	
Congressional District 2					
Charles Bass*	61,473	86.4%	Katrina Swett	24,997	78.0%
Eugene Douglass	9,486	13.3%	Norman H. "NH" Jackman	6,700	20.9%
Write-in	205	0.3%	Write-in	337	1.1%
TOTAL	71,164		TOTAL	32,034	

NEW HAMPSHIRE REPUBLICAN PRIMARY

GOVERNOR 2002

2000 Census Population	County	Total Vote	Benson	Keough	Humphrey	Other	Winner	Percentage of Total Vote			
								Benson	Keough	Humphrey	Other
56,325	BELKNAP	9,242	3,989	2,871	2,241	141	Benson	43.2%	31.1%	24.2%	1.5%
43,666	CARROLL	9,301	3,715	3,839	1,623	124	Keough	39.9%	41.3%	17.4%	1.3%
73,825	CHESHIRE	7,474	2,284	3,127	1,847	216	Keough	30.6%	41.8%	24.7%	2.9%
33,111	COOS	3,925	1,209	1,637	1,025	54	Keough	30.8%	41.7%	26.1%	1.4%
81,743	GRAFTON	10,134	4,095	2,896	2,932	211	Benson	40.4%	28.6%	28.9%	2.1%
380,841	HILLSBOROUGH	42,402	13,902	13,324	14,508	668	Humphrey	32.8%	31.4%	34.2%	1.6%
136,225	MERRIMACK	19,775	6,351	7,503	5,429	492	Keough	32.1%	37.9%	27.5%	2.5%
277,359	ROCKINGHAM	34,772	13,985	11,219	8,996	572	Benson	40.2%	32.3%	25.9%	1.6%
112,233	STRAFFORD	11,200	4,834	3,338	2,823	205	Benson	43.2%	29.8%	25.2%	1.8%
40,458	SULLIVAN	4,822	1,735	1,707	1,274	106	Benson	36.0%	35.4%	26.4%	2.2%
1,235,786	TOTAL	153,047	56,099	51,461	42,698	2,789	Benson	36.7%	33.6%	27.9%	1.8%
	City/Town										
10,769	AMHERST	2,030	666	702	634	28	Keough	32.8%	34.6%	31.2%	1.4%
6,178	ATKINSON	967	520	222	210	15	Benson	53.8%	23.0%	21.7%	1.6%
7,475	BARRINGTON	916	383	258	251	24	Benson	41.8%	28.2%	27.4%	2.6%
18,274	BEDFORD	4,016	1,153	1,553	1,279	31	Keough	28.7%	38.7%	31.8%	0.8%
6,716	BELMONT	813	362	230	202	19	Benson	44.5%	28.3%	24.8%	2.3%
10,331	BERLIN	981	263	568	138	12	Keough	26.8%	57.9%	14.1%	1.2%
7,138	BOW	1,538	464	659	392	23	Keough	30.2%	42.8%	25.5%	1.5%
13,151	CLAREMONT	1,211	510	334	318	49	Benson	42.1%	27.6%	26.3%	4.0%
40,687	CONCORD	4,811	1,491	1,958	1,226	136	Keough	31.0%	40.7%	25.5%	2.8%
8,604	CONWAY	1,219	467	586	154	12	Keough	38.3%	48.1%	12.6%	1.0%
34,021	DERRY	3,001	1,276	661	1,020	44	Benson	42.5%	22.0%	34.0%	1.5%
26,884	DOVER	2,777	1,250	853	627	47	Benson	45.0%	30.7%	22.6%	1.7%
12,664	DURHAM	792	312	310	144	26	Benson	39.4%	39.1%	18.2%	3.3%
5,476	EPPING	621	216	205	188	12	Benson	34.8%	33.0%	30.3%	1.9%
14,058	EXETER	1,945	504	1,032	382	27	Keough	25.9%	53.1%	19.6%	1.4%
5,774	FARMINGTON	544	240	151	142	11	Benson	44.1%	27.8%	26.1%	2.0%
8,405	FRANKLIN	901	404	220	256	21	Benson	44.8%	24.4%	28.4%	2.3%
6,803	GILFORD	1,404	718	433	240	13	Benson	51.1%	30.8%	17.1%	0.9%
16,929	GOFFSTOWN	2,329	693	727	871	38	Humphrey	29.8%	31.2%	37.4%	1.6%
8,297	HAMPSTEAD	1,189	503	362	310	14	Benson	42.3%	30.4%	26.1%	1.2%
14,937	HAMPTON	2,117	1,003	716	354	44	Benson	47.4%	33.8%	16.7%	2.1%
10,850	HANOVER	723	230	281	195	17	Keough	31.8%	38.9%	27.0%	2.4%
7,015	HOLLIS	1,305	484	421	381	19	Benson	37.1%	32.3%	29.2%	1.5%
11,721	HOOKSETT	1,678	562	545	554	17	Benson	33.5%	32.5%	33.0%	1.0%
22,928	HUDSON	1,867	646	512	683	26	Humphrey	34.6%	27.4%	36.6%	1.4%
5,476	JAFFREY	667	151	302	183	31	Keough	22.6%	45.3%	27.4%	4.6%
22,563	KEENE	2,021	674	914	370	63	Keough	33.3%	45.2%	18.3%	3.1%
5,862	KINGSTON	815	309	253	235	18	Benson	37.9%	31.0%	28.8%	2.2%
16,411	LACONIA	2,248	1,031	636	539	42	Benson	45.9%	28.3%	24.0%	1.9%
12,568	LEBANON	1,055	444	314	277	20	Benson	42.1%	29.8%	26.3%	1.9%
7,360	LITCHFIELD	799	261	242	288	8	Humphrey	32.7%	30.3%	36.0%	1.0%
5,845	LITTLETON	945	337	307	287	14	Benson	35.7%	32.5%	30.4%	1.5%
23,236	LONDONDERRY	2,591	899	691	972	29	Humphrey	34.7%	26.7%	37.5%	1.1%
107,006	MANCHESTER	9,874	3,136	2,840	3,761	137	Humphrey	31.8%	28.8%	38.1%	1.4%
25,119	MERRIMACK TOWN	3,010	999	860	1,105	46	Humphrey	33.2%	28.6%	36.7%	1.5%
13,535	MILFORD	1,805	570	555	640	40	Humphrey	31.6%	30.7%	35.5%	2.2%
86,605	NASHUA	6,423	2,540	1,698	2,081	104	Benson	39.5%	26.4%	32.4%	1.6%
8,027	NEWMARKET	798	307	282	187	22	Benson	38.5%	35.3%	23.4%	2.8%
6,269	NEWPORT	595	221	216	155	3	Benson	37.1%	36.3%	26.1%	0.5%
10,914	PELHAM	905	415	180	302	8	Benson	45.9%	19.9%	33.4%	0.9%
6,897	PEMBROKE	860	269	319	258	14	Keough	31.3%	37.1%	30.0%	1.6%
5,883	PETERBOROUGH	934	205	516	185	28	Keough	21.9%	55.2%	19.8%	3.0%
7,747	PLAISTOW	715	391	172	141	11	Benson	54.7%	24.1%	19.7%	1.5%
5,892	PLYMOUTH	573	247	178	133	15	Benson	43.1%	31.1%	23.2%	2.6%
20,784	PORTSMOUTH	1,966	842	696	392	36	Benson	42.8%	35.4%	19.9%	1.8%

NEW HAMPSHIRE REPUBLICAN PRIMARY

GOVERNOR 2002

2000 Census Population	City/Town	Total Vote	Benson	Keough	Humphrey	Other	Winner	Percentage of Total Vote			
								Benson	Keough	Humphrey	Other
9,674	RAYMOND	943	335	263	319	26	Benson	35.5%	27.9%	33.8%	2.8%
28,461	ROCHESTER	2,823	1,286	702	794	41	Benson	45.6%	24.9%	28.1%	1.5%
28,112	SALEM	2,573	1,250	742	544	37	Benson	48.6%	28.8%	21.1%	1.4%
7,934	SEABROOK	662	275	225	147	15	Benson	41.5%	34.0%	22.2%	2.3%
11,477	SOMERSWORTH	799	333	232	222	12	Benson	41.7%	29.0%	27.8%	1.5%
6,800	SWANZEY	685	215	285	153	32	Keough	31.4%	41.6%	22.3%	4.7%
7,776	WEARE	1,120	361	351	378	30	Humphrey	32.2%	31.3%	33.8%	2.7%
10,709	WINDHAM	1,833	841	507	462	23	Benson	45.9%	27.7%	25.2%	1.3%

NEW HAMPSHIRE DEMOCRATIC PRIMARY

GOVERNOR 2002

2000 Census Population	County	Total Vote	Fernald	Hollingworth	Other	Winner	Percentage of Total Vote		
							Fernald	Hollingworth	Other
56,325	BELKNAP	2,623	1,370	1,085	168	Fernald	52.2%	41.4%	6.4%
43,666	CARROLL	1,945	1,091	763	91	Fernald	56.1%	39.2%	4.7%
73,825	CHESHIRE	4,950	3,270	1,543	137	Fernald	66.1%	31.2%	2.8%
33,111	COOS	1,895	889	800	206	Fernald	46.9%	42.2%	10.9%
81,743	GRAFTON	4,366	2,799	1,442	125	Fernald	64.1%	33.0%	2.9%
380,841	HILLSBOROUGH	18,592	10,208	7,566	818	Fernald	54.9%	40.7%	4.4%
136,225	MERRIMACK	8,754	5,473	3,039	242	Fernald	62.5%	34.7%	2.8%
277,359	ROCKINGHAM	12,917	4,774	7,759	384	Hollingworth	37.0%	60.1%	3.0%
112,233	STRAFFORD	6,657	3,219	3,085	353	Fernald	48.4%	46.3%	5.3%
40,458	SULLIVAN	2,393	1,590	695	108	Fernald	66.4%	29.0%	4.5%
1,235,786	TOTAL	65,092	34,683	27,777	2,632	Fernald	53.3%	42.7%	4.0%

2000 Census Population	City/Town	Total Vote	Fernald	Hollingworth	Other	Winner	Fernald	Hollingworth	Other
10,769	AMHERST	515	356	136	23	Fernald	69.1%	26.4%	4.5%
6,178	ATKINSON	259	94	160	5	Hollingworth	36.3%	61.8%	1.9%
7,475	BARRINGTON	430	212	186	32	Fernald	49.3%	43.3%	7.4%
18,274	BEDFORD	761	355	358	48	Hollingworth	46.6%	47.0%	6.3%
6,716	BELMONT	227	111	91	25	Fernald	48.9%	40.1%	11.0%
10,331	BERLIN	978	435	396	147	Fernald	44.5%	40.5%	15.0%
7,138	BOW	523	309	203	11	Fernald	59.1%	38.8%	2.1%
13,151	CLAREMONT	851	543	254	54	Fernald	63.8%	29.8%	6.3%
40,687	CONCORD	3,108	1,912	1,097	99	Fernald	61.5%	35.3%	3.2%
8,604	CONWAY	301	161	116	24	Fernald	53.5%	38.5%	8.0%
34,021	DERRY	854	412	407	35	Fernald	48.2%	47.7%	4.1%
26,884	DOVER	1,754	797	875	82	Hollingworth	45.4%	49.9%	4.7%
12,664	DURHAM	794	415	372	7	Fernald	52.3%	46.9%	0.9%
5,476	EPPING	217	95	118	4	Hollingworth	43.8%	54.4%	1.8%
14,058	EXETER	965	233	717	15	Hollingworth	24.1%	74.3%	1.6%
5,774	FARMINGTON	257	133	99	25	Fernald	51.8%	38.5%	9.7%
8,405	FRANKLIN	370	198	145	27	Fernald	53.5%	39.2%	7.3%
6,803	GILFORD	320	190	109	21	Fernald	59.4%	34.1%	6.6%
16,929	GOFFSTOWN	739	397	303	39	Fernald	53.7%	41.0%	5.3%
8,297	HAMPSTEAD	284	110	166	8	Hollingworth	38.7%	58.5%	2.8%
14,937	HAMPTON	1,172	149	998	25	Hollingworth	12.7%	85.2%	2.1%
10,850	HANOVER	852	579	272	1	Fernald	68.0%	31.9%	0.1%
7,015	HOLLIS	349	196	153		Fernald	56.2%	43.8%	
11,721	HOOKSETT	487	246	212	29	Fernald	50.5%	43.5%	6.0%
22,928	HUDSON	712	317	351	44	Hollingworth	44.5%	49.3%	6.2%

307

NEW HAMPSHIRE DEMOCRATIC PRIMARY

GOVERNOR 2002

2000 Census Population	City/Town	Total Vote	Fernald	Hollingworth	Other	Winner	Percentage of Total Vote		
							Fernald	Hollingworth	Other
5,476	JAFFREY	422	339	70	13	Fernald	80.3%	16.6%	3.1%
22,563	KEENE	1,553	987	515	51	Fernald	63.6%	33.2%	3.3%
5,862	KINGSTON	179	73	97	9	Hollingworth	40.8%	54.2%	5.0%
16,411	LACONIA	756	335	363	58	Hollingworth	44.3%	48.0%	7.7%
12,568	LEBANON	849	581	258	10	Fernald	68.4%	30.4%	1.2%
7,360	LITCHFIELD	226	137	81	8	Fernald	60.6%	35.8%	3.5%
5,845	LITTLETON	267	167	71	29	Fernald	62.5%	26.6%	10.9%
23,236	LONDONDERRY	635	297	322	16	Hollingworth	46.8%	50.7%	2.5%
107,006	MANCHESTER	6,743	3,317	3,009	417	Fernald	49.2%	44.6%	6.2%
25,119	MERRIMACK TOWN	951	473	418	60	Fernald	49.7%	44.0%	6.3%
13,535	MILFORD	548	398	131	19	Fernald	72.6%	23.9%	3.5%
86,605	NASHUA	3,205	1,597	1,540	68	Fernald	49.8%	48.0%	2.1%
8,027	NEWMARKET	536	230	284	22	Hollingworth	42.9%	53.0%	4.1%
6,269	NEWPORT	287	192	78	17	Fernald	66.9%	27.2%	5.9%
10,914	PELHAM	377	148	208	21	Hollingworth	39.3%	55.2%	5.6%
6,897	PEMBROKE	351	194	145	12	Fernald	55.3%	41.3%	3.4%
5,883	PETERBOROUGH	772	653	98	21	Fernald	84.6%	12.7%	2.7%
7,747	PLAISTOW	213	79	128	6	Hollingworth	37.1%	60.1%	2.8%
5,892	PLYMOUTH	239	166	72	1	Fernald	69.5%	30.1%	0.4%
20,784	PORTSMOUTH	1,880	744	1,104	32	Hollingworth	39.6%	58.7%	1.7%
9,674	RAYMOND	279	123	137	19	Hollingworth	44.1%	49.1%	6.8%
28,461	ROCHESTER	1,396	659	660	77	Hollingworth	47.2%	47.3%	5.5%
28,112	SALEM	1,051	439	575	37	Hollingworth	41.8%	54.7%	3.5%
7,934	SEABROOK	294	60	234	0	Hollingworth	20.4%	79.6%	0.0%
11,477	SOMERSWORTH	677	339	313	25	Fernald	50.1%	46.2%	3.7%
6,800	SWANZEY	388	248	118	22	Fernald	63.9%	30.4%	5.7%
7,776	WEARE	337	192	135	10	Fernald	57.0%	40.1%	3.0%
10,709	WINDHAM	385	118	225	42	Hollingworth	30.6%	58.4%	10.9%

NEW HAMPSHIRE REPUBLICAN PRIMARY

SENATOR 2002

2000 Census Population	County	Total Vote	Sununu	Smith	Other	Winner	Percentage of Total Vote		
							Sununu	Smith	Other
56,325	BELKNAP	9,288	5,177	3,938	173	Sununu	55.7%	42.4%	1.9%
43,666	CARROLL	9,410	5,283	3,958	169	Sununu	56.1%	42.1%	1.8%
73,825	CHESHIRE	7,480	3,862	3,438	180	Sununu	51.6%	46.0%	2.4%
33,111	COOS	3,927	1,771	2,076	80	Smith	45.1%	52.9%	2.0%
81,743	GRAFTON	10,152	5,363	4,606	183	Sununu	52.8%	45.4%	1.8%
380,841	HILLSBOROUGH	42,564	22,048	19,746	770	Sununu	51.8%	46.4%	1.8%
136,225	MERRIMACK	19,874	10,045	9,405	424	Sununu	50.5%	47.3%	2.1%
277,359	ROCKINGHAM	34,795	19,797	14,309	689	Sununu	56.9%	41.1%	2.0%
112,233	STRAFFORD	11,253	5,949	5,018	286	Sununu	52.9%	44.6%	2.5%
40,458	SULLIVAN	4,842	2,625	2,114	103	Sununu	54.2%	43.7%	2.1%
1,235,786	TOTAL	153,585	81,920	68,608	3,057	Sununu	53.3%	44.7%	2.0%

NEW HAMPSHIRE REPUBLICAN PRIMARY

SENATOR 2002

2000 Census Population	City/Town	Total Vote	Sununu	Smith	Other	Winner	Percentage of Total Vote		
							Sununu	Smith	Other
10,769	AMHERST	2,045	1,166	846	33	Sununu	57.0%	41.4%	1.6%
6,178	ATKINSON	967	572	367	28	Sununu	59.2%	38.0%	2.9%
7,475	BARRINGTON	922	457	427	38	Sununu	49.6%	46.3%	4.1%
18,274	BEDFORD	4,050	2,690	1,343	17	Sununu	66.4%	33.2%	0.4%
6,716	BELMONT	809	414	377	18	Sununu	51.2%	46.6%	2.2%
10,331	BERLIN	971	368	574	29	Smith	37.9%	59.1%	3.0%
7,138	BOW	1,541	855	660	26	Sununu	55.5%	42.8%	1.7%
13,151	CLAREMONT	1,206	628	550	28	Sununu	52.1%	45.6%	2.3%
40,687	CONCORD	4,838	2,289	2,444	105	Smith	47.3%	50.5%	2.2%
8,604	CONWAY	1,226	539	664	23	Smith	44.0%	54.2%	1.9%
34,021	DERRY	3,023	1,567	1,405	51	Sununu	51.8%	46.5%	1.7%
26,884	DOVER	2,783	1,570	1,147	66	Sununu	56.4%	41.2%	2.4%
12,664	DURHAM	804	504	290	10	Sununu	62.7%	36.1%	1.2%
5,476	EPPING	611	310	289	12	Sununu	50.7%	47.3%	2.0%
14,058	EXETER	1,940	1,179	726	35	Sununu	60.8%	37.4%	1.8%
5,774	FARMINGTON	548	262	271	15	Smith	47.8%	49.5%	2.7%
8,405	FRANKLIN	912	412	475	25	Smith	45.2%	52.1%	2.7%
6,803	GILFORD	1,417	895	508	14	Sununu	63.2%	35.9%	1.0%
16,929	GOFFSTOWN	2,261	1,194	1,041	26	Sununu	52.8%	46.0%	1.1%
8,297	HAMPSTEAD	1,199	706	466	27	Sununu	58.9%	38.9%	2.3%
14,937	HAMPTON	2,125	1,225	858	42	Sununu	57.6%	40.4%	2.0%
10,850	HANOVER	742	500	232	10	Sununu	67.4%	31.3%	1.3%
7,015	HOLLIS	1,322	663	629	30	Sununu	50.2%	47.6%	2.3%
11,721	HOOKSETT	1,688	960	705	23	Sununu	56.9%	41.8%	1.4%
22,928	HUDSON	1,880	861	977	42	Smith	45.8%	52.0%	2.2%
5,476	JAFFREY	669	331	329	9	Sununu	49.5%	49.2%	1.3%
22,563	KEENE	2,021	1,141	841	39	Sununu	56.5%	41.6%	1.9%
5,862	KINGSTON	818	419	375	24	Sununu	51.2%	45.8%	2.9%
16,411	LACONIA	2,254	1,345	875	34	Sununu	59.7%	38.8%	1.5%
12,568	LEBANON	1,051	588	451	12	Sununu	55.9%	42.9%	1.1%
7,360	LITCHFIELD	265	138	120	7	Sununu	52.1%	45.3%	2.6%
5,845	LITTLETON	934	519	399	16	Sununu	55.6%	42.7%	1.7%
23,236	LONDONDERRY	2,582	1,516	1,035	31	Sununu	58.7%	40.1%	1.2%
107,006	MANCHESTER	9,951	5,319	4,469	163	Sununu	53.5%	44.9%	1.6%
25,119	MERRIMACK TOWN	3,023	1,446	1,523	54	Smith	47.8%	50.4%	1.8%
13,535	MILFORD	1,810	867	905	38	Smith	47.9%	50.0%	2.1%
86,605	NASHUA	6,437	2,918	3,378	141	Smith	45.3%	52.5%	2.2%
8,027	NEWMARKET	805	414	371	20	Sununu	51.4%	46.1%	2.5%
6,269	NEWPORT	600	314	273	13	Sununu	52.3%	45.5%	2.2%
10,914	PELHAM	901	444	444	13		49.3%	49.3%	1.4%
6,897	PEMBROKE	871	416	437	18	Smith	47.8%	50.2%	2.1%
5,883	PETERBOROUGH	927	588	329	10	Sununu	63.4%	35.5%	1.1%
7,747	PLAISTOW	716	381	323	12	Sununu	53.2%	45.1%	1.7%
5,892	PLYMOUTH	567	291	265	11	Sununu	51.3%	46.7%	1.9%
20,784	PORTSMOUTH	1,969	1,089	850	30	Sununu	55.3%	43.2%	1.5%
9,674	RAYMOND	942	468	444	30	Sununu	49.7%	47.1%	3.2%
28,461	ROCHESTER	2,832	1,348	1,406	78	Smith	47.6%	49.6%	2.8%
28,112	SALEM	2,579	1,551	973	55	Sununu	60.1%	37.7%	2.1%
7,934	SEABROOK	665	324	319	22	Sununu	48.7%	48.0%	3.3%
11,477	SOMERSWORTH	810	424	372	14	Sununu	52.3%	45.9%	1.7%
6,800	SWANZEY	677	350	308	19	Sununu	51.7%	45.5%	2.8%
7,776	WEARE	1,131	490	603	38	Smith	43.3%	53.3%	3.4%
10,709	WINDHAM	1,844	1,149	650	45	Sununu	62.3%	35.2%	2.4%

NEW JERSEY

GOVERNOR
James E. McGreevey (D). Elected 2001 to a four-year term.

SENATORS (2 Democrats)
Jon Corzine (D). Elected 2000 to a six-year term.

Frank R. Lautenberg (D). Elected 2002 to a six-year term. Previously elected 1994, 1988, 1982.

REPRESENTATIVES (7 Democrats, 6 Republicans)
1. Robert E. Andrews (D)
2. Frank A. LoBiondo (R)
3. H. James Saxton (R)
4. Christopher H. Smith (R)
5. Scott Garrett (R)
6. Frank Pallone Jr. (D)
7. Mike Ferguson (R)
8. Bill Pascrell Jr. (D)
9. Steven R. Rothman (D)
10. Donald M. Payne (D)
11. Rodney Frelinghuysen (R)
12. Rush D. Holt (D)
13. Robert Menendez (D)

POSTWAR VOTE FOR PRESIDENT

Year	Total Vote	Republican Vote	Republican Candidate	Democratic Vote	Democratic Candidate	Other Vote	Plurality	Total Vote Rep.	Total Vote Dem.	Major Vote Rep.	Major Vote Dem.
2000**	3,187,226	1,284,173	Bush, George W.	1,788,850	Gore, Al	114,203	504,677 D	40.3%	56.1%	41.8%	58.2%
1996**	3,075,807	1,103,078	Dole, Bob	1,652,329	Clinton, Bill	320,400	549,251 D	35.9%	53.7%	40.0%	60.0%
1992**	3,343,594	1,356,865	Bush, George	1,436,206	Clinton, Bill	550,523	79,341 D	40.6%	43.0%	48.6%	51.4%
1988	3,099,553	1,743,192	Bush, George	1,320,352	Dukakis, Michael S.	36,009	422,840 R	56.2%	42.6%	56.9%	43.1%
1984	3,217,862	1,933,630	Reagan, Ronald	1,261,323	Mondale, Walter F.	22,909	672,307 R	60.1%	39.2%	60.5%	39.5%
1980**	2,975,684	1,546,557	Reagan, Ronald	1,147,364	Carter, Jimmy	281,763	399,193 R	52.0%	38.6%	57.4%	42.6%
1976	3,014,472	1,509,688	Ford, Gerald R.	1,444,653	Carter, Jimmy	60,131	65,035 R	50.1%	47.9%	51.1%	48.9%
1972	2,997,229	1,845,502	Nixon, Richard M.	1,102,211	McGovern, George S.	49,516	743,291 R	61.6%	36.8%	62.6%	37.4%
1968	2,875,395	1,325,467	Nixon, Richard M.	1,264,206	Humphrey, Hubert H.	285,722	61,261 R	46.1%	44.0%	51.2%	48.8%
1964	2,847,663	964,174	Goldwater, Barry M.	1,868,231	Johnson, Lyndon B.	15,258	904,057 D	33.9%	65.6%	34.0%	66.0%
1960	2,773,111	1,363,324	Nixon, Richard M.	1,385,415	Kennedy, John F.	24,372	22,091 D	49.2%	50.0%	49.6%	50.4%
1956	2,484,312	1,606,942	Eisenhower, Dwight D.	850,337	Stevenson, Adlai E.	27,033	756,605 R	64.7%	34.2%	65.4%	34.6%
1952	2,418,554	1,373,613	Eisenhower, Dwight D.	1,015,902	Stevenson, Adlai E.	29,039	357,711 R	56.8%	42.0%	57.5%	42.5%
1948	1,949,555	981,124	Dewey, Thomas E.	895,455	Truman, Harry S.	72,976	85,669 R	50.3%	45.9%	52.3%	47.7%

In 2000 the other vote column includes 94,554 votes cast for Green (Nader). In 1996 the other vote column includes 262,134 votes cast for Perot. In 1992 the other vote column includes 521,829 votes cast for Perot. In 1980 the other vote column includes 234,632 votes for Independent (Anderson).

NEW JERSEY

POSTWAR VOTE FOR GOVERNOR

Year	Total Vote	Republican Vote	Candidate	Democratic Vote	Candidate	Other Vote	Rep.-Dem. Plurality	Rep.	Dem.	Rep.	Dem.
								Total Vote		Major Vote	
2001	2,227,165	928,174	Schundler, Bret	1,256,853	McGreevey, James E.	42,138	328,679 D	41.7%	56.4%	42.5%	57.5%
1997	2,418,344	1,133,394	Whitman, Christine T.	1,107,968	McGreevey, James E.	176,982	25,426 R	46.9%	45.8%	50.6%	49.4%
1993	2,505,964	1,236,124	Whitman, Christine T.	1,210,031	Florio, James J.	59,809	26,093 R	49.3%	48.3%	50.5%	49.5%
1989	2,253,764	838,553	Courter, James A.	1,379,937	Florio, James J.	35,274	541,384 D	37.2%	61.2%	37.8%	62.2%
1985	1,972,624	1,372,631	Kean, Thomas H.	578,402	Shapiro, Peter	21,591	794,229 R	69.6%	29.3%	70.4%	29.6%
1981	2,317,239	1,145,999	Kean, Thomas H.	1,144,202	Florio, James J.	27,038	1,797 R	49.5%	49.4%	50.0%	50.0%
1977	2,126,264	888,880	Bateman, Raymond H.	1,184,564	Byrne, Brendan T.	52,820	295,684 D	41.8%	55.7%	42.9%	57.1%
1973	2,122,009	676,235	Sandman, Charles W.	1,414,613	Byrne, Brendan T.	31,161	738,378 D	31.9%	66.7%	32.3%	67.7%
1969	2,366,606	1,411,905	Cahill, William T.	911,003	Meyner, Robert B.	43,698	500,902 R	59.7%	38.5%	60.8%	39.2%
1965	2,229,583	915,996	Dumont, Wayne	1,279,568	Hughes, Richard J.	34,019	363,572 D	41.1%	57.4%	41.7%	58.3%
1961	2,152,662	1,049,274	Mitchell, James P.	1,084,194	Hughes, Richard J.	19,194	34,920 D	48.7%	50.4%	49.2%	50.8%
1957	2,018,488	897,321	Forbes, Malcolm S.	1,101,130	Meyner, Robert B.	20,037	203,809 D	44.5%	54.6%	44.9%	55.1%
1953	1,810,812	809,068	Troast, Paul L.	962,710	Meyner, Robert B.	39,034	153,642 D	44.7%	53.2%	45.7%	54.3%
1949**	1,718,788	885,882	Driscoll, Alfred	810,022	Wene, Elmer H.	22,884	75,860 R	51.5%	47.1%	52.2%	47.8%
1946	1,414,527	807,378	Driscoll, Alfred	585,960	Hansen, Lewis G.	21,189	221,418 R	57.1%	41.4%	57.9%	42.1%

The term of office of New Jersey's Governor was increased from three to four years effective with the 1949 election.

POSTWAR VOTE FOR SENATOR

Year	Total Vote	Republican Vote	Candidate	Democratic Vote	Candidate	Other Vote	Rep.-Dem. Plurality	Rep.	Dem.	Rep.	Dem.
								Total Vote		Major Vote	
2002	2,112,604	928,439	Forrester, Douglas R.	1,138,193	Lautenberg, Frank R.	45,972	209,754 D	43.9%	53.9%	44.9%	55.1%
2000	3,015,662	1,420,267	Franks, Bob	1,511,237	Corzine, Jon	84,158	90,970 D	47.1%	50.1%	48.4%	51.6%
1996	2,884,106	1,227,817	Zimmer, Dick	1,519,328	Torricelli, Robert G.	136,961	291,511 D	42.6%	52.7%	44.7%	55.3%
1994	2,054,887	966,244	Haytaian, Garabed	1,033,487	Lautenberg, Frank R.	55,156	67,243 D	47.0%	50.3%	48.3%	51.7%
1990	1,938,454	918,874	Whitman, Christine T.	977,810	Bradley, Bill	41,770	58,936 D	47.4%	50.4%	48.4%	51.6%
1988	2,987,634	1,349,937	Dawkins, Peter M.	1,599,905	Lautenberg, Frank R.	37,792	249,968 D	45.2%	53.6%	45.8%	54.2%
1984	3,096,456	1,080,100	Mochary, Mary V.	1,986,644	Bradley, Bill	29,712	906,544 D	34.9%	64.2%	35.2%	64.8%
1982	2,193,945	1,047,626	Fenwick, Millicent	1,117,549	Lautenberg, Frank R.	28,770	69,923 D	47.8%	50.9%	48.4%	51.6%
1978	1,957,515	844,200	Bell, Jeffrey	1,082,960	Bradley, Bill	30,355	238,760 D	43.1%	55.3%	43.8%	56.2%
1976	2,771,390	1,054,508	Norcross, David F.	1,681,140	Williams, Harrison	35,742	626,632 D	38.0%	60.7%	38.5%	61.5%
1972	2,791,907	1,743,854	Case, Clifford P.	963,573	Krebs, Paul J.	84,480	780,281 R	62.5%	34.5%	64.4%	35.6%
1970	2,142,105	903,026	Gross, Nelson G.	1,157,074	Williams, Harrison	82,005	254,048 D	42.2%	54.0%	43.8%	56.2%
1966	2,131,188	1,279,343	Case, Clifford P.	788,021	Wilentz, Warren W.	63,824	491,322 R	60.0%	37.0%	61.9%	38.1%
1964	2,710,441	1,011,610	Shanley, Bernard M.	1,678,051	Williams, Harrison	20,780	666,441 D	37.3%	61.9%	37.6%	62.4%
1960	2,664,556	1,483,832	Case, Clifford P.	1,151,385	Lord, Thorn	29,339	332,447 R	55.7%	43.2%	56.3%	43.7%
1958	1,881,329	882,287	Kean, Robert W.	966,832	Williams, Harrison	32,210	84,545 D	46.9%	51.4%	47.7%	52.3%
1954	1,770,557	861,528	Case, Clifford P.	858,158	Howell, Charles R.	50,871	3,370 R	48.7%	48.5%	50.1%	49.9%
1952	2,318,232	1,286,782	Smith, H. Alexander	1,011,187	Alexander, Archibald	20,263	275,595 R	55.5%	43.6%	56.0%	44.0%
1948	1,869,882	934,720	Hendrickson, Robert	884,414	Alexander, Archibald	50,748	50,306 R	50.0%	47.3%	51.4%	48.6%
1946	1,367,155	799,808	Smith, H. Alexander	548,458	Brunner, George E.	18,889	251,350 R	58.5%	40.1%	59.3%	40.7%

NEW JERSEY

Congressional districts first established for elections held in 2002
13 members

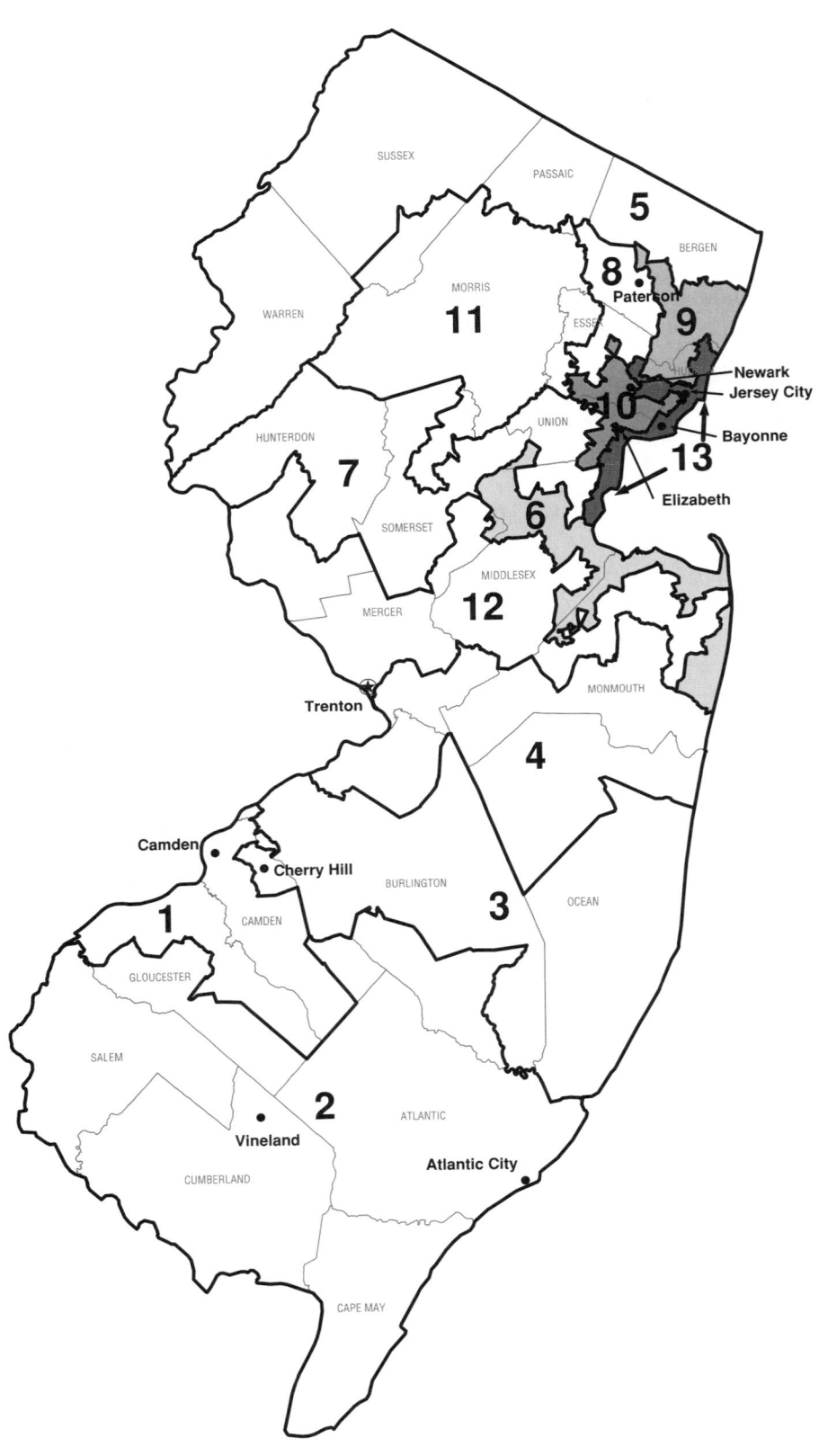

NEW JERSEY

Northern New Jersey Gateway Area

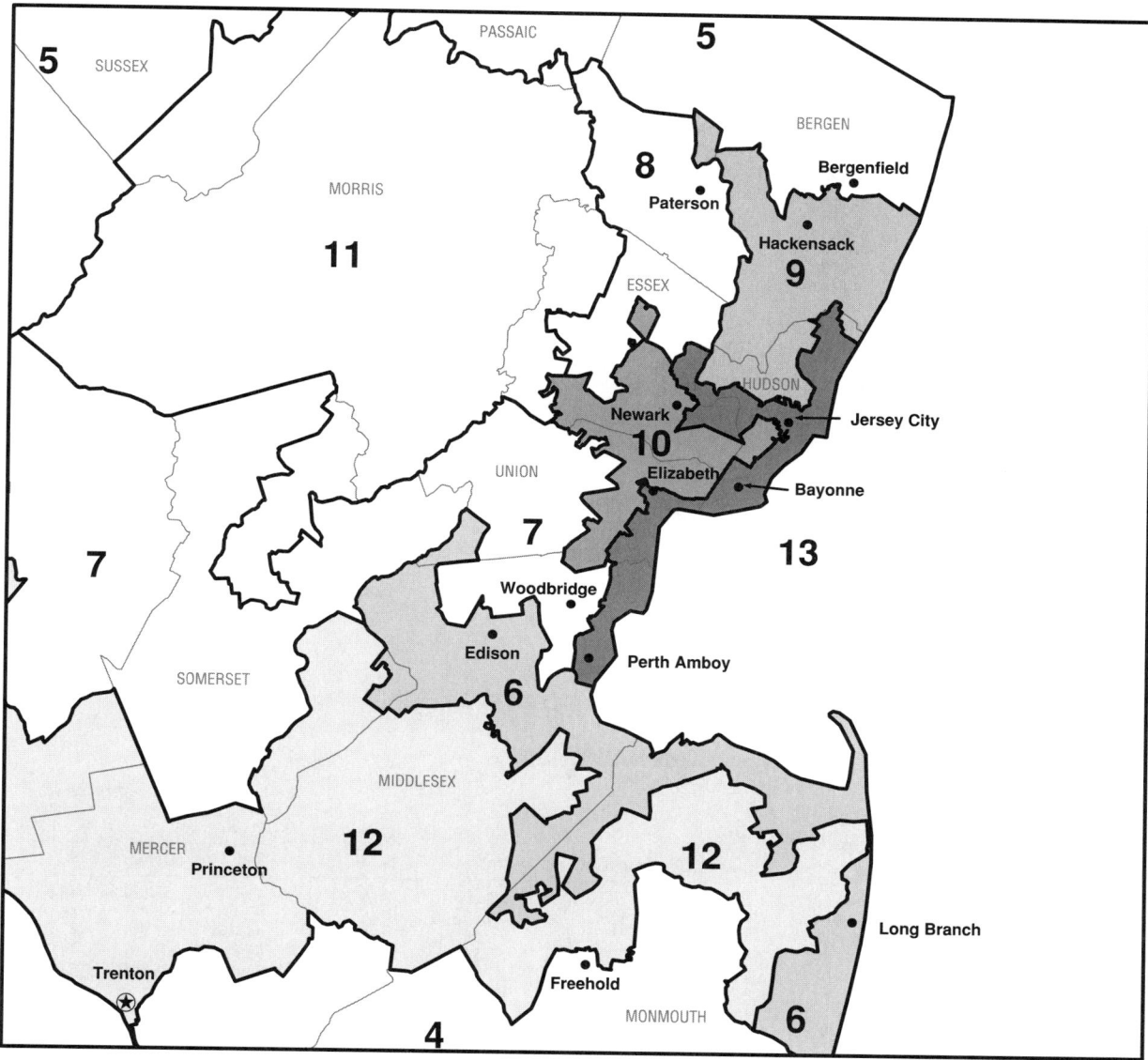

NEW JERSEY

GOVERNOR 2001

2000 Census Population	County	Total Vote	Republican	Democratic	Other	Rep.-Dem. Plurality	Percentage			
							Total Vote		Major Vote	
							Rep.	Dem.	Rep.	Dem.
252,552	ATLANTIC	67,165	27,547	38,623	995	11,076 D	41.0%	57.5%	41.6%	58.4%
884,118	BERGEN	254,542	111,221	140,215	3,106	28,994 D	43.7%	55.1%	44.2%	55.8%
423,394	BURLINGTON	113,232	48,098	62,697	2,437	14,599 D	42.5%	55.4%	43.4%	56.6%
508,932	CAMDEN	120,960	40,063	78,169	2,728	38,106 D	33.1%	64.6%	33.9%	66.1%
102,326	CAPE MAY	35,324	17,471	17,118	735	353 R	49.5%	48.5%	50.5%	49.5%
146,438	CUMBERLAND	33,696	13,583	19,445	668	5,862 D	40.3%	57.7%	41.1%	58.9%
793,633	ESSEX	180,029	48,540	129,406	2,083	80,866 D	27.0%	71.9%	27.3%	72.7%
254,673	GLOUCESTER	70,685	28,210	41,083	1,392	12,873 D	39.9%	58.1%	40.7%	59.3%
608,975	HUDSON	123,738	37,440	85,074	1,224	47,634 D	30.3%	68.8%	30.6%	69.4%
121,989	HUNTERDON	39,454	23,059	13,911	2,484	9,148 R	58.4%	35.3%	62.4%	37.6%
350,761	MERCER	94,366	31,705	57,513	5,148	25,808 D	33.6%	60.9%	35.5%	64.5%
750,162	MIDDLESEX	186,809	66,749	117,061	2,999	50,312 D	35.7%	62.7%	36.3%	63.7%
615,301	MONMOUTH	185,472	89,987	91,838	3,647	1,851 D	48.5%	49.5%	49.5%	50.5%
470,212	MORRIS	142,240	79,350	60,948	1,942	18,402 R	55.8%	42.8%	56.6%	43.4%
510,916	OCEAN	164,954	77,726	84,538	2,690	6,812 D	47.1%	51.2%	47.9%	52.1%
489,049	PASSAIC	107,434	43,806	62,390	1,238	18,584 D	40.8%	58.1%	41.3%	58.7%
64,285	SALEM	20,255	8,878	10,837	540	1,959 D	43.8%	53.5%	45.0%	55.0%
297,490	SOMERSET	85,828	44,815	39,110	1,903	5,705 R	52.2%	45.6%	53.4%	46.6%
144,166	SUSSEX	39,076	23,478	14,641	957	8,837 R	60.1%	37.5%	61.6%	38.4%
522,541	UNION	132,252	50,780	79,682	1,790	28,902 D	38.4%	60.3%	38.9%	61.1%
102,437	WARREN	29,654	15,668	12,554	1,432	3,114 R	52.8%	42.3%	55.5%	44.5%
8,414,350	TOTAL	2,227,165	928,174	1,256,853	42,138	328,679 D	41.7%	56.4%	42.5%	57.5%

NEW JERSEY

SENATOR 2002

2000 Census Population	County	Total Vote	Republican	Democratic	Other	Rep.-Dem. Plurality	Percentage			
							Total Vote		Major Vote	
							Rep.	Dem.	Rep.	Dem.
252,552	ATLANTIC	61,801	27,236	33,277	1,288	6,041 D	44.1%	53.8%	45.0%	55.0%
884,118	BERGEN	253,880	110,272	139,241	4,367	28,969 D	43.4%	54.8%	44.2%	55.8%
423,394	BURLINGTON	118,885	54,846	61,476	2,563	6,630 D	46.1%	51.7%	47.2%	52.8%
508,932	CAMDEN	122,832	41,628	77,640	3,564	36,012 D	33.9%	63.2%	34.9%	65.1%
102,326	CAPE MAY	33,098	17,751	14,760	587	2,991 R	53.6%	44.6%	54.6%	45.4%
146,438	CUMBERLAND	31,152	13,189	17,020	943	3,831 D	42.3%	54.6%	43.7%	56.3%
793,633	ESSEX	161,237	44,072	114,624	2,541	70,552 D	27.3%	71.1%	27.8%	72.2%
254,673	GLOUCESTER	73,925	31,140	41,009	1,776	9,869 D	42.1%	55.5%	43.2%	56.8%
608,975	HUDSON	101,881	25,194	74,127	2,560	48,933 D	24.7%	72.8%	25.4%	74.6%
121,989	HUNTERDON	40,177	25,124	13,890	1,163	11,234 R	62.5%	34.6%	64.4%	35.6%
350,761	MERCER	93,208	37,195	53,675	2,338	16,480 D	39.9%	57.6%	40.9%	59.1%
750,162	MIDDLESEX	167,156	65,128	98,019	4,009	32,891 D	39.0%	58.6%	39.9%	60.1%
615,301	MONMOUTH	172,432	88,424	79,730	4,278	8,694 R	51.3%	46.2%	52.6%	47.4%
470,212	MORRIS	137,982	79,984	55,592	2,406	24,392 R	58.0%	40.3%	59.0%	41.0%
510,916	OCEAN	153,235	80,592	69,328	3,315	11,264 R	52.6%	45.2%	53.8%	46.2%
489,049	PASSAIC	94,903	39,822	53,275	1,806	13,453 D	42.0%	56.1%	42.8%	57.2%
64,285	SALEM	20,275	9,487	10,232	556	745 D	46.8%	50.5%	48.1%	51.9%
297,490	SOMERSET	84,017	45,590	36,476	1,951	9,114 R	54.3%	43.4%	55.6%	44.4%
144,166	SUSSEX	39,817	25,099	13,673	1,045	11,426 R	63.0%	34.3%	64.7%	35.3%
522,541	UNION	121,402	49,243	70,085	2,074	20,842 D	40.6%	57.7%	41.3%	58.7%
102,437	WARREN	29,309	17,423	11,044	842	6,379 R	59.4%	37.7%	61.2%	38.8%
8,414,350	TOTAL	2,112,604	928,439	1,138,193	45,972	209,754 D	43.9%	53.9%	44.9%	55.1%

NEW JERSEY

HOUSE OF REPRESENTATIVES

CD	Year	Total Vote	Republican Vote	Republican Candidate	Democratic Vote	Democratic Candidate	Other Vote	Rep.-Dem. Plurality	Total Vote Rep.	Total Vote Dem.	Major Vote Rep.	Major Vote Dem.
1	2002	131,389			121,846	Andrews, Robert E.*	9,543	121,846 D		92.7%		100.0%
2	2002	168,799	116,834	LoBiondo, Frank A.*	47,735	Farkas, Steven A.	4,230	69,099 R	69.2%	28.3%	71.0%	29.0%
3	2002	189,739	123,375	Saxton, H. James*	64,364	Strada, Richard	2,000	59,011 R	65.0%	33.9%	65.7%	34.3%
4	2002	174,301	115,293	Smith, Christopher H.*	55,967	Brennan, Mary	3,041	59,326 R	66.1%	32.1%	67.3%	32.7%
5	2002	199,851	118,881	Garrett, Scott	76,504	Sumers, Anne	4,466	42,377 R	59.5%	38.3%	60.8%	39.2%
6	2002	137,495	42,479	Medrow, Ric	91,379	Pallone, Frank Jr.*	3,637	48,900 D	30.9%	66.5%	31.7%	68.3%
7	2002	183,002	106,055	Ferguson, Mike*	74,879	Carden, Tim	2,068	31,176 R	58.0%	40.9%	58.6%	41.4%
8	2002	131,819	40,318	Silverman, Jared	88,101	Pascrell, Bill Jr.*	3,400	47,783 D	30.6%	66.8%	31.4%	68.6%
9	2002	139,196	42,088	Glass, Joseph	97,108	Rothman, Steven R.*		55,020 D	30.2%	69.8%	30.2%	69.8%
10	2002	102,346	15,913	Wirtz, Andrew	86,433	Payne, Donald M.*		70,520 D	15.5%	84.5%	15.5%	84.5%
11	2002	183,678	132,938	Frelinghuysen, Rodney*	48,477	Pawar, Vij	2,263	84,461 R	72.4%	26.4%	73.3%	26.7%
12	2002	171,713	62,938	Soaries, DeForest "Buster"	104,806	Holt, Rush D.*	3,969	41,868 D	36.7%	61.0%	37.5%	62.5%
13	2002	92,731	16,852	Geron, James	72,605	Menendez, Robert*	3,274	55,753 D	18.2%	78.3%	18.8%	81.2%
Total	2002	2,006,059	933,964		1,030,204		41,891	96,240 D	46.6%	51.4%	47.6%	52.4%

An asterisk (*) denotes incumbent.

NEW JERSEY

GENERAL AND PRIMARY ELECTIONS

2002 GENERAL ELECTIONS

Governor (2001) — Other vote was 24,084 Independent (Bill Schluter); 6,238 Green (Jerry L. Coleman); 4,684 Libertarian (Mark Edgerton); 2,568 Free New Jersey (George Watson Jr.); 1,949 New Jersey Conservative (Michael W. Koontz); 1,537 Socialist (Costantino Rozzo); 1,078 Socialist Workers (Kari Sachs). All of these candidates were listed on the ballot as Independent, with their partisan designation indicated as a "Slogan."

Senator — Other vote was 24,308 Green (Ted Glick); 12,558 Libertarian (Elizabeth Macron); 6,404 New Jersey Conservative (Norman E. Wahner); 2,702 Socialist (Gregory Pason). All of these candidates were listed on the ballot as Independent, with their partisan designation indicated as a "Slogan."

House — Other vote was:

CD 1 — 9,543 Libertarian (Timothy Haas).

CD 2 — 1,739 Green (Roger Merle); 1,720 Libertarian (Michael J. Matthews Jr.); 771 Socialist (Costantino Rozzo).

CD 3 — 1,335 Libertarian (Raymond Byrne); 665 America First (Ken Feduniewicz).

CD 4 — 1,211 Libertarian (Keith Quarles); 1,063 Honesty, Humanity, Duty (Hermann Winkelmann); 767 New Jersey Conservative (Don Graham).

CD 5 — 4,466 Lower Tax Independent (Michael J. Cino).

CD 6 — 1,819 Green (Richard D. Strong); 1,206 Libertarian (Barry Allen); 612 Human Rights Advocate (Mac Dara Francis X. Lyden).

CD 7 — 2,068 Libertarian (Darren Young).

CD 8 — 3,400 Green (Joseph A. Fortunato).

CD 9

CD 10

NEW JERSEY

GENERAL AND PRIMARY ELECTIONS

2002 GENERAL ELECTIONS

CD 11	2,263 Libertarian (Richard S. Roth).
CD 12	1,871 Green (Carl J. Mayer); 1,259 Libertarian (Thomas D. Abrams); 839 New Jersey Conservative (Karen Anne Zaletel).
CD 13	1,195 Green (Pat Henry Faulkner); 774 The American Party, Anti-Corruption Doctor (Esmat Zaklama); 732 Pro Life Conservative (Dick Hester); 573 Politicians are Crooks—Politicos son Corruptos (Herbert H. Shaw).

All of these House candidates were listed on the ballot as Independent, with their partisan designation indicated as a "Slogan."

2002 PRIMARY ELECTIONS

Primary	June 26, 2001 (Governor) June 4, 2002 (Congress)	**Registration** (as of June 4, 2002)	Republican Democratic Independent Other Unaffiliated	882,168 1,149,864 13,204 323 2,570,025
			TOTAL	4,615,584

Primary Type Semi-open—Registered Democrats and Republicans could vote only in their party's primary. "Unaffiliated" voters could participate in either party's primary if they were willing to become a member of that party.

Note: An asterisk (*) denotes incumbent.

	REPUBLICAN PRIMARIES			DEMOCRATIC PRIMARIES		
Governor (2001)	Bret Schundler	193,342	57.4%	James E. McGreevey	250,404	95.5%
	Bob Franks	143,606	42.6%	Elliot Greenspan	11,682	4.5%
	TOTAL	336,948		TOTAL	262,086	
Senator	Douglas R. Forrester	97,275	44.6%	Robert G. Torricelli*	181,468	
	Diane Allen	80,476	36.9%			
	John J. Matheussen	40,549	18.6%	*Torricelli withdrew before the general election and*		
	TOTAL	218,300		*was replaced on the November ballot by Frank R. Lautenberg.*		
Congressional District 1	No Republican candidate			Robert E. Andrews*	18,362	100.0%
Congressional District 2	Frank A. LoBiondo*	25,335	100.0%	Steven A. Farkas	9,182	100.0%
Congressional District 3	H. James Saxton*	24,884	100.0%	Richard Strada	10,431	100.0%
Congressional District 4	Christopher H. Smith*	19,667	100.0%	Mary Brennan	8,589	100.0%
Congressional District 5	Scott Garrett	16,234	45.0%	Anne Sumers	6,365	100.0%
	David C. Russo	9,299	25.8%			
	Gerald Cardinale	9,109	25.2%			
	Akram Yosri Abdelrahman	773	2.1%			
	Brian Fox	665	1.8%			
	TOTAL	36,080				
Congressional District 6	Ric Medrow	6,505	100.0%	Frank Pallone Jr.*	11,005	100.0%
Congressional District 7	Mike Ferguson*	20,244	100.0%	Tim Carden	6,217	90.7%
				Tyrone Cass Ross	640	9.3%
				TOTAL	6,857	

NEW JERSEY

GENERAL AND PRIMARY ELECTIONS

	REPUBLICAN PRIMARIES			DEMOCRATIC PRIMARIES		
Congressional District 8	Jared Silverman	6,437	100.0%	Bill Pascrell Jr.*	10,462	100.0%
Congressional District 9	Joseph Glass	7,336	100.0%	Steven R. Rothman*	16,362	100.0%
Congressional District 10	Andrew Wirtz	2,005	100.0%	Donald M. Payne*	33,851	84.1%
				Edward A. Allen	3,583	8.9%
				Edmund Proctor	2,818	7.0%
				TOTAL	40,252	
Congressional District 11	Rodney Frelinghuysen*	29,691	100.0%	Vij Pawar	6,462	100.0%
Congressional District 12	DeForest "Buster" Soaries	9,596	80.6%	Rush D. Holt*	9,618	100.0%
	Deborah Jones	2,306	19.4%			
	TOTAL	11,902				
Congressional District 13	James Geron	3,420	100.0%	Robert Menendez*	37,357	100.0%

NEW JERSEY REPUBLICAN PRIMARY

GOVERNOR 2001

2000 Census Population	County	Total Vote	Schundler	Franks	Winner	Percentage of Total Vote	
						Schundler	Franks
252,552	ATLANTIC	12,852	6,831	6,021	Schundler	53.2%	46.8%
884,118	BERGEN	34,826	20,186	14,640	Schundler	58.0%	42.0%
423,394	BURLINGTON	20,003	9,696	10,307	Franks	48.5%	51.5%
508,932	CAMDEN	10,918	5,744	5,174	Schundler	52.6%	47.4%
102,326	CAPE MAY	9,234	4,272	4,962	Franks	46.3%	53.7%
146,438	CUMBERLAND	4,473	2,082	2,391	Franks	46.5%	53.5%
793,633	ESSEX	15,670	8,918	6,752	Schundler	56.9%	43.1%
254,673	GLOUCESTER	7,495	3,701	3,794	Franks	49.4%	50.6%
608,975	HUDSON	9,803	7,273	2,530	Schundler	74.2%	25.8%
121,989	HUNTERDON	10,761	7,356	3,405	Schundler	68.4%	31.6%
350,761	MERCER	10,314	5,613	4,701	Schundler	54.4%	45.6%
750,162	MIDDLESEX	15,885	10,003	5,882	Schundler	63.0%	37.0%
615,301	MONMOUTH	29,213	19,069	10,144	Schundler	65.3%	34.7%
470,212	MORRIS	39,694	23,664	16,030	Schundler	59.6%	40.4%
510,916	OCEAN	29,736	16,320	13,416	Schundler	54.9%	45.1%
489,049	PASSAIC	16,459	9,374	7,085	Schundler	57.0%	43.0%
64,285	SALEM	2,615	1,254	1,361	Franks	48.0%	52.0%
297,490	SOMERSET	18,648	10,356	8,292	Schundler	55.5%	44.5%
144,166	SUSSEX	12,310	8,151	4,159	Schundler	66.2%	33.8%
522,541	UNION	17,785	7,758	10,027	Franks	43.6%	56.4%
102,437	WARREN	8,254	5,721	2,533	Schundler	69.3%	30.7%
8,414,350	TOTAL	336,948	193,342	143,606	Schundler	57.4%	42.6%

NEW JERSEY DEMOCRATIC PRIMARY

GOVERNOR 2001

2000 Census Population	County	Total Vote	McGreevey	Greenspan	Winner	Percentage of Total Vote	
						McGreevey	Greenspan
252,552	ATLANTIC	6,921	6,672	249	McGreevey	96.4%	3.6%
884,118	BERGEN	22,437	21,295	1,142	McGreevey	94.9%	5.1%
423,394	BURLINGTON	9,006	8,790	216	McGreevey	97.6%	2.4%
508,932	CAMDEN	14,300	13,613	687	McGreevey	95.2%	4.8%
102,326	CAPE MAY	2,145	2,073	72	McGreevey	96.6%	3.4%
146,438	CUMBERLAND	3,061	2,898	163	McGreevey	94.7%	5.3%
793,633	ESSEX	43,927	42,505	1,422	McGreevey	96.8%	3.2%
254,673	GLOUCESTER	6,846	6,544	302	McGreevey	95.6%	4.4%
608,975	HUDSON	34,591	33,069	1,522	McGreevey	95.6%	4.4%
121,989	HUNTERDON	1,609	1,502	107	McGreevey	93.3%	6.7%
350,761	MERCER	8,885	8,534	351	McGreevey	96.0%	4.0%
750,162	MIDDLESEX	29,505	28,020	1,485	McGreevey	95.0%	5.0%
615,301	MONMOUTH	12,957	12,263	694	McGreevey	94.6%	5.4%
470,212	MORRIS	9,067	8,634	433	McGreevey	95.2%	4.8%
510,916	OCEAN	12,528	12,160	368	McGreevey	97.1%	2.9%
489,049	PASSAIC	14,209	13,175	1,034	McGreevey	92.7%	7.3%
64,285	SALEM	2,044	1,939	105	McGreevey	94.9%	5.1%
297,490	SOMERSET	5,490	5,199	291	McGreevey	94.7%	5.3%
144,166	SUSSEX	2,050	1,903	147	McGreevey	92.8%	7.2%
522,541	UNION	18,126	17,425	701	McGreevey	96.1%	3.9%
102,437	WARREN	2,382	2,191	191	McGreevey	92.0%	8.0%
8,414,350	TOTAL	262,086	250,404	11,682	McGreevey	95.5%	4.5%

NEW JERSEY REPUBLICAN PRIMARY

SENATOR 2002

2000 Census Population	County	Total Vote	Forrester	Allen	Matheussen	Winner	Percentage of Total Vote		
							Forrester	Allen	Matheussen
252,552	ATLANTIC	6,858	2,461	3,473	924	Allen	35.9%	50.6%	13.5%
884,118	BERGEN	25,703	14,055	8,215	3,433	Forrester	54.7%	32.0%	13.4%
423,394	BURLINGTON	18,946	3,399	13,669	1,878	Allen	17.9%	72.1%	9.9%
508,932	CAMDEN	9,128	1,782	4,195	3,151	Allen	19.5%	46.0%	34.5%
102,326	CAPE MAY	10,596	1,918	6,824	1,854	Allen	18.1%	64.4%	17.5%
146,438	CUMBERLAND	2,749	775	1,002	972	Allen	28.2%	36.4%	35.4%
793,633	ESSEX	9,569	4,382	2,961	2,226	Forrester	45.8%	30.9%	23.3%
254,673	GLOUCESTER	7,042	949	1,741	4,352	Matheussen	13.5%	24.7%	61.8%
608,975	HUDSON	4,122	1,894	1,232	996	Forrester	45.9%	29.9%	24.2%
121,989	HUNTERDON	9,290	4,674	3,448	1,168	Forrester	50.3%	37.1%	12.6%
350,761	MERCER	6,488	3,736	1,921	831	Forrester	57.6%	29.6%	12.8%
750,162	MIDDLESEX	8,466	5,616	1,649	1,201	Forrester	66.3%	19.5%	14.2%
615,301	MONMOUTH	13,839	8,331	3,760	1,748	Forrester	60.2%	27.2%	12.6%
470,212	MORRIS	25,191	11,645	7,967	5,579	Forrester	46.2%	31.6%	22.1%
510,916	OCEAN	16,242	8,283	5,368	2,591	Forrester	51.0%	33.1%	16.0%
489,049	PASSAIC	7,492	4,907	1,341	1,244	Forrester	65.5%	17.9%	16.6%
64,285	SALEM	1,976	506	994	476	Allen	25.6%	50.3%	24.1%
297,490	SOMERSET	10,611	5,715	3,373	1,523	Forrester	53.9%	31.8%	14.4%
144,166	SUSSEX	9,221	4,588	3,081	1,552	Forrester	49.8%	33.4%	16.8%
522,541	UNION	8,274	4,894	2,217	1,163	Forrester	59.1%	26.8%	14.1%
102,437	WARREN	6,497	2,765	2,045	1,687	Forrester	42.6%	31.5%	26.0%
8,414,350	TOTAL	218,300	97,275	80,476	40,549	Forrester	44.6%	36.9%	18.6%

NEW MEXICO

GOVERNOR
Bill Richardson (D). Elected 2002 to a four-year term.

SENATORS (1 Democrat, 1 Republican)
Jeff Bingaman (D). Reelected 2000 to a six-year term. Previously elected 1994, 1988, 1982.

Pete V. Domenici (R). Reelected 2002 to a six-year term. Previously elected 1996, 1990, 1984, 1978, 1972.

REPRESENTATIVES (2 Republicans, 1 Democrat)
1. Heather A. Wilson (R)   3. Tom Udall (D)
2. Steve Pearce (R)

POSTWAR VOTE FOR PRESIDENT

| | | Republican | | Democratic | | | | Percentage | | | |
| | | | | | | | | Total Vote | | Major Vote | |
Year	Total Vote	Vote	Candidate	Vote	Candidate	Other Vote	Plurality	Rep.	Dem.	Rep.	Dem.
2000**	598,605	286,417	Bush, George W.	286,783	Gore, Al	25,405	366 D	47.8%	47.9%	50.0%	50.0%
1996**	556,074	232,751	Dole, Bob	273,495	Clinton, Bill	49,828	40,744 D	41.9%	49.2%	46.0%	54.0%
1992**	569,986	212,824	Bush, George	261,617	Clinton, Bill	95,545	48,793 D	37.3%	45.9%	44.9%	55.1%
1988	521,287	270,341	Bush, George	244,497	Dukakis, Michael S.	6,449	25,844 R	51.9%	46.9%	52.5%	47.5%
1984	514,370	307,101	Reagan, Ronald	201,769	Mondale, Walter F.	5,500	105,332 R	59.7%	39.2%	60.3%	39.7%
1980**	456,971	250,779	Reagan, Ronald	167,826	Carter, Jimmy	38,366	82,953 R	54.9%	36.7%	59.9%	40.1%
1976	418,409	211,419	Ford, Gerald R.	201,148	Carter, Jimmy	5,842	10,271 R	50.5%	48.1%	51.2%	48.8%
1972	386,241	235,606	Nixon, Richard M.	141,084	McGovern, George S.	9,551	94,522 R	61.0%	36.5%	62.5%	37.5%
1968	327,350	169,692	Nixon, Richard M.	130,081	Humphrey, Hubert H.	27,577	39,611 R	51.8%	39.7%	56.6%	43.4%
1964	328,645	132,838	Goldwater, Barry M.	194,015	Johnson, Lyndon B.	1,792	61,177 D	40.4%	59.0%	40.6%	59.4%
1960	311,107	153,733	Nixon, Richard M.	156,027	Kennedy, John F.	1,347	2,294 D	49.4%	50.2%	49.6%	50.4%
1956	253,926	146,788	Eisenhower, Dwight D.	106,098	Stevenson, Adlai E.	1,040	40,690 R	57.8%	41.8%	58.0%	42.0%
1952	238,608	132,170	Eisenhower, Dwight D.	105,661	Stevenson, Adlai E.	777	26,509 R	55.4%	44.3%	55.6%	44.4%
1948	187,063	80,303	Dewey, Thomas E.	105,464	Truman, Harry S.	1,296	25,161 D	42.9%	56.4%	43.2%	56.8%

In 2000 the other vote column includes 21,251 votes cast for Green (Nader). In 1996 the other vote column includes 32,257 votes cast for Perot. In 1992 the other vote column includes 91,895 votes cast for Perot. In 1980 the other vote column includes 29,459 votes for Independent (Anderson).

NEW MEXICO

POSTWAR VOTE FOR GOVERNOR

Year	Total Vote	Republican Vote	Candidate	Democratic Vote	Candidate	Other Vote	Rep.-Dem. Plurality	Total Vote Rep.	Total Vote Dem.	Major Vote Rep.	Major Vote Dem.
2002	484,233	189,074	Sanchez, John A.	268,693	Richardson, Bill	26,466	79,619 D	39.0%	55.5%	41.3%	58.7%
1998	498,703	271,948	Johnson, Gary E.	226,755	Chavez, Martin J.		45,193 R	54.5%	45.5%	54.5%	45.5%
1994	467,621	232,945	Johnson, Gary E.	186,686	King, Bruce	47,990	46,259 R	49.8%	39.9%	55.5%	44.5%
1990	411,236	185,692	Bond, Frank M.	224,564	King, Bruce	980	38,872 D	45.2%	54.6%	45.3%	54.7%
1986	394,833	209,455	Carruthers, Garrey E.	185,378	Powell. Ray B.		24,077 R	53.0%	47.0%	53.0%	47.0%
1982	407,466	191,626	Irick, John B.	215,840	Anaya, Toney		24,214 D	47.0%	53.0%	47.0%	53.0%
1978	345,577	170,848	Skeen, Joseph R.	174,631	King, Bruce	98	3,783 D	49.4%	50.5%	49.5%	50.5%
1974	328,742	160,430	Skeen, Joseph R.	164,172	Apodaca, Jerry	4,140	3,742 D	48.8%	49.9%	49.4%	50.6%
1970**	290,375	134,640	Domenici, Pete V.	148,835	King, Bruce	6,900	14,195 D	46.4%	51.3%	47.5%	52.5%
1968	318,975	160,140	Cargo, David F.	157,230	Chavez, Fabian	1,605	2,910 R	50.2%	49.3%	50.5%	49.5%
1966	260,232	134,625	Cargo, David F.	125,587	Lusk, Thomas E.	20	9,038 R	51.7%	48.3%	51.7%	48.3%
1964	318,042	126,540	Tucker, Merle H.	191,497	Campbell, Jack M.	5	64,957 D	39.8%	60.2%	39.8%	60.2%
1962	247,135	116,184	Mechem, Edwin L.	130,933	Campbell, Jack M.	18	14,749 D	47.0%	53.0%	47.0%	53.0%
1960	305,542	153,765	Mechem, Edwin L.	151,777	Burroughs, John		1,988 R	50.3%	49.7%	50.3%	49.7%
1958	205,048	101,567	Mechem, Edwin L.	103,481	Burroughs, John		1,914 R	49.5%	50.5%	49.5%	50.5%
1956	251,751	131,488	Mechem, Edwin L.	120,263	Simms, John F.		11,225 R	52.2%	47.8%	52.2%	47.8%
1954	193,956	83,373	Stockton, Alvin	110,583	Simms, John F.		27,210 D	43.0%	57.0%	43.0%	57.0%
1952	240,150	129,116	Mechem, Edwin L.	111,034	Grantham, Everett		18,082 R	53.8%	46.2%	53.8%	46.2%
1950	180,205	96,846	Mechem, Edwin L.	83,359	Miles, John E.		13,487 R	53.7%	46.3%	53.7%	46.3%
1948	189,992	86,023	Lujan, Manuel	103,969	Mabry, Thomas J.		17,946 D	45.3%	54.7%	45.3%	54.7%
1946	132,930	62,875	Safford, Edward L.	70,055	Mabry, Thomas J.		7,180 D	47.3%	52.7%	47.3%	52.7%

The term of New Mexico's Governor was increased from two to four years effective with the 1970 election.

POSTWAR VOTE FOR SENATOR

Year	Total Vote	Republican Vote	Candidate	Democratic Vote	Candidate	Other Vote	Rep.-Dem. Plurality	Total Vote Rep.	Total Vote Dem.	Major Vote Rep.	Major Vote Dem.
2002	483,340	314,301	Domenici, Pete V.	169,039	Tristani, Gloria		145,262 R	65.0%	35.0%	65.0%	35.0%
2000	589,526	225,517	Redmond, Bill	363,744	Bingaman, Jeff	265	138,227 D	38.3%	61.7%	38.3%	61.7%
1996	551,821	357,171	Domenici, Pete V.	164,356	Trujillo, Art	30,294	192,815 R	64.7%	29.8%	68.5%	31.5%
1994	463,196	213,025	McMillan, Colin R.	249,989	Bingaman, Jeff	182	36,964 D	46.0%	54.0%	46.0%	54.0%
1990	406,938	296,712	Domenici, Pete V.	110,033	Benavides, Tom R.	193	186,679 R	72.9%	27.0%	72.9%	27.1%
1988	508,598	186,579	Valentine, William	321,983	Bingaman, Jeff	36	135,404 D	36.7%	63.3%	36.7%	63.3%
1984	502,634	361,371	Domenici, Pete V.	141,253	Pratt, Judith A.	10	220,118 R	71.9%	28.1%	71.9%	28.1%
1982	404,810	187,128	Schmitt, Harrison	217,682	Bingaman, Jeff		30,554 D	46.2%	53.8%	46.2%	53.8%
1978	343,554	183,442	Domenici, Pete V.	160,045	Anaya, Toney	67	23,397 R	53.4%	46.6%	53.4%	46.6%
1976	413,141	234,681	Schmitt, Harrison	176,382	Montoya, Joseph M.	2,078	58,299 R	56.8%	42.7%	57.1%	42.9%
1972	378,330	204,253	Domenici, Pete V.	173,815	Daniels, Jack	262	30,438 R	54.0%	45.9%	54.0%	46.0%
1970	289,906	135,004	Carter, Anderson	151,486	Montoya, Joseph M.	3,416	16,482 D	46.6%	52.3%	47.1%	52.9%
1966	258,203	120,988	Carter, Anderson	137,205	Anderson, Clinton P.	10	16,217 D	46.9%	53.1%	46.9%	53.1%
1964	325,774	147,562	Mechem, Edwin L.	178,209	Montoya, Joseph M.	3	30,647 D	45.3%	54.7%	45.3%	54.7%
1960	300,551	109,897	Colwes, William F.	190,654	Anderson, Clinton P.		80,757 D	36.6%	63.4%	36.6%	63.4%
1958	203,323	75,827	Atchley, Forrest S.	127,496	Chavez, Dennis		51,669 D	37.3%	62.7%	37.3%	62.7%
1954	194,422	83,071	Mechem, Edwin L.	111,351	Anderson, Clinton P.		28,280 D	42.7%	57.3%	42.7%	57.3%
1952	239,711	117,168	Hurley, Patrick J.	122,543	Chavez, Dennis		5,375 D	48.9%	51.1%	48.9%	51.1%
1948	188,495	80,226	Hurley, Patrick J.	108,269	Anderson, Clinton P.		28,043 D	42.6%	57.4%	42.6%	57.4%
1946	133,282	64,632	Hurley, Patrick J.	68,650	Chavez, Dennis		4,018 D	48.5%	51.5%	48.5%	51.5%

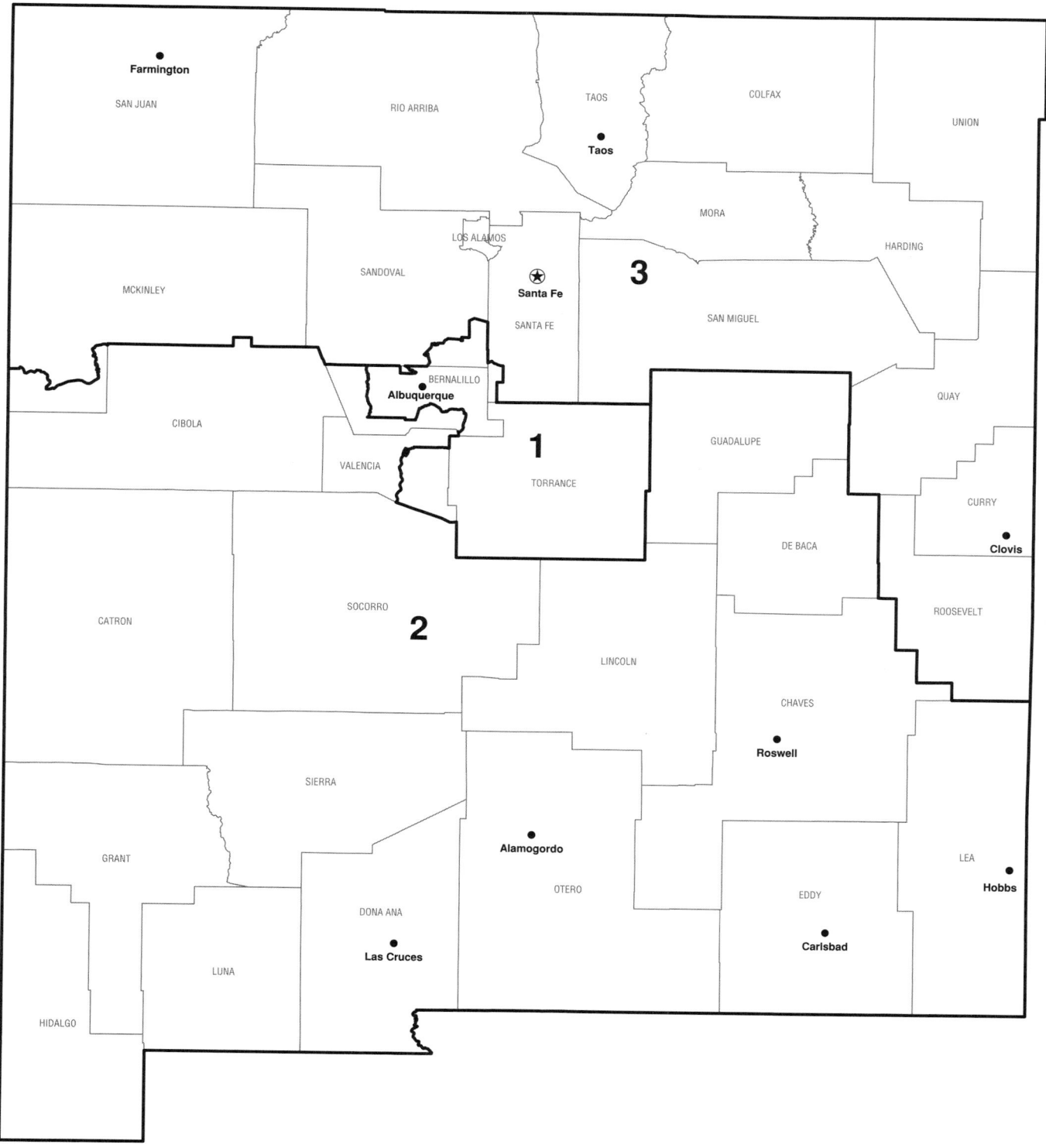

NEW MEXICO

Congressional districts first established for elections held in 2002
3 members

NEW MEXICO

GOVERNOR 2002

2000 Census Population	County	Total Vote	Republican	Democratic	Other	Rep.-Dem. Plurality	Percentage Total Vote Rep.	Dem.	Major Vote Rep.	Dem.
556,678	BERNALILLO	161,154	63,853	87,295	10,006	23,442 D	39.6%	54.2%	42.2%	57.8%
3,543	CATRON	1,656	1,069	499	88	570 R	64.6%	30.1%	68.2%	31.8%
61,382	CHAVES	14,786	7,802	6,584	400	1,218 R	52.8%	44.5%	54.2%	45.8%
25,595	CIBOLA	5,525	1,688	3,699	138	2,011 D	30.6%	67.0%	31.3%	68.7%
14,189	COLFAX	4,643	1,569	2,926	148	1,357 D	33.8%	63.0%	34.9%	65.1%
45,044	CURRY	9,301	4,182	4,851	268	669 D	45.0%	52.2%	46.3%	53.7%
2,240	DE BACA	860	389	455	16	66 D	45.2%	52.9%	46.1%	53.9%
174,682	DONA ANA	34,860	13,392	20,153	1,315	6,761 D	38.4%	57.8%	39.9%	60.1%
51,658	EDDY	13,975	6,844	6,758	373	86 R	49.0%	48.4%	50.3%	49.7%
31,002	GRANT	8,724	3,179	4,947	598	1,768 D	36.4%	56.7%	39.1%	60.9%
4,680	GUADALUPE	1,891	578	1,283	30	705 D	30.6%	67.8%	31.1%	68.9%
810	HARDING	619	253	356	10	103 D	40.9%	57.5%	41.5%	58.5%
5,932	HIDALGO	1,748	609	1,098	41	489 D	34.8%	62.8%	35.7%	64.3%
55,511	LEA	12,010	5,845	5,848	317	3 D	48.7%	48.7%	50.0%	50.0%
19,411	LINCOLN	6,135	3,303	2,575	257	728 R	53.8%	42.0%	56.2%	43.8%
18,343	LOS ALAMOS	8,232	4,097	3,612	523	485 R	49.8%	43.9%	53.1%	46.9%
25,016	LUNA	5,569	2,259	3,090	220	831 D	40.6%	55.5%	42.2%	57.8%
74,798	MCKINLEY	13,527	2,970	10,137	420	7,167 D	22.0%	74.9%	22.7%	77.3%
5,180	MORA	2,294	622	1,604	68	982 D	27.1%	69.9%	27.9%	72.1%
62,298	OTERO	13,960	7,605	5,911	444	1,694 R	54.5%	42.3%	56.3%	43.7%
10,155	QUAY	3,504	1,267	2,149	88	882 D	36.2%	61.3%	37.1%	62.9%
41,190	RIO ARRIBA	10,330	2,608	7,281	441	4,673 D	25.2%	70.5%	26.4%	73.6%
18,018	ROOSEVELT	4,333	1,943	2,241	149	298 D	44.8%	51.7%	46.4%	53.6%
89,908	SANDOVAL	26,083	10,556	14,037	1,490	3,481 D	40.5%	53.8%	42.9%	57.1%
113,801	SAN JUAN	28,144	14,237	12,765	1,142	1,472 R	50.6%	45.4%	52.7%	47.3%
30,126	SAN MIGUEL	7,849	1,577	5,910	362	4,333 D	20.1%	75.3%	21.1%	78.9%
129,292	SANTA FE	40,689	9,132	26,803	4,754	17,671 D	22.4%	65.9%	25.4%	74.6%
13,270	SIERRA	4,106	2,001	1,873	232	128 R	48.7%	45.6%	51.7%	48.3%
18,078	SOCORRO	5,937	2,157	3,492	288	1,335 D	36.3%	58.8%	38.2%	61.8%
29,979	TAOS	9,419	2,073	6,472	874	4,399 D	22.0%	68.7%	24.3%	75.7%
16,911	TORRANCE	4,192	2,004	1,944	244	60 R	47.8%	46.4%	50.8%	49.2%
4,174	UNION	1,590	731	831	28	100 D	46.0%	52.3%	46.8%	53.2%
66,152	VALENCIA	16,588	6,680	9,214	694	2,534 D	40.3%	55.5%	42.0%	58.0%
1,819,046	TOTAL	484,233	189,074	268,693	26,466	79,619 D	39.0%	55.5%	41.3%	58.7%

NEW MEXICO

SENATOR 2002

2000 Census Population	County	Total Vote	Republican	Democratic	Other	Rep.-Dem. Plurality	Percentage			
							Total Vote		Major Vote	
							Rep.	Dem.	Rep.	Dem.
556,678	BERNALILLO	160,982	103,428	57,554		45,874 R	64.2%	35.8%	64.2%	35.8%
3,543	CATRON	1,648	1,303	345		958 R	79.1%	20.9%	79.1%	20.9%
61,382	CHAVES	14,775	11,378	3,397		7,981 R	77.0%	23.0%	77.0%	23.0%
25,595	CIBOLA	5,501	3,279	2,222		1,057 R	59.6%	40.4%	59.6%	40.4%
14,189	COLFAX	4,629	3,112	1,517		1,595 R	67.2%	32.8%	67.2%	32.8%
45,044	CURRY	9,364	7,606	1,758		5,848 R	81.2%	18.8%	81.2%	18.8%
2,240	DE BACA	862	668	194		474 R	77.5%	22.5%	77.5%	22.5%
174,682	DONA ANA	34,730	21,774	12,956		8,818 R	62.7%	37.3%	62.7%	37.3%
51,658	EDDY	13,988	10,252	3,736		6,516 R	73.3%	26.7%	73.3%	26.7%
31,002	GRANT	8,694	4,925	3,769		1,156 R	56.6%	43.4%	56.6%	43.4%
4,680	GUADALUPE	1,893	1,131	762		369 R	59.7%	40.3%	59.7%	40.3%
810	HARDING	627	480	147		333 R	76.6%	23.4%	76.6%	23.4%
5,932	HIDALGO	1,734	1,139	595		544 R	65.7%	34.3%	65.7%	34.3%
55,511	LEA	12,003	9,607	2,396		7,211 R	80.0%	20.0%	80.0%	20.0%
19,411	LINCOLN	6,124	4,854	1,270		3,584 R	79.3%	20.7%	79.3%	20.7%
18,343	LOS ALAMOS	8,315	6,677	1,638		5,039 R	80.3%	19.7%	80.3%	19.7%
25,016	LUNA	5,542	3,657	1,885		1,772 R	66.0%	34.0%	66.0%	34.0%
74,798	MCKINLEY	13,452	7,746	5,706		2,040 R	57.6%	42.4%	57.6%	42.4%
5,180	MORA	2,192	1,204	988		216 R	54.9%	45.1%	54.9%	45.1%
62,298	OTERO	13,944	10,947	2,997		7,950 R	78.5%	21.5%	78.5%	21.5%
10,155	QUAY	3,497	2,567	930		1,637 R	73.4%	26.6%	73.4%	26.6%
41,190	RIO ARRIBA	10,427	5,498	4,929		569 R	52.7%	47.3%	52.7%	47.3%
18,018	ROOSEVELT	4,333	3,583	750		2,833 R	82.7%	17.3%	82.7%	17.3%
89,908	SANDOVAL	26,038	16,843	9,195		7,648 R	64.7%	35.3%	64.7%	35.3%
113,801	SAN JUAN	28,036	21,450	6,586		14,864 R	76.5%	23.5%	76.5%	23.5%
30,126	SAN MIGUEL	7,804	3,658	4,146		488 D	46.9%	53.1%	46.9%	53.1%
129,292	SANTA FE	40,562	19,074	21,488		2,414 D	47.0%	53.0%	47.0%	53.0%
13,270	SIERRA	4,120	2,999	1,121		1,878 R	72.8%	27.2%	72.8%	27.2%
18,078	SOCORRO	5,896	3,662	2,234		1,428 R	62.1%	37.9%	62.1%	37.9%
29,979	TAOS	9,359	4,509	4,850		341 D	48.2%	51.8%	48.2%	51.8%
16,911	TORRANCE	4,188	2,986	1,202		1,784 R	71.3%	28.7%	71.3%	28.7%
4,174	UNION	1,575	1,331	244		1,087 R	84.5%	15.5%	84.5%	15.5%
66,152	VALENCIA	16,506	10,974	5,532		5,442 R	66.5%	33.5%	66.5%	33.5%
1,819,046	TOTAL	483,340	314,301	169,039		145,262 R	65.0%	35.0%	65.0%	35.0%

NEW MEXICO

HOUSE OF REPRESENTATIVES

CD	Year	Total Vote	Republican		Democratic		Other Vote	Rep.-Dem. Plurality	Percentage			
			Vote	Candidate	Vote	Candidate			Total Vote		Major Vote	
									Rep.	Dem.	Rep.	Dem.
1	2002	172,945	95,711	Wilson, Heather A.*	77,234	Romero, Richard M.		18,477 R	55.3%	44.7%	55.3%	44.7%
2	2002	141,629	79,631	Pearce, Steve	61,916	Smith, John Arthur	82	17,715 R	56.2%	43.7%	56.3%	43.7%
3	2002	122,950			122,950	Udall, Tom*		122,950 D		100.0%		100.0%
Total	2002	437,524	175,342		262,100		82	86,758 D	40.1%	59.9%	40.1%	59.9%

An asterisk (*) denotes incumbent.

324

NEW MEXICO

GENERAL AND PRIMARY ELECTIONS

2002 GENERAL ELECTIONS

Governor Other vote was 26,466 Green (David E. Bacon).

Senator

House Other vote was:

CD 1
CD 2   43 write-in (George L. Dewey); 39 write-in (Padraig M. Lynch).
CD 3

2002 PRIMARY ELECTIONS

Primary June 4, 2002

Registration
(as of June 4, 2002)

Republican	303,198
Democratic	488,585
Other Parties	28,570
No Party	111,236
TOTAL	931,589

Primary Type Closed—Only registered Democrats and Republicans could vote in their party's primary.

Note: An asterisk (*) denotes incumbent.

	REPUBLICAN PRIMARIES			DEMOCRATIC PRIMARIES		
Governor	John A. Sanchez	55,102	58.5%	Bill Richardson	147,524	99.8%
	Walter D. Bradley	33,206	35.3%	Benjamin E. "Mike" Nalley (write-in)	294	0.2%
	Robert M. Burpo	3,864	4.1%			
	Gilbert S. Baca	1,979	2.1%			
	TOTAL	94,151		TOTAL	147,818	
Senator	Pete V. Domenici*	91,898	99.9%	Gloria Tristani	109,084	77.7%
	Orlin G. Cole (write-in)	62	0.1%	Francesca Lobato	31,225	22.2%
				Don E. Durham (write-in)	73	0.1%
	TOTAL	91,960		TOTAL	140,382	
Congressional District 1	Heather A. Wilson*	30,429	100.0%	Richard M. Romero	34,155	100.0%
Congressional District 2	Steve Pearce	12,317	35.0%	John Arthur Smith	22,925	53.0%
	Edward R. Tinsley	9,587	27.3%	Ruben A. Smith	20,365	47.0%
	Phelps Anderson	8,432	24.0%			
	C. Earl Greer	2,426	6.9%			
	Leo Martinez	2,389	6.8%			
	TOTAL	35,151		TOTAL	43,290	
Congressional District 3	*No Republican candidate filed for the primary. Edward F. Tsyitee received 495 write-in votes but was not a candidate in the general election.*			Tom Udall*	59,762	100.0%

NEW MEXICO REPUBLICAN PRIMARY
GOVERNOR 2002

2000 Census Population	County	Total Vote	Sanchez	Bradley	Other	Winner	Percentage of Total Vote		
							Sanchez	Bradley	Other
556,678	BERNALILLO	30,878	20,909	8,424	1,545	Sanchez	67.7%	27.3%	5.0%
3,543	CATRON	767	368	313	86	Sanchez	48.0%	40.8%	11.2%
61,382	CHAVES	5,393	3,286	1,912	195	Sanchez	60.9%	35.5%	3.6%
25,595	CIBOLA	786	506	237	43	Sanchez	64.4%	30.2%	5.5%
14,189	COLFAX	769	493	220	56	Sanchez	64.1%	28.6%	7.3%
45,044	CURRY	2,586	587	1,948	51	Bradley	22.7%	75.3%	2.0%
2,240	DE BACA	163	61	91	11	Bradley	37.4%	55.8%	6.7%
174,682	DONA ANA	5,868	2,466	3,034	368	Bradley	42.0%	51.7%	6.3%
51,658	EDDY	2,506	1,156	1,042	308	Sanchez	46.1%	41.6%	12.3%
31,002	GRANT	1,227	631	527	69	Sanchez	51.4%	43.0%	5.6%
4,680	GUADALUPE	167	129	29	9	Sanchez	77.2%	17.4%	5.4%
810	HARDING	258	139	102	17	Sanchez	53.9%	39.5%	6.6%
5,932	HIDALGO	265	98	150	17	Bradley	37.0%	56.6%	6.4%
55,511	LEA	3,842	1,639	1,752	451	Bradley	42.7%	45.6%	11.7%
19,411	LINCOLN	2,793	1,549	1,033	211	Sanchez	55.5%	37.0%	7.6%
18,343	LOS ALAMOS	1,350	810	489	51	Sanchez	60.0%	36.2%	3.8%
25,016	LUNA	1,140	536	541	63	Bradley	47.0%	47.5%	5.5%
74,798	MCKINLEY	1,247	713	393	141	Sanchez	57.2%	31.5%	11.3%
5,180	MORA	225	185	26	14	Sanchez	82.2%	11.6%	6.2%
62,298	OTERO	4,713	2,334	2,077	302	Sanchez	49.5%	44.1%	6.4%
10,155	QUAY	547	205	263	79	Bradley	37.5%	48.1%	14.4%
41,190	RIO ARRIBA	694	495	143	56	Sanchez	71.3%	20.6%	8.1%
18,018	ROOSEVELT	763	284	446	33	Bradley	37.2%	58.5%	4.3%
89,908	SANDOVAL	4,628	3,068	1,317	243	Sanchez	66.3%	28.5%	5.3%
113,801	SAN JUAN	8,061	4,384	3,129	548	Sanchez	54.4%	38.8%	6.8%
30,126	SAN MIGUEL	587	473	88	26	Sanchez	80.6%	15.0%	4.4%
129,292	SANTA FE	3,665	2,372	1,070	223	Sanchez	64.7%	29.2%	6.1%
13,270	SIERRA	1,450	805	492	153	Sanchez	55.5%	33.9%	10.6%
18,078	SOCORRO	1,461	968	375	118	Sanchez	66.3%	25.7%	8.1%
29,979	TAOS	886	709	112	65	Sanchez	80.0%	12.6%	7.3%
16,911	TORRANCE	1,114	671	373	70	Sanchez	60.2%	33.5%	6.3%
4,174	UNION	418	180	179	59	Sanchez	43.1%	42.8%	14.1%
66,152	VALENCIA	2,934	1,893	879	162	Sanchez	64.5%	30.0%	5.5%
1,819,046	TOTAL	94,151	55,102	33,206	5,843	Sanchez	58.5%	35.3%	6.2%

NEW MEXICO DEMOCRATIC PRIMARY

SENATOR 2002

2000 Census Population	County	Total Vote	Tristani	Lobato	Other	Winner	Percentage of Total Vote		
							Tristani	Lobato	Other
556,678	BERNALILLO	35,950	30,698	5,239	13	Tristani	85.4%	14.6%	
3,543	CATRON	406	312	94		Tristani	76.8%	23.2%	
61,382	CHAVES	2,667	1,967	700		Tristani	73.8%	26.2%	
25,595	CIBOLA	2,778	2,128	648	2	Tristani	76.6%	23.3%	0.1%
14,189	COLFAX	1,753	1,265	488		Tristani	72.2%	27.8%	
45,044	CURRY	2,393	1,718	668	7	Tristani	71.8%	27.9%	0.3%
2,240	DE BACA	538	411	126	1	Tristani	76.4%	23.4%	0.2%
174,682	DONA ANA	8,587	6,666	1,915	6	Tristani	77.6%	22.3%	0.1%
51,658	EDDY	4,114	3,139	966	9	Tristani	76.3%	23.5%	0.2%
31,002	GRANT	3,902	2,906	993	3	Tristani	74.5%	25.4%	0.1%
4,680	GUADALUPE	1,570	1,083	487		Tristani	69.0%	31.0%	
810	HARDING	236	167	69		Tristani	70.8%	29.2%	
5,932	HIDALGO	785	604	178	3	Tristani	76.9%	22.7%	0.4%
55,511	LEA	2,523	2,084	439		Tristani	82.6%	17.4%	
19,411	LINCOLN	906	725	180	1	Tristani	80.0%	19.9%	0.1%
18,343	LOS ALAMOS	1,239	1,024	215		Tristani	82.6%	17.4%	
25,016	LUNA	2,280	1,791	487	2	Tristani	78.6%	21.4%	0.1%
74,798	MCKINLEY	5,723	4,541	1,178	4	Tristani	79.3%	20.6%	0.1%
5,180	MORA	1,620	940	680		Tristani	58.0%	42.0%	
62,298	OTERO	2,968	2,364	604		Tristani	79.6%	20.4%	
10,155	QUAY	1,483	1,051	432		Tristani	70.9%	29.1%	
41,190	RIO ARRIBA	7,356	4,841	2,512	3	Tristani	65.8%	34.1%	
18,018	ROOSEVELT	914	715	199		Tristani	78.2%	21.8%	
89,908	SANDOVAL	6,127	4,950	1,173	4	Tristani	80.8%	19.1%	0.1%
113,801	SAN JUAN	6,377	4,681	1,690	6	Tristani	73.4%	26.5%	0.1%
30,126	SAN MIGUEL	5,087	3,504	1,581	2	Tristani	68.9%	31.1%	
129,292	SANTA FE	15,848	11,868	3,977	3	Tristani	74.9%	25.1%	
13,270	SIERRA	1,096	894	201	1	Tristani	81.6%	18.3%	0.1%
18,078	SOCORRO	2,015	1,547	468		Tristani	76.8%	23.2%	
29,979	TAOS	4,336	3,215	1,120	1	Tristani	74.1%	25.8%	
16,911	TORRANCE	1,117	842	274	1	Tristani	75.4%	24.5%	0.1%
4,174	UNION	610	396	213	1	Tristani	64.9%	34.9%	0.2%
66,152	VALENCIA	5,078	4,047	1,031		Tristani	79.7%	20.3%	
1,819,046	TOTAL	140,382	109,084	31,225	73	Tristani	77.7%	22.2%	0.1%

NEW YORK

GOVERNOR
George E. Pataki (R). Reelected 2002 to a four-year term. Previously elected 1998, 1994.

SENATORS (2 Democrats)
Hillary Rodham Clinton (D). Elected 2000 to a six-year term.

Charles E. Schumer (D). Elected 1998 to a six-year term.

REPRESENTATIVES (19 Democrats, 10 Republicans)
1. Timothy H. Bishop (D)
2. Steve Israel (D)
3. Peter T. King (R)
4. Carolyn McCarthy (D)
5. Gary L. Ackerman (D)
6. Gregory W. Meeks (D)
7. Joseph Crowley (D)
8. Jerrold Nadler (D)
9. Anthony Weiner (D)
10. Edolphus Towns (D)
11. Major R. Owens (D)
12. Nydia M. Velázquez (D)
13. Vito J. Fossella (R)
14. Carolyn B. Maloney (D)
15. Charles B. Rangel (D)
16. Jose E. Serrano (D)
17. Eliot L. Engel (D)
18. Nita M. Lowey (D)
19. Sue W. Kelly (R)
20. John E. Sweeney (R)
21. Michael R. McNulty (D)
22. Maurice D. Hinchey (D)
23. John M. McHugh (R)
24. Sherwood Boehlert (R)
25. James T. Walsh (R)
26. Thomas M. Reynolds (R)
27. Jack Quinn (R)
28. Louise M. Slaughter (D)
29. Amo Houghton (R)

POSTWAR VOTE FOR PRESIDENT

| | | Republican | | Democratic | | | | Percentage | | | |
| | | | | | | | | Total Vote | | Major Vote | |
Year	Total Vote	Vote	Candidate	Vote	Candidate	Other Vote	Plurality	Rep.	Dem.	Rep.	Dem.
2000**	6,821,999	2,403,374	Bush, George W.	4,107,697	Gore, Al	310,928	1,704,323 R	35.2%	60.2%	36.9%	63.1%
1996**	6,316,129	1,933,492	Dole, Bob	3,756,177	Clinton, Bill	626,460	1,822,685 D	30.6%	59.5%	34.0%	66.0%
1992**	6,926,925	2,346,649	Bush, George	3,444,450	Clinton, Bill	1,135,826	1,097,801 D	33.9%	49.7%	40.5%	59.5%
1988	6,485,683	3,081,871	Bush, George	3,347,882	Dukakis, Michael S.	55,930	266,011 D	47.5%	51.6%	47.9%	52.1%
1984	6,806,810	3,664,763	Reagan, Ronald	3,119,609	Mondale, Walter F.	22,438	545,154 R	53.8%	45.8%	54.0%	46.0%
1980**	6,201,959	2,893,831	Reagan, Ronald	2,728,372	Carter, Jimmy	579,756	165,459 R	46.7%	44.0%	51.5%	48.5%
1976	6,534,170	3,100,791	Ford, Gerald R.	3,389,558	Carter, Jimmy	43,821	288,767 D	47.5%	51.9%	47.8%	52.2%
1972	7,165,919	4,192,778	Nixon, Richard M.	2,951,084	McGovern, George S.	22,057	1,241,694 R	58.5%	41.2%	58.7%	41.3%
1968	6,791,688	3,007,932	Nixon, Richard M.	3,378,470	Humphrey, Hubert H.	405,286	370,538 D	44.3%	49.7%	47.1%	52.9%
1964	7,166,275	2,243,559	Goldwater, Barry M.	4,913,102	Johnson, Lyndon B.	9,614	2,669,543 D	31.3%	68.6%	31.3%	68.7%
1960	7,291,079	3,446,419	Nixon, Richard M.	3,830,085	Kennedy, John F.	14,575	383,666 D	47.3%	52.5%	47.4%	52.6%
1956	7,095,971	4,345,506	Eisenhower, Dwight D.	2,747,944	Stevenson, Adlai E.	2,521	1,597,562 R	61.2%	38.7%	61.3%	38.7%
1952	7,128,239	3,952,813	Eisenhower, Dwight D.	3,104,601	Stevenson, Adlai E.	70,825	848,212 R	55.5%	43.6%	56.0%	44.0%
1948	6,177,337	2,841,163	Dewey, Thomas E.	2,780,204	Truman, Harry S.	555,970	60,959 R	46.0%	45.0%	50.5%	49.5%

In 2000 the other vote column includes 244,030 votes cast for Green (Nader). In 1996 the other vote column includes 503,458 votes cast for Perot. In 1992 the other vote column includes 1,090,721 votes cast for Perot. In 1980 the other column includes 467,801 votes for Independent (Anderson).

NEW YORK

POSTWAR VOTE FOR GOVERNOR

| | | Republican | | Democratic | | Other | Rep.-Dem. | Percentage | | | |
| | | | | | | | | Total Vote | | Major Vote | |
Year	Total Vote	Vote	Candidate	Vote	Candidate	Vote	Plurality	Rep.	Dem.	Rep.	Dem.
2002**	4,579,078	2,262,255	Pataki, George E.	1,534,064	McCall, H. Carl	782,759	728,191 R	49.4%	33.5%	59.6%	40.4%
1998	4,735,236	2,571,991	Pataki, George E.	1,570,317	Vallone, Peter F.	592,928	1,001,674 R	54.3%	33.2%	62.1%	37.9%
1994	5,208,762	2,538,702	Pataki, George E.	2,364,904	Cuomo, Mario M.	305,156	173,798 R	48.7%	45.4%	51.8%	48.2%
1990**	4,056,896	865,948	Rinfret, Pierre A.	2,157,087	Cuomo, Mario M.	1,033,861	1,291,139 D	21.3%	53.2%	28.6%	71.4%
1986	4,294,124	1,363,810	O'Rourke, Andrew P.	2,775,229	Cuomo, Mario M.	155,085	1,411,419 D	31.8%	64.6%	32.9%	67.1%
1982	5,254,891	2,494,827	Lehrman, Lew	2,675,213	Cuomo, Mario M.	84,851	180,386 D	47.5%	50.9%	48.3%	51.7%
1978	4,768,820	2,156,404	Duryea, Perry B.	2,429,272	Carey, Hugh L.	183,144	272,868 D	45.2%	50.9%	47.0%	53.0%
1974	5,293,176	2,219,667	Wilson, Malcolm	3,028,503	Carey, Hugh L.	45,006	808,836 D	41.9%	57.2%	42.3%	57.7%
1970	6,013,064	3,151,432	Rockefeller, Nelson A.	2,421,426	Goldberg, Arthur	440,206	730,006 R	52.4%	40.3%	56.5%	43.5%
1966**	6,031,585	2,690,626	Rockefeller, Nelson A.	2,298,363	O'Connor, Frank D.	1,042,596	392,263 R	44.6%	38.1%	53.9%	46.1%
1962	5,805,631	3,081,587	Rockefeller, Nelson A.	2,552,418	Morgenthau, Robert M.	171,626	529,169 R	53.1%	44.0%	54.7%	45.3%
1958	5,712,665	3,126,929	Rockefeller, Nelson A.	2,553,895	Harriman, Averell	31,841	573,034 R	54.7%	44.7%	55.0%	45.0%
1954	5,161,942	2,549,613	Ives, Irving M.	2,560,738	Harriman, Averell	51,591	11,125 D	49.4%	49.6%	49.9%	50.1%
1950	5,308,889	2,819,523	Dewey, Thomas E.	2,246,855	Lynch, Walter A.	242,511	572,668 R	53.1%	42.3%	55.7%	44.3%
1946	4,964,552	2,825,633	Dewey, Thomas E.	2,138,482	Mead, James M.	437	687,151 R	56.9%	43.1%	56.9%	43.1%

In 2002 B. Thomas Golisano, the Independence Party candidate, received 654,016 votes (14.3 percent of the total vote). In 1990 other vote was 827,614 Conservative (London); 137,804 Right to Life (Wein); 31,089 New Alliance (Fulani); 24,611 Libertarian (Johnson) and 12,743 Socialist Workers (Gannon). In 1966 other vote was 510,023 Conservative (Adams); 507,234 Liberal (F. D. Roosevelt, Jr.); 12,730 Socialist Labor (Herder); 12,506 Socialist Workers (White) and 103 scattered.

POSTWAR VOTE FOR SENATOR

| | | Republican | | Democratic | | Other | Rep.-Dem. | Percentage | | | |
| | | | | | | | | Total Vote | | Major Vote | |
Year	Total Vote	Vote	Candidate	Vote	Candidate	Vote	Plurality	Rep.	Dem.	Rep.	Dem.
2000	6,779,839	2,915,730	Lazio, Rick A.	3,747,310	Clinton, Hillary Rodham	116,799	831,580 D	43.0%	55.3%	43.8%	56.2%
1998	4,670,805	2,058,988	D'Amato, Alfonse M.	2,551,065	Schumer, Charles E.	60,752	492,077 D	44.1%	54.6%	44.7%	55.3%
1994	4,794,601	1,988,308	Castro, Bernadette	2,646,541	Moynihan, Daniel P.	159,752	658,233 D	41.5%	55.2%	42.9%	57.1%
1992	6,458,826	3,166,994	D'Amato, Alfonse M.	3,086,200	Abrams, Robert	205,632	80,794 R	49.0%	47.8%	50.6%	49.4%
1988	6,040,980	1,875,784	McMillan, Robert	4,048,649	Moynihan, Daniel P.	116,547	2,172,865 D	31.1%	67.0%	31.7%	68.3%
1986	4,179,447	2,378,197	D'Amato, Alfonse M.	1,723,216	Green, Mark	78,034	654,981 R	56.9%	41.2%	58.0%	42.0%
1982	4,967,729	1,696,766	Sullivan, Florence M.	3,232,146	Moynihan, Daniel P.	38,817	1,535,380 D	34.2%	65.1%	34.4%	65.6%
1980	6,014,914	2,699,652	D'Amato, Alfonse M.	2,618,661	Holtzman, Elizabeth	696,601	80,991 R	44.9%	43.5%	50.8%	49.2%
1976	6,319,755	2,836,633	Buckley, James L.	3,422,594	Moynihan, Daniel P.	60,528	585,961 D	44.9%	54.2%	45.3%	54.7%
1974	5,163,600	2,340,188	Javits, Jacob K.	1,973,781	Clark, Ramsey	849,631	366,407 R	45.3%	38.2%	54.2%	45.8%
1970**	5,904,782	1,434,472	Goodell, Charles	2,171,232	Ottinger, Richard L.	2,299,078	116,958 C	24.3%	36.8%	39.8%	60.2%
1968**	6,581,587	3,269,772	Javits, Jacob K.	2,150,695	O'Dwyer, Paul	1,161,120	1,119,077 R	49.7%	32.7%	60.3%	39.7%
1964	7,151,686	3,104,056	Keating, Kenneth B.	3,823,749	Kennedy, Robert F.	223,881	719,693 D	43.4%	53.5%	44.8%	55.2%
1962	5,700,186	3,269,417	Javits, Jacob K.	2,289,341	Donovan, James B.	141,428	980,076 R	57.4%	40.2%	58.8%	41.2%
1958	5,602,088	2,842,942	Keating, Kenneth B.	2,709,950	Hogan, Frank S.	49,196	132,992 R	50.7%	48.4%	51.2%	48.8%
1956	6,991,136	3,723,933	Javits, Jacob K.	3,265,159	Wagner, Robert F.	2,044	458,774 R	53.3%	46.7%	53.3%	46.7%
1952	6,980,259	3,853,934	Ives, Irving M.	2,521,736	Cashmore, John	604,589	1,332,198 R	55.2%	36.1%	60.4%	39.6%
1950	5,228,403	2,367,353	Hanley, Joe R.	2,632,313	Lehman, Herbert H.	228,737	264,960 D	45.3%	50.3%	47.4%	52.6%
1949S	4,966,878	2,384,381	Dulles, John Foster	2,582,438	Lehman, Herbert H.	59	198,057 D	48.0%	52.0%	48.0%	52.0%
1946	4,867,564	2,559,365	Ives, Irving M.	2,308,112	Lehman, Herbert H.	87	251,253 R	52.6%	47.4%	52.6%	47.4%

In 1970 James L. Buckley, the Conservative candidate, polled 2,288,190 votes (38.8% of the total vote) and won the election with a 116,958-vote plurality. In 1968 other vote was 1,139,402 Conservative (Buckley); 8,775 Freedom and Peace (Ferguson); 7,964 Socialist Labor (Emanuel); 4,979 Socialist Workers (Garza). The 1949 election was for a short term to fill a vacancy.

NEW YORK

Congressional districts first established for elections held in 2002
29 members

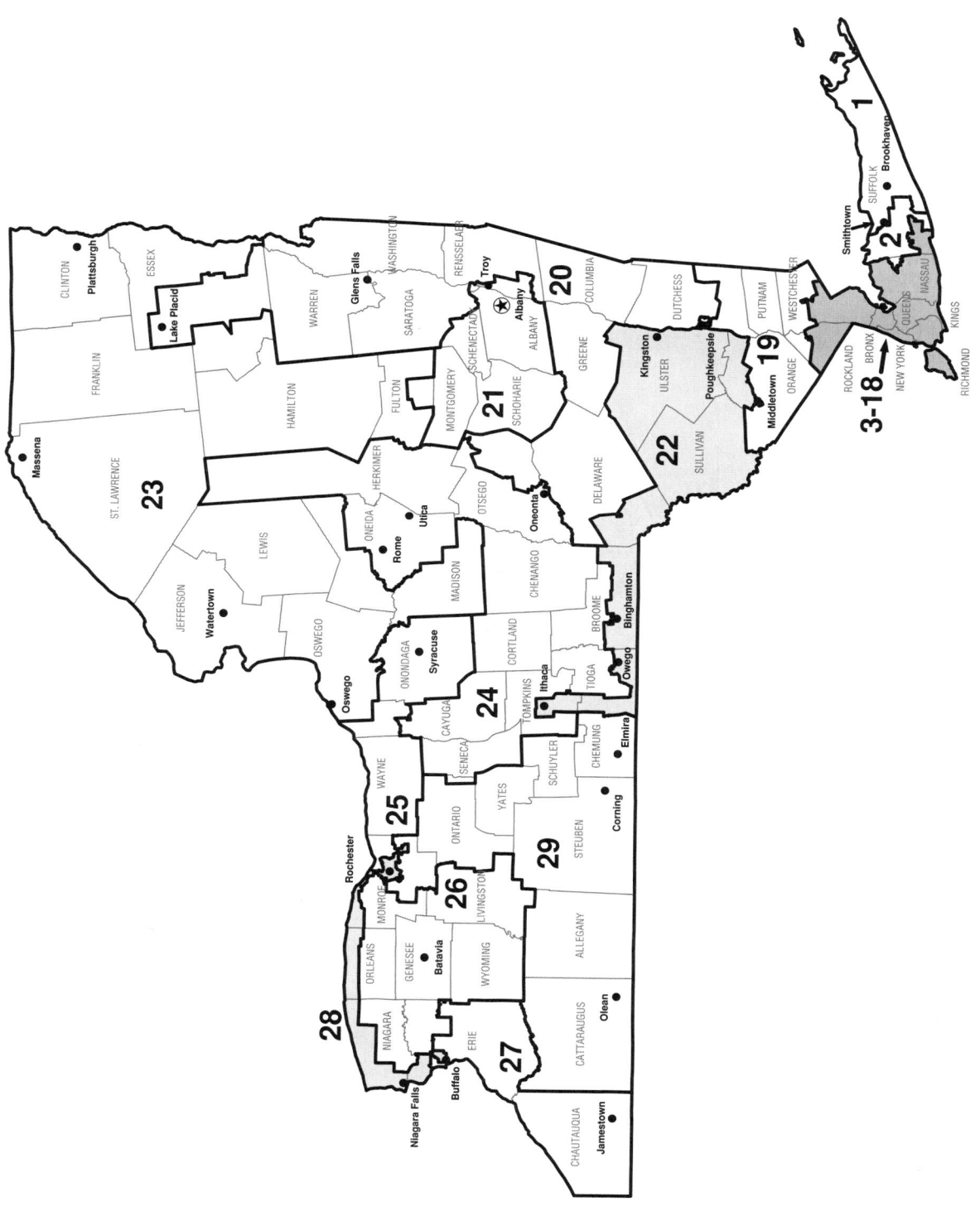

330

NEW YORK

New York City Area

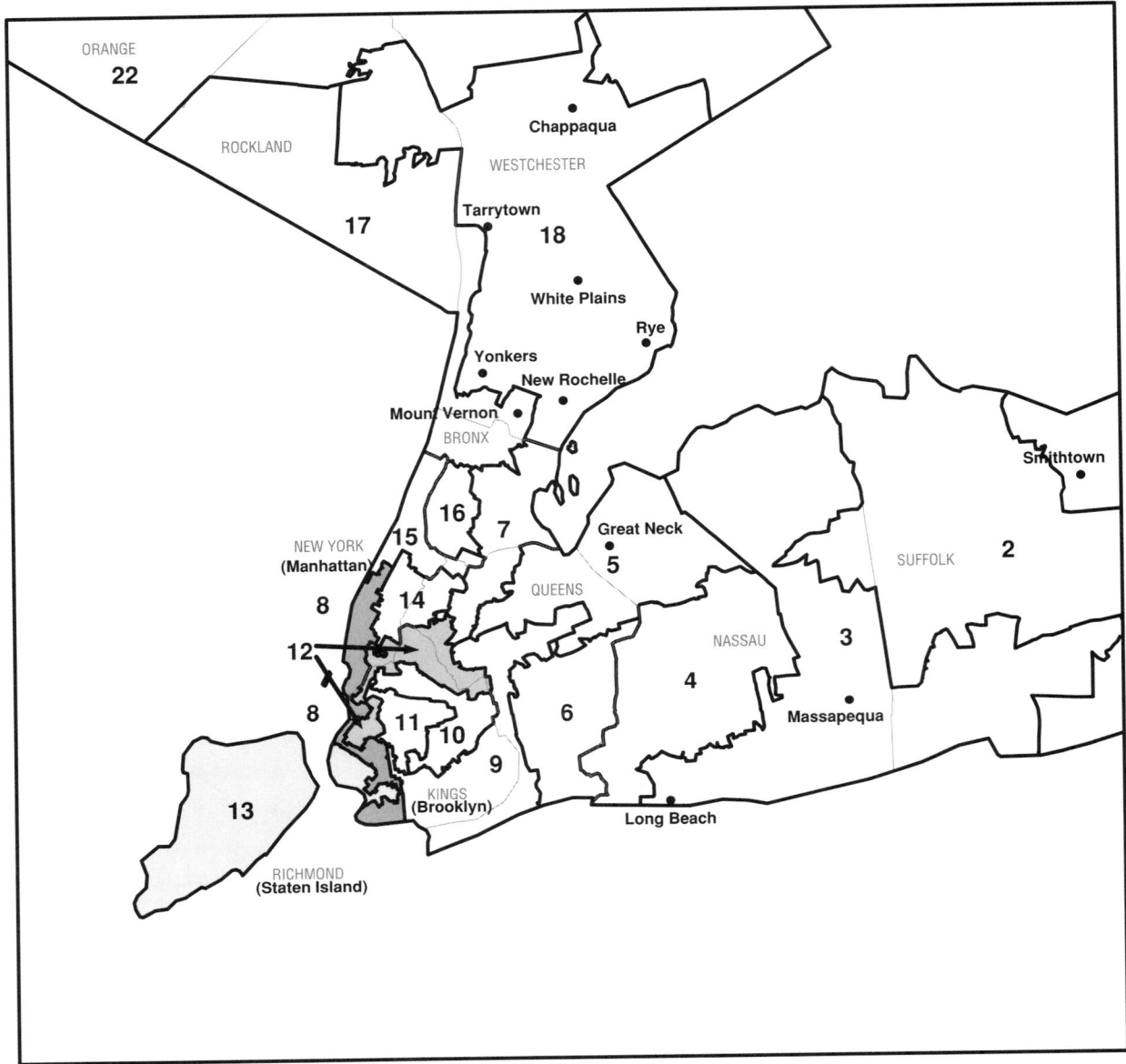

NEW YORK

GOVERNOR 2002

2000 Census Population	County	Total Vote	Republican	Democratic	Independence (Golisano)	Other	Plurality		Percentage of Total Vote		
									Rep.	Dem.	Ind.
294,565	ALBANY	111,944	45,804	45,748	17,101	3,291	56	R	40.9%	40.9%	15.3%
49,927	ALLEGANY	13,272	8,134	2,042	2,683	413	5,451	R	61.3%	15.4%	20.2%
1,332,650	BRONX	189,974	58,600	121,050	7,893	2,431	62,450	D	30.8%	63.7%	4.2%
200,536	BROOME	64,554	32,399	12,956	17,478	1,721	14,921	R	50.2%	20.1%	27.1%
83,955	CATTARAUGUS	21,673	12,400	4,302	4,287	684	8,098	R	57.2%	19.8%	19.8%
81,963	CAYUGA	24,902	14,203	5,417	4,593	689	8,786	R	57.0%	21.8%	18.4%
139,750	CHAUTAUQUA	37,810	22,869	8,323	5,747	871	14,546	R	60.5%	22.0%	15.2%
91,070	CHEMUNG	25,600	16,398	4,619	4,018	565	11,779	R	64.1%	18.0%	15.7%
51,401	CHENANGO	14,279	8,676	2,529	2,597	477	6,079	R	60.8%	17.7%	18.2%
79,894	CLINTON	22,712	17,113	3,505	1,550	544	13,608	R	75.3%	15.4%	6.8%
63,094	COLUMBIA	22,500	11,995	6,454	3,091	960	5,541	R	53.3%	28.7%	13.7%
48,599	CORTLAND	14,205	7,851	3,522	2,393	439	4,329	R	55.3%	24.8%	16.8%
48,055	DELAWARE	14,912	9,139	2,878	2,320	575	6,261	R	61.3%	19.3%	15.6%
280,150	DUTCHESS	76,025	44,289	18,606	10,671	2,459	25,683	R	58.3%	24.5%	14.0%
950,265	ERIE	293,966	130,377	85,360	68,702	9,527	45,017	R	44.4%	29.0%	23.4%
38,851	ESSEX	13,907	10,550	1,794	1,183	380	8,756	R	75.9%	12.9%	8.5%
51,134	FRANKLIN	11,943	8,628	2,009	993	313	6,619	R	72.2%	16.8%	8.3%
55,073	FULTON	15,735	9,012	3,055	3,301	367	5,711	R	57.3%	19.4%	21.0%
60,370	GENESEE	17,997	9,588	2,553	5,402	454	4,186	R	53.3%	14.2%	30.0%
48,195	GREENE	15,800	9,363	3,281	2,625	531	6,082	R	59.3%	20.8%	16.6%
5,379	HAMILTON	2,849	1,740	550	483	76	1,190	R	61.1%	19.3%	17.0%
64,427	HERKIMER	19,629	11,834	3,178	4,140	477	7,694	R	60.3%	16.2%	21.1%
111,738	JEFFERSON	26,360	17,616	3,897	4,414	433	13,202	R	66.8%	14.8%	16.7%
2,465,326	KINGS	398,536	141,846	230,040	16,787	9,863	88,194	D	35.6%	57.7%	4.2%
26,944	LEWIS	8,950	5,823	1,370	1,562	195	4,261	R	65.1%	15.3%	17.5%
64,328	LIVINGSTON	19,986	8,757	3,651	7,066	512	1,691	R	43.8%	18.3%	35.4%
69,441	MADISON	19,683	10,393	4,206	4,493	591	5,900	R	52.8%	21.4%	22.8%
735,343	MONROE	233,199	81,110	58,334	87,967	5,788	6,857	I	34.8%	25.0%	37.7%
49,708	MONTGOMERY	16,605	9,285	3,346	3,573	401	5,712	R	55.9%	20.2%	21.5%
1,334,544	NASSAU	378,511	232,785	99,865	35,860	10,001	132,920	R	61.5%	26.4%	9.5%
1,537,195	NEW YORK	353,092	117,863	202,101	19,743	13,385	84,238	D	33.4%	57.2%	5.6%
219,846	NIAGARA	65,023	32,005	12,966	18,278	1,774	13,727	R	49.2%	19.9%	28.1%
235,469	ONEIDA	70,038	40,186	13,719	14,274	1,859	25,912	R	57.4%	19.6%	20.4%
458,336	ONONDAGA	145,305	74,694	39,110	27,459	4,042	35,584	R	51.4%	26.9%	18.9%
100,224	ONTARIO	33,357	15,480	5,512	11,478	887	4,002	R	46.4%	16.5%	34.4%
341,367	ORANGE	86,391	53,950	17,866	11,914	2,661	36,084	R	62.4%	20.7%	13.8%
44,171	ORLEANS	11,092	5,426	1,568	3,869	229	1,557	R	48.9%	14.1%	34.9%
122,377	OSWEGO	32,086	17,393	6,826	7,111	756	10,282	R	54.2%	21.3%	22.2%
61,676	OTSEGO	17,623	9,846	4,109	2,824	844	5,737	R	55.9%	23.3%	16.0%
95,745	PUTNAM	28,415	19,998	4,284	3,217	916	15,714	R	70.4%	15.1%	11.3%
2,229,379	QUEENS	345,718	155,599	160,746	21,556	7,817	5,147	D	45.0%	46.5%	6.2%
152,538	RENSSELAER	54,263	27,120	15,491	9,908	1,744	11,629	R	50.0%	28.5%	18.3%
443,728	RICHMOND	87,195	59,656	18,239	7,583	1,717	41,417	R	68.4%	20.9%	8.7%
286,753	ROCKLAND	84,624	53,025	22,054	7,557	1,988	30,971	R	62.7%	26.1%	8.9%
111,931	ST. LAWRENCE	30,098	19,635	6,234	3,621	608	13,401	R	65.2%	20.7%	12.0%
200,635	SARATOGA	70,331	38,797	16,881	12,448	2,205	21,916	R	55.2%	24.0%	17.7%
146,555	SCHENECTADY	50,178	24,201	14,378	10,116	1,483	9,823	R	48.2%	28.7%	20.2%
31,582	SCHOHARIE	10,547	5,731	2,296	2,141	379	3,435	R	54.3%	21.8%	20.3%
19,224	SCHUYLER	5,802	3,535	1,043	989	235	2,492	R	60.9%	18.0%	17.0%
33,342	SENECA	10,516	5,969	1,986	2,270	291	3,699	R	56.8%	18.9%	21.6%
98,726	STEUBEN	27,414	17,523	3,419	5,721	751	11,802	R	63.9%	12.5%	20.9%
1,419,369	SUFFOLK	354,208	209,361	82,776	51,288	10,783	126,585	R	59.1%	23.4%	14.5%
73,966	SULLIVAN	19,997	11,279	4,949	3,133	636	6,330	R	56.4%	24.7%	15.7%
51,784	TIOGA	15,844	9,561	2,396	3,459	428	6,102	R	60.3%	15.1%	21.8%
96,501	TOMPKINS	27,389	10,995	10,887	3,338	2,169	108	R	40.1%	39.7%	12.2%
177,749	ULSTER	57,448	29,801	15,567	9,205	2,875	14,234	R	51.9%	27.1%	16.0%
63,303	WARREN	20,535	11,964	4,831	3,182	558	7,133	R	58.3%	23.5%	15.5%
61,042	WASHINGTON	16,799	9,491	3,767	3,012	529	5,724	R	56.5%	22.4%	17.9%
93,765	WAYNE	27,535	12,553	4,171	10,169	642	2,384	R	45.6%	15.1%	36.9%
923,459	WESTCHESTER	252,438	140,329	82,099	23,113	6,897	58,230	R	55.6%	32.5%	9.2%

NEW YORK

GOVERNOR 2002

2000 Census Population	County	Total Vote	Republican	Democratic	Independence (Golisano)	Other	Plurality	Percentage of Total Vote		
								Rep.	Dem.	Ind.
43,424	WYOMING	12,655	6,931	2,034	3,299	391	3,632 R	54.8%	16.1%	26.1%
24,621	YATES	7,104	3,781	1,319	1,768	236	2,013 R	53.2%	18.6%	24.9%
18,976,457	TOTAL	4,579,078	2,262,255	1,534,064	654,016	128,743	728,191 R	49.4%	33.5%	14.3%

Note: The plurality is based on the margin of victory of the winner over the runner-up. The Independence Party candidate, B. Thomas Golisano, finished first or second in a number of counties.

NEW YORK

HOUSE OF REPRESENTATIVES

			Republican		Democratic				Percentage			
									Total Vote		Major Vote	
CD	Year	Total Vote	Vote	Candidate	Vote	Candidate	Other Vote	Rep.-Dem. Plurality	Rep.	Dem.	Rep.	Dem.
1	2002	167,791	81,524	# Grucci, Felix J., Jr.*	84,276	# Bishop, Timothy H.	1,991	2,752 D	48.6%	50.2%	49.2%	50.8%
2	2002	146,126	59,117	# Finley, Joseph P.	85,451	# Israel, Steve*	1,558	26,334 D	40.5%	58.5%	40.9%	59.1%
3	2002	169,072	121,537	# King, Peter T.*	46,022	Finz, Stuart L.	1,513	75,515 R	71.9%	27.2%	72.5%	27.5%
4	2002	168,540	72,882	# O'Grady, Marilyn F.	94,806	# McCarthy, Carolyn*	852	21,924 D	43.2%	56.3%	43.5%	56.5%
5	2002	74,491			68,773	# Ackerman, Gary L.*	5,718	68,773 D		92.3%		100.0%
6	2002	75,431			72,799	# Meeks, Gregory W.*	2,632	72,799 D		96.5%		100.0%
7	2002	69,539	18,572	# Brawley, Kevin	50,967	# Crowley, Joseph*		32,395 D	26.7%	73.3%	26.7%	73.3%
8	2002	106,481	19,674	# Farrin, Jim	81,002	# Nadler, Jerrold*	5,805	61,328 D	18.5%	76.1%	19.5%	80.5%
9	2002	92,435	31,698	# Donohue, Alfred F.	60,737	# Weiner, Anthony*		29,039 D	34.3%	65.7%	34.3%	65.7%
10	2002	75,498			73,859	# Towns, Edolphus*	1,639	73,859 D		97.8%		100.0%
11	2002	88,864	11,149	# Cleary, Susan	76,917	# Owens, Major R.*	798	65,768 D	12.5%	86.6%	12.7%	87.3%
12	2002	50,527			48,408	# Velazquez, Nydia M.*	2,119	48,408 D		95.8%		100.0%
13	2002	103,693	72,204	# Fossella, Vito J.*	29,366	# Mattsson, Arne M.	2,123	42,838 R	69.6%	28.3%	71.1%	28.9%
14	2002	127,479	31,548	# Srdanovic, Anton	95,931	# Maloney, Carolyn B.*		64,383 D	24.7%	75.3%	24.7%	75.3%
15	2002	95,375	11,008	# Fields, Jessie A.	84,367	# Rangel, Charles B.*		73,359 D	11.5%	88.5%	11.5%	88.5%
16	2002	55,082	4,366	# Dellavalle, Frank	50,716	# Serrano, Jose E.*		46,350 D	7.9%	92.1%	7.9%	92.1%
17	2002	123,843	42,634	# Vanderhoef, C. Scott	77,535	# Engel, Eliot L.*	3,674	34,901 D	34.4%	62.6%	35.5%	64.5%
18	2002	107,515			98,957	# Lowey, Nita M.*	8,558	98,957 D		92.0%		100.0%
19	2002	173,112	121,129	# Kelly, Sue W.*	44,967	Selendy, Janine M.H.	7,016	76,162 R	70.0%	26.0%	72.9%	27.1%
20	2002	191,278	140,238	# Sweeney, John E.*	45,878	Stoppenbach, Frank	5,162	94,360 R	73.3%	24.0%	75.3%	24.7%
21	2002	214,854	53,525	Rosenstein, Charles B.	161,329	# McNulty, Michael R.*		107,804 D	24.9%	75.1%	24.9%	75.1%
22	2002	176,484	58,008	# Hall, Eric	113,280	# Hinchey, Maurice D.*	5,196	55,272 D	32.9%	64.2%	33.9%	66.1%
23	2002	124,682	124,682	# McHugh, John M.*				124,682 R	100.0%		100.0%	
24	2002	152,777	108,017	Boehlert, Sherwood*			44,760	108,017 R	70.7%		100.0%	
25	2002	200,031	144,610	# Walsh, James T.*	53,290	Aldersley, Stephanie	2,131	91,320 R	72.3%	26.6%	73.1%	26.9%

NEW YORK

HOUSE OF REPRESENTATIVES

CD	Year	Total Vote	Republican		Democratic		Other Vote	Rep.-Dem. Plurality	Percentage			
									Total Vote		Major Vote	
			Vote	Candidate	Vote	Candidate			Rep.	Dem.	Rep.	Dem.
26	2002	183,459	135,089	# Reynolds, Thomas M.*	41,140	Nariman, Ayesha F.	7,230	93,949 R	73.6%	22.4%	76.7%	23.3%
27	2002	173,919	120,117	# Quinn, Jack*	47,811	# Crotty, Peter	5,991	72,306 R	69.1%	27.5%	71.5%	28.5%
28	2002	158,604	59,547	# Wojtaszek, Henry F.	99,057	# Slaughter, Louise M.*		39,510 D	37.5%	62.5%	37.5%	62.5%
29	2002	174,631	127,657	# Houghton, Amo*	37,128	Peters, Kisun J.	9,846	90,529 R	73.1%	21.3%	77.5%	22.5%
Total	2002	3,821,613	1,770,532		1,924,769		126,312	154,237 D	46.3%	50.4%	47.9%	52.1%

A pound sign (#) indicates that the candidate received votes on the ballot line of one or more other parties. Each candidate's total vote is listed above.

An asterisk (*) denotes incumbent.

NEW YORK

GENERAL AND PRIMARY ELECTIONS

2002 GENERAL ELECTIONS

Governor   Other vote was 44,195 Right To Life (Gerard J. Cronin); 41,797 Green (Stanley Aronowitz); 21,977 Marijuana Reform (Thomas K. Leighton); 15,761 Liberal (Andrew M. Cuomo); 5,013 Libertarian (Scott Jeffrey). (The Independence Party candidate, B. Thomas Golisano, received 654,016 votes, 14.3 percent of the total vote. The Independence Party vote is listed in the county table for the 2002 gubernatorial election in New York.)

House   Other vote was:

CD 1   1,991 Green (Lorna Salzman).
CD 2   1,558 Green (John Keenan).
CD 3   1,513 Liberal (Janeen DePrima).
CD 4   852 Green (Tim Derham).
CD 5   5,718 Conservative (Perry S. Reich).
CD 6   2,632 Independence (Rey Clarke).
CD 7
CD 8   3,361 Conservative (Alan Jay Gerber); 1,918 Green (Dan Wentzel); 526 Libertarian (Joseph Dobrian).
CD 9
CD 10   1,639 Conservative (Herbert F. Ryan).
CD 11   798 Conservative (Alice Gaffney).
CD 12   2,119 Conservative (Cesar Estevez).
CD 13   1,427 Independence (Anita Lerman); 696 Green (Henry J. Bardel).
CD 14
CD 15
CD 16
CD 17   1,931 Right to Life (Arthur L. Gallagher); 1,743 Green (Elizabeth Shanklin).
CD 18   8,558 Right to Life (Michael J. Reynolds).
CD 19   4,374 Right to Life (Christine M. Tighe); 2,642 Green (Jonathan M. Wright).
CD 20   5,162 Green (Margaret Lewis).
CD 21
CD 22   2,723 Green (Steven Greenfield); 2,473 Right to Life (Paul J. Laux).
CD 23
CD 24   32,991 Conservative (David L. Walrath); 6,660 Green (Mark Dunau); 5,109 Right to Life (Kathleen M. Peters).
CD 25   2,131 Working Families (Francis J. Gavin).
CD 26   4,084 Right to Life (Shawn Harris); 3,146 Green (Paul E. Fallon).

NEW YORK

GENERAL AND PRIMARY ELECTIONS

2002 GENERAL ELECTIONS

CD 27   3,586 Right to Life (Thomas Casey); 2,405 Green (Albert N. LaBruna).
CD 28
CD 29   5,836 Right to Life (Wendy M. Johnson); 4,010 Green (Rachel Treichler).

Note: Candidates in New York can appear on the ballot line of more than one party. In the gubernatorial election, for instance, George E. Pataki received 2,085,407 votes on the Republican line and another 176,848 votes on the Conservative line, for a total of 2,262,255 votes. H. Carl McCall received 1,443,531 votes on the Democratic line and 90,533 votes on the Working Families line, for a total of 1,534,064 votes. In the New York tables, votes received by each Democratic and Republican candidate on the ballot lines of other parties are combined into one overall vote, which is credited to the major party of which they are a member.

2002 PRIMARY ELECTIONS

Primary	September 10, 2002	**Registration** (as of June 27, 2002)	Republican	3,114,972
			Democratic	5,192,717
			Independence Party	219,715
			Conservative	162,739
			Liberal	85,426
			Right to Life	49,116
			Green	26,294
			Working Families	14,771
			Other	2,208,610
			TOTAL	11,074,360

Primary Type   Closed—Only registered Democrats and Republicans could vote in their party's primary.

Note: An asterisk (*) denotes incumbent. Names of unopposed candidates did not appear on the primary ballot; therefore, no votes were cast for these candidates

	REPUBLICAN PRIMARIES			DEMOCRATIC PRIMARIES		
Governor	George E. Pataki*	Unopposed		H. Carl McCall	539,883	85.3%
				Andrew M. Cuomo	93,195	14.7%
				TOTAL	633,078	
				Cuomo withdrew a week before the primary but his name remained on the ballot.		
Congressional District 1	Felix J. Grucci Jr.*	Unopposed		Timothy H. Bishop	Unopposed	
Congressional District 2	Joseph P. Finley	Unopposed		Steve Israel*	Unopposed	
Congressional District 3	Peter T. King*	11,932	78.0%	Stuart L. Finz	Unopposed	
	Robert Previdi	3,357	22.0%			
	TOTAL	15,289				
Congressional District 4	Marilyn F. O'Grady	9,776	50.4%	Carolyn McCarthy*	Unopposed	
	Daniel Frisa	5,938	30.6%			
	Steven Irace	3,682	19.0%			
	TOTAL	19,396				
Congressional District 5	No Republican candidate			Gary L. Ackerman*	Unopposed	
Congressional District 6	No Republican candidate			Gregory W. Meeks*	22,209	78.7%
				Rey Clarke	6,024	21.3%
				Write-in	2	
				TOTAL	28,235	

NEW YORK

GENERAL AND PRIMARY ELECTIONS

	REPUBLICAN PRIMARIES			DEMOCRATIC PRIMARIES		
Congressional District 7	Kevin Brawley	Unopposed		Joseph Crowley*	15,166	64.0%
				Dennis Coleman	8,516	36.0%
				Write-in	1	
				TOTAL	23,683	
Congressional District 8	Jim Farrin	Unopposed		Jerrold Nadler*	Unopposed	
Congressional District 9	Alfred F. Donohue	Unopposed		Anthony Weiner*	Unopposed	
Congressional District 10	No Republican candidate			Edolphus Towns*	Unopposed	
Congressional District 11	Susan Cleary	Unopposed		Major R. Owens*	Unopposed	
Congressional District 12	No Republican candidate			Nydia M. Velazquez*	Unopposed	
Congressional District 13	Vito J. Fossella*	Unopposed		Arne M. Mattsson	Unopposed	
Congressional District 14	Anto Srdanovic	Unopposed		Carolyn B. Maloney*	Unopposed	
Congressional District 15	Jessie A. Fields	Unopposed		Charles B. Rangel*	Unopposed	
Congressional District 16	Frank Dellavalle	Unopposed		Jose E. Serrano*	Unopposed	
Congressional District 17	C. Scott Vanderhoef	Unopposed		Eliot L. Engel*	Unopposed	
Congressional District 18	No Republican candidate			Nita M. Lowey*	Unopposed	
Congressional District 19	Sue W. Kelly*	Unopposed		Janine M.H. Selendy	Unopposed	
Congressional District 20	John E. Sweeney*	Unopposed		Frank Stoppenbach	Unopposed	
Congressional District 21	Charles B. Rosenstein	Unopposed		Michael R. McNulty*	Unopposed	
Congressional District 22	Eric Hall	Unopposed		Maurice D. Hinchey*	Unopposed	
Congressional District 23	John M. McHugh*	Unopposed		No Democratic candidate		
Congressional District 24	Sherwood Boehlert*	21,504	53.4%	No Democratic candidate		
	David L. Walrath	18,773	46.6%			
	TOTAL	40,277				
Congressional District 25	James T. Walsh*	Unopposed		Stephanie Aldersley	Unopposed	
Congressional District 26	Thomas M. Reynolds*	Unopposed		Ayesha F. Nariman	Unopposed	
Congressional District 27	Jack Quinn*	Unopposed		Peter Crotty	Unopposed	
Congressional District 28	Henry F. Wojtaszek	Unopposed		Louise M. Slaughter*	Unopposed	
Congressional District 29	Amo Houghton*	Unopposed		Kisun J. Peters	Unopposed	

NEW YORK DEMOCRATIC PRIMARY

GOVERNOR 2002

2000 Census Population	County	Total Vote	McCall	Cuomo	Winner	Percentage of Total Vote McCall	Cuomo
294,565	ALBANY	19,590	17,444	2,146	McCall	89.0%	11.0%
49,927	ALLEGANY	591	479	112	McCall	81.0%	19.0%
1,332,650	BRONX	64,128	53,889	10,239	McCall	84.0%	16.0%
200,536	BROOME	4,527	3,847	680	McCall	85.0%	15.0%
83,955	CATTARAUGUS	1,042	794	248	McCall	76.2%	23.8%
81,963	CAYUGA	1,157	919	238	McCall	79.4%	20.6%
139,750	CHAUTAUQUA	2,081	1,641	440	McCall	78.9%	21.1%
91,070	CHEMUNG	1,119	949	170	McCall	84.8%	15.2%
51,401	CHENANGO	604	520	84	McCall	86.1%	13.9%
79,894	CLINTON	1,334	994	340	McCall	74.5%	25.5%
63,094	COLUMBIA	1,346	1,233	113	McCall	91.6%	8.4%
48,599	CORTLAND	1,181	1,037	144	McCall	87.8%	12.2%
48,055	DELAWARE	742	614	128	McCall	82.7%	17.3%
280,150	DUTCHESS	4,510	4,085	425	McCall	90.6%	9.4%
950,265	ERIE	53,541	44,153	9,388	McCall	82.5%	17.5%
38,851	ESSEX	865	671	194	McCall	77.6%	22.4%
51,134	FRANKLIN	733	543	190	McCall	74.1%	25.9%
55,073	FULTON	678	584	94	McCall	86.1%	13.9%
60,370	GENESEE	551	407	144	McCall	73.9%	26.1%
48,195	GREENE	654	578	76	McCall	88.4%	11.6%
5,379	HAMILTON	158	142	16	McCall	89.9%	10.1%
64,427	HERKIMER	933	709	224	McCall	76.0%	24.0%
111,738	JEFFERSON	1,385	1,032	353	McCall	74.5%	25.5%
2,465,326	KINGS	115,146	99,683	15,463	McCall	86.6%	13.4%
26,944	LEWIS	404	314	90	McCall	77.7%	22.3%
64,328	LIVINGSTON	1,000	863	137	McCall	86.3%	13.7%
69,441	MADISON	672	535	137	McCall	79.6%	20.4%
735,343	MONROE	16,986	14,505	2,481	McCall	85.4%	14.6%
49,708	MONTGOMERY	1,678	1,417	261	McCall	84.4%	15.6%
1,334,544	NASSAU	27,182	22,922	4,260	McCall	84.3%	15.7%
1,537,195	NEW YORK	108,250	95,078	13,172	McCall	87.8%	12.2%
219,846	NIAGARA	7,509	5,964	1,545	McCall	79.4%	20.6%
235,469	ONEIDA	3,644	2,813	831	McCall	77.2%	22.8%
458,336	ONONDAGA	7,946	6,638	1,308	McCall	83.5%	16.5%
100,224	ONTARIO	1,461	1,205	256	McCall	82.5%	17.5%
341,367	ORANGE	5,706	4,829	877	McCall	84.6%	15.4%
44,171	ORLEANS	327	255	72	McCall	78.0%	22.0%
122,377	OSWEGO	908	721	187	McCall	79.4%	20.6%
61,676	OTSEGO	854	740	114	McCall	86.7%	13.3%
95,745	PUTNAM	1,150	911	239	McCall	79.2%	20.8%
2,229,379	QUEENS	75,577	63,867	11,710	McCall	84.5%	15.5%
152,538	RENSSELAER	2,737	2,452	285	McCall	89.6%	10.4%
443,728	RICHMOND	7,321	5,849	1,472	McCall	79.9%	20.1%
286,753	ROCKLAND	11,852	9,917	1,935	McCall	83.7%	16.3%
111,931	ST. LAWRENCE	1,945	1,485	460	McCall	76.3%	23.7%
200,635	SARATOGA	2,860	2,547	313	McCall	89.1%	10.9%
146,555	SCHENECTADY	3,399	3,017	382	McCall	88.8%	11.2%
31,582	SCHOHARIE	619	544	75	McCall	87.9%	12.1%
19,224	SCHUYLER	207	172	35	McCall	83.1%	16.9%
33,342	SENECA	530	455	75	McCall	85.8%	14.2%
98,726	STEUBEN	1,061	843	218	McCall	79.5%	20.5%
1,419,369	SUFFOLK	15,689	12,759	2,930	McCall	81.3%	18.7%
73,966	SULLIVAN	1,164	989	175	McCall	85.0%	15.0%
51,784	TIOGA	643	533	110	McCall	82.9%	17.1%
96,501	TOMPKINS	4,946	4,541	405	McCall	91.8%	8.2%
177,749	ULSTER	3,034	2,679	355	McCall	88.3%	11.7%
63,303	WARREN	1,246	1,087	159	McCall	87.2%	12.8%
61,042	WASHINGTON	840	723	117	McCall	86.1%	13.9%
93,765	WAYNE	774	634	140	McCall	81.9%	18.1%
923,459	WESTCHESTER	31,519	27,418	4,101	McCall	87.0%	13.0%
43,424	WYOMING	448	358	90	McCall	79.9%	20.1%
24,621	YATES	394	357	37	McCall	90.6%	9.4%
18,976,457	TOTAL	633,078	539,883	93,195	McCall	85.3%	14.7%

NORTH CAROLINA

GOVERNOR
Michael F. Easley (D). Elected 2000 to a four-year term.

SENATORS (1 Democrat, 1 Republican)
Elizabeth Dole (R). Elected 2002 to a six-year term.

John Edwards (D). Elected 1998 to a six-year term.

REPRESENTATIVES (7 Republicans, 6 Democrats)
1. Frank W. Ballance Jr. (D)
2. Bob Etheridge (D)
3. Walter B. Jones (R)
4. David E. Price (D)
5. Richard M. Burr (R)
6. Howard Coble (R)
7. Mike McIntyre (D)
8. Robin Hayes (R)
9. Sue Myrick (R)
10. Cass Ballenger (R)
11. Charles H. Taylor (R)
12. Melvin Watt (D)
13. Brad Miller (D)

POSTWAR VOTE FOR PRESIDENT

| | | Republican | | Democratic | | | | Percentage | | | |
| | | | | | | Other | | Total Vote | | Major Vote | |
Year	Total Vote	Vote	Candidate	Vote	Candidate	Vote	Plurality	Rep.	Dem.	Rep.	Dem.
2000	2,911,262	1,631,163	Bush, George W.	1,257,692	Gore, Al	22,407	373,471 R	56.0%	43.2%	56.5%	43.5%
1996**	2,515,807	1,225,938	Dole, Bob	1,107,849	Clinton, Bill	182,020	118,089 R	48.7%	44.0%	52.5%	47.5%
1992**	2,611,850	1,134,661	Bush, George	1,114,042	Clinton, Bill	363,147	20,619 R	43.4%	42.7%	50.5%	49.5%
1988	2,134,370	1,237,258	Bush, George	890,167	Dukakis, Michael S.	6,945	347,091 R	58.0%	41.7%	58.2%	41.8%
1984	2,175,361	1,346,481	Reagan, Ronald	824,287	Mondale, Walter F.	4,593	522,194 R	61.9%	37.9%	62.0%	38.0%
1980**	1,855,833	915,018	Reagan, Ronald	875,635	Carter, Jimmy	65,180	39,383 R	49.3%	47.2%	51.1%	48.9%
1976	1,678,914	741,960	Ford, Gerald R.	927,365	Carter, Jimmy	9,589	185,405 D	44.2%	55.2%	44.4%	55.6%
1972	1,518,612	1,054,889	Nixon, Richard M.	438,705	McGovern, George S.	25,018	616,184 R	69.5%	28.9%	70.6%	29.4%
1968**	1,587,493	627,192	Nixon, Richard M.	464,113	Humphrey, Hubert H.	496,188	131,004 R	39.5%	29.2%	57.5%	42.5%
1964	1,424,983	624,844	Goldwater, Barry M.	800,139	Johnson, Lyndon B.		175,295 D	43.8%	56.2%	43.8%	56.2%
1960	1,368,556	655,420	Nixon, Richard M.	713,136	Kennedy, John F.		57,716 D	47.9%	52.1%	47.9%	52.1%
1956	1,165,592	575,062	Eisenhower, Dwight D.	590,530	Stevenson, Adlai E.		15,468 D	49.3%	50.7%	49.3%	50.7%
1952	1,210,910	558,107	Eisenhower, Dwight D.	652,803	Stevenson, Adlai E.		94,696 D	46.1%	53.9%	46.1%	53.9%
1948	791,209	258,572	Dewey, Thomas E.	459,070	Truman, Harry S.	73,567	200,498 D	32.7%	58.0%	36.0%	64.0%

In 1996 the other vote column includes 168,059 votes cast for Perot. In 1992 the other vote column includes 357,864 votes cast for Perot. In 1980 the other vote column includes 52,800 votes for Independent (Anderson). In 1968 other vote was American (Wallace).

NORTH CAROLINA

POSTWAR VOTE FOR GOVERNOR

Year	Total Vote	Republican		Democratic		Other Vote	Rep.-Dem. Plurality	Percentage			
		Vote	Candidate	Vote	Candidate			Total Vote		Major Vote	
								Rep.	Dem.	Rep.	Dem.
2000	2,942,062	1,360,960	Vinroot, Richard	1,530,324	Easley, Michael F.	50,778	169,364 D	46.3%	52.0%	47.1%	52.9%
1996	2,566,185	1,097,053	Hayes, Robin	1,436,638	Hunt, James B.	32,494	339,585 D	42.8%	56.0%	43.3%	56.7%
1992	2,595,184	1,121,955	Gardner, James C.	1,368,246	Hunt, James B.	104,983	246,291 D	43.2%	52.7%	45.1%	54.9%
1988	2,180,025	1,222,338	Martin, James G.	957,687	Jordan, Robert B.		264,651 R	56.1%	43.9%	56.1%	43.9%
1984	2,226,727	1,208,167	Martin, James G.	1,011,209	Edmisten, Rufus	7,351	196,958 R	54.3%	45.4%	54.4%	45.6%
1980	1,847,432	691,449	Lake, Beverly	1,143,145	Hunt, James B.	12,838	451,696 D	37.4%	61.9%	37.7%	62.3%
1976	1,663,824	564,102	Flaherty, David T.	1,081,293	Hunt, James B.	18,429	517,191 D	33.9%	65.0%	34.3%	65.7%
1972	1,504,785	767,470	Holshouser, James E.	729,104	Bowles, Hargrove	8,211	38,366 R	51.0%	48.5%	51.3%	48.7%
1968	1,558,308	737,075	Gardner, James C.	821,233	Scott, Robert W.		84,158 D	47.3%	52.7%	47.3%	52.7%
1964	1,396,508	606,165	Gavin, Robert L.	790,343	Moore, Dan K.		184,178 D	43.4%	56.6%	43.4%	56.6%
1960	1,350,360	613,975	Gavin, Robert L.	735,248	Sanford, Terry	1,137	121,273 D	45.5%	54.4%	45.5%	54.5%
1956	1,135,859	375,379	Hayes, Kyle	760,480	Hodges, Luther H.		385,101 D	33.0%	67.0%	33.0%	67.0%
1952	1,179,635	383,329	Seawell, H. F.	796,306	Umstead, William B.		412,977 D	32.5%	67.5%	32.5%	67.5%
1948	780,525	206,166	Pritchard, George	570,995	Scott, William Kerr	3,364	364,829 D	26.4%	73.2%	26.5%	73.5%

POSTWAR VOTE FOR SENATOR

Year	Total Vote	Republican		Democratic		Other Vote	Rep.-Dem. Plurality	Percentage			
		Vote	Candidate	Vote	Candidate			Total Vote		Major Vote	
								Rep.	Dem.	Rep.	Dem.
2002	2,331,181	1,248,664	Dole, Elizabeth	1,047,983	Bowles, Erskine B.	34,534	200,681 R	53.6%	45.0%	54.4%	45.6%
1998	2,012,143	945,943	Faircloth, Lauch	1,029,237	Edwards, John	36,963	83,294 D	47.0%	51.2%	47.9%	52.1%
1996	2,556,456	1,345,833	Helms, Jesse	1,173,875	Gantt, Harvey B.	36,748	171,958 R	52.6%	45.9%	53.4%	46.6%
1992	2,577,891	1,297,892	Faircloth, Lauch	1,194,015	Sanford, Terry	85,984	103,877 R	50.3%	46.3%	52.1%	47.9%
1990	2,069,585	1,087,331	Helms, Jesse	981,573	Gantt, Harvy B.	681	105,758 R	52.5%	47.4%	52.6%	47.4%
1986	1,591,330	767,668	Broyhill, James T.	823,662	Sanford, Terry		55,994 D	48.2%	51.8%	48.2%	51.8%
1984	2,239,051	1,156,768	Helms, Jesse	1,070,488	Hunt, James B.	11,795	86,280 R	51.7%	47.8%	51.9%	48.1%
1980	1,797,665	898,064	East, John P.	887,653	Morgan, Robert	11,948	10,411 R	50.0%	49.4%	50.3%	49.7%
1978	1,135,814	619,151	Helms, Jesse	516,663	Ingram, John		102,488 R	54.5%	45.5%	54.5%	45.5%
1974	1,020,367	377,618	Stevens, William E.	633,775	Morgan, Robert	8,974	256,157 D	37.0%	62.1%	37.3%	62.7%
1972	1,472,541	795,248	Helms, Jesse	677,293	Galifianakis, Nick		117,955 R	54.0%	46.0%	54.0%	46.0%
1968	1,437,340	566,934	Somers, Robert V.	870,406	Ervin, Sam J.		303,472 D	39.4%	60.6%	39.4%	60.6%
1966	901,978	400,502	Shallcross, John S.	501,440	Jordan, B. Everett	36	100,938 D	44.4%	55.6%	44.4%	55.6%
1962	813,155	321,635	Greene, Claude L.	491,520	Ervin, Sam J.		169,885 D	39.6%	60.4%	39.6%	60.4%
1960	1,291,485	497,964	Hayes, Kyle	793,521	Jordan, B. Everett		295,557 D	38.6%	61.4%	38.6%	61.4%
1958S	616,469	184,977	Clarke, Richard C.	431,492	Jordan, B. Everett		246,515 D	30.0%	70.0%	30.0%	70.0%
1956	1,098,828	367,475	Johnson, Joel A.	731,353	Ervin, Sam J.		363,878 D	33.4%	66.6%	33.4%	66.6%
1954	619,634	211,322	West, Paul C.	408,312	Scott, William Kerr		196,990 D	34.1%	65.9%	34.1%	65.9%
1954S	410,574		—	410,574	Ervin, Sam J.		410,574 D		100.0%		100.0%
1950	548,276	171,804	Leavitt, Halsey B.	376,472	Hoey, Clyde R.		204,668 D	31.3%	68.7%	31.3%	68.7%
1950S	544,924	177,753	Gavin, E. L.	364,912	Smith, Willis	2,259	187,159 D	32.6%	67.0%	32.8%	67.2%
1948	764,559	220,307	Wilkinson, John A.	540,762	Broughton, J. M.	3,490	320,455 D	28.8%	70.7%	28.9%	71.1%

The 1958 election and one each of the 1954 and 1950 elections were for short terms to fill vacancies.

NORTH CAROLINA

Congressional districts first established for elections held in 2002
13 members

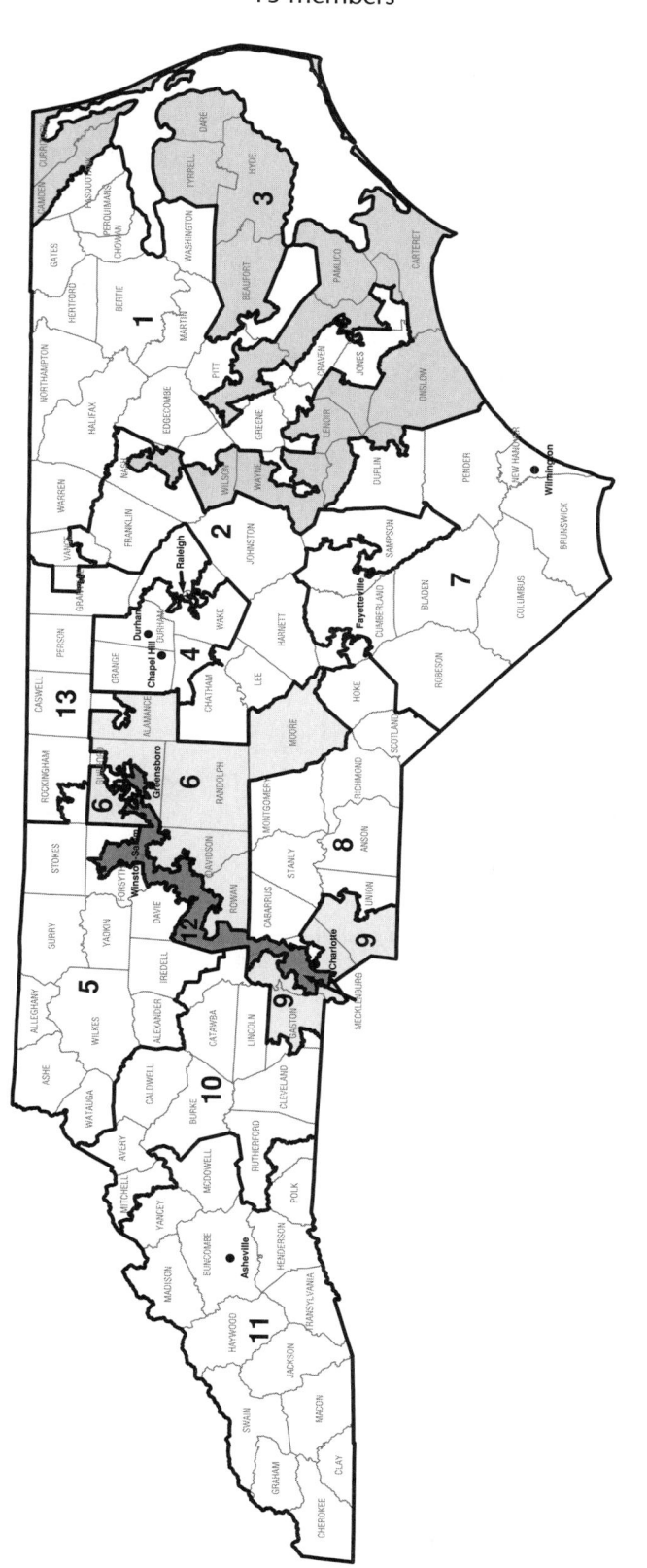

NORTH CAROLINA

Central North Carolina Area

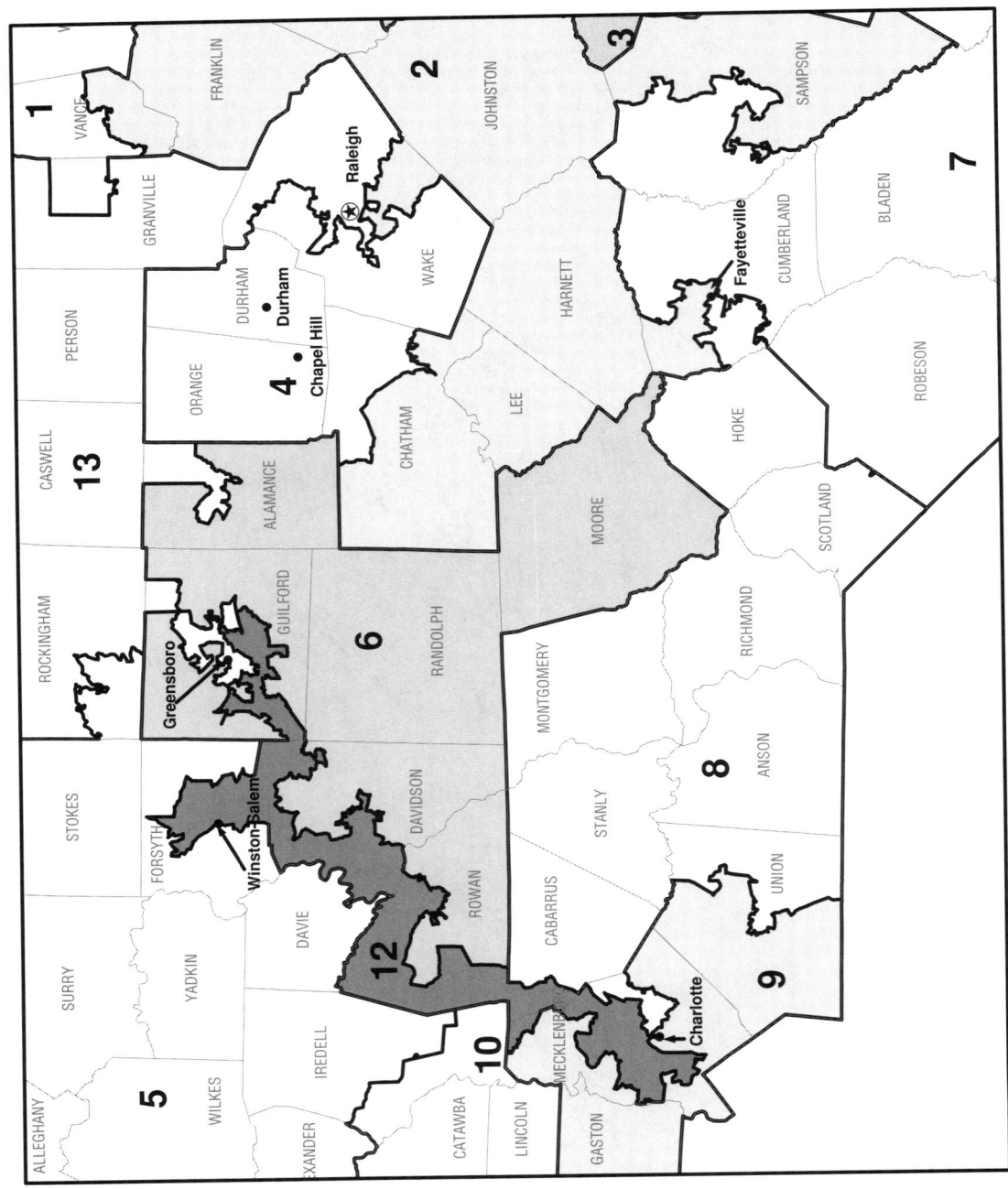

NORTH CAROLINA

SENATOR 2002

2000 Census Population	County	Total Vote	Republican	Democratic	Other	Rep.-Dem. Plurality	Total Vote Rep.	Total Vote Dem.	Major Vote Rep.	Major Vote Dem.
130,800	ALAMANCE	34,754	20,580	13,587	587	6,993 R	59.2%	39.1%	60.2%	39.8%
33,603	ALEXANDER	11,968	7,125	4,570	273	2,555 R	59.5%	38.2%	60.9%	39.1%
10,677	ALLEGHANY	3,783	1,846	1,840	97	6 R	48.8%	48.6%	50.1%	49.9%
25,275	ANSON	6,259	2,134	4,063	62	1,929 D	34.1%	64.9%	34.4%	65.6%
24,384	ASHE	9,049	4,886	3,977	186	909 R	54.0%	43.9%	55.1%	44.9%
17,167	AVERY	4,922	3,616	1,228	78	2,388 R	73.5%	24.9%	74.6%	25.4%
44,958	BEAUFORT	15,483	9,057	6,098	328	2,959 R	58.5%	39.4%	59.8%	40.2%
19,773	BERTIE	5,335	1,671	3,617	47	1,946 D	31.3%	67.8%	31.6%	68.4%
32,278	BLADEN	8,692	3,474	5,144	74	1,670 D	40.0%	59.2%	40.3%	59.7%
73,143	BRUNSWICK	26,028	14,002	11,537	489	2,465 R	53.8%	44.3%	54.8%	45.2%
206,330	BUNCOMBE	63,473	31,360	31,359	754	1 R	49.4%	49.4%	50.0%	50.0%
89,148	BURKE	26,101	14,351	11,115	635	3,236 R	55.0%	42.6%	56.4%	43.6%
131,063	CABARRUS	39,776	25,434	13,657	685	11,777 R	63.9%	34.3%	65.1%	34.9%
77,415	CALDWELL	22,324	13,245	8,511	568	4,734 R	59.3%	38.1%	60.9%	39.1%
6,885	CAMDEN	2,656	1,292	1,325	39	33 D	48.6%	49.9%	49.4%	50.6%
59,383	CARTERET	20,032	12,408	7,216	408	5,192 R	61.9%	36.0%	63.2%	36.8%
23,501	CASWELL	6,750	3,049	3,615	86	566 D	45.2%	53.6%	45.8%	54.2%
141,685	CATAWBA	39,526	25,318	13,436	772	11,882 R	64.1%	34.0%	65.3%	34.7%
49,329	CHATHAM	18,998	8,897	9,809	292	912 D	46.8%	51.6%	47.6%	52.4%
24,298	CHEROKEE	8,342	4,878	3,355	109	1,523 R	58.5%	40.2%	59.2%	40.8%
14,526	CHOWAN	3,698	1,744	1,894	60	150 D	47.2%	51.2%	47.9%	52.1%
8,775	CLAY	3,605	2,209	1,342	54	867 R	61.3%	37.2%	62.2%	37.8%
96,287	CLEVELAND	25,714	13,984	11,330	400	2,654 R	54.4%	44.1%	55.2%	44.8%
54,749	COLUMBUS	15,135	5,925	9,015	195	3,090 D	39.1%	59.6%	39.7%	60.3%
91,436	CRAVEN	25,836	15,162	10,240	434	4,922 R	58.7%	39.6%	59.7%	40.3%
302,963	CUMBERLAND	58,116	27,941	29,417	758	1,476 D	48.1%	50.6%	48.7%	51.3%
18,190	CURRITUCK	5,728	3,309	2,337	82	972 R	57.8%	40.8%	58.6%	41.4%
29,967	DARE	10,260	5,695	4,418	147	1,277 R	55.5%	43.1%	56.3%	43.7%
147,246	DAVIDSON	44,318	27,277	15,992	1,049	11,285 R	61.5%	36.1%	63.0%	37.0%
34,835	DAVIE	10,865	7,659	3,008	198	4,651 R	70.5%	27.7%	71.8%	28.2%
49,063	DUPLIN	11,581	5,476	5,912	193	436 D	47.3%	51.0%	48.1%	51.9%
223,314	DURHAM	66,943	23,841	42,350	752	18,509 D	35.6%	63.3%	36.0%	64.0%
55,606	EDGECOMBE	14,070	4,766	9,160	144	4,394 D	33.9%	65.1%	34.2%	65.8%
306,067	FORSYTH	94,852	50,867	42,696	1,289	8,171 R	53.6%	45.0%	54.4%	45.6%
47,260	FRANKLIN	14,412	7,170	6,950	292	220 R	49.8%	48.2%	50.8%	49.2%
190,365	GASTON	42,856	27,176	14,976	704	12,200 R	63.4%	34.9%	64.5%	35.5%
10,516	GATES	2,199	764	1,425	10	661 D	34.7%	64.8%	34.9%	65.1%
7,993	GRAHAM	4,166	2,220	1,906	40	314 R	53.3%	45.8%	53.8%	46.2%
48,498	GRANVILLE	11,788	5,511	6,146	131	635 D	46.8%	52.1%	47.3%	52.7%
18,974	GREENE	4,568	2,274	2,252	42	22 R	49.8%	49.3%	50.2%	49.8%
421,048	GUILFORD	130,595	64,997	64,050	1,548	947 R	49.8%	49.0%	50.4%	49.6%
57,370	HALIFAX	14,298	5,432	8,714	152	3,282 D	38.0%	60.9%	38.4%	61.6%
91,025	HARNETT	20,780	12,174	8,263	343	3,911 R	58.6%	39.8%	59.6%	40.4%
54,033	HAYWOOD	17,856	8,438	9,155	263	717 D	47.3%	51.3%	48.0%	52.0%
89,173	HENDERSON	30,111	19,283	10,575	253	8,708 R	64.0%	35.1%	64.6%	35.4%
22,601	HERTFORD	5,386	1,499	3,854	33	2,355 D	27.8%	71.6%	28.0%	72.0%
33,646	HOKE	6,272	2,513	3,665	94	1,152 D	40.1%	58.4%	40.7%	59.3%
5,826	HYDE	1,884	853	1,008	23	155 D	45.3%	53.5%	45.8%	54.2%
122,660	IREDELL	34,053	21,646	11,852	555	9,794 R	63.6%	34.8%	64.6%	35.4%
33,121	JACKSON	9,270	4,161	4,988	121	827 D	44.9%	53.8%	45.5%	54.5%
121,965	JOHNSTON	35,927	22,719	12,722	486	9,997 R	63.2%	35.4%	64.1%	35.9%
10,381	JONES	4,201	2,065	2,067	69	2 D	49.2%	49.2%	50.0%	50.0%
49,040	LEE	13,370	7,375	5,820	175	1,555 R	55.2%	43.5%	55.9%	44.1%
59,648	LENOIR	17,664	8,888	8,624	152	264 R	50.3%	48.8%	50.8%	49.2%
63,780	LINCOLN	20,432	12,309	7,649	474	4,660 R	60.2%	37.4%	61.7%	38.3%
42,151	MCDOWELL	11,290	6,202	4,901	187	1,301 R	54.9%	43.4%	55.9%	44.1%
29,811	MACON	11,613	6,383	4,932	298	1,451 R	55.0%	42.5%	56.4%	43.6%
19,635	MADISON	7,386	3,300	3,994	92	694 D	44.7%	54.1%	45.2%	54.8%
25,593	MARTIN	8,078	3,334	4,630	114	1,296 D	41.3%	57.3%	41.9%	58.1%
695,454	MECKLENBURG	201,571	100,762	98,332	2,477	2,430 R	50.0%	48.8%	50.6%	49.4%

NORTH CAROLINA

SENATOR 2002

2000 Census Population	County	Total Vote	Republican	Democratic	Other	Rep.-Dem. Plurality	Total Vote Rep.	Total Vote Dem.	Major Vote Rep.	Major Vote Dem.
15,687	MITCHELL	5,473	3,801	1,590	82	2,211 R	69.5%	29.1%	70.5%	29.5%
26,822	MONTGOMERY	7,107	3,502	3,474	131	28 R	49.3%	48.9%	50.2%	49.8%
74,769	MOORE	26,023	16,753	8,951	319	7,802 R	64.4%	34.4%	65.2%	34.8%
87,420	NASH	25,848	14,564	11,032	252	3,532 R	56.3%	42.7%	56.9%	43.1%
160,307	NEW HANOVER	52,991	29,478	22,641	872	6,837 R	55.6%	42.7%	56.6%	43.4%
22,086	NORTHAMPTON	6,637	2,006	4,564	67	2,558 D	30.2%	68.8%	30.5%	69.5%
150,355	ONSLOW	23,523	14,256	8,687	580	5,569 R	60.6%	36.9%	62.1%	37.9%
118,227	ORANGE	39,526	13,629	25,401	496	11,772 D	34.5%	64.3%	34.9%	65.1%
12,934	PAMLICO	4,936	2,734	2,112	90	622 R	55.4%	42.8%	56.4%	43.6%
34,897	PASQUOTANK	6,953	2,984	3,921	48	937 D	42.9%	56.4%	43.2%	56.8%
41,082	PENDER	12,424	6,364	5,876	184	488 R	51.2%	47.3%	52.0%	48.0%
11,368	PERQUIMANS	3,432	1,688	1,710	34	22 D	49.2%	49.8%	49.7%	50.3%
35,623	PERSON	10,476	5,873	4,444	159	1,429 R	56.1%	42.4%	56.9%	43.1%
133,798	PITT	34,234	18,514	15,446	274	3,068 R	54.1%	45.1%	54.5%	45.5%
18,324	POLK	6,750	3,939	2,713	98	1,226 R	58.4%	40.2%	59.2%	40.8%
130,454	RANDOLPH	32,065	22,134	9,366	565	12,768 R	69.0%	29.2%	70.3%	29.7%
46,564	RICHMOND	10,961	4,167	6,600	194	2,433 D	38.0%	60.2%	38.7%	61.3%
123,339	ROBESON	20,658	7,410	12,864	384	5,454 D	35.9%	62.3%	36.5%	63.5%
91,928	ROCKINGHAM	26,589	13,899	12,062	628	1,837 R	52.3%	45.4%	53.5%	46.5%
130,340	ROWAN	35,579	22,688	12,153	738	10,535 R	63.8%	34.2%	65.1%	34.9%
62,899	RUTHERFORD	17,355	10,012	7,101	242	2,911 R	57.7%	40.9%	58.5%	41.5%
60,161	SAMPSON	16,195	8,367	7,645	183	722 R	51.7%	47.2%	52.3%	47.7%
35,998	SCOTLAND	7,589	3,072	4,442	75	1,370 D	40.5%	58.5%	40.9%	59.1%
58,100	STANLY	18,689	11,680	6,643	366	5,037 R	62.5%	35.5%	63.7%	36.3%
44,711	STOKES	13,799	8,567	4,888	344	3,679 R	62.1%	35.4%	63.7%	36.3%
71,219	SURRY	18,247	10,723	7,161	363	3,562 R	58.8%	39.2%	60.0%	40.0%
12,968	SWAIN	3,616	1,636	1,940	40	304 D	45.2%	53.7%	45.7%	54.3%
29,334	TRANSYLVANIA	11,435	6,416	4,862	157	1,554 R	56.1%	42.5%	56.9%	43.1%
4,149	TYRRELL	1,196	478	701	17	223 D	40.0%	58.6%	40.5%	59.5%
123,677	UNION	36,641	24,032	12,059	550	11,973 R	65.6%	32.9%	66.6%	33.4%
42,954	VANCE	9,785	4,126	5,584	75	1,458 D	42.2%	57.1%	42.5%	57.5%
627,846	WAKE	225,623	122,445	100,371	2,807	22,074 R	54.3%	44.5%	55.0%	45.0%
19,972	WARREN	5,768	1,900	3,833	35	1,933 D	32.9%	66.5%	33.1%	66.9%
13,723	WASHINGTON	4,257	1,658	2,548	51	890 D	38.9%	59.9%	39.4%	60.6%
42,695	WATAUGA	15,729	8,832	6,561	336	2,271 R	56.2%	41.7%	57.4%	42.6%
113,329	WAYNE	27,255	16,372	10,637	246	5,735 R	60.1%	39.0%	60.6%	39.4%
65,632	WILKES	19,900	12,238	7,208	454	5,030 R	61.5%	36.2%	62.9%	37.1%
73,814	WILSON	19,137	9,756	9,230	151	526 R	51.0%	48.2%	51.4%	48.6%
36,348	YADKIN	11,566	8,128	3,139	299	4,989 R	70.3%	27.1%	72.1%	27.9%
17,774	YANCEY	8,216	3,917	4,203	96	286 D	47.7%	51.2%	48.2%	51.8%
8,049,313	TOTAL	2,331,181	1,248,664	1,047,983	34,534	200,681 R	53.6%	45.0%	54.4%	45.6%

NORTH CAROLINA

HOUSE OF REPRESENTATIVES

CD	Year	Total Vote	Republican		Democratic		Other Vote	Rep.-Dem. Plurality	Percentage			
									Total Vote		Major Vote	
			Vote	Candidate	Vote	Candidate			Rep.	Dem.	Rep.	Dem.
1	2002	146,157	50,907	Dority, Greg	93,157	Ballance, Frank W. Jr.	2,093	42,250 D	34.8%	63.7%	35.3%	64.7%
2	2002	153,184	50,965	Ellen, Joseph L.	100,121	Etheridge, Bob*	2,098	49,156 D	33.3%	65.4%	33.7%	66.3%
3	2002	144,934	131,448	Jones, Walter B.*			13,486	131,448 R	90.7%		100.0%	
4	2002	216,046	78,095	Nguyen, Tuan A.	132,185	Price, David E.*	5,766	54,090 D	36.1%	61.2%	37.1%	62.9%
5	2002	196,437	137,879	Burr, Richard M.*	58,558	Crawford, David		79,321 R	70.2%	29.8%	70.2%	29.8%
6	2002	167,497	151,430	Coble, Howard*			16,067	151,430 R	90.4%		100.0%	
7	2002	166,654	45,537	Adams, James R.	118,543	McIntyre, Mike*	2,574	73,006 D	27.3%	71.1%	27.8%	72.2%
8	2002	149,736	80,298	Hayes, Robin*	66,819	Kouri, Chris	2,619	13,479 R	53.6%	44.6%	54.6%	45.4%
9	2002	193,443	140,095	Myrick, Sue*	49,974	McGuire, Ed	3,374	90,121 R	72.4%	25.8%	73.7%	26.3%
10	2002	173,292	102,768	Ballenger, Cass*	65,587	Daugherty, Ron	4,937	37,181 R	59.3%	37.8%	61.0%	39.0%
11	2002	202,260	112,335	Taylor, Charles H.*	86,664	Neill, Sam	3,261	25,671 R	55.5%	42.8%	56.5%	43.5%
12	2002	151,239	49,588	Kish, Jeff	98,821	Watt, Melvin*	2,830	49,233 D	32.8%	65.3%	33.4%	66.6%
13	2002	183,270	77,688	Grant, Carolyn W.	100,287	Miller, Brad*	5,295	22,599 D	42.4%	54.7%	43.7%	56.3%
Total	2002	2,244,149	1,209,033		970,716		64,400	238,317 R	53.9%	43.3%	55.5%	44.5%

An asterisk (*) denotes incumbent.

NORTH CAROLINA

GENERAL AND PRIMARY ELECTIONS

2002 GENERAL ELECTIONS

Senator Other vote was 33,807 Libertarian (Sean Haugh); 727 write-in (Paul G. DeLaney).

House Other vote was:

CD 1 2,093 Libertarian (Mike Ruff).
CD 2 2,098 Libertarian (Gary Minter).
CD 3 13,486 Libertarian (Gary Goodson).
CD 4 5,766 Libertarian (Ken Nelson).
CD 5
CD 6 16,067 Libertarian (Tara Grubb).
CD 7 2,574 Libertarian (David Michael Brooks).
CD 8 2,619 Libertarian (Mark Andrew Johnson).
CD 9 3,374 Libertarian (Christopher S. Cole).
CD 10 4,937 Libertarian (Christopher M. Hill).
CD 11 3,261 Libertarian (Eric Henry).
CD 12 2,830 Libertarian (Carey Head).
CD 13 5,295 Libertarian (Alex MacDonald).

NORTH CAROLINA

GENERAL AND PRIMARY ELECTIONS

2002 PRIMARY ELECTIONS

Primary	September 10, 2002	**Registration** (as of Sept. 2, 2002)	

Republican	1,711,031
Democratic	2,427,793
Libertarian	8,552
Unaffiliated	852,348
TOTAL	4,999,724

Primary Type Semi-open—Registered Democrats and Republicans could vote only in their party's primary. Unaffiliated voters could participate in the primary of either party. The total number of registered voters was listed as 4,999,736 at the time of the 2002 primary, according to state election officials, but adds to 4,999,724.

Note: An asterisk (*) denotes incumbent. The names of unopposed candidates did not appear on the primary ballot; therefore, no votes were cast for these candidates.

	REPUBLICAN PRIMARIES			DEMOCRATIC PRIMARIES		
Senator	Elizabeth Dole	342,631	80.4%	Erskine B. Bowles	277,329	43.4%
	Jim Snyder	60,477	14.2%	Dan Blue	184,216	28.8%
	Jim Parker	8,752	2.1%	Elaine Marshall	97,392	15.2%
	Ada M. Fisher	6,045	1.4%	Cynthia D. Brown	27,799	4.4%
	Douglas J. Sellers	3,771	0.9%	Albert Lee Wiley Jr.	12,725	2.0%
	Timothy Cook	2,643	0.6%	Bob Ayers	12,326	1.9%
	Venkat Challa	1,787	0.4%	David E. Tidwell	10,510	1.6%
				Duke Underwood	9,940	1.6%
				Randy Crow	6,788	1.1%
	TOTAL	426,106		TOTAL	639,025	
Congressional District 1	Greg Dority	Unopposed		Frank W. Ballance Jr.	37,833	47.0%
				Sam Davis	20,758	25.8%
				Janice McKenzie Cole	14,410	17.9%
				Christine L. Fitch	7,526	9.3%
				TOTAL	80,527	
Congressional District 2	Joseph L. Ellen	Unopposed		Bob Etheridge*	Unopposed	
Congressional District 3	Walter B. Jones*	Unopposed		No Democratic candidate		
Congressional District 4	Tuan A. Nguyen	Unopposed		David E. Price*	Unopposed	
Congressional District 5	Richard M. Burr*	Unopposed		David Crawford	Unopposed	
Congressional District 6	Howard Coble*	Unopposed		No Democratic candidate		
Congressional District 7	James R. Adams	10,107	55.4%	Mike McIntyre*	Unopposed	
	Raymond R. Brown	8,142	44.6%			
	TOTAL	18,249				
Congressional District 8	Robin Hayes*	Unopposed		Chris Kouri	22,725	47.3%
				William O. "Billy" Richardson	15,590	32.4%
				Tripp Helms	6,062	12.6%
				Ray Warren	3,678	7.7%
				TOTAL	48,055	
Congressional District 9	Sue Myrick*	Unopposed		Ed McGuire	Unopposed	
Congressional District 10	Cass Ballenger*	Unopposed		Ron Daugherty	Unopposed	
Congressional District 11	Charles H. Taylor*	Unopposed		Sam Neill	Unopposed	

NORTH CAROLINA

GENERAL AND PRIMARY ELECTIONS

	REPUBLICAN PRIMARIES			DEMOCRATIC PRIMARIES		
Congressional District 12	Jeff Kish	Unopposed		Melvin Watt*	33,853	84.7%
				Kimberly "Kim" Holley	6,107	15.3%
				TOTAL	39,960	
Congressional District 13	Carolyn W. Grant	9,520	38.5%	Brad Miller	22,130	40.1%
	Graham Boyd	9,345	37.8%	Robin Britt	13,490	24.4%
	Paul Smith	5,840	23.6%	Bill Martin	8,021	14.5%
				Lawrence Davis	6,911	12.5%
				Gene Gay	2,459	4.5%
				Ronnie Ansley	2,168	3.9%
	TOTAL	24,705		TOTAL	55,179	

NORTH CAROLINA REPUBLICAN PRIMARY

SENATOR 2002

2000 Census Population	County	Total Vote	Dole	Snyder	Other	Winner	Percentage of Total Vote		
							Dole	Snyder	Other
130,800	ALAMANCE	6,414	4,873	1,287	254	Dole	76.0%	20.1%	4.0%
33,603	ALEXANDER	1,788	1,520	181	87	Dole	85.0%	10.1%	4.9%
10,677	ALLEGHANY	558	410	135	13	Dole	73.5%	24.2%	2.3%
25,275	ANSON	427	366	31	30	Dole	85.7%	7.3%	7.0%
24,384	ASHE	2,007	1,655	265	87	Dole	82.5%	13.2%	4.3%
17,167	AVERY	3,979	3,316	307	356	Dole	83.3%	7.7%	8.9%
44,958	BEAUFORT	3,032	2,555	340	137	Dole	84.3%	11.2%	4.5%
19,773	BERTIE	238	213	3	22	Dole	89.5%	1.3%	9.2%
32,278	BLADEN	557	487	31	39	Dole	87.4%	5.6%	7.0%
73,143	BRUNSWICK	3,885	3,269	356	260	Dole	84.1%	9.2%	6.7%
206,330	BUNCOMBE	8,317	6,278	1,444	595	Dole	75.5%	17.4%	7.2%
89,148	BURKE	4,299	3,594	403	302	Dole	83.6%	9.4%	7.0%
131,063	CABARRUS	5,817	4,568	893	356	Dole	78.5%	15.4%	6.1%
77,415	CALDWELL	5,047	4,402	393	252	Dole	87.2%	7.8%	5.0%
6,885	CAMDEN	213	177	14	22	Dole	83.1%	6.6%	10.3%
59,383	CARTERET	5,490	4,736	471	283	Dole	86.3%	8.6%	5.2%
23,501	CASWELL	594	454	111	29	Dole	76.4%	18.7%	4.9%
141,685	CATAWBA	10,924	9,157	1,132	635	Dole	83.8%	10.4%	5.8%
49,329	CHATHAM	2,961	2,452	332	177	Dole	82.8%	11.2%	6.0%
24,298	CHEROKEE	2,694	2,094	291	309	Dole	77.7%	10.8%	11.5%
14,526	CHOWAN	362	297	32	33	Dole	82.0%	8.8%	9.1%
8,775	CLAY	633	554	24	55	Dole	87.5%	3.8%	8.7%
96,287	CLEVELAND	3,429	2,966	279	184	Dole	86.5%	8.1%	5.4%
54,749	COLUMBUS	1,029	925	53	51	Dole	89.9%	5.2%	5.0%
91,436	CRAVEN	4,854	4,191	443	220	Dole	86.3%	9.1%	4.5%
302,963	CUMBERLAND	7,866	6,845	548	473	Dole	87.0%	7.0%	6.0%
18,190	CURRITUCK	603	521	37	45	Dole	86.4%	6.1%	7.5%
29,967	DARE	1,231	1,115	41	75	Dole	90.6%	3.3%	6.1%
147,246	DAVIDSON	12,297	7,060	4,942	295	Dole	57.4%	40.2%	2.4%
34,835	DAVIE	4,983	3,516	1,262	205	Dole	70.6%	25.3%	4.1%
49,063	DUPLIN	1,491	1,300	139	52	Dole	87.2%	9.3%	3.5%
223,314	DURHAM	5,972	5,156	520	296	Dole	86.3%	8.7%	5.0%
55,606	EDGECOMBE	775	672	62	41	Dole	86.7%	8.0%	5.3%
306,067	FORSYTH	22,343	16,316	5,191	836	Dole	73.0%	23.2%	3.7%
47,260	FRANKLIN	2,103	1,613	413	77	Dole	76.7%	19.6%	3.7%
190,365	GASTON	7,694	6,316	942	436	Dole	82.1%	12.2%	5.7%
10,516	GATES	151	121	14	16	Dole	80.1%	9.3%	10.6%
7,993	GRAHAM	1,378	1,164	128	86	Dole	84.5%	9.3%	6.2%
48,498	GRANVILLE	985	806	135	44	Dole	81.8%	13.7%	4.5%
18,974	GREENE	303	273	22	8	Dole	90.1%	7.3%	2.6%

NORTH CAROLINA REPUBLICAN PRIMARY

SENATOR 2002

2000 Census Population	County	Total Vote	Dole	Snyder	Other	Winner	Percentage of Total Vote		
							Dole	Snyder	Other
421,048	GUILFORD	21,025	16,360	3,780	885	Dole	77.8%	18.0%	4.2%
57,370	HALIFAX	1,090	965	34	91	Dole	88.5%	3.1%	8.3%
91,025	HARNETT	3,856	3,211	478	167	Dole	83.3%	12.4%	4.3%
54,033	HAYWOOD	2,048	1,563	340	145	Dole	76.3%	16.6%	7.1%
89,173	HENDERSON	13,585	10,712	1,960	913	Dole	78.9%	14.4%	6.7%
22,601	HERTFORD	245	224	9	12	Dole	91.4%	3.7%	4.9%
33,646	HOKE	586	475	53	58	Dole	81.1%	9.0%	9.9%
5,826	HYDE	143	118	21	4	Dole	82.5%	14.7%	2.8%
122,660	IREDELL	7,724	6,231	1,144	349	Dole	80.7%	14.8%	4.5%
33,121	JACKSON	1,034	851	91	92	Dole	82.3%	8.8%	8.9%
121,965	JOHNSTON	6,939	5,891	744	304	Dole	84.9%	10.7%	4.4%
10,381	JONES	277	219	44	14	Dole	79.1%	15.9%	5.1%
49,040	LEE	2,050	1,727	223	100	Dole	84.2%	10.9%	4.9%
59,648	LENOIR	1,802	1,651	81	70	Dole	91.6%	4.5%	3.9%
63,780	LINCOLN	6,817	5,802	630	385	Dole	85.1%	9.2%	5.6%
42,151	MCDOWELL	1,643	1,232	328	83	Dole	75.0%	20.0%	5.1%
29,811	MACON	3,596	2,913	317	366	Dole	81.0%	8.8%	10.2%
19,635	MADISON	1,295	1,038	142	115	Dole	80.2%	11.0%	8.9%
25,593	MARTIN	545	492	24	29	Dole	90.3%	4.4%	5.3%
695,454	MECKLENBURG	27,544	22,503	3,100	1,941	Dole	81.7%	11.3%	7.0%
15,687	MITCHELL	4,455	3,429	578	448	Dole	77.0%	13.0%	10.1%
26,822	MONTGOMERY	1,151	967	133	51	Dole	84.0%	11.6%	4.4%
74,769	MOORE	9,481	7,981	947	553	Dole	84.2%	10.0%	5.8%
87,420	NASH	4,864	3,999	711	154	Dole	82.2%	14.6%	3.2%
160,307	NEW HANOVER	10,064	8,116	1,651	297	Dole	80.6%	16.4%	3.0%
22,086	NORTHAMPTON	232	201	15	16	Dole	86.6%	6.5%	6.9%
150,355	ONSLOW	4,549	3,884	453	212	Dole	85.4%	10.0%	4.7%
118,227	ORANGE	3,476	2,817	452	207	Dole	81.0%	13.0%	6.0%
12,934	PAMLICO	679	610	44	25	Dole	89.8%	6.5%	3.7%
34,897	PASQUOTANK	645	547	48	50	Dole	84.8%	7.4%	7.8%
41,082	PENDER	2,233	1,889	229	115	Dole	84.6%	10.3%	5.2%
11,368	PERQUIMANS	295	245	31	19	Dole	83.1%	10.5%	6.4%
35,623	PERSON	1,566	1,372	109	85	Dole	87.6%	7.0%	5.4%
133,798	PITT	4,230	3,691	339	200	Dole	87.3%	8.0%	4.7%
18,324	POLK	2,596	2,120	271	205	Dole	81.7%	10.4%	7.9%
130,454	RANDOLPH	13,277	9,793	2,963	521	Dole	73.8%	22.3%	3.9%
46,564	RICHMOND	905	769	69	67	Dole	85.0%	7.6%	7.4%
123,339	ROBESON	1,186	958	54	174	Dole	80.8%	4.6%	14.7%
91,928	ROCKINGHAM	3,502	2,648	700	154	Dole	75.6%	20.0%	4.4%
130,340	ROWAN	10,649	8,483	1,505	661	Dole	79.7%	14.1%	6.2%
62,899	RUTHERFORD	2,175	1,809	240	126	Dole	83.2%	11.0%	5.8%
60,161	SAMPSON	4,040	3,686	195	159	Dole	91.2%	4.8%	3.9%
35,998	SCOTLAND	660	545	52	63	Dole	82.6%	7.9%	9.5%
58,100	STANLY	3,684	3,043	460	181	Dole	82.6%	12.5%	4.9%
44,711	STOKES	4,008	2,816	1,002	190	Dole	70.3%	25.0%	4.7%
71,219	SURRY	2,959	2,200	624	135	Dole	74.3%	21.1%	4.6%
12,968	SWAIN	373	302	42	29	Dole	81.0%	11.3%	7.8%
29,334	TRANSYLVANIA	2,401	1,911	341	149	Dole	79.6%	14.2%	6.2%
4,149	TYRRELL	73	67	4	2	Dole	91.8%	5.5%	2.7%
123,677	UNION	9,601	7,623	1,324	654	Dole	79.4%	13.8%	6.8%
42,954	VANCE	466	410	37	19	Dole	88.0%	7.9%	4.1%
627,846	WAKE	36,735	31,229	3,751	1,755	Dole	85.0%	10.2%	4.8%
19,972	WARREN	317	276	28	13	Dole	87.1%	8.8%	4.1%
13,723	WASHINGTON	269	229	24	16	Dole	85.1%	8.9%	5.9%
42,695	WATAUGA	4,701	3,927	450	324	Dole	83.5%	9.6%	6.9%
113,329	WAYNE	3,554	3,226	196	132	Dole	90.8%	5.5%	3.7%
65,632	WILKES	6,305	4,826	1,152	327	Dole	76.5%	18.3%	5.2%
73,814	WILSON	2,250	1,854	322	74	Dole	82.4%	14.3%	3.3%
36,348	YADKIN	6,890	4,778	1,631	481	Dole	69.3%	23.7%	7.0%
17,774	YANCEY	1,043	874	110	59	Dole	83.8%	10.5%	5.7%
8,049,313	TOTAL	426,106	342,631	60,477	22,998	Dole	80.4%	14.2%	5.4%

NORTH CAROLINA DEMOCRATIC PRIMARY

SENATOR 2002

2000 Census Population	County	Total Vote	Bowles	Blue	Marshall	Other	Winner	Percentage of Total Vote			
								Bowles	Blue	Marshall	Other
130,800	ALAMANCE	6,360	2,841	2,040	645	834	Bowles	44.7%	32.1%	10.1%	13.1%
33,603	ALEXANDER	3,501	1,988	325	431	757	Bowles	56.8%	9.3%	12.3%	21.6%
10,677	ALLEGHANY	1,218	842	132	108	136	Bowles	69.1%	10.8%	8.9%	11.2%
25,275	ANSON	4,362	1,813	1,599	399	551	Bowles	41.6%	36.7%	9.1%	12.6%
24,384	ASHE	1,402	972	112	151	167	Bowles	69.3%	8.0%	10.8%	11.9%
17,167	AVERY	329	197	26	41	65	Bowles	59.9%	7.9%	12.5%	19.8%
44,958	BEAUFORT	6,636	3,099	1,153	1,426	958	Bowles	46.7%	17.4%	21.5%	14.4%
19,773	BERTIE	4,738	1,561	1,903	572	702	Blue	32.9%	40.2%	12.1%	14.8%
32,278	BLADEN	6,514	2,361	2,026	1,137	990	Bowles	36.2%	31.1%	17.5%	15.2%
73,143	BRUNSWICK	7,025	3,464	1,193	1,308	1,060	Bowles	49.3%	17.0%	18.6%	15.1%
206,330	BUNCOMBE	11,106	5,712	1,534	1,181	2,679	Bowles	51.4%	13.8%	10.6%	24.1%
89,148	BURKE	5,272	2,644	1,120	839	669	Bowles	50.2%	21.2%	15.9%	12.7%
131,063	CABARRUS	4,794	2,973	965	408	448	Bowles	62.0%	20.1%	8.5%	9.3%
77,415	CALDWELL	2,687	1,620	402	327	338	Bowles	60.3%	15.0%	12.2%	12.6%
6,885	CAMDEN	1,408	410	214	304	480	Bowles	29.1%	15.2%	21.6%	34.1%
59,383	CARTERET	5,352	2,828	435	1,332	757	Bowles	52.8%	8.1%	24.9%	14.1%
23,501	CASWELL	4,231	1,535	1,144	336	1,216	Bowles	36.3%	27.0%	7.9%	28.7%
141,685	CATAWBA	5,433	3,025	1,137	536	735	Bowles	55.7%	20.9%	9.9%	13.5%
49,329	CHATHAM	9,633	4,256	2,642	1,703	1,032	Bowles	44.2%	27.4%	17.7%	10.7%
24,298	CHEROKEE	2,526	1,086	146	301	993	Bowles	43.0%	5.8%	11.9%	39.3%
14,526	CHOWAN	1,044	494	157	213	180	Bowles	47.3%	15.0%	20.4%	17.2%
8,775	CLAY	670	232	77	108	253	Bowles	34.6%	11.5%	16.1%	37.8%
96,287	CLEVELAND	10,350	4,859	2,509	1,475	1,507	Bowles	46.9%	24.2%	14.3%	14.6%
54,749	COLUMBUS	9,155	4,277	2,125	1,356	1,397	Bowles	46.7%	23.2%	14.8%	15.3%
91,436	CRAVEN	6,424	2,934	1,252	1,099	1,139	Bowles	45.7%	19.5%	17.1%	17.7%
302,963	CUMBERLAND	23,444	8,718	7,619	4,823	2,284	Bowles	37.2%	32.5%	20.6%	9.7%
18,190	CURRITUCK	1,221	413	164	274	370	Bowles	33.8%	13.4%	22.4%	30.3%
29,967	DARE	3,264	1,666	275	592	731	Bowles	51.0%	8.4%	18.1%	22.4%
147,246	DAVIDSON	8,064	4,830	1,509	637	1,088	Bowles	59.9%	18.7%	7.9%	13.5%
34,835	DAVIE	1,542	902	291	141	208	Bowles	58.5%	18.9%	9.1%	13.5%
49,063	DUPLIN	5,734	2,126	1,719	1,107	782	Bowles	37.1%	30.0%	19.3%	13.6%
223,314	DURHAM	26,870	8,513	12,201	3,933	2,223	Blue	31.7%	45.4%	14.6%	8.3%
55,606	EDGECOMBE	7,324	2,224	3,248	982	870	Blue	30.4%	44.3%	13.4%	11.9%
306,067	FORSYTH	22,878	10,947	8,440	1,645	1,846	Bowles	47.8%	36.9%	7.2%	8.1%
47,260	FRANKLIN	5,756	1,878	1,670	1,563	645	Bowles	32.6%	29.0%	27.2%	11.2%
190,365	GASTON	6,613	3,601	1,466	656	890	Bowles	54.5%	22.2%	9.9%	13.5%
10,516	GATES	1,648	346	276	343	683	Bowles	21.0%	16.7%	20.8%	41.4%
7,993	GRAHAM	757	390	32	66	269	Bowles	51.5%	4.2%	8.7%	35.5%
48,498	GRANVILLE	4,416	1,350	1,760	933	373	Blue	30.6%	39.9%	21.1%	8.4%
18,974	GREENE	3,123	1,390	640	668	425	Bowles	44.5%	20.5%	21.4%	13.6%
421,048	GUILFORD	27,953	14,006	10,375	1,555	2,017	Bowles	50.1%	37.1%	5.6%	7.2%
57,370	HALIFAX	9,605	2,862	4,010	1,567	1,166	Blue	29.8%	41.7%	16.3%	12.1%
91,025	HARNETT	7,797	1,640	1,371	4,338	448	Marshall	21.0%	17.6%	55.6%	5.7%
54,033	HAYWOOD	6,314	3,555	617	724	1,418	Bowles	56.3%	9.8%	11.5%	22.5%
89,173	HENDERSON	3,145	1,949	290	290	616	Bowles	62.0%	9.2%	9.2%	19.6%
22,601	HERTFORD	2,838	608	1,420	404	406	Blue	21.4%	50.0%	14.2%	14.3%
33,646	HOKE	4,714	1,410	1,914	655	735	Blue	29.9%	40.6%	13.9%	15.6%
5,826	HYDE	1,149	501	103	309	236	Bowles	43.6%	9.0%	26.9%	20.5%
122,660	IREDELL	5,195	3,113	1,040	548	494	Bowles	59.9%	20.0%	10.5%	9.5%
33,121	JACKSON	4,028	1,955	293	512	1,268	Bowles	48.5%	7.3%	12.7%	31.5%
121,965	JOHNSTON	8,929	3,109	2,259	2,820	741	Bowles	34.8%	25.3%	31.6%	8.3%
10,381	JONES	2,450	803	312	444	891	Bowles	32.8%	12.7%	18.1%	36.4%
49,040	LEE	4,705	1,532	1,036	1,877	260	Marshall	32.6%	22.0%	39.9%	5.5%
59,648	LENOIR	7,551	2,899	2,188	1,604	860	Bowles	38.4%	29.0%	21.2%	11.4%
63,780	LINCOLN	6,010	3,450	889	913	758	Bowles	57.4%	14.8%	15.2%	12.6%
42,151	MCDOWELL	1,897	922	141	431	403	Bowles	48.6%	7.4%	22.7%	21.2%
29,811	MACON	2,851	1,243	162	571	875	Bowles	43.6%	5.7%	20.0%	30.7%
19,635	MADISON	2,533	1,298	220	419	596	Bowles	51.2%	8.7%	16.5%	23.5%
25,593	MARTIN	3,929	1,681	1,147	619	482	Bowles	42.8%	29.2%	15.8%	12.3%
695,454	MECKLENBURG	33,636	19,084	10,186	1,966	2,400	Bowles	56.7%	30.3%	5.8%	7.1%

NORTH CAROLINA DEMOCRATIC PRIMARY

SENATOR 2002

2000 Census Population	County	Total Vote	Bowles	Blue	Marshall	Other	Winner	Percentage of Total Vote			
								Bowles	Blue	Marshall	Other
15,687	MITCHELL	235	132	20	25	58	Bowles	56.2%	8.5%	10.6%	24.7%
26,822	MONTGOMERY	3,016	1,459	759	367	431	Bowles	48.4%	25.2%	12.2%	14.3%
74,769	MOORE	3,981	2,078	885	632	386	Bowles	52.2%	22.2%	15.9%	9.7%
87,420	NASH	7,358	2,842	2,213	1,518	785	Bowles	38.6%	30.1%	20.6%	10.7%
160,307	NEW HANOVER	11,192	6,198	2,935	1,256	803	Bowles	55.4%	26.2%	11.2%	7.2%
22,086	NORTHAMPTON	5,878	1,505	2,674	909	790	Blue	25.6%	45.5%	15.5%	13.4%
150,355	ONSLOW	7,168	2,825	1,343	1,574	1,426	Bowles	39.4%	18.7%	22.0%	19.9%
118,227	ORANGE	14,902	6,929	4,905	1,964	1,104	Bowles	46.5%	32.9%	13.2%	7.4%
12,934	PAMLICO	2,229	982	283	305	659	Bowles	44.1%	12.7%	13.7%	29.6%
34,897	PASQUOTANK	3,169	1,037	929	627	576	Bowles	32.7%	29.3%	19.8%	18.2%
41,082	PENDER	3,868	1,628	1,226	484	530	Bowles	42.1%	31.7%	12.5%	13.7%
11,368	PERQUIMANS	1,034	503	147	190	194	Bowles	48.6%	14.2%	18.4%	18.8%
35,623	PERSON	5,643	2,197	1,519	1,089	838	Bowles	38.9%	26.9%	19.3%	14.9%
133,798	PITT	12,420	5,884	2,706	2,064	1,766	Bowles	47.4%	21.8%	16.6%	14.2%
18,324	POLK	1,732	943	106	224	459	Bowles	54.4%	6.1%	12.9%	26.5%
130,454	RANDOLPH	3,861	2,499	506	375	481	Bowles	64.7%	13.1%	9.7%	12.5%
46,564	RICHMOND	5,769	2,467	1,549	903	850	Bowles	42.8%	26.9%	15.7%	14.7%
123,339	ROBESON	19,205	4,602	8,215	2,873	3,515	Blue	24.0%	42.8%	15.0%	18.3%
91,928	ROCKINGHAM	8,067	3,754	2,121	741	1,451	Bowles	46.5%	26.3%	9.2%	18.0%
130,340	ROWAN	7,238	3,729	1,860	776	873	Bowles	51.5%	25.7%	10.7%	12.1%
62,899	RUTHERFORD	4,165	2,054	454	646	1,011	Bowles	49.3%	10.9%	15.5%	24.3%
60,161	SAMPSON	5,654	1,714	1,713	1,575	652	Bowles	30.3%	30.3%	27.9%	11.5%
35,998	SCOTLAND	4,689	1,577	1,864	568	680	Blue	33.6%	39.8%	12.1%	14.5%
58,100	STANLY	4,699	2,779	744	512	664	Bowles	59.1%	15.8%	10.9%	14.1%
44,711	STOKES	2,615	1,631	446	246	292	Bowles	62.4%	17.1%	9.4%	11.2%
71,219	SURRY	5,405	3,112	965	621	707	Bowles	57.6%	17.9%	11.5%	13.1%
12,968	SWAIN	1,426	708	70	263	385	Bowles	49.6%	4.9%	18.4%	27.0%
29,334	TRANSYLVANIA	1,519	911	165	168	275	Bowles	60.0%	10.9%	11.1%	18.1%
4,149	TYRRELL	1,128	530	162	175	261	Bowles	47.0%	14.4%	15.5%	23.1%
123,677	UNION	5,340	2,665	1,779	362	534	Bowles	49.9%	33.3%	6.8%	10.0%
42,954	VANCE	3,997	1,102	1,795	808	292	Blue	27.6%	44.9%	20.2%	7.3%
627,846	WAKE	51,037	18,434	20,535	9,507	2,561	Blue	36.1%	40.2%	18.6%	5.0%
19,972	WARREN	3,871	1,123	1,789	562	397	Blue	29.0%	46.2%	14.5%	10.3%
13,723	WASHINGTON	3,272	1,203	1,251	376	442	Blue	36.8%	38.2%	11.5%	13.5%
42,695	WATAUGA	2,544	1,428	298	468	350	Bowles	56.1%	11.7%	18.4%	13.8%
113,329	WAYNE	6,119	2,072	2,412	1,123	512	Blue	33.9%	39.4%	18.4%	8.4%
65,632	WILKES	3,029	1,929	413	328	359	Bowles	63.7%	13.6%	10.8%	11.9%
73,814	WILSON	6,343	1,910	2,523	1,307	603	Blue	30.1%	39.8%	20.6%	9.5%
36,348	YADKIN	1,312	804	244	86	178	Bowles	61.3%	18.6%	6.6%	13.6%
17,774	YANCEY	843	513	42	130	158	Bowles	60.9%	5.0%	15.4%	18.7%
8,049,313	TOTAL	639,025	277,329	184,216	97,392	80,088	Bowles	43.4%	28.8%	15.2%	12.5%

NORTH DAKOTA

GOVERNOR
John Hoeven (R). Elected 2000 to a four-year term.

SENATORS (2 Democrats)
Kent Conrad (D). Reelected 2000 to a six-year term. Previously elected 1994 and in a special election December 1992 to fill out the remaining two years of the term vacated by the death of Senator Quentin N. Burdick (D) who died in September 1992; elected 1986 to a six-year term.

Byron L. Dorgan (D). Reelected 1998 to a six-year term. Previously elected 1992.

REPRESENTATIVES (1 Democrat)
At Large. Earl Pomeroy (D)

POSTWAR VOTE FOR PRESIDENT

Year	Total Vote	Republican		Democratic		Other Vote	Plurality	Percentage			
								Total Vote		Major Vote	
		Vote	Candidate	Vote	Candidate			Rep.	Dem.	Rep.	Dem.
2000**	288,256	174,852	Bush, George W.	95,284	Gore, Al	18,120	79,568 R	60.7%	33.1%	64.7%	35.3%
1996**	266,411	125,050	Dole, Bob	106,905	Clinton, Bill	34,456	18,145 R	46.9%	40.1%	53.9%	46.1%
1992**	308,133	136,244	Bush, George	99,168	Clinton, Bill	72,721	37,076 R	44.2%	32.2%	57.9%	42.1%
1988	297,261	166,559	Bush, George	127,739	Dukakis, Michael S.	2,963	38,820 R	56.0%	43.0%	56.6%	43.4%
1984	308,971	200,336	Reagan, Ronald	104,429	Mondale, Walter F.	4,206	95,907 R	64.8%	33.8%	65.7%	34.3%
1980**	301,545	193,695	Reagan, Ronald	79,189	Carter, Jimmy	28,661	114,506 R	64.2%	26.3%	71.0%	29.0%
1976	297,188	153,470	Ford, Gerald R.	136,078	Carter, Jimmy	7,640	17,392 R	51.6%	45.8%	53.0%	47.0%
1972	280,514	174,109	Nixon, Richard M.	100,384	McGovern, George S.	6,021	73,725 R	62.1%	35.8%	63.4%	36.6%
1968	247,882	138,669	Nixon, Richard M.	94,769	Humphrey, Hubert H.	14,444	43,900 R	55.9%	38.2%	59.4%	40.6%
1964	258,389	108,207	Goldwater, Barry M.	149,784	Johnson, Lyndon B.	398	41,577 D	41.9%	58.0%	41.9%	58.1%
1960	278,431	154,310	Nixon, Richard M.	123,963	Kennedy, John F.	158	30,347 R	55.4%	44.5%	55.5%	44.5%
1956	253,991	156,766	Eisenhower, Dwight D.	96,742	Stevenson, Adlai E.	483	60,024 R	61.7%	38.1%	61.8%	38.2%
1952	270,127	191,712	Eisenhower, Dwight D.	76,694	Stevenson, Adlai E.	1,721	115,018 R	71.0%	28.4%	71.4%	28.6%
1948	220,716	115,139	Dewey, Thomas E.	95,812	Truman, Harry S.	9,765	19,327 R	52.2%	43.4%	54.6%	45.4%

In 2000 the other vote column includes 9,486 votes cast for Green (Nader). In 1996 the other vote column includes 32,515 votes cast for Perot. In 1992 the other vote column includes 71,084 votes cast for Perot. In 1980 the other vote column includes 23,640 votes for Independent (Anderson).

NORTH DAKOTA

POSTWAR VOTE FOR GOVERNOR

Year	Total Vote	Republican Vote	Republican Candidate	Democratic Vote	Democratic Candidate	Other Vote	Rep.-Dem. Plurality	Total Vote Rep.	Total Vote Dem.	Major Vote Rep.	Major Vote Dem.
2000	289,412	159,255	Hoeven, John	130,144	Heitkamp, Heidi	13	29,111 R	55.0%	45.0%	55.0%	45.0%
1996	264,298	174,937	Schafer, Edward T.	89,349	Kaldor, Lee	12	85,588 R	66.2%	33.8%	66.2%	33.8%
1992	304,861	176,398	Schafer, Edward T.	123,845	Spaeth, Nicholas	4,618	52,553 R	57.9%	40.6%	58.8%	41.2%
1988	299,080	119,986	Mallberg, Leon L.	179,094	Sinner, George		59,108 D	40.1%	59.9%	40.1%	59.9%
1984	314,382	140,460	Olson, Allen I.	173,922	Sinner, George		33,462 D	44.7%	55.3%	44.7%	55.3%
1980	302,621	162,230	Olson, Allen I.	140,391	Link, Arthur A.		21,839 R	53.6%	46.4%	53.6%	46.4%
1976	297,249	138,321	Elkin, Richard	153,309	Link, Arthur A.	5,619	14,988 D	46.5%	51.6%	47.4%	52.6%
1972	281,931	138,032	Larsen, Richard	143,899	Link, Arthur A.		5,867 D	49.0%	51.0%	49.0%	51.0%
1968	248,000	108,382	McCarney, Robert P.	135,955	Guy, William L.	3,663	27,573 D	43.7%	54.8%	44.4%	55.6%
1964**	262,661	116,247	Halcrow, Donald M.	146,414	Guy, William L.		30,167 D	44.3%	55.7%	44.3%	55.7%
1962	228,509	113,251	Andrews, Mark	115,258	Guy, William L.		2,007 D	49.6%	50.4%	49.6%	50.4%
1960	275,375	122,486	Dahl, C. P.	136,148	Guy, William L.	16,741	13,662 D	44.5%	49.4%	47.4%	52.6%
1958	210,599	111,836	Davis, John E.	98,763	Lord, John F.		13,073 R	53.1%	46.9%	53.1%	46.9%
1956	252,435	147,566	Davis, John E.	104,869	Warner, Wallace E.		42,697 R	58.5%	41.5%	58.5%	41.5%
1954	193,501	124,253	Brunsdale, C. Norman	69,248	Bymers, Cornelius		55,005 R	64.2%	35.8%	64.2%	35.8%
1952	253,934	199,944	Brunsdale, C. Norman	53,990	Johnson, Ole C.		145,954 R	78.7%	21.3%	78.7%	21.3%
1950	183,772	121,822	Brunsdale, C. Norman	61,950	Byerly, Clyde G.		59,872 R	66.3%	33.7%	66.3%	33.7%
1948	214,858	131,764	Aandahl, Fred G.	80,555	Henry, Howard	2,539	51,209 R	61.3%	37.5%	62.1%	37.9%
1946	169,391	116,672	Aandahl, Fred G.	52,719	Burdick, Quentin N.		63,953 R	68.9%	31.1%	68.9%	31.1%

The term of office of North Dakota's Governor was increased from two to four years effective with the 1964 election.

POSTWAR VOTE FOR SENATOR

Year	Total Vote	Republican Vote	Republican Candidate	Democratic Vote	Democratic Candidate	Other Vote	Rep.-Dem. Plurality	Total Vote Rep.	Total Vote Dem.	Major Vote Rep.	Major Vote Dem.
2000	287,539	111,069	Sand, Duane	176,470	Conrad, Kent		65,401 D	38.6%	61.4%	38.6%	61.4%
1998	213,358	75,013	Nalewaja, Donna	134,747	Dorgan, Byron L.	3,598	59,734 D	35.2%	63.2%	35.8%	64.2%
1994	236,547	99,390	Clayburg, Ben	137,157	Conrad, Kent		37,767 D	42.0%	58.0%	42.0%	58.0%
1992	303,957	118,162	Sydness, Steve	179,347	Dorgan, Byron L.	6,448	61,185 D	38.9%	59.0%	39.7%	60.3%
1992S	163,311	55,194	Dalrymple, Jack	103,246	Conrad, Kent	4,871	48,052 D	33.8%	63.2%	34.8%	65.2%
1988	289,170	112,937	Striden, Earl	171,899	Burdick, Quentin N.	4,334	58,962 D	39.1%	59.4%	39.6%	60.4%
1986	288,998	141,797	Andrews, Mark	143,932	Conrad, Kent	3,269	2,135 D	49.1%	49.8%	49.6%	50.4%
1982	262,465	89,304	Knorr, Gene	164,873	Burdick, Quentin N.	8,288	75,569 D	34.0%	62.8%	35.1%	64.9%
1980	299,272	210,347	Andrews, Mark	86,658	Johanneson, Kent	2,267	123,689 R	70.3%	29.0%	70.8%	29.2%
1976	283,062	103,466	Stroup, Richard	175,772	Burdick, Quentin N.	3,824	72,306 D	36.6%	62.1%	37.1%	62.9%
1974	235,661	114,117	Young, Milton R.	113,931	Guy, William L.	7,613	186 R	48.4%	48.3%	50.0%	50.0%
1970	219,560	82,996	Kleppe, Tom	134,519	Burdick, Quentin N.	2,045	51,523 D	37.8%	61.3%	38.2%	61.8%
1968	239,776	154,968	Young, Milton R.	80,815	Lashkowitz, Herschel	3,993	74,153 R	64.6%	33.7%	65.7%	34.3%
1964	258,945	109,681	Kleppe, Tom	149,264	Burdick, Quentin N.		39,583 D	42.4%	57.6%	42.4%	57.6%
1962	223,737	135,705	Young, Milton R.	88,032	Lanier, William		47,673 R	60.7%	39.3%	60.7%	39.3%
1960S	210,349	103,475	Davis, John E.	104,593	Burdick, Quentin N.	2,281	1,118 D	49.2%	49.7%	49.7%	50.3%
1958	204,635	117,070	Langer, William	84,892	Vendsel, Raymond	2,673	32,178 R	57.2%	41.5%	58.0%	42.0%
1956	244,161	155,305	Young, Milton R.	87,919	Burdick, Quentin N.	937	67,386 R	63.6%	36.0%	63.9%	36.1%
1952	237,995	157,907	Langer, William	55,347	Morrison, Harold A.	24,741	102,560 R	66.3%	23.3%	74.0%	26.0%
1950	186,716	126,209	Young, Milton R.	60,507	O'Brien, Harry		65,702 R	67.6%	32.4%	67.6%	32.4%
1946**	165,382	88,210	Langer, William	38,368	Larson, Abner B.	38,804	49,842 R	53.3%	23.2%	69.7%	30.3%
1946S	136,852	75,998	Young, Milton R.	37,507	Lanier, William	23,347	38,491 R	55.5%	27.4%	67.0%	33.0%

One of the 1992 elections was for a short term to fill a vacancy and the special election was held in December. The 1960 and 1946 special elections were held in June for short terms to fill vacancies. In 1946 other vote was for Arthur Thompson (Independent) who received 23.5% of the total vote and ran second.

NORTH DAKOTA

One member At Large

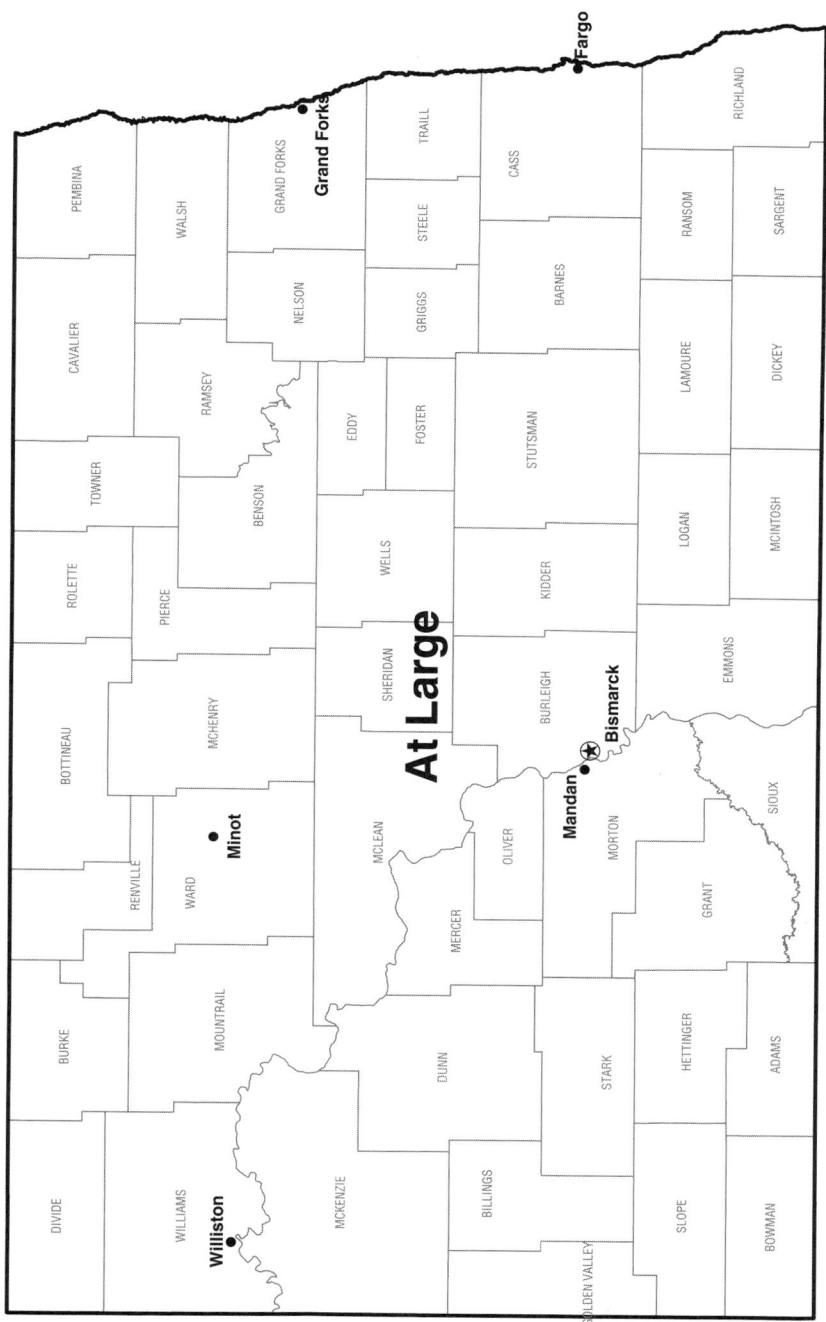

NORTH DAKOTA

HOUSE OF REPRESENTATIVES

CD	Year	Total Vote	Republican Vote	Republican Candidate	Democratic Vote	Democratic Candidate	Other Vote	Rep.-Dem. Plurality	Total Vote Rep.	Total Vote Dem.	Major Vote Rep.	Major Vote Dem.
AL	2002	231,030	109,957	Clayburgh, Rick	121,073	Pomeroy, Earl*		11,116 D	47.6%	52.4%	47.6%	52.4%
AL	2000	285,658	127,251	Dorso, John	151,173	Pomeroy, Earl*	7,234	23,922 D	44.5%	52.9%	45.7%	54.3%
AL	1998	215,469	75,013	Cramer, Kevin	134,747	Pomeroy, Earl*	5,709	59,734 D	34.8%	62.5%	35.8%	64.2%
AL	1996	263,010	113,684	Cramer, Kevin	144,833	Pomeroy, Earl*	4,493	31,149 D	43.2%	55.1%	44.0%	56.0%
AL	1994	235,389	105,988	Porter, Gary	123,134	Pomeroy, Earl*	6,267	17,146 D	45.0%	52.3%	46.3%	53.7%
AL	1992	297,898	117,442	Korsmo, John T.	169,273	Pomeroy, Earl	11,183	51,831 D	39.4%	56.8%	41.0%	59.0%
AL	1990	233,979	81,443	Schafer, Edward	152,530	Dorgan, Byron L.*	6	71,087 D	34.8%	65.2%	34.8%	65.2%
AL	1988	299,982	84,475	Sydness, Steve	212,583	Dorgan, Byron L.*	2,924	128,108 D	28.2%	70.9%	28.4%	71.6%
AL	1986	286,361	66,989	Vinje, Syver	216,258	Dorgan, Byron L.*	3,114	149,269 D	23.4%	75.5%	23.7%	76.3%
AL	1984	308,729	65,761	Altenburg, Lois I.	242,968	Dorgan, Byron L.*		177,207 D	21.3%	78.7%	21.3%	78.7%
AL	1982	260,499	72,241	Jones, Kent	186,534	Dorgan, Byron L.*	1,724	114,293 D	27.7%	71.6%	27.9%	72.1%
AL	1980	293,076	124,707	Smykowski, Jim	166,437	Dorgan, Byron L.	1,932	41,730 D	42.6%	56.8%	42.8%	57.2%
AL	1978	220,348	147,746	Andrews, Mark*	68,016	Hagen, Bruce	4,586	79,730 R	67.1%	30.9%	68.5%	31.5%
AL	1976	289,881	181,018	Andrews, Mark*	104,263	Omdahl, Lloyd B.	4,600	76,755 R	62.4%	36.0%	63.5%	36.5%
AL	1974	233,688	130,184	Andrews, Mark*	103,504	Dorgan, Byron L.		26,680 R	55.7%	44.3%	55.7%	44.3%
AL	1972	268,721	195,360	Andrews, Mark*	72,850	Ista, Richard	511	122,510 R	72.7%	27.1%	72.8%	27.2%

An asterisk (*) denotes incumbent.

NORTH DAKOTA

GENERAL AND PRIMARY ELECTIONS

2002 GENERAL ELECTIONS

House At Large   There were no other candidates and no write-in votes were included in the official returns.

2002 PRIMARY ELECTIONS

Primary   June 11, 2002   **Registration**   No Formal Registration

Primary Type   Open—Any person of voting age could participate in the primary of either party.

Note: An asterisk (*) denotes incumbent.

	REPUBLICAN PRIMARIES			DEMOCRATIC PRIMARIES		
House At Large	Rick Clayburgh	56,570	100.0%	Earl Pomeroy*	52,403	100.0%

OHIO

GOVERNOR

Bob Taft (R). Reelected 2002 to a four-year term. Previously elected 1998.

SENATORS (2 Republicans)

Mike DeWine (R). Reelected 2000 to a six-year term. Previously elected 1994.

George V. Voinovich (R). Elected 1998 to a six-year term.

REPRESENTATIVES (12 Republicans, 6 Democrats)

1. Steve Chabot (R)
2. Rob Portman (R)
3. Michael R. Turner (R)
4. Michael G. Oxley (R)
5. Paul E. Gillmor (R)
6. Ted Strickland (D)
7. David L. Hobson (R)
8. John A. Boehner (R)
9. Marcy Kaptur (D)
10. Dennis J. Kucinich (D)
11. Stephanie Tubbs Jones (D)
12. Pat Tiberi (R)
13. Sherrod Brown (D)
14. Steven C. LaTourette (R)
15. Deborah Pryce (R)
16. Ralph Regula (R)
17. Tim Ryan (D)
18. Bob Ney (R)

POSTWAR VOTE FOR PRESIDENT

| Year | Total Vote | Republican | | Democratic | | Other Vote | Plurality | Percentage | | | |
| | | Vote | Candidate | Vote | Candidate | | | Total Vote | | Major Vote | |
								Rep.	Dem.	Rep.	Dem.
2000**	4,701,998	2,350,363	Bush, George W.	2,183,628	Gore, Al	168,007	166,735 R	50.0%	46.4%	51.8%	48.2%
1996**	4,534,434	1,859,883	Dole, Bob	2,148,222	Clinton, Bill	526,329	288,339 D	41.0%	47.4%	46.4%	53.6%
1992**	4,939,967	1,894,310	Bush, George	1,984,942	Clinton, Bill	1,060,715	90,632 D	38.3%	40.2%	48.8%	51.2%
1988	4,393,699	2,416,549	Bush, George	1,939,629	Dukakis, Michael S.	37,521	476,920 R	55.0%	44.1%	55.5%	44.5%
1984	4,547,619	2,678,560	Reagan, Ronald	1,825,440	Mondale, Walter F.	43,619	853,120 R	58.9%	40.1%	59.5%	40.5%
1980**	4,283,603	2,206,545	Reagan, Ronald	1,752,414	Carter, Jimmy	324,644	454,131 R	51.5%	40.9%	55.7%	44.3%
1976	4,111,873	2,000,505	Ford, Gerald R.	2,011,621	Carter, Jimmy	99,747	11,116 D	48.7%	48.9%	49.9%	50.1%
1972	4,094,787	2,441,827	Nixon, Richard M.	1,558,889	McGovern, George S.	94,071	882,938 R	59.6%	38.1%	61.0%	39.0%
1968	3,959,698	1,791,014	Nixon, Richard M.	1,700,586	Humphrey, Hubert H.	468,098	90,428 R	45.2%	42.9%	51.3%	48.7%
1964	3,969,196	1,470,865	Goldwater, Barry M.	2,498,331	Johnson, Lyndon B.		1,027,466 D	37.1%	62.9%	37.1%	62.9%
1960	4,161,859	2,217,611	Nixon, Richard M.	1,944,248	Kennedy, John F.		273,363 R	53.3%	46.7%	53.3%	46.7%
1956	3,702,265	2,262,610	Eisenhower, Dwight D.	1,439,655	Stevenson, Adlai E.		822,955 R	61.1%	38.9%	61.1%	38.9%
1952	3,700,758	2,100,391	Eisenhower, Dwight D.	1,600,367	Stevenson, Adlai E.		500,024 R	56.8%	43.2%	56.8%	43.2%
1948	2,936,071	1,445,684	Dewey, Thomas E.	1,452,791	Truman, Harry S.	37,596	7,107 D	49.2%	49.5%	49.9%	50.1%

In 2000 the other vote column includes 117,799 votes cast for Green (Nader). In 1996 the other vote column includes 483,207 votes cast for Perot. In 1992 the other vote column includes 1,036,426 votes cast for Perot. In 1980 the other vote column includes 254,472 votes for Independent (Anderson).

OHIO

POSTWAR VOTE FOR GOVERNOR

Year	Total Vote	Republican		Democratic		Other Vote	Rep.-Dem. Plurality	Percentage			
								Total Vote		Major Vote	
		Vote	Candidate	Vote	Candidate			Rep.	Dem.	Rep.	Dem.
2002	3,228,992	1,865,007	Taft, Bob	1,236,924	Hagan, Timothy	127,061	628,083 R	57.8%	38.3%	60.1%	39.9%
1998	3,354,213	1,678,721	Taft, Bob	1,498,956	Fisher, Lee	176,536	179,765 R	50.0%	44.7%	52.8%	47.2%
1994	3,346,238	2,401,572	Voinovich, George V.	835,849	Burch, Robert L.	108,817	1,565,723 R	71.8%	25.0%	74.2%	25.8%
1990	3,477,650	1,938,103	Voinovich, George V.	1,539,416	Celebrezze, Anthony J.	131	398,687 R	55.7%	44.3%	55.7%	44.3%
1986	3,066,611	1,207,264	Rhodes, James A.	1,858,372	Celeste, Richard F.	975	651,108 D	39.4%	60.6%	39.4%	60.6%
1982	3,356,721	1,303,962	Brown, Clarence, Jr.	1,981,882	Celeste, Richard F.	70,877	677,920 D	38.8%	59.0%	39.7%	60.3%
1978	2,843,351	1,402,167	Rhodes, James A.	1,354,631	Celeste, Richard F.	86,553	47,536 R	49.3%	47.6%	50.9%	49.1%
1974	3,072,010	1,493,679	Rhodes, James A.	1,482,191	Gilligan, John J.	96,140	11,488 R	48.6%	48.2%	50.2%	49.8%
1970	3,184,133	1,382,659	Cloud, Roger	1,725,560	Gilligan, John J.	75,914	342,901 D	43.4%	54.2%	44.5%	55.5%
1966	2,887,331	1,795,277	Rhodes, James A.	1,092,054	Reams, Frazier, Jr.		703,223 R	62.2%	37.8%	62.2%	37.8%
1962	3,116,711	1,836,190	Rhodes, James A.	1,280,521	DiSalle, Michael V.		555,669 R	58.9%	41.1%	58.9%	41.1%
1958**	3,284,134	1,414,874	O'Neill, C. William	1,869,260	DiSalle, Michael V.		454,386 D	43.1%	56.9%	43.1%	56.9%
1956	3,542,091	1,984,988	O'Neill, C. William	1,557,103	DiSalle, Michael V.		427,885 R	56.0%	44.0%	56.0%	44.0%
1954	2,597,790	1,192,528	Rhodes, James A.	1,405,262	Lausche, Frank J.		212,734 D	45.9%	54.1%	45.9%	54.1%
1952	3,605,168	1,590,058	Taft, Charles P.	2,015,110	Lausche, Frank J.		425,052 D	44.1%	55.9%	44.1%	55.9%
1950	2,892,819	1,370,570	Ebright, Don H.	1,522,249	Lausche, Frank J.		151,679 D	47.4%	52.6%	47.4%	52.6%
1948	3,018,289	1,398,514	Herbert, Thomas J.	1,619,775	Lausche, Frank J.		221,261 D	46.3%	53.7%	46.3%	53.7%
1946	2,303,750	1,166,550	Herbert, Thomas J.	1,125,997	Lausche, Frank J.	11,203	40,553 R	50.6%	48.9%	50.9%	49.1%

The term of office of Ohio's Governor was increased from two to four years effective with the 1958 election.

POSTWAR VOTE FOR SENATOR

Year	Total Vote	Republican		Democratic		Other Vote	Rep.-Dem. Plurality	Percentage			
								Total Vote		Major Vote	
		Vote	Candidate	Vote	Candidate			Rep.	Dem.	Rep.	Dem.
2000	4,448,801	2,665,512	DeWine, Mike	1,595,066	Celeste, Ted	188,223	1,070,446 R	59.9%	35.9%	62.6%	37.4%
1998	3,404,351	1,922,087	Voinovich, George V.	1,482,054	Boyle, Mary O.	210	440,033 R	56.5%	43.5%	56.5%	43.5%
1994	3,436,884	1,836,556	DeWine, Mike	1,348,213	Hyatt, Joel	252,115	488,343 R	53.4%	39.2%	57.7%	42.3%
1992	4,793,953	2,028,300	DeWine, Mike	2,444,419	Glenn, John H.	321,234	416,119 D	42.3%	51.0%	45.3%	54.7%
1988	4,352,905	1,872,716	Voinovich, George V.	2,480,038	Metzenbaum, Howard	151	607,322 D	43.0%	57.0%	43.0%	57.0%
1986	3,121,189	1,171,893	Kindness, Thomas N.	1,949,208	Glenn, John H.	88	777,315 D	37.5%	62.5%	37.5%	62.5%
1982	3,395,463	1,396,790	Pfeifer, Paul E.	1,923,767	Metzenbaum, Howard	74,906	526,977 D	41.1%	56.7%	42.1%	57.9%
1980	4,027,303	1,137,695	Betts, James E.	2,770,786	Glenn, John H.	118,822	1,633,091 D	28.2%	68.8%	29.1%	70.9%
1976	3,920,613	1,823,774	Taft, Robert A., Jr.	1,941,113	Metzenbaum, Howard	155,726	117,339 D	46.5%	49.5%	48.4%	51.6%
1974	2,987,951	918,133	Perk, Ralph J.	1,930,670	Glenn, John H.	139,148	1,012,537 D	30.7%	64.6%	32.2%	67.8%
1970	3,151,274	1,565,682	Taft, Robert A., Jr.	1,495,262	Metzenbaum, Howard	90,330	70,420 R	49.7%	47.4%	51.2%	48.8%
1968	3,743,121	1,928,964	Saxbe, William B.	1,814,152	Gilligan, John J.	5	114,812 R	51.5%	48.5%	51.5%	48.5%
1964	3,830,389	1,906,781	Taft, Robert A., Jr.	1,923,608	Young, Stephen M.		16,827 D	49.8%	50.2%	49.8%	50.2%
1962	2,994,986	1,151,173	Briley, John M.	1,843,813	Lausche, Frank J.		692,640 D	38.4%	61.6%	38.4%	61.6%
1958	3,149,410	1,497,199	Bricker, John W.	1,652,211	Young, Stephen M.		155,012 D	47.5%	52.5%	47.5%	52.5%
1956	3,525,499	1,660,910	Bender, George H.	1,864,589	Lausche, Frank J.		203,679 D	47.1%	52.9%	47.1%	52.9%
1954S	2,512,778	1,257,874	Bender, George H.	1,254,904	Burke, Thomas A.		2,970 R	50.1%	49.9%	50.1%	49.9%
1952	3,442,291	1,878,961	Bricker, John W.	1,563,330	DiSalle, Michael V.		315,631 R	54.6%	45.4%	54.6%	45.4%
1950	2,860,102	1,645,643	Taft, Robert A.	1,214,459	Ferguson, Joseph T.		431,184 R	57.5%	42.5%	57.5%	42.5%
1946	2,237,269	1,275,774	Bricker, John W.	947,610	Huffman, James W.	13,885	328,164 R	57.0%	42.4%	57.4%	42.6%

The 1954 election was for a short term to fill a vacancy.

OHIO

Congressional districts first established for elections held in 2002
18 members

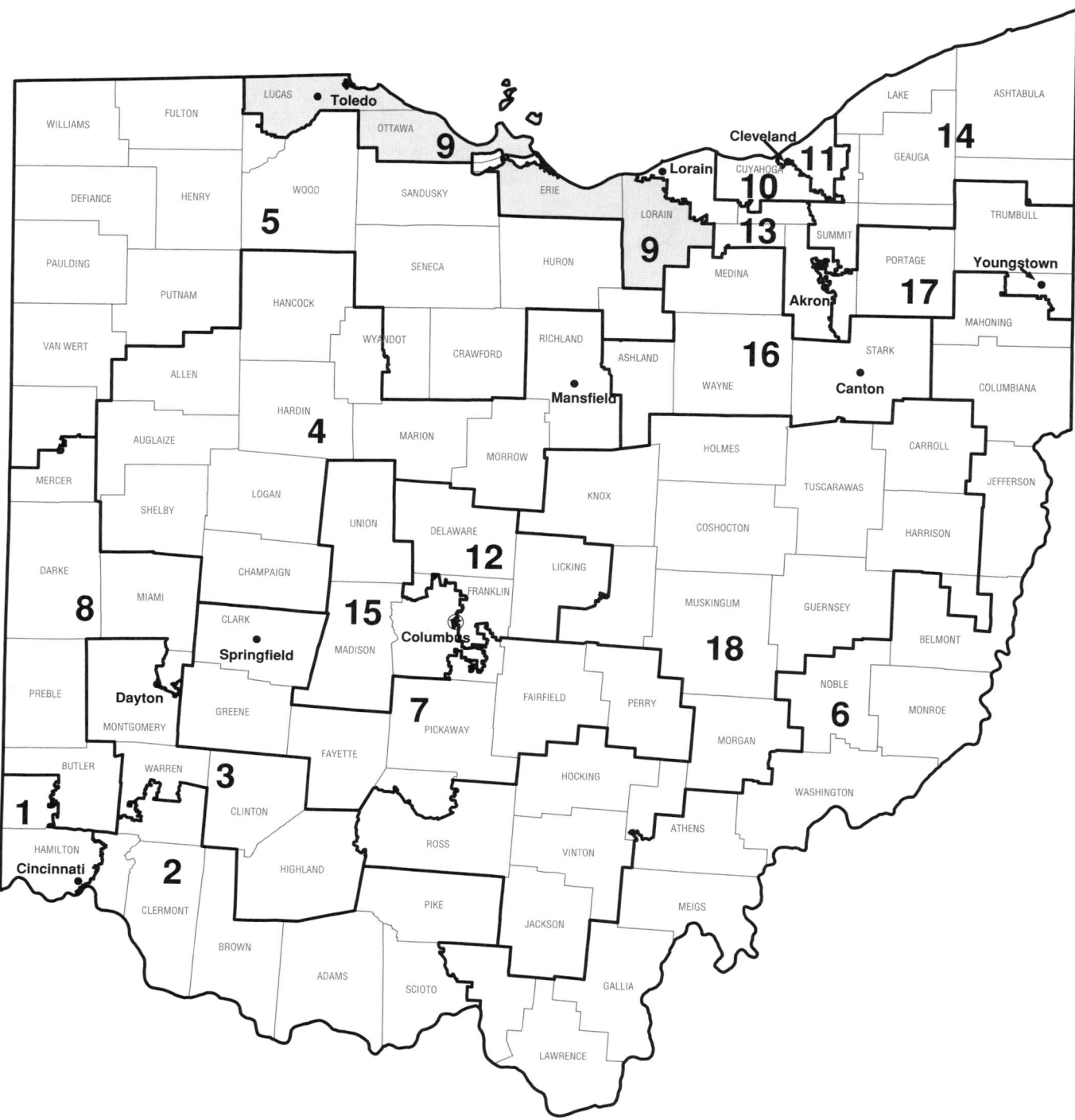

OHIO

Cleveland Area

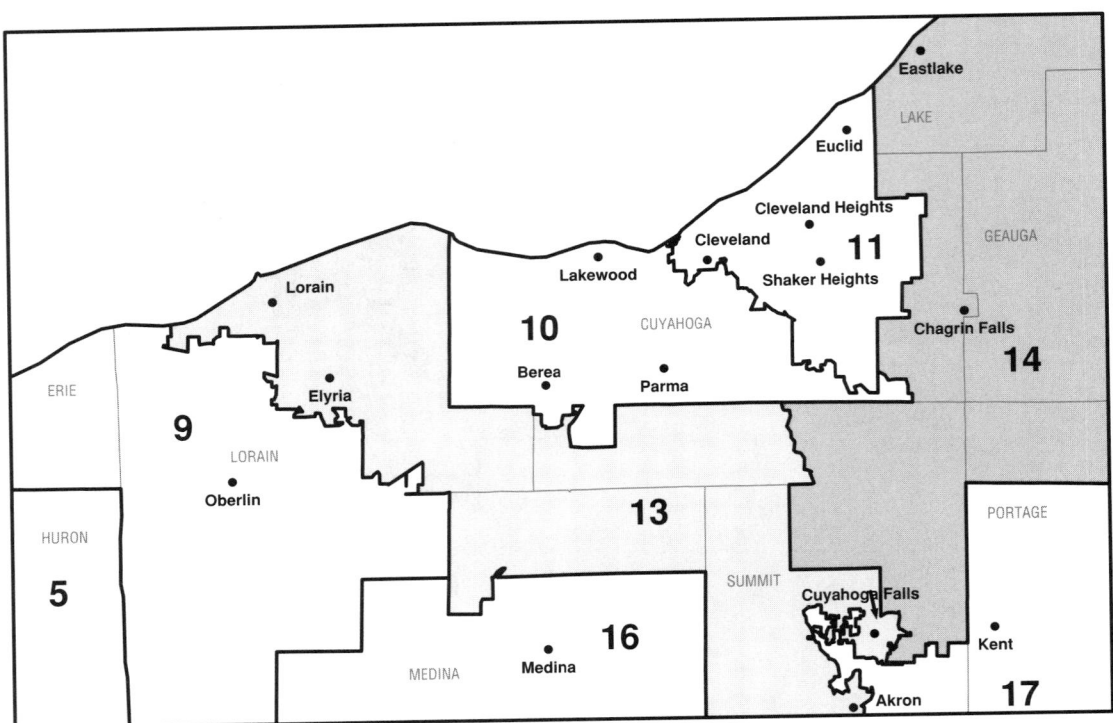

Columbus Area

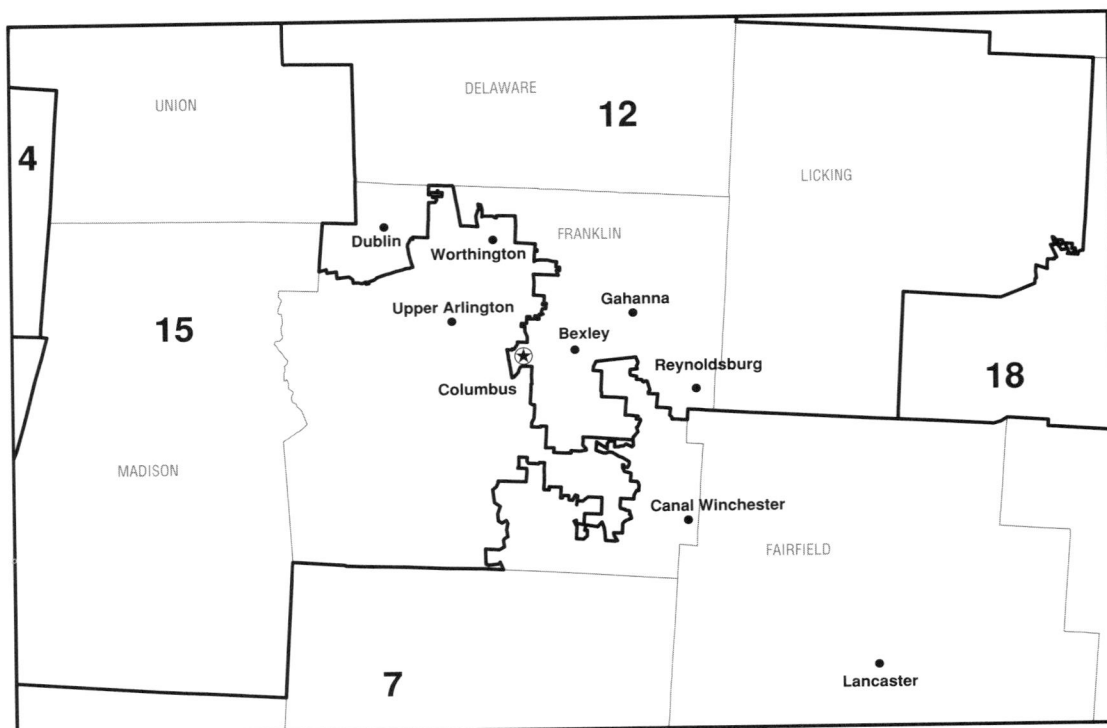

OHIO

GOVERNOR 2002

2000 Census Population	County	Total Vote	Republican	Democratic	Other	Rep.-Dem. Plurality	Percentage Total Vote Rep.	Total Vote Dem.	Major Vote Rep.	Major Vote Dem.
27,330	ADAMS	6,775	4,296	2,177	302	2,119 R	63.4%	32.1%	66.4%	33.6%
108,473	ALLEN	29,700	19,226	8,581	1,893	10,645 R	64.7%	28.9%	69.1%	30.9%
52,523	ASHLAND	15,037	9,894	4,607	536	5,287 R	65.8%	30.6%	68.2%	31.8%
102,728	ASHTABULA	27,395	14,825	11,472	1,098	3,353 R	54.1%	41.9%	56.4%	43.6%
62,223	ATHENS	16,357	7,018	8,408	931	1,390 D	42.9%	51.4%	45.5%	54.5%
46,611	AUGLAIZE	13,494	9,559	3,096	839	6,463 R	70.8%	22.9%	75.5%	24.5%
70,226	BELMONT	20,643	10,299	9,492	852	807 R	49.9%	46.0%	52.0%	48.0%
42,285	BROWN	11,550	7,881	3,181	488	4,700 R	68.2%	27.5%	71.2%	28.8%
332,807	BUTLER	86,663	62,076	20,896	3,691	41,180 R	71.6%	24.1%	74.8%	25.2%
28,836	CARROLL	8,753	5,254	3,104	395	2,150 R	60.0%	35.5%	62.9%	37.1%
38,890	CHAMPAIGN	10,605	7,067	2,880	658	4,187 R	66.6%	27.2%	71.0%	29.0%
144,742	CLARK	37,522	22,846	12,398	2,278	10,448 R	60.9%	33.0%	64.8%	35.2%
177,977	CLERMONT	42,440	31,723	9,073	1,644	22,650 R	74.7%	21.4%	77.8%	22.2%
40,543	CLINTON	10,272	7,321	2,463	488	4,858 R	71.3%	24.0%	74.8%	25.2%
112,075	COLUMBIANA	30,917	18,245	11,419	1,253	6,826 R	59.0%	36.9%	61.5%	38.5%
36,655	COSHOCTON	10,337	6,881	2,948	508	3,933 R	66.6%	28.5%	70.0%	30.0%
46,966	CRAWFORD	13,155	8,676	3,859	620	4,817 R	66.0%	29.3%	69.2%	30.8%
1,393,978	CUYAHOGA	378,952	142,874	225,582	10,496	82,708 D	37.7%	59.5%	38.8%	61.2%
53,309	DARKE	17,456	12,310	4,216	930	8,094 R	70.5%	24.2%	74.5%	25.5%
39,500	DEFIANCE	10,646	7,049	3,225	372	3,824 R	66.2%	30.3%	68.6%	31.4%
109,989	DELAWARE	39,199	28,200	9,226	1,773	18,974 R	71.9%	23.5%	75.3%	24.7%
79,551	ERIE	24,965	13,656	10,673	636	2,983 R	54.7%	42.8%	56.1%	43.9%
122,759	FAIRFIELD	38,893	26,256	10,531	2,106	15,725 R	67.5%	27.1%	71.4%	28.6%
28,433	FAYETTE	6,516	4,385	1,807	324	2,578 R	67.3%	27.7%	70.8%	29.2%
1,068,978	FRANKLIN	277,002	156,712	108,778	11,512	47,934 R	56.6%	39.3%	59.0%	41.0%
42,084	FULTON	13,008	9,600	2,995	413	6,605 R	73.8%	23.0%	76.2%	23.8%
31,069	GALLIA	9,242	6,057	2,759	426	3,298 R	65.5%	29.9%	68.7%	31.3%
90,895	GEAUGA	32,190	19,768	11,458	964	8,310 R	61.4%	35.6%	63.3%	36.7%
147,886	GREENE	42,864	28,815	11,780	2,269	17,035 R	67.2%	27.5%	71.0%	29.0%
40,792	GUERNSEY	10,846	6,348	4,042	456	2,306 R	58.5%	37.3%	61.1%	38.9%
845,303	HAMILTON	243,345	160,223	73,843	9,279	86,380 R	65.8%	30.3%	68.5%	31.5%
71,295	HANCOCK	20,593	15,757	4,151	685	11,606 R	76.5%	20.2%	79.1%	20.9%
31,945	HARDIN	8,387	5,153	2,829	405	2,324 R	61.4%	33.7%	64.6%	35.4%
15,856	HARRISON	5,708	3,131	2,327	250	804 R	54.9%	40.8%	57.4%	42.6%
29,210	HENRY	9,156	6,814	2,069	273	4,745 R	74.4%	22.6%	76.7%	23.3%
40,875	HIGHLAND	10,940	7,426	2,992	522	4,434 R	67.9%	27.3%	71.3%	28.7%
28,241	HOCKING	7,595	4,188	2,881	526	1,307 R	55.1%	37.9%	59.2%	40.8%
38,943	HOLMES	6,192	4,552	1,429	211	3,123 R	73.5%	23.1%	76.1%	23.9%
59,487	HURON	15,194	9,993	4,673	528	5,320 R	65.8%	30.8%	68.1%	31.9%
32,641	JACKSON	8,880	5,531	2,893	456	2,638 R	62.3%	32.6%	65.7%	34.3%
73,894	JEFFERSON	23,104	12,983	9,206	915	3,777 R	56.2%	39.8%	58.5%	41.5%
54,500	KNOX	14,234	9,291	4,166	777	5,125 R	65.3%	29.3%	69.0%	31.0%
227,511	LAKE	67,113	37,986	27,370	1,757	10,616 R	56.6%	40.8%	58.1%	41.9%
62,319	LAWRENCE	15,486	9,458	5,495	533	3,963 R	61.1%	35.5%	63.3%	36.7%
145,491	LICKING	47,179	32,118	12,653	2,408	19,465 R	68.1%	26.8%	71.7%	28.3%
46,005	LOGAN	12,582	8,996	2,891	695	6,105 R	71.5%	23.0%	75.7%	24.3%
284,664	LORAIN	78,466	37,423	38,515	2,528	1,092 D	47.7%	49.1%	49.3%	50.7%
455,054	LUCAS	129,486	76,572	49,648	3,266	26,924 R	59.1%	38.3%	60.7%	39.3%
40,213	MADISON	10,526	6,947	2,932	647	4,015 R	66.0%	27.9%	70.3%	29.7%
257,555	MAHONING	87,000	40,149	43,110	3,741	2,961 D	46.1%	49.6%	48.2%	51.8%
66,217	MARION	17,292	10,582	5,704	1,006	4,878 R	61.2%	33.0%	65.0%	35.0%
151,095	MEDINA	47,048	27,436	17,998	1,614	9,438 R	58.3%	38.3%	60.4%	39.6%
23,072	MEIGS	6,890	4,517	1,970	403	2,547 R	65.6%	28.6%	69.6%	30.4%
40,924	MERCER	14,834	11,001	3,237	596	7,764 R	74.2%	21.8%	77.3%	22.7%
98,868	MIAMI	29,582	20,743	7,297	1,542	13,446 R	70.1%	24.7%	74.0%	26.0%
15,180	MONROE	5,085	2,482	2,421	182	61 R	48.8%	47.6%	50.6%	49.4%
559,062	MONTGOMERY	161,283	95,891	59,584	5,808	36,307 R	59.5%	36.9%	61.7%	38.3%
14,897	MORGAN	4,634	2,975	1,378	281	1,597 R	64.2%	29.7%	68.3%	31.7%
31,628	MORROW	9,573	6,093	2,799	681	3,294 R	63.6%	29.2%	68.5%	31.5%
84,585	MUSKINGUM	22,433	14,990	6,279	1,164	8,711 R	66.8%	28.0%	70.5%	29.5%

OHIO

GOVERNOR 2002

2000 Census Population	County	Total Vote	Republican	Democratic	Other	Rep.-Dem. Plurality	Total Vote Rep.	Total Vote Dem.	Major Vote Rep.	Major Vote Dem.
14,058	NOBLE	4,283	2,438	1,628	217	810 R	56.9%	38.0%	60.0%	40.0%
40,985	OTTAWA	14,971	9,428	5,073	470	4,355 R	63.0%	33.9%	65.0%	35.0%
20,293	PAULDING	6,167	3,972	1,939	256	2,033 R	64.4%	31.4%	67.2%	32.8%
34,078	PERRY	9,064	5,102	3,422	540	1,680 R	56.3%	37.8%	59.9%	40.1%
52,727	PICKAWAY	11,883	7,432	3,775	676	3,657 R	62.5%	31.8%	66.3%	33.7%
27,695	PIKE	7,707	4,046	3,377	284	669 R	52.5%	43.8%	54.5%	45.5%
152,061	PORTAGE	41,530	19,887	19,708	1,935	179 R	47.9%	47.5%	50.2%	49.8%
42,337	PREBLE	11,646	7,832	3,112	702	4,720 R	67.3%	26.7%	71.6%	28.4%
34,726	PUTNAM	12,323	8,592	3,110	621	5,482 R	69.7%	25.2%	73.4%	26.6%
128,852	RICHLAND	36,811	21,963	13,520	1,328	8,443 R	59.7%	36.7%	61.9%	38.1%
73,345	ROSS	18,310	10,871	6,714	725	4,157 R	59.4%	36.7%	61.8%	38.2%
61,792	SANDUSKY	19,032	12,187	6,149	696	6,038 R	64.0%	32.3%	66.5%	33.5%
79,195	SCIOTO	21,845	12,161	8,867	817	3,294 R	55.7%	40.6%	57.8%	42.2%
58,683	SENECA	16,616	11,101	4,780	735	6,321 R	66.8%	28.8%	69.9%	30.1%
47,910	SHELBY	14,789	10,190	3,812	787	6,378 R	68.9%	25.8%	72.8%	27.2%
378,098	STARK	114,483	64,932	44,840	4,711	20,092 R	56.7%	39.2%	59.2%	40.8%
542,899	SUMMIT	159,246	75,340	77,928	5,978	2,588 D	47.3%	48.9%	49.2%	50.8%
225,116	TRUMBULL	71,695	33,718	35,364	2,613	1,646 D	47.0%	49.3%	48.8%	51.2%
90,914	TUSCARAWAS	25,090	13,457	10,639	994	2,818 R	53.6%	42.4%	55.8%	44.2%
40,909	UNION	12,118	8,631	2,723	764	5,908 R	71.2%	22.5%	76.0%	24.0%
29,659	VAN WERT	9,047	6,561	2,085	401	4,476 R	72.5%	23.0%	75.9%	24.1%
12,806	VINTON	3,793	2,135	1,448	210	687 R	56.3%	38.2%	59.6%	40.4%
158,383	WARREN	49,168	37,388	9,833	1,947	27,555 R	76.0%	20.0%	79.2%	20.8%
63,251	WASHINGTON	18,274	11,499	6,045	730	5,454 R	62.9%	33.1%	65.5%	34.5%
111,564	WAYNE	30,514	20,340	9,061	1,113	11,279 R	66.7%	29.7%	69.2%	30.8%
39,188	WILLIAMS	11,192	7,731	2,967	494	4,764 R	69.1%	26.5%	72.3%	27.7%
121,065	WOOD	37,887	25,172	11,521	1,194	13,651 R	66.4%	30.4%	68.6%	31.4%
22,908	WYANDOT	6,294	4,383	1,618	293	2,765 R	69.6%	25.7%	73.0%	27.0%
11,353,140	TOTAL	3,228,992	1,865,007	1,236,924	127,061	628,083 R	57.8%	38.3%	60.1%	39.9%

OHIO

HOUSE OF REPRESENTATIVES

CD	Year	Total Vote	Republican Vote	Republican Candidate	Democratic Vote	Democratic Candidate	Other Vote	Rep.-Dem. Plurality	Total Vote Rep.	Total Vote Dem.	Major Vote Rep.	Major Vote Dem.
1	2002	170,928	110,760	Chabot, Steve*	60,168	Harris, Greg		50,592 R	64.8%	35.2%	64.8%	35.2%
2	2002	188,016	139,218	Portman, Rob*	48,785	Sanders, Charles	13	90,433 R	74.0%	25.9%	74.1%	25.9%
3	2002	189,951	111,630	Turner, Michael R.	78,307	Carne, Rick	14	33,323 R	58.8%	41.2%	58.8%	41.2%
4	2002	177,727	120,001	Oxley, Michael G.*	57,726	Clark, Jim		62,275 R	67.5%	32.5%	67.5%	32.5%
5	2002	188,254	126,286	Gillmor, Paul E.*	51,872	Anderson, Roger	10,096	74,414 R	67.1%	27.6%	70.9%	29.1%
6	2002	191,615	77,643	Halleck, Mike	113,972	Strickland, Ted*		36,329 D	40.5%	59.5%	40.5%	59.5%
7	2002	167,632	113,252	Hobson, David L.*	45,568	Anastasio, Kara	8,812	67,684 R	67.6%	27.2%	71.3%	28.7%
8	2002	169,391	119,947	Boehner, John A.*	49,444	Hardenbrook, Jeff		70,503 R	70.8%	29.2%	70.8%	29.2%
9	2002	178,717	46,481	Emery, Ed	132,236	Kaptur, Marcy*		85,755 D	26.0%	74.0%	26.0%	74.0%
10	2002	175,536	41,778	Heben, Jon	129,997	Kucinich, Dennis J.*	3,761	88,219 D	23.8%	74.1%	24.3%	75.7%
11	2002	152,736	36,146	Pappano, Patrick	116,590	Jones, Stephanie Tubbs*		80,444 D	23.7%	76.3%	23.7%	76.3%
12	2002	181,689	116,982	Tiberi, Pat*	64,707	Brown, Edward		52,275 R	64.4%	35.6%	64.4%	35.6%
13	2002	178,382	55,357	Oliveros, Ed	123,025	Brown, Sherrod*		67,668 D	31.0%	69.0%	31.0%	69.0%

OHIO
HOUSE OF REPRESENTATIVES

CD	Year	Total Vote	Republican		Democratic		Other Vote	Rep.-Dem. Plurality	Percentage			
									Total Vote		Major Vote	
			Vote	Candidate	Vote	Candidate			Rep.	Dem.	Rep.	Dem.
14	2002	186,372	134,413	LaTourette, Steven C.*	51,846	Blanchard, Dale	113	82,567 R	72.1%	27.8%	72.2%	27.8%
15	2002	162,479	108,193	Pryce, Deborah*	54,286	Brown, Mark		53,907 R	66.6%	33.4%	66.6%	33.4%
16	2002	188,378	129,734	Regula, Ralph*	58,644	Rice, Jim		71,090 R	68.9%	31.1%	68.9%	31.1%
17	2002	184,674	62,188	Benjamin, Ann Womer	94,441	Ryan, Tim	28,045	32,253 D	33.7%	51.1%	39.7%	60.3%
18	2002	125,546	125,546	Ney, Bob*				125,546 R	100.0%		100.0%	
Total	2002	3,158,023	1,775,555		1,331,614		50,854	443,941 R	56.2%	42.2%	57.1%	42.9%

An asterisk (*) denotes incumbent.

OHIO
GENERAL AND PRIMARY ELECTIONS

2002 GENERAL ELECTIONS

Governor   Other vote was 126,686 Independent (John Eastman); 291 write-in (James Whitman); 84 write-in (Eva Braiman).

House   Other vote was:

CD 1	
CD 2	13 write-in (James Condit Jr.).
CD 3	14 write-in (Ronald Williamitis).
CD 4	
CD 5	10,096 Independent (John Green).
CD 6	
CD 7	8,812 Independent (Frank Doden).
CD 8	
CD 9	
CD 10	3,761 Independent (Judy Locy).
CD 11	
CD 12	
CD 13	
CD 14	113 write-in (Sid Stone).
CD 15	
CD 16	
CD 17	28,045 Independent (James A. Traficant Jr.).
CD 18	

Note: In Ohio, only the Democrats and Republicans are recognized parties. Other candidates appear on the ballot without party designation.

2002 PRIMARY ELECTIONS

Primary   May 7, 2002   **Registration** (as of May 7, 2002)   7,058,052   No Formal System of Party Registration

Primary Type   Open—Any registered voter can participate in the primary of either party. However, records are kept of voter participation in recent primaries, and in some counties voters who have cast a ballot in recent years in one party's primary can be challenged if they attempt to participate in the other party's primary.

Note: An asterisk (*) denotes incumbent.

OHIO

GENERAL AND PRIMARY ELECTIONS

	REPUBLICAN PRIMARIES			DEMOCRATIC PRIMARIES		
Governor	Bob Taft*	552,491	100.0%	Timothy Hagan	467,572	100.0%
Congressional District 1	Steve Chabot*	21,274	100.0%	Greg Harris (write-in)	339	100.0%
Congressional District 2	Rob Portman*	30,895	100.0%	Charles Sanders	5,754	46.6%
				Tony Stephens	3,383	27.4%
				Ray Mitchell	3,200	25.9%
				TOTAL	12,337	
Congressional District 3	Michael R. Turner	46,952	79.6%	Rick Carne	16,742	100.0%
	Roy Brown	8,346	14.1%			
	Gregory Hunter	3,702	6.3%			
	TOTAL	59,000				
Congressional District 4	Michael G. Oxley*	36,889	73.2%	Jim Clark	18,686	100.0%
	James Stahl	13,479	26.8%			
	TOTAL	50,368				
Congressional District 5	Paul E. Gillmor*	41,711	69.3%	Roger Anderson (write-in)	571	100.0%
	Rex Damschroder	18,498	30.7%			
	TOTAL	60,209				
Congressional District 6	Mike Halleck	19,480	58.4%	Ted Strickland*	41,351	67.5%
	Lyle Williams	13,890	41.6%	Lou D'Apolito	13,391	21.8%
				Charles Brown	6,552	10.7%
	TOTAL	33,370			61,294	
Congressional District 7	David L. Hobson*	30,367	72.7%	Kara Anastasio	16,552	100.0%
	Steven Schaefer	6,110	14.6%			
	John Mitchel	3,344	8.0%			
	Ralph Applegate	1,941	4.6%			
	TOTAL	41,762				
Congressional District 8	John A. Boehner*	27,770	85.2%	Jeff Hardenbrook	11,526	100.0%
	Roger Thomas	4,839	14.8%			
	TOTAL	32,609				
Congressional District 9	Ed Emery	14,164	100.0%	Marcy Kaptur*	26,969	100.0%
Congressional District 10	Jon Heben	16,520	100.0%	Dennis J. Kucinich*	40,205	100.0%
Congressional District 11	Patrick Pappano	6,386	100.0%	Stephanie Tubbs Jones*	37,338	100.0%
Congressional District 12	Pat Tiberi*	29,373	100.0%	Edward Brown	8,412	52.7%
				Al Warner	7,553	47.3%
				TOTAL	15,965	
Congressional District 13	Ed Oliveros	16,287	100.0%	Sherrod Brown*	25,566	100.0%
Congressional District 14	Steven C. LaTourette*	35,994	100.0%	Dale Blanchard	23,439	100.0%
Congressional District 15	Deborah Pryce*	22,048	78.0%	Mark Brown	8,439	60.9%
	Charlie Morrison	6,216	22.0%	Tabatha Cowans	5,423	39.1%
	TOTAL	28,264		TOTAL	13,862	
Congressional District 16	Ralph Regula*	44,177	100.0%	Jim Rice	27,087	100.0%
Congressional District 17	Ann Womer Benjamin	15,026	100.0%	Tim Ryan	28,922	41.3%
				Tom Sawyer*	19,247	27.5%
				Anthony Latell Jr.	13,858	19.8%
				Maridee Costanzo	5,148	7.4%
				Joe Teague	2,044	2.9%
				Bryan Taafe	787	1.1%
				TOTAL	70,006	
Congressional District 18	Bob Ney*	33,683	100.0%	No Democratic candidate		

OKLAHOMA

GOVERNOR
Brad Henry (D). Elected 2002 to a four-year term.

SENATORS (2 Republicans)
James M. Inhofe (R). Reelected 2002 to a six-year term. Previously elected 1996 and 1994 to fill out the remaining two years of the term vacated when David L. Boren (D) resigned to become president of the University of Oklahoma.

Don Nickles (R). Reelected 1998 to a six-year term. Previously elected 1992, 1986, 1980.

REPRESENTATIVES (4 Republicans, 1 Democrat)
1. John Sullivan (R)
2. Brad Carson (D)
3. Frank D. Lucas (R)
4. Tom Cole (R)
5. Ernest Istook (R)

POSTWAR VOTE FOR PRESIDENT

Year	Total Vote	Republican Vote	Republican Candidate	Democratic Vote	Democratic Candidate	Other Vote	Plurality	Total Vote Rep.	Total Vote Dem.	Major Vote Rep.	Major Vote Dem.
2000	1,234,229	744,337	Bush, George W.	474,276	Gore, Al	15,616	270,061 R	60.3%	38.4%	61.1%	38.9%
1996**	1,206,713	582,315	Dole, Bob	488,105	Clinton, Bill	136,293	94,210 R	48.3%	40.4%	54.4%	45.6%
1992**	1,390,359	592,929	Bush, George	473,066	Clinton, Bill	324,364	119,863 R	42.6%	34.0%	55.6%	44.4%
1988	1,171,036	678,367	Bush, George	483,423	Dukakis, Michael S.	9,246	194,944 R	57.9%	41.3%	58.4%	41.6%
1984	1,255,676	861,530	Reagan, Ronald	385,080	Mondale, Walter F.	9,066	476,450 R	68.6%	30.7%	69.1%	30.9%
1980**	1,149,708	695,570	Reagan, Ronald	402,026	Carter, Jimmy	52,112	293,544 R	60.5%	35.0%	63.4%	36.6%
1976	1,092,251	545,708	Ford, Gerald R.	532,442	Carter, Jimmy	14,101	13,266 R	50.0%	48.7%	50.6%	49.4%
1972	1,029,900	759,025	Nixon, Richard M.	247,147	McGovern, George S.	23,728	511,878 R	73.7%	24.0%	75.4%	24.6%
1968	943,086	449,697	Nixon, Richard M.	301,658	Humphrey, Hubert H.	191,731	148,039 R	47.7%	32.0%	59.9%	40.1%
1964	932,499	412,665	Goldwater, Barry M.	519,834	Johnson, Lyndon B.		107,169 D	44.3%	55.7%	44.3%	55.7%
1960	903,150	533,039	Nixon, Richard M.	370,111	Kennedy, John F.		162,928 R	59.0%	41.0%	59.0%	41.0%
1956	859,350	473,769	Eisenhower, Dwight D.	385,581	Stevenson, Adlai E.		88,188 R	55.1%	44.9%	55.1%	44.9%
1952	948,984	518,045	Eisenhower, Dwight D.	430,939	Stevenson, Adlai E.		87,106 R	54.6%	45.4%	54.6%	45.4%
1948	721,599	268,817	Dewey, Thomas E.	452,782	Truman, Harry S.		183,965 D	37.3%	62.7%	37.3%	62.7%

In 1996 the other vote column includes 130,788 votes cast for Perot. In 1992 the other vote column includes 319,878 votes cast for Perot. In 1980 the other vote column includes 38,284 votes for Independent (Anderson).

OKLAHOMA

POSTWAR VOTE FOR GOVERNOR

Year	Total Vote	Republican		Democratic		Other Vote	Rep.-Dem. Plurality	Percentage			
								Total Vote		Major Vote	
		Vote	Candidate	Vote	Candidate			Rep.	Dem.	Rep.	Dem.
2002**	1,035,620	441,277	Largent, Steve	448,143	Henry, Brad	146,200	6,866 D	42.6%	43.3%	49.6%	50.4%
1998	873,585	505,498	Keating, Frank	357,552	Boyd, Laura	10,535	147,946 R	57.9%	40.9%	58.6%	41.4%
1994**	995,012	466,740	Keating, Frank	294,936	Mildren, Jack	233,336	171,804 R	46.9%	29.6%	61.3%	38.7%
1990	911,314	297,584	Price, Bill	523,196	Walters, David	90,534	225,612 D	32.7%	57.4%	36.3%	63.7%
1986	909,925	431,762	Bellmon, Henry	405,295	Walters, David	72,868	26,467 R	47.5%	44.5%	51.6%	48.4%
1982	883,130	332,207	Daxon, Tom	548,159	Nigh, George	2,764	215,952 D	37.6%	62.1%	37.7%	62.3%
1978	777,414	367,055	Shotts, Ron	402,240	Nigh, George	8,119	35,185 D	47.2%	51.7%	47.7%	52.3%
1974	804,848	290,459	Inhofe, James M.	514,389	Boren, David L.		223,930 D	36.1%	63.9%	36.1%	63.9%
1970	698,790	336,157	Bartlett, Dewey F.	338,338	Hall, David	24,295	2,181 D	48.1%	48.4%	49.8%	50.2%
1966	677,258	377,078	Bartlett, Dewey F.	296,328	Moore, Preston J.	3,852	80,750 R	55.7%	43.8%	56.0%	44.0%
1962	709,763	392,316	Bellmon, Henry	315,357	Atkinson, W. P.	2,090	76,959 R	55.3%	44.4%	55.4%	44.6%
1958	538,839	107,495	Ferguson, Phil	399,504	Edmondson, J. Howard	31,840	292,009 D	19.9%	74.1%	21.2%	78.8%
1954	609,194	251,808	Sparks, Reuben K.	357,386	Gary, Raymond		105,578 D	41.3%	58.7%	41.3%	58.7%
1950	644,276	313,205	Ferguson, Jo O.	329,308	Murray, Johnston	1,763	16,103 D	48.6%	51.1%	48.7%	51.3%
1946	494,599	227,426	Flynn, Olney F.	259,491	Turner, Roy J.	7,682	32,065 D	46.0%	52.5%	46.7%	53.3%

In 2002 other vote was Independent (Richardson), which was 14.1 percent of the total vote. In 1994 other vote was Independent (Watkins), which was 23.5 percent of the total vote.

POSTWAR VOTE FOR SENATOR

Year	Total Vote	Republican		Democratic		Other Vote	Rep.-Dem. Plurality	Percentage			
								Total Vote		Major Vote	
		Vote	Candidate	Vote	Candidate			Rep.	Dem.	Rep.	Dem.
2002	1,018,424	583,579	Inhofe, James M.	369,789	Walters, David	65,056	213,790 R	57.3%	36.3%	61.2%	38.8%
1998	859,713	570,682	Nickles, Don	268,898	Carroll, Don E.	20,133	301,784 R	66.4%	31.3%	68.0%	32.0%
1996	1,183,150	670,610	Inhofe, James M.	474,162	Boren, Jim	38,378	196,448 R	56.7%	40.1%	58.6%	41.4%
1994S	982,430	542,390	Inhofe, James M.	392,488	McCurdy, Dave	47,552	149,902 R	55.2%	40.0%	58.0%	42.0%
1992	1,294,423	757,876	Nickles, Don	494,350	Lewis, Steve	42,197	263,526 R	58.5%	38.2%	60.5%	39.5%
1990	884,498	148,814	Jones, Stephen	735,684	Boren, David L.		586,870 D	16.8%	83.2%	16.8%	83.2%
1986	893,666	493,436	Nickles, Don	400,230	Jones, James R.		93,206 R	55.2%	44.8%	55.2%	44.8%
1984	1,197,937	280,638	Crozier, Will E.	906,131	Boren, David L.	11,168	625,493 D	23.4%	75.6%	23.6%	76.4%
1980	1,098,294	587,252	Nickles, Don	478,283	Coats, Andrew	32,759	108,969 R	53.5%	43.5%	55.1%	44.9%
1978	754,264	247,857	Kamm, Robert B.	493,953	Boren, David L.	12,454	246,096 D	32.9%	65.5%	33.4%	66.6%
1974	791,809	390,997	Bellmon, Henry	387,162	Edmondson, Ed	13,650	3,835 R	49.4%	48.9%	50.2%	49.8%
1972	1,005,148	516,934	Bartlett, Dewey F.	478,212	Edmondson, Ed	10,002	38,722 R	51.4%	47.6%	51.9%	48.1%
1968	909,119	470,120	Bellmon, Henry	419,658	Monroney, A. S. Mike	19,341	50,462 R	51.7%	46.2%	52.8%	47.2%
1966	638,742	295,585	Patterson, Pat J.	343,157	Harris, Fred R.		47,572 D	46.3%	53.7%	46.3%	53.7%
1964S	912,174	445,392	Wilkinson, Bud	466,782	Harris, Fred R.		21,390 D	48.8%	51.2%	48.8%	51.2%
1962	664,712	307,966	Crawford, B. Hayden	353,890	Monroney, A. S. Mike	2,856	45,924 D	46.3%	53.2%	46.5%	53.5%
1960	864,475	385,646	Crawford, B. Hayden	474,116	Kerr, Robert S.	4,713	88,470 D	44.6%	54.8%	44.9%	55.1%
1956	831,142	371,146	McKeever, Douglas	459,996	Monroney, A. S. Mike		88,850 D	44.7%	55.3%	44.7%	55.3%
1954	600,120	262,013	Mock, Fred M.	335,127	Kerr, Robert S.	2,980	73,114 D	43.7%	55.8%	43.9%	56.1%
1950	631,177	285,224	Alexander, W. H.	345,953	Monroney, A. S. Mike		60,729 D	45.2%	54.8%	45.2%	54.8%
1948	708,931	265,169	Rizley, Ross	441,654	Kerr, Robert S.	2,108	176,485 D	37.4%	62.3%	37.5%	62.5%

The 1994 and 1964 elections were for short terms to fill a vacancy.

363

OKLAHOMA

Congressional districts first established for elections held in 2002
5 members

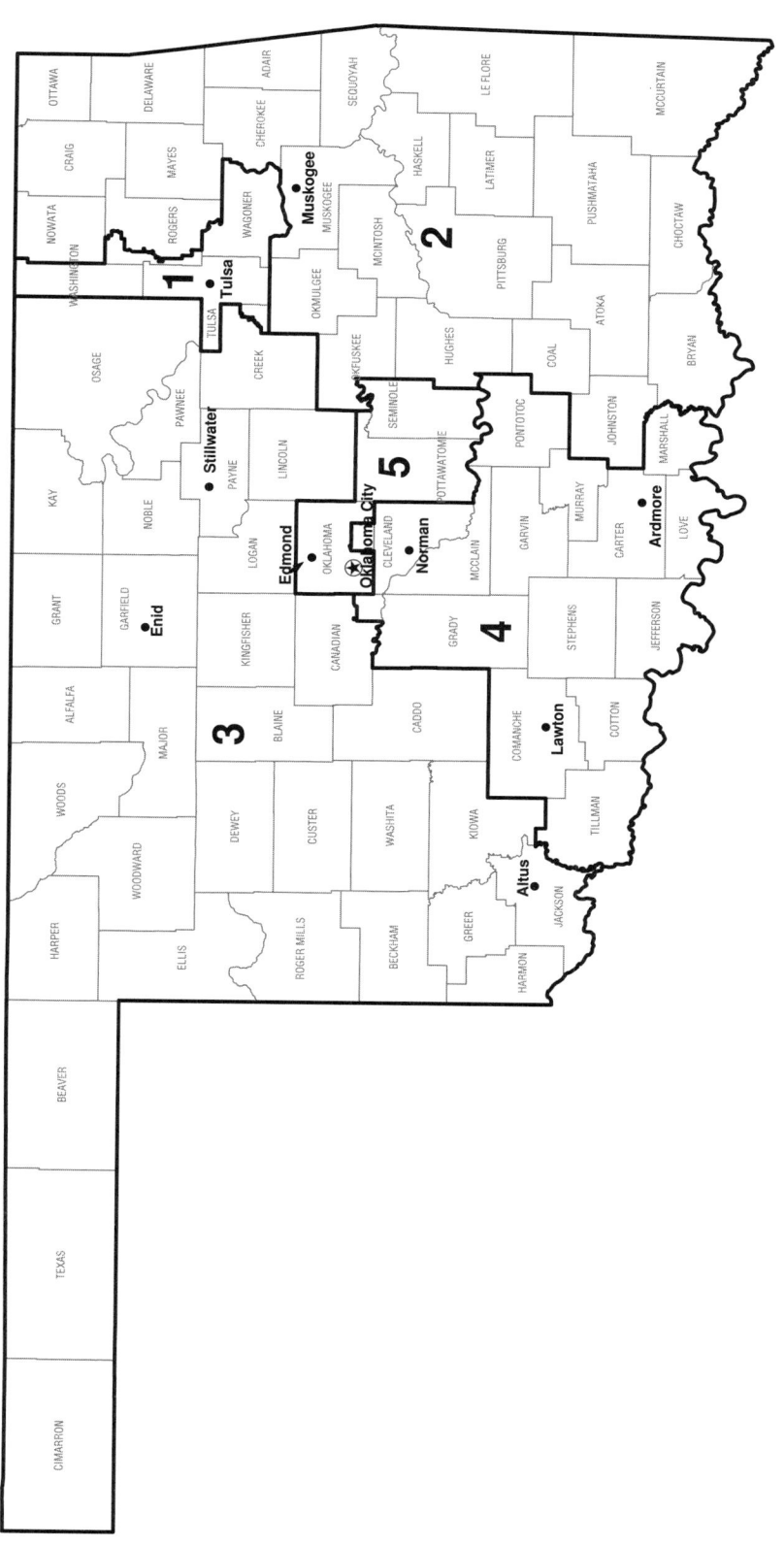

OKLAHOMA

GOVERNOR 2002

2000 Census Population	County	Total Vote	Republican	Democratic	Independent (Richardson)	Rep.-Dem. Plurality	Percentage of Total Vote		
							Rep.	Dem.	Ind.
21,038	ADAIR	6,051	2,374	2,803	874	429 D	39.2%	46.3%	14.4%
6,105	ALFALFA	2,043	964	782	297	182 R	47.2%	38.3%	14.5%
13,879	ATOKA	3,821	1,211	2,429	181	1,218 D	31.7%	63.6%	4.7%
5,857	BEAVER	1,977	1,297	561	119	736 R	65.6%	28.4%	6.0%
19,799	BECKHAM	5,265	2,105	2,511	649	406 D	40.0%	47.7%	12.3%
11,976	BLAINE	3,392	1,285	1,554	553	269 D	37.9%	45.8%	16.3%
36,534	BRYAN	9,963	3,422	6,158	383	2,736 D	34.3%	61.8%	3.8%
30,150	CADDO	7,752	2,341	3,948	1,463	1,607 D	30.2%	50.9%	18.9%
87,697	CANADIAN	28,565	14,422	9,658	4,485	4,764 R	50.5%	33.8%	15.7%
45,621	CARTER	13,457	5,458	7,099	900	1,641 D	40.6%	52.8%	6.7%
42,521	CHEROKEE	12,800	3,731	6,549	2,520	2,818 D	29.1%	51.2%	19.7%
15,342	CHOCTAW	3,868	1,183	2,472	213	1,289 D	30.6%	63.9%	5.5%
3,148	CIMARRON	1,281	909	298	74	611 R	71.0%	23.3%	5.8%
208,016	CLEVELAND	65,294	29,160	28,112	8,022	1,048 R	44.7%	43.1%	12.3%
6,031	COAL	2,046	554	1,360	132	806 D	27.1%	66.5%	6.5%
114,996	COMANCHE	21,780	9,077	8,363	4,340	714 R	41.7%	38.4%	19.9%
6,614	COTTON	1,849	717	799	333	82 D	38.8%	43.2%	18.0%
14,950	CRAIG	4,513	1,409	2,253	851	844 D	31.2%	49.9%	18.9%
67,367	CREEK	20,014	7,497	8,385	4,132	888 D	37.5%	41.9%	20.6%
26,142	CUSTER	8,043	3,438	3,426	1,179	12 R	42.7%	42.6%	14.7%
37,077	DELAWARE	10,826	4,253	4,845	1,728	592 D	39.3%	44.8%	16.0%
4,743	DEWEY	1,847	744	820	283	76 D	40.3%	44.4%	15.3%
4,075	ELLIS	1,642	739	633	270	106 R	45.0%	38.6%	16.4%
57,813	GARFIELD	17,569	8,381	6,421	2,767	1,960 R	47.7%	36.5%	15.7%
27,210	GARVIN	8,864	3,064	4,525	1,275	1,461 D	34.6%	51.0%	14.4%
45,516	GRADY	14,383	5,583	6,291	2,509	708 D	38.8%	43.7%	17.4%
5,144	GRANT	2,141	941	875	325	66 R	44.0%	40.9%	15.2%
6,061	GREER	1,939	651	957	331	306 D	33.6%	49.4%	17.1%
3,283	HARMON	889	310	446	133	136 D	34.9%	50.2%	15.0%
3,562	HARPER	1,422	642	594	186	48 R	45.1%	41.8%	13.1%
11,792	HASKELL	4,190	1,165	2,516	509	1,351 D	27.8%	60.0%	12.1%
14,154	HUGHES	4,106	1,173	2,355	578	1,182 D	28.6%	57.4%	14.1%
28,439	JACKSON	6,304	3,156	2,363	785	793 R	50.1%	37.5%	12.5%
6,818	JEFFERSON	1,968	756	1,057	155	301 D	38.4%	53.7%	7.9%
10,513	JOHNSTON	3,411	990	2,280	141	1,290 D	29.0%	66.8%	4.1%
48,080	KAY	15,614	7,264	6,071	2,279	1,193 R	46.5%	38.9%	14.6%
13,926	KINGFISHER	4,901	2,426	1,767	708	659 R	49.5%	36.1%	14.4%
10,227	KIOWA	3,115	1,000	1,742	373	742 D	32.1%	55.9%	12.0%
10,692	LATIMER	3,275	914	1,984	377	1,070 D	27.9%	60.6%	11.5%
48,109	LE FLORE	11,908	4,468	6,941	499	2,473 D	37.5%	58.3%	4.2%
32,080	LINCOLN	11,289	4,251	4,935	2,103	684 D	37.7%	43.7%	18.6%
33,924	LOGAN	11,257	5,048	4,245	1,964	803 R	44.8%	37.7%	17.4%
8,831	LOVE	2,732	884	1,753	95	869 D	32.4%	64.2%	3.5%
27,740	MCCLAIN	9,753	4,115	4,102	1,536	13 R	42.2%	42.1%	15.7%
34,402	MCCURTAIN	8,649	3,035	5,187	427	2,152 D	35.1%	60.0%	4.9%
19,456	MCINTOSH	6,797	1,809	3,631	1,357	1,822 D	26.6%	53.4%	20.0%
7,545	MAJOR	2,795	1,490	907	398	583 R	53.3%	32.5%	14.2%
13,184	MARSHALL	4,268	1,402	2,694	172	1,292 D	32.8%	63.1%	4.0%
38,369	MAYES	12,466	4,025	6,460	1,981	2,435 D	32.3%	51.8%	15.9%
12,623	MURRAY	4,450	1,325	2,662	463	1,337 D	29.8%	59.8%	10.4%
69,451	MUSKOGEE	20,274	6,132	9,867	4,275	3,735 D	30.2%	48.7%	21.1%
11,411	NOBLE	4,228	1,767	1,757	704	10 R	41.8%	41.6%	16.7%
10,569	NOWATA	3,668	1,241	1,718	709	477 D	33.8%	46.8%	19.3%
11,814	OKFUSKEE	3,510	976	1,932	602	956 D	27.8%	55.0%	17.2%
660,448	OKLAHOMA	189,076	91,270	73,236	24,570	18,034 R	48.3%	38.7%	13.0%
39,685	OKMULGEE	11,138	3,341	5,823	1,974	2,482 D	30.0%	52.3%	17.7%
44,437	OSAGE	13,886	4,696	6,843	2,347	2,147 D	33.8%	49.3%	16.9%
33,194	OTTAWA	8,662	3,018	4,508	1,136	1,490 D	34.8%	52.0%	13.1%
16,612	PAWNEE	4,969	1,814	2,251	904	437 D	36.5%	45.3%	18.2%
68,190	PAYNE	20,006	8,697	8,714	2,595	17 D	43.5%	43.6%	13.0%

OKLAHOMA

GOVERNOR 2002

2000 Census Population	County	Total Vote	Republican	Democratic	Independent (Richardson)	Rep.-Dem. Plurality	Percentage of Total Vote		
							Rep.	Dem.	Ind.
43,953	PITTSBURG	15,521	4,987	8,557	1,977	3,570 D	32.1%	55.1%	12.7%
35,143	PONTOTOC	10,458	3,904	5,447	1,107	1,543 D	37.3%	52.1%	10.6%
65,521	POTTAWATOMIE	19,539	6,674	10,740	2,125	4,066 D	34.2%	55.0%	10.9%
11,667	PUSHMATAHA	3,776	1,119	2,336	321	1,217 D	29.6%	61.9%	8.5%
3,436	ROGER MILLS	1,431	632	614	185	18 R	44.2%	42.9%	12.9%
70,641	ROGERS	24,957	10,265	10,508	4,184	243 D	41.1%	42.1%	16.8%
24,894	SEMINOLE	7,449	2,307	4,260	882	1,953 D	31.0%	57.2%	11.8%
38,972	SEQUOYAH	9,414	3,391	5,158	865	1,767 D	36.0%	54.8%	9.2%
43,182	STEPHENS	14,256	6,290	5,484	2,482	806 R	44.1%	38.5%	17.4%
20,107	TEXAS	4,914	3,208	1,424	282	1,784 R	65.3%	29.0%	5.7%
9,287	TILLMAN	2,635	1,034	1,263	338	229 D	39.2%	47.9%	12.8%
563,299	TULSA	174,728	84,187	65,383	25,158	18,804 R	48.2%	37.4%	14.4%
57,491	WAGONER	18,591	7,595	7,320	3,676	275 R	40.9%	39.4%	19.8%
48,996	WASHINGTON	17,188	8,700	5,801	2,687	2,899 R	50.6%	33.8%	15.6%
11,508	WASHITA	3,804	1,440	1,810	554	370 D	37.9%	47.6%	14.6%
9,089	WOODS	3,163	1,339	1,471	353	132 D	42.3%	46.5%	11.2%
18,486	WOODWARD	5,835	2,695	2,339	801	356 R	46.2%	40.1%	13.7%
3,450,654	TOTAL	1,035,620	441,277	448,143	146,200	6,866 D	42.6%	43.3%	14.1%

OKLAHOMA

SENATOR 2002

2000 Census Population	County	Total Vote	Republican	Democratic	Other	Rep.-Dem. Plurality	Percentage			
							Total Vote		Major Vote	
							Rep.	Dem.	Rep.	Dem.
21,038	ADAIR	5,929	2,867	2,690	372	177 R	48.4%	45.4%	51.6%	48.4%
6,105	ALFALFA	2,017	1,358	542	117	816 R	67.3%	26.9%	71.5%	28.5%
13,879	ATOKA	3,728	1,661	1,822	245	161 D	44.6%	48.9%	47.7%	52.3%
5,857	BEAVER	1,935	1,513	384	38	1,129 R	78.2%	19.8%	79.8%	20.2%
19,799	BECKHAM	5,167	2,594	2,372	201	222 R	50.2%	45.9%	52.2%	47.8%
11,976	BLAINE	3,323	2,046	1,039	238	1,007 R	61.6%	31.3%	66.3%	33.7%
36,534	BRYAN	9,757	4,394	4,769	594	375 D	45.0%	48.9%	48.0%	52.0%
30,150	CADDO	7,640	3,608	3,520	512	88 R	47.2%	46.1%	50.6%	49.4%
87,697	CANADIAN	28,188	19,493	6,947	1,748	12,546 R	69.2%	24.6%	73.7%	26.3%
45,621	CARTER	13,184	7,017	5,346	821	1,671 R	53.2%	40.5%	56.8%	43.2%
42,521	CHEROKEE	12,549	5,356	6,011	1,182	655 D	42.7%	47.9%	47.1%	52.9%
15,342	CHOCTAW	3,779	1,451	2,165	163	714 D	38.4%	57.3%	40.1%	59.9%
3,148	CIMARRON	1,268	974	255	39	719 R	76.8%	20.1%	79.3%	20.7%
208,016	CLEVELAND	64,317	39,025	21,088	4,204	17,937 R	60.7%	32.8%	64.9%	35.1%
6,031	COAL	1,996	776	1,116	104	340 D	38.9%	55.9%	41.0%	59.0%
114,996	COMANCHE	21,491	12,100	8,061	1,330	4,039 R	56.3%	37.5%	60.0%	40.0%
6,614	COTTON	1,800	886	782	132	104 R	49.2%	43.4%	53.1%	46.9%
14,950	CRAIG	4,425	2,002	1,997	426	5 R	45.2%	45.1%	50.1%	49.9%
67,367	CREEK	19,645	10,664	7,224	1,757	3,440 R	54.3%	36.8%	59.6%	40.4%
26,142	CUSTER	7,969	4,840	2,781	348	2,059 R	60.7%	34.9%	63.5%	36.5%
37,077	DELAWARE	10,646	5,463	4,400	783	1,063 R	51.3%	41.3%	55.4%	44.6%
4,743	DEWEY	1,812	1,103	586	123	517 R	60.9%	32.3%	65.3%	34.7%
4,075	ELLIS	1,607	1,057	472	78	585 R	65.8%	29.4%	69.1%	30.9%
57,813	GARFIELD	17,343	11,609	4,675	1,059	6,934 R	66.9%	27.0%	71.3%	28.7%
27,210	GARVIN	8,723	4,500	3,611	612	889 R	51.6%	41.4%	55.5%	44.5%
45,516	GRADY	14,090	8,128	4,904	1,058	3,224 R	57.7%	34.8%	62.4%	37.6%
5,144	GRANT	2,119	1,357	620	142	737 R	64.0%	29.3%	68.6%	31.4%
6,061	GREER	1,890	926	875	89	51 R	49.0%	46.3%	51.4%	48.6%
3,283	HARMON	847	397	403	47	6 D	46.9%	47.6%	49.6%	50.4%
3,562	HARPER	1,390	972	354	64	618 R	69.9%	25.5%	73.3%	26.7%

OKLAHOMA

SENATOR 2002

2000 Census Population	County	Total Vote	Republican	Democratic	Other	Rep.-Dem. Plurality		Percentage			
								Total Vote		Major Vote	
								Rep.	Dem.	Rep.	Dem.
11,792	HASKELL	4,097	1,466	2,392	239	926	D	35.8%	58.4%	38.0%	62.0%
14,154	HUGHES	4,031	1,746	2,002	283	256	D	43.3%	49.7%	46.6%	53.4%
28,439	JACKSON	6,191	4,039	1,889	263	2,150	R	65.2%	30.5%	68.1%	31.9%
6,818	JEFFERSON	1,875	804	984	87	180	D	42.9%	52.5%	45.0%	55.0%
10,513	JOHNSTON	3,285	1,399	1,613	273	214	D	42.6%	49.1%	46.4%	53.6%
48,080	KAY	15,399	9,599	4,606	1,194	4,993	R	62.3%	29.9%	67.6%	32.4%
13,926	KINGFISHER	4,807	3,553	975	279	2,578	R	73.9%	20.3%	78.5%	21.5%
10,227	KIOWA	3,039	1,415	1,453	171	38	D	46.6%	47.8%	49.3%	50.7%
10,692	LATIMER	3,193	1,234	1,771	188	537	D	38.6%	55.5%	41.1%	58.9%
48,109	LE FLORE	11,664	4,938	6,407	319	1,469	D	42.3%	54.9%	43.5%	56.5%
32,080	LINCOLN	11,095	6,472	3,802	821	2,670	R	58.3%	34.3%	63.0%	37.0%
33,924	LOGAN	11,098	7,051	3,316	731	3,735	R	63.5%	29.9%	68.0%	32.0%
8,831	LOVE	2,680	1,199	1,309	172	110	D	44.7%	48.8%	47.8%	52.2%
27,740	MCCLAIN	9,604	5,813	3,098	693	2,715	R	60.5%	32.3%	65.2%	34.8%
34,402	MCCURTAIN	8,461	3,367	4,850	244	1,483	D	39.8%	57.3%	41.0%	59.0%
19,456	MCINTOSH	6,627	2,689	3,367	571	678	D	40.6%	50.8%	44.4%	55.6%
7,545	MAJOR	2,739	1,921	660	158	1,261	R	70.1%	24.1%	74.4%	25.6%
13,184	MARSHALL	4,169	1,966	1,897	306	69	R	47.2%	45.5%	50.9%	49.1%
38,369	MAYES	12,227	5,726	5,498	1,003	228	R	46.8%	45.0%	51.0%	49.0%
12,623	MURRAY	4,355	1,999	2,028	328	29	D	45.9%	46.6%	49.6%	50.4%
69,451	MUSKOGEE	19,915	8,960	9,513	1,442	553	D	45.0%	47.8%	48.5%	51.5%
11,411	NOBLE	4,165	2,703	1,170	292	1,533	R	64.9%	28.1%	69.8%	30.2%
10,569	NOWATA	3,609	1,843	1,508	258	335	R	51.1%	41.8%	55.0%	45.0%
11,814	OKFUSKEE	3,410	1,527	1,625	258	98	D	44.8%	47.7%	48.4%	51.6%
660,448	OKLAHOMA	186,279	116,737	58,759	10,783	57,978	R	62.7%	31.5%	66.5%	33.5%
39,685	OKMULGEE	10,854	4,809	5,068	977	259	D	44.3%	46.7%	48.7%	51.3%
44,437	OSAGE	13,654	6,642	5,891	1,121	751	R	48.6%	43.1%	53.0%	47.0%
33,194	OTTAWA	8,378	3,542	4,332	504	790	D	42.3%	51.7%	45.0%	55.0%
16,612	PAWNEE	4,903	2,569	1,928	406	641	R	52.4%	39.3%	57.1%	42.9%
68,190	PAYNE	19,742	11,698	6,720	1,324	4,978	R	59.3%	34.0%	63.5%	36.5%
43,953	PITTSBURG	15,296	7,044	7,302	950	258	D	46.1%	47.7%	49.1%	50.9%
35,143	PONTOTOC	10,216	5,633	3,915	668	1,718	R	55.1%	38.3%	59.0%	41.0%
65,521	POTTAWATOMIE	19,237	10,749	7,104	1,384	3,645	R	55.9%	36.9%	60.2%	39.8%
11,667	PUSHMATAHA	3,679	1,576	1,911	192	335	D	42.8%	51.9%	45.2%	54.8%
3,436	ROGER MILLS	1,414	829	514	71	315	R	58.6%	36.4%	61.7%	38.3%
70,641	ROGERS	24,605	14,111	8,626	1,868	5,485	R	57.4%	35.1%	62.1%	37.9%
24,894	SEMINOLE	7,336	3,374	3,538	424	164	D	46.0%	48.2%	48.8%	51.2%
38,972	SEQUOYAH	9,116	4,029	4,668	419	639	D	44.2%	51.2%	46.3%	53.7%
43,182	STEPHENS	14,037	7,701	5,269	1,067	2,432	R	54.9%	37.5%	59.4%	40.6%
20,107	TEXAS	4,850	3,437	1,309	104	2,128	R	70.9%	27.0%	72.4%	27.6%
9,287	TILLMAN	2,574	1,241	1,198	135	43	R	48.2%	46.5%	50.9%	49.1%
563,299	TULSA	172,197	105,620	56,321	10,256	49,299	R	61.3%	32.7%	65.2%	34.8%
57,491	WAGONER	18,353	10,540	6,367	1,446	4,173	R	57.4%	34.7%	62.3%	37.7%
48,996	WASHINGTON	16,866	10,626	5,057	1,183	5,569	R	63.0%	30.0%	67.8%	32.2%
11,508	WASHITA	3,735	1,855	1,724	156	131	R	49.7%	46.2%	51.8%	48.2%
9,089	WOODS	3,066	1,853	1,084	129	769	R	60.4%	35.4%	63.1%	36.9%
18,486	WOODWARD	5,728	3,798	1,640	290	2,158	R	66.3%	28.6%	69.8%	30.2%
3,450,654	TOTAL	1,018,424	583,579	369,789	65,056	213,790	R	57.3%	36.3%	61.2%	38.8%

OKLAHOMA
HOUSE OF REPRESENTATIVES

CD	Year	Total Vote	Republican Vote	Republican Candidate	Democratic Vote	Democratic Candidate	Other Vote	Rep.-Dem. Plurality	Total Vote Rep.	Total Vote Dem.	Major Vote Rep.	Major Vote Dem.
1	2002	214,955	119,566	Sullivan, John*	90,649	Dodd, Doug	4,740	28,917 R	55.6%	42.2%	56.9%	43.1%
2	2002	197,982	51,234	Pharaoh, Kent	146,748	Carson, Brad*		95,514 D	25.9%	74.1%	25.9%	74.1%
3	2002	196,090	148,206	Lucas, Frank D.*			47,884	148,206 R	75.6%		100.0%	
4	2002	197,774	106,452	Cole, Tom	91,322	Roberts, Darryl		15,130 R	53.8%	46.2%	53.8%	46.2%
5	2002	195,051	121,374	Istook, Ernest*	63,208	Barlow, Lou	10,469	58,166 R	62.2%	32.4%	65.8%	34.2%
Total	2002	1,001,852	546,832		391,927		63,093	154,905 R	54.6%	39.1%	58.3%	41.7%

An asterisk (*) denotes incumbent.

OKLAHOMA
GENERAL AND PRIMARY ELECTIONS

2002 GENERAL ELECTIONS

Governor   The Independent candidate, Gary L. Richardson, received 146,200 votes, 14.1 percent of the total vote. The Independent vote is listed in the county table for the 2002 gubernatorial election in Oklahoma.

Senator   Other vote was 65,056 Independent (James Germalic).

House   Other vote was:

CD 1   4,740 Independent (Joe Cristiano).
CD 2
CD 3   47,884 Independent (Robert T. Murphy).
CD 4
CD 5   10,469 Independent (Donna C. Davis).

2002 PRIMARY ELECTIONS

Primary   August 27, 2002

Primary Runoff   September 17, 2002

Registration
(as of July, 31, 2002)

Republican	739,964
Democratic	1,084,430
Libertarian	241
Reform	15
Independent	207,242
TOTAL	2,031,892

Primary Type   Closed—Only registered Democrats and Republicans could vote in their party's primary.

Note: An asterisk (*) denotes incumbent. The names of unopposed candidates did not appear on the primary ballot; therefore, no votes were cast for these candidates.

OKLAHOMA

GENERAL AND PRIMARY ELECTIONS

	REPUBLICAN PRIMARIES			DEMOCRATIC PRIMARIES		
Governor	Steve Largent	179,631	87.3%	Vince Orza	154,263	44.0%
	Jim Denny	16,713	8.1%	Brad Henry	99,883	28.5%
	Andrew Marr Jr.	9,532	4.6%	Kelly Haney	59,044	16.9%
				Jim Dunegan	28,130	8.0%
				James E. Lamkin	9,069	2.6%
	TOTAL	205,876		TOTAL	350,389	
				PRIMARY RUNOFF		
				Brad Henry	135,336	52.4%
				Vince Orza	122,855	47.6%
				TOTAL	258,191	
Senator	James M. Inhofe*	Unopposed		David Walters	170,414	49.2%
				Tom Boettcher	118,986	34.4%
				Jim Rogers	34,217	9.9%
				George Gentry	22,770	6.6%
				TOTAL	346,387	
				PRIMARY RUNOFF		
				David Walters	146,899	56.9%
				Tom Boettcher	111,067	43.1%
				TOTAL	257,966	
Congressional District 1	John Sullivan*	39,992	84.6%	Doug Dodd	Unopposed	
	Evelyn L. Rogers	7,280	15.4%			
	TOTAL	47,272				
Congressional District 2	Kent Pharaoh	Unopposed		Brad Carson*	72,612	64.2%
				Mike Mass	34,450	30.5%
				Dorothy Vandiver	6,040	5.3%
				TOTAL	113,102	
Congressional District 3	Frank D. Lucas*	43,887	89.2%	No Democratic candidate		
	Richard Hovis	5,330	10.8%			
	TOTAL	49,217				
Congressional District 4	Tom Cole	21,789	59.7%	Darryl Roberts	34,393	48.3%
	Marc Nuttle	11,944	32.7%	Ben Odom	24,369	34.2%
	Terry Johnson	1,119	3.1%	Lance Compton	7,202	10.1%
	Tennie Rogers	648	1.8%	Brandon Clabes	5,312	7.5%
	Jerry J. Black	600	1.6%			
	Garlin Newton	426	1.2%			
	TOTAL	36,526		TOTAL	71,276	
Congressional District 5	Ernest Istook*	Unopposed		Lou Barlow	Unopposed	

OKLAHOMA REPUBLICAN PRIMARY

GOVERNOR 2002

2000 Census Population	County	Total Vote	Largent	Other	Winner	Percentage of Total Vote	
						Largent	Other
21,038	ADAIR	1,117	939	178	Largent	84.1%	15.9%
6,105	ALFALFA	1,014	864	150	Largent	85.2%	14.8%
13,879	ATOKA	185	161	24	Largent	87.0%	13.0%
5,857	BEAVER	850	718	132	Largent	84.5%	15.5%
19,799	BECKHAM	559	500	59	Largent	89.4%	10.6%
11,976	BLAINE	965	812	153	Largent	84.1%	15.9%
36,534	BRYAN	508	434	74	Largent	85.4%	14.6%
30,150	CADDO	769	669	100	Largent	87.0%	13.0%
87,697	CANADIAN	8,319	7,380	939	Largent	88.7%	11.3%
45,621	CARTER	1,173	1,045	128	Largent	89.1%	10.9%
42,521	CHEROKEE	1,221	1,070	151	Largent	87.6%	12.4%
15,342	CHOCTAW	125	112	13	Largent	89.6%	10.4%
3,148	CIMARRON	445	403	42	Largent	90.6%	9.4%
208,016	CLEVELAND	15,724	14,024	1,700	Largent	89.2%	10.8%
6,031	COAL	97	82	15	Largent	84.5%	15.5%
114,996	COMANCHE	3,551	3,158	393	Largent	88.9%	11.1%
6,614	COTTON	87	82	5	Largent	94.3%	5.7%
14,950	CRAIG	421	357	64	Largent	84.8%	15.2%
67,367	CREEK	2,842	2,414	428	Largent	84.9%	15.1%
26,142	CUSTER	1,198	1,061	137	Largent	88.6%	11.4%
37,077	DELAWARE	1,517	1,289	228	Largent	85.0%	15.0%
4,743	DEWEY	369	318	51	Largent	86.2%	13.8%
4,075	ELLIS	479	396	83	Largent	82.7%	17.3%
57,813	GARFIELD	6,412	5,510	902	Largent	85.9%	14.1%
27,210	GARVIN	934	829	105	Largent	88.8%	11.2%
45,516	GRADY	2,557	2,273	284	Largent	88.9%	11.1%
5,144	GRANT	656	548	108	Largent	83.5%	16.5%
6,061	GREER	147	134	13	Largent	91.2%	8.8%
3,283	HARMON	24	20	4	Largent	83.3%	16.7%
3,562	HARPER	521	417	104	Largent	80.0%	20.0%
11,792	HASKELL	150	139	11	Largent	92.7%	7.3%
14,154	HUGHES	209	185	24	Largent	88.5%	11.5%
28,439	JACKSON	662	605	57	Largent	91.4%	8.6%
6,818	JEFFERSON	107	89	18	Largent	83.2%	16.8%
10,513	JOHNSTON	128	102	26	Largent	79.7%	20.3%
48,080	KAY	4,765	4,161	604	Largent	87.3%	12.7%
13,926	KINGFISHER	1,447	1,257	190	Largent	86.9%	13.1%
10,227	KIOWA	305	271	34	Largent	88.9%	11.1%
10,692	LATIMER	107	93	14	Largent	86.9%	13.1%
48,109	LE FLORE	569	483	86	Largent	84.9%	15.1%
32,080	LINCOLN	2,171	1,865	306	Largent	85.9%	14.1%
33,924	LOGAN	3,461	3,034	427	Largent	87.7%	12.3%
8,831	LOVE	155	141	14	Largent	91.0%	9.0%
27,740	MCCLAIN	1,501	1,355	146	Largent	90.3%	9.7%
34,402	MCCURTAIN	374	320	54	Largent	85.6%	14.4%
19,456	MCINTOSH	444	396	48	Largent	89.2%	10.8%
7,545	MAJOR	1,212	1,011	201	Largent	83.4%	16.6%
13,184	MARSHALL	286	254	32	Largent	88.8%	11.2%
38,369	MAYES	1,457	1,240	217	Largent	85.1%	14.9%
12,623	MURRAY	324	288	36	Largent	88.9%	11.1%
69,451	MUSKOGEE	1,785	1,537	248	Largent	86.1%	13.9%
11,411	NOBLE	1,399	1,206	193	Largent	86.2%	13.8%
10,569	NOWATA	543	463	80	Largent	85.3%	14.7%
11,814	OKFUSKEE	233	192	41	Largent	82.4%	17.6%
660,448	OKLAHOMA	54,630	48,858	5,772	Largent	89.4%	10.6%
39,685	OKMULGEE	1,169	1,000	169	Largent	85.5%	14.5%
44,437	OSAGE	1,715	1,449	266	Largent	84.5%	15.5%
33,194	OTTAWA	797	674	123	Largent	84.6%	15.4%
16,612	PAWNEE	868	728	140	Largent	83.9%	16.1%
68,190	PAYNE	3,735	3,225	510	Largent	86.3%	13.7%

OKLAHOMA REPUBLICAN PRIMARY

GOVERNOR 2002

2000 Census Population	County	Total Vote	Largent	Other	Winner	Percentage of Total Vote	
						Largent	Other
43,953	PITTSBURG	996	913	83	Largent	91.7%	8.3%
35,143	PONTOTOC	1,161	1,043	118	Largent	89.8%	10.2%
65,521	POTTAWATOMIE	3,011	2,653	358	Largent	88.1%	11.9%
11,667	PUSHMATAHA	119	99	20	Largent	83.2%	16.8%
3,436	ROGER MILLS	229	200	29	Largent	87.3%	12.7%
70,641	ROGERS	3,970	3,370	600	Largent	84.9%	15.1%
24,894	SEMINOLE	885	772	113	Largent	87.2%	12.8%
38,972	SEQUOYAH	723	596	127	Largent	82.4%	17.6%
43,182	STEPHENS	1,918	1,751	167	Largent	91.3%	8.7%
20,107	TEXAS	1,837	1,588	249	Largent	86.4%	13.6%
9,287	TILLMAN	174	150	24	Largent	86.2%	13.8%
563,299	TULSA	38,432	32,444	5,988	Largent	84.4%	15.6%
57,491	WAGONER	3,683	3,154	529	Largent	85.6%	14.4%
48,996	WASHINGTON	4,288	3,781	507	Largent	88.2%	11.8%
11,508	WASHITA	400	344	56	Largent	86.0%	14.0%
9,089	WOODS	794	656	138	Largent	82.6%	17.4%
18,486	WOODWARD	1,762	1,477	285	Largent	83.8%	16.2%
3,450,654	TOTAL	205,876	179,631	26,245	Largent	87.3%	12.7%

OKLAHOMA DEMOCRATIC PRIMARY

GOVERNOR 2002

2000 Census Population	County	Total Vote	Orza	Henry	Haney	Other	Winner	Percentage of Total Vote			
								Orza	Henry	Haney	Other
21,038	ADAIR	3,337	1,145	1,222	635	335	Henry	34.3%	36.6%	19.0%	10.0%
6,105	ALFALFA	703	425	132	60	86	Orza	60.5%	18.8%	8.5%	12.2%
13,879	ATOKA	2,656	702	616	384	954	Dunegan	26.4%	23.2%	14.5%	35.9%
5,857	BEAVER	494	129	105	107	153	Orza	26.1%	21.3%	21.7%	31.0%
19,799	BECKHAM	2,565	1,183	897	298	187	Orza	46.1%	35.0%	11.6%	7.3%
11,976	BLAINE	1,113	609	265	179	60	Orza	54.7%	23.8%	16.1%	5.4%
36,534	BRYAN	6,581	804	522	385	4,870	Dunegan	12.2%	7.9%	5.9%	74.0%
30,150	CADDO	4,526	2,082	1,019	1,111	314	Orza	46.0%	22.5%	24.5%	6.9%
87,697	CANADIAN	6,421	3,308	1,828	943	342	Orza	51.5%	28.5%	14.7%	5.3%
45,621	CARTER	5,332	2,034	1,679	891	728	Orza	38.1%	31.5%	16.7%	13.7%
42,521	CHEROKEE	7,233	3,005	2,485	1,306	437	Orza	41.5%	34.4%	18.1%	6.0%
15,342	CHOCTAW	2,396	652	482	456	806	Dunegan	27.2%	20.1%	19.0%	33.6%
3,148	CIMARRON	389	68	63	96	162	Dunegan	17.5%	16.2%	24.7%	41.6%
208,016	CLEVELAND	15,127	6,651	5,464	2,453	559	Orza	44.0%	36.1%	16.2%	3.7%
6,031	COAL	1,655	470	382	337	466	Orza	28.4%	23.1%	20.4%	28.2%
114,996	COMANCHE	9,344	5,138	1,371	1,818	1,017	Orza	55.0%	14.7%	19.5%	10.9%
6,614	COTTON	757	375	93	161	128	Orza	49.5%	12.3%	21.3%	16.9%
14,950	CRAIG	2,080	1,004	635	298	143	Orza	48.3%	30.5%	14.3%	6.9%
67,367	CREEK	5,406	2,437	1,740	981	248	Orza	45.1%	32.2%	18.1%	4.6%
26,142	CUSTER	2,580	1,446	603	331	200	Orza	56.0%	23.4%	12.8%	7.8%
37,077	DELAWARE	4,637	1,920	1,432	863	422	Orza	41.4%	30.9%	18.6%	9.1%
4,743	DEWEY	745	375	186	119	65	Orza	50.3%	25.0%	16.0%	8.7%
4,075	ELLIS	480	244	124	62	50	Orza	50.8%	25.8%	12.9%	10.4%
57,813	GARFIELD	3,757	2,306	836	405	210	Orza	61.4%	22.3%	10.8%	5.6%
27,210	GARVIN	5,339	2,645	1,394	758	542	Orza	49.5%	26.1%	14.2%	10.2%
45,516	GRADY	5,688	2,749	1,530	806	603	Orza	48.3%	26.9%	14.2%	10.6%
5,144	GRANT	651	368	139	77	67	Orza	56.5%	21.4%	11.8%	10.3%
6,061	GREER	1,282	600	292	188	202	Orza	46.8%	22.8%	14.7%	15.8%
3,283	HARMON	394	205	86	33	70	Orza	52.0%	21.8%	8.4%	17.8%
3,562	HARPER	537	306	122	47	62	Orza	57.0%	22.7%	8.8%	11.5%

OKLAHOMA DEMOCRATIC PRIMARY

GOVERNOR 2002

2000 Census Population	County	Total Vote	Orza	Henry	Haney	Other	Winner	Percentage of Total Vote			
								Orza	Henry	Haney	Other
11,792	HASKELL	3,407	1,126	1,197	525	559	Henry	33.0%	35.1%	15.4%	16.4%
14,154	HUGHES	2,217	832	627	537	221	Orza	37.5%	28.3%	24.2%	10.0%
28,439	JACKSON	1,969	888	412	316	353	Orza	45.1%	20.9%	16.0%	17.9%
6,818	JEFFERSON	1,013	390	152	192	279	Orza	38.5%	15.0%	19.0%	27.5%
10,513	JOHNSTON	2,058	510	423	294	831	Dunegan	24.8%	20.6%	14.3%	40.4%
48,080	KAY	3,401	1,708	949	478	266	Orza	50.2%	27.9%	14.1%	7.8%
13,926	KINGFISHER	1,062	603	278	130	51	Orza	56.8%	26.2%	12.2%	4.8%
10,227	KIOWA	2,103	928	500	319	356	Orza	44.1%	23.8%	15.2%	16.9%
10,692	LATIMER	3,127	1,039	757	577	754	Orza	33.2%	24.2%	18.5%	24.1%
48,109	LE FLORE	6,324	1,642	1,802	1,341	1,539	Henry	26.0%	28.5%	21.2%	24.3%
32,080	LINCOLN	3,857	1,321	1,010	1,305	221	Orza	34.2%	26.2%	33.8%	5.7%
33,924	LOGAN	2,748	1,207	615	762	164	Orza	43.9%	22.4%	27.7%	6.0%
8,831	LOVE	1,220	359	341	203	317	Orza	29.4%	28.0%	16.6%	26.0%
27,740	MCCLAIN	3,057	1,385	971	470	231	Orza	45.3%	31.8%	15.4%	7.6%
34,402	MCCURTAIN	6,407	2,131	1,079	933	2,264	Orza	33.3%	16.8%	14.6%	35.3%
19,456	MCINTOSH	4,707	1,683	1,674	965	385	Orza	35.8%	35.6%	20.5%	8.2%
7,545	MAJOR	616	405	127	56	28	Orza	65.7%	20.6%	9.1%	4.5%
13,184	MARSHALL	1,817	696	413	223	485	Orza	38.3%	22.7%	12.3%	26.7%
38,369	MAYES	4,761	2,297	1,609	631	224	Orza	48.2%	33.8%	13.3%	4.7%
12,623	MURRAY	3,325	1,504	901	511	409	Orza	45.2%	27.1%	15.4%	12.3%
69,451	MUSKOGEE	9,261	4,415	2,823	1,573	450	Orza	47.7%	30.5%	17.0%	4.9%
11,411	NOBLE	1,530	769	402	260	99	Orza	50.3%	26.3%	17.0%	6.5%
10,569	NOWATA	1,297	538	483	196	80	Orza	41.5%	37.2%	15.1%	6.2%
11,814	OKFUSKEE	1,851	614	583	502	152	Orza	33.2%	31.5%	27.1%	8.2%
660,448	OKLAHOMA	50,862	25,415	14,069	8,768	2,610	Orza	50.0%	27.7%	17.2%	5.1%
39,685	OKMULGEE	5,438	2,084	1,635	1,273	446	Orza	38.3%	30.1%	23.4%	8.2%
44,437	OSAGE	5,145	2,244	1,678	921	302	Orza	43.6%	32.6%	17.9%	5.9%
33,194	OTTAWA	4,706	2,006	1,254	950	496	Orza	42.6%	26.6%	20.2%	10.5%
16,612	PAWNEE	1,888	750	648	362	128	Orza	39.7%	34.3%	19.2%	6.8%
68,190	PAYNE	5,004	2,666	1,252	849	237	Orza	53.3%	25.0%	17.0%	4.7%
43,953	PITTSBURG	9,410	3,867	3,075	1,439	1,029	Orza	41.1%	32.7%	15.3%	10.9%
35,143	PONTOTOC	5,109	2,359	1,276	1,030	444	Orza	46.2%	25.0%	20.2%	8.7%
65,521	POTTAWATOMIE	8,639	2,310	4,315	1,715	299	Henry	26.7%	49.9%	19.9%	3.5%
11,667	PUSHMATAHA	3,140	883	840	495	922	Orza	28.1%	26.8%	15.8%	29.4%
3,436	ROGER MILLS	731	306	230	101	94	Orza	41.9%	31.5%	13.8%	12.9%
70,641	ROGERS	7,199	3,286	2,652	1,005	256	Orza	45.6%	36.8%	14.0%	3.6%
24,894	SEMINOLE	4,234	1,139	917	1,968	210	Haney	26.9%	21.7%	46.5%	5.0%
38,972	SEQUOYAH	6,311	1,847	2,526	1,007	931	Henry	29.3%	40.0%	16.0%	14.8%
43,182	STEPHENS	6,322	3,501	1,153	863	805	Orza	55.4%	18.2%	13.7%	12.7%
20,107	TEXAS	1,502	362	329	255	556	Orza	24.1%	21.9%	17.0%	37.0%
9,287	TILLMAN	1,784	731	312	271	470	Orza	41.0%	17.5%	15.2%	26.3%
563,299	TULSA	31,969	17,234	9,553	4,124	1,058	Orza	53.9%	29.9%	12.9%	3.3%
57,491	WAGONER	6,447	2,897	2,291	967	292	Orza	44.9%	35.5%	15.0%	4.5%
48,996	WASHINGTON	2,921	1,468	932	374	147	Orza	50.3%	31.9%	12.8%	5.0%
11,508	WASHITA	1,920	991	586	201	142	Orza	51.6%	30.5%	10.5%	7.4%
9,089	WOODS	817	617	104	53	43	Orza	75.5%	12.7%	6.5%	5.3%
18,486	WOODWARD	1,551	925	384	166	76	Orza	59.6%	24.8%	10.7%	4.9%
3,450,654	TOTAL	350,389	154,263	99,883	59,044	37,199	Orza	44.0%	28.5%	16.9%	10.6%

OKLAHOMA DEMOCRATIC PRIMARY RUNOFF

GOVERNOR 2002

2000 Census Population	County	Total Vote	Henry	Orza	Winner	Percentage of Total Vote Henry	Orza
21,038	ADAIR	2,179	1,257	922	Henry	57.7%	42.3%
6,105	ALFALFA	453	154	299	Orza	34.0%	66.0%
13,879	ATOKA	1,593	997	596	Henry	62.6%	37.4%
5,857	BEAVER	300	174	126	Henry	58.0%	42.0%
19,799	BECKHAM	1,859	1,003	856	Henry	54.0%	46.0%
11,976	BLAINE	932	431	501	Orza	46.2%	53.8%
36,534	BRYAN	4,697	2,985	1,712	Henry	63.6%	36.4%
30,150	CADDO	3,373	1,561	1,812	Orza	46.3%	53.7%
87,697	CANADIAN	5,242	2,636	2,606	Henry	50.3%	49.7%
45,621	CARTER	4,752	2,818	1,934	Henry	59.3%	40.7%
42,521	CHEROKEE	5,364	2,945	2,419	Henry	54.9%	45.1%
15,342	CHOCTAW	1,115	668	447	Henry	59.9%	40.1%
3,148	CIMARRON	345	222	123	Henry	64.3%	35.7%
208,016	CLEVELAND	13,281	7,183	6,098	Henry	54.1%	45.9%
6,031	COAL	1,311	841	470	Henry	64.1%	35.9%
114,996	COMANCHE	5,668	2,156	3,512	Orza	38.0%	62.0%
6,614	COTTON	439	201	238	Orza	45.8%	54.2%
14,950	CRAIG	1,704	916	788	Henry	53.8%	46.2%
67,367	CREEK	3,941	2,194	1,747	Henry	55.7%	44.3%
26,142	CUSTER	2,323	964	1,359	Orza	41.5%	58.5%
37,077	DELAWARE	3,496	1,879	1,617	Henry	53.7%	46.3%
4,743	DEWEY	620	274	346	Orza	44.2%	55.8%
4,075	ELLIS	383	182	201	Orza	47.5%	52.5%
57,813	GARFIELD	3,375	1,453	1,922	Orza	43.1%	56.9%
27,210	GARVIN	4,533	2,268	2,265	Henry	50.0%	50.0%
45,516	GRADY	3,705	1,926	1,779	Henry	52.0%	48.0%
5,144	GRANT	496	214	282	Orza	43.1%	56.9%
6,061	GREER	688	317	371	Orza	46.1%	53.9%
3,283	HARMON	307	148	159	Orza	48.2%	51.8%
3,562	HARPER	398	172	226	Orza	43.2%	56.8%
11,792	HASKELL	2,399	1,530	869	Henry	63.8%	36.2%
14,154	HUGHES	1,626	932	694	Henry	57.3%	42.7%
28,439	JACKSON	1,470	657	813	Orza	44.7%	55.3%
6,818	JEFFERSON	533	280	253	Henry	52.5%	47.5%
10,513	JOHNSTON	1,132	674	458	Henry	59.5%	40.5%
48,080	KAY	3,162	1,724	1,438	Henry	54.5%	45.5%
13,926	KINGFISHER	879	368	511	Orza	41.9%	58.1%
10,227	KIOWA	1,512	754	758	Orza	49.9%	50.1%
10,692	LATIMER	2,068	1,104	964	Henry	53.4%	46.6%
48,109	LE FLORE	2,899	1,639	1,260	Henry	56.5%	43.5%
32,080	LINCOLN	3,094	1,785	1,309	Henry	57.7%	42.3%
33,924	LOGAN	2,348	1,245	1,103	Henry	53.0%	47.0%
8,831	LOVE	730	484	246	Henry	66.3%	33.7%
27,740	MCCLAIN	2,386	1,288	1,098	Henry	54.0%	46.0%
34,402	MCCURTAIN	3,111	1,482	1,629	Orza	47.6%	52.4%
19,456	MCINTOSH	4,258	2,562	1,696	Henry	60.2%	39.8%
7,545	MAJOR	457	162	295	Orza	35.4%	64.6%
13,184	MARSHALL	1,477	878	599	Henry	59.4%	40.6%
38,369	MAYES	3,430	2,052	1,378	Henry	59.8%	40.2%
12,623	MURRAY	2,177	1,199	978	Henry	55.1%	44.9%
69,451	MUSKOGEE	7,428	3,906	3,522	Henry	52.6%	47.4%
11,411	NOBLE	993	445	548	Orza	44.8%	55.2%
10,569	NOWATA	823	545	278	Henry	66.2%	33.8%
11,814	OKFUSKEE	1,304	746	558	Henry	57.2%	42.8%
660,448	OKLAHOMA	37,840	18,597	19,243	Orza	49.1%	50.9%
39,685	OKMULGEE	3,964	2,357	1,607	Henry	59.5%	40.5%
44,437	OSAGE	4,482	2,554	1,928	Henry	57.0%	43.0%
33,194	OTTAWA	4,259	2,150	2,109	Henry	50.5%	49.5%
16,612	PAWNEE	1,300	757	543	Henry	58.2%	41.8%
68,190	PAYNE	3,861	1,653	2,208	Orza	42.8%	57.2%

OKLAHOMA DEMOCRATIC PRIMARY RUNOFF

GOVERNOR 2002

2000 Census Population	County	Total Vote	Henry	Orza	Winner	Percentage of Total Vote	
						Henry	Orza
43,953	PITTSBURG	6,874	3,779	3,095	Henry	55.0%	45.0%
35,143	PONTOTOC	3,678	1,763	1,915	Orza	47.9%	52.1%
65,521	POTTAWATOMIE	6,909	4,920	1,989	Henry	71.2%	28.8%
11,667	PUSHMATAHA	2,353	1,408	945	Henry	59.8%	40.2%
3,436	ROGER MILLS	481	273	208	Henry	56.8%	43.2%
70,641	ROGERS	5,431	3,119	2,312	Henry	57.4%	42.6%
24,894	SEMINOLE	2,839	1,738	1,101	Henry	61.2%	38.8%
38,972	SEQUOYAH	2,903	1,574	1,329	Henry	54.2%	45.8%
43,182	STEPHENS	5,471	2,381	3,090	Orza	43.5%	56.5%
20,107	TEXAS	919	502	417	Henry	54.6%	45.4%
9,287	TILLMAN	730	328	402	Orza	44.9%	55.1%
563,299	TULSA	23,628	11,148	12,480	Orza	47.2%	52.8%
57,491	WAGONER	3,729	2,138	1,591	Henry	57.3%	42.7%
48,996	WASHINGTON	2,261	1,143	1,118	Henry	50.6%	49.4%
11,508	WASHITA	1,518	717	801	Orza	47.2%	52.8%
9,089	WOODS	654	161	493	Orza	24.6%	75.4%
18,486	WOODWARD	1,539	596	943	Orza	38.7%	61.3%
3,450,654	TOTAL	258,191	135,336	122,855	Henry	52.4%	47.6%

OKLAHOMA DEMOCRATIC PRIMARY

SENATOR 2002

2000 Census Population	County	Total Vote	Walters	Boettcher	Other	Winner	Percentage of Total Vote		
							Walters	Boettcher	Other
21,038	ADAIR	3,262	1,727	877	658	Walters	52.9%	26.9%	20.2%
6,105	ALFALFA	698	371	211	116	Walters	53.2%	30.2%	16.6%
13,879	ATOKA	2,592	1,307	746	539	Walters	50.4%	28.8%	20.8%
5,857	BEAVER	488	258	98	132	Walters	52.9%	20.1%	27.0%
19,799	BECKHAM	2,580	1,683	630	267	Walters	65.2%	24.4%	10.3%
11,976	BLAINE	1,106	571	405	130	Walters	51.6%	36.6%	11.8%
36,534	BRYAN	6,167	3,242	1,775	1,150	Walters	52.6%	28.8%	18.6%
30,150	CADDO	4,514	2,345	1,573	596	Walters	51.9%	34.8%	13.2%
87,697	CANADIAN	6,356	2,931	2,584	841	Walters	46.1%	40.7%	13.2%
45,621	CARTER	5,259	2,688	1,713	858	Walters	51.1%	32.6%	16.3%
42,521	CHEROKEE	7,116	3,091	2,353	1,672	Walters	43.4%	33.1%	23.5%
15,342	CHOCTAW	2,330	1,409	484	437	Walters	60.5%	20.8%	18.8%
3,148	CIMARRON	400	217	72	111	Walters	54.3%	18.0%	27.8%
208,016	CLEVELAND	14,879	7,403	5,401	2,075	Walters	49.8%	36.3%	13.9%
6,031	COAL	1,639	878	472	289	Walters	53.6%	28.8%	17.6%
114,996	COMANCHE	9,383	4,872	3,222	1,289	Walters	51.9%	34.3%	13.7%
6,614	COTTON	760	376	249	135	Walters	49.5%	32.8%	17.8%
14,950	CRAIG	2,066	886	781	399	Walters	42.9%	37.8%	19.3%
67,367	CREEK	5,360	2,206	2,305	849	Boettcher	41.2%	43.0%	15.8%
26,142	CUSTER	2,576	1,410	883	283	Walters	54.7%	34.3%	11.0%
37,077	DELAWARE	4,570	2,112	1,646	812	Walters	46.2%	36.0%	17.8%
4,743	DEWEY	749	396	236	117	Walters	52.9%	31.5%	15.6%
4,075	ELLIS	467	255	134	78	Walters	54.6%	28.7%	16.7%
57,813	GARFIELD	3,732	2,089	1,092	551	Walters	56.0%	29.3%	14.8%
27,210	GARVIN	5,275	2,427	1,784	1,064	Walters	46.0%	33.8%	20.2%
45,516	GRADY	5,642	2,675	1,947	1,020	Walters	47.4%	34.5%	18.1%
5,144	GRANT	651	342	196	113	Walters	52.5%	30.1%	17.4%
6,061	GREER	1,284	670	386	228	Walters	52.2%	30.1%	17.8%
3,283	HARMON	395	207	131	57	Walters	52.4%	33.2%	14.4%
3,562	HARPER	520	260	160	100	Walters	50.0%	30.8%	19.2%

OKLAHOMA DEMOCRATIC PRIMARY

SENATOR 2002

2000 Census Population	County	Total Vote	Walters	Boettcher	Other	Winner	Percentage of Total Vote		
							Walters	Boettcher	Other
11,792	HASKELL	3,358	1,795	769	794	Walters	53.5%	22.9%	23.6%
14,154	HUGHES	2,187	1,056	793	338	Walters	48.3%	36.3%	15.5%
28,439	JACKSON	1,959	989	642	328	Walters	50.5%	32.8%	16.7%
6,818	JEFFERSON	1,006	565	209	232	Walters	56.2%	20.8%	23.1%
10,513	JOHNSTON	2,006	917	627	462	Walters	45.7%	31.3%	23.0%
48,080	KAY	3,418	1,111	1,930	377	Boettcher	32.5%	56.5%	11.0%
13,926	KINGFISHER	1,052	482	409	161	Walters	45.8%	38.9%	15.3%
10,227	KIOWA	2,101	1,187	581	333	Walters	56.5%	27.7%	15.8%
10,692	LATIMER	3,105	1,634	814	657	Walters	52.6%	26.2%	21.2%
48,109	LE FLORE	6,336	3,770	734	1,832	Walters	59.5%	11.6%	28.9%
32,080	LINCOLN	3,806	1,765	1,407	634	Walters	46.4%	37.0%	16.7%
33,924	LOGAN	2,717	1,363	917	437	Walters	50.2%	33.8%	16.1%
8,831	LOVE	1,197	629	281	287	Walters	52.5%	23.5%	24.0%
27,740	MCCLAIN	3,027	1,352	1,131	544	Walters	44.7%	37.4%	18.0%
34,402	MCCURTAIN	6,302	3,740	1,019	1,543	Walters	59.3%	16.2%	24.5%
19,456	MCINTOSH	4,602	2,130	1,637	835	Walters	46.3%	35.6%	18.1%
7,545	MAJOR	612	369	171	72	Walters	60.3%	27.9%	11.8%
13,184	MARSHALL	1,771	802	586	383	Walters	45.3%	33.1%	21.6%
38,369	MAYES	4,738	1,990	1,885	863	Walters	42.0%	39.8%	18.2%
12,623	MURRAY	3,287	1,644	1,064	579	Walters	50.0%	32.4%	17.6%
69,451	MUSKOGEE	9,128	4,135	3,271	1,722	Walters	45.3%	35.8%	18.9%
11,411	NOBLE	1,521	691	572	258	Walters	45.4%	37.6%	17.0%
10,569	NOWATA	1,284	593	464	227	Walters	46.2%	36.1%	17.7%
11,814	OKFUSKEE	1,811	778	694	339	Walters	43.0%	38.3%	18.7%
660,448	OKLAHOMA	50,300	25,917	17,817	6,566	Walters	51.5%	35.4%	13.1%
39,685	OKMULGEE	5,382	2,176	2,306	900	Boettcher	40.4%	42.8%	16.7%
44,437	OSAGE	5,111	2,291	2,088	732	Walters	44.8%	40.9%	14.3%
33,194	OTTAWA	4,623	2,375	1,173	1,075	Walters	51.4%	25.4%	23.3%
16,612	PAWNEE	1,874	850	693	331	Walters	45.4%	37.0%	17.7%
68,190	PAYNE	4,903	2,413	1,764	726	Walters	49.2%	36.0%	14.8%
43,953	PITTSBURG	9,309	4,719	2,696	1,894	Walters	50.7%	29.0%	20.3%
35,143	PONTOTOC	5,054	2,052	2,179	823	Boettcher	40.6%	43.1%	16.3%
65,521	POTTAWATOMIE	8,482	3,807	3,293	1,382	Walters	44.9%	38.8%	16.3%
11,667	PUSHMATAHA	3,111	1,786	711	614	Walters	57.4%	22.9%	19.7%
3,436	ROGER MILLS	741	440	204	97	Walters	59.4%	27.5%	13.1%
70,641	ROGERS	7,147	3,198	2,859	1,090	Walters	44.7%	40.0%	15.3%
24,894	SEMINOLE	4,185	2,305	1,261	619	Walters	55.1%	30.1%	14.8%
38,972	SEQUOYAH	6,290	3,328	1,578	1,384	Walters	52.9%	25.1%	22.0%
43,182	STEPHENS	6,316	2,946	2,262	1,108	Walters	46.6%	35.8%	17.5%
20,107	TEXAS	1,518	962	200	356	Walters	63.4%	13.2%	23.5%
9,287	TILLMAN	1,784	918	601	265	Walters	51.5%	33.7%	14.9%
563,299	TULSA	31,542	14,506	13,268	3,768	Walters	46.0%	42.1%	11.9%
57,491	WAGONER	6,383	2,730	2,494	1,159	Walters	42.8%	39.1%	18.2%
48,996	WASHINGTON	2,906	1,255	1,278	373	Boettcher	43.2%	44.0%	12.8%
11,508	WASHITA	1,928	1,248	488	192	Walters	64.7%	25.3%	10.0%
9,089	WOODS	809	537	169	103	Walters	66.4%	20.9%	12.7%
18,486	WOODWARD	1,542	864	451	227	Walters	56.0%	29.2%	14.7%
3,450,654	TOTAL	346,387	170,414	118,986	56,987	Walters	49.2%	34.4%	16.5%

OKLAHOMA DEMOCRATIC PRIMARY RUNOFF
SENATOR 2002

2000 Census Population	County	Total Vote	Walters	Boettcher	Winner	Percentage of Total Vote	
						Walters	Boettcher
21,038	ADAIR	2,163	1,376	787	Walters	63.6%	36.4%
6,105	ALFALFA	451	288	163	Walters	63.9%	36.1%
13,879	ATOKA	1,599	904	695	Walters	56.5%	43.5%
5,857	BEAVER	313	163	150	Walters	52.1%	47.9%
19,799	BECKHAM	1,871	1,322	549	Walters	70.7%	29.3%
11,976	BLAINE	923	521	402	Walters	56.4%	43.6%
36,534	BRYAN	4,692	2,747	1,945	Walters	58.5%	41.5%
30,150	CADDO	3,391	2,033	1,358	Walters	60.0%	40.0%
87,697	CANADIAN	5,230	2,700	2,530	Walters	51.6%	48.4%
45,621	CARTER	4,765	2,653	2,112	Walters	55.7%	44.3%
42,521	CHEROKEE	5,343	2,899	2,444	Walters	54.3%	45.7%
15,342	CHOCTAW	1,117	719	398	Walters	64.4%	35.6%
3,148	CIMARRON	362	199	163	Walters	55.0%	45.0%
208,016	CLEVELAND	13,226	7,436	5,790	Walters	56.2%	43.8%
6,031	COAL	1,317	843	474	Walters	64.0%	36.0%
114,996	COMANCHE	5,692	3,475	2,217	Walters	61.1%	38.9%
6,614	COTTON	439	251	188	Walters	57.2%	42.8%
14,950	CRAIG	1,695	896	799	Walters	52.9%	47.1%
67,367	CREEK	3,936	2,166	1,770	Walters	55.0%	45.0%
26,142	CUSTER	2,320	1,424	896	Walters	61.4%	38.6%
37,077	DELAWARE	3,466	1,941	1,525	Walters	56.0%	44.0%
4,743	DEWEY	624	356	268	Walters	57.1%	42.9%
4,075	ELLIS	389	235	154	Walters	60.4%	39.6%
57,813	GARFIELD	3,386	2,107	1,279	Walters	62.2%	37.8%
27,210	GARVIN	4,541	2,297	2,244	Walters	50.6%	49.4%
45,516	GRADY	3,712	2,023	1,689	Walters	54.5%	45.5%
5,144	GRANT	494	297	197	Walters	60.1%	39.9%
6,061	GREER	693	405	288	Walters	58.4%	41.6%
3,283	HARMON	310	189	121	Walters	61.0%	39.0%
3,562	HARPER	397	212	185	Walters	53.4%	46.6%
11,792	HASKELL	2,401	1,585	816	Walters	66.0%	34.0%
14,154	HUGHES	1,628	894	734	Walters	54.9%	45.1%
28,439	JACKSON	1,476	825	651	Walters	55.9%	44.1%
6,818	JEFFERSON	533	311	222	Walters	58.3%	41.7%
10,513	JOHNSTON	1,134	586	548	Walters	51.7%	48.3%
48,080	KAY	3,178	1,388	1,790	Boettcher	43.7%	56.3%
13,926	KINGFISHER	879	437	442	Boettcher	49.7%	50.3%
10,227	KIOWA	1,514	978	536	Walters	64.6%	35.4%
10,692	LATIMER	2,069	1,258	811	Walters	60.8%	39.2%
48,109	LE FLORE	2,900	2,022	878	Walters	69.7%	30.3%
32,080	LINCOLN	3,096	1,714	1,382	Walters	55.4%	44.6%
33,924	LOGAN	2,356	1,354	1,002	Walters	57.5%	42.5%
8,831	LOVE	732	437	295	Walters	59.7%	40.3%
27,740	MCCLAIN	2,391	1,242	1,149	Walters	51.9%	48.1%
34,402	MCCURTAIN	3,130	2,037	1,093	Walters	65.1%	34.9%
19,456	MCINTOSH	4,248	2,411	1,837	Walters	56.8%	43.2%
7,545	MAJOR	461	300	161	Walters	65.1%	34.9%
13,184	MARSHALL	1,479	759	720	Walters	51.3%	48.7%
38,369	MAYES	3,421	1,829	1,592	Walters	53.5%	46.5%
12,623	MURRAY	2,179	1,182	997	Walters	54.2%	45.8%
69,451	MUSKOGEE	7,408	4,230	3,178	Walters	57.1%	42.9%
11,411	NOBLE	997	533	464	Walters	53.5%	46.5%
10,569	NOWATA	824	472	352	Walters	57.3%	42.7%
11,814	OKFUSKEE	1,304	710	594	Walters	54.4%	45.6%
660,448	OKLAHOMA	37,795	21,884	15,911	Walters	57.9%	42.1%

OKLAHOMA DEMOCRATIC PRIMARY RUNOFF

SENATOR 2002

2000 Census Population	County	Total Vote	Walters	Boettcher	Winner	Percentage of Total Vote Walters	Boettcher
39,685	OKMULGEE	3,950	1,950	2,000	Boettcher	49.4%	50.6%
44,437	OSAGE	4,470	2,333	2,137	Walters	52.2%	47.8%
33,194	OTTAWA	4,249	2,673	1,576	Walters	62.9%	37.1%
16,612	PAWNEE	1,299	727	572	Walters	56.0%	44.0%
68,190	PAYNE	3,836	2,204	1,632	Walters	57.5%	42.5%
43,953	PITTSBURG	6,857	3,900	2,957	Walters	56.9%	43.1%
35,143	PONTOTOC	3,676	1,711	1,965	Boettcher	46.5%	53.5%
65,521	POTTAWATOMIE	6,880	3,520	3,360	Walters	51.2%	48.8%
11,667	PUSHMATAHA	2,358	1,345	1,013	Walters	57.0%	43.0%
3,436	ROGER MILLS	485	289	196	Walters	59.6%	40.4%
70,641	ROGERS	5,412	3,021	2,391	Walters	55.8%	44.2%
24,894	SEMINOLE	2,845	1,593	1,252	Walters	56.0%	44.0%
38,972	SEQUOYAH	2,896	1,677	1,219	Walters	57.9%	42.1%
43,182	STEPHENS	5,492	3,051	2,441	Walters	55.6%	44.4%
20,107	TEXAS	931	624	307	Walters	67.0%	33.0%
9,287	TILLMAN	737	415	322	Walters	56.3%	43.7%
563,299	TULSA	23,522	13,671	9,851	Walters	58.1%	41.9%
57,491	WAGONER	3,713	1,966	1,747	Walters	52.9%	47.1%
48,996	WASHINGTON	2,255	1,263	992	Walters	56.0%	44.0%
11,508	WASHITA	1,522	1,108	414	Walters	72.8%	27.2%
9,089	WOODS	653	467	186	Walters	71.5%	28.5%
18,486	WOODWARD	1,538	936	602	Walters	60.9%	39.1%
3,450,654	TOTAL	257,966	146,899	111,067	Walters	56.9%	43.1%

OREGON

GOVERNOR
Theodore R. Kulongoski (D). Elected 2002 to a four-year term.

SENATORS (1 Democrat, 1 Republican)
Gordon H. Smith (R). Reelected 2002 to a six-year term. Previously elected 1996.

Ron Wyden (D). Reelected 1998 to a six-year term. Had been elected in a special election January 30, 1996, to serve the remaining three years of the term vacated when Senator Robert W. Packwood (R) resigned.

REPRESENTATIVES (4 Democrats, 1 Republican)
1. David Wu (D)
2. Greg Walden (R)
3. Earl Blumenauer (D)
4. Peter A. DeFazio (D)
5. Darlene Hooley (D)

POSTWAR VOTE FOR PRESIDENT

Year	Total Vote	Republican		Democratic		Other Vote	Plurality	Percentage			
								Total Vote		Major Vote	
		Vote	Candidate	Vote	Candidate			Rep.	Dem.	Rep.	Dem.
2000**	1,533,968	713,577	Bush, George W.	720,342	Gore, Al	100,049	6,765 D	46.5%	47.0%	49.8%	50.2%
1996**	1,377,760	538,152	Dole, Bob	649,641	Clinton, Bill	189,967	111,489 D	39.1%	47.2%	45.3%	54.7%
1992**	1,462,643	475,757	Bush, George	621,314	Clinton, Bill	365,572	145,557 D	32.5%	42.5%	43.4%	56.6%
1988	1,201,694	560,126	Bush, George	616,206	Dukakis, Michael S.	25,362	56,080 D	46.6%	51.3%	47.6%	52.4%
1984	1,226,527	685,700	Reagan, Ronald	536,479	Mondale, Walter F.	4,348	149,221 R	55.9%	43.7%	56.1%	43.9%
1980**	1,181,516	571,044	Reagan, Ronald	456,890	Carter, Jimmy	153,582	114,154 R	48.3%	38.7%	55.6%	44.4%
1976	1,029,876	492,120	Ford, Gerald R.	490,407	Carter, Jimmy	47,349	1,713 R	47.8%	47.6%	50.1%	49.9%
1972	927,946	486,686	Nixon, Richard M.	392,760	McGovern, George S.	48,500	93,926 R	52.4%	42.3%	55.3%	44.7%
1968	819,622	408,433	Nixon, Richard M.	358,866	Humphrey, Hubert H.	52,323	49,567 R	49.8%	43.8%	53.2%	46.8%
1964	786,305	282,779	Goldwater, Barry M.	501,017	Johnson, Lyndon B.	2,509	218,238 D	36.0%	63.7%	36.1%	63.9%
1960	776,421	408,060	Nixon, Richard M.	367,402	Kennedy, John F.	959	40,658 R	52.6%	47.3%	52.6%	47.4%
1956	736,132	406,393	Eisenhower, Dwight D.	329,204	Stevenson, Adlai E.	535	77,189 R	55.2%	44.7%	55.2%	44.8%
1952	695,059	420,815	Eisenhower, Dwight D.	270,579	Stevenson, Adlai E.	3,665	150,236 R	60.5%	38.9%	60.9%	39.1%
1948	524,080	260,904	Dewey, Thomas E.	243,147	Truman, Harry S.	20,029	17,757 R	49.8%	46.4%	51.8%	48.2%

In 2000 the other vote column includes 77,357 votes cast for Green (Nader). In 1996 the other vote column includes 121,221 votes cast for Perot. In 1992 the other vote column includes 354,091 votes cast for Perot. In 1980 the other vote column includes 112,389 votes for Independent (Anderson).

OREGON

POSTWAR VOTE FOR GOVERNOR

Year	Total Vote	Republican		Democratic		Other Vote	Rep.-Dem. Plurality	Percentage			
								Total Vote		Major Vote	
		Vote	Candidate	Vote	Candidate			Rep.	Dem.	Rep.	Dem.
2002	1,260,497	581,785	Mannix, Kevin L.	618,004	Kulongoski, Theodore R.	60,708	36,219 D	46.2%	49.0%	48.5%	51.5%
1998	1,113,098	334,001	Sizemore, Bill	717,061	Kitzhaber, John	62,036	383,060 D	30.0%	64.4%	31.8%	68.2%
1994	1,221,010	517,874	Smith, Denny	622,083	Kitzhaber, John	81,053	104,209 D	42.4%	50.9%	45.4%	54.6%
1990	1,112,847	444,646	Frohnmayer, Dave	508,749	Roberts, Barbara	159,452	64,103 D	40.0%	45.7%	46.6%	53.4%
1986	1,059,630	506,986	Paulus, Norma	549,456	Goldschmidt, Neil	3,188	42,470 D	47.8%	51.9%	48.0%	52.0%
1982	1,042,009	639,841	Atiyeh, Victor	374,316	Kulongoski, Theodore R.	27,852	265,525 R	61.4%	35.9%	63.1%	36.9%
1978	911,143	498,452	Atiyeh, Victor	409,411	Straub, Robert W.	3,280	89,041 R	54.7%	44.9%	54.9%	45.1%
1974	770,574	324,751	Atiyeh, Victor	444,812	Straub, Robert W.	1,011	120,061 D	42.1%	57.7%	42.2%	57.8%
1970	666,394	369,964	McCall, Tom	293,892	Straub, Robert W.	2,538	76,072 R	55.5%	44.1%	55.7%	44.3%
1966	682,862	377,346	McCall, Tom	305,008	Straub, Robert W.	508	72,338 R	55.3%	44.7%	55.3%	44.7%
1962	637,407	345,497	Hatfield, Mark	265,359	Thornton, Robert Y.	26,551	80,138 R	54.2%	41.6%	56.6%	43.4%
1958	599,994	331,900	Hatfield, Mark	267,934	Holmes, Robert D.	160	63,966 R	55.3%	44.7%	55.3%	44.7%
1956S	731,279	361,840	Smith, Elmo E.	369,439	Holmes, Robert D.		7,599 D	49.5%	50.5%	49.5%	50.5%
1954	566,701	322,522	Patterson, Paul	244,179	Carson, Joseph K.		78,343 R	56.9%	43.1%	56.9%	43.1%
1950	505,910	334,160	McKay, Douglas	171,750	Flegel, Austin F.		162,410 R	66.1%	33.9%	66.1%	33.9%
1948S	509,633	271,295	McKay, Douglas	226,958	Wallace, Lew	11,380	44,337 R	53.2%	44.5%	54.4%	45.6%
1946	344,155	237,681	Snell, Earl	106,474	Donaugh, Carl C.		131,207 R	69.1%	30.9%	69.1%	30.9%

The 1956 and 1948 elections were for short terms to fill vacancies.

POSTWAR VOTE FOR SENATOR

Year	Total Vote	Republican		Democratic		Other Vote	Rep.-Dem. Plurality	Percentage			
								Total Vote		Major Vote	
		Vote	Candidate	Vote	Candidate			Rep.	Dem.	Rep.	Dem.
2002	1,267,221	712,287	Smith, Gordon H.	501,898	Bradbury, Bill	53,036	210,389 R	56.2%	39.6%	58.7%	41.3%
1998	1,117,747	377,739	Lim, John	682,425	Wyden, Ron	57,583	304,686 D	33.8%	61.1%	35.6%	64.4%
1996	1,360,230	677,336	Smith, Gordon H.	624,370	Bruggere, Tom	58,524	52,966 R	49.8%	45.9%	52.0%	48.0%
1996S	1,196,608	553,519	Smith, Gordon H.	571,739	Wyden, Ron	71,350	18,220 D	46.3%	47.8%	49.2%	50.8%
1992	1,376,033	717,455	Packwood, Robert W.	639,851	AuCoin, Les	18,727	77,604 R	52.1%	46.5%	52.9%	47.1%
1990	1,099,255	590,095	Hatfield, Mark	507,743	Lonsdale, Harry	1,417	82,352 R	53.7%	46.2%	53.8%	46.2%
1986	1,042,555	656,317	Packwood, Robert W.	375,735	Bauman, Rick	10,503	280,582 R	63.0%	36.0%	63.6%	36.4%
1984	1,214,735	808,152	Hatfield, Mark	406,122	Hendriksen, Margie	461	402,030 R	66.5%	33.4%	66.6%	33.4%
1980	1,140,494	594,290	Packwood, Robert W.	501,963	Kulongoski, Ted	44,241	92,327 R	52.1%	44.0%	54.2%	45.8%
1978	892,518	550,165	Hatfield, Mark	341,616	Cook, Vernon	737	208,549 R	61.6%	38.3%	61.7%	38.3%
1974	766,414	420,984	Packwood, Robert W.	338,591	Roberts, Betty	6,839	82,393 R	54.9%	44.2%	55.4%	44.6%
1972	920,833	494,671	Hatfield, Mark	425,036	Morse, Wayne L.	1,126	69,635 R	53.7%	46.2%	53.8%	46.2%
1968	814,176	408,646	Packwood, Robert W.	405,353	Morse, Wayne L.	177	3,293 R	50.2%	49.8%	50.2%	49.8%
1966	685,067	354,391	Hatfield, Mark	330,374	Duncan, Robert B.	302	24,017 R	51.7%	48.2%	51.8%	48.2%
1962	636,558	291,587	Unander, Sig	344,716	Morse, Wayne L.	255	53,129 D	45.8%	54.2%	45.8%	54.2%
1960	755,875	343,009	Smith, Elmo E.	412,757	Neuberger, Maurine	109	69,748 D	45.4%	54.6%	45.4%	54.6%
1956	732,254	335,405	McKay, Douglas	396,849	Morse, Wayne L.		61,444 D	45.8%	54.2%	45.8%	54.2%
1954	569,088	283,313	Cordon, Guy	285,775	Neuberger, Richard L.		2,462 D	49.8%	50.2%	49.8%	50.2%
1950	503,455	376,510	Morse, Wayne L.	116,780	Latourette, Howard	10,165	259,730 R	74.8%	23.2%	76.3%	23.7%
1948	498,570	299,295	Cordon, Guy	199,275	Wilson, Manley J.		100,020 R	60.0%	40.0%	60.0%	40.0%

The January 1996 election was for a short term to fill a vacancy.

OREGON

Congressional districts first established for elections held in 2002
5 members

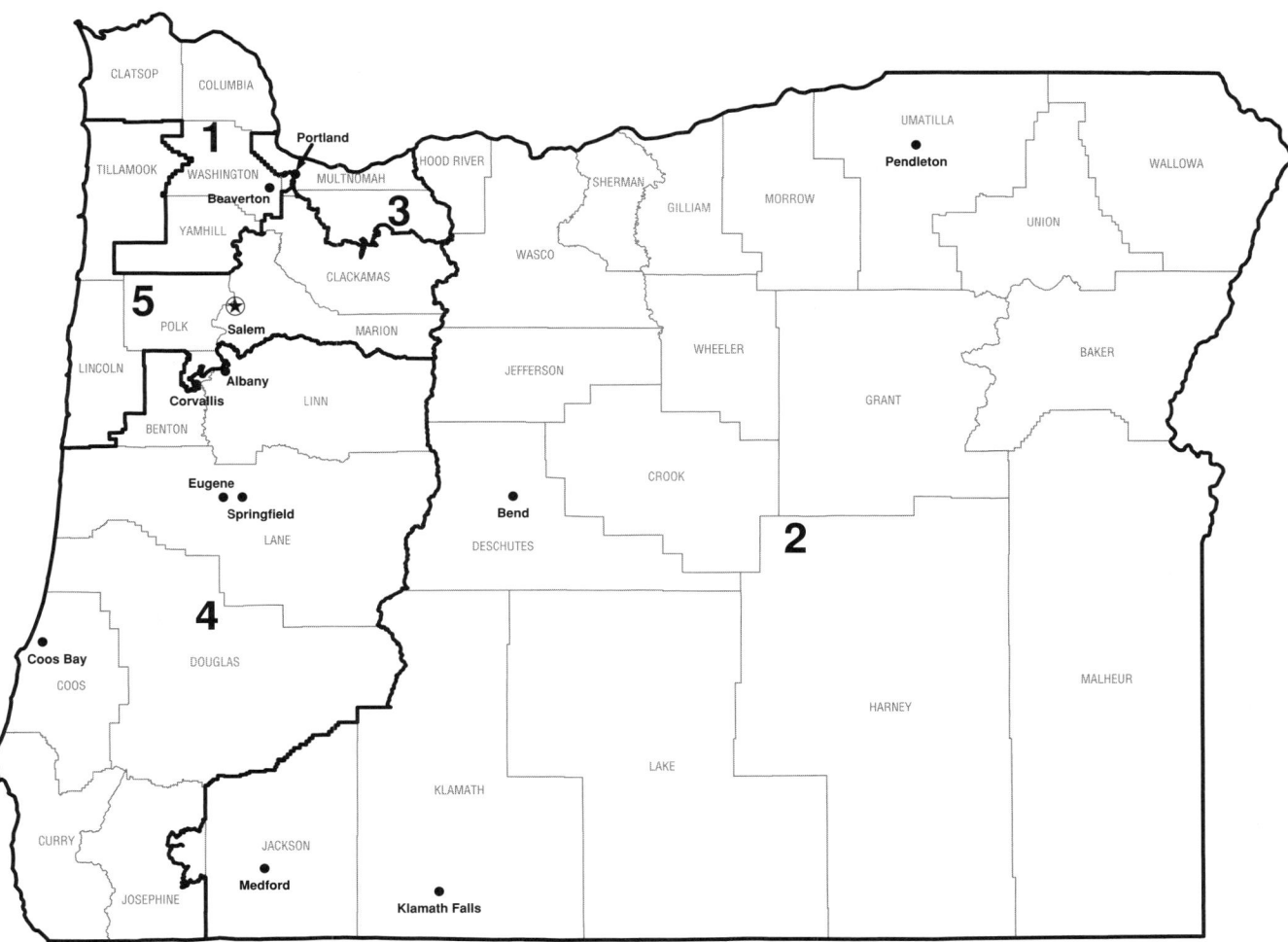

OREGON
GOVERNOR 2002

2000 Census Population	County	Total Vote	Republican	Democratic	Other	Rep.-Dem. Plurality		Percentage			
								Total Vote		Major Vote	
								Rep.	Dem.	Rep.	Dem.
16,741	BAKER	7,209	4,522	2,335	352	2,187	R	62.7%	32.4%	65.9%	34.1%
78,153	BENTON	32,214	12,769	18,226	1,219	5,457	D	39.6%	56.6%	41.2%	58.8%
338,391	CLACKAMAS	132,461	66,114	60,840	5,507	5,274	R	49.9%	45.9%	52.1%	47.9%
35,630	CLATSOP	13,720	5,606	7,347	767	1,741	D	40.9%	53.5%	43.3%	56.7%
43,560	COLUMBIA	17,855	8,000	8,465	1,390	465	D	44.8%	47.4%	48.6%	51.4%
62,779	COOS	24,899	12,463	10,968	1,468	1,495	R	50.1%	44.0%	53.2%	46.8%
19,182	CROOK	7,130	4,175	2,454	501	1,721	R	58.6%	34.4%	63.0%	37.0%
21,137	CURRY	9,472	5,154	3,816	502	1,338	R	54.4%	40.3%	57.5%	42.5%
115,367	DESCHUTES	49,408	25,189	21,544	2,675	3,645	R	51.0%	43.6%	53.9%	46.1%
100,399	DOUGLAS	38,094	22,934	12,953	2,207	9,981	R	60.2%	34.0%	63.9%	36.1%
1,915	GILLIAM	991	552	410	29	142	R	55.7%	41.4%	57.4%	42.6%
7,935	GRANT	3,441	2,615	704	122	1,911	R	76.0%	20.5%	78.8%	21.2%
7,609	HARNEY	2,972	1,970	777	225	1,193	R	66.3%	26.1%	71.7%	28.3%
20,411	HOOD RIVER	6,963	3,016	3,658	289	642	D	43.3%	52.5%	45.2%	54.8%
181,269	JACKSON	71,218	35,832	31,850	3,536	3,982	R	50.3%	44.7%	52.9%	47.1%
19,009	JEFFERSON	5,906	3,096	2,460	350	636	R	52.4%	41.7%	55.7%	44.3%
75,726	JOSEPHINE	29,711	17,462	10,462	1,787	7,000	R	58.8%	35.2%	62.5%	37.5%
63,775	KLAMATH	21,524	14,627	5,861	1,036	8,766	R	68.0%	27.2%	71.4%	28.6%
7,422	LAKE	3,093	2,202	768	123	1,434	R	71.2%	24.8%	74.1%	25.9%
322,959	LANE	121,679	46,859	69,221	5,599	22,362	D	38.5%	56.9%	40.4%	59.6%
44,479	LINCOLN	18,084	7,317	9,602	1,165	2,285	D	40.5%	53.1%	43.2%	56.8%
103,069	LINN	36,369	20,420	13,975	1,974	6,445	R	56.1%	38.4%	59.4%	40.6%
31,615	MALHEUR	8,109	5,572	2,342	195	3,230	R	68.7%	28.9%	70.4%	29.6%
284,834	MARION	96,013	50,371	41,332	4,310	9,039	R	52.5%	43.0%	54.9%	45.1%
10,995	MORROW	2,825	1,701	985	139	716	R	60.2%	34.9%	63.3%	36.7%
660,486	MULTNOMAH	241,624	70,745	159,242	11,637	88,497	D	29.3%	65.9%	30.8%	69.2%
62,380	POLK	25,046	13,128	10,956	962	2,172	R	52.4%	43.7%	54.5%	45.5%
1,934	SHERMAN	922	549	306	67	243	R	59.5%	33.2%	64.2%	35.8%
24,262	TILLAMOOK	10,458	4,818	5,025	615	207	D	46.1%	48.0%	48.9%	51.1%
70,548	UMATILLA	18,494	10,707	7,092	695	3,615	R	57.9%	38.3%	60.2%	39.8%
24,530	UNION	9,969	5,853	3,611	505	2,242	R	58.7%	36.2%	61.8%	38.2%
7,226	WALLOWA	3,457	2,283	986	188	1,297	R	66.0%	28.5%	69.8%	30.2%
23,791	WASCO	9,055	4,374	4,156	525	218	R	48.3%	45.9%	51.3%	48.7%
445,342	WASHINGTON	148,928	71,809	70,859	6,260	950	R	48.2%	47.6%	50.3%	49.7%
1,547	WHEELER	684	416	227	41	189	R	60.8%	33.2%	64.7%	35.3%
84,992	YAMHILL	30,500	16,565	12,189	1,746	4,376	R	54.3%	40.0%	57.6%	42.4%
3,421,399	TOTAL	1,260,497	581,785	618,004	60,708	36,219	D	46.2%	49.0%	48.5%	51.5%

OREGON

SENATOR 2002

2000 Census Population	County	Total Vote	Republican	Democratic	Other	Rep.-Dem. Plurality	Percentage			
							Total Vote		Major Vote	
							Rep.	Dem.	Rep.	Dem.
16,741	BAKER	7,235	5,467	1,501	267	3,966 R	75.6%	20.7%	78.5%	21.5%
78,153	BENTON	32,271	15,780	15,426	1,065	354 R	48.9%	47.8%	50.6%	49.4%
338,391	CLACKAMAS	132,742	79,735	47,704	5,303	32,031 R	60.1%	35.9%	62.6%	37.4%
35,630	CLATSOP	13,938	7,673	5,591	674	2,082 R	55.1%	40.1%	57.8%	42.2%
43,560	COLUMBIA	17,911	10,057	6,648	1,206	3,409 R	56.1%	37.1%	60.2%	39.8%
62,779	COOS	25,062	14,423	9,185	1,454	5,238 R	57.5%	36.6%	61.1%	38.9%
19,182	CROOK	7,204	5,238	1,640	326	3,598 R	72.7%	22.8%	76.2%	23.8%
21,137	CURRY	9,575	5,765	3,348	462	2,417 R	60.2%	35.0%	63.3%	36.7%
115,367	DESCHUTES	49,684	31,710	16,020	1,954	15,690 R	63.8%	32.2%	66.4%	33.6%
100,399	DOUGLAS	38,326	26,170	10,116	2,040	16,054 R	68.3%	26.4%	72.1%	27.9%
1,915	GILLIAM	1,000	730	248	22	482 R	73.0%	24.8%	74.6%	25.4%
7,935	GRANT	3,446	2,783	559	104	2,224 R	80.8%	16.2%	83.3%	16.7%
7,609	HARNEY	2,990	2,424	465	101	1,959 R	81.1%	15.6%	83.9%	16.1%
20,411	HOOD RIVER	6,976	3,894	2,815	267	1,079 R	55.8%	40.4%	58.0%	42.0%
181,269	JACKSON	71,591	41,632	27,217	2,742	14,415 R	58.2%	38.0%	60.5%	39.5%
19,009	JEFFERSON	5,953	3,993	1,716	244	2,277 R	67.1%	28.8%	69.9%	30.1%
75,726	JOSEPHINE	29,868	19,201	8,950	1,717	10,251 R	64.3%	30.0%	68.2%	31.8%
63,775	KLAMATH	21,701	16,426	4,274	1,001	12,152 R	75.7%	19.7%	79.4%	20.6%
7,422	LAKE	3,145	2,492	533	120	1,959 R	79.2%	16.9%	82.4%	17.6%
322,959	LANE	123,004	59,733	57,971	5,300	1,762 R	48.6%	47.1%	50.7%	49.3%
44,479	LINCOLN	18,142	9,469	7,795	878	1,674 R	52.2%	43.0%	54.8%	45.2%
103,069	LINN	36,588	24,490	10,367	1,731	14,123 R	66.9%	28.3%	70.3%	29.7%
31,615	MALHEUR	8,118	5,964	1,898	256	4,066 R	73.5%	23.4%	75.9%	24.1%
284,834	MARION	96,010	59,457	32,170	4,383	27,287 R	61.9%	33.5%	64.9%	35.1%
10,995	MORROW	2,862	2,106	644	112	1,462 R	73.6%	22.5%	76.6%	23.4%
660,486	MULTNOMAH	241,582	94,733	137,582	9,267	42,849 D	39.2%	57.0%	40.8%	59.2%
62,380	POLK	25,017	15,581	8,428	1,008	7,153 R	62.3%	33.7%	64.9%	35.1%
1,934	SHERMAN	931	693	196	42	497 R	74.4%	21.1%	78.0%	22.0%
24,262	TILLAMOOK	10,505	6,060	3,980	465	2,080 R	57.7%	37.9%	60.4%	39.6%
70,548	UMATILLA	18,765	13,761	4,518	486	9,243 R	73.3%	24.1%	75.3%	24.7%
24,530	UNION	10,083	7,322	2,428	333	4,894 R	72.6%	24.1%	75.1%	24.9%
7,226	WALLOWA	3,515	2,724	694	97	2,030 R	77.5%	19.7%	79.7%	20.3%
23,791	WASCO	9,125	5,715	3,042	368	2,673 R	62.6%	33.3%	65.3%	34.7%
445,342	WASHINGTON	151,012	88,740	56,555	5,717	32,185 R	58.8%	37.5%	61.1%	38.9%
1,547	WHEELER	700	502	157	41	345 R	71.7%	22.4%	76.2%	23.8%
84,992	YAMHILL	30,644	19,644	9,517	1,483	10,127 R	64.1%	31.1%	67.4%	32.6%
3,421,399	TOTAL	1,267,221	712,287	501,898	53,036	210,389 R	56.2%	39.6%	58.7%	41.3%

OREGON

HOUSE OF REPRESENTATIVES

CD	Year	Total Vote	Republican		Democratic		Other Vote	Rep.-Dem. Plurality	Percentage			
			Vote	Candidate	Vote	Candidate			Total Vote		Major Vote	
									Rep.	Dem.	Rep.	Dem.
1	2002	238,036	80,917	Greenfield, Jim	149,215	Wu, David*	7,904	68,298 D	34.0%	62.7%	35.2%	64.8%
2	2002	252,284	181,295	Walden, Greg*	64,991	Buckley, Peter	5,998	116,304 R	71.9%	25.8%	73.6%	26.4%
3	2002	234,977	62,821	Seale, Sarah	156,851	Blumenauer, Earl*	15,305	94,030 D	26.7%	66.8%	28.6%	71.4%
4	2002	263,481	90,523	VanLeeuwen, Liz	168,150	DeFazio, Peter A.*	4,808	77,627 D	34.4%	63.8%	35.0%	65.0%
5	2002	251,537	113,441	Boquist, Brian J.	137,713	Hooley, Darlene*	383	24,272 D	45.1%	54.7%	45.2%	54.8%
Total	2002	1,240,315	528,997		676,920		34,398	147,923 D	42.7%	54.6%	43.9%	56.1%

An asterisk (*) denotes incumbent.

OREGON

GENERAL AND PRIMARY ELECTIONS

2002 GENERAL ELECTIONS

Governor	Other vote was 57,760 Libertarian (Tom Cox); 2,948 write-in.
Senator	Other vote was 29,979 Libertarian (Dan Fitzgerald); 21,703 Constitution (Lon Mabon); 1,354 write-in.
House	Other vote was:

CD 1	7,639 Libertarian (Beth A. King); 265 write-in.
CD 2	5,681 Libertarian (Mike Wood); 317 write-in.
CD 3	6,588 Socialist (Walter F. "Walt" Brown); 4,704 Libertarian (Kevin Jones); 3,495 Constitution (David Brownlow); 518 write-in.
CD 4	4,602 Libertarian (Chris Bigelow); 206 write-in.
CD 5	383 write-in.

2002 PRIMARY ELECTIONS

Primary	May 21, 2002	**Registration** (as of May 21, 2002)	Republican Democratic Other Parties Non-Affiliated	669,994 720,022 58,167 390,889
			TOTAL	1,839,072

Primary Type Only registered Democrats could vote in their party's primary. Registered Republicans and Non-affiliated voters could participate in the Republican primary.

Note: An asterisk (*) denotes incumbent. The primary and general election were conducted entirely by mail.

	REPUBLICAN PRIMARIES			DEMOCRATIC PRIMARIES		
Governor	Kevin L. Mannix	117,194	35.2%	Theodore R. Kulongoski	170,799	48.2%
	Jack Roberts	98,008	29.5%	Jim Hill	92,294	26.1%
	Ron Saxton	93,484	28.1%	Bev Stein	76,517	21.6%
	W. Ames Curtright	10,986	3.3%	Peter William Allen	6,582	1.9%
	Roger Weidner	7,395	2.2%	Caleb Burns	4,167	1.2%
	Lee R. Shindler	2,266	0.7%	Write-in	3,925	1.1%
	Write-in	3,242	1.0%			
	TOTAL	332,575		TOTAL	354,284	
Senator	Gordon H. Smith*	306,504	98.9%	Bill Bradbury	279,792	85.9%
	Write-in	3,439	1.1%	Craig Hanson	27,472	8.4%
				Greg Haven	13,995	4.3%
				Write-in	4,480	1.4%
	TOTAL	309,943		TOTAL	325,739	
Congressional District 1	Jim Greenfield	43,354	99.1%	David Wu*	54,501	99.4%
	Write-in	384	0.9%	Write-in	336	0.6%
	TOTAL	43,738		TOTAL	54,837	
Congressional District 2	Greg Walden*	78,147	99.3%	Peter Buckley	29,445	63.5%
	Write-in	542	0.7%	John C. McColgan	15,779	34.0%
				Write-in	1,165	2.5%
	TOTAL	78,689		TOTAL	46,389	
Congressional District 3	Sarah Seale	28,932	98.2%	Earl Blumenauer*	68,893	87.0%
	Write-in	516	1.8%	John Sweeney	9,992	12.6%
				Write-in	279	0.4%
	TOTAL	29,448		TOTAL	79,164	

OREGON

GENERAL AND PRIMARY ELECTIONS

	REPUBLICAN PRIMARIES			DEMOCRATIC PRIMARIES		
Congressional District 4	Liz VanLeeuwen	49,976	98.6%	Peter A. DeFazio*	68,513	99.2%
	Write-in	735	1.4%	Write-in	526	0.8%
	TOTAL	50,711		TOTAL	69,039	
Congressional District 5	Brian J. Boquist	42,077	67.0%	Darlene Hooley*	59,629	98.9%
	Craig L. Schelske	20,271	32.3%	Write-in	633	1.1%
	Write-in	424	0.7%			
	TOTAL	62,772		TOTAL	60,262	

OREGON REPUBLICAN PRIMARY

GOVERNOR 2002

2000 Census Population	County	Total Vote	Mannix	Roberts	Saxton	Other	Winner	Percentage of Total Vote			
								Mannix	Roberts	Saxton	Other
16,741	BAKER	2,746	1,077	824	697	148	Mannix	39.2%	30.0%	25.4%	5.4%
78,153	BENTON	7,310	2,251	2,238	2,323	498	Saxton	30.8%	30.6%	31.8%	6.8%
338,391	CLACKAMAS	35,464	14,020	9,040	10,254	2,150	Mannix	39.5%	25.5%	28.9%	6.1%
35,630	CLATSOP	3,369	1,045	951	1,140	233	Saxton	31.0%	28.2%	33.8%	6.9%
43,560	COLUMBIA	4,101	1,552	1,274	908	367	Mannix	37.8%	31.1%	22.1%	8.9%
62,779	COOS	5,932	2,189	1,868	1,253	622	Mannix	36.9%	31.5%	21.1%	10.5%
19,182	CROOK	2,190	681	593	759	157	Saxton	31.1%	27.1%	34.7%	7.2%
21,137	CURRY	2,619	946	873	473	327	Mannix	36.1%	33.3%	18.1%	12.5%
115,367	DESCHUTES	14,541	4,914	4,405	4,216	1,006	Mannix	33.8%	30.3%	29.0%	6.9%
100,399	DOUGLAS	12,923	4,079	4,572	3,193	1,079	Roberts	31.6%	35.4%	24.7%	8.3%
1,915	GILLIAM	336	110	97	105	24	Mannix	32.7%	28.9%	31.3%	7.1%
7,935	GRANT	1,193	422	310	339	122	Mannix	35.4%	26.0%	28.4%	10.2%
7,609	HARNEY	1,227	241	437	474	75	Saxton	19.6%	35.6%	38.6%	6.1%
20,411	HOOD RIVER	1,862	512	449	775	126	Saxton	27.5%	24.1%	41.6%	6.8%
181,269	JACKSON	22,001	7,038	6,114	7,105	1,744	Saxton	32.0%	27.8%	32.3%	7.9%
19,009	JEFFERSON	1,965	498	534	777	156	Saxton	25.3%	27.2%	39.5%	7.9%
75,726	JOSEPHINE	11,680	4,526	3,285	2,713	1,156	Mannix	38.8%	28.1%	23.2%	9.9%
63,775	KLAMATH	7,490	2,778	1,862	2,263	587	Mannix	37.1%	24.9%	30.2%	7.8%
7,422	LAKE	1,358	223	559	423	153	Roberts	16.4%	41.2%	31.1%	11.3%
322,959	LANE	27,119	6,234	12,059	7,240	1,586	Roberts	23.0%	44.5%	26.7%	5.8%
44,479	LINCOLN	4,257	1,175	1,322	1,365	395	Saxton	27.6%	31.1%	32.1%	9.3%
103,069	LINN	11,292	3,655	2,992	3,970	675	Saxton	32.4%	26.5%	35.2%	6.0%
31,615	MALHEUR	2,847	930	1,135	420	362	Roberts	32.7%	39.9%	14.8%	12.7%
284,834	MARION	31,297	14,879	8,943	5,390	2,085	Mannix	47.5%	28.6%	17.2%	6.7%
10,995	MORROW	715	220	223	207	65	Roberts	30.8%	31.2%	29.0%	9.1%
660,486	MULTNOMAH	40,852	13,461	10,661	13,525	3,205	Saxton	33.0%	26.1%	33.1%	7.8%
62,380	POLK	8,011	3,604	2,537	1,431	439	Mannix	45.0%	31.7%	17.9%	5.5%
1,934	SHERMAN	337	78	111	117	31	Saxton	23.1%	32.9%	34.7%	9.2%
24,262	TILLAMOOK	2,857	1,085	733	837	202	Mannix	38.0%	25.7%	29.3%	7.1%
70,548	UMATILLA	5,180	1,625	1,594	1,604	357	Mannix	31.4%	30.8%	31.0%	6.9%
24,530	UNION	3,279	893	1,227	905	254	Roberts	27.2%	37.4%	27.6%	7.7%
7,226	WALLOWA	1,422	524	498	287	113	Mannix	36.8%	35.0%	20.2%	7.9%
23,791	WASCO	2,507	747	728	832	200	Saxton	29.8%	29.0%	33.2%	8.0%
445,342	WASHINGTON	40,549	15,149	10,296	12,666	2,438	Mannix	37.4%	25.4%	31.2%	6.0%
1,547	WHEELER	230	65	76	65	24	Roberts	28.3%	33.0%	28.3%	10.4%
84,992	YAMHILL	9,517	3,768	2,588	2,433	728	Mannix	39.6%	27.2%	25.6%	7.6%
3,421,399	TOTAL	332,575	117,194	98,008	93,484	23,889	Mannix	35.2%	29.5%	28.1%	7.2%

OREGON DEMOCRATIC PRIMARY
GOVERNOR 2002

2000 Census Population	County	Total Vote	Kulongoski	Hill	Stein	Other	Winner	Percentage of Total Vote			
								Kulongoski	Hill	Stein	Other
16,741	BAKER	1,654	824	377	341	112	Kulongoski	49.8%	22.8%	20.6%	6.8%
78,153	BENTON	8,896	4,344	2,751	1,582	219	Kulongoski	48.8%	30.9%	17.8%	2.5%
338,391	CLACKAMAS	34,168	18,450	8,617	5,928	1,173	Kulongoski	54.0%	25.2%	17.3%	3.4%
35,630	CLATSOP	4,524	2,113	1,149	1,064	198	Kulongoski	46.7%	25.4%	23.5%	4.4%
43,560	COLUMBIA	6,375	3,216	1,482	1,317	360	Kulongoski	50.4%	23.2%	20.7%	5.6%
62,779	COOS	7,266	3,235	1,623	1,883	525	Kulongoski	44.5%	22.3%	25.9%	7.2%
19,182	CROOK	1,851	887	393	410	161	Kulongoski	47.9%	21.2%	22.2%	8.7%
21,137	CURRY	2,194	958	451	612	173	Kulongoski	43.7%	20.6%	27.9%	7.9%
115,367	DESCHUTES	11,147	5,052	3,081	2,585	429	Kulongoski	45.3%	27.6%	23.2%	3.8%
100,399	DOUGLAS	9,063	3,869	2,053	2,397	744	Kulongoski	42.7%	22.7%	26.4%	8.2%
1,915	GILLIAM	340	135	108	75	22	Kulongoski	39.7%	31.8%	22.1%	6.5%
7,935	GRANT	716	303	161	117	135	Kulongoski	42.3%	22.5%	16.3%	18.9%
7,609	HARNEY	625	250	135	148	92	Kulongoski	40.0%	21.6%	23.7%	14.7%
20,411	HOOD RIVER	2,006	955	504	460	87	Kulongoski	47.6%	25.1%	22.9%	4.3%
181,269	JACKSON	17,065	8,061	4,013	4,097	894	Kulongoski	47.2%	23.5%	24.0%	5.2%
19,009	JEFFERSON	1,585	717	372	394	102	Kulongoski	45.2%	23.5%	24.9%	6.4%
75,726	JOSEPHINE	6,638	2,873	1,435	1,831	499	Kulongoski	43.3%	21.6%	27.6%	7.5%
63,775	KLAMATH	4,400	2,058	929	1,004	409	Kulongoski	46.8%	21.1%	22.8%	9.3%
7,422	LAKE	620	287	139	143	51	Kulongoski	46.3%	22.4%	23.1%	8.2%
322,959	LANE	38,666	16,013	11,184	10,380	1,089	Kulongoski	41.4%	28.9%	26.8%	2.8%
44,479	LINCOLN	5,535	2,599	1,445	1,228	263	Kulongoski	47.0%	26.1%	22.2%	4.8%
103,069	LINN	10,135	4,635	2,880	1,931	689	Kulongoski	45.7%	28.4%	19.1%	6.8%
31,615	MALHEUR	1,331	652	293	204	182	Kulongoski	49.0%	22.0%	15.3%	13.7%
284,834	MARION	26,606	12,903	8,544	3,990	1,169	Kulongoski	48.5%	32.1%	15.0%	4.4%
10,995	MORROW	569	246	177	112	34	Kulongoski	43.2%	31.1%	19.7%	6.0%
660,486	MULTNOMAH	87,313	43,838	20,630	20,446	2,399	Kulongoski	50.2%	23.6%	23.4%	2.7%
62,380	POLK	6,050	3,027	1,935	882	206	Kulongoski	50.0%	32.0%	14.6%	3.4%
1,934	SHERMAN	302	125	68	76	33	Kulongoski	41.4%	22.5%	25.2%	10.9%
24,262	TILLAMOOK	3,491	1,661	838	823	169	Kulongoski	47.6%	24.0%	23.6%	4.8%
70,548	UMATILLA	3,983	1,790	1,282	671	240	Kulongoski	44.9%	32.2%	16.8%	6.0%
24,530	UNION	2,681	1,205	691	578	207	Kulongoski	44.9%	25.8%	21.6%	7.7%
7,226	WALLOWA	860	368	211	195	86	Kulongoski	42.8%	24.5%	22.7%	10.0%
23,791	WASCO	2,763	1,336	653	618	156	Kulongoski	48.4%	23.6%	22.4%	5.6%
445,342	WASHINGTON	35,092	18,264	9,565	6,308	955	Kulongoski	52.0%	27.3%	18.0%	2.7%
1,547	WHEELER	193	85	48	40	20	Kulongoski	44.0%	24.9%	20.7%	10.4%
84,992	YAMHILL	7,581	3,465	2,077	1,647	392	Kulongoski	45.7%	27.4%	21.7%	5.2%
3,421,399	TOTAL	354,284	170,799	92,294	76,517	14,674	Kulongoski	48.2%	26.1%	21.6%	4.1%

OREGON DEMOCRATIC PRIMARY

SENATOR 2002

2000 Census Population	County	Total Vote	Bradbury	Other	Winner	Percentage of Total Vote Bradbury	Other
16,741	BAKER	1,481	1,125	356	Bradbury	76.0%	24.0%
78,153	BENTON	8,305	7,624	681	Bradbury	91.8%	8.2%
338,391	CLACKAMAS	31,014	27,134	3,880	Bradbury	87.5%	12.5%
35,630	CLATSOP	4,053	3,389	664	Bradbury	83.6%	16.4%
43,560	COLUMBIA	5,886	4,600	1,286	Bradbury	78.2%	21.8%
62,779	COOS	7,119	5,499	1,620	Bradbury	77.2%	22.8%
19,182	CROOK	1,660	1,237	423	Bradbury	74.5%	25.5%
21,137	CURRY	2,157	1,759	398	Bradbury	81.5%	18.5%
115,367	DESCHUTES	10,116	8,729	1,387	Bradbury	86.3%	13.7%
100,399	DOUGLAS	8,507	6,686	1,821	Bradbury	78.6%	21.4%
1,915	GILLIAM	303	241	62	Bradbury	79.5%	20.5%
7,935	GRANT	627	387	240	Bradbury	61.7%	38.3%
7,609	HARNEY	582	391	191	Bradbury	67.2%	32.8%
20,411	HOOD RIVER	1,838	1,560	278	Bradbury	84.9%	15.1%
181,269	JACKSON	15,796	13,547	2,249	Bradbury	85.8%	14.2%
19,009	JEFFERSON	1,424	1,195	229	Bradbury	83.9%	16.1%
75,726	JOSEPHINE	6,158	5,011	1,147	Bradbury	81.4%	18.6%
63,775	KLAMATH	4,056	3,151	905	Bradbury	77.7%	22.3%
7,422	LAKE	529	412	117	Bradbury	77.9%	22.1%
322,959	LANE	35,121	30,985	4,136	Bradbury	88.2%	11.8%
44,479	LINCOLN	5,143	4,377	766	Bradbury	85.1%	14.9%
103,069	LINN	9,146	7,258	1,888	Bradbury	79.4%	20.6%
31,615	MALHEUR	1,265	878	387	Bradbury	69.4%	30.6%
284,834	MARION	24,759	20,714	4,045	Bradbury	83.7%	16.3%
10,995	MORROW	526	423	103	Bradbury	80.4%	19.6%
660,486	MULTNOMAH	81,057	72,776	8,281	Bradbury	89.8%	10.2%
62,380	POLK	5,534	4,814	720	Bradbury	87.0%	13.0%
1,934	SHERMAN	266	187	79	Bradbury	70.3%	29.7%
24,262	TILLAMOOK	3,149	2,620	529	Bradbury	83.2%	16.8%
70,548	UMATILLA	3,630	2,806	824	Bradbury	77.3%	22.7%
24,530	UNION	2,477	1,924	553	Bradbury	77.7%	22.3%
7,226	WALLOWA	797	596	201	Bradbury	74.8%	25.2%
23,791	WASCO	2,530	2,038	492	Bradbury	80.6%	19.4%
445,342	WASHINGTON	31,536	27,949	3,587	Bradbury	88.6%	11.4%
1,547	WHEELER	174	129	45	Bradbury	74.1%	25.9%
84,992	YAMHILL	7,018	5,641	1,377	Bradbury	80.4%	19.6%
3,421,399	TOTAL	325,739	279,792	45,947	Bradbury	85.9%	14.1%

PENNSYLVANIA

GOVERNOR
Edward G. Rendell (D). Elected 2002 to a four-year term.

SENATORS (2 Republicans)
Rick Santorum (R). Reelected 2000 to a six-year term. Previously elected 1994.

Arlen Specter (R). Reelected 1998 to a six-year term. Previously elected 1992, 1986, 1980.

REPRESENTATIVES (12 Republicans, 7 Democrats)
1. Robert A. Brady (D)
2. Chaka Fattah (D)
3. Phil English (R)
4. Melissa A. Hart (R)
5. John E. Peterson (R)
6. Jim Gerlach (R)
7. Curt Weldon (R)
8. James C. Greenwood (R)
9. Bill Shuster (R)
10. Don Sherwood (R)
11. Paul E. Kanjorski (D)
12. John P. Murtha (D)
13. Joseph M. Hoeffel (D)
14. Mike Doyle (D)
15. Patrick J. Toomey (R)
16. Joe Pitts (R)
17. Tim Holden (D)
18. Tim Murphy (R)
19. Todd R. Platts (R)

POSTWAR VOTE FOR PRESIDENT

Year	Total Vote	Republican Vote	Republican Candidate	Democratic Vote	Democratic Candidate	Other Vote	Plurality	Total Vote Rep.	Total Vote Dem.	Major Vote Rep.	Major Vote Dem.
2000**	4,913,119	2,281,127	Bush, George W.	2,485,967	Gore, Al	146,025	204,840 D	46.4%	50.6%	47.9%	52.1%
1996**	4,506,118	1,801,169	Dole, Bob	2,215,819	Clinton, Bill	489,130	414,650 D	40.0%	49.2%	44.8%	55.2%
1992**	4,959,810	1,791,841	Bush, George	2,239,164	Clinton, Bill	928,805	447,323 D	36.1%	45.1%	44.5%	55.5%
1988	4,536,251	2,300,087	Bush, George	2,194,944	Dukakis, Michael S.	41,220	105,143 R	50.7%	48.4%	51.2%	48.8%
1984	4,844,903	2,584,323	Reagan, Ronald	2,228,131	Mondale, Walter F.	32,449	356,192 R	53.3%	46.0%	53.7%	46.3%
1980**	4,561,501	2,261,872	Reagan, Ronald	1,937,540	Carter, Jimmy	362,089	324,332 R	49.6%	42.5%	53.9%	46.1%
1976	4,620,787	2,205,604	Ford, Gerald R.	2,328,677	Carter, Jimmy	86,506	123,073 D	47.7%	50.4%	48.6%	51.4%
1972	4,592,106	2,714,521	Nixon, Richard M.	1,796,951	McGovern, George S.	80,634	917,570 R	59.1%	39.1%	60.2%	39.8%
1968	4,747,928	2,090,017	Nixon, Richard M.	2,259,405	Humphrey, Hubert H.	398,506	169,388 D	44.0%	47.6%	48.1%	51.9%
1964	4,822,690	1,673,657	Goldwater, Barry M.	3,130,954	Johnson, Lyndon B.	18,079	1,457,297 D	34.7%	64.9%	34.8%	65.2%
1960	5,006,541	2,439,956	Nixon, Richard M.	2,556,282	Kennedy, John F.	10,303	116,326 D	48.7%	51.1%	48.8%	51.2%
1956	4,576,503	2,585,252	Eisenhower, Dwight D.	1,981,769	Stevenson, Adlai E.	9,482	603,483 R	56.5%	43.3%	56.6%	43.4%
1952	4,580,969	2,415,789	Eisenhower, Dwight D.	2,146,269	Stevenson, Adlai E.	18,911	269,520 R	52.7%	46.9%	53.0%	47.0%
1948	3,735,348	1,902,197	Dewey, Thomas E.	1,752,426	Truman, Harry S.	80,725	149,771 R	50.9%	46.9%	52.0%	48.0%

In 2000 the other vote column includes 103,392 votes cast for Green (Nader). In 1996 the other vote column includes 430,984 votes cast for Perot. In 1992 the other vote column includes 902,667 votes cast for Perot. In 1980 the other vote column includes 292,921 votes for Independent (Anderson).

PENNSYLVANIA

POSTWAR VOTE FOR GOVERNOR

Year	Total Vote	Republican		Democratic		Other Vote	Rep.-Dem. Plurality	Percentage			
								Total Vote		Major Vote	
		Vote	Candidate	Vote	Candidate			Rep.	Dem.	Rep.	Dem.
2002	3,583,179	1,589,408	Fisher, Mike	1,913,235	Rendell, Edward G.	80,536	323,827 D	44.4%	53.4%	45.4%	54.6%
1998	3,025,152	1,736,844	Ridge, Thomas J.	938,745	Itkin, Ivan	349,563	798,099 R	57.4%	31.0%	64.9%	35.1%
1994**	3,585,526	1,627,976	Ridge, Thomas J.	1,430,099	Singel, Mark S.	527,451	197,877 R	45.4%	39.9%	53.2%	46.8%
1990	3,052,760	987,516	Hafer, Barbara	2,065,244	Casey, Robert		1,077,728 D	32.3%	67.7%	32.3%	67.7%
1986	3,388,275	1,638,268	Scranton, William W., III	1,717,484	Casey, Robert	32,523	79,216 D	48.4%	50.7%	48.8%	51.2%
1982	3,683,985	1,872,784	Thornburgh, Richard L.	1,772,353	Ertel, Allen E.	38,848	100,431 R	50.8%	48.1%	51.4%	48.6%
1978	3,741,969	1,966,042	Thornburgh, Richard L.	1,737,888	Flaherty, Peter	38,039	228,154 R	52.5%	46.4%	53.1%	46.9%
1974	3,491,234	1,578,917	Lewis, Andrew L.	1,878,252	Shapp, Milton	34,065	299,335 D	45.2%	53.8%	45.7%	54.3%
1970	3,700,060	1,542,854	Broderick, Raymond	2,043,029	Shapp, Milton	114,177	500,175 D	41.7%	55.2%	43.0%	57.0%
1966	4,050,668	2,110,349	Shafer, Raymond P.	1,868,719	Shapp, Milton	71,600	241,630 R	52.1%	46.1%	53.0%	47.0%
1962	4,378,042	2,424,918	Scranton, William W.	1,938,627	Dilworth, Richardson	14,497	486,291 R	55.4%	44.3%	55.6%	44.4%
1958	3,986,918	1,948,769	McGonigle, A. T.	2,024,852	Lawrence, David	13,297	76,083 D	48.9%	50.8%	49.0%	51.0%
1954	3,720,457	1,717,070	Wood, Lloyd H.	1,996,266	Leader, George M.	7,121	279,196 D	46.2%	53.7%	46.2%	53.8%
1950	3,540,059	1,796,119	Fine, John S.	1,710,355	Dilworth, Richardson	33,585	85,764 R	50.7%	48.3%	51.2%	48.8%
1946	3,123,994	1,828,462	Duff, James H.	1,270,947	Rice, John S.	24,585	557,515 R	58.5%	40.7%	59.0%	41.0%

In 1994 other vote was 460,269 Constitutional (Luksik); 33,602 Libertarian (Fallon); 33,235 Patriot (Holloway); 345 write-ins.

POSTWAR VOTE FOR SENATOR

Year	Total Vote	Republican		Democratic		Other Vote	Rep.-Dem. Plurality	Percentage			
								Total Vote		Major Vote	
		Vote	Candidate	Vote	Candidate			Rep.	Dem.	Rep.	Dem.
2000	4,735,504	2,481,962	Santorum, Rick	2,154,908	Klink, Ron	98,634	327,054 R	52.4%	45.5%	53.5%	46.5%
1998	2,957,772	1,814,180	Specter, Arlen	1,028,839	Lloyd, Bill	114,753	785,341 R	61.3%	34.8%	63.8%	36.2%
1994	3,513,361	1,735,691	Santorum, Rick	1,648,481	Wofford, Harris	129,189	87,210 R	49.4%	46.9%	51.3%	48.7%
1992	4,802,410	2,358,125	Specter, Arlen	2,224,966	Yeakel, Lynn	219,319	133,159 R	49.1%	46.3%	51.5%	48.5%
1991S	3,382,746	1,521,986	Thornburgh, Richard	1,860,760	Wofford, Harris		338,774 D	45.0%	55.0%	45.0%	55.0%
1988	4,366,598	2,901,715	Heinz, H. John	1,416,764	Vignola, Joseph C.	48,119	1,484,951 R	66.5%	32.4%	67.2%	32.8%
1986	3,378,226	1,906,537	Specter, Arlen	1,448,219	Edgar, Robert W.	23,470	458,318 R	56.4%	42.9%	56.8%	43.2%
1982	3,604,108	2,136,418	Heinz, H. John	1,412,965	Wecht, Cyril H.	54,725	723,453 R	59.3%	39.2%	60.2%	39.8%
1980	4,418,042	2,230,404	Specter, Arlen	2,122,391	Flaherty, Peter	65,247	108,013 R	50.5%	48.0%	51.2%	48.8%
1976	4,546,353	2,381,891	Heinz, H. John	2,126,977	Green, William J., III	37,485	254,914 R	52.4%	46.8%	52.8%	47.2%
1974	3,477,812	1,843,317	Schweiker, Richard S.	1,596,121	Flaherty, Peter	38,374	247,196 R	53.0%	45.9%	53.6%	46.4%
1970	3,644,305	1,874,106	Scott, Hugh	1,653,774	Sesler, William G.	116,425	220,332 R	51.4%	45.4%	53.1%	46.9%
1968	4,624,218	2,399,762	Schweiker, Richard S.	2,117,662	Clark, Joseph S.	106,794	282,100 R	51.9%	45.8%	53.1%	46.9%
1964	4,803,835	2,429,858	Scott, Hugh	2,359,223	Blatt, Genevieve	14,754	70,635 R	50.6%	49.1%	50.7%	49.3%
1962	4,383,475	2,134,649	Van Zandt, James E.	2,238,383	Clark, Joseph S.	10,443	103,734 D	48.7%	51.1%	48.8%	51.2%
1958	3,988,622	2,042,586	Scott, Hugh	1,929,821	Leader, George M.	16,215	112,765 R	51.2%	48.4%	51.4%	48.6%
1956	4,529,874	2,250,671	Duff, James H.	2,268,641	Clark, Joseph S.	10,562	17,970 D	49.7%	50.1%	49.8%	50.2%
1952	4,519,761	2,331,034	Martin, Edward	2,168,546	Bard, Guy Kurtz	20,181	162,488 R	51.6%	48.0%	51.8%	48.2%
1950	3,548,703	1,820,400	Duff, James H.	1,694,076	Myers, Francis J.	34,227	126,324 R	51.3%	47.7%	51.8%	48.2%
1946	3,127,860	1,853,458	Martin, Edward	1,245,338	Guffey, Joseph F.	29,064	608,120 R	59.3%	39.8%	59.8%	40.2%

The 1991 election was for a short term to fill a vacancy.

388

PENNSYLVANIA

Congressional districts first established for elections held in 2002
19 members

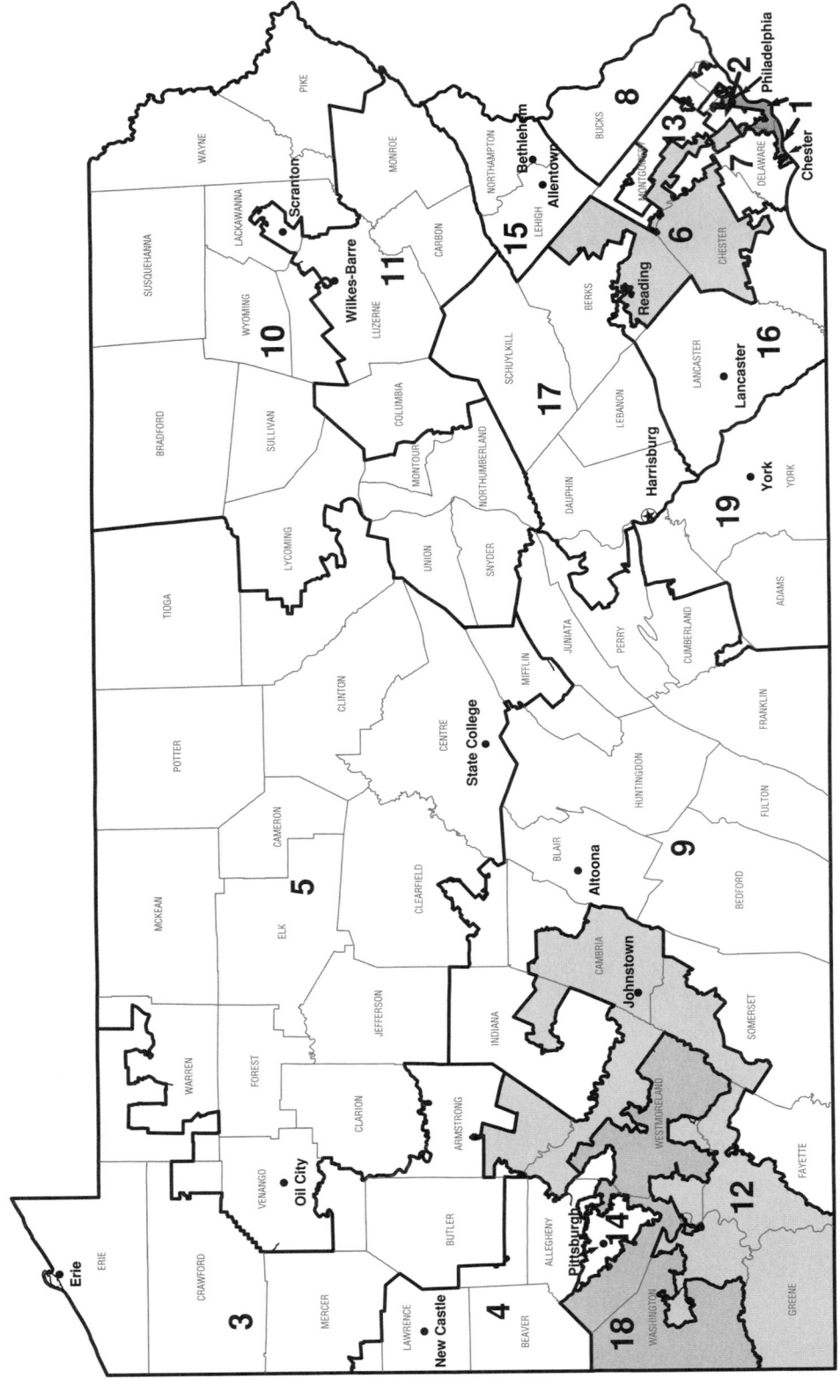

PENNSYLVANIA

Philadelphia Area

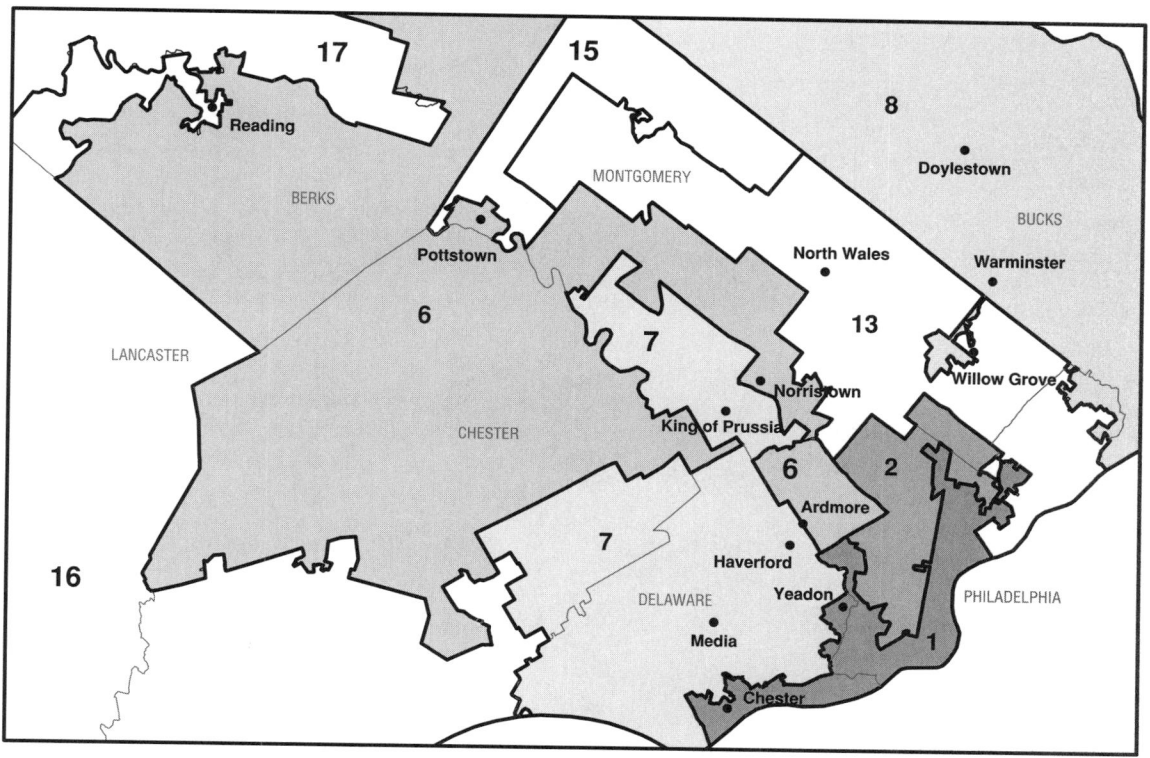

Pittsburgh Area

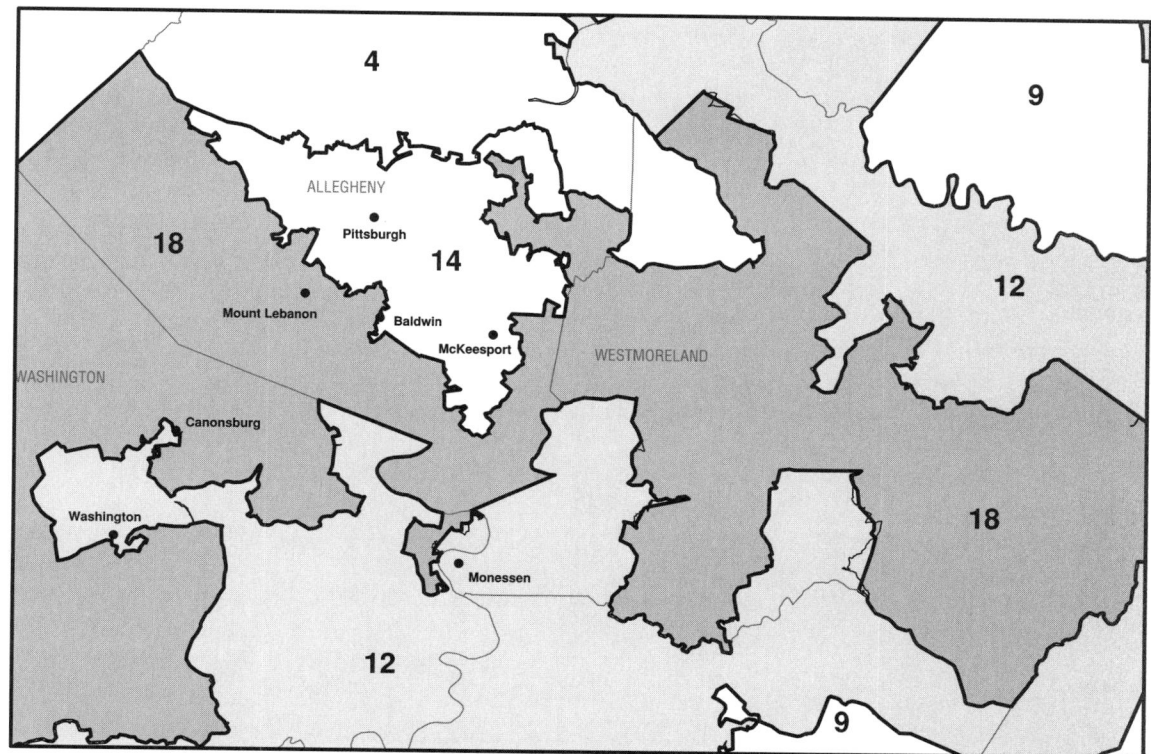

PENNSYLVANIA

GOVERNOR 2002

2000 Census Population	County	Total Vote	Republican	Democratic	Other	Rep.-Dem. Plurality	Percentage			
							Total Vote		Major Vote	
							Rep.	Dem.	Rep.	Dem.
91,292	ADAMS	24,173	15,950	7,732	491	8,218 R	66.0%	32.0%	67.4%	32.6%
1,281,666	ALLEGHENY	390,786	169,414	209,708	11,664	40,294 D	43.4%	53.7%	44.7%	55.3%
72,392	ARMSTRONG	20,364	11,898	7,965	501	3,933 R	58.4%	39.1%	59.9%	40.1%
181,412	BEAVER	52,493	23,744	27,322	1,427	3,578 R	45.2%	52.0%	46.5%	53.5%
49,984	BEDFORD	14,934	10,190	4,516	228	5,674 R	68.2%	30.2%	69.3%	30.7%
373,638	BERKS	102,528	43,790	56,592	2,146	12,802 D	42.7%	55.2%	43.6%	56.4%
129,144	BLAIR	34,529	23,530	10,356	643	13,174 R	68.1%	30.0%	69.4%	30.6%
62,761	BRADFORD	16,047	10,815	4,947	285	5,868 R	67.4%	30.8%	68.6%	31.4%
597,635	BUCKS	202,051	70,000	127,850	4,201	57,850 D	34.6%	63.3%	35.4%	64.6%
174,083	BUTLER	51,972	32,400	18,145	1,427	14,255 R	62.3%	34.9%	64.1%	35.9%
152,598	CAMBRIA	46,796	25,556	20,305	935	5,251 R	54.6%	43.4%	55.7%	44.3%
5,974	CAMERON	1,628	1,032	571	25	461 R	63.4%	35.1%	64.4%	35.6%
58,802	CARBON	15,694	6,600	8,598	496	1,998 D	42.1%	54.8%	43.4%	56.6%
135,758	CENTRE	34,899	19,027	14,557	1,315	4,470 R	54.5%	41.7%	56.7%	43.3%
433,501	CHESTER	142,814	58,669	81,996	2,149	23,327 D	41.1%	57.4%	41.7%	58.3%
41,765	CLARION	11,543	7,397	3,934	212	3,463 R	64.1%	34.1%	65.3%	34.7%
83,382	CLEARFIELD	24,544	13,822	10,221	501	3,601 R	56.3%	41.6%	57.5%	42.5%
37,914	CLINTON	9,084	4,434	4,341	309	93 R	48.8%	47.8%	50.5%	49.5%
64,151	COLUMBIA	16,718	9,304	7,004	410	2,300 R	55.7%	41.9%	57.1%	42.9%
90,366	CRAWFORD	25,615	15,551	9,155	909	6,396 R	60.7%	35.7%	62.9%	37.1%
213,674	CUMBERLAND	66,752	40,966	24,237	1,549	16,729 R	61.4%	36.3%	62.8%	37.2%
251,798	DAUPHIN	79,764	44,231	33,537	1,996	10,694 R	55.5%	42.0%	56.9%	43.1%
550,864	DELAWARE	189,070	62,649	123,117	3,304	60,468 D	33.1%	65.1%	33.7%	66.3%
35,112	ELK	9,585	5,468	3,917	200	1,551 R	57.0%	40.9%	58.3%	41.7%
280,843	ERIE	78,563	43,095	32,774	2,694	10,321 R	54.9%	41.7%	56.8%	43.2%
148,644	FAYETTE	33,736	13,878	19,082	776	5,204 D	41.1%	56.6%	42.1%	57.9%
4,946	FOREST	1,816	1,170	613	33	557 R	64.4%	33.8%	65.6%	34.4%
129,313	FRANKLIN	34,525	23,689	10,335	501	13,354 R	68.6%	29.9%	69.6%	30.4%
14,261	FULTON	3,862	2,681	1,138	43	1,543 R	69.4%	29.5%	70.2%	29.8%
40,672	GREENE	9,455	4,209	5,013	233	804 D	44.5%	53.0%	45.6%	54.4%
45,586	HUNTINGDON	11,858	7,842	3,697	319	4,145 R	66.1%	31.2%	68.0%	32.0%
89,605	INDIANA	23,986	13,462	9,897	627	3,565 R	56.1%	41.3%	57.6%	42.4%
45,932	JEFFERSON	12,923	8,745	3,879	299	4,866 R	67.7%	30.0%	69.3%	30.7%
22,821	JUNIATA	7,349	5,027	2,187	135	2,840 R	68.4%	29.8%	69.7%	30.3%
213,295	LACKAWANNA	69,061	26,099	40,206	2,756	14,107 D	37.8%	58.2%	39.4%	60.6%
470,658	LANCASTER	126,549	83,607	40,791	2,151	42,816 R	66.1%	32.2%	67.2%	32.8%
94,643	LAWRENCE	28,127	13,010	14,628	489	1,618 D	46.3%	52.0%	47.1%	52.9%
120,327	LEBANON	36,146	22,659	12,712	775	9,947 R	62.7%	35.2%	64.1%	35.9%
312,090	LEHIGH	84,896	34,738	48,150	2,008	13,412 D	40.9%	56.7%	41.9%	58.1%
319,250	LUZERNE	86,746	38,760	45,641	2,345	6,881 D	44.7%	52.6%	45.9%	54.1%
120,044	LYCOMING	31,577	20,751	9,937	889	10,814 R	65.7%	31.5%	67.6%	32.4%
45,936	MCKEAN	9,813	6,373	3,215	225	3,158 R	64.9%	32.8%	66.5%	33.5%
120,293	MERCER	31,377	16,429	14,161	787	2,268 R	52.4%	45.1%	53.7%	46.3%
46,486	MIFFLIN	10,734	7,122	3,362	250	3,760 R	66.3%	31.3%	67.9%	32.1%
138,687	MONROE	30,778	15,258	14,570	950	688 R	49.6%	47.3%	51.2%	48.8%
750,097	MONTGOMERY	260,803	81,835	175,157	3,811	93,322 D	31.4%	67.2%	31.8%	68.2%
18,236	MONTOUR	4,861	2,873	1,847	141	1,026 R	59.1%	38.0%	60.9%	39.1%
267,066	NORTHAMPTON	72,716	28,228	42,554	1,934	14,326 D	38.8%	58.5%	39.9%	60.1%
94,556	NORTHUMBERLAND	25,948	14,479	10,774	695	3,705 R	55.8%	41.5%	57.3%	42.7%
43,602	PERRY	13,038	9,286	3,426	326	5,860 R	71.2%	26.3%	73.0%	27.0%
1,517,550	PHILADELPHIA	404,025	59,223	339,697	5,105	280,474 D	14.7%	84.1%	14.8%	85.2%
46,302	PIKE	10,809	6,482	4,049	278	2,433 R	60.0%	37.5%	61.6%	38.4%
18,080	POTTER	4,905	3,471	1,357	77	2,114 R	70.8%	27.7%	71.9%	28.1%
150,336	SCHUYLKILL	49,025	22,692	25,233	1,100	2,541 D	46.3%	51.5%	47.3%	52.7%
37,546	SNYDER	9,419	6,623	2,599	197	4,024 R	70.3%	27.6%	71.8%	28.2%
80,023	SOMERSET	24,778	16,244	8,088	446	8,156 R	65.6%	32.6%	66.8%	33.2%
6,556	SULLIVAN	2,360	1,441	856	63	585 R	61.1%	36.3%	62.7%	37.3%
42,238	SUSQUEHANNA	12,724	8,175	4,244	305	3,931 R	64.2%	33.4%	65.8%	34.2%
41,373	TIOGA	11,134	7,696	3,275	163	4,421 R	69.1%	29.4%	70.1%	29.9%
41,624	UNION	9,476	6,058	3,153	265	2,905 R	63.9%	33.3%	65.8%	34.2%

PENNSYLVANIA

GOVERNOR 2002

2000 Census Population	County	Total Vote	Republican	Democratic	Other	Rep.-Dem. Plurality	Percentage			
							Total Vote		Major Vote	
							Rep.	Dem.	Rep.	Dem.
57,565	VENANGO	15,191	9,188	5,551	452	3,637 R	60.5%	36.5%	62.3%	37.7%
43,863	WARREN	11,924	6,823	4,823	278	2,000 R	57.2%	40.4%	58.6%	41.4%
202,897	WASHINGTON	59,938	28,368	30,368	1,202	2,000 D	47.3%	50.7%	48.3%	51.7%
47,722	WAYNE	12,976	8,118	4,395	463	3,723 R	62.6%	33.9%	64.9%	35.1%
369,993	WESTMORELAND	109,437	58,018	48,992	2,427	9,026 R	53.0%	44.8%	54.2%	45.8%
28,080	WYOMING	8,321	5,152	2,938	231	2,214 R	61.9%	35.3%	63.7%	36.3%
381,751	YORK	99,921	63,894	33,248	2,779	30,646 R	63.9%	33.3%	65.8%	34.2%
12,281,054	TOTAL	3,583,179	1,589,408	1,913,235	80,536	323,827 D	44.4%	53.4%	45.4%	54.6%

Note: The statewide totals for "Total Vote" and "Other" include 1,190 scattered write-in votes that were not included in the county-by-county results.

PENNSYLVANIA

HOUSE OF REPRESENTATIVES

CD	Year	Total Vote	Republican Vote	Candidate	Democratic Vote	Candidate	Other Vote	Rep.-Dem. Plurality	Percentage			
									Total Vote		Major Vote	
									Rep.	Dem.	Rep.	Dem.
1	2002	140,090	17,444	Delaney, Marie G.	121,076	Brady, Robert A.*	1,570	103,632 D	12.5%	86.4%	12.6%	87.4%
2	2002	171,611	20,988	Dougherty, Thomas G.	150,623	Fattah, Chaka*		129,635 D	12.2%	87.8%	12.2%	87.8%
3	2002	150,329	116,763	English, Phil*			33,566	116,763 R	77.7%		100.0%	
4	2002	202,218	130,534	Hart, Melissa A.*	71,674	Drobac, Stevan Jr.	10	58,860 R	64.6%	35.4%	64.6%	35.4%
5	2002	143,211	124,942	Peterson, John E.*			18,269	124,942 R	87.2%		100.0%	
6	2002	201,791	103,648	Gerlach, Jim	98,128	Wofford, Dan	15	5,520 R	51.4%	48.6%	51.4%	48.6%
7	2002	221,351	146,296	Weldon, Curt*	75,055	Lennon, Peter A.		71,241 R	66.1%	33.9%	66.1%	33.9%
8	2002	203,687	127,475	Greenwood, James C.*	76,178	Reece, Timothy T.	34	51,297 R	62.6%	37.4%	62.6%	37.4%
9	2002	174,849	124,184	Shuster, Bill*	50,558	Henry, John R.	107	73,626 R	71.0%	28.9%	71.1%	28.9%
10	2002	164,159	152,017	#Sherwood, Don*			12,142	152,017 R	92.6%		100.0%	
11	2002	168,615	71,543	Barletta, Louis J.	93,758	Kanjorksi, Paul E.*	3,314	22,215 D	42.4%	55.6%	43.3%	56.7%
12	2002	169,028	44,818	Choby, Bill	124,201	Murtha, John P.*	9	79,383 D	26.5%	73.5%	26.5%	73.5%
13	2002	211,867	100,295	Brown, Melissa	107,945	Hoeffel, Joseph M.*	3,627	7,650 D	47.3%	50.9%	48.2%	51.8%
14	2002	123,412			123,323	Doyle, Mike*	89	123,323 D		99.9%		100.0%
15	2002	171,713	98,493	Toomey, Patrick J.*	73,212	O'Brien, Edward J.	8	25,281 R	57.4%	42.6%	57.4%	42.6%
16	2002	134,597	119,046	Pitts, Joe*			15,551	119,046 R	88.4%		100.0%	
17	2002	201,291	97,802	Gekas, George W.*	103,483	Holden, Tim*	6	5,681 D	48.6%	51.4%	48.6%	51.4%
18	2002	199,349	119,885	Murphy, Tim	79,451	Machek, Jack	13	40,434 R	60.1%	39.9%	60.1%	39.9%
19	2002	157,145	143,097	Platts, Todd R.*			14,048	143,097 R	91.1%		100.0%	
Total	2002	3,310,313	1,859,270		1,348,665		102,378	510,605 R	56.2%	40.7%	58.0%	42.0%

A pound sign (#) indicates that the candidate had the endorsement of more than one party.

An asterisk (*) denotes incumbent.

PENNSYLVANIA
GENERAL AND PRIMARY ELECTIONS

2002 GENERAL ELECTIONS

Governor	Other vote was 40,923 Libertarian (Ken V. Krawchuk); 38,423 Green (Michael Morrill); 1,190 write-in.
House	Other vote was:

CD 1	1,570 Green (Mike Ewall).
CD 2	
CD 3	33,554 Green (AnnDrea M. Benson); 12 write-in.
CD 4	10 write-in.
CD 5	18,078 Libertarian (Thomas A. Martin); 191 write-in.
CD 6	15 write-in.
CD 7	
CD 8	34 write-in.
CD 9	107 write-in.
CD 10	11,613 Green (Kurt J. Shotko); 529 write-in.
CD 11	3,304 Reform (Thomas J. McLaughlin); 10 write-in.
CD 12	9 write-in.
CD 13	3,627 Constitution (John P. McDermott).
CD 14	89 write-in.
CD 15	8 write-in.
CD 16	8,720 Green (Will Todd); 6,766 Constitution (Kenneth Brenneman); 65 write-in.
CD 17	6 write-in.
CD 18	13 write-in.
CD 19	7,900 Green (Ben Price); 6,008 Libertarian (Michael Mickey Paoletta); 140 write-in.

2002 PRIMARY ELECTIONS

Primary	May 21, 2002	**Registration** (as of May 21, 2002)	Republican	3,219,730
			Democratic	3,759,201
			Green	4,611
			Other	813,850
			TOTAL	7,797,392

Primary Type   Closed—Only registered Democrats and Republicans could vote in their party's primary.

Note: An asterisk (*) denotes incumbent.

	REPUBLICAN PRIMARIES			DEMOCRATIC PRIMARIES		
Governor	Mike Fisher	538,757	99.1%	Edward G. Rendell	702,442	56.5%
	Bob Casey Jr. (write-in)	2,903	0.5%	Bob Casey Jr.	539,794	43.4%
	Write-in	2,081	0.4%	Write-in	404	
	TOTAL	543,741		TOTAL	1,242,640	
Congressional District 1	Marie G. Delaney	7,208	100.0%	Robert A. Brady*	75,798	100.0%
Congressional District 2	Thomas G. Dougherty	5,545	100.0%	Chaka Fattah*	108,589	100.0%
Congressional District 3	Phil English*	29,803	100.0%	*No Democratic candidate filed for the primary. There were 74 write-in votes.*		
	Write-in	10				
	TOTAL	29,813				
Congressional District 4	Melissa A. Hart*	26,467	99.7%	Stevan Drobac Jr.	30,413	54.2%
	Write-in	87	0.3%	Mark A. Purcell	25,634	45.7%
				Write-in	88	0.2%
	TOTAL	26,554		TOTAL	56,135	

PENNSYLVANIA

GENERAL AND PRIMARY ELECTIONS

REPUBLICAN PRIMARIES				DEMOCRATIC PRIMARIES		
Congressional District 5	John E. Peterson* Write-in TOTAL	36,659 8 36,667	100.0%	*No Democratic candidate filed for the primary. There were 189 write-in votes.*		
Congressional District 6	Jim Gerlach Write-in TOTAL	27,821 13 27,834	100.0%	Dan Wofford Frank Thomas Write-in TOTAL	30,710 18,412 7 49,129	62.5% 37.5%
Congressional District 7	Curt Weldon*	46,046	100.0%	Peter A. Lennon	27,503	100.0%
Congressional District 8	James C. Greenwood* Tom Lingenfelter Write-in TOTAL	31,327 13,981 1 45,309	69.1% 30.9%	*No Democratic candidate filed for the primary. Timothy T. Reece received 2,275 of the 2,374 write-in votes cast and qualified for the general election ballot.*		
Congressional District 9	Bill Shuster* David S. Keller David E. Bahr Write-in TOTAL	33,538 6,319 5,457 53 45,367	73.9% 13.9% 12.0% 0.1%	John R. Henry Write-in TOTAL	29,604 372 29,976	98.8% 1.2%
Congressional District 10	Don Sherwood* Write-in TOTAL	30,622 16 30,638	99.9% 0.1%	*No Democratic candidate filed for the primary. Republican Donald L. Sherwood received 1,000 of the 1,049 write-in votes cast.*		
Congressional District 11	Louis J. Barletta Write-in TOTAL	15,311 47 15,358	99.7% 0.3%	Paul E. Kanjorski* Write-in TOTAL	51,027 29 51,056	99.9% 0.1%
Congressional District 12	Bill Choby Write-in TOTAL	16,851 178 17,029	99.0% 1.0%	John P. Murtha* Frank R. Mascara* Write-in TOTAL	60,687 33,837 8 94,532	64.2% 35.8%
Congressional District 13	Melissa Brown Al Taubenberger TOTAL	19,917 16,184 36,101	55.2% 44.8%	Joseph M. Hoeffel*	62,793	100.0%
Congressional District 14	*No Republican candidate filed for the primary. There were 565 write-in votes.*			Mike Doyle* Write-in TOTAL	72,886 24 72,910	100.0%
Congressional District 15	Patrick J. Toomey* Write-in TOTAL	23,602 3 23,605	100.0%	Edward J. O'Brien Write-in TOTAL	32,671 9 32,680	100.0%
Congressional District 16	Joe Pitts* Write-in TOTAL	35,759 2 35,761	100.0%	*No Democratic candidate filed for the primary. There were 86 write-in votes.*		
Congressional District 17	George W. Gekas* Write-in TOTAL	39,734 19 39,753	100.0%	Tim Holden* Write-in TOTAL	35,940 10 35,950	100.0%
Congressional District 18	Tim Murphy Write-in TOTAL	24,324 10 24,334	100.0%	Jack Machek Larry Maggi Bob Domske Write-in TOTAL	28,565 23,392 8,756 33 60,746	47.0% 38.5% 14.4% 0.1%
Congressional District 19	Todd R. Platts* Tom Glennon Lester B. Searer Mike Johnson Write-in TOTAL	34,026 7,150 1,921 1,332 232 44,661	76.2% 16.0% 4.3% 3.0% 0.5%	*No Democratic candidate filed for the primary. There were 550 write-in votes.*		

PENNSYLVANIA DEMOCRATIC PRIMARY

GOVERNOR 2002

2000 Census Population	County	Total Vote	Rendell	Casey	Other	Winner	Percentage of Total Vote	
							Rendell	Casey
91,292	ADAMS	4,009	1,621	2,388		Casey	40.4%	59.6%
1,281,666	ALLEGHENY	174,839	80,120	94,719		Casey	45.8%	54.2%
72,392	ARMSTRONG	6,183	2,102	4,081		Casey	34.0%	66.0%
181,412	BEAVER	23,834	9,428	14,406		Casey	39.6%	60.4%
49,984	BEDFORD	3,008	863	2,145		Casey	28.7%	71.3%
373,638	BERKS	29,532	19,024	10,508		Rendell	64.4%	35.6%
129,144	BLAIR	7,008	2,806	4,202		Casey	40.0%	60.0%
62,761	BRADFORD	1,828	397	1,431		Casey	21.7%	78.3%
597,635	BUCKS	54,699	44,715	9,984		Rendell	81.7%	18.3%
174,083	BUTLER	11,132	4,311	6,821		Casey	38.7%	61.3%
152,598	CAMBRIA	26,550	8,705	17,845		Casey	32.8%	67.2%
5,974	CAMERON	575	176	399		Casey	30.6%	69.4%
58,802	CARBON	5,628	2,232	3,396		Casey	39.7%	60.3%
135,758	CENTRE	7,568	3,971	3,597		Rendell	52.5%	47.5%
433,501	CHESTER	27,308	22,564	4,744		Rendell	82.6%	17.4%
41,765	CLARION	3,090	1,085	2,005		Casey	35.1%	64.9%
83,382	CLEARFIELD	7,022	2,041	4,981		Casey	29.1%	70.9%
37,914	CLINTON	2,529	1,119	1,410		Casey	44.2%	55.8%
64,151	COLUMBIA	4,623	1,764	2,859		Casey	38.2%	61.8%
90,366	CRAWFORD	5,133	1,613	3,520		Casey	31.4%	68.6%
213,674	CUMBERLAND	12,172	5,502	6,670		Casey	45.2%	54.8%
251,798	DAUPHIN	18,592	7,279	11,313		Casey	39.2%	60.8%
550,864	DELAWARE	44,132	38,050	6,082		Rendell	86.2%	13.8%
35,112	ELK	3,546	953	2,593		Casey	26.9%	73.1%
280,843	ERIE	26,288	8,979	17,309		Casey	34.2%	65.8%
148,644	FAYETTE	20,724	5,404	15,320		Casey	26.1%	73.9%
4,946	FOREST	435	150	285		Casey	34.5%	65.5%
129,313	FRANKLIN	4,260	1,234	3,026		Casey	29.0%	71.0%
14,261	FULTON	679	147	532		Casey	21.6%	78.4%
40,672	GREENE	5,728	1,779	3,949		Casey	31.1%	68.9%
45,586	HUNTINGDON	2,378	896	1,482		Casey	37.7%	62.3%
89,605	INDIANA	7,012	2,116	4,896		Casey	30.2%	69.8%
45,932	JEFFERSON	2,970	725	2,245		Casey	24.4%	75.6%
22,821	JUNIATA	1,815	501	1,314		Casey	27.6%	72.4%
213,295	LACKAWANNA	38,654	6,085	32,569		Casey	15.7%	84.3%
470,658	LANCASTER	15,027	8,976	6,051		Rendell	59.7%	40.3%
94,643	LAWRENCE	9,220	3,378	5,842		Casey	36.6%	63.4%
120,327	LEBANON	5,341	2,233	3,108		Casey	41.8%	58.2%
312,090	LEHIGH	25,440	17,448	7,992		Rendell	68.6%	31.4%
319,250	LUZERNE	39,212	11,779	27,433		Casey	30.0%	70.0%
120,044	LYCOMING	5,847	1,760	4,087		Casey	30.1%	69.9%
45,936	MCKEAN	1,617	377	1,240		Casey	23.3%	76.7%
120,293	MERCER	8,957	3,139	5,818		Casey	35.0%	65.0%
46,486	MIFFLIN	2,350	829	1,521		Casey	35.3%	64.7%
138,687	MONROE	6,421	2,807	3,614		Casey	43.7%	56.3%
750,097	MONTGOMERY	75,472	66,712	8,760		Rendell	88.4%	11.6%
18,236	MONTOUR	1,168	304	864		Casey	26.0%	74.0%
267,066	NORTHAMPTON	22,542	14,668	7,874		Rendell	65.1%	34.9%
94,556	NORTHUMBERLAND	7,720	2,230	5,490		Casey	28.9%	71.1%
43,602	PERRY	2,391	760	1,631		Casey	31.8%	68.2%
1,517,550	PHILADELPHIA	286,100	224,635	61,465		Rendell	78.5%	21.5%
46,302	PIKE	1,082	373	709		Casey	34.5%	65.5%
18,080	POTTER	828	164	664		Casey	19.8%	80.2%
150,336	SCHUYLKILL	12,299	4,579	7,720		Casey	37.2%	62.8%
37,546	SNYDER	1,327	388	939		Casey	29.2%	70.8%

PENNSYLVANIA DEMOCRATIC PRIMARY

GOVERNOR 2002

2000 Census Population	County	Total Vote	Rendell	Casey	Other	Winner	Percentage of Total Vote	
							Rendell	Casey
80,023	SOMERSET	8,083	2,455	5,628		Casey	30.4%	69.6%
6,556	SULLIVAN	652	193	459		Casey	29.6%	70.4%
42,238	SUSQUEHANNA	2,192	428	1,764		Casey	19.5%	80.5%
41,373	TIOGA	1,315	261	1,054		Casey	19.8%	80.2%
41,624	UNION	1,440	600	840		Casey	41.7%	58.3%
57,565	VENANGO	3,061	945	2,116		Casey	30.9%	69.1%
43,863	WARREN	2,423	638	1,785		Casey	26.3%	73.7%
202,897	WASHINGTON	28,436	11,552	16,884		Casey	40.6%	59.4%
47,722	WAYNE	2,128	489	1,639		Casey	23.0%	77.0%
369,993	WESTMORELAND	46,375	19,008	27,367		Casey	41.0%	59.0%
28,080	WYOMING	1,611	452	1,159		Casey	28.1%	71.9%
381,751	YORK	18,676	7,425	11,251		Casey	39.8%	60.2%
12,281,054	TOTAL	1,242,640	702,442	539,794	404	Rendell	56.5%	43.4%

Note: The statewide total for "Total Vote" and "Other" includes 404 scattered write-in votes that were not included in the county-by-county results.

RHODE ISLAND

GOVERNOR
Donald L. Carcieri (R). Elected 2002 to a four-year term.

SENATORS (1 Democrat, 1 Republican)
Lincoln Chafee (R). Elected 2000 to a six-year term. Previously appointed to complete the term of his late father, John Chafee, beginning Nov. 4, 1999.

Jack Reed (D). Reelected 2002 to a six-year term. Previously elected 1996.

REPRESENTATIVES (2 Democrats)
1. Patrick J. Kennedy (D) 2. Jim Langevin (D)

POSTWAR VOTE FOR PRESIDENT

| | | Republican | | Democratic | | Other | | Percentage | | | |
| | Total | | | | | | | Total Vote | | Major Vote | |
Year	Vote	Vote	Candidate	Vote	Candidate	Vote	Plurality	Rep.	Dem.	Rep.	Dem.
2000**	409,047	130,555	Bush, George W.	249,508	Gore, Al	28,984	118,953 D	31.9%	61.0%	34.4%	65.6%
1996**	390,284	104,683	Dole, Bob	233,050	Clinton, Bill	52,551	128,367 D	26.8%	59.7%	31.0%	69.0%
1992**	453,477	131,601	Bush, George	213,299	Clinton, Bill	108,577	81,698 D	29.0%	47.0%	38.2%	61.8%
1988	404,620	177,761	Bush, George	225,123	Dukakis, Michael S.	1,736	47,362 D	43.9%	55.6%	44.1%	55.9%
1984	410,492	212,080	Reagan, Ronald	197,106	Mondale, Walter F.	1,306	14,974 R	51.7%	48.0%	51.8%	48.2%
1980**	416,072	154,793	Reagan, Ronald	198,342	Carter, Jimmy	62,937	43,549 D	37.2%	47.7%	43.8%	56.2%
1976	411,170	181,249	Ford, Gerald R.	227,636	Carter, Jimmy	2,285	46,387 D	44.1%	55.4%	44.3%	55.7%
1972	415,808	220,383	Nixon, Richard M.	194,645	McGovern, George S.	780	25,738 R	53.0%	46.8%	53.1%	46.9%
1968	385,000	122,359	Nixon, Richard M.	246,518	Humphrey, Hubert H.	16,123	124,159 D	31.8%	64.0%	33.2%	66.8%
1964	390,091	74,615	Goldwater, Barry M.	315,463	Johnson, Lyndon B.	13	240,848 D	19.1%	80.9%	19.1%	80.9%
1960	405,535	147,502	Nixon, Richard M.	258,032	Kennedy, John F.	1	110,530 D	36.4%	63.6%	36.4%	63.6%
1956	387,609	225,819	Eisenhower, Dwight D.	161,790	Stevenson, Adlai E.		64,029 R	58.3%	41.7%	58.3%	41.7%
1952	414,498	210,935	Eisenhower, Dwight D.	203,293	Stevenson, Adlai E.	270	7,642 R	50.9%	49.0%	50.9%	49.1%
1948	327,702	135,787	Dewey, Thomas E.	188,736	Truman, Harry S.	3,179	52,949 D	41.4%	57.6%	41.8%	58.2%

In 2000 the other vote column includes 25,052 votes cast for Green (Nader). In 1996 the other vote column includes 43,723 votes cast for Perot. In 1992 the other vote column includes 105,045 votes cast for Perot. In 1980 the other vote column includes 59,819 votes for Independent (Anderson).

RHODE ISLAND

POSTWAR VOTE FOR GOVERNOR

Year	Total Vote	Republican Vote	Candidate	Democratic Vote	Candidate	Other Vote	Rep.-Dem. Plurality	Total Vote Rep.	Total Vote Dem.	Major Vote Rep.	Major Vote Dem.
2002	332,655	181,827	Carcieri, Donald L.	150,229	York, Myrth	599	31,598 R	54.7%	45.2%	54.8%	45.2%
1998	306,445	156,180	Almond, Lincoln C.	129,105	York, Myrth	21,160	27,075 R	51.0%	42.1%	54.7%	45.3%
1994**	361,377	171,194	Almond, Lincoln C.	157,361	York, Myrth	32,822	13,833 R	47.4%	43.5%	52.1%	47.9%
1992	425,026	145,590	Leonard, Elizabeth Ann	261,484	Sundlun, Bruce G.	17,952	115,894 D	34.3%	61.5%	35.8%	64.2%
1990	356,672	92,177	DiPrete, Edward	264,411	Sundlun, Bruce G.	84	172,234 D	25.8%	74.1%	25.8%	74.2%
1988	400,516	203,550	DiPrete, Edward	196,936	Sundlun, Bruce G.	30	6,614 R	50.8%	49.2%	50.8%	49.2%
1986	322,724	208,822	DiPrete, Edward	104,508	Sundlun, Bruce G.	9,394	104,314 R	64.7%	32.4%	66.6%	33.4%
1984	408,375	245,059	DiPrete, Edward	163,311	Solomon, Anthony J.	5	81,748 R	60.0%	40.0%	60.0%	40.0%
1982	337,259	79,602	Marzullo, Vincent	247,208	Garrahy, J. Joseph	10,449	167,606 D	23.6%	73.3%	24.4%	75.6%
1980	405,916	106,729	Cianci, Vincent A.	299,174	Garrahy, J. Joseph	13	192,445 D	26.3%	73.7%	26.3%	73.7%
1978	314,363	96,596	Almond, Lincoln	197,386	Garrahy, J. Joseph	20,381	100,790 D	30.7%	62.8%	32.9%	67.1%
1976	398,683	178,254	Taft, James L.	218,561	Garrahy, J. Joseph	1,868	40,307 D	44.7%	54.8%	44.9%	55.1%
1974	321,660	69,224	Nugent, James W.	252,436	Noel, Philip W.		183,212 D	21.5%	78.5%	21.5%	78.5%
1972	412,866	194,315	DeSimone, Herbert F.	216,953	Noel, Philip W.	1,598	22,638 D	47.1%	52.5%	47.2%	52.8%
1970	346,342	171,549	DeSimone, Herbert F.	173,420	Licht, Frank	1,373	1,871 D	49.5%	50.1%	49.7%	50.3%
1968	383,725	187,958	Chafee, John H.	195,766	Licht, Frank	1	7,808 D	49.0%	51.0%	49.0%	51.0%
1966	332,064	210,202	Chafee, John H.	121,862	Hobbs, Horace E.		88,340 R	63.3%	36.7%	63.3%	36.7%
1964	391,668	239,501	Chafee, John H.	152,165	Gallogly, Edward P.	2	87,336 R	61.1%	38.9%	61.1%	38.9%
1962	327,506	163,952	Chafee, John H.	163,554	Notte, John A.		398 R	50.1%	49.9%	50.1%	49.9%
1960	401,362	174,044	Del Sesto, Christopher	227,318	Notte, John A.		53,274 D	43.4%	56.6%	43.4%	56.6%
1958	346,780	176,505	Del Sesto, Christopher	170,275	Roberts, Dennis J.		6,230 R	50.9%	49.1%	50.9%	49.1%
1956	383,919	191,604	Del Sesto, Christopher	192,315	Roberts, Dennis J.		711 D	49.9%	50.1%	49.9%	50.1%
1954	328,670	137,131	Lewis, Dean J.	189,595	Roberts, Dennis J.	1,944	52,464 D	41.7%	57.7%	42.0%	58.0%
1952	409,689	194,102	Archambault, Raoul	215,587	Roberts, Dennis J.		21,485 D	47.4%	52.6%	47.4%	52.6%
1950	296,809	120,684	Lachapelle, E. T.	176,125	Roberts, Dennis J.		55,441 D	40.7%	59.3%	40.7%	59.3%
1948	323,863	124,441	Ruerat, Albert P.	198,056	Pastore, John O.	1,366	73,615 D	38.4%	61.2%	38.6%	61.4%
1946	275,341	126,456	Murphy, John G.	148,885	Pastore, John O.		22,429 D	45.9%	54.1%	45.9%	54.1%

The term of office of Rhode Island's Governor was increased to four from two years effective with the 1994 election.

POSTWAR VOTE FOR SENATOR

Year	Total Vote	Republican Vote	Candidate	Democratic Vote	Candidate	Other Vote	Rep.-Dem. Plurality	Total Vote Rep.	Total Vote Dem.	Major Vote Rep.	Major Vote Dem.
2002	323,912	69,881	Tingle, Robert G.	253,922	Reed, Jack	109	184,041 D	21.6%	78.4%	21.6%	78.4%
2000	391,537	222,588	Chafee, Lincoln	161,023	Weygand, Bob	7,926	61,565 R	56.8%	41.1%	58.0%	42.0%
1996	363,378	127,368	Mayer, Nancy	230,676	Reed, Jack	5,334	103,308 D	35.1%	63.5%	35.6%	64.4%
1994	345,388	222,856	Chafee, John H.	122,532	Kushner, Linda J.		100,324 R	64.5%	35.5%	64.5%	35.5%
1990	364,062	138,947	Schneider, Claudine	225,105	Pell, Claiborne	10	86,158 D	38.2%	61.8%	38.2%	61.8%
1988	397,996	217,273	Chafee, John H.	180,717	Licht, Richard A.	6	36,556 R	54.6%	45.4%	54.6%	45.4%
1984	395,285	108,492	Leonard, Barbara	286,780	Pell, Claiborne	13	178,288 D	27.4%	72.6%	27.4%	72.6%
1982	342,779	175,495	Chafee, John H.	167,283	Michaelson, Julius C.	1	8,212 R	51.2%	48.8%	51.2%	48.8%
1978	305,618	76,061	Reynolds, James G.	229,557	Pell, Claiborne		153,496 D	24.9%	75.1%	24.9%	75.1%
1976	398,906	230,329	Chafee, John H.	167,665	Lorber, Richard P.	912	62,664 R	57.7%	42.0%	57.9%	42.1%
1972	413,432	188,990	Chafee, John H.	221,942	Pell, Claiborne	2,500	32,952 D	45.7%	53.7%	46.0%	54.0%
1970	341,222	107,351	McLaughlin, John	230,469	Pastore, John O.	3,402	123,118 D	31.5%	67.5%	31.8%	68.2%
1966	324,173	104,838	Briggs, Ruth M.	219,331	Pell, Claiborne	4	114,493 D	32.3%	67.7%	32.3%	67.7%
1964	386,322	66,715	Lagueux, Ronald R.	319,607	Pastore, John O.		252,892 D	17.3%	82.7%	17.3%	82.7%
1960	399,983	124,408	Archambault, Raoul	275,575	Pell, Claiborne		151,167 D	31.1%	68.9%	31.1%	68.9%
1958	344,519	122,353	Ewing, Bayard	222,166	Pastore, John O.		99,813 D	35.5%	64.5%	35.5%	64.5%
1954	326,624	132,970	Sundlun, Walter I.	193,654	Green, Theodore F.		60,684 D	40.7%	59.3%	40.7%	59.3%
1952	410,978	185,850	Ewing, Bayard	225,128	Pastore, John O.		39,278 D	45.2%	54.8%	45.2%	54.8%
1950S	297,909	114,184	Levy, Austin T.	183,725	Pastore, John O.		69,541 D	38.3%	61.7%	38.3%	61.7%
1948	320,420	130,262	Hazard, Thomas P.	190,158	Green, Theodore F.		59,896 D	40.7%	59.3%	40.7%	59.3%
1946	273,528	122,780	Dyer, W. Gurnee	150,748	McGrath, J. Howard		27,968 D	44.9%	55.1%	44.9%	55.1%

The 1950 election was for a short term to fill a vacancy.

RHODE ISLAND

Congressional districts first established for elections held in 2002
2 members

PROVIDENCE

1

Pawtucket •

Providence

Cranston
•

BRISTOL

Warwick
•

KENT

Bristol
•

2

NEWPORT

1

WASHINGTON

Newport
•

Kingston
•

Westerly
•

New Shoreham
•
2

RHODE ISLAND

GOVERNOR 2002

2000 Census Population	County	Total Vote	Republican	Democratic	Other	Rep.-Dem. Plurality	Percentage			
							Total Vote		Major Vote	
							Rep.	Dem.	Rep.	Dem.
50,648	BRISTOL	18,262	10,707	7,555		3,152 R	58.6%	41.4%	58.6%	41.4%
167,090	KENT	60,609	36,470	24,139		12,331 R	60.2%	39.8%	60.2%	39.8%
85,433	NEWPORT	29,416	17,008	12,408		4,600 R	57.8%	42.2%	57.8%	42.2%
621,602	PROVIDENCE	177,515	89,697	87,818		1,879 R	50.5%	49.5%	50.5%	49.5%
123,546	WASHINGTON	46,254	27,945	18,309		9,636 R	60.4%	39.6%	60.4%	39.6%
1,048,319	TOTAL	332,655	181,827	150,229	599	31,598 R	54.7%	45.2%	54.8%	45.2%

Note: The statewide totals for "Total Vote" and "Other" include 599 scattered write-in votes that are not included in the county-by-county returns.

2000 Census Population	City/Town	Total Vote	Republican	Democratic	Other	Rep.-Dem. Plurality	Rep.	Dem.	Rep.	Dem.
16,819	BARRINGTON	7,432	4,817	2,615		2,202 R	64.8%	35.2%	64.8%	35.2%
22,469	BRISTOL TOWN	7,241	3,961	3,280		681 R	54.7%	45.3%	54.7%	45.3%
15,796	BURRILLVILLE	4,570	2,510	2,060		450 R	54.9%	45.1%	54.9%	45.1%
18,928	CENTRAL FALLS	2,431	771	1,660		889 D	31.7%	68.3%	31.7%	68.3%
7,859	CHARLESTOWN	3,128	1,781	1,347		434 R	56.9%	43.1%	56.9%	43.1%
33,668	COVENTRY	11,809	6,811	4,998		1,813 R	57.7%	42.3%	57.7%	42.3%
79,269	CRANSTON	28,887	16,959	11,928		5,031 R	58.7%	41.3%	58.7%	41.3%
31,840	CUMBERLAND	11,584	6,867	4,717		2,150 R	59.3%	40.7%	59.3%	40.7%
12,948	EAST GREENWICH	5,797	4,582	1,215		3,367 R	79.0%	21.0%	79.0%	21.0%
48,688	EAST PROVIDENCE	15,591	7,230	8,361		1,131 D	46.4%	53.6%	46.4%	53.6%
6,045	EXETER	2,277	1,438	839		599 R	63.2%	36.8%	63.2%	36.8%
4,274	FOSTER	1,779	1,087	692		395 R	61.1%	38.9%	61.1%	38.9%
9,948	GLOCESTER	3,498	2,128	1,370		758 R	60.8%	39.2%	60.8%	39.2%
7,836	HOPKINTON	2,359	1,325	1,034		291 R	56.2%	43.8%	56.2%	43.8%
5,622	JAMESTOWN	2,829	1,675	1,154		521 R	59.2%	40.8%	59.2%	40.8%
28,195	JOHNSTON	10,574	5,931	4,643		1,288 R	56.1%	43.9%	56.1%	43.9%
20,898	LINCOLN	8,887	5,746	3,141		2,605 R	64.7%	35.3%	64.7%	35.3%
3,593	LITTLE COMPTON	1,769	1,099	670		429 R	62.1%	37.9%	62.1%	37.9%
17,334	MIDDLETOWN	5,390	3,170	2,220		950 R	58.8%	41.2%	58.8%	41.2%
16,361	NARRAGANSETT	6,698	4,184	2,514		1,670 R	62.5%	37.5%	62.5%	37.5%
26,475	NEWPORT CITY	6,960	3,757	3,203		554 R	54.0%	46.0%	54.0%	46.0%
1,010	NEW SHOREHAM	949	479	470		9 R	50.5%	49.5%	50.5%	49.5%
26,326	NORTH KINGSTOWN	11,066	7,546	3,520		4,026 R	68.2%	31.8%	68.2%	31.8%
32,411	NORTH PROVIDENCE	12,231	6,520	5,711		809 R	53.3%	46.7%	53.3%	46.7%
10,618	NORTH SMITHFIELD	4,491	2,678	1,813		865 R	59.6%	40.4%	59.6%	40.4%
72,958	PAWTUCKET	16,152	7,025	9,127		2,102 D	43.5%	56.5%	43.5%	56.5%
17,149	PORTSMOUTH	7,317	4,592	2,725		1,867 R	62.8%	37.2%	62.8%	37.2%
173,618	PROVIDENCE CITY	35,913	12,019	23,894		11,875 D	33.5%	66.5%	33.5%	66.5%
7,222	RICHMOND	2,431	1,355	1,076		279 R	55.7%	44.3%	55.7%	44.3%
10,324	SCITUATE	4,492	3,087	1,405		1,682 R	68.7%	31.3%	68.7%	31.3%
20,613	SMITHFIELD	7,573	4,666	2,907		1,759 R	61.6%	38.4%	61.6%	38.4%
27,921	SOUTH KINGSTOWN	9,730	5,511	4,219		1,292 R	56.6%	43.4%	56.6%	43.4%
15,260	TIVERTON	5,151	2,715	2,436		279 R	52.7%	47.3%	52.7%	47.3%
11,360	WARREN	3,589	1,929	1,660		269 R	53.7%	46.3%	53.7%	46.3%
85,808	WARWICK	32,261	19,023	13,238		5,785 R	59.0%	41.0%	59.0%	41.0%
22,966	WESTERLY	7,616	4,326	3,290		1,036 R	56.8%	43.2%	56.8%	43.2%
5,085	WEST GREENWICH	1,996	1,314	682		632 R	65.8%	34.2%	65.8%	34.2%
29,581	WEST WARWICK	8,746	4,740	4,006		734 R	54.2%	45.8%	54.2%	45.8%
43,224	WOONSOCKET	8,862	4,473	4,389		84 R	50.5%	49.5%	50.5%	49.5%
1,048,319	TOTAL	332,655	181,827	150,229	599	31,598 R	54.7%	45.2%	54.8%	45.2%

Note: The statewide totals for "Total Vote" and "Other" include 599 scattered write-in votes that are not included in the city/town returns.

RHODE ISLAND

SENATOR 2002

2000 Census Population	County	Total Vote	Republican	Democratic	Other	Rep.-Dem. Plurality	Percentage			
							Total Vote		Major Vote	
							Rep.	Dem.	Rep.	Dem.
50,648	BRISTOL	17,797	4,308	13,489		9,181 D	24.2%	75.8%	24.2%	75.8%
167,090	KENT	59,590	14,209	45,381		31,172 D	23.8%	76.2%	23.8%	76.2%
85,433	NEWPORT	28,780	7,435	21,345		13,910 D	25.8%	74.2%	25.8%	74.2%
621,602	PROVIDENCE	172,391	31,948	140,443		108,495 D	18.5%	81.5%	18.5%	81.5%
123,546	WASHINGTON	45,245	11,981	33,264		21,283 D	26.5%	73.5%	26.5%	73.5%
1,048,319	TOTAL	323,912	69,881	253,922	109	184,041 D	21.6%	78.4%	21.6%	78.4%

Note: The statewide totals for "Total Vote" and "Other" include 109 scattered write-in votes that are not included in the county-by-county returns.

	City/Town									
16,819	BARRINGTON	7,275	2,007	5,268		3,261 D	27.6%	72.4%	27.6%	72.4%
22,469	BRISTOL TOWN	7,034	1,526	5,508		3,982 D	21.7%	78.3%	21.7%	78.3%
15,796	BURRILLVILLE	4,474	1,064	3,410		2,346 D	23.8%	76.2%	23.8%	76.2%
18,928	CENTRAL FALLS	2,300	296	2,004		1,708 D	12.9%	87.1%	12.9%	87.1%
7,859	CHARLESTOWN	3,060	913	2,147		1,234 D	29.8%	70.2%	29.8%	70.2%
33,668	COVENTRY	11,630	2,841	8,789		5,948 D	24.4%	75.6%	24.4%	75.6%
79,269	CRANSTON	28,129	5,575	22,554		16,979 D	19.8%	80.2%	19.8%	80.2%
31,840	CUMBERLAND	11,252	2,639	8,613		5,974 D	23.5%	76.5%	23.5%	76.5%
12,948	EAST GREENWICH	5,672	1,867	3,805		1,938 D	32.9%	67.1%	32.9%	67.1%
48,688	EAST PROVIDENCE	15,191	2,522	12,669		10,147 D	16.6%	83.4%	16.6%	83.4%
6,045	EXETER	2,239	742	1,497		755 D	33.1%	66.9%	33.1%	66.9%
4,274	FOSTER	1,776	528	1,248		720 D	29.7%	70.3%	29.7%	70.3%
9,948	GLOCESTER	3,445	926	2,519		1,593 D	26.9%	73.1%	26.9%	73.1%
7,836	HOPKINTON	2,307	687	1,620		933 D	29.8%	70.2%	29.8%	70.2%
5,622	JAMESTOWN	2,800	675	2,125		1,450 D	24.1%	75.9%	24.1%	75.9%
28,195	JOHNSTON	10,224	1,898	8,326		6,428 D	18.6%	81.4%	18.6%	81.4%
20,898	LINCOLN	8,693	2,110	6,583		4,473 D	24.3%	75.7%	24.3%	75.7%
3,593	LITTLE COMPTON	1,733	571	1,162		591 D	32.9%	67.1%	32.9%	67.1%
17,334	MIDDLETOWN	5,277	1,277	4,000		2,723 D	24.2%	75.8%	24.2%	75.8%
16,361	NARRAGANSETT	6,530	1,490	5,040		3,550 D	22.8%	77.2%	22.8%	77.2%
26,475	NEWPORT CITY	6,808	1,529	5,279		3,750 D	22.5%	77.5%	22.5%	77.5%
1,010	NEW SHOREHAM	948	222	726		504 D	23.4%	76.6%	23.4%	76.6%
26,326	NORTH KINGSTOWN	10,821	2,972	7,849		4,877 D	27.5%	72.5%	27.5%	72.5%
32,411	NORTH PROVIDENCE	11,829	1,994	9,835		7,841 D	16.9%	83.1%	16.9%	83.1%
10,618	NORTH SMITHFIELD	4,321	1,054	3,267		2,213 D	24.4%	75.6%	24.4%	75.6%
72,958	PAWTUCKET	15,734	2,493	13,241		10,748 D	15.8%	84.2%	15.8%	84.2%
17,149	PORTSMOUTH	7,181	2,039	5,142		3,103 D	28.4%	71.6%	28.4%	71.6%
173,618	PROVIDENCE CITY	34,622	3,991	30,631		26,640 D	11.5%	88.5%	11.5%	88.5%
7,222	RICHMOND	2,383	639	1,744		1,105 D	26.8%	73.2%	26.8%	73.2%
10,324	SCITUATE	4,438	1,537	2,901		1,364 D	34.6%	65.4%	34.6%	65.4%
20,613	SMITHFIELD	7,421	1,849	5,572		3,723 D	24.9%	75.1%	24.9%	75.1%
27,921	SOUTH KINGSTOWN	9,549	2,197	7,352		5,155 D	23.0%	77.0%	23.0%	77.0%
15,260	TIVERTON	4,981	1,344	3,637		2,293 D	27.0%	73.0%	27.0%	73.0%
11,360	WARREN	3,488	775	2,713		1,938 D	22.2%	77.8%	22.2%	77.8%
85,808	WARWICK	31,721	7,025	24,696		17,671 D	22.1%	77.9%	22.1%	77.9%
22,966	WESTERLY	7,408	2,119	5,289		3,170 D	28.6%	71.4%	28.6%	71.4%
5,085	WEST GREENWICH	1,952	652	1,300		648 D	33.4%	66.6%	33.4%	66.6%
29,581	WEST WARWICK	8,615	1,824	6,791		4,967 D	21.2%	78.8%	21.2%	78.8%
43,224	WOONSOCKET	8,542	1,472	7,070		5,598 D	17.2%	82.8%	17.2%	82.8%
1,048,319	TOTAL	323,912	69,881	253,922	109	184,041 D	21.6%	78.4%	21.6%	78.4%

Note: The statewide totals for "Total Vote" and "Other" include 109 scattered write-in votes that are not included in the city/town returns.

RHODE ISLAND

HOUSE OF REPRESENTATIVES

CD	Year	Total Vote	Republican Vote	Republican Candidate	Democratic Vote	Democratic Candidate	Other Vote	Rep.-Dem. Plurality	Percentage Total Vote Rep.	Total Vote Dem.	Major Vote Rep.	Major Vote Dem.
1	2002	159,066	59,370	Rogers, David W.	95,286	Kennedy, Patrick J.*	4,410	35,916 D	37.3%	59.9%	38.4%	61.6%
2	2002	169,580	37,767	Matson, John O.	129,390	Langevin, Jim*	2,423	91,623 D	22.3%	76.3%	22.6%	77.4%
Total	2002	328,646	97,137		224,676		6,833	127,539 D	29.6%	68.4%	30.2%	69.8%

An asterisk (*) denotes incumbent.

RHODE ISLAND

GENERAL AND PRIMARY ELECTIONS

2002 GENERAL ELECTIONS

Governor   Other vote was 599 write-in.

Senator   Other vote was 109 write-in.

House   Other vote was:

CD 1   4,318 Independent (Frank Carter); 92 write-in.
CD 2   2,327 Independent (Dorman J. Hayes); 96 write-in.

2002 PRIMARY ELECTIONS

Primary   September 10, 2002   **Registration** (as of Sept. 10, 2002)   665,012   Party registration totals traditionally have been kept only at the local level.

Primary Type   Semi-open—Registered Democrats and Republicans could vote only in their party's primary. Unaffiliated voters could participate in either party's primary if they were willing to become a member of that party.

Note: An asterisk (*) denotes incumbent.

	REPUBLICAN PRIMARIES			DEMOCRATIC PRIMARIES		
Governor	Donald L. Carcieri	17,227	66.9%	Myrth York	46,806	39.2%
	James S. Bennett	8,518	33.1%	Sheldon Whitehouse	45,880	38.4%
				Antonio J. Pires	26,838	22.5%
	TOTAL	25,745		TOTAL	119,524	
Senator	Robert G. Tingle	16,041	100.0%	Jack Reed*	85,315	100.0%
Congressional District 1	David W. Rogers	4,691	40.1%	Patrick J. Kennedy*	43,470	100.0%
	Michael J. Battles	3,900	33.4%			
	Christine C. Ferguson	3,094	26.5%			
	TOTAL	11,685				
Congressional District 2	John O. Matson	6,934	61.1%	Jim Langevin*	41,702	100.0%
	Rod Driver	4,419	38.9%			
	TOTAL	11,353				

RHODE ISLAND REPUBLICAN PRIMARY

GOVERNOR 2002

2000 Census Population	County	Total Vote	Carcieri	Bennett	Winner	Percentage of Total Vote	
						Carcieri	Bennett
50,648	BRISTOL	1,821	1,246	575	Carcieri	68.4%	31.6%
167,090	KENT	5,881	4,529	1,352	Carcieri	77.0%	23.0%
85,433	NEWPORT	3,509	2,055	1,454	Carcieri	58.6%	41.4%
621,602	PROVIDENCE	9,824	6,091	3,733	Carcieri	62.0%	38.0%
123,546	WASHINGTON	4,710	3,306	1,404	Carcieri	70.2%	29.8%
1,048,319	TOTAL	25,745	17,227	8,518	Carcieri	66.9%	33.1%
	City/Town						
16,819	BARRINGTON	1,131	796	335	Carcieri	70.4%	29.6%
22,469	BRISTOL TOWN	523	344	179	Carcieri	65.8%	34.2%
15,796	BURRILLVILLE	224	121	103	Carcieri	54.0%	46.0%
18,928	CENTRAL FALLS	68	44	24	Carcieri	64.7%	35.3%
7,859	CHARLESTOWN	297	130	167	Bennett	43.8%	56.2%
33,668	COVENTRY	721	490	231	Carcieri	68.0%	32.0%
79,269	CRANSTON	1,845	1,229	616	Carcieri	66.6%	33.4%
31,840	CUMBERLAND	615	366	249	Carcieri	59.5%	40.5%
12,948	EAST GREENWICH	1,591	1,431	160	Carcieri	89.9%	10.1%
48,688	EAST PROVIDENCE	839	539	300	Carcieri	64.2%	35.8%
6,045	EXETER	402	288	114	Carcieri	71.6%	28.4%
4,274	FOSTER	162	113	49	Carcieri	69.8%	30.2%
9,948	GLOCESTER	202	145	57	Carcieri	71.8%	28.2%
7,836	HOPKINTON	179	88	91	Bennett	49.2%	50.8%
5,622	JAMESTOWN	440	300	140	Carcieri	68.2%	31.8%
28,195	JOHNSTON	200	134	66	Carcieri	67.0%	33.0%
20,898	LINCOLN	1,924	1,089	835	Carcieri	56.6%	43.4%
3,593	LITTLE COMPTON	246	164	82	Carcieri	66.7%	33.3%
17,334	MIDDLETOWN	496	309	187	Carcieri	62.3%	37.7%
16,361	NARRAGANSETT	611	438	173	Carcieri	71.7%	28.3%
26,475	NEWPORT CITY	690	381	309	Carcieri	55.2%	44.8%
1,010	NEW SHOREHAM	45	11	34	Bennett	24.4%	75.6%
26,326	NORTH KINGSTOWN	1,618	1,380	238	Carcieri	85.3%	14.7%
32,411	NORTH PROVIDENCE	326	244	82	Carcieri	74.8%	25.2%
10,618	NORTH SMITHFIELD	460	223	237	Bennett	48.5%	51.5%
72,958	PAWTUCKET	582	328	254	Carcieri	56.4%	43.6%
17,149	PORTSMOUTH	1,300	704	596	Carcieri	54.2%	45.8%
173,618	PROVIDENCE CITY	981	629	352	Carcieri	64.1%	35.9%
7,222	RICHMOND	216	149	67	Carcieri	69.0%	31.0%
10,324	SCITUATE	454	316	138	Carcieri	69.6%	30.4%
20,613	SMITHFIELD	580	377	203	Carcieri	65.0%	35.0%
27,921	SOUTH KINGSTOWN	846	543	303	Carcieri	64.2%	35.8%
15,260	TIVERTON	337	197	140	Carcieri	58.5%	41.5%
11,360	WARREN	167	106	61	Carcieri	63.5%	36.5%
85,808	WARWICK	2,829	2,046	783	Carcieri	72.3%	27.7%
22,966	WESTERLY	496	279	217	Carcieri	56.3%	43.8%
5,085	WEST GREENWICH	272	207	65	Carcieri	76.1%	23.9%
29,581	WEST WARWICK	468	355	113	Carcieri	75.9%	24.1%
43,224	WOONSOCKET	362	194	168	Carcieri	53.6%	46.4%
1,048,319	TOTAL	25,745	17,227	8,518	Carcieri	66.9%	33.1%

RHODE ISLAND DEMOCRATIC PRIMARY

GOVERNOR 2002

2000 Census Population	County	Total Vote	York	Whitehouse	Pires	Winner	Percentage of Total Vote		
							York	Whitehouse	Pires
50,648	BRISTOL	4,615	1,656	1,682	1,277	Whitehouse	35.9%	36.4%	27.7%
167,090	KENT	15,612	6,333	6,265	3,014	York	40.6%	40.1%	19.3%
85,433	NEWPORT	6,699	2,724	2,943	1,032	Whitehouse	40.7%	43.9%	15.4%
621,602	PROVIDENCE	80,402	30,687	30,311	19,404	York	38.2%	37.7%	24.1%
123,546	WASHINGTON	12,196	5,406	4,679	2,111	York	44.3%	38.4%	17.3%
1,048,319	TOTAL	119,524	46,806	45,880	26,838	York	39.2%	38.4%	22.5%
	City/Town								
16,819	BARRINGTON	1,592	622	692	278	Whitehouse	39.1%	43.5%	17.5%
22,469	BRISTOL TOWN	1,999	647	642	710	Pires	32.4%	32.1%	35.5%
15,796	BURRILLVILLE	1,098	468	436	194	York	42.6%	39.7%	17.7%
18,928	CENTRAL FALLS	1,477	522	362	593	Pires	35.3%	24.5%	40.1%
7,859	CHARLESTOWN	472	229	168	75	York	48.5%	35.6%	15.9%
33,668	COVENTRY	2,791	1,153	1,061	577	York	41.3%	38.0%	20.7%
79,269	CRANSTON	9,367	3,706	3,818	1,843	Whitehouse	39.6%	40.8%	19.7%
31,840	CUMBERLAND	5,029	1,325	1,699	2,005	Pires	26.3%	33.8%	39.9%
12,948	EAST GREENWICH	854	362	337	155	York	42.4%	39.5%	18.1%
48,688	EAST PROVIDENCE	6,017	2,114	1,878	2,025	York	35.1%	31.2%	33.7%
6,045	EXETER	377	170	146	61	York	45.1%	38.7%	16.2%
4,274	FOSTER	238	112	85	41	York	47.1%	35.7%	17.2%
9,948	GLOCESTER	515	200	219	96	Whitehouse	38.8%	42.5%	18.6%
7,836	HOPKINTON	292	131	136	25	Whitehouse	44.9%	46.6%	8.6%
5,622	JAMESTOWN	894	396	348	150	York	44.3%	38.9%	16.8%
28,195	JOHNSTON	6,200	2,190	2,817	1,193	Whitehouse	35.3%	45.4%	19.2%
20,898	LINCOLN	2,388	716	902	770	Whitehouse	30.0%	37.8%	32.2%
3,593	LITTLE COMPTON	295	111	136	48	Whitehouse	37.6%	46.1%	16.3%
17,334	MIDDLETOWN	962	404	420	138	Whitehouse	42.0%	43.7%	14.3%
16,361	NARRAGANSETT	2,974	1,103	1,208	663	Whitehouse	37.1%	40.6%	22.3%
26,475	NEWPORT CITY	2,275	846	1,171	258	Whitehouse	37.2%	51.5%	11.3%
1,010	NEW SHOREHAM	93	58	20	15	York	62.4%	21.5%	16.1%
26,326	NORTH KINGSTOWN	2,411	1,064	915	432	York	44.1%	38.0%	17.9%
32,411	NORTH PROVIDENCE	5,884	1,891	2,830	1,163	Whitehouse	32.1%	48.1%	19.8%
10,618	NORTH SMITHFIELD	1,249	419	567	263	Whitehouse	33.5%	45.4%	21.1%
72,958	PAWTUCKET	8,785	2,546	1,891	4,348	Pires	29.0%	21.5%	49.5%
17,149	PORTSMOUTH	1,483	638	587	258	York	43.0%	39.6%	17.4%
173,618	PROVIDENCE CITY	26,175	12,414	10,035	3,726	York	47.4%	38.3%	14.2%
7,222	RICHMOND	369	189	128	52	York	51.2%	34.7%	14.1%
10,324	SCITUATE	586	231	214	141	York	39.4%	36.5%	24.1%
20,613	SMITHFIELD	1,967	704	810	453	Whitehouse	35.8%	41.2%	23.0%
27,921	SOUTH KINGSTOWN	3,496	1,708	1,213	575	York	48.9%	34.7%	16.4%
15,260	TIVERTON	790	329	281	180	York	41.6%	35.6%	22.8%
11,360	WARREN	1,024	387	348	289	York	37.8%	34.0%	28.2%
85,808	WARWICK	9,009	3,719	3,571	1,719	York	41.3%	39.6%	19.1%
22,966	WESTERLY	1,712	754	745	213	York	44.0%	43.5%	12.4%
5,085	WEST GREENWICH	282	112	113	57	Whitehouse	39.7%	40.1%	20.2%
29,581	WEST WARWICK	2,676	987	1,183	506	Whitehouse	36.9%	44.2%	18.9%
43,224	WOONSOCKET	3,427	1,129	1,748	550	Whitehouse	32.9%	51.0%	16.0%
1,048,319	TOTAL	119,524	46,806	45,880	26,838	York	39.2%	38.4%	22.5%

SOUTH CAROLINA

GOVERNOR
Mark Sanford (R). Elected 2002 to a four-year term.

SENATORS (1 Democrat, 1 Republican)
Ernest F. Hollings (D). Reelected 1998 to a six-year term. Previously elected 1992, 1986, 1980, 1974, 1968 and in 1966 to fill out term vacated by the death of Senator Olin D. Johnston (D).

Lindsey Graham (R). Elected 2002 to a six-year term.

REPRESENTATIVES (4 Republicans, 2 Democrats)
1. Henry E. Brown Jr. (R)
2. Joe Wilson (R)
3. J. Gresham Barrett (R)
4. Jim DeMint (R)
5. John M. Spratt Jr. (D)
6. James E. Clyburn (D)

POSTWAR VOTE FOR PRESIDENT

Year	Total Vote	Republican		Democratic		Other Vote	Plurality	Percentage			
		Vote	Candidate	Vote	Candidate			Total Vote		Major Vote	
								Rep.	Dem.	Rep.	Dem.
2000**	1,382,717	785,937	Bush, George W.	565,561	Gore, Al	31,219	220,376 R	56.8%	40.9%	58.2%	41.8%
1996**	1,151,689	573,458	Dole, Bob	506,283	Clinton, Bill	71,948	67,175 R	49.8%	44.0%	53.1%	46.9%
1992**	1,202,527	577,507	Bush, George	479,514	Clinton, Bill	145,506	97,993 R	48.0%	39.9%	54.6%	45.4%
1988	986,009	606,443	Bush, George	370,554	Dukakis, Michael S.	9,012	235,889 R	61.5%	37.6%	62.1%	37.9%
1984	968,529	615,539	Reagan, Ronald	344,459	Mondale, Walter F.	8,531	271,080 R	63.6%	35.6%	64.1%	35.9%
1980**	894,071	441,841	Reagan, Ronald	430,385	Carter, Jimmy	21,845	11,456 R	49.4%	48.1%	50.7%	49.3%
1976	802,583	346,149	Ford, Gerald R.	450,807	Carter, Jimmy	5,627	104,658 D	43.1%	56.2%	43.4%	56.6%
1972	673,960	477,044	Nixon, Richard M.	186,824	McGovern, George S.	10,092	290,220 R	70.8%	27.7%	71.9%	28.1%
1968**	666,978	254,062	Nixon, Richard M.	197,486	Humphrey, Hubert H.	215,430	38,632 R	38.1%	29.6%	56.3%	43.7%
1964	524,779	309,048	Goldwater, Barry M.	215,723	Johnson, Lyndon B.	8	93,325 R	58.9%	41.1%	58.9%	41.1%
1960	386,688	188,558	Nixon, Richard M.	198,129	Kennedy, John F.	1	9,571 D	48.8%	51.2%	48.8%	51.2%
1956**	300,583	75,700	Eisenhower, Dwight D.	136,372	Stevenson, Adlai E.	88,511	47,863 D	25.2%	45.4%	35.7%	64.3%
1952	341,087	168,082	Eisenhower, Dwight D.	173,004	Stevenson, Adlai E.	1	4,922 D	49.3%	50.7%	49.3%	50.7%
1948**	142,571	5,386	Dewey, Thomas E.	34,423	Truman, Harry S.	102,762	68,184 SR	3.8%	24.1%	13.5%	86.5%

In 2000 the other vote column includes 20,200 votes cast for Green (Nader). In 1996 the other vote column includes 64,386 votes cast for Perot. In 1992 the other vote column includes 138,872 votes cast for Perot. In 1980 the other vote column includes 14,153 votes for Independent (Anderson). In 1968 other vote was Independent (Wallace). In 1956 other vote was 88,509 Independent (Uncommitted States Rights) and 2 scattered. In 1948 other vote was 102,607 States Rights; 154 Progressive and 1 Socialist.

SOUTH CAROLINA

POSTWAR VOTE FOR GOVERNOR

Year	Total Vote	Republican		Democratic		Other Vote	Rep.-Dem. Plurality	Percentage			
								Total Vote		Major Vote	
		Vote	Candidate	Vote	Candidate			Rep.	Dem.	Rep.	Dem.
2002	1,107,725	585,422	Sanford, Mark	521,140	Hodges, Jim	1,163	64,282 R	52.8%	47.0%	52.9%	47.1%
1998	1,070,869	484,088	Beasley, David	570,070	Hodges, Jim	16,711	85,982 D	45.2%	53.2%	45.9%	54.1%
1994	933,850	470,756	Beasley, David	447,002	Theodore, Nick A.	16,092	23,754 R	50.4%	47.9%	51.3%	48.7%
1990	760,965	528,831	Campbell, Carroll	212,034	Mitchell, Theo	20,100	316,797 R	69.5%	27.9%	71.4%	28.6%
1986	753,751	384,565	Campbell, Carroll	361,325	Daniel, Mike	7,861	23,240 R	51.0%	47.9%	51.6%	48.4%
1982	671,625	202,806	Workman, W. D.	468,819	Riley, Richard W.		266,013 D	30.2%	69.8%	30.2%	69.8%
1978	627,182	236,946	Young, Edward L.	384,898	Riley, Richard W.	5,338	147,952 D	37.8%	61.4%	38.1%	61.9%
1974	523,199	266,109	Edwards, James B.	248,938	Dorn, W. J. Bryan	8,152	17,171 R	50.9%	47.6%	51.7%	48.3%
1970	484,857	221,233	Watson, Albert W.	250,551	West, John C.	13,073	29,318 D	45.6%	51.7%	46.9%	53.1%
1966	439,942	184,088	Rogers, Joseph O.	255,854	McNair, Robert E.		71,766 D	41.8%	58.2%	41.8%	58.2%
1962	253,721		—	253,704	Russell, Donald S.	17	253,704 D		100.0%		100.0%
1958	77,740		—	77,714	Hollings, Ernest F.	26	77,714 D		100.0%		100.0%
1954	214,212		—	214,204	Timmerman, George B.	8	214,204 D		100.0%		100.0%
1950	50,642		—	50,633	Byrnes, James F.	9	50,633 D		100.0%		100.0%
1946	26,520		—	26,520	Thurmond, Strom		26,520 D		100.0%		100.0%

POSTWAR VOTE FOR SENATOR

Year	Total Vote	Republican		Democratic		Other Vote	Rep.-Dem. Plurality	Percentage			
								Total Vote		Major Vote	
		Vote	Candidate	Vote	Candidate			Rep.	Dem.	Rep.	Dem.
2002	1,102,948	600,010	Graham, Lindsey	487,359	Sanders, Alex	15,579	112,651 R	54.4%	44.2%	55.2%	44.8%
1998	1,068,367	488,132	Inglis, Robert D.	562,791	Hollings, Ernest F.	17,444	74,659 D	45.7%	52.7%	46.4%	53.6%
1996	1,161,372	619,859	Thurmond, Strom	510,951	Close, Elliott Springs	30,562	108,908 R	53.4%	44.0%	54.8%	45.2%
1992	1,180,438	554,175	Hartnett, Thomas F.	591,030	Hollings, Ernest F.	35,233	36,855 D	46.9%	50.1%	48.4%	51.6%
1990	750,716	482,032	Thurmond, Strom	244,112	Cunningham, Bob	24,572	237,920 R	64.2%	32.5%	66.4%	33.6%
1986	737,962	262,886	McMaster, Henry D.	465,500	Hollings, Ernest F.	9,576	202,614 D	35.6%	63.1%	36.1%	63.9%
1984	965,130	644,815	Thurmond, Strom	306,982	Purvis, Melvin	13,333	337,833 R	66.8%	31.8%	67.7%	32.3%
1980	870,594	257,946	Mays, Marshall T.	612,554	Hollings, Ernest F.	94	354,608 D	29.6%	70.4%	29.6%	70.4%
1978	632,852	351,733	Thurmond, Strom	281,119	Ravenel, Charles D.		70,614 R	55.6%	44.4%	55.6%	44.4%
1974	512,397	146,645	Bush, Gwenyfred	356,126	Hollings, Ernest F.	9,626	209,481 D	28.6%	69.5%	29.2%	70.8%
1972	672,246	426,601	Thurmond, Strom	245,457	Zeigler, Eugene N.	188	181,144 R	63.5%	36.5%	63.5%	36.5%
1968	652,855	248,780	Parker, Marshall	404,060	Hollings, Ernest F.	15	155,280 D	38.1%	61.9%	38.1%	61.9%
1966	436,252	271,297	Thurmond, Strom	164,955	Morrah, Bradley		106,342 R	62.2%	37.8%	62.2%	37.8%
1966S	435,822	212,032	Parker, Marshall	223,790	Hollings, Ernest F.		11,758 D	48.7%	51.3%	48.7%	51.3%
1962	312,647	133,930	Workman, W. D.	178,712	Johnston, Olin D.	5	44,782 D	42.8%	57.2%	42.8%	57.2%
1960	330,266		—	330,164	Thurmond, Strom	102	330,164 D		100.0%		100.0%
1956	279,845	49,695	Crawford, Leon P.	230,150	Johnston, Olin D.		180,455 D	17.8%	82.2%	17.8%	82.2%
1956S	251,907		—	251,907	Thurmond, Strom		251,907 D		100.0%		100.0%
1954**	227,232		—	83,525	Brown, Edgar A.	143,707	59,919 ID		36.8%		100.0%
1950	50,277		—	50,240	Johnston, Olin D.	37	50,240 D		99.9%		100.0%
1948	141,006	5,008	Gerald, J. Bates	135,998	Maybank, Burnet R.		130,990 D	3.6%	96.4%	3.6%	96.4%

One each of the 1966 and 1956 elections was for a short term to fill a vacancy. In 1954 Strom Thurmond polled 143,444 votes as an Independent Democratic write-in candidate (63.1% of the total vote) and won the election with a 59,919-vote plurality.

SOUTH CAROLINA

Congressional districts first established for elections held in 2002
6 members

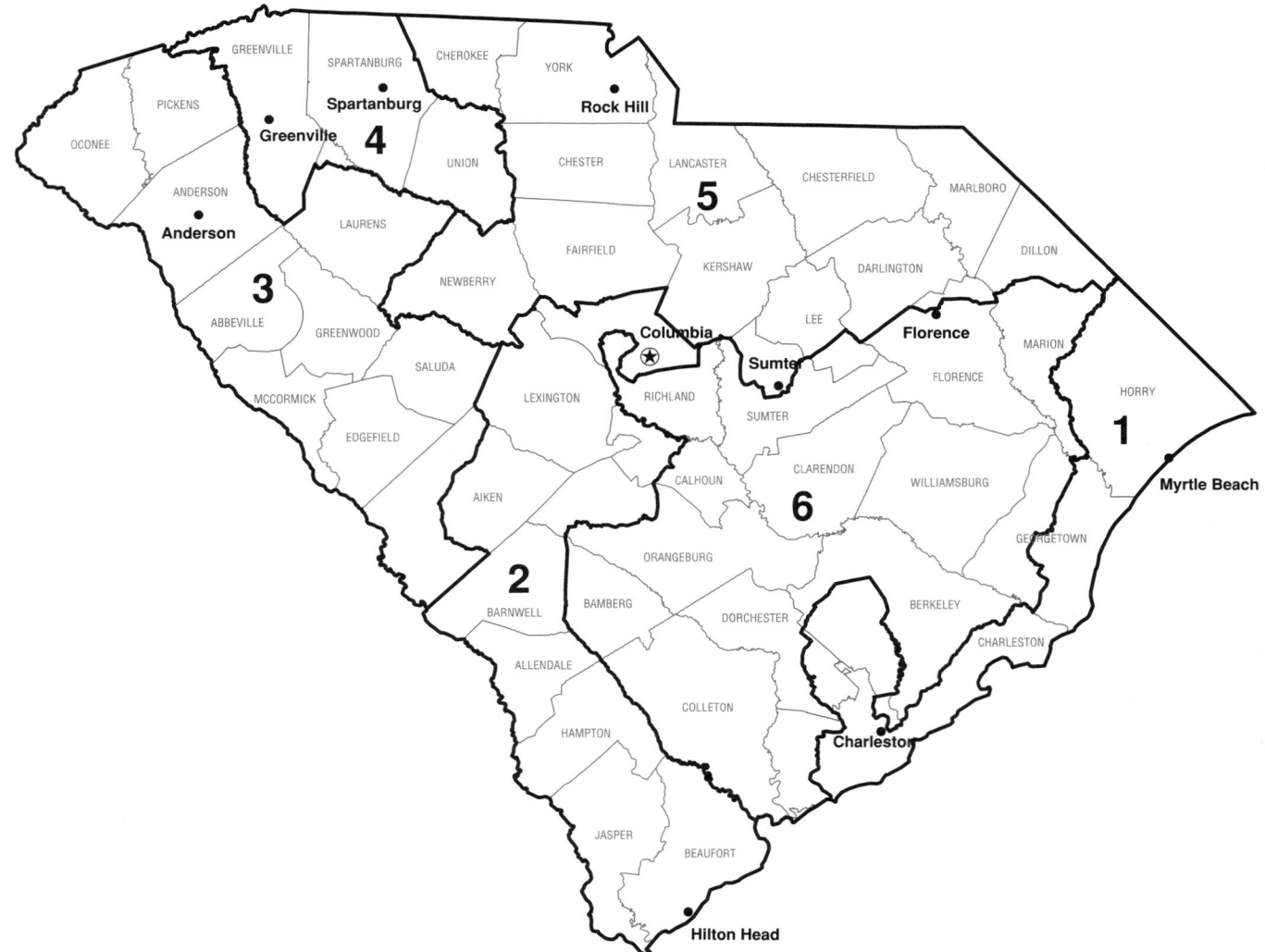

SOUTH CAROLINA

GOVERNOR 2002

2000 Census Population	County	Total Vote	Republican	Democratic	Other	Rep.-Dem. Plurality		Percentage			
								Total Vote		Major Vote	
								Rep.	Dem.	Rep.	Dem.
26,167	ABBEVILLE	7,599	3,327	4,270	2	943	D	43.8%	56.2%	43.8%	56.2%
142,552	AIKEN	39,687	25,746	13,938	3	11,808	R	64.9%	35.1%	64.9%	35.1%
11,211	ALLENDALE	2,396	646	1,750		1,104	D	27.0%	73.0%	27.0%	73.0%
165,740	ANDERSON	43,838	23,582	20,242	14	3,340	R	53.8%	46.2%	53.8%	46.2%
16,658	BAMBERG	4,420	1,481	2,938	1	1,457	D	33.5%	66.5%	33.5%	66.5%
23,478	BARNWELL	6,085	3,061	3,024		37	R	50.3%	49.7%	50.3%	49.7%
120,937	BEAUFORT	37,569	22,164	15,381	24	6,783	R	59.0%	40.9%	59.0%	41.0%
142,651	BERKELEY	34,653	20,018	14,624	11	5,394	R	57.8%	42.2%	57.8%	42.2%
15,185	CALHOUN	5,382	2,494	2,884	4	390	D	46.3%	53.6%	46.4%	53.6%
309,969	CHARLESTON	93,300	51,917	41,352	31	10,565	R	55.6%	44.3%	55.7%	44.3%
52,537	CHEROKEE	12,899	6,621	6,270	8	351	R	51.3%	48.6%	51.4%	48.6%
34,068	CHESTER	7,955	2,963	4,983	9	2,020	D	37.2%	62.6%	37.3%	62.7%
42,768	CHESTERFIELD	8,971	3,449	5,522		2,073	D	38.4%	61.6%	38.4%	61.6%
32,502	CLARENDON	10,641	4,015	6,626		2,611	D	37.7%	62.3%	37.7%	62.3%
38,264	COLLETON	10,218	4,991	5,218	9	227	D	48.8%	51.1%	48.9%	51.1%
67,394	DARLINGTON	18,146	8,509	9,630	7	1,121	D	46.9%	53.1%	46.9%	53.1%
30,722	DILLON	6,381	2,419	3,960	2	1,541	D	37.9%	62.1%	37.9%	62.1%
96,413	DORCHESTER	27,846	16,933	10,906	7	6,027	R	60.8%	39.2%	60.8%	39.2%
24,595	EDGEFIELD	6,847	3,506	3,341		165	R	51.2%	48.8%	51.2%	48.8%
23,454	FAIRFIELD	7,194	2,313	4,878	3	2,565	D	32.2%	67.8%	32.2%	67.8%
125,761	FLORENCE	32,021	16,581	15,396	44	1,185	R	51.8%	48.1%	51.9%	48.1%
55,797	GEORGETOWN	16,745	8,606	8,130	9	476	R	51.4%	48.6%	51.4%	48.6%
379,616	GREENVILLE	110,264	68,657	41,367	240	27,290	R	62.3%	37.5%	62.4%	37.6%
66,271	GREENWOOD	16,634	9,073	7,525	36	1,548	R	54.5%	45.2%	54.7%	45.3%
21,386	HAMPTON	6,538	1,886	4,652		2,766	D	28.8%	71.2%	28.8%	71.2%
196,629	HORRY	53,509	28,971	24,519	19	4,452	R	54.1%	45.8%	54.2%	45.8%
20,678	JASPER	5,357	1,832	3,521	4	1,689	D	34.2%	65.7%	34.2%	65.8%
52,647	KERSHAW	15,774	8,567	7,139	68	1,428	R	54.3%	45.3%	54.5%	45.5%
61,351	LANCASTER	13,578	5,196	8,372	10	3,176	D	38.3%	61.7%	38.3%	61.7%
69,567	LAURENS	17,953	9,082	8,818	53	264	R	50.6%	49.1%	50.7%	49.3%
20,119	LEE	6,041	2,008	4,033		2,025	D	33.2%	66.8%	33.2%	66.8%
216,014	LEXINGTON	69,554	45,835	23,664	55	22,171	R	65.9%	34.0%	66.0%	34.0%
9,958	MCCORMICK	3,531	1,647	1,884		237	D	46.6%	53.4%	46.6%	53.4%
35,466	MARION	9,125	2,971	6,153	1	3,182	D	32.6%	67.4%	32.6%	67.4%
28,818	MARLBORO	5,970	1,747	4,218	5	2,471	D	29.3%	70.7%	29.3%	70.7%
36,108	NEWBERRY	9,748	5,145	4,579	24	566	R	52.8%	47.0%	52.9%	47.1%
66,215	OCONEE	19,258	11,776	7,480	2	4,296	R	61.1%	38.8%	61.2%	38.8%
91,582	ORANGEBURG	28,860	9,280	19,534	46	10,254	D	32.2%	67.7%	32.2%	67.8%
110,757	PICKENS	26,949	17,650	9,220	79	8,430	R	65.5%	34.2%	65.7%	34.3%
320,677	RICHLAND	95,841	40,484	55,103	254	14,619	D	42.2%	57.5%	42.4%	57.6%
19,181	SALUDA	5,861	3,160	2,701		459	R	53.9%	46.1%	53.9%	46.1%
253,791	SPARTANBURG	60,606	35,558	24,980	68	10,578	R	58.7%	41.2%	58.7%	41.3%
104,646	SUMTER	26,837	11,729	15,108		3,379	D	43.7%	56.3%	43.7%	56.3%
29,881	UNION	8,759	4,244	4,515		271	D	48.5%	51.5%	48.5%	51.5%
37,217	WILLIAMSBURG	10,602	3,207	7,386	9	4,179	D	30.2%	69.7%	30.3%	69.7%
164,614	YORK	39,783	20,375	19,406	2	969	R	51.2%	48.8%	51.2%	48.8%
4,012,012	TOTAL	1,107,725	585,422	521,140	1,163	64,282	R	52.8%	47.0%	52.9%	47.1%

SOUTH CAROLINA

SENATOR 2002

2000 Census Population	County	Total Vote	Republican	Democratic	Other	Rep.-Dem. Plurality	Percentage			
							Total Vote		Major Vote	
							Rep.	Dem.	Rep.	Dem.
26,167	ABBEVILLE	7,595	3,687	3,774	134	87 D	48.5%	49.7%	49.4%	50.6%
142,552	AIKEN	39,680	26,667	12,583	430	14,084 R	67.2%	31.7%	67.9%	32.1%
11,211	ALLENDALE	2,356	649	1,686	21	1,037 D	27.5%	71.6%	27.8%	72.2%
165,740	ANDERSON	43,807	26,455	16,543	809	9,912 R	60.4%	37.8%	61.5%	38.5%
16,658	BAMBERG	4,348	1,463	2,846	39	1,383 D	33.6%	65.5%	34.0%	66.0%
23,478	BARNWELL	6,105	3,123	2,913	69	210 R	51.2%	47.7%	51.7%	48.3%
120,937	BEAUFORT	37,304	22,738	14,086	480	8,652 R	61.0%	37.8%	61.7%	38.3%
142,651	BERKELEY	34,252	20,188	13,607	457	6,581 R	58.9%	39.7%	59.7%	40.3%
15,185	CALHOUN	5,365	2,481	2,839	45	358 D	46.2%	52.9%	46.6%	53.4%
309,969	CHARLESTON	91,949	48,773	41,955	1,221	6,818 R	53.0%	45.6%	53.8%	46.2%
52,537	CHEROKEE	12,828	7,079	5,488	261	1,591 R	55.2%	42.8%	56.3%	43.7%
34,068	CHESTER	7,887	3,330	4,418	139	1,088 D	42.2%	56.0%	43.0%	57.0%
42,768	CHESTERFIELD	8,976	3,795	5,099	82	1,304 D	42.3%	56.8%	42.7%	57.3%
32,502	CLARENDON	10,638	4,204	6,353	81	2,149 D	39.5%	59.7%	39.8%	60.2%
38,264	COLLETON	10,262	5,155	5,010	97	145 R	50.2%	48.8%	50.7%	49.3%
67,394	DARLINGTON	18,033	8,774	9,051	208	277 D	48.7%	50.2%	49.2%	50.8%
30,722	DILLON	6,364	2,606	3,711	47	1,105 D	40.9%	58.3%	41.3%	58.7%
96,413	DORCHESTER	27,533	16,942	10,237	354	6,705 R	61.5%	37.2%	62.3%	37.7%
24,595	EDGEFIELD	6,822	3,730	3,035	57	695 R	54.7%	44.5%	55.1%	44.9%
23,454	FAIRFIELD	6,997	2,170	4,748	79	2,578 D	31.0%	67.9%	31.4%	68.6%
125,761	FLORENCE	32,037	16,685	14,614	738	2,071 R	52.1%	45.6%	53.3%	46.7%
55,797	GEORGETOWN	16,905	8,534	8,246	125	288 R	50.5%	48.8%	50.9%	49.1%
379,616	GREENVILLE	110,169	70,149	38,026	1,994	32,123 R	63.7%	34.5%	64.8%	35.2%
66,271	GREENWOOD	16,706	9,554	6,935	217	2,619 R	57.2%	41.5%	57.9%	42.1%
21,386	HAMPTON	6,119	1,961	4,080	78	2,119 D	32.0%	66.7%	32.5%	67.5%
196,629	HORRY	52,638	29,406	22,460	772	6,946 R	55.9%	42.7%	56.7%	43.3%
20,678	JASPER	5,372	1,927	3,383	62	1,456 D	35.9%	63.0%	36.3%	63.7%
52,647	KERSHAW	15,698	8,619	6,872	207	1,747 R	54.9%	43.8%	55.6%	44.4%
61,351	LANCASTER	13,669	6,612	6,818	239	206 D	48.4%	49.9%	49.2%	50.8%
69,567	LAURENS	17,970	9,778	7,852	340	1,926 R	54.4%	43.7%	55.5%	44.5%
20,119	LEE	6,024	2,018	3,960	46	1,942 D	33.5%	65.7%	33.8%	66.2%
216,014	LEXINGTON	69,620	45,671	22,915	1,034	22,756 R	65.6%	32.9%	66.6%	33.4%
9,958	MCCORMICK	3,729	1,724	1,770	235	46 D	46.2%	47.5%	49.3%	50.7%
35,466	MARION	8,957	3,157	5,711	89	2,554 D	35.2%	63.8%	35.6%	64.4%
28,818	MARLBORO	5,949	1,825	4,028	96	2,203 D	30.7%	67.7%	31.2%	68.8%
36,108	NEWBERRY	9,825	5,247	4,371	207	876 R	53.4%	44.5%	54.6%	45.4%
66,215	OCONEE	19,237	13,392	5,613	232	7,779 R	69.6%	29.2%	70.5%	29.5%
91,582	ORANGEBURG	28,879	9,583	19,134	162	9,551 D	33.2%	66.3%	33.4%	66.6%
110,757	PICKENS	26,956	19,142	7,334	480	11,808 R	71.0%	27.2%	72.3%	27.7%
320,677	RICHLAND	95,394	37,413	56,977	1,004	19,564 D	39.2%	59.7%	39.6%	60.4%
19,181	SALUDA	5,884	3,335	2,508	41	827 R	56.7%	42.6%	57.1%	42.9%
253,791	SPARTANBURG	60,096	36,237	22,937	922	13,300 R	60.3%	38.2%	61.2%	38.8%
104,646	SUMTER	26,718	12,563	13,878	277	1,315 D	47.0%	51.9%	47.5%	52.5%
29,881	UNION	8,803	4,503	4,172	128	331 R	51.2%	47.4%	51.9%	48.1%
37,217	WILLIAMSBURG	10,535	3,453	6,989	93	3,536 D	32.8%	66.3%	33.1%	66.9%
164,614	YORK	39,958	23,513	15,794	651	7,719 R	58.8%	39.5%	59.8%	40.2%
4,012,012	TOTAL	1,102,948	600,010	487,359	15,579	112,651 R	54.4%	44.2%	55.2%	44.8%

SOUTH CAROLINA

HOUSE OF REPRESENTATIVES

| | | | Republican | | Democratic | | | | Percentage | | | |
| | | | | | | | | | Total Vote | | Major Vote | |
CD	Year	Total Vote	Vote	Candidate	Vote	Candidate	Other Vote	Rep.-Dem. Plurality	Rep.	Dem.	Rep.	Dem.
1	2002	142,425	127,562	Brown, Henry E. Jr.*			14,863	127,562 R	89.6%		100.0%	
2	2002	171,359	144,149	Wilson, Joe*			27,210	144,149 R	84.1%		100.0%	
3	2002	178,195	119,644	Barrett, J. Gresham	55,743	Brightharp, George L.	2,808	63,901 R	67.1%	31.3%	68.2%	31.8%
4	2002	177,417	122,422	DeMint, Jim*	52,635 #	Ashy, Peter J.	2,360	69,787 R	69.0%	29.7%	69.9%	30.1%
5	2002	141,972			121,912	Spratt, John M. Jr.*	20,060	121,912 D		85.9%		100.0%
6	2002	174,066	55,760	McLeod, Gary	116,586	Clyburn, James E.*	1,720	60,826 D	32.0%	67.0%	32.4%	67.6%
Total	2002	985,434	569,537		346,876		69,021	222,661 R	57.8%	35.2%	62.1%	37.9%

A pound sign (#) indicates that a candidate received votes on the ballot line of another party.

An asterisk (*) denotes incumbent.

SOUTH CAROLINA

GENERAL AND PRIMARY ELECTIONS

2002 GENERAL ELECTIONS

Governor   Other vote was 1,163 write in.

Senator   Other vote was 8,228 Constitution (Ted Adams); 6,684 Libertarian (Victor Kocher); 667 write-in.

House   Other vote was:

CD 1   9,841 United Citizens (James E. Dunn); 4,965 Natural Law (Joe Innella); 57 write-in.
CD 2   17,189 United Citizens (Mark Whittington); 9,650 Libertarian (James R. "Jim" Legg); 371 write-in.
CD 3   2,785 Libertarian (Mike Boerste); 23 write-in.
CD 4   2,176 Natural Law (C. Faye Walters); 184 write-in. (Democrat Peter J. Ashy received 1,173 votes on the ballot line of United Citizens.)
CD 5   11,013 Libertarian (Doug Kendall); 8,930 Constitution (Steve Lefemine); 117 write-in.
CD 6   1,680 Libertarian (R. Craig Augenstein); 40 write-in.

2002 PRIMARY ELECTIONS

Primary   June 11, 2002   **Registration**   2,005,671   No Party Registration
                                      (as of June 11, 2002)

Primary Runoff June 25, 2002

Primary Type   Open—Any registered voter could participate in either the Democratic or Republican primary, although if they voted in one party's primary they could not vote in a primary runoff of the other party.

Note: An asterisk (*) denotes incumbent. The names of unopposed candidates did not appear on the primary ballot; therefore, no votes were cast for these candidates.

SOUTH CAROLINA

GENERAL AND PRIMARY ELECTIONS

	REPUBLICAN PRIMARIES			DEMOCRATIC PRIMARIES		
Governor	Mark Sanford	122,143	38.6%	Jim Hodges*	Unopposed	
	Bob Peeler	119,026	37.6%			
	Charlie Condon	49,469	15.6%			
	Ken Wingate	12,366	3.9%			
	Jim Miles	8,566	2.7%			
	Reb Sutherland	2,770	0.9%			
	Bill Branton	1,915	0.6%			
	TOTAL	316,255				
	PRIMARY RUNOFF					
	Mark Sanford	183,820	60.1%			
	Bob Peeler	121,881	39.9%			
	TOTAL	305,701				
Senator	Lindsey Graham	Unopposed		Alex Sanders	Unopposed	
Congressional District 1	Henry E. Brown Jr.*	47,084	78.8%	No Democratic candidate		
	Bob Batchelder	12,680	21.2%			
	TOTAL	59,764				
Congressional District 2	Joe Wilson*	Unopposed		No Democratic candidate		
Congressional District 3	J. Gresham Barrett	27,499	43.5%	George L. Brightharp	Unopposed	
	Jim Klauber	13,865	21.9%			
	George Ducworth	13,836	21.9%			
	Bob Waldrep	3,983	6.3%			
	Stan Jackson	2,702	4.3%			
	Michael Thompson	1,360	2.2%			
	TOTAL	63,245				
	PRIMARY RUNOFF					
	J. Gresham Barrett	38,366	65.2%			
	Jim Klauber	20,505	34.8%			
	TOTAL	58,871				
Congressional District 4	Jim DeMint*	39,142	61.6%	Peter J. Ashy	Unopposed	
	Phil Bradley	24,423	38.4%			
	TOTAL	63,565				
Congressional District 5	No Republican candidate			John M. Spratt Jr.*	Unopposed	
Congressional District 6	Gary McLeod	Unopposed		James E. Clyburn*	34,106	88.8%
				Ben Frasier	4,304	11.2%
				TOTAL	38,410	

SOUTH CAROLINA REPUBLICAN PRIMARY

GOVERNOR 2002

2000 Census Population	County	Total Vote	Sanford	Peeler	Condon	Other	Winner	Percentage of Total Vote			
								Sanford	Peeler	Condon	Other
26,167	ABBEVILLE	1,754	339	1,096	243	76	Peeler	19.3%	62.5%	13.9%	4.3%
142,552	AIKEN	10,428	3,820	4,071	1,362	1,175	Peeler	36.6%	39.0%	13.1%	11.3%
11,211	ALLENDALE	68	1	30	3	34	Peeler	1.5%	44.1%	4.4%	50.0%
165,740	ANDERSON	17,403	3,694	9,560	2,647	1,502	Peeler	21.2%	54.9%	15.2%	8.6%
16,658	BAMBERG	674	254	261	93	66	Peeler	37.7%	38.7%	13.8%	9.8%
23,478	BARNWELL	1,111	388	378	243	102	Sanford	34.9%	34.0%	21.9%	9.2%
120,937	BEAUFORT	10,460	5,612	2,209	1,847	792	Sanford	53.7%	21.1%	17.7%	7.6%
142,651	BERKELEY	14,131	7,864	2,426	3,095	746	Sanford	55.7%	17.2%	21.9%	5.3%
15,185	CALHOUN	1,292	410	588	227	67	Peeler	31.7%	45.5%	17.6%	5.2%
309,969	CHARLESTON	28,954	18,395	3,330	5,940	1,289	Sanford	63.5%	11.5%	20.5%	4.5%
52,537	CHEROKEE	3,853	338	3,084	336	95	Peeler	8.8%	80.0%	8.7%	2.5%
34,068	CHESTER	891	160	445	228	58	Peeler	18.0%	49.9%	25.6%	6.5%
42,768	CHESTERFIELD	557	119	252	145	41	Peeler	21.4%	45.2%	26.0%	7.4%
32,502	CLARENDON	1,210	378	466	296	70	Peeler	31.2%	38.5%	24.5%	5.8%
38,264	COLLETON	3,060	1,570	693	661	136	Sanford	51.3%	22.6%	21.6%	4.4%
67,394	DARLINGTON	3,157	1,060	1,387	557	153	Peeler	33.6%	43.9%	17.6%	4.8%
30,722	DILLON	509	165	181	134	29	Peeler	32.4%	35.6%	26.3%	5.7%
96,413	DORCHESTER	8,359	4,975	1,243	1,663	478	Sanford	59.5%	14.9%	19.9%	5.7%
24,595	EDGEFIELD	1,770	481	970	212	107	Peeler	27.2%	54.8%	12.0%	6.0%
23,454	FAIRFIELD	1,133	393	450	184	106	Peeler	34.7%	39.7%	16.2%	9.4%
125,761	FLORENCE	8,005	2,679	3,453	1,332	541	Peeler	33.5%	43.1%	16.6%	6.8%
55,797	GEORGETOWN	3,940	2,551	587	520	282	Sanford	64.7%	14.9%	13.2%	7.2%
379,616	GREENVILLE	40,223	12,191	17,902	5,929	4,201	Peeler	30.3%	44.5%	14.7%	10.4%
66,271	GREENWOOD	6,163	1,749	3,290	782	342	Peeler	28.4%	53.4%	12.7%	5.5%
21,386	HAMPTON	220	93	39	70	18	Sanford	42.3%	17.7%	31.8%	8.2%
196,629	HORRY	17,237	9,996	3,672	2,314	1,255	Sanford	58.0%	21.3%	13.4%	7.3%
20,678	JASPER	189	61	32	78	18	Condon	32.3%	16.9%	41.3%	9.5%
52,647	KERSHAW	4,306	1,687	1,826	549	244	Peeler	39.2%	42.4%	12.7%	5.7%
61,351	LANCASTER	1,425	356	554	407	108	Peeler	25.0%	38.9%	28.6%	7.6%
69,567	LAURENS	6,199	1,284	3,557	954	404	Peeler	20.7%	57.4%	15.4%	6.5%
20,119	LEE	668	4	175	11	478	Miles	0.6%	26.2%	1.6%	71.6%
216,014	LEXINGTON	26,973	10,212	10,681	3,723	2,357	Peeler	37.9%	39.6%	13.8%	8.7%
9,958	MCCORMICK	851	214	487	91	59	Peeler	25.1%	57.2%	10.7%	6.9%
35,466	MARION	876	258	372	202	44	Peeler	29.5%	42.5%	23.1%	5.0%
28,818	MARLBORO	497	167	180	130	20	Peeler	33.6%	36.2%	26.2%	4.0%
36,108	NEWBERRY	3,015	993	1,445	409	168	Peeler	32.9%	47.9%	13.6%	5.6%
66,215	OCONEE	7,930	2,070	4,309	1,002	549	Peeler	26.1%	54.3%	12.6%	6.9%
91,582	ORANGEBURG	4,456	1,375	1,884	939	258	Peeler	30.9%	42.3%	21.1%	5.8%
110,757	PICKENS	12,234	2,879	6,729	1,703	923	Peeler	23.5%	55.0%	13.9%	7.5%
320,677	RICHLAND	21,946	11,134	5,606	2,084	3,122	Sanford	50.7%	25.5%	9.5%	14.2%
19,181	SALUDA	1,871	455	1,035	303	78	Peeler	24.3%	55.3%	16.2%	4.2%
253,791	SPARTANBURG	23,896	6,037	12,268	3,597	1,994	Peeler	25.3%	51.3%	15.1%	8.3%
104,646	SUMTER	4,906	1,558	2,434	625	289	Peeler	31.8%	49.6%	12.7%	5.9%
29,881	UNION	1,654	323	958	296	77	Peeler	19.5%	57.9%	17.9%	4.7%
37,217	WILLIAMSBURG	344	122	93	115	14	Sanford	35.5%	27.0%	33.4%	4.1%
164,614	YORK	5,457	1,279	2,338	1,188	652	Peeler	23.4%	42.8%	21.8%	11.9%
4,012,012	TOTAL	316,255	122,143	119,026	49,469	25,617	Sanford	38.6%	37.6%	15.6%	8.1%

SOUTH CAROLINA REPUBLICAN PRIMARY RUNOFF
GOVERNOR 2002

2000 Census Population	County	Total Vote	Sanford	Peeler	Winner	Percentage of Total Vote Sanford	Peeler
26,167	ABBEVILLE	1,526	554	972	Peeler	36.3%	63.7%
142,552	AIKEN	9,912	6,447	3,465	Sanford	65.0%	35.0%
11,211	ALLENDALE	65	52	13	Sanford	80.0%	20.0%
165,740	ANDERSON	15,059	6,145	8,914	Peeler	40.8%	59.2%
16,658	BAMBERG	705	434	271	Sanford	61.6%	38.4%
23,478	BARNWELL	1,018	595	423	Sanford	58.4%	41.6%
120,937	BEAUFORT	8,486	6,735	1,751	Sanford	79.4%	20.6%
142,651	BERKELEY	13,249	10,959	2,290	Sanford	82.7%	17.3%
15,185	CALHOUN	1,233	648	585	Sanford	52.6%	47.4%
309,969	CHARLESTON	30,937	27,314	3,623	Sanford	88.3%	11.7%
52,537	CHEROKEE	4,629	678	3,951	Peeler	14.6%	85.4%
34,068	CHESTER	750	279	471	Peeler	37.2%	62.8%
42,768	CHESTERFIELD	418	171	247	Peeler	40.9%	59.1%
32,502	CLARENDON	1,150	569	581	Peeler	49.5%	50.5%
38,264	COLLETON	2,663	2,167	496	Sanford	81.4%	18.6%
67,394	DARLINGTON	2,863	1,630	1,233	Sanford	56.9%	43.1%
30,722	DILLON	330	186	144	Sanford	56.4%	43.6%
96,413	DORCHESTER	8,607	7,373	1,234	Sanford	85.7%	14.3%
24,595	EDGEFIELD	1,432	773	659	Sanford	54.0%	46.0%
23,454	FAIRFIELD	1,153	630	523	Sanford	54.6%	45.4%
125,761	FLORENCE	7,230	3,791	3,439	Sanford	52.4%	47.6%
55,797	GEORGETOWN	3,792	3,230	562	Sanford	85.2%	14.8%
379,616	GREENVILLE	38,423	19,812	18,611	Sanford	51.6%	48.4%
66,271	GREENWOOD	6,646	3,266	3,380	Peeler	49.1%	50.9%
21,386	HAMPTON	173	131	42	Sanford	75.7%	24.3%
196,629	HORRY	14,214	11,035	3,179	Sanford	77.6%	22.4%
20,678	JASPER	229	188	41	Sanford	82.1%	17.9%
52,647	KERSHAW	4,318	2,436	1,882	Sanford	56.4%	43.6%
61,351	LANCASTER	1,234	561	673	Peeler	45.5%	54.5%
69,567	LAURENS	5,809	2,170	3,639	Peeler	37.4%	62.6%
20,119	LEE	666	267	399	Peeler	40.1%	59.9%
216,014	LEXINGTON	28,322	15,997	12,325	Sanford	56.5%	43.5%
9,958	MCCORMICK	814	396	418	Peeler	48.6%	51.4%
35,466	MARION	758	394	364	Sanford	52.0%	48.0%
28,818	MARLBORO	414	244	170	Sanford	58.9%	41.1%
36,108	NEWBERRY	3,121	1,477	1,644	Peeler	47.3%	52.7%
66,215	OCONEE	7,958	3,843	4,115	Peeler	48.3%	51.7%
91,582	ORANGEBURG	4,422	2,470	1,952	Sanford	55.9%	44.1%
110,757	PICKENS	11,082	4,865	6,217	Peeler	43.9%	56.1%
320,677	RICHLAND	23,577	16,683	6,894	Sanford	70.8%	29.2%
19,181	SALUDA	1,898	804	1,094	Peeler	42.4%	57.6%
253,791	SPARTANBURG	21,456	9,897	11,559	Peeler	46.1%	53.9%
104,646	SUMTER	5,477	2,222	3,255	Peeler	40.6%	59.4%
29,881	UNION	1,507	521	986	Peeler	34.6%	65.4%
37,217	WILLIAMSBURG	296	210	86	Sanford	70.9%	29.1%
164,614	YORK	5,680	2,571	3,109	Peeler	45.3%	54.7%
4,012,012	TOTAL	305,701	183,820	121,881	Sanford	60.1%	39.9%

SOUTH DAKOTA

GOVERNOR
Mike Rounds (R). Elected 2002 to a four-year term.

SENATORS (2 Democrats)
Tom Daschle (D). Reelected 1998 to a six-year term. Previously elected 1992, 1986.

Tim Johnson (D). Reelected 2002 to a six-year term. Previously elected 1996.

REPRESENTATIVE (1 Republican)
At Large. Bill Janklow (R)

POSTWAR VOTE FOR PRESIDENT

Year	Total Vote	Republican		Democratic		Other Vote	Plurality	Percentage			
								Total Vote		Major Vote	
		Vote	Candidate	Vote	Candidate			Rep.	Dem.	Rep.	Dem.
2000	316,269	190,700	Bush, George W.	118,804	Gore, Al	6,765	71,896 R	60.3%	37.6%	61.6%	38.4%
1996**	323,826	150,543	Dole, Bob	139,333	Clinton, Bill	33,950	11,210 R	46.5%	43.0%	51.9%	48.1%
1992**	336,254	136,718	Bush, George	124,888	Clinton, Bill	74,648	11,830 R	40.7%	37.1%	52.3%	47.7%
1988	312,991	165,415	Bush, George	145,560	Dukakis, Michael S.	2,016	19,855 R	52.8%	46.5%	53.2%	46.8%
1984	317,867	200,267	Reagan, Ronald	116,113	Mondale, Walter F.	1,487	84,154 R	63.0%	36.5%	63.3%	36.7%
1980**	327,703	198,343	Reagan, Ronald	103,855	Carter, Jimmy	25,505	94,488 R	60.5%	31.7%	65.6%	34.4%
1976	300,678	151,505	Ford, Gerald R.	147,068	Carter, Jimmy	2,105	4,437 R	50.4%	48.9%	50.7%	49.3%
1972	307,415	166,476	Nixon, Richard M.	139,945	McGovern, George S.	994	26,531 R	54.2%	45.5%	54.3%	45.7%
1968	281,264	149,841	Nixon, Richard M.	118,023	Humphrey, Hubert H.	13,400	31,818 R	53.3%	42.0%	55.9%	44.1%
1964	293,118	130,108	Goldwater, Barry M.	163,010	Johnson, Lyndon B.		32,902 D	44.4%	55.6%	44.4%	55.6%
1960	306,487	178,417	Nixon, Richard M.	128,070	Kennedy, John F.		50,347 R	58.2%	41.8%	58.2%	41.8%
1956	293,857	171,569	Eisenhower, Dwight D.	122,288	Stevenson, Adlai E.		49,281 R	58.4%	41.6%	58.4%	41.6%
1952	294,283	203,857	Eisenhower, Dwight D.	90,426	Stevenson, Adlai E.		113,431 R	69.3%	30.7%	69.3%	30.7%
1948	250,105	129,651	Dewey, Thomas E.	117,653	Truman, Harry S.	2,801	11,998 R	51.8%	47.0%	52.4%	47.6%

In 1996 the other vote column includes 31,250 votes cast for Perot. In 1992 the other vote column includes 73,295 votes cast for Perot. In 1980 the other votes column includes 21,431 votes for Independent (Anderson).

SOUTH DAKOTA

POSTWAR VOTE FOR GOVERNOR

Year	Total Vote	Republican		Democratic		Other Vote	Rep.-Dem. Plurality	Percentage			
								Total Vote		Major Vote	
		Vote	Candidate	Vote	Candidate			Rep.	Dem.	Rep.	Dem.
2002	334,559	189,920	Rounds, Mike	140,263	Abbott, Jim	4,376	49,657 R	56.8%	41.9%	57.5%	42.5%
1998	260,187	166,621	Janklow, Bill	85,473	Hunhoff, Bernie	8,093	81,148 R	64.0%	32.9%	66.1%	33.9%
1994	311,613	172,515	Janklow, Bill	126,273	Beddow, Jim	12,825	46,242 R	55.4%	40.5%	57.7%	42.3%
1990	256,723	151,198	Mickelson, George S.	105,525	Samuelson, Bob L.		45,673 R	58.9%	41.1%	58.9%	41.1%
1986	294,441	152,543	Mickelson, George S.	141,898	Herseth, R. Lars		10,645 R	51.8%	48.2%	51.8%	48.2%
1982	278,562	197,426	Janklow, Bill	81,136	O'Connor, Michael J.		116,290 R	70.9%	29.1%	70.9%	29.1%
1978	259,795	147,116	Janklow, Bill	112,679	McKellips, Roger		34,437 R	56.6%	43.4%	56.6%	43.4%
1974**	278,228	129,077	Olson, John E.	149,151	Kneip, Richard F.		20,074 D	46.4%	53.6%	46.4%	53.6%
1972	308,177	123,165	Thompson, Carveth	185,012	Kneip, Richard F.		61,847 D	40.0%	60.0%	40.0%	60.0%
1970	239,963	108,347	Farrar, Frank	131,616	Kneip, Richard F.		23,269 D	45.2%	54.8%	45.2%	54.8%
1968	276,906	159,646	Farrar, Frank	117,260	Chamberlin, Robert		42,386 R	57.7%	42.3%	57.7%	42.3%
1966	228,214	131,710	Boe, Nils A.	96,504	Chamberlin, Robert		35,206 R	57.7%	42.3%	57.7%	42.3%
1964	290,570	150,151	Boe, Nils A.	140,419	Lindley, John F.		9,732 R	51.7%	48.3%	51.7%	48.3%
1962	256,120	143,682	Gubbrud, Archie M.	112,438	Herseth, Ralph		31,244 R	56.1%	43.9%	56.1%	43.9%
1960	304,625	154,530	Gubbrud, Archie M.	150,095	Herseth, Ralph		4,435 R	50.7%	49.3%	50.7%	49.3%
1958	258,281	125,520	Saunders, Phil	132,761	Herseth, Ralph		7,241 D	48.6%	51.4%	48.6%	51.4%
1956	292,017	158,819	Foss, Joe J.	133,198	Herseth, Ralph		25,621 R	54.4%	45.6%	54.4%	45.6%
1954	236,255	133,878	Foss, Joe J.	102,377	Martin, Ed C.		31,501 R	56.7%	43.3%	56.7%	43.3%
1952	289,515	203,102	Anderson, Sigurd	86,413	Iverson, Sherman A.		116,689 R	70.2%	29.8%	70.2%	29.8%
1950	253,316	154,254	Anderson, Sigurd	99,062	Robbie, Joseph		55,192 R	60.9%	39.1%	60.9%	39.1%
1948	245,372	149,883	Mickelson, George	95,489	Volz, Harold J.		54,394 R	61.1%	38.9%	61.1%	38.9%
1946	162,292	108,998	Mickelson, George	53,294	Haeder, Richard		55,704 R	67.2%	32.8%	67.2%	32.8%

The term of office of South Dakota's Governor was increased from two to four years effective with the 1974 election.

POSTWAR VOTE FOR SENATOR

Year	Total Vote	Republican		Democratic		Other Vote	Rep.-Dem. Plurality	Percentage			
								Total Vote		Major Vote	
		Vote	Candidate	Vote	Candidate			Rep.	Dem.	Rep.	Dem.
2002	337,508	166,957	Thune, John	167,481	Johnson, Tim	3,070	524 D	49.5%	49.6%	49.9%	50.1%
1998	262,111	95,431	Schmidt, Ron	162,884	Daschle, Tom	3,796	67,453 D	36.4%	62.1%	36.9%	63.1%
1996	324,487	157,954	Pressler, Larry	166,533	Johnson, Tim		8,579 D	48.7%	51.3%	48.7%	51.3%
1992	334,495	108,733	Haar, Charlene	217,095	Daschle, Tom	8,667	108,362 D	32.5%	64.9%	33.4%	66.6%
1990	258,976	135,682	Pressler, Larry	116,727	Muenster, Ted	6,567	18,955 R	52.4%	45.1%	53.8%	46.2%
1986	295,830	143,173	Abdnor, James	152,657	Daschle, Tom		9,484 D	48.4%	51.6%	48.4%	51.6%
1984	315,713	235,176	Pressler, Larry	80,537	Cunningham, George V.		154,639 R	74.5%	25.5%	74.5%	25.5%
1980	327,478	190,594	Abdnor, James	129,018	McGovern, George S.	7,866	61,576 R	58.2%	39.4%	59.6%	40.4%
1978	255,599	170,832	Pressler, Larry	84,767	Barnett, Don		86,065 R	66.8%	33.2%	66.8%	33.2%
1974	278,884	130,955	Thorsness, Leo K.	147,929	McGovern, George S.		16,974 D	47.0%	53.0%	47.0%	53.0%
1972	306,386	131,613	Hirsch, Robert W.	174,773	Abourezk, James		43,160 D	43.0%	57.0%	43.0%	57.0%
1968	279,912	120,951	Gubbrud, Archie M.	158,961	McGovern, George S.		38,010 D	43.2%	56.8%	43.2%	56.8%
1966	227,080	150,517	Mundt, Karl E.	76,563	Wright, Donn H.		73,954 R	66.3%	33.7%	66.3%	33.7%
1962	254,319	126,861	Bottum, Joe H.	127,458	McGovern, George S.		597 D	49.9%	50.1%	49.9%	50.1%
1960	305,442	160,181	Mundt, Karl E.	145,261	McGovern, George S.		14,920 R	52.4%	47.6%	52.4%	47.6%
1956	290,622	147,621	Case, Francis	143,001	Holum, Kenneth		4,620 R	50.8%	49.2%	50.8%	49.2%
1954	235,745	135,071	Mundt, Karl E.	100,674	Holum, Kenneth		34,397 R	57.3%	42.7%	57.3%	42.7%
1950	251,362	160,670	Case, Francis	90,692	Engel, John A.		69,978 R	63.9%	36.1%	63.9%	36.1%
1948	242,833	144,084	Mundt, Karl E.	98,749	Engel, John A.		45,335 R	59.3%	40.7%	59.3%	40.7%

SOUTH DAKOTA

One member At Large

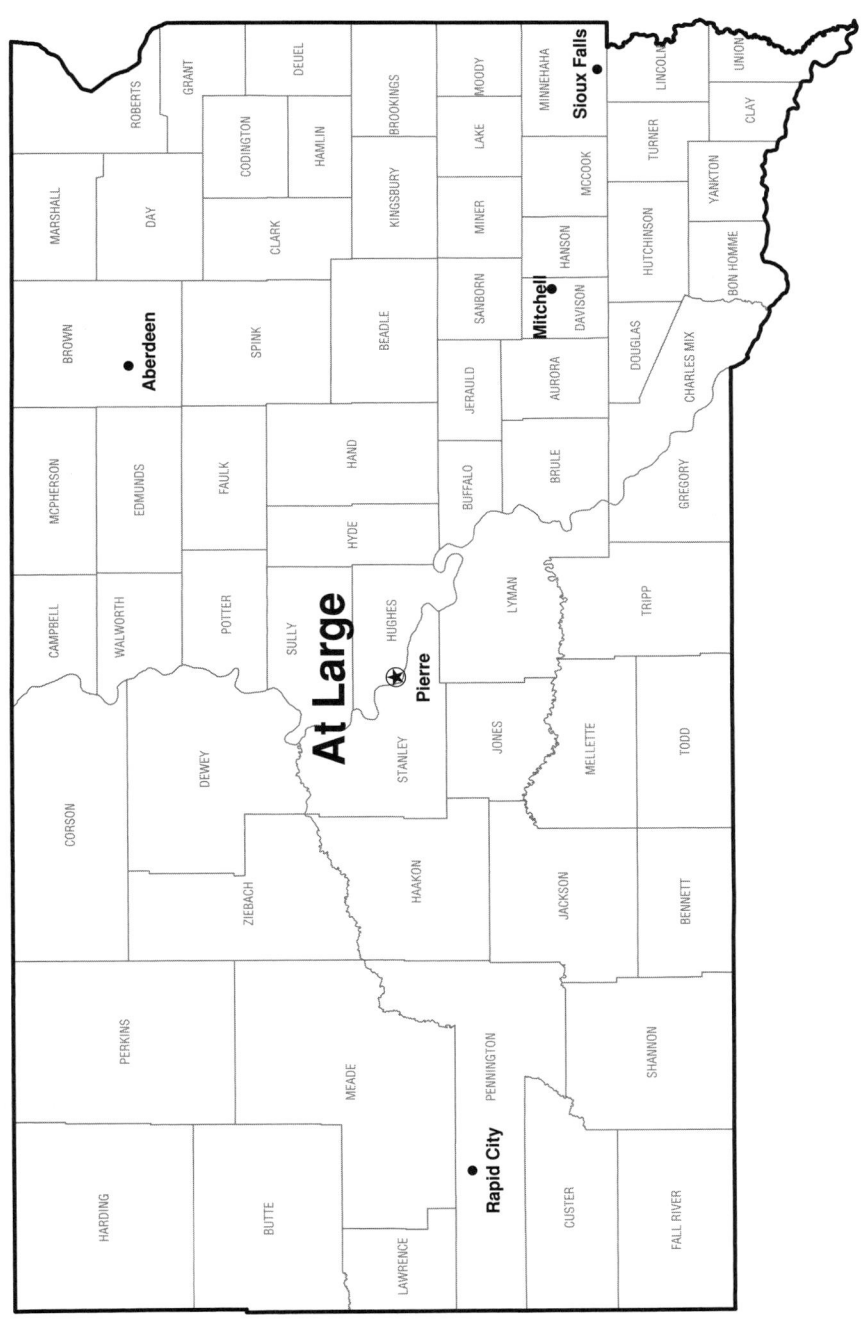

SOUTH DAKOTA

GOVERNOR 2002

2000 Census Population	County	Total Vote	Republican	Democratic	Other	Rep.-Dem. Plurality	Percentage Total Vote Rep.	Dem.	Major Vote Rep.	Dem.
3,058	AURORA	1,577	791	767	19	24 R	50.2%	48.6%	50.8%	49.2%
17,023	BEADLE	7,890	4,876	2,946	68	1,930 R	61.8%	37.3%	62.3%	37.7%
3,574	BENNETT	1,506	670	789	47	119 D	44.5%	52.4%	45.9%	54.1%
7,260	BON HOMME	3,220	1,665	1,511	44	154 R	51.7%	46.9%	52.4%	47.6%
28,220	BROOKINGS	11,404	6,409	4,859	136	1,550 R	56.2%	42.6%	56.9%	43.1%
35,460	BROWN	17,107	9,398	7,520	189	1,878 R	54.9%	44.0%	55.6%	44.4%
5,364	BRULE	2,476	1,463	997	16	466 R	59.1%	40.3%	59.5%	40.5%
2,032	BUFFALO	774	177	583	14	406 D	22.9%	75.3%	23.3%	76.7%
9,094	BUTTE	3,572	2,257	1,248	67	1,009 R	63.2%	34.9%	64.4%	35.6%
1,782	CAMPBELL	965	707	247	11	460 R	73.3%	25.6%	74.1%	25.9%
9,350	CHARLES MIX	4,253	2,345	1,880	28	465 R	55.1%	44.2%	55.5%	44.5%
4,143	CLARK	2,215	1,318	879	18	439 R	59.5%	39.7%	60.0%	40.0%
13,537	CLAY	5,239	2,014	3,135	90	1,121 D	38.4%	59.8%	39.1%	60.9%
25,897	CODINGTON	11,302	6,519	4,692	91	1,827 R	57.7%	41.5%	58.1%	41.9%
4,181	CORSON	1,527	653	819	55	166 D	42.8%	53.6%	44.4%	55.6%
7,275	CUSTER	3,593	2,339	1,162	92	1,177 R	65.1%	32.3%	66.8%	33.2%
18,741	DAVISON	7,884	4,616	3,187	81	1,429 R	58.5%	40.4%	59.2%	40.8%
6,267	DAY	3,354	1,551	1,772	31	221 D	46.2%	52.8%	46.7%	53.3%
4,498	DEUEL	2,186	1,122	1,036	28	86 R	51.3%	47.4%	52.0%	48.0%
5,972	DEWEY	2,247	812	1,380	55	568 D	36.1%	61.4%	37.0%	63.0%
3,458	DOUGLAS	1,849	1,372	463	14	909 R	74.2%	25.0%	74.8%	25.2%
4,367	EDMUNDS	2,201	1,416	758	27	658 R	64.3%	34.4%	65.1%	34.9%
7,453	FALL RIVER	3,138	1,852	1,150	136	702 R	59.0%	36.6%	61.7%	38.3%
2,640	FAULK	1,357	903	443	11	460 R	66.5%	32.6%	67.1%	32.9%
7,847	GRANT	3,847	2,019	1,762	66	257 R	52.5%	45.8%	53.4%	46.6%
4,792	GREGORY	2,354	1,448	884	22	564 R	61.5%	37.6%	62.1%	37.9%
2,196	HAAKON	1,214	900	302	12	598 R	74.1%	24.9%	74.9%	25.1%
5,540	HAMLIN	2,867	1,798	1,035	34	763 R	62.7%	36.1%	63.5%	36.5%
3,741	HAND	2,340	1,348	974	18	374 R	57.6%	41.6%	58.1%	41.9%
3,139	HANSON	1,838	1,198	612	28	586 R	65.2%	33.3%	66.2%	33.8%
1,353	HARDING	783	651	122	10	529 R	83.1%	15.6%	84.2%	15.8%
16,481	HUGHES	8,372	6,144	2,190	38	3,954 R	73.4%	26.2%	73.7%	26.3%
8,075	HUTCHINSON	3,766	2,435	1,303	28	1,132 R	64.7%	34.6%	65.1%	34.9%
1,671	HYDE	905	618	280	7	338 R	68.3%	30.9%	68.8%	31.2%
2,930	JACKSON	1,130	667	429	34	238 R	59.0%	38.0%	60.9%	39.1%
2,295	JERAULD	1,257	651	577	29	74 R	51.8%	45.9%	53.0%	47.0%
1,193	JONES	717	537	173	7	364 R	74.9%	24.1%	75.6%	24.4%
5,815	KINGSBURY	2,952	1,876	1,037	39	839 R	63.6%	35.1%	64.4%	35.6%
11,276	LAKE	5,481	2,897	2,529	55	368 R	52.9%	46.1%	53.4%	46.6%
21,802	LAWRENCE	9,692	5,747	3,731	214	2,016 R	59.3%	38.5%	60.6%	39.4%
24,131	LINCOLN	12,476	7,529	4,856	91	2,673 R	60.3%	38.9%	60.8%	39.2%
3,895	LYMAN	1,953	1,103	837	13	266 R	56.5%	42.9%	56.9%	43.1%
5,832	MCCOOK	2,941	1,586	1,326	29	260 R	53.9%	45.1%	54.5%	45.5%
2,904	MCPHERSON	1,578	1,212	345	21	867 R	76.8%	21.9%	77.8%	22.2%
4,576	MARSHALL	2,146	1,083	1,052	11	31 R	50.5%	49.0%	50.7%	49.3%
24,253	MEADE	9,010	5,816	3,045	149	2,771 R	64.6%	33.8%	65.6%	34.4%
2,083	MELLETTE	857	469	359	29	110 R	54.7%	41.9%	56.6%	43.4%
2,884	MINER	1,409	756	636	17	120 R	53.7%	45.1%	54.3%	45.7%
148,281	MINNEHAHA	65,233	35,923	28,617	693	7,306 R	55.1%	43.9%	55.7%	44.3%
6,595	MOODY	3,038	1,678	1,325	35	353 R	55.2%	43.6%	55.9%	44.1%
88,565	PENNINGTON	35,844	21,634	13,672	538	7,962 R	60.4%	38.1%	61.3%	38.7%
3,363	PERKINS	1,578	1,069	455	54	614 R	67.7%	28.8%	70.1%	29.9%
2,693	POTTER	1,592	1,125	452	15	673 R	70.7%	28.4%	71.3%	28.7%
10,016	ROBERTS	4,365	1,919	2,379	67	460 D	44.0%	54.5%	44.6%	55.4%
2,675	SANBORN	1,411	724	671	16	53 R	51.3%	47.6%	51.9%	48.1%
12,466	SHANNON	2,946	256	2,535	155	2,279 D	8.7%	86.0%	9.2%	90.8%
7,454	SPINK	3,599	2,036	1,543	20	493 R	56.6%	42.9%	56.9%	43.1%
2,772	STANLEY	1,484	974	503	7	471 R	65.6%	33.9%	65.9%	34.1%
1,556	SULLY	946	676	263	7	413 R	71.5%	27.8%	72.0%	28.0%
9,050	TODD	2,415	533	1,825	57	1,292 D	22.1%	75.6%	22.6%	77.4%

SOUTH DAKOTA

GOVERNOR 2002

2000 Census Population	County	Total Vote	Republican	Democratic	Other	Rep.-Dem. Plurality	Percentage			
							Total Vote		Major Vote	
							Rep.	Dem.	Rep.	Dem.
6,430	TRIPP	3,009	1,903	1,082	24	821 R	63.2%	36.0%	63.8%	36.2%
8,849	TURNER	4,274	2,433	1,801	40	632 R	56.9%	42.1%	57.5%	42.5%
12,584	UNION	5,253	2,795	2,358	100	437 R	53.2%	44.9%	54.2%	45.8%
5,974	WALWORTH	2,689	1,783	873	33	910 R	66.3%	32.5%	67.1%	32.9%
21,652	YANKTON	9,217	4,334	4,768	115	434 D	47.0%	51.7%	47.6%	52.4%
2,519	ZIEBACH	945	392	522	31	130 D	41.5%	55.2%	42.9%	57.1%
754,844	TOTAL	334,559	189,920	140,263	4,376	49,657 R	56.8%	41.9%	57.5%	42.5%

SOUTH DAKOTA

SENATOR 2002

2000 Census Population	County	Total Vote	Republican	Democratic	Other	Rep.-Dem. Plurality	Percentage			
							Total Vote		Major Vote	
							Rep.	Dem.	Rep.	Dem.
3,058	AURORA	1,591	698	875	18	177 D	43.9%	55.0%	44.4%	55.6%
17,023	BEADLE	7,974	3,499	4,381	94	882 D	43.9%	54.9%	44.4%	55.6%
3,574	BENNETT	1,609	694	899	16	205 D	43.1%	55.9%	43.6%	56.4%
7,260	BON HOMME	3,329	1,444	1,858	27	414 D	43.4%	55.8%	43.7%	56.3%
28,220	BROOKINGS	11,428	5,128	6,208	92	1,080 D	44.9%	54.3%	45.2%	54.8%
35,460	BROWN	17,223	7,226	9,868	129	2,642 D	42.0%	57.3%	42.3%	57.7%
5,364	BRULE	2,518	1,157	1,343	18	186 D	45.9%	53.3%	46.3%	53.7%
2,032	BUFFALO	793	153	631	9	478 D	19.3%	79.6%	19.5%	80.5%
9,094	BUTTE	3,573	2,321	1,193	59	1,128 R	65.0%	33.4%	66.1%	33.9%
1,782	CAMPBELL	954	581	365	8	216 R	60.9%	38.3%	61.4%	38.6%
9,350	CHARLES MIX	4,320	2,031	2,264	25	233 D	47.0%	52.4%	47.3%	52.7%
4,143	CLARK	2,239	984	1,232	23	248 D	43.9%	55.0%	44.4%	55.6%
13,537	CLAY	5,264	1,786	3,455	23	1,669 D	33.9%	65.6%	34.1%	65.9%
25,897	CODINGTON	11,439	5,630	5,732	77	102 D	49.2%	50.1%	49.6%	50.4%
4,181	CORSON	1,579	573	983	23	410 D	36.3%	62.3%	36.8%	63.2%
7,275	CUSTER	3,649	2,337	1,249	63	1,088 R	64.0%	34.2%	65.2%	34.8%
18,741	DAVISON	7,937	3,937	3,930	70	7 R	49.6%	49.5%	50.0%	50.0%
6,267	DAY	3,391	1,196	2,175	20	979 D	35.3%	64.1%	35.5%	64.5%
4,498	DEUEL	2,203	902	1,280	21	378 D	40.9%	58.1%	41.3%	58.7%
5,972	DEWEY	2,299	598	1,678	23	1,080 D	26.0%	73.0%	26.3%	73.7%
3,458	DOUGLAS	1,879	1,257	610	12	647 R	66.9%	32.5%	67.3%	32.7%
4,367	EDMUNDS	2,281	1,109	1,156	16	47 D	48.6%	50.7%	49.0%	51.0%
7,453	FALL RIVER	3,211	1,873	1,276	62	597 R	58.3%	39.7%	59.5%	40.5%
2,640	FAULK	1,373	727	626	20	101 R	52.9%	45.6%	53.7%	46.3%
7,847	GRANT	3,877	1,783	2,064	30	281 D	46.0%	53.2%	46.3%	53.7%
4,792	GREGORY	2,346	1,226	1,092	28	134 R	52.3%	46.5%	52.9%	47.1%
2,196	HAAKON	1,217	860	347	10	513 R	70.7%	28.5%	71.3%	28.7%
5,540	HAMLIN	2,888	1,444	1,421	23	23 R	50.0%	49.2%	50.4%	49.6%
3,741	HAND	2,358	1,128	1,196	34	68 D	47.8%	50.7%	48.5%	51.5%
3,139	HANSON	1,856	1,047	790	19	257 R	56.4%	42.6%	57.0%	43.0%
1,353	HARDING	790	614	164	12	450 R	77.7%	20.8%	78.9%	21.1%
16,481	HUGHES	8,392	4,703	3,626	63	1,077 R	56.0%	43.2%	56.5%	43.5%
8,075	HUTCHINSON	3,934	2,231	1,678	25	553 R	56.7%	42.7%	57.1%	42.9%
1,671	HYDE	897	510	374	13	136 R	56.9%	41.7%	57.7%	42.3%
2,930	JACKSON	1,167	598	552	17	46 R	51.2%	47.3%	52.0%	48.0%
2,295	JERAULD	1,286	504	770	12	266 D	39.2%	59.9%	39.6%	60.4%
1,193	JONES	723	517	201	5	316 R	71.5%	27.8%	72.0%	28.0%
5,815	KINGSBURY	3,004	1,298	1,678	28	380 D	43.2%	55.9%	43.6%	56.4%
11,276	LAKE	5,496	2,248	3,198	50	950 D	40.9%	58.2%	41.3%	58.7%
21,802	LAWRENCE	9,756	5,822	3,762	172	2,060 R	59.7%	38.6%	60.7%	39.3%

SOUTH DAKOTA

SENATOR 2002

2000 Census Population	County	Total Vote	Republican	Democratic	Other	Rep.-Dem. Plurality	Total Vote Rep.	Dem.	Major Vote Rep.	Dem.
24,131	LINCOLN	12,483	6,808	5,614	61	1,194 R	54.5%	45.0%	54.8%	45.2%
3,895	LYMAN	1,968	832	1,118	18	286 D	42.3%	56.8%	42.7%	57.3%
5,832	MCCOOK	2,927	1,428	1,475	24	47 D	48.8%	50.4%	49.2%	50.8%
2,904	MCPHERSON	1,590	1,007	571	12	436 R	63.3%	35.9%	63.8%	36.2%
4,576	MARSHALL	2,165	845	1,311	9	466 D	39.0%	60.6%	39.2%	60.8%
24,253	MEADE	9,065	5,840	3,075	150	2,765 R	64.4%	33.9%	65.5%	34.5%
2,083	MELLETTE	894	399	483	12	84 D	44.6%	54.0%	45.2%	54.8%
2,884	MINER	1,410	541	857	12	316 D	38.4%	60.8%	38.7%	61.3%
148,281	MINNEHAHA	65,538	31,261	33,903	374	2,642 D	47.7%	51.7%	48.0%	52.0%
6,595	MOODY	3,094	1,169	1,910	15	741 D	37.8%	61.7%	38.0%	62.0%
88,565	PENNINGTON	35,976	21,790	13,732	454	8,058 R	60.6%	38.2%	61.3%	38.7%
3,363	PERKINS	1,637	1,032	579	26	453 R	63.0%	35.4%	64.1%	35.9%
2,693	POTTER	1,597	900	687	10	213 R	56.4%	43.0%	56.7%	43.3%
10,016	ROBERTS	4,454	1,737	2,683	34	946 D	39.0%	60.2%	39.3%	60.7%
2,675	SANBORN	1,422	612	789	21	177 D	43.0%	55.5%	43.7%	56.3%
12,466	SHANNON	3,118	248	2,856	14	2,608 D	8.0%	91.6%	8.0%	92.0%
7,454	SPINK	3,613	1,519	2,064	30	545 D	42.0%	57.1%	42.4%	57.6%
2,772	STANLEY	1,484	802	668	14	134 R	54.0%	45.0%	54.6%	45.4%
1,556	SULLY	939	561	364	14	197 R	59.7%	38.8%	60.6%	39.4%
9,050	TODD	2,508	464	2,027	17	1,563 D	18.5%	80.8%	18.6%	81.4%
6,430	TRIPP	3,039	1,682	1,331	26	351 R	55.3%	43.8%	55.8%	44.2%
8,849	TURNER	4,297	2,201	2,056	40	145 R	51.2%	47.8%	51.7%	48.3%
12,584	UNION	5,278	2,715	2,518	45	197 R	51.4%	47.7%	51.9%	48.1%
5,974	WALWORTH	2,721	1,519	1,177	25	342 R	55.8%	43.3%	56.3%	43.7%
21,652	YANKTON	9,270	4,350	4,804	116	454 D	46.9%	51.8%	47.5%	52.5%
2,519	ZIEBACH	978	321	649	8	328 D	32.8%	66.4%	33.1%	66.9%
754,844	TOTAL	337,508	166,957	167,481	3,070	524 D	49.5%	49.6%	49.9%	50.1%

SOUTH DAKOTA

HOUSE OF REPRESENTATIVES

CD	Year	Total Vote	Republican Vote	Candidate	Democratic Vote	Candidate	Other Vote	Rep.-Dem. Plurality	Total Vote Rep.	Dem.	Major Vote Rep.	Dem.
AL	2002	336,807	180,023	Janklow, Bill	153,656	Herseth, Stephanie	3,128	26,367 R	53.4%	45.6%	54.0%	46.0%
AL	2000	314,761	231,083	Thune, John*	78,321	Hohn, Curt	5,357	152,762 R	73.4%	24.9%	74.7%	25.3%
AL	1998	258,590	194,157	Thune, John*	64,433	Moser, Jeff		129,724 R	75.1%	24.9%	75.1%	24.9%
AL	1996	323,203	186,393	Thune, John	119,547	Weiland, Rick	17,263	66,846 R	57.7%	37.0%	60.9%	39.1%
AL	1994	305,922	112,054	Berkhout, Jan	183,036	Johnson, Tim*	10,832	70,982 D	36.6%	59.8%	38.0%	62.0%
AL	1992	332,902	89,375	Timmer, John	230,070	Johnson, Tim*	13,457	140,695 D	26.8%	69.1%	28.0%	72.0%
AL	1990	257,298	83,484	Frankenfeld, Don	173,814	Johnson, Tim*		90,330 D	32.4%	67.6%	32.4%	67.6%
AL	1988	311,916	88,157	Volk, David	223,759	Johnson, Tim*		135,602 D	28.3%	71.7%	28.3%	71.7%
AL	1986	289,723	118,261	Bell, Dale	171,462	Johnson, Tim		53,201 D	40.8%	59.2%	40.8%	59.2%
AL	1984	316,222	134,821	Bell, Dale	181,401	Daschle, Tom*		46,580 D	42.6%	57.4%	42.6%	57.4%
AL	1982	275,652	133,530	Roberts, Clint	142,122	Daschle, Tom*		8,592 D	48.4%	51.6%	48.4%	51.6%

An asterisk (*) denotes incumbent.

SOUTH DAKOTA

GENERAL AND PRIMARY ELECTIONS

2002 GENERAL ELECTIONS

Governor   Other vote was 2,393 Independent (James P. Carlson); 1,983 Libertarian (Nathan A. Barton).

Senator   Other vote was 3,070 Libertarian (Kurt Evans).

House   Other vote was:

  At Large   3,128 Libertarian (Terry Begay).

2002 PRIMARY ELECTIONS

Primary	June 4, 2002	**Registration**	Republican	219,292
		(active registrants as	Democratic	171,956
		of June 4, 2002)	Libertarian	1,072
			Reform	120
			Other	59,478
			TOTAL	451,918

Primary Type   Closed—Only registered Democrats and Republicans could vote in their party's primary. In addition to the active registered voters, there were 54,376 inactive voters at the time of the 2002 primary.

Note: An asterisk (*) denotes incumbent. The names of unopposed candidates did not appear on the primary ballot; therefore, no votes were cast for these candidates.

	REPUBLICAN PRIMARIES			DEMOCRATIC PRIMARIES		
Governor	Mike Rounds	49,331	44.3%	Jim Abbott	46,794	68.8%
	Mark Barnett	32,868	29.5%	Ron Volesky	11,481	16.9%
	Steve Kirby	29,065	26.1%	Jim Hutmacher	8,847	13.0%
				Robert Hockett	915	1.3%
	TOTAL	111,264		TOTAL	68,037	
Senator	John Thune	Unopposed		Tim Johnson*	65,438	94.8%
				Herman Eilers	3,558	5.2%
				TOTAL	68,996	
House	Bill Janklow	60,575	54.9%	Stephanie Herseth	39,576	58.1%
At Large	Larry Pressler	29,992	27.2%	Rick Weiland	22,083	32.4%
	Tim Amdahl	10,593	9.6%	Dick Casey	4,732	7.0%
	Roger Hunt	7,799	7.1%	Denny Pierson	1,671	2.5%
	Bert Tollefson Jr.	1,311	1.2%			
	TOTAL	110,270		TOTAL	68,062	

SOUTH DAKOTA REPUBLICAN PRIMARY

GOVERNOR 2002

2000 Census Population	County	Total Vote	Rounds	Barnett	Kirby	Winner	Percentage of Total Vote		
							Rounds	Barnett	Kirby
3,058	AURORA	490	238	97	155	Rounds	48.6%	19.8%	31.6%
17,023	BEADLE	2,214	1,380	457	377	Rounds	62.3%	20.6%	17.0%
3,574	BENNETT	429	111	196	122	Barnett	25.9%	45.7%	28.4%
7,260	BON HOMME	1,130	559	296	275	Rounds	49.5%	26.2%	24.3%
28,220	BROOKINGS	3,461	1,967	787	707	Rounds	56.8%	22.7%	20.4%
35,460	BROWN	4,459	1,936	1,437	1,086	Rounds	43.4%	32.2%	24.4%
5,364	BRULE	691	321	260	110	Rounds	46.5%	37.6%	15.9%
2,032	BUFFALO	92	17	57	18	Barnett	18.5%	62.0%	19.6%
9,094	BUTTE	1,799	585	672	542	Barnett	32.5%	37.4%	30.1%
1,782	CAMPBELL	519	185	153	181	Rounds	35.6%	29.5%	34.9%
9,350	CHARLES MIX	1,109	344	509	256	Barnett	31.0%	45.9%	23.1%
4,143	CLARK	857	487	250	120	Rounds	56.8%	29.2%	14.0%
13,537	CLAY	1,078	462	337	279	Rounds	42.9%	31.3%	25.9%
25,897	CODINGTON	3,339	1,393	1,005	941	Rounds	41.7%	30.1%	28.2%
4,181	CORSON	299	81	103	115	Kirby	27.1%	34.4%	38.5%
7,275	CUSTER	1,719	614	625	480	Barnett	35.7%	36.4%	27.9%
18,741	DAVISON	2,204	1,024	661	519	Rounds	46.5%	30.0%	23.5%
6,267	DAY	809	394	242	173	Rounds	48.7%	29.9%	21.4%
4,498	DEUEL	629	329	167	133	Rounds	52.3%	26.6%	21.1%
5,972	DEWEY	445	140	150	155	Kirby	31.5%	33.7%	34.8%
3,458	DOUGLAS	1,097	521	271	305	Rounds	47.5%	24.7%	27.8%
4,367	EDMUNDS	717	356	201	160	Rounds	49.7%	28.0%	22.3%
7,453	FALL RIVER	1,266	409	500	357	Barnett	32.3%	39.5%	28.2%
2,640	FAULK	544	280	147	117	Rounds	51.5%	27.0%	21.5%
7,847	GRANT	1,162	502	395	265	Rounds	43.2%	34.0%	22.8%
4,792	GREGORY	795	404	231	160	Rounds	50.8%	29.1%	20.1%
2,196	HAAKON	774	341	194	239	Rounds	44.1%	25.1%	30.9%
5,540	HAMLIN	994	600	211	183	Rounds	60.4%	21.2%	18.4%
3,741	HAND	910	533	201	176	Rounds	58.6%	22.1%	19.3%
3,139	HANSON	412	220	83	109	Rounds	53.4%	20.1%	26.5%
1,353	HARDING	484	225	133	126	Rounds	46.5%	27.5%	26.0%
16,481	HUGHES	4,868	2,882	1,288	698	Rounds	59.2%	26.5%	14.3%
8,075	HUTCHINSON	2,290	1,095	736	459	Rounds	47.8%	32.1%	20.0%
1,671	HYDE	434	235	107	92	Rounds	54.1%	24.7%	21.2%
2,930	JACKSON	481	185	168	128	Rounds	38.5%	34.9%	26.6%
2,295	JERAULD	439	226	133	80	Rounds	51.5%	30.3%	18.2%
1,193	JONES	460	234	106	120	Rounds	50.9%	23.0%	26.1%
5,815	KINGSBURY	1,262	790	325	147	Rounds	62.6%	25.8%	11.6%
11,276	LAKE	1,794	1,003	443	348	Rounds	55.9%	24.7%	19.4%
21,802	LAWRENCE	3,919	1,310	1,243	1,366	Kirby	33.4%	31.7%	34.9%
24,131	LINCOLN	4,007	1,690	1,043	1,274	Rounds	42.2%	26.0%	31.8%
3,895	LYMAN	776	448	185	143	Rounds	57.7%	23.8%	18.4%
5,832	MCCOOK	1,082	504	337	241	Rounds	46.6%	31.1%	22.3%
2,904	MCPHERSON	893	395	276	222	Rounds	44.2%	30.9%	24.9%
4,576	MARSHALL	525	241	178	106	Rounds	45.9%	33.9%	20.2%
24,253	MEADE	3,330	1,184	1,057	1,089	Rounds	35.6%	31.7%	32.7%
2,083	MELLETTE	345	104	142	99	Barnett	30.1%	41.2%	28.7%
2,884	MINER	384	213	116	55	Rounds	55.5%	30.2%	14.3%
148,281	MINNEHAHA	19,486	8,206	5,000	6,280	Rounds	42.1%	25.7%	32.2%
6,595	MOODY	743	362	206	175	Rounds	48.7%	27.7%	23.6%
88,565	PENNINGTON	12,891	4,948	4,256	3,687	Rounds	38.4%	33.0%	28.6%
3,363	PERKINS	628	202	232	194	Barnett	32.2%	36.9%	30.9%
2,693	POTTER	849	427	258	164	Rounds	50.3%	30.4%	19.3%
10,016	ROBERTS	810	324	287	199	Rounds	40.0%	35.4%	24.6%
2,675	SANBORN	509	255	169	85	Rounds	50.1%	33.2%	16.7%
12,466	SHANNON	92	15	39	38	Barnett	16.3%	42.4%	41.3%
7,454	SPINK	1,093	557	359	177	Rounds	51.0%	32.8%	16.2%
2,772	STANLEY	685	399	171	115	Rounds	58.2%	25.0%	16.8%
1,556	SULLY	445	231	111	103	Rounds	51.9%	24.9%	23.1%
9,050	TODD	230	61	112	57	Barnett	26.5%	48.7%	24.8%

SOUTH DAKOTA REPUBLICAN PRIMARY

GOVERNOR 2002

2000 Census Population	County	Total Vote	Rounds	Barnett	Kirby	Winner	Percentage of Total Vote		
							Rounds	Barnett	Kirby
6,430	TRIPP	1,158	517	350	291	Rounds	44.6%	30.2%	25.1%
8,849	TURNER	1,736	839	485	412	Rounds	48.3%	27.9%	23.7%
12,584	UNION	1,276	373	473	430	Barnett	29.2%	37.1%	33.7%
5,974	WALWORTH	1,290	545	357	388	Rounds	42.2%	27.7%	30.1%
21,652	YANKTON	2,924	1,292	1,017	615	Rounds	44.2%	34.8%	21.0%
2,519	ZIEBACH	203	81	75	47	Rounds	39.9%	36.9%	23.2%
754,844	TOTAL	111,264	49,331	32,868	29,065	Rounds	44.3%	29.5%	26.1%

SOUTH DAKOTA DEMOCRATIC PRIMARY

GOVERNOR 2002

2000 Census Population	County	Total Vote	Abbott	Volesky	Hutmacher	Hockett	Winner	Percentage of Total Vote			
								Abbott	Volesky	Hutmacher	Hockett
3,058	AURORA	596	276	92	220	8	Abbott	46.3%	15.4%	36.9%	1.3%
17,023	BEADLE	2,317	968	1,189	152	8	Volesky	41.8%	51.3%	6.6%	0.3%
3,574	BENNETT	627	324	248	25	30	Abbott	51.7%	39.6%	4.0%	4.8%
7,260	BON HOMME	925	653	75	187	10	Abbott	70.6%	8.1%	20.2%	1.1%
28,220	BROOKINGS	2,030	1,462	381	161	26	Abbott	72.0%	18.8%	7.9%	1.3%
35,460	BROWN	4,259	3,059	668	474	58	Abbott	71.8%	15.7%	11.1%	1.4%
5,364	BRULE	1,080	215	41	820	4	Hutmacher	19.9%	3.8%	75.9%	0.4%
2,032	BUFFALO	302	53	156	89	4	Volesky	17.5%	51.7%	29.5%	1.3%
9,094	BUTTE	406	346	25	27	8	Abbott	85.2%	6.2%	6.7%	2.0%
1,782	CAMPBELL	69	38	13	15	3	Abbott	55.1%	18.8%	21.7%	4.3%
9,350	CHARLES MIX	1,270	493	164	597	16	Hutmacher	38.8%	12.9%	47.0%	1.3%
4,143	CLARK	558	365	116	70	7	Abbott	65.4%	20.8%	12.5%	1.3%
13,537	CLAY	1,328	1,038	179	103	8	Abbott	78.2%	13.5%	7.8%	0.6%
25,897	CODINGTON	2,661	1,893	440	293	35	Abbott	71.1%	16.5%	11.0%	1.3%
4,181	CORSON	288	88	145	44	11	Volesky	30.6%	50.3%	15.3%	3.8%
7,275	CUSTER	435	342	37	44	12	Abbott	78.6%	8.5%	10.1%	2.8%
18,741	DAVISON	1,654	1,143	211	271	29	Abbott	69.1%	12.8%	16.4%	1.8%
6,267	DAY	943	650	170	110	13	Abbott	68.9%	18.0%	11.7%	1.4%
4,498	DEUEL	532	337	107	87	1	Abbott	63.3%	20.1%	16.4%	0.2%
5,972	DEWEY	612	167	372	51	22	Volesky	27.3%	60.8%	8.3%	3.6%
3,458	DOUGLAS	225	145	19	53	8	Abbott	64.4%	8.4%	23.6%	3.6%
4,367	EDMUNDS	550	395	77	70	8	Abbott	71.8%	14.0%	12.7%	1.5%
7,453	FALL RIVER	422	346	34	31	11	Abbott	82.0%	8.1%	7.3%	2.6%
2,640	FAULK	320	214	56	44	6	Abbott	66.9%	17.5%	13.8%	1.9%
7,847	GRANT	812	589	112	101	10	Abbott	72.5%	13.8%	12.4%	1.2%
4,792	GREGORY	636	233	36	359	8	Hutmacher	36.6%	5.7%	56.4%	1.3%
2,196	HAAKON	215	164	21	22	8	Abbott	76.3%	9.8%	10.2%	3.7%
5,540	HAMLIN	561	395	98	58	10	Abbott	70.4%	17.5%	10.3%	1.8%
3,741	HAND	612	381	125	99	7	Abbott	62.3%	20.4%	16.2%	1.1%
3,139	HANSON	440	269	45	115	11	Abbott	61.1%	10.2%	26.1%	2.5%
1,353	HARDING	73	38	20	11	4	Abbott	52.1%	27.4%	15.1%	5.5%
16,481	HUGHES	1,364	1,041	169	125	29	Abbott	76.3%	12.4%	9.2%	2.1%
8,075	HUTCHINSON	692	450	89	145	8	Abbott	65.0%	12.9%	21.0%	1.2%
1,671	HYDE	210	126	35	46	3	Abbott	60.0%	16.7%	21.9%	1.4%
2,930	JACKSON	155	88	51	15	1	Abbott	56.8%	32.9%	9.7%	0.6%
2,295	JERAULD	379	193	97	82	7	Abbott	50.9%	25.6%	21.6%	1.8%
1,193	JONES	114	65	11	37	1	Abbott	57.0%	9.6%	32.5%	0.9%
5,815	KINGSBURY	551	344	145	58	4	Abbott	62.4%	26.3%	10.5%	0.7%
11,276	LAKE	1,351	1,018	202	121	10	Abbott	75.4%	15.0%	9.0%	0.7%
21,802	LAWRENCE	1,296	1,096	113	72	15	Abbott	84.6%	8.7%	5.6%	1.2%

SOUTH DAKOTA DEMOCRATIC PRIMARY

GOVERNOR 2002

2000 Census Population	County	Total Vote	Abbott	Volesky	Hutmacher	Hockett	Winner	Percentage of Total Vote			
								Abbott	Volesky	Hutmacher	Hockett
24,131	LINCOLN	1,854	1,414	243	185	12	Abbott	76.3%	13.1%	10.0%	0.6%
3,895	LYMAN	403	119	68	211	5	Hutmacher	29.5%	16.9%	52.4%	1.2%
5,832	MCCOOK	794	554	120	104	16	Abbott	69.8%	15.1%	13.1%	2.0%
2,904	MCPHERSON	166	110	22	28	6	Abbott	66.3%	13.3%	16.9%	3.6%
4,576	MARSHALL	636	506	65	57	8	Abbott	79.6%	10.2%	9.0%	1.3%
24,253	MEADE	1,144	926	136	68	14	Abbott	80.9%	11.9%	5.9%	1.2%
2,083	MELLETTE	204	111	42	31	20	Abbott	54.4%	20.6%	15.2%	9.8%
2,884	MINER	517	343	81	81	12	Abbott	66.3%	15.7%	15.7%	2.3%
148,281	MINNEHAHA	12,697	9,861	1,634	1,106	96	Abbott	77.7%	12.9%	8.7%	0.8%
6,595	MOODY	863	571	203	83	6	Abbott	66.2%	23.5%	9.6%	0.7%
88,565	PENNINGTON	5,447	4,617	517	259	54	Abbott	84.8%	9.5%	4.8%	1.0%
3,363	PERKINS	185	119	36	27	3	Abbott	64.3%	19.5%	14.6%	1.6%
2,693	POTTER	265	190	32	42	1	Abbott	71.7%	12.1%	15.8%	0.4%
10,016	ROBERTS	1,120	772	182	132	34	Abbott	68.9%	16.3%	11.8%	3.0%
2,675	SANBORN	378	220	86	65	7	Abbott	58.2%	22.8%	17.2%	1.9%
12,466	SHANNON	588	210	335	22	21	Volesky	35.7%	57.0%	3.7%	3.6%
7,454	SPINK	962	613	245	96	8	Abbott	63.7%	25.5%	10.0%	0.8%
2,772	STANLEY	351	263	26	55	7	Abbott	74.9%	7.4%	15.7%	2.0%
1,556	SULLY	189	144	16	26	3	Abbott	76.2%	8.5%	13.8%	1.6%
9,050	TODD	587	140	408	26	13	Volesky	23.9%	69.5%	4.4%	2.2%
6,430	TRIPP	582	380	45	138	19	Abbott	65.3%	7.7%	23.7%	3.3%
8,849	TURNER	782	575	102	94	11	Abbott	73.5%	13.0%	12.0%	1.4%
12,584	UNION	938	734	96	86	22	Abbott	78.3%	10.2%	9.2%	2.3%
5,974	WALWORTH	331	201	80	45	5	Abbott	60.7%	24.2%	13.6%	1.5%
21,652	YANKTON	1,998	1,547	170	258	23	Abbott	77.4%	8.5%	12.9%	1.2%
2,519	ZIEBACH	186	54	107	18	7	Volesky	29.0%	57.5%	9.7%	3.8%
754,844	TOTAL	68,037	46,794	11,481	8,847	915	Abbott	68.8%	16.9%	13.0%	1.3%

SOUTH DAKOTA DEMOCRATIC PRIMARY

SENATOR 2002

2000 Census Population	County	Total Vote	Johnson	Eilers	Winner	Percentage of Total Vote	
						Johnson	Eilers
3,058	AURORA	594	555	39	Johnson	93.4%	6.6%
17,023	BEADLE	2,314	2,193	121	Johnson	94.8%	5.2%
3,574	BENNETT	649	598	51	Johnson	92.1%	7.9%
7,260	BON HOMME	931	888	43	Johnson	95.4%	4.6%
28,220	BROOKINGS	2,065	2,002	63	Johnson	96.9%	3.1%
35,460	BROWN	4,363	4,197	166	Johnson	96.2%	3.8%
5,364	BRULE	1,064	1,012	52	Johnson	95.1%	4.9%
2,032	BUFFALO	306	292	14	Johnson	95.4%	4.6%
9,094	BUTTE	418	377	41	Johnson	90.2%	9.8%
1,782	CAMPBELL	70	65	5	Johnson	92.9%	7.1%
9,350	CHARLES MIX	1,271	1,197	74	Johnson	94.2%	5.8%
4,143	CLARK	584	566	18	Johnson	96.9%	3.1%
13,537	CLAY	1,345	1,302	43	Johnson	96.8%	3.2%
25,897	CODINGTON	2,742	2,624	118	Johnson	95.7%	4.3%
4,181	CORSON	297	258	39	Johnson	86.9%	13.1%
7,275	CUSTER	458	417	41	Johnson	91.0%	9.0%
18,741	DAVISON	1,664	1,587	77	Johnson	95.4%	4.6%
6,267	DAY	970	936	34	Johnson	96.5%	3.5%
4,498	DEUEL	541	522	19	Johnson	96.5%	3.5%
5,972	DEWEY	643	591	52	Johnson	91.9%	8.1%

SOUTH DAKOTA DEMOCRATIC PRIMARY

SENATOR 2002

2000 Census Population	County	Total Vote	Johnson	Eilers	Winner	Percentage of Total Vote	
						Johnson	Eilers
3,458	DOUGLAS	215	201	14	Johnson	93.5%	6.5%
4,367	EDMUNDS	557	524	33	Johnson	94.1%	5.9%
7,453	FALL RIVER	432	407	25	Johnson	94.2%	5.8%
2,640	FAULK	336	311	25	Johnson	92.6%	7.4%
7,847	GRANT	847	813	34	Johnson	96.0%	4.0%
4,792	GREGORY	629	588	41	Johnson	93.5%	6.5%
2,196	HAAKON	213	177	36	Johnson	83.1%	16.9%
5,540	HAMLIN	573	556	17	Johnson	97.0%	3.0%
3,741	HAND	618	585	33	Johnson	94.7%	5.3%
3,139	HANSON	446	422	24	Johnson	94.6%	5.4%
1,353	HARDING	76	69	7	Johnson	90.8%	9.2%
16,481	HUGHES	1,392	1,344	48	Johnson	96.6%	3.4%
8,075	HUTCHINSON	687	662	25	Johnson	96.4%	3.6%
1,671	HYDE	218	204	14	Johnson	93.6%	6.4%
2,930	JACKSON	159	146	13	Johnson	91.8%	8.2%
2,295	JERAULD	374	347	27	Johnson	92.8%	7.2%
1,193	JONES	113	99	14	Johnson	87.6%	12.4%
5,815	KINGSBURY	559	543	16	Johnson	97.1%	2.9%
11,276	LAKE	1,366	1,333	33	Johnson	97.6%	2.4%
21,802	LAWRENCE	1,340	1,220	120	Johnson	91.0%	9.0%
24,131	LINCOLN	1,870	1,781	89	Johnson	95.2%	4.8%
3,895	LYMAN	402	386	16	Johnson	96.0%	4.0%
5,832	MCCOOK	795	750	45	Johnson	94.3%	5.7%
2,904	MCPHERSON	171	165	6	Johnson	96.5%	3.5%
4,576	MARSHALL	664	639	25	Johnson	96.2%	3.8%
24,253	MEADE	1,154	1,062	92	Johnson	92.0%	8.0%
2,083	MELLETTE	210	195	15	Johnson	92.9%	7.1%
2,884	MINER	517	486	31	Johnson	94.0%	6.0%
148,281	MINNEHAHA	12,754	12,212	542	Johnson	95.8%	4.2%
6,595	MOODY	892	842	50	Johnson	94.4%	5.6%
88,565	PENNINGTON	5,542	5,126	416	Johnson	92.5%	7.5%
3,363	PERKINS	215	196	19	Johnson	91.2%	8.8%
2,693	POTTER	268	257	11	Johnson	95.9%	4.1%
10,016	ROBERTS	1,175	1,104	71	Johnson	94.0%	6.0%
2,675	SANBORN	378	353	25	Johnson	93.4%	6.6%
12,466	SHANNON	608	582	26	Johnson	95.7%	4.3%
7,454	SPINK	966	915	51	Johnson	94.7%	5.3%
2,772	STANLEY	352	330	22	Johnson	93.8%	6.3%
1,556	SULLY	195	182	13	Johnson	93.3%	6.7%
9,050	TODD	595	556	39	Johnson	93.4%	6.6%
6,430	TRIPP	581	549	32	Johnson	94.5%	5.5%
8,849	TURNER	794	759	35	Johnson	95.6%	4.4%
12,584	UNION	935	884	51	Johnson	94.5%	5.5%
5,974	WALWORTH	337	313	24	Johnson	92.9%	7.1%
21,652	YANKTON	1,997	1,909	88	Johnson	95.6%	4.4%
2,519	ZIEBACH	190	175	15	Johnson	92.1%	7.9%
754,844	TOTAL	68,996	65,438	3,558	Johnson	94.8%	5.2%

TENNESSEE

GOVERNOR
Phil Bredesen (D). Elected 2002 to a four-year term.

SENATORS (2 Republicans)
Lamar Alexander (R). Elected 2002 to a six-year term.

Bill Frist (R). Reelected 2000 to a six-year term. Previously elected 1994.

REPRESENTATIVES (5 Democrats, 4 Republicans)
1. Bill Jenkins (R)
2. John J. "Jimmy" Duncan Jr. (R)
3. Zach Wamp (R)
4. Lincoln Davis (D)
5. Jim Cooper (D)
6. Bart Gordon (D)
7. Marsha Blackburn (R)
8. John Tanner (D)
9. Harold E. Ford Jr. (D)

POSTWAR VOTE FOR PRESIDENT

Year	Total Vote	Republican Vote	Candidate	Democratic Vote	Candidate	Other Vote	Plurality	Rep.	Dem.	Rep.	Dem.
2000**	2,076,181	1,061,949	Bush, George W.	981,720	Gore, Al	32,512	80,229 R	51.1%	47.3%	52.0%	48.0%
1996**	1,894,105	863,530	Dole, Bob	909,146	Clinton, Bill	121,429	45,616 D	45.6%	48.0%	48.7%	51.3%
1992**	1,982,638	841,300	Bush, George	933,521	Clinton, Bill	207,817	92,221 D	42.4%	47.1%	47.4%	52.6%
1988	1,636,250	947,233	Bush, George	679,794	Dukakis, Michael S.	9,223	267,439 R	57.9%	41.5%	58.2%	41.8%
1984	1,711,994	990,212	Reagan, Ronald	711,714	Mondale, Walter F.	10,068	278,498 R	57.8%	41.6%	58.2%	41.8%
1980**	1,617,616	787,761	Reagan, Ronald	783,051	Carter, Jimmy	46,804	4,710 R	48.7%	48.4%	50.1%	49.9%
1976	1,476,345	633,969	Ford, Gerald R.	825,879	Carter, Jimmy	16,497	191,910 D	42.9%	55.9%	43.4%	56.6%
1972	1,201,182	813,147	Nixon, Richard M.	357,293	McGovern, George S.	30,742	455,854 R	67.7%	29.7%	69.5%	30.5%
1968**	1,248,617	472,592	Nixon, Richard M.	351,233	Humphrey, Hubert H.	424,792	47,800 R	37.8%	28.1%	57.4%	42.6%
1964	1,143,946	508,965	Goldwater, Barry M.	634,947	Johnson, Lyndon B.	34	125,982 D	44.5%	55.5%	44.5%	55.5%
1960	1,051,792	556,577	Nixon, Richard M.	481,453	Kennedy, John F.	13,762	75,124 R	52.9%	45.8%	53.6%	46.4%
1956	939,404	462,288	Eisenhower, Dwight D.	456,507	Stevenson, Adlai E.	20,609	5,781 R	49.2%	48.6%	50.3%	49.7%
1952	892,553	446,147	Eisenhower, Dwight D.	443,710	Stevenson, Adlai E.	2,696	2,437 R	50.0%	49.7%	50.1%	49.9%
1948	550,283	202,914	Dewey, Thomas E.	270,402	Truman, Harry S.	76,967	67,488 D	36.9%	49.1%	42.9%	57.1%

In 2000 the other vote column includes 19,781 votes cast for Green (Nader). In 1996 the other vote column includes 105,918 votes cast for Perot. In 1992 the other vote column includes 199,968 votes cast for Perot. In 1980 the other vote column includes 35,991 votes for Independent (Anderson). In 1968 other vote was American (Wallace).

TENNESSEE

POSTWAR VOTE FOR GOVERNOR

Year	Total Vote	Republican Vote	Republican Candidate	Democratic Vote	Democratic Candidate	Other Vote	Rep.-Dem. Plurality	Total Vote Rep.	Total Vote Dem.	Major Vote Rep.	Major Vote Dem.
2002	1,653,167	786,803	Hilleary, Van	837,284	Bredesen, Phil	29,080	50,481 D	47.6%	50.6%	48.4%	51.6%
1998	976,236	669,973	Sundquist, Don	287,750	Hooker, John J.	18,513	382,223 R	68.6%	29.5%	70.0%	30.0%
1994	1,487,130	807,104	Sundquist, Don	664,252	Bredesen, Phil	15,774	142,852 R	54.3%	44.7%	54.9%	45.1%
1990	790,441	289,348	Henry, Dwight	480,885	McWherter, Ned	20,208	191,537 D	36.6%	60.8%	37.6%	62.4%
1986	1,210,339	553,449	Dunn, Winfield	656,602	McWherter, Ned	288	103,153 D	45.7%	54.2%	45.7%	54.3%
1982	1,238,927	737,963	Alexander, Lamar	500,937	Tyree, Randy	27	237,026 R	59.6%	40.4%	59.6%	40.4%
1978	1,189,695	661,959	Alexander, Lamar	523,495	Butcher, Jake	4,241	138,464 R	55.6%	44.0%	55.8%	44.2%
1974	1,040,714	455,467	Alexander, Lamar	576,833	Blanton, Ray	8,414	121,366 D	43.8%	55.4%	44.1%	55.9%
1970	1,108,247	575,777	Dunn, Winfield	509,521	Hooker, John J.	22,949	66,256 R	52.0%	46.0%	53.1%	46.9%
1966**	656,566			532,998	Ellington, Buford	123,568	532,998 D		81.2%		100.0%
1962**	621,064	100,190	Patty, Hubert D.	315,648	Clement, Frank G.	205,226	215,458 D	16.1%	50.8%	24.1%	75.9%
1958**	432,545	35,938	Wall, Thomas P.	248,874	Ellington, Buford	147,733	212,936 D	8.3%	57.5%	12.6%	87.4%
1954**	322,586		—	281,291	Clement, Frank G.	41,295	281,291 D		87.2%		100.0%
1952	806,771	166,377	Witt, R. Beecher	640,290	Clement, Frank G.	104	473,913 D	20.6%	79.4%	20.6%	79.4%
1950	236,194		—	184,437	Browning, Gordon	51,757	184,437 D		78.1%		100.0%
1948	543,881	179,957	Acuff, Roy	363,903	Browning, Gordon	21	183,946 D	33.1%	66.9%	33.1%	66.9%
1946	229,456	73,222	Lowe, W. O.	149,937	McCord, Jim Nance	6,297	76,715 D	31.9%	65.3%	32.8%	67.2%

In 1966 other vote was 64,602 H. L. Crawford (Independent); 50,221 Charles Moffett (Independent); 8,407 Charles G. Vick (Independent) and 338 scattered. In 1962 other vote was 203,765 William R. Anderson (Independent) who finished second; 1,441 E. B. Bowles (Independent) and 20 scattered. In 1958 Jim Nance McCord (Independent) received 136,399 votes (31.5% of the total vote) and finished second. The term of office of Tennessee's Governor was increased from two to four years effective with the 1954 election.

POSTWAR VOTE FOR SENATOR

Year	Total Vote	Republican Vote	Republican Candidate	Democratic Vote	Democratic Candidate	Other Vote	Rep.-Dem. Plurality	Total Vote Rep.	Total Vote Dem.	Major Vote Rep.	Major Vote Dem.
2002	1,642,421	891,420	Alexander, Lamar	728,295	Clement, Bob	22,706	163,125 R	54.3%	44.3%	55.0%	45.0%
2000	1,928,613	1,255,444	Frist, Bill	621,152	Clark, Jeff	52,017	634,292 R	65.1%	32.2%	66.9%	33.1%
1996	1,778,664	1,091,554	Thompson, Fred	654,937	Gordon, Houston	32,173	436,617 R	61.4%	36.8%	62.5%	37.5%
1994	1,480,391	834,226	Frist, Bill	623,164	Sasser, James R.	23,001	211,062 R	56.4%	42.1%	57.2%	42.8%
1994S	1,465,862	885,998	Thompson, Fred	565,930	Cooper, Jim	13,934	320,068 R	60.4%	38.6%	61.0%	39.0%
1990	783,922	233,703	Hawkins, William R.	530,898	Gore, Albert, Jr.	19,321	297,195 D	29.8%	67.7%	30.6%	69.4%
1988	1,567,181	541,033	Anderson, Bill	1,020,061	Sasser, James R.	6,087	479,028 D	34.5%	65.1%	34.7%	65.3%
1984	1,648,064	557,016	Ashe, Victor	1,000,607	Gore, Albert, Jr.	90,441	443,591 D	33.8%	60.7%	35.8%	64.2%
1982	1,259,785	479,642	Beard, Robin L.	780,113	Sasser, James R.	30	300,471 D	38.1%	61.9%	38.1%	61.9%
1978	1,157,094	642,644	Baker, Howard H., Jr.	466,228	Eskind, Jane	48,222	176,416 R	55.5%	40.3%	58.0%	42.0%
1976	1,432,046	673,231	Brock, William E.	751,180	Sasser, James R.	7,635	77,949 D	47.0%	52.5%	47.3%	52.7%
1972	1,164,195	716,539	Baker, Howard H., Jr.	440,599	Blanton, Ray	7,057	275,940 R	61.5%	37.8%	61.9%	38.1%
1970	1,097,041	562,645	Brock, William E.	519,858	Gore, Albert	14,538	42,787 R	51.3%	47.4%	52.0%	48.0%
1966	866,961	483,063	Baker, Howard H., Jr.	383,843	Clement, Frank G.	55	99,220 R	55.7%	44.3%	55.7%	44.3%
1964	1,064,018	493,475	Kuykendall, Daniel H.	570,542	Gore, Albert	1	77,067 D	46.4%	53.6%	46.4%	53.6%
1964S	1,091,093	517,330	Baker, Howard H., Jr.	568,905	Bass, Ross	4,858	51,575 D	47.4%	52.1%	47.6%	52.4%
1960	828,519	234,053	Frazier, A. Bradley	594,460	Kefauver, Estes	6	360,407 D	28.2%	71.7%	28.2%	71.8%
1958	401,666	76,371	Atkins, Hobart F.	317,324	Gore, Albert	7,971	240,953 D	19.0%	79.0%	19.4%	80.6%
1954	356,094	106,971	Wall, Thomas P.	249,121	Kefauver, Estes	2	142,150 D	30.0%	70.0%	30.0%	70.0%
1952	735,219	153,479	Atkins, Hobart F.	545,432	Gore, Albert	36,308	391,953 D	20.9%	74.2%	22.0%	78.0%
1948	499,218	166,947	Reece, B. Carroll	326,142	Kefauver, Estes	6,129	159,195 D	33.4%	65.3%	33.9%	66.1%
1946	218,714	57,238	Ladd, William B.	145,654	McKellar, Kenneth	15,822	88,416 D	26.2%	66.6%	28.2%	71.8%

One each of the 1994 and 1964 elections was for a short term to fill a vacancy.

TENNESSEE

Congressional districts first established for elections held in 2002
9 members

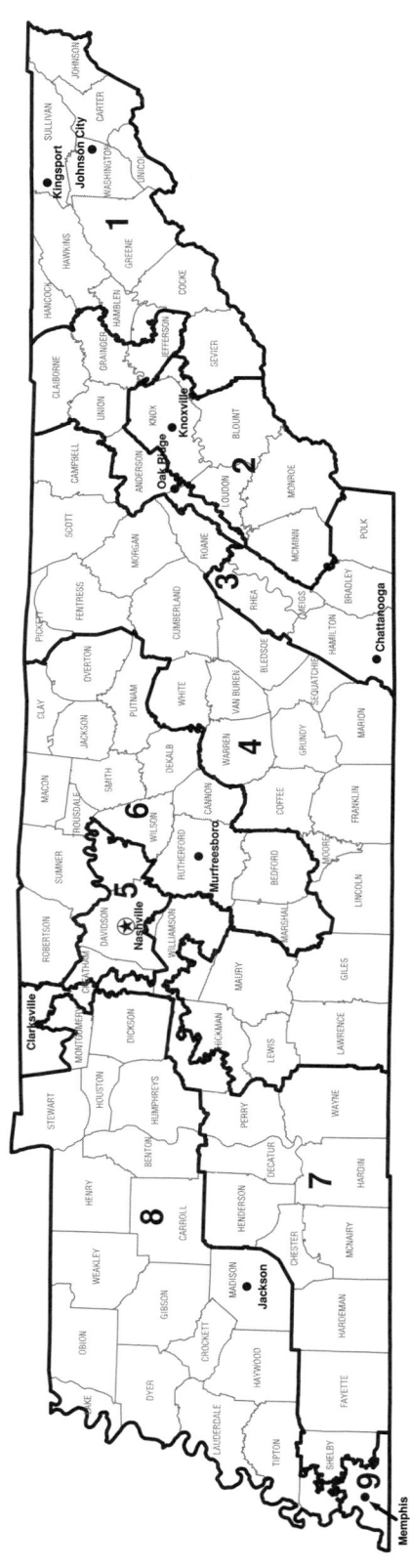

TENNESSEE

GOVERNOR 2002

2000 Census Population	County	Total Vote	Republican	Democratic	Other	Rep.-Dem. Plurality	Percentage Total Vote Rep.	Dem.	Major Vote Rep.	Dem.
71,330	ANDERSON	22,997	10,153	12,526	318	2,373 D	44.1%	54.5%	44.8%	55.2%
37,586	BEDFORD	10,114	4,860	5,098	156	238 D	48.1%	50.4%	48.8%	51.2%
16,537	BENTON	5,627	1,863	3,640	124	1,777 D	33.1%	64.7%	33.9%	66.1%
12,367	BLEDSOE	3,575	1,795	1,722	58	73 R	50.2%	48.2%	51.0%	49.0%
105,823	BLOUNT	32,706	18,189	13,908	609	4,281 R	55.6%	42.5%	56.7%	43.3%
87,965	BRADLEY	24,440	14,756	9,178	506	5,578 R	60.4%	37.6%	61.7%	38.3%
39,854	CAMPBELL	9,244	4,129	5,020	95	891 D	44.7%	54.3%	45.1%	54.9%
12,826	CANNON	4,057	1,654	2,346	57	692 D	40.8%	57.8%	41.4%	58.7%
29,475	CARROLL	9,119	3,982	4,957	180	975 D	43.7%	54.4%	44.5%	55.5%
56,742	CARTER	15,862	9,656	5,877	329	3,779 R	60.9%	37.1%	62.2%	37.8%
35,912	CHEATHAM	11,041	5,305	5,538	198	233 D	48.0%	50.2%	48.9%	51.1%
15,540	CHESTER	4,516	2,544	1,900	72	644 R	56.3%	42.1%	57.2%	42.8%
29,862	CLAIBORNE	7,045	3,483	3,469	93	14 R	49.4%	49.2%	50.1%	49.9%
7,976	CLAY	2,407	932	1,436	39	504 D	38.7%	59.7%	39.4%	60.6%
33,565	COCKE	8,524	4,114	4,219	191	105 D	48.3%	49.5%	49.4%	50.6%
48,014	COFFEE	15,061	7,286	7,613	162	327 D	48.4%	50.5%	48.9%	51.1%
14,532	CROCKETT	4,304	1,951	2,265	88	314 D	45.3%	52.6%	46.3%	53.7%
46,802	CUMBERLAND	16,911	9,235	7,437	239	1,798 R	54.6%	44.0%	55.4%	44.6%
569,891	DAVIDSON	165,897	63,176	97,048	5,673	33,872 D	38.1%	58.5%	39.4%	60.6%
11,731	DECATUR	4,194	1,738	2,375	81	637 D	41.4%	56.6%	42.3%	57.7%
17,423	DE KALB	5,017	2,025	2,929	63	904 D	40.4%	58.4%	40.9%	59.1%
43,156	DICKSON	13,700	5,673	7,810	217	2,137 D	41.4%	57.0%	42.1%	57.9%
37,279	DYER	10,081	4,740	5,114	227	374 D	47.0%	50.7%	48.1%	51.9%
28,806	FAYETTE	9,270	5,306	3,798	166	1,508 R	57.2%	41.0%	58.3%	41.7%
16,625	FENTRESS	5,030	2,832	2,155	43	677 R	56.3%	42.8%	56.8%	43.2%
39,270	FRANKLIN	11,835	5,364	6,312	159	948 D	45.3%	53.3%	45.9%	54.1%
48,152	GIBSON	14,628	6,639	7,700	289	1,061 D	45.4%	52.6%	46.3%	53.7%
29,447	GILES	7,883	3,616	4,167	100	551 D	45.9%	52.9%	46.5%	53.5%
20,659	GRAINGER	5,315	2,809	2,432	74	377 R	52.9%	45.8%	53.6%	46.4%
62,909	GREENE	16,271	9,280	6,739	252	2,541 R	57.0%	41.4%	57.9%	42.1%
14,332	GRUNDY	3,720	1,154	2,524	42	1,370 D	31.0%	67.8%	31.4%	68.6%
58,128	HAMBLEN	16,716	9,069	7,424	223	1,645 R	54.3%	44.4%	55.0%	45.0%
307,896	HAMILTON	88,183	46,109	40,864	1,210	5,245 R	52.3%	46.3%	53.0%	47.0%
6,786	HANCOCK	1,958	1,097	829	32	268 R	56.0%	42.3%	57.0%	43.0%
28,105	HARDEMAN	6,885	2,822	3,891	172	1,069 D	41.0%	56.5%	42.0%	58.0%
25,578	HARDIN	7,476	3,820	3,594	62	226 R	51.1%	48.1%	51.5%	48.5%
53,563	HAWKINS	14,083	7,893	5,921	269	1,972 R	56.0%	42.0%	57.1%	42.9%
19,797	HAYWOOD	5,104	1,986	3,028	90	1,042 D	38.9%	59.3%	39.6%	60.4%
25,522	HENDERSON	7,173	3,933	3,098	142	835 R	54.8%	43.2%	55.9%	44.1%
31,115	HENRY	9,482	3,598	5,672	212	2,074 D	37.9%	59.8%	38.8%	61.2%
22,295	HICKMAN	6,514	2,477	3,931	106	1,454 D	38.0%	60.3%	38.7%	61.3%
8,088	HOUSTON	2,770	750	1,970	50	1,220 D	27.1%	71.1%	27.6%	72.4%
17,929	HUMPHREYS	6,066	2,023	3,944	99	1,921 D	33.3%	65.0%	33.9%	66.1%
10,984	JACKSON	3,680	1,135	2,483	62	1,348 D	30.8%	67.5%	31.4%	68.6%
44,294	JEFFERSON	11,922	6,453	5,293	176	1,160 R	54.1%	44.4%	54.9%	45.1%
17,499	JOHNSON	4,520	2,802	1,641	77	1,161 R	62.0%	36.3%	63.1%	36.9%
382,032	KNOX	116,852	57,683	57,726	1,443	43 D	49.4%	49.4%	50.0%	50.0%
7,954	LAKE	1,586	400	1,128	58	728 D	25.2%	71.1%	26.2%	73.8%
27,101	LAUDERDALE	6,437	2,662	3,621	154	959 D	41.4%	56.3%	42.4%	57.6%
39,926	LAWRENCE	12,420	6,430	5,835	155	595 R	51.8%	47.0%	52.4%	47.6%
11,367	LEWIS	3,821	1,700	2,026	95	326 D	44.5%	53.0%	45.6%	54.4%
31,340	LINCOLN	8,831	4,877	3,808	146	1,069 R	55.2%	43.1%	56.2%	43.8%
39,086	LOUDON	14,180	8,036	5,995	149	2,041 R	56.7%	42.3%	57.3%	42.7%
49,015	MCMINN	13,587	7,407	5,919	261	1,488 R	54.5%	43.6%	55.6%	44.4%
24,653	MCNAIRY	7,657	3,849	3,677	131	172 R	50.3%	48.0%	51.1%	48.9%
20,386	MACON	5,140	2,516	2,554	70	38 D	48.9%	49.7%	49.6%	50.4%
91,837	MADISON	27,846	13,770	13,614	462	156 R	49.5%	48.9%	50.3%	49.7%
27,776	MARION	8,054	3,062	4,856	136	1,794 D	38.0%	60.3%	38.7%	61.3%
26,767	MARSHALL	7,524	3,065	4,323	136	1,258 D	40.7%	57.5%	41.5%	58.5%
69,498	MAURY	20,553	9,313	10,862	378	1,549 D	45.3%	52.8%	46.2%	53.8%

TENNESSEE

GOVERNOR 2002

2000 Census Population	County	Total Vote	Republican	Democratic	Other	Rep.-Dem. Plurality	Percentage Total Vote Rep.	Dem.	Major Vote Rep.	Dem.
11,086	MEIGS	2,819	1,282	1,486	51	204 D	45.5%	52.7%	46.3%	53.7%
38,961	MONROE	10,964	5,709	5,081	174	628 R	52.1%	46.3%	52.9%	47.1%
134,768	MONTGOMERY	31,998	12,723	18,714	561	5,991 D	39.8%	58.5%	40.5%	59.5%
5,740	MOORE	2,071	1,070	950	51	120 R	51.7%	45.9%	53.0%	47.0%
19,757	MORGAN	5,424	2,252	3,128	44	876 D	41.5%	57.7%	41.9%	58.1%
32,450	OBION	10,272	4,083	5,928	261	1,845 D	39.7%	57.7%	40.8%	59.2%
20,118	OVERTON	6,125	1,999	4,027	99	2,028 D	32.6%	65.7%	33.2%	66.8%
7,631	PERRY	2,306	871	1,379	56	508 D	37.8%	59.8%	38.7%	61.3%
4,945	PICKETT	2,071	1,221	831	19	390 R	59.0%	40.1%	59.5%	40.5%
16,050	POLK	4,535	1,925	2,539	71	614 D	42.4%	56.0%	43.1%	56.9%
62,315	PUTNAM	18,835	8,241	10,241	353	2,000 D	43.8%	54.4%	44.6%	55.4%
28,400	RHEA	8,190	5,383	2,727	80	2,656 R	65.7%	33.3%	66.4%	33.6%
51,910	ROANE	17,612	7,478	9,873	261	2,395 D	42.5%	56.1%	43.1%	56.9%
54,433	ROBERTSON	17,323	7,944	9,089	290	1,145 D	45.9%	52.5%	46.6%	53.4%
182,023	RUTHERFORD	51,171	25,750	24,683	738	1,067 R	50.3%	48.2%	51.1%	48.9%
21,127	SCOTT	4,848	2,480	2,326	42	154 R	51.2%	48.0%	51.6%	48.4%
11,370	SEQUATCHIE	3,644	1,582	2,020	42	438 D	43.4%	55.4%	43.9%	56.1%
71,170	SEVIER	20,378	12,477	7,642	259	4,835 R	61.2%	37.5%	62.0%	38.0%
897,472	SHELBY	237,393	100,261	133,084	4,048	32,823 D	42.2%	56.1%	43.0%	57.0%
17,712	SMITH	5,940	2,086	3,741	113	1,655 D	35.1%	63.0%	35.8%	64.2%
12,370	STEWART	4,066	1,260	2,709	97	1,449 D	31.0%	66.6%	31.7%	68.3%
153,048	SULLIVAN	42,515	24,118	17,760	637	6,358 R	56.7%	41.8%	57.6%	42.4%
130,449	SUMNER	41,518	21,032	19,860	626	1,172 R	50.7%	47.8%	51.4%	48.6%
51,271	TIPTON	13,460	8,015	5,192	253	2,823 R	59.5%	38.6%	60.7%	39.3%
7,259	TROUSDALE	2,302	753	1,515	34	762 D	32.7%	65.8%	33.2%	66.8%
17,667	UNICOI	4,795	2,739	1,975	81	764 R	57.1%	41.2%	58.1%	41.9%
17,808	UNION	4,681	2,319	2,307	55	12 R	49.5%	49.3%	50.1%	49.9%
5,508	VAN BUREN	1,860	654	1,178	28	524 D	35.2%	63.3%	35.7%	64.3%
38,276	WARREN	12,037	4,743	7,137	157	2,394 D	39.4%	59.3%	39.9%	60.1%
107,198	WASHINGTON	29,835	17,290	12,012	533	5,278 R	58.0%	40.3%	59.0%	41.0%
16,842	WAYNE	4,180	2,462	1,685	33	777 R	58.9%	40.3%	59.4%	40.6%
34,895	WEAKLEY	10,706	4,680	5,821	205	1,141 D	43.7%	54.4%	44.6%	55.4%
23,102	WHITE	7,328	3,564	3,653	111	89 D	48.6%	49.8%	49.4%	50.6%
126,638	WILLIAMSON	51,777	29,965	21,358	454	8,607 R	57.9%	41.2%	58.4%	41.6%
88,809	WILSON	30,777	15,416	14,854	507	562 R	50.1%	48.3%	50.9%	49.1%
5,689,283	TOTAL	1,653,167	786,803	837,284	29,080	50,481 D	47.6%	50.6%	48.4%	51.6%

TENNESSEE

SENATOR 2002

2000 Census Population	County	Total Vote	Republican	Democratic	Other	Rep.-Dem. Plurality	Percentage Total Vote Rep.	Dem.	Major Vote Rep.	Dem.
71,330	ANDERSON	22,999	12,700	9,957	342	2,743 R	55.2%	43.3%	56.1%	43.9%
37,586	BEDFORD	9,976	4,898	4,918	160	20 D	49.1%	49.3%	49.9%	50.1%
16,537	BENTON	5,664	2,030	3,530	104	1,500 D	35.8%	62.3%	36.5%	63.5%
12,367	BLEDSOE	3,591	1,934	1,603	54	331 R	53.9%	44.6%	54.7%	45.3%
105,823	BLOUNT	32,943	21,061	11,471	411	9,590 R	63.9%	34.8%	64.7%	35.3%
87,965	BRADLEY	23,667	16,489	6,782	396	9,707 R	69.7%	28.7%	70.9%	29.1%
39,854	CAMPBELL	9,036	4,392	4,527	117	135 D	48.6%	50.1%	49.2%	50.8%
12,826	CANNON	4,033	1,671	2,292	70	621 D	41.4%	56.8%	42.2%	57.8%
29,475	CARROLL	9,238	4,540	4,518	180	22 R	49.1%	48.9%	50.1%	49.9%
56,742	CARTER	15,711	10,798	4,542	371	6,256 R	68.7%	28.9%	70.4%	29.6%

TENNESSEE

SENATOR 2002

2000 Census Population	County	Total Vote	Republican	Democratic	Other	Rep.-Dem. Plurality	Total Vote Rep.	Total Vote Dem.	Major Vote Rep.	Major Vote Dem.
35,912	CHEATHAM	10,980	5,647	5,209	124	438 R	51.4%	47.4%	52.0%	48.0%
15,540	CHESTER	4,379	2,518	1,809	52	709 R	57.5%	41.3%	58.2%	41.8%
29,862	CLAIBORNE	6,859	3,666	3,045	148	621 R	53.4%	44.4%	54.6%	45.4%
7,976	CLAY	2,325	1,004	1,277	44	273 D	43.2%	54.9%	44.0%	56.0%
33,565	COCKE	8,356	4,859	3,298	199	1,561 R	58.1%	39.5%	59.6%	40.4%
48,014	COFFEE	15,037	7,541	7,322	174	219 R	50.1%	48.7%	50.7%	49.3%
14,532	CROCKETT	4,318	2,071	2,171	76	100 D	48.0%	50.3%	48.8%	51.2%
46,802	CUMBERLAND	16,901	9,942	6,714	245	3,228 R	58.8%	39.7%	59.7%	40.3%
569,891	DAVIDSON	165,601	70,974	92,994	1,633	22,020 D	42.9%	56.2%	43.3%	56.7%
11,731	DECATUR	4,140	1,802	2,258	80	456 D	43.5%	54.5%	44.4%	55.6%
17,423	DE KALB	4,918	1,973	2,869	76	896 D	40.1%	58.3%	40.7%	59.3%
43,156	DICKSON	13,758	5,910	7,731	117	1,821 D	43.0%	56.2%	43.3%	56.7%
37,279	DYER	10,299	5,475	4,610	214	865 R	53.2%	44.8%	54.3%	45.7%
28,806	FAYETTE	9,462	5,744	3,589	129	2,155 R	60.7%	37.9%	61.5%	38.5%
16,625	FENTRESS	4,856	2,653	2,131	72	522 R	54.6%	43.9%	55.5%	44.5%
39,270	FRANKLIN	11,683	5,499	5,994	190	495 D	47.1%	51.3%	47.8%	52.2%
48,152	GIBSON	14,596	7,326	6,947	323	379 R	50.2%	47.6%	51.3%	48.7%
29,447	GILES	7,682	3,559	3,941	182	382 D	46.3%	51.3%	47.5%	52.5%
20,659	GRAINGER	5,265	3,085	2,102	78	983 R	58.6%	39.9%	59.5%	40.5%
62,909	GREENE	15,879	10,414	5,131	334	5,283 R	65.6%	32.3%	67.0%	33.0%
14,332	GRUNDY	3,701	1,220	2,439	42	1,219 D	33.0%	65.9%	33.3%	66.7%
58,128	HAMBLEN	16,427	10,115	6,058	254	4,057 R	61.6%	36.9%	62.5%	37.5%
307,896	HAMILTON	87,516	53,070	33,433	1,013	19,637 R	60.6%	38.2%	61.4%	38.6%
6,786	HANCOCK	1,882	1,180	666	36	514 R	62.7%	35.4%	63.9%	36.1%
28,105	HARDEMAN	6,400	3,002	3,266	132	264 D	46.9%	51.0%	47.9%	52.1%
25,578	HARDIN	7,416	3,895	3,425	96	470 R	52.5%	46.2%	53.2%	46.8%
53,563	HAWKINS	13,833	8,658	4,893	282	3,765 R	62.6%	35.4%	63.9%	36.1%
19,797	HAYWOOD	5,268	2,274	2,929	65	655 D	43.2%	55.6%	43.7%	56.3%
25,522	HENDERSON	7,099	4,096	2,858	145	1,238 R	57.7%	40.3%	58.9%	41.1%
31,115	HENRY	9,537	4,097	5,263	177	1,166 D	43.0%	55.2%	43.8%	56.2%
22,295	HICKMAN	6,530	2,560	3,885	85	1,325 D	39.2%	59.5%	39.7%	60.3%
8,088	HOUSTON	2,595	763	1,794	38	1,031 D	29.4%	69.1%	29.8%	70.2%
17,929	HUMPHREYS	6,035	2,073	3,891	71	1,818 D	34.3%	64.5%	34.8%	65.2%
10,984	JACKSON	3,432	1,133	2,247	52	1,114 D	33.0%	65.5%	33.5%	66.5%
44,294	JEFFERSON	11,771	7,266	4,269	236	2,997 R	61.7%	36.3%	63.0%	37.0%
17,499	JOHNSON	4,414	3,101	1,227	86	1,874 R	70.3%	27.8%	71.6%	28.4%
382,032	KNOX	114,524	70,793	42,106	1,625	28,687 R	61.8%	36.8%	62.7%	37.3%
7,954	LAKE	1,319	506	778	35	272 D	38.4%	59.0%	39.4%	60.6%
27,101	LAUDERDALE	6,491	2,904	3,456	131	552 D	44.7%	53.2%	45.7%	54.3%
39,926	LAWRENCE	11,916	6,381	5,380	155	1,001 R	53.5%	45.1%	54.3%	45.7%
11,367	LEWIS	3,879	1,730	2,073	76	343 D	44.6%	53.4%	45.5%	54.5%
31,340	LINCOLN	8,659	4,523	3,967	169	556 R	52.2%	45.8%	53.3%	46.7%
39,086	LOUDON	14,219	9,398	4,668	153	4,730 R	66.1%	32.8%	66.8%	33.2%
49,015	MCMINN	13,666	8,410	4,989	267	3,421 R	61.5%	36.5%	62.8%	37.2%
24,653	MCNAIRY	7,601	3,954	3,533	114	421 R	52.0%	46.5%	52.8%	47.2%
20,386	MACON	5,060	2,476	2,495	89	19 D	48.9%	49.3%	49.8%	50.2%
91,837	MADISON	27,864	15,640	11,879	345	3,761 R	56.1%	42.6%	56.8%	43.2%
27,776	MARION	8,047	3,640	4,281	126	641 D	45.2%	53.2%	46.0%	54.0%
26,767	MARSHALL	7,469	3,355	3,971	143	616 D	44.9%	53.2%	45.8%	54.2%
69,498	MAURY	20,566	10,240	10,053	273	187 R	49.8%	48.9%	50.5%	49.5%
11,086	MEIGS	2,805	1,541	1,210	54	331 R	54.9%	43.1%	56.0%	44.0%
38,961	MONROE	11,009	6,469	4,396	144	2,073 R	58.8%	39.9%	59.5%	40.5%
134,768	MONTGOMERY	31,901	15,824	15,645	432	179 R	49.6%	49.0%	50.3%	49.7%
5,740	MOORE	2,034	1,031	984	19	47 R	50.7%	48.4%	51.2%	48.8%
19,757	MORGAN	5,421	2,575	2,811	35	236 D	47.5%	51.9%	47.8%	52.2%
32,450	OBION	10,108	4,593	5,319	196	726 D	45.4%	52.6%	46.3%	53.7%
20,118	OVERTON	5,712	2,071	3,565	76	1,494 D	36.3%	62.4%	36.7%	63.3%
7,631	PERRY	2,190	857	1,273	60	416 D	39.1%	58.1%	40.2%	59.8%
4,945	PICKETT	2,032	1,162	844	26	318 R	57.2%	41.5%	57.9%	42.1%
16,050	POLK	4,546	2,259	2,215	72	44 R	49.7%	48.7%	50.5%	49.5%

TENNESSEE

SENATOR 2002

2000 Census Population	County	Total Vote	Republican	Democratic	Other	Rep.-Dem. Plurality	Total Vote Rep.	Total Vote Dem.	Major Vote Rep.	Major Vote Dem.
62,315	PUTNAM	18,516	9,340	8,829	347	511 R	50.4%	47.7%	51.4%	48.6%
28,400	RHEA	7,767	5,115	2,561	91	2,554 R	65.9%	33.0%	66.6%	33.4%
51,910	ROANE	17,399	9,693	7,445	261	2,248 R	55.7%	42.8%	56.6%	43.4%
54,433	ROBERTSON	17,254	7,948	9,110	196	1,162 D	46.1%	52.8%	46.6%	53.4%
182,023	RUTHERFORD	51,179	29,018	21,613	548	7,405 R	56.7%	42.2%	57.3%	42.7%
21,127	SCOTT	4,703	2,414	2,202	87	212 R	51.3%	46.8%	52.3%	47.7%
11,370	SEQUATCHIE	3,640	1,765	1,826	49	61 D	48.5%	50.2%	49.2%	50.8%
71,170	SEVIER	20,459	13,979	6,223	257	7,756 R	68.3%	30.4%	69.2%	30.8%
897,472	SHELBY	238,402	117,929	117,629	2,844	300 R	49.5%	49.3%	50.1%	49.9%
17,712	SMITH	5,759	2,137	3,555	67	1,418 D	37.1%	61.7%	37.5%	62.5%
12,370	STEWART	3,837	1,317	2,436	84	1,119 D	34.3%	63.5%	35.1%	64.9%
153,048	SULLIVAN	42,121	28,495	12,872	754	15,623 R	67.7%	30.6%	68.9%	31.1%
130,449	SUMNER	41,760	23,638	17,650	472	5,988 R	56.6%	42.3%	57.3%	42.7%
51,271	TIPTON	13,756	8,821	4,678	257	4,143 R	64.1%	34.0%	65.3%	34.7%
7,259	TROUSDALE	2,275	786	1,461	28	675 D	34.5%	64.2%	35.0%	65.0%
17,667	UNICOI	4,617	3,189	1,335	93	1,854 R	69.1%	28.9%	70.5%	29.5%
17,808	UNION	4,446	2,413	1,984	49	429 R	54.3%	44.6%	54.9%	45.1%
5,508	VAN BUREN	1,760	673	1,063	24	390 D	38.2%	60.4%	38.8%	61.2%
38,276	WARREN	11,846	5,219	6,414	213	1,195 D	44.1%	54.1%	44.9%	55.1%
107,198	WASHINGTON	29,725	20,195	8,994	536	11,201 R	67.9%	30.3%	69.2%	30.8%
16,842	WAYNE	3,953	2,421	1,486	46	935 R	61.2%	37.6%	62.0%	38.0%
34,895	WEAKLEY	10,776	5,138	5,434	204	296 D	47.7%	50.4%	48.6%	51.4%
23,102	WHITE	7,341	3,373	3,831	137	458 D	45.9%	52.2%	46.8%	53.2%
126,638	WILLIAMSON	51,669	36,272	15,044	353	21,228 R	70.2%	29.1%	70.7%	29.3%
88,809	WILSON	30,415	17,122	12,904	389	4,218 R	56.3%	42.4%	57.0%	43.0%
5,689,283	TOTAL	1,642,421	891,420	728,295	22,706	163,125 R	54.3%	44.3%	55.0%	45.0%

TENNESSEE

HOUSE OF REPRESENTATIVES

CD	Year	Total Vote	Republican Vote	Republican Candidate	Democratic Vote	Democratic Candidate	Other Vote	Rep.-Dem. Plurality	Total Vote Rep.	Total Vote Dem.	Major Vote Rep.	Major Vote Dem.
1	2002	128,886	127,300	Jenkins, Bill*			1,586	127,300 R	98.8%		100.0%	
2	2002	185,981	146,887	Duncan, John J. "Jimmy" Jr.*	37,035	Greene, John	2,059	109,852 R	79.0%	19.9%	79.9%	20.1%
3	2002	173,921	112,254	Wamp, Zach*	58,824	Wolfe, John	2,843	53,430 R	64.5%	33.8%	65.6%	34.4%
4	2002	184,300	85,680	Bowling, Janice	95,989	Davis, Lincoln	2,631	10,309 D	46.5%	52.1%	47.2%	52.8%
5	2002	170,886	56,825	Duvall, Robert	108,903	Cooper, Jim	5,158	52,078 D	33.3%	63.7%	34.3%	65.7%
6	2002	177,547	57,401	Garrison, Robert L.	117,034	Gordon, Bart*	3,112	59,633 D	32.3%	65.9%	32.9%	67.1%
7	2002	195,558	138,314	Blackburn, Marsha	51,790	Barron, Tim	5,454	86,524 R	70.7%	26.5%	72.8%	27.2%
8	2002	167,970	45,853	McClain, Mat	117,811	Tanner, John*	4,306	71,958 D	27.3%	70.1%	28.0%	72.0%
9	2002	144,260			120,904	Ford, Harold E. Jr.*	23,356	120,904 D		83.8%		100.0%
Total	2002	1,529,309	770,514		708,290		50,505	62,224 R	50.4%	46.3%	52.1%	47.9%

An asterisk (*) denotes incumbent.

TENNESSEE
GENERAL AND PRIMARY ELECTIONS

2002 GENERAL ELECTIONS

Governor Other vote was 7,749 Independent (Edwin C. Sanders); 5,308 Independent (Carl Two Feathers Whitaker); 4,577 Independent (John Jay Hooker); 2,991 Independent (David Gatchell); 1,591 Independent (Gabriel Givens); 1,589 Independent (Ray Ledford); 1,210 Independent (James E. Herren); 898 Independent (Charles V. Wilhoit Jr.); 645 Independent (Marivuana Stout Leinoff); 635 Independent (Francis E. Waldron); 630 Independent (Ronny Simmons); 579 Independent (Robert O. Watson); 302 Independent (Basil J. Marceaux I); 376 write-in.

Senator Other vote was 6,407 Independent (John Jay Hooker); 6,105 Independent (Wesley M. Baker); 5,346 Independent (Connie Gammon); 2,216 Independent (Karl Stanley Davidson); 1,173 Independent (Basil J. Marceaux I); 1,103 Independent (H. Gary Keplinger); 356 write-in.

House Other vote was:

CD 1	1,586 write-in.
CD 2	1,110 Independent (Joshua Williamson); 940 Independent (George Njezic); 9 write-in.
CD 3	1,743 Independent (William C. Bolen); 947 Independent (Timothy A. Sevier); 153 write-in.
CD 4	1,073 Independent (William Tharon Chandler); 605 Independent (John Ray); 504 Independent (Bert Mason); 399 Independent (Ed Wellmann); 50 write-in.
CD 5	3,063 Independent (John Jay Hooker); 1,205 Independent (Jonathan D. Farley); 877 Independent (Jesse Turner); 13 write-in.
CD 6	3,065 Independent (J. Patrick Lyons); 47 write-in.
CD 7	5,423 Independent (Rick Patterson); 31 write-in.
CD 8	4,288 Independent (James L. Hart); 18 write-in.
CD 9	23,208 Independent (Tony Rush); 148 write-in.

Note: In Tennessee all third-party candidates were listed as Independents regardless of party affiliation.

2002 PRIMARY ELECTIONS

Primary	August 1, 2002	**Registration** (as of June 1, 2002—includes 320,856 inactive registrants)	3,358,681 No Party Registration

Primary Type Open—Any registered voter could participate in either the Democratic or Republican primary.

Note: An asterisk (*) denotes incumbent.

	REPUBLICAN PRIMARIES			DEMOCRATIC PRIMARIES		
Governor	Van Hilleary	343,543	64.3%	Phil Bredesen	426,418	79.0%
	James M. "Jim" Henry	159,862	29.9%	Randy Nichols	38,322	7.1%
	Bob Tripp	17,156	3.2%	Charles E. Smith	34,547	6.4%
	Dave Kelley	8,581	1.6%	Charles V. Brown	17,506	3.2%
	Jessie D. McDonald	4,682	0.9%	L. Best	16,007	3.0%
	Write-in	389	0.1%	Floyd R. Conover	6,218	1.2%
				Write-in	420	0.1%
	TOTAL	534,213		TOTAL	539,438	

TENNESSEE

GENERAL AND PRIMARY ELECTIONS

	REPUBLICAN PRIMARIES			DEMOCRATIC PRIMARIES		
Senator	Lamar Alexander	295,052	53.8%	Bob Clement	418,172	82.2%
	Ed Bryant	233,678	42.6%	Gary G. Davis	50,563	9.9%
	Mary Taylor-Shelby	5,589	1.0%	Cher A. Hopkey	14,481	2.8%
	June Griffin	4,930	0.9%	Michael L. Hampstead	12,940	2.5%
	Michael Brent Todd	4,002	0.7%	Alvin M. Strauss	12,241	2.4%
	James E. DuBose	3,572	0.7%	Write-in	478	0.1%
	Christopher G. Fenner	1,552	0.3%			
	Write-in	107				
	TOTAL	548,482		TOTAL	508,875	
Congressional District 1	Bill Jenkins*	65,421	88.2%	*No Democratic candidate filed for the primary. There were 494 write-in votes.*		
	Larry P. Edgell	8,740	11.8%			
	Write-in	50	0.1%			
	TOTAL	74,211				
Congressional District 2	John J. "Jimmy" Duncan Jr.*	67,582	91.7%	John Greene	23,885	100.0%
	Jim Pendergrass	6,095	8.3%	Write-in	3	
	Write-in	3				
	TOTAL	73,680		TOTAL	23,888	
Congressional District 3	Zach Wamp*	59,410	99.3%	John Wolfe	22,731	66.1%
	Write-in	392	0.7%	John Norman E. Knott Jr.	11,517	33.5%
				Write-in	150	0.4%
	TOTAL	59,802		TOTAL	34,398	
Congressional District 4	Janice Bowling	20,709	37.1%	Lincoln Davis	48,843	57.0%
	Mike Greene	13,563	24.3%	Fran F. Marcum	36,779	42.9%
	Andy Ogles	8,201	14.7%	Write-in	64	0.1%
	John Bumpus	7,245	13.0%			
	Mike Coffield	4,991	8.9%			
	Harvey Howard	1,063	1.9%			
	Write-in	41	0.1%			
	TOTAL	55,813		TOTAL	85,686	
Congressional District 5	Robert Duvall	11,572	45.3%	Jim Cooper	32,651	46.7%
	Thomas W. Lawless	5,759	22.5%	John Arriola	16,878	24.2%
	Kevin Wilkinson	5,608	21.9%	Gayle Ray	16,087	23.0%
	Remo Circo	2,009	7.9%	David C. Mills	1,657	2.4%
	Ben J. Tomeo	600	2.3%	Carlton Cornett	1,096	1.6%
	Write-in	23	0.1%	Ronnie Steine	901	1.3%
				Adam Cox	593	0.8%
				Write-in	21	
	TOTAL	25,571		TOTAL	69,884	
Congressional District 6	Robert L. Garrison	34,329	99.6%	Bart Gordon*	69,121	91.6%
	Write-in	147	0.4%	Harvey Howard	6,255	8.3%
				Write-in	99	0.1%
	TOTAL	34,476		TOTAL	75,475	
Congressional District 7	Marsha Blackburn	36,633	40.3%	Tim Barron	22,789	71.0%
	David Kustoff	18,392	20.2%	Omer R. Hayden	9,262	28.9%
	Brent Taylor	14,139	15.6%	Write-in	25	0.1%
	Mark Norris	13,104	14.4%			
	Forrest Shoaf	7,319	8.1%			
	Sonny Carlota	642	0.7%			
	Randy Starkey	628	0.7%			
	Write-in	9				
	TOTAL	90,866		TOTAL	32,076	
Congressional District 8	Mat McClain	18,878	56.5%	John Tanner*	66,015	86.8%
	Bill Warren	14,531	43.5%	Richard Ward	10,069	13.2%
	Write-in	26	0.1%	Write-in	12	
	TOTAL	33,435		TOTAL	76,096	
Congressional District 9	*No Republican candidate filed for the primary. There were 5 write-in votes.*			Harold E. Ford Jr.*	79,146	99.9%
				Write-in	46	0.1%
				TOTAL	79,192	

TENNESSEE REPUBLICAN PRIMARY
GOVERNOR 2002

2000 Census Population	County	Total Vote	Hilleary	Henry	Other	Winner	Percentage of Total Vote		
							Hilleary	Henry	Other
71,330	ANDERSON	9,010	5,010	3,493	507	Hilleary	55.6%	38.8%	5.6%
37,586	BEDFORD	1,763	1,618	123	22	Hilleary	91.8%	7.0%	1.2%
16,537	BENTON	1,240	752	316	172	Hilleary	60.6%	25.5%	13.9%
12,367	BLEDSOE	1,444	1,113	247	84	Hilleary	77.1%	17.1%	5.8%
105,823	BLOUNT	11,437	5,912	5,053	472	Hilleary	51.7%	44.2%	4.1%
87,965	BRADLEY	10,280	5,769	3,925	586	Hilleary	56.1%	38.2%	5.7%
39,854	CAMPBELL	3,759	2,949	675	135	Hilleary	78.5%	18.0%	3.6%
12,826	CANNON	1,054	875	116	63	Hilleary	83.0%	11.0%	6.0%
29,475	CARROLL	2,448	1,366	790	292	Hilleary	55.8%	32.3%	11.9%
56,742	CARTER	10,165	5,170	3,983	1,012	Hilleary	50.9%	39.2%	10.0%
35,912	CHEATHAM	3,572	2,911	503	158	Hilleary	81.5%	14.1%	4.4%
15,540	CHESTER	1,772	1,291	317	164	Hilleary	72.9%	17.9%	9.3%
29,862	CLAIBORNE	3,703	2,981	583	139	Hilleary	80.5%	15.7%	3.8%
7,976	CLAY	657	491	107	59	Hilleary	74.7%	16.3%	9.0%
33,565	COCKE	4,556	2,538	1,788	230	Hilleary	55.7%	39.2%	5.0%
48,014	COFFEE	3,364	3,081	230	53	Hilleary	91.6%	6.8%	1.6%
14,532	CROCKETT	827	538	203	86	Hilleary	65.1%	24.5%	10.4%
46,802	CUMBERLAND	7,439	5,807	1,432	200	Hilleary	78.1%	19.2%	2.7%
569,891	DAVIDSON	29,245	22,443	6,092	710	Hilleary	76.7%	20.8%	2.4%
11,731	DECATUR	1,211	608	447	156	Hilleary	50.2%	36.9%	12.9%
17,423	DE KALB	950	802	117	31	Hilleary	84.4%	12.3%	3.3%
43,156	DICKSON	3,677	3,033	478	166	Hilleary	82.5%	13.0%	4.5%
37,279	DYER	3,342	1,921	976	445	Hilleary	57.5%	29.2%	13.3%
28,806	FAYETTE	4,437	2,389	1,444	604	Hilleary	53.8%	32.5%	13.6%
16,625	FENTRESS	2,393	2,227	121	45	Hilleary	93.1%	5.1%	1.9%
39,270	FRANKLIN	2,757	2,446	228	83	Hilleary	88.7%	8.3%	3.0%
48,152	GIBSON	1,952	1,330	403	219	Hilleary	68.1%	20.6%	11.2%
29,447	GILES	2,699	2,395	215	89	Hilleary	88.7%	8.0%	3.3%
20,659	GRAINGER	1,954	1,352	519	83	Hilleary	69.2%	26.6%	4.2%
62,909	GREENE	9,698	5,460	3,749	489	Hilleary	56.3%	38.7%	5.0%
14,332	GRUNDY	386	311	57	18	Hilleary	80.6%	14.8%	4.7%
58,128	HAMBLEN	7,703	5,728	1,714	261	Hilleary	74.4%	22.3%	3.4%
307,896	HAMILTON	26,761	15,448	10,336	977	Hilleary	57.7%	38.6%	3.7%
6,786	HANCOCK	1,620	908	439	273	Hilleary	56.0%	27.1%	16.9%
28,105	HARDEMAN	2,002	1,219	550	233	Hilleary	60.9%	27.5%	11.6%
25,578	HARDIN	3,138	2,777	225	136	Hilleary	88.5%	7.2%	4.3%
53,563	HAWKINS	6,092	3,706	2,069	317	Hilleary	60.8%	34.0%	5.2%
19,797	HAYWOOD	1,707	614	537	556	Hilleary	36.0%	31.5%	32.6%
25,522	HENDERSON	2,156	1,285	641	230	Hilleary	59.6%	29.7%	10.7%
31,115	HENRY	740	414	259	67	Hilleary	55.9%	35.0%	9.1%
22,295	HICKMAN	1,656	1,325	208	123	Hilleary	80.0%	12.6%	7.4%
8,088	HOUSTON	580	463	85	32	Hilleary	79.8%	14.7%	5.5%
17,929	HUMPHREYS	1,251	1,003	164	84	Hilleary	80.2%	13.1%	6.7%
10,984	JACKSON	791	501	205	85	Hilleary	63.3%	25.9%	10.7%
44,294	JEFFERSON	5,651	3,539	1,796	316	Hilleary	62.6%	31.8%	5.6%
17,499	JOHNSON	2,979	1,673	952	354	Hilleary	56.2%	32.0%	11.9%
382,032	KNOX	42,629	22,413	17,978	2,238	Hilleary	52.6%	42.2%	5.2%
7,954	LAKE	266	109	102	55	Hilleary	41.0%	38.3%	20.7%
27,101	LAUDERDALE	1,700	1,066	393	241	Hilleary	62.7%	23.1%	14.2%
39,926	LAWRENCE	4,311	3,851	378	82	Hilleary	89.3%	8.8%	1.9%
11,367	LEWIS	1,432	1,146	201	85	Hilleary	80.0%	14.0%	5.9%
31,340	LINCOLN	3,107	2,772	222	113	Hilleary	89.2%	7.1%	3.6%
39,086	LOUDON	5,731	3,140	2,354	237	Hilleary	54.8%	41.1%	4.1%
49,015	MCMINN	6,601	3,983	2,229	389	Hilleary	60.3%	33.8%	5.9%
24,653	MCNAIRY	3,198	2,106	737	355	Hilleary	65.9%	23.0%	11.1%
20,386	MACON	1,685	1,377	197	111	Hilleary	81.7%	11.7%	6.6%
91,837	MADISON	10,281	7,200	2,389	692	Hilleary	70.0%	23.2%	6.7%
27,776	MARION	1,716	1,149	414	153	Hilleary	67.0%	24.1%	8.9%
26,767	MARSHALL	2,042	1,679	273	90	Hilleary	82.2%	13.4%	4.4%
69,498	MAURY	6,266	4,937	1,045	284	Hilleary	78.8%	16.7%	4.5%

TENNESSEE REPUBLICAN PRIMARY

GOVERNOR 2002

2000 Census Population	County	Total Vote	Hilleary	Henry	Other	Winner	Percentage of Total Vote		
							Hilleary	Henry	Other
11,086	MEIGS	1,603	938	552	113	Hilleary	58.5%	34.4%	7.0%
38,961	MONROE	5,417	2,395	2,784	238	Henry	44.2%	51.4%	4.4%
134,768	MONTGOMERY	7,759	5,566	1,653	540	Hilleary	71.7%	21.3%	7.0%
5,740	MOORE	990	924	51	15	Hilleary	93.3%	5.2%	1.5%
19,757	MORGAN	1,986	1,298	609	79	Hilleary	65.4%	30.7%	4.0%
32,450	OBION	1,378	720	493	165	Hilleary	52.2%	35.8%	12.0%
20,118	OVERTON	828	670	119	39	Hilleary	80.9%	14.4%	4.7%
7,631	PERRY	321	263	38	20	Hilleary	81.9%	11.8%	6.2%
4,945	PICKETT	1,268	1,055	174	39	Hilleary	83.2%	13.7%	3.1%
16,050	POLK	1,210	686	427	97	Hilleary	56.7%	35.3%	8.0%
62,315	PUTNAM	4,435	3,278	1,005	152	Hilleary	73.9%	22.7%	3.4%
28,400	RHEA	4,623	4,199	348	76	Hilleary	90.8%	7.5%	1.6%
51,910	ROANE	8,485	2,721	5,532	232	Henry	32.1%	65.2%	2.7%
54,433	ROBERTSON	4,810	3,912	674	224	Hilleary	81.3%	14.0%	4.7%
182,023	RUTHERFORD	13,237	10,938	1,903	396	Hilleary	82.6%	14.4%	3.0%
21,127	SCOTT	2,626	2,238	283	105	Hilleary	85.2%	10.8%	4.0%
11,370	SEQUATCHIE	907	569	232	106	Hilleary	62.7%	25.6%	11.7%
71,170	SEVIER	7,059	4,095	2,596	368	Hilleary	58.0%	36.8%	5.2%
897,472	SHELBY	79,822	43,179	30,152	6,491	Hilleary	54.1%	37.8%	8.1%
17,712	SMITH	1,139	902	171	66	Hilleary	79.2%	15.0%	5.8%
12,370	STEWART	755	531	129	95	Hilleary	70.3%	17.1%	12.6%
153,048	SULLIVAN	13,670	7,075	5,857	738	Hilleary	51.8%	42.8%	5.4%
130,449	SUMNER	11,298	9,315	1,575	408	Hilleary	82.4%	13.9%	3.6%
51,271	TIPTON	5,548	3,346	1,467	735	Hilleary	60.3%	26.4%	13.2%
7,259	TROUSDALE	546	427	83	36	Hilleary	78.2%	15.2%	6.6%
17,667	UNICOI	2,179	1,114	642	423	Hilleary	51.1%	29.5%	19.4%
17,808	UNION	2,309	1,721	499	89	Hilleary	74.5%	21.6%	3.9%
5,508	VAN BUREN	508	456	34	18	Hilleary	89.8%	6.7%	3.5%
38,276	WARREN	2,767	2,427	275	65	Hilleary	87.7%	9.9%	2.3%
107,198	WASHINGTON	12,061	6,057	5,096	908	Hilleary	50.2%	42.3%	7.5%
16,842	WAYNE	2,288	2,038	181	69	Hilleary	89.1%	7.9%	3.0%
34,895	WEAKLEY	1,229	590	550	89	Hilleary	48.0%	44.8%	7.2%
23,102	WHITE	1,717	1,571	105	41	Hilleary	91.5%	6.1%	2.4%
126,638	WILLIAMSON	19,763	14,602	4,708	453	Hilleary	73.9%	23.8%	2.3%
88,809	WILSON	8,689	7,307	1,043	339	Hilleary	84.1%	12.0%	3.9%
5,689,283	TOTAL	534,213	343,543	159,862	30,808	Hilleary	64.3%	29.9%	5.8%

TENNESSEE DEMOCRATIC PRIMARY

GOVERNOR 2002

2000 Census Population	County	Total Vote	Bredesen	Other	Winner	Percentage of Total Vote	
						Bredesen	Other
71,330	ANDERSON	8,577	6,225	2,352	Bredesen	72.6%	27.4%
37,586	BEDFORD	4,206	3,656	550	Bredesen	86.9%	13.1%
16,537	BENTON	5,882	4,990	892	Bredesen	84.8%	15.2%
12,367	BLEDSOE	1,742	1,434	308	Bredesen	82.3%	17.7%
105,823	BLOUNT	3,198	2,500	698	Bredesen	78.2%	21.8%
87,965	BRADLEY	3,823	3,206	617	Bredesen	83.9%	16.1%
39,854	CAMPBELL	4,053	3,160	893	Bredesen	78.0%	22.0%
12,826	CANNON	2,894	2,499	395	Bredesen	86.4%	13.6%
29,475	CARROLL	3,788	2,783	1,005	Bredesen	73.5%	26.5%
56,742	CARTER	2,649	2,060	589	Bredesen	77.8%	22.2%

TENNESSEE DEMOCRATIC PRIMARY

GOVERNOR 2002

2000 Census Population	County	Total Vote	Bredesen	Other	Winner	Percentage of Total Vote	
						Bredesen	Other
35,912	CHEATHAM	4,972	4,145	827	Bredesen	83.4%	16.6%
15,540	CHESTER	1,283	1,082	201	Bredesen	84.3%	15.7%
29,862	CLAIBORNE	3,332	2,655	677	Bredesen	79.7%	20.3%
7,976	CLAY	1,546	1,366	180	Bredesen	88.4%	11.6%
33,565	COCKE	1,306	1,103	203	Bredesen	84.5%	15.5%
48,014	COFFEE	6,308	5,342	966	Bredesen	84.7%	15.3%
14,532	CROCKETT	1,529	1,267	262	Bredesen	82.9%	17.1%
46,802	CUMBERLAND	5,563	4,342	1,221	Bredesen	78.1%	21.9%
569,891	DAVIDSON	60,347	47,660	12,687	Bredesen	79.0%	21.0%
11,731	DECATUR	2,096	1,816	280	Bredesen	86.6%	13.4%
17,423	DE KALB	2,894	2,560	334	Bredesen	88.5%	11.5%
43,156	DICKSON	6,534	5,696	838	Bredesen	87.2%	12.8%
37,279	DYER	4,829	3,807	1,022	Bredesen	78.8%	21.2%
28,806	FAYETTE	2,380	1,442	938	Bredesen	60.6%	39.4%
16,625	FENTRESS	2,754	2,283	471	Bredesen	82.9%	17.1%
39,270	FRANKLIN	5,777	4,781	996	Bredesen	82.8%	17.2%
48,152	GIBSON	6,266	5,049	1,217	Bredesen	80.6%	19.4%
29,447	GILES	4,391	3,567	824	Bredesen	81.2%	18.8%
20,659	GRAINGER	953	770	183	Bredesen	80.8%	19.2%
62,909	GREENE	3,410	2,706	704	Bredesen	79.4%	20.6%
14,332	GRUNDY	2,155	1,818	337	Bredesen	84.4%	15.6%
58,128	HAMBLEN	3,900	3,121	779	Bredesen	80.0%	20.0%
307,896	HAMILTON	18,291	14,898	3,393	Bredesen	81.4%	18.6%
6,786	HANCOCK	422	275	147	Bredesen	65.2%	34.8%
28,105	HARDEMAN	2,980	2,127	853	Bredesen	71.4%	28.6%
25,578	HARDIN	3,052	2,227	825	Bredesen	73.0%	27.0%
53,563	HAWKINS	2,229	1,705	524	Bredesen	76.5%	23.5%
19,797	HAYWOOD	3,068	1,963	1,105	Bredesen	64.0%	36.0%
25,522	HENDERSON	948	808	140	Bredesen	85.2%	14.8%
31,115	HENRY	4,486	3,575	911	Bredesen	79.7%	20.3%
22,295	HICKMAN	4,018	3,381	637	Bredesen	84.1%	15.9%
8,088	HOUSTON	2,104	1,918	186	Bredesen	91.2%	8.8%
17,929	HUMPHREYS	3,470	3,052	418	Bredesen	88.0%	12.0%
10,984	JACKSON	3,129	2,738	391	Bredesen	87.5%	12.5%
44,294	JEFFERSON	1,816	1,465	351	Bredesen	80.7%	19.3%
17,499	JOHNSON	1,229	975	254	Bredesen	79.3%	20.7%
382,032	KNOX	20,968	13,507	7,461	Bredesen	64.4%	35.6%
7,954	LAKE	1,434	1,149	285	Bredesen	80.1%	19.9%
27,101	LAUDERDALE	3,598	2,766	832	Bredesen	76.9%	23.1%
39,926	LAWRENCE	5,699	4,656	1,043	Bredesen	81.7%	18.3%
11,367	LEWIS	2,330	1,999	331	Bredesen	85.8%	14.2%
31,340	LINCOLN	3,793	2,628	1,165	Bredesen	69.3%	30.7%
39,086	LOUDON	2,159	1,629	530	Bredesen	75.5%	24.5%
49,015	MCMINN	3,117	2,577	540	Bredesen	82.7%	17.3%
24,653	MCNAIRY	3,037	2,503	534	Bredesen	82.4%	17.6%
20,386	MACON	1,784	1,563	221	Bredesen	87.6%	12.4%
91,837	MADISON	9,062	7,563	1,499	Bredesen	83.5%	16.5%
27,776	MARION	4,607	3,747	860	Bredesen	81.3%	18.7%
26,767	MARSHALL	4,132	3,701	431	Bredesen	89.6%	10.4%
69,498	MAURY	5,856	5,219	637	Bredesen	89.1%	10.9%
11,086	MEIGS	1,107	865	242	Bredesen	78.1%	21.9%
38,961	MONROE	3,753	3,137	616	Bredesen	83.6%	16.4%
134,768	MONTGOMERY	10,719	9,781	938	Bredesen	91.2%	8.8%
5,740	MOORE	1,540	1,293	247	Bredesen	84.0%	16.0%
19,757	MORGAN	3,270	2,603	667	Bredesen	79.6%	20.4%
32,450	OBION	4,095	3,091	1,004	Bredesen	75.5%	24.5%
20,118	OVERTON	4,254	3,782	472	Bredesen	88.9%	11.1%
7,631	PERRY	1,035	859	176	Bredesen	83.0%	17.0%
4,945	PICKETT	1,038	926	112	Bredesen	89.2%	10.8%
16,050	POLK	2,404	2,091	313	Bredesen	87.0%	13.0%

TENNESSEE DEMOCRATIC PRIMARY

GOVERNOR 2002

2000 Census Population	County	Total Vote	Bredesen	Other	Winner	Percentage of Total Vote Bredesen	Other
62,315	PUTNAM	9,912	8,628	1,284	Bredesen	87.0%	13.0%
28,400	RHEA	2,679	2,067	612	Bredesen	77.2%	22.8%
51,910	ROANE	6,266	4,926	1,340	Bredesen	78.6%	21.4%
54,433	ROBERTSON	8,394	7,254	1,140	Bredesen	86.4%	13.6%
182,023	RUTHERFORD	14,246	12,167	2,079	Bredesen	85.4%	14.6%
21,127	SCOTT	2,429	1,752	677	Bredesen	72.1%	27.9%
11,370	SEQUATCHIE	2,562	2,106	456	Bredesen	82.2%	17.8%
71,170	SEVIER	1,810	1,495	315	Bredesen	82.6%	17.4%
897,472	SHELBY	87,211	61,476	25,735	Bredesen	70.5%	29.5%
17,712	SMITH	4,026	3,584	442	Bredesen	89.0%	11.0%
12,370	STEWART	2,595	2,331	264	Bredesen	89.8%	10.2%
153,048	SULLIVAN	8,047	6,056	1,991	Bredesen	75.3%	24.7%
130,449	SUMNER	11,083	9,734	1,349	Bredesen	87.8%	12.2%
51,271	TIPTON	3,877	2,659	1,218	Bredesen	68.6%	31.4%
7,259	TROUSDALE	1,881	1,573	308	Bredesen	83.6%	16.4%
17,667	UNICOI	409	313	96	Bredesen	76.5%	23.5%
17,808	UNION	1,865	1,474	391	Bredesen	79.0%	21.0%
5,508	VAN BUREN	1,464	1,236	228	Bredesen	84.4%	15.6%
38,276	WARREN	6,979	5,976	1,003	Bredesen	85.6%	14.4%
107,198	WASHINGTON	3,959	3,123	836	Bredesen	78.9%	21.1%
16,842	WAYNE	1,505	1,227	278	Bredesen	81.5%	18.5%
34,895	WEAKLEY	3,437	2,158	1,279	Bredesen	62.8%	37.2%
23,102	WHITE	4,705	3,088	1,617	Bredesen	65.6%	34.4%
126,638	WILLIAMSON	5,725	5,060	665	Bredesen	88.4%	11.6%
88,809	WILSON	11,002	9,322	1,680	Bredesen	84.7%	15.3%
5,689,283	TOTAL	539,438	426,418	113,020	Bredesen	79.0%	21.0%

TENNESSEE REPUBLICAN PRIMARY

SENATOR 2002

2000 Census Population	County	Total Vote	Alexander	Bryant	Other	Winner	Percentage of Total Vote Alexander	Bryant	Other
71,330	ANDERSON	9,245	6,153	2,761	331	Alexander	66.6%	29.9%	3.6%
37,586	BEDFORD	1,712	950	700	62	Alexander	55.5%	40.9%	3.6%
16,537	BENTON	1,354	758	472	124	Alexander	56.0%	34.9%	9.2%
12,367	BLEDSOE	1,477	1,037	347	93	Alexander	70.2%	23.5%	6.3%
105,823	BLOUNT	11,699	7,531	3,919	249	Alexander	64.4%	33.5%	2.1%
87,965	BRADLEY	10,422	6,700	3,257	465	Alexander	64.3%	31.3%	4.5%
39,854	CAMPBELL	3,669	2,502	961	206	Alexander	68.2%	26.2%	5.6%
12,826	CANNON	1,088	711	310	67	Alexander	65.3%	28.5%	6.2%
29,475	CARROLL	2,686	1,345	1,226	115	Alexander	50.1%	45.6%	4.3%
56,742	CARTER	10,911	7,246	3,163	502	Alexander	66.4%	29.0%	4.6%
35,912	CHEATHAM	3,667	1,650	1,916	101	Bryant	45.0%	52.2%	2.8%
15,540	CHESTER	2,044	282	1,719	43	Bryant	13.8%	84.1%	2.1%
29,862	CLAIBORNE	3,635	2,637	809	189	Alexander	72.5%	22.3%	5.2%
7,976	CLAY	735	530	108	97	Alexander	72.1%	14.7%	13.2%
33,565	COCKE	4,697	3,019	1,448	230	Alexander	64.3%	30.8%	4.9%
48,014	COFFEE	3,299	2,234	941	124	Alexander	67.7%	28.5%	3.8%
14,532	CROCKETT	888	316	548	24	Bryant	35.6%	61.7%	2.7%
46,802	CUMBERLAND	7,308	4,637	2,237	434	Alexander	63.5%	30.6%	5.9%
569,891	DAVIDSON	29,693	15,930	13,024	739	Alexander	53.6%	43.9%	2.5%
11,731	DECATUR	1,306	417	846	43	Bryant	31.9%	64.8%	3.3%

TENNESSEE REPUBLICAN PRIMARY
SENATOR 2002

2000 Census Population	County	Total Vote	Alexander	Bryant	Other	Winner	Percentage of Total Vote		
							Alexander	Bryant	Other
17,423	DE KALB	950	557	362	31	Alexander	58.6%	38.1%	3.3%
43,156	DICKSON	3,783	1,435	2,254	94	Bryant	37.9%	59.6%	2.5%
37,279	DYER	3,627	2,031	1,389	207	Alexander	56.0%	38.3%	5.7%
28,806	FAYETTE	4,751	1,352	3,238	161	Bryant	28.5%	68.2%	3.4%
16,625	FENTRESS	2,225	1,654	408	163	Alexander	74.3%	18.3%	7.3%
39,270	FRANKLIN	2,676	1,789	746	141	Alexander	66.9%	27.9%	5.3%
48,152	GIBSON	2,071	742	1,247	82	Bryant	35.8%	60.2%	4.0%
29,447	GILES	2,571	1,631	647	293	Alexander	63.4%	25.2%	11.4%
20,659	GRAINGER	1,923	1,288	579	56	Alexander	67.0%	30.1%	2.9%
62,909	GREENE	10,294	6,273	3,692	329	Alexander	60.9%	35.9%	3.2%
14,332	GRUNDY	390	257	102	31	Alexander	65.9%	26.2%	7.9%
58,128	HAMBLEN	7,624	4,981	2,383	260	Alexander	65.3%	31.3%	3.4%
307,896	HAMILTON	27,321	16,872	9,699	750	Alexander	61.8%	35.5%	2.7%
6,786	HANCOCK	1,567	1,059	349	159	Alexander	67.6%	22.3%	10.1%
28,105	HARDEMAN	2,433	674	1,670	89	Bryant	27.7%	68.6%	3.7%
25,578	HARDIN	3,090	1,507	1,360	223	Alexander	48.8%	44.0%	7.2%
53,563	HAWKINS	6,319	4,288	1,776	255	Alexander	67.9%	28.1%	4.0%
19,797	HAYWOOD	1,752	752	952	48	Bryant	42.9%	54.3%	2.7%
25,522	HENDERSON	2,352	582	1,699	71	Bryant	24.7%	72.2%	3.0%
31,115	HENRY	782	441	280	61	Alexander	56.4%	35.8%	7.8%
22,295	HICKMAN	1,693	631	985	77	Bryant	37.3%	58.2%	4.5%
8,088	HOUSTON	591	326	233	32	Alexander	55.2%	39.4%	5.4%
17,929	HUMPHREYS	1,288	618	622	48	Bryant	48.0%	48.3%	3.7%
10,984	JACKSON	762	484	204	74	Alexander	63.5%	26.8%	9.7%
44,294	JEFFERSON	5,722	3,492	2,015	215	Alexander	61.0%	35.2%	3.8%
17,499	JOHNSON	3,156	2,315	606	235	Alexander	73.4%	19.2%	7.4%
382,032	KNOX	42,993	22,821	18,947	1,225	Alexander	53.1%	44.1%	2.8%
7,954	LAKE	309	161	115	33	Alexander	52.1%	37.2%	10.7%
27,101	LAUDERDALE	1,853	928	810	115	Alexander	50.1%	43.7%	6.2%
39,926	LAWRENCE	4,043	2,674	1,138	231	Alexander	66.1%	28.1%	5.7%
11,367	LEWIS	1,462	655	728	79	Bryant	44.8%	49.8%	5.4%
31,340	LINCOLN	2,930	1,970	552	408	Alexander	67.2%	18.8%	13.9%
39,086	LOUDON	5,766	3,552	2,060	154	Alexander	61.6%	35.7%	2.7%
49,015	MCMINN	6,918	4,128	2,527	263	Alexander	59.7%	36.5%	3.8%
24,653	MCNAIRY	3,481	744	2,621	116	Bryant	21.4%	75.3%	3.3%
20,386	MACON	1,735	1,043	615	77	Alexander	60.1%	35.4%	4.4%
91,837	MADISON	11,055	2,311	8,559	185	Bryant	20.9%	77.4%	1.7%
27,776	MARION	1,837	1,311	419	107	Alexander	71.4%	22.8%	5.8%
26,767	MARSHALL	1,980	1,238	622	120	Alexander	62.5%	31.4%	6.1%
69,498	MAURY	6,582	2,409	3,664	509	Bryant	36.6%	55.7%	7.7%
11,086	MEIGS	1,680	1,162	406	112	Alexander	69.2%	24.2%	6.7%
38,961	MONROE	5,529	3,959	1,407	163	Alexander	71.6%	25.4%	2.9%
134,768	MONTGOMERY	8,223	2,890	5,078	255	Bryant	35.1%	61.8%	3.1%
5,740	MOORE	925	604	251	70	Alexander	65.3%	27.1%	7.6%
19,757	MORGAN	1,978	1,456	433	89	Alexander	73.6%	21.9%	4.5%
32,450	OBION	1,456	671	704	81	Bryant	46.1%	48.4%	5.6%
20,118	OVERTON	797	507	241	49	Alexander	63.6%	30.2%	6.1%
7,631	PERRY	336	92	228	16	Bryant	27.4%	67.9%	4.8%
4,945	PICKETT	1,119	815	205	99	Alexander	72.8%	18.3%	8.8%
16,050	POLK	1,270	924	307	39	Alexander	72.8%	24.2%	3.1%
62,315	PUTNAM	4,512	2,636	1,689	187	Alexander	58.4%	37.4%	4.1%
28,400	RHEA	4,258	3,163	810	285	Alexander	74.3%	19.0%	6.7%
51,910	ROANE	8,227	5,765	2,101	361	Alexander	70.1%	25.5%	4.4%
54,433	ROBERTSON	4,916	2,565	2,186	165	Alexander	52.2%	44.5%	3.4%
182,023	RUTHERFORD	13,378	7,295	5,724	359	Alexander	54.5%	42.8%	2.7%
21,127	SCOTT	2,554	1,576	851	127	Alexander	61.7%	33.3%	5.0%
11,370	SEQUATCHIE	943	587	268	88	Alexander	62.2%	28.4%	9.3%
71,170	SEVIER	7,191	3,971	3,036	184	Alexander	55.2%	42.2%	2.6%
897,472	SHELBY	84,941	34,755	48,159	2,027	Bryant	40.9%	56.7%	2.4%
17,712	SMITH	1,154	760	335	59	Alexander	65.9%	29.0%	5.1%

TENNESSEE REPUBLICAN PRIMARY

SENATOR 2002

2000 Census Population	County	Total Vote	Alexander	Bryant	Other	Winner	Percentage of Total Vote		
							Alexander	Bryant	Other
12,370	STEWART	787	401	319	67	Alexander	51.0%	40.5%	8.5%
153,048	SULLIVAN	14,044	8,788	4,868	388	Alexander	62.6%	34.7%	2.8%
130,449	SUMNER	11,485	5,874	5,323	288	Alexander	51.1%	46.3%	2.5%
51,271	TIPTON	5,648	2,532	2,810	306	Bryant	44.8%	49.8%	5.4%
7,259	TROUSDALE	556	339	194	23	Alexander	61.0%	34.9%	4.1%
17,667	UNICOI	2,313	1,646	586	81	Alexander	71.2%	25.3%	3.5%
17,808	UNION	2,336	1,429	814	93	Alexander	61.2%	34.8%	4.0%
5,508	VAN BUREN	494	336	113	45	Alexander	68.0%	22.9%	9.1%
38,276	WARREN	2,643	1,820	698	125	Alexander	68.9%	26.4%	4.7%
107,198	WASHINGTON	12,695	8,115	4,111	469	Alexander	63.9%	32.4%	3.7%
16,842	WAYNE	2,125	1,311	652	162	Alexander	61.7%	30.7%	7.6%
34,895	WEAKLEY	1,238	498	686	54	Bryant	40.2%	55.4%	4.4%
23,102	WHITE	1,666	1,026	556	84	Alexander	61.6%	33.4%	5.0%
126,638	WILLIAMSON	20,068	9,454	10,209	405	Bryant	47.1%	50.9%	2.0%
88,809	WILSON	8,805	4,769	3,734	302	Alexander	54.2%	42.4%	3.4%
5,689,283	TOTAL	548,482	295,052	233,678	19,752	Alexander	53.8%	42.6%	3.6%

TENNESSEE DEMOCRATIC PRIMARY

SENATOR 2002

2000 Census Population	County	Total Vote	Clement	Other	Winner	Percentage of Total Vote	
						Clement	Other
71,330	ANDERSON	7,856	6,238	1,618	Clement	79.4%	20.6%
37,586	BEDFORD	4,043	3,579	464	Clement	88.5%	11.5%
16,537	BENTON	7,484	6,514	970	Clement	87.0%	13.0%
12,367	BLEDSOE	1,574	1,242	332	Clement	78.9%	21.1%
105,823	BLOUNT	2,999	2,509	490	Clement	83.7%	16.3%
87,965	BRADLEY	3,611	2,352	1,259	Clement	65.1%	34.9%
39,854	CAMPBELL	3,601	2,679	922	Clement	74.4%	25.6%
12,826	CANNON	2,724	2,417	307	Clement	88.7%	11.3%
29,475	CARROLL	3,553	3,011	542	Clement	84.7%	15.3%
56,742	CARTER	2,474	1,775	699	Clement	71.7%	28.3%
35,912	CHEATHAM	4,890	4,341	549	Clement	88.8%	11.2%
15,540	CHESTER	1,168	1,033	135	Clement	88.4%	11.6%
29,862	CLAIBORNE	2,889	2,076	813	Clement	71.9%	28.1%
7,976	CLAY	1,362	1,205	157	Clement	88.5%	11.5%
33,565	COCKE	1,197	882	315	Clement	73.7%	26.3%
48,014	COFFEE	5,988	5,102	886	Clement	85.2%	14.8%
14,532	CROCKETT	1,413	1,188	225	Clement	84.1%	15.9%
46,802	CUMBERLAND	5,241	4,044	1,197	Clement	77.2%	22.8%
569,891	DAVIDSON	59,795	54,744	5,051	Clement	91.6%	8.4%
11,731	DECATUR	2,018	1,774	244	Clement	87.9%	12.1%
17,423	DE KALB	2,819	2,526	293	Clement	89.6%	10.4%
43,156	DICKSON	6,506	6,017	489	Clement	92.5%	7.5%
37,279	DYER	4,478	3,515	963	Clement	78.5%	21.5%
28,806	FAYETTE	2,197	1,528	669	Clement	69.5%	30.5%
16,625	FENTRESS	2,524	1,890	634	Clement	74.9%	25.1%
39,270	FRANKLIN	5,505	4,612	893	Clement	83.8%	16.2%
48,152	GIBSON	5,705	4,671	1,034	Clement	81.9%	18.1%
29,447	GILES	4,131	3,219	912	Clement	77.9%	22.1%
20,659	GRAINGER	903	744	159	Clement	82.4%	17.6%
62,909	GREENE	3,067	2,272	795	Clement	74.1%	25.9%
14,332	GRUNDY	2,042	1,637	405	Clement	80.2%	19.8%
58,128	HAMBLEN	3,635	2,817	818	Clement	77.5%	22.5%
307,896	HAMILTON	17,449	13,289	4,160	Clement	76.2%	23.8%
6,786	HANCOCK	376	272	104	Clement	72.3%	27.7%
28,105	HARDEMAN	2,520	1,888	632	Clement	74.9%	25.1%

TENNESSEE DEMOCRATIC PRIMARY
SENATOR 2002

2000 Census Population	County	Total Vote	Clement	Other	Winner	Percentage of Total Vote Clement	Other
25,578	HARDIN	2,794	2,271	523	Clement	81.3%	18.7%
53,563	HAWKINS	2,097	1,626	471	Clement	77.5%	22.5%
19,797	HAYWOOD	2,908	2,094	814	Clement	72.0%	28.0%
25,522	HENDERSON	931	840	91	Clement	90.2%	9.8%
31,115	HENRY	4,331	3,781	550	Clement	87.3%	12.7%
22,295	HICKMAN	3,975	3,491	484	Clement	87.8%	12.2%
8,088	HOUSTON	2,048	1,930	118	Clement	94.2%	5.8%
17,929	HUMPHREYS	3,447	3,171	276	Clement	92.0%	8.0%
10,984	JACKSON	2,918	2,596	322	Clement	89.0%	11.0%
44,294	JEFFERSON	1,681	1,284	397	Clement	76.4%	23.6%
17,499	JOHNSON	1,098	726	372	Clement	66.1%	33.9%
382,032	KNOX	18,684	15,173	3,511	Clement	81.2%	18.8%
7,954	LAKE	1,112	853	259	Clement	76.7%	23.3%
27,101	LAUDERDALE	3,219	2,516	703	Clement	78.2%	21.8%
39,926	LAWRENCE	5,353	4,543	810	Clement	84.9%	15.1%
11,367	LEWIS	2,256	1,949	307	Clement	86.4%	13.6%
31,340	LINCOLN	3,719	2,681	1,038	Clement	72.1%	27.9%
39,086	LOUDON	1,952	1,652	300	Clement	84.6%	15.4%
49,015	MCMINN	2,991	2,432	559	Clement	81.3%	18.7%
24,653	MCNAIRY	2,915	2,467	448	Clement	84.6%	15.4%
20,386	MACON	1,711	1,570	141	Clement	91.8%	8.2%
91,837	MADISON	8,547	7,162	1,385	Clement	83.8%	16.2%
27,776	MARION	4,313	3,217	1,096	Clement	74.6%	25.4%
26,767	MARSHALL	3,979	3,597	382	Clement	90.4%	9.6%
69,498	MAURY	5,841	5,220	621	Clement	89.4%	10.6%
11,086	MEIGS	1,002	666	336	Clement	66.5%	33.5%
38,961	MONROE	3,536	2,926	610	Clement	82.7%	17.3%
134,768	MONTGOMERY	10,251	9,120	1,131	Clement	89.0%	11.0%
5,740	MOORE	1,386	1,127	259	Clement	81.3%	18.7%
19,757	MORGAN	3,020	2,349	671	Clement	77.8%	22.2%
32,450	OBION	3,639	2,973	666	Clement	81.7%	18.3%
20,118	OVERTON	3,804	3,334	470	Clement	87.6%	12.4%
7,631	PERRY	987	890	97	Clement	90.2%	9.8%
4,945	PICKETT	988	814	174	Clement	82.4%	17.6%
16,050	POLK	2,302	1,823	479	Clement	79.2%	20.8%
62,315	PUTNAM	9,080	7,793	1,287	Clement	85.8%	14.2%
28,400	RHEA	2,269	1,782	487	Clement	78.5%	21.5%
51,910	ROANE	5,888	4,318	1,570	Clement	73.3%	26.7%
54,433	ROBERTSON	8,404	7,728	676	Clement	92.0%	8.0%
182,023	RUTHERFORD	13,750	12,244	1,506	Clement	89.0%	11.0%
21,127	SCOTT	2,201	1,446	755	Clement	65.7%	34.3%
11,370	SEQUATCHIE	2,350	1,685	665	Clement	71.7%	28.3%
71,170	SEVIER	1,648	1,283	365	Clement	77.9%	22.1%
897,472	SHELBY	78,641	56,358	22,283	Clement	71.7%	28.3%
17,712	SMITH	3,839	3,460	379	Clement	90.1%	9.9%
12,370	STEWART	2,448	2,139	309	Clement	87.4%	12.6%
153,048	SULLIVAN	7,400	5,624	1,776	Clement	76.0%	24.0%
130,449	SUMNER	10,852	9,981	871	Clement	92.0%	8.0%
51,271	TIPTON	3,682	2,932	750	Clement	79.6%	20.4%
7,259	TROUSDALE	1,792	1,638	154	Clement	91.4%	8.6%
17,667	UNICOI	371	270	101	Clement	72.8%	27.2%
17,808	UNION	1,531	1,149	382	Clement	75.0%	25.0%
5,508	VAN BUREN	1,406	1,197	209	Clement	85.1%	14.9%
38,276	WARREN	6,640	5,602	1,038	Clement	84.4%	15.6%
107,198	WASHINGTON	3,698	2,740	958	Clement	74.1%	25.9%
16,842	WAYNE	1,402	1,157	245	Clement	82.5%	17.5%
34,895	WEAKLEY	3,210	2,710	500	Clement	84.4%	15.6%
23,102	WHITE	4,495	3,799	696	Clement	84.5%	15.5%
126,638	WILLIAMSON	5,599	5,082	517	Clement	90.8%	9.2%
88,809	WILSON	10,807	9,589	1,218	Clement	88.7%	11.3%
5,689,283	TOTAL	508,875	418,172	90,703	Clement	82.2%	17.8%

TEXAS

GOVERNOR
Rick Perry (R). Elected 2002 to a four-year term. Assumed office Dec. 21, 2000, following the resignation of president-elect George W. Bush.

SENATORS (2 Republicans)
John Cornyn (R). Elected 2002 to a six-year term.

Kay Bailey Hutchison (R). Reelected 2000 to a six-year term. Previously elected 1994 and in a special election June 5, 1993, to fill out the remaining year and a half of the term vacated when Senator Lloyd Bentsen (D) resigned to become Secretary of the Treasury.

REPRESENTATIVES (17 Democrats, 15 Republicans)
1. Max Sandlin (D)
2. Jim Turner (D)
3. Sam Johnson (R)
4. Ralph M. Hall (D)
5. Jeb Hensarling (R)
6. Joe L. Barton (R)
7. John Culberson (R)
8. Kevin Brady (R)
9. Nick Lampson (D)
10. Lloyd Doggett (D)
11. Chet Edwards (D)
12. Kay Granger (R)
13. William M. "Mac" Thornberry (R)
14. Ron Paul (R)
15. Ruben Hinojosa (D)
16. Silvestre Reyes (D)
17. Charles W. Stenholm (D)
18. Sheila Jackson-Lee (D)
19. Larry Combest (R)
20. Charlie Gonzalez (D)
21. Lamar Smith (R)
22. Tom DeLay (R)
23. Henry Bonilla (R)
24. Martin Frost (D)
25. Chris Bell (D)
26. Michael C. Burgess (R)
27. Solomon P. Ortiz (D)
28. Ciro D. Rodriguez (D)
29. Gene Green (D)
30. Eddie Bernice Johnson (D)
31. John Carter (R)
32. Pete Sessions (R)

POSTWAR VOTE FOR PRESIDENT

Year	Total Vote	Republican Vote	Republican Candidate	Democratic Vote	Democratic Candidate	Other Vote	Plurality	Total Vote Rep.	Total Vote Dem.	Major Vote Rep.	Major Vote Dem.
2000**	6,407,637	3,799,639	Bush, George W.	2,433,746	Gore, Al	174,252	1,365,893 R	59.3%	38.0%	61.0%	39.0%
1996**	5,611,644	2,736,167	Dole, Bob	2,459,683	Clinton, Bill	415,794	276,484 R	48.8%	43.8%	52.7%	47.3%
1992**	6,154,018	2,496,071	Bush, George	2,281,815	Clinton, Bill	1,376,132	214,256 R	40.6%	37.1%	52.2%	47.8%
1988	5,427,410	3,036,829	Bush, George	2,352,748	Dukakis, Michael S.	37,833	684,081 R	56.0%	43.3%	56.3%	43.7%
1984	5,397,571	3,433,428	Reagan, Ronald	1,949,276	Mondale, Walter F.	14,867	1,484,152 R	63.6%	36.1%	63.8%	36.2%
1980**	4,541,636	2,510,705	Reagan, Ronald	1,881,147	Carter, Jimmy	149,784	629,558 R	55.3%	41.4%	57.2%	42.8%
1976	4,071,884	1,953,300	Ford, Gerald R.	2,082,319	Carter, Jimmy	36,265	129,019 D	48.0%	51.1%	48.4%	51.6%
1972	3,471,281	2,298,896	Nixon, Richard M.	1,154,289	McGovern, George S.	18,096	1,144,607 R	66.2%	33.3%	66.6%	33.4%
1968**	3,079,216	1,227,844	Nixon, Richard M.	1,266,804	Humphrey, Hubert H.	584,568	38,960 D	39.9%	41.1%	49.2%	50.8%
1964	2,626,811	958,566	Goldwater, Barry M.	1,663,185	Johnson, Lyndon B.	5,060	704,619 D	36.5%	63.3%	36.6%	63.4%
1960	2,311,084	1,121,310	Nixon, Richard M.	1,167,567	Kennedy, John F.	22,207	46,257 D	48.5%	50.5%	49.0%	51.0%
1956	1,955,168	1,080,619	Eisenhower, Dwight D.	859,958	Stevenson, Adlai E.	14,591	220,661 R	55.3%	44.0%	55.7%	44.3%
1952	2,075,946	1,102,878	Eisenhower, Dwight D.	969,228	Stevenson, Adlai E.	3,840	133,650 R	53.1%	46.7%	53.2%	46.8%
1948	1,249,577	303,467	Dewey, Thomas E.	824,235	Truman, Harry S.	121,875	520,768 D	24.3%	66.0%	26.9%	73.1%

In 2000 the other vote column includes 137,994 votes cast for Green (Nader). In 1996 the other vote column includes 378,537 votes cast for Perot. In 1992 the other vote column includes 1,354,781 votes cast for Perot. In 1980 the other vote column includes 111,613 votes for Independent (Anderson). In 1968 other vote was 584,269 American (Wallace) and 299 scattered.

TEXAS

POSTWAR VOTE FOR GOVERNOR

Year	Total Vote	Republican		Democratic		Other Vote	Rep.-Dem. Plurality	Percentage			
		Vote	Candidate	Vote	Candidate			Total Vote		Major Vote	
								Rep.	Dem.	Rep.	Dem.
2002	4,553,987	2,632,591	Perry, Rick	1,819,798	Sanchez, Tony	101,598	812,793 R	57.8%	40.0%	59.1%	40.9%
1998	3,738,483	2,551,454	Bush, George W.	1,165,444	Mauro, Garry	21,585	1,386,010 R	68.2%	31.2%	68.6%	31.4%
1994	4,396,242	2,350,994	Bush, George W.	2,016,928	Richards, Ann	28,320	334,066 R	53.5%	45.9%	53.8%	46.2%
1990	3,892,746	1,826,431	Williams, Clayton	1,925,670	Richards, Ann	140,645	99,239 D	46.9%	49.5%	48.7%	51.3%
1986	3,441,460	1,813,779	Clements, William P.	1,584,515	White, Mark	43,166	229,264 R	52.7%	46.0%	53.4%	46.6%
1982	3,191,091	1,465,937	Clements, William P.	1,697,870	White, Mark	27,284	231,933 D	45.9%	53.2%	46.3%	53.7%
1978	2,369,764	1,183,839	Clements, William P.	1,166,979	Hill, John	18,946	16,860 R	50.0%	49.2%	50.4%	49.6%
1974**	1,654,984	514,725	Granberry, Jim	1,016,334	Briscoe, Dolph	123,925	501,609 D	31.1%	61.4%	33.6%	66.4%
1972	3,410,128	1,534,060	Grover, Henry C.	1,633,970	Briscoe, Dolph	242,098	99,910 D	45.0%	47.9%	48.4%	51.6%
1970	2,235,847	1,037,723	Eggers, Paul W.	1,197,726	Smith, Preston	398	160,003 D	46.4%	53.6%	46.4%	53.6%
1968	2,916,509	1,254,333	Eggers, Paul W.	1,662,019	Smith, Preston	157	407,686 D	43.0%	57.0%	43.0%	57.0%
1966	1,425,861	368,025	Kennerly, T. E.	1,037,517	Connally, John B.	20,319	669,492 D	25.8%	72.8%	26.2%	73.8%
1964	2,544,753	661,675	Crichton, Jack	1,877,793	Connally, John B.	5,285	1,216,118 D	26.0%	73.8%	26.1%	73.9%
1962	1,569,181	715,025	Cox, Jack	847,036	Connally, John B.	7,120	132,011 D	45.6%	54.0%	45.8%	54.2%
1960	2,250,718	612,963	Steger, William M.	1,637,755	Daniel, Price		1,024,792 D	27.2%	72.8%	27.2%	72.8%
1958	789,133	94,098	Mayer, Edwin S.	695,035	Daniel, Price		600,937 D	11.9%	88.1%	11.9%	88.1%
1956	1,828,161	271,088	Bryant, William R.	1,433,051	Daniel, Price	124,022	1,161,963 D	14.8%	78.4%	15.9%	84.1%
1954	636,892	66,154	Adams, Tod R.	569,533	Shivers, Allan	1,205	503,379 D	10.4%	89.4%	10.4%	89.6%
1952	1,881,202		—	1,844,530	Shivers, Allan	36,672	1,844,530 D		98.1%		100.0%
1950	394,747	39,737	Currie, Ralph W.	355,010	Shivers, Allan		315,273 D	10.1%	89.9%	10.1%	89.9%
1948	1,208,860	177,399	Lane, Alvin H.	1,024,160	Jester, Beauford	7,301	846,761 D	14.7%	84.7%	14.8%	85.2%
1946	378,744	33,231	Nolte, Eugene	345,513	Jester, Beauford		312,282 D	8.8%	91.2%	8.8%	91.2%

The term of office of Texas' Governor was increased from two to four years effective with the 1974 election.

POSTWAR VOTE FOR SENATOR

Year	Total Vote	Republican		Democratic		Other Vote	Rep.-Dem. Plurality	Percentage			
		Vote	Candidate	Vote	Candidate			Total Vote		Major Vote	
								Rep.	Dem.	Rep.	Dem.
2002	4,514,012	2,496,243	Cornyn, John	1,955,758	Kirk, Ron	62,011	540,485 R	55.3%	43.3%	56.1%	43.9%
2000	6,276,652	4,082,091	Hutchison, Kay Bailey	2,030,315	Kelly, Gene	164,246	2,051,776 R	65.0%	32.3%	66.8%	33.2%
1996	5,527,441	3,027,680	Gramm, Phil	2,428,776	Morales, Victor M.	70,985	598,904 R	54.8%	43.9%	55.5%	44.5%
1994	4,279,940	2,604,218	Hutchison, Kay Bailey	1,639,615	Fisher, Richard	36,107	964,603 R	60.8%	38.3%	61.4%	38.6%
1993S	1,765,254	1,188,716	Hutchison, Kay Bailey	576,538	Krueger, Robert		612,178 R	67.3%	32.7%	67.3%	32.7%
1990	3,822,157	2,302,357	Gramm, Phil	1,429,986	Parmer, Hugh	89,814	872,371 R	60.2%	37.4%	61.7%	38.3%
1988	5,323,606	2,129,228	Boulter, Beau	3,149,806	Bentsen, Lloyd	44,572	1,020,578 D	40.0%	59.2%	40.3%	59.7%
1984	5,319,178	3,116,348	Gramm, Phil	2,202,557	Doggett, Lloyd	273	913,791 R	58.6%	41.4%	58.6%	41.4%
1982	3,103,167	1,256,759	Collins, James M.	1,818,223	Bentsen, Lloyd	28,185	561,464 D	40.5%	58.6%	40.9%	59.1%
1978	2,312,540	1,151,376	Tower, John G.	1,139,149	Krueger, Robert	22,015	12,227 R	49.8%	49.3%	50.3%	49.7%
1976	3,874,516	1,636,370	Steelman, Alan	2,199,956	Bentsen, Lloyd	38,190	563,586 D	42.2%	56.8%	42.7%	57.3%
1972	3,413,903	1,822,877	Tower, John G.	1,511,985	Sanders, Barefoot	79,041	310,892 R	53.4%	44.3%	54.7%	45.3%
1970	2,231,671	1,035,794	Bush, George	1,194,069	Bentsen, Lloyd	1,808	158,275 D	46.4%	53.5%	46.5%	53.5%
1966	1,493,182	842,501	Tower, John G.	643,855	Carr, Waggoner	6,826	198,646 R	56.4%	43.1%	56.7%	43.3%
1964	2,603,856	1,134,337	Bush, George	1,463,958	Yarborough, Ralph	5,561	329,621 D	43.6%	56.2%	43.7%	56.3%
1961S	886,091	448,217	Tower, John G.	437,874	Blakley, William A.		10,343 R	50.6%	49.4%	50.6%	49.4%
1960	2,253,784	926,653	Tower, John G.	1,306,625	Johnson, Lyndon B.	20,506	379,972 D	41.1%	58.0%	41.5%	58.5%
1958	787,128	185,926	Whittenburg, Roy	587,030	Yarborough, Ralph	14,172	401,104 D	23.6%	74.6%	24.1%	75.9%
1957S	957,298		[See note below]				D				
1954	636,475	94,131	Watson, Carlos G.	539,319	Johnson, Lyndon B.	3,025	445,188 D	14.8%	84.7%	14.9%	85.1%
1952	1,895,192		—	1,895,192	Daniel, Price		1,895,192 D		100.0%		100.0%
1948	1,061,563	349,665	Porter, Jack	702,985	Johnson, Lyndon B.	8,913	353,320 D	32.9%	66.2%	33.2%	66.8%
1946	380,681	43,750	Sells, Murray C.	336,931	Connally, Tom		293,181 D	11.5%	88.5%	11.5%	88.5%

The June 1993 election was for a short term to fill a vacancy; the vote above was for the special election runoff. The May 1961 and April 1957 elections were for short terms to fill vacancies. Although neither vote was held with official party designations, the 1961 vote above was a runoff contest between unofficial party candidates. In 1957 there was a single ballot without a runoff and Ralph Yarborough polled 364,605 votes (38.1% of the total vote) and won the election with a 73,802-vote plurality.

TEXAS

Congressional districts first established for elections held in 2002
32 members

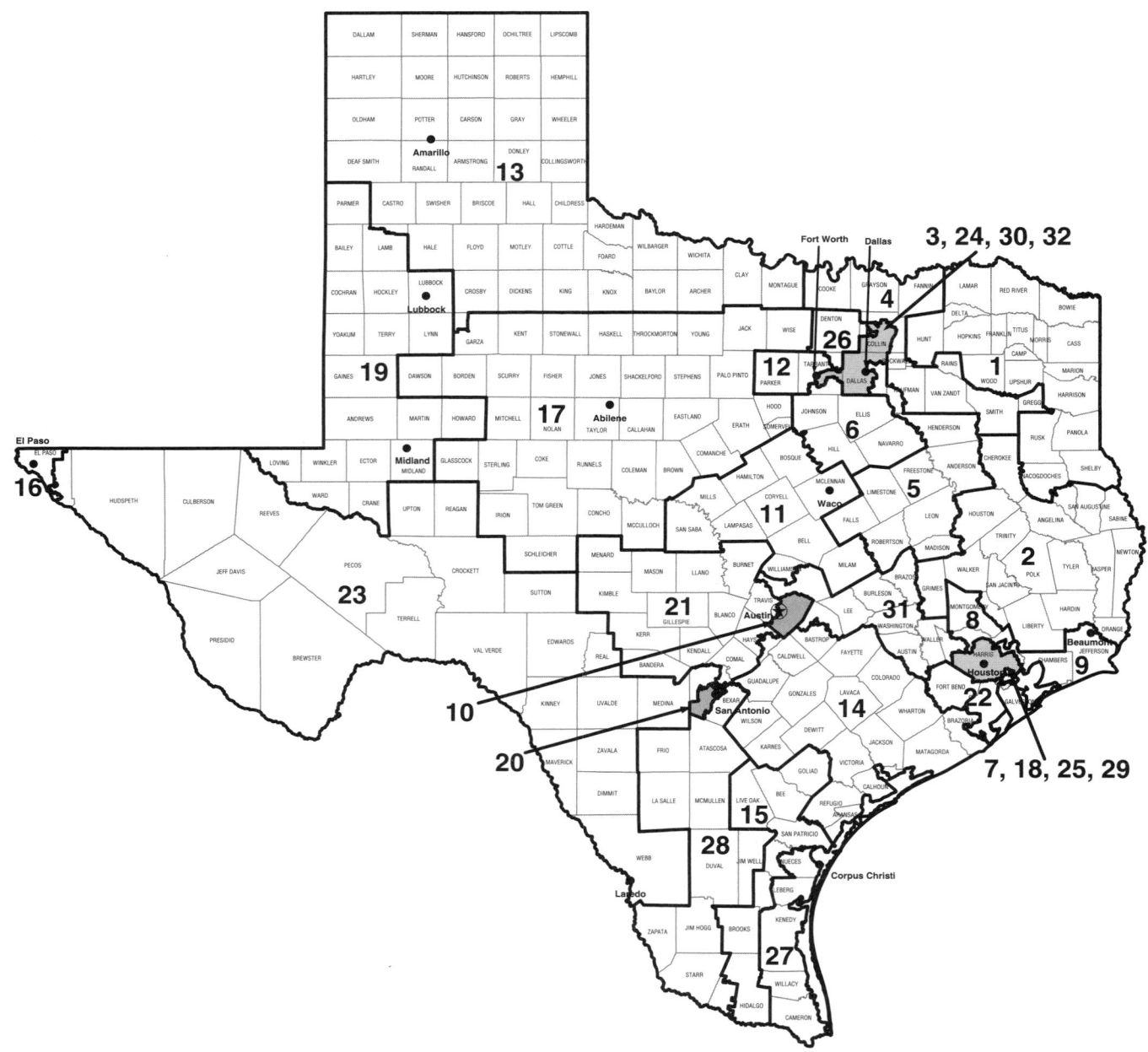

TEXAS

Houston Area

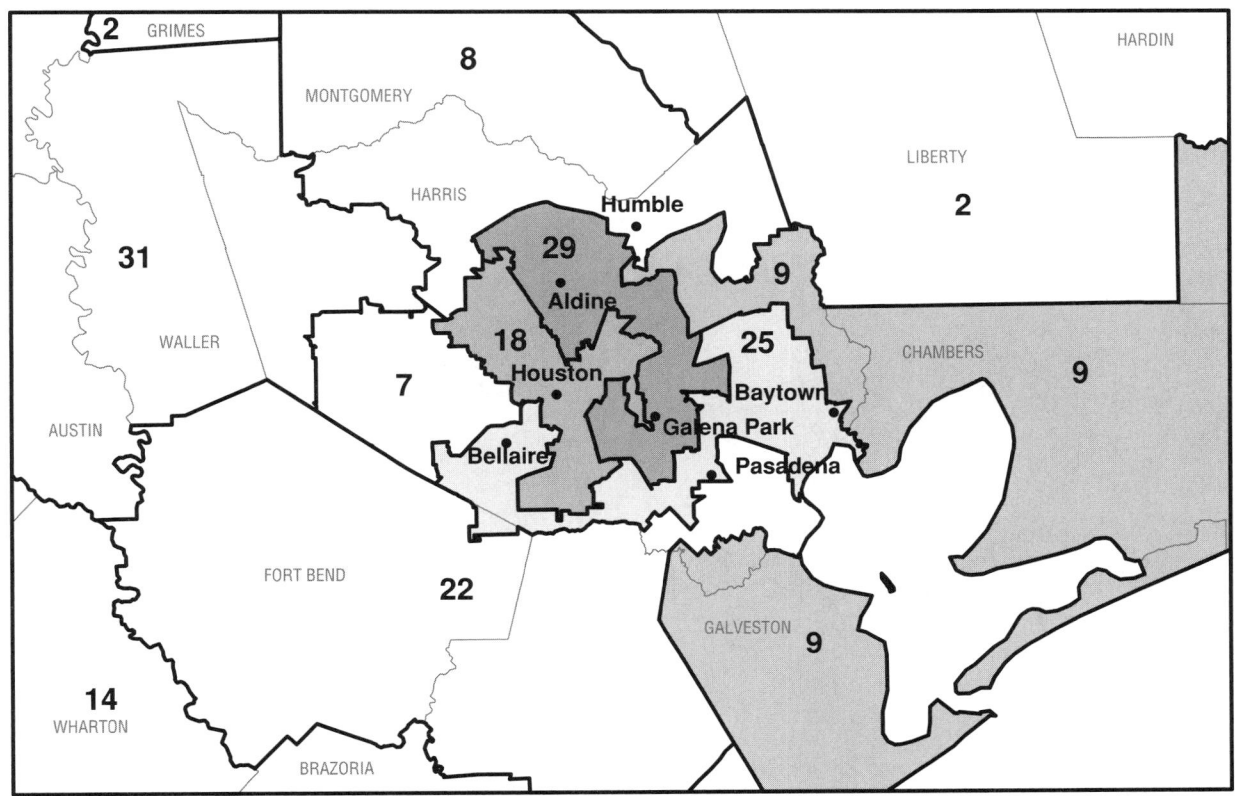

TEXAS

Dallas-Fort Worth Area

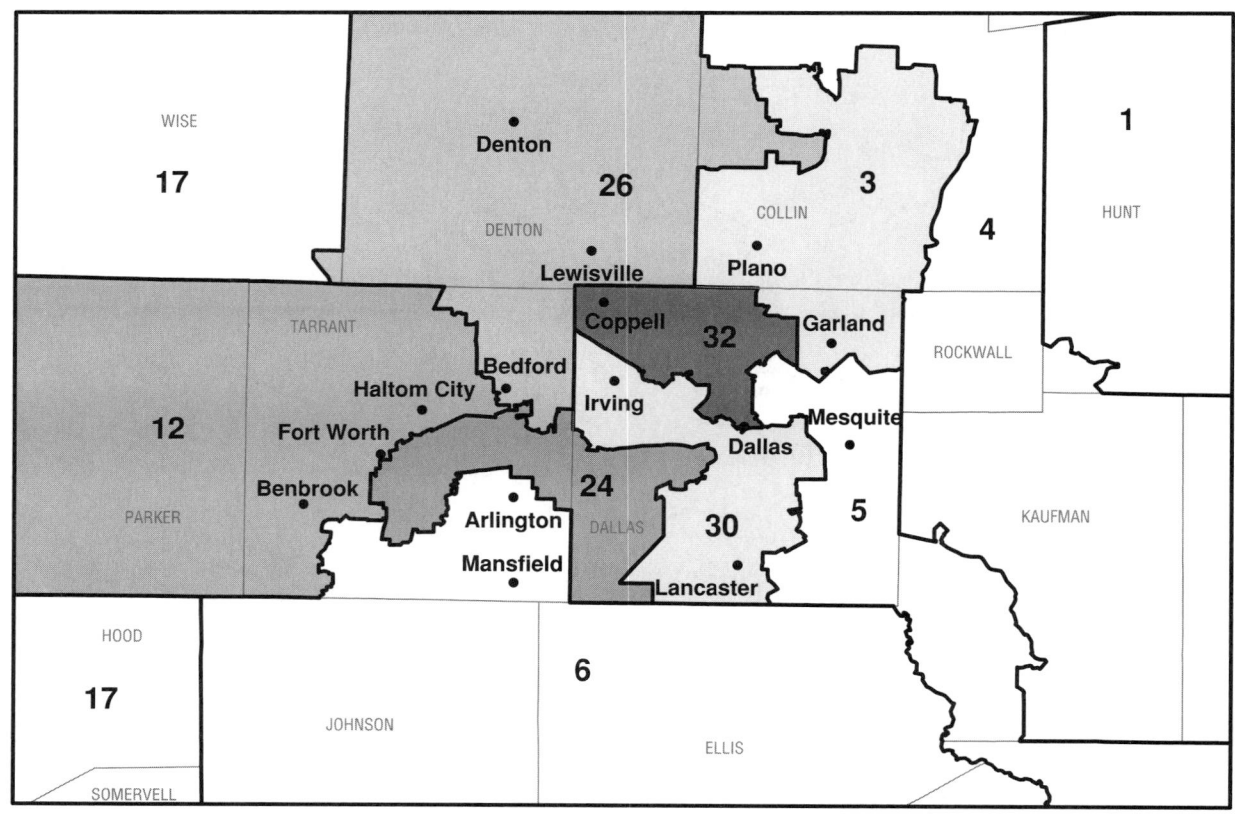

TEXAS

GOVERNOR 2002

2000 Census Population	County	Total Vote	Republican	Democratic	Other	Rep.-Dem. Plurality		Percentage			
								Total Vote		Major Vote	
								Rep.	Dem.	Rep.	Dem.
55,109	ANDERSON	10,297	6,386	3,758	153	2,628	R	62.0%	36.5%	63.0%	37.0%
13,004	ANDREWS	2,990	2,018	877	95	1,141	R	67.5%	29.3%	69.7%	30.3%
80,130	ANGELINA	19,035	10,892	7,760	383	3,132	R	57.2%	40.8%	58.4%	41.6%
22,497	ARANSAS	5,945	3,966	1,798	181	2,168	R	66.7%	30.2%	68.8%	31.2%
8,854	ARCHER	2,903	2,115	730	58	1,385	R	72.9%	25.1%	74.3%	25.7%
2,148	ARMSTRONG	753	566	157	30	409	R	75.2%	20.8%	78.3%	21.7%
38,628	ATASCOSA	8,252	4,446	3,649	157	797	R	53.9%	44.2%	54.9%	45.1%
23,590	AUSTIN	6,976	5,285	1,582	109	3,703	R	75.8%	22.7%	77.0%	23.0%
6,594	BAILEY	1,568	1,111	437	20	674	R	70.9%	27.9%	71.8%	28.2%
17,645	BANDERA	5,596	4,363	1,053	180	3,310	R	78.0%	18.8%	80.6%	19.4%
57,733	BASTROP	15,086	8,932	5,392	762	3,540	R	59.2%	35.7%	62.4%	37.6%
4,093	BAYLOR	1,189	809	360	20	449	R	68.0%	30.3%	69.2%	30.8%
32,359	BEE	7,514	3,107	4,272	135	1,165	D	41.3%	56.9%	42.1%	57.9%
237,974	BELL	43,593	27,451	15,307	835	12,144	R	63.0%	35.1%	64.2%	35.8%
1,392,931	BEXAR	273,604	142,137	125,434	6,033	16,703	R	51.9%	45.8%	53.1%	46.9%
8,418	BLANCO	3,051	2,274	678	99	1,596	R	74.5%	22.2%	77.0%	23.0%
729	BORDEN	275	228	37	10	191	R	82.9%	13.5%	86.0%	14.0%
17,204	BOSQUE	5,447	3,840	1,490	117	2,350	R	70.5%	27.4%	72.0%	28.0%
89,306	BOWIE	20,302	10,921	9,173	208	1,748	R	53.8%	45.2%	54.3%	45.7%
241,767	BRAZORIA	53,059	34,645	17,063	1,351	17,582	R	65.3%	32.2%	67.0%	33.0%
152,415	BRAZOS	28,828	20,313	7,905	610	12,408	R	70.5%	27.4%	72.0%	28.0%
8,866	BREWSTER	2,475	1,254	1,121	100	133	R	50.7%	45.3%	52.8%	47.2%
1,790	BRISCOE	806	488	293	25	195	R	60.5%	36.4%	62.5%	37.5%
7,976	BROOKS	2,387	338	2,022	27	1,684	D	14.2%	84.7%	14.3%	85.7%
37,674	BROWN	9,065	6,629	2,233	203	4,396	R	73.1%	24.6%	74.8%	25.2%
16,470	BURLESON	4,829	2,992	1,767	70	1,225	R	62.0%	36.6%	62.9%	37.1%
34,147	BURNET	11,025	7,834	2,834	357	5,000	R	71.1%	25.7%	73.4%	26.6%
32,194	CALDWELL	7,558	4,000	3,294	264	706	R	52.9%	43.6%	54.8%	45.2%
20,647	CALHOUN	5,443	2,742	2,590	111	152	R	50.4%	47.6%	51.4%	48.6%
12,905	CALLAHAN	3,743	2,787	859	97	1,928	R	74.5%	22.9%	76.4%	23.6%
335,227	CAMERON	45,754	17,716	27,374	664	9,658	D	38.7%	59.8%	39.3%	60.7%
11,549	CAMP	2,934	1,539	1,354	41	185	R	52.5%	46.1%	53.2%	46.8%
6,516	CARSON	2,142	1,562	514	66	1,048	R	72.9%	24.0%	75.2%	24.8%
30,438	CASS	7,396	3,527	3,787	82	260	D	47.7%	51.2%	48.2%	51.8%
8,285	CASTRO	2,030	1,277	729	24	548	R	62.9%	35.9%	63.7%	36.3%
26,031	CHAMBERS	7,034	4,716	2,171	147	2,545	R	67.0%	30.9%	68.5%	31.5%
46,659	CHEROKEE	10,192	6,616	3,410	166	3,206	R	64.9%	33.5%	66.0%	34.0%
7,688	CHILDRESS	1,572	1,048	497	27	551	R	66.7%	31.6%	67.8%	32.2%
11,006	CLAY	3,355	2,244	1,014	97	1,230	R	66.9%	30.2%	68.9%	31.1%
3,730	COCHRAN	1,099	612	461	26	151	R	55.7%	41.9%	57.0%	43.0%
3,864	COKE	1,153	898	227	28	671	R	77.9%	19.7%	79.8%	20.2%
9,235	COLEMAN	2,572	1,786	727	59	1,059	R	69.4%	28.3%	71.1%	28.9%
491,675	COLLIN	129,092	95,680	30,903	2,509	64,777	R	74.1%	23.9%	75.6%	24.4%
3,206	COLLINGSWORTH	1,121	673	435	13	238	R	60.0%	38.8%	60.7%	39.3%
20,390	COLORADO	5,891	4,178	1,623	90	2,555	R	70.9%	27.6%	72.0%	28.0%
78,021	COMAL	24,186	18,560	5,047	579	13,513	R	76.7%	20.9%	78.6%	21.4%
14,026	COMANCHE	3,757	2,428	1,269	60	1,159	R	64.6%	33.8%	65.7%	34.3%
3,966	CONCHO	783	555	204	24	351	R	70.9%	26.1%	73.1%	26.9%
36,363	COOKE	9,595	7,218	2,210	167	5,008	R	75.2%	23.0%	76.6%	23.4%
74,978	CORYELL	9,733	6,214	3,257	262	2,957	R	63.8%	33.5%	65.6%	34.4%
1,904	COTTLE	544	340	191	13	149	R	62.5%	35.1%	64.0%	36.0%
3,996	CRANE	1,351	868	434	49	434	R	64.2%	32.1%	66.7%	33.3%
4,099	CROCKETT	963	558	387	18	171	R	57.9%	40.2%	59.0%	41.0%
7,072	CROSBY	1,636	939	662	35	277	R	57.4%	40.5%	58.7%	41.3%
2,975	CULBERSON	611	200	401	10	201	D	32.7%	65.6%	33.3%	66.7%
6,222	DALLAM	904	622	260	22	362	R	68.8%	28.8%	70.5%	29.5%
2,218,899	DALLAS	445,683	229,820	208,022	7,841	21,798	R	51.6%	46.7%	52.5%	47.5%
14,985	DAWSON	3,770	2,328	1,395	47	933	R	61.8%	37.0%	62.5%	37.5%
18,561	DEAF SMITH	3,648	2,387	1,189	72	1,198	R	65.4%	32.6%	66.8%	33.2%
5,327	DELTA	1,296	826	454	16	372	R	63.7%	35.0%	64.5%	35.5%

TEXAS
GOVERNOR 2002

2000 Census Population	County	Total Vote	Republican	Democratic	Other	Rep.-Dem. Plurality		Percentage Total Vote Rep.	Dem.	Major Vote Rep.	Dem.
432,976	DENTON	104,514	74,431	27,682	2,401	46,749	R	71.2%	26.5%	72.9%	27.1%
20,013	DE WITT	4,420	3,220	1,156	44	2,064	R	72.9%	26.2%	73.6%	26.4%
2,762	DICKENS	762	470	269	23	201	R	61.7%	35.3%	63.6%	36.4%
10,248	DIMMIT	2,590	671	1,896	23	1,225	D	25.9%	73.2%	26.1%	73.9%
3,828	DONLEY	1,406	1,035	343	28	692	R	73.6%	24.4%	75.1%	24.9%
13,120	DUVAL	3,170	377	2,772	21	2,395	D	11.9%	87.4%	12.0%	88.0%
18,297	EASTLAND	5,065	3,630	1,298	137	2,332	R	71.7%	25.6%	73.7%	26.3%
121,123	ECTOR	23,438	15,239	7,614	585	7,625	R	65.0%	32.5%	66.7%	33.3%
2,162	EDWARDS	696	475	216	5	259	R	68.2%	31.0%	68.7%	31.3%
111,360	ELLIS	28,376	20,107	7,749	520	12,358	R	70.9%	27.3%	72.2%	27.8%
679,622	EL PASO	102,347	35,324	64,702	2,321	29,378	D	34.5%	63.2%	35.3%	64.7%
33,001	ERATH	8,150	5,954	1,996	200	3,958	R	73.1%	24.5%	74.9%	25.1%
18,576	FALLS	4,239	2,371	1,807	61	564	R	55.9%	42.6%	56.7%	43.3%
31,242	FANNIN	6,999	4,109	2,760	130	1,349	R	58.7%	39.4%	59.8%	40.2%
21,804	FAYETTE	7,393	5,406	1,850	137	3,556	R	73.1%	25.0%	74.5%	25.5%
4,344	FISHER	1,449	704	716	29	12	D	48.6%	49.4%	49.6%	50.4%
7,771	FLOYD	1,984	1,403	558	23	845	R	70.7%	28.1%	71.5%	28.5%
1,622	FOARD	372	186	182	4	4	R	50.0%	48.9%	50.5%	49.5%
354,452	FORT BEND	87,861	52,068	34,344	1,449	17,724	R	59.3%	39.1%	60.3%	39.7%
9,458	FRANKLIN	3,021	2,032	942	47	1,090	R	67.3%	31.2%	68.3%	31.7%
17,867	FREESTONE	5,263	3,331	1,819	113	1,512	R	63.3%	34.6%	64.7%	35.3%
16,252	FRIO	3,166	1,082	2,057	27	975	D	34.2%	65.0%	34.5%	65.5%
14,467	GAINES	2,472	1,704	698	70	1,006	R	68.9%	28.2%	70.9%	29.1%
250,158	GALVESTON	61,066	33,409	26,289	1,368	7,120	R	54.7%	43.1%	56.0%	44.0%
4,872	GARZA	1,169	836	307	26	529	R	71.5%	26.3%	73.1%	26.9%
20,814	GILLESPIE	7,918	6,502	1,262	154	5,240	R	82.1%	15.9%	83.7%	16.3%
1,406	GLASSCOCK	426	381	42	3	339	R	89.4%	9.9%	90.1%	9.9%
6,928	GOLIAD	2,275	1,399	847	29	552	R	61.5%	37.2%	62.3%	37.7%
18,628	GONZALES	4,177	2,850	1,281	46	1,569	R	68.2%	30.7%	69.0%	31.0%
22,744	GRAY	6,057	4,572	1,328	157	3,244	R	75.5%	21.9%	77.5%	22.5%
110,595	GRAYSON	27,802	18,075	9,093	634	8,982	R	65.0%	32.7%	66.5%	33.5%
111,379	GREGG	26,870	17,847	8,713	310	9,134	R	66.4%	32.4%	67.2%	32.8%
23,552	GRIMES	5,292	3,293	1,879	120	1,414	R	62.2%	35.5%	63.7%	36.3%
89,023	GUADALUPE	21,708	15,457	5,812	439	9,645	R	71.2%	26.8%	72.7%	27.3%
36,602	HALE	7,671	4,802	2,695	174	2,107	R	62.6%	35.1%	64.1%	35.9%
3,782	HALL	1,005	578	407	20	171	R	57.5%	40.5%	58.7%	41.3%
8,229	HAMILTON	2,861	1,930	863	68	1,067	R	67.5%	30.2%	69.1%	30.9%
5,369	HANSFORD	1,472	1,269	185	18	1,084	R	86.2%	12.6%	87.3%	12.7%
4,724	HARDEMAN	993	622	354	17	268	R	62.6%	35.6%	63.7%	36.3%
48,073	HARDIN	10,725	6,840	3,726	159	3,114	R	63.8%	34.7%	64.7%	35.3%
3,400,578	HARRIS	648,077	355,293	280,077	12,707	75,216	R	54.8%	43.2%	55.9%	44.1%
62,110	HARRISON	16,217	8,684	7,331	202	1,353	R	53.5%	45.2%	54.2%	45.8%
5,537	HARTLEY	1,508	1,143	323	42	820	R	75.8%	21.4%	78.0%	22.0%
6,093	HASKELL	1,991	1,264	687	40	577	R	63.5%	34.5%	64.8%	35.2%
97,589	HAYS	27,805	15,919	10,508	1,378	5,411	R	57.3%	37.8%	60.2%	39.8%
3,351	HEMPHILL	1,110	791	295	24	496	R	71.3%	26.6%	72.8%	27.2%
73,277	HENDERSON	19,379	12,444	6,498	437	5,946	R	64.2%	33.5%	65.7%	34.3%
569,463	HIDALGO	71,844	22,108	48,964	772	26,856	D	30.8%	68.2%	31.1%	68.9%
32,321	HILL	8,185	5,476	2,576	133	2,900	R	66.9%	31.5%	68.0%	32.0%
22,716	HOCKLEY	4,831	3,426	1,275	130	2,151	R	70.9%	26.4%	72.9%	27.1%
41,100	HOOD	13,402	9,571	3,507	324	6,064	R	71.4%	26.2%	73.2%	26.8%
31,960	HOPKINS	7,505	4,716	2,678	111	2,038	R	62.8%	35.7%	63.8%	36.2%
23,185	HOUSTON	5,864	3,627	2,163	74	1,464	R	61.9%	36.9%	62.6%	37.4%
33,627	HOWARD	6,855	4,324	2,386	145	1,938	R	63.1%	34.8%	64.4%	35.6%
3,344	HUDSPETH	727	310	403	14	93	D	42.6%	55.4%	43.5%	56.5%
76,596	HUNT	17,053	11,547	5,174	332	6,373	R	67.7%	30.3%	69.1%	30.9%
23,857	HUTCHINSON	5,894	4,410	1,311	173	3,099	R	74.8%	22.2%	77.1%	22.9%
1,771	IRION	633	468	142	23	326	R	73.9%	22.4%	76.7%	23.3%
8,763	JACK	2,202	1,551	610	41	941	R	70.4%	27.7%	71.8%	28.2%
14,391	JACKSON	3,429	2,302	1,071	56	1,231	R	67.1%	31.2%	68.2%	31.8%

TEXAS

GOVERNOR 2002

2000 Census Population	County	Total Vote	Republican	Democratic	Other	Rep.-Dem. Plurality	Percentage			
							Total Vote		Major Vote	
							Rep.	Dem.	Rep.	Dem.
35,604	JASPER	7,356	4,178	3,062	116	1,116 R	56.8%	41.6%	57.7%	42.3%
2,207	JEFF DAVIS	980	570	379	31	191 R	58.2%	38.7%	60.1%	39.9%
252,051	JEFFERSON	55,456	23,991	30,751	714	6,760 D	43.3%	55.5%	43.8%	56.2%
5,281	JIM HOGG	1,614	307	1,301	6	994 D	19.0%	80.6%	19.1%	80.9%
39,326	JIM WELLS	8,991	2,757	6,149	85	3,392 D	30.7%	68.4%	31.0%	69.0%
126,811	JOHNSON	27,269	18,710	7,937	622	10,773 R	68.6%	29.1%	70.2%	29.8%
20,785	JONES	4,574	2,961	1,460	153	1,501 R	64.7%	31.9%	67.0%	33.0%
15,446	KARNES	3,317	1,933	1,342	42	591 R	58.3%	40.5%	59.0%	41.0%
71,313	KAUFMAN	18,188	12,063	5,760	365	6,303 R	66.3%	31.7%	67.7%	32.3%
23,743	KENDALL	8,631	7,074	1,367	190	5,707 R	82.0%	15.8%	83.8%	16.2%
414	KENEDY	116	51	64	1	13 D	44.0%	55.2%	44.3%	55.7%
859	KENT	429	279	134	16	145 R	65.0%	31.2%	67.6%	32.4%
43,653	KERR	14,147	11,152	2,726	269	8,426 R	78.8%	19.3%	80.4%	19.6%
4,468	KIMBLE	1,164	905	244	15	661 R	77.7%	21.0%	78.8%	21.2%
356	KING	119	100	18	1	82 R	84.0%	15.1%	84.7%	15.3%
3,379	KINNEY	1,104	688	409	7	279 R	62.3%	37.0%	62.7%	37.3%
31,549	KLEBERG	6,411	2,525	3,785	101	1,260 D	39.4%	59.0%	40.0%	60.0%
4,253	KNOX	1,281	830	433	18	397 R	64.8%	33.8%	65.7%	34.3%
48,499	LAMAR	10,515	6,454	3,914	147	2,540 R	61.4%	37.2%	62.2%	37.8%
14,709	LAMB	4,210	2,280	1,875	55	405 R	54.2%	44.5%	54.9%	45.1%
17,762	LAMPASAS	4,815	3,366	1,324	125	2,042 R	69.9%	27.5%	71.8%	28.2%
5,866	LA SALLE	1,493	481	1,001	11	520 D	32.2%	67.0%	32.5%	67.5%
19,210	LAVACA	6,071	4,398	1,559	114	2,839 R	72.4%	25.7%	73.8%	26.2%
15,657	LEE	4,532	3,123	1,312	97	1,811 R	68.9%	28.9%	70.4%	29.6%
15,335	LEON	4,662	3,275	1,322	65	1,953 R	70.2%	28.4%	71.2%	28.8%
70,154	LIBERTY	12,832	7,766	4,750	316	3,016 R	60.5%	37.0%	62.0%	38.0%
22,051	LIMESTONE	5,422	3,192	2,142	88	1,050 R	58.9%	39.5%	59.8%	40.2%
3,057	LIPSCOMB	970	732	222	16	510 R	75.5%	22.9%	76.7%	23.3%
12,309	LIVE OAK	2,741	1,864	827	50	1,037 R	68.0%	30.2%	69.3%	30.7%
17,044	LLANO	7,153	5,420	1,566	167	3,854 R	75.8%	21.9%	77.6%	22.4%
67	LOVING	63	49	14	0	35 R	77.8%	22.2%	77.8%	22.2%
242,628	LUBBOCK	55,581	38,097	15,935	1,549	22,162 R	68.5%	28.7%	70.5%	29.5%
6,550	LYNN	1,739	1,113	592	34	521 R	64.0%	34.0%	65.3%	34.7%
8,205	MCCULLOCH	2,117	1,476	606	35	870 R	69.7%	28.6%	70.9%	29.1%
213,517	MCLENNAN	52,044	32,219	18,788	1,037	13,431 R	61.9%	36.1%	63.2%	36.8%
851	MCMULLEN	391	288	102	1	186 R	73.7%	26.1%	73.8%	26.2%
12,940	MADISON	2,501	1,611	847	43	764 R	64.4%	33.9%	65.5%	34.5%
10,941	MARION	2,574	1,125	1,404	45	279 D	43.7%	54.5%	44.5%	55.5%
4,746	MARTIN	1,450	917	505	28	412 R	63.2%	34.8%	64.5%	35.5%
3,738	MASON	1,320	1,009	276	35	733 R	76.4%	20.9%	78.5%	21.5%
37,957	MATAGORDA	8,426	4,945	3,309	172	1,636 R	58.7%	39.3%	59.9%	40.1%
47,297	MAVERICK	6,397	1,249	5,103	45	3,854 D	19.5%	79.8%	19.7%	80.3%
39,304	MEDINA	9,763	6,578	2,967	218	3,611 R	67.4%	30.4%	68.9%	31.1%
2,360	MENARD	924	583	310	31	273 R	63.1%	33.5%	65.3%	34.7%
116,009	MIDLAND	29,100	21,866	6,634	600	15,232 R	75.1%	22.8%	76.7%	23.3%
24,238	MILAM	6,156	3,689	2,341	126	1,348 R	59.9%	38.0%	61.2%	38.8%
5,151	MILLS	1,589	1,157	400	32	757 R	72.8%	25.2%	74.3%	25.7%
9,698	MITCHELL	1,933	1,271	622	40	649 R	65.8%	32.2%	67.1%	32.9%
19,117	MONTAGUE	4,798	3,212	1,478	108	1,734 R	66.9%	30.8%	68.5%	31.5%
293,768	MONTGOMERY	74,329	57,743	15,055	1,531	42,688 R	77.7%	20.3%	79.3%	20.7%
20,121	MOORE	4,283	3,004	1,169	110	1,835 R	70.1%	27.3%	72.0%	28.0%
13,048	MORRIS	3,519	1,582	1,901	36	319 D	45.0%	54.0%	45.4%	54.6%
1,426	MOTLEY	592	448	132	12	316 R	75.7%	22.3%	77.2%	22.8%
59,203	NACOGDOCHES	12,854	8,128	4,379	347	3,749 R	63.2%	34.1%	65.0%	35.0%
45,124	NAVARRO	10,728	6,724	3,833	171	2,891 R	62.7%	35.7%	63.7%	36.3%
15,072	NEWTON	3,351	1,490	1,813	48	323 D	44.5%	54.1%	45.1%	54.9%
15,802	NOLAN	3,619	2,318	1,209	92	1,109 R	64.1%	33.4%	65.7%	34.3%
313,645	NUECES	68,841	33,152	34,001	1,688	849 D	48.2%	49.4%	49.4%	50.6%
9,006	OCHILTREE	2,108	1,819	253	36	1,566 R	86.3%	12.0%	87.8%	12.2%
2,185	OLDHAM	623	489	123	11	366 R	78.5%	19.7%	79.9%	20.1%

TEXAS

GOVERNOR 2002

2000 Census Population	County	Total Vote	Republican	Democratic	Other	Rep.-Dem. Plurality	Percentage			
							Total Vote		Major Vote	
							Rep.	Dem.	Rep.	Dem.
84,966	ORANGE	18,270	10,050	7,895	325	2,155 R	55.0%	43.2%	56.0%	44.0%
27,026	PALO PINTO	6,337	3,944	2,260	133	1,684 R	62.2%	35.7%	63.6%	36.4%
22,756	PANOLA	6,036	3,505	2,465	66	1,040 R	58.1%	40.8%	58.7%	41.3%
88,495	PARKER	25,522	18,352	6,629	541	11,723 R	71.9%	26.0%	73.5%	26.5%
10,016	PARMER	1,977	1,473	477	27	996 R	74.5%	24.1%	75.5%	24.5%
16,809	PECOS	3,905	1,791	2,032	82	241 D	45.9%	52.0%	46.8%	53.2%
41,133	POLK	11,180	6,261	4,684	235	1,577 R	56.0%	41.9%	57.2%	42.8%
113,546	POTTER	18,764	11,701	6,537	526	5,164 R	62.4%	34.8%	64.2%	35.8%
7,304	PRESIDIO	1,343	322	997	24	675 D	24.0%	74.2%	24.4%	75.6%
9,139	RAINS	2,768	1,730	966	72	764 R	62.5%	34.9%	64.2%	35.8%
104,312	RANDALL	31,139	23,770	6,627	742	17,143 R	76.3%	21.3%	78.2%	21.8%
3,326	REAGAN	765	526	224	15	302 R	68.8%	29.3%	70.1%	29.9%
3,047	REAL	1,096	846	235	15	611 R	77.2%	21.4%	78.3%	21.7%
14,314	RED RIVER	3,554	1,957	1,562	35	395 R	55.1%	44.0%	55.6%	44.4%
13,137	REEVES	2,523	782	1,716	25	934 D	31.0%	68.0%	31.3%	68.7%
7,828	REFUGIO	1,924	1,065	827	32	238 R	55.4%	43.0%	56.3%	43.7%
887	ROBERTS	402	339	53	10	286 R	84.3%	13.2%	86.5%	13.5%
16,000	ROBERTSON	5,639	2,673	2,865	101	192 D	47.4%	50.8%	48.3%	51.7%
43,080	ROCKWALL	14,087	10,999	2,833	255	8,166 R	78.1%	20.1%	79.5%	20.5%
11,495	RUNNELS	2,916	2,200	637	79	1,563 R	75.4%	21.8%	77.5%	22.5%
47,372	RUSK	11,085	7,371	3,598	116	3,773 R	66.5%	32.5%	67.2%	32.8%
10,469	SABINE	2,838	1,604	1,182	52	422 R	56.5%	41.6%	57.6%	42.4%
8,946	SAN AUGUSTINE	2,910	1,481	1,383	46	98 R	50.9%	47.5%	51.7%	48.3%
22,246	SAN JACINTO	5,804	3,440	2,228	136	1,212 R	59.3%	38.4%	60.7%	39.3%
67,138	SAN PATRICIO	13,602	7,123	6,199	280	924 R	52.4%	45.6%	53.5%	46.5%
6,186	SAN SABA	1,793	1,283	483	27	800 R	71.6%	26.9%	72.7%	27.3%
2,935	SCHLEICHER	819	556	246	17	310 R	67.9%	30.0%	69.3%	30.7%
16,361	SCURRY	3,725	2,727	918	80	1,809 R	73.2%	24.6%	74.8%	25.2%
3,302	SHACKELFORD	940	762	147	31	615 R	81.1%	15.6%	83.8%	16.2%
25,224	SHELBY	6,524	3,882	2,574	68	1,308 R	59.5%	39.5%	60.1%	39.9%
3,186	SHERMAN	833	651	157	25	494 R	78.2%	18.8%	80.6%	19.4%
174,706	SMITH	46,969	32,763	13,609	597	19,154 R	69.8%	29.0%	70.7%	29.3%
6,809	SOMERVELL	2,492	1,674	757	61	917 R	67.2%	30.4%	68.9%	31.1%
53,597	STARR	6,240	663	5,556	21	4,893 D	10.6%	89.0%	10.7%	89.3%
9,674	STEPHENS	2,857	1,972	787	98	1,185 R	69.0%	27.5%	71.5%	28.5%
1,393	STERLING	448	352	85	11	267 R	78.6%	19.0%	80.5%	19.5%
1,693	STONEWALL	600	372	210	18	162 R	62.0%	35.0%	63.9%	36.1%
4,077	SUTTON	1,057	699	344	14	355 R	66.1%	32.5%	67.0%	33.0%
8,378	SWISHER	2,097	1,163	885	49	278 R	55.5%	42.2%	56.8%	43.2%
1,446,219	TARRANT	337,032	200,486	129,861	6,685	70,625 R	59.5%	38.5%	60.7%	39.3%
126,555	TAYLOR	29,631	21,723	7,271	637	14,452 R	73.3%	24.5%	74.9%	25.1%
1,081	TERRELL	404	192	207	5	15 D	47.5%	51.2%	48.1%	51.9%
12,761	TERRY	2,921	1,966	897	58	1,069 R	67.3%	30.7%	68.7%	31.3%
1,850	THROCKMORTON	679	497	168	14	329 R	73.2%	24.7%	74.7%	25.3%
28,118	TITUS	5,630	3,256	2,288	86	968 R	57.8%	40.6%	58.7%	41.3%
104,010	TOM GREEN	24,808	17,158	6,876	774	10,282 R	69.2%	27.7%	71.4%	28.6%
812,280	TRAVIS	220,043	102,914	103,127	14,002	213 D	46.8%	46.9%	49.9%	50.1%
13,779	TRINITY	4,135	2,210	1,863	62	347 R	53.4%	45.1%	54.3%	45.7%
20,871	TYLER	4,631	2,436	2,123	72	313 R	52.6%	45.8%	53.4%	46.6%
35,291	UPSHUR	9,066	5,507	3,368	191	2,139 R	60.7%	37.1%	62.1%	37.9%
3,404	UPTON	859	604	241	14	363 R	70.3%	28.1%	71.5%	28.5%
25,926	UVALDE	6,210	3,159	2,965	86	194 R	50.9%	47.7%	51.6%	48.4%
44,856	VAL VERDE	7,674	3,197	4,403	74	1,206 D	41.7%	57.4%	42.1%	57.9%
48,140	VAN ZANDT	13,296	9,168	3,867	261	5,301 R	69.0%	29.1%	70.3%	29.7%
84,088	VICTORIA	19,228	11,385	7,494	349	3,891 R	59.2%	39.0%	60.3%	39.7%
61,758	WALKER	10,444	6,448	3,807	189	2,641 R	61.7%	36.5%	62.9%	37.1%
32,663	WALLER	7,965	4,765	3,071	129	1,694 R	59.8%	38.6%	60.8%	39.2%
10,909	WARD	3,211	1,697	1,399	115	298 R	52.8%	43.6%	54.8%	45.2%
30,373	WASHINGTON	9,440	7,020	2,270	150	4,750 R	74.4%	24.0%	75.6%	24.4%
193,117	WEBB	39,241	3,958	35,101	182	31,143 D	10.1%	89.4%	10.1%	89.9%

TEXAS

GOVERNOR 2002

2000 Census Population	County	Total Vote	Republican	Democratic	Other	Rep.-Dem. Plurality		Total Vote Rep.	Dem.	Major Vote Rep.	Dem.
41,188	WHARTON	9,409	6,002	3,245	162	2,757	R	63.8%	34.5%	64.9%	35.1%
5,284	WHEELER	1,568	1,122	425	21	697	R	71.6%	27.1%	72.5%	27.5%
131,664	WICHITA	26,179	16,930	8,518	731	8,412	R	64.7%	32.5%	66.5%	33.5%
14,676	WILBARGER	2,993	2,086	857	50	1,229	R	69.7%	28.6%	70.9%	29.1%
20,082	WILLACY	3,664	1,004	2,615	45	1,611	D	27.4%	71.4%	27.7%	72.3%
249,967	WILLIAMSON	75,096	51,326	20,822	2,948	30,504	R	68.3%	27.7%	71.1%	28.9%
32,408	WILSON	9,071	5,614	3,294	163	2,320	R	61.9%	36.3%	63.0%	37.0%
7,173	WINKLER	1,667	1,036	581	50	455	R	62.1%	34.9%	64.1%	35.9%
48,793	WISE	11,766	8,212	3,309	245	4,903	R	69.8%	28.1%	71.3%	28.7%
36,752	WOOD	11,136	7,852	3,124	160	4,728	R	70.5%	28.1%	71.5%	28.5%
7,322	YOAKUM	1,872	1,292	516	64	776	R	69.0%	27.6%	71.5%	28.5%
17,943	YOUNG	5,313	3,804	1,422	87	2,382	R	71.6%	26.8%	72.8%	27.2%
12,182	ZAPATA	2,454	366	2,082	6	1,716	D	14.9%	84.8%	15.0%	85.0%
11,600	ZAVALA	2,653	430	2,195	28	1,765	D	16.2%	82.7%	16.4%	83.6%
20,851,820	TOTAL	4,553,987	2,632,591	1,819,798	101,598	812,793	R	57.8%	40.0%	59.1%	40.9%

TEXAS

SENATOR 2002

2000 Census Population	County	Total Vote	Republican	Democratic	Other	Rep.-Dem. Plurality		Total Vote Rep.	Dem.	Major Vote Rep.	Dem.
55,109	ANDERSON	10,340	6,347	3,882	111	2,465	R	61.4%	37.5%	62.0%	38.0%
13,004	ANDREWS	2,929	1,869	1,000	60	869	R	63.8%	34.1%	65.1%	34.9%
80,130	ANGELINA	18,885	10,623	7,991	271	2,632	R	56.3%	42.3%	57.1%	42.9%
22,497	ARANSAS	5,968	3,597	2,298	73	1,299	R	60.3%	38.5%	61.0%	39.0%
8,854	ARCHER	2,815	1,811	967	37	844	R	64.3%	34.4%	65.2%	34.8%
2,148	ARMSTRONG	742	554	180	8	374	R	74.7%	24.3%	75.5%	24.5%
38,628	ATASCOSA	8,090	4,261	3,693	136	568	R	52.7%	45.6%	53.6%	46.4%
23,590	AUSTIN	6,915	5,006	1,836	73	3,170	R	72.4%	26.6%	73.2%	26.8%
6,594	BAILEY	1,557	1,079	472	6	607	R	69.3%	30.3%	69.6%	30.4%
17,645	BANDERA	5,563	4,246	1,171	146	3,075	R	76.3%	21.0%	78.4%	21.6%
57,733	BASTROP	15,030	7,862	6,734	434	1,128	R	52.3%	44.8%	53.9%	46.1%
4,093	BAYLOR	1,139	675	455	9	220	R	59.3%	39.9%	59.7%	40.3%
32,359	BEE	7,189	2,918	4,168	103	1,250	D	40.6%	58.0%	41.2%	58.8%
237,974	BELL	43,283	25,728	17,013	542	8,715	R	59.4%	39.3%	60.2%	39.8%
1,392,931	BEXAR	271,785	138,936	128,577	4,272	10,359	R	51.1%	47.3%	51.9%	48.1%
8,418	BLANCO	3,043	2,106	876	61	1,230	R	69.2%	28.8%	70.6%	29.4%
729	BORDEN	273	195	74	4	121	R	71.4%	27.1%	72.5%	27.5%
17,204	BOSQUE	5,399	3,456	1,880	63	1,576	R	64.0%	34.8%	64.8%	35.2%
89,306	BOWIE	19,981	11,075	8,719	187	2,356	R	55.4%	43.6%	56.0%	44.0%
241,767	BRAZORIA	52,884	33,645	18,329	910	15,316	R	63.6%	34.7%	64.7%	35.3%
152,415	BRAZOS	27,855	17,963	9,543	349	8,420	R	64.5%	34.3%	65.3%	34.7%
8,866	BREWSTER	2,395	1,173	1,157	65	16	R	49.0%	48.3%	50.3%	49.7%
1,790	BRISCOE	748	446	299	3	147	R	59.6%	40.0%	59.9%	40.1%
7,976	BROOKS	2,208	291	1,865	52	1,574	D	13.2%	84.5%	13.5%	86.5%
37,674	BROWN	8,992	6,284	2,588	120	3,696	R	69.9%	28.8%	70.8%	29.2%
16,470	BURLESON	4,756	2,625	2,070	61	555	R	55.2%	43.5%	55.9%	44.1%
34,147	BURNET	10,960	7,221	3,525	214	3,696	R	65.9%	32.2%	67.2%	32.8%
32,194	CALDWELL	7,463	3,575	3,714	174	139	D	47.9%	49.8%	49.0%	51.0%
20,647	CALHOUN	5,273	2,494	2,691	88	197	D	47.3%	51.0%	48.1%	51.9%
12,905	CALLAHAN	3,674	2,571	1,042	61	1,529	R	70.0%	28.4%	71.2%	28.8%

TEXAS

SENATOR 2002

2000 Census Population	County	Total Vote	Republican	Democratic	Other	Rep.-Dem. Plurality		Percentage			
								Total Vote		Major Vote	
								Rep.	Dem.	Rep.	Dem.
335,227	CAMERON	44,426	14,836	28,903	687	14,067	D	33.4%	65.1%	33.9%	66.1%
11,549	CAMP	2,922	1,485	1,414	23	71	R	50.8%	48.4%	51.2%	48.8%
6,516	CARSON	2,132	1,559	551	22	1,008	R	73.1%	25.8%	73.9%	26.1%
30,438	CASS	7,278	3,708	3,488	82	220	R	50.9%	47.9%	51.5%	48.5%
8,285	CASTRO	1,934	1,188	726	20	462	R	61.4%	37.5%	62.1%	37.9%
26,031	CHAMBERS	6,984	4,401	2,420	163	1,981	R	63.0%	34.7%	64.5%	35.5%
46,659	CHEROKEE	10,106	6,391	3,582	133	2,809	R	63.2%	35.4%	64.1%	35.9%
7,688	CHILDRESS	1,543	1,051	484	8	567	R	68.1%	31.4%	68.5%	31.5%
11,006	CLAY	3,271	1,932	1,317	22	615	R	59.1%	40.3%	59.5%	40.5%
3,730	COCHRAN	1,017	588	410	19	178	R	57.8%	40.3%	58.9%	41.1%
3,864	COKE	1,124	770	343	11	427	R	68.5%	30.5%	69.2%	30.8%
9,235	COLEMAN	2,475	1,613	829	33	784	R	65.2%	33.5%	66.1%	33.9%
491,675	COLLIN	126,403	88,315	36,810	1,278	51,505	R	69.9%	29.1%	70.6%	29.4%
3,206	COLLINGSWORTH	1,080	662	409	9	253	R	61.3%	37.9%	61.8%	38.2%
20,390	COLORADO	5,707	3,629	1,999	79	1,630	R	63.6%	35.0%	64.5%	35.5%
78,021	COMAL	24,213	18,158	5,696	359	12,462	R	75.0%	23.5%	76.1%	23.9%
14,026	COMANCHE	3,720	2,273	1,415	32	858	R	61.1%	38.0%	61.6%	38.4%
3,966	CONCHO	762	515	242	5	273	R	67.6%	31.8%	68.0%	32.0%
36,363	COOKE	9,561	6,835	2,649	77	4,186	R	71.5%	27.7%	72.1%	27.9%
74,978	CORYELL	9,640	5,734	3,782	124	1,952	R	59.5%	39.2%	60.3%	39.7%
1,904	COTTLE	534	283	240	11	43	R	53.0%	44.9%	54.1%	45.9%
3,996	CRANE	1,272	828	412	32	416	R	65.1%	32.4%	66.8%	33.2%
4,099	CROCKETT	913	531	369	13	162	R	58.2%	40.4%	59.0%	41.0%
7,072	CROSBY	1,604	848	741	15	107	R	52.9%	46.2%	53.4%	46.6%
2,975	CULBERSON	557	176	367	14	191	D	31.6%	65.9%	32.4%	67.6%
6,222	DALLAM	897	666	217	14	449	R	74.2%	24.2%	75.4%	24.6%
2,218,899	DALLAS	447,289	217,923	224,705	4,661	6,782	D	48.7%	50.2%	49.2%	50.8%
14,985	DAWSON	3,492	2,182	1,279	31	903	R	62.5%	36.6%	63.0%	37.0%
18,561	DEAF SMITH	3,531	2,418	1,063	50	1,355	R	68.5%	30.1%	69.5%	30.5%
5,327	DELTA	1,301	778	513	10	265	R	59.8%	39.4%	60.3%	39.7%
432,976	DENTON	104,900	70,684	32,931	1,285	37,753	R	67.4%	31.4%	68.2%	31.8%
20,013	DE WITT	4,375	3,045	1,295	35	1,750	R	69.6%	29.6%	70.2%	29.8%
2,762	DICKENS	725	413	307	5	106	R	57.0%	42.3%	57.4%	42.6%
10,248	DIMMIT	2,430	581	1,808	41	1,227	D	23.9%	74.4%	24.3%	75.7%
3,828	DONLEY	1,365	962	380	23	582	R	70.5%	27.8%	71.7%	28.3%
13,120	DUVAL	3,072	373	2,660	39	2,287	D	12.1%	86.6%	12.3%	87.7%
18,297	EASTLAND	4,966	3,249	1,607	110	1,642	R	65.4%	32.4%	66.9%	33.1%
121,123	ECTOR	23,340	15,378	7,576	386	7,802	R	65.9%	32.5%	67.0%	33.0%
2,162	EDWARDS	651	447	199	5	248	R	68.7%	30.6%	69.2%	30.8%
111,360	ELLIS	99,768	28,649	69,491	1,628	40,842	D	28.7%	69.7%	29.2%	70.8%
679,622	EL PASO	28,353	19,285	8,774	294	10,511	R	68.0%	30.9%	68.7%	31.3%
33,001	ERATH	8,086	5,478	2,514	94	2,964	R	67.7%	31.1%	68.5%	31.5%
18,576	FALLS	4,268	2,121	2,115	32	6	R	49.7%	49.6%	50.1%	49.9%
31,242	FANNIN	7,004	3,810	3,120	74	690	R	54.4%	44.5%	55.0%	45.0%
21,804	FAYETTE	7,303	4,827	2,395	81	2,432	R	66.1%	32.8%	66.8%	33.2%
4,344	FISHER	1,408	579	817	12	238	D	41.1%	58.0%	41.5%	58.5%
7,771	FLOYD	1,915	1,268	627	20	641	R	66.2%	32.7%	66.9%	33.1%
1,622	FOARD	364	136	227	1	91	D	37.4%	62.4%	37.5%	62.5%
354,452	FORT BEND	87,636	49,459	37,320	857	12,139	R	56.4%	42.6%	57.0%	43.0%
9,458	FRANKLIN	3,004	1,903	1,056	45	847	R	63.3%	35.2%	64.3%	35.7%
17,867	FREESTONE	5,254	3,117	2,065	72	1,052	R	59.3%	39.3%	60.2%	39.8%
16,252	FRIO	3,010	1,044	1,929	37	885	D	34.7%	64.1%	35.1%	64.9%
14,467	GAINES	2,417	1,628	754	35	874	R	67.4%	31.2%	68.3%	31.7%
250,158	GALVESTON	60,822	32,193	27,741	888	4,452	R	52.9%	45.6%	53.7%	46.3%
4,872	GARZA	1,168	801	337	30	464	R	68.6%	28.9%	70.4%	29.6%
20,814	GILLESPIE	7,840	6,268	1,461	111	4,807	R	79.9%	18.6%	81.1%	18.9%
1,406	GLASSCOCK	411	339	71	1	268	R	82.5%	17.3%	82.7%	17.3%
6,928	GOLIAD	2,174	1,281	865	28	416	R	58.9%	39.8%	59.7%	40.3%
18,628	GONZALES	4,058	2,536	1,478	44	1,058	R	62.5%	36.4%	63.2%	36.8%
22,744	GRAY	6,013	4,634	1,303	76	3,331	R	77.1%	21.7%	78.1%	21.9%

TEXAS

SENATOR 2002

2000 Census Population	County	Total Vote	Republican	Democratic	Other	Rep.-Dem. Plurality	Percentage — Total Vote Rep.	Dem.	Percentage — Major Vote Rep.	Dem.
110,595	GRAYSON	27,624	16,613	10,661	350	5,952 R	60.1%	38.6%	60.9%	39.1%
111,379	GREGG	26,778	18,310	8,250	218	10,060 R	68.4%	30.8%	68.9%	31.1%
23,552	GRIMES	5,202	3,053	2,076	73	977 R	58.7%	39.9%	59.5%	40.5%
89,023	GUADALUPE	21,695	14,993	6,376	326	8,617 R	69.1%	29.4%	70.2%	29.8%
36,602	HALE	7,544	4,719	2,727	98	1,992 R	62.6%	36.1%	63.4%	36.6%
3,782	HALL	980	551	425	4	126 R	56.2%	43.4%	56.5%	43.5%
8,229	HAMILTON	2,829	1,774	1,024	31	750 R	62.7%	36.2%	63.4%	36.6%
5,369	HANSFORD	1,461	1,264	195	2	1,069 R	86.5%	13.3%	86.6%	13.4%
4,724	HARDEMAN	975	530	437	8	93 R	54.4%	44.8%	54.8%	45.2%
48,073	HARDIN	10,635	6,598	3,918	119	2,680 R	62.0%	36.8%	62.7%	37.3%
3,400,578	HARRIS	640,791	337,774	294,673	8,344	43,101 R	52.7%	46.0%	53.4%	46.6%
62,110	HARRISON	15,970	8,948	6,821	201	2,127 R	56.0%	42.7%	56.7%	43.3%
5,537	HARTLEY	1,518	1,168	336	14	832 R	76.9%	22.1%	77.7%	22.3%
6,093	HASKELL	1,916	946	954	16	8 D	49.4%	49.8%	49.8%	50.2%
97,589	HAYS	27,865	14,813	12,286	766	2,527 R	53.2%	44.1%	54.7%	45.3%
3,351	HEMPHILL	1,219	913	294	12	619 R	74.9%	24.1%	75.6%	24.4%
73,277	HENDERSON	19,267	12,082	6,928	257	5,154 R	62.7%	36.0%	63.6%	36.4%
569,463	HIDALGO	68,108	18,862	48,367	879	29,505 D	27.7%	71.0%	28.1%	71.9%
32,321	HILL	8,170	5,068	3,020	82	2,048 R	62.0%	37.0%	62.7%	37.3%
22,716	HOCKLEY	4,756	3,365	1,334	57	2,031 R	70.8%	28.0%	71.6%	28.4%
41,100	HOOD	13,426	9,462	3,779	185	5,683 R	70.5%	28.1%	71.5%	28.5%
31,960	HOPKINS	7,433	4,413	2,944	76	1,469 R	59.4%	39.6%	60.0%	40.0%
23,185	HOUSTON	5,733	3,385	2,276	72	1,109 R	59.0%	39.7%	59.8%	40.2%
33,627	HOWARD	6,807	4,169	2,523	115	1,646 R	61.2%	37.1%	62.3%	37.7%
3,344	HUDSPETH	650	280	359	11	79 D	43.1%	55.2%	43.8%	56.2%
76,596	HUNT	16,978	10,835	5,948	195	4,887 R	63.8%	35.0%	64.6%	35.4%
23,857	HUTCHINSON	5,969	4,507	1,379	83	3,128 R	75.5%	23.1%	76.6%	23.4%
1,771	IRION	623	423	189	11	234 R	67.9%	30.3%	69.1%	30.9%
8,763	JACK	2,170	1,419	730	21	689 R	65.4%	33.6%	66.0%	34.0%
14,391	JACKSON	3,375	2,138	1,210	27	928 R	63.3%	35.9%	63.9%	36.1%
35,604	JASPER	7,248	3,954	3,202	92	752 R	54.6%	44.2%	55.3%	44.7%
2,207	JEFF DAVIS	904	513	359	32	154 R	56.7%	39.7%	58.8%	41.2%
252,051	JEFFERSON	55,146	23,217	31,272	657	8,055 D	42.1%	56.7%	42.6%	57.4%
5,281	JIM HOGG	1,544	260	1,269	15	1,009 D	16.8%	82.2%	17.0%	83.0%
39,326	JIM WELLS	8,692	2,381	6,212	99	3,831 D	27.4%	71.5%	27.7%	72.3%
126,811	JOHNSON	27,228	18,190	8,675	363	9,515 R	66.8%	31.9%	67.7%	32.3%
20,785	JONES	4,466	2,540	1,847	79	693 R	56.9%	41.4%	57.9%	42.1%
15,446	KARNES	3,216	1,796	1,387	33	409 R	55.8%	43.1%	56.4%	43.6%
71,313	KAUFMAN	18,122	11,531	6,385	206	5,146 R	63.6%	35.2%	64.4%	35.6%
23,743	KENDALL	8,605	6,883	1,596	126	5,287 R	80.0%	18.5%	81.2%	18.8%
414	KENEDY	110	47	63		16 D	42.7%	57.3%	42.7%	57.3%
859	KENT	406	200	199	7	1 R	49.3%	49.0%	50.1%	49.9%
43,653	KERR	14,074	10,884	2,997	193	7,887 R	77.3%	21.3%	78.4%	21.6%
4,468	KIMBLE	1,111	807	294	10	513 R	72.6%	26.5%	73.3%	26.7%
356	KING	98	74	23	1	51 R	75.5%	23.5%	76.3%	23.7%
3,379	KINNEY	1,029	650	371	8	279 R	63.2%	36.1%	63.7%	36.3%
31,549	KLEBERG	6,248	2,156	4,001	91	1,845 D	34.5%	64.0%	35.0%	65.0%
4,253	KNOX	1,221	668	543	10	125 R	54.7%	44.5%	55.2%	44.8%
48,499	LAMAR	10,543	6,205	4,246	92	1,959 R	58.9%	40.3%	59.4%	40.6%
14,709	LAMB	3,156	2,121	1,009	26	1,112 R	67.2%	32.0%	67.8%	32.2%
17,762	LAMPASAS	4,774	3,137	1,568	69	1,569 R	65.7%	32.8%	66.7%	33.3%
5,866	LA SALLE	1,349	425	902	22	477 D	31.5%	66.9%	32.0%	68.0%
19,210	LAVACA	5,890	3,792	2,033	65	1,759 R	64.4%	34.5%	65.1%	34.9%
15,657	LEE	4,502	2,713	1,736	53	977 R	60.3%	38.6%	61.0%	39.0%
15,335	LEON	4,582	3,001	1,536	45	1,465 R	65.5%	33.5%	66.1%	33.9%
70,154	LIBERTY	12,699	7,308	5,145	246	2,163 R	57.5%	40.5%	58.7%	41.3%
22,051	LIMESTONE	5,361	2,863	2,432	66	431 R	53.4%	45.4%	54.1%	45.9%
3,057	LIPSCOMB	952	706	238	8	468 R	74.2%	25.0%	74.8%	25.2%
12,309	LIVE OAK	2,704	1,757	925	22	832 R	65.0%	34.2%	65.5%	34.5%
17,044	LLANO	7,123	5,056	1,960	107	3,096 R	71.0%	27.5%	72.1%	27.9%

TEXAS
SENATOR 2002

2000 Census Population	County	Total Vote	Republican	Democratic	Other	Rep.-Dem. Plurality	Percentage Total Vote		Major Vote	
							Rep.	Dem.	Rep.	Dem.
67	LOVING	58	42	16		26 R	72.4%	27.6%	72.4%	27.6%
242,628	LUBBOCK	55,267	38,217	16,248	802	21,969 R	69.1%	29.4%	70.2%	29.8%
6,550	LYNN	1,677	1,038	625	14	413 R	61.9%	37.3%	62.4%	37.6%
8,205	MCCULLOCH	2,065	1,387	670	8	717 R	67.2%	32.4%	67.4%	32.6%
213,517	MCLENNAN	52,044	29,608	21,904	532	7,704 R	56.9%	42.1%	57.5%	42.5%
851	MCMULLEN	359	263	89	7	174 R	73.3%	24.8%	74.7%	25.3%
12,940	MADISON	2,479	1,496	944	39	552 R	60.3%	38.1%	61.3%	38.7%
10,941	MARION	2,546	1,216	1,303	27	87 D	47.8%	51.2%	48.3%	51.7%
4,746	MARTIN	1,317	877	426	14	451 R	66.6%	32.3%	67.3%	32.7%
3,738	MASON	1,297	917	352	28	565 R	70.7%	27.1%	72.3%	27.7%
37,957	MATAGORDA	8,270	4,722	3,427	121	1,295 R	57.1%	41.4%	57.9%	42.1%
47,297	MAVERICK	5,984	1,124	4,721	139	3,597 D	18.8%	78.9%	19.2%	80.8%
39,304	MEDINA	9,588	6,268	3,151	169	3,117 R	65.4%	32.9%	66.5%	33.5%
2,360	MENARD	855	540	301	14	239 R	63.2%	35.2%	64.2%	35.8%
116,009	MIDLAND	28,898	21,761	6,815	322	14,946 R	75.3%	23.6%	76.2%	23.8%
24,238	MILAM	6,131	3,172	2,879	80	293 R	51.7%	47.0%	52.4%	47.6%
5,151	MILLS	1,592	1,048	532	12	516 R	65.8%	33.4%	66.3%	33.7%
9,698	MITCHELL	1,852	1,062	767	23	295 R	57.3%	41.4%	58.1%	41.9%
19,117	MONTAGUE	4,775	3,005	1,715	55	1,290 R	62.9%	35.9%	63.7%	36.3%
293,768	MONTGOMERY	73,904	56,068	16,750	1,086	39,318 R	75.9%	22.7%	77.0%	23.0%
20,121	MOORE	4,171	3,054	1,065	52	1,989 R	73.2%	25.5%	74.1%	25.9%
13,048	MORRIS	3,441	1,534	1,879	28	345 D	44.6%	54.6%	44.9%	55.1%
1,426	MOTLEY	564	395	159	10	236 R	70.0%	28.2%	71.3%	28.7%
59,203	NACOGDOCHES	12,681	7,776	4,690	215	3,086 R	61.3%	37.0%	62.4%	37.6%
45,124	NAVARRO	10,711	6,225	4,382	104	1,843 R	58.1%	40.9%	58.7%	41.3%
15,072	NEWTON	3,289	1,331	1,922	36	591 D	40.5%	58.4%	40.9%	59.1%
15,802	NOLAN	3,568	2,038	1,480	50	558 R	57.1%	41.5%	57.9%	42.1%
313,645	NUECES	68,432	29,423	38,184	825	8,761 D	43.0%	55.8%	43.5%	56.5%
9,006	OCHILTREE	2,098	1,837	250	11	1,587 R	87.6%	11.9%	88.0%	12.0%
2,185	OLDHAM	628	471	153	4	318 R	75.0%	24.4%	75.5%	24.5%
84,966	ORANGE	18,102	9,380	8,463	259	917 R	51.8%	46.8%	52.6%	47.4%
27,026	PALO PINTO	6,305	3,796	2,418	91	1,378 R	60.2%	38.4%	61.1%	38.9%
22,756	PANOLA	5,933	3,580	2,291	62	1,289 R	60.3%	38.6%	61.0%	39.0%
88,495	PARKER	25,434	17,803	7,283	348	10,520 R	70.0%	28.6%	71.0%	29.0%
10,016	PARMER	1,929	1,454	455	20	999 R	75.4%	23.6%	76.2%	23.8%
16,809	PECOS	3,615	1,748	1,764	103	16 D	48.4%	48.8%	49.8%	50.2%
41,133	POLK	11,035	5,745	5,067	223	678 R	52.1%	45.9%	53.1%	46.9%
113,546	POTTER	18,496	11,962	6,300	234	5,662 R	64.7%	34.1%	65.5%	34.5%
7,304	PRESIDIO	1,212	323	856	33	533 D	26.7%	70.6%	27.4%	72.6%
9,139	RAINS	2,770	1,647	1,077	46	570 R	59.5%	38.9%	60.5%	39.5%
104,312	RANDALL	31,064	24,360	6,452	252	17,908 R	78.4%	20.8%	79.1%	20.9%
3,326	REAGAN	724	517	198	9	319 R	71.4%	27.3%	72.3%	27.7%
3,047	REAL	1,114	865	234	15	631 R	77.6%	21.0%	78.7%	21.3%
14,314	RED RIVER	3,514	1,817	1,667	30	150 R	51.7%	47.4%	52.2%	47.8%
13,137	REEVES	2,415	827	1,538	50	711 D	34.2%	63.7%	35.0%	65.0%
7,828	REFUGIO	1,852	897	934	21	37 D	48.4%	50.4%	49.0%	51.0%
887	ROBERTS	396	321	68	7	253 R	81.1%	17.2%	82.5%	17.5%
16,000	ROBERTSON	5,576	2,277	3,249	50	972 D	40.8%	58.3%	41.2%	58.8%
43,080	ROCKWALL	14,080	10,566	3,390	124	7,176 R	75.0%	24.1%	75.7%	24.3%
11,495	RUNNELS	2,814	1,911	879	24	1,032 R	67.9%	31.2%	68.5%	31.5%
47,372	RUSK	10,890	7,185	3,605	100	3,580 R	66.0%	33.1%	66.6%	33.4%
10,469	SABINE	2,755	1,514	1,197	44	317 R	55.0%	43.4%	55.8%	44.2%
8,946	SAN AUGUSTINE	2,807	1,306	1,450	51	144 D	46.5%	51.7%	47.4%	52.6%
22,246	SAN JACINTO	5,711	3,194	2,406	111	788 R	55.9%	42.1%	57.0%	43.0%
67,138	SAN PATRICIO	13,430	6,228	7,050	152	822 D	46.4%	52.5%	46.9%	53.1%
6,186	SAN SABA	1,742	1,172	551	19	621 R	67.3%	31.6%	68.0%	32.0%
2,935	SCHLEICHER	786	508	269	9	239 R	64.6%	34.2%	65.4%	34.6%
16,361	SCURRY	3,650	2,324	1,254	72	1,070 R	63.7%	34.4%	65.0%	35.0%
3,302	SHACKELFORD	918	689	212	17	477 R	75.1%	23.1%	76.5%	23.5%
25,224	SHELBY	6,332	3,695	2,555	82	1,140 R	58.4%	40.4%	59.1%	40.9%

TEXAS

SENATOR 2002

2000 Census Population	County	Total Vote	Republican	Democratic	Other	Rep.-Dem. Plurality		Total Vote Rep.	Dem.	Major Vote Rep.	Dem.
3,186	SHERMAN	813	624	182	7	442	R	76.8%	22.4%	77.4%	22.6%
174,706	SMITH	46,969	32,537	13,984	448	18,553	R	69.3%	29.8%	69.9%	30.1%
6,809	SOMERVELL	2,499	1,593	875	31	718	R	63.7%	35.0%	64.5%	35.5%
53,597	STARR	5,536	535	4,934	67	4,399	D	9.7%	89.1%	9.8%	90.2%
9,674	STEPHENS	2,775	1,767	967	41	800	R	63.7%	34.8%	64.6%	35.4%
1,393	STERLING	439	351	84	4	267	R	80.0%	19.1%	80.7%	19.3%
1,693	STONEWALL	581	288	283	10	5	R	49.6%	48.7%	50.4%	49.6%
4,077	SUTTON	1,016	698	315	3	383	R	68.7%	31.0%	68.9%	31.1%
8,378	SWISHER	2,077	1,050	1,010	17	40	R	50.6%	48.6%	51.0%	49.0%
1,446,219	TARRANT	338,264	195,111	139,596	3,557	55,515	R	57.7%	41.3%	58.3%	41.7%
126,555	TAYLOR	29,072	20,701	8,051	320	12,650	R	71.2%	27.7%	72.0%	28.0%
1,081	TERRELL	355	149	194	12	45	D	42.0%	54.6%	43.4%	56.6%
12,761	TERRY	2,852	1,794	1,011	47	783	R	62.9%	35.4%	64.0%	36.0%
1,850	THROCKMORTON	630	376	245	9	131	R	59.7%	38.9%	60.5%	39.5%
28,118	TITUS	5,517	3,065	2,395	57	670	R	55.6%	43.4%	56.1%	43.9%
104,010	TOM GREEN	24,752	16,649	7,761	342	8,888	R	67.3%	31.4%	68.2%	31.8%
812,280	TRAVIS	221,222	92,270	122,639	6,313	30,369	D	41.7%	55.4%	42.9%	57.1%
13,779	TRINITY	4,067	2,056	1,959	52	97	R	50.6%	48.2%	51.2%	48.8%
20,871	TYLER	4,559	2,249	2,235	75	14	R	49.3%	49.0%	50.2%	49.8%
35,291	UPSHUR	8,934	5,338	3,458	138	1,880	R	59.7%	38.7%	60.7%	39.3%
3,404	UPTON	841	575	253	13	322	R	68.4%	30.1%	69.4%	30.6%
25,926	UVALDE	6,026	3,057	2,887	82	170	R	50.7%	47.9%	51.4%	48.6%
44,856	VAL VERDE	7,443	3,184	4,153	106	969	D	42.8%	55.8%	43.4%	56.6%
48,140	VAN ZANDT	13,173	8,836	4,200	137	4,636	R	67.1%	31.9%	67.8%	32.2%
84,088	VICTORIA	18,540	11,171	7,121	248	4,050	R	60.3%	38.4%	61.1%	38.9%
61,758	WALKER	10,432	6,448	3,807	177	2,641	R	61.8%	36.5%	62.9%	37.1%
32,663	WALLER	7,883	4,498	3,282	103	1,216	R	57.1%	41.6%	57.8%	42.2%
10,909	WARD	3,073	1,621	1,375	77	246	R	52.7%	44.7%	54.1%	45.9%
30,373	WASHINGTON	9,325	6,639	2,568	118	4,071	R	71.2%	27.5%	72.1%	27.9%
193,117	WEBB	37,331	4,922	31,714	695	26,792	D	13.2%	85.0%	13.4%	86.6%
41,188	WHARTON	9,294	5,658	3,545	91	2,113	R	60.9%	38.1%	61.5%	38.5%
5,284	WHEELER	1,542	1,094	437	11	657	R	70.9%	28.3%	71.5%	28.5%
131,664	WICHITA	26,130	16,171	9,602	357	6,569	R	61.9%	36.7%	62.7%	37.3%
14,676	WILBARGER	2,945	1,841	1,088	16	753	R	62.5%	36.9%	62.9%	37.1%
20,082	WILLACY	3,586	865	2,681	40	1,816	D	24.1%	74.8%	24.4%	75.6%
249,967	WILLIAMSON	75,159	47,305	26,306	1,548	20,999	R	62.9%	35.0%	64.3%	35.7%
32,408	WILSON	8,870	5,333	3,416	121	1,917	R	60.1%	38.5%	61.0%	39.0%
7,173	WINKLER	1,559	987	542	30	445	R	63.3%	34.8%	64.6%	35.4%
48,793	WISE	11,702	7,716	3,831	155	3,885	R	65.9%	32.7%	66.8%	33.2%
36,752	WOOD	11,036	7,563	3,367	106	4,196	R	68.5%	30.5%	69.2%	30.8%
7,322	YOAKUM	1,779	1,215	530	34	685	R	68.3%	29.8%	69.6%	30.4%
17,943	YOUNG	5,278	3,490	1,747	41	1,743	R	66.1%	33.1%	66.6%	33.4%
12,182	ZAPATA	2,261	341	1,896	24	1,555	D	15.1%	83.9%	15.2%	84.8%
11,600	ZAVALA	2,441	380	2,030	31	1,650	D	15.6%	83.2%	15.8%	84.2%
20,851,820	TOTAL	4,514,012	2,496,243	1,955,758	62,011	540,485	R	55.3%	43.3%	56.1%	43.9%

TEXAS

HOUSE OF REPRESENTATIVES

CD	Year	Total Vote	Republican Vote	Republican Candidate	Democratic Vote	Democratic Candidate	Other Vote	Rep.-Dem. Plurality	Percentage Total Vote Rep.	Dem.	Major Vote Rep.	Dem.
1	2002	153,038	66,654	Lawrence, John	86,384	Sandlin, Max*		19,730 D	43.6%	56.4%	43.6%	56.4%
2	2002	140,501	53,656	Brookshire, Van	85,492	Turner, Jim*	1,353	31,836 D	38.2%	60.8%	38.6%	61.4%
3	2002	154,133	113,974	Johnson, Sam*	37,503	Molera, Manny	2,656	76,471 R	73.9%	24.3%	75.2%	24.8%
4	2002	168,285	67,939	Graves, John	97,304	Hall, Ralph M.*	3,042	29,365 D	40.4%	57.8%	41.1%	58.9%
5	2002	139,908	81,439	Hensarling, Jeb	56,330	Chapman, Ron	2,139	25,109 R	58.2%	40.3%	59.1%	40.9%
6	2002	164,037	115,396	Barton, Joe L.*	45,404	Alvarado, Felix	3,237	69,992 R	70.3%	27.7%	71.8%	28.2%
7	2002	108,527	96,795	Culberson, John*			11,732	96,795 R	89.2%		100.0%	
8	2002	150,926	140,575	Brady, Kevin*			10,351	140,575 R	93.1%		100.0%	
9	2002	147,958	59,635	Williams, Paul	86,710	Lampson, Nick*	1,613	27,075 D	40.3%	58.6%	40.7%	59.3%
10	2002	135,624			114,428	Doggett, Lloyd*	21,196	114,428 D		84.4%		100.0%
11	2002	144,857	68,236	Farley, Ramsey	74,678	Edwards, Chet*	1,943	6,442 D	47.1%	51.6%	47.7%	52.3%
12	2002	131,931	121,208	Granger, Kay*			10,723	121,208 R	91.9%		100.0%	
13	2002	150,619	119,401	Thornberry, William M. "Mac"*	31,218	Reese, Zane		88,183 R	79.3%	20.7%	79.3%	20.7%
14	2002	151,129	102,905	Paul, Ron*	48,224	Windham, Corby		54,681 R	68.1%	31.9%	68.1%	31.9%
15	2002	66,311			66,311	Hinojosa, Ruben*		66,311 D		100.0%		100.0%
16	2002	72,383			72,383	Reyes, Silvestre*		72,383 D		100.0%		100.0%
17	2002	163,804	77,622	Beckham, Rob	84,136	Stenholm, Charles W.*	2,046	6,514 D	47.4%	51.4%	48.0%	52.0%
18	2002	128,926	27,980	Abbott, Phillip J.	99,161	Jackson-Lee, Sheila*	1,785	71,181 D	21.7%	76.9%	22.0%	78.0%
19	2002	127,776	117,092	Combest, Larry*			10,684	117,092 R	91.6%		100.0%	
20	2002	68,685			68,685	Gonzalez, Charlie*		68,685 D		100.0%		100.0%
21	2002	222,093	161,836	Smith, Lamar*	56,206	Courage, John	4,051	105,630 R	72.9%	25.3%	74.2%	25.8%
22	2002	159,084	100,499	DeLay, Tom*	55,716	Riley, Tim	2,869	44,783 R	63.2%	35.0%	64.3%	35.7%
23	2002	150,552	77,573	Bonilla, Henry*	71,067	Cuellar, Henry	1,912	6,506 R	51.5%	47.2%	52.2%	47.8%
24	2002	112,894	38,332	Ortega, Mike Rivera	73,002	Frost, Martin*	1,560	34,670 D	34.0%	64.7%	34.4%	65.6%
25	2002	116,126	50,041	Reiser, Tom	63,590	Bell, Chris	2,495	13,549 D	43.1%	54.8%	44.0%	56.0%
26	2002	164,678	123,195	Burgess, Michael C.	37,485	LeBon, Paul William	3,998	85,710 R	74.8%	22.8%	76.7%	23.3%
27	2002	112,209	41,004	Ahumada, Pat	68,559	Ortiz, Solomon P.*	2,646	27,555 D	36.5%	61.1%	37.4%	62.6%
28	2002	100,420	26,973	Perales, Gabriel Jr.	71,393	Rodriguez, Ciro D.*	2,054	44,420 D	26.9%	71.1%	27.4%	72.6%
29	2002	58,593			55,760	Green, Gene*	2,833	55,760 D		95.2%		100.0%
30	2002	119,817	28,981	Bush, Ron	88,980	Johnson, Eddie Bernice*	1,856	59,999 D	24.2%	74.3%	24.6%	75.4%
31	2002	161,484	111,556	Carter, John	44,183	Bagley, David	5,745	67,373 R	69.1%	27.4%	71.6%	28.4%
32	2002	147,902	100,226	Sessions, Pete*	44,886	Dixon, Pauline K.	2,790	55,340 R	67.8%	30.3%	69.1%	30.9%
Total	2002	4,295,210	2,290,723		1,885,178		119,309	405,545 R	53.3%	43.9%	54.9%	45.1%

An asterisk (*) denotes incumbent.

TEXAS

GENERAL AND PRIMARY ELECTIONS

2002 GENERAL ELECTIONS

Governor Other vote was 66,720 Libertarian (Jeff Daiell); 32,187 Green (Rahul Mahajan); 1,715 write-in (Elaine Eure Henderson); 976 write-in (Earl W. "Bill" O'Neil).

Senator Other vote was 35,538 Libertarian (Scott Lanier Jameson); 25,051 Green (Roy H. Williams); 1,422 write-in (James W. "Jim" Wright).

House Other vote was:

CD 1
CD 2 1,353 Libertarian (Peter Beach).
CD 3 2,656 Libertarian (John Davis).
CD 4 3,042 Libertarian (Barbara Robinson).
CD 5 1,283 Libertarian (Dan Michalski); 856 Green (Thomas J. Kemper).
CD 6 1,992 Libertarian (Frank Brady); 1,245 Green (B.J. Armstrong).
CD 7 11,674 Libertarian (Drew Parks); 58 write-in (John R. Skone-Palmer).
CD 8 10,351 Libertarian (Gil Guillory).
CD 9 1,613 Libertarian (Dean L. Tucker).
CD 10 21,196 Libertarian (Michele Messina).
CD 11 1,943 Libertarian (Andrew Paul Farris).
CD 12 10,723 Libertarian (Edward A. Hanson).
CD 13
CD 14
CD 15
CD 16
CD 17 2,046 Libertarian (Fred Jones).
CD 18 1,785 Libertarian (Brent Sullivan).
CD 19 10,684 Libertarian (Larry Johnson).
CD 20
CD 21 4,051 Libertarian (DG Roberts).
CD 22 1,612 Libertarian (Gerald W. "Jerry" LaFleur); 1,257 Green (Joel West).
CD 23 1,106 Libertarian (Jeffrey C. Blunt); 806 Green (Ed Scharf).
CD 24 1,560 Libertarian (Ken Ashby).
CD 25 1,399 Green (George Reiter); 1,096 Libertarian (Guy McLendon).
CD 26 2,367 Libertarian (David Wallace Croft); 1,631 Green (Gary R. Page).
CD 27 2,646 Libertarian (Christopher J. Claytor).
CD 28 2,054 Libertarian (William A. "Bill" Stallknecht).
CD 29 2,833 Libertarian (Paul Hansen).
CD 30 1,856 Libertarian (Lance Flores).
CD 31 2,037 Libertarian (Clark Simmons); 1,992 Green (John S. Petersen); 1,716 Independent (R.C. Crawford).
CD 32 1,582 Libertarian (Steve Martin); 1,208 Green (Carla Hubbell).

2002 PRIMARY ELECTIONS

Primary March 12, 2002   **Registration**   12,218,164 No Party Registration
Primary Runoff April 9, 2002   (as of March 12, 2002)

Primary Type Open—Any registered voter could participate in the primary of either party, although if they voted in the primary of one party they could not vote in the runoff of the other party.

Note: An asterisk (*) denotes incumbent.

TEXAS

GENERAL AND PRIMARY ELECTIONS

	REPUBLICAN PRIMARIES			DEMOCRATIC PRIMARIES		
Governor	Rick Perry*	620,463	100.0%	Tony Sanchez	609,383	60.7%
				Dan Morales	330,873	33.0%
				Bill Lyon	43,011	4.3%
				John Worldpeace	20,121	2.0%
				TOTAL	1,003,388	
Senator	John Cornyn	478,825	77.3%	Victor Morales	317,048	33.2%
	Bruce Rusty Lang	46,907	7.6%	Ron Kirk	316,052	33.1%
	Douglas G. Deffenbaugh	43,611	7.0%	Ken Bentsen	255,501	26.8%
	Dudley F. Mooney	32,202	5.2%	Gene Kelly	44,038	4.6%
	Lawrence Cranberg	17,757	2.9%	Ed Cunningham	22,016	2.3%
	TOTAL	619,302		TOTAL	954,655	
				PRIMARY RUNOFF		
				Ron Kirk	370,878	59.8%
				Victor Morales	249,423	40.2%
				TOTAL	620,301	
Congressional District 1	John Lawrence	13,875	100.0%	Max Sandlin*	51,009	100.0%
Congressional District 2	Van Brookshire	10,962	100.0%	Jim Turner*	50,387	100.0%
Congressional District 3	Sam Johnson*	17,153	84.3%	Manny Molera	5,363	100.0%
	Thomas "Tom" Caiazzo	3,184	15.7%			
	TOTAL	20,337				
Congressional District 4	John Graves	21,781	69.3%	Ralph M. Hall*	17,404	100.0%
	Edward G. Conger	9,627	30.7%			
	TOTAL	31,408				
Congressional District 5	Jeb Hensarling	10,475	53.6%	Ron Chapman	18,298	70.8%
	Dan Hagood	3,628	18.6%	Bill Bernstein	5,902	22.8%
	Mike Armour	3,247	16.6%	Wayne Raasch	1,635	6.3%
	Phil Sudan	1,632	8.3%			
	Fred A. Wood	574	2.9%			
	TOTAL	19,556		TOTAL	25,835	
Congressional District 6	Joe L. Barton*	23,758	100.0%	Felix Alvarado	13,604	100.0%
Congressional District 7	John Culberson*	17,843	100.0%	No Democratic candidate		
Congressional District 8	Kevin Brady*	31,116	100.0%	No Democratic candidate		
Congressional District 9	Paul Williams	10,782	100.0%	Nick Lampson*	32,700	100.0%
Congressional District 10	No Republican candidate			Lloyd Doggett*	33,083	90.3%
				Jennifer Gale	3,554	9.7%
				TOTAL	36,637	
Congressional District 11	Ramsey Farley	17,985	66.1%	Chet Edwards*	17,191	100.0%
	Rob Curnock	5,792	21.3%			
	James "Dub" Maines	3,452	12.7%			
	TOTAL	27,229				
Congressional District 12	Kay Granger*	20,769	87.1%	No Democratic candidate		
	Philip Hillery	3,067	12.9%			
	TOTAL	23,836				
Congressional District 13	William M. "Mac" Thornberry*	35,367	100.0%	Zane Reese	15,564	100.0%
Congressional District 14	Ron Paul*	22,715	100.0%	Corby Windham	21,335	56.8%
				Sergio Martinez	16,207	43.2%
				TOTAL	37,542	
Congressional District 15	No Republican candidate			Ruben Hinojosa*	46,688	86.7%
				Mel Hawkins	7,138	13.3%
				TOTAL	53,826	

TEXAS

GENERAL AND PRIMARY ELECTIONS

	REPUBLICAN PRIMARIES			DEMOCRATIC PRIMARIES		
Congressional District 16	No Republican candidate			Silvestre Reyes*	33,904	100.0%
Congressional District 17	Rob Beckham	21,662	100.0%	Charles W. Stenholm*	30,426	100.0%
Congressional District 18	Phillip J. Abbott	4,252	100.0%	Sheila Jackson-Lee*	31,563	94.4%
				Lenwood Johnson	1,871	5.6%
				TOTAL	33,434	
Congressional District 19	Larry Combest*	30,440	100.0%	No Democratic candidate		
Congressional District 20	No Republican candidate			Charlie Gonzalez*	25,645	100.0%
Congressional District 21	Lamar Smith*	49,752	100.0%	John Courage	14,654	100.0%
Congressional District 22	Tom DeLay*	22,379	79.9%	Tim Riley	4,606	51.6%
	Mike Fjetland	5,645	20.1%	Frank "Chip" Briscoe	4,316	48.4%
	TOTAL	28,024		TOTAL	8,922	
Congressional District 23	Henry Bonilla*	12,881	100.0%	Henry Cuellar	51,495	100.0%
Congressional District 24	Mike Rivera Ortega	5,770	100.0%	Martin Frost*	17,963	100.0%
Congressional District 25	Tom Reiser	10,995	100.0%	Chris Bell	7,443	36.1%
				Carroll G. Robinson	5,597	27.1%
				Paul Colbert	4,307	20.9%
				Stephen King	3,274	15.9%
				TOTAL	20,621	
				PRIMARY RUNOFF		
				Chris Bell	9,572	54.3%
				Carroll G. Robinson	8,056	45.7%
				TOTAL	17,628	
Congressional District 26	Scott Armey	11,493	45.4%	Paul William LeBon	5,182	100.0%
	Michael C. Burgess	5,703	22.5%			
	Keith A. Self	5,610	22.2%			
	Roger Sessions	1,630	6.4%			
	Dave Kovatch	675	2.7%			
	David Gulling	204	0.8%			
	TOTAL	25,315				
	PRIMARY RUNOFF					
	Michael C. Burgess	10,522	54.6%			
	Scott Armey	8,737	45.4%			
	TOTAL	19,259				
Congressional District 27	Pat Ahumada	9,614	100.0%	Solomon P. Ortiz*	41,574	100.0%
Congressional District 28	Gabriel Perales Jr.	4,422	100.0%	Ciro D. Rodriguez*	41,152	100.0%
Congressional District 29	No Republican candidate			Gene Green*	11,891	100.0%
Congressional District 30	Ron Bush	3,958	75.3%	Eddie Bernice Johnson*	27,670	100.0%
	Zach Rader	1,296	24.7%			
	TOTAL	5,254				

TEXAS

GENERAL AND PRIMARY ELECTIONS

	REPUBLICAN PRIMARIES			DEMOCRATIC PRIMARIES		
Congressional	Peter Wareing	12,987	36.9%	David Bagley	11,741	100.0%
District 31	John Carter	9,144	26.0%			
	Brad Barton	5,751	16.4%			
	C. Patrick Meece	3,653	10.4%			
	Flynn Adcock	1,117	3.2%			
	Eric Whitfield	1,014	2.9%			
	Roy Streckfuss	898	2.6%			
	Terry S. Ward	600	1.7%			
	TOTAL	35,164				
	PRIMARY RUNOFF					
	John Carter	13,150	56.8%			
	Peter Wareing	9,986	43.2%			
	TOTAL	23,136				
Congressional	Pete Sessions*	19,973	93.5%	Pauline K. Dixon	9,384	72.4%
District 32	Danny Davis	1,391	6.5%	Walter W. Hofheinz	3,572	27.6%
	TOTAL	21,364		TOTAL	12,956	

TEXAS DEMOCRATIC PRIMARY

GOVERNOR 2002

2000 Census Population	County	Total Vote	Sanchez	D. Morales	Other	Winner	Percentage of Total Vote		
							Sanchez	D. Morales	Other
55,109	ANDERSON	4,576	2,019	2,058	499	D. Morales	44.1%	45.0%	10.9%
13,004	ANDREWS	1,378	657	478	243	Sanchez	47.7%	34.7%	17.6%
80,130	ANGELINA	8,226	4,255	2,922	1,049	Sanchez	51.7%	35.5%	12.8%
22,497	ARANSAS	1,047	623	298	126	Sanchez	59.5%	28.5%	12.0%
8,854	ARCHER	793	468	250	75	Sanchez	59.0%	31.5%	9.5%
2,148	ARMSTRONG	90	46	37	7	Sanchez	51.1%	41.1%	7.8%
38,628	ATASCOSA	4,493	2,447	1,706	340	Sanchez	54.5%	38.0%	7.6%
23,590	AUSTIN	595	292	267	36	Sanchez	49.1%	44.9%	6.1%
6,594	BAILEY	230	130	73	27	Sanchez	56.5%	31.7%	11.7%
17,645	BANDERA	313	137	152	24	D. Morales	43.8%	48.6%	7.7%
57,733	BASTROP	4,550	2,031	2,074	445	D. Morales	44.6%	45.6%	9.8%
4,093	BAYLOR	950	508	327	115	Sanchez	53.5%	34.4%	12.1%
32,359	BEE	2,511	1,683	628	200	Sanchez	67.0%	25.0%	8.0%
237,974	BELL	3,810	2,246	1,266	298	Sanchez	59.0%	33.2%	7.8%
1,392,931	BEXAR	62,600	36,398	24,779	1,423	Sanchez	58.1%	39.6%	2.3%
8,418	BLANCO	234	109	109	16		46.6%	46.6%	6.8%
729	BORDEN	134	43	56	35	D. Morales	32.1%	41.8%	26.1%
17,204	BOSQUE	1,731	705	840	186	D. Morales	40.7%	48.5%	10.7%
89,306	BOWIE	10,036	5,137	3,933	966	Sanchez	51.2%	39.2%	9.6%
241,767	BRAZORIA	4,555	2,652	1,616	287	Sanchez	58.2%	35.5%	6.3%
152,415	BRAZOS	3,423	1,936	1,241	246	Sanchez	56.6%	36.3%	7.2%
8,866	BREWSTER	969	439	408	122	Sanchez	45.3%	42.1%	12.6%
1,790	BRISCOE	384	195	142	47	Sanchez	50.8%	37.0%	12.2%
7,976	BROOKS	3,113	2,184	836	93	Sanchez	70.2%	26.9%	3.0%
37,674	BROWN	980	439	441	100	D. Morales	44.8%	45.0%	10.2%
16,470	BURLESON	1,232	601	506	125	Sanchez	48.8%	41.1%	10.1%
34,147	BURNET	1,522	647	736	139	D. Morales	42.5%	48.4%	9.1%
32,194	CALDWELL	2,016	1,068	763	185	Sanchez	53.0%	37.8%	9.2%
20,647	CALHOUN	2,398	1,090	971	337	Sanchez	45.5%	40.5%	14.1%
12,905	CALLAHAN	939	368	456	115	D. Morales	39.2%	48.6%	12.2%

TEXAS DEMOCRATIC PRIMARY
GOVERNOR 2002

2000 Census Population	County	Total Vote	Sanchez	D. Morales	Other	Winner	Percentage of Total Vote		
							Sanchez	D. Morales	Other
335,227	CAMERON	23,574	15,608	7,085	881	Sanchez	66.2%	30.1%	3.7%
11,549	CAMP	1,539	836	543	160	Sanchez	54.3%	35.3%	10.4%
6,516	CARSON	301	149	123	29	Sanchez	49.5%	40.9%	9.6%
30,438	CASS	5,197	2,649	1,951	597	Sanchez	51.0%	37.5%	11.5%
8,285	CASTRO	388	203	152	33	Sanchez	52.3%	39.2%	8.5%
26,031	CHAMBERS	2,450	1,219	980	251	Sanchez	49.8%	40.0%	10.2%
46,659	CHEROKEE	3,671	1,938	1,237	496	Sanchez	52.8%	33.7%	13.5%
7,688	CHILDRESS	548	280	204	64	Sanchez	51.1%	37.2%	11.7%
11,006	CLAY	825	460	289	76	Sanchez	55.8%	35.0%	9.2%
3,730	COCHRAN	335	201	107	27	Sanchez	60.0%	31.9%	8.1%
3,864	COKE	792	320	315	157	Sanchez	40.4%	39.8%	19.8%
9,235	COLEMAN	1,172	528	487	157	Sanchez	45.1%	41.6%	13.4%
491,675	COLLIN	6,118	3,059	2,805	254	Sanchez	50.0%	45.8%	4.2%
3,206	COLLINGSWORTH	685	328	284	73	Sanchez	47.9%	41.5%	10.7%
20,390	COLORADO	866	424	385	57	Sanchez	49.0%	44.5%	6.6%
78,021	COMAL	1,742	877	769	96	Sanchez	50.3%	44.1%	5.5%
14,026	COMANCHE	1,820	745	773	302	D. Morales	40.9%	42.5%	16.6%
3,966	CONCHO	268	113	117	38	D. Morales	42.2%	43.7%	14.2%
36,363	COOKE	730	338	326	66	Sanchez	46.3%	44.7%	9.0%
74,978	CORYELL	1,075	577	421	77	Sanchez	53.7%	39.2%	7.2%
1,904	COTTLE	541	232	183	126	Sanchez	42.9%	33.8%	23.3%
3,996	CRANE	577	293	202	82	Sanchez	50.8%	35.0%	14.2%
4,099	CROCKETT	454	279	138	37	Sanchez	61.5%	30.4%	8.1%
7,072	CROSBY	1,761	650	414	697	Sanchez	36.9%	23.5%	39.6%
2,975	CULBERSON	312	36	262	14	D. Morales	11.5%	84.0%	4.5%
6,222	DALLAM	147	83	51	13	Sanchez	56.5%	34.7%	8.8%
2,218,899	DALLAS	75,670	47,458	24,834	3,378	Sanchez	62.7%	32.8%	4.5%
14,985	DAWSON	1,553	794	537	222	Sanchez	51.1%	34.6%	14.3%
18,561	DEAF SMITH	470	331	110	29	Sanchez	70.4%	23.4%	6.2%
5,327	DELTA	892	332	428	132	D. Morales	37.2%	48.0%	14.8%
432,976	DENTON	5,152	2,725	2,234	193	Sanchez	52.9%	43.4%	3.7%
20,013	DE WITT	656	273	316	67	D. Morales	41.6%	48.2%	10.2%
2,762	DICKENS	692	326	259	107	Sanchez	47.1%	37.4%	15.5%
10,248	DIMMIT	3,191	2,128	939	124	Sanchez	66.7%	29.4%	3.9%
3,828	DONLEY	238	131	80	27	Sanchez	55.0%	33.6%	11.3%
13,120	DUVAL	5,812	3,969	1,752	91	Sanchez	68.3%	30.1%	1.6%
18,297	EASTLAND	1,249	514	567	168	D. Morales	41.2%	45.4%	13.5%
121,123	ECTOR	3,393	2,605	600	188	Sanchez	76.8%	17.7%	5.5%
2,162	EDWARDS	615	289	222	104	Sanchez	47.0%	36.1%	16.9%
111,360	ELLIS	2,540	1,267	1,047	226	Sanchez	49.9%	41.2%	8.9%
679,622	EL PASO	47,990	34,069	12,008	1,913	Sanchez	71.0%	25.0%	4.0%
33,001	ERATH	1,496	604	735	157	D. Morales	40.4%	49.1%	10.5%
18,576	FALLS	1,757	874	655	228	Sanchez	49.7%	37.3%	13.0%
31,242	FANNIN	3,117	1,069	1,577	471	D. Morales	34.3%	50.6%	15.1%
21,804	FAYETTE	2,571	1,008	1,240	323	D. Morales	39.2%	48.2%	12.6%
4,344	FISHER	1,089	462	506	121	D. Morales	42.4%	46.5%	11.1%
7,771	FLOYD	889	486	263	140	Sanchez	54.7%	29.6%	15.7%
1,622	FOARD	232	97	100	35	D. Morales	41.8%	43.1%	15.1%
354,452	FORT BEND	9,071	7,227	1,576	268	Sanchez	79.7%	17.4%	3.0%
9,458	FRANKLIN	893	350	478	65	D. Morales	39.2%	53.5%	7.3%
17,867	FREESTONE	2,450	977	1,171	302	D. Morales	39.9%	47.8%	12.3%
16,252	FRIO	3,391	2,275	921	195	Sanchez	67.1%	27.2%	5.8%
14,467	GAINES	1,662	837	551	274	Sanchez	50.4%	33.2%	16.5%
250,158	GALVESTON	13,709	7,890	4,768	1,051	Sanchez	57.6%	34.8%	7.7%
4,872	GARZA	433	226	150	57	Sanchez	52.2%	34.6%	13.2%
20,814	GILLESPIE	314	120	172	22	D. Morales	38.2%	54.8%	7.0%
1,406	GLASSCOCK	18	11	5	2	Sanchez	61.1%	27.8%	11.1%
6,928	GOLIAD	963	588	310	65	Sanchez	61.1%	32.2%	6.7%
18,628	GONZALES	1,809	731	816	262	D. Morales	40.4%	45.1%	14.5%
22,744	GRAY	386	226	126	34	Sanchez	58.5%	32.6%	8.8%

TEXAS DEMOCRATIC PRIMARY

GOVERNOR 2002

2000 Census Population	County	Total Vote	Sanchez	D. Morales	Other	Winner	Percentage of Total Vote		
							Sanchez	D. Morales	Other
110,595	GRAYSON	2,468	1,169	1,106	193	Sanchez	47.4%	44.8%	7.8%
111,379	GREGG	3,834	2,558	1,109	167	Sanchez	66.7%	28.9%	4.4%
23,552	GRIMES	1,990	1,027	688	275	Sanchez	51.6%	34.6%	13.8%
89,023	GUADALUPE	1,849	1,017	740	92	Sanchez	55.0%	40.0%	5.0%
36,602	HALE	984	656	243	85	Sanchez	66.7%	24.7%	8.6%
3,782	HALL	877	409	355	113	Sanchez	46.6%	40.5%	12.9%
8,229	HAMILTON	785	356	350	79	Sanchez	45.4%	44.6%	10.1%
5,369	HANSFORD								
4,724	HARDEMAN	751	313	332	106	D. Morales	41.7%	44.2%	14.1%
48,073	HARDIN	3,925	2,098	1,452	375	Sanchez	53.5%	37.0%	9.6%
3,400,578	HARRIS	87,215	63,955	21,121	2,139	Sanchez	73.3%	24.2%	2.5%
62,110	HARRISON	7,648	4,282	2,766	600	Sanchez	56.0%	36.2%	7.8%
5,537	HARTLEY	175	110	44	21	Sanchez	62.9%	25.1%	12.0%
6,093	HASKELL	1,168	514	536	118	D. Morales	44.0%	45.9%	10.1%
97,589	HAYS	4,368	2,391	1,767	210	Sanchez	54.7%	40.5%	4.8%
3,351	HEMPHILL	83	33	39	11	D. Morales	39.8%	47.0%	13.3%
73,277	HENDERSON	4,681	2,149	2,022	510	Sanchez	45.9%	43.2%	10.9%
569,463	HIDALGO	49,317	37,800	10,239	1,278	Sanchez	76.6%	20.8%	2.6%
32,321	HILL	2,968	1,204	1,343	421	D. Morales	40.6%	45.2%	14.2%
22,716	HOCKLEY	377	228	114	35	Sanchez	60.5%	30.2%	9.3%
41,100	HOOD	1,089	476	492	121	D. Morales	43.7%	45.2%	11.1%
31,960	HOPKINS	2,989	1,288	1,423	278	D. Morales	43.1%	47.6%	9.3%
23,185	HOUSTON	1,813	879	762	172	Sanchez	48.5%	42.0%	9.5%
33,627	HOWARD	767	489	214	64	Sanchez	63.8%	27.9%	8.3%
3,344	HUDSPETH	612	380	133	99	Sanchez	62.1%	21.7%	16.2%
76,596	HUNT	2,591	1,172	1,157	262	Sanchez	45.2%	44.7%	10.1%
23,857	HUTCHINSON	486	287	161	38	Sanchez	59.1%	33.1%	7.8%
1,771	IRION	383	160	151	72	Sanchez	41.8%	39.4%	18.8%
8,763	JACK	733	314	346	73	D. Morales	42.8%	47.2%	10.0%
14,391	JACKSON	1,729	653	831	245	D. Morales	37.8%	48.1%	14.2%
35,604	JASPER	3,764	1,939	1,517	308	Sanchez	51.5%	40.3%	8.2%
2,207	JEFF DAVIS	540	226	220	94	Sanchez	41.9%	40.7%	17.4%
252,051	JEFFERSON	22,659	13,719	7,814	1,126	Sanchez	60.5%	34.5%	5.0%
5,281	JIM HOGG	2,473	1,753	671	49	Sanchez	70.9%	27.1%	2.0%
39,326	JIM WELLS	7,701	5,552	1,756	393	Sanchez	72.1%	22.8%	5.1%
126,811	JOHNSON	2,172	1,105	915	152	Sanchez	50.9%	42.1%	7.0%
20,785	JONES	2,001	829	893	279	D. Morales	41.4%	44.6%	13.9%
15,446	KARNES	2,655	1,255	1,033	367	Sanchez	47.3%	38.9%	13.8%
71,313	KAUFMAN	2,684	1,232	1,169	283	Sanchez	45.9%	43.6%	10.5%
23,743	KENDALL	396	151	230	15	D. Morales	38.1%	58.1%	3.8%
414	KENEDY	169	121	42	6	Sanchez	71.6%	24.9%	3.6%
859	KENT	425	164	162	99	Sanchez	38.6%	38.1%	23.3%
43,653	KERR	891	344	496	51	D. Morales	38.6%	55.7%	5.7%
4,468	KIMBLE	467	200	195	72	Sanchez	42.8%	41.8%	15.4%
356	KING	95	25	51	19	D. Morales	26.3%	53.7%	20.0%
3,379	KINNEY	948	475	342	131	Sanchez	50.1%	36.1%	13.8%
31,549	KLEBERG	3,644	2,405	1,017	222	Sanchez	66.0%	27.9%	6.1%
4,253	KNOX	337	142	160	35	D. Morales	42.1%	47.5%	10.4%
48,499	LAMAR	3,713	1,594	1,788	331	D. Morales	42.9%	48.2%	8.9%
14,709	LAMB	1,822	913	640	269	Sanchez	50.1%	35.1%	14.8%
17,762	LAMPASAS	478	258	190	30	Sanchez	54.0%	39.7%	6.3%
5,866	LA SALLE	2,028	1,393	539	96	Sanchez	68.7%	26.6%	4.7%
19,210	LAVACA	3,471	1,163	1,822	486	D. Morales	33.5%	52.5%	14.0%
15,657	LEE	1,791	684	918	189	D. Morales	38.2%	51.3%	10.6%
15,335	LEON	724	337	303	84	Sanchez	46.5%	41.9%	11.6%
70,154	LIBERTY	6,278	3,386	2,121	771	Sanchez	53.9%	33.8%	12.3%
22,051	LIMESTONE	1,311	615	526	170	Sanchez	46.9%	40.1%	13.0%
3,057	LIPSCOMB	257	112	105	40	Sanchez	43.6%	40.9%	15.6%
12,309	LIVE OAK	709	377	219	113	Sanchez	53.2%	30.9%	15.9%
17,044	LLANO	832	290	445	97	D. Morales	34.9%	53.5%	11.7%

TEXAS DEMOCRATIC PRIMARY

GOVERNOR 2002

2000 Census Population	County	Total Vote	Sanchez	D. Morales	Other	Winner	Percentage of Total Vote		
							Sanchez	D. Morales	Other
67	LOVING	39	17	16	6	Sanchez	43.6%	41.0%	15.4%
242,628	LUBBOCK	4,590	3,120	1,261	209	Sanchez	68.0%	27.5%	4.6%
6,550	LYNN	1,074	579	340	155	Sanchez	53.9%	31.7%	14.4%
8,205	MCCULLOCH	954	437	379	138	Sanchez	45.8%	39.7%	14.5%
213,517	MCLENNAN	6,858	3,667	2,681	510	Sanchez	53.5%	39.1%	7.4%
851	MCMULLEN	178	78	69	31	Sanchez	43.8%	38.8%	17.4%
12,940	MADISON	642	308	265	69	Sanchez	48.0%	41.3%	10.7%
10,941	MARION	1,289	769	407	113	Sanchez	59.7%	31.6%	8.8%
4,746	MARTIN	682	365	240	77	Sanchez	53.5%	35.2%	11.3%
3,738	MASON	87	50	36	1	Sanchez	57.5%	41.4%	1.1%
37,957	MATAGORDA	1,722	905	624	193	Sanchez	52.6%	36.2%	11.2%
47,297	MAVERICK	7,514	5,151	2,131	232	Sanchez	68.6%	28.4%	3.1%
39,304	MEDINA	2,990	1,398	1,330	262	Sanchez	46.8%	44.5%	8.8%
2,360	MENARD	196	117	55	24	Sanchez	59.7%	28.1%	12.2%
116,009	MIDLAND	1,399	923	409	67	Sanchez	66.0%	29.2%	4.8%
24,238	MILAM	1,811	847	767	197	Sanchez	46.8%	42.4%	10.9%
5,151	MILLS	921	353	428	140	D. Morales	38.3%	46.5%	15.2%
9,698	MITCHELL	444	205	168	71	Sanchez	46.2%	37.8%	16.0%
19,117	MONTAGUE	1,607	766	668	173	Sanchez	47.7%	41.6%	10.8%
293,768	MONTGOMERY	2,937	1,716	1,042	179	Sanchez	58.4%	35.5%	6.1%
20,121	MOORE	353	208	112	33	Sanchez	58.9%	31.7%	9.3%
13,048	MORRIS	2,265	1,021	1,001	243	Sanchez	45.1%	44.2%	10.7%
1,426	MOTLEY	191	72	81	38	D. Morales	37.7%	42.4%	19.9%
59,203	NACOGDOCHES	2,223	1,379	668	176	Sanchez	62.0%	30.0%	7.9%
45,124	NAVARRO	5,188	2,005	2,595	588	D. Morales	38.6%	50.0%	11.3%
15,072	NEWTON	2,824	1,449	1,005	370	Sanchez	51.3%	35.6%	13.1%
15,802	NOLAN	1,018	412	482	124	D. Morales	40.5%	47.3%	12.2%
313,645	NUECES	29,009	20,557	6,710	1,742	Sanchez	70.9%	23.1%	6.0%
9,006	OCHILTREE								
2,185	OLDHAM	294	148	108	38	Sanchez	50.3%	36.7%	12.9%
84,966	ORANGE	9,751	5,089	3,752	910	Sanchez	52.2%	38.5%	9.3%
27,026	PALO PINTO	3,345	1,353	1,545	447	D. Morales	40.4%	46.2%	13.4%
22,756	PANOLA	3,401	1,620	1,427	354	Sanchez	47.6%	42.0%	10.4%
88,495	PARKER	2,232	1,021	1,033	178	D. Morales	45.7%	46.3%	8.0%
10,016	PARMER	323	187	92	44	Sanchez	57.9%	28.5%	13.6%
16,809	PECOS	2,403	1,516	668	219	Sanchez	63.1%	27.8%	9.1%
41,133	POLK	3,326	2,038	1,006	282	Sanchez	61.3%	30.2%	8.5%
113,546	POTTER	2,221	1,461	623	137	Sanchez	65.8%	28.1%	6.2%
7,304	PRESIDIO	1,116	719	335	62	Sanchez	64.4%	30.0%	5.6%
9,139	RAINS	1,458	580	645	233	D. Morales	39.8%	44.2%	16.0%
104,312	RANDALL	1,419	942	398	79	Sanchez	66.4%	28.0%	5.6%
3,326	REAGAN	23	16	7	0	Sanchez	69.6%	30.4%	0.0%
3,047	REAL	44	22	16	6	Sanchez	50.0%	36.4%	13.6%
14,314	RED RIVER	2,445	983	1,154	308	D. Morales	40.2%	47.2%	12.6%
13,137	REEVES	3,027	1,981	839	207	Sanchez	65.4%	27.7%	6.8%
7,828	REFUGIO	1,561	816	480	265	Sanchez	52.3%	30.7%	17.0%
887	ROBERTS								
16,000	ROBERTSON	3,196	1,808	1,060	328	Sanchez	56.6%	33.2%	10.3%
43,080	ROCKWALL	708	332	340	36	D. Morales	46.9%	48.0%	5.1%
11,495	RUNNELS	1,344	529	585	230	D. Morales	39.4%	43.5%	17.1%
47,372	RUSK	2,152	1,186	775	191	Sanchez	55.1%	36.0%	8.9%
10,469	SABINE	810	406	296	108	Sanchez	50.1%	36.5%	13.3%
8,946	SAN AUGUSTINE	2,064	1,060	685	319	Sanchez	51.4%	33.2%	15.5%
22,246	SAN JACINTO	3,352	1,634	1,302	416	Sanchez	48.7%	38.8%	12.4%
67,138	SAN PATRICIO	5,597	3,882	1,157	558	Sanchez	69.4%	20.7%	10.0%
6,186	SAN SABA	278	148	106	24	Sanchez	53.2%	38.1%	8.6%
2,935	SCHLEICHER	349	166	122	61	Sanchez	47.6%	35.0%	17.5%
16,361	SCURRY	599	273	219	107	Sanchez	45.6%	36.6%	17.9%
3,302	SHACKELFORD	546	208	239	99	D. Morales	38.1%	43.8%	18.1%
25,224	SHELBY	2,117	1,129	739	249	Sanchez	53.3%	34.9%	11.8%

TEXAS DEMOCRATIC PRIMARY
GOVERNOR 2002

2000 Census Population	County	Total Vote	Sanchez	D. Morales	Other	Winner	Sanchez	D. Morales	Other
3,186	SHERMAN	116	58	46	12	Sanchez	50.0%	39.7%	10.3%
174,706	SMITH	4,224	2,833	1,230	161	Sanchez	67.1%	29.1%	3.8%
6,809	SOMERVELL	886	373	425	88	D. Morales	42.1%	48.0%	9.9%
53,597	STARR	8,777	7,396	1,246	135	Sanchez	84.3%	14.2%	1.5%
9,674	STEPHENS	1,858	719	824	315	D. Morales	38.7%	44.3%	17.0%
1,393	STERLING	41	18	19	4	D. Morales	43.9%	46.3%	9.8%
1,693	STONEWALL	548	204	256	88	D. Morales	37.2%	46.7%	16.1%
4,077	SUTTON	143	91	42	10	Sanchez	63.6%	29.4%	7.0%
8,378	SWISHER	1,211	510	536	165	D. Morales	42.1%	44.3%	13.6%
1,446,219	TARRANT	36,779	22,804	12,867	1,108	Sanchez	62.0%	35.0%	3.0%
126,555	TAYLOR	2,619	1,279	1,178	162	Sanchez	48.8%	45.0%	6.2%
1,081	TERRELL	445	152	214	79	D. Morales	34.2%	48.1%	17.8%
12,761	TERRY	1,136	578	404	154	Sanchez	50.9%	35.6%	13.6%
1,850	THROCKMORTON	389	154	176	59	D. Morales	39.6%	45.2%	15.2%
28,118	TITUS	3,255	1,270	1,618	367	D. Morales	39.0%	49.7%	11.3%
104,010	TOM GREEN	2,627	1,649	799	179	Sanchez	62.8%	30.4%	6.8%
812,280	TRAVIS	44,152	24,566	17,658	1,928	Sanchez	55.6%	40.0%	4.4%
13,779	TRINITY	2,962	1,360	1,239	363	Sanchez	45.9%	41.8%	12.3%
20,871	TYLER	2,563	1,288	1,053	222	Sanchez	50.3%	41.1%	8.7%
35,291	UPSHUR	6,049	2,739	2,542	768	Sanchez	45.3%	42.0%	12.7%
3,404	UPTON	394	158	151	85	Sanchez	40.1%	38.3%	21.6%
25,926	UVALDE	4,830	2,641	1,610	579	Sanchez	54.7%	33.3%	12.0%
44,856	VAL VERDE	2,417	1,766	543	108	Sanchez	73.1%	22.5%	4.5%
48,140	VAN ZANDT	3,362	1,476	1,487	399	D. Morales	43.9%	44.2%	11.9%
84,088	VICTORIA	6,307	3,260	2,248	799	Sanchez	51.7%	35.6%	12.7%
61,758	WALKER	1,404	763	536	105	Sanchez	54.3%	38.2%	7.5%
32,663	WALLER	1,654	1,044	504	106	Sanchez	63.1%	30.5%	6.4%
10,909	WARD	2,627	1,392	815	420	Sanchez	53.0%	31.0%	16.0%
30,373	WASHINGTON	693	323	328	42	D. Morales	46.6%	47.3%	6.1%
193,117	WEBB	31,378	26,383	4,647	348	Sanchez	84.1%	14.8%	1.1%
41,188	WHARTON	3,098	1,446	1,255	397	Sanchez	46.7%	40.5%	12.8%
5,284	WHEELER	743	329	299	115	Sanchez	44.3%	40.2%	15.5%
131,664	WICHITA	2,714	1,730	821	163	Sanchez	63.7%	30.3%	6.0%
14,676	WILBARGER	1,491	688	635	168	Sanchez	46.1%	42.6%	11.3%
20,082	WILLACY	3,502	2,276	1,024	202	Sanchez	65.0%	29.2%	5.8%
249,967	WILLIAMSON	6,228	3,122	2,797	309	Sanchez	50.1%	44.9%	5.0%
32,408	WILSON	4,607	2,463	1,730	414	Sanchez	53.5%	37.6%	9.0%
7,173	WINKLER	262	170	65	27	Sanchez	64.9%	24.8%	10.3%
48,793	WISE	1,915	801	907	207	D. Morales	41.8%	47.4%	10.8%
36,752	WOOD	2,254	1,090	892	272	Sanchez	48.4%	39.6%	12.1%
7,322	YOAKUM	325	166	104	55	Sanchez	51.1%	32.0%	16.9%
17,943	YOUNG	1,490	702	608	180	Sanchez	47.1%	40.8%	12.1%
12,182	ZAPATA	3,010	2,371	577	62	Sanchez	78.8%	19.2%	2.1%
11,600	ZAVALA	3,228	2,282	835	111	Sanchez	70.7%	25.9%	3.4%
20,851,820	TOTAL	1,003,388	609,383	330,873	63,132	Sanchez	60.7%	33.0%	6.3%

TEXAS REPUBLICAN PRIMARY
SENATOR 2002

2000 Census Population	County	Total Vote	Cornyn	Other	Winner	Percentage of Total Vote	
						Cornyn	Other
55,109	ANDERSON	1,042	706	336	Cornyn	67.8%	32.2%
13,004	ANDREWS	158	113	45	Cornyn	71.5%	28.5%
80,130	ANGELINA	1,054	764	290	Cornyn	72.5%	27.5%
22,497	ARANSAS	2,214	1,250	964	Cornyn	56.5%	43.5%
8,854	ARCHER	170	95	75	Cornyn	55.9%	44.1%
2,148	ARMSTRONG	188	145	43	Cornyn	77.1%	22.9%
38,628	ATASCOSA	686	509	177	Cornyn	74.2%	25.8%
23,590	AUSTIN	2,665	2,031	634	Cornyn	76.2%	23.8%
6,594	BAILEY	355	192	163	Cornyn	54.1%	45.9%
17,645	BANDERA	1,513	1,105	408	Cornyn	73.0%	27.0%
57,733	BASTROP	1,617	1,260	357	Cornyn	77.9%	22.1%
4,093	BAYLOR	26	21	5	Cornyn	80.8%	19.2%
32,359	BEE	811	539	272	Cornyn	66.5%	33.5%
237,974	BELL	6,816	5,094	1,722	Cornyn	74.7%	25.3%
1,392,931	BEXAR	36,032	30,310	5,722	Cornyn	84.1%	15.9%
8,418	BLANCO	886	641	245	Cornyn	72.3%	27.7%
729	BORDEN	17	14	3	Cornyn	82.4%	17.6%
17,204	BOSQUE	564	408	156	Cornyn	72.3%	27.7%
89,306	BOWIE	988	592	396	Cornyn	59.9%	40.1%
241,767	BRAZORIA	8,898	7,054	1,844	Cornyn	79.3%	20.7%
152,415	BRAZOS	9,856	7,965	1,891	Cornyn	80.8%	19.2%
8,866	BREWSTER	98	72	26	Cornyn	73.5%	26.5%
1,790	BRISCOE	106	77	29	Cornyn	72.6%	27.4%
7,976	BROOKS	4	4		Cornyn	100.0%	
37,674	BROWN	939	718	221	Cornyn	76.5%	23.5%
16,470	BURLESON	725	532	193	Cornyn	73.4%	26.6%
34,147	BURNET	2,792	2,156	636	Cornyn	77.2%	22.8%
32,194	CALDWELL	1,205	896	309	Cornyn	74.4%	25.6%
20,647	CALHOUN	340	209	131	Cornyn	61.5%	38.5%
12,905	CALLAHAN	256	190	66	Cornyn	74.2%	25.8%
335,227	CAMERON	2,401	1,484	917	Cornyn	61.8%	38.2%
11,549	CAMP	167	129	38	Cornyn	77.2%	22.8%
6,516	CARSON	382	280	102	Cornyn	73.3%	26.7%
30,438	CASS	208	133	75	Cornyn	63.9%	36.1%
8,285	CASTRO	127	96	31	Cornyn	75.6%	24.4%
26,031	CHAMBERS	498	370	128	Cornyn	74.3%	25.7%
46,659	CHEROKEE	707	534	173	Cornyn	75.5%	24.5%
7,688	CHILDRESS	72	50	22	Cornyn	69.4%	30.6%
11,006	CLAY	231	147	84	Cornyn	63.6%	36.4%
3,730	COCHRAN	88	57	31	Cornyn	64.8%	35.2%
3,864	COKE	60	44	16	Cornyn	73.3%	26.7%
9,235	COLEMAN	73	52	21	Cornyn	71.2%	28.8%
491,675	COLLIN	16,089	11,542	4,547	Cornyn	71.7%	28.3%
3,206	COLLINGSWORTH	59	35	24	Cornyn	59.3%	40.7%
20,390	COLORADO	395	314	81	Cornyn	79.5%	20.5%
78,021	COMAL	8,587	6,871	1,716	Cornyn	80.0%	20.0%
14,026	COMANCHE	155	109	46	Cornyn	70.3%	29.7%
3,966	CONCHO	73	47	26	Cornyn	64.4%	35.6%
36,363	COOKE	1,371	1,010	361	Cornyn	73.7%	26.3%
74,978	CORYELL	1,202	879	323	Cornyn	73.1%	26.9%
1,904	COTTLE	1	1		Cornyn	100.0%	
3,996	CRANE	163	92	71	Cornyn	56.4%	43.6%
4,099	CROCKETT	15	12	3	Cornyn	80.0%	20.0%
7,072	CROSBY	51	22	29	Cornyn	43.1%	56.9%
2,975	CULBERSON	4	2	2		50.0%	50.0%
6,222	DALLAM	285	167	118	Cornyn	58.6%	41.4%
2,218,899	DALLAS	47,031	38,587	8,444	Cornyn	82.0%	18.0%
14,985	DAWSON	531	319	212	Cornyn	60.1%	39.9%
18,561	DEAF SMITH	2,173	1,386	787	Cornyn	63.8%	36.2%
5,327	DELTA	35	24	11	Cornyn	68.6%	31.4%

TEXAS REPUBLICAN PRIMARY

SENATOR 2002

2000 Census Population	County	Total Vote	Cornyn	Other	Winner	Percentage of Total Vote	
						Cornyn	Other
432,976	DENTON	15,758	11,079	4,679	Cornyn	70.3%	29.7%
20,013	DE WITT	750	572	178	Cornyn	76.3%	23.7%
2,762	DICKENS	7	6	1	Cornyn	85.7%	14.3%
10,248	DIMMIT	9	4	5	Cornyn	44.4%	55.6%
3,828	DONLEY	148	109	39	Cornyn	73.6%	26.4%
13,120	DUVAL	2	1	1		50.0%	50.0%
18,297	EASTLAND	676	486	190	Cornyn	71.9%	28.1%
121,123	ECTOR	3,428	2,516	912	Cornyn	73.4%	26.6%
2,162	EDWARDS	26	19	7	Cornyn	73.1%	26.9%
111,360	ELLIS	6,547	4,783	1,764	Cornyn	73.1%	26.9%
679,622	EL PASO	7,310	4,673	2,637	Cornyn	63.9%	36.1%
33,001	ERATH	1,424	1,039	385	Cornyn	73.0%	27.0%
18,576	FALLS	214	174	40	Cornyn	81.3%	18.7%
31,242	FANNIN	293	186	107	Cornyn	63.5%	36.5%
21,804	FAYETTE	794	627	167	Cornyn	79.0%	21.0%
4,344	FISHER	7	5	2	Cornyn	71.4%	28.6%
7,771	FLOYD	144	98	46	Cornyn	68.1%	31.9%
1,622	FOARD						
354,452	FORT BEND	14,723	12,012	2,711	Cornyn	81.6%	18.4%
9,458	FRANKLIN	528	321	207	Cornyn	60.8%	39.2%
17,867	FREESTONE	462	324	138	Cornyn	70.1%	29.9%
16,252	FRIO	29	23	6	Cornyn	79.3%	20.7%
14,467	GAINES	210	131	79	Cornyn	62.4%	37.6%
250,158	GALVESTON	5,755	4,318	1,437	Cornyn	75.0%	25.0%
4,872	GARZA	36	22	14	Cornyn	61.1%	38.9%
20,814	GILLESPIE	3,004	2,190	814	Cornyn	72.9%	27.1%
1,406	GLASSCOCK	189	107	82	Cornyn	56.6%	43.4%
6,928	GOLIAD	377	226	151	Cornyn	59.9%	40.1%
18,628	GONZALES	580	442	138	Cornyn	76.2%	23.8%
22,744	GRAY	2,125	1,454	671	Cornyn	68.4%	31.6%
110,595	GRAYSON	4,256	3,078	1,178	Cornyn	72.3%	27.7%
111,379	GREGG	8,672	7,080	1,592	Cornyn	81.6%	18.4%
23,552	GRIMES	954	667	287	Cornyn	69.9%	30.1%
89,023	GUADALUPE	7,673	5,683	1,990	Cornyn	74.1%	25.9%
36,602	HALE	912	642	270	Cornyn	70.4%	29.6%
3,782	HALL	26	20	6	Cornyn	76.9%	23.1%
8,229	HAMILTON	648	485	163	Cornyn	74.8%	25.2%
5,369	HANSFORD	852	609	243	Cornyn	71.5%	28.5%
4,724	HARDEMAN	13	10	3	Cornyn	76.9%	23.1%
48,073	HARDIN	1,040	697	343	Cornyn	67.0%	33.0%
3,400,578	HARRIS	83,573	72,910	10,663	Cornyn	87.2%	12.8%
62,110	HARRISON	1,952	1,219	733	Cornyn	62.4%	37.6%
5,537	HARTLEY	437	302	135	Cornyn	69.1%	30.9%
6,093	HASKELL	37	27	10	Cornyn	73.0%	27.0%
97,589	HAYS	4,478	3,478	1,000	Cornyn	77.7%	22.3%
3,351	HEMPHILL	670	449	221	Cornyn	67.0%	33.0%
73,277	HENDERSON	2,725	2,135	590	Cornyn	78.3%	21.7%
569,463	HIDALGO	1,845	1,010	835	Cornyn	54.7%	45.3%
32,321	HILL	796	595	201	Cornyn	74.7%	25.3%
22,716	HOCKLEY	1,278	737	541	Cornyn	57.7%	42.3%
41,100	HOOD	5,595	3,822	1,773	Cornyn	68.3%	31.7%
31,960	HOPKINS	348	251	97	Cornyn	72.1%	27.9%
23,185	HOUSTON	365	260	105	Cornyn	71.2%	28.8%
33,627	HOWARD	1,236	761	475	Cornyn	61.6%	38.4%
3,344	HUDSPETH	14	7	7	Cornyn	50.0%	50.0%
76,596	HUNT	2,971	2,176	795	Cornyn	73.2%	26.8%
23,857	HUTCHINSON	1,745	1,282	463	Cornyn	73.5%	26.5%
1,771	IRION	48	29	19	Cornyn	60.4%	39.6%
8,763	JACK	109	80	29	Cornyn	73.4%	26.6%
14,391	JACKSON	205	143	62	Cornyn	69.8%	30.2%

TEXAS REPUBLICAN PRIMARY

SENATOR 2002

2000 Census Population	County	Total Vote	Cornyn	Other	Winner	Percentage of Total Vote Cornyn	Other
35,604	JASPER	231	168	63	Cornyn	72.7%	27.3%
2,207	JEFF DAVIS	26	12	14	Cornyn	46.2%	53.8%
252,051	JEFFERSON	3,265	2,118	1,147	Cornyn	64.9%	35.1%
5,281	JIM HOGG	7	7		Cornyn	100.0%	
39,326	JIM WELLS	177	114	63	Cornyn	64.4%	35.6%
126,811	JOHNSON	5,829	4,128	1,701	Cornyn	70.8%	29.2%
20,785	JONES	154	92	62	Cornyn	59.7%	40.3%
15,446	KARNES	107	76	31	Cornyn	71.0%	29.0%
71,313	KAUFMAN	2,725	2,007	718	Cornyn	73.7%	26.3%
23,743	KENDALL	3,176	2,349	827	Cornyn	74.0%	26.0%
414	KENEDY	3	3		Cornyn	100.0%	
859	KENT	4	1	3		25.0%	75.0%
43,653	KERR	4,719	3,676	1,043	Cornyn	77.9%	22.1%
4,468	KIMBLE	122	92	30	Cornyn	75.4%	24.6%
356	KING	7	4	3	Cornyn	57.1%	42.9%
3,379	KINNEY	49	29	20	Cornyn	59.2%	40.8%
31,549	KLEBERG	205	152	53	Cornyn	74.1%	25.9%
4,253	KNOX	50	42	8	Cornyn	84.0%	16.0%
48,499	LAMAR	765	582	183	Cornyn	76.1%	23.9%
14,709	LAMB	62	49	13	Cornyn	79.0%	21.0%
17,762	LAMPASAS	1,159	865	294	Cornyn	74.6%	25.4%
5,866	LA SALLE						
19,210	LAVACA	331	235	96	Cornyn	71.0%	29.0%
15,657	LEE	287	224	63	Cornyn	78.0%	22.0%
15,335	LEON	807	614	193	Cornyn	76.1%	23.9%
70,154	LIBERTY	1,165	776	389	Cornyn	66.6%	33.4%
22,051	LIMESTONE	643	486	157	Cornyn	75.6%	24.4%
3,057	LIPSCOMB	190	130	60	Cornyn	68.4%	31.6%
12,309	LIVE OAK	256	173	83	Cornyn	67.6%	32.4%
17,044	LLANO	1,759	1,428	331	Cornyn	81.2%	18.8%
67	LOVING						
242,628	LUBBOCK	15,601	10,814	4,787	Cornyn	69.3%	30.7%
6,550	LYNN	39	20	19	Cornyn	51.3%	48.7%
8,205	MCCULLOCH	191	143	48	Cornyn	74.9%	25.1%
213,517	MCLENNAN	10,310	7,986	2,324	Cornyn	77.5%	22.5%
851	MCMULLEN	44	29	15	Cornyn	65.9%	34.1%
12,940	MADISON	413	298	115	Cornyn	72.2%	27.8%
10,941	MARION	50	39	11	Cornyn	78.0%	22.0%
4,746	MARTIN	76	45	31	Cornyn	59.2%	40.8%
3,738	MASON	637	463	174	Cornyn	72.7%	27.3%
37,957	MATAGORDA	339	275	64	Cornyn	81.1%	18.9%
47,297	MAVERICK	13	12	1	Cornyn	92.3%	7.7%
39,304	MEDINA	896	704	192	Cornyn	78.6%	21.4%
2,360	MENARD	296	179	117	Cornyn	60.5%	39.5%
116,009	MIDLAND	5,252	4,188	1,064	Cornyn	79.7%	20.3%
24,238	MILAM	446	374	72	Cornyn	83.9%	16.1%
5,151	MILLS	39	31	8	Cornyn	79.5%	20.5%
9,698	MITCHELL	126	95	31	Cornyn	75.4%	24.6%
19,117	MONTAGUE	304	196	108	Cornyn	64.5%	35.5%
293,768	MONTGOMERY	18,984	14,246	4,738	Cornyn	75.0%	25.0%
20,121	MOORE	1,243	955	288	Cornyn	76.8%	23.2%
13,048	MORRIS	75	48	27	Cornyn	64.0%	36.0%
1,426	MOTLEY	172	95	77	Cornyn	55.2%	44.8%
59,203	NACOGDOCHES	3,480	2,616	864	Cornyn	75.2%	24.8%
45,124	NAVARRO	1,221	950	271	Cornyn	77.8%	22.2%
15,072	NEWTON	80	57	23	Cornyn	71.3%	28.8%
15,802	NOLAN	76	58	18	Cornyn	76.3%	23.7%
313,645	NUECES	9,656	6,643	3,013	Cornyn	68.8%	31.2%
9,006	OCHILTREE	1,476	1,024	452	Cornyn	69.4%	30.6%
2,185	OLDHAM	71	50	21	Cornyn	70.4%	29.6%

TEXAS REPUBLICAN PRIMARY

SENATOR 2002

2000 Census Population	County	Total Vote	Cornyn	Other	Winner	Percentage of Total Vote Cornyn	Other
84,966	ORANGE	1,356	785	571	Cornyn	57.9%	42.1%
27,026	PALO PINTO	320	194	126	Cornyn	60.6%	39.4%
22,756	PANOLA	223	154	69	Cornyn	69.1%	30.9%
88,495	PARKER	6,134	4,530	1,604	Cornyn	73.9%	26.1%
10,016	PARMER	620	448	172	Cornyn	72.3%	27.7%
16,809	PECOS	242	130	112	Cornyn	53.7%	46.3%
41,133	POLK	949	584	365	Cornyn	61.5%	38.5%
113,546	POTTER	4,512	3,431	1,081	Cornyn	76.0%	24.0%
7,304	PRESIDIO	14	8	6	Cornyn	57.1%	42.9%
9,139	RAINS	188	121	67	Cornyn	64.4%	35.6%
104,312	RANDALL	9,923	7,855	2,068	Cornyn	79.2%	20.8%
3,326	REAGAN	551	295	256	Cornyn	53.5%	46.5%
3,047	REAL	410	246	164	Cornyn	60.0%	40.0%
14,314	RED RIVER	44	19	25	Cornyn	43.2%	56.8%
13,137	REEVES						
7,828	REFUGIO	44	31	13	Cornyn	70.5%	29.5%
887	ROBERTS	288	211	77	Cornyn	73.3%	26.7%
16,000	ROBERTSON	281	205	76	Cornyn	73.0%	27.0%
43,080	ROCKWALL	3,093	2,321	772	Cornyn	75.0%	25.0%
11,495	RUNNELS	117	85	32	Cornyn	72.6%	27.4%
47,372	RUSK	1,124	873	251	Cornyn	77.7%	22.3%
10,469	SABINE	141	109	32	Cornyn	77.3%	22.7%
8,946	SAN AUGUSTINE	23	12	11	Cornyn	52.2%	47.8%
22,246	SAN JACINTO	505	340	165	Cornyn	67.3%	32.7%
67,138	SAN PATRICIO	1,197	671	526	Cornyn	56.1%	43.9%
6,186	SAN SABA	208	158	50	Cornyn	76.0%	24.0%
2,935	SCHLEICHER	148	108	40	Cornyn	73.0%	27.0%
16,361	SCURRY	805	567	238	Cornyn	70.4%	29.6%
3,302	SHACKELFORD	86	75	11	Cornyn	87.2%	12.8%
25,224	SHELBY	707	487	220	Cornyn	68.9%	31.1%
3,186	SHERMAN	65	55	10	Cornyn	84.6%	15.4%
174,706	SMITH	12,592	10,078	2,514	Cornyn	80.0%	20.0%
6,809	SOMERVELL	357	241	116	Cornyn	67.5%	32.5%
53,597	STARR	5	2	3	Cornyn	40.0%	60.0%
9,674	STEPHENS	124	98	26	Cornyn	79.0%	21.0%
1,393	STERLING	201	130	71	Cornyn	64.7%	35.3%
1,693	STONEWALL	8	6	2	Cornyn	75.0%	25.0%
4,077	SUTTON	61	41	20	Cornyn	67.2%	32.8%
8,378	SWISHER	61	39	22	Cornyn	63.9%	36.1%
1,446,219	TARRANT	35,225	28,462	6,763	Cornyn	80.8%	19.2%
126,555	TAYLOR	4,415	3,487	928	Cornyn	79.0%	21.0%
1,081	TERRELL	7	5	2	Cornyn	71.4%	28.6%
12,761	TERRY	136	97	39	Cornyn	71.3%	28.7%
1,850	THROCKMORTON	25	23	2	Cornyn	92.0%	8.0%
28,118	TITUS	400	296	104	Cornyn	74.0%	26.0%
104,010	TOM GREEN	7,045	5,125	1,920	Cornyn	72.7%	27.3%
812,280	TRAVIS	20,310	16,844	3,466	Cornyn	82.9%	17.1%
13,779	TRINITY	118	88	30	Cornyn	74.6%	25.4%
20,871	TYLER	158	114	44	Cornyn	72.2%	27.8%
35,291	UPSHUR	681	415	266	Cornyn	60.9%	39.1%
3,404	UPTON						
25,926	UVALDE	224	154	70	Cornyn	68.8%	31.3%
44,856	VAL VERDE	438	312	126	Cornyn	71.2%	28.8%
48,140	VAN ZANDT	1,710	1,246	464	Cornyn	72.9%	27.1%
84,088	VICTORIA	1,875	1,292	583	Cornyn	68.9%	31.1%
61,758	WALKER	2,324	1,689	635	Cornyn	72.7%	27.3%
32,663	WALLER	1,839	1,284	555	Cornyn	69.8%	30.2%
10,909	WARD	52	31	21	Cornyn	59.6%	40.4%
30,373	WASHINGTON	1,949	1,401	548	Cornyn	71.9%	28.1%
193,117	WEBB	600	221	379	Cornyn	36.8%	63.2%

TEXAS REPUBLICAN PRIMARY

SENATOR 2002

2000 Census Population	County	Total Vote	Cornyn	Other	Winner	Percentage of Total Vote Cornyn	Other
41,188	WHARTON	1,773	1,148	625	Cornyn	64.7%	35.3%
5,284	WHEELER	54	44	10	Cornyn	81.5%	18.5%
131,664	WICHITA	4,087	2,597	1,490	Cornyn	63.5%	36.5%
14,676	WILBARGER	186	117	69	Cornyn	62.9%	37.1%
20,082	WILLACY	20	14	6	Cornyn	70.0%	30.0%
249,967	WILLIAMSON	13,208	10,579	2,629	Cornyn	80.1%	19.9%
32,408	WILSON	918	664	254	Cornyn	72.3%	27.7%
7,173	WINKLER	349	208	141	Cornyn	59.6%	40.4%
48,793	WISE	1,336	861	475	Cornyn	64.4%	35.6%
36,752	WOOD	1,800	1,260	540	Cornyn	70.0%	30.0%
7,322	YOAKUM	557	276	281	Cornyn	49.6%	50.4%
17,943	YOUNG	509	365	144	Cornyn	71.7%	28.3%
12,182	ZAPATA	31	16	15	Cornyn	51.6%	48.4%
11,600	ZAVALA	47	34	13	Cornyn	72.3%	27.7%
20,851,820	TOTAL	619,302	478,825	140,477	Cornyn	77.3%	22.7%

TEXAS DEMOCRATIC PRIMARY

SENATOR 2002

2000 Census Population	County	Total Vote	V. Morales	Kirk	Bentsen	Other	Winner	Percentage of Total Vote V. Morales	Kirk	Bentsen	Other
55,109	ANDERSON	4,558	1,582	1,488	1,157	331	V. Morales	34.7%	32.6%	25.4%	7.3%
13,004	ANDREWS	1,314	325	234	558	197	Bentsen	24.7%	17.8%	42.5%	15.0%
80,130	ANGELINA	7,987	1,265	1,827	3,850	1,045	Bentsen	15.8%	22.9%	48.2%	13.1%
22,497	ARANSAS	988	381	237	172	198	V. Morales	38.6%	24.0%	17.4%	20.0%
8,854	ARCHER	781	175	178	351	77	Bentsen	22.4%	22.8%	44.9%	9.9%
2,148	ARMSTRONG	90	10	29	41	10	Bentsen	11.1%	32.2%	45.6%	11.1%
38,628	ATASCOSA	4,297	2,573	813	541	370	V. Morales	59.9%	18.9%	12.6%	8.6%
23,590	AUSTIN	596	81	85	395	35	Bentsen	13.6%	14.3%	66.3%	5.9%
6,594	BAILEY	220	54	42	97	27	Bentsen	24.5%	19.1%	44.1%	12.3%
17,645	BANDERA	301	85	118	63	35	Kirk	28.2%	39.2%	20.9%	11.6%
57,733	BASTROP	4,469	1,133	2,061	907	368	Kirk	25.4%	46.1%	20.3%	8.2%
4,093	BAYLOR	895	332	140	304	119	V. Morales	37.1%	15.6%	34.0%	13.3%
32,359	BEE	2,302	1,415	374	264	249	V. Morales	61.5%	16.2%	11.5%	10.8%
237,974	BELL	3,684	808	1,477	1,047	352	Kirk	21.9%	40.1%	28.4%	9.6%
1,392,931	BEXAR	58,735	27,648	20,613	7,458	3,016	V. Morales	47.1%	35.1%	12.7%	5.1%
8,418	BLANCO	222	59	110	42	11	Kirk	26.6%	49.5%	18.9%	5.0%
729	BORDEN	127	30	22	46	29	Bentsen	23.6%	17.3%	36.2%	22.8%
17,204	BOSQUE	1,738	467	545	588	138	Bentsen	26.9%	31.4%	33.8%	7.9%
89,306	BOWIE	9,774	1,913	3,583	3,160	1,118	Kirk	19.6%	36.7%	32.3%	11.4%
241,767	BRAZORIA	4,364	875	672	2,582	235	Bentsen	20.1%	15.4%	59.2%	5.4%
152,415	BRAZOS	3,362	1,341	1,115	743	163	V. Morales	39.9%	33.2%	22.1%	4.8%
8,866	BREWSTER	893	443	128	198	124	V. Morales	49.6%	14.3%	22.2%	13.9%
1,790	BRISCOE	361	91	54	141	75	Bentsen	25.2%	15.0%	39.1%	20.8%
7,976	BROOKS	2,897	2,099	270	229	299	V. Morales	72.5%	9.3%	7.9%	10.3%
37,674	BROWN	963	221	337	326	79	Kirk	22.9%	35.0%	33.9%	8.2%
16,470	BURLESON	1,193	321	372	394	106	Bentsen	26.9%	31.2%	33.0%	8.9%
34,147	BURNET	1,491	319	686	346	140	Kirk	21.4%	46.0%	23.2%	9.4%
32,194	CALDWELL	1,963	715	735	383	130	Kirk	36.4%	37.4%	19.5%	6.6%
20,647	CALHOUN	2,345	748	296	966	335	Bentsen	31.9%	12.6%	41.2%	14.3%
12,905	CALLAHAN	871	278	164	290	139	Bentsen	31.9%	18.8%	33.3%	16.0%

TEXAS DEMOCRATIC PRIMARY

SENATOR 2002

2000 Census Population	County	Total Vote	V. Morales	Kirk	Bentsen	Other	Winner	Percentage of Total Vote			
								V. Morales	Kirk	Bentsen	Other
335,227	CAMERON	21,222	11,259	3,141	5,453	1,369	V. Morales	53.1%	14.8%	25.7%	6.5%
11,549	CAMP	1,503	251	724	422	106	Kirk	16.7%	48.2%	28.1%	7.1%
6,516	CARSON	302	63	64	127	48	Bentsen	20.9%	21.2%	42.1%	15.9%
30,438	CASS	5,031	1,128	1,383	1,925	595	Bentsen	22.4%	27.5%	38.3%	11.8%
8,285	CASTRO	387	106	55	188	38	Bentsen	27.4%	14.2%	48.6%	9.8%
26,031	CHAMBERS	2,415	381	202	1,523	309	Bentsen	15.8%	8.4%	63.1%	12.8%
46,659	CHEROKEE	3,595	731	1,021	1,290	553	Bentsen	20.3%	28.4%	35.9%	15.4%
7,688	CHILDRESS	522	121	109	215	77	Bentsen	23.2%	20.9%	41.2%	14.8%
11,006	CLAY	781	165	182	359	75	Bentsen	21.1%	23.3%	46.0%	9.6%
3,730	COCHRAN	307	128	39	121	19	V. Morales	41.7%	12.7%	39.4%	6.2%
3,864	COKE	705	177	157	218	153	Bentsen	25.1%	22.3%	30.9%	21.7%
9,235	COLEMAN	1,127	427	203	344	153	V. Morales	37.9%	18.0%	30.5%	13.6%
491,675	COLLIN	6,193	1,432	3,745	945	71	Kirk	23.1%	60.5%	15.3%	1.1%
3,206	COLLINGSWORTH	625	173	89	221	142	Bentsen	27.7%	14.2%	35.4%	22.7%
20,390	COLORADO	864	186	122	510	46	Bentsen	21.5%	14.1%	59.0%	5.3%
78,021	COMAL	1,701	565	674	381	81	Kirk	33.2%	39.6%	22.4%	4.8%
14,026	COMANCHE	1,806	509	589	506	202	Kirk	28.2%	32.6%	28.0%	11.2%
3,966	CONCHO	256	66	81	64	45	Kirk	25.8%	31.6%	25.0%	17.6%
36,363	COOKE	743	181	373	159	30	Kirk	24.4%	50.2%	21.4%	4.0%
74,978	CORYELL	1,081	218	313	494	56	Bentsen	20.2%	29.0%	45.7%	5.2%
1,904	COTTLE	515	122	72	202	119	Bentsen	23.7%	14.0%	39.2%	23.1%
3,996	CRANE	537	163	88	174	112	Bentsen	30.4%	16.4%	32.4%	20.9%
4,099	CROCKETT	375	257	40	41	37	V. Morales	68.5%	10.7%	10.9%	9.9%
7,072	CROSBY	1,203	357	227	426	193	Bentsen	29.7%	18.9%	35.4%	16.0%
2,975	CULBERSON	237	145	36	32	24	V. Morales	61.2%	15.2%	13.5%	10.1%
6,222	DALLAM	135	39	22	49	25	Bentsen	28.9%	16.3%	36.3%	18.5%
2,218,899	DALLAS	77,938	14,998	54,373	8,083	484	Kirk	19.2%	69.8%	10.4%	0.6%
14,985	DAWSON	1,466	551	182	567	166	Bentsen	37.6%	12.4%	38.7%	11.3%
18,561	DEAF SMITH	433	262	40	89	42	V. Morales	60.5%	9.2%	20.6%	9.7%
5,327	DELTA	989	270	335	282	102	Kirk	27.3%	33.9%	28.5%	10.3%
432,976	DENTON	5,191	1,310	3,184	606	91	Kirk	25.2%	61.3%	11.7%	1.8%
20,013	DE WITT	660	184	237	184	55	Kirk	27.9%	35.9%	27.9%	8.3%
2,762	DICKENS	658	146	109	317	86	Bentsen	22.2%	16.6%	48.2%	13.1%
10,248	DIMMIT	2,830	1,995	311	244	280	V. Morales	70.5%	11.0%	8.6%	9.9%
3,828	DONLEY	226	33	23	128	42	Bentsen	14.6%	10.2%	56.6%	18.6%
13,120	DUVAL	5,098	3,982	295	578	243	V. Morales	78.1%	5.8%	11.3%	4.8%
18,297	EASTLAND	1,231	346	381	339	165	Kirk	28.1%	31.0%	27.5%	13.4%
121,123	ECTOR	2,636	1,106	545	796	189	V. Morales	42.0%	20.7%	30.2%	7.2%
2,162	EDWARDS	517	228	100	97	92	V. Morales	44.1%	19.3%	18.8%	17.8%
111,360	ELLIS	2,567	729	1,360	410	68	Kirk	28.4%	53.0%	16.0%	2.6%
679,622	EL PASO	44,602	23,527	9,249	8,947	2,879	V. Morales	52.7%	20.7%	20.1%	6.5%
33,001	ERATH	1,507	518	558	351	80	Kirk	34.4%	37.0%	23.3%	5.3%
18,576	FALLS	1,780	312	643	661	164	Bentsen	17.5%	36.1%	37.1%	9.2%
31,242	FANNIN	3,139	1,066	1,194	596	283	Kirk	34.0%	38.0%	19.0%	9.0%
21,804	FAYETTE	2,494	480	691	997	326	Bentsen	19.2%	27.7%	40.0%	13.1%
4,344	FISHER	994	355	158	340	141	V. Morales	35.7%	15.9%	34.2%	14.2%
7,771	FLOYD	856	205	214	308	129	Bentsen	23.9%	25.0%	36.0%	15.1%
1,622	FOARD	207	47	40	85	35	Bentsen	22.7%	19.3%	41.1%	16.9%
354,452	FORT BEND	8,930	1,378	3,159	3,985	408	Bentsen	15.4%	35.4%	44.6%	4.6%
9,458	FRANKLIN	844	212	273	291	68	Bentsen	25.1%	32.3%	34.5%	8.1%
17,867	FREESTONE	2,492	883	917	510	182	Kirk	35.4%	36.8%	20.5%	7.3%
16,252	FRIO	2,916	1,536	498	520	362	V. Morales	52.7%	17.1%	17.8%	12.4%
14,467	GAINES	1,609	504	191	726	188	Bentsen	31.3%	11.9%	45.1%	11.7%
250,158	GALVESTON	13,459	2,628	2,762	7,162	907	Bentsen	19.5%	20.5%	53.2%	6.7%
4,872	GARZA	390	105	68	161	56	Bentsen	26.9%	17.4%	41.3%	14.4%
20,814	GILLESPIE	317	48	155	98	16	Kirk	15.1%	48.9%	30.9%	5.0%
1,406	GLASSCOCK	18	1	2	14	1	Bentsen	5.6%	11.1%	77.8%	5.6%
6,928	GOLIAD	872	451	169	127	125	V. Morales	51.7%	19.4%	14.6%	14.3%
18,628	GONZALES	1,709	458	606	451	194	Kirk	26.8%	35.5%	26.4%	11.4%
22,744	GRAY	381	79	78	161	63	Bentsen	20.7%	20.5%	42.3%	16.5%

TEXAS DEMOCRATIC PRIMARY

SENATOR 2002

2000 Census Population	County	Total Vote	V. Morales	Kirk	Bentsen	Other	Winner	Percentage of Total Vote			
								V. Morales	Kirk	Bentsen	Other
110,595	GRAYSON	2,509	616	1,417	349	127	Kirk	24.6%	56.5%	13.9%	5.1%
111,379	GREGG	3,738	560	2,349	617	212	Kirk	15.0%	62.8%	16.5%	5.7%
23,552	GRIMES	1,938	358	364	979	237	Bentsen	18.5%	18.8%	50.5%	12.2%
89,023	GUADALUPE	1,794	796	631	248	119	V. Morales	44.4%	35.2%	13.8%	6.6%
36,602	HALE	960	310	228	347	75	Bentsen	32.3%	23.8%	36.1%	7.8%
3,782	HALL	806	238	119	272	177	Bentsen	29.5%	14.8%	33.7%	22.0%
8,229	HAMILTON	772	216	277	219	60	Kirk	28.0%	35.9%	28.4%	7.8%
5,369	HANSFORD										
4,724	HARDEMAN	714	157	125	283	149	Bentsen	22.0%	17.5%	39.6%	20.9%
48,073	HARDIN	3,482	636	467	2,077	302	Bentsen	18.3%	13.4%	59.6%	8.7%
3,400,578	HARRIS	82,418	14,204	23,483	41,112	3,619	Bentsen	17.2%	28.5%	49.9%	4.4%
62,110	HARRISON	7,320	1,550	2,572	2,087	1,111	Kirk	21.2%	35.1%	28.5%	15.2%
5,537	HARTLEY	170	31	29	73	37	Bentsen	18.2%	17.1%	42.9%	21.8%
6,093	HASKELL	1,081	309	161	434	177	Bentsen	28.6%	14.9%	40.1%	16.4%
97,589	HAYS	4,212	1,758	1,687	563	204	V. Morales	41.7%	40.1%	13.4%	4.8%
3,351	HEMPHILL	81	15	15	37	14	Bentsen	18.5%	18.5%	45.7%	17.3%
73,277	HENDERSON	4,785	1,586	1,835	1,012	352	Kirk	33.1%	38.3%	21.1%	7.4%
569,463	HIDALGO	41,045	22,925	6,716	9,333	2,071	V. Morales	55.9%	16.4%	22.7%	5.0%
32,321	HILL	3,033	814	1,021	1,024	174	Bentsen	26.8%	33.7%	33.8%	5.7%
22,716	HOCKLEY	363	125	47	156	35	Bentsen	34.4%	12.9%	43.0%	9.6%
41,100	HOOD	1,121	395	428	196	102	Kirk	35.2%	38.2%	17.5%	9.1%
31,960	HOPKINS	3,088	681	1,356	944	107	Kirk	22.1%	43.9%	30.6%	3.5%
23,185	HOUSTON	1,750	292	397	793	268	Bentsen	16.7%	22.7%	45.3%	15.3%
33,627	HOWARD	739	196	165	303	75	Bentsen	26.5%	22.3%	41.0%	10.1%
3,344	HUDSPETH	531	249	103	82	97	V. Morales	46.9%	19.4%	15.4%	18.3%
76,596	HUNT	2,622	706	1,428	388	100	Kirk	26.9%	54.5%	14.8%	3.8%
23,857	HUTCHINSON	481	91	80	224	86	Bentsen	18.9%	16.6%	46.6%	17.9%
1,771	IRION	329	100	89	70	70	V. Morales	30.4%	27.1%	21.3%	21.3%
8,763	JACK	746	173	245	233	95	Kirk	23.2%	32.8%	31.2%	12.7%
14,391	JACKSON	1,720	297	215	928	280	Bentsen	17.3%	12.5%	54.0%	16.3%
35,604	JASPER	3,685	684	743	2,023	235	Bentsen	18.6%	20.2%	54.9%	6.4%
2,207	JEFF DAVIS	497	191	82	113	111	V. Morales	38.4%	16.5%	22.7%	22.3%
252,051	JEFFERSON	21,643	4,257	5,810	10,262	1,314	Bentsen	19.7%	26.8%	47.4%	6.1%
5,281	JIM HOGG	2,227	1,640	167	217	203	V. Morales	73.6%	7.5%	9.7%	9.1%
39,326	JIM WELLS	7,019	4,297	1,088	724	910	V. Morales	61.2%	15.5%	10.3%	13.0%
126,811	JOHNSON	2,174	780	914	407	73	Kirk	35.9%	42.0%	18.7%	3.4%
20,785	JONES	1,856	597	295	594	370	V. Morales	32.2%	15.9%	32.0%	19.9%
15,446	KARNES	2,473	782	586	817	288	Bentsen	31.6%	23.7%	33.0%	11.6%
71,313	KAUFMAN	2,739	996	1,305	371	67	Kirk	36.4%	47.6%	13.5%	2.4%
23,743	KENDALL	384	122	148	96	18	Kirk	31.8%	38.5%	25.0%	4.7%
414	KENEDY	146	85	20	15	26	V. Morales	58.2%	13.7%	10.3%	17.8%
859	KENT	399	82	58	134	125	Bentsen	20.6%	14.5%	33.6%	31.3%
43,653	KERR	875	222	353	228	72	Kirk	25.4%	40.3%	26.1%	8.2%
4,468	KIMBLE	429	134	85	110	100	V. Morales	31.2%	19.8%	25.6%	23.3%
356	KING	94	29	16	25	24	V. Morales	30.9%	17.0%	26.6%	25.5%
3,379	KINNEY	832	340	170	149	173	V. Morales	40.9%	20.4%	17.9%	20.8%
31,549	KLEBERG	3,433	2,134	639	406	254	V. Morales	62.2%	18.6%	11.8%	7.4%
4,253	KNOX	314	83	58	110	63	Bentsen	26.4%	18.5%	35.0%	20.1%
48,499	LAMAR	3,693	1,159	1,236	990	308	Kirk	31.4%	33.5%	26.8%	8.3%
14,709	LAMB	1,824	402	337	779	306	Bentsen	22.0%	18.5%	42.7%	16.8%
17,762	LAMPASAS	526	190	107	185	44	V. Morales	36.1%	20.3%	35.2%	8.4%
5,866	LA SALLE	1,601	957	232	235	177	V. Morales	59.8%	14.5%	14.7%	11.1%
19,210	LAVACA	3,354	791	833	1,356	374	Bentsen	23.6%	24.8%	40.4%	11.2%
15,657	LEE	1,744	369	707	458	210	Kirk	21.2%	40.5%	26.3%	12.0%
15,335	LEON	723	212	177	270	64	Bentsen	29.3%	24.5%	37.3%	8.9%
70,154	LIBERTY	6,297	747	886	4,009	655	Bentsen	11.9%	14.1%	63.7%	10.4%
22,051	LIMESTONE	1,328	301	503	420	104	Kirk	22.7%	37.9%	31.6%	7.8%
3,057	LIPSCOMB	243	52	43	87	61	Bentsen	21.4%	17.7%	35.8%	25.1%
12,309	LIVE OAK	686	243	191	138	114	V. Morales	35.4%	27.8%	20.1%	16.6%
17,044	LLANO	823	207	361	178	77	Kirk	25.2%	43.9%	21.6%	9.4%

470

TEXAS DEMOCRATIC PRIMARY
SENATOR 2002

2000 Census Population	County	Total Vote	V. Morales	Kirk	Bentsen	Other	Winner	Percentage of Total Vote			
								V. Morales	Kirk	Bentsen	Other
67	LOVING	33	3	6	15	9	Bentsen	9.1%	18.2%	45.5%	27.3%
242,628	LUBBOCK	4,420	1,751	1,124	1,297	248	V. Morales	39.6%	25.4%	29.3%	5.6%
6,550	LYNN	1,011	251	180	436	144	Bentsen	24.8%	17.8%	43.1%	14.2%
8,205	MCCULLOCH	881	296	203	257	125	V. Morales	33.6%	23.0%	29.2%	14.2%
213,517	MCLENNAN	6,897	1,199	2,861	2,575	262	Kirk	17.4%	41.5%	37.3%	3.8%
851	MCMULLEN	160	61	32	25	42	V. Morales	38.1%	20.0%	15.6%	26.3%
12,940	MADISON	617	184	86	261	86	Bentsen	29.8%	13.9%	42.3%	13.9%
10,941	MARION	1,285	206	399	532	148	Bentsen	16.0%	31.1%	41.4%	11.5%
4,746	MARTIN	632	226	98	255	53	Bentsen	35.8%	15.5%	40.3%	8.4%
3,738	MASON	84	32	23	23	6	V. Morales	38.1%	27.4%	27.4%	7.1%
37,957	MATAGORDA	1,692	419	282	869	122	Bentsen	24.8%	16.7%	51.4%	7.2%
47,297	MAVERICK	6,391	4,722	432	600	637	V. Morales	73.9%	6.8%	9.4%	10.0%
39,304	MEDINA	2,779	1,071	812	590	306	V. Morales	38.5%	29.2%	21.2%	11.0%
2,360	MENARD	162	86	20	34	22	V. Morales	53.1%	12.3%	21.0%	13.6%
116,009	MIDLAND	1,320	438	360	457	65	Bentsen	33.2%	27.3%	34.6%	4.9%
24,238	MILAM	1,781	435	421	792	133	Bentsen	24.4%	23.6%	44.5%	7.5%
5,151	MILLS	934	245	188	362	139	Bentsen	26.2%	20.1%	38.8%	14.9%
9,698	MITCHELL	409	117	96	144	52	Bentsen	28.6%	23.5%	35.2%	12.7%
19,117	MONTAGUE	1,565	411	435	581	138	Bentsen	26.3%	27.8%	37.1%	8.8%
293,768	MONTGOMERY	2,922	595	361	1,774	192	Bentsen	20.4%	12.4%	60.7%	6.6%
20,121	MOORE	335	104	53	133	45	Bentsen	31.0%	15.8%	39.7%	13.4%
13,048	MORRIS	2,175	494	646	840	195	Bentsen	22.7%	29.7%	38.6%	9.0%
1,426	MOTLEY	168	35	27	54	52	Bentsen	20.8%	16.1%	32.1%	31.0%
59,203	NACOGDOCHES	2,194	488	713	826	167	Bentsen	22.2%	32.5%	37.6%	7.6%
45,124	NAVARRO	5,310	1,502	2,572	884	352	Kirk	28.3%	48.4%	16.6%	6.6%
15,072	NEWTON	2,694	719	459	1,160	356	Bentsen	26.7%	17.0%	43.1%	13.2%
15,802	NOLAN	975	258	251	295	171	Bentsen	26.5%	25.7%	30.3%	17.5%
313,645	NUECES	27,263	13,362	7,363	3,840	2,698	V. Morales	49.0%	27.0%	14.1%	9.9%
9,006	OCHILTREE										
2,185	OLDHAM	282	53	52	129	48	Bentsen	18.8%	18.4%	45.7%	17.0%
84,966	ORANGE	9,441	1,968	1,263	5,441	769	Bentsen	20.8%	13.4%	57.6%	8.1%
27,026	PALO PINTO	3,413	1,237	1,223	739	214	V. Morales	36.2%	35.8%	21.7%	6.3%
22,756	PANOLA	3,311	662	806	1,394	449	Bentsen	20.0%	24.3%	42.1%	13.6%
88,495	PARKER	2,250	864	853	449	84	V. Morales	38.4%	37.9%	20.0%	3.7%
10,016	PARMER	301	94	56	107	44	Bentsen	31.2%	18.6%	35.5%	14.6%
16,809	PECOS	2,134	1,184	204	535	211	V. Morales	55.5%	9.6%	25.1%	9.9%
41,133	POLK	3,228	456	620	1,849	303	Bentsen	14.1%	19.2%	57.3%	9.4%
113,546	POTTER	2,193	621	596	770	206	Bentsen	28.3%	27.2%	35.1%	9.4%
7,304	PRESIDIO	957	582	97	160	118	V. Morales	60.8%	10.1%	16.7%	12.3%
9,139	RAINS	1,464	500	552	319	93	Kirk	34.2%	37.7%	21.8%	6.4%
104,312	RANDALL	1,403	320	393	534	156	Bentsen	22.8%	28.0%	38.1%	11.1%
3,326	REAGAN	23	9	5	5	4	V. Morales	39.1%	21.7%	21.7%	17.4%
3,047	REAL	42	12	12	14	4	Bentsen	28.6%	28.6%	33.3%	9.5%
14,314	RED RIVER	2,485	594	686	919	286	Bentsen	23.9%	27.6%	37.0%	11.5%
13,137	REEVES	2,571	1,662	160	406	343	V. Morales	64.6%	6.2%	15.8%	13.3%
7,828	REFUGIO	1,463	593	419	233	218	V. Morales	40.5%	28.6%	15.9%	14.9%
887	ROBERTS										
16,000	ROBERTSON	3,177	880	1,071	836	390	Kirk	27.7%	33.7%	26.3%	12.3%
43,080	ROCKWALL	719	226	352	128	13	Kirk	31.4%	49.0%	17.8%	1.8%
11,495	RUNNELS	1,284	338	349	324	273	Kirk	26.3%	27.2%	25.2%	21.3%
47,372	RUSK	2,114	362	789	770	193	Kirk	17.1%	37.3%	36.4%	9.1%
10,469	SABINE	782	137	124	388	133	Bentsen	17.5%	15.9%	49.6%	17.0%
8,946	SAN AUGUSTINE	2,013	395	458	724	436	Bentsen	19.6%	22.8%	36.0%	21.7%
22,246	SAN JACINTO	3,297	490	337	2,086	384	Bentsen	14.9%	10.2%	63.3%	11.6%
67,138	SAN PATRICIO	5,219	2,643	1,037	658	881	V. Morales	50.6%	19.9%	12.6%	16.9%
6,186	SAN SABA	265	76	85	85	19		28.7%	32.1%	32.1%	7.2%
2,935	SCHLEICHER	316	128	77	67	44	V. Morales	40.5%	24.4%	21.2%	13.9%
16,361	SCURRY	572	137	130	212	93	Bentsen	24.0%	22.7%	37.1%	16.3%
3,302	SHACKELFORD	530	153	99	169	109	Bentsen	28.9%	18.7%	31.9%	20.6%
25,224	SHELBY	2,071	316	442	942	371	Bentsen	15.3%	21.3%	45.5%	17.9%

TEXAS DEMOCRATIC PRIMARY

SENATOR 2002

2000 Census Population	County	Total Vote	V. Morales	Kirk	Bentsen	Other	Winner	Percentage of Total Vote			
								V. Morales	Kirk	Bentsen	Other
3,186	SHERMAN	115	21	24	44	26	Bentsen	18.3%	20.9%	38.3%	22.6%
174,706	SMITH	4,160	759	2,391	833	177	Kirk	18.2%	57.5%	20.0%	4.3%
6,809	SOMERVELL	894	315	346	150	83	Kirk	35.2%	38.7%	16.8%	9.3%
53,597	STARR	6,057	3,728	407	1,388	534	V. Morales	61.5%	6.7%	22.9%	8.8%
9,674	STEPHENS	1,809	585	476	463	285	V. Morales	32.3%	26.3%	25.6%	15.8%
1,393	STERLING	39	12	10	12	5		30.8%	25.6%	30.8%	12.8%
1,693	STONEWALL	512	173	85	136	118	V. Morales	33.8%	16.6%	26.6%	23.0%
4,077	SUTTON	140	82	20	22	16	V. Morales	58.6%	14.3%	15.7%	11.4%
8,378	SWISHER	1,190	252	265	515	158	Bentsen	21.2%	22.3%	43.3%	13.3%
1,446,219	TARRANT	36,812	10,003	22,733	3,631	445	Kirk	27.2%	61.8%	9.9%	1.2%
126,555	TAYLOR	2,522	890	568	808	256	V. Morales	35.3%	22.5%	32.0%	10.2%
1,081	TERRELL	383	195	32	85	71	V. Morales	50.9%	8.4%	22.2%	18.5%
12,761	TERRY	1,125	323	180	491	131	Bentsen	28.7%	16.0%	43.6%	11.6%
1,850	THROCKMORTON	384	128	65	123	68	V. Morales	33.3%	16.9%	32.0%	17.7%
28,118	TITUS	3,178	525	1,071	1,291	291	Bentsen	16.5%	33.7%	40.6%	9.2%
104,010	TOM GREEN	2,534	1,016	844	395	279	V. Morales	40.1%	33.3%	15.6%	11.0%
812,280	TRAVIS	44,163	10,065	27,601	5,300	1,197	Kirk	22.8%	62.5%	12.0%	2.7%
13,779	TRINITY	2,815	553	251	1,708	303	Bentsen	19.6%	8.9%	60.7%	10.8%
20,871	TYLER	2,431	446	303	1,405	277	Bentsen	18.3%	12.5%	57.8%	11.4%
35,291	UPSHUR	5,853	1,262	1,320	2,633	638	Bentsen	21.6%	22.6%	45.0%	10.9%
3,404	UPTON	377	96	84	138	59	Bentsen	25.5%	22.3%	36.6%	15.6%
25,926	UVALDE	4,414	2,315	708	874	517	V. Morales	52.4%	16.0%	19.8%	11.7%
44,856	VAL VERDE	2,232	1,461	364	293	114	V. Morales	65.5%	16.3%	13.1%	5.1%
48,140	VAN ZANDT	3,402	1,002	1,277	965	158	Kirk	29.5%	37.5%	28.4%	4.6%
84,088	VICTORIA	5,704	2,438	1,291	1,462	513	V. Morales	42.7%	22.6%	25.6%	9.0%
61,758	WALKER	1,395	334	297	685	79	Bentsen	23.9%	21.3%	49.1%	5.7%
32,663	WALLER	1,636	263	516	719	138	Bentsen	16.1%	31.5%	43.9%	8.4%
10,909	WARD	2,449	921	374	752	402	V. Morales	37.6%	15.3%	30.7%	16.4%
30,373	WASHINGTON	694	117	139	405	33	Bentsen	16.9%	20.0%	58.4%	4.8%
193,117	WEBB	27,927	15,638	7,347	3,204	1,738	V. Morales	56.0%	26.3%	11.5%	6.2%
41,188	WHARTON	3,084	670	319	1,850	245	Bentsen	21.7%	10.3%	60.0%	7.9%
5,284	WHEELER	698	197	78	277	146	Bentsen	28.2%	11.2%	39.7%	20.9%
131,664	WICHITA	2,682	799	845	884	154	Bentsen	29.8%	31.5%	33.0%	5.7%
14,676	WILBARGER	1,390	314	222	637	217	Bentsen	22.6%	16.0%	45.8%	15.6%
20,082	WILLACY	3,257	1,756	392	815	294	V. Morales	53.9%	12.0%	25.0%	9.0%
249,967	WILLIAMSON	6,196	1,512	3,205	1,229	250	Kirk	24.4%	51.7%	19.8%	4.0%
32,408	WILSON	4,188	1,924	1,094	727	443	V. Morales	45.9%	26.1%	17.4%	10.6%
7,173	WINKLER	247	87	35	87	38		35.2%	14.2%	35.2%	15.4%
48,793	WISE	1,918	662	704	447	105	Kirk	34.5%	36.7%	23.3%	5.5%
36,752	WOOD	2,240	537	799	753	151	Kirk	24.0%	35.7%	33.6%	6.7%
7,322	YOAKUM	312	113	45	126	28	Bentsen	36.2%	14.4%	40.4%	9.0%
17,943	YOUNG	1,458	388	377	566	127	Bentsen	26.6%	25.9%	38.8%	8.7%
12,182	ZAPATA	2,400	1,410	588	158	244	V. Morales	58.8%	24.5%	6.6%	10.2%
11,600	ZAVALA	2,516	1,820	255	184	257	V. Morales	72.3%	10.1%	7.3%	10.2%
20,851,820	TOTAL	954,655	317,048	316,052	255,501	66,054	V. Morales	33.2%	33.1%	26.8%	6.9%

TEXAS DEMOCRATIC PRIMARY RUNOFF

SENATOR 2002

2000 Census Population	County	Total Vote	Kirk	V. Morales	Winner	Percentage of Total Vote	
						Kirk	V. Morales
55,109	ANDERSON	2,017	1,045	972	Kirk	51.8%	48.2%
13,004	ANDREWS	675	372	303	Kirk	55.1%	44.9%
80,130	ANGELINA	2,091	1,392	699	Kirk	66.6%	33.4%
22,497	ARANSAS	215	145	70	Kirk	67.4%	32.6%
8,854	ARCHER	116	56	60	V. Morales	48.3%	51.7%
2,148	ARMSTRONG	21	15	6	Kirk	71.4%	28.6%
38,628	ATASCOSA	1,262	229	1,033	V. Morales	18.1%	81.9%
23,590	AUSTIN	187	134	53	Kirk	71.7%	28.3%
6,594	BAILEY	53	36	17	Kirk	67.9%	32.1%
17,645	BANDERA	140	83	57	Kirk	59.3%	40.7%
57,733	BASTROP	2,023	1,262	761	Kirk	62.4%	37.6%
4,093	BAYLOR	49	24	25	V. Morales	49.0%	51.0%
32,359	BEE	2,115	619	1,496	V. Morales	29.3%	70.7%
237,974	BELL	2,429	1,956	473	Kirk	80.5%	19.5%
1,392,931	BEXAR	21,894	11,978	9,916	Kirk	54.7%	45.3%
8,418	BLANCO	127	85	42	Kirk	66.9%	33.1%
729	BORDEN	96	53	43	Kirk	55.2%	44.8%
17,204	BOSQUE	557	264	293	V. Morales	47.4%	52.6%
89,306	BOWIE	3,048	2,480	568	Kirk	81.4%	18.6%
241,767	BRAZORIA	2,387	1,556	831	Kirk	65.2%	34.8%
152,415	BRAZOS	1,882	1,062	820	Kirk	56.4%	43.6%
8,866	BREWSTER	222	98	124	V. Morales	44.1%	55.9%
1,790	BRISCOE	177	91	86	Kirk	51.4%	48.6%
7,976	BROOKS	2,369	270	2,099	V. Morales	11.4%	88.6%
37,674	BROWN	462	246	216	Kirk	53.2%	46.8%
16,470	BURLESON	374	249	125	Kirk	66.6%	33.4%
34,147	BURNET	508	332	176	Kirk	65.4%	34.6%
32,194	CALDWELL	1,392	696	696		50.0%	50.0%
20,647	CALHOUN	411	182	229	V. Morales	44.3%	55.7%
12,905	CALLAHAN	386	197	189	Kirk	51.0%	49.0%
335,227	CAMERON	12,534	3,803	8,731	V. Morales	30.3%	69.7%
11,549	CAMP	494	387	107	Kirk	78.3%	21.7%
6,516	CARSON	97	54	43	Kirk	55.7%	44.3%
30,438	CASS	2,596	1,522	1,074	Kirk	58.6%	41.4%
8,285	CASTRO	52	42	10	Kirk	80.8%	19.2%
26,031	CHAMBERS	392	218	174	Kirk	55.6%	44.4%
46,659	CHEROKEE	2,878	1,598	1,280	Kirk	55.5%	44.5%
7,688	CHILDRESS	246	129	117	Kirk	52.4%	47.6%
11,006	CLAY	258	111	147	V. Morales	43.0%	57.0%
3,730	COCHRAN	79	42	37	Kirk	53.2%	46.8%
3,864	COKE	46	32	14	Kirk	69.6%	30.4%
9,235	COLEMAN	1,084	501	583	V. Morales	46.2%	53.8%
491,675	COLLIN	6,127	4,269	1,858	Kirk	69.7%	30.3%
3,206	COLLINGSWORTH	41	20	21	V. Morales	48.8%	51.2%
20,390	COLORADO	344	183	161	Kirk	53.2%	46.8%
78,021	COMAL	585	363	222	Kirk	62.1%	37.9%
14,026	COMANCHE	1,343	648	695	V. Morales	48.3%	51.7%
3,966	CONCHO	63	45	18	Kirk	71.4%	28.6%
36,363	COOKE	411	218	193	Kirk	53.0%	47.0%
74,978	CORYELL	327	230	97	Kirk	70.3%	29.7%
1,904	COTTLE	453	226	227	V. Morales	49.9%	50.1%
3,996	CRANE	172	73	99	V. Morales	42.4%	57.6%
4,099	CROCKETT	67	35	32	Kirk	52.2%	47.8%
7,072	CROSBY	615	331	284	Kirk	53.8%	46.2%
2,975	CULBERSON	22	5	17	V. Morales	22.7%	77.3%
6,222	DALLAM	28	6	22	V. Morales	21.4%	78.6%
2,218,899	DALLAS	92,408	69,927	22,481	Kirk	75.7%	24.3%
14,985	DAWSON	339	208	131	Kirk	61.4%	38.6%
18,561	DEAF SMITH	71	31	40	V. Morales	43.7%	56.3%
5,327	DELTA	677	310	367	V. Morales	45.8%	54.2%

TEXAS DEMOCRATIC PRIMARY RUNOFF

SENATOR 2002

2000 Census Population	County	Total Vote	Kirk	V. Morales	Winner	Percentage of Total Vote	
						Kirk	V. Morales
432,976	DENTON	5,029	3,547	1,482	Kirk	70.5%	29.5%
20,013	DE WITT	180	116	64	Kirk	64.4%	35.6%
2,762	DICKENS	101	47	54	V. Morales	46.5%	53.5%
10,248	DIMMIT	3,132	632	2,500	V. Morales	20.2%	79.8%
3,828	DONLEY	65	32	33	V. Morales	49.2%	50.8%
13,120	DUVAL	2,009	914	1,095	V. Morales	45.5%	54.5%
18,297	EASTLAND	279	133	146	V. Morales	47.7%	52.3%
121,123	ECTOR	674	532	142	Kirk	78.9%	21.1%
2,162	EDWARDS	398	207	191	Kirk	52.0%	48.0%
111,360	ELLIS	1,807	1,144	663	Kirk	63.3%	36.7%
679,622	EL PASO	20,023	8,809	11,214	V. Morales	44.0%	56.0%
33,001	ERATH	446	239	207	Kirk	53.6%	46.4%
18,576	FALLS	998	648	350	Kirk	64.9%	35.1%
31,242	FANNIN	834	421	413	Kirk	50.5%	49.5%
21,804	FAYETTE	1,377	793	584	Kirk	57.6%	42.4%
4,344	FISHER	670	334	336	V. Morales	49.9%	50.1%
7,771	FLOYD	96	66	30	Kirk	68.8%	31.3%
1,622	FOARD	23	13	10	Kirk	56.5%	43.5%
354,452	FORT BEND	7,003	6,097	906	Kirk	87.1%	12.9%
9,458	FRANKLIN	733	393	340	Kirk	53.6%	46.4%
17,867	FREESTONE	2,231	1,181	1,050	Kirk	52.9%	47.1%
16,252	FRIO	2,703	954	1,749	V. Morales	35.3%	64.7%
14,467	GAINES	466	220	246	V. Morales	47.2%	52.8%
250,158	GALVESTON	9,101	5,877	3,224	Kirk	64.6%	35.4%
4,872	GARZA	27	8	19	V. Morales	29.6%	70.4%
20,814	GILLESPIE	143	118	25	Kirk	82.5%	17.5%
1,406	GLASSCOCK	6	4	2	Kirk	66.7%	33.3%
6,928	GOLIAD	693	274	419	V. Morales	39.5%	60.5%
18,628	GONZALES	850	552	298	Kirk	64.9%	35.1%
22,744	GRAY	114	45	69	V. Morales	39.5%	60.5%
110,595	GRAYSON	1,613	1,091	522	Kirk	67.6%	32.4%
111,379	GREGG	3,196	2,868	328	Kirk	89.7%	10.3%
23,552	GRIMES	660	341	319	Kirk	51.7%	48.3%
89,023	GUADALUPE	723	424	299	Kirk	58.6%	41.4%
36,602	HALE	186	113	73	Kirk	60.8%	39.2%
3,782	HALL	727	391	336	Kirk	53.8%	46.2%
8,229	HAMILTON	572	288	284	Kirk	50.3%	49.7%
5,369	HANSFORD						
4,724	HARDEMAN	759	358	401	V. Morales	47.2%	52.8%
48,073	HARDIN	1,358	604	754	V. Morales	44.5%	55.5%
3,400,578	HARRIS	63,598	49,133	14,465	Kirk	77.3%	22.7%
62,110	HARRISON	2,037	1,623	414	Kirk	79.7%	20.3%
5,537	HARTLEY	42	22	20	Kirk	52.4%	47.6%
6,093	HASKELL	237	118	119	V. Morales	49.8%	50.2%
97,589	HAYS	2,524	1,401	1,123	Kirk	55.5%	44.5%
3,351	HEMPHILL	18	12	6	Kirk	66.7%	33.3%
73,277	HENDERSON	3,728	1,734	1,994	V. Morales	46.5%	53.5%
569,463	HIDALGO	40,187	15,562	24,625	V. Morales	38.7%	61.3%
32,321	HILL	761	349	412	V. Morales	45.9%	54.1%
22,716	HOCKLEY	34	14	20	V. Morales	41.2%	58.8%
41,100	HOOD	521	262	259	Kirk	50.3%	49.7%
31,960	HOPKINS	1,530	862	668	Kirk	56.3%	43.7%
23,185	HOUSTON	1,109	488	621	V. Morales	44.0%	56.0%
33,627	HOWARD	256	161	95	Kirk	62.9%	37.1%
3,344	HUDSPETH	213	95	118	V. Morales	44.6%	55.4%
76,596	HUNT	1,666	1,071	595	Kirk	64.3%	35.7%
23,857	HUTCHINSON	85	40	45	V. Morales	47.1%	52.9%
1,771	IRION	52	37	15	Kirk	71.2%	28.8%
8,763	JACK	225	106	119	V. Morales	47.1%	52.9%
14,391	JACKSON	208	107	101	Kirk	51.4%	48.6%

TEXAS DEMOCRATIC PRIMARY RUNOFF

SENATOR 2002

2000 Census Population	County	Total Vote	Kirk	V. Morales	Winner	Percentage of Total Vote	
						Kirk	V. Morales
35,604	JASPER	807	565	242	Kirk	70.0%	30.0%
2,207	JEFF DAVIS	593	250	343	V. Morales	42.2%	57.8%
252,051	JEFFERSON	9,521	7,836	1,685	Kirk	82.3%	17.7%
5,281	JIM HOGG	2,442	369	2,073	V. Morales	15.1%	84.9%
39,326	JIM WELLS	7,008	2,095	4,913	V. Morales	29.9%	70.1%
126,811	JOHNSON	1,117	532	585	V. Morales	47.6%	52.4%
20,785	JONES	1,562	799	763	Kirk	51.2%	48.8%
15,446	KARNES	2,210	1,257	953	Kirk	56.9%	43.1%
71,313	KAUFMAN	1,916	1,021	895	Kirk	53.3%	46.7%
23,743	KENDALL	169	119	50	Kirk	70.4%	29.6%
414	KENEDY	20	12	8	Kirk	60.0%	40.0%
859	KENT	265	129	136	V. Morales	48.7%	51.3%
43,653	KERR	390	286	104	Kirk	73.3%	26.7%
4,468	KIMBLE	61	34	27	Kirk	55.7%	44.3%
356	KING	117	62	55	Kirk	53.0%	47.0%
3,379	KINNEY	854	395	459	V. Morales	46.3%	53.7%
31,549	KLEBERG	2,092	682	1,410	V. Morales	32.6%	67.4%
4,253	KNOX	132	56	76	V. Morales	42.4%	57.6%
48,499	LAMAR	1,705	963	742	Kirk	56.5%	43.5%
14,709	LAMB	1,317	752	565	Kirk	57.1%	42.9%
17,762	LAMPASAS	150	92	58	Kirk	61.3%	38.7%
5,866	LA SALLE	1,511	374	1,137	V. Morales	24.8%	75.2%
19,210	LAVACA	445	265	180	Kirk	59.6%	40.4%
15,657	LEE	450	282	168	Kirk	62.7%	37.3%
15,335	LEON	196	110	86	Kirk	56.1%	43.9%
70,154	LIBERTY	3,704	2,048	1,656	Kirk	55.3%	44.7%
22,051	LIMESTONE	954	680	274	Kirk	71.3%	28.7%
3,057	LIPSCOMB	170	83	87	V. Morales	48.8%	51.2%
12,309	LIVE OAK	320	205	115	Kirk	64.1%	35.9%
17,044	LLANO	296	187	109	Kirk	63.2%	36.8%
67	LOVING	18	7	11	V. Morales	38.9%	61.1%
242,628	LUBBOCK	1,408	840	568	Kirk	59.7%	40.3%
6,550	LYNN	42	26	16	Kirk	61.9%	38.1%
8,205	MCCULLOCH	362	155	207	V. Morales	42.8%	57.2%
213,517	MCLENNAN	4,151	3,328	823	Kirk	80.2%	19.8%
851	MCMULLEN	81	29	52	V. Morales	35.8%	64.2%
12,940	MADISON	100	52	48	Kirk	52.0%	48.0%
10,941	MARION	333	257	76	Kirk	77.2%	22.8%
4,746	MARTIN	251	75	176	V. Morales	29.9%	70.1%
3,738	MASON	28	19	9	Kirk	67.9%	32.1%
37,957	MATAGORDA	778	474	304	Kirk	60.9%	39.1%
47,297	MAVERICK	6,451	1,035	5,416	V. Morales	16.0%	84.0%
39,304	MEDINA	1,879	1,067	812	Kirk	56.8%	43.2%
2,360	MENARD	21	7	14	V. Morales	33.3%	66.7%
116,009	MIDLAND	426	318	108	Kirk	74.6%	25.4%
24,238	MILAM	558	302	256	Kirk	54.1%	45.9%
5,151	MILLS	1,068	532	536	V. Morales	49.8%	50.2%
9,698	MITCHELL	128	67	61	Kirk	52.3%	47.7%
19,117	MONTAGUE	336	153	183	V. Morales	45.5%	54.5%
293,768	MONTGOMERY	1,137	728	409	Kirk	64.0%	36.0%
20,121	MOORE	20	13	7	Kirk	65.0%	35.0%
13,048	MORRIS	652	459	193	Kirk	70.4%	29.6%
1,426	MOTLEY	166	95	71	Kirk	57.2%	42.8%
59,203	NACOGDOCHES	551	479	72	Kirk	86.9%	13.1%
45,124	NAVARRO	2,809	1,544	1,265	Kirk	55.0%	45.0%
15,072	NEWTON	1,570	847	723	Kirk	53.9%	46.1%
15,802	NOLAN	283	151	132	Kirk	53.4%	46.6%
313,645	NUECES	25,597	11,734	13,863	V. Morales	45.8%	54.2%
9,006	OCHILTREE						
2,185	OLDHAM	161	101	60	Kirk	62.7%	37.3%

TEXAS DEMOCRATIC PRIMARY RUNOFF
SENATOR 2002

2000 Census Population	County	Total Vote	Kirk	V. Morales	Winner	Percentage of Total Vote Kirk	V. Morales
84,966	ORANGE	4,444	2,300	2,144	Kirk	51.8%	48.2%
27,026	PALO PINTO	1,948	854	1,094	V. Morales	43.8%	56.2%
22,756	PANOLA	1,574	787	787		50.0%	50.0%
88,495	PARKER	1,135	526	609	V. Morales	46.3%	53.7%
10,016	PARMER	33	23	10	Kirk	69.7%	30.3%
16,809	PECOS	861	195	666	V. Morales	22.6%	77.4%
41,133	POLK	1,632	865	767	Kirk	53.0%	47.0%
113,546	POTTER	564	364	200	Kirk	64.5%	35.5%
7,304	PRESIDIO	724	531	193	Kirk	73.3%	26.7%
9,139	RAINS	1,052	552	500	Kirk	52.5%	47.5%
104,312	RANDALL	326	189	137	Kirk	58.0%	42.0%
3,326	REAGAN	8	2	6	V. Morales	25.0%	75.0%
3,047	REAL	22	11	11		50.0%	50.0%
14,314	RED RIVER	1,242	696	546	Kirk	56.0%	44.0%
13,137	REEVES	615	231	384	V. Morales	37.6%	62.4%
7,828	REFUGIO	502	227	275	V. Morales	45.2%	54.8%
887	ROBERTS						
16,000	ROBERTSON	3,470	2,094	1,376	Kirk	60.3%	39.7%
43,080	ROCKWALL	578	327	251	Kirk	56.6%	43.4%
11,495	RUNNELS	564	279	285	V. Morales	49.5%	50.5%
47,372	RUSK	1,053	687	366	Kirk	65.2%	34.8%
10,469	SABINE	174	102	72	Kirk	58.6%	41.4%
8,946	SAN AUGUSTINE	1,909	1,085	824	Kirk	56.8%	43.2%
22,246	SAN JACINTO	2,150	1,125	1,025	Kirk	52.3%	47.7%
67,138	SAN PATRICIO	2,534	1,182	1,352	V. Morales	46.6%	53.4%
6,186	SAN SABA	93	48	45	Kirk	51.6%	48.4%
2,935	SCHLEICHER	39	23	16	Kirk	59.0%	41.0%
16,361	SCURRY	76	54	22	Kirk	71.1%	28.9%
3,302	SHACKELFORD	706	111	595	V. Morales	15.7%	84.3%
25,224	SHELBY	405	255	150	Kirk	63.0%	37.0%
3,186	SHERMAN	25	18	7	Kirk	72.0%	28.0%
174,706	SMITH	3,218	2,812	406	Kirk	87.4%	12.6%
6,809	SOMERVELL	523	211	312	V. Morales	40.3%	59.7%
53,597	STARR	5,452	1,714	3,738	V. Morales	31.4%	68.6%
9,674	STEPHENS	683	346	337	Kirk	50.7%	49.3%
1,393	STERLING	4	2	2		50.0%	50.0%
1,693	STONEWALL	239	122	117	Kirk	51.0%	49.0%
4,077	SUTTON	32	6	26	V. Morales	18.8%	81.3%
8,378	SWISHER	151	101	50	Kirk	66.9%	33.1%
1,446,219	TARRANT	39,094	28,707	10,387	Kirk	73.4%	26.6%
126,555	TAYLOR	789	466	323	Kirk	59.1%	40.9%
1,081	TERRELL	501	191	310	V. Morales	38.1%	61.9%
12,761	TERRY	90	62	28	Kirk	68.9%	31.1%
1,850	THROCKMORTON	55	19	36	V. Morales	34.5%	65.5%
28,118	TITUS	963	610	353	Kirk	63.3%	36.7%
104,010	TOM GREEN	714	441	273	Kirk	61.8%	38.2%
812,280	TRAVIS	33,583	25,764	7,819	Kirk	76.7%	23.3%
13,779	TRINITY	982	456	526	V. Morales	46.4%	53.6%
20,871	TYLER	413	244	169	Kirk	59.1%	40.9%
35,291	UPSHUR	5,129	2,860	2,269	Kirk	55.8%	44.2%
3,404	UPTON	52	30	22	Kirk	57.7%	42.3%
25,926	UVALDE	1,508	376	1,132	V. Morales	24.9%	75.1%
44,856	VAL VERDE	399	80	319	V. Morales	20.1%	79.9%
48,140	VAN ZANDT	1,342	548	794	V. Morales	40.8%	59.2%
84,088	VICTORIA	1,539	868	671	Kirk	56.4%	43.6%
61,758	WALKER	588	401	187	Kirk	68.2%	31.8%
32,663	WALLER	551	408	143	Kirk	74.0%	26.0%
10,909	WARD	2,100	948	1,152	V. Morales	45.1%	54.9%
30,373	WASHINGTON	344	233	111	Kirk	67.7%	32.3%
193,117	WEBB	11,135	3,704	7,431	V. Morales	33.3%	66.7%

TEXAS DEMOCRATIC PRIMARY RUNOFF

SENATOR 2002

2000 Census Population	County	Total Vote	Kirk	V. Morales	Winner	Percentage of Total Vote	
						Kirk	V. Morales
41,188	WHARTON	551	302	249	Kirk	54.8%	45.2%
5,284	WHEELER	433	224	209	Kirk	51.7%	48.3%
131,664	WICHITA	1,062	668	394	Kirk	62.9%	37.1%
14,676	WILBARGER	93	54	39	Kirk	58.1%	41.9%
20,082	WILLACY	3,312	963	2,349	V. Morales	29.1%	70.9%
249,967	WILLIAMSON	3,872	2,816	1,056	Kirk	72.7%	27.3%
32,408	WILSON	1,863	543	1,320	V. Morales	29.1%	70.9%
7,173	WINKLER	15	12	3	Kirk	80.0%	20.0%
48,793	WISE	658	279	379	V. Morales	42.4%	57.6%
36,752	WOOD	1,623	821	802	Kirk	50.6%	49.4%
7,322	YOAKUM	175	97	78	Kirk	55.4%	44.6%
17,943	YOUNG	1,139	549	590	V. Morales	48.2%	51.8%
12,182	ZAPATA	933	367	566	V. Morales	39.3%	60.7%
11,600	ZAVALA	2,512	477	2,035	V. Morales	19.0%	81.0%
20,851,820	TOTAL	620,301	370,878	249,423	Kirk	59.8%	40.2%

UTAH

GOVERNOR
Michael O. Leavitt (R). Reelected 2000 to a four-year term. Previously elected 1996, 1992.

SENATORS (2 Republicans)
Robert F. Bennett (R). Reelected 1998 to a six-year term. Previously elected 1992.

Orrin G. Hatch (R). Reelected 2000 to a six-year term. Previously elected 1994, 1988, 1982, 1976.

REPRESENTATIVES (2 Republicans, 1 Democrat)
1. Rob Bishop (R)   2. Jim Matheson (D)   3. Chris Cannon (R)

POSTWAR VOTE FOR PRESIDENT

Year	Total Vote	Republican		Democratic		Other Vote	Plurality	Percentage			
		Vote	Candidate	Vote	Candidate			Total Vote		Major Vote	
								Rep.	Dem.	Rep.	Dem.
2000**	770,754	515,096	Bush, George W.	203,053	Gore, Al	52,605	312,043 R	66.8%	26.3%	71.7%	28.3%
1996**	665,629	361,911	Dole, Bob	221,633	Clinton, Bill	82,085	140,278 R	54.4%	33.3%	62.0%	38.0%
1992**	743,999	322,632	Bush, George	183,429	Clinton, Bill	237,938	119,232 R	43.4%	24.7%	63.8%	36.2%
1988	647,008	428,442	Bush, George	207,343	Dukakis, Michael S.	11,223	221,099 R	66.2%	32.0%	67.4%	32.6%
1984	629,656	469,105	Reagan, Ronald	155,369	Mondale, Walter F.	5,182	313,736 R	74.5%	24.7%	75.1%	24.9%
1980**	604,222	439,687	Reagan, Ronald	124,266	Carter, Jimmy	40,269	315,421 R	72.8%	20.6%	78.0%	22.0%
1976	541,198	337,908	Ford, Gerald R.	182,110	Carter, Jimmy	21,180	155,798 R	62.4%	33.6%	65.0%	35.0%
1972	478,476	323,643	Nixon, Richard M.	126,284	McGovern, George S.	28,549	197,359 R	67.6%	26.4%	71.9%	28.1%
1968	422,568	238,728	Nixon, Richard M.	156,665	Humphrey, Hubert H.	27,175	82,063 R	56.5%	37.1%	60.4%	39.6%
1964	401,413	181,785	Goldwater, Barry M.	219,628	Johnson, Lyndon B.		37,843 D	45.3%	54.7%	45.3%	54.7%
1960	374,709	205,361	Nixon, Richard M.	169,248	Kennedy, John F.	100	36,113 R	54.8%	45.2%	54.8%	45.2%
1956	333,995	215,631	Eisenhower, Dwight D.	118,364	Stevenson, Adlai E.		97,267 R	64.6%	35.4%	64.6%	35.4%
1952	329,554	194,190	Eisenhower, Dwight D.	135,364	Stevenson, Adlai E.		58,826 R	58.9%	41.1%	58.9%	41.1%
1948	276,306	124,402	Dewey, Thomas E.	149,151	Truman, Harry S.	2,753	24,749 D	45.0%	54.0%	45.5%	54.5%

In 2000 the other vote column includes 35,850 votes cast for Green (Nader). In 1996 the other vote column includes 66,461 votes cast for Perot. In 1992 the other vote column includes 203,400 votes cast for Perot who came in second. In 1980 the other vote column includes 30,284 votes for Independent (Anderson).

UTAH

POSTWAR VOTE FOR GOVERNOR

Year	Total Vote	Republican Vote	Republican Candidate	Democratic Vote	Democratic Candidate	Other Vote	Rep.-Dem. Plurality	Total Vote Rep.	Total Vote Dem.	Major Vote Rep.	Major Vote Dem.
2000	761,806	424,837	Leavitt, Michael O.	321,979	Orton, Bill	14,990	102,858 R	55.8%	42.3%	56.9%	43.1%
1996	671,879	503,693	Leavitt, Michael O.	156,616	Bradley, Jim	11,570	347,077 R	75.0%	23.3%	76.3%	23.7%
1992**	762,549	321,713	Leavitt, Michael O.	177,181	Hanson, Stewart	263,655	65,960 R	42.2%	23.2%	64.5%	35.5%
1988**	649,114	260,462	Bangerter, Norman H.	249,321	Wilson, Ted	139,331	11,141 R	40.1%	38.4%	51.1%	48.9%
1984	629,619	351,792	Bangerter, Norman H.	275,669	Owens, Wayne	2,158	76,123 R	55.9%	43.8%	56.1%	43.9%
1980	600,019	266,578	Wright, Bob	330,974	Matheson, Scott M.	2,467	64,396 D	44.4%	55.2%	44.6%	55.4%
1976	539,649	248,027	Romney, Vernon B.	280,706	Matheson, Scott M.	10,916	32,679 D	46.0%	52.0%	46.9%	53.1%
1972	476,447	144,449	Strike, Nicholas L.	331,998	Rampton, Calvin L.		187,549 D	30.3%	69.7%	30.3%	69.7%
1968	421,012	131,729	Buehner, Carl W.	289,283	Rampton, Calvin L.		157,554 D	31.3%	68.7%	31.3%	68.7%
1964	398,256	171,300	Melich, Mitchell	226,956	Rampton, Calvin L.		55,656 D	43.0%	57.0%	43.0%	57.0%
1960	371,489	195,634	Clyde, George D.	175,855	Barlocker, W. A.		19,779 R	52.7%	47.3%	52.7%	47.3%
1956**	332,889	127,164	Clyde, George D.	111,297	Romney, L. C.	94,428	15,867 R	38.2%	33.4%	53.3%	46.7%
1952	327,704	180,516	Lee, J. Bracken	147,188	Glade, Earl J.		33,328 R	55.1%	44.9%	55.1%	44.9%
1948	275,067	151,253	Lee, J. Bracken	123,814	Maw, Herbert B.		27,439 R	55.0%	45.0%	55.0%	45.0%

In 1992 other vote was 255,753 Independent (Cook); 3,593 Populist (Gum); 1,492 American (Van Horn); 1,158 Socialist Workers (Garcia); 917 Independent (Metzger-Agin); 729 Independent American (Richins) and 13 scattered; Cook finished second. In 1988 other vote was 136,651 Independent (Cook); 1,661 Libertarian (Burton) and 1,019 American (Pedersen). In 1956 other vote was Independent (Lee).

POSTWAR VOTE FOR SENATOR

Year	Total Vote	Republican Vote	Republican Candidate	Democratic Vote	Democratic Candidate	Other Vote	Rep.-Dem. Plurality	Total Vote Rep.	Total Vote Dem.	Major Vote Rep.	Major Vote Dem.
2000	769,704	504,803	Hatch, Orrin G.	242,569	Howell, Scott N.	22,332	262,234 R	65.6%	31.5%	67.5%	32.5%
1998	494,909	316,652	Bennett, Robert F.	163,172	Leckman, Scott	15,085	153,480 R	64.0%	33.0%	66.0%	34.0%
1994	519,323	357,297	Hatch, Orrin G.	146,938	Shea, Patrick A.	15,088	210,359 R	68.8%	28.3%	70.9%	29.1%
1992	758,479	420,069	Bennett, Robert F.	301,228	Owens, Wayne	37,182	118,841 R	55.4%	39.7%	58.2%	41.8%
1988	640,702	430,089	Hatch, Orrin G.	203,364	Moss, Brian H.	7,249	226,725 R	67.1%	31.7%	67.9%	32.1%
1986	435,111	314,608	Garn, E. J.	115,523	Oliver, Craig	4,980	199,085 R	72.3%	26.6%	73.1%	26.9%
1982	530,802	309,332	Hatch, Orrin G.	219,482	Wilson, Ted	1,988	89,850 R	58.3%	41.3%	58.5%	41.5%
1980	594,298	437,675	Garn, E. J.	151,454	Berman, Dan	5,169	286,221 R	73.6%	25.5%	74.3%	25.7%
1976	540,108	290,221	Hatch, Orrin G.	241,948	Moss, Frank E.	7,939	48,273 R	53.7%	44.8%	54.5%	45.5%
1974	420,642	210,299	Garn, E. J.	185,377	Owens, Wayne	24,966	24,922 R	50.0%	44.1%	53.1%	46.9%
1970	374,303	159,004	Burton, Laurence J.	210,207	Moss, Frank E.	5,092	51,203 D	42.5%	56.2%	43.1%	56.9%
1968	419,262	225,075	Bennett, Wallace F.	192,168	Weilenmann, Milton	2,019	32,907 R	53.7%	45.8%	53.9%	46.1%
1964	397,384	169,562	Wilkinson, Ernest L.	227,822	Moss, Frank E.		58,260 D	42.7%	57.3%	42.7%	57.3%
1962	318,411	166,755	Bennett, Wallace F.	151,656	King, David S.		15,099 R	52.4%	47.6%	52.4%	47.6%
1958**	291,311	101,471	Watkins, Arthur V.	112,827	Moss, Frank E.	77,013	11,356 D	34.8%	38.7%	47.4%	52.6%
1956	330,381	178,261	Bennett, Wallace F.	152,120	Hopkin, Alonzo F.		26,141 R	54.0%	46.0%	54.0%	46.0%
1952	327,033	177,435	Watkins, Arthur V.	149,598	Granger, Walter K.		27,837 R	54.3%	45.7%	54.3%	45.7%
1950	264,440	142,427	Bennett, Wallace F.	121,198	Thomas, Elbert D.	815	21,229 R	53.9%	45.8%	54.0%	46.0%
1946	197,399	101,142	Watkins, Arthur V.	96,257	Murdock, Abe		4,885 R	51.2%	48.8%	51.2%	48.8%

In 1958 other vote was Independent (Lee).

UTAH

Congressional districts first established for elections held in 2002
3 members

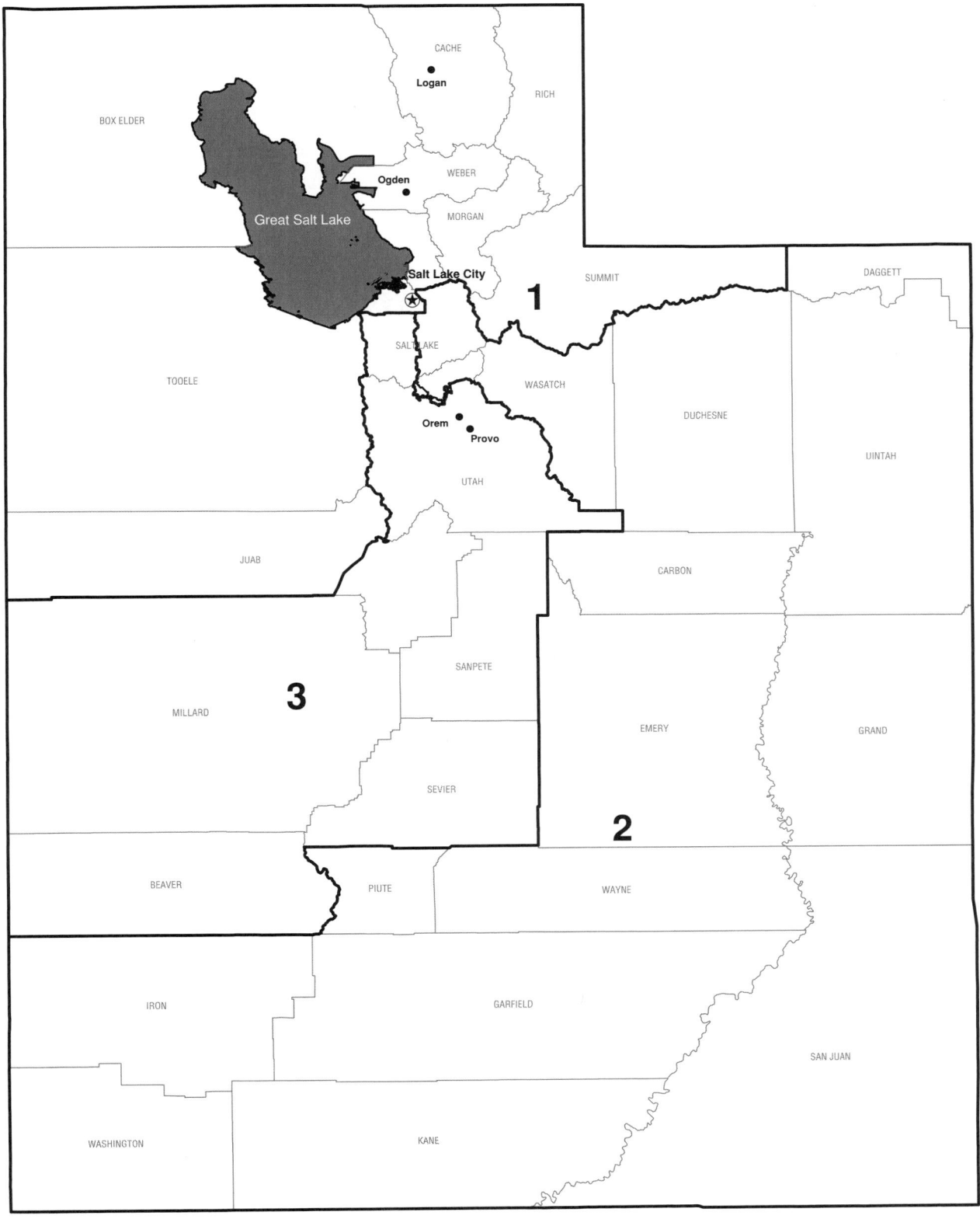

UTAH
HOUSE OF REPRESENTATIVES

CD	Year	Total Vote	Republican Vote	Candidate	Democratic Vote	Candidate	Other Vote	Rep.-Dem. Plurality	Total Vote Rep.	Dem.	Major Vote Rep.	Dem.
1	2002	179,412	109,265	Bishop, Rob	66,104	Thomas, Dave	4,043	43,161 R	60.9%	36.8%	62.3%	37.7%
2	2002	224,098	109,123	Swallow, John	110,764	Matheson, Jim*	4,211	1,641 D	48.7%	49.4%	49.6%	50.4%
3	2002	153,643	103,598	Cannon, Chris*	44,533	Woodside, Nancy Jane	5,512	59,065 R	67.4%	29.0%	69.9%	30.1%
Total	2002	557,153	321,986		221,401		13,766	100,585 R	57.8%	39.7%	59.3%	40.7%

An asterisk (*) denotes incumbent.

UTAH
GENERAL AND PRIMARY ELECTIONS

2002 GENERAL ELECTIONS

House   Other vote was:

CD 1   4,027 Green (Craig Axford); 8 write-in (Cody Judy); 7 write-in (Charles Johnston); 1 write-in (Susan Howard).
CD 2   2,589 Green (Patrick Diehl); 1,622 Libertarian (Ron Copier).
CD 3   5,511 Libertarian (Kitty K. Burton); 1 write-in (John William Maurin).

2002 PRIMARY ELECTIONS

Primary   June 25, 2002   **Registration** (as of June 25, 2002)   1,070,571 In process of instituting registration by party

Primary Type   Any registered voter could participate in the Democratic primary. Only registered Republicans could vote in the Republican primary. (As of July 8, 2003, there were 289,722 registered Republicans in Utah, 74,349 registered Democrats.)

Note: An asterisk (*) denotes incumbent. Candidates in Utah are usually nominated by convention. It is up to each party to determine the percentage of the convention vote that is needed to force a primary.

REPUBLICAN PRIMARIES			DEMOCRATIC PRIMARIES		
Congressional District 1	Rob Bishop Kevin S. Garn TOTAL	25,280 16,957 42,237	59.9% 40.1%	Dave Thomas Donald Dunn TOTAL	7,294 6,665 13,959	52.3% 47.7%
Congressional District 2	John Swallow Tim Bridgewater TOTAL	22,689 20,705 43,394	52.3% 47.7%	Jim Matheson*	Unopposed	
Congressional Diastrict 3	Chris Cannon*	Nominated by convention		Nancy Jane Woodside	Nominated by convention	

VERMONT

GOVERNOR

Jim Douglas (R). Elected January 2003 by the State Legislature to a two-year term. Douglas had finished first in the general election but failed to win a majority of the vote as required by Vermont law.

SENATORS (1 Democrat, 1 Independent)

James M. Jeffords (I). Reelected 2000 to a six-year term. Previously elected 1994, 1988. Announced switch in party affiliation from Republican to Independent May 24, 2001, effective at the close of business June 5, 2001.

Patrick J. Leahy (D). Reelected 1998 to a six-year term. Previously elected 1992, 1986, 1980, 1974.

REPRESENTATIVES (1 Independent)

At Large. Bernard Sanders (I)

POSTWAR VOTE FOR PRESIDENT

| | | Republican | | Democratic | | Other | | Percentage | | | |
| | | | | | | | | Total Vote | | Major Vote | |
Year	Total Vote	Vote	Candidate	Vote	Candidate	Vote	Plurality	Rep.	Dem.	Rep.	Dem.
2000**	294,308	119,775	Bush, George W.	149,022	Gore, Al	25,511	29,247 D	40.7%	50.6%	44.6%	55.4%
1996**	258,449	80,352	Dole, Bob	137,894	Clinton, Bill	40,203	57,542 D	31.1%	53.4%	36.8%	63.2%
1992**	289,701	88,122	Bush, George	133,592	Clinton, Bill	67,987	45,470 D	30.4%	46.1%	39.7%	60.3%
1988	243,328	124,331	Bush, George	115,775	Dukakis, Michael S.	3,222	8,556 R	51.1%	47.6%	51.8%	48.2%
1984	234,561	135,865	Reagan, Ronald	95,730	Mondale, Walter F.	2,966	40,135 R	57.9%	40.8%	58.7%	41.3%
1980**	213,299	94,628	Reagan, Ronald	81,952	Carter, Jimmy	36,719	12,676 R	44.4%	38.4%	53.6%	46.4%
1976	187,765	102,085	Ford, Gerald R.	80,954	Carter, Jimmy	4,726	21,131 R	54.4%	43.1%	55.8%	44.2%
1972	186,947	117,149	Nixon, Richard M.	68,174	McGovern, George S.	1,624	48,975 R	62.7%	36.5%	63.2%	36.8%
1968	161,404	85,142	Nixon, Richard M.	70,255	Humphrey, Hubert H.	6,007	14,887 R	52.8%	43.5%	54.8%	45.2%
1964	163,089	54,942	Goldwater, Barry M.	108,127	Johnson, Lyndon B.	20	53,185 D	33.7%	66.3%	33.7%	66.3%
1960	167,324	98,131	Nixon, Richard M.	69,186	Kennedy, John F.	7	28,945 R	58.6%	41.3%	58.6%	41.4%
1956	152,978	110,390	Eisenhower, Dwight D.	42,549	Stevenson, Adlai E.	39	67,841 R	72.2%	27.8%	72.2%	27.8%
1952	153,557	109,717	Eisenhower, Dwight D.	43,355	Stevenson, Adlai E.	485	66,362 R	71.5%	28.2%	71.7%	28.3%
1948	123,382	75,926	Dewey, Thomas E.	45,557	Truman, Harry S.	1,899	30,369 R	61.5%	36.9%	62.5%	37.5%

In 2000 the other vote column includes 20,374 votes cast for Green (Nader). In 1996 the other vote column includes 31,024 votes cast for Perot. In 1992 the other vote column includes 65,991 votes cast for Perot. In 1980 the other vote column includes 31,761 votes for Independent (Anderson).

VERMONT

POSTWAR VOTE FOR GOVERNOR

Year	Total Vote	Republican		Democratic		Other Vote	Rep.-Dem. Plurality	Percentage			
		Vote	Candidate	Vote	Candidate			Total Vote		Major Vote	
								Rep.	Dem.	Rep.	Dem.
2002**	230,161	103,436	Douglas, Jim	97,565	Racine, Doug	29,160	5,871 R	44.9%	42.4%	51.5%	48.5%
2000	293,473	111,359	Dwyer, Ruth	148,059	Dean, Howard B.	34,055	36,700 D	37.9%	50.5%	42.9%	57.1%
1998	218,120	89,726	Dwyer, Ruth	121,425	Dean, Howard B.	6,969	31,699 D	41.1%	55.7%	42.5%	57.5%
1996	254,648	57,161	Gropper, John L.	179,544	Dean, Howard B.	17,943	122,383 D	22.4%	70.5%	24.1%	75.9%
1994	212,046	40,292	Kelley, David F.	145,661	Dean, Howard B.	26,093	105,369 D	19.0%	68.7%	21.7%	78.3%
1992	285,728	65,837	McClaughry, John	213,523	Dean, Howard B.	6,368	147,686 D	23.0%	74.7%	23.6%	76.4%
1990	211,422	109,540	Snelling, Richard A.	97,321	Welch, Peter	4,561	12,219 R	51.8%	46.0%	53.0%	47.0%
1988	243,130	105,319	Bernhardt, Michael	134,594	Kunin, Madeleine M.	3,253	29,275 D	43.3%	55.4%	43.9%	56.1%
1986**	196,716	75,162	Smith, Peter	92,379	Kunin, Madeleine M.	29,175	17,217 D	38.2%	47.0%	44.9%	55.1%
1984	233,753	113,264	Easton, John J.	116,938	Kunin, Madeleine M.	3,551	3,674 D	48.5%	50.0%	49.2%	50.8%
1982	169,251	93,111	Snelling, Richard A.	74,394	Kunin, Madeleine M.	1,746	18,717 R	55.0%	44.0%	55.6%	44.4%
1980	210,381	123,229	Snelling, Richard A.	77,363	Diamond, J. Jerome	9,789	45,866 R	58.6%	36.8%	61.4%	38.6%
1978	124,482	78,181	Snelling, Richard A.	42,482	Granai, Edwin C.	3,819	35,699 R	62.8%	34.1%	64.8%	35.2%
1976	185,929	99,268	Snelling, Richard A.	75,262	Hackel, Stella B.	11,399	24,006 R	53.4%	40.5%	56.9%	43.1%
1974	141,156	53,672	Kennedy, Walter L.	79,842	Salmon, Thomas P.	7,642	26,170 D	38.0%	56.6%	40.2%	59.8%
1972	189,237	82,491	Hackett, Luther F.	104,533	Salmon, Thomas P.	2,213	22,042 D	43.6%	55.2%	44.1%	55.9%
1970	153,528	87,458	Davis, Deane C.	66,028	O'Brien, Leo	42	21,430 R	57.0%	43.0%	57.0%	43.0%
1968	161,089	89,387	Davis, Deane C.	71,656	Daley, John J.	46	17,731 R	55.5%	44.5%	55.5%	44.5%
1966	136,262	57,577	Snelling, Richard A.	78,669	Hoff, Philip H.	16	21,092 D	42.3%	57.7%	42.3%	57.7%
1964	164,199	57,576	Foote, Ralph A.	106,611	Hoff, Philip H.	12	49,035 D	35.1%	64.9%	35.1%	64.9%
1962	121,422	60,035	Keyser, F. Ray	61,383	Hoff, Philip H.	4	1,348 D	49.4%	50.6%	49.4%	50.6%
1960	164,632	92,861	Keyser, F. Ray	71,755	Niquette, Russell F.	16	21,106 R	56.4%	43.6%	56.4%	43.6%
1958	123,728	62,222	Stafford, Robert T.	61,503	Leddy, Bernard J.	3	719 R	50.3%	49.7%	50.3%	49.7%
1956	153,809	88,379	Johnson, Joseph B.	65,420	Branon, E. Frank	10	22,959 R	57.5%	42.5%	57.5%	42.5%
1954	114,360	59,778	Johnson, Joseph B.	54,554	Branon, E. Frank	28	5,224 R	52.3%	47.7%	52.3%	47.7%
1952	150,862	78,338	Emerson, Lee E.	60,051	Larrow, Robert W.	12,473	18,287 R	51.9%	39.8%	56.6%	43.4%
1950	87,155	64,915	Emerson, Lee E.	22,227	Moran, J. Edward	13	42,688 R	74.5%	25.5%	74.5%	25.5%
1948	120,183	86,394	Gibson, Ernest W., Jr.	33,588	Ryan, Charles F.	201	52,806 R	71.9%	27.9%	72.0%	28.0%
1946	72,044	57,849	Gibson, Ernest W., Jr.	14,096	Coburn, Berthold	99	43,753 R	80.3%	19.6%	80.4%	19.6%

In 2002 and 1986, in the absence of a majority for any candidate, the State Legislature elected the governor—Republican Jim Douglas in January 2003, Democrat Madeleine M. Kunin in January 1987.

POSTWAR VOTE FOR SENATOR

Year	Total Vote	Republican		Democratic		Other Vote	Rep.-Dem. Plurality	Percentage			
		Vote	Candidate	Vote	Candidate			Total Vote		Major Vote	
								Rep.	Dem.	Rep.	Dem.
2000	288,500	189,133	Jeffords, James M.	73,352	Flanagan, Ed	26,015	115,781 R	65.6%	25.4%	72.1%	27.9%
1998	214,036	48,051	Tuttle, Fred H.	154,567	Leahy, Patrick J.	11,418	106,516 D	22.4%	72.2%	23.7%	76.3%
1994	211,672	106,505	Jeffords, James M.	85,868	Backus, Jan	19,299	20,637 R	50.3%	40.6%	55.4%	44.6%
1992	285,739	123,854	Douglas, James H.	154,762	Leahy, Patrick J.	7,123	30,908 D	43.3%	54.2%	44.5%	55.5%
1988	240,111	163,203	Jeffords, James M.	71,469	Gray, William	5,439	91,736 R	68.0%	29.8%	69.5%	30.5%
1986	196,532	67,798	Snelling, Richard A.	124,123	Leahy, Patrick J.	4,611	56,325 D	34.5%	63.2%	35.3%	64.7%
1982	168,003	84,450	Stafford, Robert T.	79,340	Guest, James A.	4,213	5,110 R	50.3%	47.2%	51.6%	48.4%
1980	209,124	101,421	Ledbetter, Stewart M.	104,176	Leahy, Patrick J.	3,527	2,755 D	48.5%	49.8%	49.3%	50.7%
1976	189,060	94,481	Stafford, Robert T.	85,682	Salmon, Thomas P.	8,897	8,799 R	50.0%	45.3%	52.4%	47.6%
1974	142,772	66,223	Mallary, Richard W.	70,629	Leahy, Patrick J.	5,920	4,406 D	46.4%	49.5%	48.4%	51.6%
1972S	71,348	45,888	Stafford, Robert T.	23,842	Major, Randolph T.	1,618	22,046 R	64.3%	33.4%	65.8%	34.2%
1970	154,899	91,198	Prouty, Winston L.	62,271	Hoff, Philip H.	1,430	28,927 R	58.9%	40.2%	59.4%	40.6%
1968**	157,375	157,154	Aiken, George D.	—		221	157,154 R	99.9%		100.0%	
1964	164,350	87,879	Prouty, Winston L.	76,457	Fayette, Frederick J.	14	11,422 R	53.5%	46.5%	53.5%	46.5%
1962	121,571	81,241	Aiken, George D.	40,134	Johnson, W. Robert	196	41,107 R	66.8%	33.0%	66.9%	33.1%
1958	124,442	64,900	Prouty, Winston L.	59,536	Fayette, Frederick J.	6	5,364 R	52.2%	47.8%	52.2%	47.8%
1956	155,289	103,101	Aiken, George D.	52,184	O'Shea, Bernard G.	4	50,917 R	66.4%	33.6%	66.4%	33.6%
1952	154,052	111,406	Flanders, Ralph E.	42,630	Johnston, Allan R.	16	68,776 R	72.3%	27.7%	72.3%	27.7%
1950	89,171	69,543	Aiken, George D.	19,608	Bigelow, James E.	20	49,935 R	78.0%	22.0%	78.0%	22.0%
1946	73,340	54,729	Flanders, Ralph E.	18,594	McDevitt, Charles P.	17	36,135 R	74.6%	25.4%	74.6%	25.4%

The January 1972 election was for a short term to fill a vacancy. In 1968 the Republican candidate won both major party nominations.

VERMONT

One member At Large

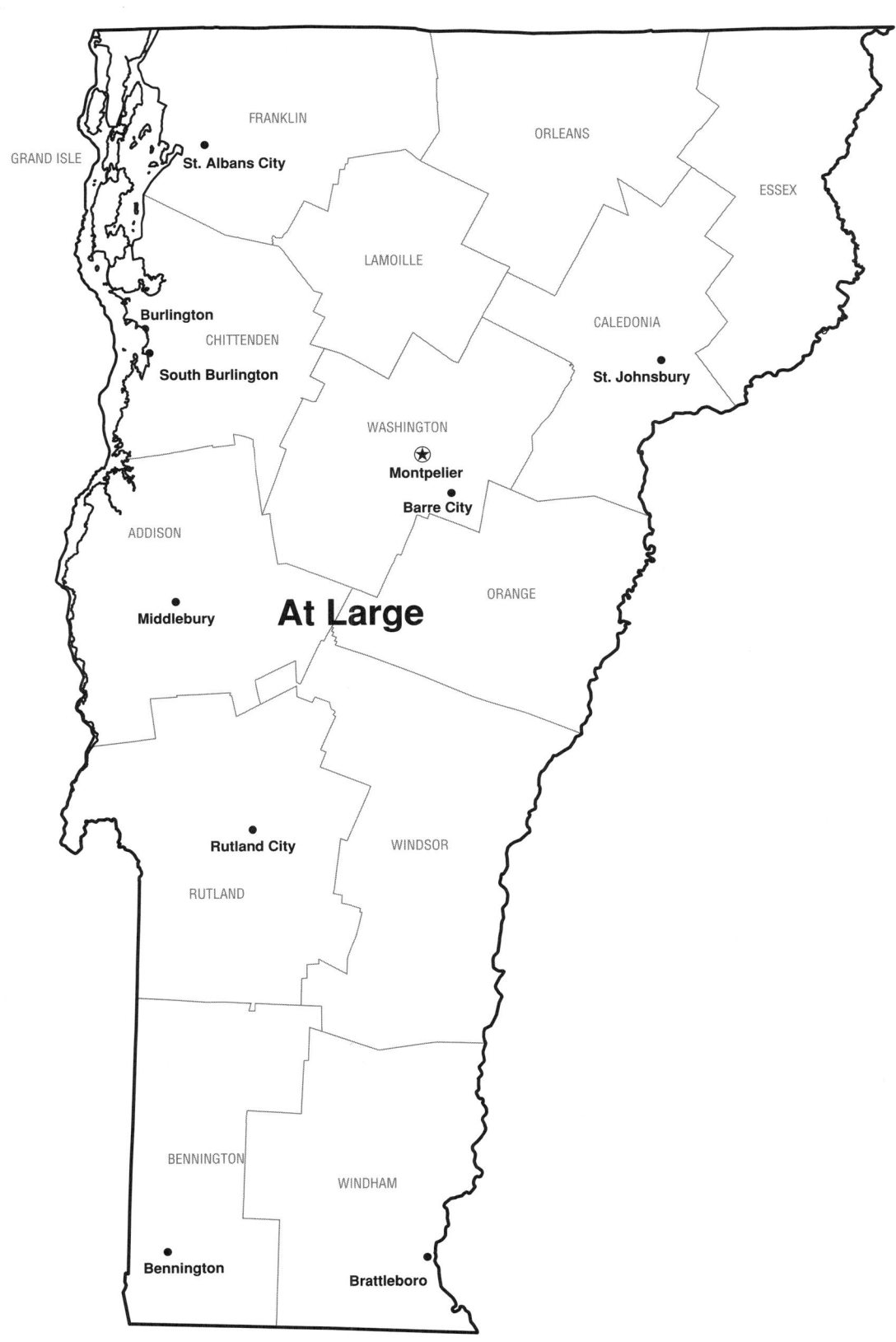

VERMONT

GOVERNOR 2002

2000 Census Population	County	Total Vote	Republican	Democratic	Other	Rep.-Dem. Plurality	Percentage			
							Total Vote		Major Vote	
							Rep.	Dem.	Rep.	Dem.
35,974	ADDISON	15,070	7,305	6,354	1,411	951 R	48.5%	42.2%	53.5%	46.5%
36,994	BENNINGTON	13,238	6,440	5,125	1,673	1,315 R	48.6%	38.7%	55.7%	44.3%
29,702	CALEDONIA	9,903	5,501	3,321	1,081	2,180 R	55.5%	33.5%	62.4%	37.6%
146,571	CHITTENDEN	56,612	24,536	26,249	5,827	1,713 D	43.3%	46.4%	48.3%	51.7%
6,459	ESSEX	2,026	1,269	540	217	729 R	62.6%	26.7%	70.1%	29.9%
45,417	FRANKLIN	14,912	7,383	5,677	1,852	1,706 R	49.5%	38.1%	56.5%	43.5%
6,901	GRAND ISLE	3,166	1,577	1,180	409	397 R	49.8%	37.3%	57.2%	42.8%
23,233	LAMOILLE	9,049	3,854	3,508	1,687	346 R	42.6%	38.8%	52.3%	47.7%
28,226	ORANGE	11,254	5,035	4,634	1,585	401 R	44.7%	41.2%	52.1%	47.9%
26,277	ORLEANS	9,129	4,734	2,900	1,495	1,834 R	51.9%	31.8%	62.0%	38.0%
63,400	RUTLAND	22,744	11,883	8,538	2,323	3,345 R	52.2%	37.5%	58.2%	41.8%
58,039	WASHINGTON	24,568	9,015	10,151	5,402	1,136 D	36.7%	41.3%	47.0%	53.0%
44,216	WINDHAM	16,851	6,054	8,884	1,913	2,830 D	35.9%	52.7%	40.5%	59.5%
57,418	WINDSOR	21,639	8,850	10,504	2,285	1,654 D	40.9%	48.5%	45.7%	54.3%
608,827	TOTAL	230,161	103,436	97,565	29,160	5,871 R	44.9%	42.4%	51.5%	48.5%
	City/Town									
9,291	BARRE CITY	2,895	1,263	976	656	287 R	43.6%	33.7%	56.4%	43.6%
7,602	BARRE TOWN	3,142	1,573	832	737	741 R	50.1%	26.5%	65.4%	34.6%
15,737	BENNINGTON	4,711	1,916	2,008	787	92 D	40.7%	42.6%	48.8%	51.2%
12,005	BRATTLEBORO	4,216	1,154	2,697	365	1,543 D	27.4%	64.0%	30.0%	70.0%
38,889	BURLINGTON	13,309	3,752	7,939	1,618	4,187 D	28.2%	59.7%	32.1%	67.9%
16,986	COLCHESTER	5,518	2,634	2,302	582	332 R	47.7%	41.7%	53.4%	46.6%
4,604	DERBY	1,701	881	576	244	305 R	51.8%	33.9%	60.5%	39.5%
18,626	ESSEX	7,515	4,242	2,612	661	1,630 R	56.4%	34.8%	61.9%	38.1%
10,367	HARTFORD	3,116	1,283	1,623	210	340 D	41.2%	52.1%	44.2%	55.8%
5,015	JERICHO	2,348	1,114	1,046	188	68 R	47.4%	44.5%	51.6%	48.4%
5,448	LYNDON	1,524	947	460	117	487 R	62.1%	30.2%	67.3%	32.7%
4,180	MANCHESTER	1,579	953	497	129	456 R	60.4%	31.5%	65.7%	34.3%
8,183	MIDDLEBURY	2,836	1,289	1,358	189	69 D	45.5%	47.9%	48.7%	51.3%
9,479	MILTON	3,150	1,779	1,053	318	726 R	56.5%	33.4%	62.8%	37.2%
8,035	MONTPELIER	3,939	994	2,128	817	1,134 D	25.2%	54.0%	31.8%	68.2%
5,139	MORRISTOWN	1,911	725	789	397	64 D	37.9%	41.3%	47.9%	52.1%
5,791	NORTHFIELD	1,760	731	656	373	75 R	41.5%	37.3%	52.7%	47.3%
4,853	RANDOLPH	1,878	848	796	234	52 R	45.2%	42.4%	51.6%	48.4%
4,090	RICHMOND	1,836	699	971	166	272 D	38.1%	52.9%	41.9%	58.1%
5,309	ROCKINGHAM	1,655	546	937	172	391 D	33.0%	56.6%	36.8%	63.2%
17,292	RUTLAND CITY	5,743	2,842	2,379	522	463 R	49.5%	41.4%	54.4%	45.6%
4,038	RUTLAND TOWN	1,903	1,176	566	161	610 R	61.8%	29.7%	67.5%	32.5%
6,944	SHELBURNE	3,527	1,699	1,475	353	224 R	48.2%	41.8%	53.5%	46.5%
15,814	SOUTH BURLINGTON	6,462	2,971	2,893	598	78 R	46.0%	44.8%	50.7%	49.3%
9,078	SPRINGFIELD	3,173	1,297	1,582	294	285 D	40.9%	49.9%	45.1%	54.9%
7,650	ST. ALBANS CITY	2,063	960	825	278	135 R	46.5%	40.0%	53.8%	46.2%
5,086	ST. ALBANS TOWN	1,862	968	640	254	328 R	52.0%	34.4%	60.2%	39.8%
7,571	ST. JOHNSBURY	2,067	1,242	640	185	602 R	60.1%	31.0%	66.0%	34.0%
2,548	SWANTON	1,861	943	699	219	244 R	50.7%	37.6%	57.4%	42.6%
4,915	WATERBURY	2,114	814	942	358	128 D	38.5%	44.6%	46.4%	53.6%
7,650	WILLISTON	3,811	1,994	1,441	376	553 R	52.3%	37.8%	58.0%	42.0%
6,561	WINOOSKI	1,662	621	862	179	241 D	37.4%	51.9%	41.9%	58.1%
3,232	WOODSTOCK	1,438	553	644	241	91 D	38.5%	44.8%	46.2%	53.8%

VERMONT

HOUSE OF REPRESENTATIVES

| | | | Republican | | Democratic | | Other | | Percentage | | | |
| | | Total | | | | | | | Total Vote | | Major Vote | |
CD	Year	Vote	Vote	Candidate	Vote	Candidate	Vote	Plurality	Rep.	Dem.	Rep.	Dem.
AL	2002	225,476	72,813	Meub, William "Bill"			152,663	72,067 I	32.3%	64.3%		
AL	2000	283,366	51,977	Kerin, Karen Ann	14,918	#Diamondstone, Pete	216,471	144,141 I	18.3%	69.2%		
AL	1998	215,133	70,740	Candon, Mark			144,393	65,663 I	32.9%	63.4%		
AL	1996	254,706	83,021	Sweetser, Susan W.	23,830	Long, Jack	147,855	57,657 I	32.6%	55.2%		
AL	1994	211,449	98,523	Carroll, John			112,926	6,979 I	46.6%	49.9%		
AL	1992	281,626	86,901	Philbin, Timothy	22,279	Young, Lewis E.	172,446	75,823 I	30.9%	57.8%		
AL	1990	209,856	82,938	Smith, Peter*	6,315	Sandoval, Dolores	120,603	34,584 I	39.5%	56.0%		
AL	1988	240,131	98,937	Smith, Peter	45,330	Poirier, Paul N.	95,864	53,607 R	41.2%	18.9%	68.6%	31.4%
AL	1986	188,954	168,403	#Jeffords, James M.*			20,551	168,403 R	89.1%		100.0%	
AL	1984	226,297	148,025	Jeffords, James M.*	60,360	Pollina, Anthony	17,912	87,665 R	65.4%	26.7%	71.0%	29.0%
AL	1982	164,951	114,191	Jeffords, James M.*	38,296	Kaplan, Mark A.	12,464	75,895 R	69.2%	23.2%	74.9%	25.1%
AL	1980	194,697	154,274	Jeffords, James M.*			40,423	154,274 R	79.2%		100.0%	
AL	1978	120,502	90,688	Jeffords, James M.*	23,228	Dietz, S. Marie	6,586	67,460 R	75.3%	19.3%	79.6%	20.4%
AL	1976	184,783	124,458	Jeffords, James M.*	60,202	#Burgess, John A.	123	64,256 R	67.4%	32.6%	67.4%	32.6%
AL	1974	140,899	74,561	Jeffords, James M.*	56,342	#Cain, Francis J.	9,996	18,219 R	52.9%	40.0%	57.0%	43.0%
AL	1972	186,028	120,924	Mallary, Richard W.	65,062	Meyer, William H.	42	55,862 R	65.0%	35.0%	65.0%	35.0%
AL	1970	152,557	103,806	Stafford, Robert T.*	44,415	O'Shea, Bernard G.	4,336	59,391 R	68.0%	29.1%	70.0%	30.0%
AL	1968	157,133	156,956	#Stafford, Robert T.*			177	156,956 R	99.9%		100.0%	
AL	1966	135,748	89,097	Stafford, Robert T.*	46,643	Ryan, William J.	8	42,454 R	65.6%	34.4%	65.6%	34.4%
AL	1964	163,452	92,252	Stafford, Robert T.*	71,193	O'Shea, Bernard G.	7	21,059 R	56.4%	43.6%	56.4%	43.6%
AL	1962	121,381	68,822	Stafford, Robert T.*	52,535	Raynolds, Harold	24	16,287 R	56.7%	43.3%	56.7%	43.3%
AL	1960	166,035	94,905	Stafford, Robert T.	71,111	Meyer, William H.	19	23,794 R	57.2%	42.8%	57.2%	42.8%
AL	1958	122,702	59,536	Arthur, Harold J.	63,131	Meyer, William H.	35	3,595 D	48.5%	51.5%	48.5%	51.5%
AL	1956	154,536	103,736	Prouty, Winston L.*	50,797	St. Amour, Camille	3	52,939 R	67.1%	32.9%	67.1%	32.9%
AL	1954	114,289	70,143	Prouty, Winston L.*	44,141	Baylan, John J.	5	26,002 R	61.4%	38.6%	61.4%	38.6%
AL	1952	153,060	109,871	Prouty, Winston L.*	43,187	Comings, Herbert B.	2	66,684 R	71.8%	28.2%	71.8%	28.2%
AL	1950	88,851	65,248	Prouty, Winston L.	22,709	Comings, Herbert B.	894	42,539 R	73.4%	25.6%	74.2%	25.8%
AL	1948	121,968	74,076	Plumley, Charles A.*	47,767	Ready, Robert W.	125	26,309 R	60.7%	39.2%	60.8%	39.2%
AL	1946	73,066	46,985	Plumley, Charles A.*	26,056	Caldbeck, Matthew J.	25	20,929 R	64.3%	35.7%	64.3%	35.7%

An asterisk (*) denotes incumbent. Seat was won in 1990, 1992, 1994, 1996, 1998, 2000 and 2002 by Bernard Sanders, an Independent. "Other" Vote for those years includes the total for Sanders and other independent and minor party candidates. However, plurality and percent of total vote figures since 1990 compare the Republican candidate and Sanders only. For earlier years the comparison is between the Republican and Democratic candidates. A pound sign (#) indicates that a candidate received votes from another party.

Pete Diamondstone received 5.3 percent of the vote in 2000 as the candidate of the Democratic and Liberty Union parties. In the 1990s, Democratic candidates received the following shares of the total vote: Jack Long, 9.4 percent in 1996; Lewis E. Young, 7.9 percent in 1992; Dolores Sandoval, 3.0 percent in 1990.

VERMONT

GENERAL AND PRIMARY ELECTIONS

2002 GENERAL ELECTIONS

Governor Other vote was 22,353 Independent (Cornelius "Con" Hogan); 1,737 Make Marijuana Legal (Cris Ericson); 1,380 Progressive (Michael J. Badamo); 938 Libertarian (Joel Williams); 771 Vermont Grassroots (Patricia Hejny); 638 Restore Justice-Freedom (Marilynn "Mom" Christian); 625 Liberty Union (Pete Diamondstone); 569 Independent (Brian Pearl); 149 write-in.

House Other vote was:

At Large 144,880 Independent (Bernard Sanders); 3,185 Liberty Union/Progressive (Jane Newton); 2,344 Vermont Grassroots (Fawn Skinner); 2,033 Libertarian (Daniel H. Krymkowski); 221 write-in. (Sanders was elected with 64.3 percent of the total vote.)

VERMONT

GENERAL AND PRIMARY ELECTIONS

2002 PRIMARY ELECTIONS

Primary   September 10, 2002   **Registration**   409,240   No Party Registration
(as of Sept. 10, 2002)

Primary Type   Open—Any registered voter could participate in the Democratic or Republican primary.

Note: An asterisk (*) denotes incumbent.

	REPUBLICAN PRIMARIES			DEMOCRATIC PRIMARIES		
Governor	Jim Douglas	23,366	96.7%	Doug Racine	25,522	99.1%
	Write-in	789	3.3%	Write-in	232	0.9%
	TOTAL	24,155		TOTAL	25,754	
House	William "Bill" Meub	14,105	57.6%	*No Democratic candidate filed for the primary.*		
At Large	Greg Parke	5,467	22.3%	*There were a total of 3,965 write-in votes cast,*		
	Karen A. Kerin	4,643	19.0%	*2,583 for incumbent Bernard Sanders, an*		
	Write-in	252	1.0%	*Independent, and 1,382 scattered write-ins.*		
	TOTAL	24,467				

VIRGINIA

GOVERNOR
Mark Warner (D). Elected 2001 to a four-year term.

SENATORS (2 Republicans)
George Allen (R). Elected 2000 to a six-year term.

John W. Warner (R). Reelected 2002 to a six-year term. Previously elected 1996, 1990, 1984, 1978.

REPRESENTATIVES (8 Republicans, 3 Democrats)
1. Jo Ann Davis (R)
2. Ed Schrock (R)
3. Robert C. Scott (D)
4. J. Randy Forbes (R)
5. Virgil H. Goode Jr. (R)
6. Robert W. Goodlatte (R)
7. Eric Cantor (R)
8. James P. Moran (D)
9. Rick Boucher (D)
10. Frank R. Wolf (R)
11. Thomas M. Davis III (R)

POSTWAR VOTE FOR PRESIDENT

		Republican		Democratic		Other		Total Vote		Major Vote	
Year	Total Vote	Vote	Candidate	Vote	Candidate	Vote	Plurality	Rep.	Dem.	Rep.	Dem.
2000**	2,739,447	1,437,490	Bush, George W.	1,217,290	Gore, Al	84,667	220,200 R	52.5%	44.4%	54.1%	45.9%
1996**	2,416,642	1,138,350	Dole, Bob	1,091,060	Clinton, Bill	187,232	47,290 R	47.1%	45.1%	51.1%	48.9%
1992**	2,558,665	1,150,517	Bush, George	1,038,650	Clinton, Bill	369,498	111,867 R	45.0%	40.6%	52.6%	47.4%
1988	2,191,609	1,309,162	Bush, George	859,799	Dukakis, Michael S.	22,648	449,363 R	59.7%	39.2%	60.4%	39.6%
1984	2,146,635	1,337,078	Reagan, Ronald	796,250	Mondale, Walter F.	13,307	540,828 R	62.3%	37.1%	62.7%	37.3%
1980**	1,866,032	989,609	Reagan, Ronald	752,174	Carter, Jimmy	124,249	237,435 R	53.0%	40.3%	56.8%	43.2%
1976	1,697,094	836,554	Ford, Gerald R.	813,896	Carter, Jimmy	46,644	22,658 R	49.3%	48.0%	50.7%	49.3%
1972	1,457,019	988,493	Nixon, Richard M.	438,887	McGovern, George S.	29,639	549,606 R	67.8%	30.1%	69.3%	30.7%
1968**	1,361,491	590,319	Nixon, Richard M.	442,387	Humphrey, Hubert H.	328,785	147,932 R	43.4%	32.5%	57.2%	42.8%
1964	1,042,267	481,334	Goldwater, Barry M.	558,038	Johnson, Lyndon B.	2,895	76,704 D	46.2%	53.5%	46.3%	53.7%
1960	771,449	404,521	Nixon, Richard M.	362,327	Kennedy, John F.	4,601	42,194 R	52.4%	47.0%	52.8%	47.2%
1956	697,978	386,459	Eisenhower, Dwight D.	267,760	Stevenson, Adlai E.	43,759	118,699 R	55.4%	38.4%	59.1%	40.9%
1952	619,689	349,037	Eisenhower, Dwight D.	268,677	Stevenson, Adlai E.	1,975	80,360 R	56.3%	43.4%	56.5%	43.5%
1948	419,256	172,070	Dewey, Thomas E.	200,786	Truman, Harry S.	46,400	28,716 D	41.0%	47.9%	46.1%	53.9%

In 2000 the other vote column includes 59,398 votes cast for Green (Nader). In 1996 the other vote column includes 159,861 votes cast for Perot. In 1992 the other vote column includes 348,639 votes cast for Perot. In 1980 the other vote column includes 95,418 votes for Independent (Anderson). In 1968 other vote was 321,833 American Independent (Wallace); 4,671 Socialist Labor; 1,680 Peace and Freedom; and 601 Prohibition.

VIRGINIA

POSTWAR VOTE FOR GOVERNOR

Year	Total Vote	Republican		Democratic		Other Vote	Rep.-Dem. Plurality	Percentage			
								Total Vote		Major Vote	
		Vote	Candidate	Vote	Candidate			Rep.	Dem.	Rep.	Dem.
2001	1,886,721	887,234	Earley, Mark L.	984,177	Warner, Mark	15,310	96,943 D	47.0%	52.2%	47.4%	52.6%
1997	1,736,314	969,062	Gilmore, James S., III	738,971	Beyer, Donald S., Jr.	28,281	230,091 R	55.8%	42.6%	56.7%	43.3%
1993	1,793,916	1,045,319	Allen, George	733,527	Terry, Mary Sue	15,070	311,792 R	58.3%	40.9%	58.8%	41.2%
1989	1,789,078	890,195	Coleman, J. Marshall	896,936	Wilder, L. Douglas	1,947	6,741 D	49.8%	50.1%	49.8%	50.2%
1985	1,343,243	601,652	Durrette, Wyatt B.	741,438	Baliles, Gerald L.	153	139,786 D	44.8%	55.2%	44.8%	55.2%
1981	1,420,611	659,398	Coleman, J. Marshall	760,357	Robb, Charles S.	856	100,959 D	46.4%	53.5%	46.4%	53.6%
1977	1,250,940	699,302	Dalton, John	541,319	Howell, Henry	10,319	157,983 R	55.9%	43.3%	56.4%	43.6%
1973**	1,035,495	525,075	Godwin, Mills E.	—		510,420	14,972 R	50.7%		100.0%	
1969	915,764	480,869	Holton, Linwood	415,695	Battle, William C.	19,200	65,174 R	52.5%	45.4%	53.6%	46.4%
1965	562,789	212,207	Holton, Linwood	269,526	Godwin, Mills E.	81,056	57,319 D	37.7%	47.9%	44.1%	55.9%
1961	394,490	142,567	Pearson, H. Clyde	251,861	Harrison, Albertis	62	109,294 D	36.1%	63.8%	36.1%	63.9%
1957	517,655	188,628	Dalton, Ted	326,921	Almond, J. Lindsay	2,106	138,293 D	36.4%	63.2%	36.6%	63.4%
1953	414,025	183,328	Dalton, Ted	226,998	Stanley, Thomas B.	3,699	43,670 D	44.3%	54.8%	44.7%	55.3%
1949	262,350	71,991	Johnson, Walter	184,772	Battle, John S.	5,587	112,781 D	27.4%	70.4%	28.0%	72.0%
1945	168,783	52,386	Landreth, S. Floyd	112,355	Tuck, William M.	4,042	59,969 D	31.0%	66.6%	31.8%	68.2%

In 1973 other vote was 510,103 Independent (Howell) and 317 scattered. In 1973 the plurality reflects the difference between the Republican and Independent vote. In other elections, the plurality is the difference between the Republican and Democratic vote.

POSTWAR VOTE FOR SENATOR

Year	Total Vote	Republican		Democratic		Other Vote	Rep.-Dem. Plurality	Percentage			
								Total Vote		Major Vote	
		Vote	Candidate	Vote	Candidate			Rep.	Dem.	Rep.	Dem.
2002	1,489,422	1,229,894	Warner, John W.	—		259,528	1,229,894 R	82.6%		100.0%	
2000	2,718,301	1,420,460	Allen, George	1,296,093	Robb, Charles S.	1,748	124,367 R	52.3%	47.7%	52.3%	47.7%
1996	2,354,715	1,235,744	Warner, John W.	1,115,982	Warner, Mark R.	2,989	119,762 R	52.5%	47.4%	52.5%	47.5%
1994**	2,057,463	882,213	North, Oliver L.	938,376	Robb, Charles S.	236,874	56,163 D	42.9%	45.6%	48.5%	51.5%
1990	1,083,690	876,782	Warner, John W.	—		206,908	876,782 R	80.9%		100.0%	
1988	2,068,897	593,652	Dawkins, Maurice A.	1,474,086	Robb, Charles S.	1,159	880,434 D	28.7%	71.2%	28.7%	71.3%
1984	2,007,487	1,406,194	Warner, John W.	601,142	Harrison, Edythe C.	151	805,052 R	70.0%	29.9%	70.1%	29.9%
1982	1,415,622	724,571	Trible, Paul	690,839	Davis, Richard	212	33,732 R	51.2%	48.8%	51.2%	48.8%
1978	1,222,256	613,232	Warner, John W.	608,511	Miller, Andrew P.	513	4,721 R	50.2%	49.8%	50.2%	49.8%
1976**	1,557,500	—		596,009	Zumwalt, Elmo R.	961,491	294,769 I		38.3%		100.0%
1972	1,396,268	718,337	Scott, William L.	643,963	Spong, William B.	33,968	74,374 R	51.4%	46.1%	52.7%	47.3%
1970**	946,751	145,031	Garland, Ray	295,057	Rawlings, George C.	506,663	211,576 I	15.3%	31.2%	33.0%	67.0%
1966	733,879	245,681	Ould, James P.	429,855	Spong, William B.	58,343	184,174 D	33.5%	58.6%	36.4%	63.6%
1966S	729,839	272,804	Traylor, Lawrence M.	389,028	Byrd, Harry Flood, Jr.	68,007	116,224 D	37.4%	53.3%	41.2%	58.8%
1964	928,363	176,624	May, Richard A.	592,260	Byrd, Harry Flood	159,479	415,636 D	19.0%	63.8%	23.0%	77.0%
1960	622,820		—	506,169	Robertson, A. Willis	116,651	506,169 D		81.3%		100.0%
1958	457,640		—	317,221	Byrd, Harry Flood	140,419	317,221 D		69.3%		100.0%
1954	306,510		—	244,844	Robertson, A. Willis	61,666	244,844 D		79.9%		100.0%
1952	543,516		—	398,677	Byrd, Harry Flood	144,839	398,677 D		73.4%		100.0%
1948	386,178	118,546	Woods, Robert	253,865	Robertson, A. Willis	13,767	135,319 D	30.7%	65.7%	31.8%	68.2%
1946	252,863	77,005	Parsons, Lester S.	163,960	Byrd, Harry Flood	11,898	86,955 D	30.5%	64.8%	32.0%	68.0%
1946S	248,962	72,253	Woods, Robert	169,680	Robertson, A. Willis	7,029	97,427 D	29.0%	68.2%	29.9%	70.1%

In 1994 J. Marshall Coleman ran as an Independent candidate and received 235,324 votes, 11.4 percent of the total vote. In 1970 Harry Flood Byrd Jr. ran as an Independent candidate and received 506,633 votes (53.5% of the total vote) and won the election with a 211,576-vote plurality. In 1976 Harry Flood Byrd Jr. polled 890,778 votes as an Independent candidate (57.2% of the total vote) and won the election with a 294,769-vote plurality. In the 1970 and 1976 elections Byrd's plurality is listed. In other elections, the plurality is the difference between the Republican and Democratic vote. One each of the 1966 and 1946 elections was for a short term to fill a vacancy.

VIRGINIA

Congressional districts first established for elections held in 2002
11 members

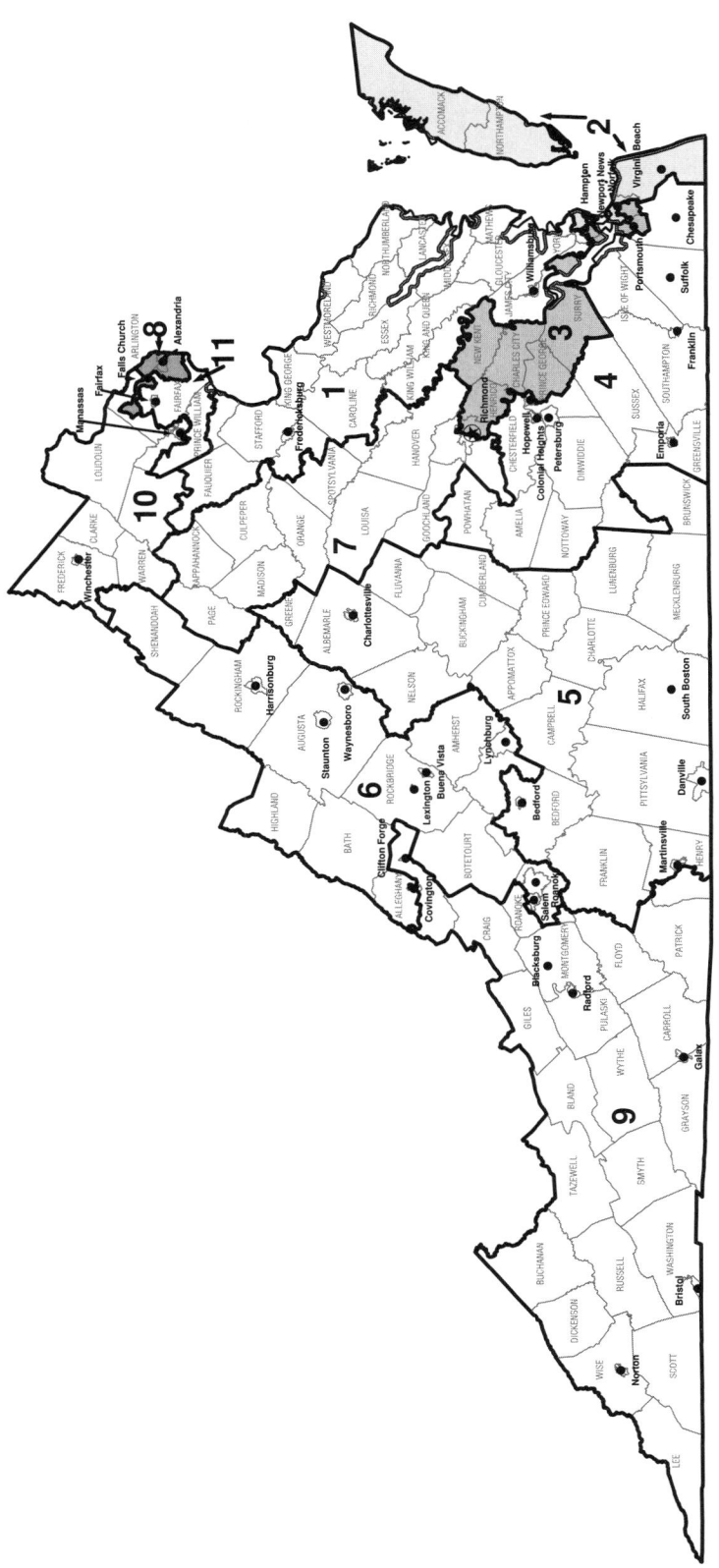

VIRGINIA

Northern Virginia Area

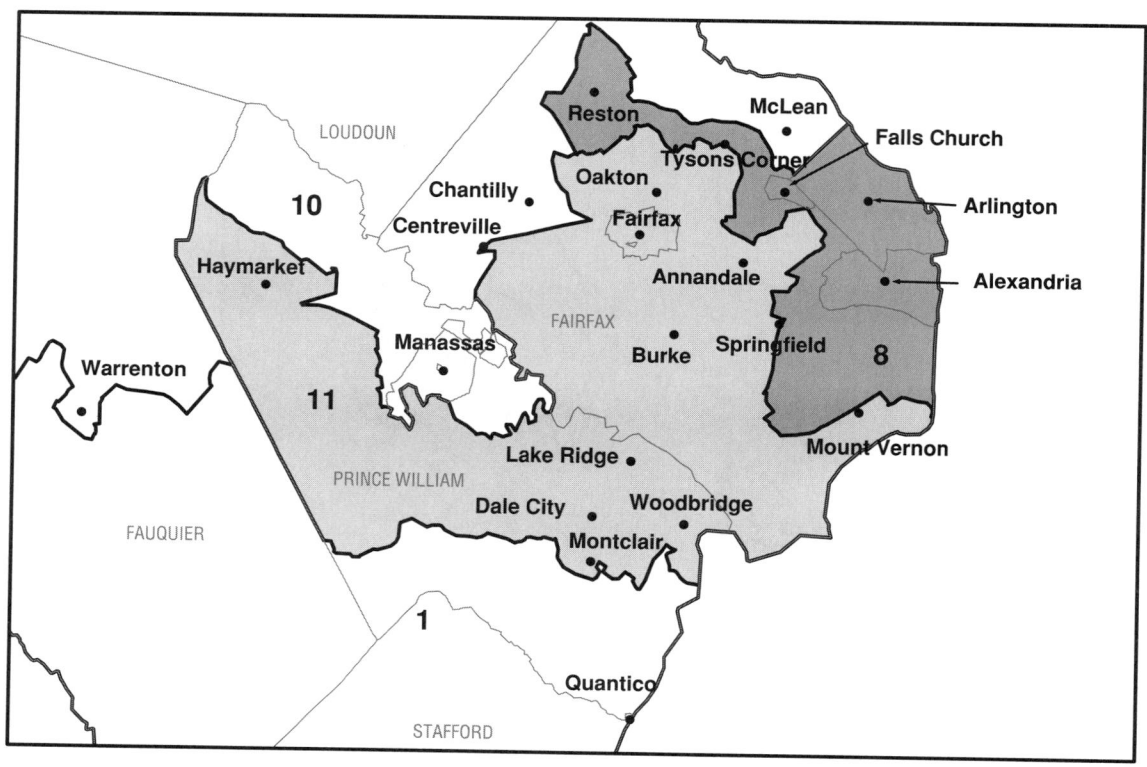

Hampton Roads, Virginia Beach Area

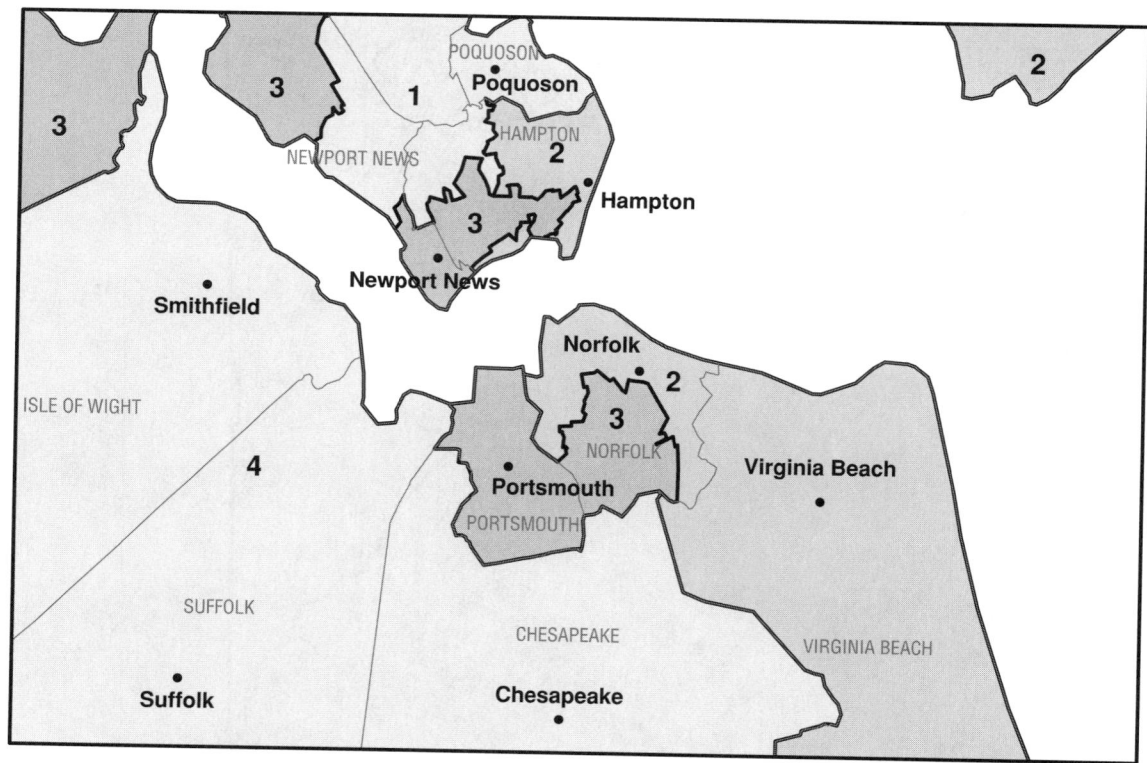

VIRGINIA

GOVERNOR 2001

2000 Census Population	County	Total Vote	Republican	Democratic	Other	Rep.-Dem. Plurality	Percentage			
							Total Vote		Major Vote	
							Rep.	Dem.	Rep.	Dem.
38,305	ACCOMACK	7,374	3,575	3,710	89	135 D	48.5%	50.3%	49.1%	50.9%
79,236	ALBEMARLE	26,428	11,143	14,891	394	3,748 D	42.2%	56.3%	42.8%	57.2%
17,215	ALLEGHANY	5,118	2,044	3,018	56	974 D	39.9%	59.0%	40.4%	59.6%
11,400	AMELIA	3,565	1,880	1,665	20	215 R	52.7%	46.7%	53.0%	47.0%
31,894	AMHERST	8,266	4,031	4,198	37	167 D	48.8%	50.8%	49.0%	51.0%
13,705	APPOMATTOX	4,420	2,090	2,268	62	178 D	47.3%	51.3%	48.0%	52.0%
189,453	ARLINGTON	52,719	16,214	35,990	515	19,776 D	30.8%	68.3%	31.1%	68.9%
65,615	AUGUSTA	17,974	11,133	6,673	168	4,460 R	61.9%	37.1%	62.5%	37.5%
5,048	BATH	1,553	721	804	28	83 D	46.4%	51.8%	47.3%	52.7%
60,371	BEDFORD COUNTY	19,547	11,298	8,035	214	3,263 R	57.8%	41.1%	58.4%	41.6%
6,871	BLAND	1,734	888	835	11	53 R	51.2%	48.2%	51.5%	48.5%
30,496	BOTETOURT	10,602	5,872	4,629	101	1,243 R	55.4%	43.7%	55.9%	44.1%
18,419	BRUNSWICK	4,350	1,491	2,840	19	1,349 D	34.3%	65.3%	34.4%	65.6%
26,978	BUCHANAN	5,706	1,921	3,746	39	1,825 D	33.7%	65.7%	33.9%	66.1%
15,623	BUCKINGHAM	3,997	1,601	2,364	32	763 D	40.1%	59.1%	40.4%	59.6%
51,078	CAMPBELL	15,743	8,366	7,187	190	1,179 R	53.1%	45.7%	53.8%	46.2%
22,121	CAROLINE	5,902	2,274	3,590	38	1,316 D	38.5%	60.8%	38.8%	61.2%
29,245	CARROLL	7,830	4,481	3,309	40	1,172 R	57.2%	42.3%	57.5%	42.5%
6,926	CHARLES CITY	2,391	631	1,747	13	1,116 D	26.4%	73.1%	26.5%	73.5%
12,472	CHARLOTTE	4,287	2,012	2,202	73	190 D	46.9%	51.4%	47.7%	52.3%
259,903	CHESTERFIELD	80,598	46,160	33,810	628	12,350 R	57.3%	41.9%	57.7%	42.3%
12,652	CLARKE	3,727	1,851	1,839	37	12 R	49.7%	49.3%	50.2%	49.8%
5,091	CRAIG	1,825	887	918	20	31 D	48.6%	50.3%	49.1%	50.9%
34,262	CULPEPER	8,849	5,054	3,721	74	1,333 R	57.1%	42.0%	57.6%	42.4%
9,017	CUMBERLAND	2,632	1,255	1,315	62	60 D	47.7%	50.0%	48.8%	51.2%
16,395	DICKENSON	4,763	1,837	2,907	19	1,070 D	38.6%	61.0%	38.7%	61.3%
24,533	DINWIDDIE	6,836	3,202	3,578	56	376 D	46.8%	52.3%	47.2%	52.8%
9,989	ESSEX	2,651	1,203	1,436	12	233 D	45.4%	54.2%	45.6%	54.4%
969,749	FAIRFAX COUNTY	269,014	120,799	146,537	1,678	25,738 D	44.9%	54.5%	45.2%	54.8%
55,139	FAUQUIER	16,472	9,420	6,952	100	2,468 R	57.2%	42.2%	57.5%	42.5%
13,874	FLOYD	4,493	2,331	2,093	69	238 R	51.9%	46.6%	52.7%	47.3%
20,047	FLUVANNA	6,630	3,425	3,118	87	307 R	51.7%	47.0%	52.3%	47.7%
47,286	FRANKLIN COUNTY	13,996	6,703	7,182	111	479 D	47.9%	51.3%	48.3%	51.7%
59,209	FREDERICK	16,499	9,947	6,433	119	3,514 R	60.3%	39.0%	60.7%	39.3%
16,657	GILES	5,432	2,276	3,071	85	795 D	41.9%	56.5%	42.6%	57.4%
34,780	GLOUCESTER	9,196	5,010	4,116	70	894 R	54.5%	44.8%	54.9%	45.1%
16,863	GOOCHLAND	6,537	3,394	3,091	52	303 R	51.9%	47.3%	52.3%	47.7%
17,917	GRAYSON	5,371	2,824	2,507	40	317 R	52.6%	46.7%	53.0%	47.0%
15,244	GREENE	3,944	2,244	1,644	56	600 R	56.9%	41.7%	57.7%	42.3%
11,560	GREENSVILLE	2,709	841	1,859	9	1,018 D	31.0%	68.6%	31.1%	68.9%
37,355	HALIFAX	10,051	4,366	5,506	179	1,140 D	43.4%	54.8%	44.2%	55.8%
86,320	HANOVER	30,691	18,757	11,713	221	7,044 R	61.1%	38.2%	61.6%	38.4%
262,300	HENRICO	81,903	39,215	42,089	599	2,874 D	47.9%	51.4%	48.2%	51.8%
57,930	HENRY	16,085	5,942	9,872	271	3,930 D	36.9%	61.4%	37.6%	62.4%
2,536	HIGHLAND	1,110	568	533	9	35 R	51.2%	48.0%	51.6%	48.4%
29,728	ISLE OF WIGHT	9,471	4,708	4,727	36	19 D	49.7%	49.9%	49.9%	50.1%
48,102	JAMES CITY	17,251	8,654	8,505	92	149 R	50.2%	49.3%	50.4%	49.6%
6,630	KING AND QUEEN	2,074	872	1,188	14	316 D	42.0%	57.3%	42.3%	57.7%
16,803	KING GEORGE	4,291	2,151	2,110	30	41 R	50.1%	49.2%	50.5%	49.5%
13,146	KING WILLIAM	3,929	1,960	1,942	27	18 R	49.9%	49.4%	50.2%	49.8%
11,567	LANCASTER	4,432	2,373	2,025	34	348 R	53.5%	45.7%	54.0%	46.0%
23,589	LEE	5,484	2,536	2,923	25	387 D	46.2%	53.3%	46.5%	53.5%
169,599	LOUDOUN	45,609	24,372	20,907	330	3,465 R	53.4%	45.8%	53.8%	46.2%
25,627	LOUISA	7,902	3,568	4,244	90	676 D	45.2%	53.7%	45.7%	54.3%
13,146	LUNENBURG	3,652	1,634	1,996	22	362 D	44.7%	54.7%	45.0%	55.0%
12,520	MADISON	3,992	2,121	1,794	77	327 R	53.1%	44.9%	54.2%	45.8%
9,207	MATHEWS	3,265	1,712	1,516	37	196 R	52.4%	46.4%	53.0%	47.0%
32,380	MECKLENBURG	7,541	3,898	3,519	124	379 R	51.7%	46.7%	52.6%	47.4%
9,932	MIDDLESEX	3,692	1,861	1,757	74	104 R	50.4%	47.6%	51.4%	48.6%
83,629	MONTGOMERY	20,034	8,639	11,154	241	2,515 D	43.1%	55.7%	43.6%	56.4%

VIRGINIA

GOVERNOR 2001

2000 Census Population	County	Total Vote	Republican	Democratic	Other	Rep.-Dem. Plurality	Percentage Total Vote Rep.	Dem.	Major Vote Rep.	Dem.
14,445	NELSON	4,513	1,763	2,681	69	918 D	39.1%	59.4%	39.7%	60.3%
13,462	NEW KENT	4,737	2,532	2,161	44	371 R	53.5%	45.6%	54.0%	46.0%
13,093	NORTHAMPTON	3,610	1,236	2,316	58	1,080 D	34.2%	64.2%	34.8%	65.2%
12,259	NORTHUMBERLAND	4,355	2,159	2,166	30	7 D	49.6%	49.7%	49.9%	50.1%
15,725	NOTTOWAY	4,381	1,824	2,513	44	689 D	41.6%	57.4%	42.1%	57.9%
25,881	ORANGE	7,613	3,902	3,617	94	285 R	51.3%	47.5%	51.9%	48.1%
23,177	PAGE	5,757	3,292	2,443	22	849 R	57.2%	42.4%	57.4%	42.6%
19,407	PATRICK	5,483	2,775	2,651	57	124 R	50.6%	48.3%	51.1%	48.9%
61,745	PITTSYLVANIA	17,568	9,831	7,462	275	2,369 R	56.0%	42.5%	56.8%	43.2%
22,377	POWHATAN	6,957	4,338	2,558	61	1,780 R	62.4%	36.8%	62.9%	37.1%
19,720	PRINCE EDWARD	4,905	1,967	2,874	64	907 D	40.1%	58.6%	40.6%	59.4%
33,047	PRINCE GEORGE	7,570	4,104	3,414	52	690 R	54.2%	45.1%	54.6%	45.4%
280,813	PRINCE WILLIAM	58,342	30,543	27,297	502	3,246 R	52.4%	46.8%	52.8%	47.2%
35,127	PULASKI	9,639	4,411	5,109	119	698 D	45.8%	53.0%	46.3%	53.7%
6,983	RAPPAHANNOCK	2,675	1,369	1,284	22	85 R	51.2%	48.0%	51.6%	48.4%
8,809	RICHMOND COUNTY	2,242	1,124	1,101	17	23 R	50.1%	49.1%	50.5%	49.5%
85,778	ROANOKE COUNTY	31,917	16,713	14,993	211	1,720 R	52.4%	47.0%	52.7%	47.3%
20,808	ROCKBRIDGE	5,903	2,885	2,972	46	87 D	48.9%	50.3%	49.3%	50.7%
67,725	ROCKINGHAM	18,472	11,723	6,642	107	5,081 R	63.5%	36.0%	63.8%	36.2%
30,308	RUSSELL	7,467	2,907	4,507	53	1,600 D	38.9%	60.4%	39.2%	60.8%
23,403	SCOTT	6,727	3,772	2,877	78	895 R	56.1%	42.8%	56.7%	43.3%
35,075	SHENANDOAH	11,263	6,653	4,531	79	2,122 R	59.1%	40.2%	59.5%	40.5%
33,081	SMYTH	9,130	4,354	4,691	85	337 D	47.7%	51.4%	48.1%	51.9%
17,482	SOUTHAMPTON	4,632	1,827	2,790	15	963 D	39.4%	60.2%	39.6%	60.4%
90,395	SPOTSYLVANIA	21,283	11,447	9,742	94	1,705 R	53.8%	45.8%	54.0%	46.0%
92,446	STAFFORD	21,422	12,019	9,248	155	2,771 R	56.1%	43.2%	56.5%	43.5%
6,829	SURRY	2,365	801	1,550	14	749 D	33.9%	65.5%	34.1%	65.9%
12,504	SUSSEX	3,124	1,134	1,924	66	790 D	36.3%	61.6%	37.1%	62.9%
44,598	TAZEWELL	9,661	4,335	5,250	76	915 D	44.9%	54.3%	45.2%	54.8%
31,584	WARREN	7,959	4,311	3,546	102	765 R	54.2%	44.6%	54.9%	45.1%
51,103	WASHINGTON	14,808	7,972	6,703	133	1,269 R	53.8%	45.3%	54.3%	45.7%
16,718	WESTMORELAND	4,293	1,759	2,471	63	712 D	41.0%	57.6%	41.6%	58.4%
40,123	WISE	9,421	3,816	5,509	96	1,693 D	40.5%	58.5%	40.9%	59.1%
27,599	WYTHE	7,869	3,991	3,822	56	169 R	50.7%	48.6%	51.1%	48.9%
56,297	YORK	16,718	9,083	7,530	105	1,553 R	54.3%	45.0%	54.7%	45.3%
	City									
128,283	ALEXANDRIA	34,802	10,810	23,739	253	12,929 D	31.1%	68.2%	31.3%	68.7%
6,299	BEDFORD CITY	1,813	747	1,031	35	284 D	41.2%	56.9%	42.0%	58.0%
17,367	BRISTOL	4,458	2,268	2,166	24	102 R	50.9%	48.6%	51.2%	48.8%
6,349	BUENA VISTA	1,455	572	853	30	281 D	39.3%	58.6%	40.1%	59.9%
45,049	CHARLOTTESVILLE	9,306	2,316	6,781	209	4,465 D	24.9%	72.9%	25.5%	74.5%
199,184	CHESAPEAKE	52,633	28,328	24,087	218	4,241 R	53.8%	45.8%	54.0%	46.0%
16,897	COLONIAL HEIGHTS	5,473	3,660	1,758	55	1,902 R	66.9%	32.1%	67.6%	32.4%
6,303	COVINGTON	1,709	597	1,071	41	474 D	34.9%	62.7%	35.8%	64.2%
48,411	DANVILLE	13,730	6,150	7,346	234	1,196 D	44.8%	53.5%	45.6%	54.4%
5,665	EMPORIA	1,535	616	912	7	296 D	40.1%	59.4%	40.3%	59.7%
21,498	FAIRFAX CITY	6,724	3,203	3,478	43	275 D	47.6%	51.7%	47.9%	52.1%
10,377	FALLS CHURCH	3,985	1,326	2,623	36	1,297 D	33.3%	65.8%	33.6%	66.4%
8,346	FRANKLIN CITY	2,222	781	1,434	7	653 D	35.1%	64.5%	35.3%	64.7%
19,279	FREDERICKSBURG	4,456	1,679	2,717	60	1,038 D	37.7%	61.0%	38.2%	61.8%
6,837	GALAX	1,605	733	866	6	133 D	45.7%	54.0%	45.8%	54.2%
146,437	HAMPTON	32,392	11,592	20,627	173	9,035 D	35.8%	63.7%	36.0%	64.0%
40,468	HARRISONBURG	6,468	3,334	3,083	51	251 R	51.5%	47.7%	52.0%	48.0%
22,354	HOPEWELL	4,994	2,435	2,467	92	32 D	48.8%	49.4%	49.7%	50.3%
6,867	LEXINGTON	1,629	552	1,053	24	501 D	33.9%	64.6%	34.4%	65.6%
65,269	LYNCHBURG	17,568	8,132	9,314	122	1,182 D	46.3%	53.0%	46.6%	53.4%

VIRGINIA

GOVERNOR 2001

2000 Census Population	City	Total Vote	Republican	Democratic	Other	Rep.-Dem. Plurality	Percentage Total Vote Rep.	Dem.	Major Vote Rep.	Dem.
35,135	MANASSAS	6,543	3,520	2,992	31	528 R	53.8%	45.7%	54.1%	45.9%
10,290	MANASSAS PARK	1,494	790	691	13	99 R	52.9%	46.3%	53.3%	46.7%
15,416	MARTINSVILLE	4,132	1,346	2,769	17	1,423 D	32.6%	67.0%	32.7%	67.3%
180,150	NEWPORT NEWS	37,422	15,920	21,318	184	5,398 D	42.5%	57.0%	42.8%	57.2%
234,403	NORFOLK	43,293	14,741	28,244	308	13,503 D	34.0%	65.2%	34.3%	65.7%
3,904	NORTON	1,144	366	773	5	407 D	32.0%	67.6%	32.1%	67.9%
33,740	PETERSBURG	8,559	1,509	7,018	32	5,509 D	17.6%	82.0%	17.7%	82.3%
11,566	POQUOSON	4,171	2,656	1,489	26	1,167 R	63.7%	35.7%	64.1%	35.9%
100,565	PORTSMOUTH	26,374	8,922	17,336	116	8,414 D	33.8%	65.7%	34.0%	66.0%
15,859	RADFORD	3,183	1,280	1,876	27	596 D	40.2%	58.9%	40.6%	59.4%
197,790	RICHMOND CITY	48,537	12,432	35,558	547	23,126 D	25.6%	73.3%	25.9%	74.1%
94,911	ROANOKE CITY	24,699	9,147	15,348	204	6,201 D	37.0%	62.1%	37.3%	62.7%
24,747	SALEM	8,175	4,042	4,067	66	25 D	49.4%	49.7%	49.8%	50.2%
23,853	STAUNTON	6,437	3,256	3,141	40	115 R	50.6%	48.8%	50.9%	49.1%
63,677	SUFFOLK	17,181	7,996	9,124	61	1,128 D	46.5%	53.1%	46.7%	53.3%
425,257	VIRGINIA BEACH	93,890	49,800	43,495	595	6,305 R	53.0%	46.3%	53.4%	46.6%
19,520	WAYNESBORO	4,911	2,777	2,109	25	668 R	56.5%	42.9%	56.8%	43.2%
11,998	WILLIAMSBURG	2,566	1,067	1,475	24	408 D	41.6%	57.5%	42.0%	58.0%
23,585	WINCHESTER	6,133	2,928	3,155	50	227 D	47.7%	51.4%	48.1%	51.9%
7,078,515	TOTAL	1,886,721	887,234	984,177	15,310	96,943 D	47.0%	52.2%	47.4%	52.6%

VIRGINIA

SENATOR 2002

2000 Census Population	County	Total Vote	Republican	Democratic	Other	Rep.-Dem. Plurality	Percentage Total Vote Rep.	Dem.	Major Vote Rep.	Dem.
38,305	ACCOMACK	6,022	4,903		1,119	4,903 R	81.4%		100.0%	
79,236	ALBEMARLE	22,351	17,647		4,704	17,647 R	79.0%		100.0%	
17,215	ALLEGHANY	3,400	2,706		694	2,706 R	79.6%		100.0%	
11,400	AMELIA	1,879	1,633		246	1,633 R	86.9%		100.0%	
31,894	AMHERST	6,953	5,957		996	5,957 R	85.7%		100.0%	
13,705	APPOMATTOX	2,680	2,147		533	2,147 R	80.1%		100.0%	
189,453	ARLINGTON	49,752	36,508		13,244	36,508 R	73.4%		100.0%	
65,615	AUGUSTA	10,629	8,507		2,122	8,507 R	80.0%		100.0%	
5,048	BATH	996	794		202	794 R	79.7%		100.0%	
60,371	BEDFORD COUNTY	14,156	11,802		2,354	11,802 R	83.4%		100.0%	
6,871	BLAND	1,597	1,376		221	1,376 R	86.2%		100.0%	
30,496	BOTETOURT	6,422	5,188		1,234	5,188 R	80.8%		100.0%	
18,419	BRUNSWICK	2,424	1,958		466	1,958 R	80.8%		100.0%	
26,978	BUCHANAN	3,447	2,824		623	2,824 R	81.9%		100.0%	
15,623	BUCKINGHAM	2,510	2,081		429	2,081 R	82.9%		100.0%	
51,078	CAMPBELL	10,064	8,554		1,510	8,554 R	85.0%		100.0%	
22,121	CAROLINE	3,522	2,844		678	2,844 R	80.7%		100.0%	
29,245	CARROLL	6,386	5,308		1,078	5,308 R	83.1%		100.0%	
6,926	CHARLES CITY	1,168	943		225	943 R	80.7%		100.0%	
12,472	CHARLOTTE	2,189	1,738		451	1,738 R	79.4%		100.0%	
259,903	CHESTERFIELD	58,649	51,052		7,597	51,052 R	87.0%		100.0%	
12,652	CLARKE	3,059	2,484		575	2,484 R	81.2%		100.0%	
5,091	CRAIG	1,357	1,091		266	1,091 R	80.4%		100.0%	
34,262	CULPEPER	6,249	5,149		1,100	5,149 R	82.4%		100.0%	
9,017	CUMBERLAND	1,520	1,249		271	1,249 R	82.2%		100.0%	

VIRGINIA

SENATOR 2002

2000 Census Population	County	Total Vote	Republican	Democratic	Other	Rep.-Dem. Plurality	Percentage			
							Total Vote		Major Vote	
							Rep.	Dem.	Rep.	Dem.
16,395	DICKENSON	3,338	2,635		703	2,635 R	78.9%		100.0%	
24,533	DINWIDDIE	3,521	2,967		554	2,967 R	84.3%		100.0%	
9,989	ESSEX	1,526	1,329		197	1,329 R	87.1%		100.0%	
969,749	FAIRFAX COUNTY	251,142	205,276		45,866	205,276 R	81.7%		100.0%	
55,139	FAUQUIER	12,542	10,669		1,873	10,669 R	85.1%		100.0%	
13,874	FLOYD	3,070	2,382		688	2,382 R	77.6%		100.0%	
20,047	FLUVANNA	5,071	4,191		880	4,191 R	82.6%		100.0%	
47,286	FRANKLIN COUNTY	12,154	10,167		1,987	10,167 R	83.7%		100.0%	
59,209	FREDERICK	11,215	9,565		1,650	9,565 R	85.3%		100.0%	
16,657	GILES	3,403	2,797		606	2,797 R	82.2%		100.0%	
34,780	GLOUCESTER	6,984	5,935		1,049	5,935 R	85.0%		100.0%	
16,863	GOOCHLAND	4,829	4,253		576	4,253 R	88.1%		100.0%	
17,917	GRAYSON	3,992	3,328		664	3,328 R	83.4%		100.0%	
15,244	GREENE	2,707	2,229		478	2,229 R	82.3%		100.0%	
11,560	GREENSVILLE	1,446	1,132		314	1,132 R	78.3%		100.0%	
37,355	HALIFAX	6,001	4,874		1,127	4,874 R	81.2%		100.0%	
86,320	HANOVER	22,909	20,461		2,448	20,461 R	89.3%		100.0%	
262,300	HENRICO	59,933	51,167		8,766	51,167 R	85.4%		100.0%	
57,930	HENRY	10,530	8,566		1,964	8,566 R	81.3%		100.0%	
2,536	HIGHLAND	731	589		142	589 R	80.6%		100.0%	
29,728	ISLE OF WIGHT	8,439	7,372		1,067	7,372 R	87.4%		100.0%	
48,102	JAMES CITY	16,565	14,266		2,299	14,266 R	86.1%		100.0%	
6,630	KING AND QUEEN	1,250	1,021		229	1,021 R	81.7%		100.0%	
16,803	KING GEORGE	2,652	2,287		365	2,287 R	86.2%		100.0%	
13,146	KING WILLIAM	2,499	2,200		299	2,200 R	88.0%		100.0%	
11,567	LANCASTER	2,965	2,645		320	2,645 R	89.2%		100.0%	
23,589	LEE	4,261	3,471		790	3,471 R	81.5%		100.0%	
169,599	LOUDOUN	48,621	40,196		8,425	40,196 R	82.7%		100.0%	
25,627	LOUISA	5,137	4,176		961	4,176 R	81.3%		100.0%	
13,146	LUNENBURG	2,368	2,010		358	2,010 R	84.9%		100.0%	
12,520	MADISON	2,658	2,117		541	2,117 R	79.6%		100.0%	
9,207	MATHEWS	2,260	1,858		402	1,858 R	82.2%		100.0%	
32,380	MECKLENBURG	4,823	3,854		969	3,854 R	79.9%		100.0%	
9,932	MIDDLESEX	2,252	1,958		294	1,958 R	86.9%		100.0%	
83,629	MONTGOMERY	16,138	12,834		3,304	12,834 R	79.5%		100.0%	
14,445	NELSON	3,466	2,607		859	2,607 R	75.2%		100.0%	
13,462	NEW KENT	4,693	4,122		571	4,122 R	87.8%		100.0%	
13,093	NORTHAMPTON	2,548	2,135		413	2,135 R	83.8%		100.0%	
12,259	NORTHUMBERLAND	3,143	2,732		411	2,732 R	86.9%		100.0%	
15,725	NOTTOWAY	2,044	1,717		327	1,717 R	84.0%		100.0%	
25,881	ORANGE	5,427	4,369		1,058	4,369 R	80.5%		100.0%	
23,177	PAGE	4,646	3,767		879	3,767 R	81.1%		100.0%	
19,407	PATRICK	4,832	4,080		752	4,080 R	84.4%		100.0%	
61,745	PITTSYLVANIA	11,428	9,372		2,056	9,372 R	82.0%		100.0%	
22,377	POWHATAN	4,774	4,200		574	4,200 R	88.0%		100.0%	
19,720	PRINCE EDWARD	2,889	2,398		491	2,398 R	83.0%		100.0%	
33,047	PRINCE GEORGE	5,490	4,723		767	4,723 R	86.0%		100.0%	
280,813	PRINCE WILLIAM	53,263	43,375		9,888	43,375 R	81.4%		100.0%	
35,127	PULASKI	6,754	5,638		1,116	5,638 R	83.5%		100.0%	
6,983	RAPPAHANNOCK	2,438	1,880		558	1,880 R	77.1%		100.0%	
8,809	RICHMOND COUNTY	1,261	1,122		139	1,122 R	89.0%		100.0%	
85,778	ROANOKE COUNTY	23,527	20,261		3,266	20,261 R	86.1%		100.0%	
20,808	ROCKBRIDGE	5,049	4,322		727	4,322 R	85.6%		100.0%	
67,725	ROCKINGHAM	12,698	10,305		2,393	10,305 R	81.2%		100.0%	
30,308	RUSSELL	4,094	3,381		713	3,381 R	82.6%		100.0%	
23,403	SCOTT	4,203	3,608		595	3,608 R	85.8%		100.0%	
35,075	SHENANDOAH	6,864	5,811		1,053	5,811 R	84.7%		100.0%	
33,081	SMYTH	5,587	4,659		928	4,659 R	83.4%		100.0%	
17,482	SOUTHAMPTON	2,952	2,490		462	2,490 R	84.3%		100.0%	
90,395	SPOTSYLVANIA	14,753	12,513		2,240	12,513 R	84.8%		100.0%	

VIRGINIA

SENATOR 2002

2000 Census Population	County	Total Vote	Republican	Democratic	Other	Rep.-Dem. Plurality	Total Vote Rep.	Total Vote Dem.	Major Vote Rep.	Major Vote Dem.
92,446	STAFFORD	15,732	13,264		2,468	13,264 R	84.3%		100.0%	
6,829	SURRY	1,322	1,100		222	1,100 R	83.2%		100.0%	
12,504	SUSSEX	1,620	1,317		303	1,317 R	81.3%		100.0%	
44,598	TAZEWELL	6,450	5,411		1,039	5,411 R	83.9%		100.0%	
31,584	WARREN	5,036	4,192		844	4,192 R	83.2%		100.0%	
51,103	WASHINGTON	9,532	8,280		1,252	8,280 R	86.9%		100.0%	
16,718	WESTMORELAND	2,159	1,779		380	1,779 R	82.4%		100.0%	
40,123	WISE	5,673	4,923		750	4,923 R	86.8%		100.0%	
27,599	WYTHE	5,989	5,178		811	5,178 R	86.5%		100.0%	
56,297	YORK	16,370	14,213		2,157	14,213 R	86.8%		100.0%	
	City									
128,283	ALEXANDRIA	29,477	22,289		7,188	22,289 R	75.6%		100.0%	
6,299	BEDFORD CITY	1,213	988		225	988 R	81.5%		100.0%	
17,367	BRISTOL	3,475	2,914		561	2,914 R	83.9%		100.0%	
6,349	BUENA VISTA	1,017	898		119	898 R	88.3%		100.0%	
45,049	CHARLOTTESVILLE	7,315	4,701		2,614	4,701 R	64.3%		100.0%	
199,184	CHESAPEAKE	44,811	37,892		6,919	37,892 R	84.6%		100.0%	
16,897	COLONIAL HEIGHTS	3,316	3,020		296	3,020 R	91.1%		100.0%	
6,303	COVINGTON	1,118	872		246	872 R	78.0%		100.0%	
48,411	DANVILLE	8,060	6,793		1,267	6,793 R	84.3%		100.0%	
5,665	EMPORIA	837	716		121	716 R	85.5%		100.0%	
21,498	FAIRFAX CITY	5,945	4,829		1,116	4,829 R	81.2%		100.0%	
10,377	FALLS CHURCH	3,675	2,837		838	2,837 R	77.2%		100.0%	
8,346	FRANKLIN CITY	1,488	1,278		210	1,278 R	85.9%		100.0%	
19,279	FREDERICKSBURG	2,638	2,108		530	2,108 R	79.9%		100.0%	
6,837	GALAX	1,240	1,076		164	1,076 R	86.8%		100.0%	
146,437	HAMPTON	28,274	22,888		5,386	22,888 R	81.0%		100.0%	
40,468	HARRISONBURG	4,520	3,528		992	3,528 R	78.1%		100.0%	
22,354	HOPEWELL	2,527	2,039		488	2,039 R	80.7%		100.0%	
6,867	LEXINGTON	1,397	1,130		267	1,130 R	80.9%		100.0%	
65,269	LYNCHBURG	11,801	9,873		1,928	9,873 R	83.7%		100.0%	
35,135	MANASSAS	5,714	4,766		948	4,766 R	83.4%		100.0%	
10,290	MANASSAS PARK	1,163	910		253	910 R	78.2%		100.0%	
15,416	MARTINSVILLE	3,182	2,670		512	2,670 R	83.9%		100.0%	
180,150	NEWPORT NEWS	32,285	27,017		5,268	27,017 R	83.7%		100.0%	
234,403	NORFOLK	33,700	27,002		6,698	27,002 R	80.1%		100.0%	
3,904	NORTON	823	688		135	688 R	83.6%		100.0%	
33,740	PETERSBURG	3,619	2,789		830	2,789 R	77.1%		100.0%	
11,566	POQUOSON	4,062	3,640		422	3,640 R	89.6%		100.0%	
100,565	PORTSMOUTH	18,920	15,472		3,448	15,472 R	81.8%		100.0%	
15,859	RADFORD	2,538	2,056		482	2,056 R	81.0%		100.0%	
197,790	RICHMOND CITY	32,743	25,496		7,247	25,496 R	77.9%		100.0%	
94,911	ROANOKE CITY	15,966	12,730		3,236	12,730 R	79.7%		100.0%	
24,747	SALEM	5,499	4,682		817	4,682 R	85.1%		100.0%	
23,853	STAUNTON	3,528	2,878		650	2,878 R	81.6%		100.0%	
63,677	SUFFOLK	13,756	11,849		1,907	11,849 R	86.1%		100.0%	
425,257	VIRGINIA BEACH	90,375	76,293		14,082	76,293 R	84.4%		100.0%	
19,520	WAYNESBORO	3,113	2,593		520	2,593 R	83.3%		100.0%	
11,998	WILLIAMSBURG	2,237	1,807		430	1,807 R	80.8%		100.0%	
23,585	WINCHESTER	4,036	3,423		613	3,423 R	84.8%		100.0%	
7,078,515	TOTAL	1,489,422	1,229,894		259,528	1,229,894 R	82.6%		100.0%	

VIRGINIA

HOUSE OF REPRESENTATIVES

CD	Year	Total Vote	Republican Vote	Candidate	Democratic Vote	Candidate	Other Vote	Rep.-Dem. Plurality	Percentage Total Vote Rep.	Dem.	Major Vote Rep.	Dem.
1	2002	117,997	113,168	Davis, Jo Ann*			4,829	113,168 R	95.9%		100.0%	
2	2002	124,846	103,807	Schrock, Ed*			21,039	103,807 R	83.1%		100.0%	
3	2002	91,073			87,521	Scott, Robert C.*	3,552	87,521 D		96.1%		100.0%
4	2002	111,041	108,733	Forbes, J. Randy*			2,308	108,733 R	97.9%		100.0%	
5	2002	150,233	95,360	Goode, Virgil H. Jr.*	54,805	Richards, Meredith M.	68	40,555 R	63.5%	36.5%	63.5%	36.5%
6	2002	108,732	105,530	Goodlatte, Robert W.*			3,202	105,530 R	97.1%		100.0%	
7	2002	163,665	113,658	Cantor, Eric*	49,854	Jones, Ben L. "Cooter"	153	63,804 R	69.4%	30.5%	69.5%	30.5%
8	2002	171,799	64,121	Tate, Scott C.	102,759	Moran, James P.*	4,919	38,638 D	37.3%	59.8%	38.4%	61.6%
9	2002	152,183	52,076	Katzen, Jay K.	100,075	Boucher, Rick*	32	47,999 D	34.2%	65.8%	34.2%	65.8%
10	2002	161,615	115,917	Wolf, Frank R.*	45,464	Stevens, John B. Jr.	234	70,453 R	71.7%	28.1%	71.8%	28.2%
11	2002	163,298	135,379	Davis, Thomas M. III*			27,919	135,379 R	82.9%		100.0%	
Total	2002	1,516,482	1,007,749		440,478		68,255	567,271 R	66.5%	29.0%	69.6%	30.4%

An asterisk (*) denotes incumbent.

VIRGINIA

GENERAL AND PRIMARY ELECTIONS

2002 GENERAL ELECTIONS

Governor (2001) Other vote was 14,497 Libertarian (William B. Redpath); 813 write-in.

Senator Other vote was 145,102 Independent (Nancy B. Spannaus); 106,055 Independent (Jacob G. Hornberger Jr.); 8,371 write-in.

House Other vote was:

CD 1 4,829 write-in.
CD 2 20,589 Green (D.C. Amarasinghe); 450 write-in.
CD 3 3,552 write-in.
CD 4 2,308 write-in.
CD 5 68 write-in.
CD 6 3,202 write-in.
CD 7 153 write-in.
CD 8 4,558 Independent (Ronald V. Crickenberger); 361 write-in.
CD 9 32 write-in.
CD 10 234 write-in.
CD 11 26,892 Constitution (Frank W. Creel); 1,027 write-in.

VIRGINIA

GENERAL AND PRIMARY ELECTIONS

2001–2002 PRIMARY ELECTIONS

Primary	June 12, 2001 (Governor) June 11, 2002 (Congress)

Registration (as of June 1, 2002)	4,181,667	No Party Registration

Primary Type   Open—Any registered voter could participate in the primary of either party.

Note: An asterisk (*) denotes incumbent. The state parties and local party committees have the option of holding a primary or nominating candidates by convention or committee. If a primary was called and only one candidate filed to run in it, then no primary was held.

	REPUBLICAN PRIMARIES		DEMOCRATIC PRIMARIES	
Governor (2001)	Mark L. Earley	Nominated by convention	Mark Warner	Unopposed
Senator	John W. Warner*	Unopposed	No Democratic candidate	
Congressional District 1	Jo Ann Davis*	Unopposed	No Democratic candidate	
Congressional District 2	Ed Schrock*	Unopposed	No Democratic candidate	
Congressional District 3	No Republican candidate		Robert C. Scott*	Unopposed
Congressional District 4	J. Randy Forbes*	Unopposed	*L. Louise Lucas ran unopposed in the Democratic primary but subsequently withdrew from the race. There was no Democratic candidate on the general election ballot.*	
Congressional District 5	Virgil H. Goode Jr.*	Unopposed	Meredith M. Richards	Nominated by convention
Congressional District 6	Robert W. Goodlatte*	Unopposed	No Democratic candidate	
Congressional District 7	Eric Cantor*	Unopposed	Ben L. "Cooter" Jones	Nominated by convention
Congressional District 8	Scott C. Tate	Nominated by convention	James P. Moran*	Nominated by convention
Congressional District 9	Jay K. Katzen	Nominated by convention	Rick Boucher*	Nominated by convention
Congressional District 10	Frank R. Wolf*	Unopposed	John B. Stevens Jr.	Nominated by committee
Congressional District 11	Thomas M. Davis III*	Unopposed	No Democratic candidate	

WASHINGTON

GOVERNOR
Gary Locke (D). Reelected 2000 to a four-year term. Previously elected 1996.

SENATORS (2 Democrats)
Maria Cantwell (D). Elected 2000 to a six-year term.

Patty Murray (D). Reelected 1998 to a six-year term. Previously elected 1992.

REPRESENTATIVES (6 Democrats, 3 Republicans)
1. Jay Inslee (D)
2. Rick Larsen (D)
3. Brian Baird (D)
4. Doc Hastings (R)
5. George Nethercutt (R)
6. Norm Dicks (D)
7. Jim McDermott (D)
8. Jennifer Dunn (R)
9. Adam Smith (D)

POSTWAR VOTE FOR PRESIDENT

| Year | Total Vote | Republican | | Democratic | | Other Vote | Plurality | Percentage | | | |
| | | Vote | Candidate | Vote | Candidate | | | Total Vote | | Major Vote | |
								Rep.	Dem.	Rep.	Dem.
2000**	2,487,433	1,108,864	Bush, George W.	1,247,652	Gore, Al	130,917	138,788 D	44.6%	50.2%	47.1%	52.9%
1996**	2,253,837	840,712	Dole, Bob	1,123,323	Clinton, Bill	289,802	282,611 D	37.3%	49.8%	42.8%	57.2%
1992**	2,288,230	731,234	Bush, George	993,037	Clinton, Bill	563,959	261,803 D	32.0%	43.4%	42.4%	57.6%
1988	1,865,253	903,835	Bush, George	933,516	Dukakis, Michael S.	27,902	29,681 D	48.5%	50.0%	49.2%	50.8%
1984	1,883,910	1,051,670	Reagan, Ronald	807,352	Mondale, Walter F.	24,888	244,318 R	55.8%	42.9%	56.6%	43.4%
1980**	1,742,394	865,244	Reagan, Ronald	650,193	Carter, Jimmy	226,957	215,051 R	49.7%	37.3%	57.1%	42.9%
1976	1,555,534	777,732	Ford, Gerald R.	717,323	Carter, Jimmy	60,479	60,409 R	50.0%	46.1%	52.0%	48.0%
1972	1,470,847	837,135	Nixon, Richard M.	568,334	McGovern, George S.	65,378	268,801 R	56.9%	38.6%	59.6%	40.4%
1968	1,304,281	588,510	Nixon, Richard M.	616,037	Humphrey, Hubert H.	99,734	27,527 D	45.1%	47.2%	48.9%	51.1%
1964	1,258,556	470,366	Goldwater, Barry M.	779,881	Johnson, Lyndon B.	8,309	309,515 D	37.4%	62.0%	37.6%	62.4%
1960	1,241,572	629,273	Nixon, Richard M.	599,298	Kennedy, John F.	13,001	29,975 R	50.7%	48.3%	51.2%	48.8%
1956	1,150,889	620,430	Eisenhower, Dwight D.	523,002	Stevenson, Adlai E.	7,457	97,428 R	53.9%	45.4%	54.3%	45.7%
1952	1,102,708	599,107	Eisenhower, Dwight D.	492,845	Stevenson, Adlai E.	10,756	106,262 R	54.3%	44.7%	54.9%	45.1%
1948	905,058	386,314	Dewey, Thomas E.	476,165	Truman, Harry S.	42,579	89,851 D	42.7%	52.6%	44.8%	55.2%

In 2000 the other vote column includes 103,002 votes cast for Green (Nader). In 1996 the other vote column includes 201,003 votes cast for Perot. In 1992 the other vote column includes 541,780 votes cast for Perot. In 1980 the other vote column includes 185,073 votes for Independent (Anderson).

WASHINGTON

POSTWAR VOTE FOR GOVERNOR

Year	Total Vote	Republican Vote	Republican Candidate	Democratic Vote	Democratic Candidate	Other Vote	Rep.-Dem. Plurality	Percentage Total Vote Rep.	Percentage Total Vote Dem.	Percentage Major Vote Rep.	Percentage Major Vote Dem.
2000	2,469,852	980,060	Carlson, John	1,441,973	Locke, Gary	47,819	461,913 D	39.7%	58.4%	40.5%	59.5%
1996	2,237,030	940,538	Craswell, Ellen	1,296,492	Locke, Gary		355,954 D	42.0%	58.0%	42.0%	58.0%
1992	2,270,826	1,086,216	Eikenberry, Ken	1,184,315	Lowry, Mike	295	98,099 D	47.8%	52.2%	47.8%	52.2%
1988	1,874,929	708,481	Williams, Bob	1,166,448	Gardner, Booth		457,967 D	37.8%	62.2%	37.8%	62.2%
1984	1,888,987	881,994	Spellman, John D.	1,006,993	Gardner, Booth		124,999 D	46.7%	53.3%	46.7%	53.3%
1980	1,730,896	981,083	Spellman, John D.	749,813	McDermott, James A.		231,270 R	56.7%	43.3%	56.7%	43.3%
1976	1,546,382	687,039	Spellman, John D.	821,797	Ray, Dixy Lee	37,546	134,758 D	44.4%	53.1%	45.5%	54.5%
1972	1,472,542	747,825	Evans, Daniel J.	630,613	Rosellini, Albert D.	94,104	117,212 R	50.8%	42.8%	54.3%	45.7%
1968	1,265,355	692,378	Evans, Daniel J.	560,262	O'Connell, John J.	12,715	132,116 R	54.7%	44.3%	55.3%	44.7%
1964	1,250,274	697,256	Evans, Daniel J.	548,692	Rosellini, Albert D.	4,326	148,564 R	55.8%	43.9%	56.0%	44.0%
1960	1,215,748	594,122	Andrews, Lloyd J.	611,987	Rosellini, Albert D.	9,639	17,865 D	48.9%	50.3%	49.3%	50.7%
1956	1,128,977	508,041	Anderson, Emmett T.	616,773	Rosellini, Albert D.	4,163	108,732 D	45.0%	54.6%	45.2%	54.8%
1952	1,078,497	567,822	Langlie, Arthur B.	510,675	Mitchell, Hugh B.		57,147 R	52.6%	47.4%	52.6%	47.4%
1948	883,141	445,958	Langlie, Arthur B.	417,035	Wallgren, Mon C.	20,148	28,923 R	50.5%	47.2%	51.7%	48.3%

POSTWAR VOTE FOR SENATOR

Year	Total Vote	Republican Vote	Republican Candidate	Democratic Vote	Democratic Candidate	Other Vote	Rep.-Dem. Plurality	Percentage Total Vote Rep.	Percentage Total Vote Dem.	Percentage Major Vote Rep.	Percentage Major Vote Dem.
2000	2,461,379	1,197,208	Gorton, Slade	1,199,437	Cantwell, Maria	64,734	2,229 D	48.6%	48.7%	50.0%	50.0%
1998	1,888,561	785,377	Smith, Linda	1,103,184	Murray, Patty		317,807 D	41.6%	58.4%	41.6%	58.4%
1994	1,700,173	947,821	Gorton, Slade	752,352	Sims, Ron		195,469 R	55.7%	44.3%	55.7%	44.3%
1992	2,219,162	1,020,829	Chandler, Rod	1,197,973	Murray, Patty	360	177,144 D	46.0%	54.0%	46.0%	54.0%
1988	1,848,542	944,359	Gorton, Slade	904,183	Lowry, Mike		40,176 R	51.1%	48.9%	51.1%	48.9%
1986	1,337,367	650,931	Gorton, Slade	677,471	Adams, Brock	8,965	26,540 D	48.7%	50.7%	49.0%	51.0%
1983S	1,213,307	672,326	Evans, Daniel J.	540,981	Lowry, Mike		131,345 R	55.4%	44.6%	55.4%	44.6%
1982	1,368,476	332,273	Jewett, Doug	943,655	Jackson, Henry M.	92,548	611,382 D	24.3%	69.0%	26.0%	74.0%
1980	1,728,369	936,317	Gorton, Slade	792,052	Magnuson, Warren G.		144,265 R	54.2%	45.8%	54.2%	45.8%
1976	1,491,111	361,546	Brown, George M.	1,071,219	Jackson, Henry M.	58,346	709,673 D	24.2%	71.8%	25.2%	74.8%
1974	1,007,847	363,626	Metcalf, Jack	611,811	Magnuson, Warren G.	32,410	248,185 D	36.1%	60.7%	37.3%	62.7%
1970	1,066,807	170,790	Elicker, Charles W.	879,385	Jackson, Henry M.	16,632	708,595 D	16.0%	82.4%	16.3%	83.7%
1968	1,236,063	435,894	Metcalf, Jack	796,183	Magnuson, Warren G.	3,986	360,289 D	35.3%	64.4%	35.4%	64.6%
1964	1,213,088	337,138	Andrews, Lloyd J.	875,950	Jackson, Henry M.		538,812 D	27.8%	72.2%	27.8%	72.2%
1962	943,229	446,204	Christensen, Richard G.	491,365	Magnuson, Warren G.	5,660	45,161 D	47.3%	52.1%	47.6%	52.4%
1958	886,822	278,271	Bantz, William B.	597,040	Jackson, Henry M.	11,511	318,769 D	31.4%	67.3%	31.8%	68.2%
1956	1,122,217	436,652	Langlie, Arthur B.	685,565	Magnuson, Warren G.		248,913 D	38.9%	61.1%	38.9%	61.1%
1952	1,058,735	460,884	Cain, Harry P.	595,288	Jackson, Henry M.	2,563	134,404 D	43.5%	56.2%	43.6%	56.4%
1950	744,783	342,464	Williams, Walter	397,719	Magnuson, Warren G.	4,600	55,255 D	46.0%	53.4%	46.3%	53.7%
1946	660,342	358,847	Cain, Harry P.	298,683	Mitchell, Hugh B.	2,812	60,164 R	54.3%	45.2%	54.6%	45.4%

The 1983 election was for a short term to fill a vacancy.

WASHINGTON

Congressional districts first established for elections held in 2002
9 members

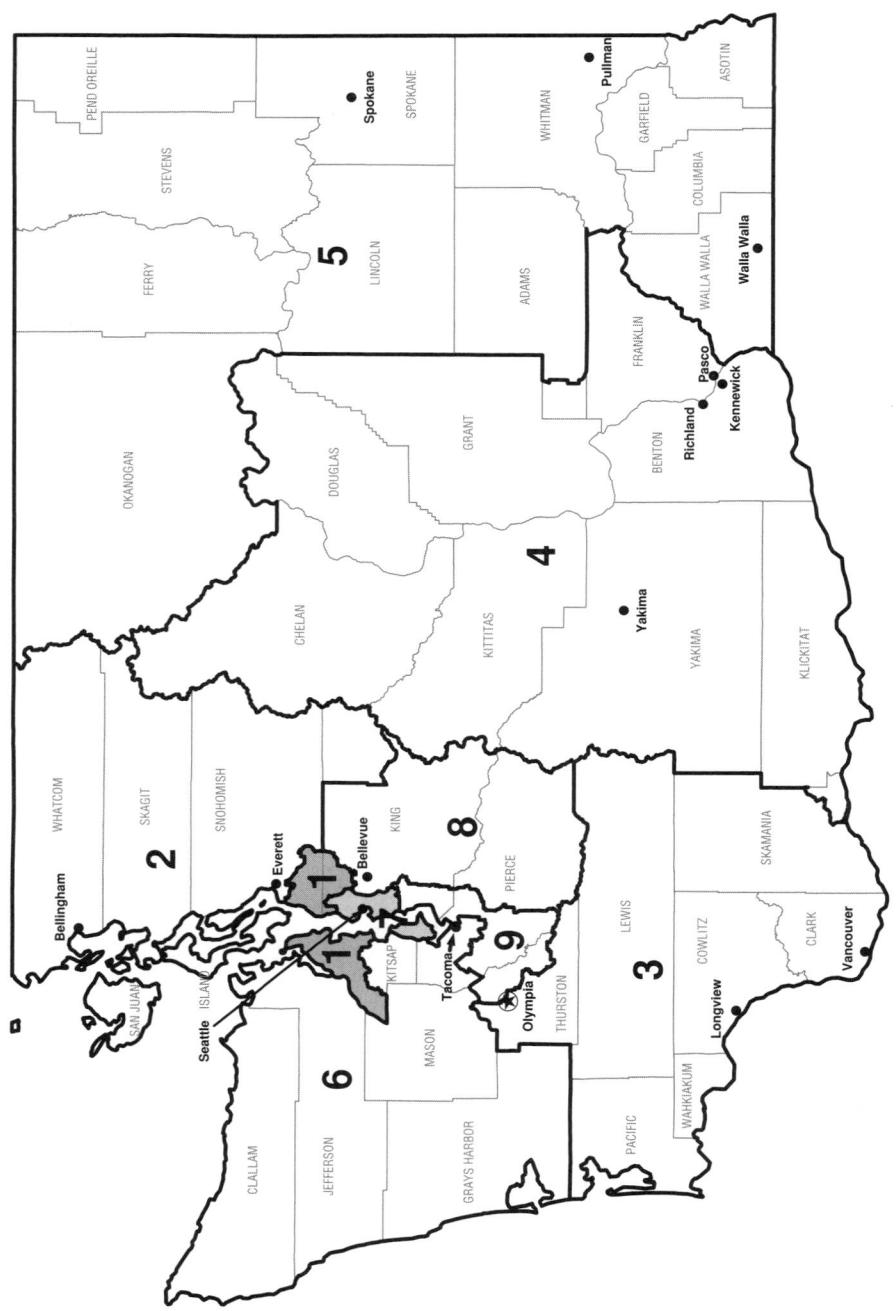

WASHINGTON

Seattle, Puget Sound Area

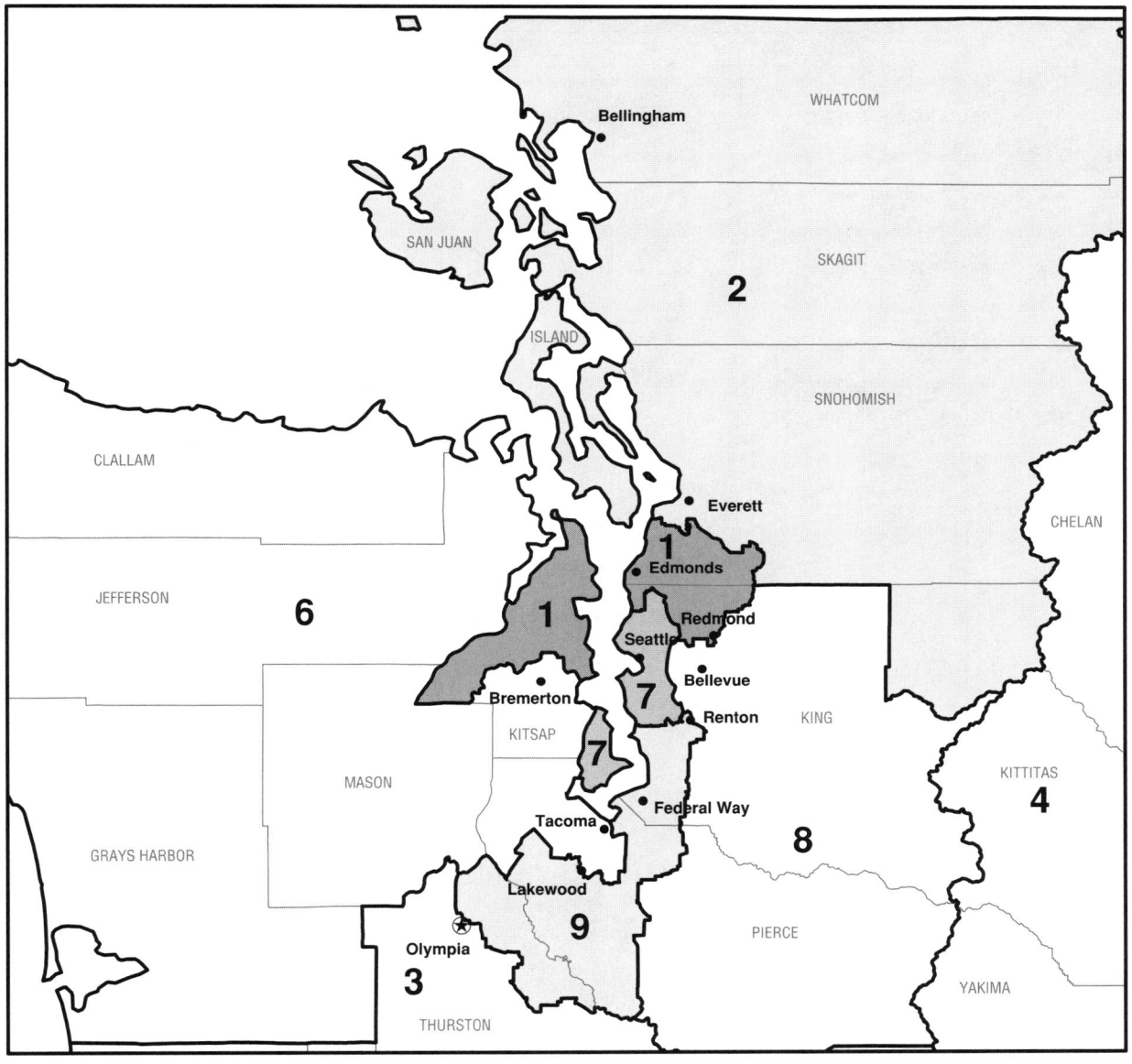

WASHINGTON

HOUSE OF REPRESENTATIVES

CD	Year	Total Vote	Republican Vote	Republican Candidate	Democratic Vote	Democratic Candidate	Other Vote	Rep.-Dem. Plurality	Percentage Total Vote Rep.	Dem.	Major Vote Rep.	Dem.
1	2002	205,034	84,696	Marine, Joe	114,087	Inslee, Jay*	6,251	29,391 D	41.3%	55.6%	42.6%	57.4%
2	2002	202,150	92,528	Smith, Norma	101,219	Larsen, Rick*	8,403	8,691 D	45.8%	50.1%	47.8%	52.2%
3	2002	193,329	74,065	Zarelli, Joseph	119,264	Baird, Brian*		45,199 D	38.3%	61.7%	38.3%	61.7%
4	2002	161,829	108,257	Hastings, Doc*	53,572	Mason, Craig		54,685 R	66.9%	33.1%	66.9%	33.1%
5	2002	202,282	126,757	Nethercutt, George*	65,146	Haggin, Bart	10,379	61,611 R	62.7%	32.2%	66.1%	33.9%
6	2002	196,444	61,584	Lawrence, Bob	126,116	Dicks, Norm*	8,744	64,532 D	31.3%	64.2%	32.8%	67.2%
7	2002	211,003	46,256	Cassady, Carol Thorne	156,300	McDermott, Jim*	8,447	110,044 D	21.9%	74.1%	22.8%	77.2%
8	2002	203,335	121,633	Dunn, Jennifer*	75,931	Behrens-Benedict, Heidi	5,771	45,702 R	59.8%	37.3%	61.6%	38.4%
9	2002	163,710	63,146	Casada, Sarah	95,805	Smith, Adam*	4,759	32,659 D	38.6%	58.5%	39.7%	60.3%
Total	2002	1,739,116	778,922		907,440		52,754	128,518 D	44.8%	52.2%	46.2%	53.8%

An asterisk (*) denotes incumbent.

WASHINGTON

GENERAL AND PRIMARY ELECTIONS

2002 GENERAL ELECTIONS

House   Other vote was:

CD 1   6,251 Libertarian (Mark B. Wilson).
CD 2   4,326 Libertarian (Bruce Guthrie); 4,077 Green (Bernard Patrick "Bern" Haggerty).
CD 3
CD 4
CD 5   10,379 Libertarian (Rob Chase).
CD 6   8,744 Libertarian (John A. Bennett).
CD 7   8,447 Libertarian (Stan Lippmann).
CD 8   5,771 Libertarian (Mark A. Taff).
CD 9   4,759 Libertarian (J. Mills).

2002 PRIMARY ELECTIONS

Primary   September 17, 2002   **Registration**   3,239,122   No Party Registration
(as of Sept. 17, 2002)

Primary Type   Open—For each office, candidates ran on a single, all-party ballot, and the primary was open to all registered voters. The nominations went to the candidate with the highest vote in each party, providing the winner received at least 1 percent of the total votes cast for that office.

Note: An asterisk (*) denotes incumbent.

WASHINGTON

GENERAL AND PRIMARY ELECTIONS

			Overall Percentage	Republican Percentage	Democratic Percentage
Congressional District 1	Jay Inslee (D)*	65,368	56.3%		92.5%
	Joe Marine (R)	42,473	36.6%	100.0%	
	Mike The Mover (D)	5,291	4.6%		7.5%
	Mark B. Wilson (Libertarian)	3,025	2.6%		
	TOTAL	116,157			
	Republican Total	42,473			
	Democratic Total	70,659			
Congressional District 2	Rick Larsen (D)*	59,238	48.4%		100.0%
	Norma Smith (R)	26,365	21.5%	46.2%	
	Herb Meyer (R)	22,168	18.1%	38.8%	
	Warren E. Hanson (R)	8,541	7.0%	15.0%	
	Bernard Patrick "Bern" Haggerty (Green)	3,233	2.6%		
	Bruce Guthrie (Libertarian)	2,854	2.3%		
	TOTAL	122,399			
	Republican Total	57,074			
	Democratic Total	59,238			
Congressional District 3	Brian Baird (D)*	77,540	56.8%		100.0%
	Joseph Zarelli (R)	58,939	43.2%	100.0%	
	TOTAL	136,479			
	Republican Total	58,939			
	Democratic Total	77,540			
Congressional District 4	Doc Hastings (R)*	75,745	69.9%	92.1%	
	Craig Mason (D)	18,726	17.3%		71.8%
	Thor Amundson (D)	7,342	6.8%		28.2%
	Gordon Allen Pross (R)	6,500	6.0%	7.9%	
	TOTAL	108,313			
	Republican Total	82,245			
	Democratic Total	26,068			
Congressional District 5	George Nethercutt (R)*	83,972	64.4%	100.0%	
	Bart Haggin (D)	38,630	29.6%		100.0%
	Rob Chase (Libertarian)	7,700	5.9%		
	TOTAL	130,302			
	Republican Total	83,972			
	Democratic Total	38,630			
Congressional District 6	Norm Dicks (D)*	83,455	63.0%		89.5%
	Bob Lawrence (R)	35,639	26.9%	100.0%	
	Douglas Milholland (D)	9,758	7.4%		10.5%
	John A. Bennett (Libertarian)	3,549	2.7%		
	TOTAL	132,401			
	Republican Total	35,639			
	Democratic Total	93,213			
Congressional District 7	Jim McDermott (D)*	84,876	77.4%		100.0%
	Carol Thorne Cassady (R)	20,688	18.9%	100.0%	
	Stan Lippmann (Libertarian)	2,238	2.0%		
	Brien Bartels (Libertarian)	1,874	1.7%		
	TOTAL	109,676			
	Republican Total	20,688			
	Democratic Total	84,876			

WASHINGTON

GENERAL AND PRIMARY ELECTIONS

			Overall Percentage	Republican Percentage	Democratic Percentage
Congressional District 8	Jennifer Dunn (R)*	68,199	64.0%	100.0%	
	Heidi Behrens-Benedict (D)	35,681	33.5%		100.0%
	Mark A. Taff (Libertarian)	2,606	2.4%		
	TOTAL	106,486			
	Republican Total	68,199			
	Democratic Total	35,681			
Congressional District 9	Adam Smith (D)*	57,250	59.5%		100.0%
	Sarah Casada (R)	36,368	37.8%	100.0%	
	J. Mills (Libertarian)	2,555	2.7%		
	TOTAL	96,173			
	Republican Total	36,368			
	Democratic Total	57,250			

WEST VIRGINIA

GOVERNOR
Bob Wise (D). Elected 2000 to a four-year term.

SENATORS (2 Democrats)
Robert C. Byrd (D). Reelected 2000 to a six-year term. Previously elected 1994, 1988, 1982, 1976, 1970, 1964, 1958.

John D. Rockefeller IV (D). Reelected 2002 to a six-year term. Previously elected 1996, 1990, 1984.

REPRESENTATIVES (2 Democrats, 1 Republican)
1. Alan B. Mollohan (D)   2. Shelley Moore Capito (R)   3. Nick J. Rahall II (D)

POSTWAR VOTE FOR PRESIDENT

| | | Republican | | Democratic | | Other | | Percentage | | | |
| | | | | | | | | Total Vote | | Major Vote | |
Year	Total Vote	Vote	Candidate	Vote	Candidate	Vote	Plurality	Rep.	Dem.	Rep.	Dem.
2000**	648,124	336,475	Bush, George W.	295,497	Gore, Al	16,152	40,978 R	51.9%	45.6%	53.2%	46.8%
1996**	636,459	233,946	Dole, Bob	327,812	Clinton, Bill	74,701	93,866 D	36.8%	51.5%	41.6%	58.4%
1992**	683,762	241,974	Bush, George	331,001	Clinton, Bill	110,787	89,027 D	35.4%	48.4%	42.2%	57.8%
1988	653,311	310,065	Bush, George	341,016	Dukakis, Michael S.	2,230	30,951 D	47.5%	52.2%	47.6%	52.4%
1984	735,742	405,483	Reagan, Ronald	328,125	Mondale, Walter F.	2,134	77,358 R	55.1%	44.6%	55.3%	44.7%
1980**	737,715	334,206	Reagan, Ronald	367,462	Carter, Jimmy	36,047	33,256 D	45.3%	49.8%	47.6%	52.4%
1976	750,964	314,760	Ford, Gerald R.	435,914	Carter, Jimmy	290	121,154 D	41.9%	58.0%	41.9%	58.1%
1972	762,399	484,964	Nixon, Richard M.	277,435	McGovern, George S.		207,529 R	63.6%	36.4%	63.6%	36.4%
1968	754,206	307,555	Nixon, Richard M.	374,091	Humphrey, Hubert H.	72,560	66,536 D	40.8%	49.6%	45.1%	54.9%
1964	792,040	253,953	Goldwater, Barry M.	538,087	Johnson, Lyndon B.		284,134 D	32.1%	67.9%	32.1%	67.9%
1960	837,781	395,995	Nixon, Richard M.	441,786	Kennedy, John F.		45,791 D	47.3%	52.7%	47.3%	52.7%
1956	830,831	449,297	Eisenhower, Dwight D.	381,534	Stevenson, Adlai E.	67,763	67,763 D	54.1%	45.9%	54.1%	45.9%
1952	873,548	419,970	Eisenhower, Dwight D.	453,578	Stevenson, Adlai E.		33,608 D	48.1%	51.9%	48.1%	51.9%
1948	748,750	316,251	Dewey, Thomas E.	429,188	Truman, Harry S.	3,311	112,937 D	42.2%	57.3%	42.4%	57.6%

In 2000 the other vote column includes 10,680 votes cast for Green (Nader). In 1996 the other vote column includes 71,639 votes cast for Perot. In 1992 the other vote column includes 108,829 votes cast for Perot. In 1980 the other vote column includes 31,691 votes for Independent (Anderson).

POSTWAR VOTE FOR GOVERNOR

| | | Republican | | Democratic | | Other | Rep.-Dem. | Percentage | | | |
| | | | | | | | | Total Vote | | Major Vote | |
Year	Total Vote	Vote	Candidate	Vote	Candidate	Vote	Plurality	Rep.	Dem.	Rep.	Dem.
2000	648,047	305,926	Underwood, Cecil H.	324,822	Wise, Bob	17,299	18,896 D	47.2%	50.1%	48.5%	51.5%
1996	628,559	324,518	Underwood, Cecil H.	287,870	Pritt, Charlotte	16,171	36,648 R	51.6%	45.8%	53.0%	47.0%
1992	657,193	240,390	Benedict, Cleveland K.	368,302	Caperton, Gaston	48,501	127,912 D	36.6%	56.0%	39.5%	60.5%
1988	649,593	267,172	Moore, Arch A.	382,421	Caperton, Gaston		115,249 D	41.1%	58.9%	41.1%	58.9%
1984	741,502	394,937	Moore, Arch A.	346,565	See, Clyde M.		48,372 R	53.3%	46.7%	53.3%	46.7%
1980	742,150	337,240	Moore, Arch A.	401,863	Rockefeller, John D.	3,047	64,623 D	45.4%	54.1%	45.6%	54.4%
1976	749,270	253,420	Underwood, Cecil H.	495,661	Rockefeller, John D.	189	242,241 D	33.8%	66.2%	33.8%	66.2%
1972	774,279	423,817	Moore, Arch A.	350,462	Rockefeller, John D.		73,355 R	54.7%	45.3%	54.7%	45.3%
1968	743,845	378,315	Moore, Arch A.	365,530	Sprouse, James M.		12,785 R	50.9%	49.1%	50.9%	49.1%
1964	788,582	355,559	Underwood, Cecil H.	433,023	Smith, Hulett C.		77,464 D	45.1%	54.9%	45.1%	54.9%
1960	827,420	380,665	Neely, Harold E.	446,755	Barron, W. W.		66,090 D	46.0%	54.0%	46.0%	54.0%
1956	817,623	440,502	Underwood, Cecil H.	377,121	Mollohan, Robert H.		63,381 R	53.9%	46.1%	53.9%	46.1%
1952	882,527	427,629	Holt, Rush D.	454,898	Marland, William C.		27,269 D	48.5%	51.5%	48.5%	51.5%
1948	768,061	329,309	Boreman, Herbert	438,752	Patteson, Okey L.		109,443 D	42.9%	57.1%	42.9%	57.1%

WEST VIRGINIA

POSTWAR VOTE FOR SENATOR

Year	Total Vote	Republican		Democratic		Other Vote	Rep.-Dem. Plurality	Percentage			
								Total Vote		Major Vote	
		Vote	Candidate	Vote	Candidate			Rep.	Dem.	Rep.	Dem.
2002	436,183	160,902	Wolfe, Jay	275,281	Rockefeller, John D. IV		114,379 D	36.9%	63.1%	36.9%	63.1%
2000	603,477	121,635	Gallaher, David T.	469,215	Byrd, Robert C.	12,627	347,580 D	20.2%	77.8%	20.6%	79.4%
1996	595,614	139,088	Burks, Betty A.	456,526	Rockefeller, John D. IV		317,438 D	23.4%	76.6%	23.4%	76.6%
1994	420,936	130,441	Klos, Stan	290,495	Byrd, Robert C.		160,054 D	31.0%	69.0%	31.0%	69.0%
1990	404,305	128,071	Yoder, John	276,234	Rockefeller, John D. IV		148,163 D	31.7%	68.3%	31.7%	68.3%
1988	634,547	223,564	Wolfe, M. Jay	410,983	Byrd, Robert C.		187,419 D	35.2%	64.8%	35.2%	64.8%
1984	722,212	344,680	Raese, John R.	374,233	Rockefeller, John D. IV	3,299	29,553 D	47.7%	51.8%	47.9%	52.1%
1982	565,314	173,910	Benedict, Cleveland K.	387,170	Byrd, Robert C.	4,234	213,260 D	30.8%	68.5%	31.0%	69.0%
1978	493,351	244,317	Moore, Arch A.	249,034	Randolph, Jennings		4,717 D	49.5%	50.5%	49.5%	50.5%
1976	566,790		—	566,423	Byrd, Robert C.	367	566,423 D		99.9%		100.0%
1972	731,841	245,531	Leonard, Louise	486,310	Randolph, Jennings		240,779 D	33.5%	66.5%	33.5%	66.5%
1970	445,623	99,658	Dodson, Elmer H.	345,965	Byrd, Robert C.		246,307 D	22.4%	77.6%	22.4%	77.6%
1966	491,216	198,891	Love, Francis J.	292,325	Randolph, Jennings		93,434 D	40.5%	59.5%	40.5%	59.5%
1964	761,087	246,072	Benedict, Cooper P.	515,015	Byrd, Robert C.		268,943 D	32.3%	67.7%	32.3%	67.7%
1960	828,292	369,935	Underwood, Cecil H.	458,355	Randolph, Jennings	2	88,420 D	44.7%	55.3%	44.7%	55.3%
1958	644,917	263,172	Revercomb, Chapman	381,745	Byrd, Robert C.		118,573 D	40.8%	59.2%	40.8%	59.2%
1958S	630,677	256,510	Hoblitzell, John D.	374,167	Randolph, Jennings		117,657 D	40.7%	59.3%	40.7%	59.3%
1956S	805,174	432,123	Revercomb, Chapman	373,051	Marland, William C.		59,072 R	53.7%	46.3%	53.7%	46.3%
1954	593,329	268,066	Sweeney, Tom	325,263	Neely, Matthew M.		57,197 D	45.2%	54.8%	45.2%	54.8%
1952	876,573	406,554	Revercomb, Chapman	470,019	Kilgore, Harley M.		63,465 D	46.4%	53.6%	46.4%	53.6%
1948	763,888	328,534	Revercomb, Chapman	435,354	Neely, Matthew M.		106,820 D	43.0%	57.0%	43.0%	57.0%
1946	542,768	269,617	Sweeney, Tom	273,151	Kilgore, Harley M.		3,534 D	49.7%	50.3%	49.7%	50.3%

One of the 1958 elections and the 1956 election were for short terms to fill vacancies.

WEST VIRGINIA

Congressional districts first established for elections held in 2002
3 members

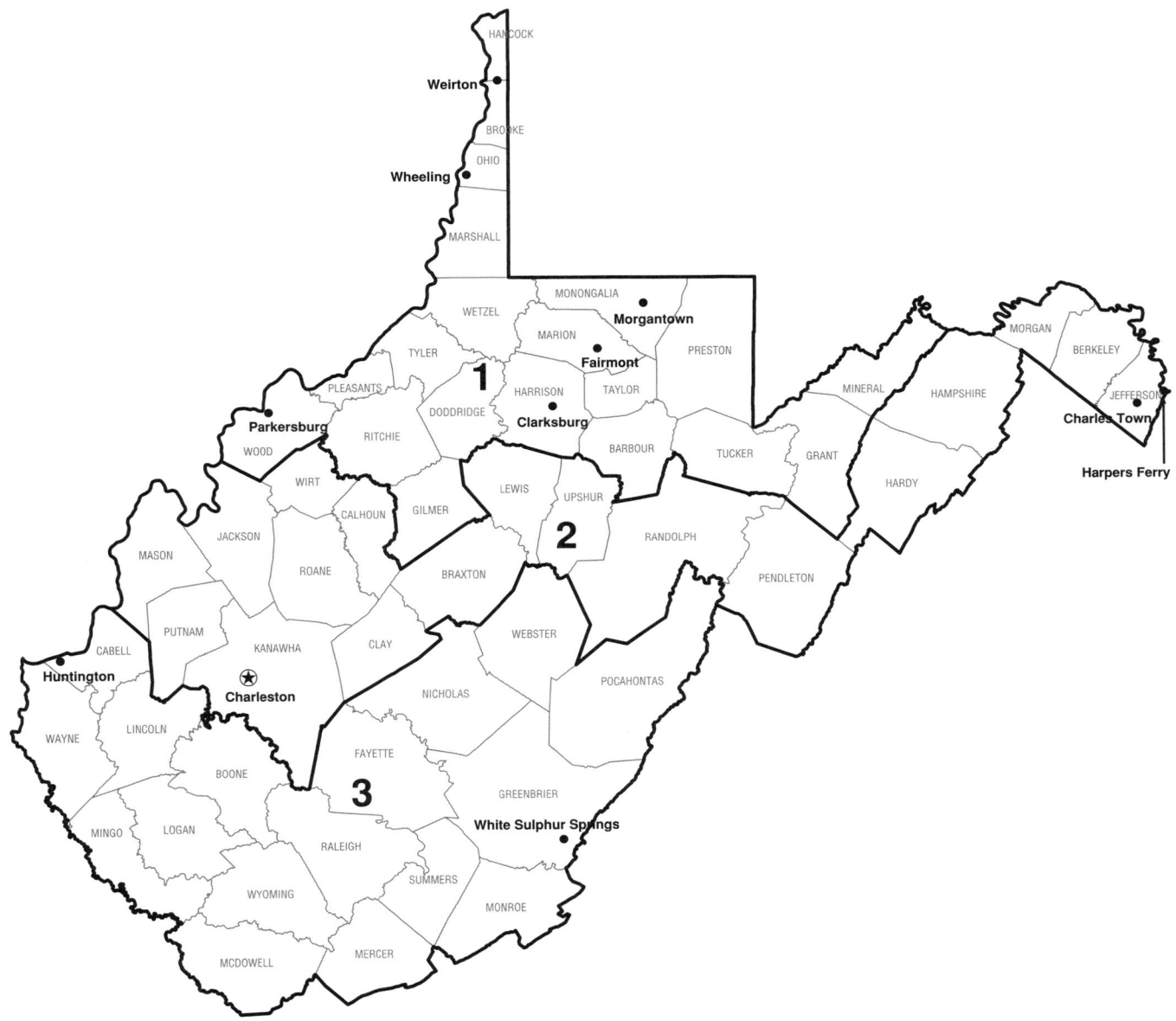

WEST VIRGINIA

SENATOR 2002

2000 Census Population	County	Total Vote	Republican	Democratic	Other	Rep.-Dem. Plurality		Percentage			
								Total Vote		Major Vote	
								Rep.	Dem.	Rep.	Dem.
15,557	BARBOUR	4,384	1,693	2,691		998	D	38.6%	61.4%	38.6%	61.4%
75,905	BERKELEY	16,962	8,088	8,874		786	D	47.7%	52.3%	47.7%	52.3%
25,535	BOONE	5,725	1,163	4,562		3,399	D	20.3%	79.7%	20.3%	79.7%
14,702	BRAXTON	3,539	1,247	2,292		1,045	D	35.2%	64.8%	35.2%	64.8%
25,447	BROOKE	4,835	1,405	3,430		2,025	D	29.1%	70.9%	29.1%	70.9%
96,784	CABELL	22,479	8,324	14,155		5,831	D	37.0%	63.0%	37.0%	63.0%
7,582	CALHOUN	1,940	701	1,239		538	D	36.1%	63.9%	36.1%	63.9%
10,330	CLAY	2,513	838	1,675		837	D	33.3%	66.7%	33.3%	66.7%
7,403	DODDRIDGE	1,988	1,250	738		512	R	62.9%	37.1%	62.9%	37.1%
47,579	FAYETTE	9,866	2,723	7,143		4,420	D	27.6%	72.4%	27.6%	72.4%
7,160	GILMER	1,789	702	1,087		385	D	39.2%	60.8%	39.2%	60.8%
11,299	GRANT	2,724	1,628	1,096		532	R	59.8%	40.2%	59.8%	40.2%
34,453	GREENBRIER	9,341	3,473	5,868		2,395	D	37.2%	62.8%	37.2%	62.8%
20,203	HAMPSHIRE	4,573	2,170	2,403		233	D	47.5%	52.5%	47.5%	52.5%
32,667	HANCOCK	6,416	1,959	4,457		2,498	D	30.5%	69.5%	30.5%	69.5%
12,669	HARDY	3,277	1,092	2,185		1,093	D	33.3%	66.7%	33.3%	66.7%
68,652	HARRISON	17,192	6,612	10,580		3,968	D	38.5%	61.5%	38.5%	61.5%
28,000	JACKSON	8,848	3,509	5,339		1,830	D	39.7%	60.3%	39.7%	60.3%
42,190	JEFFERSON	10,734	4,165	6,569		2,404	D	38.8%	61.2%	38.8%	61.2%
200,073	KANAWHA	57,848	20,169	37,679		17,510	D	34.9%	65.1%	34.9%	65.1%
16,919	LEWIS	4,598	1,941	2,657		716	D	42.2%	57.8%	42.2%	57.8%
22,108	LINCOLN	4,944	1,417	3,527		2,110	D	28.7%	71.3%	28.7%	71.3%
37,710	LOGAN	7,548	1,439	6,109		4,670	D	19.1%	80.9%	19.1%	80.9%
27,329	MCDOWELL	3,670	540	3,130		2,590	D	14.7%	85.3%	14.7%	85.3%
56,598	MARION	14,510	4,631	9,879		5,248	D	31.9%	68.1%	31.9%	68.1%
35,519	MARSHALL	8,925	2,889	6,036		3,147	D	32.4%	67.6%	32.4%	67.6%
25,957	MASON	7,447	2,534	4,913		2,379	D	34.0%	66.0%	34.0%	66.0%
62,980	MERCER	12,302	4,435	7,867		3,432	D	36.1%	63.9%	36.1%	63.9%
27,078	MINERAL	6,343	3,108	3,235		127	D	49.0%	51.0%	49.0%	51.0%
28,253	MINGO	5,485	935	4,550		3,615	D	17.0%	83.0%	17.0%	83.0%
81,866	MONONGALIA	16,961	6,024	10,937		4,913	D	35.5%	64.5%	35.5%	64.5%
14,583	MONROE	3,676	1,448	2,228		780	D	39.4%	60.6%	39.4%	60.6%
14,943	MORGAN	3,893	1,953	1,940		13	R	50.2%	49.8%	50.2%	49.8%
26,562	NICHOLAS	6,067	2,021	4,046		2,025	D	33.3%	66.7%	33.3%	66.7%
47,427	OHIO	11,147	3,654	7,493		3,839	D	32.8%	67.2%	32.8%	67.2%
8,196	PENDLETON	2,163	838	1,325		487	D	38.7%	61.3%	38.7%	61.3%
7,514	PLEASANTS	2,017	847	1,170		323	D	42.0%	58.0%	42.0%	58.0%
9,131	POCAHONTAS	2,364	830	1,534		704	D	35.1%	64.9%	35.1%	64.9%
29,334	PRESTON	7,522	3,153	4,369		1,216	D	41.9%	58.1%	41.9%	58.1%
51,589	PUTNAM	16,464	6,891	9,573		2,682	D	41.9%	58.1%	41.9%	58.1%
79,220	RALEIGH	15,648	6,634	9,014		2,380	D	42.4%	57.6%	42.4%	57.6%
28,262	RANDOLPH	7,110	2,578	4,532		1,954	D	36.3%	63.7%	36.3%	63.7%
10,343	RITCHIE	2,738	1,551	1,187		364	R	56.6%	43.4%	56.6%	43.4%
15,446	ROANE	4,329	1,650	2,679		1,029	D	38.1%	61.9%	38.1%	61.9%
12,999	SUMMERS	3,227	1,282	1,945		663	D	39.7%	60.3%	39.7%	60.3%
16,089	TAYLOR	4,171	1,470	2,701		1,231	D	35.2%	64.8%	35.2%	64.8%
7,321	TUCKER	2,428	939	1,489		550	D	38.7%	61.3%	38.7%	61.3%
9,592	TYLER	2,166	1,074	1,092		18	D	49.6%	50.4%	49.6%	50.4%
23,404	UPSHUR	6,176	3,016	3,160		144	D	48.8%	51.2%	48.8%	51.2%
42,903	WAYNE	9,305	2,951	6,354		3,403	D	31.7%	68.3%	31.7%	68.3%
9,719	WEBSTER	2,303	536	1,767		1,231	D	23.3%	76.7%	23.3%	76.7%
17,693	WETZEL	3,693	1,261	2,432		1,171	D	34.1%	65.9%	34.1%	65.9%
5,873	WIRT	1,681	727	954		227	D	43.2%	56.8%	43.2%	56.8%
87,986	WOOD	21,827	9,603	12,224		2,621	D	44.0%	56.0%	44.0%	56.0%
25,708	WYOMING	4,362	1,191	3,171		1,980	D	27.3%	72.7%	27.3%	72.7%
1,808,344	TOTAL	436,183	160,902	275,281		114,379	D	36.9%	63.1%	36.9%	63.1%

WEST VIRGINIA

HOUSE OF REPRESENTATIVES

			Republican		Democratic		Other	Rep.-Dem.	Percentage			
									Total Vote		Major Vote	
CD	Year	Total Vote	Vote	Candidate	Vote	Candidate	Vote	Plurality	Rep.	Dem.	Rep.	Dem.
1	2002	111,261			110,941	Mollohan, Alan B.*	320	110,941 D		99.7%		100.0%
2	2002	163,676	98,276	Capito, Shelley Moore*	65,400	Humphreys, Jim		32,876 R	60.0%	40.0%	60.0%	40.0%
3	2002	125,012	37,229	Chapman, Paul E.	87,783	Rahall, Nick J. II*		50,554 D	29.8%	70.2%	29.8%	70.2%
Total	2002	399,949	135,505		264,124		320	128,619 D	33.9%	66.0%	33.9%	66.1%

An asterisk (*) denotes incumbent.

WEST VIRGINIA

GENERAL AND PRIMARY ELECTIONS

2002 GENERAL ELECTIONS

Senator

House

CD 1   Other vote was:
CD 2
CD 3   320 write-in (Louis "Lou" Davis).

2002 PRIMARY ELECTIONS

Primary   May 14, 2002

Registration (as of May 14, 2002)		
Republican	305,063
Democratic	639,368
Other Parties	11,959
Nonpartisan	93,620
TOTAL	1,050,010

Primary Type   Only registered Democrats could vote in the Democratic primary. Registered Republicans and those with no party registration could vote in the Republican primary.

Note: An asterisk (*) denotes incumbent.

	REPUBLICAN PRIMARIES			DEMOCRATIC PRIMARIES		
Senator	Jay Wolfe	46,096	61.0%	John D. Rockefeller IV*	198,327	89.9%
	Hiram C. "Bucky" Lewis IV	29,417	39.0%	Bruce Barilla	11,178	5.1%
				William "Bill" Galloway	11,173	5.1%
	TOTAL	75,513		TOTAL	220,678	
Congressional District 1	No Republican candidate			Alan B. Mollohan*	60,443	100.0%
Congressional District 2	Shelley Moore Capito*	32,655	100.0%	Jim Humphreys	31,597	51.4%
				Margaret L. Workman	29,888	48.6%
				TOTAL	61,485	
Congressional District 3	*No Republican candidate filed for the primary. Paul E. Chapman was named to fill the vacancy on the general election ballot.*			Nick J. Rahall II*	72,655	86.7%
				Theodore W. Hamb	11,110	13.3%
				TOTAL	83,765	

WEST VIRGINIA REPUBLICAN PRIMARY

SENATOR 2002

2000 Census Population	County	Total Vote	Wolfe	Lewis	Winner	Percentage of Total Vote	
						Wolfe	Lewis
15,557	BARBOUR	1,288	855	433	Wolfe	66.4%	33.6%
75,905	BERKELEY	2,840	1,070	1,770	Lewis	37.7%	62.3%
25,535	BOONE	410	222	188	Wolfe	54.1%	45.9%
14,702	BRAXTON	321	229	92	Wolfe	71.3%	28.7%
25,447	BROOKE	687	269	418	Lewis	39.2%	60.8%
96,784	CABELL	4,079	2,703	1,376	Wolfe	66.3%	33.7%
7,582	CALHOUN	279	221	58	Wolfe	79.2%	20.8%
10,330	CLAY	347	173	174	Lewis	49.9%	50.1%
7,403	DODDRIDGE	1,018	943	75	Wolfe	92.6%	7.4%
47,579	FAYETTE	893	402	491	Lewis	45.0%	55.0%
7,160	GILMER	316	255	61	Wolfe	80.7%	19.3%
11,299	GRANT	1,349	685	664	Wolfe	50.8%	49.2%
34,453	GREENBRIER	1,338	806	532	Wolfe	60.2%	39.8%
20,203	HAMPSHIRE	848	475	373	Wolfe	56.0%	44.0%
32,667	HANCOCK	762	379	383	Lewis	49.7%	50.3%
12,669	HARDY	256	123	133	Lewis	48.0%	52.0%
68,652	HARRISON	3,342	2,894	448	Wolfe	86.6%	13.4%
28,000	JACKSON	1,853	1,122	731	Wolfe	60.6%	39.4%
42,190	JEFFERSON	1,113	528	585	Lewis	47.4%	52.6%
200,073	KANAWHA	7,818	5,585	2,233	Wolfe	71.4%	28.6%
16,919	LEWIS	1,433	1,209	224	Wolfe	84.4%	15.6%
22,108	LINCOLN	465	312	153	Wolfe	67.1%	32.9%
37,710	LOGAN	288	181	107	Wolfe	62.8%	37.2%
27,329	MCDOWELL	150	49	101	Lewis	32.7%	67.3%
56,598	MARION	2,650	1,502	1,148	Wolfe	56.7%	43.3%
35,519	MARSHALL	1,702	606	1,096	Lewis	35.6%	64.4%
25,957	MASON	1,579	978	601	Wolfe	61.9%	38.1%
62,980	MERCER	1,377	669	708	Lewis	48.6%	51.4%
27,078	MINERAL	1,442	592	850	Lewis	41.1%	58.9%
28,253	MINGO	240	144	96	Wolfe	60.0%	40.0%
81,866	MONONGALIA	3,107	1,142	1,965	Lewis	36.8%	63.2%
14,583	MONROE	786	389	397	Lewis	49.5%	50.5%
14,943	MORGAN	1,087	462	625	Lewis	42.5%	57.5%
26,562	NICHOLAS	803	390	413	Lewis	48.6%	51.4%
47,427	OHIO	1,728	709	1,019	Lewis	41.0%	59.0%
8,196	PENDLETON	411	244	167	Wolfe	59.4%	40.6%
7,514	PLEASANTS	455	352	103	Wolfe	77.4%	22.6%
9,131	POCAHONTAS	478	314	164	Wolfe	65.7%	34.3%
29,334	PRESTON	2,602	957	1,645	Lewis	36.8%	63.2%
51,589	PUTNAM	2,617	1,592	1,025	Wolfe	60.8%	39.2%
79,220	RALEIGH	1,904	1,085	819	Wolfe	57.0%	43.0%
28,262	RANDOLPH	907	599	308	Wolfe	66.0%	34.0%
10,343	RITCHIE	1,266	1,086	180	Wolfe	85.8%	14.2%
15,446	ROANE	1,191	733	458	Wolfe	61.5%	38.5%
12,999	SUMMERS	359	221	138	Wolfe	61.6%	38.4%
16,089	TAYLOR	1,075	637	438	Wolfe	59.3%	40.7%
7,321	TUCKER	509	310	199	Wolfe	60.9%	39.1%
9,592	TYLER	664	548	116	Wolfe	82.5%	17.5%
23,404	UPSHUR	2,563	2,027	536	Wolfe	79.1%	20.9%
42,903	WAYNE	1,072	531	541	Lewis	49.5%	50.5%
9,719	WEBSTER	133	89	44	Wolfe	66.9%	33.1%
17,693	WETZEL	508	273	235	Wolfe	53.7%	46.3%
5,873	WIRT	474	352	122	Wolfe	74.3%	25.7%
87,986	WOOD	5,765	4,577	1,188	Wolfe	79.4%	20.6%
25,708	WYOMING	566	296	270	Wolfe	52.3%	47.7%
1,808,344	TOTAL	75,513	46,096	29,417	Wolfe	61.0%	39.0%

WEST VIRGINIA DEMOCRATIC PRIMARY

SENATOR 2002

2000 Census Population	County	Total Vote	Rockefeller	Other	Winner	Percentage of Total Vote	
						Rockefeller	Other
15,557	BARBOUR	2,482	2,211	271	Rockefeller	89.1%	10.9%
75,905	BERKELEY	4,028	3,574	454	Rockefeller	88.7%	11.3%
25,535	BOONE	6,468	6,077	391	Rockefeller	94.0%	6.0%
14,702	BRAXTON	2,385	2,146	239	Rockefeller	90.0%	10.0%
25,447	BROOKE	3,585	2,851	734	Rockefeller	79.5%	20.5%
96,784	CABELL	9,858	8,982	876	Rockefeller	91.1%	8.9%
7,582	CALHOUN	1,172	1,045	127	Rockefeller	89.2%	10.8%
10,330	CLAY	1,614	1,504	110	Rockefeller	93.2%	6.8%
7,403	DODDRIDGE	503	447	56	Rockefeller	88.9%	11.1%
47,579	FAYETTE	7,059	6,397	662	Rockefeller	90.6%	9.4%
7,160	GILMER	1,346	1,183	163	Rockefeller	87.9%	12.1%
11,299	GRANT	334	301	33	Rockefeller	90.1%	9.9%
34,453	GREENBRIER	4,840	4,060	780	Rockefeller	83.9%	16.1%
20,203	HAMPSHIRE	2,170	1,873	297	Rockefeller	86.3%	13.7%
32,667	HANCOCK	3,469	2,826	643	Rockefeller	81.5%	18.5%
12,669	HARDY	1,830	1,610	220	Rockefeller	88.0%	12.0%
68,652	HARRISON	10,759	9,795	964	Rockefeller	91.0%	9.0%
28,000	JACKSON	2,934	2,725	209	Rockefeller	92.9%	7.1%
42,190	JEFFERSON	2,950	2,614	336	Rockefeller	88.6%	11.4%
200,073	KANAWHA	22,640	20,546	2,094	Rockefeller	90.8%	9.2%
16,919	LEWIS	2,179	1,958	221	Rockefeller	89.9%	10.1%
22,108	LINCOLN	3,833	3,589	244	Rockefeller	93.6%	6.4%
37,710	LOGAN	7,964	7,450	514	Rockefeller	93.5%	6.5%
27,329	MCDOWELL	2,973	2,801	172	Rockefeller	94.2%	5.8%
56,598	MARION	11,165	10,063	1,102	Rockefeller	90.1%	9.9%
35,519	MARSHALL	4,107	3,666	441	Rockefeller	89.3%	10.7%
25,957	MASON	3,198	2,985	213	Rockefeller	93.3%	6.7%
62,980	MERCER	6,204	5,454	750	Rockefeller	87.9%	12.1%
27,078	MINERAL	1,735	1,524	211	Rockefeller	87.8%	12.2%
28,253	MINGO	7,542	7,169	373	Rockefeller	95.1%	4.9%
81,866	MONONGALIA	8,822	7,605	1,217	Rockefeller	86.2%	13.8%
14,583	MONROE	2,061	1,822	239	Rockefeller	88.4%	11.6%
14,943	MORGAN	903	827	76	Rockefeller	91.6%	8.4%
26,562	NICHOLAS	3,753	3,347	406	Rockefeller	89.2%	10.8%
47,427	OHIO	3,213	2,677	536	Rockefeller	83.3%	16.7%
8,196	PENDLETON	1,381	1,247	134	Rockefeller	90.3%	9.7%
7,514	PLEASANTS	1,074	962	112	Rockefeller	89.6%	10.4%
9,131	POCAHONTAS	1,262	1,105	157	Rockefeller	87.6%	12.4%
29,334	PRESTON	2,968	2,571	397	Rockefeller	86.6%	13.4%
51,589	PUTNAM	5,324	4,835	489	Rockefeller	90.8%	9.2%
79,220	RALEIGH	8,761	7,839	922	Rockefeller	89.5%	10.5%
28,262	RANDOLPH	4,611	4,021	590	Rockefeller	87.2%	12.8%
10,343	RITCHIE	741	679	62	Rockefeller	91.6%	8.4%
15,446	ROANE	1,861	1,741	120	Rockefeller	93.6%	6.4%
12,999	SUMMERS	2,650	2,298	352	Rockefeller	86.7%	13.3%
16,089	TAYLOR	1,933	1,720	213	Rockefeller	89.0%	11.0%
7,321	TUCKER	1,172	1,023	149	Rockefeller	87.3%	12.7%
9,592	TYLER	559	507	52	Rockefeller	90.7%	9.3%
23,404	UPSHUR	1,926	1,715	211	Rockefeller	89.0%	11.0%
42,903	WAYNE	6,940	6,381	559	Rockefeller	91.9%	8.1%
9,719	WEBSTER	2,006	1,874	132	Rockefeller	93.4%	6.6%
17,693	WETZEL	2,185	1,969	216	Rockefeller	90.1%	9.9%
5,873	WIRT	933	834	99	Rockefeller	89.4%	10.6%
87,986	WOOD	6,760	6,008	752	Rockefeller	88.9%	11.1%
25,708	WYOMING	3,553	3,294	259	Rockefeller	92.7%	7.3%
1,808,344	TOTAL	220,678	198,327	22,351	Rockefeller	89.9%	10.1%

WISCONSIN

GOVERNOR
James E. Doyle (D). Elected 2002 to a four-year term.

SENATORS (2 Democrats)
Russell D. Feingold (D). Reelected 1998 to a six-year term. Previously elected 1992.

Herb Kohl (D). Reelected 2000 to a six-year term. Previously elected 1994, 1988.

REPRESENTATIVES (4 Democrats, 4 Republicans)
1. Paul D. Ryan (R)
2. Tammy Baldwin (D)
3. Ron Kind (D)
4. Gerald D. Kleczka (D)
5. F. James Sensenbrenner Jr. (R)
6. Tom Petri (R)
7. David R. Obey (D)
8. Mark Green (R)

POSTWAR VOTE FOR PRESIDENT

| | | Republican | | Democratic | | Other | | Percentage | | | |
| | | | | | | | | Total Vote | | Major Vote | |
Year	Total Vote	Vote	Candidate	Vote	Candidate	Vote	Plurality	Rep.	Dem.	Rep.	Dem.
2000**	2,598,607	1,237,279	Bush, George W.	1,242,987	Gore, Al	118,341	5,708 D	47.6%	47.8%	49.9%	50.1%
1996**	2,196,169	845,029	Dole, Bob	1,071,971	Clinton, Bill	279,169	226,942 D	38.5%	48.8%	44.1%	55.9%
1992**	2,531,114	930,855	Bush, George	1,041,066	Clinton, Bill	559,193	110,211 D	36.8%	41.1%	47.2%	52.8%
1988	2,191,608	1,047,499	Bush, George	1,126,794	Dukakis, Michael S.	17,315	79,295 D	47.8%	51.4%	48.2%	51.8%
1984	2,211,689	1,198,584	Reagan, Ronald	995,740	Mondale, Walter F.	17,365	202,844 R	54.2%	45.0%	54.6%	45.4%
1980**	2,273,221	1,088,845	Reagan, Ronald	981,584	Carter, Jimmy	202,792	107,261 R	47.9%	43.2%	52.6%	47.4%
1976	2,104,175	1,004,987	Ford, Gerald R.	1,040,232	Carter, Jimmy	58,956	35,245 D	47.8%	49.4%	49.1%	50.9%
1972	1,852,890	989,430	Nixon, Richard M.	810,174	McGovern, George S.	53,286	179,256 R	53.4%	43.7%	55.0%	45.0%
1968	1,691,538	809,997	Nixon, Richard M.	748,804	Humphrey, Hubert H.	132,737	61,193 R	47.9%	44.3%	52.0%	48.0%
1964	1,691,815	638,495	Goldwater, Barry M.	1,050,424	Johnson, Lyndon B.	2,896	411,929 D	37.7%	62.1%	37.8%	62.2%
1960	1,729,082	895,175	Nixon, Richard M.	830,805	Kennedy, John F.	3,102	64,370 R	51.8%	48.0%	51.9%	48.1%
1956	1,550,558	954,844	Eisenhower, Dwight D.	586,768	Stevenson, Adlai E.	8,946	368,076 R	61.6%	37.8%	61.9%	38.1%
1952	1,607,370	979,744	Eisenhower, Dwight D.	622,175	Stevenson, Adlai E.	5,451	357,569 R	61.0%	38.7%	61.2%	38.8%
1948	1,276,800	590,959	Dewey, Thomas E.	647,310	Truman, Harry S.	38,531	56,351 D	46.3%	50.7%	47.7%	52.3%

In 2000 the other vote column includes 94,070 votes cast for Green (Nader). In 1996 the other vote column includes 227,339 votes cast for Perot. In 1992 the other vote column includes 544,479 votes cast for Perot. In 1980 the other vote column includes 160,657 votes for Independent (Anderson).

WISCONSIN

POSTWAR VOTE FOR GOVERNOR

Year	Total Vote	Republican Vote	Republican Candidate	Democratic Vote	Democratic Candidate	Other Vote	Rep.-Dem. Plurality	Percentage Total Vote Rep.	Percentage Total Vote Dem.	Percentage Major Vote Rep.	Percentage Major Vote Dem.
2002**	1,775,349	734,779	McCallum, Scott	800,515	Doyle, James E.	240,055	65,736 D	41.4%	45.1%	47.9%	52.1%
1998	1,756,014	1,047,716	Thompson, Tommy G.	679,553	Garvey, Edward R.	28,745	368,163 R	59.7%	38.7%	60.7%	39.3%
1994	1,563,835	1,051,326	Thompson, Tommy G.	482,850	Chvala, Chuck	29,659	568,476 R	67.2%	30.9%	68.5%	31.5%
1990	1,379,727	802,321	Thompson, Tommy G.	576,280	Loftus, Thomas	1,126	226,041 R	58.2%	41.8%	58.2%	41.8%
1986	1,526,960	805,090	Thompson, Tommy G.	705,578	Earl, Anthony S.	16,292	99,512 R	52.7%	46.2%	53.3%	46.7%
1982	1,580,344	662,838	Kohler, Terry J.	896,812	Earl, Anthony S.	20,694	233,974 D	41.9%	56.7%	42.5%	57.5%
1978	1,500,996	816,056	Dreyfus, Lee S.	673,813	Schreiber, Martin J.	11,127	142,243 R	54.4%	44.9%	54.8%	45.2%
1974	1,181,976	497,195	Dyke, William D.	628,639	Lucey, Patrick J.	56,142	131,444 D	42.1%	53.2%	44.2%	55.8%
1970**	1,343,160	602,617	Olson, Jack B.	728,403	Lucey, Patrick J.	12,140	125,786 D	44.9%	54.2%	45.3%	54.7%
1968	1,689,738	893,463	Knowles, Warren P.	791,100	LaFollette, Bronson C.	5,175	102,363 R	52.9%	46.8%	53.0%	47.0%
1966	1,170,173	626,041	Knowles, Warren P.	539,258	Lucey, Patrick J.	4,874	86,783 R	53.5%	46.1%	53.7%	46.3%
1964	1,694,887	856,779	Knowles, Warren P.	837,901	Reynolds, John W.	207	18,878 R	50.6%	49.4%	50.6%	49.4%
1962	1,265,900	625,536	Kuehn, Philip G.	637,491	Reynolds, John W.	2,873	11,955 D	49.4%	50.4%	49.5%	50.5%
1960	1,728,009	837,123	Kuehn, Philip G.	890,868	Nelson, Gaylord A.	18	53,745 D	48.4%	51.6%	48.4%	51.6%
1958	1,202,219	556,391	Thomson, Vernon W.	644,296	Nelson, Gaylord A.	1,532	87,905 D	46.3%	53.6%	46.3%	53.7%
1956	1,557,788	808,273	Thomson, Vernon W.	749,421	Proxmire, William	94	58,852 R	51.9%	48.1%	51.9%	48.1%
1954	1,158,666	596,158	Kohler, Walter J.	560,747	Proxmire, William	1,761	35,411 R	51.5%	48.4%	51.5%	48.5%
1952	1,615,214	1,009,171	Kohler, Walter J.	601,844	Proxmire, William	4,199	407,327 R	62.5%	37.3%	62.6%	37.4%
1950	1,138,148	605,649	Kohler, Walter J.	525,319	Thompson, Carl W.	7,180	80,330 R	53.2%	46.2%	53.6%	46.4%
1948	1,266,139	684,839	Rennebohm, Oscar	558,497	Thompson, Carl W.	22,803	126,342 R	54.1%	44.1%	55.1%	44.9%
1946	1,040,444	621,970	Goodland, Walter	406,499	Hoan, Daniel W.	11,975	215,471 R	59.8%	39.1%	60.5%	39.5%

In 2002 Ed Thompson, the Libertarian Party candidate, received 185,455 votes (10.4 percent of the total vote). The term of office of Wisconsin's Governor was increased from two to four years effective with the 1970 election.

POSTWAR VOTE FOR SENATOR

Year	Total Vote	Republican Vote	Republican Candidate	Democratic Vote	Democratic Candidate	Other Vote	Rep.-Dem. Plurality	Percentage Total Vote Rep.	Percentage Total Vote Dem.	Percentage Major Vote Rep.	Percentage Major Vote Dem.
2000	2,540,083	940,744	Gillespie, John	1,563,238	Kohl, Herb	36,101	622,494 D	37.0%	61.5%	37.6%	62.4%
1998	1,760,836	852,272	Neumann, Mark W.	890,059	Feingold, Russell D.	18,505	37,787 D	48.4%	50.5%	48.9%	51.1%
1994	1,565,628	636,989	Welch, Robert T.	912,662	Kohl, Herb	15,977	175,673 D	40.7%	58.3%	41.1%	58.9%
1992	2,455,124	1,129,599	Kasten, Robert W.	1,290,662	Feingold, Russell D.	34,863	161,063 D	46.0%	52.6%	46.7%	53.3%
1988	2,168,190	1,030,440	Engeleiter, Susan	1,128,625	Kohl, Herb	9,125	98,185 D	47.5%	52.1%	47.7%	52.3%
1986	1,483,174	754,573	Kasten, Robert W.	702,963	Garvey, Edward R.	25,638	51,610 R	50.9%	47.4%	51.8%	48.2%
1982	1,544,981	527,355	McCallum, Scott	983,311	Proxmire, William	34,315	455,956 D	34.1%	63.6%	34.9%	65.1%
1980	2,204,202	1,106,311	Kasten, Robert W.	1,065,487	Nelson, Gaylord A.	32,404	40,824 R	50.2%	48.3%	50.9%	49.1%
1976	1,935,183	521,902	York, Stanley	1,396,970	Proxmire, William	16,311	875,068 D	27.0%	72.2%	27.2%	72.8%
1974	1,199,495	429,327	Petri, Thomas E.	740,700	Nelson, Gaylord A.	29,468	311,373 D	35.8%	61.8%	36.7%	63.3%
1970	1,338,967	381,297	Erickson, John E.	948,445	Proxmire, William	9,225	567,148 D	28.5%	70.8%	28.7%	71.3%
1968	1,654,861	633,910	Leonard, Jerris	1,020,931	Nelson, Gaylord A.	20	387,021 D	38.3%	61.7%	38.3%	61.7%
1964	1,673,776	780,116	Renk, Wilbur N.	892,013	Proxmire, William	1,647	111,897 D	46.6%	53.3%	46.7%	53.3%
1962	1,260,168	594,846	Wiley, Alexander	662,342	Nelson, Gaylord A.	2,980	67,496 D	47.2%	52.6%	47.3%	52.7%
1958	1,194,678	510,398	Steinle, Roland J.	682,440	Proxmire, William	1,840	172,042 D	42.7%	57.1%	42.8%	57.2%
1957S	772,620	312,931	Kohler, Walter J.	435,985	Proxmire, William	23,704	123,054 D	40.5%	56.4%	41.8%	58.2%
1956	1,523,356	892,473	Wiley, Alexander	627,903	Maier, Henry W.	2,980	264,570 R	58.6%	41.2%	58.7%	41.3%
1952	1,605,228	870,444	McCarthy, Joseph R.	731,402	Fairchild, Thomas E.	3,382	139,042 R	54.2%	45.6%	54.3%	45.7%
1950	1,116,135	595,283	Wiley, Alexander	515,539	Fairchild, Thomas E.	5,313	79,744 R	53.3%	46.2%	53.6%	46.4%
1946	1,014,594	620,430	McCarthy, Joseph R.	378,772	McMurray, Howard J.	15,392	241,658 R	61.2%	37.3%	62.1%	37.9%

The August 1957 election was for a short term to fill a vacancy.

514

WISCONSIN

Congressional districts first established for elections held in 2002
8 members

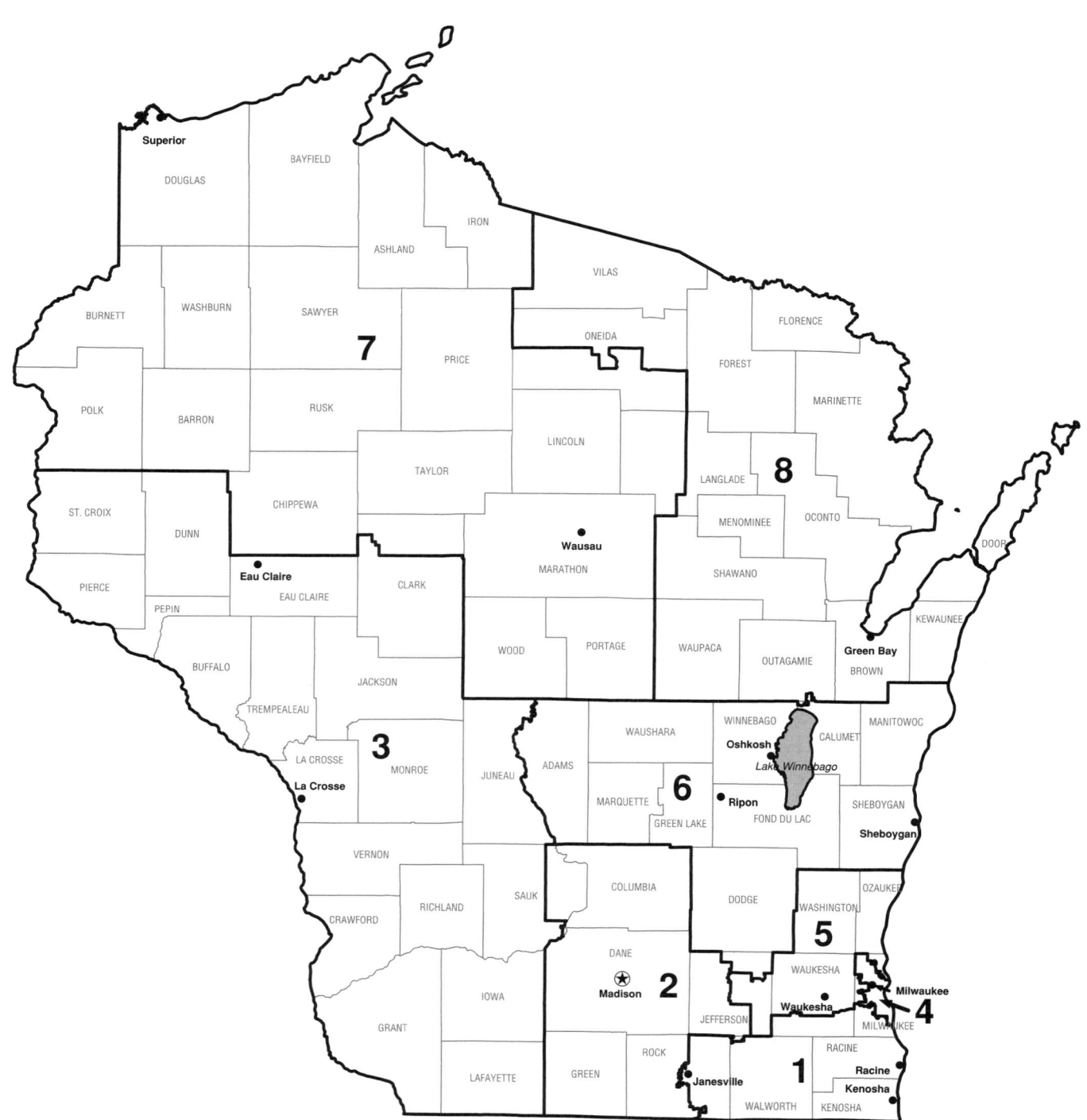

WISCONSIN

GOVERNOR 2002

2000 Census Population	County	Total Vote	Republican	Democratic	Libertarian (Thompson)	Other	Plurality	Percentage of Total Vote		
								Rep.	Dem.	Libertarian
18,643	ADAMS	6,844	2,168	3,160	1,355	161	992 D	31.7%	46.2%	19.8%
16,866	ASHLAND	5,120	1,572	3,092	296	160	1,520 D	30.7%	60.4%	5.8%
44,963	BARRON	14,206	6,239	6,540	1,074	353	301 D	43.9%	46.0%	7.6%
15,013	BAYFIELD	6,299	1,948	3,752	379	220	1,804 D	30.9%	59.6%	6.0%
226,778	BROWN	70,830	32,368	29,949	5,860	2,653	2,419 R	45.7%	42.3%	8.3%
13,804	BUFFALO	4,558	1,706	2,225	499	128	519 D	37.4%	48.8%	10.9%
15,674	BURNETT	6,454	3,142	3,004	205	103	138 R	48.7%	46.5%	3.2%
40,631	CALUMET	14,021	6,844	5,528	1,198	451	1,316 R	48.8%	39.4%	8.5%
55,195	CHIPPEWA	18,614	7,592	7,539	2,868	615	53 R	40.8%	40.5%	15.4%
33,557	CLARK	10,359	4,031	3,826	2,221	281	205 R	38.9%	36.9%	21.4%
52,468	COLUMBIA	18,117	6,308	7,581	3,585	643	1,273 D	34.8%	41.8%	19.8%
17,243	CRAWFORD	5,183	1,879	2,296	791	217	417 D	36.3%	44.3%	15.3%
426,526	DANE	172,033	41,810	97,084	22,477	10,662	55,274 D	24.3%	56.4%	13.1%
85,897	DODGE	26,396	12,761	8,607	4,416	612	4,154 R	48.3%	32.6%	16.7%
27,961	DOOR	11,481	5,333	4,647	849	652	686 R	46.5%	40.5%	7.4%
43,287	DOUGLAS	14,557	4,153	9,291	732	381	5,138 D	28.5%	63.8%	5.0%
39,858	DUNN	11,403	4,560	5,525	911	407	965 D	40.0%	48.5%	8.0%
93,142	EAU CLAIRE	32,736	11,946	15,958	3,241	1,591	4,012 D	36.5%	48.7%	9.9%
5,088	FLORENCE	1,533	842	609	70	12	233 R	54.9%	39.7%	4.6%
97,296	FOND DU LAC	31,347	17,653	10,394	2,540	760	7,259 R	56.3%	33.2%	8.1%
10,024	FOREST	3,206	1,332	1,435	371	68	103 D	41.5%	44.8%	11.6%
49,597	GRANT	14,337	5,946	6,175	1,832	384	229 D	41.5%	43.1%	12.8%
33,647	GREEN	11,047	3,581	5,148	1,930	388	1,567 D	32.4%	46.6%	17.5%
19,105	GREEN LAKE	6,432	3,322	2,232	685	193	1,090 R	51.6%	34.7%	10.6%
22,780	IOWA	7,626	2,234	3,606	1,422	364	1,372 D	29.3%	47.3%	18.6%
6,861	IRON	2,836	900	1,461	413	62	561 D	31.7%	51.5%	14.6%
19,100	JACKSON	6,321	2,101	2,770	1,271	179	669 D	33.2%	43.8%	20.1%
74,021	JEFFERSON	25,179	11,237	9,243	3,912	787	1,994 R	44.6%	36.7%	15.5%
24,316	JUNEAU	7,173	2,118	2,249	2,629	177	380 L	29.5%	31.4%	36.7%
149,577	KENOSHA	39,611	14,833	21,922	2,179	677	7,089 D	37.4%	55.3%	5.5%
20,187	KEWAUNEE	6,736	2,989	2,584	682	481	405 R	44.4%	38.4%	10.1%
107,120	LA CROSSE	35,186	12,578	15,255	6,075	1,278	2,677 D	35.7%	43.4%	17.3%
16,137	LAFAYETTE	5,335	1,648	2,313	1,244	130	665 D	30.9%	43.4%	23.3%
20,740	LANGLADE	7,571	3,238	3,320	843	170	82 D	42.8%	43.9%	11.1%
29,641	LINCOLN	10,190	3,664	4,379	1,872	275	715 D	36.0%	43.0%	18.4%
82,887	MANITOWOC	27,031	11,533	11,993	2,650	855	460 D	42.7%	44.4%	9.8%
125,834	MARATHON	43,173	16,904	18,940	5,989	1,340	2,036 D	39.2%	43.9%	13.9%
43,384	MARINETTE	13,919	6,627	6,032	900	360	595 R	47.6%	43.3%	6.5%
15,832	MARQUETTE	5,048	1,862	2,034	986	166	172 D	36.9%	40.3%	19.5%
4,562	MENOMINEE	939	171	681	61	26	510 D	18.2%	72.5%	6.5%
940,164	MILWAUKEE	267,725	95,015	150,877	15,891	5,942	55,862 D	35.5%	56.4%	5.9%
40,899	MONROE	12,787	3,433	3,275	5,809	270	2,376 L	26.8%	25.6%	45.4%
35,634	OCONTO	11,478	5,420	4,561	1,170	327	859 R	47.2%	39.7%	10.2%
36,776	ONEIDA	13,479	5,226	5,748	2,143	362	522 D	38.8%	42.6%	15.9%
160,971	OUTAGAMIE	50,478	23,695	21,158	3,799	1,826	2,537 R	46.9%	41.9%	7.5%
82,317	OZAUKEE	33,505	20,486	10,542	1,891	586	9,944 R	61.1%	31.5%	5.6%
7,213	PEPIN	2,377	870	1,234	203	70	364 D	36.6%	51.9%	8.5%
36,804	PIERCE	11,857	5,290	5,855	401	311	565 D	44.6%	49.4%	3.4%
41,319	POLK	14,509	6,789	6,901	422	397	112 D	46.8%	47.6%	2.9%
67,182	PORTAGE	23,974	7,157	11,954	3,265	1,598	4,797 D	29.9%	49.9%	13.6%
15,822	PRICE	6,378	2,324	2,670	1,219	165	346 D	36.4%	41.9%	19.1%
188,831	RACINE	58,868	26,654	27,859	3,442	913	1,205 D	45.3%	47.3%	5.8%
17,924	RICHLAND	5,410	1,958	1,961	1,307	184	3 D	36.2%	36.2%	24.2%
152,307	ROCK	50,301	14,929	26,648	7,418	1,306	11,719 D	29.7%	53.0%	14.7%
15,347	RUSK	6,020	2,208	2,305	1,345	162	97 D	36.7%	38.3%	22.3%
63,155	ST. CROIX	21,132	11,076	8,803	739	514	2,273 R	52.4%	41.7%	3.5%
55,225	SAUK	17,709	5,629	7,286	3,953	841	1,657 D	31.8%	41.1%	22.3%
16,196	SAWYER	6,097	2,890	2,626	434	147	264 R	47.4%	43.1%	7.1%
40,664	SHAWANO	12,018	5,734	4,752	1,203	329	982 R	47.7%	39.5%	10.0%
112,646	SHEBOYGAN	41,250	19,634	17,521	3,360	735	2,113 R	47.6%	42.5%	8.1%

WISCONSIN

GOVERNOR 2002

2000 Census Population	County	Total Vote	Republican	Democratic	Libertarian (Thompson)	Other	Plurality	Percentage of Total Vote		
								Rep.	Dem.	Libertarian
19,680	TAYLOR	6,782	2,426	2,498	1,708	150	72 D	35.8%	36.8%	25.2%
27,010	TREMPEALEAU	8,988	2,818	4,196	1,678	296	1,378 D	31.4%	46.7%	18.7%
28,056	VERNON	8,801	2,813	3,410	2,229	349	597 D	32.0%	38.7%	25.3%
21,033	VILAS	8,962	4,305	3,320	1,075	262	985 R	48.0%	37.0%	12.0%
93,759	WALWORTH	26,162	13,319	9,764	2,395	684	3,555 R	50.9%	37.3%	9.2%
16,036	WASHBURN	6,141	2,593	2,895	495	158	302 D	42.2%	47.1%	8.1%
117,493	WASHINGTON	41,465	25,592	11,480	3,765	628	14,112 R	61.7%	27.7%	9.1%
360,767	WAUKESHA	142,114	88,661	42,327	8,846	2,280	46,334 R	62.4%	29.8%	6.2%
51,731	WAUPACA	15,059	7,369	5,672	1,481	537	1,697 R	48.9%	37.7%	9.8%
23,154	WAUSHARA	7,280	3,371	2,909	799	201	462 R	46.3%	40.0%	11.0%
156,763	WINNEBAGO	51,275	23,110	22,425	3,708	2,032	685 R	45.1%	43.7%	7.2%
75,555	WOOD	23,981	8,312	10,704	4,349	616	2,392 D	34.7%	44.6%	18.1%
5,363,675	TOTAL	1,775,349	734,779	800,515	185,455	54,600	65,736 D	41.4%	45.1%	10.4%

Note: The plurality is based on the margin of victory of the winner over the runner up. The Libertarian Party candidate, Ed Thompson, carried two counties but ran third elsewhere, where the plurality reflects the difference between the Democratic and Republican vote.

WISCONSIN

HOUSE OF REPRESENTATIVES

CD	Year	Total Vote	Republican		Democratic		Other Vote	Rep.-Dem. Plurality	Percentage			
			Vote	Candidate	Vote	Candidate			Total Vote		Major Vote	
									Rep.	Dem.	Rep.	Dem.
1	2002	208,613	140,176	Ryan, Paul D.*	63,895	Thomas, Jeffrey C.	4,542	76,281 R	67.2%	30.6%	68.7%	31.3%
2	2002	247,410	83,694	Greer, Ron	163,313	Baldwin, Tammy*	403	79,619 D	33.8%	66.0%	33.9%	66.1%
3	2002	208,581	69,955	Arndt, Bill	131,038	Kind, Ron*	7,588	61,083 D	33.5%	62.8%	34.8%	65.2%
4	2002	141,367			122,031	Kleczka, Gerald D.*	19,336	122,031 D		86.3%		100.0%
5	2002	222,012	191,224	Sensenbrenner, F. James Jr.*			30,788	191,224 R	86.1%		100.0%	
6	2002	171,161	169,834	Petri, Tom*			1,327	169,834 R	99.2%		100.0%	
7	2002	227,955	81,518	Rothbauer, Joe	146,364	Obey, David R.*	73	64,846 D	35.8%	64.2%	35.8%	64.2%
8	2002	210,447	152,745	Green, Mark*	50,284	Becker, Andrew M.	7,418	102,461 R	72.6%	23.9%	75.2%	24.8%
Total	2002	1,637,546	889,146		676,925		71,475	212,221 R	54.3%	41.3%	56.8%	43.2%

An asterisk (*) denotes incumbent.

WISCONSIN

GENERAL AND PRIMARY ELECTIONS

2002 GENERAL ELECTIONS

Governor Other vote was 44,111 Wisconsin Greens (Jim Young); 2,847 Independent (Alan D. Eisenberg); 2,637 Independent (Ty A. Bollerud); 1,710 Independent (Mike Mangan); 929 Independent (Aneb Jah Rasta Sensas-Utcha-Nefer-I); 2,366 write-in. (The Libertarian Party candidate, Ed Thompson, received 185,455 votes, 10.4 percent of the total vote. The Libertarian vote is listed in the county table for the 2002 gubernatorial election in Wisconsin.)

House Other vote was:

CD 1 4,406 Libertarian (George Meyers); 136 write-in.
CD 2 403 write-in.
CD 3 6,674 Libertarian (Jeff Zastrow); 914 write-in.
CD 4 18,324 Wisconsin Greens (Brian Verdin); 1,012 write-in.
CD 5 29,567 Independent (Robert Raymond); 1,221 write-in.
CD 6 1,327 write-in.
CD 7 73 write-in.
CD 8 7,338 Wisconsin Greens (Dick Kaiser); 80 write-in.

2002 PRIMARY ELECTIONS

Primary September 10, 2002   No Statewide Registration

Primary Type Open—Any registered voter could participate in the primary of either party in municipalities where registration was required. Elsewhere, a voter had merely be a resident of voting age.

Note: An asterisk (*) denotes incumbent.

	REPUBLICAN PRIMARIES			DEMOCRATIC PRIMARIES		
Governor	Scott McCallum*	198,525	86.2%	James E. Doyle	212,066	38.3%
	Bill Lorge	18,852	8.2%	Thomas M. Barrett	190,605	34.4%
	George Pobuda	12,452	5.4%	Kathleen Falk	150,161	27.1%
	Write-in	403	0.2%	Write-in	803	0.1%
	TOTAL	230,232		TOTAL	553,635	
Congressional District 1	Paul D. Ryan*	18,791	99.9%	Jeffrey C. Thomas	31,144	65.0%
	Write-in	12	0.1%	Dale Moore	16,724	34.9%
				Write-in	74	0.2%
	TOTAL	18,803		TOTAL	47,942	
Congressional District 2	Ron Greer	13,422	61.2%	Tammy Baldwin*	75,458	99.6%
	Phil Alfonsi	8,491	38.7%	Write-in	333	0.4%
	Write-in	17	0.1%			
	TOTAL	21,930		TOTAL	75,791	
Congressional District 3	Bill Arndt	14,371	99.9%	Ron Kind*	41,406	99.8%
	Write-in	14	0.1%	Write-in	89	0.2%
	TOTAL	14,385		TOTAL	41,495	
Congressional District 4	No Republican candidate			Gerald D. Kleczka*	54,258	71.7%
				Nathaniel J. Stampley	21,244	28.1%
				Write-in	165	0.2%
				TOTAL	75,667	
Congressional District 5	F. James Sensenbrenner Jr.*	40,235	99.8%	*No Democratic candidate filed for the*		
	Write-in	66	0.2%	*primary. There was 1 write-in vote.*		
	TOTAL	40,301				
Congressional District 6	Tom Petri*	45,042	99.8%	*No Democratic candidate filed for the*		
	Write-in	84	0.2%	*primary. There were 11 write-in votes.*		
	TOTAL	45,126				

WISCONSIN

GENERAL AND PRIMARY ELECTIONS

	REPUBLICAN PRIMARIES			DEMOCRATIC PRIMARIES		
Congressional District 7	Joe Rothbauer	17,711	99.9%	David R. Obey*	60,367	99.8%
	Write-in	17	0.1%	Write-in	114	0.2%
	TOTAL	17,728		TOTAL	60,481	
Congressional District 8	Mark Green*	37,857	99.8%	Andrew M. Becker	31,784	99.8%
	Write-in	60	0.2%	Write-in	66	0.2%
	TOTAL	37,917		TOTAL	31,850	

WISCONSIN REPUBLICAN PRIMARY

GOVERNOR 2002

2000 Census Population	County	Total Vote	McCallum	Other	Winner	Percentage of Total Vote	
						McCallum	Other
18,643	ADAMS	1,135	884	251	McCallum	77.9%	22.1%
16,866	ASHLAND	278	239	39	McCallum	86.0%	14.0%
44,963	BARRON	765	684	81	McCallum	89.4%	10.6%
15,013	BAYFIELD	346	301	45	McCallum	87.0%	13.0%
226,778	BROWN	14,396	11,735	2,661	McCallum	81.5%	18.5%
13,804	BUFFALO	267	229	38	McCallum	85.8%	14.2%
15,674	BURNETT	1,563	1,278	285	McCallum	81.8%	18.2%
40,631	CALUMET	1,350	1,192	158	McCallum	88.3%	11.7%
55,195	CHIPPEWA	2,560	2,118	442	McCallum	82.7%	17.3%
33,557	CLARK	858	768	90	McCallum	89.5%	10.5%
52,468	COLUMBIA	4,384	3,418	966	McCallum	78.0%	22.0%
17,243	CRAWFORD	215	189	26	McCallum	87.9%	12.1%
426,526	DANE	11,051	10,212	839	McCallum	92.4%	7.6%
85,897	DODGE	8,741	7,167	1,574	McCallum	82.0%	18.0%
27,961	DOOR	3,517	2,912	605	McCallum	82.8%	17.2%
43,287	DOUGLAS	495	430	65	McCallum	86.9%	13.1%
39,858	DUNN	626	539	87	McCallum	86.1%	13.9%
93,142	EAU CLAIRE	1,532	1,391	141	McCallum	90.8%	9.2%
5,088	FLORENCE	910	665	245	McCallum	73.1%	26.9%
97,296	FOND DU LAC	9,169	7,954	1,215	McCallum	86.7%	13.3%
10,024	FOREST	134	122	12	McCallum	91.0%	9.0%
49,597	GRANT	2,463	1,957	506	McCallum	79.5%	20.5%
33,647	GREEN	1,469	1,191	278	McCallum	81.1%	18.9%
19,105	GREEN LAKE	2,436	1,888	548	McCallum	77.5%	22.5%
22,780	IOWA	1,553	1,206	347	McCallum	77.7%	22.3%
6,861	IRON	82	75	7	McCallum	91.5%	8.5%
19,100	JACKSON	292	266	26	McCallum	91.1%	8.9%
74,021	JEFFERSON	5,962	5,061	901	McCallum	84.9%	15.1%
24,316	JUNEAU	686	565	121	McCallum	82.4%	17.6%
149,577	KENOSHA	2,018	1,739	279	McCallum	86.2%	13.8%
20,187	KEWAUNEE	1,031	902	129	McCallum	87.5%	12.5%
107,120	LA CROSSE	1,878	1,745	133	McCallum	92.9%	7.1%
16,137	LAFAYETTE	989	743	246	McCallum	75.1%	24.9%
20,740	LANGLADE	2,363	1,793	570	McCallum	75.9%	24.1%
29,641	LINCOLN	4,121	2,726	1,395	McCallum	66.1%	33.9%
82,887	MANITOWOC	1,652	1,534	118	McCallum	92.9%	7.1%
125,834	MARATHON	2,239	1,979	260	McCallum	88.4%	11.6%
43,384	MARINETTE	3,477	2,737	740	McCallum	78.7%	21.3%
15,832	MARQUETTE	510	444	66	McCallum	87.1%	12.9%
4,562	MENOMINEE	29	23	6	McCallum	79.3%	20.7%
940,164	MILWAUKEE	18,962	17,993	969	McCallum	94.9%	5.1%
40,899	MONROE	746	670	76	McCallum	89.8%	10.2%
35,634	OCONTO	2,976	2,371	605	McCallum	79.7%	20.3%
36,776	ONEIDA	771	636	135	McCallum	82.5%	17.5%
160,971	OUTAGAMIE	5,016	4,347	669	McCallum	86.7%	13.3%

WISCONSIN REPUBLICAN PRIMARY

GOVERNOR 2002

2000 Census Population	County	Total Vote	McCallum	Other	Winner	McCallum	Other
						Percentage of Total Vote	
82,317	OZAUKEE	8,531	7,759	772	McCallum	91.0%	9.0%
7,213	PEPIN	362	293	69	McCallum	80.9%	19.1%
36,804	PIERCE	545	469	76	McCallum	86.1%	13.9%
41,319	POLK	739	669	70	McCallum	90.5%	9.5%
67,182	PORTAGE	864	778	86	McCallum	90.0%	10.0%
15,822	PRICE	773	653	120	McCallum	84.5%	15.5%
188,831	RACINE	7,042	6,549	493	McCallum	93.0%	7.0%
17,924	RICHLAND	1,706	1,415	291	McCallum	82.9%	17.1%
152,307	ROCK	3,467	3,018	449	McCallum	87.0%	13.0%
15,347	RUSK	611	513	98	McCallum	84.0%	16.0%
63,155	ST. CROIX	1,367	1,174	193	McCallum	85.9%	14.1%
55,225	SAUK	1,487	1,314	173	McCallum	88.4%	11.6%
16,196	SAWYER	1,942	1,576	366	McCallum	81.2%	18.8%
40,664	SHAWANO	3,180	2,405	775	McCallum	75.6%	24.4%
112,646	SHEBOYGAN	9,044	8,030	1,014	McCallum	88.8%	11.2%
19,680	TAYLOR	1,321	987	334	McCallum	74.7%	25.3%
27,010	TREMPEALEAU	370	325	45	McCallum	87.8%	12.2%
28,056	VERNON	2,908	2,190	718	McCallum	75.3%	24.7%
21,033	VILAS	626	521	105	McCallum	83.2%	16.8%
93,759	WALWORTH	3,409	3,072	337	McCallum	90.1%	9.9%
16,036	WASHBURN	797	684	113	McCallum	85.8%	14.2%
117,493	WASHINGTON	4,459	4,130	329	McCallum	92.6%	7.4%
360,767	WAUKESHA	27,527	25,914	1,613	McCallum	94.1%	5.9%
51,731	WAUPACA	2,577	2,002	575	McCallum	77.7%	22.3%
23,154	WAUSHARA	2,634	2,079	555	McCallum	78.9%	21.1%
156,763	WINNEBAGO	11,297	8,720	2,577	McCallum	77.2%	22.8%
75,555	WOOD	2,634	2,268	366	McCallum	86.1%	13.9%
5,363,675	TOTAL	230,232	198,525	31,707	McCallum	86.2%	13.8%

WISCONSIN DEMOCRATIC PRIMARY

GOVERNOR 2002

2000 Census Population	County	Total Vote	Doyle	Barrett	Falk	Other	Winner	Doyle	Barrett	Falk	Other
								Percentage of Total Vote			
18,643	ADAMS	2,338	1,254	628	452	4	Doyle	53.6%	26.9%	19.3%	0.2%
16,866	ASHLAND	1,528	453	816	258	1	Barrett	29.6%	53.4%	16.9%	0.1%
44,963	BARRON	5,773	2,280	2,282	1,210	1	Barrett	39.5%	39.5%	21.0%	
15,013	BAYFIELD	2,591	832	1,122	636	1	Barrett	32.1%	43.3%	24.5%	
226,778	BROWN	15,541	6,992	4,929	3,608	12	Doyle	45.0%	31.7%	23.2%	0.1%
13,804	BUFFALO	1,098	437	374	287		Doyle	39.8%	34.1%	26.1%	
15,674	BURNETT	1,560	732	583	245		Doyle	46.9%	37.4%	15.7%	
40,631	CALUMET	3,100	1,427	838	835		Doyle	46.0%	27.0%	26.9%	
55,195	CHIPPEWA	4,638	1,610	1,922	1,101	5	Barrett	34.7%	41.4%	23.7%	0.1%
33,557	CLARK	3,166	1,267	1,200	697	2	Doyle	40.0%	37.9%	22.0%	0.1%
52,468	COLUMBIA	4,545	2,152	786	1,605	2	Doyle	47.3%	17.3%	35.3%	
17,243	CRAWFORD	3,272	1,591	768	910	3	Doyle	48.6%	23.5%	27.8%	0.1%
426,526	DANE	74,389	24,156	12,845	37,369	19	Falk	32.5%	17.3%	50.2%	
85,897	DODGE	4,519	2,225	876	1,417	1	Doyle	49.2%	19.4%	31.4%	
27,961	DOOR	2,233	913	757	563		Doyle	40.9%	33.9%	25.2%	
43,287	DOUGLAS	6,886	2,270	3,859	753	4	Barrett	33.0%	56.0%	10.9%	0.1%
39,858	DUNN	2,816	1,090	1,053	673		Doyle	38.7%	37.4%	23.9%	
93,142	EAU CLAIRE	8,905	3,096	3,389	2,403	17	Barrett	34.8%	38.1%	27.0%	0.2%
5,088	FLORENCE	140	94	23	23		Doyle	67.1%	16.4%	16.4%	
97,296	FOND DU LAC	5,305	2,440	1,415	1,439	11	Doyle	46.0%	26.7%	27.1%	0.2%

WISCONSIN DEMOCRATIC PRIMARY

GOVERNOR 2002

2000 Census Population	County	Total Vote	Doyle	Barrett	Falk	Other	Winner	Percentage of Total Vote			
								Doyle	Barrett	Falk	Other
10,024	FOREST	1,613	730	704	179		Doyle	45.3%	43.6%	11.1%	
49,597	GRANT	3,026	1,536	556	931	3	Doyle	50.8%	18.4%	30.8%	0.1%
33,647	GREEN	2,867	1,393	435	1,038	1	Doyle	48.6%	15.2%	36.2%	
19,105	GREEN LAKE	1,059	498	268	289	4	Doyle	47.0%	25.3%	27.3%	0.4%
22,780	IOWA	2,120	1,052	292	776		Doyle	49.6%	13.8%	36.6%	
6,861	IRON	1,259	385	660	214		Barrett	30.6%	52.4%	17.0%	
19,100	JACKSON	2,891	1,069	1,219	601	2	Barrett	37.0%	42.2%	20.8%	0.1%
74,021	JEFFERSON	5,552	2,567	1,143	1,833	9	Doyle	46.2%	20.6%	33.0%	0.2%
24,316	JUNEAU	1,782	833	494	455		Doyle	46.7%	27.7%	25.5%	
149,577	KENOSHA	13,250	5,331	4,824	3,094	1	Doyle	40.2%	36.4%	23.4%	
20,187	KEWAUNEE	2,954	1,137	1,128	688	1	Doyle	38.5%	38.2%	23.3%	
107,120	LA CROSSE	9,538	3,681	3,563	2,259	35	Doyle	38.6%	37.4%	23.7%	0.4%
16,137	LAFAYETTE	1,309	680	256	372	1	Doyle	51.9%	19.6%	28.4%	0.1%
20,740	LANGLADE	1,962	942	733	276	11	Doyle	48.0%	37.4%	14.1%	0.6%
29,641	LINCOLN	1,614	739	635	240		Doyle	45.8%	39.3%	14.9%	
82,887	MANITOWOC	10,552	4,497	3,459	2,575	21	Doyle	42.6%	32.8%	24.4%	0.2%
125,834	MARATHON	11,958	4,650	4,527	2,780	1	Doyle	38.9%	37.9%	23.2%	
43,384	MARINETTE	2,566	1,255	851	455	5	Doyle	48.9%	33.2%	17.7%	0.2%
15,832	MARQUETTE	1,661	867	344	450		Doyle	52.2%	20.7%	27.1%	
4,562	MENOMINEE	535	257	128	146	4	Doyle	48.0%	23.9%	27.3%	0.7%
940,164	MILWAUKEE	132,617	42,643	62,687	26,802	485	Barrett	32.2%	47.3%	20.2%	0.4%
40,899	MONROE	2,638	1,002	990	641	5	Doyle	38.0%	37.5%	24.3%	0.2%
35,634	OCONTO	2,458	1,122	765	550	21	Doyle	45.6%	31.1%	22.4%	0.9%
36,776	ONEIDA	3,859	1,246	1,922	674	17	Barrett	32.3%	49.8%	17.5%	0.4%
160,971	OUTAGAMIE	11,788	5,508	3,076	3,202	2	Doyle	46.7%	26.1%	27.2%	
82,317	OZAUKEE	6,904	2,497	2,719	1,685	3	Barrett	36.2%	39.4%	24.4%	
7,213	PEPIN	538	242	170	125	1	Doyle	45.0%	31.6%	23.2%	0.2%
36,804	PIERCE	1,393	691	461	241		Doyle	49.6%	33.1%	17.3%	
41,319	POLK	2,554	1,075	1,035	444		Doyle	42.1%	40.5%	17.4%	
67,182	PORTAGE	13,074	5,174	5,827	2,061	12	Barrett	39.6%	44.6%	15.8%	0.1%
15,822	PRICE	2,968	1,126	1,294	547	1	Barrett	37.9%	43.6%	18.4%	
188,831	RACINE	17,669	7,821	5,236	4,596	16	Doyle	44.3%	29.6%	26.0%	0.1%
17,924	RICHLAND	1,216	582	177	457		Doyle	47.9%	14.6%	37.6%	
152,307	ROCK	15,995	7,166	3,869	4,951	9	Doyle	44.8%	24.2%	31.0%	0.1%
15,347	RUSK	1,960	705	798	457		Barrett	36.0%	40.7%	23.3%	
63,155	ST. CROIX	2,052	998	718	335	1	Doyle	48.6%	35.0%	16.3%	
55,225	SAUK	5,071	2,567	841	1,663		Doyle	50.6%	16.6%	32.8%	
16,196	SAWYER	1,061	489	318	254		Doyle	46.1%	30.0%	23.9%	
40,664	SHAWANO	2,600	1,253	851	495	1	Doyle	48.2%	32.7%	19.0%	
112,646	SHEBOYGAN	11,164	4,332	3,402	3,415	15	Doyle	38.8%	30.5%	30.6%	0.1%
19,680	TAYLOR	1,852	803	755	294		Doyle	43.4%	40.8%	15.9%	
27,010	TREMPEALEAU	2,609	1,040	953	613	3	Doyle	39.9%	36.5%	23.5%	0.1%
28,056	VERNON	1,594	707	464	422	1	Doyle	44.4%	29.1%	26.5%	0.1%
21,033	VILAS	2,086	747	921	416	2	Barrett	35.8%	44.2%	19.9%	0.1%
93,759	WALWORTH	5,442	2,360	1,425	1,656	1	Doyle	43.4%	26.2%	30.4%	
16,036	WASHBURN	1,720	711	689	319	1	Doyle	41.3%	40.1%	18.5%	0.1%
117,493	WASHINGTON	8,396	3,115	2,952	2,329		Doyle	37.1%	35.2%	27.7%	
360,767	WAUKESHA	31,753	11,649	11,104	8,979	21	Doyle	36.7%	35.0%	28.3%	0.1%
51,731	WAUPACA	3,515	1,658	971	884	2	Doyle	47.2%	27.6%	25.1%	0.1%
23,154	WAUSHARA	1,680	856	474	350		Doyle	51.0%	28.2%	20.8%	
156,763	WINNEBAGO	10,932	5,067	2,830	3,034	1	Doyle	46.4%	25.9%	27.8%	
75,555	WOOD	8,066	3,704	3,227	1,135		Doyle	45.9%	40.0%	14.1%	
5,363,675	TOTAL	553,635	212,066	190,605	150,161	803	Doyle	38.3%	34.4%	27.1%	0.1%

WYOMING

GOVERNOR
Dave Freudenthal (D). Elected 2002 to a four-year term.

SENATORS (2 Republicans)
Michael B. Enzi (R). Reelected 2002 to a six-year term. Previously elected 1996.

Craig Thomas (R). Elected 2000 to a six-year term. Previously elected 1994.

REPRESENTATIVE (1 Republican)
At Large. Barbara Cubin (R)

POSTWAR VOTE FOR PRESIDENT

Year	Total Vote	Republican Vote	Republican Candidate	Democratic Vote	Democratic Candidate	Other Vote	Plurality	Total Vote Rep.	Total Vote Dem.	Major Vote Rep.	Major Vote Dem.
2000**	218,351	147,947	Bush, George W.	60,481	Gore, Al	9,923	87,466 R	67.8%	27.7%	71.0%	29.0%
1996**	211,571	105,388	Dole, Bob	77,934	Clinton, Bill	28,249	27,454 R	49.8%	36.8%	57.5%	42.5%
1992**	200,598	79,347	Bush, George	68,160	Clinton, Bill	53,091	11,187 R	39.6%	34.0%	53.8%	46.2%
1988	176,551	106,867	Bush, George	67,113	Dukakis, Michael S.	2,571	39,754 R	60.5%	38.0%	61.4%	38.6%
1984	188,968	133,241	Reagan, Ronald	53,370	Mondale, Walter F.	2,357	79,871 R	70.5%	28.2%	71.4%	28.6%
1980**	176,713	110,700	Reagan, Ronald	49,427	Carter, Jimmy	16,586	61,273 R	62.6%	28.0%	69.1%	30.9%
1976	156,343	92,717	Ford, Gerald R.	62,239	Carter, Jimmy	1,387	30,478 R	59.3%	39.8%	59.8%	40.2%
1972	145,570	100,464	Nixon, Richard M.	44,358	McGovern, George S.	748	56,106 R	69.0%	30.5%	69.4%	30.6%
1968	127,205	70,927	Nixon, Richard M.	45,173	Humphrey, Hubert H.	11,105	25,754 R	55.8%	35.5%	61.1%	38.9%
1964	142,716	61,998	Goldwater, Barry M.	80,718	Johnson, Lyndon B.		18,720 D	43.4%	56.6%	43.4%	56.6%
1960	140,782	77,451	Nixon, Richard M.	63,331	Kennedy, John F.		14,120 R	55.0%	45.0%	55.0%	45.0%
1956	124,127	74,573	Eisenhower, Dwight D.	49,554	Stevenson, Adlai E.		25,019 R	60.1%	39.9%	60.1%	39.9%
1952	129,253	81,049	Eisenhower, Dwight D.	47,934	Stevenson, Adlai E.	270	33,115 R	62.7%	37.1%	62.8%	37.2%
1948	101,425	47,947	Dewey, Thomas E.	52,354	Truman, Harry S.	1,124	4,407 D	47.3%	51.6%	47.8%	52.2%

In 2000 the other vote column includes 4,625 votes cast for Green (Nader). In 1996 the other vote column includes 25,928 votes cast for Perot. In 1992 the other vote column includes 51,263 votes cast for Perot. In 1980 the other vote column includes 12,072 votes for Independent (Anderson).

POSTWAR VOTE FOR GOVERNOR

Year	Total Vote	Republican Vote	Republican Candidate	Democratic Vote	Democratic Candidate	Other Vote	Rep.-Dem. Plurality	Total Vote Rep.	Total Vote Dem.	Major Vote Rep.	Major Vote Dem.
2002	185,459	88,873	Bebout, Eli	92,662	Freudenthal, Dave	3,924	3,789 D	47.9%	50.0%	49.0%	51.0%
1998	174,888	97,235	Geringer, Jim	70,754	Vinich, John P.	6,899	26,481 R	55.6%	40.5%	57.9%	42.1%
1994	200,990	118,016	Geringer, Jim	80,747	Karpan, Kathy	2,227	37,269 R	58.7%	40.2%	59.4%	40.6%
1990	160,109	55,471	Mead, Mary	104,638	Sullivan, Mike		49,167 D	34.6%	65.4%	34.6%	65.4%
1986	164,720	75,841	Simpson, Peter	88,879	Sullivan, Mike		13,038 D	46.0%	54.0%	46.0%	54.0%
1982	168,555	62,128	Morton, Warren A.	106,427	Herschler, Ed		44,299 D	36.9%	63.1%	36.9%	63.1%
1978	137,567	67,595	Ostlund, John C.	69,972	Herschler, Ed		2,377 D	49.1%	50.9%	49.1%	50.9%
1974	128,386	56,645	Jones, Dick	71,741	Herschler, Ed		15,096 D	44.1%	55.9%	44.1%	55.9%
1970	118,257	74,249	Hathaway, Stan	44,008	Rooney, John J.		30,241 R	62.8%	37.2%	62.8%	37.2%
1966	120,873	65,624	Hathaway, Stan	55,249	Wilkerson, Ernest		10,375 R	54.3%	45.7%	54.3%	45.7%
1962	119,268	64,970	Hansen, Clifford P.	54,298	Gage, Jack R.		10,672 R	54.5%	45.5%	54.5%	45.5%
1958	112,537	52,488	Simpson, Milward L.	55,070	Hickey, J. J.	4,979	2,582 D	46.6%	48.9%	48.8%	51.2%
1954	111,438	56,275	Simpson, Milward L.	55,163	Jack, William		1,112 R	50.5%	49.5%	50.5%	49.5%
1950	96,959	54,441	Barrett, Frank A.	42,518	McIntyre, John J.		11,923 R	56.1%	43.9%	56.1%	43.9%
1946	81,353	38,333	Wright, Earl	43,020	Hunt, Lester C.		4,687 D	47.1%	52.9%	47.1%	52.9%

WYOMING

POSTWAR VOTE FOR SENATOR

Year	Total Vote	Republican Vote	Republican Candidate	Democratic Vote	Democratic Candidate	Other Vote	Rep.-Dem. Plurality	Percentage Total Vote Rep.	Percentage Total Vote Dem.	Percentage Major Vote Rep.	Percentage Major Vote Dem.
2002	183,280	133,710	Enzi, Michael B.	49,570	Corcoran, Joyce Jansa		84,140 R	73.0%	27.0%	73.0%	27.0%
2000	213,659	157,622	Thomas, Craig	47,087	Logan, Mel	8,950	110,535 R	73.8%	22.0%	77.0%	23.0%
1996	211,077	114,116	Enzi, Michael B.	89,103	Karpan, Kathy	7,858	25,013 R	54.1%	42.2%	56.2%	43.8%
1994	201,710	118,754	Thomas, Craig	79,287	Sullivan, Mike	3,669	39,467 R	58.9%	39.3%	60.0%	40.0%
1990	157,632	100,784	Simpson, Alan K.	56,848	Helling, Kathy		43,936 R	63.9%	36.1%	63.9%	36.1%
1988	180,964	91,143	Wallop, Malcolm	89,821	Vinich, John P.		1,322 R	50.4%	49.6%	50.4%	49.6%
1984	186,898	146,373	Simpson, Alan K.	40,525	Ryan, Victor A.		105,848 R	78.3%	21.7%	78.3%	21.7%
1982	167,191	94,725	Wallop, Malcolm	72,466	McDaniel, Rodger		22,259 R	56.7%	43.3%	56.7%	43.3%
1978	133,364	82,908	Simpson, Alan K.	50,456	Whitaker, Raymond B.		32,452 R	62.2%	37.8%	62.2%	37.8%
1976	155,368	84,810	Wallop, Malcolm	70,558	McGee, Gale		14,252 R	54.6%	45.4%	54.6%	45.4%
1972	142,067	101,314	Hansen, Clifford P.	40,753	Vinich, Mike		60,561 R	71.3%	28.7%	71.3%	28.7%
1970	120,486	53,279	Wold, John S.	67,207	McGee, Gale		13,928 D	44.2%	55.8%	44.2%	55.8%
1966	122,689	63,548	Hansen, Clifford P.	59,141	Roncalio, Teno		4,407 R	51.8%	48.2%	51.8%	48.2%
1964	141,670	65,185	Wold, John S.	76,485	McGee, Gale		11,300 D	46.0%	54.0%	46.0%	54.0%
1962S	119,372	69,043	Simpson, Milward L.	50,329	Hickey, J. J.		18,714 R	57.8%	42.2%	57.8%	42.2%
1960	138,550	78,103	Thomson, E. Keith	60,447	Whitaker, Ray		17,656 R	56.4%	43.6%	56.4%	43.6%
1958	114,157	56,122	Barrett, Frank A.	58,035	McGee, Gale		1,913 D	49.2%	50.8%	49.2%	50.8%
1954	112,252	54,407	Harrison, William H.	57,845	O'Mahoney, Joseph C.		3,438 D	48.5%	51.5%	48.5%	51.5%
1952	130,097	67,176	Barrett, Frank A.	62,921	O'Mahoney, Joseph C.		4,255 R	51.6%	48.4%	51.6%	48.4%
1948	101,480	43,527	Robertson, Edward V.	57,953	Hunt, Lester C.		14,426 D	42.9%	57.1%	42.9%	57.1%
1946	81,557	35,714	Henderson, Harry B.	45,843	O'Mahoney, Joseph C.		10,129 D	43.8%	56.2%	43.8%	56.2%

The 1962 election was for a short term to fill a vacancy.

WYOMING

One member At Large

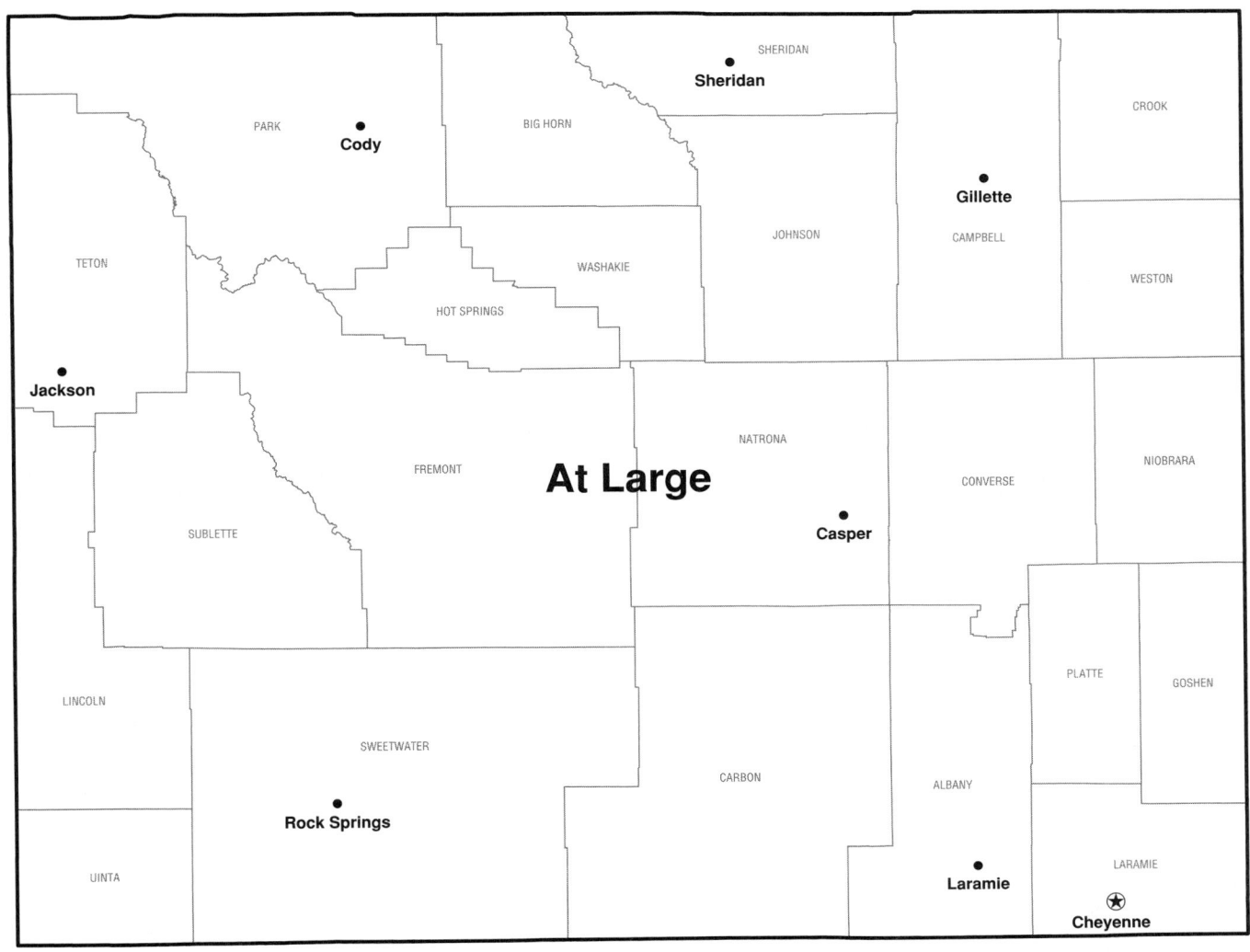

WYOMING

GOVERNOR 2002

2000 Census Population	County	Total Vote	Republican	Democratic	Other	Rep.-Dem. Plurality	Percentage Total Vote Rep.	Dem.	Major Vote Rep.	Dem.
32,014	ALBANY	11,381	4,404	6,772	205	2,368 D	38.7%	59.5%	39.4%	60.6%
11,461	BIG HORN	4,178	2,579	1,438	161	1,141 R	61.7%	34.4%	64.2%	35.8%
33,698	CAMPBELL	10,234	6,501	3,498	235	3,003 R	63.5%	34.2%	65.0%	35.0%
15,639	CARBON	5,986	2,345	3,493	148	1,148 D	39.2%	58.4%	40.2%	59.8%
12,052	CONVERSE	4,471	2,281	2,092	98	189 R	51.0%	46.8%	52.2%	47.8%
5,887	CROOK	2,819	1,807	931	81	876 R	64.1%	33.0%	66.0%	34.0%
35,804	FREMONT	13,866	8,108	5,500	258	2,608 R	58.5%	39.7%	59.6%	40.4%
12,538	GOSHEN	4,693	2,718	1,893	82	825 R	57.9%	40.3%	58.9%	41.1%
4,882	HOT SPRINGS	2,181	942	1,212	27	270 D	43.2%	55.6%	43.7%	56.3%
7,075	JOHNSON	3,140	1,829	1,263	48	566 R	58.2%	40.2%	59.2%	40.8%
81,607	LARAMIE	30,435	11,487	18,563	385	7,076 D	37.7%	61.0%	38.2%	61.8%
14,573	LINCOLN	5,546	3,520	1,887	139	1,633 R	63.5%	34.0%	65.1%	34.9%
66,533	NATRONA	23,610	9,825	13,175	610	3,350 D	41.6%	55.8%	42.7%	57.3%
2,407	NIOBRARA	1,217	774	411	32	363 R	63.6%	33.8%	65.3%	34.7%
25,786	PARK	10,748	6,287	4,192	269	2,095 R	58.5%	39.0%	60.0%	40.0%
8,807	PLATTE	3,868	1,645	2,122	101	477 D	42.5%	54.9%	43.7%	56.3%
26,560	SHERIDAN	11,266	5,567	5,510	189	57 R	49.4%	48.9%	50.3%	49.7%
5,920	SUBLETTE	2,610	1,539	1,025	46	514 R	59.0%	39.3%	60.0%	40.0%
37,613	SWEETWATER	13,163	5,026	7,809	328	2,783 D	38.2%	59.3%	39.2%	60.8%
18,251	TETON	7,564	3,128	4,281	155	1,153 D	41.4%	56.6%	42.2%	57.8%
19,742	UINTA	6,314	3,125	3,004	185	121 R	49.5%	47.6%	51.0%	49.0%
8,289	WASHAKIE	3,387	1,805	1,533	49	272 R	53.3%	45.3%	54.1%	45.9%
6,644	WESTON	2,782	1,631	1,058	93	573 R	58.6%	38.0%	60.7%	39.3%
493,782	TOTAL	185,459	88,873	92,662	3,924	3,789 D	47.9%	50.0%	49.0%	51.0%

WYOMING

SENATOR 2002

2000 Census Population	County	Total Vote	Republican	Democratic	Rep.-Dem. Plurality	Percentage Total Vote Rep.	Dem.	Major Vote Rep.	Dem.
32,014	ALBANY	11,235	7,017	4,218	2,799 R	62.5%	37.5%	62.5%	37.5%
11,461	BIG HORN	4,142	3,406	736	2,670 R	82.2%	17.8%	82.2%	17.8%
33,698	CAMPBELL	10,240	8,938	1,302	7,636 R	87.3%	12.7%	87.3%	12.7%
15,639	CARBON	5,951	4,091	1,860	2,231 R	68.7%	31.3%	68.7%	31.3%
12,052	CONVERSE	4,446	3,520	926	2,594 R	79.2%	20.8%	79.2%	20.8%
5,887	CROOK	2,819	2,440	379	2,061 R	86.6%	13.4%	86.6%	13.4%
35,804	FREMONT	13,646	10,262	3,384	6,878 R	75.2%	24.8%	75.2%	24.8%
12,538	GOSHEN	4,663	3,555	1,108	2,447 R	76.2%	23.8%	76.2%	23.8%
4,882	HOT SPRINGS	1,902	1,503	399	1,104 R	79.0%	21.0%	79.0%	21.0%
7,075	JOHNSON	2,947	2,540	407	2,133 R	86.2%	13.8%	86.2%	13.8%
81,607	LARAMIE	30,203	21,169	9,034	12,135 R	70.1%	29.9%	70.1%	29.9%
14,573	LINCOLN	5,523	4,319	1,204	3,115 R	78.2%	21.8%	78.2%	21.8%
66,533	NATRONA	23,335	16,229	7,106	9,123 R	69.5%	30.5%	69.5%	30.5%
2,407	NIOBRARA	1,205	1,036	169	867 R	86.0%	14.0%	86.0%	14.0%
25,786	PARK	10,704	8,723	1,981	6,742 R	81.5%	18.5%	81.5%	18.5%
8,807	PLATTE	3,859	2,817	1,042	1,775 R	73.0%	27.0%	73.0%	27.0%
26,560	SHERIDAN	11,210	8,357	2,853	5,504 R	74.5%	25.5%	74.5%	25.5%
5,920	SUBLETTE	2,584	2,146	438	1,708 R	83.0%	17.0%	83.0%	17.0%
37,613	SWEETWATER	12,918	7,986	4,932	3,054 R	61.8%	38.2%	61.8%	38.2%
18,251	TETON	7,504	4,153	3,351	802 R	55.3%	44.7%	55.3%	44.7%
19,742	UINTA	6,254	4,569	1,685	2,884 R	73.1%	26.9%	73.1%	26.9%
8,289	WASHAKIE	3,210	2,644	566	2,078 R	82.4%	17.6%	82.4%	17.6%
6,644	WESTON	2,780	2,290	490	1,800 R	82.4%	17.6%	82.4%	17.6%
493,782	TOTAL	183,280	133,710	49,570	84,140 R	73.0%	27.0%	73.0%	27.0%

WYOMING
HOUSE OF REPRESENTATIVES

CD	Year	Total Vote	Republican Vote	Candidate	Democratic Vote	Candidate	Other Vote	Rep.-Dem. Plurality	Total Vote Rep.	Dem.	Major Vote Rep.	Dem.
AL	2002	182,152	110,229	Cubin, Barbara*	65,961	Akin, Ron	5,962	44,268 R	60.5%	36.2%	62.6%	37.4%
AL	2000	212,312	141,848	Cubin, Barbara*	60,638	Green, Michael Allen	9,826	81,210 R	66.8%	28.6%	70.1%	29.9%
AL	1998	174,219	100,687	Cubin, Barbara*	67,399	Farris, Scott	6,133	33,288 R	57.8%	38.7%	59.9%	40.1%
AL	1996	209,983	116,004	Cubin, Barbara*	85,724	Maxfield, Pete	8,255	30,280 R	55.2%	40.8%	57.5%	42.5%
AL	1994	196,197	104,426	Cubin, Barbara	81,022	Schuster, Bob	10,749	23,404 R	53.2%	41.3%	56.3%	43.7%
AL	1992	196,977	113,882	Thomas, Craig*	77,418	Herschler, Jon	5,677	36,464 R	57.8%	39.3%	59.5%	40.5%
AL	1990	158,055	87,078	Thomas, Craig*	70,977	Maxfield, Pete		16,101 R	55.1%	44.9%	55.1%	44.9%
AL	1988	177,651	118,350	Cheney, Richard*	56,527	Sharratt, Bryan	2,774	61,823 R	66.6%	31.8%	67.7%	32.3%
AL	1986	159,787	111,007	Cheney, Richard*	48,780	Gilmore, Rick		62,227 R	69.5%	30.5%	69.5%	30.5%
AL	1984	187,904	138,234	Cheney, Richard*	45,857	McFadden, Hugh B.	3,813	92,377 R	73.6%	24.4%	75.1%	24.9%
AL	1982	159,277	113,236	Cheney, Richard*	46,041	Hommel, Theodore H.		67,195 R	71.1%	28.9%	71.1%	28.9%
AL	1980	169,699	116,361	Cheney, Richard*	53,338	Rogers, Jim		63,023 R	68.6%	31.4%	68.6%	31.4%
AL	1978	129,377	75,855	Cheney, Richard	53,522	Bagley, Bill		22,333 R	58.6%	41.4%	58.6%	41.4%
AL	1976	151,868	66,147	Hart, Larry	85,721	Roncalio, Tino*		19,574 D	43.6%	56.4%	43.6%	56.4%
AL	1974	126,933	57,499	Strook, Tom	69,434	Roncalio, Tino*		11,935 D	45.3%	54.7%	45.3%	54.7%
AL	1972	146,299	70,667	Kidd, William	75,632	Roncalio, Tino*		4,965 D	48.3%	51.7%	48.3%	51.7%
AL	1970	116,304	57,848	Roberts, Harry	58,456	Roncalio, Tino		608 D	49.7%	50.3%	49.7%	50.3%
AL	1968	123,313	77,363	Wold, John S.	45,950	Linford, Velma		31,413 R	62.7%	37.3%	62.7%	37.3%
AL	1966	119,426	62,984	Harrison, William H.*	56,442	Christian, Al		6,542 R	52.7%	47.3%	52.7%	47.3%
AL	1964	139,175	68,482	Harrison, William H.*	70,693	Roncalio, Tino		2,211 D	49.2%	50.8%	49.2%	50.8%
AL	1962	116,474	71,489	Harrison, William H.*	44,985	Mankus, Louis A.		26,504 R	61.4%	38.6%	61.4%	38.6%
AL	1960	134,331	70,241	Harrison, William H.	64,090	Armstrong, H.T.		6,151 R	52.3%	47.7%	52.3%	47.7%
AL	1958	111,780	59,894	Thomson, E. Keith*	51,886	Whitaker, Ray		8,008 R	53.6%	46.4%	53.6%	46.4%
AL	1956	120,128	69,903	Thomson, E. Keith*	50,225	O'Callaghan, Jerry		19,678 R	58.2%	41.8%	58.2%	41.8%
AL	1954	108,771	61,111	Thomson, E. Keith	47,660	Tully, Sam		13,451 R	56.2%	43.8%	56.2%	43.8%
AL	1952	126,720	76,161	Harrison, William H.*	50,559	Rose, Robert R.		25,602 R	60.1%	39.9%	60.1%	39.9%
AL	1950	93,348	50,865	Harrison, William H.	42,483	Clark, John B.		8,382 R	54.5%	45.5%	54.5%	45.5%
AL	1948	97,464	50,218	Barrett, Frank A.*	47,246	Flannery, L. G.		2,972 R	51.5%	48.5%	51.5%	48.5%
AL	1946	79,438	44,482	Barrett, Frank A.*	34,956	McIntyre, John J.		9,526 R	56.0%	44.0%	56.0%	44.0%

An asterisk (*) denotes incumbent.

WYOMING
GENERAL AND PRIMARY ELECTIONS

2002 GENERAL ELECTIONS

Governor — Other vote was 3,924 Libertarian (Dave Dawson).

Senator

House

At Large — Other vote was: 5,962 Libertarian (Lewis Stock).

2002 PRIMARY ELECTIONS

Primary August 20, 2002

Registration (as of Aug. 13, 2002)

Republican	137,156
Democratic	62,805
Libertarian	307
Natural Law	26
Wyoming Reform	7
Other	29,076
TOTAL	229,377

WYOMING

GENERAL AND PRIMARY ELECTIONS

2002 PRIMARY ELECTIONS

Primary Type   Only registered Democrats and Republicans could vote in their party's primary, although on primary day any new voter could register in the party of their choice and any previously registered voter could participate in another party's primary by changing their registration to that party.

Note: An asterisk (*) denotes incumbent.

	REPUBLICAN PRIMARIES			DEMOCRATIC PRIMARIES		
Governor	Eli Bebout	44,417	49.0%	Dave Freudenthal	19,732	53.6%
	Ray Hunkins	25,363	28.0%	Paul J. Hickey	13,793	37.5%
	Bill Sniffin	13,633	15.0%	Toby Simpson	1,918	5.2%
	Steve Watt	5,724	6.3%	Kenneth R. Casner	1,356	3.7%
	John H. Self	1,548	1.7%			
	TOTAL	90,685		TOTAL	36,799	
Senator	Michael B. Enzi*	78,612	85.9%	Joyce Jansa Corcoran	30,548	100.0%
	Crosby "Cros" Allen	12,931	14.1%			
	TOTAL	91,543				
House At Large	Barbara Cubin*	75,169	100.0%	Ron Akin	20,068	63.7%
				John A. Swett	11,426	36.3%
				TOTAL	31,494	

WYOMING REPUBLICAN PRIMARY

GOVERNOR 2002

2000 Census Population	County	Total Vote	Bebout	Hunkins	Sniffin	Other	Winner	Percentage of Total Vote			
								Bebout	Hunkins	Sniffin	Other
32,014	ALBANY	3,047	1,435	1,035	385	192	Bebout	47.1%	34.0%	12.6%	6.3%
11,461	BIG HORN	3,308	1,555	972	567	214	Bebout	47.0%	29.4%	17.1%	6.5%
33,698	CAMPBELL	7,816	4,355	1,755	1,018	688	Bebout	55.7%	22.5%	13.0%	8.8%
15,639	CARBON	2,139	946	585	253	355	Bebout	44.2%	27.3%	11.8%	16.6%
12,052	CONVERSE	2,834	1,223	977	429	205	Bebout	43.2%	34.5%	15.1%	7.2%
5,887	CROOK	1,840	887	457	240	256	Bebout	48.2%	24.8%	13.0%	13.9%
35,804	FREMONT	8,634	6,050	1,038	1,253	293	Bebout	70.1%	12.0%	14.5%	3.4%
12,538	GOSHEN	2,348	1,062	925	219	142	Bebout	45.2%	39.4%	9.3%	6.0%
4,882	HOT SPRINGS	1,562	824	373	223	142	Bebout	52.8%	23.9%	14.3%	9.1%
7,075	JOHNSON	2,600	1,159	921	401	119	Bebout	44.6%	35.4%	15.4%	4.6%
81,607	LARAMIE	10,686	4,479	4,018	1,697	492	Bebout	41.9%	37.6%	15.9%	4.6%
14,573	LINCOLN	2,685	1,069	759	513	344	Bebout	39.8%	28.3%	19.1%	12.8%
66,533	NATRONA	10,240	5,444	2,676	1,579	541	Bebout	53.2%	26.1%	15.4%	5.3%
2,407	NIOBRARA	940	422	312	141	65	Bebout	44.9%	33.2%	15.0%	6.9%
25,786	PARK	6,994	3,614	2,064	986	330	Bebout	51.7%	29.5%	14.1%	4.7%
8,807	PLATTE	1,995	426	1,283	201	85	Hunkins	21.4%	64.3%	10.1%	4.3%
26,560	SHERIDAN	5,517	2,457	1,499	1,020	541	Bebout	44.5%	27.2%	18.5%	9.8%
5,920	SUBLETTE	1,677	754	526	254	143	Bebout	45.0%	31.4%	15.1%	8.5%
37,613	SWEETWATER	3,472	1,573	627	498	774	Bebout	45.3%	18.1%	14.3%	22.3%
18,251	TETON	2,984	1,427	571	550	436	Bebout	47.8%	19.1%	18.4%	14.6%
19,742	UINTA	2,737	1,090	854	410	383	Bebout	39.8%	31.2%	15.0%	14.0%
8,289	WASHAKIE	2,424	1,234	558	502	130	Bebout	50.9%	23.0%	20.7%	5.4%
6,644	WESTON	2,206	932	578	294	402	Bebout	42.2%	26.2%	13.3%	18.2%
493,782	TOTAL	90,685	44,417	25,363	13,633	7,272	Bebout	49.0%	28.0%	15.0%	8.0%

WYOMING DEMOCRATIC PRIMARY

GOVERNOR 2002

2000 Census Population	County	Total Vote	Freudenthal	Hickey	Other	Winner	Percentage of Total Vote		
							Freudenthal	Hickey	Other
32,014	ALBANY	3,275	2,062	920	293	Freudenthal	63.0%	28.1%	8.9%
11,461	BIG HORN	392	185	95	112	Freudenthal	47.2%	24.2%	28.6%
33,698	CAMPBELL	705	378	167	160	Freudenthal	53.6%	23.7%	22.7%
15,639	CARBON	1,684	693	792	199	Hickey	41.2%	47.0%	11.8%
12,052	CONVERSE	582	347	161	74	Freudenthal	59.6%	27.7%	12.7%
5,887	CROOK	253	140	53	60	Freudenthal	55.3%	20.9%	23.7%
35,804	FREMONT	2,573	1,463	893	217	Freudenthal	56.9%	34.7%	8.4%
12,538	GOSHEN	900	555	231	114	Freudenthal	61.7%	25.7%	12.7%
4,882	HOT SPRINGS	323	262	40	21	Freudenthal	81.1%	12.4%	6.5%
7,075	JOHNSON	170	103	50	17	Freudenthal	60.6%	29.4%	10.0%
81,607	LARAMIE	7,905	3,854	3,698	353	Freudenthal	48.8%	46.8%	4.5%
14,573	LINCOLN	722	340	291	91	Freudenthal	47.1%	40.3%	12.6%
66,533	NATRONA	5,146	3,124	1,652	370	Freudenthal	60.7%	32.1%	7.2%
2,407	NIOBRARA	67	27	26	14	Freudenthal	40.3%	38.8%	20.9%
25,786	PARK	625	327	166	132	Freudenthal	52.3%	26.6%	21.1%
8,807	PLATTE	939	422	409	108	Freudenthal	44.9%	43.6%	11.5%
26,560	SHERIDAN	2,023	1,279	568	176	Freudenthal	63.2%	28.1%	8.7%
5,920	SUBLETTE	188	70	88	30	Hickey	37.2%	46.8%	16.0%
37,613	SWEETWATER	5,892	2,876	2,622	394	Freudenthal	48.8%	44.5%	6.7%
18,251	TETON	570	312	139	119	Freudenthal	54.7%	24.4%	20.9%
19,742	UINTA	1,233	505	612	116	Hickey	41.0%	49.6%	9.4%
8,289	WASHAKIE	391	297	50	44	Freudenthal	76.0%	12.8%	11.3%
6,644	WESTON	241	111	70	60	Freudenthal	46.1%	29.0%	24.9%
493,782	TOTAL	36,799	19,732	13,793	3,274	Freudenthal	53.6%	37.5%	8.9%

WYOMING REPUBLICAN PRIMARY

SENATOR 2002

2000 Census Population	County	Total Vote	Enzi	Allen	Winner	Percentage of Total Vote	
						Enzi	Allen
32,014	ALBANY	3,086	2,765	321	Enzi	89.6%	10.4%
11,461	BIG HORN	3,299	2,701	598	Enzi	81.9%	18.1%
33,698	CAMPBELL	8,078	7,363	715	Enzi	91.1%	8.9%
15,639	CARBON	2,179	1,903	276	Enzi	87.3%	12.7%
12,052	CONVERSE	2,823	2,455	368	Enzi	87.0%	13.0%
5,887	CROOK	1,911	1,694	217	Enzi	88.6%	11.4%
35,804	FREMONT	8,549	6,588	1,961	Enzi	77.1%	22.9%
12,538	GOSHEN	2,359	2,007	352	Enzi	85.1%	14.9%
4,882	HOT SPRINGS	1,573	1,352	221	Enzi	86.0%	14.0%
7,075	JOHNSON	2,597	2,238	359	Enzi	86.2%	13.8%
81,607	LARAMIE	10,828	9,620	1,208	Enzi	88.8%	11.2%
14,573	LINCOLN	2,792	2,300	492	Enzi	82.4%	17.6%
66,533	NATRONA	10,147	8,938	1,209	Enzi	88.1%	11.9%
2,407	NIOBRARA	941	808	133	Enzi	85.9%	14.1%
25,786	PARK	6,939	6,001	938	Enzi	86.5%	13.5%
8,807	PLATTE	1,970	1,758	212	Enzi	89.2%	10.8%
26,560	SHERIDAN	5,693	5,003	690	Enzi	87.9%	12.1%
5,920	SUBLETTE	1,744	1,404	340	Enzi	80.5%	19.5%
37,613	SWEETWATER	3,469	2,989	480	Enzi	86.2%	13.8%
18,251	TETON	3,180	2,524	656	Enzi	79.4%	20.6%
19,742	UINTA	2,792	2,337	455	Enzi	83.7%	16.3%
8,289	WASHAKIE	2,359	2,009	350	Enzi	85.2%	14.8%
6,644	WESTON	2,235	1,855	380	Enzi	83.0%	17.0%
493,782	TOTAL	91,543	78,612	12,931	Enzi	85.9%	14.1%

HOUSE CONTESTED AND UNCONTESTED ELECTIONS 2002

	Contested House Seats 2002								Uncontested House Seats 2002								
	Republican win	Democratic win	Independent win	Total contested	Republican vote	Democratic vote	Other vote	Total votes contested seats	Republican win	Democratic win	Total uncontested	Republican vote	Democratic vote	Other vote	Total vote uncontested seats	Total vote	Total seats
Alabama	3	1		4	376,730	353,382	12,934	743,046	2	1	3	317,876	153,735	54,145	525,756	1,268,802	7
Alaska	1	—		1	169,685	39,357	18,683	227,725			—					227,725	1
Arizona	6	2		8	681,922	472,135	40,343	1,194,400			—					1,194,400	8
Arkansas	—	2		2	142,261	249,334	—	391,595	1	1	2	141,478	142,752	12,451	296,681	688,276	4
California	19	32		51	3,131,072	3,604,691	232,960	6,968,723	1	1	2	94,594	126,390	68,710	289,694	7,258,417	53
Colorado	5	2		7	752,998	589,463	54,609	1,397,070			—					1,397,070	7
Connecticut	3	2		5	465,982	509,036	14,291	989,309			—					989,309	5
Delaware	1	—		1	164,605	61,011	2,789	228,405			—					228,405	1
Florida	12	4		16	1,814,026	1,423,375	20,334	3,257,735	6	3	9	347,323	113,749	47,751	508,823	3,766,558	25
Georgia	7	3		10	974,891	594,865	111	1,569,867	1	2	3	129,242	219,155	—	348,397	1,918,264	13
Hawaii	—	2		2	116,693	232,344	10,947	359,984			—					359,984	2
Idaho	2	—		2	256,348	138,038	10,637	405,023			—					405,023	2
Illinois	9	8		17	1,464,616	1,584,499	31,412	3,080,527	1	1	2	192,567	156,042	—	348,609	3,429,136	19
Indiana	6	3		9	840,694	640,568	40,091	1,521,353			—					1,521,353	9
Iowa	4	1		5	546,382	453,550	12,690	1,012,622			—					1,012,622	5
Kansas	2	1		3	346,050	259,911	15,368	621,329	1	—	1	189,976	—	18,585	208,561	829,890	4
Kentucky	4	1		5	578,238	350,924	4,392	933,554	1	—	1	115,622	—	45,066	160,688	1,094,242	6
Louisiana	1	2		3	215,833	219,368	39,510	474,711	3	1	4	424,372	138,659	—	665,452	1,140,163	7
Maine	—	2		2	205,780	289,514	—	495,294			—					495,294	2
Maryland	2	6		8	752,911	904,250	4,757	1,661,918			—					1,661,918	8
Massachusetts	4	—		4	290,484	602,541	12,388	905,413	—	6	6	—	926,093	9,365	935,458	1,840,871	10
Michigan	9	4		13	1,474,178	1,227,596	48,843	2,750,617	—	2	2	—	279,578	25,702	305,280	3,055,897	15
Minnesota	4	4		8	1,029,612	1,097,911	74,115	2,201,638			—					2,201,638	8
Mississippi	2	2		4	338,817	320,157	18,662	677,636			—					677,636	4
Missouri	5	4		9	985,905	829,177	38,481	1,853,563			—					1,853,563	9
Montana	1	—		1	214,100	108,233	8,988	331,321			—					331,321	1
Nebraska	1	—		1	89,917	46,843	5,254	142,014	2	—	2	296,952	—	34,848	331,800	473,814	3
Nevada	2	1		3	301,100	171,160	27,648	499,908			—					499,908	3
New Hampshire	2	—		2	254,797	175,905	12,741	443,443			—					443,443	2
New Jersey	6	6		12	933,964	908,358	32,348	1,874,670	—	1	1	—	121,846	9,543	131,389	2,006,059	13
New Mexico	2	—		2	175,342	139,150	82	314,574			—		122,950		122,950	437,524	3
New York	8	14		22	1,537,833	1,561,973	60,886	3,160,692	2	5	7	232,699	362,796	65,426	660,921	3,821,613	29
North Carolina	5	6		11	926,155	970,716	34,847	1,931,718	2	—	2	282,878	—	29,553	312,431	2,244,149	13
North Dakota	—	1		1	109,957	121,073	—	231,030			—					231,030	1
Ohio	11	6		17	1,650,009	1,331,614	50,854	3,032,477	1	—	1	125,546	—		125,546	3,158,023	18
Oklahoma	3	1		4	398,626	391,927	15,209	805,762	1	—	1	148,206	—	47,884	196,090	1,001,852	5
Oregon	1	4		5	528,997	676,920	34,398	1,240,315			—					1,240,315	5
Pennsylvania	7	6		13	1,203,405	1,225,342	8,713	2,437,460	5	1	6	655,865	123,323	93,665	872,853	3,310,313	19
Rhode Island	—	2		2	97,137	224,676	6,833	328,646			—					328,646	2
South Carolina	2	1		3	297,826	224,964	6,888	529,678	2	1	3	271,711	121,912	62,133	455,756	985,434	6
South Dakota	1	—		1	180,023	153,656	3,128	336,807			—					336,807	1
Tennessee	3	4		7	643,214	587,386	25,563	1,256,163	1	1	2	127,300	120,904	24,942	273,146	1,529,309	9
Texas	11	12		23	1,815,053	1,507,611	51,790	3,374,454	4	5	9	475,670	377,567	67,519	920,756	4,295,210	32
Utah	2	1		3	321,986	221,401	13,766	557,153			—					557,153	3
Vermont			1	1	72,813		152,663	225,476			—					225,476	1
Virginia	3	2		5	441,132	352,957	5,406	799,495	5	1	6	566,617	87,521	62,849	716,987	1,516,482	11
Washington	3	6		9	778,922	907,440	52,754	1,739,116			—					1,739,116	9
West Virginia	1	1		2	135,505	153,183	—	288,688	—	1	1	—	110,941	320	111,261	399,949	3
Wisconsin	2	3		5	528,088	554,894	20,024	1,103,006	2	1	3	361,058	122,031	51,451	534,540	1,637,546	8
Wyoming	1	—		1	110,229	65,961	5,962	182,152			—					182,152	1
	189	165	1	355	31,862,872	29,830,344	1,396,092	63,089,308	44	36	80	5,497,552	3,927,944	934,329	10,359,825	73,449,100	435

Note: The Vermont seat was won by Bernard Sanders. His vote, shown in the Other Vote column, was 144,880; the remainder of the Other Vote went to other third-party candidates.